The SAGE Handbook of

Modern
Japanese Studies

The SAGE Handbook of

Modern
Japanese Studies

Edited by
James Babb

$SAGE reference

Los Angeles | London | New Delhi
Singapore | Washington DC

Los Angeles | London | New Delhi
Singapore | Washington DC

SAGE Publications Ltd
1 Oliver's Yard
55 City Road
London EC1Y 1SP

SAGE Publications Inc.
2455 Teller Road
Thousand Oaks, California 91320

SAGE Publications India Pvt Ltd
B 1/I 1 Mohan Cooperative Industrial Area
Mathura Road
New Delhi 110 044

SAGE Publications Asia-Pacific Pte Ltd
3 Church Street
#10-04 Samsung Hub
Singapore 049483

Editor: Chris Rojek
Assistant editor: Colette Wilson
Production editor: Sushant Nailwal
Copyeditor: Sunrise Setting Limited
Proofreader: Sunrise Setting Limited
Indexer: Cathryn Pritchard
Marketing manager: Michael Ainsley
Cover design: Wendy Scott
Typeset by: Cenveo Publisher Services
Printed and bound by CPI Group (UK) Ltd,
Croydon, CR0 4YY [for Antony Rowe]

MIX
Paper from
responsible sources
FSC® C013604

At SAGE we take sustainability seriously.
Most of our products are printed in the UK
using FSC papers and boards. When we
print overseas we ensure sustainable
papers are used as measured by the
Egmont grading system. We undertake an
annual audit to monitor our sustainability.

Editorial arrangement © James Babb, 2015

Chapter 1 © Andrew Cobbing, 2015
Chapter 2 © Carolyn S. Stevens, 2015
Chapter 3 © Lucia Dolce, 2015
Chapter 4 © Katja Valaskivi, 2015
Chapter 5 © Noriaki Nishiyama, 2015
Chapter 6 © Mary McDonald, 2015
Chapter 7 © Anthony Rausch, 2015
Chapter 8 © Robert W. Aspinall, 2015
Chapter 9 © Vera Mackie, 2015
Chapter 10 © Mark McLelland, 2015
Chapter 11 © Joyce Gelb, 2015
Chapter 12 © David T. Johnson, 2015
Chapter 13 © Peter Hill, 2015
Chapter 14 © Izumi Yokoyama and Michael D. Fetters, 2015
Chapter 15 © Jonathan E. Rodnick, Izumi Yokoyama and Michael D. Fetters, 2015
Chapter 16 © Michael D. Fetters and Izumi Yokoyama, 2015
Chapter 17 © Michael D. Fetters, 2015
Chapter 18 © Denise St Arnault, 2015
Chapter 19 © James Babb, 2015
Chapter 20 © Kenneth Mori McElwain, 2015
Chapter 21 © Sherry Martin Murphy, 2015
Chapter 22 © Yuko Kawato, Robert J. Pekkanen and Hidehiro Yamamoto, 2015
Chapter 23 © Christopher W. Hughes, 2015
Chapter 24 © Hugo Dobson, 2015
Chapter 25 © Paul Midford, 2015
Chapter 26 © Caroline Rose, 2015
Chapter 27 © Marcus Rebick, 2015
Chapter 28 © Parissa Haghirian, 2015
Chapter 29 © Parissa Haghirian, 2015
Chapter 30 © Akira Suzuki, 2015
Chapter 31 © Gabriele Vogt, 2015
Chapter 32 © Aurelia George Mulgan, 2015
Chapter 33 © Alexandru P. Luta and Paul Midford, 2015

Library of Congress Control Number: 2014938537

British Library Cataloguing in Publication data

A catalogue record for this book is available from the British Library

ISBN 978-1-84860-663-0

Contents

List of Figures

List of Tables

Notes on the Editor and Contributors

THE EDITOR

James Babb is Senior Lecturer in Politics at the University of Newcastle-upon-Tyne. He holds an MA in East Asian Studies and PhD in Political Science from Stanford University. He is also currently the Newcastle University representative for the Japan Foundation Endowment Committee (UK) and a member of the inte rnational advisory board for the British Association of Japanese Studies journal *Japan Forum*. He has published a number of journal articles on Japan and is the author of *Tanaka and the Making of Post-war Japan* (Longman, 2000), *Business and Politics in Japan* (Manchester University Press, 2001) and co-author of *Empirical Political Analysis* (Longman, 2012), a textbook of political science methodology.

THE CONTRIBUTORS

Robert W. Aspinall is Professor in the Faculty of Economics, Shiga University. He was a secondary school history teacher in England before coming to Japan on the JET programme. After completing a DPhil doctoral degree at St Antony's, College, Oxford he worked at Nagoya University as a visiting lecturer before taking up his present position. He is the author of *Teachers' Unions and the Politics of Education in Japan* (SUNY Press, 2001) and *International Education Policy in Japan in an Age of Globalisation and Risk* (Global Oriental, 2013) as well as numerous articles on Japanese educational politics and policy.

Andrew Cobbing received his first degree in History from the University of Bristol before completing his Masters at Kyushu University and PhD at SOAS, University of London. He then spent several years working at Kyushu University and is now an Associate Professor at the University of Nottingham. He is the author of, among other works, *The Japanese Discovery of Victorian Britain* (Routledge, 1998) and *Kyushu: Gateway to Japan* (Global Oriental Ltd., 2009). He has also been involved in some major translation projects including Volume Three in Kume Kunitake's official account of the Iwakura Embassy (The Japan Documents, 2002) and, most recently, the last volume of Shiba Ryōtarō's *Clouds Above the Hill* (Routledge, 2014).

Hugo Dobson is Professor of Japan's International Relations at the National Institute of Japanese Studies and School of East Asian Studies at the University of Sheffield, UK. His research interests focus on global governance, especially the G8 and G20 and Japan's role therein, as well as the role of images in shaping our understanding of international relations. He is the author of various books and articles including *Japan and the G7/G8, 1975–2002* (Routledge, 2004), *The Group of 7/8* (Routledge, 2007) and *Japan's International Relations: Politics, Economics and Security* (Routledge, 2012, 3rd ed.).

Lucia Dolce is Numata Reader in Japanese Buddhism at SOAS, University of London, where she also directs the Centre for the Study of Japanese Religions. Her research has explored hermeneutical and ritual practices of religion in Japan, including Buddhist traditions, from the Tendai and Nichiren schools to Tantric Buddhism, combinatory cults, ritual iconography and ritual performance. Among her recent publications are *Shinbutsu shûgō saikō* [*Rethinking Syncretism in Japanese Religion*] (Bensei shuppan, 2013, co-editor); *Japanese Religions*, 4 vols. (SAGE, 2012, editor); *Girei no chikara–chûsei shûkyō no jissen sekai* [*The Power of Ritual: The World of Religious Practice in Medieval Japan*] (Hôzôkan, 2010, co-editor).

Michael D. Fetters (MD, MPH, MA) is Professor of Family Medicine at the University of Michigan in Ann Arbor, Michigan. His undergraduate degree in Japanese studies was followed by his medical degree at Ohio State University. His academic interests focus on US–Japan comparisons in medical ethics, medical education, family medicine and on the influence of culture on medical decision making. Bilingual in Japanese and English, he founded and directs the University of Michigan Japanese Family Health Program. He has authored over 150 scholarly articles, chapters and editorials and serves as Associate Editor, *Journal of Mixed Methods Research*.

Joyce Gelb is Professor Emerita of Political Science at City College and the Graduate Center, City University of NY. She has been a visiting professor in recent years at Yale University, Doshisha and Tokyo Universities in Japan, Queens University in Belfast in Northern Ireland, Stockholm University in Sweden, Shanghai University in China, and National Taiwan University and Tsinghua University in Taiwan. Her research and publications deal primarily with comparative politics and policy on women's issues. She is the author of *Women and Public Policies: Reassessing Gender Politics* (Princeton, 1987; University of Virginia Press, 1996, 2nd ed., with Marian Palley) and *Gender Policies in Japan and the United States: Comparing Women's Movements, Rights and Politics* (St Martin's Press, 2003) as well as numerous articles in edited volumes and journals. Recent publications include an article on the anti-feminist backlash in Japan and the USA published in Grey and Sawyer, *Women's Movements Worldwide* (2008), *Women and Politics Around the World*, co-edited with Marian Palley (ABC-CLIO, 2009) and 'Women and politics in Japan and Taiwan' in O'Connor ed. *Gender and Women's Leadership* (SAGE, 2010).

Aurelia George Mulgan is Professor of Politics at the University of New South Wales, Canberra, Australia. She is the author of six books on Japanese politics and political economy including *Ozawa Ichiro and Japanese Politics: Old Versus New* (Routledge, 2014), *Japan's Interventionist State: The Role of the MAFF* (Routledge, 2005), *Power and Pork: A Japanese Political Life* (ANU Press, 2006) and *Japan's Failed Revolution: Koizumi and the Politics of Economic Reform* (ANU Press, 2002). In 2001 she won an Ohira Memorial Prize for *The Politics of Agriculture in Japan* (Routledge, 2000) and in 2010 the Toshiba Prize from the British Association of Japanese Studies.

Parissa Haghirian is Professor of International Management at the Faculty of Liberal Arts at Sophia University in Tokyo, Japan. She obtained her MA in Japanese studies from Vienna University (1998). She was awarded an MA (2000) and PhD in International Management (2003) by Vienna University of Business, Austria. Since joining Sophia University Parissa has taught undergraduate, graduate and MBA-level classes on the subject of Japanese management and researched and consulted on numerous aspects of Japanese business practices with Western and native Japanese companies in Tokyo. She has published several books and articles on the topic and is the author of *Understanding Japanese Management Practices* (Business Expert Press, 2010) and the editor of *Innovation and Change in Japanese Management* (Palgrave Macmillan, 2010) and *Japanese Consumer Dynamics* (Palgrave Macmillan, 2011).

Peter Hill received his PhD in 2000 from the Scottish Centre for Japanese Studies at the University of Stirling for his research on the effect of the *Bôryokudan* countermeasures law on Japanese crime syndicates. From 2000 to 2003 he was a British Academy Postdoctoral Fellow in Sociology at the University of Oxford. During his fieldwork he was a visiting researcher at the Institute of Social Science at the University of Tokyo. His publications include *The Japanese Mafia: Yakuza, Law and the State* (Oxford

University Press, 2003) and 'Kamikaze 1943–5' in Gambetta ed. *Making Sense of Suicide Missions* (Oxford University Press, 2005).

Christopher W. Hughes (BA Oxford University; MA Rochester University; PhD Sheffield University) is Professor of International Politics and Japanese Studies, Chair of the Department of Politics and International Studies and Chair of the Faculty of Social Sciences at the University of Warwick, UK. He was formerly Research Associate, University of Hiroshima; Asahi Shimbun Visiting Professor of Mass Media and Politics, University of Tokyo; and Edwin O. Reischauer Visiting Professor of Japanese Studies, Department of Government, Harvard University. He holds adjunct/associate positions at Hiroshima, Waseda and Harvard universities. His most recent book publications include *Japan's Remilitarisation* (Routledge, 2009) and *Japan's Reemergence as a 'Normal' Military Power* (Oxford University Press, 2004). He is Joint Editor of *The Pacific Review*. He was President of the British Association of Japanese Studies from 2009 to 2013.

David T. Johnson is Professor of Sociology at the University of Hawaii at Manoa and a former co-editor of *Law and Society Review*. He is the author of *The Japanese Way of Justice: Prosecuting Crime in Japan* (Oxford University Press, 2002), co-author of *The Next Frontier: National Development, Political Change, and the Death Penalty in Asia* (Oxford University Press, 2009, with Franklin Zimring), and co-author of *Koritsu Suru Nihon no Shikei* [Japan's Isolated Death Penalty] (Gendai Jinbunsha, 2012, with Maiko Tagusari).

Yuko Kawato (PhD University of Washington, 2010) is Research Fellow at the Asia Centre, a think-tank in Paris, France. Her expertise is on Japan's civil society and foreign policy. Her publications include a book chapter on civil society in Kingston (ed.) *Natural Disaster and Nuclear Crisis in Japan: Response and Recovery after 3/11* (Routledge, 2012, with Robert J. Pekkanen and Yutaka Tsujinaka), an article about the politics of nuclear energy in *Outre-Terre Revue Européenne de Géopolitique* (2013) and articles on Japan's foreign policy in Asia Centre's *Japan Analysis*. Her book *Protests against U.S. Military Base Policy in Asia: Persuasion and Its Limits in Base Politics* is forthcoming from Stanford University Press in 2015.

Alexandru P. Luta is a policy analyst and campaigner for the Sandbag Climate Campaign, an advocacy group lobbying for a stronger EU climate-mitigation policy. He is finalizing his PhD on comparative renewable-energy policy at the Tokyo Institute of Technology. In the past he has been a researcher on Japanese climate and energy policy for the Finnish Institute of International Affairs, and the Tokyo representative of Enersense International, a resource management company for energy construction projects.

Vera Mackie is Senior Professor of Asian Studies at the University of Wollongong. Her publications include *Creating Socialist Women in Japan: Gender, Labour and Activism, 1900–1937* (Cambridge, 1997); *Feminism in Modern Japan: Citizenship, Embodiment and Sexuality* (Cambridge, 2003); *Gurōbaruka to Jendā Hyōshō* [*Globalisation and Representations of Gender*] (Ochanomizu Shobō, 2003); *The Routledge Handbook of Sexuality Studies in East Asia* (Routledge, 2015, co-edited with Mark McLelland); *Gender, Nation and State in Modern Japan* (Routledge, 2014, co-edited with Andrea Germer and Ulrike Wöhr); *and Human Rights and Gender Politics: Asia–Pacific Perspectives* (Routledge, 2000, co-edited with Anne-Marie Hilsdon, Martha Macintyre and Maila Stivens).

Sherry Martin Murphy is Foreign Affairs Research Analyst in the US Department of State. She was Associate Professor at Cornell University holding a joint appointment in both the Government Department and the Program in Feminist, Gender, and Sexuality Studies. Her research has been published in the *Social Science Japan Journal* and the *Journal of Women, Politics and Policy*, and she has published the monograph *Popular Democracy in Japan: How Gender and Community are Changing Modern Electoral Politics* (Cornell University Press, 2011) and *Democratic Reform in Japan: Assessing the Impact* (Lynne Rienner, 2008, co-edited with Gill Steel). Her undergraduate degree in Politics is from Princeton University and her PhD in Political Science from the University of Michigan.

Mary McDonald is Director of the Center for Japanese Studies (2012–2015) and Associate Professor of Geography at the University of Hawaii at Mānoa. She holds a BA from Oberlin College and MA and PhD from University of California, Berkeley. Her research interests include industrial change in Japan's rural regions, farm labor, farmland, rice improvement, food trade, tourism and trans-Pacific economic linkages. She served on the editorial board of *The Geographical Review of Japan*. She led a student year abroad at Kōnan University in Kōbe. Her research hosts in Japan have included Tōhoku University and Kyōto University.

Kenneth Mori McElwain is Assistant Professor of Political Science at the University of Michigan, Ann Arbor. His research focuses on institutional design, including the manipulation of electoral rules, the democratization of political parties and the evolution of national constitutions. He received his PhD in Political Science from Stanford University, and an AB in Public Policy and International Affairs from Princeton University. He is a co-editor of *Political Change in Japan* (Stanford APARC, 2009), and his research has been published in the *American Journal of Political Science*, *Journal of East Asian Studies*, *Journal of Social Science* and in numerous edited volumes.

Mark McLelland is Professor of Gender and Sexuality Studies at the University of Wollongong and a former Toyota Visiting Professor of Japanese at the University of Michigan. He has written extensively on the cultural history of sex and sexuality in Japan, most recently in *Love, Sex and Democracy in Japan during the American Occupation* (Palgrave, 2012) and in *The Routledge Handbook of Sexuality Studies in East Asia* (Routledge, 2014, co-edited with Vera Mackie).

Paul Midford is Professor and Director of the Japan Program at the Norwegian University for Science and Technology (NTNU) in Trondheim. Midford received his PhD in Political Science from Columbia University in 2001. His research interests include Japanese foreign and defense policies, the impact of public opinion on policy, renewable energy and energy security and East Asian security multilateralism. He has published in *International Organization*, *International Studies Quarterly, Security Studies*, *Pacific Review*, *Asian Survey*, *Japan Forum* and *International Relations of the Asia-Pacific*. Midford is the author of *Rethinking Japanese Public Opinion and Security: From Pacifism to Realism?* (Stanford University Press, 2011).

Noriaki Nishiyama received his Doctor of Engineering from Kyoto University Graduate School of Engineering and was Professor at Kyushu Institute of Design, Kyushu University. He assumed his current position as Director of the Center for Advanced Tourism Studies at Hokkaido University in 2014. His areas of specialization are in architecture, urban planning, tourism, and cultural heritage management. He is Expert Advisor for the Culture Advisory Committee of the Agency for Cultural Affairs, Advisor for the Tourism Development Sector, Japan International Cooperation Agency (JICA), Deputy Chief of the Japan Society of Urban Planning Hokkaido Branch and President of the Shirakawa Village Landscape Committee. One of his major publications is *Building a Sustainable Relationship between Cultural Heritage Management and Tourism* (National Museum of Ethnology, 2006, editor).

Robert J. Pekkanen (PhD Harvard, 2002) is Professor at the Henry M. Jackson School of International Studies, Adjunct Professor of Political Science and Adjunct Professor of Sociology at the University of Washington. He has published articles in journals including *The American Political Science Review*, *The British Journal of Political Science* and *Comparative Political Studies*. He has authored, co-authored or co-edited six books on topics of Japanese civil society, American nonprofit advocacy and Japanese elections and political parties. His first book, *Japan's Dual Civil Society: Members without Advocates* (Stanford University Press, 2006), won the Masayoshi Ohira Prize in 2008 and also an award from the Japanese Nonprofit Research Association (JANPORA).

Anthony Rausch is Professor at Hirosaki University, Japan. His research interests focus on rural Japan and he is the author of *A Year With the Local Newspaper: Understanding the Times in Aomori, Japan* (University Press of America, 2001), *Cultural Commodities in Japanese Rural Revitalization: Tsugaru*

Nuri Lacquerware and Tsugaru Shamisen (Brill, 2010) and *Japan's Local Newspapers: Chihoshi and Revitalization Journalism* (Routledge, 2012) and co-author of *Japan's Shrinking Regions in the 21st Century: Contemporary Responses to Depopulation and Socioeconomic Decline* (Cambria Press, 2011).

Marcus Rebick is a former Nissan Lecturer in the Japanese Economy at Oxford University and fellow of St Antony's College. He has taught at the Industrial and Labor Relations School at Cornell University and been a visiting researcher at Tokyo, Nagoya and Gakushuin Universities in Japan as well as several Japanese government institutions. He is a labor economist who has written numerous articles on Japan's labour market and institutions. He received his doctorate in Economics from Harvard in 1990.

Jonathan 'Jack' Rodnick (MD) earned his undergraduate degree at Yale University and medical degree at the University of California, Los Angeles. He died unexpectedly on 26 January 2008 while vacationing in Hawaii. Under his 14-year tenure as Chair, Department of Family and Community Medicine, University of California, San Francisco, he led a student-run homeless clinic, the national HIV 'Warmline', the Center on Social Disparities in Health and the Family and Community Medicine Collaborative Research Network. His research focused on global development of family-medicine and primary-care education and clinical programs, particularly in health systems in African and Asian countries.

Caroline Rose is Professor of Sino-Japanese Relations in the School of Modern Languages and Cultures at the University of Leeds, Executive Director of the White Rose East Asia Centre and President of the British Association of Japanese Studies. Her teaching and research focus on Sino-Japanese relations, with a particular interest in the history problem and reconciliation, and history and citizenship education in China and Japan. She has published two monographs on Sino-Japanese relations (both with Routledge) in addition to various articles and chapters on such issues as Japan's relations with Latin America, Japan and China in Africa, Japanese nationalism and changing representations of Japan in Chinese school textbooks. She is currently working on a monograph on educational reforms in China and Japan and their implications for China-Japan relations.

Denise St Arnault has studied the cultural variables that influence illness and help-seeking for over 20 years using a variety of qualitative and quantitative methods including photo-elicitation, card sorts, life-lines, event calendars, body maps, structured and semi-structured interviewing, fieldwork, participant observation, grounded theory and clinical ethnography. She has carried out research in India, Japan, Korea and Ireland, and has worked with African Americans, Native Americans and East Asian immigrants. She is an Association of American Colleges and Universities (AACU) Japan scholar, has been a consultant on several grants in Japan and has received federal funding for her research on Japanese immigrant women.

Carolyn S. Stevens is Professor of Japanese Studies and Director of the Japanese Studies Centre at Monash University. Trained as an anthropologist, she teaches and conducts research on Japanese popular culture as well as social problems in Japan. Recent major publications include *Disability in Japan* (Routledge, 2013) and the co-edited volumes *Sound, Space and Sociality in Modern Japan* (Routledge, 2014) and *Internationalising Japan: Discourse and Practice* (Routledge, 2014).

Akira Suzuki is Professor at the Ohara Institute for Social Research, Hosei University. His major research interests include social-movement unionism and the historical analysis of union involvement in environmental issues. He has edited volumes on social-movement unionism and recent trends in Japanese labor movements, most recently *Cross-National Comparisons of Social Movement Unionism: Diversities of Labour Movement Revitalization in Japan, Korea and the United States* (Peter Lang, 2012).

Katja Valaskivi is Senior Research Fellow and Reader (Docent) at the University of Tampere, School of Communication, Media and Theatre. Her first speciality back in the 1990s was Japanese media and popular culture, television drama in particular. Her current research interests include the social construction of knowledge and belief, media and promotional culture. She is writing a book for Routledge on nation branding and the concept of 'Cool'. She has worked as a visiting researcher at Goldsmiths College, University of London, as well as Sophia University, Tokyo and the National Institute of Informatics, Tokyo. Between 2002 and 2005 she headed the Finnish Institute in Japan, Tokyo. Her recent publications in English include 'A brand new future? Cool Japan and social imaginary of the branded nation' in *Japan Forum* (2013).

Gabriele Vogt is Professor of Japanese Politics at the University of Hamburg. Her previous appointments include positions at Chūō University, Sophia University and the German Institute for Japanese Studies (all in Tokyo), the University of the Ryūkyūs in Okinawa and Cornell University in Ithaca, NY. Her research interest lies with Japan's demographic change and international migration to Japan. She is co-editor of *The Demographic Challenge: A Handbook about Japan* (Brill, 2008) and *Migration and Integration. Japan in Comparative Perspective* (iudicium, 2011). She also served as a guest editor to *Contemporary Japan* and *ASIEN, The German Journal on Contemporary Asia*.

Hidehiro Yamamoto is Associate Professor of Yamagata University. He received his PhD in sociology from Tohoku University. His research interests are in civil society, social movement and interest-group politics. He is co-author of *Neighborhood Associations and Local Governance in Japan* (Routledge, 2014).

Izumi Yokoyama obtained her PhD in economics from the University of Michigan in 2013 and is currently Assistant Professor at Hitotsubashi University teaching applied econometrics and microeconomics. Her research interests include wage inequalities and impacts on public policies related to labor markets, such as spousal exemptions and standard hours' effects on wages and work hours. Her current research focuses on evaluating policies using empirical methodologies. She is the author of 'Wage distribution in Japan: 1989–2003' in *Canadian Journal of Economics* (2008, with Daiji Kawaguchi and Ryo Kambayashi).

Acknowledgements

It has taken a long time to bring this volume to publication but the wait was worth it because it has resulted in a major contribution to Japanese studies including chapters that are unique and insightful.

Funding from the Jitsukōkai Foundation supported Mike Fetters' and Izumi Yokoyama's research and writing of Chapters 14 to 17, and they would like to thank Susan O. Long, Akira Akabayashi, John C. Campbell, and Robert B. Leflar for helpful comments, corrections and embellishments on earlier drafts of their chapters. Some of the research for Denise Saint Arnault's chapter was funded by the NIH Office of Behavioral and Social Sciences Research, the NIH Office of Research on Women's Health and the National Institute of Mental Health (MH071307). Aurelia George Mulgan's research was made possible in part by the Australian Research Council. Vera Mackie would like to acknowledge Australian Research Council grants DP0450753 and FT0992328. Carolyn Stevens gratefully acknowledges feedback on early drafts from Laura Miller and research assistance provided by Anika Ervin-Ward. Alexandru Luta and Paul Midford would like to acknowledge Paul J. Scalise for reading over a draft of their energy chapter. Paul Midford would also like to thank Professor Koji Murata and the Faculty of Law at Doshisha University who hosted him during his writing of Japan–US chapter.

The chapter on Religion was originally published as the introductory essay to the 2012 SAGE major work, *Japanese Religions* (Volumes I – IV), edited by Lucia Dolce. This was chosen based on the advice of Louella Matsunaga who sacrificed her perfectly acceptable chapter on Religion in Japan in deference to this one because she thought it would better cover all aspects of the topic. Thanks to Lucia Dolce and SAGE for agreeing to republish the chapter with amendments here and to Louella for the suggestion.

My particular thanks go to those contributors who persevered. Special thanks are due to the contributors who were patient throughout this process, especially those, such as Robert Aspinall and Caroline Rose, who were consistently supportive and kind. Others, such as Andrew Cobbing, Paul Midford and Mike Fetters, who went beyond the call of duty to offer excellent chapters at relatively short notice also need to be acknowledged.

Martine Jonsrud, formerly of SAGE, was only an editor a short time but did the most to get the project back on track. The sympathetic and professional assistance of Delia Martinez-Alfonso and Colette Wilson helped to move the project seamlessly through final production.

I should also thank my wife who will hopefully never have to hear me talk about this project again.

James Babb

Historical Timeline of Modern Japan

MEIJI ERA (1868–1912)

1868	Meiji Restoration
1873	Military Conscription
1874–89	Freedom and Popular Rights Movement
1881	Matsukata Deflation Begins
1889	The Constitution of the Empire of Japan Promulgated
1894–95	First Sino–Japanese War
1898	Meiji Civil Code Implemented
1904–05	Russo–Japanese War
1910	Korea Annexed by Japan

TAISHO ERA (1912–1926)

1914–18	World War I (Japan Allied with USA and UK)
1918	First 'Commoner' Prime Minister Hara
1922	Japanese Communist Party Formed
1923	Great Kantō Earthquake

SHOWA ERA: PRE-WAR AND WARTIME (1926–1945)

1925	Universal [Manhood] Suffrage and Peace Preservation Laws Passed
1928	First Election after passing of Universal [Manhood] Suffrage Law
1931	Manchurian Incident (Japan Occupies Manchuria)
1932	Assassination of Prime Minister Inukai Tsuyoshi
1936	Attempted Military Coup d'État
1937	Second Sino–Japanese War Begins
1940	Tripartite Pact (Japan Allies with Germany and Italy)
1941	Pacific War Begins (World War II)

SHOWA ERA: POSTWAR (1945–1989)

1945	End of World War II: Allied Occupation of Japan Begins
1952	Allied Occupation of Japan Ends
1955	Formation of the Liberal Democratic Party
1960	Renewal of the US–Japan Mutual Security Treaty
1964	Tokyo Olympics
1971	Nixon 'Dollar' Shock
1973	First Oil Crisis

1976	Former LDP Prime Minister Tanaka Kakuei Arrested for Bribery
1979	Second Oil Crisis
1982–87	LDP President Nakasone Yasuhiro Prime Minister

HEISEI ERA (1989–PRESENT)

1989	Peak of the Economic Bubble (Nikkei 225 Index at Nearly 39,000)
1993	LDP Loses Power Temporarily
1994	Political Reform Laws Pass Parliament
1995	Kobe Earthquake/Sarin Gas Terrorist Attack in Tokyo
2001–06	LDP President Koizumi Jun'ichirō Prime Minister
2009	LDP Loses Power Completely
2011	North East Japan Earthquake and Tsunami
2012	LDP Back in Power

Introduction

James Babb

Japanese studies is an important interdisciplinary field with relevance to scholars in many countries. The field covers the exciting and sometimes provocative combination of modern and traditional Japanese approaches to the world. It is informed by and has an impact on the range of disciplines, particularly in the social sciences. This *Handbook* is intended to serve as a major reference work and a seminal text, both rigorous and accessible, in assisting students and scholars in understanding one of the major nations of the world.

After over 100 years of interaction with the West, Japan continues to be an important comparator for advanced and developing nations alike. Despite the growth of China, the Japanese economy is still important to the global economy and China is still dependent on foreign technology, much of which has been developed in Japan. Indeed, Japan is competing with other advanced industrial countries at the cutting edge of research, outpacing her East Asian neighbors. More importantly, the Japanese experience is likely to inform the future of both Western industrialized countries and the new industrial countries in Asia. Japan is interesting precisely because its experience speaks both to the developed and the developing alike. It has already experienced the rapid economic growth that is spreading through Asia and is the aim of many other countries. It has the same problems and prospects as other advanced industrial countries but it has often sought its own solutions with dramatic results.

There is a close connection between economic development and environmental problems, rapid social change, political innovation, and the marketing of 'culture'. Most of the major pollution-related illnesses were discovered in Japan and its anti-pollution technology and energy-saving devices are going to be important to the future of the economies of many nations as concern over the global environment spreads. Rapid social change has produced an ageing society and a low birth rate, both of which defy easy solutions due to issues related to gender and lifestyle. The politics of Japan shares much with Western democracies but also contains features similar to one-party regimes in Asia and elsewhere. Finally, modern Japanese culture is not only growing in popularity in the West but is already a dominant force in the markets of East Asia and beyond. This modern Japanese culture reflects an embracing of new technology, traditional values, and often complex identity issues in a powerful combination attractive to many.

In order to secure the background necessary to understand Japan, this volume provides an authoritative overview of the field of Japanese studies. Japanese studies has grown dramatically over the past 30 years and has spread throughout the globe with all major universities employing Japan specialists both in East Asian studies and discipline-specific academic departments. The origins of the field are in Oriental studies but in the aftermath of World War II a large number of those formerly involved in the Allied Occupation of Japan (1945–1952) in a social-science capacity took up academic posts, especially in the US. When economic friction between Japan and its major trading partners intensified in the 1980s a new cohort of academic specialists were trained and funded by the Japanese and other governments. It is primarily those scholars trained in the 1980s and 1990s, often themselves students of the Occupation generation, who occupy the numerous posts in Japanese studies at academic institutions around the world. This volume aims to help meet the needs of these scholars and their students.

This volume focuses on what has traditionally been called the social sciences. It provides an overview of classic and current research in each of the major disciplines and an examination of the major issues facing Japan today. In addition, experts in all areas have been sought out so as to uncover those disciplines and issues that have less prominence but have continuing or future importance, especially in relation to other disciplines. It aims to be a comprehensive treatment of the major work in the social sciences.

The chapters have been written by the experts in each area who have conducted research and published substantial work on the subjects. The contributors have the knowledge and authority recognized by others in the same field. A conscious attempt was made to solicit contributions from across the globe but the priority was to secure the best expert possible for each chapter. As is obvious from the list of contributors, the diversity and level of expertise of the chapter authors is impressive.

This *Handbook* has the academic rigor and depth required for advanced research without losing accessibility for an educated readership. Most handbooks of this type expect to be read only by researchers, professors, and advanced students, but this *Handbook* can also be an important resource for undergraduates at all levels, as well as for interested members of the general public. Given the nature of the field, there is less need for technical jargon, and chapters have been written clearly to be attractive to a wide audience. It provides a useful background to each of the relevant fields of study and adjacent subject areas. It will help students at the beginning of their studies, facilitate access to the research and deepen understanding.

In the past few years, there have been similar volumes on Japanese studies but they have tended to be narrower in focus. For example, *The Routledge Handbook of Japanese Culture and Society* (2011) focuses primarily on sociology and anthropology, and *The Routledge Handbook of Japanese Politics* (2011) is focused only on politics. This SAGE *Handbook* covers the key topics raised in the Routledge volumes but also contains many unique contributions found nowhere else. In addition, this *Handbook* is more up-to-date because it reflects the dramatic changes in Japan in recent years as a result of events such as the fall of the Liberal Democratic Party after almost 55 years in power and the disasters which followed the massive earthquake in the north-east of Japan in 2011. Overall, this volume is more well rounded and at the cutting edge of developments than any other handbook.

ORGANIZATION OF THE HANDBOOK

The slightly archaic title of the first section, Land, History and Culture, is a light-hearted reference to travel guides to exotic locations which began to be popular in the late nineteenth century. The need to include the 'Land' is occasioned by the chapter on the geography of Japan, which is a contribution unique to this type of handbook. As might be expected from a geographer, the chapter is largely organized by geographic location of scholars, though there are a large number of resources on geography, such as links to maps and data, to be found in the chapter as well. The chapter on Regionalism and the Local reinforces this theme and is an important issue in Japanese studies in its own right. The chapter on Religion is more typical of this genre but a valuable overview of the field in its own right. Heritage management, in contrast, is a new area of research and this volume is privileged to have a chapter by one of the pioneering scholars in this field. A number of other chapters could have been added to this section but as the *Handbook* is primarily focused on social science it had to be limited in focus. The chapter on the mass media covers some of this ground as an excellent overview of a range of topics from newspapers to film. From the social science point of view, the key chapter in the section is the one on anthropology, which makes clear that the role of culture in Japan is not as straightforward as commonly thought. This is reinforced throughout this work.

The second section, Society, explores the most important issues in Japanese society today. The educational system in Japan is still considered to be successful by many policy makers in the West a good model to emulate; but as the chapter on the subject shows there are problems and challenges in Japan which suggest it is not the best model for imitation. The next three chapters look at sexuality, gender equality, and feminism. It might be curious to some that there are three closely related chapters but this is an area of Japan and Japanese studies with profound importance. A colleague once joked that at conferences in the United States conversations on the state of US society always ended in a discussion of race; in the United Kingdom conversations on the state of UK society ended in a discussion of social class; but in Japan conversations on the state of Japanese society ended in a discussion of gender. There is some truth to this statement even though it was said in jest. The chapter on Japanese organized crime, or the yakuza, is also in the Society section but could have easily been part of a discussion of culture or even the Japanese economy. Here it is paired with an important chapter on policing in modern Japan.

The third section, devoted to Medicine and Health Care in Japan, is an encyclopedic overview of the topic which has no parallel in English and is full of useful facts and insights. There are five chapters in this section. The first examines the historical background of Japanese medicine. The second gives an overview of medical education, including its historical roots, key figures in the development of the system and medical-education reforms. The third chapter looks more comprehensively at Japan's health-care system as a whole, specifically the lessons that other countries can learn from its technologically similar but culturally very different society. The fourth chapter provides a background to and discussion of biomedical ethics and related legal issues in Japan. The final chapter covers mental health in Japan.

The fourth section of this *Handbook*, Politics and Foreign Relations, focuses on key areas of Japanese politics. The introductory chapter to the section provides a crucial overview of the development of political studies, both in Japan and elsewhere, to put current research in context. This is followed by three chapters focusing on areas of politics which are most important to understanding Japanese politics today. First there is the role of parties and elections, which has become the dominant focus of scholarship on Japanese politics in the past two decades. Then, there is an overview of the implications of the changes in Japanese politics in recent years for the state of democracy in Japan. Finally, there is an important chapter covers the role of civil society and raises a wide range of issues about the organization of political society in Japan. The chapters on Japan's international relations include two overviews, one on international relations themselves and the other on globalization. There is also one chapter each on Japan's relations with two major countries, the USA and China, which seem set to determine the fate of Japan for the foreseeable future.

The fifth and final section on the Economy contains outstanding contributions on key areas of concern. There is an excellent overview of the significance of the Japanese economic experience and the relevance of Japan to the study of economics. There are useful chapters on both Japanese business and Japanese consumerism as well as chapters on labor, the labor movement in Japan and the issue of foreign workers. A key sector of the economy, Agriculture, has a chapter dedicated to it because it has an influence on Japanese political economy and international economic relations far out of proportion to its role in the economy in terms of simple numbers employed or the value of its output. The final chapter on Energy is also an important one because it is intimately related to Japan's future. In the aftermath of the Fukushima nuclear disaster Japan has been forced to radically reassess its energy supply and needs. Energy supply is essential to the Japanese economy but innovation in energy saving and production could also benefit Japanese industry and the economy.

As can be seen from the chapters summarized above this is an up-to-date and comprehensive *Handbook* of Modern Japanese Studies which will serve the needs of scholars for many years. It has taken considerable time and effort to compile but on behalf of the contributors I am certain you will find this to be a rewarding study.

PART I

Land, History and Culture

Modern Japan in History

Andrew Cobbing

How and when did modern Japan begin? Conventionally, histories of this topic embark with the Meiji Restoration in 1868 and the advent of a modern nation state that more or less endures to this day. Alternatively, they depart from 1853, when the arrival of Commodore Perry's 'Black Ships' signaled the 'Opening' of Japan and, with it, a notional leap forward into something called modernity. To those inhabitants who were not yet aware that their islands needed opening this came as a surprise; something was clearly afoot, but apart from the fear of upheaval who knew what it meant? The Americans and Europeans, however, thought they knew exactly what was going on. Now that commercial treaties – subsequently decried as 'unequal' – had been imposed on the ailing Tokugawa shogunate in 1858, to them it stood to reason that they were standing on the threshold of a new modern chapter in Japan's history.

So began their story and, by extension, ours as well (at least in part). Steeped in the values of the Enlightenment and emboldened by the achievements of the industrial age, their brave new world was driven by an absolute faith in the march of progress (and their own leading role). They had every right to be there, of course, since their civilizing influence would help to lift the Japanese people out of the relatively primitive state they must have endured to date. Central to their mission

was also a desire to rescue Japan from the self-imposed isolation which they had been told kept the population sealed off from the outside world (and Western progress in particular). It took a few rounds of gunboat diplomacy, an arms race, civil war and regime change to carry this argument, but Japan under the new Meiji state would turn out to be a precocious pupil. Complete with railroads and telegraph lines, the rapid progress of the 1870s was hailed by Western observers as near miraculous, their praise reflecting as much on their own excellent tutelage as Japanese efforts to embrace this new modern era.

Essentially, these observers viewed Japan and its history through the prism of their own experience, including a romantic nostalgia for traditional cultures then being swept away by the onslaught of the industrial revolution. To them the Japan they had 'unlocked' recalled a feudal society from the distant past; few readers of Walter Scott's popular *Ivanhoe*, for example, failed to compare the two-sworded samurai they encountered with medieval knights. Robert Louis Stevenson conveyed this outlook vividly in his biographical portrait of Yoshida Shōin, the celebrated Chōshū activist. Describing a trip that Yoshida made overland to Nagasaki in 1853, he told readers how the hero of his tale had 'travelled through the Middle Ages on his journey into the nineteenth century'

(Stevenson, 1882). In his view, then, the Dutch trading post at Nagasaki, for centuries the only point of contact with the West, made it seem like a beachhead of modernity on the shore of medieval Japan.

Before long such historical imagery would transform perspectives on this country's past. In Japan itself the custom for measuring the passage of time had been to count years by the imperial era in which they fell; in recent generations, for example, Meiji, Taishō, Shōwa and now Heisei. Alternatively, eras were labeled according to the seat of power of the regime then in charge, such as Heian, Kamakura, Muromachi or Edo. The notion of a 'middle' age being superseded by a modern era had not really featured before, but the idea took hold and has now come to frame the way that everyone views the history of these islands. So a European model for measuring historical time was projected onto Japan's past; everything up to and including the Edo period came to be known as pre-modern, and modern Japan just described everything after that.

At this stage our story seemed to be literally straightforward. In the event it was less so, partly due to the complex train of events that followed, and also because people today do not necessarily look upon this process in quite the same unequivocal light as Western observers in the nineteenth century. Questions that often surface include: What is the nature of modernity anyway? And what exactly *is* Japan? Historians usually make it their business, for example, to try and identify key turning points, the discontinuities that signal epochal change in the continuous river of time. 1868 (or 1853) may have been singled out early on as the start of Japan's modern age, but as we shall see this outlook has since come under review. Similarly, in the twentieth century, postwar historians immediately saw 1945 as a key turning point signaling the end of Japan's empire (and the start of the Allied Occupation), but even this perspective has now been questioned to some extent. And more recently 1990 has attracted attention as possibly marking the high watermark of Japan's postwar recovery, although this is still so fresh in contemporary memory that historians struggle to pin down the significance of changes that practically feel like yesterday. For want of any more definitive turning points, however, these dates will frame the parameters of the timeframe under discussion here.

EARLY HISTORIES OF MODERN JAPAN

Historical accounts of these islands had been written before, of course, mainly in Japanese. Notable examples were influenced by Chinese dynastic histories, such as the *Kojiki* (Record of Ancient Matters) produced as early as 712, which charted the imperial lineage from its inception in the 'Age of the Gods'. A more recent project was the *Dai Nihon Shi* (Great History of Japan), a multi-volume narrative of the imperial line commissioned in the seventeenth century by Tokugawa Mitsukuni, daimyo of the Mito domain and a nephew of Ieyasu, founder of the new regime. Originally compiled by a Ming refugee who fled China during the Manchu invasions, this was developed by subsequent generations of Mito School scholars until its eventual completion in the Meiji period and publication in 1906. While Marco Polo had mentioned Japan briefly in his *Travels* as a land of gold, the first European historical account was probably *Historia de Japam*, written in Portugese by the Jesuit missionary Luis Frois in the late sixteenth century. Subsequent histories were occasionally produced by European employees of the Dutch East India Company stationed at Dejima in Nagasaki. The most extensive projects in this mould were written by two German doctors, the *History of Japan* by Engelbert Kaempfer (1727) and *Nippon* by Phillip Franz von Siebold (1832–52). Although written a hundred years apart, between them these works contributed much of the knowledge that Europeans and Americans had about Japan in the mid-nineteenth century.

For our purposes, though, we should focus on those histories that describe the new 'modern' Japan that captured the imagination following the onset of Meiji. At first these were typically written by one-time *oyatoi*, the foreign experts employed by the government to help jump-start the process of modernization, especially those who found the experience more rewarding. An early example was *The Mikado's Empire* (Griffis, 1876), and subsequently British engineers also remembered their time there when heralding Japan's rise to great power status, such as in *Advance Japan* (Morris, 1895) and *Dai Nippon: The Britain of the East* (Dyer, 1904).

Appropriately, in this age of nationalism, due weight was often given to a narrative of nationhood. In Japan, meanwhile, as the Meiji oligarchs passed away one by one, committees were formed to compile biographies in the 'Great Man of History' mould, often comprising several volumes each and including letters written over the course of decades. Notable examples include the biographies of Katsura, Yamagata and Matsukata by the prodigious writer Tokutomi Sohō (Duus, 1974).

The commemoration of the Meiji Restoration was underway. Tokutomi, for example, is seen as the founder of the Min'yūsha, a group of historians that had begun to assess the recent changes as the dust settled on the constitutional and institutional reforms of the 1880s. Imagining the past before the onset of Meiji, moreover, he described the preceding Edo period as the *kinsei* ('early modern') era, suggesting that Tokugawa society had not been quite as backward as Western observers assumed. This new generation of Japanese scholars, some with experience of overseas travel themselves, faced the challenge of representing their own history while accommodating the Western concepts that had been flooding in during the Meiji Enlightenment. Although full of pride at the epochal achievements of the Meiji Restoration, already there was a sense of ambivalence and anxiety over Japan's future.

As the half century loomed since the abolition of the domains there also emerged a certain nostalgia for *han* nationalism; Suematsu Kenchō, who had studied at Cambridge, was commissioned by Itō Hirobumi to write a twelve-volume history of the Meiji Restoration based on the letters of the Mōri family and the exploits of Itō's compatriots in his native Chōshū (1920). A history of the Mito domain based on the letters of the Tokugawa house had already been published (Takeguma, 1915), and this would set the tone for similar works. The next year, for example, there appeared a six-volume biography of Nabeshima Naomasa, daimyo of the Saga domain (Kume and Nakano, 1921). And, arguably, only in Japan would you find naval histories for individual domains, as now happened in the case of Saga and Satsuma (Hideshima, 1917; Kōshaku Shimazu-ke Henshūsho, 1928–9).

Nabeshima's biography was initially overseen by Kume Kunitake, whose career as a modern historian had taken off in the 1870s in his role as secretary to Iwakura Tomomi and official chronicler of the Iwakura Embassy's travels (Kume, 1878). His experience deserves special mention here as it exemplifies some of the problems that faced Japanese scholars in the Meiji period. Following his service with Iwakura he rose to the prestigious post of Professor of History at the Imperial University in Tokyo. Committed to a rational approach to history, he drew on the influence of European authorities such as Leopold von Ranke in trying to impose a greater emphasis on empirical evidence. In 1892, however, he was ordered to resign by the Ministry of Education following a storm of protest against his article 'Shintō wa saiten no kozoku' ('Shinto is an ancient custom of heaven worship'), in which he argued that the 'Age of the Gods' inscribed in the *Kojiki* should not be understood too literally (Brownlee, 1997).

Despite such occasional state interference, the culture of modern archiving was well in train, both in government ministries and at regional level. Several decades into their existence already, the local institutions ordained by the Meiji government to replace the old domains now had a history of their own to celebrate, giving rise to the multi-volume *kenshi* and *shishi* compilations of prefectural and municipal histories that, with updates every generation or so, continue to line the shelves of libraries in Japan today. A scientific imprint was also visible in the huge volume of data being systematically collated across Japan. Adherents of another modern school of thought, the Marxists, were now drawing on these records to challenge existing narratives of state building by developing their own overarching interpretations of Japan's historical past.

In the 1920s and 1930s, for example, two competing Marxist factions argued at length over the nature of the Meiji Restoration. With the changes of the mid-nineteenth century now a fading memory, their legacy was increasingly contested given the climate of uncertainty as the brittle Taishō democracy creaked under economic pressures and militarist expansion. On the one hand, contributors to the *Rōnō* (*Workers and Peasants*) journal tried to present Meiji as a bourgeois revolution, placing Japan within a universal framework of historical development and revolution from below. On the other, the Kōzaha (Lecture Faction) viewed Japan as an exceptional case, with an alliance of lower-ranking samurai and wealthy peasantry somehow colluding to impose more of a revolution from above (Sims, 2001). By extension, it could also be seen as a flawed revolution, which might help to explain the unusual path from colonial victim to imperialist power that Japan was following en route to the Asia Pacific War. Already present here was the impression that Japan had somehow deviated from a normative path of modernization, whatever that path may be (Hoston, 1991).

This early Japanese Marxist scholarship had a profound impact on Western perspectives as well. Although not a Marxist himself, George B. Sansom drew on their research to construct a grander conceptual overview of Japanese society and culture (Sansom, 1931, 1958) than anything attained in previous general narrative histories (e.g. Murdoch, 1926). It was E. Herbert Norman, however, who employed a Marxist approach to expose the apparent failings of recent decades in *Japan's Emergence as a Modern State* (1940). Describing social development in terms of class struggle, not only did he emphasize the oppression of the peasantry under a feudal Tokugawa state, he argued that semi-feudal structures had survived into the modern era as well under a system of still ongoing 'absolutism'. A controversial figure also in his career in the Canadian diplomatic service, Norman was viewed with suspicion by the US Occupation authorities for his sympathetic treatment of the Japanese Communist Party. His apparent suicide in 1957, when he jumped off an eight-story building in Cairo, is still shrouded in mystery amid claims that it was the work of a CIA conspiracy (Bowen, 1986).

POSTWAR SCHOLARSHIP

The end of the Asia Pacific War in 1945 framed the thoughts of the next generation. Taking stock of the collapse of Japan's colonial adventure, historians tried to work out what had gone so wrong. Whether Japanese commentators reflecting on their country's errors, or Western observers justifying those occupation reforms designed to correct them, a recurring theme was the apparently deviant route that Japan had taken since encountering modernity. Such an outlook was not confined to historians. In her influential *The Chrysanthemum and the Sword* (1946), for example, Ruth Benedict, an American anthropologist hired by the US Government shortly before the onset of the Allied Occupation, highlighted cultural differences to focus on the Japanese national character by isolating particular patterns of behavior. Similarly, Japan's supposedly distinctive history of 'isolationism' was subjected to scrutiny (Voss, 1945). Addressing a Japanese audience, meanwhile, philosopher Watsuji Tetsurō (1950) also lamented the so-called *sakoku* policy of self-imposed isolation which he argued had created the environment for the 'tragedy of Japan'.

During the 1950s critics of E. H. Norman's vision of flawed modernization responded by drawing on 'modernization theory', a body of thought developed by Western (mainly American) social scientists in an effort to build stable capitalist systems in the postwar world. With US Ambassador Edwin O. Reischauer in their ranks, they looked for signs that Japan could yet become more like a liberal democracy by highlighting the achievements of the Meiji state and precursors of modernization under Tokugawa rule. Notable contributions to this field included *Tanuma Okitsugu* (Hall, 1955), *The Agrarian Roots of Modern Japan* (Smith, 1965), *Education in Tokugawa Japan* (Dore, 1965), *Toward Restoration* (Harootunian, 1970) and *Treasures Among Men* (Bolitho, 1974). From this perspective it was possible to view the 1930s as more of an aberration than the norm, within a wider ongoing process of development (Hall, 1965a). Modernization theory would subsequently come under fire during the 1970s from various quarters, including the New Left, for what was increasingly seen as its rose-tinted vision of a linear path toward a brighter future. The framework of class conflict expounded by Norman, meanwhile, also continued to inform subsequent works, such as Thomas Huber's *The*

Revolutionary Origins of Modern Japan (1981). Even so, the influence of modernization theory is still reflected in studies that chart wider developments spanning the early to mid-twentieth century (Garon, 1994).

More than any other postwar Japanese scholar, however, it was the political scientist Maruyama Masao who did most to raise awareness of the structural problems that had beset the government during the 'Dark Tunnel' of recent decades. Faced with the challenge of recovery, there was now a vigorous debate on the issue of Japanese identity, and how, with the wartime regime dismantled, this might be reconfigured in the new environment. In Maruyama's view, the aim was to foster a sense of civic national consciousness *(kokumin shugi)*. On the other hand, members of the Japanese Historical Science Association *(Rekiken)* championed an ethnic national consciousness *(minzoku shugi)*, to some extent influenced by Benedict's *The Chrysanthemum and the Sword*, which was now available in Japanese translation.

The emergence of Japanese national consciousness has, of course, been traced back to the growing interest in classical literature during the eighteenth century by Motoori Norinaga and other influential scholars of *kokugaku*, or 'national studies', to use a now contested translation. For example, Burns (2004) argues that any awareness of a Japanese nation was still so vague during Motoori's time that it would be more appropriate to render *kokugaku* as 'study of our country'. It was more the coining of the term *kokutai* (national polity) by Aizawa Seishisai in the nineteenth century that prefigured the conceptualization of the Meiji state as an extended family under the paternal authority of the emperor. The state education system in place by the onset of the twentieth century – in part enabled by the communications revolution of the modern era – also lent itself to the 'emperor worship' that would go on to stoke the fanaticism associated with militant groups intent on protecting and projecting Japan's power in Asia. It was a narrative that shone through in English postwar studies on the subject such as *Nationalism in Japan* (Brown, 1955). Nationalist narratives have continued to attract interest in recent years as well, given the changing shape of this and other nation states in the twentieth century (Doak, 1997, 1998).

In the postwar period the most conspicuous theme in this vein was the rising prominence of *nihonjinron* discourse on the nature of Japanese identity. Following the symbolic achievements of economic recovery and then Tokyo hosting the 1964 Olympic Games, commentators began to look beyond the disastrous experience of the Asia Pacific War and reflect on more positive aspects of Japan's development as a modern state. In the late 1960s, for example, this agenda was apparent in popular historian Shiba Ryōtarō's serialized account on the background and course of the Russo-Japanese War, now available in English translation (Shiba, 2013). With the country's emergence as an industrial superpower by the 1980s, *nihonjinron* discourse also became a highly topical theme as an explanation of the economic miracle. Once again there was a focus on Japanese exceptionalism and claims to a unique cultural heritage fundamentally different from that experienced elsewhere. Critics were quick to respond to the often emotive rhetoric employed, however, describing it as more of a political tool for enforcing social conformity (Befu, 1984), or dismissing it outright as a 'myth of homogeneity' (Dale, 1986).

To return to the immediate postwar world, one burning question was whether or not this all meant that the government of Japan in the 1930s had become a fascist regime. It certainly exhibited some features reminiscent of Mussolini's Italy and Nazi Germany, quite apart from the Axis pact that united them. The comparison often featured in Japanese commentaries, notably Maruyama's article on 'The Logic and Psychology of Ultranationalism' (1946), which was subsequently translated into English (Morris, 1963). In response, others have warned against applying such a Western construct in an East Asian context, pointing out that Japan's government never really developed the more revolutionary features that were such hallmarks of fascist regimes in Europe (Large, 2009: 167–8). Traits of racism did exist in pre-war Japan, though, notably in the case of Tanabe Hajime, a prominent member of the Kyoto School of Philosophy, who attempted to explain Japanese racial superiority through his theory on the 'Logic of Species'. A loosely organized group that drew on Western philosophical teachings in an East Asian cultural context, this organization has come under scrutiny from claims that its 'fascistic' outlook was in effect complicit with the militarist state (Harootunian, 2000a; 2000b). In their defense, others have pointed out that these scholars did not actually support the war effort and tried to mobilize intellectual resistance to Tōjō's government (Parkes, 2011). Their opposition to Western imperialism, moreover, did not in itself imply support for the reactionary politics of their government (Williams, 2004). And over and above any ideological persuasion, the school's founder Nishida Kitarō and his disciples seem to have still treasured the pursuit of academic rigor throughout (Goto-Jones, 2005).

Framing the colonial adventure more broadly, the theme of Japanese imperialism also received close attention in the postwar period (e.g. Ward, 1968). Some overviews trace Japan's intervention in East Asia back to 1895 and the acquisition of Taiwan after the First Sino-Japanese War (Beasley, 1987; Myers and Peattie, 1987; Duus et al., 1989; 1996). Other studies with a focus on expansionism in Korea go back as far as the early Meiji period (e.g. Conroy, 1960; Calman, 1992; Duus, 1998). Given the volatile international climate in the region at the time, it is not hard to identify a self-fulfilling 'long fuse' of Japanese expansionism from the onset of the modern state. At what point this became a systematic agenda, however, is far from clear, and arguably it is not until the collapse of the Taishō democracy or even beyond that the road to war became irreversible (Iriye, 1997).

Recently, there has also been growing interest in justifications of empire, whether in the shape of a 'civilizing mission' in Taiwan or Korea, or the growth of pan-Asianist thought which sought to place Japan at the head of a wider campaign to roll back the tide of Western imperialism. To some extent this was itself a by-product of the modern outlook on historical progress introduced by the Western intrusion in East Asia in the nineteenth century. For example, the Meiji intellectual Fukuzawa Yukichi was influenced by political economists such as Adam Smith and Henry Thomas Buckle when he articulated his theory on the stages of civilization, strategically placing Japan still behind the West but ahead of her continental neighbors (Craig, 2008). Fukuzawa's call in 1885 for Japan to 'leave Asia' (*datsu-A ron*) even helped to position the Meiji state as a quasi-Western power by the turn of the century (Lu, 1996). Once faced by direct competition with those same powers – first Russia then the USA – it was a short mental leap to appeal to Japan's continental neighbors for a show of regional solidarity, while still retaining this newly configured superiority complex (Takeuchi, 1993). And now that the Cold War divisions which fractured dialogue in East Asia for so much of the twentieth century have begun to subside, further studies are emerging on the pan-Asianist outlook of Japanese politicians and intellectuals, from ultranationalist groups to cultural nationalists like Okakura Tenshin (e.g. Saaler and Koschmann, 2006).

In the immediate aftermath of war, with the Tokyo Military Tribunal and execution of seven defendants still fresh in the memory, there was also the vexed question of war guilt. Maruyama described the entire pre-war government structure as a 'system of irresponsibility'. The recent publication of the complete proceedings of the tribunal has given this research new impetus (Pritchard, 1998–2005). In particular, the emperor's own agency in leading Japan into war received fresh attention following his death in 1989, in some cases receiving sympathetic treatment (Large, 1992), while others claim he was sufficiently aware of the situation to shoulder some responsibility

(Bix, 2000). The issue of the Tokyo trials has to some extent been clouded not just by the exoneration of the commander-in-chief of the Imperial Army, but by the lack of US contrition over the atomic bombings of Hiroshima and Nagasaki, and the curious failure to prosecute leaders of Unit 731 for laboratory experiments on human subjects in Manchuria (Maga, 2001).

In recent years, Japan's memories of its wartime past more generally have become the subject of further controversy, drawing comparisons with the experience in Germany (Buruma, 1994), and prompting descriptions ranging from 'amnesia or concealment' (Hicks, 1997b) to the notion of 'memory rifts' (Seaton, 2007). At the heart of this debate has been the long-running textbook controversy of the late twentieth century in which Ienaga Saburō campaigned to ensure that schoolchildren are confronted with their country's wartime legacy (Ienaga, 1993/94). While Ienaga's activities were reaching the attention of the English-reading world in *The Pacific War* (1978), journalist Honda Katsuichi had been traveling through China and investigating Japanese wartime atrocities, notably *The Nanjing Massacre* (Honda, 1999). It was at the turn of the millennium that this issue became the subject of notoriety following the publication of Iris Chang's polemical *The Rape of Nanking* (1997), prompting some qualification as the accuracy of some her sources were questioned in *The Nanjing Massacre in History and Historiography* (Fogel, 2000).

Meanwhile, from 1982 onwards the debate over textbooks became an issue of growing public interest (Rose, 1999). A key theme in this long-running saga has been the efforts of neo-nationalist groups, exemplified by the Liberal School of History, to repackage the presentation of Japan's recent past (Kersten, 1999). The debate has increasingly drawn in museum curators as well, in the course of preparing exhibitions designed to commemorate war events, notably in the case of the Smithsonian Institute's controversial plans to exhibit the Enola Gay airplane in 1995 (Jeans, 2005).

Moving on from memories of wartime itself, later in the twentieth century the role of the USA in the postwar Occupation also became the subject of interest as historians tried to place Japan's rehabilitation in context. Former ambassador Edwin O. Reischauer was a prominent advocate of US policy in, for example, *Japan: Story of a Nation* (1970). Other apologists included Robert Ward (1968) and later T. A. Bisson (1989), although from the 1960s revisionist scholars were already beginning to criticize the Occupation regime. Questions were asked, for example, about the rationale for deploying nuclear weapons in the first place in *Atomic Diplomacy* (Alperovitz, 1965), and accusations were made about the so-called 'Reverse Course'

in which Occupation authorities allegedly tailored their agenda to make Japan what MacArthur described as a 'bastion of democracy'. Three main stances emerged in this debate: the conservatives, progressives and the New Left (Schonberger, 1989). More recently both Japanese and Western scholarship has been synthesized to focus more on the human experience and the collaborative links forged between the occupying forces and Japanese government authorities (Dower, 2000).

By the mid 1970s, however, an increasingly dominant theme was not so much the disaster of defeat, but the success of the economic miracle. The role of MITI in shaping this process, for example, was the subject of considerable interest (Johnson, 1982). And despite the immediate impact of the oil shocks there was even a work on *Japan as Number One* (Vogel, 1979). At the same time, many of these studies tended to focus on the supply side of the Japanese economy with the burgeoning growth of Japanese industry and its role in setting the pace in global export markets. Only more recently has attention shifted to the role of the Japanese consumer in fostering growth (Bailey, 1996). Drawing also on research into 'the legacy of material culture in premodern Japan' (Hanley, 1997), this has prompted efforts to explore an 'alternative perspective on Japanese economic history' (Francks, 2009), and the role of 'the Japanese consumer in history' more broadly (Hunter, 2012).

Besides Japan's postwar economic growth itself, attention has also turned to some of the more conspicuous attending features, among them the effects of rapid urbanization and the problems surrounding industrial pollution that emerged during the 1960s. Urban growth was hardly a new phenomenon – the disparity between town and country had been a feature of modernization since the Meiji period – but the rapid changes and accompanying social dislocation became a key theme in the postwar era, as evoked in Ozu Yasujirō's 1952 film *Tokyo Story*. Just as with recent studies on consumerism, there has been some interest in urbanization during the early modern period as well, especially the prodigious growth and cosmopolitan culture of Edo, Osaka and Kyoto, collectively the 'Three Great Cities' *(san-daitoshi)* of Tokugawa Japan. After all, Edo emerged to become the largest city in the world with a population of over one million by the turn of the eighteenth century (McClain et al., 1994), and a number of works have traced the subsequent development of Tokyo (e.g. Seidensticker, 1991; Richie, 1999), and recently modern Osaka as well (Hanes, 2002). Broader historical overviews on urban Japan are also now charting the growth of cities into the twenty-first century (Sorensen, 2002).

Interest in environmental history was to some extent a response to the pollution disasters of the 1960s, the most notorious case being the mercury poisoning at Minamata (George, 2001). Again harking back to earlier industrial growth in the Meiji period, such incidents were nothing new, given the scale of the environmental disaster at the Ashio copper mine (Notehelfer, 1975). More broadly, Conrad Totman developed an environmental approach to looking at Japan's past, initially through the perspective of forestry (1989), but more recently in an overarching survey of the archipelago's history structured according to land use and ecology (2000). In a similar vein with a focus on the Meiji period, recent studies also explore the manner in which nature has been viewed in the modern era (Thomas, 2001) and the role of animals in Japan's history (Plugfelder and Walker, 2005).

SOME POSTMODERN REFLECTIONS

In the last decades of the twentieth century the influence of postmodernist ideas on the formulation of power and knowledge began to shape perspectives on the past in new ways, and our historical outlook on modern Japan was no exception. Among those to draw on these influences were scholars already mentioned in the previous section, but who feature there inasmuch as their work mainly addresses historical events of the pre- and postwar era. While an empirical approach to the modern science of studying the past had for long dominated the field, fresh questions were now being raised over agency in the production of historical knowledge. Through a combination of systematic administration, control of archives and propaganda, for example, politicians and other state officials may have shaped or distorted representations of their country's past. A more deconstructive approach to historical texts, therefore, might expose alternative angles of inquiry that could challenge some of the familiar discourses in Japan's modern development. Even such apparently timeless structures as the nation state itself might be reconsidered. The impact this had was to blur some of the boundaries that had previously formed the basis of historical narratives on modern Japan. New light was shed also on some of the key turning points that, in the past, had been considered as almost set in stone. It would transform the subject of modern Japan itself into more contested, fluid territory, with further scope for interpretative exploration.

Take, for example, the received wisdom that our story of modern Japan starts in 1868 (or 1853). Viewed collectively, much of the historical

research from the last few decades seems to point not so much to an abrupt discontinuity as Japan jumps into the modern era, but to more of a continuous, even smooth, transition. Already we have come across features identified in pre-Meiji times that, by most measures of development, have a distinctly modern tone, among them rapid urbanization, the world's largest city and a vibrant consumer society. Advocates of modernization theory also highlighted, for example, the increasing specialization in cash crops (Smith, 1965) and a relatively high literacy rate (Dore, 1965). More recently other remarkable features of Tokugawa society have emerged, such as its highly regulated transport network and thriving tourist industry (Vaporis, 1995).

All of this informs the way we interpret the Meiji period that followed. What appeared at the time to be miraculous progress may, in hindsight, appear less surprising, given that Japanese society was more dynamic than the static feudal world many Western observers imagined and, in some respects, was already primed for major change. At the same time, despite the outward appearance of social reforms during the Meiji period, many cultural features more reminiscent of the bygone Tokugawa world would still be present at the end of the nineteenth century (Howell, 2005) and in some cases persisted through much of the twentieth century and beyond.

As Carol Gluck noted in 'The People in History' (1978), moreover, in the 1960s influential Japanese scholars such as Irokawa Daikichi and Kano Masanao broke with Marxism and modernization theory to develop a more populist 'view from below'. Themes such as people's history and this sense of a smoother transition from late Tokugawa through Meiji would subsequently feature prominently in volume 5 of the *Cambridge History of Japan,* a landmark collection of essays tracing historical developments in the nineteenth century (Jansen, 1989). As one review suggests, it helps to understand events not so much 'from above' through the state-centered ruling elites, but rather by tapping into voices in the wider population through an emphasis on 'history from below' (Notehelfer, 1990). This focus on people's history has become a recurring theme in recent research, including a four-volume collection on Meiji Japan (Kornicki, 1998). In relation to the overthrow of the Tokugawa state, for example, it offers fresh insight on *eejanaika* riots, the apparently spontaneous street parties that contributed to crippling the Tokugawa economy in central Honshu in the summer of 1867 (Wilson, 1992).

The emergence of people's history has also introduced a certain skepticism over structures that hitherto occupied central places in the history of modern Japan. A number of studies, for example, have begun to chip away at the representations of nation, state and culture as unassailable edifices handed down since time immemorial. Drawing on seminal works such as *Imagined Communities* (Anderson, 1983), Gluck (1985) pointed out that the state ideology developed in the late Meiji period and imposed on the population had a profound influence in shaping Japan's modern history. Arguably, therefore, it was the 1890s rather than any date in the mid-nineteenth century that really signaled the onset of a modern society. After all, this was the stage when, through the combined influence of a national education system, the escalating scale of industrialization and the Meiji press (Huffman, 1997), the population at large increasingly shared a communal experience of state coercion and control.

Further studies on reinventing traditions and the shaping of cultural constructs have increasingly undermined the previous monolithic representations of Japan's history and culture (Morris-Suzuki, 1998; Vlastos, 1998). Such was the degree of creative state planning this apparently entailed that it has even been described as *Inventing Japan* (Buruma, 2003). And even such time-honored traditions as Bushidō (Friday, 1994) and the tea ceremony (Cross, 2009) have, on closer scrutiny, been identified as not just a legacy of ancient practices but also the product of some imaginative thinking in the modern era. Needless to say, these and other canons of quintessentially Japanese cultural tradition continue to find expression in terms of the 'soft power' essential to projecting international influence. They certainly reach a global audience, helped in no small measure by Hollywood productions like *The Last Samurai*, but in terms of historical perspectives this realm of traditional cultures is now very much contested ground.

Moving on to key events of the twentieth century, the clearest turning point would have to be 1945, marking the end of the wartime regime and, with the onset of the Allied Occupation, the departure point for postwar Japan. While in many respects this does represent a useful divide, at the same time some studies on twentieth-century Japan have begun to place more emphasis on strands of continuity between the pre- and postwar worlds (Duus, 1988; Large, 1998). Again, such trans-war perspectives can help to explain some of the developments that followed, among them patterns of consumer culture (Gordon, 2007) and the economic miracle of postwar Japan (Garon & Maclachlan, 2006).

Finally, studies on contemporary history have now advanced so far into the world of living memory that they compete for space, as ever, with fields like politics and economics (even if methodology sets them apart). As Japan's experience since 1945 has often been characterized as an era of postwar

recovery, the question then arises, when, if at all, does that era end? It takes only a cursory look at the 'lost decade' of the 1990s and the ongoing economic gloom that has followed to suggest that this recovery is now a thing of the past. Such a shift, however, was not yet fully apparent when Gordon (1993) was developing his influential *Postwar Japan as History*. Now into the twenty-first century there are perhaps signs that some 'quiet transformation' may be underway (Kingston, 2004), and historical perspectives on the post-industrial, post-bubble era are beginning to emerge on what can arguably be thought of as a postmodern Japan (George and Gerteis, 2012).

Beyond these immediate questions of identifying key events, there is also a growing body of research that interrogates deep-seated issues in Japanese history more broadly. The focus of such studies is not necessarily confined to the modern era as such, but they merit inclusion here as they go to the heart of what we understand the history of modern Japan, and Japan itself, to be. In many respects, these efforts to problematize the very concept of 'Japan' have led to some of the most interesting developments in postwar historical work. A survey of modern Japan, therefore, requires some detail on these themes, among them cultural homogeneity and diversity, perspectives to be found at subnational levels and interpretations of Japanese identity. Looking outwards beyond the archipelago as well, we need to consider the increasingly prevalent research on transnational and transcultural networks. Also worth mentioning in passing is the influence of post-colonial studies in relation to Japan. First, however, we should address the recurring theme of 'isolationism' and the still enduring belief that Japan's foreign relations in the past amounted to a 'closed country' policy known as *sakoku*. It is a theme essential to framing all the other issues that follow since, for so much of the last century, to a large extent the legacy of this apparently self-imposed isolation shaped our outlook on modern Japan.

REVISITING *SAKOKU*: THE OPEN/CLOSED PARADIGM

In the minds of the early Western observers we met in the introduction Japan in the mid nineteenth century was unquestionably 'closed'. Everything they had ever read about this part of the world reinforced their understanding that Commodore Perry and others were engaged in the business of 'opening' Japan. It was not just this first generation of Western pioneers who subscribed to this outlook: Meiji officials were also apt to invoke the memory of *sakoku* policy as a convenient stick with which to beat the Tokugawa regime they had replaced. As early as 1868 the Charter Oath tried to distance the new regime from 'evil practices of the past', and even if this vague gesture pointed more specifically to the recent campaign of *jōi* (expel the barbarian), it could also be taken as a swipe at Tokugawa foreign policy more generally.

The cumulative effect was to introduce 'the idea of an open/closed rhythm to Japanese history' (Massarella, 1996; 135). Not only did it determine views of the past, but the concept informed perspectives on the new modern Japan as well. In the early twentieth century, for example, scholars tried to justify the country's colonial expansion in East Asia by accusing *sakoku* of retarding what they saw as Japan's natural growth. The memory of a 'closed' mentality borne of a culture of isolation would also resurface sporadically whenever traces of an insular outlook appeared. The most conspicuous case was in the build-up to war in the 1930s when, diplomatically isolated, Japanese government officials turned their backs on Western culture, decrying its influence as symptomatic of the West's imperialist hegemony in East Asia. True to form, critics might argue, Japan had reverted to type and a *sakoku* reflex response cultivated over centuries. Through this lens, moreover, the more 'open' engagement with the West since the Meiji period could seem like a temporary blip, even an aberration rather than the norm. In this context it was hardly surprising that General Macarthur should liken himself to Commodore Perry in some ways, seeing his mission as an opportunity for the second 'opening' of Japan. And in the reflective postwar years some Japanese commentators also railed against the destructive shackles of their 'closed' cultural heritage, among them, as we have seen, Watsuji Tetsurō (1950) when he lamented 'the tragedy of Japan'.

Not only did this open/closed paradigm set the tone for much of the postwar scholarship on modern Japan, but it has resurfaced more recently in the context of flashpoints in the late twentieth century. During the 1980s, for example, when anger erupted over the restrictive trading practices employed by this new economic superpower, the *keiretsu* network of domestic suppliers that locked foreign firms out of the Japanese market were slated as a new *sakoku*. A similar argument has been applied to Japanese universities, whose reputation for excluding foreign academics has even been labeled 'academic apartheid' and described as an 'intellectual closed shop' (Hall, 1997). Still today, accusations of an embedded 'closed' mentality are never far from view when discussing current affairs, for example in relation to immigration policy in the wake of the North Korean refugee crisis.

What such perspectives often overlook is the fact that *sakoku* is not originally a Japanese idea at all, but a European construct first articulated by Engelbert Kaempfer in Appendix VI of his *History of Japan* (1727). In this polemical essay he claimed it was 'breaking through the laws of nature' for 'the Japanese Empire, to keep [the land] shut up, as it now is, and not to suffer its inhabitants to have any Commerce with foreign nations, either at home or abroad'. Not until 1801, however, was the essay translated into Japanese by a Nagasaki interpreter called Shizuki Tadao who, as Itazawa Takeo (1940) first pointed out, in the process coined this new term by giving it the title of *sakoku-ron*. And it was not until the 1850s that the word *sakoku* appeared in government documents.

Despite its tenuous place in the Tokugawa record, for more than thirty years after the Asia Pacific War *sakoku* was still very much at the heart of postwar historians' perspectives on Japan's foreign relations. From the 1960s onward, though, new avenues of research began to suggest a more nuanced outlook. Iwao Seiichi (1963; 1976), for example, explored the Nihon-machi (Japantown) settlements in South East Asia that lasted well into the seventeenth century, in the process questioning the view that the principle of Tokugawa law was to exclude foreigners totally. Robert Sakai (1964) highlighted the indirect trade orchestrated through the Ryukyu kingdom which, although, nominally independent, was to some extent controlled by the Satsuma domain while still maintaining its tributary relations with China.

It was in the late 1970s, however, that a series of articles challenged the long-accepted paradigm, notably 'Reopening the Question of Sakoku' (Toby, 1977). After all, Kaempfer's information had been based on his own experience in the 1690s, spent mostly confined to the man-made island of Dejima, which hardly afforded him a broad overview of Tokugawa foreign policy. Pointing out that *sakoku* did not even feature in Japanese officials' vocabulary for much of the period, Toby argued that if they did conceptualize the foreign policy prescribed by Iemitsu's seclusion edicts in the 1630s it would be seen instead in such terms as *kaikin* (maritime prohibition). The practice of regulating overseas trade by confining ships to designated enclaves, moreover, was hardly unusual in the context of East Asian international relations. The Qing regime had much the same approach with the Canton System that lasted up to the First Opium War. Similarly, in a singular exception to the ruling that no Japanese were allowed overseas, the Joseon kingdom in Korea confined merchants from the Tsushima domain to the Waegwan (*wakan*), the 'Japan House' in Busan (Lewis, 2003). In a former age, Japan had also operated a comparable system during the Heian period. And even in Europe before free trade became the norm the mercantilist policies of some states featured trading restrictions that could throw doubt on Kaempfer's perception of Japan's case as so unusual that it transgressed the laws of nature.

Around the same time there were also challenges to the prevailing assumption that Nagasaki had been Japan's sole window on the outside world. It was argued, for example, that at one stage the volume of silver exported to Korea from Tsushima – payment for luxury goods like ginseng – was far in excess of the outflow through Nagasaki and might be thought of as the 'Silver Road' (Tashiro and Videen, 1982). Another colorful expression used to describe Tokugawa seclusion policy was to portray the drive to channel energies inward to a thorough exercise in 'house-painting', in contrast to the slapdash approach of European colonial expansion (Kato, 1981). Intriguingly, this also drew comparison between Japan's experience in the seventeenth century and the programs of decolonization that took hold some three centuries later in twentieth-century Europe.

Rather than being viewed as isolated and on the periphery of European trading networks, moreover, Toby (1984) contended that the Tokugawa regime had carved out its own niche at the heart of a new 'Japan-centric' international network, modeled on but designed to work separately from the traditional tribute system centered on China. This would help to explain the carefully choreographed stream of high-ranking foreign guests from Korea, Ryukyu and Holland who, much like the processions of daimyo lords, journeyed to Edo to pay homage, or at least their respects, to the shogun. Tokugawa suspicions of a Christian threat to their temporal authority may have resulted in the expulsion of the Catholic Spanish and Portuguese, but, as Jansen points out, 'it is Western ethnocentrism to think that a country that has chosen to cut itself off from Westerners has cut itself off from the world' (2000: 87).

No longer so tenable either is the notion that a single policy could really describe Japan's foreign relations for a period of over two hundred years, as there are signs that this ebbed and flowed from one generation to the next. Besides the 'Silver Road' to Korea, for example, the volume of trade with China also showed a significant increase some decades after the imposition of the seclusion edicts. With civil war on the continent now over, the influx of Chinese traders to Nagasaki in the 1680s was on such a scale that a new enclave called the Tōjin yashiki was built with space for around 5,000 people (Jansen, 2000). Another example sometimes mentioned is the relatively courteous treatment accorded to three Russian ships that appeared off the Japanese coast in 1739. So if there ever was a policy of *sakoku* in the sense that Europeans understood Kaempfer's (or Shizuki's) concept,

then probably this only really took effect in the 1790s in response to Russian encroachment in the north (Wakabayashi, 1986). It was this approach that would frame the notorious directive of 1825 – described variously as 'don't think twice' or 'shoot on sight' – that underlined the determination of late Tokugawa officials to uphold what they now, somewhat creatively, called 'ancestral law'.

On the other hand, in search of balance, it has been pointed out that the seclusion decrees were not just illusory and did have a measurable impact on trade. After all, there was a significant dip in the volume of shipping in the immediate aftermath of the seclusion edicts, and trading levels in the early decades of the seventeenth century still look remarkable by comparison with the quieter traffic of, say, the eighteenth century (Batten, 2006). Furthermore, the system was not just about trade levels and gateways like Satsuma, Tsushima and Matsumae, but served also as a demonstration of state control, which may partly explain why the apparent capitulation in the 1850s had such a disastrous effect on Tokugawa legitimacy (Cullen, 2003). Even so, Japanese foreign relations now look a lot more complex than originally imagined by early European observers. As Jansen (2000; 64) neatly summed up, 'the famous decrees that closed the country were more of a bamboo blind than a Berlin wall'. The latest research in this field continues to erode Kaempfer's model by suggesting an evolutionary rather than revolutionary process, and situating Tokugawa foreign relations in a global context (Hellyer, 2009).

Nevertheless, the idea of *sakoku* continues to hold a powerful grip on the popular imagination. Perhaps its resilience is due to a certain romance at the thought of a hermetically sealed society locked away from the outside world. Alternatively, the concept may have survived due to the habit among historians of trying to divide the past into distinct periods since it so 'neatly delineates the line between Japan's early modern and modern worlds' (Walker, 2012: 205). Either way, in popular histories at least, *sakoku* continues to define Japan's past before its 'opening' to the modernizing influence of the West in the nineteenth century. And this in spite of the fact that, as we have seen, in some respects the seeds of Japan's modern growth had already been sown.

A HOMOGENEOUS OR DIVERSE CULTURE?

A theme closely linked to the enduring perception of Japan's 'isolationist' past is a long-standing and still prevalent conception of the islands' inhabitants as an unusually homogeneous society.

Inextricably bound up with questions of Japanese identity, and by extension *nihonjinron* discourse, this idea is manifest in various guises too numerous to pursue in detail here, although striking examples from the early twentieth century include the invocation of Yamato racial purity and the sense of discipline that was instilled through state education under the imperial system.

The vision of a homogenous society has also been central to some historical representations of modern Japan, particularly those with an emphasis on the growth and development of the state. After all, the impact of mass communications and the education system are key themes in the Japanese people's experience of modernity since the mid-Meiji period. In the late twentieth century, however, the works of Amino Yoshihiko began to undermine this assumption, even though his field of inquiry was often confined mainly to medieval and sometimes early modern history. Amino argued that Japanese society was actually far more heterogeneous than previously assumed, and, although few of his works were translated into Western languages at the time, a collection of his writings has recently appeared in English (Amino, 2012).

At the risk of encroaching on the field of sociology, in postwar Japan another recurring theme of population surveys was a tendency for the vast majority of people to categorize themselves as middle class. Historical reasons sometimes cited for this include their collective rural heritage spent working the fields in times past. Under Tokugawa rule, for example, more than 80 per cent of the population was affiliated to the status group of *nōmin* (peasants).

This invites a reading of the past that suggests a romantic vision of rural communities standing ankle-deep together in flooded paddy fields planting rice. No doubt this did occur – planting rice is incredibly labor-intensive – but Amino contended that there was actually far greater occupational diversity in pre-modern Japan. Even if they were classified as *nomin,* he pointed out, as many as half of these peasants (or farmers) did not spend their working lives in the fields. And even those that did would spend much of their time growing crops other than rice, such as wheat, millet or sweet potato; after all, due to rapid urban growth in the seventeenth century, most of the rice was supplied to the towns anyway, while in country villages it might appear on the table only once a month. In the rice belts, moreover, many *nōmin* might not be in the fields at all, but engaged instead in, for example, breweries, water mills, or manning river ferries. In coastal villages, of course, they would be just as likely to spend their time fishing, making nets, producing salt, manning trade vessels or even whaling. In mountain areas, meanwhile, large numbers were engaged in logging, mining and producing ceramic ware.

In short, the notion of a homogeneous Japanese society borne of a common heritage of life experiences no longer seems so convincing. Besides occupational diversity, a growing tendency to err on the side of caution when describing cultural features specific to Japan has also challenged some familiar narratives of modern history. The notion of class, for example, is itself a European construct, so instead the idea of 'status groups' is increasingly used in the context of Tokugawa Japan, allowing historians to view social relations in terms of mutual obligation – what John Whitney Hall (1965b) described as a 'container society' – rather than the traditional Marxist approach of class oppression (White, 1995). In this perspective the widespread peasant protests in the Edo period, therefore, do not necessarily signify a growing sense of class conflict (Vlastos, 1986). More detailed studies of rural spatial organization also suggest that village representatives had a far greater say in controlling their own communities than has often been assumed (Ooms, 1996).

The influence of postmodernism, moreover, has encouraged researchers to look beyond the hegemonic discourse of state-centered narratives of history and search for marginalized voices that previously may have been suppressed or considered peripheral by the ruling elites. One example is a focus on peasant narratives (Walthall, 1991). This trend has also brought into closer view a host of minorities, among them 'peasants, rebels, women, and outcastes' (Hane, 1982). Collectively, their experiences can serve to demystify any 'illusion of homogeneity' in Japanese society (Weiner, 1997). A number of studies, for example, have embarked on the task of reconceptualizing women's place in Japan's history (Bernstein, 1991). In some cases these explore case studies of family histories over several generations (e.g. Bernstein, 2005; Yamakawa, 2001). Accompanied by developments in gender studies more broadly (Lebra, 2007), other research explores the boundaries of social roles, for example by addressing the topic of women and class (Tonomura et al., 1999) or the emergence of the 'New Woman' in interwar Japan (Sato, 2003).

Excavating histories of these social minorities brings research into contested territory, so there is naturally some crossover here with political science, for example in the case of research on Japan's Burakumin communities (e.g. Neary, 1989). English studies on this issue date to before the Pacific War (Ninomiya, 1933), but it was in the 1960s that they gained prominence (DeVos and Wagatsuma, 1967), together with work on the Korean minority in Japan (Mitchell, 1967) and the Ainu communities in Hokkaido (Hilger, 1967).

More recently, as interest in multiculturalism grew during the 1990s, further studies appeared on the Burakumin (Kariya, 1995), Koreans (Hicks, 1997a) and the Ainu (Kayano, 1994; Howell, 1994). In an interesting departure, there is also now research on how Burakumin emigré communities fared after crossing the Pacific Ocean to America (Geiger, 2011). The Ainu experience, meanwhile, has been treated from various angles, in one case viewed within a framework of resistance (Siddle, 1996), in another with more of a focus on the environmental impact of Japanese northward expansion (Walker, 2001).

Rather than being treated separately, the experiences of these minorities have also started appearing together in collections exploring concepts such as *Diversity in Japanese Culture* (Maher and Macdonald, 1995), or *Multicultural Japan* (Denoon et al., 1996). Now in this post-industrial age with the effects of globalization everywhere, Japan's demographic complexion is clearly more varied than the state acknowledged for much of the twentieth century. Besides the Korean labor force that was imported in wartime as part of the colonial experiment, in the last decades of the twentieth century several new waves of foreign workers arrived, ranging from Sri Lankan wives destined to help their husbands fight rural depopulation to graduates from America and Europe on the JET Program, Iranian construction workers and *nikkei* Brazilians of Japanese heritage. All of these groups have contributed to the increasingly rich tapestry that has been described as *Multiethnic Japan* (Lie, 2001).

Similarly, following on a pioneering postwar study by George Kerr (1958), some research explores the historical experience of the Ryukyu Islands and the complex nature of their inhabitants' relations with the 'mainland' (e.g. Smits, 1991; Beillevaire, 2000, 2002). Whether addressing Hokkaido or Okinawa, moreover, these reinterpretations of communities based in notionally 'outlying' islands begin to encroach on questions of Japan's own identity by undermining the state's claims to sovereignty encompassing the entire archipelago stretching from near Taiwan to close to Kamchatka. Historically, this is untenable, for as Batten (2006) shows in *To the Ends of Japan,* these national borders are human constructs that have been extended since ancient times in accordance with state expansion, subjugating various populations in the process. In this context, a thought-provoking anthropological study, *The Ruins of Identity,* discusses evidence of migrations and agricultural colonization before going on to examine the cultural construction of Japanese ethnicity (Hudson 1999). The cumulative effect of such research is to erode the belief that there is or ever has been an innate territory on these islands inhabited by one Japanese people. Instead, it invites the perspective of many peoples and many Japans.

MULTIPLE JAPANS

The prefectural and municipal histories compiled in modern Japan reflect the diverse heritage and civic spirit in communities across the archipelago. Given this rich variety, it is surprising that studies exploring what may be called a regional or subnational level are a relatively recent phenomenon. Early examples include a groundbreaking case study by John Whitney Hall (1956) on records in Bizen, which examined political control at provincial level in early modern Japan. Into the 1960s there were also some detailed histories of political movements at a domainal level, charting the roles played in the Meiji Restoration by Chōshū (Craig, 1961) and Tosa (Jansen, 1961), even if these were framed within more of a nation-building narrative.

More recently the focus has been to explore how relations between regions and the center feature in the modern history of Japan. Even as the new Meiji state was being developed, for example, there was still a conspicuous patchwork of fragmented loyalties and affiliations across these islands, as Howell (2005) has shown in *Geographies of Identity.* Regional studies such as *Kyushu* (Cobbing, 2009) and *Hokkaido* (Irish, 2009) have revisited the distinctive cultural legacies on individual islands and their often ambivalent relations with the political center. Closer to the ground, Wigen (1995) examined the changing spatial order in one province near the heartland of Tokugawa control and, following research on the 'mapping of early modern Japan' (Yonemoto, 2003), used a rich seam of cartographical evidence to show how Shinano Province was creatively represented by state level and regional stakeholders (Wigen, 2010). Another study on mercantilism traces the theme of economic growth in the Tosa domain (Roberts, 1998, 2012). Similarly, Baxter (1994) analyzes the process and effects of the 'Meiji unification' at provincial level 'through the lens of Ishikawa Prefecture', while, in the case of Toyama, Lewis (2000) extends his study of 'national power and local politics' up to the end of the Asia Pacific War. Studies at an even more local level include *Shinohata: A Portrait of a Japanese Village.* (Dore, 1978), while more recently *Hard Times in the Hometown* has traced the experience of one community through modern times (Dusinberre, 2012).

Increasingly, studies of core-periphery relations emphasize not just links between these regions and the metropole within Japan, but take a wider view by exploring connections beyond the archipelago. Ongoing efforts to re-evaluate the Japanese empire, for example, are uncovering not so much the monolithic structure that was portrayed in postwar representations, but rather multipolar networks influenced by diverse agents. Mimura (2011), for example, addresses the roles played by bureaucrats, Townsend (2000) traces a pacifist academic's outlook on colonial policy, while the experience of ordinary colonialists has also been highlighted (Uchida, 2011). Other works focus on a particular territory within this broader empire, such as the colony of Manchuria (Young, 1998). A current project by Barak Kushner on the process of decolonization in postwar East Asia should also help to place the aftermath of empire in a wider context.

Collectively, these ventures can be seen as part of a growing trend to explore transnational and transcultural networks. Such projects open up new interpretive possibilities, transcending the 'national labeling' that characterized much of the twentieth-century scholarship on the history of modern Japan. To some extent they also reflect current socio-political changes globally. In the Cold War era especially, national labels often seemed like an obvious approach to the modern history of countries like Japan. With access to the internet now enabling less restricted flows of information across borders, however, researchers have more opportunities to look beyond national and cultural barriers when examining Japan's past. One example is a study on the culture of savings in an international context (Garon, 2011). Again, these projects examine aspects of not just Japan's modern history, but encompass older periods as well, legacies of which, to varying extents, may still be evident today. Two collections that address ancient and medieval networks, for example, are *Heian Japan: Centers and Peripheries* (Adolphson et al., 2007) and *Tools of Culture* (Goble et al., 2005).

Finally, another trend in historical research not to be overlooked is the influence of post-colonial studies. Arguably, Japan features only marginally in a field often dominated by researchers focusing on the legacies of European colonial empires. It also occupies a somewhat ambivalent position in this context, having been both an imperial power and also perhaps a victim of Western imperialism in East Asia (even if it was never officially a colony as such). In a theme that draws together empire, conflicted identity and issues of representation, post-colonial theory can explore other Japans altogether by undermining the chimerical constructs imagined by a subjective colonial gaze. Often the target here is the Western-centric misrepresentation of the Other. In some respects, therefore, it coincides with the recent debate on *sakoku* that identified the notion of Japan's 'closed' mentality as a European construct dating back to the Edo period. Similarly, the increasing tendency to guard

against a Western-centric outlook has gravitated against using such culturally specific and loaded terms as class, feudalism or fascism in the context of Japan. Scholars have even become circumspect, for example, about employing the term feudalism when discussing medieval Europe, let alone in relation to Japan, although Howell (1998) has bucked the trend by making a case for retaining this idea as a helpful way to understand the logic behind the mode of production under Tokugawa rule.

How, then, does Japan fit into the world of Orientalism that Edward Said (1978) so provocatively expounded over thirty years ago? A cursory look through representations of Japan in Western art, for example, soon demonstrates that this is a theme highly relevant to Japan as well. The objectification of Japanese women often described as *musume* is never far from view in nineteenth-century works such as *Madame Chrysanthème, Madam Butterfly* and the *Mikado*. Much like other critical reviews of Said, however, Japan's particular cultural experience has made it difficult to fit seamlessly within his oversimplified binary model of the Orient and the West, suggesting scope instead for imagining multiple Orients (Minear, 1980). Even so, Said's imagery has had a powerful effect on various strands of historical research, influencing explorations of how the Japanese were viewed by Americans (Miyoshi, 1979), or the British (Yokoyama, 1987) in the nineteenth century. There have also been attempts to apply some of Said's ideas within an East Asian setting, as in the case of *Japan's Orient* (Tanaka, 1995).

CONCLUSION

This chapter has tried to chart some of the main trends in historical scholarship on Japan since the onset of the modern era. In the process it has hopefully underlined how fluid and often contested this field can be, as fresh perspectives open up new avenues for interpretive exploration from one generation to the next. The first histories of modern Japan to appear in the Meiji period demonstrated an unshakable belief in the march of progress. Little did they know then how tortuous the encounters with modernity would be as this new modern state grew up into a somewhat old-fashioned empire in twentieth-century East Asia. From another modernist perspective Marxist historiography had a significant impact on Japanese academia, at times trying to find theories to explain why this modern project had gone off the rails. In postwar scholarship some reflective soul-searching in Japan and a renewed sense of Western triumphalism were both in evidence as the region settled into the tense environment of the

Cold War era. With the onset of the economic miracle, however, fresh initiatives in *nihonjinron* discourse put more emphasis on Japan's arguably 'unique' modern experience.

In the last few decades it is fair to say that the historical goalposts have been rapidly moving once again. Postmodernist insights have helped to portray the state as more of a recent construct than has often been presented in the past, while to varying extents supposedly time-honored traditions, it emerges, are the products of creative reinvention. Key dates that were once set in stone, such as 1868 as the starting point of the modern era, have been re-evaluated as historians find traces or precursors of modern culture and society stretching back into the Edo period, and features of fragmented Tokugawa social identities lingering into Meiji and beyond. Similarly, transwar histories have found continuities stretching through the twentieth century as well. Not only have turning points been reconsidered, but the nature of Japan itself, or in the light of the plural perspectives now on view, multiple Japans. To some extent the daunting task of navigating this complex field has been assisted by the appearance, besides the cursory overview here, of voluminous collections presented as readers (Megarry, 1995) or companions (Tsutsui, 2010) of Japanese history. With the effects of globalization in train, new initiatives to explore transnational and transcultural networks also offer fresh opportunities to reconceptualize the past. Interpreting Modern Japan, therefore, is not just something to be imbibed from history books or readers, despite the formative influence of numerous works, but a contested, evolving field of inquiry still very much in the making.

REFERENCES

Adolphson, M., Kamens, E. and Matsumoto, S. (eds.) (2007). *Heian Japan: Centers and Peripheries.* Honolulu: University of Hawaii Press.

Alperovitz, G. (1965). *Atomic Diplomacy: Hiroshima and Potsdam.* New York: Simon and Schuster.

Amino, Y. (2012). *Rethinking Japanese History* (translated and with an introduction by Alan S. Christy). Ann Arbor: Center for Japanese Studies, University of Michigan.

Anderson, B. (1983). *Imagined Communities: Reflections on the Origins and Spread of Nationalism.* London: Verso.

Bailey, P. (1996). *Postwar Japan: 1945 to the Present.* Oxford: Blackwell.

Batten, B. L. (2006). *To the Ends of Japan: Premodern Frontiers, Boundaries, and Interactions.* Honolulu: University of Hawaii Press.

Baxter, J.C. (1994). *The Meiji Unification through the Lens of Ishikawa Prefecture.* Cambridge, MA: Harvard University Press.

Beasley, W. G. (1987). *Japanese Imperialism, 1894–1945.* Oxford: Clarendon Press.

Befu, H. (1984). *Ideorogī toshite no nihonbunkaron [Nihonjinron as an Ideology].* Tokyo: Shisō no Kagakusha.

Beillevaire. P. (2000; 2002). *Ryukyu Studies to 1854: Western Encounter* (parts 1 and 2: 10 volumes). London: Routledge.

Benedict, R. (1946). *The Chrysanthemum and the Sword: Patterns of Japanese Culture.* Boston: Houghton Mifflin.

Bernstein, G. L. (1991). *Recreating Japanese Women, 1600–1945.* Berkeley: University of California Press.

Bernstein, G. L. (2005). *Isami's House: Three Generations of a Japanese Family.* Berkeley: University of California Press.

Bisson, T. A. (1989). The Limits of Reform, in H. Schonberger (ed.), *Aftermath of War: Americans and the Remaking of Japan, 1945–1952.* Kent, OH: Kent State University Press. pp. 90–110.

Bix, H. P. (2000). *Hirohito and the Making of Modern Japan.* London: HarperCollins.

Bolitho, H. (1974). *Treasures among Men: Fudai Daimyo in Tokugawa Japan.* New Haven: Yale University Press.

Bowen, R. W. (1986). *Innocence Is Not Enough: The Life and Death of Herbert Norman.* Vancouver: Douglas and McIntyre.

Brown, D. (1955). *Nationalism in Japan: An Introductory Analysis.* Berkeley: University of California Press.

Brownlee, J. S. (1997). *Japanese Historians and the National Myths, 1600–1945: The Age of the Gods and Emperor Jimmu.* Vancouver: University of British Columbia Press.

Burns, S. L. (2004). *Before the Nation: Kokugaku and the Imagining of Community in Early Modern Japan.* Durham, NC: Duke University Press.

Buruma, I. (1994). *The Wages of Guilt: Memories of War in Germany and Japan.* New York: Farrar, Strauss and Giroux.

Buruma, I. (2003). *Inventing Japan, 1853–1964.* New York: Modern Library.

Calman, D. (1992). *The Nature and Origins of Japanese Imperialism: A Reinterpretation of the Great Crisis of 1873.* London: Routledge.

Chang, I. (1997). *The Rape of Nanking: The Forgotten Holocaust of World War II.* New York: Basic Books.

Cobbing, A. (2009). *Kyushu: Gateway to Japan – A Concise History.* Folkestone: Global Oriental.

Conroy, H. (1960). *The Japanese Seizure of Korea, 1868–1910: A Study of Realism and Idealism in International Relations.* Philadelphia and Oxford: Pennsylvania University Press and Oxford University Press.

Craig, A. M. (1961). *Chōshū in the Meiji Restoration*. Cambridge, MA: Harvard University Press.

Craig, A. M. (2008). *Civilization and Enlightenment: The Early Thought of Fukuzawa Yukichi*. Cambridge, MA: Harvard University Press.

Cross, T. (2009). *The Ideologies of Japanese Tea: Subjectivity, Transience and National Identity*. Folkestone: Global Oriental.

Cullen, L. M. (2003). *A History of Japan, 1582–1941: Internal and External Worlds*. Cambridge: Cambridge University Press.

Dale, P. (1986). *The Myth of Japanese Uniqueness*. Oxford and London: Nissan Institute/Routledge.

Denoon, D., Hudson, M., McCormack, G. and Morris-Suzuki, T. (eds.) (1996). *Multicultural Japan: Palaeolithic to Postmodern*. Cambridge: Cambridge University Press.

DeVos, G. A. and Wagatsuma, H. (eds.) (1967). *Japan's Invisible Race: Caste in Culture and Personality*. Berkeley: University of California Press.

Doak, K. M. (1997). What is a Nation and Who Belongs? National Narratives and the Ethnic Imagination in Twentieth Century Japan, *American Historical Review*, 102(2): 283–309.

Doak, K. M. (1998). Culture, Ethnicity, and the State in Early Twentieth Century Japan, in S. Minichiello (ed.), *Japan's Competing Modernities: Issues in Culture and Democracy, 1900–1930*. Honolulu: University of Hawaii Press. pp. 181–205.

Dore, R. P. (1965). *Education in Tokugawa Japan*. Berkeley: University of California Press.

Dore, R. P. (1978). *Shinohata: A Portrait of a Japanese Village*. New York: Pantheon Books.

Dower, J. W. (2000). *Embracing Defeat: Japan in the Wake of World War II*. New York: W. W. Norton and Co.

Dusinberre, M. (2012). *Hard Times in the Hometown: A History of Community Survival in Modern Japan*. Honolulu: University of Hawaii Press.

Duus, P. (1974). Whig History, Japanese Style: The Min'yusha Historians and the Meiji Restoration, *The Journal of Asian Studies*, 33(3): 415–436.

Duus, P. (1998). *The Abacus and the Sword: The Japanese Penetration of Korea, 1895–1910*. Berkeley: University of California Press.

Duus, P. (ed.) (1988). *The Cambridge History of Japan, Volume 6: The Twentieth Century*. Cambridge: Cambridge University Press.

Duus, P., Myers, R. H. and Peattie, M. R. (eds.) (1989). *The Japanese Informal Empire in China, 1895–1937*. Princeton: Princeton University Press.

Duus, P., Myers, R. H. and Peattie, M. R. (eds.) (1996). *The Japanese Wartime Empire in China, 1931–1945*. Princeton: Princeton University Press.

Dyer, H. (1904). *Dai Nippon: The Britain of the East – A Study in National Evolution*. London: Blackie and Son Ltd.

Fogel, J. (ed.) (2000). *The Nanjing Massacre in History and Historiography*. Berkeley: University of California Press.

Francks, P. (2009). *The Japanese Consumer: An Alternative Economic History of Modern Japan*. Cambridge: Cambridge University Press.

Friday, K. (1994). Bushidō or Bull? A Medieval Historian's Perspective on the Imperial Army and the Japanese Warrior Tradition, *The History Teacher*, 27(3): 339–349.

Garon, S. (1994). Rethinking Modernization and Modernity in Japanese History: A Focus on State-Society Relations, *The Journal of Asian Studies*, 53(2): 346–366.

Garon, S. (2011). *Beyond Our Means: Why America Spends and the World Saves*. Princeton: Princeton University Press.

Garon, S., and Maclachlan, P. (eds.) (2006). *The Ambivalent Consumer: Questioning Consumption in East Asia and the West*. Ithaca: Cornell University Press.

Geiger, A. (2011). *Subverting Exclusion: Transpacific Encounters with Race, Caste, and Borders, 1885–1928*. New Haven: Yale University Press.

George, T. S. (2001). *Minamata: Pollution and the Struggle for Democracy in postwar Japan*. Cambridge, MA: Harvard University Press.

George, T. S., and Gerteis, C. (2012). *Japan since 1945: From Postwar to Post-Bubble*. London: Bloomsbury Academic.

Gluck, C. (1978). The People in History: Recent Trends in Japanese Historiography, *The Journal of Asian Studies*, 38(1): 25–50.

Gluck, C. (1985). *Japan's Modern Myths: Ideology in the Late Meiji Period*. Princeton: Princeton University Press.

Goble, A., Robinson, K. and Wakabayashi, H. (eds.) (2005). *Tools of Culture: Japan's Cultural, Intellectual, Medical, and Technological Contacts in East Asia, 1000s–1500s*. Ann Arbor: Association of Asian Studies.

Gordon, A. (1993). *Postwar Japan as History*. Berkeley: University of California Press.

Gordon, A. (2007). Consumption, Leisure and the Middle Class in Transwar Japan, *Social Science Japan Journal*, 10(1): 1–21.

Goto-Jones, C. (2005). Political Philosophy in Japan: Nishida, the Kyoto School, and Co-Prosperity. London and New York: Routledge.

Griffis, W. E. (1876). *The Mikado's Empire*. New York: Harper and Brothers, Publishers.

Hall, I. P. (1997). *Cartels of the Mind: Japan's Intellectual Closed Shop*. New York and London: Norton.

Hall, J. W. (1955). *Tanuma Okitsugu, 1719–1788: Forerunner of Modern Japan*. Cambridge, MA: Harvard University Press.

Hall, J. W. (1956). *Government and Local Power in Japan, 500–1700: A Study Based on Bizen Province*. Princeton: Princeton University Press.

Hall, J. W. (1965a). Changing Conceptions of the Modernization of Japan, in M. B. Jansen (ed.), *Changing Japanese Attitudes toward Modernization.* Princeton: Princeton University Press. pp. 7–41.

Hall, J. W. (1965b). Rule by Status in Tokugawa Japan, *Journal of Japanese Studies,* 1(1): 39–49.

Hane, M. (1982). *Peasants, Women, Rebels and Outcastes: The Underside of Modern Japan.* New York: Pantheon Books.

Hanes, J. E. (2002). *The City as Subject: Seki Hajime and the Reinvention of Modern Osaka.* Berkeley: University of California Press.

Hanley, S. (1997). *Everyday Things in Premodern Japan: The Hidden Legacy of Material Culture.* Berkeley: University of California Press.

Harootunian, H.D. (1970). *Toward Restoration: Growth of Political Consciousness in Tokugawa Japan.* Berkeley: University of California Press.

Harootunian, H. D. (2000a). *History's Disquiet: Modernity, Cultural Practice and the Question of Everyday Life.* New York: Columbia University Press.

Harootunian, H. D. (2000b). *Overcome by Modernity: History, Culture, and Community in Interwar Japan.* Princeton: Princeton University Press.

Hellyer, R. I. (2009). *Defining Engagement: Japan and Global Contexts, 1640–1868.* Cambridge, MA: Harvard University Press.

Hicks, G. (1997a). *Japan's Hidden Apartheid: The Korean Minority and the Japanese.* Aldershot: Ashgate.

Hicks, G. (1997b). *Japan's War Memories: Amnesia or Concealment.* Aldershot: Ashgate.

Hideshima. N. (1917). *Saga han kaigun shi [History of the Saga domain navy].* Tokyo: Chishinkai.

Hilger, M. I. (1967). Japan's 'Sky People': The Vanishing Ainu, *National Geographic,* 131(2): 268–295.

Honda, K. (1999). *The Nanjing Massacre: A Japanese Journalist Confronts Japan's National Shame.* Armonk: M. E. Sharpe.

Howell, D. L. (1994). Ainu Ethnicity and the Boundaries of the Early Modern Japanese State, *Past and Present,* 142(1): 69–93.

Howell. D. L. (1998). Territoriality and Collective Identity in Tokugawa Japan, *Daedalus,* 127(3): 105–132.

Howell, D. L. (2005). *Geographies of Identity in Nineteenth-Century Japan.* Berkeley: University of California Press.

Hoston, G. (1991). Conceptualizing Bourgeois Revolution: The Pre-War Japanese Left and the Meiji Restoration, *Comparative Studies in Society and History,* 33(3): 539–581.

Huber, T. (1981). *The Revolutionary Origins of Modern Japan.* Stanford: Stanford University Press.

Hudson, M. J. (1999). *The Ruins of Identity: Ethnogenesis in the Japanese Islands.* Honolulu: University of Hawaii Press.

Hunter, J. (ed.) (2012). *The Historical Consumer: Consumption and Everyday Life in Japan, 1850–2000.* Basingstoke: Palgrave Macmillan.

Huffman, J. L. (1997). *Creating a Public: People and Press in Meiji Japan.* Honolulu: University of Hawaii Press.

Ienaga, S. (1978). *The Pacific War, 1931–1945: A Critical Perspective on Japan's Role in World War II.* New York: Pantheon Press.

Ienaga, S. (1993/4). The Glorification of War in Japanese Education, *International Security* 18(3): 113–133.

Irish, A. B. (2009). *Hokkaido: A History of Ethnic Transition and Development on Japan's Northern Island.* Jefferson, NC and London: McFarland.

Iriye, A. (1997). *Japan and the Wider World: From the Mid-Nineteenth Century to the Present.* London and New York: Longman.

Itazawa, T. (1940). *Mukashi no nanyō to nihon [The South Seas and Japan in olden days].* Tokyo: Nihon Hōsō Shuppan Kyōkai.

Iwao, S. (1963). Reopening of the Diplomatic and Commercial Relations between Japan and Siam during the Tokugawa Period, *Acta Asiatica,* 4: 1–31.

Iwao, S. (1976). Japanese Foreign Trade in the 16th and 17th Centuries, *Acta Asiatica,* 30: 1–18.

Jansen, M. B. (1961). *Sakamoto Ryoma and the Meiji Restoration.* Princeton: Princeton University Press.

Jansen, M. B. (ed.). (1989). *The Cambridge History of Japan, Vol. 5: The Nineteenth Century.* Cambridge: Cambridge University Press.

Jansen, M. B. (1992). *China in the Tokugawa World.* Cambridge MA: Harvard University Press.

Jansen, M. B. (2000). *The Making of Modern Japan.* Cambridge, MA: Harvard University Press.

Jeans, R. (2005). Victims or Victimizers? Museums, Textbooks, and the War Debate in Contemporary Japan, *The Journal of Military History,* 69(1): 149–195.

Johnson, C. (1982). *MITI and the Japanese 'Miracle'.* Stanford: Stanford University Press.

Kaempfer, E. (1727). *The History of Japan: written in High-Dutch by Engelbertus Kaempfer and translated by J.G. Scheuchzer.* London: Printed for the Translator.

Kariya, R. (1995). The Confidence to Live! Experiencing the Buraku Liberation Movement, in J. C. Maher and G. M. Macdonald (eds.), *Diversity in Japanese Culture and Language.* London: Kegan Paul International. pp. 178–201.

Kato, H. (1981). The Significance of the Period of National Seclusion Reconsidered, *Journal of Japanese Studies,* 7(1): 85–109.

Kayano, S. (1994). *Our Land Was a Forest: An Ainu Memoir.* Boulder, CO: Westview Press.

Kerr, G. (1958). *Okinawa: The History of an Island People.* Tokyo: C. E. Tuttle Co.

Kersten, R. (1999). Neo-nationalism and the 'Liberal School of History', *Japan Forum* 11(2): 191–203.

Kingston, J. (2004). *Japan's Quiet Transformation: Social Change and Civil Society in the 21st Century*. London: Routledge Courzon.

Kornicki, P. (ed.) (1998). *Meiji Japan: Political, Economic and Social History, 1868–1912* (4 volumes). London and New York: Routledge.

Kōshaku Shimazu-ke Henshūsho (1928–9). *Sappan kaigun shi [History of the Satsuma domain navy]*. Tokyo: Hara Shobō.

Kume, K. (1878). *Tokumei Zenken Taishi Bei-ō Kairan Jikki*. English translation: Healey, G. and Tsuzuki, C. (eds.) (2002). *The Iwakura Embassy, 1871–73: A True Account of the Ambassador Extraordinary and Plenipotentiary's Journey of Observation through the United States of America and Europe*. Tokyo: The Japan Documents.

Kume, K. and Nakano, R. (eds.) (1921). *Nabeshima Naomasa Kōden [Biography of Lord Nabeshima Naomasa]*. Tokyo: Kōshaku Nabeshima Hensansho.

Kushner, B. *The Dissolution of the Japanese Empire and the Struggle for Legitimacy in Postwar East Asia, 1945–1965* (current ERC Research Project).

Large, S. (1992). *Emperor Hirohito and Showa Japan: A Political Biography*. London: Nissan Institute/ Routledge.

Large, S. (ed.) (1998). *Showa Japan: Political, Economic and Social History, 1926–1989* (4 volumes). London and New York: Routledge.

Large, S. (2009). Oligarchy, Democracy and Fascism in W. M. Tsutsui (ed.), *A Companion to Japanese History*. Oxford: Wiley-Blackwell. pp. 156–171.

Lebra, T. (2007). *Collected Papers of Takie Lebra: Identity, Gender and Status in Japan*. Folkestone: Global Oriental.

Lewis, J. B. (2003). *Frontier Contact Between Choson Korea and Tokugawa Japan*. London: Routledge.

Lewis, M. (2000). *Becoming Apart: National Power and Local Politics in Toyama, 1868–1945*. Cambridge, MA: Harvard University Press.

Lie, J. (2001). *Multiethnic Japan*. Cambridge, MA: Harvard University Press.

Lu, D. (ed.) (1996). *Japan: A Documentary History, vol.2: The Late Tokugawa Period to the Present*. Armonk, NY: M. E. Sharpe.

Maga, T. (2001). *Judgment at Tokyo: The Japanese War Crimes Trials*. Lexington: The University Press of Kentucky.

Maher J. C., and Macdonald G. M. (eds.) (1995). *Diversity in Japanese Culture and Language*. London: Kegan Paul International.

Maruyama M. (1946). Chōkokka-shugi no ronri to shisō [The Logic and Psychology of Ultranationalism], *Sekai*. May edition.

Massarella, D. (1996). Some Reflections on Identity Formation in East Asia in the Sixteenth and Seventeenth Centuries, in D. Denoon, M. Hudson, G. McCormack, and T. Morris-Suzuki (eds.), *Multicultural Japan: Palaeolithic to Postmodern*. Cambridge: Cambridge University. pp. 135–152.

McClain, J., Merriman, J. and Ugawa, K. (eds). (1994). *Edo and Paris: Urban Life and the State in the Early-Modern Era*. Ithaca: Cornell University Press.

Megarry, T. (ed.) (1995). *The Making of Modern Japan: A Reader*. Dartford: Greenwich University Press.

Mimura, J. (2011). *Planning for Empire: Reform Bureaucrats and the Japanese Wartime State*. Ithaca, NY: Cornell University Press.

Minear, R. H. (1980). Orientalism and the Study of Japan, *Journal of Asian Studies*, 39(3): 507–517.

Mitchell, R. H. (1967). *The Korean Minority in Japan*. Berkeley: University of California Press.

Miyoshi, M. (1979). *As We Saw Them: The First Japanese Embassy to the United States*. Berkeley: University of California Press.

Morris, I. (ed.) (1963). *Thought and Behavior in Modern Japanese Politics*. London: Oxford University Press.

Morris, J. (1895). *Advance Japan: A Nation Thoroughly in Earnest*. London: Wyman and Sons Ltd.

Morris-Suzuki, T. (1998). *Re-inventing Japan: Time, Space, Nation*. Armonk, NY: M. E. Sharpe.

Murdoch, J. (1926). *A History of Japan* (3 volumes). London: Routledge.

Myers, R. H., and Peattie, M. R. (1987). *The Japanese Colonial Empire, 1895–1945*. Princeton: Princeton University Press.

Neary, I. (1989). *Political Protest and Social Control in Pre-war Japan: The Origins of Buraku Liberation*. Manchester: Manchester University Press.

Ninomiya, S. (1933). An Inquiry Concerning the Origin, Development, and Present Situation of the Eta in Relation to the History of Social Classes in Japan, *The Transactions of the Asiatic Society of Japan*, 10 (Second Series): 47–145.

Norman, E. H. (1940). *Japan's Emergence as a Modern State: Political and Economic Problems of the Meiji Period*. International Secretariat: Institute of Pacific Relations.

Notehelfer, F. G. (1990). Review: Meiji in the Rear-View Mirror: Top Down vs. Bottom Up History, *Monumenta Nipponica*, 45(2): 207–228.

Notehelfer, F. G. (1975). Japan's First Pollution Incident, *Journal of Japanese Studies*, 1(2): 351–383.

Ooms, H. (1996). *Tokugawa Village Practice: Class, Status, Power, Law*. Berkeley: University of California Press.

Parkes, G. (2011). Heidegger and Japanese Fascism: An Unsubstantiated Connection, in B. W. Davis, B. Schroeder, and J. Wirth (eds.), *Japanese and Continental Philosophy: Conversations with the Kyoto School*. Bloomington: Indiana University Press.

Plugfelder, G. M., and Walker, B. W. (2005). *Japanimals: History and Culture in Japan's Animal Life*. Ann Arbor: Center for Japanese Studies, University of Michigan.

Pritchard, J. R. (eds.) (1998–2005). *The Tokyo Major War Crimes Trial: The Complete Transcripts of the Proceedings of the International Military Tribunal for the Far East* (124 volumes). Lewiston: Mellen Press.

Reischauer, E. O. (1970). *Japan: Story of a Nation* (1970). New York: Alfred A. Knopf Inc.

Richie, D. (1999). *Tokyo*. London: Reaktion Books.

Roberts, L. S. (1998). *Mercantilism in a Japanese Domain: The Merchant Origins of Economic Nationalism in 18th-Century Tosa*. Cambridge: Cambridge University Press.

Roberts, L. S. (2012). *Performing the Great Peace: Political Space and Open Secrets in Tokugawa Japan*. Honolulu: University of Hawaii Press.

Rose, C. (1999). The Textbook Issue: Domestic Sources of Japan's Foreign Policy, *Japan Forum* 11(2): 205–216.

Saaler, S. and J. V. Koschmann (2006). *Pan-Asianism in Modern Japanese History: Colonialism, Regionalism and Borders*. London and New York: Routledge.

Said, E. (1978). *Orientalism: Western Representations of the Orient*. Harmondsworth: Penguin.

Sakai, R. K. (1964). The Satsuma-Ryukyu Trade and the Tokugawa Seclusion Policy, *Journal of Asian Studies*, 23(3): 391–403.

Sansom, G. B. (1931). *Japan: A Short Cultural History*. London: Cresset Press, and New York: D. Appleton.

Sansom, G. B. (1958). *A History of Japan* (3 volumes). Stanford: Stanford University Press.

Sato, B. (2003). *The New Japanese Woman: Modernity, Media and Women in Interwar Japan*. Durham, NC: Duke University Press.

Schonberger, H. (ed.) (1989). *Aftermath of War: Americans and the Remaking of Japan, 1945–1952*. Kent, OH: Kent State University Press.

Seaton, P. (2007). *Japan's Contested War Memories: The 'Memory' Rifts in Historical Consciousness of World War II*. London and New York: Routledge.

Seidensticker, E. (1991). *Low City, High City: Tokyo from Edo to the Earthquake – How the Shogun's Ancient Capital Became a Great Modern City, 1867–1923*. Cambridge, MA: Harvard University Press.

Siebold, P. F. von (1832–52). *Nippon, Archiv zur Beschreibung von Japan und Dessen neben- und Schutzlandern*. Leiden: C. C. van der Hoek.

Shiba, R. (2013). *Clouds above the Hill* (4 volumes). Tokyo and London: Japan Documents and Routledge.

Siddle. R. M. (1996). *Race, Resistance and the Ainu of Japan*. London: Routledge.

Sims, R. L. (2001). *Japanese Political History since the Meiji Renovation*. London: C. Hurst and Co.

Smith, T. C. (1965). *The Agrarian Origins of Modern Japan*. Stanford: Stanford University Press.

Smits, G. (1991). *Visions of Ryukyu: Identity and Ideology in Early Modern Thought and Politics*. Honolulu: University of Hawaii Press.

Sorensen, A. (2002). *The Making of Urban Japan: Cities and Planning from Edo to the Twenty-First Century*. London: Blackwell Publishing.

Stevenson, R. L. (1882). *Familiar Studies of Men and Books*. London: Chatto and Windus.

Suematsu, K. (ed.) (1920). *Bōchō kaiten shi*. Tokyo: Yoshikawa Kōbunkan.

Takeguma, T. (ed.) (1915). *Mito han shiryō [Records of the Mito domain]*. Tokyo: Yoshikawa Kōbunkan.

Takeuchi, Y. (1993). *Nihon to Ajia [Japan and Asia]*. Tokyo: Chikuma Gakugei Bunko.

Tanaka, S. (1995). *Japan's Orient: Rendering Pasts into History*. Berkeley: University of California Press.

Tashiro, K., and Videen, S. D. (1982). Foreign Relations during the Edo Period: Sakoku Reexamined, *Journal of Japanese Studies*, 8(2): 283–306.

Thomas, J. A. (2001). *Reconfiguring Modernity: Concepts of Nature in Japanese Political Ideology*. Berkeley: University of California Press.

Toby, R. P. (1977). Reopening the Question of Sakoku: Diplomacy in the Legitimation of the Tokugawa Bakufu, *Journal of Japanese Studies*, 3(2): 323–363.

Toby, R. P. (1984). *State and Diplomacy in Early Modern Japan: Asia in the Development of the Tokugawa Bakufu*. Stanford: Stanford University Press.

Tonomura, H., Walthall, A. and Wakita, H. (eds.) (1999). *Women and Class in Japanese History*. Ann Arbor: Center for Japanese Studies, University of Michigan.

Totman, C. (1989). *The Green Archipelago: Forestry in Preindustrial Japan*. Berkeley: University of California Press.

Totman, C. (2000). *History of Japan*. Oxford: Wiley-Blackwell.

Townsend, S. C. (2000). *Yanaihara Tadao and Japanese Colonial Policy: Redeeming Empire*. Richmond: Curzon.

Tsutsui, W. M. (ed.) (2009). *A Companion to Japanese History*. Oxford: Wiley-Blackwell.

Uchida, J. (2011). *Brokers of Empire: Japanese Settler Colonialism in Korea, 1876–1945*. Cambridge, MA: Harvard University Asia Center.

Vaporis, C. (1995). *Breaking Barriers: Travel and the State in Early Modern Japan*. Cambridge, MA: Harvard University Press.

Vlastos, S. (1986). *Peasant Protests and Uprisings in Tokugawa Society*. Berkeley: University of California Press.

Vlastos, S. (ed.) (1998), *Mirror of Modernity: Invented Traditions of Modern Japan*. Berkeley: University of California Press.

Vogel, E. (1979). *Japan as Number One: Lessons for Americans.* Cambridge, MA: Harvard University Press.

Voss, G. (1945). Early Japanese Isolationism, *Pacific Historical Review,* 14(1): 13–35.

Wakabayashi, B. T. (1986). *Anti-Foreignism and Western Learning in Early Modern Japan: The New Theses of 1825.* Cambridge, MA: Harvard University Press.

Walker, B. L. (2001). *The Conquest of Ainu Lands: Ecology and Culture in Japanese Expansion, 1590–1800.* Berkeley: University of California Press.

Walker, B. (2012). *Review: Hellyer, R. Defining Engagement: Japan and Global Context, 1640–1868.* Harvard Journal of Asiatic Studies, 72(1): 205–210.

Walthall, A. (ed.) (1991). *Peasant Uprisings in Japan: A Critical Anthology of Peasant Histories.* Chicago: University of Chicago Press.

Ward, R. (1968). Reflections of the Allied occupation and Planned Political Change in Japan, in Robert Ward (ed.), *Political Development in Modern Japan.* pp. 477–535.

Watsuji, T. (1950). *Sakoku Nihon no higeki [Sakoku: the tragedy of Japan].* Tokyo: Chikuma Shob⁻o.

Weiner, M. (1994). *Race and Migration in Imperial Japan.* London and New York: Routledge.

Weiner, M. (1997). *Japan's Minorities: The Illusion of Homogeneity.* London and New York: Routledge.

White, J. W. (1995). *Ikki: Social Conflict and Political Protest in Early Modern Japan.* Ithaca: Cornell University Press.

Wigen, K. (2010). A *Malleable Map: Geographies of Restoration in Central Japan, 1600–1912.* Berkeley: University of California Press.

Wigen, K. (1995). *The Making of a Japanese Periphery, 1750–1920.* Berkeley: University of California Press.

Williams, D. (2004). *Defending Japan: Pacific War, the Kyoto School Philosophers and Post-White Power.* London and New York: Routledge Curzon.

Wilson, G. M. (1992). *Patriots and Redeemers in Japan: Motives in the Meiji Restoration.* Chicago: University of Chicago Press. 1992.

Yamakawa, K. (2001). *Women of the Mito Domain: Recollections of Samurai Family Life* (translated by Kate Wildman Nakai). Stanford: Stanford University Press.

Yokoyama, T. (1987). *Japan in the Victorian Mind: A Study of Stereotyped Images of a Nation, 1850–80.* London: Macmillan.

Yonemoto, M. (2003). *Mapping Early Modern Japan: Space, Place and Culture in the Tokugawa Period, 1603–1868.* Berkeley: University of California Press.

Young. L. (1998). *Japan's Total Empire: Manchuria and the Culture of Wartime Imperialism.* Berkeley: University of California Press.

2

Anthropology of Modern Japan

Carolyn S. Stevens

INTRODUCTION

The discipline of social and cultural anthropology and the study of Japan have a long, well documented history.[1] What are the strengths and the accompanying weaknesses of anthropological research of Japan? This chapter attempts to encapsulate some of the methodological approaches and thematic issues that have dominated the field in the post-war era, offer an explanation as to why anthropology makes an important contribution to Japanese studies and give a snapshot of some of the predominant themes in anthropological research in the post-war era.

At the forefront of most anthropological research is a concern for 'human culture': describing it, interpreting it and using it to understand social relationships and practices, and to explain how and why certain events occurred around the world. Despite this, anthropologists rarely agree on what the term means; it can be seen as distinct from nature (as in the 'nature versus nurture' debate) as well as from society (structures that form relationships between people and groups, as well as institutions like the family, the workplace, the community and the nation-state). Robert LeVine wrote:

Anthropologists who converse with scholars in other disciplines are often asked what culture is, sometimes with the implication that the concept is outdated and ambiguous and that its use is an indicator of obscurantism in anthropology. Indeed, culture is often treated in quantitative social science as representing the unexplained residuum of rigorous empirical analysis, an area of darkness beyond the reach of currently available scientific searchlights... For many anthropologists... culture is a source of illumination, not a veil of obscurity... [C]ulture is a shared organization of ideas that includes the intellectual, moral, and aesthetic standards prevalent in a community and the meanings of communicative actions. But formal definitions do little to clarify the nature of culture; clarification is only possible through ethnography. (1984: 67)

LeVine's definition touches on the nature versus nurture debate (in that culture is outside 'scientific searchlights'); his basic description of culture as a 'shared organization of ideas... and the meanings of communicative actions' seems reasonable to most observers of Japan. While the notion of culture as shared is important we must be mindful not to allow this idea of an ideal 'shared' culture to overrun the diverse realities of everyday life in every society. Japanese culture in particular has been described by Japanese and foreign scholars alike as a rather fixed and monolithic entity (see Babb, Chapter 19, this volume), yet this is rarely the case. As these chapters demonstrate, Japanese society and culture has changed tremendously in the past century. Culture changes over time just as society and values do. Culture is something both tangible and intangible, and something that is able to shift and change while maintaining some links from the present to the past. These links include a consistent and shared 'message' that we get from cultural icons and institutions but also their critiques. Understanding culture is the main intellectual goal of anthropology and, as LeVine remarks, culture is understood through ethnographic fieldwork, the method of choice for anthropologists. Therefore, any discussion of the anthropology of Japan must begin with a conversation about ethnographic methods.

ETHNOGRAPHY: BACKGROUND AND METHODS

Visions of past figures of anthropology – the young cultural anthropologist Margaret Mead wrapped in a grass skirt and beads in Samoa, or the dashing but fictional archaeologist/treasure hunter Indiana Jones – romanticise the study of other cultures as exotic, exciting, undiscovered and even dangerous; in the past anthropology was always about knowing the 'Other'. This is not always the case today. Anthropologists study 'first world', urban, industralised societies just as often as they do the developing world. Romantic icons aside, the most important distinguishing characteristic of anthropological studies is its methodological focus on extended, in-depth fieldwork: 'participant-observation'. As a senior colleague once quipped, this difference is made most plain when comparing the cognate fields of anthropology and sociology: 'sociologists know a little about a lot of people. Anthropologists know a lot about few people'. Implied here, however, is that what they do know is deep and complex. They have shared days and nights with these individuals, living together in a particular social and physical environment, breathing the same air, eating the same food, speaking the same language, scratching the same insect bites... this focus on the 'lived experience' – both of the people being studied as well as of the researcher him/herself – is what separates anthropology from other kindred disciplines like sociology. This lived experience – more commonly expressed by academics as 'ethnographic fieldwork' – is the hallmark of anthropological research and writing. Living in the field, speaking the same language when necessary (steep learning curves often accompany this

kind of research; translators are not unheard of but are not considered best practice) creates understanding as no survey snapshot ever could.

Despite this physical, emotional and linguistic closeness, there has always been distance between the anthropologist and the informant. Ahmed notes that '[a]nthropology, it has often been said, served as a handmaid to colonialism' (1992: 155). Many past (and some current) ethnographic contexts involve researchers who are not in equal socioeconomic relationships with their informers. This is the nature of knowledge as power, where the society with capital to spare deems it important to learn about others, partly to preserve its own position of privilege and partly to further extend its influence, as Ahmed writes, through colonial and neo-colonial projects. This history is not absent from the Japanese anthropological research but the discipline has followed its own particular path, which charts the rise of Japanese global influence.

Japan's place in the anthropological landscape seems to be contested. On the one hand, cultural anthropological research on Japan, as we will see below, has had enduring influence in the discipline, as evidenced by very long print runs of classic monographs. On the other hand, as Jennifer Robertson notes, '[i]t... appears that anthropologists in general do not regard Japan as a geographical "prestige zone"; that is... they do not regard Japan as a cultural area of choice and theoretical cachet' (2005: 4). This is because Japan was 'somehow perceived as too much like "us"' and any information yielded about Japan or about the West (via comparative analysis) would be uninteresting and weak. Furthermore, Japan does not fit into a simplified 'West and the rest' or core-periphery model, which has dominated our diplomatic and academic understandings of international relations since the 1970s.[2] Yet, as this exchange between veteran anthropologists demonstrates, there is still a great deal to be learned from the study of Japan:

D. Plath: Are [the Japanese] different?

K. Brown: They are, in fact... I got into this question thirty years ago. And I was not so sure. And I thought maybe when Japan 'catches up', they will look like those of us from the Western world. They don't. . . and that was a dumb assumption.

...

D. Plath: It all looks familiar at least on the surface and then you go around the corner and it's not the same. It's not opposite; it's not topsy-turvy land. I tell students all the time: don't think of Japan as 180 degrees out from American life, where everything is different and everything is opposite.

If anything, what is fascinating to me is that it's 18 degrees different – not 180 degrees. (Plath, 1992)

As these two veteran anthropologists note, many scholars' original interest in Japan was rooted in a desire to see if modernisation theory (in other words, the 'catch up' game to the West) would prove true in Japan. To some extent there are similarities between contemporary Japanese society and other societies in Europe and North America; but it is the gradation of difference (the '18 degrees') that intrigues today's scholars. Furthermore, it is precisely that fine detail of 18 degrees that one could argue requires the 'thick description' that only long term ethnographic fieldwork can convey. Broad paint strokes may capture a 180-degree difference, but they are less capable of communicating subtleties. Clifford Geertz notes that 180-degree differences in human cultures may yield defensible but somewhat disheartening results when he writes that 'there is a difference between difference and a dichotomy. The first is a comparison and it relates; the second is a severance and it isolates' (1995: 28). It seems that many initial inquiries into Japan find it in the latter category, but after careful consideration place it in the former. That is the true intellectual contribution of anthropology in the study of any culture: to connect and relate ideas from another culture to shed light on the understanding of one's own. Even though the anthropological research cited in the essay below is mostly focused on a single site (in some cases a location such as a particular village, school or company; for others a genre of music or a particular industry, for example), implicit in all of these cases are the comparative lessons. While we learn about Japan we learn about ourselves, and others around the world.[3]

THE ANTHROPOLOGY OF JAPAN: BEGINNINGS

The study of Japan through foreign anthropological research has had many intellectual outcomes over the years. In its early days it transformed the study of anthropology by presenting a complex picture of a nation that had undergone drastic economic, social and military transformations. When John Embree first began his fieldwork in 1935, Japan was already well on its path of industrialisation; his book *Suye Mura: A Japanese Village* (1939) was the first systematic study of prewar Japan. The Japan he encountered had moved on from the quaint stories he might have read by his foreign predecessors, British traveller Isabella Bird (whose *Unbeaten Tracks in Japan* was published

in 1880) or American journalist Lafcadio Hearn (the densely ethnographic travelogue, *Glimpses of Unfamiliar Japan*, was published in 1894). Bird and Hearn (the latter naturalised as Japanese) were early Anglophone writers who sought to 'capture' the difference of Japan from North America and Europe, while Embree strived to understand how 1930s rural Japan worked, both literally and figuratively, through his mapping of cooperative social structures and emphasis on political and semi-professional or social organisations.

The next major anthropologist's work on Japan was of such great influence it has been called 'the master narrative' by those in the field (Ryang, 2004: 28). Ruth Benedict was commissioned by the US Government in 1944 to write a psychological profile of the 'enemy', resulting in the much criticised, but still in print, volume *The Chrysanthemum and the Sword: Patterns of Japanese Culture* (1946, 1974). Benedict, a successful anthropologist in her own right who had established herself as an expert on south-west Native American culture, was unable to carry out direct field work due to the hostilities between Japan and the USA and based much of her writing on secondary sources (in particular, she notes a debt to Embree's work (1974: 6) and to Japanese films (1974: 7)), supplemented by interviews with Japanese Americans, particularly those who had been born and educated in Japan. Many of these interviewees, including her main informant Robert Hashima, were internees at 'War Relocation Camps', individuals who Benedict herself describes with some sympathy as being in 'a most difficult position' (1974: frontispiece). Lummis, a scholar who has recently studied Benedict's interview notes for this volume, has written:

given that the research was mainly done during World War II and the book published shortly after, it seems remarkably liberal and tolerant. Perhaps it was the best American liberalism could have produced under those circumstances. Nevertheless judged by the criterion that matters most – whether it helps or hinders understanding of Japanese culture – it is deeply flawed. (2007)

The flaws Lummis describe centre not so much on Benedict's inability to speak Japanese or visit Japan directly (which would be expected), but on the fact that she 'took the ideology of a class for the culture of a people, a state of acute social dislocation for a normal condition, and an extraordinary moment in a nation's history as an unvarying norm of social behavior'. Her classification of Japan as a 'shame culture', one which primarily motivates the individual to acceptable behaviour through external rather than internal means (Benedict, 1974: 177–194), has been critiqued by both Japanese and non-Japanese scholars; but, on the other hand, some of her observations remain 'useful' (Lummis, 2007). William W. Kelly recognised that Benedict 'portrayed the Japanese as oriented to multiple social positions and thus caught in culturally marked, exclusive circles of obligation and duty that forced painful choices in normative behavior' (1991: 400). While the stakes of the painful choices are may be radical today than in the days of wartime Japan, some of the struggle between 'obligation' (*giri*) and 'duty' (*on*) are still culturally resonant in observing contemporary dilemmas that the Japanese face, such as family responsibilities versus professional requirements. Takami Kuwayama,[4] a Japanese anthropologist who was trained in the USA, notes that one of the most important lessons we have gained from *The Chrysanthemum and the Sword* is not necessarily about Japan but rather about the USA. His essay 'Ethnographic Reading in Reverse: *The Chrysanthemum and the Sword* as a Study of the American Character' (2004: 87–114) suggests that it is an American bias towards a necessary moral and psychological 'unity' and 'absoluteness' that created the concept of a Japanese 'duality' and perceived 'contradictions' in behaviour. Lastly, the American privileging of an ideology of egalitarianism finds its reverse in the complex hierarchical relations described by Benedict's chart of duty and obligation. Kuwayama's analysis of the 'ethnography in reverse', notably, attempts to bridge the gap between Geertz's 'difference' versus 'dichotomy'. In *The Chrysanthemum and the Sword* we find valuable lessons if we read the text as an exercise in the delineation of the important and emerging, if dichotomous, relationship between the USA and Japan.

The next set of anthropological tomes were dominated by English-speaking scholars but, interestingly, also included those that were penned by Japanese scholars such as Nakane Chie (a Japanese anthropologist who had, during her postgraduate career, studied England and Italy, conducting fieldwork in India.). Post-war Japan differed significantly from 'classic' anthropological sites. Not only was it competing with the first world in economic terms, Japan also had its own educated and articulate class of scholars who made important contributions to the anthropological debate. As William W. Kelly wrote in his 1991 review of the field:

> We Japan specialists ... are actually caught between rival polemics. We are dealing with a nation whose power in many respects equals our own: It has a more potent economy, a more literate citizenry, a massive cultural industry and a distinguished and independent academic establishment. (1991: 396)

This constant shifting (balancing) between the prominence of Western scholars of Japan and the Japanese scholar (plus further permutations, which include the Japanese American scholar, and the Resident Korean scholar, whose perspectives give them an interesting and different voice) has been an important intellectual phenomenon over the post-war era. Furthermore, unlike anthropological research in less developed nations, published work on Japan is open to review and criticism by Japanese readers and scholars due to its highly developed publishing industry that includes many translated books from English to Japanese. In this sense, it is important to note that the non-Japanese ethnographer can no longer claim sole privilege of bringing Japanese society to a wider audience.

MAJOR THEMES IN ANTHROPOLOGICAL RESEARCH IN JAPAN

The Self: Individual in Society

Introductory students of Japan often focus on the conformity of Japanese society because they see it as an immediate contrast to the individualism they prioritise in their own cultural values: the expected 180-degree difference appears and represents 'difference' to be mastered and understood. Professional scholars of Japan, however, in anthropology have frequently sought to do the opposite: to find similarities and to clarify and de-bunk this myth of the monolithic 'group-ism' of Japan by focusing on different conceptualisations of the individual in Japanese society and how they relate to others in groups. Research in the area of selfhood and Japanese society peaked in the early post-war period when research by Japanese and American psychologists and anthropologists built an image of the Japanese 'self', as expressed through 'personality'. Work by Caudill (1963), Doi (1981, 1986), and Lebra (see Lebra and Lebra, 1974; 1986) epitomised this period's focus on childrearing, family relations and psychological strategies in the home, which were then projected into adult relationships. Much like Benedict's work early research on the Japanese self was of great interest to those who wanted to figure out 'what made the Japanese tick' during the period of Japan's high economic growth. Doi (1981) was a psychologist who posited that much of adult interaction in Japanese society could be explained by a dependency theory that was ingrained in the mother-child relationship (note the continuity with Benedict's work). According to his theory of dependency in the book *The Anatomy of Independence* (1981) (*amae* in Japanese, also translated as 'passive love') he posited that the indulgent dependency experienced by children in the family sets the tone for relationships in other social contexts. For example, personal relationships between spouses, and employees and employers, could be analysed based on an understanding of socially accepted levels of one party's *amaeru* (seeking indulgence; creating a dependent, emotive relationship) and the corresponding other's *amaesaseru* (to indulge another person as an expression of love). His interest in *amae* stemmed from his position as a psychologist: *amae*, when it worked, created stable families and corporate groups; when it went wrong it resulted in clinical neuroses (Doi, 1986: 122). In other words, *amae* seemed to be 'what made the Japanese tick', much as Benedict's *on* and *giri* had seemed to be.

Doi's psychological model provided the emotional glue that made another Japanese anthropologist's argument hold water: Nakane Chie's theory of vertical society (*tateshakai*) stated that hierarchical relationships were more psychologically dynamic than horizontal ones. She published this idea first in Japanese and then in English in the slim but influential book *Japanese Society* (1970). Although her work focused on the hierarchical aspect of Japanese society, many took home the message that Japanese society was a 'group-based' society, and this 'group model' stuck in the popular imagination of the non-Japanese world. From Ruth Benedict's *on-giri* model through Doi's *amae* to Nakane's pyramid of hierarchical relationships non-Japanese people began to see Japan as a set of nested and triangle-shaped 'groups' that from the outside appeared to be interacting a sometimes 'irrational' way, but when considered in light of anthropological research the cultural logic made sense. This was the way for the 'Other' to understand the mysteries of Japanese behaviour.

Westerners (the 'Other' in the above sentence) were bent on figuring out what motivated the Japanese in both political and economic terms; understanding their 'culture' and their 'personalities' was deemed crucial to successful business negotiations. The Japanese were more than obliged to help the 'Other' learn about them and in the process created a national mythology of self-definition. *Nihonjinron*, or theories of the Japanese people, serves as a useful interlude to the discussion of Japanese cultural anthropology. This body of work, which arose from both popular and academic presses in Japan, rested on the idea that the Japanese culture, language and even race are unique compared to other societies. Thus, it is difficult, if not impossible, for an outsider to penetrate Japan's meaning or to master its manoeuvres. *Nihonjinron*'s emergence is thought to have been instigated not only by indigenous Japanese thought but by the initial isolating gaze of the foreign observer: '[i]n particular, though the

debt is rarely acknowledged, virtually the entire discourse of that branch of Japanese studies called *Nihonjinron* has been carried out within the framework established by Benedict's book' (Lummis, 2007). More succinctly William W. Kelly writes: '*Nihonjinron* is the Occidentalist retort to our Orientalist illusions' (1991: 396).

In the 1970s and 1980s the ideas of Japan as 'unique' and a 'collective society' have had resonance with scholars as well as general readers interested in the phenomenon of 'Japan Inc' (Japan's spectacular rise to economic power in the post-war era). Many wrestled with it, but perhaps the most powerful critique of this set of ideas was that made by two sociologists based in Australia, Ross Mouer and Yoshio Sugimoto. Their book *Images of Japanese Society: A Study in the Social Construction of Reality* (1986) was a methodological debunking of the myths that had gradually accumulated about Japan's special place in the world, simply by noting that their research had

> raise[d] doubts whether, in comparison with people in other societies, the Japanese are *more* group oriented, place *more* emphasis and social harmony, value *more* deeply group membership or social solidarity, or are more accustomed to 'vertical' forms of organization. Certainly every society is unique; but is Japanese society as 'uniquely unique' in terms of its levels of consensus and social integration as so many seem to suggest? (1986: 11, original emphasis)

Mouer and Sugimoto gave many examples of a more diverse and even disruptive Japanese society, which weakened the hold that the many theorists, culminating in the *Nihonjinron* and group-model supporters, had held for many years. For example, they noted variation and conflict in Japanese society on all levels and throughout history; the constant comparison between Japan with the West skewed its meaning (1986: 13–14, 16). Their ideas consolidated and gave voice to the discomfort other scholars felt regarding the popularity of the group model. Anthropologist Harumi Befu had argued similarly in 1980 that, amongst other things, historical evidence of enduring conflict, 'paternalistic neglect', strife that led to labour movements and scholarly 'failure to distinguish between ideology and behaviour' (1980: 31–36) had led him to believe that Nakane's group model was not a valid way to think of Japan as 'different' or 'unified'. This was mostly a kind of *kireigoto* ('nice things in Japan which Japanese find it comfortable to discuss with outsiders whose approval they seek' (1980: 39)) rather than an empirical description of social life in Japan.

While Mouer and Sugimoto were not card-carrying anthropologists, their challenge to the hegemonic view of Japanese society as a unified entity that could be understood only on its own terms had wide reaching influence on anthropological research. In the 1980s, concern with diversity in Japanese society grew: anthropologists conducted fieldwork that yielded messages about gender, identity, tradition and change. For example, the exploration of the Japanese 'self' was revisited with the publication of Dorinne Kondo's *Crafting Selves: Power, Gender and Discourses of Identity in a Japanese Workplace* (1990). Rather than focusing on the family or the individual's relationship to the corporate state or other entity, Kondo took a more nuanced approach to the understanding of Japanese social interaction in a variety of contexts. In her informative first chapter entitled 'The Eye/I' (1990: 3–48) she uses a discussion of the first person pronoun ('I') in Japanese to demonstrate the fractured but sensible 'wholeness' of the Japanese self (1990: 26). Kondo used the phrase 'referential solidarity' to refer the way the self is defined through a 'spatialized ideology of meaning as reference'; these referents are primarily determined by relationships to other conversational partners (1990: 35). While these discussions are not new in the field of Japanese social linguistics, this book did much to elevate anthropological studies of the self out of old binaries, and her reflective focus on her own selfhood not as a Japanese scholar or an American or British scholar but as an Asian American scholar further disrupted old mind sets about 'studying the "Other"'. The flourishing of Asian American studies was close to follow.

My own work on social marginality hinges on another aspect of the Japanese self: its interaction with others. As a student I was interested in Harumi Befu's previously mentioned essay 'A Critique of the Group Model of Japanese Society' (1980), where he convincingly argued against the group model as the main descriptor of Japanese society and instead offered the social-exchange model. In other words, the 'I'll scratch your back if you scratch mine' motto was more of a motivator than 'I have been programmed to respect people hierarchically superior to me in ways that no one else can understand'. Japanese people (like most humans on the planet) were equally motivated by 'individual self interest' (1980: 39) and thus were not any more 'unique' or more impenetrable than any other human beings. This made sense to me, but then I also wondered if Japanese people were strongly motivated by reciprocity why did volunteers working with the disadvantaged and homeless residents of Kotobuki-chô in Yokohama offer their time, energy and labour in an environment where there was little if any possibility for return? In *On the Margins of Japanese Society: Volunteers and the Welfare of the Urban Underclass* (1997), I observed that

the fundamental inequality of the economic and social status of the volunteers and residents in Kotobuki prevents their relationship from becoming truly reciprocal. [Yet, i]nequality is what brings the groups together... Volunteer activities provide an opportunity for Japanese to overstep social boundaries and have an impact on the underclass. (244)

In other words, though the 'self' in Japan had been previously bound to a group to which an individual was not only hierarchically embedded but was also caught up in a 'give-and-take' relationship, there was significant activity by some Japanese against the strong borders that separate individual or corporate interests. It was precisely this kind of against-the-grain activity that arose from the unrest and dissatisfaction described by Befu, Mouer and Sugimoto in their criticisms of Japan as a serene homogenous society. The Japanese self was fractured and relational but also one that was active and took risks rather than staying within the status quo.

Another more contemporary view of the self offers a different perspective on the relationship between individual will and self-expression. While Benedict's or Doi's model had portrayed the Japanese self as bound by certain theoretical concepts that 'stuck' the individual in certain roles with specific expectations during their life stages, Laura Miller's work on the beauty industry in contemporary Japan eloquently illustrated that the self (as seen through the body) in Japan is not merely a static, nature-given object. In *Beauty Up: Exploring Contemporary Japanese Body Aesthetics* (2006) Miller saw the body as a concrete example of the self, certainly gendered, but that its expression and aesthetic values could be molded and contoured (literally as well as figuratively!) to create a self-image that appealed to the individual's sense of beauty as well as discipline, as a pleasingly expressed face and figure was equivalent to a well disciplined mind (2006: 3).

Lastly, while identity has been discussed in many fruitful ways, another interesting recent approach by an anthropologist is the work of Karen Nakamura on the deaf community in Japan. Her book *Deaf in Japan: Signing and the Politics of Identity* (2006) proposed that deaf people, like any other ethnic group in Japan, such as the Ainu or the Resident Koreans, constituted an ethnic minority which has its own language and which experiences limited access to mainstream positions of power and status. Like race, deafness is thought to be biological, but there is socio-historical construction behind deaf identity that varies immensely (2006: 11–12). The self has an undeniable physicality but Nakamura demonstrates that the social, economic and political landscape of the deaf culture in Japan has a great deal in common with other attributes such as gender, ethnicity or class.

Modernity and Tradition

A strong interest in the changes Japan was experiencing during the reconstruction period (beginning in 1945 and ending with the 1964 Tokyo Olympics) and the ensuing 'rapid growth period' (1955–1973), with all its economic, social and ideological reforms, resulted in a great many monographs on Japan's transition from a pre-war imperial state to a democratic consumerist nation. Befu notes that anthropologists have been particularly 'interested in the generalized cultural patterns, social practices, and personality traits which have contributed to Japan's *modernization*' (1971: 183, emphasis added), implicitly referring to the Benedict Doi Nakane legacy mentioned above. He continues by noting that anthropologists have looked at modern Japan using a number of tropes; one of interest here is the 'Japan as a Borrower' (1971: 183–4). He notes that Japan 'has not been simply a copier... [but] has devoted her energy to making refinements' (1971: 183). This idea of 'refining', or, in other words, an active change to an existing cultural or social form intended to produce a desired effect or benefit, is a focal point for research on the social and cultural changes that Japan underwent in the post-war period.

While Thomas P. Rohlen's *For Harmony and Strength: Japanese White-Collar Organization in Anthropological Perspective* (1974) and Ronald P. Dore's *Shinohata: A Portrait of a Japanese Village* (1978) were some of the earlier examples of this concern with a transforming society (the former has been considered closely aligned with Nakane's model of vertical society), other scholars have looked at Japan's progress to, through and perhaps out of modernity in a multitude of innovative ways. For example, Theodore C. Bestor, who undertook fieldwork in an 'old' Tokyo neighbourhood, found that the historical evidence behind some of the 'traditions' was actually rather thin. Instead, Japanese community leaders and other participants relied on

the use of social idioms or metaphors that seek to clothe the present in a mantle of venerable antiquity... [where] residents construct and manipulate ideas about what are supposed... to be historical patterns of community organization so as to shape the present to their own advantage. (1989: 258)

Jennifer Robertson's book *Native and Newcomer: Making and Remaking a Japanese City* (1991) is a more recent example of the re-examination of community construction in wider metropolitan Tokyo. Both these ethnographies showed the importance of 'history' and 'tradition' in Japanese society, but delved deeper into the social consequences as to what 'history' meant to real people in their real lives.

Another ethnography that addresses contemporary manifestations of tradition and modernity in Japanese society is Scott Schnell's *The Rousing Drum: Ritual Practice in a Japanese Community* (1999). Schnell tracks the 'unruly' drum performances in a communal festival in Furukawa, Gifu Prefecture. Schnell argues that the ritual meaning within this festival is 'continually amended, reinterpreted, or transformed according to the needs of its practitioners – needs that clearly change over time in response to changing sociopolitical and economic conditions' (1999: 4). While the festival dates back to the early 1830s, the 'traditional' aspects of this ritual are manipulated by current performers to express resistance and to legitimate change in this community.

The use of the term 'history' in inverted commas is deliberate. Anthropologists have examined the use and the manipulation of this term extensively in recent scholarship. Marilyn Ivy's essay 'Itineraries of Knowledge: Trans-figuring Japan' in her book *Discourses of the Vanishing: Modernity, Phantasm, Japan* (1995: 29–97) argues that postwar cultural expressions of 'Japanese-ness' have been seen through the prisms of the past, the present and even through 'Other'-ed geographic references. 'Traditional' Japan had become as 'exotic' to its own urbanised inhabitants as a trip to a foreign country. By essentialising 'Japan' as historic and exotic, the full-speed-ahead pace of postmodern Japan was allowed a space to preserve the idea of a past, even as it left that idea behind. This creatively strategic malleability of Japanese historical traditions continues to capture our attention: Christine R. Yano's ethnography of the musical genre of *enka, Tears of Longing: Nostalgia and the Nation in Popular Song* (2002), focuses on looking back (and forward) through popular music. *Enka*, she notes, is not 'mere nostalgia', idealising a cultural past that has been lost or has never truly existed; instead, it

is always newly created ... enka denies that the past is past and provides a space within the present where the values, interactions, and emotions associated with the past can continue to exist. (26–27)

Globalisation and Consumption

As previously noted, Japan has been seen as a geographical area with little to offer theoretical advancements in the field (Robertson, 2005: 4). Recent research in the area of globalisation and consumption, however, trumps this long-held position that anthropologists of Japan have little to contribute to theoretical understanding of global phenomena.

Japan's own preoccupation with globalisation's linguistic predecessor 'internationalisation' (*koku-saika*) means that there is a wealth of published research on transnational issues concerning Japan, even before 'globalisation' became a catchword in academia (see 'Japan and Globalization' by Dobson, this volume). For example, Roger Goodman's long-term research on the internationalisation of education in Japan covers many aspects of globalisation as seen from an anthropological perspective, from his first ethnography on *kikokushijo* (returnee students) (1993) to his more recent work on internationalisation as an aspect of educational reform, and wider issues of globalisation in Japan (for example, Goodman et al. 2003).

Another anthropologist who has written convincingly about globalisation in the Japanese context is the veteran scholar Harumi Befu. His article 'Globalisation Theory from the Bottom Up: Japan's Contribution' (2003) argues that the diffusion of Japanese culture around the world provides an empirical 'bottom up' approach that challenges the assumption that globalisation is a Westernising process (2003: 4–5).[5] This idea (globalisation equals Westernisation) has been most directly challenged by evidence provided by voluminous Japanese cultural flows to other parts of Asia and the West, making Japanese popular culture an important decentring force in the contemporary global landscape (Iwabuchi, 2002). In particular, the transnational consumption of Japanese popular culture (in the form of food, consumer electronics, anime films, fashion and so on) has been at the heart of these globalisation processes. Ian Condry's book *Hip-hop Japan: Rap and the Paths of Cultural Globalization* (2006) is of great interest in this discussion not only because of its timely topic but also because of its strong reliance on anthropological methods to analyse a complex cultural phenomenon in Japan. Condry employs cultural-studies theory but privileges the ethnographic context, using the emic term *genba* to describe the 'scene' (coincidentally, I often heard this same term in the context of day labouring, referring to the construction site – obviously, whatever the context, the *genba* is 'where it's at'). Condry's major contribution is that he gives a concrete context that demonstrates that the development of globalisation and its counterpart, localisation, proceed simultaneously and cannot be examined separately.

While Japanese products have been enormously successful in overseas markets, despite ongoing recessions since 1991, Japan's domestic consumption patterns of both domestically and internationally produced goods are also highly developed. Whether Japan is selling high-tech electronics or automobiles to international trade partners, or importing foreign luxury goods, everyday basics or basic food stuffs, Japanese society itself has developed into an intensely consumerist environment. Consuming is empowering, both for the individual and the collective nation: my research on Japanese popular music industry recounts a reflected rise in the 'positional power' of Japan vis-à-vis the USA, which is seen as the leader of a constructed 'West', from 'conquered' nation to 'valued consumer' in a global market (2008: 37). Popular cultural production and consumption is the main arena in which everyday citizens could participate in this shifting cultural relationship, merely by choosing (or not choosing) to buy certain products.

While consumer electronics, computer games, *manga*, and *anime* (and the music associated with these latter two products) have been the most significant cultural exports to Japan, food culture is an emerging subgenre in scholarship about Japanese cultural consumption. With the success of sushi and other Japanese food products overseas, interest has been focused on what Japanese culinary culture means in Japan as well as abroad. Food purchasing, preparation and consumption, all of which constitute a total social event in the daily lives of every Japanese citizen, have potent cultural meaning. Theodore C. Bestor's *Tsukiji: The Fish Market at the Center of the World* (2004) is another important anthropological monograph that demonstrates that the raw materials of Japan's beloved cuisine of sashimi, sushi and other seafood dishes are globally traded yet internally quite powerful in their ability to convey meaning to consumers. Merry I. White, who has written extensively on the Japanese family, zeroes in on this communicative ability of food culture to convey powerful messages. Her essay 'Ladies Who Lunch: Young Women and the Domestic Fallacy in Japan' (2001) demonstrates that consumption patterns of Japanese young women show how the consumption of food (both in restaurants and in shops) conveys changing notions of femininity in Japanese society. White argues that the 'self-expressive bond between young women and food' works to create 'unfeminine acts and expression, which one might see as small resistances to the contradictions of the "domestic fallacy"' (2001: 64).

Within the scholarship on consumption, a focus on specialised consumption, or fandom, has also emerged as a subset of interest in Japanese practices. William W. Kelly's edited volume *Fanning the Flames: Fandom and Consumer Culture in Contemporary Japan* (2004) made convincing arguments that fandom as a kind of active and intimate consumption was a useful tool for understanding the dynamics of a variety of social relationships and a number of aesthetic preferences in Japan; meanwhile, the concomitant explosion of the popularity of 'Japan's Gross National Cool' (a phrase coined by American journalist Douglas McGray in 2002) meant that English-speaking audiences were no longer interested in 'what made Japan tick' in terms of winning or losing military wars, but rather 'what made them make such cool stuff?'. Yet in this maelstrom of interest and fascination lies judgement: the predictable and defensive reaction to the initial Western fascination with Japan's 'soft power' is a kind of cultural put-down of consumers of Japanese pop culture (both Japanese and non-Japanese) as 'deviant' (Stevens, 2010). Further studies of Japanese popular culture are necessary, I believe, to 'rescue' fandom from its current association with social ostracism, placing it instead in a logical structure of a historical consumer culture in Japan and in the West.

CONCLUSION

In this essay I have necessarily narrowed a rich and lengthy disciplinary 'story' in two ways: first by interrogating its methods and then by focusing on a selected portion of its content. The latter part of the story (here described under the rubrics of 'studies of the self', 'tradition and modernity' and 'globalisation and consumption') is crucial because it provides important, if debatable, insight into an empirical reality we hope to know as 'Japan'. In terms of other disciplinary contributions to this volume, information about Japan as supplied by anthropologists (versus sociologists or political scientists, for example) demonstrates its methodological priorities as it focuses on particular aspects: the self, social interaction and social ideologies of identity.

Perhaps then we can say that while the content is interesting and valuable, anthropology's singular contribution is in its methods. Ethnographic fieldwork, as an epistemological philosophy, underpins all of the research I have mentioned above (though I note there are many more worthy volumes omitted by space constraint rather than by quality). Laura Miller underwent many of the '*esute*' procedures she describes in her book, physically experiencing the same sensations to better understand why her informants sought to shape their bodies in certain ways; Karen Nakamura is fluent in both ASL and Japanese *shuwa* (sign language). Fieldwork, where this kind of first hand experience is embedded, results in what anthropologists hope is a better an understanding of the 'Other', hopefully at an 'intimate "grass roots" level' (Hendry, 2003: 3) rather than one which is distant and described with broad brush strokes. The detail that intrigues us is also the detail that informs us to consider our own selves as an object of inquiry and reflection. Robertson's statement that 'anthropologists... [have] continued to work *both through and against*

a conventionalized conception of Japan as a mirror image of... the United States [and more generically] "the West"' (2005: 6, emphasis added) demonstrates this struggle to understand the differences between 'Self' and 'Other'.

NOTES

1. See Robertson (2005) and Ryang (2004) for critical reviews of the history of Western anthropologists of Japan, and Kuwayama (2004) for a review of how Western anthropologists' work has interacted with those whom he refers to as 'native' scholars. A definitional caveat: this chapter focuses on socio-cultural anthropology, although studies of the linguistic anthropology and archaeology of Japan are present in the wider field. Also, for reasons of scope and space, I am limiting my focus to works published in English by scholars from North America, Europe, Australia and Asia.

2. This stance is illustrated by Immanuel Wallerstein's influential world-systems theory (1974).

3. One anthropologist in particular who has made this point explicit in many of her publications is Joy Hendry: for example, her book *Wrapping Culture: Politeness, Presentation, and Power in Japan and Other Societies* (1993) is clearly about Japan, but gives attention to related customs of wrapping in the Middle East and Africa.

4. Generally, Japanese names in this chapter are presented in the Japanese fashion (family name first, personal name second) except in the case where the author has published extensively in English, such as Takami Kuwayama, Yoshio Sugimoto and Harumi Befu.

5. This article followed his co-edited volume with Sylvie Guichard-Anguis entitled *Globalizing Japan: Ethnography of the Japanese Presence in Asia, Europe and America* (2001), an earlier collection of essays on globalisation and Japan.

FURTHER READING

Bestor, T. C., Steinhoff, P. and Lyon-Bestor, V. (eds.) (2003) *Doing Fieldwork in Japan*. Honolulu: University of Hawaii Press.

Caudill, W. (1963) Patterns of Emotion in Modern Japan, in R. J. Smith and R. K. Beardsley (eds.) *Japanese Culture: Its Development and Characteristics*. London: Methuen, 115–131.

Hendry, J. (1999) *An Anthropologist in Japan: Glimpses of Life in the Field*. London and New York: Routledge.

Hendry, J. and Wong, H. W. (eds) (2006) *Dismantling the East–West Dichotomy: Essays in Honour of Jan van Bremen*. London: Routledge.

Lebra, T.S. and Lebra, W. P. (eds) (1974, 1986) *Japanese Culture and Behavior*. Honolulu: University of Hawaii Press.

REFERENCES

Ahmed, L. (1992) *Women and Gender in Islam: Historical Roots of a Modern Debate*. New Haven: Yale University Press.

Befu, H. (1971) *Japan: An Anthropological Introduction*. New York: Harper and Row.

Befu, H. (1980) A Critique of the Group Model of Japanese Society, *Social Analysis*, 5/6:29–43.

Befu, H. (2003) Globalization Theory from the Bottom Up: Japan's Contribution, *Japanese Studies*, 23(1):3–22.

Befu, H. and Guichard-Anguis, S. (eds) (2001) *Globalizing Japan: Ethnography of the Japanese Presence in Asia, Europe and America*. London: RoutledgeCurzon.

Benedict, R. (1946, 1974) *The Chrysanthemum and the Sword: Patterns of Japanese Culture*. New York: Houghton Mifflin.

Bestor, T. C. (1989) *Neighborhood Tokyo*. Stanford: Stanford University Press.

Bestor, T. C. (2004) *Tsukiji: The Fish Market at the Center of the World*. Berkeley: University of California Press.

Bird, I. (1880, 1984) *Unbeaten Tracks in Japan: An Account of Travels in the Interior including Visits to the Aborigines of Yezo and the Shrines of Nikkō and Isé*. London: Virago.

Condry, I. (2006) *Hip-hop Japan: Rap and the Paths of Cultural Globalization*. Durham and London: Duke University Press.

Doi, T. (trans. by J. Bester) (1981) *The Anatomy of Dependence*. Tokyo: Kodansha.

Doi, T. (1986) Amae: A Key Concept for Understanding Japanese Personality Structure, in T.S. Lebra and W.P. Lebra (eds) *Japanese Culture and Behavior*. Honolulu: University of Hawaii Press, 121–129.

Dore, R. P. (1978) *Shinohata: A Portrait of a Japanese Village*. New York: Pantheon.

Embree, J. F. (1939) *Suye Mura: A Japanese Village*. Chicago: University of Chicago Press.

Geertz, C. (1995) *After the Fact: Two Countries, Four Decades, One Anthropologist*. Cambridge MA: Harvard University Press.

Goodman, R. (1993) *Japan's 'International Journal': The Emergence of a New Class of Schoolchildren*. Oxford: Clarendon Press.

Goodman, R., Peach, C., Takenaka, A. and White, P. (eds) (2003) *Global Japan: The Experiences of Japan's New Immigrants and Overseas Communities*. London: Routledge.

Hearn, L. (1894) *Glimpses of Unfamiliar Japan*. Tokyo: Kodansha.

Hendry, J. (1993) *Wrapping Culture: Politeness, Presentation, and Power in Japan and Other Societies*. Oxford: Oxford University Press.

Hendry, J. (2003) *Understanding Japanese Society* (3rd ed.). New York: Routledge.

Ivy, M. (1995) *Discourses of the Vanishing: Modernity, Phantasm, Japan*. Chicago: University of Chicago Press.

Iwabuchi, K. (2002) *Recentering Globalization: Popular Culture and Japanese Transnationalism*. Durham: Duke University Press.

Kelly, W. W. (1991) Directions in the Anthropology of Contemporary Japan, *Annual Review of Anthropology*, 20, 395–431.

Kelly, W. W. (ed) (2004) *Fanning the Flames: Fandom and Consumer Culture in Contemporary Japan*. Albany: State University of New York Press.

Kondo, D. (1990) *Crafting Selves: Power, Gender and Discourses of Identity in a Japanese Workplace*. Chicago: University of Chicago Press.

Kuwayama, T. (2004) *Native Anthropology: The Japanese Challenge to Western Academic Hegemony*. Melbourne: Trans Pacific Press.

LeVine, Robert A. (1984, 1994) Properties of Culture: An Ethnographic View, in R. A. Shweder and R. A. LeVine (eds) *Culture Theory: Essays on Mind, Self and Emotion*. Cambridge: Cambridge University Press, 67–87.

Lummis, C. L. (2007) Ruth Benedict's Obituary for Japanese Culture, *Japan Focus*. Online: http://www.japanfocus.org/-C__Douglas-Lummis/2474

McGray, D. (2002) Japan's Gross National Cool, *Foreign Policy*, May/June, 45–54.

Miller, L. (2006) *Beauty Up: Exploring Contemporary Japanese Body Aesthetics*. Berkeley: University of California Press.

Mouer, R. and Sugimoto, Y. (1986) *Images of Japanese Society: A Study in the Social Construction of Reality*. London: Kegan Paul International.

Nakane, C. (1970) *Japanese Society*. Berkeley and Los Angeles: University of California Press.

Nakamura, K. (2006) *Deaf in Japan: Signing and the Politics of Identity*. Ithaca NY: Cornell University Press.

Plath, D. (1992) *What's an Anthropologist Doing in Japan?* VHS video. Richmond, in Earlham College, Institute for Education on Japan, Media Production Group.

Robertson, J. (1991) *Native and Newcomer: Making and Remaking a Japanese City*. Berkeley: University of California Press.

Robertson, J. (2005) Introduction: Putting and Keeping Japan in Anthropology, in J. Robertson (ed) *A*

Companion to the Anthropology of Japan. Malden, MA and Oxford, UK: Blackwell Publishing, 3–16.

Rohlen, T.P. (1974) *For Harmony and Strength: Japanese White-Collar Organization in Anthropological Perspective*. Berkeley: University of California.

Ryang, S. (2004) *Japan and National Anthropology: A Critique*. Abingdon: RoutledgeCurzon.

Schnell, S. (1999) *The Rousing Drum: Ritual Practice in a Japanese Community*. Honolulu: University of Hawaii Press.

Stevens, C. S. (1997) *On the Margins of Japanese Society: Volunteers and the Welfare of the Urban Underclass*. London: Routledge.

Stevens, C. S. (2008) *Japanese Popular Music: Culture, Authenticity and Power*. London: Routledge.

Stevens, C. S. (2010) You are what you buy: consumption and fandom in (Post) Modern Japan, *Japanese Studies*, 30(2): 199–214.

Wallerstein, I. (1974) *The Modern World System I: Capitalist Agriculture and the Origins of the European World Economy in the Sixteenth Century*. Orlando FL: Academic Press, Inc.

White, M. I. (2001) Ladies Who Lunch: Young Women and the Domestic Fallacy in Japan, in K. Cwiertka and B. Walraven (eds) *Asian Food: The Global and the Local*. Honolulu: University of Hawaii Press, 63–75.

Yano, C. R. (2002) *Tears of Longing: Nostalgia and the Nation in Popular Song*. Cambridge MA: Harvard University Press.

3

The Practice of Religion in Japan: An Exploration of the State of the Field

Lucia Dolce

Banshōji 万松寺 is an ancient Buddhist temple in the Osu district of central Nagoya, affiliated to the Sōtō denomination of Zen.[1] Squeezed within the streets of an extensive shopping arcade lined with small shops selling traditional goods and amusement parlours, it looks like many other temples in the middle of a bustling modern city. Its illustrious pedigree is attested by the grave of the Oda family, kept in a small back yard accessible from the street. The temple was originally built in Ōwari province by the father of Oda Nobunaga, the famous sixteenth-century daimyō, and moved to this area in 1610. Its main hall was rebuilt in 1994 as a five-floor concrete building, and the third floor now houses a postmodern reinterpretation of the memorial hall: the Suishōden 水晶殿, or Crystal Palace. Designed by Tokyo architect Fujimura Masuo in 2008, this charnel house makes use of the latest technology, glass and stainless steel to fill the space with light. A stylised altar is placed at the centre of the hall. The curved walls contain small drawers enshrining the ashes of departed parishioners, on which small images of Buddha have been carved. Entrance to the chamber is by a secure identification system that ensures only family members with identity cards can access it. When a visitor swipes the card on the sensor reader a drawer lights up and its little Buddha emits a halo of white light that

expands in circles, thus identifying the visitor's own ancestor. Samples of ground on which to scatter the ashes are displayed on a small table in the corridor outside the hall. The bereaved may choose from different types of grass, mountain stones and sand to mirror the departed's favourite landscape.[2] Although it belongs to the Zen school, the temple welcomes anyone to acquire a 'lot' in the chamber, regardless of one's Buddhist sectarian affiliation or indeed one's religion.

Such a modern interpretation of the memorial hall may seem at odds with traditional modes of caring for the ancestors. Yet Banshōji is but one example of the dynamic integration of the past and contemporary that characterises the religious landscape of today's Japan. Continuity and creativity, postmodern crisis and kitsch unfold in asymmetric patterns and shifting translocal modes. Monks in black robes rush through the muggy Tokyo streets in August to offer ancestral prayers at their parishioners' homes; children in coloured kimonos celebrate their coming of age at Shinto shrines in cities as in the countryside; centuries-old apotropaic liturgies attract crowds to Nara in the cold winter nights; ascetic practitioners train under a mountain waterfall on Sunday and return to be businessmen on Monday – all these practices attest to the resilience of ritual traditions, albeit with added layers and adaptations. A shrine dedicated to war criminals, the subject of yearly protests throughout Asia, and a political party sponsored by a lay Buddhist organisation echo the complex relation that religion continues to entertain with the state. The animation films of new religious groups connecting humankind to the universe and the 'vows bars' run by Buddhist priests to appeal to young people reveal the concern of new and old institutions with finding alternative ways of impacting on society. A bewildering spectrum of organisations, sites, performances, narratives, beliefs and material culture reveals a diverse participation in religious life, at the official and community-wide as well as the informal and individual level.

How do we make sense of the plurality of expressions that constitutes 'religion' in Japan today? How have scholars approached and analysed the complexity and fluidity of this religious landscape? The following pages explore the state of the field, highlighting a number of methodological issues that have confronted scholars and the paradigms that currently inform the field.

RELIGION, RELIGIONS, NO RELIGION: THE DILEMMA OF DEFINITIONS

The ambiguity inherent in the use of 'religion' as a universal category has affected the understanding of belief systems in Japan since the beginning of its modern era. During the Meiji period (1868–1912) a specific term, shūkyō 宗教 (literally 'the teachings of a school'), was adopted to identify a variety of phenomena related to the practice of religion (Pye, 2003). This term translated the idea of a text-centred, distinctively doctrinal and cognitive religion, modelled after Christian Protestantism. Yet conceptually this formulation of religion was, and has altogether remained, alien to the great majority of the Japanese engaged in religious practices.

The figures that statistical surveys give for the religious composition of the population testify to the difficulty of defining religion in terms of (exclusive) commitment to a creed. Quantitative data, collected by the government or other research institutions, indicate that most Japanese people simultaneously belong to at least two religious traditions, Shinto and Buddhism. At the same time a large part of the population professes to be non-religious. Young people, in particular, claim to have no interest in religion, although they also appear to believe that some gods or other forms of invisible beings exist. Furthermore, religion comes last among the social institutions afforded trust (Kisala, 1999). A number of interconnected factors are behind these apparently idiosyncratic results. Firstly, the language used in analysing religious

identity draws from interpretative parameters rooted in the early modern, north-European experience of religion. This language places religion within the narrow field of individual belief, rather than practice, which, by contrast, has a cultural, historical and socio-political dimension. Secondly, the post-war policies aimed at separating state and church, which were a reaction to the deployment of religion during the Second World War to sustain the imperialist regime, helped on the one hand to affirm freedom of religion and erect privileges for all religious bodies (Abe, 1968–70) but on the other marginalised religion within distinct boundaries. The lack of conceptualisation of religion in formal education (Fujiwara, 2005), together with what one may call a 'will to secularism' that has reformulated religious activities in cultural terms, have precipitated the difficulty of recognising specific acts performed within the family or society as religious actions. Finally, the religious pluralism that characterises Japan as an integral part of its historical make-up poses interpretive problems to the monotheistic model of religion.

This last point is of crucial importance if one examines the way in which the Japanese religious landscape is described. Should one speak of a 'Japanese religion' in the singular, in which the peculiarities of religious practice in Japan can be subsumed and exalted, or rather of 'Japanese religions' in the plural? If the latter, how many 'religions' should this rubric include? The expression 'Japanese religion' first appeared as an academic term in the English-language publications of Anesaki Masaharu (1873–1949), the founder of modern religious studies in Japan. It is still employed in introductory works that are widely used in English-speaking classrooms (Earhart, 2004; Ellwood, 2007). Yet the use of the singular has come under critical scrutiny, for it does not just emphasise a region-specific focus but suggests a type of religious experience that is unique to Japan and is endowed with uniform features. It ultimately engenders an essentialised, idealised and therefore inevitably ahistorical view of religion (Isomae, 2005), often with nationalistic overtones.[3]

By contrast, the use of the plural stresses the multivocal presence of religious beliefs, making Japan 'a hybrid space where religions have both emerged and been introduced, and have then influenced one another' (Isomae, 2005). The question here, however, is that of the nature of each of these 'religions' and the dynamics of their interaction. While the co-existence of diverse traditions and segments of traditions, autochthonous or of continental origin, is widely acknowledged, each of them has traditionally been treated as a discrete object of enquiry, following a (monotheistic) model of religion. Overviews of the religious landscape of Japan describe it as consisting of four, five or six traditions, with Shinto and Buddhism at its core and other traditions, such as Confucianism, Christianity or Daoism, variously added depending on the position and interest of the writer. The inventory expands to include 'traditions' of ambiguous status, such as new religions and folk religion. For instance, one of the survey books mentioned above lists five religious strands, Shinto, Buddhism, Confucianism, Daoism and folk religion, and mentions a sixth, Christianity (which, however, it does not consider to have contributed to the formation of traditional Japanese religion; Earhart, 2004: 2). A more recent and undoubtedly excellent guide to Japanese religions lists Shinto, Buddhism, Folk Religion, New Religions and Christianity (Swanson and Chilson, 2006). These traditions are differentiated on the basis of their geographical origins, with Shinto embodying the 'indigenous' religion of Japan, Buddhism the Indian religio-philosophical system that reached Japan at the dawn of its (written) history, Confucianism and Daoism the 'quasi-religions' imported from China, and Christianity the religion from the West. Other distinctions are built on the social functions that each strand is perceived to fulfil today, often disregarding their historical evolution. Thus Shinto is presented as concerned with the positive stages of the life cycle, such as births and weddings, Buddhism with its darker aspects, such as funerals; new religions are seen as eclectic (and therefore suspicious) practices catering to the individual needs of well-being and success; Christianity is a minority creed for intellectuals; Confucianism informs the ethical dimension of social life. Furthermore, the received description of each tradition is not uniform, for historical traditions are identified by their philosophical and cultural assets, while new religions or folk religion by their socio-political organisation or by their rituals. This is also due to the different training of the scholars working on each of these two areas, as we shall see. In short, the attempt at organising the religious landscape of Japan according to categories borrowed from other cultural contexts has favoured the depiction of its religious strands as self-contained units with discrete moments of interaction. At best, the image conveyed is that of a division of labour, crystallised in mottos such as 'born Shinto and die Buddhist'.

PLURALITY AND THE COMBINATORY PARADIGM

There are practical and heuristic reasons for drawing borders. The problem with a compartmentalised representation is that it obscures the reciprocal and multiple relations that determine each religious strand. The differences in the possible lists of Japanese religions already hint at the difficulties of formulating the relevance of a single tradition independently from the place it occupies within a combinatory system. Other factors need to be taken into account too. Firstly, the interaction between two or more traditions is not static: it needs to be historicised. For instance, the simplistic division between Shinto and Buddhism outlined above might be reassessed when one considers that most of the rites performed at shrines today have not existed for much more than a century. Shinto weddings are a recent ritual invention, which dates back only to the beginning of the twentieth century and was part of the adoption of Western customs in the wave of modernisation (Antoni, 2001). By contrast, Shinto funerals were created in the Edo period, became available to the larger population at the end of the nineteenth century – that is, before the first 'Shinto' wedding was celebrated – and are still performed today (Kenney, 1996–7, 2000). Secondly, the compartimentalisation of religious traditions is not a neutral, descriptive taxonomy. It implies a judgment of value expressed in binaries such as indigenous/imported, old/new, orthodox/heterodox, pure/eclectic, where one tradition is played against the other according to agencies that are different every time.

The study of religion in Japan thus continues to struggle with a double question: how to formulate the interdependencies between differently originated traditions and the dynamics of discrete processes of transfer, and how to do so with a language developed in a perspective of the monotheistic religions. From the latter perspective the Japanese approach to religion(s) appears so peculiar that indigenous practices have been described as 'syncretic religion' (shūgō shūkyō 習合宗教) (Shinno, 1993), and this characterisation is often extended to most religious forms developed in Japan. A similar impasse has occurred in the study of Chinese religions. Received scholarship has put the syncretic label on the interaction between traditions that do not fit the model of neatly distinguished and independent religions (Sharf, 2002: 21–25). Yet the notion of syncretism is born of modern theological concerns. It implies the existence of a self-contained system around a core set of beliefs, which is understood as 'pure, orthodox religion'. As in the example of the practices that characterised the Mediterranean basin in the Hellenistic period, syncretism constitutes a hegemonic system in a vertical relation of power with weaker, popular systems, which are progressively absorbed in it (Martin, 1983). Syncretism is also associated with popular practices, vis-à-vis institutional and official practices (Shaw and Stewart, 1994). Neither of these characterisations, and the negative connotations they bear, reflects the religious phenomena in Japan.

Historically, the combinatory system in Japan was a complex and creative discourse that affected ideology, economics and social practices. It belonged to the elite, religious and lay, as much as to the common people. One of the best illustrations of how the system worked is the relation between kami[4] cults (that is, Shinto) and Buddhism. Their combination was expressed in linguistic strategies, grounded in the Buddhist textual tradition and its meditational techniques (Grapard, 1987), narratives and miraculous tales (MacWilliams, 1990) as well as visual representations that depicted the kami in the guise of Buddhist deities (Guth Kanda, 1985; Bocking, 2001; Dolce, 2006–07 [2009]) (see Figure 3.3). A relational logic was developed, which connected religious institutions, myths and politics in a web of analogies, and affected the ways of legitimising political power, from the emperor[5] to the shogun. The medieval discourse on the combination of Buddhist and kami-related practices has been well researched in the last twenty years, both in Japan and in the West, and important studies have appeared in English, starting with the pioneering work of Allan Grapard.[6] In these studies terms that refer to isomorphic systems, such as 'associative' or 'combinatory', have emerged to describe the relation between Shinto and Buddhism in the attempt to overcome the inadequacies of the term 'syncretism'. Albeit more generic, this terminology indicates that the 'religions' that developed on Japanese soil intersected at multiple points and even shared the ontological identity of their deities, but at the same time

maintained clear distinctions in segments of their physical space and ritual modalities.

Recent research has demonstrated that the combinatory nature of Japanese religious practice was not just as a characteristic of a specific historical period (the medieval) or of distinct social groups, as post-war scholars had argued. It pervaded Japanese history in a variety of ways. The extent to which it was overcome by modernity and by the adoption of western models of religion also needs to be reconsidered. At the end of the nineteenth century the Meiji government imposed a forced separation of Buddhism and kami worship (*shinbutsu bunri*), which amounted to Japan's cultural revolution (Grapard, 1984) and is often regarded as the starting point of modern religion in Japan. This movement no doubt destroyed many of the rituals, places and arts of the combinatory system. Yet current field evidence shows that it did not mark the end of combinatory practices. Combinatory beliefs have continued in everyday practice (Smyers, 1991; Reader and Tanabe, 1999). Shugendō, the tradition of mountain asceticism that embodies the system, has been maintained, albeit on a smaller scale and in a different institutional format, and is having a resurgence in contemporary Japan (Bouchy, 2000a, 2005; Sekimori, 2009; *Cahiers d'Extrême-Asie*, 2009 [2011]). Historic combinatory rituals have been reintroduced at major shrines (see Figures 3.1 and 3.2). New rituals that associate well known shrines and temples have recently been created to publicise the symbiotic worship of kami and Buddha as the essence of Japanese spirituality, and

Figure 3.1   Tendai monks, led by the *zasu*, enter Hiyoshi Shrine to perform Buddhist rituals for the kami during the Sannō festival (Photo: Lucia Dolce)

Figure 3.2   Monks from Mt Hiei debate the *Lotus Sutra* in front of the kami of Hiyoshi Shrine (*Sannô raihai*) (Photo: Lucia Dolce)

the media coverage that these have received suggests that a return to 'pre-Meiji religion' may become a new marketing element for these institutions (Dolce, 2007b). These trends oblige us to rethink the combinatory phenomenon beyond a historically confined time, and beyond the binary Shinto-Buddhism model.

One may argue that what is today called 'religious pluralism' has been part of the religious history of Japan since its beginning, and has affected the very definition of its 'indigenous' religion. The combinatory system was and still appears to be the 'main paradigm' of Japanese religiosity, rather than the exception. To read the religious phenomenon in Japan through a combinatory perspective may thus offer a key to decode the apparent ambiguity and the overlaps between traditions. Such a perspective implies a hermeneutical paradigm that employs plurality and inclusiveness as analytical categories, rather than just descriptive terms, as an alternative to the predominant model based on purity and alterity[7]. It is here, then, where the study of Japanese religion could contribute to the study of religion in general.

INSTITUTIONS AND DISCIPLINES: THE BOUNDARIES OF THE ACADEMIC STUDY OF JAPANESE RELIGIONS

The modern study of religion in Japan started relatively early. In 1905 the first Department of Religion was established in a state university, the then Tokyo Imperial University. Its pioneer scholars, Anesaki Masaharu and Kishimoto Hideo (1903–64), both conversant with contemporary north European and American notions of religion, exerted an enduring influence on the field (Isomae, 2002; Pye, 2003). Yet religion as a field of study has maintained an ambiguous status in post-war Japan. This is perhaps reflected in the small number of departments of religion. Indeed critics have pointed out that the contribution of religious studies (*shūkyōgaku* 宗教学) to the theoretical understanding of religion in Japan has been less significant in post-War Japan than in its beginnings (Isomae, 2003: 55–64).

As an academic field, the enquiry into Japanese religions reflects the methodological diversification that characterises the study of religion in general, but also brings questions specific to the Japanese case to the fore. Firstly, there is a conspicuous division of tasks and knowledge between experts belonging to the different disciplines interested in the religious phenomenon, from theology (in its meaning of systematic theory of the divine, including Buddhist and Shinto doctrines) to history, sociology, literature, anthropology and folklore. While each subject area has hugely contributed to our (factual) understanding of the specifics of religious life in Japan, the traditional boundaries between disciplines and the consequent extremely specialised nature of Japanese scholarship have hindered a comprehensive approach to the study of religion.

Secondly, departments of religion in Japan have been characterised by a sociological approach that favours a quantitative analysis of religion and a focus on current, socially relevant practices. Throughout the second half of the twentieth century religious studies have, by and large, concentrated on documenting the impact of New Religious movements. The success of these groups triggered scholarly attention on their organisational structures and socio-economic context (Shimazono, 1998 and 2004). At the same time it allowed scholars to draw parallels between Japan and Western societies, and explore the tension between the expected secularisation of a modern, industrialised society and the numeric and financial growth of religious groups. Further, their extraordinary expansion abroad offered the possibility of studying Japanese religions in a global context, addressing issues of diaspora and translocality (*JJRS*, 1991).

By contrast, a systematic study of historical religions such as Buddhism or Shinto is not usually part of the curriculum of departments of religion. As belief systems, these traditions have typically been studied by philologists, intellectual historians and theologians in other institutional contexts: the confessional departments of universities run by Buddhist or Shinto lineages on the one hand[8] and the departments of Oriental Thought, Indian and Buddhist studies or National Literature on the other. Similarly, Christian doctrine is studied mainly in Christian institutions, and Confucianism as part of intellectual history or of Chinese studies. Thus, while programmes in religion have concentrated on contemporary practices, and on emerging groups in particular, the study of established traditions has revolved around the knowledge of their historical and philosophical context and predominantly of their pre-modern sources.

This split reflects another division, that between the study of modern and contemporary religion on one side and pre-modern religion on the other. This dichotomy, which appears more pronounced in Japan than in other academic cultures, draws on the methodological antithesis between the use of textual sources and ethnographic fieldwork, but it goes beyond the question of the specific linguistic training needed to approach pre-modern material. It embodies a superfluous distinction between doctrine and practices, written sources and material culture, which has had repercussions on how the dynamics of development of religious traditions in Japan have been represented (Hubbard, 1992; Sharf, 1995b). I shall return to this point.

PARADIGM SHIFTS AND TURNING POINTS

Given this divided academic context, the shifts that have occurred in the field of Japanese

religions in the last decades necessitate a different analysis according to the rubric and tradition.

Sociological Reorientation

Recent trends in the study of contemporary religious practices have been profoundly influenced by the social and political situation created by the sarin gas attack on the Tokyo underground by members of a new religion, Aum Shinrikyō, in 1995. The Aum affair, as it was called, may indeed be considered as the most important turning point in the perception of religion in post-war Japan (Pye, 1996a). Many Japanese suddenly became aware that 'religion' existed in Japan, and the incident triggered a new, disparaging association of the word with danger, violence and politics. The role of the media in shaping the public discourse about religion and in fostering religious groups' identity changed (Baffelli, 2007). In the academic world, it caused a shift of focus away from the study of new religious movements (Kisala and Mullins, 2001; Reader, 2001). Instead, the importance of reassessing the relation between politics and religion in modern times came to the fore, precipitated by the revisions in the law that regulated religious bodies as juridical persons (*shūkyō hōjin*) and the restrictions on the activities of such religious bodies (Kisala, 1996; Reader, 2002; Hardacre, 2005), as well as by the resurgence of nationalist policies. The latter have been most prominently explored in relation to the official worship at Yasukuni shrine, where war criminals are enshrined (Nelson, 2003; Breen, 2004). An emerging area of inquiry addresses the ethical aspects of current social practices, in particular the issue of organ donation and post-life destiny (Shimazono, 2007; Steineck, 2003).[9] Another line of research has turned to the cultural practices of religion, including those of the New Religions (McLaughlin, 2003; Stalker, 2003), and to the visual and virtual channels of postmodern spirituality, such as anime (Thomas, 2007), manga (MacWilliams, 1999), films (Reider, 2007) and the internet (Baffelli et al., 2010). Less attention has been paid to the transformations that are occurring within the historical traditions, both at the hermeneutical and at the institutional level (Covell, 2005). This is a promising area of enquiry that may help bridge the gap between modern and pre-modern practices. For instance, the radical reinterpretation of Buddhist doctrines that occurred in the late 1990s, known as critical Buddhism (hihan bukkyō), was triggered by contemporary social problems but put into discussion notions that were considered the quintessence of Japanese Buddhism, such as that of original enlightenment (Bodiford, 1996; Stone, 1999b;

Swanson, 1993). Similarly, the current engagement of Buddhist temples and clerics with questions of social responsibility, such as welfare and terminal care, and their search for new spaces of proselytising, from NGOs to night bars (*JJRS*, 2004; Licha, 2009), calls for a more comprehensive reassessment of the patterns of Buddhist presence in contemporary society. Among the traditional practices that have undergone tremendous growth and permutations only pilgrimages and funerals have received sustained attention (Reader, 2007; Rowe, 2008).

Historiographical Shifts

The study of pre-modern religion has been characterised by other paradigm shifts. Here historians have played the leading role in readdressing the axioms of post-war scholarship. To understand the import of this reorientation of the field one needs to recall that the received narrative on the historical development of Japanese religion was based on a chronological division that followed that of Japanese political history. In very broad outlines, it highlighted four stages, each with an internal progression of climax and decay: a period of formation, when Buddhism was imported from China and kami practices took their definitive shape, which parallels the creation of the Japanese state under the centralised ruling of a king; a period of expansion, which saw the establishment

of Chinese forms of Buddhism with the support of the aristocratic court (Heian period); a period of creativity when new Buddhist schools emerged, paralleling the rise of the new warrior classes to power (medieval period); and a period of rationalisation and secularisation corresponding to the long peace under shogun rule when Confucianism came to dominate over and above the superstition and corruption of Buddhism (early modern period, better known as Tokugawa or Edo).[10] In this narrative one notes, firstly, the disjuncture between periods, which fixes the significance of each stage in a few traits with contrasting terms (aristocratic rituality versus military-style commitment, Confucianism versus Buddhism), dismissing the complexity of the interaction between old and new. Secondly, this view assumes a linear development according to an evolutionary model that saw the next stage as an improvement on the previous in ethical, theological or spiritual terms, with great breakthroughs and turning points. Thirdly, the representation of each period is affected by an anachronistic reading of religious history through the lens of institutional models developed later. Thus the Tokugawa period, for instance, was studied for its Confucian ideologies and nativistic thought (*kokugaku*), with the result that the study of Buddhism was almost completely dismissed. The theory of the decadence of Tokugawa Buddhism was affected by the economic and ideological blow that Buddhist institutions suffered in the aftermath of the Meiji

Figure 3.3 Amaterasu in the guise of a Buddhist young male deity called Uhō dōji. Hand-coloured print on paper. Edo period. Private collection (© Lucia Dolce)

Restoration and by a reading of the Meiji Restoration as the overthrowing of the ancient military regime in favour of modernity and progress, as well as religious freedom (Ienaga, 1965; Klautau, 2008).

The grand theories of historical development fragmented in the 1970s. The idea that religious innovation occurs only in periods of dramatic change also found its critics.[11] Scholars turned from macro political history to micro socio-economic history. A seminal figure in the formulation of new paradigms to interpret the development of Shinto and Buddhism was the late Kuroda Toshio (1926–1993). As a medieval historian with a Marxist perspective, Kuroda focused on the economic and institutional aspects of Buddhism. Previous scholars had maintained a reformist and ethical reading of the new schools of Buddhism that began in the early medieval period, projecting on them the idea of religion as an individual and interiorised experience, which aspired to the transcendental and was based on faith rather than on the performance of rituals – an interpretation clearly influenced by Protestant notions, which served to set medieval Buddhism apart from the state-related religion of the previous periods. Kuroda, by contrast, demonstrated that the shrines and temples of the 'old institutions' had maintained a hegemonic position through the political changes of the period and indeed constituted the dominant discourse in doctrinal and socio-political terms throughout the middle ages. In Kuroda's paradigm (called *kenmon taisei*, system of power structures) religious institutions were one of the three power blocks that ruled pre-modern Japan, together with the court and the warriors (Kuroda, 1996a; Sueki, 2006). The theory also proved that the understanding of medieval Buddhism as a Japanese type of 'Protestant religion' was at fault, and helped shift the focus to a variety of devotional (as well as exorcistic) practices that were upheld across borders (*JJRS*, 1996). Finally, drawing on medieval sources, Kuroda called attention to the extent to which Shinto was inextricably linked to and depended on Buddhism throughout the pre-modern period (Kuroda, 1981). As we shall see shortly, this instigated a groundbreaking rethinking of the terms in which it was possible to speak of Shinto as a historical category.

The impact of the socio-economic paradigm and a re-evaluation of institutional history have also helped reorient the discourse on Tokugawa religion. The work of the historian Tamamuro Fumio has been noteworthy for articulating the significance of Buddhism anew. It has demonstrated that in this period Buddhism became a de facto national religion in institutional terms, for every Japanese was required to be affiliated to a Buddhist temple. Such affiliation popularised devotional practices that would remain enduring features of Japanese Buddhism, above all the ways of dealing with the ancestors (Tamamuro, 2001). Scholars now acknowledge that Buddhism continued to legitimise the authority of the ruling elites, including the shogun (Sonehara, 2006), and from them received significant support that allowed the physical expansion of Buddhism with new temples and halls of worship (Graham, 2007). The rise of urban merchant culture did not mean the demise of the combinatory practices that characterised medieval religious culture but their spread among wider strata of the population. Tamamuro also turned attention to local religion and to local sources dug out of temple and private archives. (*JJRS*, 2001) Far from being stagnant the Tokugawa period now appears as an era of extraordinary ferment which saw a surge in devotional activities, such as pilgrimages, and a proliferation of local religious associations (Sawada, 2002). Such wealth of research on Buddhism has eclipsed the centrality of Confucianism, the place of which in the religious landscape of Japan needs to be reconsidered. It is true that Confucianism became a more influential intellectual force during the Tokugawa era and was described as one of the three 'ways' upheld in the country, the others being Buddhism and Shinto. Further, neo-Confucian forms of self-cultivation informed several religious practices, not only of the elite (Sawada, 2004, 1998). Yet Confucianism in Japan never developed a ritual system broadly adopted by the population as it did in other Asian countries, such as in Korea. The rites for the ancestors, for example, which are a fundamental feature of Confucian practice, in Japan took a Buddhist format even at the moment of greatest influence of Confucianism. The worship of Confucius, too, was a circumscribed phenomenon (McMullen, 1996). Thus the question remains of what should be included in the rubric of Confucianism and to what extent Confucianism in Japan may be regarded as a religious tradition (Boot, 2007; Tucker, 1998).[12]

More recently the early period of Japanese religious history has undergone review.[13] Here the issues are twofold. Firstly, there is a problem of sources. While the Tokugawa period has an excess of sources, the early period is characterised by a paucity of records and the problematic nature of the extant ones. Then there is an ideological question concerning the interpretation of foreign influences on early Japan, connected with the origin of the Japanese kingship – a politically sensitive topic reflected, for instance, in the post-war limitation of access to the imperial tombs (Edwards, 2000). The post-war depiction of early historical religion was that of a uniform and homogeneous religiosity sponsored and controlled by the emerging state through the organised worship of indigenous deities and a centralised form of Buddhism. In recent decades scholars have started challenging such presumptions, drawing on extraordinary archaeological discoveries as well the work of historians such as the late Amino Yoshihiko (Amino, 1992). These findings have questioned the Japanese ethnic origins of indigenous practices and pointed at their East Asian root. Recent studies have substantially reconstructed the influence that immigrant lineages from the Korean peninsula exerted on the development of Buddhism and Shinto alike (Yoshida, 2003; Como, 2008). This perspective has shifted the focus from state Buddhism to an understanding of Buddhism as a more disseminated tradition in various local areas. The role played by women, lay and ordained, in the performance of religion has come to the fore (Ruch, 2002; Nishiguchi, 2009), as has that of religious figures not officially ordained (Kleine, 1997; Kleine and Kohn, 1999). On the other hand the historical existence of Shōtoku Taishi as the pious statesman, who received scholarship had posited as the emblem of state Buddhism, has been questioned (Yoshida, 2006). Scholars have started unveiling the extent to which continental ideas shaped the conception of the indigenous deities, further demonstrating that religious knowledge moved around not necessarily through religious specialists but through the dissemination of technology and the practices of service groups, such as artisans and skilled craftsmen (Como, 2009). Such compelling reorientation of the field calls into question the nature of practices that have long been thought to be native or pre-Buddhist, and variously defined as Shinto or Daoist, for want of a better interpretative framework. I shall discuss the question of Shinto shortly. Here I would like to point out the impact of the current historiographical perspective on the understanding of the role that another Chinese tradition, Daoism, played in shaping Japanese religion. Daoism never took on an institutional dimension in Japan, nor was there a systematic appropriation of Daoist liturgies. In this sense it is difficult to include it in the classification of Japanese religions, where it sometimes figures, as we have seen above. Scholars have looked for the Daoist roots of practices that could not easily be placed within the received boundaries of Buddhism and Shinto (Kohn, 1995) (see Figure 3.4). Daoist ideas may indeed be found in the early conception of kingship (Barrett, 2000) and ancient Japanese court symbolism (Ooms, 2008). However, recent research has made clear that notions included under the rubric of Daoism, such as the doctrines of yin and yang and Five Phases, divination, geomancy, astrology and calendar calculations, were seen as intrinsic component of a general Chinese religiosity and were transmitted to Japan not as Daoism but as part of Chinese culture. The Bureau of Yin and Yang, for instance, an important institution in early

Japan that compiled the calendar, was adopted as part of Chinese-style state administration (Bock, 1985; Butler, 1996). At a later phase Daoist deities and practices were transmitted together with Buddhist texts and as a component of Buddhism. Such is the influential cult of the Northern Dipper (Dolce, 2006d) or of Kōshin (Kohn, 1993–1995). Techniques of longevity and immortality, originally inspired by Daoist religious practice, were also incorporated in Buddhist medical knowledge. Does it then make sense to speak of Daoism as a separate, perhaps liminal, category of Japanese religion? Once again, a reassessment of practices performed across the borders of institutional Daoism, Buddhism or Shinto may help to reshape understanding of how the combinatory system worked in the ancient period (*Cahiers d'Extrême-Asie, 2012*).[14]

Buddhist Studies and the Sectarian Nature of Japanese Buddhism

While recent historiographical directions have shifted the interest of scholars towards the institutional aspects of Japanese Buddhism, scholarship on the doctrinal development of Buddhism in Japan is still by and large produced within the narrow confines of the field of 'buddhology' (*bukkyōgaku*). This idiosyncratic English term was traditionally used in European languages to indicate the scientific study of Buddhist texts, namely a philological-critical approach devoid of faith-based concerns, which Japanese scholars embraced at the beginning of the modern era.[15] In recent decades Buddhist Studies in Western academia have shown a great extent of self-reflection and awareness of the methodological problems that affected the field, in particular the concentration on textual material, and have produced a remarkable amount of inter-disciplinary research, opening new avenues of enquiry into Buddhist thought (Cabezón, 1995, 2007 [2009]; Gomez 2007 [2009]). By contrast, the Japanese world of buddhology has been slow in articulating new methodological positions and the theoretical awareness that could encourage new directions of research. The study of Japanese Buddhist thought continues to suffer from the division of the Japanese tradition into discrete schools. The textual heritage of Japanese Buddhism is identified by distinct scriptural and commentarial corpora, each representing a school or lineage, according to the institutional make-up of contemporary Buddhism. Each school has its own canon, propounds linguistically independent representations of Buddhist soteriology, and is authenticated by different genealogies of patriarchs, with hardly any transversal concern for the whole of Buddhism.[16] The establishment of

(a)

(b)

Figure 3.4   (a) Astrological amulets sold at Daishōgun shrine and (b) the shrine to the yin-yang master Abe no Seimei in Kyoto (Photo: Lucia Dolce)

textual and hermeneutical lineages along the lines of sectarian genealogies has favoured the study of the Chinese precursors of each Japanese schools and their interaction more than a cross-sectarian analysis of hermeneutical patterns or soteriological tropes developed in the context of Japanese Buddhism. Even the meetings of the Japanese Association of Religious Studies reiterate the sectarian configuration by maintaining separate sections for each denomination, so that little theoretical conversation takes place between specialists of two or more forms of Buddhism. As a result it has become impossible to narrate a single history of Japanese Buddhist doctrine. Received scholarship speaks of the history of Tendai, Shingon, Pure Land, Zen Buddhism (and, 'more accurately', of Rinzai Zen, Sōtō Zen and Ōbaku Zen). Further, thanks to the fact that post-war

Japanese buddhology flourished remarkably and played a leading role in the study of Buddhism, compared with other Asian countries, this sectarian model was exported and projected onto other forms of East Asian Buddhism. Chinese Buddhism, for instance, has been understood to have developed within a similar sectarian structure, a problematic interpretation that scholars have begun to revisit only in recent years.

This sectarian approach has remained wedded to the academic study of Buddhist thought for the additional reason that the majority of doctrinal scholars work in denominational institutions, the successors of the monastic training seminars (*danrin*) of the Tokugawa period, and frequently belong to the tradition they study.[17] Such institutional affiliation on the one hand has assured the availability of resources to address doctrinal problems. On the other hand, it has accentuated the concern with sectarian agendas and the need to support the legitimacy of a denomination while at the same time pursuing an 'objective' enquiry. This tension has engendered a strategic concentration of the academic enquiry on specific topics. Much important work has been produced on the doctrinal sources that enjoy a privileged status in today's orthodox definition of each lineage. By contrast, little has been done on textual material that does not reflect such orthodoxy. The grey areas of Buddhist thought – those hermeneutical patterns that are no longer upheld, such as one finds in medieval Zen Buddhism, and those notions that the modernisation of Buddhism during the Meiji period relinquished in the sphere of superstition, such as ritual or divination – have been left in the shadows. Similarly, cross-sectarian connections, which would help untangle notions specific to Japan, have received little attention. The theories of original enlightenment, which shed light on Japanese conceptions of liberation and practice are one of the few topics that have undergone sustained analysis across sectarian borders (Stone, 1999a). The interpretation that different schools have given of the *vinaya*, the monastic rules that define the Buddhist clergy (Bodiford, 2005); the significance of the esoteric paradigm beyond the boundaries of the Tantric schools (Teeuwen and Scheid, 2006); and the reformulation of Buddhism carried out in the Meiji period under the aim of religious unity (Mohr, 2005) are only now starting to be explored.

The limit of Japanese buddhology thus lies in the nature of sectarian identities not having been put under due scrutiny. Sectarian forms of identity clearly existed throughout the history of Japanese Buddhism and in the early modern period were imposed institutionally on Buddhist lineages by the Tokugawa government (Sonehara, 2006). Yet the distinction between lineages rarely implied a coherent and exclusive affiliation to the doctrine that is today

assimilated to a single school. There was a rhetoric of legitimation at which the sectarian discourse was carried out, and a historical reality where monks moved freely between centres of learning and received instructions from multiple masters, which were then fed into the formulation of their doctrinal interpretations. Recent research has clearly proven that major figures of Japanese Buddhism, which received scholarship incontrovertibly located with a single school, were trained in more than one tradition. The textual body authored by Yōsai (or Eisai), known as the founder of Rinzai Zen, mainly consists of Tantric commentaries, and attest to his role as the initiator of a Tendai Tantric lineage (Mano, 2011). Nichiren, another medieval thinker, infamous for his fierce critique of Tantric forms of Buddhism, undoubtedly operated within esoteric circles (Dolce, 1999). To rewrite the mainstream narrative of Japanese Buddhism taking these links into account is the challenge of future Buddhist studies.

Between Politics and Cultural Identity: 'Shinto'

The study of Shinto has undergone an extraordinary revision in the last two decades, which has problematised the status that Shinto has held in the religious landscape of Japan. Today scholars agree that Shinto should be considered a flexible label applied to phenomena as diverse as the physical existence of shrines throughout the national territory, imperial ideology and folk practices, each of which represents an aspect of the engagement with the world of the native deities (*kami*), but not as the elements of a coherent and uniform religious system. The Shinto that has been presented as one of the religions of Japan is, by and large the product of late-nineteenth-century government policies, and it is necessary to take into account its modern beginnings to understand the problems that its study poses to present-day researchers.

The Meiji government actively campaigned to separate the spaces and rites of native gods from those devoted to Buddhist deities, dismantling the combinatory system that, as we have seen, formed the core of Japanese religion. The aim of Meiji ideologues was not to promote every shrine and every kami but to construct a 'national' faith that would serve as the backbone of a new and modern national identity, centred on the emperor. In fact, they conceived Shinto as a 'civic creed', and prohibited shrines from performing traditional rites of communication with the unseen world as well as other devotional practices that catered to the individual's need, focusing instead on reverence of the emperor and celebration of the nation. In this sense the new Shinto was the 'invention of a new religion', as an illustrious commentator

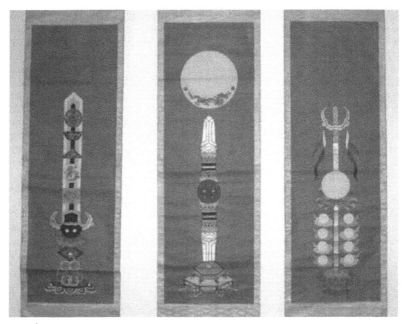

Figure 3.5   Buddhist shape of the three regalia that legitimised the Japanese rulers. Hanging scrolls, ink and colour on silk. Eighteenth century (© Trustees of the British Museum)

of the time, Basil H. Chamberlain, noted in 1912 (Chamberlain, 1912). Selective use of historical material and textual exegesis transformed the notion of kami into an ideological force at the service of the state, though the way in which this took place did not necessarily reflect the concerns of individual priests nor the interests of individual shrines (Breen, 2000).[18] At the same time, however, the possibility opened up for construing Shinto as a tradition in its own right, vis à vis Buddhism, Confucianism or Christianity, a status that Shinto had never occupied before in either institutional or cultural terms. It is this tradition that was resurrected after the Second World War.

Post-war studies of Shinto were mostly carried out by scholars, who often were also Shinto priests, descended by blood or academic lineage from the creators and administrators of state Shinto (Hardacre, 1989). Their narrative of the historical development of Shinto reflected a certain version of political history. It privileged the periods considered to be formative for the Japanese state, and later the nation: the ancient period as the moment of constitution of sacral kingship, when the myth of the divine origin of the Japanese rulers was formulated; and the late Tokugawa period as the precursor to the Meiji state, for at this time nativistic interpretations of the world of the kami emerged, which would be reused by Meiji ideologues. The rupture between these two 'beginnings', more than a millennium of cultural and institutional practices, was essentially left unaccounted for.

The continuity of the present with the ancient past was propounded on the basis of two, not necessarily consistent, self-definitions of Shinto. The first posited it as the 'indigenous' religion of Japan, which emerged in Japan's ancient past and has continued in an unbroken line from prehistoric times down to the present. The second elevated Shinto to embody the spirit of the Japanese, suggesting that Shinto was 'more than a religious faith' and encompassed the attitudes, ideas and ways of doing things that have become part of the way of the Japanese people (Ono, 1962).[19] The genealogy of such definitions is to be sought in the concern with recovering the identity of Japan along lines pretty much set in the Meiji period, that is, by exploiting the indigenous/foreign binary paradigm and by de-sacralising religion. Interestingly, historians shared this understanding of Shinto with scholars of folklore, who, albeit in a methodologically different way, were interested in kami cultic practices as the common substratum of the Japanese and the origins of their uniqueness.

The notion of the enduring existence of Shinto as a religious system was challenged in the late 1970s by the historian Kuroda Toshio. Kuroda shifted scholarly attention to the long span of history between the ancient period and the late Tokugawa period, which had been neglected by Shinto scholars, and argued that Shinto institutions and forms of worship had not existed independently from Buddhism before the Meiji period. As noted earlier, Kuroda's research became a turning point in many ways. It stimulated new archival research and a new interpretative framework, which has allowed us to uncover a wealth of material and document the variety of interaction between kami rites, institutions, notions and Buddhism (Grapard, 1984, 1987, 1992a, 1992b; Teeuwen and Rambelli, 2003; *JJRS*, 2002; *Cahiers d'Extrême-Asie*, 2006–07 [2009]; Breen and Teeuwen, 2010) (see Figure 3.5). It has also initiated a critical discussion of what constituted Shinto and at what point in history the word Shinto could be used as an appropriate term to describe the discourse on the kami that was produced in pre-modern Japan (Teeuwen, 2002, 2007). In fact, the term Shinto has become so loaded with difficulties (and vagueness) that religious historians often prefer the expression 'worship of kami' (*jingi sūhai*) instead.

The fundamental question of what was indigenous beyond the continental accretions remains under discussion. Recent research has demonstrated that even if one looks at ancient Shinto as a distinct liturgical system the rituals systematised between the seventh and ninth centuries (at the beginning of Japanese history) had little in common with those of the prehistorical period. They were adapted from contemporary Chinese codes (Okada, 1983) and were formulated after the encounter with Buddhism and the development of Japanese territorial awareness, at the same time Buddhist practices related to the afterlife were created (Mitsuhashi, 2010). For example, the specificity of the early kami cult, characterised by a complex, prescriptive but temporary, ritual purity, could be conceived only because Buddhism existed in symbiotic relation with it.

The other component of the received notion of Shinto as indigenous tradition, mythology, has also undergone a critical rereading. Myth was central to the interpretation of Shinto throughout history because the 'sacred corpus' of Shinto consisted of the historical chronicles of the early state originating in a mythical age of the gods. After the war the controversial historian Tsuda Sōkichi (1873–1961) pointed out the political nature of Japanese mythology, arguing that it had nothing to do with religion but was the creation of the intellectual elite of the time in which it was compiled (Tsuda, 1966). Today scholars have demonstrated that, whether expressed in the stories of the ancestral deities that legitimate the imperial persona as a divinely consecrated ruler, or in the romanticised notion of the emotional and aesthetic feelings of the people of Japan put forward by the nativist reading of Motoori Norinaga, the myth represents the narrative construction of the state and later of the nation (Isomae, 2010). Further, many of the features that characterise its deities, the depiction of the imperial ancestor Amaterasu as a weaver, for instance, are not immune to continental influences either (Como, 2009). Thus, what was conceptualised as

'indigenous' has been proven to have emerged and taken shape only through a negotiating process with imported elements. Rather than representing the enduring essence of what is 'Japanese' the indigenous may be rationalised, as Sidney Pollock has eloquently suggested in relation to the Indian cultural context, as that 'prior to which it is impossible to historicize – but not anything essential to the ethnos' (Pollock, 1996: 234).

Contemporary Shinto as a religious organisation, however, continues to rely on the definition of Shinto that scholars are deconstructing. The National Association of Shinto Shrines (Jinja honchō), an umbrella organisation constituted immediately after the war (Teeuwen, 1996), has attempted to articulate a consistent form of belief that could unify the diverse practices at shrines. It has Amaterasu as its central deity and reasserts the everlasting presence of shrines and kami, and at the same time speaks of a spiritual teaching based on respect for nature, exploiting the features of shrine geography (the sacred woods that often surround shrine buildings) and reinterpreting them in line with contemporary concern for the environment.[20] In this way the notion of indigenous is recreated and revamped in terms of cultural values. Yet some important shrines are not part of the National Association or have left it, and others proclaim that the nature of Japanese belief is combinatory. Anthropological fieldwork has documented the tensions between the organisation and individual priests (Nelson, 1997, 2000). Other organisations lay claims to Shinto and put forward its idealised values as universal values to be shared globally.[21] Who and what represent Shinto in the twenty-first century? Future scholars will no doubt need to decode the interactions and conflicts between the contemporary users and producers of 'Shinto' and the alternative visions of Shinto as a new religion which are borne out of its continuous search for identity.

Liminal Categories or Liminal Religion? Folk Religion

The rubric of folk religion has occupied a very important space in Japanese scholarship on religion and accordingly cannot be ignored in an overview of the field. Its area of enquiry traditionally covered a range of beliefs and practices that did not fall under institutionalised religion. In the words of the 'father' of folklore studies, Yanagita Kunio (1875–1962), these were the customs and beliefs preserved mainly in rural areas, a timeless 'faith of the ordinary people', unique to Japan. Yanagita focused on kami-related beliefs and on the practices concerning the ancestors, thus contributing to the definition of Shinto that I have noted above. Another ethnographer, Gorai Shigeru

(1908–93), pioneered the field of 'Buddhist folklore', aimed at understanding how Buddhism actually worked within the lives of ordinary people. Framed in these terms, the existence of a 'folk' class of religious practice in itself instituted the distinction between theoretically systematic religions, understood as orthodox and the domain of clerical and intellectual elites, and other interspersed, loosely structured practices, lacking in explicit doctrinal foci and accordingly described vaguely as magical, superstitious and, of course, inherently 'popular'. Recent Japanese scholarship has debated the meaning of folklore studies and the appropriate terminology that could give this discipline a broader respite (Shinno, 1993; Kawahashi, 2005), but the field does not seem to have overcome the circumscribed and introspective nativism that has characterised it (Schnell and Hashimoto, 2003). Scholarship in English, on the other hand, has insightfully attempted to find a different rubric that would do justice to the variety of practices shared across the borders of elite and folk, clergy and laity. Pye has advocated a new understanding of the notion of 'primal religion' (1996b), while Reader and Tanabe have developed the idea of 'common religion' (1999). Nevertheless, the reflection on the limits of the category of folk has not eradicated the rubric of folk religion as one of the distinct 'traditions' of Japanese religious landscape.[22]

Many of the practices that the rubric of folk religion encompasses are at the intersection of traditions (when these are defined as monothetic systems), but by no means of popular origin, or performed by casual or 'common' practitioners alone. A case in point is the mountain tradition of Shugendō, which among its lineages counts two of imperial origin (*monzeki*). Another example is asceticism, a category of practice that in other religious cultures is treated as part of the mainstream tradition.[23] These practices have been included in the rubric of folk religion primarily because they express combinatory forms of belief. In turn, by the very fact of being considered 'folk religion' their institutional aspects, the dynamics of power and identity that have helped their growth through the centuries, as well as the changes that they have undergone, have all been dismissed. Yet the mountain entry rituals of Shugendō, for instance, are institutionalised practices which have historically taken specific forms (Sekimori, 1995), are rooted in the Tantric formulation of soteriological ways and have evolved to the present day to include an entirely invented Shinto version (Lobetti, 2011). The same may be said of ascetic practices, some of which are performed in an institutional context. Examples are the thousand-day walking practice of the monks of Mt Hiei (Rhodes, 1987; Covell, 2004; Lobetti, 2011) and the winter practice of the Nichiren school (*aragyō*), a staggering hundred-day retreat held within institutional space, having as one result the acquisition of healing powers, which are in turn deployed within an institutional framework.

Interestingly, ascetic practices have often been linked to and read as shamanic practices, perhaps

Figure 3.6   Spirit possession on Mt Ontake (Photo: Lucia Dolce)

because of the healing effects that both produce. One may say that asceticism and shamanism are both academic categories imported into the religious scene of Japan. It is difficult to identify practices that correspond perfectly to the phenomena indicated by these terms. Let us take shamanism, which has been more studied. Japanese scholars have used this Western category to define a number of Japanese practices and have spoken of the religious specialists who perform them as shamans who enter into direct contact with different types of spirits by undergoing an altered state of consciousness. Certainly, communication between the world of the living and the invisible forces of the 'other' world is the main space of action of a shaman, who acts as an intermediary between these two worlds. Yet the current debate in religious studies has criticised the use of the term shamanism in the sense of a universal tradition embodied in different local realities (Knecht, 2003). This raises the question as to whether the diverse – mainly female – religious specialists that constitute the broad category of shamans in Japan may indeed be called such. Indigenous categories are not necessary helpful, given the diversity of the vernacular terms that are used to refer to these figures according to their geographical expansion (*miko*, *itako*, *dai*, *yuta*). How different these then are from other figures of 'specialists of possession', such as the (mainly male) leaders of the Ontakekyō confraternities (see Figure 3.6), is a point that needs to be explored. (The latter are often categorised in a different rubric because Ontakekyō is officially a new religion with Shinto origins.) A valuable interpretation, which promises to unveil the links between different historical agencies, focuses on the nature of these figures as oracular specialists (Bouchy, 2000b). Anne Bouchy has carried out a compelling study of one of such specialist from the Osaka area (1992). Scholars have also explored the language of the oracles of the *itako* of northern Japan (Neumann, 1992), as well as the adaptations that their oracular rituals have undergone to fit the contemporary space in which these specialists operate (Ivy, 1995; Knecht, 2004) (see Figure 3.7). The specific ways in which they are trained have also been surveyed (Blacker, 1975; Kawamura, 1994), but much needs to be done to understand their techniques, the cosmological system that informs them and the institutions that have supported them.

One very important shift in the areas of enquiry comprised by 'folk religion' is the turn from ethnographic studies to a historical and sociopolitical analysis. This new direction has allowed research to blossom, as the study of Shugendō attests (Sekimori, 2009; Bouchy, 2000a, 2005; Ambros, 2009; *Cahiers d'Extrême-Asie*, 2009 [2011]). Scholars have also started to explore the changes over time that affected religious occupations considered shamanic, in particular the *miko* (Goodwin, 2007; Meeks, 2011) and the *itako* (Groemer, 2007). This is important to understand the nature of their social role and the reason for their enduring presence in the landscape of Japanese religions. More importantly perhaps, this research highlights the relation of mutual influence, rather than opposition, and even physical closeness that these practices entertained with religious and political institutions. In this sense the current direction of research may ultimately help us reconsider the category of folk religion and suggest that it may be unnecessary in a perspective that takes religion as practice, that is, constructed out of both a discursive and performative dimension.

Liminal Categories or Liminal Religion? New Religions

The rubric of New Religions has been used as a descriptive category to indicate a variety of religious groups formed after 1868 as well as to emphasise the diverse characteristics that these groups share, such as their being lay movements, focusing on material and physical benefits and miraculous interactions with the spirit world, or expressing millenarian expectations (Shimazono, 1995). Contrary to their Western counterparts, Japanese new religious movements cannot be regarded as a marginal and transient phenomenon. They have been part of the modern fabric of religion in Japan for more than a century, several of them count a considerable membership and, as mentioned above, have had a noticeable influence on Japanese society. In this sense they are better considered as alternatives to established religions (Reader, 2005), which may amplify aspects that are present in the latter, for instance a vitalist worldview that encourages self-cultivation (Hardacre, 1986), but are not substantially different from established religions. Do we then need a separate academic category for them and a distinct place in the inventory of Japanese religious traditions?

The ambiguous status of New Religions is evinced by the disparate contextualisation that scholars have made. Some have presented them as part of a global new–age movement (Shimazono, 1993). Others have linked them to folk traditions, comparing their exorcistic practices to the shamanic techniques found in local expressions of religion (Davis, 1980). Scholars have also noted the close relation many of these groups have with established religions in terms of the language they use to define practices, beliefs and gods (Hubbard, 1998) or of their very practice (Hardacre, 1982). This is an important point that is often dismissed, partly because the study of these movements has primarily addressed their social dimension, partly because their followers are often thought not to be interested in doctrinal matters. Yet not only could some of these groups be included within one of the established traditions – Buddhism, say – because of theological or ritual similarities; they present themselves as Buddhist. Such is the case of Sōka Gakkai, Shinnyoen and Agonshū, among others. The 'appropriation' of a Buddhist identity against the more topical association with 'Japanese new religions' is even more explicit abroad, where these groups emphasise the Buddhist essence of their practice.[24]

Thus, the category of New Religions remains a scholarly rubric. The explosion of research in this field throughout the second half of the twentieth century, in Japan and in the West, has perhaps made inevitable that the 'new' and 'new new' movements were construed as a 'new tradition'. Yet the self-perception of the groups that constitute the rubric remains fluid and fluctuating. Different mechanisms of identity construction are at work, which need to be explored further. The tension between the local and often nationalistic basis on which the new religious groups were originally grounded, and their aspirations to represent the universal message of religion, which has been exploited in their pursuit of international visibility, is one area that has not received sufficient attention. The redefinition of religion that is taking place in Japan since the Aum affair (mentioned earlier) will no doubt further affect the categories in which new religious groups are understood.

A PRACTICE-CENTRED APPROACH

Having surveyed problems and expectation of the field, I would like to sketch an alternative perspective from where it may be possible to reread Japanese religions beyond the traditional sectorialised approach of disciplines and fields. This approach takes practice as its object of enquiry. The focus on practice not only attests to the shift from text-centred analysis to context, which has occurred widely in religious studies, it puts emphasis on the different ways of apprehending the religious.[25] I understand practice in a broad sense that encompasses the textual and discursive, as well the political, institutional, ritual and narrative, that is, practice as an interpretative paradigm that does not privilege one level of analysis but is constructed on the interplay between different levels. Scholars have long contended that the prominence given to systems of belief implies a narrowly prescriptive definition of what counts as religion, which privileges the written expressions of elites, usually male, and thereby eliminates from consideration the vast majority of what religious people actually do (McMullin, 1989: 10–12). By contrast, a practice-centred approach draws attention to the ways in which the facts of religion are expressed through laws, objects, places, narratives and performances, namely, that which constitutes the materiality of religion. In this sense materiality does not consist exclusively of the world of objects that are produced for and by religious practice. It also embraces the liturgical procedures that regulate the communication with the unseen world as well as the physical gestures that are acted out as ways to resolve the problems of the mind. Purity, for instance, is considered a condition of the sacred in all religious forms in Japan. If one analyses it from the perspective of practice, however, purity needs to be understood through the spatial constructions that implement it (it delimits the sacred and accordingly the access to it), in the physical conduct prescribed to manifest it (washing one's hands before enter a shrine) and in the performative movements to achieve it (chanting the phrase 'purification of the six senses' while ascending a sacred mountain, enacting repentance through running and virtuous jumps). Insofar as these are material expressions they have each their own history, and are, like other historical phenomena, subject to change. Focusing on the dynamics of practice thus allows us to explore religion as a process (rather than a product of either symbolic or economic systems) and as embodied and emplaced experience (Vasquez, 2010) – a paradigm that necessarily privileges fluidity, translocativity and asymmetric uses.

Among the conceptual components of a practice-focused perspective three deserve particular attention as interpretative parameters: agency, emplacement and media. The notion of an agency was traditionally connected to the role of individual experts in the development of rituals. Ritual-studies scholars have reinterpreted the concept in a more complex fashion, relating it more broadly to notions of authority, legitimacy and efficacy. In particular, they have emphasised that agency does not only deal with supernatural and divine (or virtual) intervention, whether from gods, spirits, ancestors or prophecies, it also comprehends human agency, manifested in a variety of modes (Sax, 2008). One example of the latter, of great importance for interpreting the development of religious practice in Japan, is political agency. It occupies a central role in the growth of the institutions that carry out religious practice and often determines the systematisation of the latter (Okada, 1983; Sonehara, 2006). It shapes the discourse on religion as a contested space for the assertion of or the resistance to power, whether in ideological terms (Paramore, 2009), nationalistic or pacifist terms (Ives, 2001; Stone, 2003) or legal terms (Hardacre, 2005). I shall return to these modalities shortly. At the opposite spectrum of the political mode is another type of agency that I have called gendered agency. This serves as a valuable viewpoint to explore the discrete meanings that are moulded into a given practice because of the gender and social status of religious actors. Here the focus on women's agency is particularly interesting, not only because it has recently emerged conspicuously in scholarship on religion (Nishiguchi, 2009; Ruch, 2002; *JJRS*, 2003), but also because the social position of women in Japan allows for a shift of attention towards practices that are often perceived as marginal. Women's agency reveals how their engagement in religious activities has created new meanings for religious practices as well as new practices themselves. A case in point are the rituals for aborted foetuses, often interpreted as practices that exploit women's emotionality (Hardacre, 1997; Underwood, 2009), or the 'shamanic' rituals performed by *itako* and *miko*, considered to exploit women's ability to communicate with the invisible world (Kawamura, 1994; Meeks, 2011). The focus on agency also allows us to understand how women have negotiated or challenged practices that have limited their participation in religion, such as the historical denial of access to sacred places (Fowler, 1998; Miyazaki, 2005; Suzuki, M., 2007) or the idea of bodily hindrances to the achievement of perfect enlightenment (Groner, 1992). It is important to bear in mind that the notion of agency does not imply a single agent in relation to a specific practice. On the contrary, practice entails multiple agencies. It is this property that allows continuous negotiations between actors and recipients and produces the tension between, for instance, institutions and individuals. The dynamics of control and patronage that are generated by political agency well illustrate this aspect. Multiple agency also implies that practices that are presented as unchanged since old times do not remain invariable but are transformed and are the subject of constant innovation by new users (Inoue, 2000; Reader, 2007).

The second parameter that I would like to consider, emplacement, addresses the strategies by which beliefs and soteriologies are embedded in time and space. Time and space have been key categories in religious studies and, as such, have been analysed through a variety of approaches from philosophical to sociological and phenomenological. In a perspective focused on practice they are crucial not as terms of the historical and geographical contextualisation of religious practices but as active elements that shape practice themselves. Emplacement emphasises the flow of time and the construction of space; it allows us to consider the possibility of a soteriology of time. In Buddhism, for instance, temporality is an agent of awakening, as one finds in the interpretations of the stories of the *Lotus Sutra* (Groner, 1992), or in the philosophy of time of the Zen master Dōgen (Heine, 1986). The language of prophecy, in the past as in the present (Dolce, 2003; Kisala, 1998), and the writing of history and the remaking of myths (Isomae, 2010; MacWilliams, 1999) demonstrate that practices related to time are entwined with the formulation of space as part of the process of constructing identities, both individual and collective. These dynamics

Figure 3.7 A female oracular specialists (*itako*) channels the spirits of the dead at Osorezan (Photo: Lucia Dolce)

provide an insight into notions such as the end of Buddhism (*mappō*), which inspired many religious practices in medieval Japan and was related to a specific conception of the national territory (Dolce, 1992, 2007a). In this perspective space is postulated not as the container in which individuals and societies perform their activities but as an element that is appropriated and construed as the place of practice, be it physical territory or imagined geography. Scholarship on Japanese religion has produced compelling redefinitions of sacred space, pioneered by the studies of Allan Grapard on cultic sites (1982, 1984, 1992a, 1994), and has explored a remarkable number of temples, shrines and sacred areas. This research has unveiled how the configuration of religious space responds to historically determined agendas, as we see in the medieval creation of Kōyasan, the mountains which would become the sacred place of Tantric Buddhism (Londo, 2002; Gardiner, 1996), or in the politically loaded modernist constructions of Ise as a Shinto place (Reynolds, 2001), as well as in the transformation of Buddhist temples into places that display the modernisation of Japan (Jaffe, 2006). The analysis of emplaced practices proves that sacred geography is made of boundaries, centres and peripheries, liminality and hierarchies (of places and of the individuals who use them, and even of the deities who abide

therein), and that political and economic power needs to be taken into account in the articulation of religious space.

Finally, let us turn to the media of religious discourse. The appreciation of the visual and material as categories of analysis of religious phenomena has grown immensely in the last twenty years, influenced both by an interest for the practice of the quotidian and by the acknowledgment that visual and material sources can elucidate what people thought and did better than written sources. This turn has helped focus on issues of representation and performance of religion, drawing on different areas of literary and artistic production. It has brought to the fore, for instance, the role that legends and miracle stories have played in the construction of religious views and the strategies of legitimation and proselytisation that unfold in text-image material, from the precious medieval scrolls explaining hell (Hirasawa, 2008) to contemporary manga (MacWilliams, 1999; Eynon, 1997). At the same time visual sources often attest to the conceptualisations of the soteriological discourse in a more compelling way than written sources, which are bound by the rhetoric of sectarian legitimation. The paintings representing the deity Amaterasu as a variety of Buddhist figures (Dolce, 2006-07 [2009]), or the several statues of kami wearing Buddhist robes (see Figure 3.8) which

Figure 3.8   Stone at the entrance of the temple complex on Mt Hiei, carved with the word 'Protecting the state' (*chingo kokka*) (Photo: Lucia Dolce)

emerged from the shrine repositories of Kanagawa Prefecture a few years ago (Kanagawa kenritsu shiryō hakubutsukan, 2006), offer incontrovertible evidence to the devotional nature of the combinatory cult of the kami (see Figure 3.3). In some cases visual sources also present alternative and even heretical readings of doctrinal questions, which the received orthodox and standardised interpretations have buried away (Dolce, 2006a, 2010a). The ritual context offers other ways to reconsider the importance of material sources. Objects such as the Buddhist statues used as main objects of worship during liturgical performances play a specific function that goes beyond the decorative and the didactic. Scholars have produced compelling analyses of these icons as living embodiments of divine agency and religious authority, and as agents in the transmission of religious hierarchies (Faure, 1998; Sharf and Sharf, 2001; Levine, 2001). Here the relationship between icons and the normative texts that prescribe their ritual use needs to be re-evaluated in the light of the disagreements between the two, which emerges both from a close analysis of records of ritual procedures and the observation of ritual performances. The link of the material media to political agency is also fundamental: artistic and architectural projects as well as ritual performances serve to impress the significance and effectiveness of religion as well as the power of its sponsors. In turn, religious patronage entails a substantial investment of resources for the creation and maintenance of religious buildings, the provision of offerings and the commission of rituals. Japanese history offers plenty of evidence of this strategic alliance between religious materiality and power, from the construction of the Great Buddha of Tōdaiji in the early times of the Japanese state to the shogunal reconstruction of Buddhist temples in the early modern period (Graham, 2007). Similar dynamics are at work in the case of private sponsorship. Finally, visual agency has distinct repurcussions. The metamorphoses of religious objects into cultural artefacts, which ensue from the placement of icons in spaces of display, whether at the temple itself or in a museum, suggest yet another interplay between users and producers. (Levine, 2001; Stalker, 2003; Suzuki, Y., 2007; Dolce, 2006b).

The Performance of Religion

Within a perspective on practice, ritual occupies a crucial place. The ritual landscape of Japan is difficult to map because of the bewildering quantity and diversity of liturgical performances, both contemporary and historical. The terminology employed to name them offers some distinction according to the institutional framework in which rituals are performed. For instance, the terms that refer to kami-related liturgies (*saishi, sairei, matsuri*) are different from those indicating Buddhist liturgies (*hōe, shūhō, hōyō, jisō*). Further distinctions may be made within single traditions: Buddhists liturgists use the two emic categories of exoteric and esoteric to indicate rituals belonging to different systems of Buddhism. Yet these characterisations are not always consistent: there are kami rituals performed by the Buddhist clergy (see Figure 3.1), as there are liturgies that include elements of both the exoteric and esoteric systems (Payne, 2006). An alternative way of exploring religious performance which highlights its dynamics is to employ broader paradigms based on agency. Here I shall outline three: denominational rituals, public rituals of political agency and private rituals.

The first paradigm draws on rituals that define one religious tradition as liturgically distinct from another and thus serve to legitimise its position in inter-sectarian and intra-sectarian terms. These rituals embody the doctrinal specificity of a lineage and shape the training curriculum of its clergy. Examples are the initiation rituals of the mandalas of the two worlds in the Buddhist Tantric schools (Sharf, 2003), the meditation sessions of the Zen school or the mountain entry practices of the Shugendō lineages (Sekimori, 1995). Yet if one considers the individual practitioner's agency these liturgical procedures may also become rituals of individual empowerment and are described as the experiential space of close interaction with the unseen or divine world (Sharf, 1995a). Received scholarship has seen these rituals as the patrimony of distinct hermeneutical traditions. Recent research, however, suggests that the historical process that established them as unique to a tradition was more complex: different levels of exchange can occur between lineages, and many elements of these liturgies may be indeed shared between ritualists officially belonging to different traditions. (Dolce, 2011) Further, some elements considered inherently constitutive of these rituals may be portable, i.e. they may be used in a different institutional or non-institutional context with complex strategies of adoption and recreation. The new religion Agonshū, for example, employs a typical element of Tantric and Shugendō liturgies, the fire altar, but with a completely revisited meaning that no longer depends on the Tantric understanding (the two fire altars are said to represent the worlds of the dead and of the living) (see Figure 3.9).

The second paradigm of analysis brings public agency into play to explore community rituals and institutional rituals in support of the state or nation. The first have traditionally been embodied by festivals conducted at local shrines (*matsuri*), in particular in villages and rural areas. These were the focus of the early studies of ritual in Japan, which

(a)

(b)

Figure 3.9   (a) Agonshū Star Festival: members dressed as *yamabushi* and (b) the two *goma* platforms (Photo: Lucia Dolce)

emphasised the continuity of the celebrations for the kami as an example of an enduring popular rituality that gave cohesion to the community. There are Buddhist rituals that also play this role. Some examples are the propitiatory rituals (*shunie*) performed at Tōdaiji and Yakushiji as part of the annual calendar of those temples, or the rituals performed for the commemoration of the founder in temples belonging to Nichiren Buddhism. Although these events also have a separate clerical dimension, it is the agency of local groups that

makes possible their performance as public rituals (Dolce, 2010b). The historical continuity of this type of ritual, albeit often invented, has been seen as an important factor in understanding the role that ritual plays in the maintenance of authority and expression of political hierarchies. Yet these rituals may also become critical sites for the struggle over authority (Schnell, 1995). State-supporting rituals, on the other hand, historically constituted one of the main activities of selected shrines and temples and embodied the symbiotic relation between ruling elites and religion (see Figure 3.8). Religious institutions and individual clerics invested in and were legitimised by the provision of a range of ritual benefits that protected the state from enemies or natural disasters, assured a good harvest or rain (Okada, 1983; Ruppert, 2002) and guaranteed the health of the emperor and empowered him as ruler (Rambelli, 2002–2003). This ritual dynamic produced the notion of Buddhism as a religion that 'appeases and safeguards the state' (*chingo kokka*), which defined Japanese Buddhism from the beginning of its history (Kuroda, 1996b) and was in the background of the involvement of all religious lineages in the modern wars fought by Japan (Ives, 2001). Historical evidence shows that political sponsors supported religious institutions in a non-exclusive way. Apotropaic and exorcistic liturgies for the benefit of the state were simultaneously commissioned from diverse religious specialists, from Buddhist monks to shrine ritualists and yin-yang masters. Further, combinatory practices were at the core of the public agency. The parallel performance of two enthronement rites may be recalled here as a remarkable example. For much of pre-modern history the Japanese emperor received a double liturgical legitimisation, with a rite of enthronement in Shinto mode and one in Buddhist fashion. The first, the *daijōsai*, enacted the mythic ancestry of the ruler from the gods, and is still performed by a new emperor at the time of his accession to the throne albeit with some adaptations as to its meaning (Blacker, 1990). The second, called *sokui kanjō*, took place until 1846; it drew on Tantric liturgies of consecration and confirmed the emperor as a follower of Buddhism (Kamikawa, 1990).[26] Today the relevance of public agency is affected by the post-war political redefinition of the relation between state and religion.[27] Article 20 of the Constitution imposed a separation between state and church, forbidding the state and its representatives from engaging in religious activities. At the same time the Religious Corporations Law promoted the idea that religion is primarily an internal affair of individuals (Covell, 2000). Thus the state is no longer an official sponsor of religious institutions for their performance of rituals. The performance of religious rituals by public officials is understood, albeit controversially, as a private matter.

The last and perhaps broader paradigm of ritual agency is offered by private rituals. This rubric includes rites of empowerment of individual practitioners, such as ascetic rituals and healing practices, as well as apotropaic rituals for good luck and success in business or in life, and the variety of memorial rites for the dead. Fundamentally, these rituals are cross-institutional, may be performed by a range of religious specialists, clerical or not, with similar patterns, and draw on a variety of doctrinal sources. Let us look at some examples. Healing rituals are often regarded to be typical of new religious movements (Stroupe, 1983; Becker, 1990; Hardacre, 1982) and to display the new-age inclinations of these movements. Yet healing has historically been integral to Buddhist medicine, and a variety of Buddhist rituals today address the needs of physical and spiritual health (Winfield, 2005). Further, procedures for divinatory and exorcistic practices, closely related to healing techniques, may be found in abundance in the Japanese Buddhist canon, having been transmitted together with Buddhist texts and formulated by Buddhist monks (Dolce, 2006c). Similar considerations may be made for the rituals for the dead. Buddhism historically played a major part in the management of death, supplying a cosmology of the afterlife and the ritual expertise to create funerary liturgies (Bodiford, 1992; Stone and Walter, 2008). Yet the care for the ancestors also takes other forms, Christian, Shinto or non-religious (Mullins, 2004; Kenney, 1996–1997; Rowe, 2008) and includes liminal practices that, albeit subsumed within a Buddhist framework, draw from a broad range of understanding of the divide between the world of the living and the world of the dead (Schattschneider, 2001). Finally, when seen in relation to divine agency, private rituals often involve deities who have ambiguous institutional identities and are not the monopoly of a specific group of ritualists. The popular god of rice and wealth, Inari, conspicuously exemplifies this type of agency. While Inari little red shrines may be encountered in their thousands across the country, its three major worshipping sites, located in different areas of Japan, consist of a Shinto shrine and two Buddhist temples. Accordingly, Inari ritualists may be Shinto and Buddhist priests of different denominations, as well as female shamans and other unofficial religionists (Smyers, 1991).

It is important to emphasise that the paradigms presented above are interpretative strategies to navigate the multivocality of ritual practice and not to set the boundaries between agencies. As hinted earlier on it is multiple agency that ultimately defines the meaning of ritual performance. Spirit pacification may seem to address the sphere of private emotions when one considers the practices related to unborn children (Underwood, 1999). Yet the pacification of vengeful spirits deemed to cause epidemics and unrest was a great display of public agency in the past (McMullin, 1988) and may still be considered so in the present if one sees the practices towards recent war dead at Yasukuni shrine as pacification rituals (Nelson, 2003; Breen, 2004). The multilayered meaning produced by performance is perhaps crystallised best in the dynamics of ascetic practices. Ascetic practices may be at once construed as institutional rituals (when they are performed only by selected members of a denomination), personal challenges to find liberation in overcoming bodily limitations, and benefits-granting practices for an audience of devotees who support the ascetics. This is the case of the already mentioned hundred-day retreat of the Nichirenshū or the thousand-day walking marathon of Mt Hiei. In fact the meaning of ascetic practices is always expressed in the interaction between the self and the community (Lobetti, 2011). Ascetic practices articulate the potentiality of individual bodies but are not limited to the pursuit of the practitioners' own aims, whether that is self-mummification (Hori, 1961; Raveri, 1990, 1992) or self-cultivation (Sawada, 1998, 2004).[28]

In recent years scholars from different fields have produced a wealth of empirical data unveiling the details and specific contexts of several rituals. Yet ritual practice in Japan is still a young area of enquiry. The performative aspect of ritual in particular (namely, the meaning and efficacy each performance produces) needs to be articulated in a sustained fashion, and the theoretical discussion that has transformed ritual studies needs to be incorporated into and measured against Japanese cases. These are the tasks of future scholarship on Japanese religion.

NOTES

1 I follow the established convention in English publications of referring to religious buildings dedicated to Buddhist deities as 'temples' and to those that enshrine Shinto deities as 'shrines,' although historically the difference between the two was not so demarcated.

2 I am grateful to the temple assistant who answered my questions during a field visit in 2010. Photos of the building are available on the architect's website (www.fujimura-ds.com/). See also Peter Yeoh's reportage in *Glass* (spring 2010): www.theglassmagazine.com/forum/article.asp?tid=1099#title.

3 The distinct development of Japanese religious traditions has often generated the notion of the country's superiority based on its spiritual achievements. This tendency has affected the interpretation of single religious forms, from Shinto to Buddhism. Zen Buddhism is perhaps its most striking example. Zen has been the most successful cultural export of Japan and the only form of Buddhism where the contact with the West has triggered a further development of ritual modes (Sharf, 1995b). Yet Zen was first presented to the West as a 'legitimate development' of Buddhism which 'has been achieved in order to meet the requirements peculiarly characteristic of the psychology of the Far-Eastern

people… and especially of the Japanese' (Suzuki, 1949: 37; on the nationalistic tendencies in his thought see Sharf, 1993).

4 Kami is the general term for the deities of Shinto.

5 I use the English term 'emperor' to translate the Japanese title of *tennō* for the sake of convenience, but the two terms do not fully correspond.

6 See the discussion of Shinto below.

7 I am here referring to the methodological use of the notion of purity, by which purity becomes a discriminatory category exploited to construct the identity and legitimacy of a tradition.

8 Japanese confessional universities are different from theological seminars in that they also offer regular curricula in subjects other than religion. Similar private universities are also sponsored by New Religions, such as Sōka Gakkai and Tenrikyō.

9 Representative of this trend is the government sponsored ten-year project on Life and Death Studies at the University of Tokyo, lead by Shimazono Susumu (www.l.u-tokyo.ac.jp/shiseigaku/en/overview.htm).

10 Space does not allow for a discussion of the developments of Christianity. For an overview of the questions see Higashibaba (1999) and Mullins (2003).

11 Michel de Certeau, for instance, contended that innovation takes place in the process of consumption of religion by the introduction of potentially heretical interpretations (Certeau, 1980).

12 Whether Confucianism should be considered a religion or not has been discussed extensively by scholars of Chinese thought. For a review see Boot (2007).

13 Space constraints do not permit me to discuss the Heian period here. Current views of historians of religion have virtually crushed this period between the newly conceived ancient and medieval periods, of which the divide runs along the tenth century.

14 Interestingly, a new input to the question of Daoist knowledge has come from the recent interest in yin-yang practices, following the commercial success of manga and films dedicated to an early historical figure of yin-yang specialist, Abe no Seimei (Reider, 2007).

15 A similar term, *shintōgaku*, is used for textual Shinto studies, although this is a field much smaller than 'buddhology'.

16 This is also reflected in devotional practices. In the calendar of most Japanese temples the commemoration of the founder of each lineage is more important than the demise of the Buddha.

17 In fact, most Buddhist universities count two departments devoted to religious studies: a

department of Buddhist Studies, where the history of Buddhism outside Japan, Buddhist art, Buddhist literature and similar broader subjects are usually studied, and a department of Sectarian Studies (*shūgaku*), which concentrates on the specific tradition upheld by the lineage that runs the university. The latter also serves as a training course for Buddhist priests.

18 It should be remembered that 'Shinto' was not the only religion involved in shaping the ideology of the new state. The role of Buddhist thinkers and of Confucian ideas developed in the late Tokugawa period was crucial (Paramore, 2009).

19 Importantly, these are the definitions of Shinto given today in the literature produced by the Association of Shinto Shrines. See www.jinja-honcho.or.jp/en/shinto/index.html.

20 www.jinjahoncho.or.jp/en/spiritual/index.html. The Japanese pages of the site, however, do not put such emphasis on nature.

21 A case in point is the International Shinto Foundation, an NGO recognised by the UN and very active on the international scene, which claims not to be a religious organisation aimed to propagate Shinto and yet has an office in New York where Shinto weddings and other rites are celebrated. www.shinto.org/isf/index.html.

22 It may be interesting here to compare with Western Catholicism, where a range of practices similar to those included in the rubric of folk religion, from the rituals for the dead to the blessing of a new car or a new house, are performed. These are understood to be proper acts of Christian devotion, rather than apotropaic gestures, and therefore do not necessitate the label of folk practices. On the other hand the rubric of folk Catholicism is used to describe similar phenomena in non-European countries, in Latin America for instance, suggesting a Eurocentric bias in its application.

23 Asceticism does not appear as a specific category of practice in Japanese sources, but the existence of practices of the body that employ parameters that other cultures define ascetic makes it viable as a paradigm of analysis.

24 This does not necessarily correspond to an endorsement by the related Buddhist schools, with whom actual relations may be confrontational. Sōka Gakkai, for instance, has notoriously had long disputes with the Nichiren school from which it originated. On the other hand, another group with origins in the same form of Buddhism, Risshō kōsekai, has not. Similarly, Shinnyoen entertains amicable relations with the Buddhist Shingon school of Daigoji, to which lineage it claims to belong. One should also note that other groups, such as Tenrikyō and Konkōkyō, which were originally classified as 'Shinto' lineages, have found the association

with their 'source' tradition problematic. Indeed, today Tenrikyō rejects it completely.

25 I draw here on Narayanan's insightful notion of 'epistemic diversity' in the approach to religion (2003).

26 These practices are in sharp contrast to the ritual definition of Western rulers. The Emperor of the medieval Sacred Roman Empire could not have been enthroned with both a Christian and a Muslim rite. The current image of the Japanese emperor, however, is shaped by the Shinto purist parameters established by Meiji ideologues, when all the official links between the imperial house and Buddhism were severed.

27 Attempts to redefine it had already occurred in the Meiji period. A case in point is Mokurai Shimaji's movement for the separation of church and state in 1872 (Ienaga, 1965). Their influence on the modern conception of religion needs to be explored further.

28 Ascetic practitioners also display a complex understanding of tradition as source of authority: they internalise tradition by inscribing it on the body through their actions (Flood, 2004), but they also combine different traditions (Tyler, 1993; Sawada, 2004).

REFERENCES

Abe, Yoshiya. 1968–1970. Religious Freedom under the Meiji constitution, Part I–V. *Contemporary Religion in Japan* 9(4): 268–338; 10(1-2): 57–98; 10(3–4): 181–203; 11(1–2): 27–79; 11(3–4): 223–266.

Ambros, Barbara. 2009. Clerical Demographics in the Edo-Meiji Transition: Shingon and Tōzanha Shugendō in Western Sagami. *Monumenta Nipponica* 64(1): 83–125.

Amino, Yoshihiko. 1992. Deconstructing 'Japan'. *East Asian History* 3: 121–142.

Antoni, Klaus. 2001. Religion and Commercialization: The Shintō Wedding Ritual (*shinzenshiki*) as an 'Invented Tradition' in Japan. *Japanese Religions* 26(1): 45–54.

Baffelli, Erica. 2007. Mass Media and Religion in Japan: Mediating the Leader's Image. *Westminster Paper in Communication and Culture* 4(1): 83–99.

Baffelli, Erica, Ian Reader, and Birgit Staemmler, eds. 2010. *Japanese Religions on the Internet: Innovation, Representation, and Authority.* London and New York: Routledge.

Barrett, Timothy. 2000. Shinto and Taoism in Early Japan. In John Breen and Mark Teeuwen (eds.) *Shinto in History: Ways of the Kami.* Richmond: Curzon Press. pp. 13–31.

de Bary, Theodore, Keene, Donald, Tanabe, George and Varley, Paul, eds. 2001. *Source of Japanese Tradition Vol. 1,* 2nd ed. New York: Columbia University Press.

de Bary, Theodore, Gluck, Carol and Tiedemann, Arthur, eds. 2005. *Source of Japanese Tradition Vol. 2*, 2nd ed. New York: Columbia University Press.

Becker, Carl. 1990. Religious Healing in 19th Century 'New Religions': The Cases of Tenrikyō and Christian Science. *Religion* 20: 199–215.

Blacker, Carmen. 1975. *The Catalpa Bow: A Study of Shamanistic Practices in Japan*. London: George Allen and Unwin.

Blacker, Carmen. 1990. The Shinza or God-Seat in the Daijōsai: Throne, Bed, or Incubation Couch? *Japanese Journal of Religious Studies* 17(2–3): 179–197.

Bock, Felicia. 1985. *Classical Learning and Taoist Practice in Early Japan*. Tucson: Arizona State University Press.

Bocking, Brian. 2001. *The Oracle of the Three Shrines: Windows on Japanese Religion*. Richmond: Curzon Press.

Bodiford, William, 1992. Zen in the Art of Funerals: Ritual Salvation in Japanese Buddhism. *History of Religions* 32(2): 146–164.

Bodiford, William, 1996. Zen and the Art of Religious Prejudice Efforts to Reform a Tradition of Social Discrimination. *Japanese Journal of Religious Studies* 23(1–2): 1–27.

Bodiford, William, ed. 2005. *Going Forth: Visions of Buddhist Vinaya*. Honolulu: University of Hawaii Press.

Boot, Wim. 2007. Should Confucianism be Studied as a Religious Tradition? In Remco E. Breuker (ed.) *Korea in the Middle: Korean Studies and Area Studies. Essays in Honour of Boudewijn Walraven*. Leiden: CNWS Publications. pp. 288–312.

Bouchy, Anne. 1992. *Les oracles de Shirataka, ou, La sibylle d'Ōsaka: vie d'une femme specialist de la possession dans le Japon du XXe siècle*. Arles: Editions Picquier.

Bouchy, Anne. 2000a. La cascade et l'écritoire. Dynamique de l'histoire du fait religieux et de l'ethnologie du Japon: le cas du shugendō. *Bulletin de l' École francaise d'Extrême Orient* 87(1): 341–366.

Bouchy, Anne. 2000b. Quand je est l'Autre – Altérité et identité dans la possession au Japon. *L' Homme* 153: 207–230.

Bouchy, Anne. 2005. Du légitime et de l'illégitime dans le shugendō ou 'Sang de buddha', 'sang des êtres des montagnes'. In Anne Bouchy, Guillaume Carré, and François Lachaud (eds.) *Légitimités, légitimations – La construction de l'autorité au Japon*. Paris: EFEO. pp. 111–177.

Breen, John. 2000. Ideologues, Bureaucrats and Priests: On Shinto and Buddhism in Early Meiji Japan. In John Breen and M. Teeuwen (eds.) *Shinto in History: Ways of the kami*. Richmond: Curzon Press. pp. 230–251.

Breen, John. 2004. The Dead and the Living in the Land of Peace: A Sociology of the Yasukuni Shrine. *Mortality* 9(1): 76–93.

Breen, John, and Mark Teeuwen. 2010. *A New History of Shinto*. Chichester: Wiley-Blackwell.

Butler, Lee. 1996. The Way of Yin and Yang. A Tradition Revived, Sold, Adopted. *Monumenta Nipponica* 51–2: 189–217.

Cabezón, José Ignacio. 1995. Buddhist Studies as a Discipline and the Role of Theory. *Journal of the International Association of Buddhist Studies* 18: 183–230.

Cabezón, José Ignacio. 2007 [2009]. The Changing Field of Buddhist Studies in North America. *Journal of the International Association of Buddhist Studies* 30(1–2): 283–298.

Cahiers d'Extrême-Asie 2006–07 [2009]. Medieval Shinto, special issue of *Cahiers d'Extrême-Asie* 16.

Cahiers d'Extrême-Asie 2009 [2011]. Shugendō, special issue of *Cahiers d'Extrême-Asie* 18.

Cahiers d'Extrême Asie 2012: The Way of Yin and Yang. Divinatory Techniques and Religious Practices, special issue of *Cahiers d'Extrême Asie* 21.

Certeau, Michel de. 1980. *L'invention du quotidien*. Paris: Union générale d'éditions.

Chamberlain, Basil Hall. 1912. *The Invention of a New Religion*. London: Watts &Co.

Como, Michael. 2008. *Shōtoku: Ethnicity, Ritual and Violence in the Formation of Japanese Buddhism*. New York: Oxford University Press.

Como, Michael. 2009. *Weaving and Binding: Immigrant Gods and Female Immortals in Ancient Japan*. Honolulu: University of Hawaii Press.

Covell, Stephen. 2000. The Temple/Juridical Person: Law and the Temple in Japan. *Asian Cultural Studies* アジア文化研究 26: 7–23.

Covell, Stephen. 2004. Learning to Persevere: The Popular Teachings of Tendai Ascetics. *Japanese Journal of Religious Studies* 31(2): 255–87.

Covell, Stephen. 2005. *Japanese Temple Buddhism*. Honolulu: University of Hawaii Press.

Davis, Winston. 1980. *Dōjō: Magic and Exorcism in Modern Japan*. Stanford: Stanford University Press.

Dolce, Lucia. 1992. Awareness of Mappō. Soteriological Interpretations of Time in Nichiren. *Transactions of the Asiatic Society of Japan* (fourth series) 7: 81–106.

Dolce, Lucia. 1999. Criticism and Appropriation: Ambiguities in Nichiren's Attitude Towards Esoteric Buddhism. *Japanese Journal of Religious Studies* 26(3–4): 349–382.

Dolce, Lucia. 2003. On the Use of Prophecy in Mediaeval Japan: Nichiren, the Future of Buddhism and the Country of Japan. In Watanabe Hōyō sensei koki kinen ronbunshū kankōkai (ed.) *Hokke bukkyō bunkashi ronsō [Essays on the Cultural History of Lotus Buddhism]*. Kyoto: Heirakuji Shoten. pp. 59–90.

Dolce, Lucia. 2006a. Reconsidering the Taxonomy of the 'Esoteric': Taimitsu Hermeneutical and Ritual Practices. In Mark Teeuwen and Bernard Scheid (eds.) *The Culture of Secrecy in Japanese Religion*. London and New York: Routledge. pp. 130–171.

Dolce, Lucia. 2006b. Icons, Scriptures, and their Ritual Use: Reflections on Nineteenth-Century European Understandings of Japanese Buddhism. In *La rencontre du Japon et de l'Europe: Images d'une découverte*. Paris: Publication Orientalistes de France: 57–78.

Dolce, Lucia, ed. 2006c. *The Worship of Stars in Japanese Religious Practice*, special issue of *Culture and Cosmos: A Journal of the History of Astrology and Cultural Astronomy* 10(1–2).

Dolce, Lucia. 2006d. The Worship of Celestial Bodies in Japan: Politics, Rituals and Icons. *Culture and Cosmos: A Journal of the History of Astrology and Cultural Astronomy*, 10(1–2): 3–43.

Dolce, Lucia. 2006–07 [2009]. Duality and the Kami: The Ritual Iconography and Visual Constructions of Medieval Shinto. *Cahiers d'Extrême-Asie* 16 (special issue: *Medieval Shinto*). pp. 119–150.

Dolce, Lucia. 2007a. Mapping the 'Divine Country:' Sacred Geography and International Concerns in Mediaeval Japan. In Remco E. Breuker (ed.) *Korea in the Middle: Korean Studies and Area Studies. Essays in Honour of Boudewijn Walraven*. Leiden: CNWS Publications. pp. 288–312.

Dolce, Lucia. 2007b. Did *shinbutsu bunri* Irremediably Change Japanese Religion? Perspectives on Contemporary Forms of Associative Practices. Paper presented at the American Academy of Religion, San Diego.

Dolce, Lucia. 2010a. Nigenteki genri no girei: Fudō Aizen to chikara no hizō [Ritualizing Duality: Fudō, Aizen and the Secret Iconography of Empowerment]. In Lucia Dolce and Matsumoto Ikuyo (eds.) *Girei no chikara: chikara –chûsei shûkyô no jissen sekai*. Kyoto: Hōzōkan. pp. 159–206.

Dolce, Lucia. 2010b. The Contested Space of Buddhist Public Rituals: The *shūnie* of the Nara Temples. In Lucia Dolce, Gil Raz, and Katja Triplett (eds.) *Ritual Debates, Ritual Performances: Rituals in China and Japan*. (Part II of *Grammars and Morphologies of Ritual Practices in Asia*) Wiesbaden: Harrassowitz. pp. 439–464.

Dolce, Lucia. 2011. Taimitsu Rituals in Medieval Japan: Sectarian Competition and the Dynamics of Tantric Performance. In Istvan Keul (ed.) *Transformations and Transfer of Tantra in Asia and Beyond*. Berlin/New York: Walter de Gruyter Publishers. pp. 311–344.

Earhart, H. Byron. 2004. [reprint] *Japanese Religion: Unity and Diversity*. Thomson/Wadsworth.

Edwards, Walter. 2000. Contested Access: The Imperial Tombs in the Post-War Period. *Journal of Japanese Studies* 26: 371–397.

Ellwood, Robert. 2007. *Introducing Japanese Religion*. London: Routledge.

Eynon, Matthew. 1997. Japanese Modern Religious Manga: An Ancient Tradition in New Clothing. *Tenri Journal of Religion,* 25: 77–111.

Faure, Bernard. 1998. The Buddhist Icon and the Modern Gaze. *Critical Inquiry* 24(3): 768–813.

Flood, Gavin. 2004. *The Ascetic Self: Subjectivity, Memory and Tradition*. Cambridge: Cambridge University Press.

Fowler, Sherry. 1998. Setting Foot on the Mountain: Mt. Muro as a Women's Alternative to Mt. Koya. *Asian Journal of Women's Studies* 3(4): 52–73.

Fujiwara, Satoko. 2005. Survey on Religion and Higher Education in Japan. *Japanese Journal of Religious Studies* 32(2): 353–370.

Gardiner, David. 1996. Mandala, Mandala on the Wall: Variations of Usage in the Shingon School. *Journal of the International Association of Buddhist Studies* 19(2): 245–279.

Goodwin, Janet. 2007. *Selling Songs and Smiles: The Sex Trade in Heian and Kamakura Japan*. Honolulu: University of Hawaii Press.

Gomez, Luis. 2007 [2009]. Studying Buddhism as If It Were Not One More Among the Religions. *Journal of the International Association of Buddhist Studies* 30(1–2): 319–343.

Graham, Patricia. 2007. *Faith and Power in Japanese Buddhist Art 1600–2005*. Honolulu: Hawai University Press.

Grapard, Allan. 1982. Flying Mountains and Walkers of Emptiness: Toward a Definition of Sacred Space in Japanese Religions. *History of Religions* 21:195–221.

Grapard, Allan. 1984. Japan's Ignored Cultural Revolution: The Separation of Shinto and Buddhist Divinities in Meiji (*shimbutsu bunri*) and a Case Study: Tōnomine'. *History of Religion*, 23(3): 240–265.

Grapard, Allan. 1987. Linguistic Cubism: A Singularity of Pluralism in the Sannō Cult. *Japanese Journal of Religious Studies* 14(2–3): 211–234.

Grapard, Allan. 1992a. *The Protocol of the Gods. A Study of the Kasuga Cult in Japanese History*. Berkeley: University of California Press.

Grapard, Allan. 1992b. The Shinto of Yoshida Kanetomo. *Monumenta Nipponica* 47(1): 27–58.

Grapard, Allan. 1994. Geosophia, Geognosis, and Geopiety: Orders of Significance in Japanese Representations of Space. In Roger Friedland and Deirdre Boden (eds.) *Nowhere: Space, Time, and Modernity*. Berkeley, CA: University of California Press. pp. 372–401.

Groemer, Gerald. 2007. Female Shamans in Eastern Japan During the Edo Period. *Asian Folklore Studies* 66: 27–53.

Groner, Paul. 1992. Shortening the Path: Early Tendai Interpretations of the Realization of Buddhahood with This Very Body (*Sokushin Jōbutsu*). In Robert Buswell and Robert Gimello (eds.) *Paths to Liberation: The Marga and Its Transformation in Buddhist Thought*. Honolulu: University of Hawaii Press. pp. 439–471.

Guth Kanda, Christine. 1985. *Shinzō*: Hachiman Imagery and its Development. Cambridge: Harvard University Press.

Hardacre, Helen. 1982. The Transformation of Healing in the Japanese New Religions. *History of Religions* 21(4): 305–320.

Hardacre, Helen. 1986. *Kurozumikyō and the New Religions of Japan*. Princeton: Princeton University Press.

Hardacre, Helen. 1989. *Shintō and the State, 1868-1988*. Princeton: Princeton University Press.

Hardacre, Helen. 1997. *Marketing the Menacing Fetus in Japan*. Berkeley: University of California Press.

Hardacre, Helen. 2005. Constitutional Revision and Japanese Religions. *Japanese Studies* 25(3): 235–247.

Heine, Steven. 1986. *Essential and Ontological Dimensions of Time in Heidegger and Dōgen*. Albany: State University of New York Press.

Higashibaba, Ikuo. 1999. Historiographical Issues in the Studies of the 'Christian Century' in Japan. *Japanese Religions* 24(1): 29–50.

Hirasawa, Caroline. 2008. The Inflatable, Collapsible Kingdom of Retribution: A Primer on Japanese Hell Imagery and Imagination. *Monumenta Nipponica*, 63(1): 1–50.

Hori, Ichirō. 1961. Self-Mummified Buddhas in Japan. An Aspect of the Shugendō ("Mountain Asceticism"). *History of Religions* 1(2): 222–242.

Hubbard, Jamie. 1992. Premodern, Modern, and Postmodern: Doctrine and the Study of Japanese Religion. *Japanese Journal of Religious Studies* 19(1): 3–27.

Hubbard, Jamie. 1998. Embarrassing Superstitions, Doctrine, and the Study of New Religious Movements. *Journal of the American Academy of Religion* 66(1): 59–92.

Ienaga, Saburo. 1965. Japan's Modernization and Buddhism. *Contemporary Religions in Japan* 6: 1–41.

Inoue, Nobutaka. 2000. From Religious Conformity to Innovation: New Ideas of Religious Journey and Holy Places. *Social Compass* 47(1): 21–32.

Isomae, Jun'ichi. 2002. The Discursive Position of Religious Studies in Japan: Masaharu Anesaki and the Origins of Religious Studies. *Method and Theory in the Study of Religion* 14(1): 21–46.

Isomae, Jun'ichi. 2003. *Kindai Nihon no shukyō gensetsu to sono keifu*. Tokyo: Iwanami Shoten.

Isomae, Jun'ichi. 2005. Deconstructing "Japanese Religion": A Historical Survey. *Japanese Journal of Religious Studies* 32(2): 235–248.

Isomae, Jun'ichi. 2010. *Japanese Mythology: Hermeneutics on Scripture*. London: Equinox.

Ives, Christopher. 2001. Protect the Dharma, Protect the Country: Buddhist War Responsibility and Social Ethics. *The Eastern Buddhist* (NS), XXXIII(2): 15–34.

Ivy, Marilyn. 1995. *Discourses of the Vanishing: Modernity, Phantasm, Japan*. Chicago: University of Chicago Press.

Jaffe, Richard M. 2006. Buddhist Material Culture, 'Indianism,' and the Construction of Pan-Asian Buddhism in Prewar Japan. *Material Religion: The Journal of Objects, Art and Belief*, 2(3): 268–292.

JJRS. 1991. *Japanese New Religions Abroad*, special issue of *Japanese Journal of Religious Studies* 18(2–3).

JJRS. 1995. *The New Age in Japan*, special issue of *Japanese Journal of Religious Studies* 22(3–4).

JJRS. 1996. *The Legacy of Kuroda Toshio*, special issue of *Japanese Journal of Religious Studies* 23(3–4).

JJRS. 2001. *Local Religion in Tokugawa History*, special issue of *Japanese Journal of Religious Studies* 28(3–4).

JJRS. 2002. *Tracing Shinto in the History of Kami Worship*, special issue of *Japanese Journal of Religious Studies* 29(3–4).

JJRS. 2003. *Feminism and Religion in Contemporary Japan*, special issue of *Japanese Journal of Religious Studies* 30(3–4).

JJRS. 2004. *Traditional Buddhism in Contemporary Japan*, special issue of *Japanese Journal of Religious Studies* 31(2): 245–254.

Kamikawa, Michio. 1990. Accession Rituals and Buddhism in Medieval Japan. *Japanese Journal of Religious Studies* 17(2–3): 243–280.

Kanagawa kenritsu shiryō hakubutsukan, ed. 2006. *Kamigami to deau*. Kanagawa-Ken Jinjachō.

Kawahashi, Noriko. 2005. Folk Religion and Its Contemporary Issues. In Jennifer Robertson (ed.) *A Companion to the Anthropology of Japan*. Malden: Blackwell. pp. 452–466.

Kawamura, Kunimitsu. 1994. The Life of a Shamaness: Scenes from the Shamanism of Northeastern Japan. Originally published in *Contemporary Papers on Japanese Religion* 3, Inoue Nobutaka, General Editor.

Kenney, Elizabeth. 1996–1997. Shintō Mortuary Rites in Contemporary Japan. *Cahiers d'Extrême-Asie* 9: 397–436.

Kenney, Elizabeth. 2000. Shinto Funerals in the Edo Period. *Japanese Journal of Religious Studies* 27(3–4): 239–271.

Kisala, Robert. 1996. Living in a Post-Aum World. *Bulletin of the Nanzan Institute for Religion and Culture* 20: 7–18.

Kisala, Robert. 1998. 1999 and Beyond: The Use of Nostradamus' Prophecies by Japanese Religions. *Japanese Religions*, 23(1–2): 143–157.

Kisala, Robert. 1999. Asian Values Study. *Bulletin of the Nanzan Institute for Religion and Culture* 23: 59–73.

Kisala, Robert, and Mark Mullins, eds. 2001. *Religion and Social Crisis in Japan. Understanding Japanese Society through the Aum Affair*. New York: Palgrave.

Klautau, Orion. 2008. Against the Ghosts of Recent Past: Meiji Scholarship and the Discourse on Edo-Period Buddhist Decadence. *Japanese Journal of Religious Studies* 35(2): 263–303.

Kleine, Christoph. 1997. Hermits and Ascetics in Ancient Japan: The Concept of Hijiri Reconsidered. *Japanese Religions* 22(2): 1–46.

Kleine, Christoph, and Livia Kohn. 1999. Daoist Immortality and Buddhist Holiness: A Study and Translation of the *Honchō shinsen-den*. *Japanese Religions* 24(2): 119–196.

Knecht, Peter. 2003. Aspects of Shamanism: An Introduction. In Clark Chilson and Peter Knecht (eds.) *Shamans in Asia*. London: RoutledgeCurzon. pp. 1–30.

Knecht, Peter. 2004. Kuchiyose: Enacting the Encounter of this World with the Other World. In Susanne Formanek and William LaFleur (eds.) *Practicing the Afterlife: Perspectives from Japan*. Wien: Verlag der Österreichischen Akademie der Wissenschaften. pp. 179–201.

Kohn, Livia. 1993–1995. Kōshin: A Taoist Cult in Japan, Part I: Contemporary Practices; Part II: Historical Development; Part III: The Scripture: A Translation of the *Kōshinkyō*. *Japanese Religions* 18(2) (1993): 113–139; 20(1) (1995): 34–55; 20(2) (1995): 123–142.

Kohn, Livia. 1995. Taoism in Japan: Positions and Evaluations. *Cahiers d'Extrême-Asie* 8: 389–412.

Kuroda, Toshio. 1981. Shinto in the History of Japanese Religion. *Journal of Japanese Studies* 7(1): 1–21.

Kuroda, Toshio. 1996a. The Development of the Kenmitsu System as Japan's Medieval Orthodoxy. *Japanese Journal of Religious Studies* 23(3–4): 233–269.

Kuroda Toshio. 1996b. The Imperial Law and the Buddhist Law. *Japanese Journal of Religious Studies* 23(3–4): 271–286.

Levine, Gregory. 2001. Switching Sites and Identity: The Founder's Statue at the Buddhist Temple Kōrin' in. *The Art Bulletin*, LXXXIII(1): 72–104.

Licha, Kigensan. 2009. Serving Dharma: A Report on the Vow's Bar, Nakano, Tokyo. *CSJR Newsletter* 18–19: 24–26. (www.soas.ac.uk/csjr/newsletter/file55523.pdf)

Lobetti, Tullio. 2011. Faith in the Flesh: Body and Ascetic Practices in a Contemporary Japanese Religious Context. PhD Dissertation, SOAS, University of London.

Londo, William. 2002. The 11th Century Revival of Mt. Kōya: Its Genesis as a Popular Religious Site. *Japanese Religion* 27(1): 10–40.

MacWilliams, Mark. 1990. Kannon-engi: The Reijō and the Concept of Kechien as Strategies of Indigenization in Buddhist Sacred Narratives. *Transactions of the Asiatic Society of Japan*, Fourth Series 5: 53–70.

MacWilliams, Mark. 1999. Revisioning Japanese Religiosity: Tezuka Osamu's *Hi no Tori* (The Phoenix). *Japanese Religions* 24(1): 73–100.

Mano, Shinya. 2011. Yōsai and Esoteric Buddhism. In Charles Orzech general (ed.) *Esoteric Buddhism and the Tantras in East Asia*. Leiden: Brill. pp. 827–834.

Martin, Luther. 1983. Why Cecropian Minerva? Hellenistic Religious Syncretism as System. *Numen* 30(2): 131–145.

McLaughlin, Levi. 2003. Faith and Practice: Bringing Religion, Music and Beethoven to Life in Soka Gakkai. *Social Science Japan Journal* 6(2): 161–179.

McMullen, James. 1996. The Worship of Confucius in Ancient Japan. In Peter Francis Kornicki and Ian James McMullen (eds.) *Religion in Japan: Arrows to Heaven and Earth*. Cambridge: Cambridge University Press. pp. 39–77.

McMullin, Neil. 1989. Historical and Historiographical Issues in the Study of Pre-Modern Japanese Religion. *Japanese Journal of Religious Studies* 16(1): 3–40.

McMullin, Neil. 1988. On Placating the Gods and Pacifying the Populace: The Case of the Gion *Goryō* Cult. *History of Religions* 27(3): 270–293.

Meeks, Lori. 2011. The Disappearing Medium: Reassessing the Place of Miko in the Religious Landscape of Premodern Japan. *History of Religions* 50(3): 208–260.

Miyazaki, Fumiko. 2005. Female Pilgrims and Mt. Fuji: Changing Perspectives on the Exclusion of Women. *Monumenta Nipponica* 60(3): 339–391.

Mitsuhashi, Tadashi. 2010. *Nihon kodai jingi girei no keisei to tenkai*. Kyoto: Hōzōkan.

Mohr, Michel, ed. 2005. Buddhist and Non-Buddhist Trends Towards Religious Unity in Meiji Japan, special feature of *The Eastern Buddhist*, n.s. 37(1–2).

Mullins, Mark. 2003. *Handbook of Christianity in Japan*. Leiden: Brill.

Mullins, Mark. 2004. Japanese Christians and the World of the Dead. *Mortality* 9(1): 61–75.

Narayanan, Vasudha. 2003. Embodied Cosmologies: Sights of Piety, Sites of Power. *Journal of the American Academic of Religion* 71(3): 495–520.

Nelson, John. 1997. Warden + Virtuoso + Salaryman = Priest: Paradigms within Japanese Shinto for Religious Specialists and Institutions. *The Journal of Asian Studies,* 56(3): 678–707.

Nelson, John. 2000. *Enduring Identities: The Guise of Shinto in Contemporary Japan*. Honolulu: University of Hawaii Press.

Nelson, John. 2003. Social Memory as Ritual Practice: Commemorating Spirits of the Military Dead at Yasukuni Shinto Shrine. *Journal of Asian Studies* 62: 443–467.

Neumann, Nelly. 1992. The *itako* of North-eastern Japan and Their Chants. *Nachrichten der Gesellschaft für Natur- und Völkerkunde Ostasiens* 152: 21–37.

Nishiguchi, Junko. 2009. Trends in the Study of Women and Buddhism. *Acta Asiatica*, 97 (Special issue: *Women in Japanese Buddhism: Focusing on the Ancient and Medieval Period*). pp. 75–93.

Okada, Shōji. 1983. The Development of State Ritual in Ancient Japan. *Acta Asiatica* 51: 22–41.

Ooms, Herman. 2008. *Imperial Politics and Symbolics in Ancient Japan: The Tenmu dynasty, 650–800*. Honolulu: University of Hawaii Press.

Ono Sokyo. 1962. *Shinto: The Kami Way*. Rutland and Tokyo: Charles E. Tuttle for Bridgeway Press.

Paramore, Kiri. 2009. Sectarianism as Ideology: Anti-Christian Discourse and the Politicization of Religious History in Modern Japan. *Sungkyun Journal of East Asian Studies*, 9(1): 107–144.

Payne, Richard K. 2006. The Shingon Subordinating Fire Offering for Amitābha, 'Amida Kei Ai Goma'. *Pacific World: Journal of the Institute of Buddhist Studies* Third Series, 8: 191–207 and 229–236.

Piggott, Joan. 1989. Sacral Kingship and Confederacy in Early Izumo. *Monumenta Nipponica* 44(1): 45–74

Pollock, Sheldon. 1996. The Sanskrit Cosmopolis, 300–1300 CE: Transculturation, Vernacularization and the Question of Ideology. In Jan Houben (ed.) *Ideology and Status of Sanskrit*. Leiden: Brill. pp. 197–248.

Pye, Michael. 1996a. Aum Shinrikyō. Can Religious Studies Cope? *Religion* 26: 261–270.

Pye, Michael. 1996b. Shinto, Primal Religion and International Identity. *Marburg Journal of Religion* 1(1): 1–14.

Pye, Michael. 2003. Modern Japan and the Science of Religions. *Method & Theory in the Study of Religion* 15(1): 1–27.

Rambelli, Fabio. 2002–2003. The Emperor's New Robes: Processes of Resignification in Shingon Imperial Rituals. *Cahiers d'Extrême-Asie* 13: 427–453.

Raveri, Massimo. 1990. In Search of a New Interpretation of Ascetic Experience. In Adriana Boscaro, Franco Gatti and Massimo Raveri (eds.) *Rethinking Japan*. Folkestone: Routledge. pp. 250–261 and 378–379.

Raveri, Massimo. 1992. *Il corpo e il paradiso*. Venezia: Marsilio.

Reader, Ian. 2001. Consensus Shattered: Japanese Paradigm Shifts and Moral Panic in the Post-Aum Era. *Nova Religio: The Journal of Alternative and Emergent Religions* 4(2): 225–234.

Reader, Ian. 2002. Spectres and Shadows: Aum Shinrikyō and the Road to Megiddo. *Terrorism and Political Violence* (Special issue: Millennial Violence, Past, Present and Future) 14(1): 147–186.

Reader, Ian. 2005. Chronologies, Commonalities and Alternative Status in Japanese New Religious Movements: Defining NRMs outside the Western Cul-de-sac. *Nova Religio: The Journal of Alternative and Emergent Religions* 9(2):84–96.

Reader, Ian. 2007. Positively Promoting Pilgrimages: Media Representations of Pilgrimage in Japan. *Nova Religio: The Journal of Alternative and Emergent Religions* 10(3): 13–31.

Reader, Ian, and George Tanabe. 1999. *Practically Religious: Worldly Benefits and the Common Religion of Japan*. Honolulu: University of Hawai'i Press.

Reider, Noriko. 2007. *Onmyōji*: Sex, Pathos, and Grotesquery in Yumemakura Baku's *Oni*. *Asian Folklore Studies* 66: 107–124.

Reynolds, Jonathan. 2001. Ise Shrine and a Modernist Construction of Japanese Tradition. *The Art Bulletin* 83(2): 316–341.

Rhodes, Robert. 1987. The *kaihōgyō* Practice of Mt. Hiei. *Japanese Journal of Religious Studies* 14(2–3): 185–202.

Rowe, Mark. 2008. Death, Burial, and the Study of Contemporary Japanese Buddhism. *Religion Compass* 3(1): 18–30.

Ruch, Barbara, ed. 2002. *Engendering Faith. Women and Buddhism in Premodern Japan*. University of Michigan.

Ruppert, Brian. 2002. Buddhist Rainmaking in Early Japan: The Dragon King and the Ritual Careers of Esoteric Monks. *History of Religions* 42(2): 143–174.

Sax, William. 2008. Agency. In Jens Kreinath, Jan Snoek, and Michael Stausberg (eds.) *Theorizing Rituals: Issues, Topics, Approaches, Concepts*. Leiden: Brill. pp. 473–481.

Sawada, Janine Anderson. 1998. Mind and Morality in Nineteenth-Century Japanese Religions: Misogi-kyō and Maruyama-kyō. *Philosophy East & West*, 48(1): 108–136.

Sawada, Janine Tasca. 2002. Tokugawa Religious History: Studies in Western Languages. *Early Modern Japan: An Interdisciplinary Journal* 10(1): 39–64.

Sawada, Janine Tasca. 2004. *Practical Pursuits: Religion, Politics, and Personal Cultivation in Nineteenth-Century Japan*. Honolulu: University of Hawaii Press.

Schattschneider, Ellen. 2001. 'Buy Me a Bride': Death and Exchange in Northern Japanese Bride-Doll Marriage. *American Ethnologist* 28(4): 854–880.

Schnell, Scott. 1995. Ritual as an Instrument of Political Resistance in Rural Japan. *Journal of Anthropological Research* 51(4): 301–328.

Schnell, Scott, and Hashimoto Hiroyuki. 2003. Revitalizing Japanese Folklore. *Asian Folklore Studies* 62: 185–194.

Sekimori, Gaynor. 1995. The Akinomine of Haguro Shugendō: A Historical Perspective. *Transactions of the International Conference of Eastern Studies* 40: 163–186.

Sekimori, Gaynor. 2009. Shugendo: Japanese Mountain Religion – State of the Field and Bibliographic Review. *Religion Compass* 3(1): 31–57.

Sharf, Robert. 1993. The Zen of Japanese Nationalism. *History of Religions* 33(1): 1–43.

Sharf, Robert. 1995a. Buddhist Modernism and the Rhetoric of Meditative Experience. *Numen* 42(3): 228–283.

Sharf, Robert. 1995b. Sanbōkyōdan: Zen and the Way of the New Religions. *Japanese Journal of Religious Studies* 22(3–4): 417–458.

Sharf, Robert. 2002. *Coming to Terms with Chinese Buddhism: A Reading of the Treasure Store Treatise.* Honolulu: University of Hawaii Press.

Sharf, Robert. 2003. Thinking through Shingon Ritual. *Journal of the International Association of Buddhist Studies* 26(1): 51–96.

Sharf, Robert, and Elisabeth Horton Sharf, eds. 2001. *Living Images: Japanese Buddhist Icons in Context.* Stanford: Stanford University Press.

Shaw, Rosalind, and Charles, Stewart. 1994. Introduction: Problematizing Syncretism. In Rosalind Shaw and Charles Stewart (eds.) *Syncretism/Anti-Syncretism: The Politics of Religious Synthesis.* London: Routledge.

Shimazono, Susumu. 1993. New Age and New Spiritual Movements: The Role of Spiritual Intellectuals. *Syzygy: Journal of Alternative Religion and Culture* 2(12): 9–22.

Shimazono, Susumu. 1995. New New Religions and This World: Religious Movements in Japan after the 1970s and their Beliefs about Salvation. *Social Compass* 42(2): 193–205.

Shimazono, Susumu. 1998. The Commercialization of the Sacred: The Structural Evolution of Religious Communities in Japan. *Social Science Japan Journal,* 1(2): 181–198.

Shimazono, Susumu. 2004. *From Salvation to Spirituality.* Melbourne: Trans Pacific Press.

Shimazono, Susumu. 2007. Bioethics on the Beginning of Life: Bioscience and Religious Culture in an Age of Crisis. *Journal of Oriental Studies* 17: 57–80.

Shinno, Toshikazu. 1993. From *minkan shinkō* to *minzoku shūkyō*: Reflections on the Study of Folk Buddhism. *Japanese Journal of Religious Studies* 20(2–3): 187–206.

Smyers, Karen. 1991. Of Foxes, Buddhas, and Shinto Kami: The Syncretic Nature of Inari Beliefs. *Japanese Religions* 16(3): 60–75.

Sonehara, Satoshi. 2006. The Establishment of Early Modern Buddhism. *Acta Asiatica*, 91 (The Cutting Edge of Research on Japanese Buddhism): 65–83.

Stalker, Nancy. 2003. Art and the New Religions: From Deguchi Onisaburō to the Miho Museum. *Japanese Religions,* 28(2): 151–166.

Steineck, Christian. 2003. Brain Death, Death, and Personal Identity. *KronoScope* 3(2): 226–249.

Stone, Jacqueline. 1999a. *Original Enlightenment and the Transformation of Medieval Japanese Buddhism.* Honolulu: University of Hawaii Press.

Stone, Jacqueline. 1999b. Review: Some Reflections on Critical Buddhism. *Japanese Journal of Religious Studies* 26(1–2): 159–188.

Stone, Jacqueline. 2003. Nichiren's Activist Heirs: Sōka Gakkai, Risshō Kōseikai and Nipponzan Myōhōji. In Christopher Queen, Charles Prebish and Damien Keown (eds.) *Action Dharma: New Studies in Engaged Buddhism.* New York: Routledge Curzon. pp. 63–94.

Stone, Jacqueline, and Mariko Namba Walter, eds. 2008. *Death and the Afterlife in Japanese Buddhism.* Honolulu: University of Hawaii Press.

Stroupe, Bart. 1983. Healing in the History of Tenrikyō, the Religion of Divine Wisdom. *Tenri Journal of Religion* 17: 79–132.

Sueki, Fumihiko. 2006. Buddhism in the History of Japanese Religion: Research History and Research Methods. *Acta Asiatica*, 91 (Special issue: The Cutting Edge of Research on Japanese Buddhism): 85–103.

Suzuki, Daisetsu T. 1949. *An Introduction to Zen Buddhism.* London: Rider and Company.

Suzuki, Masataka. 2007. Mountain Religion and Gender. *Sangaku Shugen.* pp. 57–83.

Suzuki, Yui. 2007. Temple as Museum, Buddha as Art: Hōryūji's Kudara Kannon and its Great Repository. *Res* 52: 128–140.

Swanson, Paul. 1993. Zen Is Not Buddhism: Recent Japanese Critiques of Buddha-Nature. *Numen* 40(2): 115–140.

Swanson, Paul, and Clark Chilson, eds. 2006. *Nanzan Guide to Japanese Religions.* Honolulu: University of Hawaii Press.

Tamamuro, Fumio. 2001. Local Society and the Temple-Parishioner Relationship within the Bakufu's Governance Structure. *Japanese Journal of Religious Studies* 28(3–4): 261–292.

Tanabe, George, ed. 1999. *Religions of Japan in Practice.* Princeton: Princeton University Press.

Teeuwen, Mark. 1996. Jinja Honchō and Shrine Shintō Policy. *Japan Forum* 8(2): 177–188.

Teeuwen, Mark. 2002. From Jindō to Shinto: A Concept Takes Shape. *Japanese Journal of Religious Studies* 29(3–4): 233–263.

Teeuwen, Mark. 2007. Comparative Perspectives on the Emergence of Jindō and Shinto. *Bulletin of the School of Oriental and African Studies* 70(2): 373–402.

Teeuwen, Mark, and Fabio Rambelli, eds. 2003. *Buddhas and Kami in Japan: Honji suijaku as a Combinatory Paradigm.* London: RoutledgeCurzon.

Teeuwen, Mark, and Bernhard Scheid, eds. 2006. *The Culture of Secrecy in Japanese Religion.* London: Routledge.

Thomas, Jolyon Baraka. 2007. Shūkyō Asobi and Miyazaki Hayao's Anime. *Nova Religio* 10(3): 73–95.

Tsuda, Sokichi. 1966. The Idea of Kami in Ancient Japanese Classics. *T'oung Pao* 52(4–5): 293–304.

Tucker, Mary Evelyn. 1998. Religious Dimensions of Confucianism: Cosmology and Cultivation. *Philosophy East & West,* 48(1): 5–45.

Tyler, Royall. 1981. A Glimpse of Mt. Fuji in Legend and Cult. *Journal of the Association of Teachers of Japanese* 16(2): 140–165.

Tyler, Royall. 1993. "The Book of the Great Practice": The Life of the Mt. Fuji Ascetic Kakugyō Tobutsū Kū. *Asian Folklore Studies* 52: 251–331.

Underwood, Meredith. 1999. Strategies of Survival: Women, Abortion, and Popular Religion in Contemporary Japan. *Journal of the American Academy of Religion* 67(4): 739–768.

Vasquez, Manuel. 2010. *More Than Belief: A Materialist Theory of Religion*. New York: Oxford University Press.

Winfield, Pamela. 2005. Curing with Kaji: Healing and Esoteric Empowerment in Japan. *Japanese Journal of Religious Studies* 32(1): 107–130.

Yoshida, Kazuhiko. 2003. Revisioning Religion in Ancient Japan. *Japanese Journal of Religious Studies* 30(1–2): 1–26.

Yoshida, Kazuhiko. 2006. The Thesis that Prince Shōtoku did not Exist. *Acta Asiatica* 91: 1–20.

Online sources

www.fujimura-ds.com/
www.jinjahoncho.or.jp/en/shinto/index.html
www.jinjahoncho.or.jp/en/spiritual/index.html
www.l.u-tokyo.ac.jp/shiseigaku/en/overview.htm
www.shinto.org/isf/index.html
www.theglassmagazine.com/forum/article.asp?tid=1099#title
(All sites last accessed 15 April 2011)

4

Mass Media in Japan

Katja Valaskivi

Research into mass media in Japan has mostly been separate from the Japanese studies discipline. Although Japanese studies has become increasingly interested in issues involving media, mass-media studies, particularly studies of audience reception, seem to keep their distance from Japanese studies (for a recent example see Takahashi, 2010). For media studies, obviously, media is the focus. However, in Japanese studies media is not the object of study itself, it is simply a source of research material on Japan or the medium through which research on Japanese politics, social phenomena, international relations or history can be studied.

One could argue that for Japanese studies mass media has largely been a window to look into Japan rather than a focus of study as such. For instance, the media system and media institutions of Japan have mostly been defined in comparative projects that describe media systems in different parts of the world. An extensive example of this kind is *The Handbook of the Media in Asia*, edited by Shelton Gunaratne in 2000. Books focusing only on mass media in Japan include Anne Cooper-Chen's and Miiko Kodama's *Mass Communication in Japan* (1997) and this writer's report on media and communication research in Japan, which describes the Japanese media landscape (Valaskivi, 2007). In addition, mass media from different perspectives

has systematically been covered at the Department of Japanology in the University of Trier's Center for East Asian and Pacific Studies. Its published work includes Gössmann's and Waldenberger's (as editors) *Medien in Japan* (2003). A refreshing and rare example of a study focusing on media as business is Westney, 1996. Westney's earlier work (1987) is an intriguing analysis of the interplay of Western influences and Japanese inventions in the development of Japanese journalism and Japan's newspaper industry.

This chapter has three main objectives. Firstly, it describes the main themes of research on media within Japanese studies. These themes are: Japanese society and social phenomena through media texts; research of media reception and role of media in the society; gender and media; and ethnographic and other approaches to popular culture, including film, television, manga, anime etc. Since research of mass media within Japanese studies comprises only part of the research into Japanese mass media, the second objective of the chapter is to look into research of mass media conducted in Japan within media and communication studies.[1] The third objective is to give a general outline of the Japanese media system and its development. The chapter ends with a discussion of changes and challenges for media and cultural studies within Japanese studies.

As the concept of 'mass media' has become outdated with the development of internet and social media, in this chapter it is used historically. For more general purposes 'media' is used.

MEDIA IN JAPAN

The history of Japanese media has been told in many ways and from different perspectives. In Japanese studies media is often approached from a historical perspective and the attempt is, quite obviously, to state something about Japan rather than about media. This is apparent in a variety of books from James Huffman's *Creating a Public: People and Press in Meiji Japan* (1997) to Barbara Hamill Sato's *The New Japanese Woman: Modernity, Media, and Women in Interwar Japan* (2003) and Scott Nygren's *Time Frames: Japanese Cinema and the Unfolding of History* (2007).

Originating in Germany, *Zeitung-swissenschaft* – newspaper studies – was the beginning of media studies in Japan. It was typical at the time in Japan to look to Germany for scholarly influences, and Professor Hideo Ono established the research field in Japan in the 1920s and 1930s. Small research groups were first established at Tokyo University, Sophia University and Meiji University. A rare contemporary account of the relationship between politics and journalism in Japan was written in English by Kisaburo Kawabe, who defended his dissertation *The Press and Politics in Japan* at the University of Chicago. The book ends with an optimistic note emphasizing that the 'awakening of the masses' in Japan has led to democratization and the diminishing power of 'bureaucrats and militarists' (Kawabe, 1921).

After the Second World War the source of influences shifted from Germany to the USA, and theoretical approaches, methodology, teaching methods and curriculums at universities were reformulated after American empirical science and positivism. In the study of mass media in Japan this meant a shift from journalism to mass communication and from studies of newspapers to mass media (Tamura, 2004). According to Ishikawa (1998), scientific mass-communication research in Japan began in 1951 when the Japanese Society for the Study of Journalism and Mass Communication was founded. The Japan Broadcasting Company NHK (Nippon Hoso Kyokai) founded the Broadcasting Culture Research Institute in 1946.

The mass media in Japan has even older roots. The prototype newspaper in Japan was the *kawara-ban*, or 'tile block print', which appeared during the Tokugawa era in 1615. *Kawaraban* were one-page flyers, which were printed using roof tiles of houses as negatives. They were published irregularly and contained information on lovers' suicides, disasters and other sensational events. The tone was mostly scandalous (Moeran, 1996; Huffman, 1997). Huffman notes that although *kawaraban* were the precursors of modern newspapers there were also other means of mass communication in Tokugawa Japan:

> Scholars have catalogued an astonishing variety of media through which Tokugawa-era Japanese told each other about things curious and important: courier networks that linked the villages of each *han* and communicated not only official decrees but political messages people wanted to get to each other; streetside sermons of Buddhist priests, called *dangibon*; kabuki and puppet theater shows; shadow plays (*kage e*) and the later *kami shibai* or picture card shows, which remain popular to this day; traveling storytellers; and *tozaiya* (town criers), who advertised all manners of merchandise. During the lively Genroku era (1688–1704), singing couples (*tsurebushi*) would roam the streets, hiding if necessary behind large straw hats or folding fans, and singing to a lively beat the juicy details of some illicit love affair or of the revenge of the forty-seven *ronin*. When the ever-vigilant morality police tried to suppress *the tsurebushi*, the same material would appear in different media, particularly *share-bon* (jokebooks) and *kibuyoshi* (yellow-covered storybooks), many of which disguised their salacious material about the court or *bakufu* in thinly veiled stories about "the past." (1997: 23)

The multiplicity of mass-communication forms in Japan is shown by the research. Alongside mass-media research there has been a steady thread of research into different forms of popular culture. This is inseparable from the growing media saturation of society. As Kogawa (1988) notes: 'Today's Japanese popular culture manifests itself through the medium of... electronic devices'. This topic will be discussed in more detail later.

The first modern private newspaper, *Nagasaki Shipping List and Advertiser*, was published in English, in Nagasaki in 1861. It appeared twice a week. The first Japanese-language newspapers appeared in 1862 and the first daily, *Yokohama Mainichi*, appeared on 28 January 1871 (Moeran, 1996; Huffman, 1997).

The current newspaper market in Japan has been described as having a dual structure (Löhr, 2003). There are five national quality newspapers (*zenkokushi*) with distinct regional editions. There are also four regional (or multi-prefectural) papers and a variety of prefectural dailies (*chihoushi*). Most of the papers publish two editions a day (Cooper-Chen and Kodama, 1997; Fujitake, 2005).

Japan's magazine market is also huge, although it has been diminishing since the early 1990s. During the 1990s more than a third of published magazines were *manga*. The proportion of *manga* is still significant although sales of *manga* have been diminishing since the mid 1990s; of the ten largest magazines with circulations of more than a million eight are *manga* magazines. Segmentation is the governing feature of magazine markets, and the women's magazine market, like that for *manga*, is carefully segmented (Valaskivi, 2007; Fujitake, 2005).

Newspaper circulations are diminishing globally and Japan's are no exception. In 1997 the total circulation of Japanese newspapers was 53.8 million; in 2011 the number had declined to 46.8 million (Tanaka, 2012). But this decline in comparison with those in the USA or the UK is fairly modest and slow. The reasons for Japanese newspapers' relative strength include the fact that newspapers are mostly delivered to the door (only a small amount of newspapers' income comes from newsstand sales) and the strong tradition of newspaper readership in Japan (together with Finland and Iceland Japan is one of the world's leading newspaper-reading nations (Valaskivi, 2007)). Research into newspapers and journalism has been strongly connected to politics and issues of democracy (Feldman, 1993; Pharr and Krauss, 1996). The history of Japanese journalism has been explored, although not recently (de Lange, 1998). The *kisha kurabu*, or press-club system, in Japan has been discussed frequently and identified as a major problem in developing impartial journalistic reporting in Japan (de Lange, 1998; Freeman, 2000, 2003). The issue of the possible partiality of Japanese media in general and NHK in particular has also been discussed in these studies (Krauss, 1996, 2000).

The relationship between media and politicians appears to be a topic that has been easier to approach from outside of Japan than inside. However, the outsider's view can also be biased. Japanese journalism, for instance, is frequently compared with US journalism without deeper elaboration of the development and structure of Japanese society and media system as a whole. This is particularly apparent with Freeman (2000), who seems determined to prove that Japanese journalism is lacking because of its deviance from the US norm. In her analysis of the *kisha*-club system she ignores with all but a mention those forms of journalism that are not tied to the system. The *kisha* clubs – literally, journalist clubs – are affiliated with all Japan's major organizations (the ministries, the police, the municipalities and large corporations). The clubs are officially maintained by the Japan Newspaper Association (*Nihon Shimbun Kyoukai*) and membership is institutional: only the most influential newspapers and television-company news departments can join. Media companies assign journalists to particular clubs, which means that they have their office space in the *kisha* club, which is located in the relevant ministry, local-government office etc. The main critique of the system is that it restricts independent information gathering and leads to too close ties between decision makers and journalists – and among journalists (Yada, 2007).

However, there are ways in which journalism can challenge the *kisha*-club system and the internal ties of the elite. For instance, Hayashi (1998) describes the 'home and family sections' *(katei)* of the largest nationwide newspapers and the particular role of these sections in generating an alternative public sphere in Japan. Journalists working in the *katei* sections of newspapers are not part of the *kisha*-club system. There are also the weekly magazines, sports magazines and other forms of journalism that remain outside the system. Until recently foreign journalists could not become members of *kisha* clubs (Valaskivi, 2007).

There are also many Japanese researchers (and decision makers) who see the *kisha*-club system as outdated, and this number is steadily growing. Because of this some organizations have already opened their *kisha* clubs to all journalists or given up the system altogether (Yada, 2007). The 2011 triple catastrophe – the Tohoku earthquake, tsunami and Fukushima nuclear-power-plant disaster (3/11) – has dramatically changed the Japanese media landscape, including the re-evalution of the *kisha*-club system – and the system has become significantly looser simply because alternative sources of information via the internet have multiplied (Tanaka, 2012).

Within the Japanese tradition of mass-media research there is a strand that has had almost no impact on Japanese studies although it is of crucial importance within Japan. Research into natural-disaster communications – information dissemination, panic and rumor, journalism and the role of media – has been and still is vast in Japan (Ishikawa, 1998). In Japanese studies these issues had hardly been touched before the March 2011 earthquake. One of the rare cases is MacLachlan (2001), who studied television news production after the Kobe earthquake. Since 3/11, though, there has been a surge of articles and books studying the role of media in the disaster (see Slater, 2011; Leavitt, 2013). In Japan the focus has been on research evaluating the performance of media in the disaster and the possibility of developing better media-based warnings and information-dissemination systems in situations of crisis (Fukunaga, 2013).

The Japanese research of crisis communication has traditionally been close to the media industry and aims at developing new and more efficient ways of information dissemination in times of natural disaster. The results of this work can be seen in the tsunami and earthquake warnings disseminated through the media quickly, accurately and effectively. In the case of environmental catastrophes generated by the industry the weaknesses of the *kisha*-club system and close ties between the media and environmental decision-makers become evident. It is not difficult to see parallels in the coverage of the Fukushima Dai-ichi nuclear crisis and the so-called Minamata lead-poisoning case, which slowly unwound from the 1960s and has been described by Ishikawa (1990). The lead-pollution illnesses of the inhabitants of Minamata in Kumamoto prefecture took 20–30 years to become public knowledge. In the case of the Fukushima Dai-ichi nuclear crisis (from March 2011 onwards) the cover-up was much more difficult because of social media and the easy access of private activists to the media. Independent information was spread quickly, some of which was rumour (see Slater, 2011). The Japanese government, convinced of the country's dependence on nuclear energy, is fighting back with extraordinary measures: it issued a call for a private tender to find and correct 'untrue' and 'economically harmful information' on social media and Twitter (MEXT, 2011). Independent documentary film makers and video journalists have become an important source of alternative information since the Japanese government has been more and more keen on restricting information dissemination on the matter since Tokyo was selected in Sept 2013 to be the Olympic city in 2020.

Radio broadcasts in Japan were begun in 1925 by the semi-governmental Tokyo Broadcasting Station, the predecessor of NHK. Before and during the Second World War NHK was a vehicle for military propaganda (Cooper-Chen and Kodama, 1997). Commercial radio broadcasts began in 1950. By the 1990s Japan had more than 300 radio stations, the majority of them AM stations. Since then the number has multiplied, in particular because of the growth of FM community radio since the turn of the century (Fujitake, 2005). Research on radio in Japanese studies has been marginal, and it has not been the focus of interest in media studies either.

Despite the internet's rapid growth in Japan, not least mobile internet use, television is still the strongest medium both in terms of viewing time and advertising revenue. The current television system with its strong public-service broadcaster (NHK) and competing private broadcasters was formed after the Second World War. It is perhaps paradoxical that the strength of public broadcasting in Japan is a result of the Occupation. Instead of trying to dissolve NHK, a mainstay of imperial Japan, the USA reinforced its national role. It was considered an efficient and quick way of communicating matters to Japanese citizens (Luther and Boyd, 1997). As for private broadcasting, Japanese television resembles the US network model more than the strong public-service television of European countries such as the UK or Finland and other Nordic countries (Valaskivi and Ruoho, 2006).

As noted, Japanese studies has not focused very much on the media industry or media economy; but in Japanese media research these are central topics. Research approaches include historical descriptions of developments in particular sectors of the media, comparisons of industry features with corresponding ones abroad and policy developments. Issues of media convergence in terms of technology, economy, legislation and use are currently among the hot topics of media research in Japan (Valaskivi, 2007).

The rapid change of the media industry has further shifted focus towards technological changes and their effects on the media economy and the development of the industry (Sugaya, 2005; Minami and Nakata, 2007). Research into convergence and its effects on markets, legislation and policy decision-making is being conducted in many research institutions in Japan including the Research Institute of Telecommunication and Economics and Keio University MediaCom. (Valaskivi, 2007: 76).

In Japan most internet use is through mobile phones, of which almost 90 percent have internet access (Valaskivi, 2007: 30–3). Japan was one of the early adopters of the internet, but it was the mobile phone (*keitai*) that brought the internet to the whole population (Coates and Holroyd, 2003: 140). The internet changes media markets, the role of media in society and everyday life and the ways in which media is used. In a survey published in 2011 respondents for the first time pointed to the internet as more important than newspapers in the 'value of media' category (Tanaka, 2012: 30). Newspapers came in second place together with television.

The 3/11 earthquake, tsunami and nuclear crisis has made the impact of social media in society more visible than before. Some descriptions of the situation have already appeared. For instance, the Hot Spots collection of texts by Japanese-studies specialists, published by the journal *Cultural Anthropology*, describes the anti-nuclear demonstrations and the use of social media in activism (Slater, 2011). Twitter use in and after the disaster has also been studied (Leavitt, 2013).

SOCIAL PHENOMENA IN MEDIA TEXTS

As noted, Japanese studies has often considered media as something transparent. Within Japanese studies, media texts have been perceived as handy sources of material when the attempt is to grasp social phenomena in Japan. At its extreme this has meant that, for instance, television drama has been perceived not as a scripted text but as a suitable place for studying Japanese behaviour in situations where 'the observational methods... affect(s) the behavior observed' (Niyekawa, 1984: 62). Niyekawa analysed conflict as an interpersonal situation and used television drama as material, since 'television home drama enables an outsider to have a close look, so to speak, into personal and private aspects of life in Japan, particularly since these home dramas are characterized as down to earth' (Niyekawa, 1984).

Television programmes are also used as proof of certain features in Japanese society. This approach requires a belief in the 'down to earth' or realistic nature of the programmes under study; 'realistic' programmes are then considered revealing of the unique nature of the Japanese phenomenon under investigation. For instance, Stephen D. Miller (1997) emphasizes in his article on the Japanese television serial *Reunion* that the gay culture depicted demonstrates how the social structure of Japanese gay bars is unlike that in the USA. Like Niyekawa, Miller gets into trouble claiming that the programme tells us about the unique nature of Japan because of its realism. Television texts are scripted and their relationship to 'real life' is more complicated than is often presumed in Japanese-studies research that focuses on media texts. When the focus is on Japan rather than media features of televisual texts testify to societal features. Corresponding simplified interpretations would hardly be possible if the writer was discussing cultural texts closer to home.

Emphasising or discussing the uniqueness of Japan and the Japanese has been apparent in studies of media. Similarly, the Japanese in relation to others is and has been a central theme. A legendary case is the failure in Japan of the iconic American television series *Dallas,* which has been discussed in Katz, et al. (1991). They concluded that *Dallas* failed because of 'cultural incompatibility' between the two countries (1991: 100), although they did consider other explanations: marginal broadcasting time, incompetent PR and no market for a long-running foreign serial. Another case is the reception of *The Lion King* in Japan (Kuwahara, 1997). In these articles both the underlying starting point and the final finding assumes a Japanese uniqueness or essential difference in comparison to the USA.

The relationship of Japan and 'Japaneseness' is also one of the underlying themes in work focusing on fandom of Japanese popular culture outside of Japan (Allison, 2000a; Napier, 2001, 2006; Mikhailova, 2006; Valaskivi, 2009), which will be more thoroughly discussed later. Probably the most systematic description of the historical relationship between Japan and 'the West' in terms of popular-culture influences is by Napier (2007). She leads the reader into an interesting exploration of Western perceptions of Japanese popular and media culture since the mid nineteenth century starting with the impressionists – for whom Japan was a newly found land with authentic and playful culture – and ending with contemporary fans of anime and manga. Napier describes in detail how Japanese influences have affected artists, thinkers and enthusiasts in Europe and the USA since the forceful opening of Japan.

RESEARCH OF MEDIA RECEPTION AND THE ROLE OF MEDIA IN SOCIETY

Use of media, radio, television and, currently, the internet has been of interest for researchers from early on. In Japan research of radio audiences began in the 1930s when NHK started audience surveys. The aim was to analyse audience interest and responses. In the 1940s NHK introduced the diary method in audience research (Ishikawa, 1998: 63). The NHK Broadcasting Culture Institute (*Housou Bunka Kenkyuujo*) continues to research television and radio audiences and uses various methods in so doing. The longitudinal Time Use Survey, conducted for decades, includes a media-use section and provides useful comparative data.[2] Because of strong interest in audience responses most user, audience and consumer research in Japan is conducted by commercial bodies, such as advertising agencies and subcontractors catering for the needs of various media-related companies.

In Japanese studies research of audiences began in the late 1960s when several studies were conducted at Sophia University. These studies followed the then current approach of media-uses and gratifications research, which focused on how audiences used media and the gratifications those media provided (Katz et al., 1973). In other words, these studies focused on the meanings of television viewing in people's lives. An influential publishing channel for these studies was the Sophia University *Monumenta Nipponica* series together with the *Monumenta Nipponica Monographs.* Assistant professor of mass media and later the chairman of the Socio-Economic Institute at the Sophia University, Jose Maria de Vera was the most active researcher in the field. His studies on television viewing (de Vera, undated; 1968) and educational television in Japan (de Vera, 1967) have almost been forgotten, probably in part because of the uncomfortable fact that de Vera belongs to the Society of Jesus, i.e. he is a Jesuit,[3] but also because the uses and gratifications approach has been seen as old-fashioned in mass-media research and never really took on in Japanese studies. Despite the limited setting of the research, de Vera's work and that of his colleagues contains interesting findings, such as viewership patterns of different gender and age groups (de Vera, 1968; Furu, 1971).

It appears, nevertheless, that research on media audiences within Japanese studies ceased at the beginning of the 1970s with the uses and gratifications approach. Nor does there seem to be any research on newspaper audiences within Japanese studies, nor on television- and radio-news audiences. However, research on the role of media in civil society, and newspapers in particular, has been published (Kawato, et al., 2011).

In Japan there is a fairly strong tradition of critical studies of journalism, and the study of the public sphere has been of continuous interest among Japanese scholars of journalism and media. Habermas's theory of the public sphere has been discussed in numerous works, the majority of them in Japanese. In Japan, like elsewhere, applying the Habermasian conception of the public sphere has led to observations of insufficient possibilities of citizen participation and the need for a more inclusive public sphere (Hanada, 1997; Hayashi, 2002; Ishikawa, 1998.) Before the breakthrough of the internet, interest focused on the role of journalism and public service in creating the public sphere (Ishikawa, 1998), but with the growing importance of the internet, theoretical and empirical studies on the possibilities for the new media to create the public sphere and public debate have been increasing (Nakamura and Yonekura, 2008; Suzuki et al., 2008). The government has funded research on media literacy since the 1990s, but its concept of media literacy has often been exclusively technical, meaning access to and ability to use various forms of media. Researchers, however, quickly began to emphasize the importance of critical reading abilities and the right to participate (Suzuki, 1997: 8; Shibata, 2002).

Research on the role of media in society has also been central. Through effect studies and tests of the cognitive (or other) effects of mass communication researchers have attempted to understand the impact of media in social processes. For instance, Takeshita (1981, 1990) has discussed the so-called agenda-setting function of mass communication and focused on the social and political effects of mass communication. Japanese scholars have also often applied the effect hypothesis to general political processes and focused on media effects (television in particular) on audiences (Ishikawa,

1998: 62; Valaskivi, 2007: 67). The effects have been studied empirically, surveys being among the most popular methods (Gatzen, 2001).

In Japanese studies audience research reappeared in the 1990s, when interest towards Japanese media and popular culture outside of Japan started to grow (Rosenberger, 1996; Kinsella, 1996; Valaskivi, 1999, 2000; Takahashi, 2010). However, the great surge of interest in media audiences and media use has come with the explosion of the internet. Interest in internet and mobile media use has grown steadily. Fairly recent examples are Coates and Holroyd (2003: 139–40) and Ito et al. (2005). Coates and Holroyd give a detailed historical account of the interconnectedness of technological development and economic growth in Japan. Their focus is more on the gadgets, technologies and business than content, analysing the consumer-driven nature of the computer and internet business in Japan and demonstrating the interconnectedness of business, government and industry in creating the Japanese success story of mobile internet consumer products. Coates and Holroyd wrote during the time when Japan was considered one of the strong drivers of internet-content business development and this shows in the writers' great enthusiasm in describing the 'essence of contemporary Japan' as 'young, aggressive, male, female, wired, motivated, capitalistic and creative' (2003: 7).

Ito et al. carefully consider everyday meanings and uses of the mobile phone (*keitai*) in Japan. In the book Misa Matsuda suggests that *keitai* was first approached by researchers from the perspective of business and business use before interest shifted to youth relationships. Finally, Matsuda claims, (some) researchers joined a 'technonationalistic celebration of Japan's leadership in the *keitai* arena' (Matsuda, 2005: 6).

Matsuda's article appeared in Ito et al.'s book, a collection of the work of Japanese scholars. These scholars are an example of the growing trend of Japanese academics publishing their work in English for international audiences. This trend is particularly strong in areas of media, popular culture and new-media use. The trend is boosted not only by the global nature of the internet, burgeoning social media and interest in media trends around the world but by the global boom of Japanese popular culture since the late 1990s, which will be discussed later.

GENDER AND MEDIA CULTURE

Research of gender in media has been one of the central topics in Japanese studies since the late 1980s. Within Japan the area has been marginal;

however, Muramatsu Yasuko and Suzuki Midori were pioneers in the field, publishing research in Japanese in the 1970s and in English since the 1980s. Their research focused on images of the roles of men and women in TV programmes and advertising (Muramatsu, 1982, 1986, 1991; Suzuki, 1985). Quite obviously, they found that the roles of women tended to be related to homemaking or looks, whereas men were represented in active and professional roles. Together with Hilaria Gössmann, one of the pioneers in the field in Europe, in 1998 Muramatsu published *Media ga Tsukuru Jendā*, or *Media Making Gender*, in which they emphasized the current perception of media as a technology that constructs gender rather than reflects 'the world'. Muramatsu (2002) has also published research on how gender is constructed through the relationship of the media and audience, and Gössmann has edited an anthology on the representations of family in Japanese television (1993). The current writer's publications on television drama also have gender and family relationships as one of their themes (Valaskivi, 1995, 1999, 2000). Gender in television drama is one of the focuses also in Lukacs (2010).

When studying gender the focus on television, and television drama in particular, is typical of media and cultural studies outside of Japanese studies. However, many studies of television drama and soap opera focus on the female audience rather than the programmes (Brunsdon, 1981; Ang, 1985; Geraghty, 1991), while in the case of Japan the study of women as television viewers has not had a major role in academic research (however, see Valaskivi, 1999).

In addition to television, women's magazines have been a frequent focus of research on gender. Among those who have studied women's magazines from different perspectives are Neuss (1971), Wöhr (1997), Sakamoto (1999), Wöhr et al. (1998) and Sato (2003). Perspectives vary from historical to textual analysis. Women's magazines have also been used as sources for studying particular phenomena. The articles in the influential anthology of this field, Skov and Moeran's (1995) *Women, Media and Consumption in Japan*, focus mostly on women's magazines, print media and advertising. Textual analysis is their most used method. The focus is on media representations of women in media that are targeted at women. A general finding of the book is summed up in an article by John Clammer (1995: 213): gender and class intersect in Japanese media and so do age and class. Concerns of 'Japaneseness' and a preoccupation with social distinctions define representations of the female body in Japanese print media.

Until the mid 1990s research of media and gender meant, in practice, 'women', which is underlined in the choice of media and genres under study. However, since the late 1990s issues of gender have been widened to include men, homosexuals and other genders (McLelland, 1999; Darling-Wolf, 2004).

The study of gender in Japanese popular culture is plentiful and multifaceted. It varies from studies of women's genres, such as *shoujou* (girl's manga) and *yaoi* (homosexual manga pornography drawn by women for women), and pornography (Allison, 2000b; Kangasvuo, 2007; Saito, 2008) to analysis of female characters (Napier, 1998). Research of gender has widened into themes of otherness (Miller, 1995; Gössmann, 2001; Iwabuchi, 2005) and limits of the human (Lunning, 2008).

RESEARCH OF POPULAR CULTURE

In Japan research of popular culture has deep roots in the research of popular entertainment of the 1920s and 1930s. Early researchers were sociologists who focused on popular performances or on movie and theatre audiences. In the 1930s the focus shifted to radio, which at the time was perceived through conceptions of national identity (Yoshimi, 1998: 66).

From the 1940s to the 1960s the *Shisou no Kagaku*, or Institute of Science of Thought, developed research of popular culture further. From the beginning the group was interested in actual daily practices of media and popular-culture use and the meaning made from the texts. This kind of approach took on in the West much later (Yoshimi, 1998). The group also translated its work into English to make it accessible outside of Japan. Hidetoshi Kato edited and translated the first English anthology on Japanese popular culture in 1953. This anthology was, apparently, an effort to make Japanese communication and popular culture more accessible to Americans. It is interesting that it makes no clear-cut division between 'journalism' and 'popular culture', which are discussed within the same frame of reference (Kato, 1973 [1953]).

Kato continued to act as a bridge between Japanese and English scholars in decades to come, writing himself and translating Japanese colleagues' work into English. He took part in editing the *Handbook of Japanese Popular Culture* (Powers et al., 1989), in the introduction to which he (Kato, 1989: xvii–xviii) explains Japanese popular culture to the international (academic) audience, starting from the differences of the concept of popular culture: 'The term "popular" is not popular in Japan. To be more precise, there is no proper Japanese word that corresponds to "popular" in English, especially in its American use and, more particularly, in the context of "popular culture'". He continues with concepts of *taishu bunka* (mass culture), *minshu bunka* (public culture) and *minzoku bunkai* (folk culture), and notes that American 'pop art' became *poppu aato* because of difficulties in translation. One of the rare anthologies of the field in the 1980s, Powers et al. discusses the hybrid interplay of influences between Japan and the West. The book's chapters discuss music, television, film, comics and literature. The articles are written by Japanese, American and European scholars. In his conclusion Kato (1989: 316) notes: 'Japanese popular culture is unique, and its research methodology requires that special consideration be given to this singularity'.

The first form of modern popular media of interest to researchers outside of Japan was film. It is probably also the most researched part of Japanese mass media outside of Japan, although *manga* and *anime* may take over shortly. Japanese film has an important role in film studies in general. Yoshimoto (2000: 8) goes as far as to state that 'the position of Japanese cinema is inseparable from the question of how film studies has constituted itself, legitimated its existence, and maintained its institutional territoriality through the double process of inclusion and exclusion'. In his refreshingly critical text Yoshimoto (2000: 8) divides the history of American scholarship on Japanese cinema into three stages, which follow the general developments of research in film studies in the USA.

The first stage was the humanistic celebration of Japanese cinemas's great auteurs, such as Kurosawa and Ozu, in the 1960s, which started with the commercial success of their movies in the USA. According to Yoshimoto (2000: 10), Donald Richie was a typical representative of the humanistic phase of research. This phase emphasized the 'Japanese national character' as a particular case for representing ideal humanistic values. Research and critiques used cultural stereotypes and cultural essence to explain formal features, thematic motifs and contextual background in Japanese films.

At the second stage, in the 1970s, film criticism and research focused on the formalistic and Marxist celebration of Japanese cinema as an alternative to Hollywood. Formalism was interested in the ideology of film form, although its influence on the study of Japanese cinema was fleeting and the humanistic approach far more influential throughout. According to Yoshimoto (2000: 19–20), one of the most important scholars of formalism in the study of Japanese cinema was Noel Burch, who emphasized the essential difference between Western (Hollywood) and Japanese cinematic expression – needless to say, favouring the Japanese. He made constant juxtapositions between the two: Western cinema is representational and Japanese cinema is presentational;

Western artists aim at creating a sense of depth and Japanese artists make the viewer pay attention to the surface; Western texts conceal construction, Japanese texts foreground the construction of meaning, and so on. Yoshimoto (2000: 21) concludes that Burch's approach was Orientalist in its idealized and arbitrary attempt to construct a model of Japanese culture.

At the third stage film research turned to a 'critical reexamination of the preceding approaches through the introduction of discourse of Otherness and cross-cultural analysis in the 1980s' (Yoshimoto 2000: 8). Interest shifted to cross-cultural influences between Western and Japanese cinema. Yoshimoto quotes Scott Nygren, who sees modern Japan and the West as inverted mirror images of each other because 'each culture turns to the other for traditional values which function to deconstruct its own dominant ideology' (Yoshimoto 2000: 24).

In an interesting way there is an interdependency between the fame of Japanese popular culture outside Japan and the amount and depth of research into it. The celebration of Akira Kurosawa and Yasujiro Ozu in film studies in the 1960s came after their popularity in the 1950s. In 1959 Anderson and Richie published their collection *The Japanese Film: Art and Industry* with a foreword from Kurosawa. A similar kind of surge of enthusiasm can be seen in the *Mechademia* journal which, since 2005, has been focusing on Japanese popular culture (Lunning, 2006, 2007, 2008, 2009, 2010, 2011). This surge has followed the steadily growing interest in Japanese popular culture since the late 1980s and throughout the 1990s in the USA and Europe.

With the new interest in popular culture and new generations of researchers, Japan is no longer predominantly the Other, always scrutinized as the deviant culture. Not only has Japanese popular culture become a part of everyday experience in the USA and Europe but it has also become a shared experience with Japanese researchers. In the *Mechademia* project an exceptional and profound dialogue takes place, where researchers (and media makers) from different (although mainly Anglo-American or Japanese) backgrounds come together.

Japanese film has received more attention than television. Anderson and Richie's historical account is only one example of this. Film and fiction (including literature) have their own strand of research in Japanese studies. In this humanistic orientation myths, beliefs and religious influences have been an inspiration for analysis (Buruma, 1985; Barrett, 1989). In *Behind the Mask* Ian Buruma focuses on one of the main paradoxes for outsiders of Japan: the polite and organized everyday life and the violent, obsene imagery of popular culture. He analyses the gender roles of men and women and concludes that Shintoism with its reverence for the strong female and mother has contributed to some of the mythic imagery of contemporary popular culture. In this strand of research, strong connection with both the French film-study tradition and psychoanalytical approaches have been apparent (Yoshimoto, 1993b). These ideas have their continuum in twenty-first-century studies of *anime* and *manga*, in the science-fiction genre in particular, which analyse popular-culture texts in the context of myths and beliefs (Lunning, 2008). The continuum between film and anime research has to some extent been explicated by Steven T. Brown (2006).

Psychoanalytical approaches have spilled over from film studies not only to *anime* and *manga* research but to analysis of the *otaku* phenomenon (LaMarre, 2006). The word *otaku* has different meanings depending on the context. In everyday Japanese it is a honorific form of the pronoun *you*, which also refers to household and family. Sometime in the late 1980s the word began to be used among nerdish male *manga* and *anime* fans when referring to each other. Gradually the word has come to mean a male nerd who is a frantic enthusiast of any form of popular culture, usually something sexually loaded. Female *otaku* are often called *fuyoshi*, a word hadly ever used outside Japan.

In Japan the term *otaku* still has a somewhat dubious tone. The word circulated widely in the late 1980s when Tsutomu Miyazaki, an introverted video fan who had no human contacts outside of his home, was revealed to have raped, murdered and dismembered four very young girls. Miyazaki, who was executed in 2008, was called the '*otaku* murderer' (Schodt, 1996: 33; Kondo, 1993: 42–45).

Outside Japan *otaku* has come to mean, simply, a fan – male of female – of Japanese popular culture, usually *manga* and/or *anime* (Schodt, 1996: 33; Valaskivi, 2009). Since the so-called Cool Japan phenomenon in the 2000s and the Japanese government's official strategies in boosting Japanese popular culture outside of Japan the term *otaku* has also become less stigmatized in the country of origin. The former prime minister Taro Aso made a point of calling himself *otaku* on several occasions in 2006. After all, he likes to read *manga*.

There is also a strand of artists, researchers and enthusiasts who call themselves the *otaku* movement. Outside Japan the movement's best-known proponent is Hiroki Azuma, who writes:

... the postmodern social structure is based not on the invisible ideology but the also invisible information like the Internet. Our society is losing the grand Narrative but constructing the grand database in its place and the simulacra covering the postmodern surfaces are actually controlled and regulated by the database. As postmodernists often say, all the postmodern works (not only fine art but literature, music and many pop cultural works) are created not by being led by an idea, not an authorship nor an ideology, but by deconstructing and reconstructing the preceding works or rereading them in a different way. In other words, postmodern artists or authors prefer dismantling the preceding works into some elements or fragments and reassembling them repeatedly rather than expressing their own authorship or originality. The accumulation of those fragments (CDs, video clips, web sites...) now becomes a kind of anonymous database from where new works emerge. I believe you can find this tendency in almost all genres including the recent Hollywood movies and techno/house music. (2001)

As Azuma, one of the leading philosophers of Japanese popular culture describes, the *otaku* culture is based on a multiplicity of narratives, readily available in the 'database' of the internet, not only to be consumed and used but recycled, produced, reproduced, rewritten and redrawn. Azuma connects his theory with the concept of Superflat by Takashi Murakami (2001). For Murakami the concept describes the two-dimensionality of society, customs, art and culture (Brehm, 2002: 036, 040).

In his analysis Azuma sees *otaku* culture as an expression and integral phenomenon of contemporary Japanese culture rather than a sector or a fad of 'the youth'. It uses and interprets media but in a more profound way – as a way of being in the world, of seeing and interpreting society. Connections used to be made with the world through ideology – now they are made through invisible information, and affection (Azuma, 2009).

Both Azuma and Murakami emphasize that the Superflat is not solely a Japanese phenomenon but a global one. It can also be used as a description of the experience of a Western fan, who sees the 'Japaneseness' of Japanese popular art in a two-dimensional reflection through the media.

Reflecting on the Japanese enthusiasm of the *otaku* movement and the Superflat phenomenon, Thomas LaMarre (2007) notes that focusing on the active internet use of fans can be a redemptive project – an attempt to justify the fandom itself. The psychoanalytically oriented LaMarre (2007: 383–384) emphasizes that the Japanese writers who have discussed *otaku* culture tend to exaggerate the importance of the media at the expense of the fact that, for many (male) *otaku*, the object of affection is not the *media* but the *woman* who can be reached through the media, if not in real life.

According to LaMarre, protagonists of the *otaku* movement claim (Azuma, 2007, 2009; Okada, 1995) that the *otaku* are attracted to the media rather than its contents. The media is explained as both the source of pleasure and the affect. Media is a socially acceptable and even preferable target of fandom, at least, more so than sex or the woman. Thus, media becomes an acceptable justification for fandom and, through this justification, fandom is redeemed from the deviant and unclear into the category of acceptable and innovative.

For LaMarre (2007), the idea that, for the *otaku*, the affect is the media (rather than women) reinforces the *otaku* image as an inverted, unsocial (male) nerd, withdrawn into a dark room with a computer. At the same time it emphasizes homosocial bonds, the power of men over women, and refuses female creativity.

Study of Japanese non-animated television has never been as popular as study of film and *manga/anime*, although the popularity of Japanese television drama outside Japan during the late 1980s probably contributed to the research interest in television drama during the 1990s. At least, this was the case with *Oshin*, the most popular Japanese television drama internationally. *Oshin*'s success was discussed in NHK International (1991), Mowlana and Rad (1992) and Harvey (1996). The Japan Association of Broadcasting Art capitalized on the interest in television drama by publishing in English *A History of Japanese Television Drama* (Gotou et al., 1990). However, television drama unknown to Western audiences was also studied. For instance, Valaskivi (1995, 1999) focused on a Japanese *houmu dorama* (home drama) hit, which later became popular in South East and East Asia, but has not been broadcast on television in Europe or the USA. Since the 1990s most of the popular Japanese television programmes broadcast outside Japan have been redone formats or quiz shows. The writer has tracked down the route of one format (TBS's *Happy Family Plan*) through Holland and Denmark to Finland and compared the similarities and differences in the representations of the family (Valaskivi, 2004).

Mostly, however, research into television and Japanese television formats in Europe and the USA has been sidetracked by research into *anime* and *manga* fandom on the one hand and the internet and *keitai* culture on the other.

The popularity of *manga* and *anime* began to steadily grow outside of Japan from the late 1980s. During the 1990s Japanese studies also turned its eye to *manga* and *anime*. The first research book on the phenomenon was Sharon Kinsella's *Adult Manga. Culture and Power in Contemporary Japanese Society* in 1997. Around the same time, Dolores Martinez edited a collection of articles titled *The Worlds of Japanese Popular Culture* (1998). Like Kinsella, other writers in this book were mostly interested in questions of gender. A couple of years later Anne Allison (2000b) in her

ethnographic work elaborated on and discussed extensively the intertwined relationship of gender, censorship and comics. The main red thread of the book is about mothers: how they take part in defining and teaching the borderline between performing according to the rules and discipline and performances of desire in media texts, *manga* in particular. In Kinsella, Martinez and Allison the focus was still on Japanese popular culture within Japan. And this was also the case in the Curzon Press's (currently University of Hawaii Press) *ConsumAsiaN* series, which published several anthologies on media and consumption in Asia and Japan in the late 1990s and early 2000s, mostly from the international research network of *Consumption in Asia* (Skov and Moeran, 1995; Treat, 1996). Despite its name, the network was also interested in the production of media and popular culture in Japan and Asia (Moeran, 2001), and conducted ethnographical research and fieldwork (Painter, 1991; Moeran, 1996, 2001). The ethnographic approach to media production aimed at describing in detail how television production companies (Painter, 1991) and advertising agencies (Moeran, 1996) worked.

Only since the late 1990s has research into Japanese popular culture undergone a gradual shift from focusing on a particular medium to focusing on fantasy, story or the wider phenomena of media and popular culture use; but there has also been a shift from looking at Japanese popular culture as a phenomenon inside Japan to seeing it as a global phenomenon. This shift reimagines the globalized popular culture industry, where characters and storylines are multimodal and produced in all kinds of media at the same time and marketed to consumers translocally. Originally a character in all kinds of products, Kitty-chan becomes a heroine in *manga* and *anime*, while the Game Boy game *Pokémon* becomes first *anime* and then playing cards, soft toys, small plastic characters – you name it. In this multimodality, research focusing on one form of media fails to grasp the scope of the phenomena. Consequently, a growing proportion of media and popular-culture research does not focus on a particular medium but rather plotlines across media or the vastness of the phenomenon itself – and it becomes increasingly difficult to distinguish between media research and popular culture research. An inspiring, American example of describing and analysing the multiplicity of Japanese popular culture and its global spread is Anne Allison's (2006) *Millennial Monsters. Japanese Toys and the Global Imagination.* Allison successfully illuminates the consumer culture and spread of Japanese popular culture in the global context of national interests, competition and changing power relations. She discusses the change in perceptions of Japan throughout the world through the spread of consumer culture branded as Japanese. Firstly, Allison sees the global influence of Japanese popular culture as a challenge to the American hegemonic center of global culture. Secondly, the attraction of Japanese popular culture does not directly translate into political power or signify Japan as a place that is signified: '"Japan" operates more as a signifier for a particular brand and blend of fantasy-ware' (Allison, 2006: 277). Thirdly, the Cool Japan phenomenon – the global boom of Japanese popular culture – can be explained with its productivity in capitalistic marketing of the new millennium: the 'got to catch them all' mode, with its constant changing of products and the stretching of them into new zones of media, develops what Allison calls 'polymorphous perversity'. Constantly shifting fantasy becomes addictive in the capitalism of endless innovation, information and acquisition (Allison, 2006: 277).

A European perspective on Japanese popular culture is provided by Marco Pellitteri (2010). In his *The Dragon and the Dazzle* he analyses the phenomenon in four European countries: Italy, France, Spain and Germany. He sees the influences of Japanese popular culture as particularly strong in France, but also in Italy, where not only fans but also politicians, television programmers, educators and artists acknowledge the impact of Japanese popular culture in discussions. According to Pelliteri, the influence of Japanese popular culture came in two phases: the first was between 1975 and 1995 (which Pellitteri calls the Dragon phase) and the second started in 1996 (the Dazzle phase). The first came through localized television animations, the second through heavily commercialized multimodal product families, such as *Pokémon*. Pellitteri sees three main motifs that have travelled to Europe in Japanese popular culture: 'machine', 'infant' (*kawaii*; literally, cute) and 'mutation' (Pellitteri, 2010: 5–10).

SHIFTING OBJECTS

Dialogue between Japanese studies and media research has taken place throughout history. However, this dialogue has not necessarily been very knowledgeable of research traditions or media research approaches. For instance, in 1994 Andrew A. Painter called for 'anthropology of television'. Painter's argument was that television is a cultural phenomenon and thus has to be studied in relation to culture rather than attempting to grasp 'ideological' aspects of television. For him, an anthropological approach to television would be broad, comparative and cross-cultural, 'relating television to matters of lived

experience' as opposed to research that tries to prove a conspiracy theory in which television producers and sponsors are manipulative 'captains of consciousness' (Painter, 1994: 71). Painter refers to Stuart Ewen's classic book *Captains of Consciousness: Advertising and the Social Roots of Consumer Culture* from 1976 to dismiss much media research as 'ignoring culture and labelling [sic] virtually everything on TV as "ideological"'. Although Painter demonstrated fairly thin knowledge of media research and made gross simplifications, he was right to emphasize a cultural and anthropological approach to media. This way of approaching media – in Japan and elsewhere – has become more and more common in recent years.

Currently, Japanese studies faces the question of what Japan is. Already by 1998 the issue had been discussed by Ryuuichi Narita, Tessa Morris-Suzuki and Souchou Yao: '… until recently within Japanese studies Japan was not a problem… in studying Japan few people paused to think what "Japan" meant' (Narita et al., 1998: 76). Since the turn of the millennium research has began to take this question seriously, and with the spread of Japanese media and popular culture around the world the question of 'Japaneseness' has been seen from different perspectives. For instance, Koichi Iwabuchi (2002b) has written about 'Japanese transnationalism' in East and South East Asia and the spread of Japanese popular culture, television dramas in particular (Iwabuchi, 2001, 2002a). He uses the concept of Japanese transnationalism to explain Japan's nationalistic uses of the global spread of Japanese popular culture (2002b). He explores the relationship between commercialization, capitalist culture and brand nationalism. He claims that the image of Japan outside of the country, moulded by the Cool Japan phenomenon, and utilized for political purposes by Japanese elites, obscures inequalities and contradictions within Japanese society. In order to create wider perspectives for understanding he sees the necessity of creating well formulated public pedagogy programmes that make use of the dialogic potential of media cultures (Iwabuchi, 2010: 95).

The internet poses growing challenges to all research into media. As noted, the internet has changed the media industry, economy and media use in unexpected ways. Fans of Japanese popular culture are leading the way in peer-to-peer fan subtitling since most of the interesting film and *anime* material will never be licensed in the USA, let alone Europe. The phenomenon has hardly been scratched in research (Hu, 2005; Valaskivi, 2009, 2011) but raises questions about media markets, intellectual-property rights and media-use patterns and Big Data, to mention just a few. The relationship of these practices with the 'Japaneseness' brand brings the phenomenon within the scope of Japanese studies. In Japan the attempt to grasp this issue is the so called 'socio-information' (*shakai jouhou*) approach, which aims to combine research from humanistic, societal and sociological perspectives (Valaskivi, 2007: 77).

Schäfer (2009, 36) suggests that embedding the cultural studies approach more deeply into Japanese studies would provide the self-reflexivity necessary for the discipline. He argues for an even deeper inclusion of mass media and popular culture in research into Japan in order to discover 'the complex mechanisms of nationalism and the constructions of collective national identities within modern Japanese society'. The Rabinowian (1986) idea of 'anthropologizing the West' fits into Schäfer's suggestion of an attempt to 'provincialize' cultural studies by the constant reflux of critical thought from 'marginalized' re-articulations of cultural studies into hegemonic Anglo-American centers. In addition – and most importantly – Schäfer emphasizes that Japanese studies must 'open itself towards the post-colonial condition of, and the power-relations within, the East Asian region' to overcome methodological nationalism, in which 'Japan' is presumed as self-evident and unquestioned.

To some extent Japanese studies has shifted its focus outside of Japan, to popular Japanese phenomena in East Asia and the West (the USA, in particular). For the fans of and participants in the Japanese popular-culture wave, 'Japaneseness' is a brand, a point of identification and affect (Allison, 2006; Nikunen, 2006; Napier, 2007; Valaskivi, 2009, 2011; Pellitteri, 2010). At the same time the growing interest in and actual lived experience of Japanese popular culture outside Japan has given birth to a rich and fruitful multicultural dialogue – mostly in the English language – about Japanese popular culture in which Japanese researchers also take part in. This can be seen in the Mechademia project as well as in other publications (Bolton et al., 2007) and translations of Japanese thinkers into English (Azuma, 2009).

The enthusiasm over the availability of Japanese popular culture calls also for alternative, critical approaches that see Japan as part of circulating transnational trends (Valaskivi, 2013). These approaches would analyse the 'millennial capitalism' (Allison, 2006) of (Japanese) popular culture, opening eyes to inequalities (Iwabuchi, 2005), as well as analysing the political attempts to use popular culture to raise national pride (Iwabuchi, 2007, 2010) and the politics of representation in media. These approaches are already under consideration in many studies, but there is room for more.

NOTES

1 The discussion on Japanese media and communication research is based on the research project 'Mapping media and communication research', which was conducted at the University of Helsinki's Communication Research Center in 2007 and funded by the Helsingin Sanomat Foundation. The project outlined the media landscape and media and communication research in six countries: Japan, the USA, France, Germany, Estonia and Finland. The writer was in charge of the study in relation to Japan (Valaskivi, 2007).

2 Currently available in English at www.nhk.or.jp/bunken/english/reports/ and in Japanese at www.nhk.or.jp/bunken/research/index.html (Accessed 29 April, 2013).

3 The Jesuits of Sophia University aspired to convert the Japanese into Christianity, at least in the 1960s. Interesting traces of this aspiration can be seen in research. Sophia University library contains *Jesuit sociological surveys*, including *A socio-politico-economic survey of broadcasting media in Japan* by Chugo Koito with an appendix by de Vera: *UHF: A change and a challenge for the Church in Japan* (Koito, 1968). Although currently openly available, at the time of their completion they were considered delicate, and marked 'for private circulation only'.

REFERENCES

Allison, A. (2000a). A challenge to Hollywood? Japanese character goods hit the US. *Japanese Studies* 20(1), 67–88.

Allison, A. (2000b). *Permitted and prohibited Desires. Mothers, comics, and censorship in Japan.* Berkeley: University of California Press.

Allison, A. (2006). *Millennial monsters. Japanese toys and the global imagination.* Berkeley: University of California Press.

Anderson, J. L. and Richie, D. (1982[1959]). *The Japanese film: Art and industry.* Expanded edition, Princeton: Princeton University Press.

Ang, I. (1985). *Watching Dallas. Soap opera and the melodramatic imagination.* London: Methuen.

Azuma, H. (2001). Superflat Japanese postmodernity. Lecture at the MOCA gallery, The Pacific Design Center, West Hollywood, April 5, 2001. Retrieved on 4 February 2008 from www.hirokiazuma.com/en/texts/superflat_en2.html.

Azuma, H. (2007). The Animalization of Otaku Culture. In F. Lunning (Ed.) *Mechademia* 2, 177–89. Minneapolis: University of Minnesota Press.

Azuma, H. (2009). *Otaku. Japan's database animals.* Minneapolis: University of Minnesota Press.

Barrett, G. (1989). *Archetypes in Japanese film. The sociopolitical and religious significance of the principal heroes and heroines.* London: Associated University Presses Inc.

Bolton C., Cscsery-Ronay, I. Jr. and Tatsumi, T. (Eds.) (2007). *Robot ghosts and wired dreams. Japanese science fiction and the origins of anime.* Minneapolis: University of Minnesota press.

Brown, S. T. (2006). *Cinema anime.* New York: Palgrave Macmillan.

Brunsdon, C. (1981) Crossroads. Notes on soap opera. Screen 22(4).

Brehm, M. (2002) Takashi Murakami. A lesson in strategy (morphed double loop). In Brehm (Ed.) *The Japanese experience – inevitable.* Ostfildern-Ruit: Hatje Cantz Verlag.

Buruma, I. (1985). *Behind the mask. On sexual demons, sacred mothers, transvestites, gangsters, and other Japanese cultural heroes.* New York: Meridian, Penguin books.

Clammer, J. (1995). Consuming bodies: Constructing and representing the female body in contemporary Japanese print media. In L. Skov and B. Moeran (Eds.) *Women, media and consumption in Japan.* ConsumAsiaN series. Richmond: Curzon Press.

Coates, K. and Holroyd, C. (2003). *Japan and the Internet revolution.* New York: Palgrave Macmillan.

Cooper-Chen, A. and Kodama, M. (1997). *Mass communication in Japan.* Ames: Iowa State University Press.

Darling-Wolf, F. (2004). Women and new men: negotiating masculinity in the Japanese media. *The Communication Review* 7, 285–303.

Ewen, S. (1976). *Captains of consciousness: Advertising and the social roots of the consumer culture.* New York: McGraw-Hill.

Feldman, O. (1993). *Politics and news media in Japan.* Ann Arbor: The University of Michigan Press.

Freeman, L. A. (2000). *Closing the shop: Information cartels and Japan's mass media.* New Jersey: Princeton University Press.

Freeman, L. A. (2003). Mobilizing and demobilizing the Japanese public sphere: Mass media and the internet in Japan. In F. J. Schwartz and S. J. Pharr (Eds.) *The state of civil society in Japan.* Cambridge: Cambridge University Press.

Fujitake, A. (2005). *Nihon no masumedia: The second edition.* Tokyo: Nihon housou shuppan kyoukai.

Fukunaga, H. (2013) Expected Tsunami Heights and Emergency Communication: What Changes will the revised tsunami warnings/advisories bring? NHK Broadcasting Culture Research Centre Reports 3/2013. Full version in Japanese at www.nhk.or.jp/bunken/summary/research/report/2013_03/20130301.pdf Retrieved on 30 April 2013.

Furu, T. (1971). The function of television for children and adolescents. *Monumenta Nipponica Monographs.* Tokyo: Sophia University.

Gatzen, B. (2001). Media and communication in Japan. Current issues and future research. *Electronic Journal of Contemporary Japanese Studies.* Retrieved July 4, 2014 from www.japanesestudies.org.uk/discussionpapers/Gatzen.html

Geraghty, C. (1991). *Women and soap opera: a study of prime time soaps.* Cambridge: Polity Press.

Gotou, K., Hirahara, H., Ouyama, K. and Sata, M. (1990). *A history of Japanese television drama. Modern Japan and the Japanese.* Tokyo: The Japan Association of Broadcasting Art. Sophia University.

Gössmann, H. (Ed.) (1993). *Das Bild der Familie in den japanischen Medien.* München: Deutschen Institut fur Japanstudien, 20.

Gössmann, H. (2001). Introduction to the panel 'Images of Asia in Japanese mass media, popular culture and literature'. *Electronic Journal of Japanese Studies.* Retrieved July 4, 2014 from www.japanesestudies.org.uk/ICAS2/contents.pdf

Gössmann, H. and Waldenberger, F. (Eds.) (2003). *Medien in Japan. Gesellschafts- und kulturwissenschaftliche Perspektiven.* Mitteilungen des Instituts für Asienkunde Hamburg 372. Hamburg: Verbund Stiftung Deutsches Übersee-Institut.

Gunaratne, S. A. (2000). *Handbook of the media in Asia.* London: Sage.

Hanada, T. (1997). Can there be a public sphere in Japan? *Review of Media, Information and Society* 2, 1–23.

Harvey, P. A. S. (1996). Interpreting Oshin – war, history and women in Japan. In L. Skov and B. Moeran (Eds.) *Women, media and consumption in Japan.* ConsumAsiaN series. Richmond: Curzon Press.

Hayashi, K. (1998). The home and family section in Japanese newspapers. *The Public* 5(3), 51–63.

Hayashi, K. (2002). *Masumedia no shuuen, jaanarisumu no kakushin.* Tokyo: Shinyo-sha.

Hu, K. (2005). The power of circulation: digital technologies and the online Chinese fans of Japanese TV drama. *Inter-Asia Cultural Studies* 6(2), 171–186.

Huffman, J. L. (1997). *Creating a public: People and press in Meiji Japan.* Honolulu: University of Hawaii Press.

Ishii, K. and Jarkey, N. (2002). The housewife is born: The establishment of the notion and identity of the shufu in modern Japan. *Japanese Studies* 22(1), 35–47.

Ishikawa, S. (1990). Mass-generated minorities: The role of Japan's mass media in pollution disasters. *Studies of Broadcasting* 26, 105–120.

Ishikawa, S. (1998). Mass communication research in Japan. *The Public* 5 (1), 59–69.

Ishita, S. (2002). Media and cultural studies in Japanese sociology: An introduction. *International journal of Japanese sociology* 11, 2–4.

Ito, M., Okabe, D. and Matsuda, M. (2005) (Eds.) *Personal, portable, pedestrian. Mobile phones in Japanese life.* Cambridge: MIT Press.

Ito, T. (2005). Public journalism and journalism in Japan. *Keio Communication Review* 27, 43–63.

Iwabuchi, K. (2001). Uses of Japanese popular culture: Trans/nationalism and postcolonial desire for 'Asia'. *Emergences* 11, 199–222.

Iwabuchi, K. (2002a). Nostalgia for a (different) Asian modernity: media consumption of 'Asia' in Japan. *Positions* 10(3), 547–573.

Iwabuchi, K. (2002b). *Recentering globalization. Popular culture and Japanese transnationalism.* Durham NC: Duke University Press.

Iwabuchi, K. (2005). Multinationalizing the multicultural: The commodification of 'ordinary foreign residents' in a Japanese TV talk show. *Japanese Studies* 25(2), 103–18.

Iwabuchi, K. (2007). *Bunka no taiwaryoku. Softo pawaa to brando nachionalisumu.* Tokyo: Nihon Keizai Shimbun Shuppansha.

Iwabuchi, K. (2010). Undoing Inter-national Fandom in the Age of Brand Nationalism. In F. Lunning (Ed.) *Mechademia* 5, 87–95. Minneapolis: University of Minnesota Press.

Kangasvuo, J. (2007). Halun leikkiä ja pervoja fantasioita japanilaisessa naisten pornosarjakuvassa. In H. Kalha (Ed.) *Pornoakatemia!* Eetos-julkaisuja (Ethos-publications) Tampere: Juvenes Print.

Kato, H. (1973 [1953]). *Japanese popular culture. Studies in mass communication and cultural change.* Westport: Greenwood Press, Publishers.

Kato, H. (1989). Some thoughts on Japanese popular culture. In R. G. Powers, H. Kato and B. Stronach (Eds.) *Handbook of Japanese Popular Culture.* London: Greenwood Press.

Katz, E., Blumler, J. G. and Gurevitch, M. (1973). Uses and gratifications research. *Public opinion quarterly,* 37(4), 509–523.

Katz, E., Liebes, T. and Iwao, S. (1991). Neither here nor there: Why 'Dallas' failed in Japan. *Communication* 12, 99–110.

Kawabe, K. (1921) *The press and politics in Japan. A study of the relation between the newspaper and the political development of modern Japan.* Chicago: University of Chicago Press.

Kawato, Y., Pekkanen, R. and Yamamoto, H. (2011). State and Civil Society in Japan. In A. Gaunder (Ed.) *The Routledge handbook of Japanese politics* (pp. 117–129). London: Routledge.

Kinsella, S. (1996). Cuties in Japan. In Lise Skov and Brian Moeran (Eds.) *Women, media and consumption in Japan.* ConsumAsiaN series. Richmond: Curzon Press.

Kinsella, S. (1997) *Adult manga. Culture and power in contemporary Japanese Society.* ConsumAsiaN Series. Richmond: Curzon Press.

Kogawa, T. (1988). New trends in Japanese popular culture. In G. McCormack and Y. Sugimoto (Eds.)

The Japanese trajectory: modernization and beyond. Cambridge: Cambridge University Press.

Koito, C. (1968) A socio-politico-economic survey of broadcasting media in Japan with an appendix by J. M. de Vera, UHF: A change and a challenge for the Church in Japan in the field of TV. *Jesuit sociological survey: Japan* 11. The Socio-Economic Institute of Sophia University. Unpublished copy.

Kondo, M. (1993). The impersonalization of the self in an image society. *Iris* 16, 37–48.

Krauss, E. S. (1996). Portraying the state: NHK television news and politics. In S. J. Pharr, E. S. Krauss. *Media and politics in Japan.* Honolulu: University of Hawaii Press.

Krauss, E. S. (2000). *Broadcasting politics in Japan. NHK and television news.* New York: Cornell University Press.

Kuwahara, Y. (1997). Japanese culture and popular consciousness: Disney's Lion King vs. Tezuka's Jungle Emperor. *Journal of Popular Culture* 31(1), 37–48.

de Lange, W. (1998). *A history of Japanese journalism. Japan's press club as the last obstacle to mature press.* Surrey: Japan Library.

LaMarre, T. (2006). The otaku movement. In T. Yoda and H. Harootunian (Eds.) *Japan after Japan. Social and cultural life from the recessionary 1990s to the present.* Durham: Duke University Press.

LaMarre, T. (2007). Introduction to the Azuma Hiroyuki article The Animalization of Otaku Culture. In F. Lunning (Ed.) *Mechademia* 2, 175–177. Minneapolis: University of Minnesota Press.

Leavitt, Alex (2013) Tsubuyaite kudasai: Twitter's Networks in Japan. *Social Flow* 25 April 2013. Retrieved on 30 April 2013 from www.blog.socialflow.com/.

Löhr, M. (2003). Zeitung machen in Japan – Historische Entwicklung und gegenwärtige Tendenzen. In H. Gössmann and F. Waldenberger (Eds.) *Medien in Japan. Gesellschafts- und kulturwissenschafliche Perspektiven.* Mitteilungen des Instituts für Asienkunde Hamburg 372. Hamburg: Verbund Stiftung Deutsches Übersee-Institut.

Lukacs, G. (2010) *Scripted Affects, Branded Selves: Television, Subjectivity, and Capitalism in 1990s Japan.* Duke University Press.

Lunning, F. (2006). *Mechademia 1. Emerging worlds of manga and anime.* Mechademia Series. Minneapolis: University of Minnesota Press.

Lunning, F. (2007). *Mechademia 2: Networks of desire.* Minneapolis: University of Minnesota Press.

Lunning, F. (2008). *Mechademia 3: Limits of the human.* Minneapolis: University of Minnesota Press.

Lunning, F. (2009). *Mechademia 4: War / Time.* Minneapolis: University of Minnesota Press.

Lunning, F. (2010). *Mechademia 5: Fanthropologies.* Minneapolis: University of Minnesota Press.

Lunning, F. (2011). *Mechademia 6: User Enhanced.* Minneapolis: University of Minnesota Press.

Luther, C. A. and Boyd, D. A. (1997). American occupation control over broadcasting in Japan, 1945–1952. *Journal of communication* 47(2), 39–59.

MacLachlan, E. (2001). Turning seeing into believing: Producing credibility in the television news coverage of the Kobe earthquake. In B. Moeran (Ed.) *Asian Media Productions.* Surrey: Curzon.

Martinez, D. (1998). *The worlds of Japanese popular culture. Gender, shifting boundaries and global cultures.* Cambridge: Cambridge University Press.

Matsuda, M. (2005). Discourses of *keitai* in Japan. In M. Ito, D. Okabe and M Matsuda (Eds.) *Personal, portable, pedestrian: Mobile phones in Japanese life.* Cambridge MA: MIT Press.

McLelland, M. (1999). How to be a nice gay: The stereotyping of gay men in Japanese media. *New Zealand Journal of Asian Studies.* 1(1), 42–59.

MEXT 2011. Retrieved on 12 April, 2013 from www.enecho.meti.go.jp/info/tender/tenddata/1106/110624b/110624b.htm (in Japanese).

Mikhailova, J. (2006). *In Godzilla's footsteps: Japanese pop culture icons on the global stage.* New York: Palgrave Macmillan.

Miller, L. (1995). Crossing ethnolinguistic boundaries: A preliminary look at the gaijin tarento in Japan. In J. A. Lent (Ed.) *Asian popular culture.* Boulder: Westview Press.

Miller, S. D. (1997). The Reunion of history and popular culture: Japan 'comes out' on TV. *Journal of Popular Culture* 31(2), 161–176.

Minami, K. and Nakata, K. (2007). Overview of the media content market in Japan. *Keio Communication Review* 29, 25–59.

Moeran, B. (1996). *A Japanese advertising agency. An anthropology of media and markets.* Surrey: Curzon Press.

Moeran, B. (Ed.) (2001). *Asian media productions.* ConsumAsiaN series. Honolulu: University of Hawaii Press.

Mowlana, H. and Rad, M. M. (1992). International flow of Japanese television programs: The 'Oshin' phenomenon. *Keio Communication Review* 14, 51–68.

Muramatsu Y. (1982). Images of man and woman in Japanese TV and sex-role attitude of people. Based on a comparative study on five countries on TV and sex-role socialization. *Housou Bunka Foundation Newsletter* 14: 14–26. Tokyo: Housou Bunka Foundation.

Muramatsu, Y. (1986). For wives on Friday: Women's roles in TV dramas. In *Japan Quarterly* 33(2), 158–63.

Muramatsu, Y. (1991). Of women by women for women? Japanese media today. *NHK Studies of Broadcasting* 27, 83–104.

Muramatsu, Y. (2002). Gender construction through interactions between the media and audience in Japan. *International Journal of Japanese Sociology* (11), 72–87.

Muramatsu, Y. and Gössmann, H. (Eds.) (1998). *Media ga tsukuru jendaa.* Tokyo: Shinyousha.

Nakamura, Y. and Yonekura, R. (2008). Public broadcasting and changing audiences in the digital era: services and social mission. *NHK Broadcasting Studies* 6, 103–50.

Napier, S. J. (1998). Vampires, psychic girls, flying women and sailor scouts. Four faces of the young female in Japanese popular culture. In D. P. Martinez (Ed.) *The worlds of Japanese popular culture. Gender, shifting boundaries and global cultures.* Cambridge: Cambridge University Press.

Napier, S. J. (2001). *Anime. From Akira to Howl's moving castle. Experiencing contemporary Japanese animation.* New York: Palgrave Macmillan.

Napier, S. J. (2006). The world of anime fandom in America. In F. Lunning (Ed.) *Mechademia 1,* 47–65.

Napier, S. J. (2007). *From impressionism to anime. Japan as fantasy and fan cult in the mind of the West.* New York: Palgrave Macmillan.

Narita, R., Morris-Suzuki, T. and Yao, S. (1998). Zadankai: On cultural studies, Japanese studies, area studies. *Japanese Studies* 18(1), 73–87.

NHK International (Eds.) (1991). *The world's view of Japan through 'Oshin'. Japanese TV programs in the world media market. An international symposium.* Tokyo: NHK International Inc.

Neuss, M. (1971). Die *Seitousha. Oriens Extemus* 18, 1–66 and 137–201.

Nikunen, K. (2006). Animellista faniutta. Internet ja japanilaisen piirroskulttuurin fanit. In Katja Valaskivi (Ed.) *Vauriauden lapset. Näkökulmia suomalaiseen ja japanilaiseen nykykulttuuriin.* Tampere: Vastapaino.

Niyekawa, A. (1984). Analysis of conflict in a television home drama. In Ellis S. Krauss, T. P. Rohlen and P. G. Steinhoff (Eds.) *Conflict in Japan.* Honolulu: University of Hawaii Press.

Nygren, S. (2007). *Time frames: Japanese cinema and the unfolding of history.* Minneapolis MN: University of Minnesota Press.

Okada, T. (1995). Anime bunka wa chou kakkouii. *Aera* 2 October: 43–44.

Painter, A. A. (1991). The creation of Japanese television and culture. Doctoral dissertation, University of Michigan.

Painter, A. A. (1994). On the anthropology of television: A perspective from Japan. *Visual Anthropology Review* 10(1), 70–84.

Pellitteri, M. (2010). *The dragon and the dazzle. Models, strategies, and identities of Japanese imagination. A European perspective.* Latina: Tunué International.

Pharr, S. J. and Krauss, E. S. (1996). *Media and politics in Japan.* Honolulu: University of Hawaii Press.

Powers, R. G., Kato, H. and Stronach, B. (Eds.) (1989). *Handbook of Japanese popular culture*. New York: Greenwood Press.

Rabinow, P. (1986). Representations are social facts: Modernity and post-modernity in anthropology. In James Clifford and George E. Marcus (eds.) *The poetics and politics of ethnography*. Berkeley: University of California Press.

Rosenberger, N. (1996). Antiphonal performances? Japanese women's magazines and women's voices. In L. Skov and B. Moeran (Eds.) *Women, media and consumption in Japan*. ConsumAsiaN series. Richmond: Curzon Press.

Saito, Tamaki (2008). Otaku sexuality. In C. Bolton, I. Csicsery-Ronay Jr. and T. Tatsumi (Eds.) *Robot ghosts and wired dreams. Japanese science fiction from origins to anime*. Minneapolis: University of Minnesota Press.

Sakamoto, K. (1999). Reading Japanese women's magazines: The construction of new identities in the 1970s and 1980s. *Media, culture & society* 21(2): 173–193.

Sato, B. H. (2003). *The new Japanese woman: modernity, media, and women in interwar Japan*. Durham NC: Duke Unversity Press.

Schäfer, F. (2009). The re-articulation of cultural studies in Japan and its consequences for Japanese studies. *International Journal of Cultural Studies* 12(1): 23–41.

Schodt, F. L. (1996). *Dreamland Japan. Writings of modern manga. Japanese Comics for Otaku*. Berkeley: Stone Bridge Press.

Shibata, K. (2002). Analysis of 'critical' approach in media literacy. Comparative studies between Japan and Canada. *Keio Communication Review* 24, 93–110.

Skov, L. and Moeran, B. (1995). *Women, media and consumption in Japan*. Richmond: Curzon Press.

Slater, D. (Ed.) (2011). 3.11 Politics in disaster Japan: Fear and anger, possibility and hope. Cultural anthropology hot spots. Retrieved on 4 July 2014 from www.culanth.org/? q=node/409

Sugaya, M. (2005). From earth to sky: Open doors, hurdles for Japan's broadcasters. *Japan Media Review*. Retrieved on May 20, 2005 from www.japanmediareview.com/japan/stories/050505Sugaya

Suzuki, M. (1985). Portrayal of families and gender roles in Japan's TV advertising. *The Japan Christian Quarterly*, Winter, 19–23.

Suzuki, M. (1997). (Ed.) *Media literashii wo manabu hito no tame ni*. Tokyo: Sekai shiso sha.

Suzuki, Y., Yonekura R., Nakano S and Nishimura, N. (2008) Mobile phones as multiple information terminals: from the research project 'People and media usage in Japan'. *NHK Broadcasting Studies* 6, 151–74.

Takahashi, T. (2010). *Audience studies. A Japanese perspective*. London: Routledge.

Takeshita, T. (1981). Mass media no gidaisettei kasetsu kento. *The Bulletin of the Institute of Journalism and Communication Studies* 31, 101–143.

Takeshita, T. (1990). *Mass communication no shakai katei*. Tokyo: University of Tokyo Press.

Tamura, N. (Ed.) (2004). *Gendai jaanarisumu wo manabu hito no tame ni*. Kyoto: Sekaishisousha.

Tanaka, M. (2012) Japan: Journo-based and journo-oriented. In Sirkkunen, E. and Cook, C. (Eds.) *Chasing Sustainability on the Net*. Tampere: Tampere University Research Centre for Journalism, Media and Communication.

Treat, J. W. (1996). *Contemporary Japan and popular culture*. ConsumAsiaN. Richmond: Curzon Press.

Valaskivi, K. (1995). *Wataru seken wa oni bakari. Mothers-in-law and daughters-in-law in a Japanese television drama*. Research unit for contemporary culture, 46. Jyväskylä: Jyväskylä University Print.

Valaskivi, K. (1999). Relations of television. Genre and gender in the production, reception and text of a Japanese family drama. *Acta Universitatis Tamperensis* 689. Tampere: University of Tampere. *Acta Electronica Universitatis Tamperensis*, 1. Retrieved on Jan 22, 2014 from www.acta.uta.fi/pdf/951-44-4674-7.pdf

Valaskivi, K. (2000). Being a/part of the family? Genre, gender and production in a Japanese TV drama. *Media, culture and society*, May.

Valaskivi, K. (2004). Onnellinen perhe mahdottoman tehtävän edessä. Japanilainen ja suomalainen tapa esittää isän ja äidin rooli television viihdeohjelmassa. In Annamari Konttinen and Seija Jalagin (Eds.) *Japanilainen nainen. Kuvissa ja kuvien takana*. Tampere: Vastapaino.

Valaskivi, K. (2007). *Mapping media and communication research in Japan*. Communication research center, Department of communication, University of Helsinki. Retrieved on 4 July 2014 from www.valt.helsinki.fi/blogs/crc/ReportJapan.pdf

Valaskivi, K. (2009). *Pokemonin perilliset. Japanilainen populaarikulttuuri Suomessa*. Department of Journalism and Mass Communication Series A 110. Tampere: Unversity of Tampere. Retrieved on 4, July 2014 from www.ncom.nordicom.gu.se/ncom/ research/pokemonin_perilliset(128927)/

Valaskivi, K. (2011) 'Everything is there' – Internet in the lives of Japanese popular culture fans in Finland. In Sonja Kangas (Ed.) Digital Pioneers. Tracing the cultural drivers of future media culture. *Publications in the Net by the Youth Research Association* 49, 2011. Retrieved on 30 April 2013 from www.nuorisotutkimusseura.fi/julkaisuja/ digitalpioneers.pdf.

Valaskivi, K. (2013) A brand new future? Cool Japan and the social imaginary of the branded nation. *Japan Forum*. Retrieved on 30 April 2013 from DOI: 10.1080/09555803. 2012.756538.

Valaskivi, K. and Ruoho, I. (2006). Television murros: Yhteinäiskulttuurista tilattaviin palveluihin. In Katja Valaskivi (Ed.) *Vaurauden lapset. Näkökulmia suomalaiseen ja japanilaiseen nykykulttuuriin.* Tampere: Vastapaino.

de Vera, J. M. (undated). *Television viewing in Japan. Its pattern and its effectiveness.* Tokyo: Sophia University Socio-Economic Institute.

de Vera, J. M. (1967). Educational television in Japan. *Monumenta Nipponica Monographs.* Tokyo: Sophia University.

de Vera, J. M. (1968). Serious television drama: The Japanese audience, its composition and characteristics. *Monumenta Nipponica* 23, 90–101.

Westney, E. D. (1987). *Imitation and innovation: The transfer of Western organizational patterns to Meiji Japan.* Cambridge: Harvard University Press.

Westney, E. D. (1996). Mass media as business organizations: A US–Japanese comparison. In S. J. Pharr, and E. S. Krauss, *Media and politics in Japan.* Honolulu: University of Hawaii Press.

Wöhr, U. (1997). *Frauen zwischen Rollenerwartung und Selbsdeutung. Ehe, Mutterschaft und Liebe im Spiegel der japanischen Zeitschrift Shin shin fujin von 1913 bis 1916.* Wiesbaden: Harrassowitz.

Wöhr, U., Sato Hamill, B. and Suzuki, S. (Eds.) (1998). *Gender and modernity. Rereading Japanese women's magazines.* International symposium in Europe. International Research Center for Japanese Studies.

Yada, Y. (2007). Journalism in Japan. In P. J. Anderson and G. Ward (Eds.) *The future of journalism in the advanced democracies.* Surrey: Ashgate.

Yoshimi, S. (1998). *The condition of cultural studies in Japan. Japanese Studies* 18(1), 65–72.

Yoshimoto, M. (1993a). Melodrama, postmodernism, and Japanese cinema. In W. Dissanayake (Ed.) *Melodrama and Asian Cinema.* Cambridge: Cambridge University Press.

Yoshimoto, M. (1993b). Le postmoderne at les images de masse au Japon. *Iris* 16, 145–164.

Yoshimoto, M. (2000). *Kurosawa. Film studies and Japanese cinema.* Durham: Duke University Press.

5

Heritage Management in Present-day Japan

Noriaki Nishiyama

INTRODUCTION

In order to understand current research trends in heritage management one must first understand how heritage, the target of this management, is regarded in present-day Japan. In Japan the concept of cultural-properties protection emerged in modern times; however, the background to the birth of the idea is unique and different from that of the West. This warrants a separate review, which is given below. I then describe the current status of heritage management, including a discussion of the providers of the management, the recent depletion of heritage and its causes, and efforts toward World Heritage protection. Finally, I examine research trends in heritage management in two parts: research into existing preservation methods, valuation and protection systems; and research into new trends in heritage management.

HISTORY OF HERITAGE MANAGEMENT

Protection of Cultural Heritage

Fostering Heritage during the Feudal Era and Meiji Restoration

In pre-modern Japan the idea of management or protection of cultural heritage by the state (by today's definition) did not exist. Cultural heritage was the private property of court nobles, including the Emperor's family, and feudal lords, including the Tokugawa Shogunate, which managed to control Japan peacefully for 260 years without any drastic changes of the boundaries between over 300 domains. Similarly, the Meiji Restoration, a revolution that opened the door of Japan's modernisation, did not entail widespread destruction of cities or most regions, as symbolised in the bloodless takeover of Edo Castle. Therefore, samurai, merchants, farmers and artisans were also able to accumulate a considerable amount of tangible/intangible or movable/immovable cultural assets.

However, since the Restoration in 1868, in part due to the efforts of the Meiji administration to modernise the nation by adopting aspects of Western culture, there has been a tendency to make light of old things, which has led to the destruction of specific types of cultural heritage across Japan. Representative of this is the *haibutsu–kishaku* movement: when Shintoism was, essentially, made the state religion Buddhist buildings and objects in Shinto-shrine precincts were destroyed where previously they had coexisted with their Shinto surroundings. The movement spread nationwide and numerous Buddhist temples, statues and fixtures were destroyed. Many castles where feudal lords and retainers resided were destroyed or fell into ruin too, as they were considered to symbolise the old feudal system. In addition, the 1867 Paris Expo and 1873 Vienna Expo gave rise to 'Japonism' among European art and craft collectors, which suited the Meiji administration's intent to advertise Japanese culture and expand foreign trade (art for the national interest's sake). As a result, aggressive purchasing by foreign collectors and Japanese art dealers triggered a drain of cultural assets overseas (Nishiyama, 2004b).

Emergence of the Idea of Protection

Intellectuals at universities decried the destruction and sale of cultural assets which should have been cherished as national treasures. This, they argued, was equal to abandoning the nation's claim to traditional Japanese culture. They insisted it harmed the national interest and that Japan should be embarrassed as a modern nation state to ignore its cultural assets. In response the Japanese government enacted a law directed at the protection of cultural assets (*koki-kyūbutsu-hozon-kata*) in 1871. This law identified 31 types of tangible properties that are thought to be important for studying changes in Japanese history, institutions and popular culture (such as ritual utensils, precious stones, paintings and calligraphic works, antiques, folk crafts, ceramics and tea sets, Buddhist statues and fittings) and requested local governments to submit lists of holdings. This was the first law in modern Japan related to cultural property protection. In addition, as measures to provide protection, expo venues were turned into more permanent facilities to serve as museums to pursue the collection and protection of cultural properties. In 1872 Japan's first museum (Nishiyama, 2004b) was born.

Protection of Property Heritage

In contrast to movable heritage protection, buildings and places of scenic and historical interest were made the first target for national preservation. The Ministry of Home Affairs' law of 1874 stipulated protection of places of scenic and historical interest as one of its duties. Based on this policy, gardens, renowned mythical mountains, historical ruins and graves of historically important figures were made public properties in order to preserve them – and places of scenic beauty and castle ruins were preserved as parks. One outstanding feature of Japan's heritage are *kofun*, or ancient burial mounds. The 1874 law, which restricted *kofun* excavations and made it obligatory to report to the authority any discovery of a *kofun*, was the first of its kind to promote protection of ancient sites. However, it should be noted that the law's true intent was to preserve information to identify emperors' graves as the basis for

bolstering the national unifying power of the Emperor rather than to protect cultural heritage per se. Nonetheless, other laws and regulations, including the concept of the 'beauty of the scenery', was introduced in 1882 in an attempt to prohibit reckless cutting down of renowned, beautiful trees on the grounds of temples and shrines.

Preservation of Old Buildings

Old buildings were also recognized as important heritage properties, though it took several more years before attention was paid to their protection. There were several causes for the delay. In addition to the destruction of Buddhist temples by the above-mentioned *haibutsu kishaku* movement, in 1871 the government attempted to nationalise territories owned by temples and shrines outside of their immediate grounds as part of *hanseki hokan* (policy of returning the land and people to the emperor), an initiative undertaken to repair high-ranking Shinto shrines using tax money, which had an impact on shrine grounds and building alterations. In this context the Ministry of Home Affairs issued (1878) a definition of 'old shrines and temples' in an attempt to first identify shrines and temples which should be preserved, and this triggered a string of moves to protect them. Shrines and temples established before 1486 (year 18 of the Bunmei reign) in the late Muromachi period were classified as being ancient. A notable point here was the specification that shrines and temples had to be 'established' 400 years ago or earlier, focusing primarily on historical background. However, the age of the buildings was not the only standard for judgment. The first of the actual protection measures was provided by the Shrines and Temples Preservation Rules (Ministry of Home Affairs, 1880), which indicated the requirements for the old shrines and temples to be protected, and established a preservation fund allocated to 539 of them, including Horyu-ji Temple, the oldest wooden structure built in the seventh century, for their maintenance and repair regardless of age.

Old Temples and Shrines Preservation Act and National Treasure Preservation Act

The enactment of the Old Temples and Shrines Preservation Act of 1897 provided a legal foundation for the protection policies for historical buildings. Although the scope of the act was limited only to old shrines and temples, it covered not only real properties (buildings) but also movable properties owned by the shrines and temples. Naming movable properties 'national treasures' and real properties 'buildings under special protection', the act was noteworthy as it unified protection policies for both, and established the basis for protection of 'places of scenic and historical interest'. The Act put 1,081 buildings under special protection in 845 locations and named 3,705 objects as national treasures. However, the method of protection remained the same and money for preservation was granted only to shrines and temples that met the Act's criteria.

Later, the National Treasure Preservation Act, established in 1929, unified and absorbed the 'buildings under special protection' into 'national treasures'. The National Treasure Preservation Act served as a prototype for the Cultural Properties Protection Act that is currently in force because it introduced a 'designation system', which formed the core of today's cultural properties-protection system in Japan. The designation system expanded the range of subjects to be protected from properties owned by shrines and temples to those owned by the nation, public organisations and individuals, including castles, mausoleums, *shoin* (residential architecture), tea rooms and stone pagodas, etc., and, in principle, banned export or transfer of items designated as national treasures. The act designated 6,933 items (including 1,109 buildings) as national treasures to be protected.

Aiming to provide protection to a wider range of buildings, the act targeted cultural assets up to the Meiji Restoration. The age-prorated valuation standard established the principle that the older the building the more worthless it was. However, buildings older than approximately 50 years, that is prior to the Meiji Restroration, were considered as potential targets for preservation. This established the basis for the following 50 years of Japanese thinking and practices that 'cultural assets are items from the period prior to Meiji Restoration'.

Historic Sites, Places of Scenic Beauty, or Natural Monument Preservation Act

Places of scenic and historical interest, which are heritage properties, enjoyed the nation's protection from early days after the Meiji Restoration as described above, but no particular progress in protection measures was seen until 1919. During the interim period, it should be noted, the preservation activities for historic sites emerged spontaneously across Japan as part of patriotic or love- your-hometown movements to foster nationalism. The love-your-hometown movements tried to protect plants, such as renowned trees, to preserve local characteristics, and these movements merged with the historical-site-protection movements. Furthermore, the idea of 'place of scenic beauty', which is the precursor of the current idea of 'cultural landscape', emerged, and together with moves to protect national monuments, led to the promotion of a legal system to protect each of these three targets. The result was the Historic Sites, Places of Scenic Beauty, or Natural Monument Preservation Act of 1919.

Cultural properties associated with the emperor's family and with imperial history, such as citadel or castle ruins and palaces, attained positive valuation as historic sites that were classed as 'artificial national treasures'. Natural monuments that were classed as 'natural national treasures' included animals, plants and geology/minerals, and, in order to provide protection for these, natural protection areas were introduced and established. Places of Scenic Beauty encompassed a variety of categories such as artificially created gardens, bridges and natural objects, including uniquely shaped rocks and various combinations of these. This was a precursor for today's Cultural Landscape by the UNESCO World Heritage Convention, and Japan was the first nation in the world to designate this category as a target for protection.

Heritage Protection during World War II

During the war (1941–1945) resource-poor Japan had no choice but to mobilise everything it had to produce weapons. As a result, the policy measures for cultural-heritage protection that had been gradually developing up until the beginning of the war began to be suspended. By around 1943, when the war was at its peak, all cultural-heritage-protection measures had to be abandoned, apart from 'holy sites' or historic sites related to the Emperor or 'sacred grounds', such as Ise Shrine or Kashiwara Shrine. In addition, the Metal Recovery Act of 1941 mandated that all metallic items, regardless of whether they were privately or publicly owned, had to be submitted for weapon production, which resulted in a great loss of cultural properties. Many trees in the protected forests were also cut down. Two hundred and fifteen cities were subjected to air raids towards the end of the war and a total of 64,500 hectares of land was burnt down. Only a handful of cities, such as Kyoto, Nara and Kanazawa, were spared the damage. The majority of the stock of heritage properties from the modern period was lost during the raids. It was recorded that the war damaged 292 national treasures and 44 historic sites, places of scenic beauty and natural monuments. The most noteworthy protective action carried out during the war was the compilation of the 'Warner List', a list of Japanese art and cultural items that warranted protection from war damage, by intellectuals such as Langdon Warner and Edwin Reischauer of the USA, the enemy country. Most of the listed items, such as shrines, temples and castles of Kyoto and Nara, or university libraries, were spared damage during the war.

Enactment of the Cultural Properties Protection Act

The framework for the current Japanese heritage-protection system was forged in 1950 by the establishment of the Cultural Properties Protection Act. The development was directly triggered by the loss of wall paintings from the Golden Pavilion in Horyu-ji Temple in 1949. The destruction of the crown jewel of Japanese culture by a fire, under the dire social conditions wrought by the war when Japan was filled with victims of the war and those repatriated from overseas, highlighted the urgent need for a renewed heritage protection system.

The Act was significant in that it established the definition of the concept of 'cultural asset'. The existing categories of national treasure, historic sites, places of scenic beauty and natural monuments were unified under the concept of cultural assets. Further, the idea of 'intangible cultural assets' was added. Specifically, Article 2 of the Act categorised properties included in existing national treasures such as 'buildings, paintings, sculptures, crafts, pieces of calligraphy, brush calligraphy, books, old documents, folklore documents and other tangible cultural properties that are highly valuable for Japan historically or artistically, and archaeological documents' as 'tangible cultural property'; it categorised 'plays, music, craftsmanship, and other intangible cultural properties that are highly valuable for Japan historically or artistically' as 'intangible cultural property'; and it reconfirmed the concept of 'historic sites, places of scenic beauty and natural monuments'. These three categories formed the notion of 'cultural properties'. It is only in recent years that the expression 'World Heritage' has become well known and the word 'heritage' widely used; but up until the 1980s the general term used to describe such heritage was 'cultural properties'. For the Japanese the term 'cultural properties' had been in general use since the Meiji era, but it had not been established as a legal term until the enactment of the Cultural Properties Protection Act.

Originally, the concept of cultural properties, according to the Act, did not include National Parks (in Japanese literally Natural Parks or *shizen kōen*) which is more narrowly focused on preservation of the natural environment, but did include 'natural' scenery that has been artificially created and had value added by humans, such as viewing platforms for scenic sites or gardens as 'place of scenic beauty'. However, the new post-war Cultural Properties Protection Act now included 'National Monuments', natural heritage sites of special scientific value, such as primeval forests, giant trees, old trees, rare plants, wildlife such as birds, beasts and insects, and uniquely shaped rocks and geological materials. This is a unique forerunner anywhere in the world for this type of heritage-protection system.

In addition, a new valuation framework was introduced so that heritage of superior quality can be selected for protection and limited funds provided for its protection from the national treasury. This included all tangible cultural properties classed as 'national treasures' and important cultural properties (designated by the national government)'; and historic sites, places of scenic beauty and natural monuments were classed as 'special historical sites, special places of scenic beauty and special natural monuments' or 'historic sites, places of scenic beauty and natural monuments (designated by the national government)'.

Another important point was the abolition of pre-war protection measures that were slanted toward 'holy sites' and 'sacred grounds' based on imperial history. Protection policies took a new course based on scientific evaluation.

As for the administrative organisation for cultural-property-protection policies, the Cultural Properties Protection Committee was established as an extra-ministerial bureau of the Ministry of Education (now the Ministry of Education, Culture, Sports, Science and Technology). Although the committee aimed to achieve independence, expertise and consistency in administration, it did not function well on a practical level so in the structural reform of 1968 the Agency for Cultural Affairs was created, which still is in service today.

Amendment of the Cultural Properties Protection Act in 1954

Since the initial establishment of the Protection Act in 1950 several amendments have been made, expanding the concept of cultural properties and enhancing protection measures. The amendment of 1954 upgraded and expanded the system for intangible cultural properties. This law introduced grant-in-aid, that is, central funding for the protection of items not owned by the state, the requirement to make the items available for public viewing, a system to designate 'intangible cultural properties' and a legal basis for the organisations possessing the properties so that they would be eligible for funding and legally responsible for the protection of the cultural properties. This essentially completed the protection system we have today.

While 'buried cultural properties', in effect archaeological sites, were stipulated as one of the important cultural assets, the Act emphasised that their significance was in the 'condition' of burial, introducing the concept of the 'land containing buried cultural properties'. A new distribution survey in 1960–62 revealed approximately

140,000 locations of buried cultural properties nationwide, which were published as the 'National Map of Historical Remains'. The map ensured the status of 'publicly known land containing buried cultural properties' and made it an obligation to report to the authorities when developing or excavating the relevant land. After 1964 it became customary for the developers to cover the cost for emergency investigative excavation for new developments, and, coupled with the fact that the period coincided with Japan's high economic growth, the number of excavations grew dramatically. As of 2006 over 450,000 (457,290) locations for buried cultural properties have been identified and approximately 9,000 investigative excavations are now being carried out annually (Agency for Cultural Affairs, 2012b). These excavations are ordinarily supervised by the municipal boards of education (and their departments for the protection of cultural properties), which means each municipality needs to have at least one person in charge of buried cultural properties. In fact, many excavation specialists are stationed at local municipalities. As a result, most of the people in charge of cultural-property protection at municipalities nationwide are specialists in buried properties, and it has become a problem that an extremely small number of them specialise in architecture, civil engineering, folk culture, history or arts and crafts considering the actual number of these properties and the need for a range of skills to evaluate them.

Another important aspect of the amendment of 1954 was that it allowed local governments to play a role in cultural-property protection, which up until that point had been a task exclusively for central government. Each prefecture as well as cities, towns and villages stipulated their own local ordinances for the protection of cultural properties, leading to a three-tier system for protection consisting of cultural properties designated at the national, prefectural and municipal levels.

In addition, the term 'historic sites, places of scenic beauty and natural monuments' was replaced by a general term, 'monuments', which contained three separate types of heritage: 'historic sites', 'place of scenic beauty' and 'natural monuments'.

The 1954 amendment of the Act was significant in that two new categories of cultural properties, 'folk-cultural properties' and 'group of historic buildings', were introduced. The original three categories – 'tangible', 'intangible' and 'monuments' – were now increased to five.

Folklore documents and related objects, which used to be considered part of tangible cultural properties, were made into a category on their own called 'folk-cultural property'. It consisted of 'tangible folk-cultural property' and 'intangible folk-cultural property', and the relevant properties were required to be designated to either of the two categories. Folk-cultural properties were defined as 'manners and customs regarding food, clothing and shelter, livelihood, faith, and annual events, etc., folk entertainment and clothes that are used for performances, instruments, houses and other objects or matters that were created by people in their daily lives and inherited by subsequent generations as tangible or intangible tradition, and that represent changes in people's lives.

Amendment of the Cultural Properties Protection Act in 1975

In 1975 the Act was amended again to create a new category of cultural property called 'group of historic buildings' defined as a 'traditional group of buildings that forms historic scenery in integration with the surrounding environment and of high value'. It targets the castle towns, post towns or temple towns that still remain nationwide, and attempts to capture the value of historic villages and towns and protect them. In order to achieve the goal each municipality establishes its own ordinance for preservation and designates 'preservation districts for groups of historic buildings' that are the 'districts designated by municipalities based on the Cultural Properties Protection Act in order to preserve groups of historic buildings and the integrated surrounding environment that forms its value'. Further, municipalities are required to create a preservation plan. The system is set up so that upon proposal of candidate districts from municipalities the state can 'select (not designate)' 'important preservation districts for groups of historic buildings' that are judged to be of high value for the nation.

The idea here is that local governments on the level of each municipality will first make a decision (based on absolute value) of their local historic communities and streets, and provide protection. Then, among them, the national government will judge (based on relative value) their merit at the national level and select the most important as cultural properties. It can be said that this system sums up the development of administration of cultural properties in Japan. Most of the communities and streets that are subject to protection are made up of buildings that are privately owned (by individual residents or private business operators). The repairs and work required to preserve them are carried out as a grant provided for extensions to alterations of new constructions in privately owned properties while the owners live in them. The system is set up so that being selected by the state as an important property will bring in half of the grant money for preservation from the state. The selection by the state is an important financial factor for local government, which is why most of the time municipalities designate preservation districts on the premise that they will be selected by the state.

As of 20 June 2011 there are 91 important preservation districts for groups of historic buildings in 77 municipalities (a total of 3,322ha) and approximately 18,000 traditional buildings have been identified to be preserved.

Amendment of the Cultural Properties Protection Act in 1996

The main purpose of a further amendment in 1996 was to introduce a cultural-property-registry system. Cultural properties designated or selected under previous cultural-property-protection systems were under tight controls so that any changes to the property had to be approved. Moving to a registry system meant a more lenient protection system based on guidance, advice and recommendations to achieve more appropriate preservation through the cooperation with the owners. Specifically, the registry system warrants that the Minister of Education can register buildings, other than those designated by the state or local government, as cultural properties that require preservation and use the cultural-property registry ledger. Once a building is registered an application must be made for any repair or alteration work. There will be no direct grant for the repair construction work but, for instance, there may be a supplementary grant for the design fee for repairs. The 2004 amendment to the Act expanded the application of the system to tangible cultural properties, intangible cultural properties and monuments.

Around the time of the amendment of the Act a survey report was made by the Survey Study Cooperative Committee regarding the preservation and use of modern cultural properties. Based on the characteristics of modern cultural properties with the prerequisite of being 50 years or older, standard criteria for valuation and repairs/ alterations were indicated separately for buildings or civil-engineering works, and other man-made structures. As a result, the range of designation was successfully widened by the review of standards for historic sites and buildings rather than by amending the law. Since the introduction of the National Treasure Preservation Act described above this has largely changed the existing philosophy of cultural-property protection, which tacitly valued individual tangible properties from the modern era or older.

Amendment of the Cultural Properties Protection Act in 2004

This amendment focuses on the addition of cultural landscape as a sixth category of cultural property. Landscape that has been developed by humans interacting with nature for a long period of time is newly defined as 'cultural landscape'. From the cultural landscapes proposed by prefectures and municipalities the state will select particularly significant locations as important cultural landscapes and provide protective measures. As described in fuller detail later, this concept is based on the new idea of 'cultural landscape' that forms a part of World Heritage, which emerged during the review of operational guidelines for the 1992 UNESCO World Heritage Convention. However, in comparison to the UNESCO case, it was very difficult to position the new idea of cultural landscape in Japan's Cultural Properties Protection Act, which already had overlapping concepts of cultural properties, such as places of scenic beauty, historic sites and groups of historic buildings (conservation districts). Even now the operation of protective measures for cultural landscape or efforts to make its value more widely known can sometimes meet with an attitude of bewilderment or perplexity.

Protection of Natural Heritage

Grasping Heritage as Natural Parks

The fact that a concept similar to 'cultural heritage' – even partially, such as national treasures, buildings under special protection and cultural properties – existed from early on throughout the development of cultural-heritage protection in modern Japan has already been explained. In comparison, when looking for the birth in modern Japanese history of the idea of 'nature as a target for protection', something similar to 'natural heritage' as defined by UNESCO, we must wait until the enactment of the National Parks Law in 1931. Based upon this law, Setonaikai National Park, Unzen National Park (currently Unzen-Amakusa National Park) and Kirishima National Park (later Kirishima-Yaku National Park) were designated the first Japanese National Parks in 1934. These were vast areas (natural heritage) which could not have been covered by the concepts of places of scenic beauty or Natural Monuments.

Up until then there had been the idea of managing (but not preserving) gardens, famous mountains, places of scenic beauty and castle ruins as artificial parks (including publicly owned parks managed as public facilities). The National Parks Law was the first vehicle to provide measures based on this management ideal. One method of protection offered by the law was to keep control by setting up special areas within the park where any change to the current status had to be approved by the relevant minister (of the Ministry of Finance or Ministry of Home Affairs). In Japan it was not possible to publicly own the entire land area within a park, therefore a 'regional zoning park' system (providing protection by designating an area regardless of it being publicly or privately owned) was the only option available for setting up protective areas. If any private owners suffered damages as a result of these protection measures then compensation was paid out from the national treasury. Incidentally, in Japan, examples of above mentioned regional zoning parks are Shinjuku Imperial Garden and the Outer Gardens of the Imperial Palace. These are set up as urban parks and each park in its entirety is managed on the concept that it is such a facility.

The law defines National Parks as 'parks set up by the state to protect and develop great natural sceneries and contribute to the health, rest and education of the people'. Even though it may be a large-scale natural area it has to be open for public use and easily accessible. The clear intention is to re-evaluate suitability, prepare and offer areas for public-recreation activities. Further, allowing access to places of natural beauty that are unique to Japan, and not only inviting Japanese but also foreign visitors, is important in boosting national prestige and for acquiring foreign currency.

Protection by Natural Parks Act

The National Parks Law of 1931 was fundamentally amended and re-enacted as the Natural Parks Act in 1957. The Act aims to 'further health, rest and education of the people as well as contributing to securing biodiversity by protecting locations of great natural scenery and promote active usage of them' (Article 1). Natural parks are currently under the jurisdiction of the Ministry of Environment and divided into three systems: national parks, quasi-national parks and prefectural natural parks, with each having its own stipulations for designation, planning and protective rules. Today the total area of the combined designated parks covers 14 per cent of the national land and forms the core of Japan's nature conservation.

The 150-year History of Cultural Properties Protection Administration

As described above, the relatively peaceful nature of the Meiji Restoration, the modernisation revolution in Japan which did not bring about the large-scale destruction of cities and local spaces, enabled a rich variety of cultural heritage to be passed down to modern Japan. Japan's initial heritage management can be described as a movement to protect cultural heritage relatively quickly after the initial policies of the Meiji government mistakenly invited destruction or and the sale of heritage overseas. Although Japan was largely behind the West in industrial development, it succeeded in rapid modernisation by industrial revolution under the policy of 'rich country, strong army'. During that process Japan was fully aware that losing cultural heritage would hurt the national interest, and, in an attempt to enhance national prestige and support the imperial historical legacy, Japan launched state-led initiatives for heritage protection.

Having survived the Pacific War, the post-war Japanese administration of cultural-property protection began to form a firm concept of 'cultural property'. An objective evaluation system not skewed by philosophy or politics was established and substantive protection measures were introduced. However, the efforts were reliant on limited funds and, as a result, so-called, 'benefiting-a-select-few' protection measures were developed; in other words, only a handful of elite objects and locations were amply protected by tax money. This tended to drive cultural properties away from the space of ordinary citizens' lives to unreachable places, which was against the original intention of the protection legislation.

In an attempt to deal with such criticisms, changes were made to increase the categories of cultural properties to extend protection to more varied types of assets and introduced the registry system with more lenient protective measures to widen the range of properties brought into the scope of protection. However, the ongoing loss of non-designated or non-registered cultural properties in the regional towns and communities has been devastating, and further state measures to save them are expected in earnest.

On the other hand there has been a shift in thinking from national-park legislation to nature-reserve legislation to provide places of leisure and recreation for the Japanese public and foreign visitors with the goals of enhancing national prestige and obtaining foreign exchange in mind. In this regard, one can see a difference in that in national-park protection more priority was given to providing benefits for the nation whereas cultural-property protection, initially at least, prioritised protection of the select few (current figures and trends for the designation of cultural assets can be found on the website of the Agency for Cultural Affairs).

STATUS OF HERITAGE MANAGEMENT

Administration of Heritage Management

One could debate the types of heritage that should be the target of protection by society. The history

Table 5.1   Number of designated cultural properties (as of 1 June 2012)

1. National Treasure/ Important Cultural Properties

		National Treasures	Important Cultural Properties
Arts and Crafts	Pictures	158	1,974
	Sculpture	126	2,654
	Craft Objects	252	2,428
	Calligraphy and Books	223	1,882
	Old Documents	60	739
	Archaeological Specimens	44	586
	Historical Materials	3	167
Total		866	10,430
Buildings		216	2,386
Grand Total		1,082	12,816

Note: The number of Important Cultural Properties also includes National Treasures.

2. Historic sites, places of scenic beauty and natural monuments

Special Historic Sites	60	Historic Sites	1,668
Special Places of Scenic Beauty	30	Places of Scenic Beauty	331
Special Natural Monuments	72	Natural Monuments	953
Total	162	Total	2,952

Note: Historic sites, places of scenic beauty and natural monuments includes special historic sites, places of scenic beauty and natural monuments as well.

3. Important Intangible Cultural Properties

	Individual Recognized		Recognition of Holding Body	
	Number	Individuals	Number	Holding Bodies
Entertainment	38	56 (56)	12	12
Craft Skills	42	57 (56)	14	14
Total	80	113 (112)	26	26

Note: An individual may possession more than one recognized skill; actual number of individuals in brackets.

Other

4. Important Tangible Folk Cultural Properties: 212

5. Important Intangible Folk Cultural Properties: 278

6. Special Designations
  – Important Cultural Scenery: 30
  – Important Traditional Architectural Building Group Preservation District: 93
  – Special Preserved Techniques

Special Preserved Techniques

	Holding Individuals		Holding Groups	
Total Recognized	Number	Individuals	Number	Groups
68	46	52	29	31 (29)

Note: Groups may possess more than one technique; actual number of groups in brackets.

7. Registrations

Buildings: 8,826

Arts and Crafts: 13

Folk Culture: 25

Memorials: 61

Source: Agency for Cultural Affairs, Retrieved from: http://www.bunka.go.jp/bunkazai/shoukai/shitei.html

of the protection of cultural properties and natural parks in Japan described above is that heritage that has been the target of protection of Japanese by central and local governments. A private heritage-protection movement, with the state's heritage-protection administration, something similar to the National Trust in UK, has not emerged in Japan. The earliest example, if it can be described as such, was the *Mingei* (folk art) movement, started by the first issue of 'Prospectus for the establishment of the Japanese Folk Crafts Museum' in 1926. The *Mingei* movement aims to discover the beauty of folk arts and crafts such as ceramic ware, dyed and woven materials, lacquer ware and woodwork/bamboo-work for daily use, or Buddhist statues by unknown craftsmen from across Japan, which in 1926 had not been fairly evaluated in the history of art, and introduce these to the wider world. The movement is still active. It is said that the Arts and Crafts movement in the UK had some influence, but, if we examine the content, it is a movement unique to Japan. However, as discussed, the interest of Japanese mass society since the modern era leaned toward 'rich country, strong army' or economic development first. While the scrap-and-build urban development and mass-consumption society destroyed innumerable pieces of cultural and natural heritage, civilian-led heritage-protection movements, often seen in the West, did not spread in Japan. It cannot be denied that citizens valued heritage protection for the appearance and prestige of the nation or the specific regions, but the tendency was to believe that central and local governments were responsible for providing protection. Of course, it must be mentioned that a handful of trust movements, inspired by the National Trust, emerged in Japan and are still active (Kihara, 1984), but they never really attained a position of widespread influence. Either way, mass society in Japan has always regarded cultural property as a treasure of the elite, and as something that commoners were not supposed to come into contact with; something that was inaccessible. As a result, ordinary citizens came to a tacit understanding that those things that were not selected for protection could be lost and nothing could be done about it.

The state or local administration has been burdened with such responsibilities that it is necessary to touch upon their attitude towards cultural-property protection. Looking at its development since the enactment of the Cultural Properties Protection Act of 1950, cultural properties were first divided into three categories by the state: tangible cultural property, intangible cultural property and monument. As we have seen, this was increased to six categories by adding folk-cultural properties, groups of historic buildings and cultural landscapes, and property-identification criteria were

also expanded from designation alone to include selection and registration. In order to include relevant properties in wider ranges, the central government has lowered the barrier for selection and made prefectures and municipalities more central in the designation process. The fact is that the state budget for cultural-property protection has steadily grown (Agency for Cultural Affairs, 2012b) and so have the activities made by the state and local governments. Having said that, the increasing number of cultural properties through designation and other methods naturally meant an increase in cost and expertise needed to provide protection. If we look deeper at the breakdown of the budget for cultural-property protection, it shows the budget for investigating and designation of new cultural properties has not been particularly generous. In fact governments have been trying hard just to secure sufficient budget for maintaining existing cultural properties.

In short, the nature of cultural-property protection in Japan, where the philosophy of 'cultural property protection is a responsibility of the authorities (the state and local governments)' is prevalent, means that it has always been the responsibility of the state in the modern era to increase the targets for protection; but this has meant that the process has been consistently top-down.

Rapid Depletion of Cultural Heritage in Recent Years

As has already been described, Japan has a protective system in place for buried cultural properties that prevents them from being destroyed before identification. However, for heritage on the surface only a few cultural properties are designated, selected and registered for protection. Many other items, which originally should have been protected, are rapidly being lost without their value as a heritage being widely known.

To list some examples, a survey report revealed that in the former castle town of Hagi City in Yamaguchi Prefecture the number of traditional buildings decreased from 1,604 to 1,434 (decrease rate of 10.6 per cent) during the six years between 1998 and 2004, and the number of other traditional scenic elements, such as trees, walls and hedges decreased from 3,825 to 3,460 (decrease rate of 9.5 per cent).[1] In Yanaka, Taito Ward, which is one of the few areas spared war destruction in Tokyo, during the 15 years between 1986 and 2001 'pre-war residences', consisting mainly of regular houses and shops where people also lived, decreased from 537 to 369 (decrease rate of 31.3 per cent).[2] Furthermore, in Kanazawa City, Ishikawa Prefecture, a representative local historic town in Japan, it was reported that during the five years between 1999 and 2004 historic buildings decreased from 21,496 to 19,037 (decrease rate of 11.4 per cent) in the entire city area, and from 10,877 to 9,506 in the historic city-centre area (decrease rate of 12.6 per cent).[3] Despite the fact that each of these three examples comes from a completely different type of community – and their context in current society varies, as one is a local main city, another is a local small town and one is within the Tokyo Metropolitan area – they all demonstrate that more than 20 per cent of historic buildings were lost in 10 years. Let us discuss the background of such rapid losses of traditional buildings.

Formation and Destruction of Cities Built with Wood

Apart from Kyoto, Nara and Kamakura, the majority of Japanese cities including Tokyo, Osaka, Nagoya and Fukuoka, have their origin in castle towns established in the modern era (early seventeenth century onwards). These castle towns were unique phenomena in the world as they were not surrounded by walls and built using wood in a low-rise and high-density style. Obviously, these wooden cities were susceptible to fire, and were destroyed periodically by large fires. However, as it will be described in more detail later, private buildings evolved structurally in the nineteenth century and through appropriate maintenance were built to last almost permanently. Walls were plastered and roofs covered by baked tiles; they had also become fire-resistant. From the Meiji to the early Showa Era, while some Western-style stone or concrete buildings emerged in some city-centre districts, most of the early Showa cities were filled with this durable, low-rise wooden architecture. During the air raids toward the end of World War II most of these structures were reduced to ashes, but a sizable number of them survived the war and fires. Kyoto and some local cities that were spared from air raids inherited dense districts filled with groups of wooden buildings.

Thus, the highly sophisticated architectural culture, including common people's residences, which are rare in the world, survived. However, during the high economic growth era which started in the 1960s, and the bubble economy, which lasted up to the 1990s, many of these buildings were aggressively destroyed in city-development projects without their value being reviewed at all. While the end of the bubble economy put a hold on the waves of city development for a while, the unfavourable social conditions, which will be explained below, left many private wooden buildings unattended, and the number of them continued to decrease rapidly, as described above.

The Japanese Valuation and Inheritance System for Land and Buildings and Loss of Historic Property

Much of the wealth created by the high economic growth and the bubble economy was poured in to land transactions, causing land prices to skyrocket in Japan. One of the trial calculations indicated that if all the land area in Japan was converted into currency in the early 1990s, immediately before the bubble economy burst, you could buy the entire land of the USA four times. Although land prices dropped after the bubble economy collapsed, the generally high level of land prices rarely seen in the world still continues in metropolitan areas and in local cities. In addition, the asset-valuation system in Japan, which sets the building depreciation period to be 47 years for steel reinforced-concrete buildings, 34 years for heavy steel-framed structures and 22 years for wooden buildings, does not grant any value to older buildings. Therefore, when a person inherits an expensive piece of land often he or she cannot afford to pay the inheritance tax and chooses to demolish the worthless house and sell the land. Not allowing buildings to be inherited is a situation unique to Japan. This is in sharp contrast to the European value system where the land is relatively cheap but well tended buildings are highly valued.

The argument is that Japanese buildings do not last long because they are built using vulnerable wood, but this is at least partly wrong. Japan is affected by monsoons and high-temperature/humidity and sub-tropical climates so closed-style houses made of stones with small openings were not popular, and open and airy wooden houses were much preferred. Initially, Japanese architecture adopted the 'pit and pillar' structure, where the residents dug a pit and stood pillars in the soil piled around the pit to support the roof. They lived on the dirt floor. It was true that those pillars were prone to rotting at the bottom ends in the earth and the houses did not last too long, but residents soon buried a foundation stone in the ground on which the pillars stood. Once they introduced floorboards over the dirt floor the life of buildings was extended to a remarkable degree. The fact that the five-storied pagoda at Horyu-ji Temple has stood for 1,300 years to this day serves as proof of the durability of wooden structures. Having said that, for a long period from the remote past up to the mid-nineteenth century most ordinary residential houses never managed to escape from the 'pit and pillar' structure, and they were usually renewed every ten years or, at most, every few decades. Private houses had to wait until the end of modern times, around the last days of the Shogunate, to enjoy the durable structure described above, and the same went for farm houses and town houses. We must remember that those that have been maintained and repaired continuously and evaded destruction by recent urban development are being inherited without impairment to their functions, and still stand to this day.

The adoption of the Nara Document in 1994, which will be explained later, has given Asian wooden architecture authenticity as World Heritage. The significance is that the value of wood-built culture, whose functionality and form are maintained by replacing parts through careful repair, has been recognised.

The system for the preservation districts for groups of historic buildings described earlier came into existence on the premise that private houses that constitute cities, towns and farm villages are valuable as permanent assets and can be preserved and maintained by continuous repair work.

Ratification of World Heritage Convention and the Nara Document

The UNESCO World Heritage Convention came into effect in 1972, but the Japanese government delayed its ratification for 20 years until 1992. Possible reasons why the Japanese government, which professes to be a cultural power, chose not to ratify it for so long are as follows. The registration criteria for World Heritage, which evolved centring on European regions, are based on the concept of stone-built culture, and the idea of 'authenticity', in particular, was not compatible with that of Japan in the wood-built-culture region. In contrast to placing value on the original constituent materials having existed in the same space continuously, Japanese wooden buildings are inherited by repeated replacement of parts, sometimes involving partial or total dismantling repairs. Therefore, even if Japan ratified the convention, Japan's proud wooden cultural properties may not be approved for registration because of the fact that they lack authenticity according to the then standard, and there may be no merit for Japan to justify the contribution required by the World Heritage Fund.

In order to overcome this issue, the Japanese government held the Nara Conference soon after its ratification of the Convention in 1992. At the Conference additions were made to the authenticity-evaluation criteria to allow for wooden structures in Japan, and incorporated into the Nara Document on Authenticity. The Japanese temple and shrine construction is carried out by *miyadaiku*, or temple and shrine carpenters, who inherit superb and specialised techniques going back beyond a thousand years. *Gassho*-style, or steep-rafter roofed houses in the historic villages

of Shirakawa and Gokayama, are maintained by a mutual labour cooperative system called *yui* among the residents that inherits thatching techniques for the roof. These systems ensure the exact same construction of the original, which is what the Nara Document declares for the proof of authenticity of the shape and technology of the buildings.

The philosophy agreed with the global strategy of the World Heritage Committee at the time, which intended to rectify the imbalance of the number of registered cultural heritage sites across the world. The significance of the Nara Document is well demonstrated by the fact that registration of World Heritage sites whose constituent assets are wooden structures followed one after another in China, Vietnam and other Asian nations.

Protection of World Heritage

After Japan ratified the UNESCO World Heritage Convention in 1992 the first registration of Japanese assets in the list of World Heritage sites was made in the following year, namely, two cultural heritage sites of 'Buddhist Monuments in the Horyu-ji Area' and 'Himeji-jo Castle', and two natural heritage sites in Shirakami-Sanchi and Yakushima. Then followed registrations of cultural heritage in the list of World Heritage sites: 'Historic Monuments of Ancient Kyoto (Kyoto, Uji and Otsu Cities)' in 1994; 'Historic Villages of Shirakawa-go and Gokayama' in 1995; 'Hiroshima Peace Memorial (Genbaku Dome)' and 'Itsukushima Shinto Shrine' in 1996; 'Historic Monuments of Ancient Nara' in 1998; 'Shrines and Temples of Nikko' in 1999; 'Gusuku Sites and Related Properties of the Kingdom of Ryukyu' in 2000; 'Sacred Sites and Pilgrimage Routes in the Kii Mountain Range' in 2004; 'Iwami Ginzan Silver Mine and its Cultural Landscape' in 2007; and 'Hiraizumi – Temples, Gardens and Archaeological Sites Representing the Buddhist Pure Land' in 2011.

The selection process for the candidates for registration was as follows: the Agency for Cultural Affairs judged the suitability of each item listed in the state-designated or selected cultural properties (groups) and itemised them in priority order in the provisional domestic list, then, starting with a site where preparations were completed, an application was made to the World Heritage Committee. It can be safely said that the selection process was dictated by the central government. Due to the growing concern that more attention should be given to the views of the regions that host the sites, the Agency for Cultural Affairs established a special committee on World Cultural Heritage under the subcommittee on cultural assets in the Council for Cultural Affairs in September 2006, and invited candidates proposed by local governments to be listed in the provisional list of applicants to the World Heritage committee.

As a result, by November of the same year, 24 sites had applied through local governments nation-wide (subsequently four sites were shortlisted by the initial selection process) and submitted to the special committee. Many of the applications included features that went beyond the original imagination of the Agency for Cultural Affairs in terms of unexpected and varied themes or stories of heritage, or the wider region to be grouped as a heritage site. The process inadvertently revealed the fact that heritage that could not have been described by the existing six categories (tangible, intangible, folk-cultural, monument, cultural landscape and groups of historic buildings). The administrative bodies of cultural-property protection were faced with the requirement to provide a more comprehensive framework or even a completely new framework for the concept of cultural property (cultural heritage). The agenda should not have been contained within the discussion for World Cultural Heritage alone, but debated for the ideal state of cultural-property protection in general in Japan but this did not happen. The agenda was subsequently inherited by the 2006–7 subcommittee on cultural assets in the Council for Cultural Affairs, which will be described later.

Cultural Landscape

The last category to appear in the system of Japanese cultural-property protection is the cultural landscape. The concept is to recognise the value of regional scenery produced by the continuing efforts of ordinary citizens interacting with the natural environment, and to keep creating new scenery by continuing those efforts.

An amendment to the Cultural Properties Protection Act in 2004 enabled the introduction of cultural landscape, which includes scenery in the following eight categories: 'farming', 'mowing and grazing', 'use of forest', 'fishing', 'use of water', 'mining and manufacturing', 'transport and traffic' and 'dwellings'. When we look at the land in Japan, it is difficult to discover scenery that has nothing to do with any of the categories, and the definition is exhaustive.

The conceptual diagram that was used by the Agency for Cultural Affairs to spread the idea of cultural landscape in Japan is explicit and significant (see Figure 5.1 below).

Up until then the Cultural Properties Protection Act only allowed identification of specific areas in regions as a cultural property (or a preservation district) to be protected as one of the following categories: historic sites, places of scenic beauty, Natural Monuments, or preservation districts for groups of historic buildings. Therefore, it was appropriate to introduce a new concept to enlist landscape, such as terraced paddy fields, that could not have been protected under the existing framework. This diagram indicates that the new concept is cultural landscape. Cultural landscapes, whose value as a cultural property can be clearly described, are classed as 'cultural landscape in the narrow sense' and consist of elite sites selected by the state. It is an easy-to-understand reform of the system that further enhances the entries for cultural protection and covers precious treasures of the people without omission. However, the concept of 'cultural landscape in the wider sense' is more important. While they may not necessarily

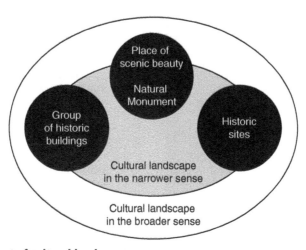

Figure 5.1 Concept of cultural landscape

Source: Author.

be as spectacular as those selected as cultural properties, the wider concept indicates that each region in Japan has precious and inherent cultural landscape, and the awareness of its existence will eventually lead to the identification of true cultural landscape as a cultural property. It is important to understand that the oval of 'cultural landscape in the wider sense' represents each and every form of 'cultural' scenery that is developed in Japan. Most of the large and medium-sized local cities in Japan originate in historic castle towns from the modern era. Many old post towns, port towns, rural towns, farming, logging or fishing villages and surrounding pastoral areas boast rich residential or land-use histories, and, if needed, they can always identify their own cultural landscapes and provide descriptions for them.

Nevertheless, the administrative work for the protection of cultural landscape is still in its infancy and is faced with many issues. Under this system, which assumes such a wide range of targets for valuation, as of February 2012 a total of 30 properties had been selected (Agency for Cultural Affairs, 2012c). Due to the expansiveness of selected areas and the fact that many people still live and work in them, it is difficult to form a consensus among local governments, residents and private businesses about what should be targeted for protection. Perhaps the management of Cultural Landscape stipulated in the World Heritage Convention is experiencing the same kind of difficulty. The effort to maintain the inherited value of scenery, while allowing for the inevitable changes that happen in any inhabited area, is an extremely difficult undertaking.

The approach to comprehensively grasp the cultural heritage (cultural properties) that exists in local regions as they are, of the basic concept of history and culture which will be described in detail below, is in line with the above attempt to place a value on cultural landscape. Such an integrated approach shapes the frontline of cultural-heritage management in Japan, and the optimal-protection method to realise such an approach will be the focus for future endeavours.

HERITAGE MANAGEMENT: RESEARCH TRENDS

The Cultural Properties Protection Act states that it is important to preserve, as well as utilise, cultural properties, and the concept of 'protection' combines both. However, the majority of people's understanding of the idea of cultural-properties protection is the preservation of the select-few elite properties.

The actual process of cultural-properties protection involves: excavation (investigation) of

heritage, valuation (analysis), sifting through and registering targets for protection (designation, selection and registration, etc.), repair and restoration for retaining value and maintenance, opening them to the public and holding exhibitions (utilisation) so that the people can share them, and monitoring the state of preservation. All of these activities form a cycle of administrative work in cultural-properties protection.

In contrast, the author inclusively defines 'Heritage Management' as follows: not only preserving and maintaining the precious natural, historic or cultural properties in each region but also attempting to rediscover them from a variety of viewpoints; endeavouring to reproduce what is lost or newly create things that would inherit the lost values; utilising them in daily lives, production activities or tourism; and close monitoring of the cycle of identification, investigation, valuation, preservation, maintenance, recreation, new creation, maintenance, inheritance and utilisation.

In other words, as shown in the examples in Europe, preservation, maintenance and utilisation of cultural heritage would go far beyond what used to be covered by cultural-property administration and is now developing as the main agenda for urban policies (such as making cities attractive) with strong ties to city-planning and tourism-policy divisions. In short, in order to build a sustainable relationship between heritage management and urban development/tourism, not only is preserving the select-few cultural properties with utmost care required but also paying attention to a wider range of cultural heritage. The management process described above will have to be put into practice as a part of urban policies.

The 'publicly known cultural properties' defined in the Protection Act represent only a small part of the cultural heritage that such a management style should be focusing on, and our environment is filled with far more cultural properties and heritage (in the original sense) than the act specifies. Full and proper management of those items is clearly beyond the control of the existing cultural-property administration. The Japanese government has openly admitted this fact, and, as stated in the 'Basic Concept of History and Culture' and the 'Historic Town Planning Act', which are explained in detail later, the Agency for Cultural Affairs has changed its policy to protect and pass down our precious cultural heritage to future generations in cooperation from various other agencies such as the Ministry of Land, Infrastructure, Transport and Tourism and the Ministry of Agriculture, Forestry and Fisheries.

Looking at this proposition from the standpoint of local governments and regions, the era of leaving cultural heritage up to the central administration has passed and it is now time to move on to the age of taking initiatives to actively incorporate heritage management into urban planning. Identifying the hidden cultural heritage of regions and how best to develop them it are unmistakably the most important items on the agenda for today's urban policy for many towns and regions, especially in the current context of competition among cities. It is no exaggeration to say that whether Japan can be counted among developed nations as a cultural centre depends on the aggregated efforts of local governments and municipalities.

From this perspective it is true that the research on cultural-property protection has been developed mainly by governmental-research institutes rather than by university or academic research organisations. Furthermore, it can be said that studies of heritage management, in the sense discussed above, have mostly been developed within the context of research for urban planning and town planning for tourism. Therefore, the recent Japanese research trends in the field is discussed in two sections below: research trends in cultural-property protection and research trends in heritage management.

Research Trends in Cultural Property Protection

The study of techniques for cultural-property protection is most advanced in the public organisations where the actual fieldwork is carried out. Specifically, the system for protective measures cascading from the Agency for Cultural Affairs represents the body of the research. Designation, selection and registration of cultural properties are carried out by the Ministry of Education, Culture, Sports, Science and Technology based on advice from the Council for Cultural Affairs (Agency for Cultural Affairs, 2012d).

The Council for Cultural Affairs consists of subcommittees on each category of cultural properties to be considered: (1) arts and crafts; (2) buildings and preservation districts for groups of historic buildings; (3) monuments, cultural landscape and buried cultural properties; (4) intangible cultural properties and methods for their preservation; (5) folk-cultural properties; (6) policies for implementing the Convention Concerning the Protection of World Heritage; and (7) policies for implementing the Convention Concerning the Protection of Intangible Cultural Properties. The Council pulls together the wisdom of specialists in evaluating and protecting cultural heritage in Japan, and the academic authorities in each field (researchers of related universities and academic societies, such as the Japanese Archaeological Association, the Japanese Society for Cultural Heritage, the Architectural Institute of Japan, the Japan Society of Civil Engineers and the Japanese

Institute of Landscape Architecture) constitute the members of the Council and its subcommittees. For the practical work of evaluating cultural heritage by prefectures and municipalities a similar system to that at state level is duplicated for the subordinate organisations. In order to provide advice to prefectural governors, mayors of municipalities or heads of municipal education committees many of these local governments have established their own Council for Cultural Affairs.

Apart from researchers affiliated to universities and other educational organisations that send members to the Council and its Committees, governmental institutes that employ researchers specialising in valuation of cultural properties are the 'Incorporated Administrative Agency National Research Institute for Cultural Properties, Tokyo (www.tobunken. go.jp)' which focuses mainly on tangible properties and intangible heritage, and the 'Incorporated Administrative Agency Nara National Research Institute for Cultural Properties (www.nabunken. go.jp)', which focuses mainly on real estate heritage.

The National Research Institute for Cultural Properties, Tokyo, consists of four departments, namely, the 'Department of Art Research, Archives and Information Systems', which conducts research on art history; the 'Department of Intangible Cultural Heritage', which covers intangible cultural properties and folk entertainment, such as traditional music and theatre or applied fine arts; the 'Center for Conservation Science and Restoration Techniques', which handles the establishment of protective environments for the maintenance of cultural properties and carries out preservative repairs to cultural properties, such as Kofun wall drawings; and the 'Japan Center for International Cooperation in Conservation', which deals with Japan's international contribution to cultural-heritage protection.

Nara National Research Institute for Cultural Properties is also made up of four departments, namely, the 'Department of Planning and Coordination', which is responsible for the comprehensive planning and coordination of research activities; the 'Department of Cultural Heritage', which conducts research on tangible cultural properties such as arts and crafts or buildings, groups of historic buildings, cultural landscape and monuments (places of scenic beauty and historic sites); the 'Department of Imperial Palace Sites Investigations', whose members include researchers specialising in investigative excavation of ancient capitals and castles in the disciplines of archaeology, history of literature, architecture and gardens, conservation and restoration science, dendrochronology and environmental studies, among others; and the 'Center for Archaeological Operations', which studies and develops methods for investigating buried cultural properties.

The National Institute for Cultural Heritage (www.nich.go.jp/) is an umbrella organisation for both institutes as well as the four National Museums of Tokyo, Kyoto, Nara and Kyushu. In particular, Kyushu National Museum, the newest of the four, is conducting the most advanced research on methods to protect tangible cultural properties. Further, the National Institute established the 'International Research Centre for Intangible Cultural Heritage in the Asia-Pacific Region (IRCI)' (www.irci.jp/62.html) in October 2011 as a base for enhancing protection of intangible cultural heritage in Asia Pacific region.

As stated above, movements of private citizens for registration or protection of heritage in Japan is historically scarce. Apart from the *Mingei* (folk art) movement described earlier, Dazaifu Citizens Heritage Conference (Daizaifu Shi Keikan/Shimin Isan Kaigi 2014), one of the recent developments to emerge in response to the Basic Concept of History and Culture and that conducts excavation, preservation and utilisation of cultural heritage by citizens, has attracted attention with its initiative for a 'citizens' heritage registration system'. Another system that attracted the attention of the general public is the NPO Hokkaido Heritage Council. It registers heritage as a tourism resource for Hokkaido and has proposed 'A Plan for Hokkaido Heritage' (2001) and other initiatives. However, its plans did not get beyond these proposals and– no actual system for protection was included – and it failed to gain sufficient effectiveness as a heritage-management operation.

Research Trends in Heritage Management

Comprehensive Understanding of Local Cultural Heritage and Cultural Assets

The following studies deserve to be mentioned at this point, as they represent the expanding concept of heritage that is not limited by the so-called cultural-properties-protection administration in Japan.

First, Koji Nishikawa, proposed a concept of 'regional cultural property', stating that many important cultural properties exist in regional areas, albeit they do not qualify for the state designation and other formal criteria. Nishikawa defined that 'regional cultural property is something that constitutes the life space of a town or a village in an area in a given region, and is devised to make the space attractive and lively' (Nishikawa, 1986) and called for protection and utilisation of cultural properties in local areas and regions that cannot be protected by the cultural-property administration for the select-few elite properties.

The Architectural Institute of Japan, in its report entitled 'Survey Research Report on the Ideal Townscapes and Landscapes of Japan: Towards Historic and Cultural Town Planning' (Architectural Institute of Japan, 1997), proposed that local governments survey local historic and cultural properties exhaustively, without being limited by the existing concept of cultural property, and that they establish a 'History and Culture Master Plan' to enable the utilisation of the identified cultural properties as landscape resources to promote town planning.

Similarly, Hiroshi Mimura went beyond the highly visible elements called 'urban space cultural property', which signifies the historical context, and presented a concept of space patterns, weaved by historically formed elements to give values to the urban space itself as heritage (Mimura, 1997).

These all came from the accumulation of studies in architectural planning, and are the origin of the philosophy that the cultural properties are better protected by utilising them and not merely protecting them. It has taken longer than 20 years for such thinking to be reflected in cultural-properties-protection administration. The 2007 Agency for Cultural Affairs Report (Agency for Cultural Affairs, 2007) asserted the need to understand cultural assets in their locality as they are, and in a comprehensive manner, without being limited by the existing six categories (tangible, intangible, folk-culture, monument, cultural landscape and groups of historic buildings) of cultural properties. It proposed a new policy to build a system to support such cultural properties by society as a whole, and not leave them to the administration or to private organisations.

As a result, the 'Basic Concept of History and Culture' (Agency for Cultural Affairs, 2012a), which can be regarded as the Agency for Cultural Affairs' version of the earlier described 'History and Culture Master Plan', was published. The concept was drawn up as an actual plan on a trial basis in 20 local cities nationwide in the 'Model Project on Comprehensive Understanding of Cultural Property' (Fiscal, 2008–2010). In addition, in order to develop the concept into actual projects, three ministries – the Agency for Cultural Affairs, the Ministry of Land, Infrastructure, Transport and Tourism and the Ministry of Agriculture, Forestry and Fisheries – jointly established the Act Concerning the Maintenance and Improvement of Historic Scenery (enacted 2008) (commonly called the Historic Town Planning Act). The Act which calls for the creation of a favourable environment, based on the unique local history and culture of each locality, including its 'historic scenery', clearly defines its value for each city and aims to maintain/improve it for future generations. In order for local governments to take advantage of the act, each of them has to develop the 'historic scene maintenance enhancement plan', which specifies a concrete business plan for the above-mentioned 'Basic Concept of History and Culture' and must be authorised by the state (Ministry of Land, Infrastructure, Transport and Tourism, 2014). As of June 2012 a total of 35 local governments are authorised for this scheme, and it has rapidly spread within a short period of time.

Preservation, Conservation and Utilisation Integral with the Surrounding Heritage Environment

The cultural-property-protection-administration system in Japan has its drawbacks in not having a measure that acts as a buffer zone, which is present in the protection system for World Heritage. The challenge of maintaining the environment surrounding cultural properties is addressed by some of the historic cities using legal means, such as architectural regulations based on urban planning. These are: the Act on Special Measures Concerning Conservation of Historic Natural Features of Ancient Cities (*Koto Hozon Ho*, or the Ancient Capitals Preservation Law), enacted in 1996, and the Asuka Village Special Measures Law, enacted in 1980.

The Ancient Capitals Preservation Law defines the state of the land where historic buildings and ruins of the 'ancient capitals' (municipalities that used to play important historic roles as centres of politics and culture in Japanese history) are blended with natural surroundings, to embody the tradition and culture of the old capital as an 'historic landscape', and stipulates measures for the state and other authorities to adopt in order to protect them as cultural assets to be shared by the Japanese people and inherited by future generations. At present 10 municipalities – Kyoto City; Nara City; Kamakura City; Tenri City; Kashihara City; Sakurai City; Ikaruga Town of Ikoma County, Nara Prefecture; Asuka Village of Takaichi County, Nara Prefecture; Zushi City; and Otsu City – are designated as 'ancient capitals' by the Ancient Capitals Preservation Law. In these municipalities preservation areas of historic landscapes are designated and urban planning is carried out to protect special historic natural features in conservation zones. Also, it restricts development activities within the area to preserve historic scenery in the ancient capitals (Ministry of Land, Infrastructure, Transport and Tourism, 2012a).

As for the Asuka Village Special Measures Law, it defines Asuka Village of Takaichi County, Nara Prefecture, as the centre of politics and culture in ancient Japan, and its incomparably precious historical scenery has been preserved where numerous historic and cultural assets spread across the area in perfect unity with the surrounding environment. To this end the village is deemed a special case in the Ancient Capitals Preservation Law and activity restrictions are enforced in the entire village. At the same time projects to develop a living environment and basis for industry, as well as projects sponsored by the Asuka Village Development Fund, are implemented based on the Asuka Development Plan. These special measures attempt to harmonise the preservation of the precious historic scenery of Asuka Village, the stability of the residents' lives and the promotion of industry (Ministry of Land, Infrastructure, Transport and Tourism, 2012b).

These schemes are in force in the special municipalities, as described above, in order for the urban planning administration to maintain historic scenery that contains cultural heritage. However, they are not really applicable universally to cities and regions across Japan as a cultural-heritage-management system.

Originally, the buffer zone for a World Heritage site was a zone set around the periphery of the heritage, which 'has no value' and 'should be sacrificed' to maintain the environment of the core zone which carries the value of the heritage. Existing debates surrounding cultural properties in Japan have mostly focused on the cultural properties themselves that form the core, and it is usually only on a secondary level that consideration is given to the sacrifice of the surrounding area (restrictions on development) required to protect them. Thus it has always been assumed that it is difficult to set up buffer zones (force sacrifice) in Japanese urban areas where the incentives for development are always at the maximum level.

On the other hand, the Japanese urban areas often are historic urban areas to begin with, in varying degrees, and hence the idea of making a set area surrounding a cultural property sacrifice itself in order to preserve the value of the cultural property is not feasible. Instead, by positively evaluating the historic and cultural significance of those urban areas and their surrounding environment, and by arranging the environment and forming a landscape that will enhance the surrounding area's inherent characteristics, the adjacent environment, as well as the important cultural property, can be maintained well, and this will be more agreeable in the Japanese context.

As a result of such debates, the Historic Town Planning Law was established to target not only ancient capitals but also other local cities. It aims to clearly define historic scenery that is unique to each city and improve the characteristics of the cultural heritage which forms the nucleus of the scenery, together with the surrounding environment.

Building a Sustainable Relationship between Heritage and Tourism

Lastly, we need to consider the relationship between heritage protection and tourism, which has been the weakest aspect in heritage-management studies in Japan. A new research field that aims to establish a sustainable relationship between heritage and tourism has emerged and been discussed in Japanese academic circles (the National Museum of Ethnology, the Center for Advanced Tourism Studies (CATS) at Hokkaido National University and the University of Tsukuba World Heritage Studies, among others) since the beginning of the twenty-first century.

As long as there are people to enjoy it heritage will always be a target for tourism. The 1976 'ICOMOS Charter on Cultural Tourism' adopted by the International Council on Monuments and Sites (ICOMOS) regarded tourists as physical threat to the integrity of heritage and its surrounding environment, and it mainly focused on the management of the tension between tourists visiting heritage sites and those attempting to protect the heritage. However, a quarter of a century later in 1999, the charter was revised as the 'ICOMOS International Cultural Tourism Charter', which set forth its main purpose of protection as adopting management techniques that can promote positive access so that visitors can truly understand the significance of the heritage. ICOMOS understood that unless heritage protection attracts a high level of recognition and support from the general public it will not be supported as a policy and financial backing will not be secured. This demonstrates that 'the control over the relationship between heritage (object) and visitors (tourists)' has moved to 'building a relationship between heritage (event), local communities (host) and visitors (guests)'. A great paradigm shift in the conceptual relationship between heritage and tourism has occurred.

The role of tourism is to skilfully interpret the value (meaning) of the identified heritage, first for local residents and the nation, then for tourists who visit the sites. In other words, it allows access to the value, which in turn will deepen the understanding of the tourism resource (heritage) and increase the number of people who understand and provide support. True protection cannot be provided simply by building a fence which keeps the heritage safe from physical destruction. The first step of heritage-tourism development is to offer a comprehensive and thorough explanation of the universal value of the heritage and to work on the utilisation method that can enhance the authenticity and completeness of the heritage.

The aforementioned Agency for Cultural Affairs report (by the subcommittee on cultural assets in the Council for Cultural Affairs) lists eco-tourism, geo-parks and eco-museums, which have recently attracted attention as a maintenance and utilisation technique for local natural or cultural resources, as examples for successful heritage management methods. The report places museums, fine-art museums and history and folk-culture resource centres that hold collections of local significance as a core in the basic concept and promotes their utilisation as bases to transmit information. By recognising heritage as a tourism resource in the wider context of cultural exchange that goes beyond the target of simple economic activity, or by classing it as a resource for scenic town planning, cultural properties, once thought to have finished their useful roles and left unattended to perish, are given a new lease of life and value. These cultural properties will be utilised and inherited by future generations.

This trend, at the same time, requires liaison within the administrative organisation involved in urban planning, scenic landscape, tourism, agriculture and fisheries, education, etc., and cooperation between the administration and private operators engaged in tourism and town building or citizens' movements. The culmination of such collective activities will bring about the development of a successful tourism business, great town building and industrial promotion. In summary, the cultural-property administration will not only be limited to designation/selection and protection but will take on a new role recognising the existence and value of many other cultural properties, which they failed to identify using the existing framework. Although the administration may no longer be able to provide protection directly, it has taken a giant step towards offering indirect support to preservation/maintenance and utilization in cooperation with other administrative and private organisations. Of course, such development is no doubt closely connected to the enactment of the Historic Town Planning Act, which was jointly established by the Agency for Cultural Affairs, the Ministry of Land, Infrastructure, Transport and Tourism and the Ministry of Agriculture, Forestry and Fisheries.

CONCLUSION

Japanese cultural heritage was built up from the ancient period and through medieval times to reach a climax during the 260-year period of the Tokugawa regime when, under its *sakoku* policy, all regions of Japan were closed both to the world and to other parts of Japan as well. Then suddenly Japan was opened up as a result of the Meiji Restoration. The accompanying dramatic and rapid modernization led to a sense of national crisis over the loss of cultural heritage. These were the conditions which gave birth to policies of cultural-heritage protection and are characteristic of the beginnings of cultural-heritage management.

From this point and until recent years Japanese cultural-heritage management proceeded on the path symbolised by the words 'protection of the select few' and, fundamentally, it took the form of protection of cultural assets by the public sector (national and local governments). Many types of cultural assets and cultural-asset-protection schedules were created and, in the context of a fixed environment of monsoon and wooden-structure culture, Japan has been able to develop a high level of protection technology, even when viewed from a global perspective.

As we have entered the twenty-first century, however, it is necessary to call attention to cultural heritage which is not designated as such, and to the need for enhanced cultural-resource management. Therefore, along with starting to engage in research on the subject, cultural-heritage management is beginning to put in place national and local legal arrangements, town and landscape planning, tourism, and private-sector cooperative partnerships which go beyond existing forms of the administration of cultural heritage. Movement in this area is still very much in its beginning stages and one must avoid clearly stating the direction that Japan might take in the future. Nonetheless, as the key words 'Japanese pop culture' and 'cool Japan' have recently become a hot topic of discussion, one might suggest that this points to a phenomenon which might be built upon by future research into Japanese cultural-heritage management.

NOTES

1 This survey was carried out by the Department of Environmental Design, Graduate School of Design, Kyushu University, where the author was formerly affiliated.
2 This survey was carried out by the Graduate School of Conservation, Tokyo University of the Arts, Buildings and Districts and Taito Cultural and Historical Society.
3 This survey was carried out by the Property Tax Division of Kanazawa City.

FURTHER READING

Agency for Cultural Affairs, Monuments and Sites Division, Cultural Properties Department (2005). *Shisekitō Seibi no Tebiki – Hozon to Katsuyō no tame ni.* Tokyo: Dōseisha.

Daizaifu Shi Keikan/Shimin Isan Kaigi. (2014). *Daizaifu Shi Keikan/Shimin Isan Kaigi.* www.市民遺産.jp/

Miyamoto, M. (2000). Rekishiteki Shūraku Machinami no Chōsa to Hozonkeikaku. *Gekkan Bunkazai*, 444: 13–18.

Miyamoto, M. (2001). Rekishiteki Machinami no Mezasumono. *Mirai e Tsuzuku Rekishi no Machinami Denken Chiku to Machizukuri.* Tokyo: Zenkoku Dentōteki Kenzōbutsugun Hozonchiku Kyōgikai.

Miyamoto, M. (2006). *Toshikūkan no Kinseishi Kenkyū.* Tokyo: Chūōkōron Bijyutsu Shuppan.

Miyamoto, M. (2010). Dentōchiku ni okeru Shūri to Shūkei. *Gekkan Bukazai*, 559: 24–27.

Miyamoto, M. and Nishiyama, N. (1998). *Yame Fukushima - Yameshi Fukushima Dentōteki Kenzōbutsugun Hozontaisaku Chōsahōkoku.* Yameshi: Yameshi Kyōiku Iinkai.

Miyamoto, M. and Nishiyama, N. (2000). *Hagi Hamazaki: Hagishi Hamazakichiku Dentōteki Kenzōbutugun Hozon Taisaku Chōsa Hōkoku.* Hagi: Hagi Shi Kyōiku Iinkai.

Nishiyama, N. (2004c). *Hagi Machijū Hakubutsukan Kihon Keikaku Kōdō Keikaku.* Hagi: Hagi Machijū Hakubutsukan Seibi Kentō Iinkai.

Nishiyama, N. (2007). Bunka Isan kara Hajimaru Machizukuri. Tokushū: Chiiki Isan to Machizukuri. *Kikan Machizukuri*, 15: 65–68.

Nishiyama, N. (2008). Shichōson ni okeru Bunkazai no Sōgō teki Haaku no Torikumi. *Bunka Chō Geppo*, 480: 16–19

Nishiyama, N. (2009). Waga Kuni no Bunkazai no Ataratan Tenkai – Bunkazai no Sōgōteki Haaku to Reki Bunka Kihon Kōsō Yakuwari ni Tsuite. *Kikan Machizukuri*, 25: 20–29.

Nishiyama, N. (2012). Rekishi Bunka o ikashite Machizukuri no Koremade to Sōrai. *Shintoshi*, 66 (3): 12–16.

Nishiyama, U. (1990). *Rekishiteki Keikan to Machizukuri.* Tokyo: Toshi Bunka Sha.

Ohara, K. (1999). *Eco-Myūziamu e no Tabi.* Tokyo: Kajima Shuppan Sha.

Okawa, N. (Ed.) (1995). *Toshi no Rekishi to Machizukuri.* Tokyo: Gakugei Shuppan Sha.

Okawa, N. (Ed.) (1997). *Rekishi Isan no Hozon/ Katsuyō.* Gakugei Shuppan Sha.

Ota, H. (1981). *Rekishi Fūdo no Hozon.* Tokyo; Shōkokusha.

Ota, H. et al. (Eds.) (1982). *Zukan Nihon no Machi Nami.* 12 volumes. Tokyo: Daiichi Hōki Shuppan Sha.

REFERENCES

Agency for Cultural Affairs [Japan] (2007). Bunka Shingi Kai Bunka Zai Bukakai Kikaku Chosakai Hōkokusho.

Agency for Cultural Affairs [Japan] (2012a). Rekishi Bunka Kihon Kōsō Sakutei Gijutsu Shishin. Last retrieved on 5 August 2014 from: www.bunka.go.jp/bunkazai/rekishibunka/ pdf/guideline.pdf

Agency for Cultural Affairs [Japan] (2012b). Bunka Kankei Yosan. Last retrieved on 5 August 2014 from: www.bunka.go.jp/bunka_gyousei/yosan/index.html

Agency for Cultural Affairs [Japan] (2012c). Bunkateki Keikan. Last retrieved on 5 August 2014 from: www.bunka.go.jp/bunkazai/shoukai/keikan.html

Agency for Cultural Affairs [Japan] (2012d). Bunka Shingikai Sōshiki Zu. Last retrieved on 5 August 2014 from: www.bunka.go.jp/bunkashingikai/about/sosikizu.html.

Agency for Cultural Affairs [Japan] (2014). Bunka Zai Shitei Nado no Kensu. Last retrieved on 5 August 2014 from: www.bunka.go.jp/bunkazai/shoukai/shitei.html

Architectural Institute of Japan, Survey Research Report on the Ideal Townscapes and Landscapes of Japan: Towards Historic and Cultural Town Planning, (1997). *Wagakuni ni okeru Machinami Keikan no Arikata ni kansuru Chōsa Kenkyū Hōkokusyo Rekishi to Bunkano Machizukuri e mukete.* Tokyo: Nihon Kenchiku Gakkai.

City of Hagi (2004). *Hagi Machijū Hakubutsukan Kihon Keikaku/Kōdō Keikaku.*

Council for National Preservation Districts for Historic Buildings (Zenkoku Dentōteki Kenzōbutsu Hozon Chiku Kyōgikai) (Eds.) (2001). *Mirai e Tsuzuku Rekishi no Machinami – Denken Chiku to Machizukuri.* Tokyo: Kyōsei.

Foundation for Tourism Resource Protection [now known as Japan National Trust] (1981). *Rekishiteki Machinami Jiten.* Tokyo: Kashiwa Shobō.

Kihara, K. (1984). *Nashonaru Torasuto.* Tokyo: Sanseido.

Mimura, H. (1997). Toshikūkan Bunkazai no Chiriteki Seisō Bunseki to Moderu karuchā Dezain ni Kansuru Kenkyū. *Jyūtaku Sōgō Kenkyū Zaidan Kenkyū Hōkoku.* Tokyo: Jyūtaku Sōgō Kenkyū Zaidan.

Ministry of Land, Infrastructure, Transport and Tourism (2012a). Koto Hozon Hō. Retrieved from www.mlit.go.jp/crd/rekimachi/koto_hozon/index.html

Ministry of Land, Infrastructure, Transport and Tourism (2012b). Asuka Mura Tokubetsu Soki Hō. Retrieved from: www.mlit.go.jp/crd/rekimachi/asuka_law/index.html.

Ministry of Land, Infrastructure, Transport and Tourism (2014). Rekishiteki Fūchi Iji Kōjō Keikaku. Last retrieved on 5 August 2014 from www.mlit.go.jp/crd/rekimachi/nintei/nintei.html

Nishikawa, K. (1986). *21 Seki no Shisaku: Chiiki no Bunzai.* Kyushu Daigaku Shuppankai.

Nishiyama, N. (2004a). *Hagi Monogatari Vol. 4: Hagi Machijū Hakubutsukan.* Hagi: Yūgen Sekinin Chūkan Hōjin Hagi Monogatari Jimu Kyoku.

Nishiyama, N. (2004b). Chiiki Shigen no Hakkutsu to Katsuyō: Kihonteki na Kangaekata to Chōsa Keikaku Shuhō. In Nihon Kenchiku Gakkai (Eds.) *Machinami Hozongata Machizukuri Machizukuri Kyōkasho Dai 2 Kan*, pp. 36–59.

6

Geography's Contributions to Japanese Studies

Mary McDonald

Human geography takes many approaches and methods, reflecting the twentieth-century arc of paradigms in the social sciences. Environmental determinism held sway in the early twentieth century, giving way to views of environments as products of human action, that is, as anthropogenic cultural products. Scientific positivism drove the 'quantitative revolution', emphasizing numerical data and statistical methods. This stream survives in approaches to regional science through behavioralism, quantitative modeling, and econometric analysis of abstract 'space'. Reactions against quantitative methods came from phenomenologists and humanists stressing 'place', and seeking a grasp of the lifeworld through experience and consciousness. This raised questions of epistemologies of place rooted in culture, gender, and locality. Alternatively, structuralism and political economy illuminated underlying power relations, especially the roles of land and territory in regime legitimation, capital accumulation, and social differentiation. Post-structuralism diffused analyses of power to realms of language and representations: the aesthetic processes of place making. Space and place could be ideological products and identity strategies of weak and strong alike. Postmodern geographers debate the merits and hazards of throwing away the maps of modernity. The discipline of geography, like other

social sciences, acknowledges its role in empire and tries to be post-colonial and anti-colonial. Yet geography serves geopolitics and the 'colonial present' as much now as ever. Human geographers try to understand world regions such as Japan and East Asia, even as they debate the ontology of regions under globalization. In recent decades David Harvey has called on the field of geography for a more critical engagement with the questions of social justice through the lenses of flexible accumulation and dispossession. Japan has been the subject of all of these projects of geography.

WHAT IS JAPAN?

Though chorography is quite outdated as a pursuit in academic geography, the what and where of Japan are not so simply answered. Facts and figures on Japan's geography in the opening sections of the *Japan Statistical Yearbook* (Statistics Bureau, 2011) show that Hokkaidō, Honshū, Shikoku, and Kyūshū are just the start of Japan's 6,852 islands, 314 of which are inhabited, including Lake Biwa's Okishima (Nihon Ritō Sentaa, 2004). Japan's remote-island territorial claims such as Okinotori-shima and Minami-torishima give Japan extensive claims on the earth's surface

(Akiyama, 1995). Etorofu and Kunashiri in the Northern Territories are each larger than the island of Okinawa. Discussion of territory, islands, and names soon brings us to disputes between Japan and her neighbors concerning the Senkaku Islands, Takeshima, the Sea of Japan, and the Northern Territories that belie the simple 'facts' of geography (Eyre, 1968; Suganuma, 2000). Japan's Ministry of Foreign Affairs gives Japan's positions on nomenclature and sovereignty on its web pages, as do the neighboring nations.

The Geospatial Information Authority of Japan, known until 2010 as the Geographical Survey Institute, draws Japan's basic geodetic map. The Coast Guard's Hydrographic and Oceanographic Department has issued navigational charts since 1871 and still produces Japan's nautical and aeronautical charts. Both these mapping authorities reside within the MLIT, the Ministry of Land, Infrastructure, Transport, and Tourism, the old Ministry of Construction.

Today's national mapping institutions evolved from the regime change of 1868. Cartographers and topographers such as Kawada Takeshi continued from shogunate service into the new Meiji government (Shimazu, 2004). The Geographical Survey Institute began in 1869 as the Geography Section of the Civil Service Ministry, for cadastral mapping and land registration. In 1888 this office became Japan's Imperial Land Survey under the Army. Army maps of the former external territories of Japan have been digitized by Tōhoku University. In 1945 the Imperial Army cartographers became the Geographical Survey Institute. The GSI publishes maps of Japan's islands and cities, such as 1:25,000 topographic maps of Japan in 4,300 sheets.

Japan's century of topographic maps supports detailed analysis of historical land-use change (Himiyama, 1999; Himiyama et al., 2002). Cadastral mapping (*chiseki chōsa*) of Japan continues today, still aiming toward standardization across the prefectures. Japan's Meteorological Agency, dating from 1875, now under the MLIT, maps the ever present effects of earthquakes, tsunami and climate change. The March 2011 earthquake and tsunami have been the central concern of the JMA recently. Mitigating and preventing such human losses is the aim. The JMA ceased its annual forecast of the cherry blossom front in 2010; a bit of magic went out of the world. A dimension of Japan's unstable geography has been the township mergers of recent years, the *Heisei Dai Gappei* (Rausch, 2006). Place names of yesterday are no more. Amalgamation has reduced 3,200 townships ten years ago to 1,700 today. Even Tōkyō changes size according to the definition used in each study (Forstall, et al., 2009).

SCIENTIFIC REPORTS AND EARLY ACADEMIC GEOGRAPHY

Geographical reports about Japan from missionaries, diplomats, and scientists began to reach an eager Europe in the sixteenth century. Publishers printed nineteenth-century accounts of the Japanese islands from Portuguese, Dutch, French, and Russian observers. The Royal Geographical Society in London published the 1861 trip by her majesty's envoy Rutherford Alcock that began 'The empire of Japan has so long been a sealed book'. Alcock described his ascent of Mt Fuji, believed himself the first foreigner to make the climb, and provided a map to inspire others. Geologist Edmund Naumann described Japan's physical geography in the proceedings of the Royal Society. Henry Brunton mapped Japan with Romanized place names (Griffis, 1878; Brunton, 1991: 53–54). Isabella Bird published her 1878 travels as the two-volume *Unbeaten Tracks in Japan* (Bird, 1880; Elliott, 2008). The late nineteenth century brought a stream of physical and human geographies of Japan to distant readers. Scientific societies promoted scholarly and popular geographic knowledge. Academic geography appeared first in continental Europe. Karl Ritter held a chair at the University of Berlin from the 1820s. From 1887 England began to add academic chairs and departments (Scargill, 1976). The USA and Japan followed this trend in subsequent decades.

In Japan the Chinese loan word *chiri* had meant geography for a thousand years. In the Bakumatsu and early Meiji periods geographical knowledge about the world was a growth industry. World knowledge had reached Edo partially via returning castaways (Ninomiya, 1972). Fukuzawa Yukichi and Shiga Shigetaka wrote about regions of the world and calibrated Japan's place in it (Gavin, 2001; Bonnett, 2002; Yonechi, 1999). In the Meiji Period *chiri* also meant earth science. The Tōkyō Chigaku Kyōkai, or the Tōkyō Geographical Society, was founded in 1879 as the first group in Japan (and the first outside the West) to parallel the geographical societies in Russia, Italy, Berlin, and London (Takeuchi, 1980, 2003, 2006). The Tōkyō Geographical Society promoted exploration, including Shirase's expedition to Antarctica in 1910–1912. The society's journal took the English name *Journal of Geography* in 1889. This is the *Chigaku Zasshi*, today a journal of physical geography or geology, but still bearing the English name *Journal of Ge.ography*. The 1899 study group for the historical geography of Japan, the Nihon Rekishi Chiri Kenkyūkai, became the forerunner of the Nihon Rekishi Chiri Gakkai, the national association for academic historical geography in Japan.

ACADEMIC GEOGRAPHY IN JAPAN

Japan's first academic geography department began in 1907 at Kyōto University when the university was ten years old. That year Ogawa Takuji (1870–1941) became the first head of the department. Ogawa had studied geology at Tōkyō University and worked for the Government Survey Bureau in Tōkyō. At Kyōto, Ogawa and Ishibashi Gorō founded the broad-based field of geography. Ogawa eventually moved to geology at Kyōto (and was father of Nobel laureate Yukawa Hideki). Ishibashi became the second head of the geography department.

Kyōto University's third chair of geography was Komaki Saneshige (1898–1990), historical geographer. Komaki was one of the Kyōto geographers providing the intellectual scaffolding of *chiseigaku*, or geopolitics, to Japan's military expansion and war (Takagi, 1998; Shibata, Y., 2006). Takeuchi (2000a) takes stock of geopolitical theorists, their relation to German geopolitics, their publications and influence during and after the war. Though Kearns (2009: 20–21) now says that geopolitics of the German and Japanese varieties were not radically detached from political-geography thinking in Europe and North America, the Allied Occupation purged geographers such as Komaki, Yonekura and Kawanishi from public positions for a number of years. Many returned to other universities, but Kyōto geography functioned without a chair for a time after the war (United States Cultural Science Mission to Japan, 1949). The field of political geography in Japan maintained a long silence about geopolitics. Geographers in the 1950s breathed a new kind of internationalism (Takeuchi, 2000a).

Kyōto remains a strong center for human and historical geography, with geographers in the Faculty of Letters and in the new Graduate School of Human and Environmental Studies. The Human Geographical Society of Japan, or Jinbun Chiri Gakkai, was established in 1948 in Kyōto. Its 1400 members maintain four specialty groups and hold seasonal meetings. Important publications include the serial *Jinbun Chiri/Japanese Journal of Human Geography* and the annual *Chirigaku Bunken Mokuroku/Bibliography of Geographical Research*, issued from 1953 to the present. An annual review essay in the journal *Jinbun Chiri* summarizes the year's content in English (Stradford, 2005). Volume 56(4) in 2004 was the first number of the journal wholly in English. *Jinbun Chiri* reviewed geography across Asia: Singapore, Taiwan, Korea, and Vietnam in 2006 (Kanasaka et al., 2006) and Malaysia, India, and Hong Kong in 2008 (Mizuuchi, 2008). Academic geography in Japan is sometimes said to have its own

geography, with human geography dominant in western Japan in faculties of letters, and physical geography dominant in eastern Japan in science faculties. Though an oversimplification, it is true that Kyōto University leads in human geography.

In eastern Japan geography became an independent department in the Faculty of Science in Tōkyō Imperial University in 1918. Yamasaki Naomasa (1870–1928) was its first chair. Yamasaki trained in geology at Tōkyō University then spent four years from 1898 studying in Europe. He taught in other faculties until he was able to open a distinct Department of Geography in 1918. His research on physical processes and his department's location in the Faculty of Science lent to the focus on physical geography at Tōkyō University. In 1925–26 Yamasaki organized the Nippon Chiri Gakkai/Association of Japanese Geographers and its journal *Chirigaku Hyōron/Geographical Review of Japan*. In the 1950s Tōkyō University added human geography. Today Tōkyō University's Komaba campus is the location of the Jinbun Chirigaku Kyōshitsu, or Human Geography Department, granting undergraduate and graduate degrees. The department's journal is *Komaba Studies in Human Geography/Tōkyō Daigaku Jinbun Chirigaku Kenkyū*.

Tsukuba University (first Tōkyō Higher Normal School then Tōkyō University of Education) opened its Geography Department in 1926. Tsukuba University has the largest Geography Department in Japan today, and Hiroshima University the second largest. Tōhoku University in Sendai has been an important regional geography department for the north-east. With both earth science and human geography foci, Tōhoku geographers have led regional research and publication through the Tōhoku Geographical Association since 1947. *Kikan Chirigaku* is its journal.

The society most central to the wide discipline of geography in Japan today remains the Nihon Chiri Gakkai, Association of Japanese Geographers, established in 1925. The association holds annual spring meetings in the Tōkyō area and fall meetings in outlying prefectures. *The Geographical Review of Japan/Chirigaku Hyōron* added a parallel English series in 1984. Both series of *The Geographical Review of Japan* reside on the J-stage website of Japan's Science and Technology Agency. AJG also publishes the e-journal *GEO*. The association has 19 specialty groups, or *kenkyū guruppu*, focusing on subfields. The *Geographical Review of Japan* publishes periodic surveys of subfields of literature by geographers in Japan. In 2008, Volume 81(5) carried reviews of progress in eleven subfields by geographers in Japan, valuable especially for their English summaries of research in Japanese. In 2013, for the regional conference of the International Geographical Union in Kyōto,

Volume 86(1) contained eleven articles reviewing recent progress in subfields, summarizing much research in Japanese (Yagasaki, 2013). The English language is still a very narrow window on the world (Harris, 2001); geographers in Japan help open the window with these essays.

Japanese geographers are scattered across departments not always bearing the name 'geography'. Recent university reforms have combined geographers into interdisciplinary groupings (Ogawa, 2002). The Association of Japanese Geographers (2011) counts 38 departments named 'geography' and 66 other departments where geographers teach. In 2001 women comprised only 8 percent of the membership of the two main academic societies for geography (Mitsuhashi, 1992; Murata, 2005). Takeuchi (2000b) traces *Modern Japanese Geography: An Intellectual History* in terms of events, ideas, thinkers, and byways of the discipline. Saito and Mizuoka (2009) add further chapters on six important Japanese geographers in *The International Encyclopedia of Human Geography*. Bio-bibliographies published by the International Geographical Union contain summaries of several Japanese scholars, such as Vidalian human-geographer Iizuka Kōji (Okada, 2009).

THE CONTEXT FOR GEOGRAPHY OF JAPAN IN SEVERAL COUNTRIES

In the UK organizations of geographers include The Royal Geographical Society and the Institute of British Geographers, which merged in 1995 into the RGS-IBG. Journals of the RGS-IBG are *Area, The Geographical Journal*, and *Transactions of the Institute of British Geographers*. Counterparts in Scotland are the Royal Scottish Geographical Society and *The Scottish Geographical Journal*. Geographers are also members of the British Association for Japanese Studies, publisher of *Japan Forum*.

Geographers in the UK count early geographers of Asia such as Dudley Stamp (1929) among those who shaped the academic discipline. Yet by 1993, when John Sargent looked for geographers of Japan in the UK, he could find very few. Sargent joined SOAS (The School of Oriental and African Studies, University of London) in 1966 and Richard Wiltshire did so in 1979 (Sargent, 1993). These two geographers of Japan at SOAS were the core of the field when Sargent wrote in 1993. John Sargent attended the founding conference of the European Association for Japanese Studies in April 1973, presenting research on Prime Minister Tanaka's famous plan for his archipelago (Sargent, 1975). SOAS hosted the first Anglo-Japanese geographical seminar across three locales in 1988: SOAS, Sheffield, and Durham (Sargent and Wiltshire, 1989). Sargent and Wiltshire (1993) edited the papers into a conference volume, *Geographical Studies and Japan*. A third of the papers in the volume dealt with Japan. Urban geographer Paul Waley, with a background in Japanese language and area studies, joined University of Leeds' 48 geographers to complement institutional strength in East Asian studies.

Many geographers in Australia and New Zealand have broad Pacific Rim interests. *Geographical Research*, the journal of the Institute of Australian Geographers, published recent articles on land use in Kamakura (Iwata and Oguchi, 2009) and on knowledge about indigenous people in Japan (Nakamura, 2010). *Japanese Studies* is the journal of the Japanese Studies Association of Australia. New Zealand has launched leading scholars of Asia such as Terry McGee (Watters et al., 1997; McGee and Edgington, 2004; Edgington, 2007). The Geography Department at the University of Victoria, Wellington, is the home of the journal *Asia Pacific Viewpoint*.

The Japan Society for New Zealand Studies includes several Kansai-based geographers such as George Ohshima (1991) and Yukiko Numata Bedford. The group published the *Japanese Encyclopedia of New Zealand* in 2007 (Aoyagi et al., 2007). The society has alternated meetings between Japan and New Zealand, and has published the *Journal of New Zealand Studies* in Japan for twenty years.

Dutch studies of Japan, along with those of the Portuguese, comprise arguably the oldest institutional study outside Asia, notably at the University of Leiden, founded 1575. Academic geography is strong today at the universities of Utrecht, Amsterdam, Groningen, and Nijmegen (Pellenbarg and Van Steen, 2009). The Royal Dutch Geographical Society publishes two academic series. Their *Tijdschrift voor economische en sociale geografie (Journal of economic and social geography)* carries research related to Japan by Dutch and international geographers in the English language.

Sweden is home to geography at universities such as Uppsala, Lund, Stockholm, and Gothenburg (or Göteborg). The journal of the Swedish Society for Anthropology and Geography is *Geografiska Annaler, Series B, Human Geography* (and *Series A, Physical Geography*). A 1921 paper reported climate records at Lake Suwa; several subsequent papers have addressed Japan. Sweden lists new dissertations on www.dissertations.se. French social science on Japan includes geographers associated with the Maison Franco-Japonaise, or *Nichi-Futsu Kaikan*, in Tōkyō, and the Institut français du Japon in several cities (Aveline, 2008).

The *Boletín* of Spain's royal geographical society is a window into the Asia-Pacific expertise of geographers in Europe and Latin America.

German-language scholars from several countries have researched Japan from the field of geography. Shulman's (1970) bibliography lists several nineteenth- and early-twentieth-century German-language dissertations on Japan and the Ryūkyūs. Professor J.J. Rein (1884) traveled for the Prussian government in 1874–75 to report on Japanese development, duly recording observations of 'Hondo, Shikoku, Kiushiu, and Amakusa'. Rein was teaching in Frankfurt when dispatched to Japan and became Professor of Geography at Marburg upon his return. Karl Haushofer spent 1909–1910 in Japan as an army officer. He later wrote his dissertation at the University of Munich on the geopolitics of the Pacific Ocean and a text on Japan.

German geographers of Japan have enjoyed the support of two institutions. First is the Japanese-German Geographical Conference, *Nichi-Doku Chiri Gakkai*, held ten times since 1969. Conference volumes have included Flüchter (1995) and Feldhoff et al. (2005). The tenth meeting took place at Ōsaka City University and Wakayama in March 2010 on the theme 'Making New Cultural Landscapes in the Era of Growing Disparities'. The *Nichi-Doku* geographers' meetings have been a venue of sustained research exchange. The Deutsches Institut für Japanstudien, or DIJ, in Tōkyō is the second. The DIJ Tōkyō staff has included geographers of Japan working in comparative demography, regional economies, and social conditions.

Two recent reviews of German geographical studies of Japan discuss works in German and English. Winfried Flüchter (2000) discusses writers of past centuries and twentieth-century geographers of Japan in Germany. He includes geographers active at the time of his writing, their institutional settings, their Japanese language skills, and their contributions to subthemes. Ralph Lützeler (2008a) wrote the second useful review of German-language geographies of Japan. Lützeler mentions early academic figures and surveys work from 1962 in three periods: high-growth years and urbanization, internationalized Japan with socio-economic challenges similar to Europe's, and, from 2005, the reality of population decline. Lützeler also notes the relevance of Netherlands-born sociologist Saskia Sassen (1991) and her global-city framework in his own social analysis of Tōkyō (Lützeler, 2011).

Geography is a broadly established discipline in Canada, Australia, and New Zealand as a legacy of the curriculum in the 'British System'. The Canadian Association of Geographers is the main professional organization, publishing *The Canadian Geographer*. The Geographies of Asia Study Group of the CAG organizes papers at each annual meeting, as in Newfoundland in 2013.

Geographers with Japan interests also join the Japan Studies Association of Canada, an organization of 25 years' standing. Geographers have edited and published the proceedings of this meeting (Millward and Morrison, 1997; Bowles and Woods, 2000). The University of British Columbia has a strong history of Asian studies, Japan studies, and geography. The journal *Pacific Affairs*, a legacy of the Institute of Pacific Relations, is edited at UBC.

Several international professional associations unite geographers inside and outside Japan. The International Geographical Union, based in Rome, consists of country-level organizations and individual members. Asian, North American, and European members actively promote the IGU's research exchanges and publications. IGU Commission meetings produce edited volumes of Asia-Pacific research, as in Tsukuba in 1995 (Sasaki et al., 1996) and in Vancouver in 2003 (LeHeron and Harrington, 2005). IGU meetings also result in Japan-focused papers in comparative volumes (Aoyama, 2000a). Japan hosted a 2013 Regional IGU conference in Kyōto in August 2013, chaired by Ishikawa Yoshitaka of Kyōto University.

A newer association is EARCAG, the East Asia Regional Conference on Alternative Geographies, formed in the 1990s by participants in the International Critical Geography Group. EARCAG's first meeting was in Taegu in 1999, with subsequent meetings in Hong Kong, Ōsaka, Taipei, Seoul, and Malaysia. As the name implies, alternative or critical approaches are the emphasis. Asia is both the focus and the home base of this new group. Collaboration among critical geographers resulted in a critical look at East Asia by Tang and Mizuoka (2010).

Another new research venue has been the Global Conference on Economic Geography, held first in Singapore in 2000, second in Beijing in 2007, and third in Seoul in 2011. Hundreds of economic geographers have come to these meetings, including about 25 participants from Japan or reporting about Japan. The leadership of these meetings has emerged from geographers in Asia and of Asia. The Asian location of the three global meetings is significant. Longstanding pan-Asian journals, such as *Asian Geographer* from Hong Kong and the *Singapore Journal of Tropical Geography* from the National University of Singapore, provide further region-wide communications.

US GEOGRAPHERS OF JAPAN FROM THE EARLY TWENTIETH CENTURY

In the USA today a total of 230 universities offer geography degrees: 86 the undergraduate degree only, 72 up to the master's degree, and 72 through the PhD degree. In Canada 25 universities offer doctoral degrees in geography (Association of American Geographers, 2011). The Association of American Geographers has over 10,000 members. President of the AAG in 2011 was Audrey Kobayashi (Queens University, Ontario), a geographer of Japan and the Japanese diaspora.

Most geographers with Japan interests belong to the AAG Asian Geography Specialty Group. *The Bulletin of Asian Geography* has been the newsletter of the AGSG for 35 years. In 2014 the editor is Japan-geographer Todd Stradford at the University of Wisconsin, Platteville. The AAG organizes *Geography in America* volumes about once per decade, reviewing progress in the sub-discipline of Asian geography (Shrestha et al., 2003). Roughly 50 to 60 geographers in US and Canadian universities have research experience in Japan.

The Asian Geography Specialty Group sponsors panels on all parts of Asia at the annual meetings of the AAG. International colleagues add to reports of new research at the AAG. The 2014 AAG meeting in Tampa, Florida, included six panels on the Fukushima disaster, organized by Daisaku Yamamoto (Colgate) and Fujimoto Noritsugu (Fukushima University). Another panel in Tampa addressed Japanese Cities in their Global Context under organizers David Edgington and Carola Hein, following from their two panels on the same theme at the 2013 AAG meeting in Los Angeles. Two of the 2013 papers addressed the damage done by the 2011 Tōhoku tsunami. A third panel in Los Angeles, organized by Karl Hoarau, addressed the Fukushima disaster. The 2012 meeting in New York offered 34 papers on Japan, including five panels on Japanese Cities in Global Networks, organized by Carola Hein, Paul Waley and Cary Karacas. The New York AAG papers about Japan were more international and interdisciplinary than ever. At the 2011 AAG meeting in Seattle a special session examined the effects of the March 11 tsunami and earthquake.

The American Geographical Society was born in 1851, a decade of great world interest in Japan. The first volume of the society's journal lists Townsend Harris, US Consul in Hakodate, Japan, as a corresponding member (American Geographical and Statistical Society, 1859). Japanese ambassadors of the Iwakura Embassy visited a meeting of the society in New York on 16 April 1872. Associate Justice E. S. Hiraka of Yeddo thanked the society in English (American Geographical Society of New York, 1873: 40–41).

American geography grew as a subject for teachers of higher and commercial schools, with journals now associated with undergraduate education. The *Journal of Geography*, for example, carried articles about Japan by Whitbeck (1911)

on teaching about Asia, Lacy (1917) on Nagasaki's cheap coal for steamers, and Cowen (1918) on Japan's silk for American consumers. The Association of American Geographers, today's premier academic organization, dates from 1904. One of the first articles on Japan in its *Annals* was by a commercial-high-school teacher who observed Japan's physical geography en route from India (Cushing, 1913).

An early American academic geographer to observe Japan was Ellen Churchill Semple, from the University of Chicago. Semple gained wide entrée through her Vassar classmate Yamakawa Sutematsu, wife of War Minister Ōyama Iwao. Semple (1912) attributed Japanese agricultural forms to environment, landforms, and population, based on her field observations. She evaluated Japanese settlement planning in the expanding empire (Semple, 1913). Semple's colleague at Chicago, Wellington D. Jones, visited Hokkaidō in July 1916, guided by geographer Tanakadate Hidezō of Tōhoku Imperial University in Sendai (Jones, 1921).

Geographers also tried to analyze Japan's spatial patterns from afar. Mark Jefferson, Harvard Geography MA and influential teacher at Michigan State, mapped population densities across the prefectures and colonies using 1913 population data from Tōkyō University geographer N. Yamasaki (Jefferson, 1916). John Wesley Coulter, ultimately a geographer of the Pacific, published a population map of Japan in 1926, the year of his PhD from Chicago. He also drew his dot map from 1913 data, using Japanese topographic maps and advice from Professor Wellington Jones (Coulter, 1926). The maps in these publications began to illustrate the concentration of Japan's population in three urban areas.

In the 1920s and 1930s Japan commanded more attention from several American geographers. The Orchards, Trewartha, Hall, and Davis broke new ground. None of these had done dissertation research on Japan, none was a scholar of the language, but all extended to Japan their interests in regional economies. These were notable as early studies of rural production, cities, population, and industries. John E. Orchard, a 1923 Harvard PhD in the economics of coal, taught in the geography department in the Columbia School of Business. Orchard and his political-scientist wife Dorothy surveyed manufacturing in Japan in 1926 and published *Japan's Economic Position* in 1930, a work strong on the small-scale producers of Japan. Orchard wrote on questions of population and economic development in Japan (Orchard, 1928, 1929) and went on to study such questions in China and India. When elected Honorary President of the Association of American Geographers, Orchard foresaw the 'world implications' of industrialization in Japan, China, and India (Orchard, 1960).

Glenn Trewartha went to Harvard for his Geography MA then returned to Wisconsin to complete his PhD in 1925. As a new member of the Wisconsin faculty, he was induced by the first Guggenheim Fellowships to spend a post-doctoral year in Japan, with a short trip to China, in 1926–27. During his year in Japan he traveled widely and collected maps, relying on interpreters to interview and understand. This was the first of three trips to Japan pre-war. His findings are local studies of Japan: Shizuoka (1928), tea (1929), Iwaki in Aomori (1930a), and Suwa in Nagano (1930b). A Manchuria article (Murakoshi and Trewartha, 1930) shows Trewartha's interest in Japanese economic influence along the South Manchurian Railroad. He analyzed cities next (1934b). He compiled these findings from the 1920s and 30s into his first book on Japan, *A Reconnaissance Geography of Japan* (Trewartha, 1934a), which required a careful physical map of Japan (Trewartha, 1934c).

A second key geographer was Robert B. Hall at the University of Michigan, active as a scholar, founder of interdisciplinary area studies, and supervisor of a number of mid-century dissertations on Japan. Hall's dissertation was on the landscape of Haiti. He wrote about Quelpart Island, Jeju or Cheju-do, sight unseen (Hall, 1926). For postdoctoral research, Hall made his first trip to Japan in 1929 with Social Science Research Council (SSRC) funding (Hall, 1931: 93). Hall's pre-war papers covered Manchuria (1930), rural settlements in four regions of Japan (1931), landforms (Hall and Watanabe, 1932), the Nara basin (1932), and cities (1934a, 1934b). He published a three-part treatise on Japan's agriculture across the empire in *Economic Geography* (1934, 1935a, 1935b). He walked the old and new Tōkaidō road with Watanabe Akira (Eyre, 1994), recording its stations, inns, rivers, economies, and industrial areas (Hall, 1937). Hall encouraged Michigan students to visit Japan and took some graduate students with him to Japan in the 1930s. Joseph A. Russell studied tea production in Ogura Mura near Kyōto (Russell, 1940), though his 1937 PhD was not on Japan. Russell became an economic geographer at Syracuse and later at Illinois.

Also studying Japan in the 1930s was geographer Darrell Haug Davis. Davis was a Michigan PhD who went on to establish the University of Minnesota Geography Department in 1925. At Minnesota Davis won university funds to travel to Japan in 1932. His three publications in 1934 report his observations of Hokkaidō agriculture and settlement (Davis, 1934a, 1934b, 1934c). Despite this surge of attention in Japan, there was yet no dissertation on Japan; that would not

happen until the late 1940s. In 1921 Stanislaus Novakovsky wrote his Yale geography dissertation on the climate of the Russian Far East. Clyde Cooper wrote his 1927 Clark dissertation on Luzon and later taught at Ohio University. Floy Hurlbut wrote her Nebraska dissertation on China in 1930 and spent her career at Ball State. George Cressey wrote his Clark dissertation on China in 1931 and taught at Syracuse. Shannon McCune wrote his dissertation at Clark in 1939 on the climate of Korea (McCune, 1939, 1941). These were the first US geography dissertations on East Asia.

The 1940s brought catastrophic world war that diverted careers into intelligence about and occupation of Japan (Barnes and Crampton, 2011). US geographers of Japan served government roles during this decade, much more directly involved in war efforts than Japanese counterparts (United States Cultural Science Mission to Japan, 1949: 58). Geographers mapped Japanese urban bombing targets for the OSS, the War Department, and the Army Map Service (Fedman and Karacas, 2012). The US National Archives' records of the Office of Strategic Services (1942–1945) lists eight geographers mentioned in this review as employed by the OSS: Ackerman, Trewartha, Bowers, Harris, Russell, Kiss, Titiev, and R.B Hall, Junior (Office of Strategic Services Personnel Files, 2011). Trewartha, a veteran of World War I, was not in military service in the 1940s but advised the OSS (Smith, N., 2003). At the start of the Pacific War the Department of the Navy came to borrow his maps of Japan, and kept them in Washington for the duration (Trewartha, 1982). Trewartha remained on the Wisconsin campus training military climatologists. He greatly revised his book under the new title *Japan: A Physical, Cultural, and Regional Geography* (Trewartha, 1945). The 1945 print run was so small the press could not fill a large order from the Supreme Commander for the Allied Powers (SCAP). Trewartha wrote an overview of geography in Japan for SCAP (1949) and served on the five-member Cultural Science Mission, *Jimbun Kagaku Komon Dan*, to advise SCAP on university policy in Japan (United States Cultural Science Mission to Japan, 1949). This panel surveyed Japanese humanities and social sciences and recommended greater support for social research on contemporary needs. Trewartha's teammate Edwin O. Reischauer gossiped that Trewartha was a 'stuffed shirt' who 'did not enter Horyuji when we finally got there but wandered off to take pictures of Japanese agriculture' (Packard, 2010: 90). The team met with MacArthur to present their findings but MacArthur did all the talking. The team met the Emperor of Japan, who remarked that Trewartha had seen more of Japan than he had (Trewartha, 1982). Trewartha weighed postwar agrarian land questions (1949a, 1949b 1950).

He abandoned plans to study Chinese cities due to civil war there (Trewartha, 1952). He taught climatology, population, and Japan for the rest of his career at Wisconsin. He was 1953 president of the Association of American Geographers. His third revision of *Japan, A Geography* (1965) was his last.

Robert B. Hall's trajectory in geography and Japanese studies also detoured during the war. Hall was in South America studying Japanese settlements in late 1941 as war broke out (Titiev, 1951). During the war Hall directed the Pacific Coast Office of the Office of Strategic Services then worked in China and Burma (University of Michigan Faculty History Project, 2011a). The US State Department copied Hall's volumes of the Japanese census as the only set they could find during the war (Harris, 1997: 253–4). When Hall returned to academic functions two of his Michigan graduate students were able to finish their dissertations about Japan, the first two in US geography. Douglas Crary completed a 1947 dissertation on Iga-no-kuni from pre-war fieldwork conducted in the Tōkaidō Region with Hall. Crary became a long-time member of the Michigan geography faculty. When Crary married Hall's wife's sister Crary and Hall became brothers-in-law into the bargain (Eyre, 1994).

Curtis Manchester, who had studied in Japan and Manchuria in the late 1930s, also finished his Michigan dissertation in 1947, on Edo-period highway checkpoints, or *sekisho*. Manchester went to the Geography Department at the University of Hawaii where he taught Japan for many years (Manchester, 1947, 1958, 1962). Manchester supervised the Michigan Okayama field station at times, and R.B. Hall was a frequent visitor in the Hawaii Geography Department. Two more Michigan geography doctoral candidates, Neal and Rohma (Leverton) Bowers, spent 1947–48 on Saipan studying the transition in the Northern Mariana Islands post-Japanese Mandate and post-warfare (Bowers, 1950). Neal and Rohma joined Manchester in teaching geography at Hawaii. One more dissertation about Japan was completed in the late 1940s at University of Chicago, Norton Ginsburg's (1949a) research into pre-war Japanese trade and shipping.

Michigan and other universities saw an influx of individuals with interests in Japan, Japanese language skills from armed-services language schools, experience in research for agencies like the OSS, and the GI Bill for education. The postwar Japanese academic boom extended to geography. The Association of American Geographers found that 48 of its members had 'first-hand experience' in Japan (Association of American Geographers, 1949). The AAG formed a Committee on Asian Studies, chaired first by

Shannon McCune (McCune, 1950). The AAG and the Far Eastern Association, forerunner of the Association for Asian Studies, held a joint meeting in Cleveland in April 1953 (Trewartha, 1953). The Michigan geography department developed faculty who knew Japan. George Kish (né Kiss) earned a 1945 Michigan Geography PhD with a dissertation on the Danube Basin then, as a faculty member at Michigan, took up the history of Japanese cartography (Kiss, 1947; Kish, 1949, 1951, 1966).

To institutionalize this wide focus on Japan at Michigan R.B. Hall envisioned an interdisciplinary Area Studies center and a field station focused on Japan. Hall founded Michigan's Center for Japanese Studies in 1947. He parlayed his position on the SSRC into advising the Carnegie Foundation on how America should know Asia better. Hall surveyed major universities in 1946 and found only six with graduate programs in study areas relating to China or Japan (Hall, 1947). The Carnegie Foundation agreed to fund field stations in several countries and R.B. Hall won the field station for Japan for the University of Michigan. Hall located this in Okayama City and administered the project at Michigan from 1950 to 1955.

The University of Michigan's field station in Okayama was the first non-military group allowed into occupied Japan. As Japan had no offices abroad in those years, Michigan had to get permission to work in Japan from SCAP. SCAP itself had employed a number of academics as analysts, such as geographer Edward Ackerman (1949, 1953) on natural resources, geographer Ada Espenshade (1947, 1949) on fisheries, and rural sociologist Arthur F. Raper (1950) on land reform. These SCAP functions were wrapped up before the Michigan scholars arrived and there was no contact between the research groups (Eyre, 1994).

The first entourage of Michigan scholars arrived in Tōkyō by ship and had a meeting with MacArthur. In Okayama research and teaching proceeded through a rotation of faculty and students from Michigan, with cooperative work on one large joint research project, and individual research projects toward degrees. While the center received core funding from Carnegie, each student was an SSRC-fellowship recipient who contributed funds to food and lodging at the Okayama Center (Pitts, 1992). Geographer John Doug Eyre was the first of the geography graduate students to go in this initial group. With Beardsley, Eyre chose Niike as the site of the group study, the 'village' of the book *Village Japan* (Beardsley et al., 1959). Eyre conducted his own research for his dissertation on coastal salt production (1950, 1951, 1952b). After his Michigan degree Eyre went to the University of Washington then spent a long career at the University of North Carolina. His publications document his return to Japan in 1953 under Ford Foundation support and many subsequent periods of fieldwork in Japan over the decades. His research followed Japan's rural production (Eyre, 1952a, 1955a, 1955b, 1956a, 1956b, 1959, 1962a, 1962b). Then Eyre saw industrialization in the 1960s (1963a, 1963b, 1964, 1965, 1970) and later wrote on the metropolitan giant of Nagoya (1982).

The second Michigan geography PhD student rotating to the Okayama Field Station in Japan was Forrest R. 'Woody' Pitts. He had written his MA thesis on Mt Fuji in Ann Arbor. His doctoral fieldwork in towns such as Kawaoka, Kagawa Prefecture, comprised his 1955 dissertation on land fertility in four prefectures. This work was the basis for Pitts' views of rural prosperity (Pitts, 1964). Among the sites he compared Kagawa rice farmers got the highest yields, an average of 2.6 *koku* per *tan*, the richer farmers using fertilizers. Pitts resurveyed some of his field sites in the 1980s (Pitts, 1985). Pitts joined an Okinawan survey, reported as *Postwar Okinawa* (Pitts et al., 1955). He wrote a social-studies textbook about Japan (1960), taught at the University of Oregon, and joined rural-development projects in Korea. Later he went to the University of Hawaii, where he was active in Korean studies, Japanese studies, and geography (Pitts, 2002).

The third Michigan geography graduate student rotating to Okayama was David Kornhauser, specialist in urban geography. Kornhauser's 1955 dissertation traced the rise of Japan's cities. Throughout his career at the University of Hawaii he taught Geography of Japan. His contributions in the urban geography of Japan grew out of his dissertation into two books and one study of city densities (1976, 1982, 1989). Kornhauser also published bibliographic works useful to geographers (1979, 1984).

Though the Okayama Field Station closed in 1955, Michigan's Center for Japanese Studies still makes publications of that era available on the web (University of Michigan, 2011b). Important work on the geography of Japan continued to come from the Michigan geography department after the field station closed. George Kakiuchi completed his dissertation on fruit production in Okayama, and went to the University of Washington to spend a career teaching geography (Kakiuchi, 1958, 1960, 1962; Kakiuchi and Murakami, 1961). Robert B. Hall's son and namesake, Robert B. Hall, Junior, became an economic geographer in his own right, heralding the theme of his generation with studies of Japanese industrialization (Hall, Jr., 1958, 1963). Hall, Junior, taught for many years at the University of Rochester, held two Fulbright grants to Japan, and headed Rochester's new East Asian Language and Area Center in 1967 (University of

Rochester Library, 2011). Michigan-trained geographers of Japan filled faculty posts around the nation and remained in those jobs into the 1980s. Robert B. Hall, Senior, retired from Michigan to head the Tōkyō office of the Asia Foundation late in his career. The Tōkyō Geographical Society and the Japanese government awarded him distinctions for his work.

Strong ties between Michigan geographers and Japanese geographers lasted long after the Okayama Field Station closed. Watanabe Akira, who had helped R.B. Hall in his earliest studies, became head of Japan's Geographical Survey Institute and later a professor at Ochanomizu University. Ishida Hiroshi, who assisted the Okayama station, built a career at Hiroshima University dedicated to international research and exchange (Ishida, 1980; Ishida, et al., 1982). Ishida received an American Geographical Society medal in 1989. The Michigan geography department hosted Japanese geographers, including Noh Toshio from Tōhoku University. Hall and Noh's bibliographic guide (1956, 1970) is still useful for its handwritten *kanji* and Romanizations for over 1200 Japanese works. Noh later co-authored geography textbooks about Japan in Teikoku Shoin's English-language series (Noh and Gordon, 1974; Noh and Kimura, 1983, 1989).

The post-SCAP US administration of Okinawa under the United States Civil Administration of the Ryūkyūs (USCAR) until 1972 meant many years of attention from US geographers. Clarence Glacken on the Berkeley geography faculty produced *Studies of Okinawan Village Life* for the Pacific Science Board of the National Research Council, National Academy of Sciences (Glacken, 1953). This became *The Great Loochoo: A Study of Okinawan Village Life* (Glacken, 1955). Glacken taught a course on Japan's geography at Berkeley for some years thereafter. Geographer Shannon McCune's upbringing in Korea and his Clark dissertation (1939) made him a lifelong scholar of Korea (McCune, 1941, 1949, 1956, 1966), but he also wrote about Japan (Smith et al., 1943). In wartime he worked in the US Foreign Economic Administration, analyzing Japan's diminishing economic lifelines (McCune, 1989). McCune became civil administrator for the US government of Okinawa from 1962 to 1964. His USCAR years and later academic research at the University of Florida yielded many studies of the Ryūkyū Islands (McCune, 1970, 1975a, 1975b, 1984).

Norton S. Ginsburg came through three geography degrees at Chicago, an old and strong department. He worked in the Army Map Service and the US Naval Reserve in the 1940s, studied Japanese at the Naval Language School in Boulder, Colorado (Harris, 1997), and worked in the State Department's Office of Research and Intelligence

(Ginsburg, 1950). Ginsburg wrote his 1949 dissertation on pre-war Japanese shipping and took an early interest in transportation (Ginsburg, 1949a, 1949b). He joined the geography faculty at Chicago in 1951, chaired the department from 1978 to 1985, and researched every part of Asia. He led both the Association of American Geographers and the Association for Asian Studies. After retirement from Chicago in 1986 he served at the East-West Center in Honolulu for five years. Ginsburg took the broad view of comparative Asian urbanism and land-use change over recent decades (Ginsburg, 1990; Ginsburg et al., 1991).

Three other geographers with interests in Japan finished dissertations in the 1950s. Midori Nishi focused on Japanese settlement in North and South America and aspects of the cultural geography of Japan. Nishi was removed from her undergraduate studies at University of California Los Angeles to internment with her family at Manzanar in 1942. She managed to finish her BA in the Midwest, her geography MA at Clark in 1946, and her geography PhD at the University of Washington in 1955. Her dissertation and early publications treated Japanese immigrants in Los Angeles and Latin America (Nishi, 1955, 1958, 1962; Nishi and Kim, 1964; Miyares et al., 2000). Nishi studied cultural geographies within Japan, notably rural house types (Nishi, 1967). Her father's relatives in Wakayama Prefecture aided her Japan fieldwork (Monk, 2011; Bedford, 2011). Nishi appraised Japanese economic development in Micronesia using National Diet Library archives (1968). Nishi taught at California State College at Los Angeles, now California State University Los Angeles, and pioneered East Asian Studies there.

Robert L. Anstey completed his geography PhD at the University of Maryland in 1957 with research on agricultural land use in Kumamoto Prefecture, comparing uplands and lowlands. Masaharu George Inaba completed his geography PhD at Columbia in 1959 with research on Japan's industrialization (Inaba, 1959). Inaba taught geography at Hofstra from 1960 to 1991 and chaired the department. He took Adelphi-Hofstra students to Japan for summer study at Sophia University in the 1960s, and introduced his students to Japanese language (Adelphi Goes Japanese, 1969; Adelphi Appoints New Supervisor for Japan Program, 1969).

Geographers with Japan experience during the 1940s but with dissertations unrelated to Japan sometimes turned back to Japan in later decades. Such was John H. Thompson, economic geographer, a 1949 PhD from the University of Washington who taught at Syracuse University from 1949 to 1981. Thompson had studied Japanese at the Navy Language School at Boulder, Colorado, and worked in naval intelligence during the war (University of Colorado

at Boulder Library, 2009). In 1954 he received Fulbright support for a year and a half at Kōbe University. Thompson researched the economy of western Japan, watching urbanization displace agriculture on the Ōsaka Plain, and the spread of industrialization in Kyūshū (Thompson, 1957, 1959; Thompson and Miyazaki, 1959).

The pace of postwar research on Japan was positive: geographers with research experience in Japan were filling posts in universities, colleges, and government. Japan's booming economic significance in the past two decades commanded wide attention. Geography departments strengthened their Japan offerings inside and outside departments through institutional cooperation with their universities' Japan-studies centers. Several US universities got federally funded Title VI National Resource Centers for East Asia and FLAS fellowships for language study, relying on geography courses to teach contemporary Japan. States have advanced local goals in business, technologies, or arts relating to Japan. The University of Kentucky deliberately grew its Japan studies offerings in 1988 when Toyota began producing autos in the state. Support from the Japanese government through fellowships from the *Monbukagakushō* (Ministry of Education, Culture, Sports, Science and Technology), the Japan Foundation, and the Japan Society for the Promotion of Science also encouraged geography graduate students.

The good news was mitigated, however, by a background sense of crisis in the discipline. A basic problem for geographers of Japan was that geography departments themselves were being eliminated from US universities from the 1940s through the 1980s. The future of the field was in some doubt. Harvard closed Geography in 1948, Edward Ackerman of the SCAP natural-resources study one of the casualties. Stanford eliminated Geography. Michigan itself, home of R.B. Hall and many Michigan geographers of Japan, closed its department in 1982. The University of Chicago closed its geography department in 1986, under the decision of Dean Edward Laumann who had also closed Michigan's department (Barnes, 2004). Northwestern closed geography in the 1980s and closed regional science in 1993. Columbia closed its geography department in 1986 (De Bres, 1989). The Ivy League schools all had geography in the period 1900–1920, but only Dartmouth retains its geography program today, an undergraduate degree. Many US universities with outstanding programs in Japanese studies are no longer places one can pursue any degree in geography. This did some damage, but it was by no means the end of advanced study or graduate degrees focusing on Japan from the discipline of geography. Dissertations about Japan in North American geography departments in the 1980s numbered about a dozen, continuing to view Japan and Japanese in the wider world. About half of the dissertations had a field-research component within Japan, yet all were arguably about Japan in the broadest perspective.

European examples of geography-department closure could also be seen. The decision of SOAS to close its geography department in 2001 subtracted one more university from the list of schools offering geography degrees alongside Japanese language, social sciences and humanities. Geography had been one of the 15 departments of SOAS. Its faculty and students merged into the geography department of King's College London, a sister institution under University College London. Thus Richard Wiltshire, originally in SOAS Geography, is now on the staff of King's College London.

CONTRIBUTIONS BY GEOGRAPHERS TO SUB-FIELDS

For the purposes of teaching about Japan, some research has addressed pedagogy (Marchetti, 1993; Taylor, 2009, 2011). Textbooks include Noh and Kimura (1983, 1989), MacDonald (1985), Karan and Gilbreath (2005), Weightman (2011), and Yagasaki (2002). Regional geographers teach Japan broadly and also contribute research in distinct subfields.

Environment 1: Physical Geography

Early twentieth-century environmental determinism, or the attribution of social characteristics to landforms and climate, gave way to a view of the earth as everywhere modified by human action and an approach to places through the lens of human-environment interaction. The destructive forces of nature appear in the earliest geographical journals, such the 1891 Nobi earthquake in *The Geographical Journal* (Koto, 1894). Tsunami science has evolved through the decades since John Milne (1896) described Japan's 'great sea-waves'. Though geography departed from geology long ago, physical geographers have continued to contribute to understandings of the physical systems around Japan. John Kimura wrote an MA with Trewartha in 1956 on climatology then did doctoral studies at Tōkyō Metropolitan University on Japan's fall rainy season (Kimura, 1966). Michael Grossman (2003) researched flooding on the Arakawa. Past earthquakes and sea levels in Hokkaidō were analyzed by Thomson (2009).

Natural and artificial processes erode Japanese islands while humans armor coastlines with concrete (Walker and Mossa, 1986; Walker, 2012). In Japan both sides of the human-environment equation are formidable shapers.

Environment 2: Hazards and Disaster-risk Reduction

Tsunami risk and preparedness in Tōhoku and Hawaii was the theme of Morgan (1978, 1979). Cultural attitudes and behavior toward earthquake risk were compared in Yokohama and Los Angeles by Palm (1998). Kōbe's 1995 earthquake spurred a decade of discussion of earthquake vulnerability in Japanese cities (Uitto, 1998; Takahashi, 1998; Takahashi and Uitto, 2004; Wisner and Uitto, 2009). Investigators offered lessons from the Kōbe earthquake (Harada, 2000), including the ways we should think about earthquake risk in Japan's urban structure (Flüchter, 2003). Tanaka Kazuko of Kyōto University (2005) showed that specific education makes a great difference in earthquake preparedness. The Kōbe earthquake was also a time to gauge social responses (Childs, 2008). It was the topic of the UBC planning dissertation by Yasui Etsuko (2007) on earthquake recovery, and the Sheffield work of Neil Evans. Great local differences were seen in neighborhood power under national planners in *machizukuri, or town planning* (Evans, 2001, 2002). Edgington (2010) tells the story of the planning response to the 1995 Kōbe earthquake in *Reconstructing Kobe: The Geography of Crisis and Opportunity*.

The 2004 Indian Ocean tsunami drew comparative work citing the exemplary tsunami preparations in Tarō, part of Iwate's Miyako City (Yamazaki and Yamazaki, 2011). Sadly, just as this was published, Tarō's high sea wall was overswept by the tsunami of March 11, 2011. The March 2011 earthquake and tsunami have been the focus of geographers of all ilks. Tōhoku geographers came to the fore with research and activities addressing the March 2011 disasters. Online reports by Professors Sugiura, Sakaida, Takano, Miyahara, Hino, Ueda, Isoda, Murayama, Sekine, Higaki, Tsuchiya, Tsushima, Suzuki, Miyazawa, Abe, Oda, Hidaka, Nakamura, Iwafune, and Iwahana show geographers responding to the immediate emergency (Tōhoku Geographical Association, 2011). A 2012 symposium of 25 speakers at J. F. Oberlin University in Machida addressed The 2011 Japanese Tsunami: Disaster, Response, and Recovery. Organizers were Suganuma Unryū of J. F. Oberlin University and P.P. Karan of the University of Kentucky, with support from The Association of Japanese Geographers.

Environment 3: Pollution Abatement and Conservation Movements

In the mid 1970s geographers at SOAS were attuned to the environmental crises accompanying Japan's industrial success (Fisher and Sargent, 1975). Japan's islands come into focus in environmental studies of economic practices. Reforestation campaigns began in the 1950s (Nakashima, 2010). Sugimura Ken (1987) researched conservation on the Amami Ōshima islands south-west of Kyūshū and measured the implications to wildlife of forest clearing under logging subsidies (Sugimura, 1988; Sugimura et al., 2003). The growth of nature-centered conservation is seen in Cusick's (2003) study of protections for Yakushima, and studies of the Ogasawara Islands (Guo, 2009; Guo and McCormack, 2001). A doctoral thesis on the development fate of Inland Sea islands led Philippe Pelletier at Lumière-Lyon 2 University to see Japan's environment in the broadest context of the contemporary political economy of Asia (Pelletier, 1997, 2004, 2007, 2008, 2011). The environment is an arena of struggle in local controversies, many of which end badly for the cause of conservation (Karan and Suganuma, 2008). Preserving wetlands from industrialization is still an uphill battle (Ikeguchi and Okamoto, 2008; Yamazaki and Yamazaki, 2008). Okinawa's environment is subject to military designs and grassroots movements (Taylor, 2000, 2001, 2002, 2007, 2008). Environmental activists themselves are one focus of analysis (Mason, 1999). The question of the location of civil society and its relation to the state becomes central to the analysis of river-conservation activists (Waley, 2005b).

Environment 4: Global Environment and Climate Change

Japan's global environmental policies and resource practices invited doubts about equity and sustainability (Taylor, 1999; Seo and Taylor, 2003). In the arena of environmental practices to reduce greenhouse-gas emissions a Mie Prefecture study shows mixed progress (Puppim de Oliveira, 2011). Kusaka (2008) notes that Tōkyō's urban heat-island effect is now calculated into local weather maps. Japan's plant biogeography also shows the effects of climate warming (Yoshida, 2008). Despite slow progress on problems at many scales, Japanese youth now say environment is more important than economy, so Japan may be moving toward a new environmental paradigm (Barrett et al., 2000).

HISTORICAL GEOGRAPHY

Historical geography has sought to reveal spatial systems and places of the past, and to analyze ideological uses of the past for purposes of modern control. The horizon of 'geographic thought' in Japan begins at the dawn of history and the topic is never far from the regime of the day. Landscape perception, cartographic representation, site choices, and construction planning contain elements of Japanese nativism, Chinese knowledge, and European conventions. Archaeological and literary sources reveal worlds of the early people that became the Japanese (Palmer, 1991, 1994, 1996, 2005, 2007). Japan's context in East Asia holds an enduring and central value in historical understanding (Waley, 2012). Chinese paradigms of *fu sui*, or *feng shui*, dominate landscape perception, dwelling construction, and urban planning. Geomancy informs the planning of T'ang-style *ritsuryō* cities, castle towns, and modern communities. Yoon (2006) reveals the workings of *feng shui* and contested ideologies of place in Japan and Japanese-colonial Seoul. Japan's archives and scholars have been one foundation of historical studies of urban China (Whitehand and Gu, 2006). Spatial perception and principles of the past undergird today's Japanese cities, as Waley and Fiévé (2003) show in their introduction to capital planning. The work of the historical geographer in capturing the material production of place is exemplified by the case of Nagano's late nineteenth-century economic peripheralization (Wigen, 1990, 1992, 1995).

Kyōto University geographers have been active in probing the spatial perception of the past and in reconstructing past landscapes (Kinda, 1997, 2010). Japanese cartography of recent centuries shows the march of rationalization (Kawamura, 1989; Unno, 1991, 1994). Historical maps in Japan are an artistic heritage as well as an archive of data (Potter, 2001a, 2001b, 2003a, 2003b, 2003c, 2007). The map and forms of local data about the *kuni*, or province, helped promoted both localism and nationalism in Shinshū through the restoration years (Wigen, 2010). Perceptions of distance and place are also mapped in a figurative sense through texts and narratives from the years of early Japan-US encounters (Hones and Endo, 2006). Historical geographers now turn to postcolonial analysis of the Gaihōzu, maps of external territories produced by and for the Japanese empire. These maps are only now being organized (Wigen, 2012; Kobayashi, 2012) and utilized to understand control of Manchuria (Matsusaka, 2012), Korea (Fedman, 2012) and the Pacific (Ngo, 2012).

CULTURAL GEOGRAPHY

Cultural geography has asked what are each culture's perceptions of nature and expressions of values in the landscape. After the literary turn landscape became text for cultural geographers. Materialist cultural geographers ask how places are produced commercially to appeal to consumers. Some have explicated essential Japanese attitudes toward nature (Saito, 1985, 1992, 2002). In this vein, Senda (1992) showed traditional ways of thinking about nature. Literary works such as a Kawabata novel could also evince Japanese perceptions of nature (Childs, 1991b). A post-structural approach to nature charts changing meanings corresponding to projects of modernity, as Wigen (2005) demonstrates for mountains and the creation of the 'Japanese Alps'.

A corollary concern has been that of cultural landscape, or the expression of cultural values on the land. One of the first Canadian dissertations about Japan was by Hiroshi Tanaka (1975) at Simon Fraser University. His sacred site studies are a contribution to the cultural geography of Japan and of Buddhism's landscapes (Tanaka, 1977, 1981, 1984). Religious places still structure pilgrimage and tourism at sacred mountains, shrines, and temples (Matsui, 2008, 2014). Even stereotypical 'natural' sceneries, such as Japan's pine-beach landscapes, are human creations (Ikagawa, 1993). 'Vernacular' landscapes of ordinary places were photographed by Mather, Karan and Iijima (1998).

Japanese gardens have always been a part of the cultural landscape (Shimazaki, 1992). Japan has transported its landscapes via plants and gardens abroad, as found in Honolulu (Ikagawa, 1994, 1996) and in Britain (Tachibana et al., 2004). In Japan, lest nowhere looks like Japan anymore, the Kyōto landscape has become something managed with aesthetics in mind (Fukamachi et al., 2000).

Cultural geography of Japan has been one focus of French geographers. Jacques Pezeu-Massabuau (1968, 1978) wrote his doctoral dissertation at Université de Paris IV (Sorbonne) in 1973 on the Japanese house and argued a connection across scales, seeing the house and construction system as a fundamental socio-spatial organizer of Japanese life. Kyōto's International Research Center for Japanese Studies, or *Nichibunken*, gathered Jacques Pezeu-Massabuau, Augustin Berque, Nicolas Fiévé, Corinne Tiry, and architectural historians from France and Japan for its 43rd International Research Symposium 'Toward a Vocabulary of Japanese Spatiality' in May 2012. Pezeu-Massabuau and others discussed notions at the heart of Japanese spatialities, such as *ie, aida, ma, meisho, shinden-zukuri, niwa, shataku, jinja,*

sandō, hiroba, danchi, both etymologically and as expressed in the built environment (Bonnin et al., 2013).

Augustin Berque began studying Japanese culture by looking at its limits in Hokkaidō (1974) and the spread of Japanese settlement with the success of rice. He also represents philosophical humanism as a scholar of Watsuji Tetsuro. Berque uses Watsuji's *fūdo* in his own theory of milieu, not simply as climate but as the unitary space-time of being. Berque's cross-cultural and cross-language philosophy of place is influenced by his years of residence in and breadth of cultural knowledge of Japan (1994). He has argued an inter-subjective understanding of relations to nature (Berque, 1992). He has focused on the ontology of social space and milieu (Berque, 1996, 1997c, 2004). This leads to an inter-subjective view of cities through social bonds (Berque, 1997a) and an argument that nature, artifice, and culture are one in each structural moment (Berque, 1997b). Berque (2011) reviews his trajectory from years of fieldwork through these philosophical topics in *Cultural Geographies*.

Cultural geography now also reflects cultural studies and the world of cool Japan. At the University of Edinburgh Lesley Anne Gallacher (2011) researched practices of reading boys' *manga*. In Uppsala's Department of Social and Economic Geography Jakob Nobuoka has written a dissertation on the Tōkyō electronic-goods district, Akihabara, with *manga, anime,* and places that create new Japanese cultural products (Nobuoka, 2010a, 2010b).

RURAL GEOGRAPHIES AND PRIMARY PRODUCTION

Japan's tuna-fishing rights were studied by Keen (1965) and informed his policy suggestions (1988). Japan now plays a major role in distant resources and environments, as in Pacific salmon fisheries (Augerot, 2000). Japanese fishers and seafood firms innovated to compensate for supply problems, with new products such as *surimi,* imitation crab (Mansfield, 2001, 2003a, 2003b, 2003c).

Studying inputs and outputs of agriculture, Ueda (1983) compared rice farmers' efficiency in Japan to that in the Philippines, finding that Japanese efficiency peaked in 1930. Nevertheless, the dominant staple continued to serve as the foundation of Japan's geography (Rutherford, 1984).

A coherent, functional, and modernizing rural community was the finding of studies in Wakayama (Bedford, 1978, 1980a, 1980b). Farming played a regional development role, as in the Tōhoku dairy industry (Oshiro, 1972). Yet by the 1980s farm households in the north-east were earning income from seasonal migration (Oshiro, 1984) and were reallocating labor concomitant with farm mechanization (Oshiro, 1985). In contrast with the slow-to-change views of Japanese agriculture, dissertation research in the late 1980s and 1990s found rapid change, as in Tōhoku rice districts (McDonald, 1990), among Kōchi Prefecture rice and vegetable producers (Stradford, 1994), and in apple-growing Aomori (Brucklacher, 1999). Even among relatively large-scale farms in Hokkaidō, restructuring differentiated the off-farm income strategies of south Hokkaidō from the industrialization strategies of farms farther north (Millward, 1995).

In the 2000s other products and their survival struggles came into focus. Farmers invested in hydroponic technologies in Chiba (Iguchi et al., 2007). Convention theory applied to genetic modification helped Yamamoto (2007) see how domestic soybean producers competed with imports. Grape and wine producers struggled to renew their place-based industry in Yamanashi (Kingsbury, 2012, 2013, 2014).

Agriculture was not unaffected by expanding industrial and urban land use. Latz (1986) researched pressures on urban-fringe agriculture in Japan within Ginsburg's conceptual framework. He found the Land Improvement District managing to stabilize water allocations to agriculture (Latz, 1989, 1991) even on the edge of Tōkyō. Farmland secured to the tillers at land reform was steadily reregulated and rezoned (McDonald, 1997). The developing urban fringe remained satisfactory as a lifeworld to residents (Waldichuk, 1995, 1998, 2009; Waldichuk and Whitney, 1997). A comparison of constraints on urban-fringe farmland conversion in Japan, Canada, and Britain showed generally strong regulation in Japan but with differing real effects on residential growth in Asahikawa and Hakodate (Millward, 2006). Regional cities such as Sapporo and Sendai feel great demand for land at their fringe even with the post-bubble decline of land values (Oshiro 2003). Farm households supplied labor to manufacturing firms seeking low-wage labor (McDonald, 1996a), and farmtowns offered themselves as greenfield sites for industrial restructuring (McDonald, 1996b).

Despite urbanization and transitions in Japanese agriculture, Japanese citizens still wish to grow and consume local food. Japan has re-engineered the smallest scale of farming into community food gardens (Wiltshire, 1992b; Wiltshire and Azuma, 2000; Azuma and Wiltshire, 2001; Wiltshire et al., 2002). City dwellers seek local farm products, green areas, and want to protect Japan's farmland

(Kikuchi, 2008; Yagasaki and Nakamura, 2008). Farms near Nagoya advertise their 'rurality' to appeal to city consumers (Kingsbury et al., 2010). Today's concerns for eating locally draw studies of urban-fringe food supply (Kurita et al., 2009) and proposals for food production within the urban footprint (Yokohari and Bolthouse, 2011).

Despite consumer activism, rural communities struggle while Japan imports more food from Asian neighbors (Araki, 2002, 2003, 2005). Japan's food-supply lines extend far offshore and food processors seek wider import streams (McDonald, 2000). Australia supplies dairy products (Pritchard and Curtis, 2004) and beef (Oro and Pritchard, 2011). To address scandals in false food labeling MAFF has tried to promote traceability to trusted producers (Hall, D. 2010).

Imazato (2008) reviews many studies of the globalization of rural villages, and sees globalization as the new frame for researchers. Lieba Faier paints a globalized view of rural Japan in terms of brides from the Philippines (Faier, 2003, 2009, 2011, 2013). One future for the rural might be tourism, in which the rural is the commodity. McMorran's fieldwork in Kyūshū has showed the workings of rural tourism (McMorran, 2005, 2008a, 2008b, 2012). Another rural future may be larger production organizations operating the farmland of whole villages. Miyake (2014) describes policy pressures on farmers to join larger incorporated land pools in Tōhoku.

Sustainability is a current theme and question (Tabayashi et al., 2000; Koganezawa, 2007, 2009). Yokoyama (2013) surveys recent rural geography from approaches of cultural and political ecology, or nature and society, showing human-environment interactions in Japan and Asia.

URBAN GEOGRAPHY

Urban geographers have approached Japan historically with the rise of commerce, services, industry, capital, and the state. The quantitative revolution and its spatial interaction models had a passing effect on approaches to Japan. The 1960s and 1970s viewed Japan under rapid urbanization. Masai Yasuo (1960) compared Lansing and Shizuoka in terms of areal functional organization. Two of the last Michigan geography dissertations about Japan were Robert Douglas Robertson (1972, 1975) on Ōsaka's water supply from Lake Biwa, and Yukiko Numata Bedford (1967) on *danchi* apartment life in the new vertical suburbs. Kanno (1977) compared land use in Shizuoka and Atlanta. Job growth drove migration even among cities (Glickman and McHone, 1977). Glickman analyzed Japanese cites as a managed 'urban system' (Glickman, 1979). Kornhauser (1976, 1982) stressed the rise of cities before factory industrialization and intensification under it (1989). Urban geography in Japan may also be moving more toward the question of spatial practices. Abe (2008) reviews publications and finds evidence for the collapse and reorganization of urban geography as practiced in Japan. Taira (2008) surveys new themes in the social geography of the city such as quality of life and neighborhood diversity. Older approaches such as urban morphology are now more likely to be questions of urban public space (Cybriwsky, 1999; Sakai, 2005, 2011).

Particular historical geographies distinguish old and new Japanese capitals over a millennium (Waley, 2003a; Waley and Fiévé, 2003). In the 1990s urban decline hit Okayama's Saidaiji temple town, or *monzenmachi* (Yoon, 1997), and Ashio, a mountain mining town (Cybriwsky and Shimizu,1993). The 'Japanese city' was many diverging places facing great economic and environmental challenges (Karan and Stapleton, 1997) In the bubble years Japan's banks and construction firms fanned voracious resort development (Rimmer, 1992). Real-estate investment and golf-course construction reached Australia (Rimmer, 1990, 1994). Tōkyō's urban land market boomed and sagged along with that of other Asian cities (Aveline, 2004a, 2004b, 2004c.).

New technologies helped visualize the twentieth-century growth of Tōkyō (Siebert, 1997, 2000, 2003, 2004). Once distinct and distant cities such as Chiba reflected concomitant growth as edge cities (Robinson, 2010). McGee (1991) offered the Japanese term *konjuka* for his influential model of interspersed rural-urban land use between cities in Japan and across Asia.

The World City or Global City idea (Friedmann and Wolff, 1982; Friedmann, 1986; Sassen, 1991), that a few cities such as Tōkyō serve as global nodes rather than national ones, engendered debate across many disciplines (Fujita, 1991; Fujita and Hill, 1993). Whether Tōkyō really fits the World City descriptions was in doubt from the outset (Rimmer, 1986). The role of the state in capital formation and in the manufacturing base in Japan's largest cities, not to mention relatively thin immigrant populations, set Japanese cities apart (Hill and Kim, 2000). Tōkyō nevertheless enjoyed inflated financial power (Douglass, 1993) and adopted World City discourse in over-reaching financial gambles in the bubble era that left the national and metropolitan governments indebted (Fujita, 2011; Saito and Thornley, 2003). In the aftermath finance capital and construction firms are arguably the drivers of urban development in Tōkyō-as-World City (Waley, 2007).

The books of Cybriwsky (1991, 1998, 2011a) were the first to survey Tōkyō's distinct 'epitome

districts' at the time of the bubble and after. A decade later Cybriwsky (2005, 2010) observed megastructure redevelopment again continuing in Tōkyō's forever ephemeral physical form. Continuous construction and simulation of foreign places were simply 'new twists on old patterns'. The space of Tōkyō is everywhere the medium of the real-estate, finance, and construction economies. Cybriwsky (2011b) treats these processes in depth in the case of redevelopment in Roppongi.

Further understanding of Tōkyō comes from the historical urban geography of Paul Waley. With three prior books on the history of Tōkyō to his credit, Waley completed doctoral research at SOAS in 1994 on *Symbolic Space and Urban Change in the Japanese City: The Edo-Tokyo Periphery, 1800–1930*. Transformations in the waterways and environments of Edo are among the displacements of modernity (Waley, 2000a, 2000c, 2002a, 2003b; Waley and Purvis, 2004). Urban accretions to Edo in centuries past remain parts of Tōkyō (Waley and Tinios, 1999). Waley explains efforts to green Tōkyō (2005a) and the consequences of industrializing atop pre-existing density (2009). He shows the discursive and material replacings of Tōkyō's city center today (Waley, 2002b, 2006). These processes occur in an era of a limited state, reproducing socio-spatial differentiation (Waley, 2000b, 2013).

The last two decades have brought a wealth of studies of urban planning in Japan, many focused on conditions in the recessionary years since the bubble (Hebbert and Nakai, 1988; Hebbert, 1994; Shapira et al., 1994; Edgington, 2000, 2003). Hein researched key urban planners in Japan (Hein, 2003). She organized a 2001 colloquium on the rebuilding of Japan's cities destroyed by air raids (Hein, 2010; Hein et al., 2003). Hein further drew together European, Japanese, and North American scholars on civic and city questions under Japan's decentralization policies (Hein and Pelletier, 2006a). Hein shows that Tōkyō neighborhoods embody the *machi* as the enduring premise, while absorbing international concepts into land development (Hein, 2008, 2010).

André Sorensen developed case studies in planning history that showed incremental improvisation at the urban fringe (2001a, 2001b) and frequent failure of land readjustment due to local opposition (2000). Such cases built his 2002 book on urban growth and planning from the Edo era to the present. Sorensen interpreted urban sprawl as evidence of a weak civil society and weak local state in relation to the national developmental institutions (2005, 2006a, 2007a, 2007b). Gaubatz (2004) accepted that Japanese suburbs, developed before the era of the auto, had a logic and convenience of their own.

Carolin Funck and Sorensen further examined the effectiveness of *machizukuri* governance, planning at town and neighborhood levels (Sorensen and Funck, 2007). Meanings and strengths of citizen participation varied in terms of spatial outcomes from *machizukuri* in Kōbe (Funck, 2007). Sorensen finds recent popular support for better planning (2011) and sees population decline as an opportunity for more livable cities (2006b). Urban shrinkage in Ōsaka brings its own set of planning problems (Buhnik, 2011). International comparisons continue to place Japanese cities among the world's largest (Sorensen et al., 2004; Sorensen and Okata, 2011).

Local autonomy and decentralization were new trends in urban governance (Hein and Pelletier, 2006a). Tensions between global and local actors affected Kyōto and Tōkyō (Hein and Pelletier, 2006b). Uta Hohn wrote on the preservation of historic districts (Hohn, 1997, 1998) and city planning in Japan (Hohn, 2000). Shibata Kuniko (2006, 2008a, 2008b) researched the planning ideologies of Japan's developmental modernity. Saitō Asato examined the interaction of developmental state with global city planning in Tōkyō, with attention to the scales of state imperatives in urban redevelopment (Saito, 2002, 2003, 2006, 2012; Saito and Thornley, 2003). Urban brownfield-site redevelopment in Ōsaka and Manchester provided a comparative study (Dixon et al., 2011).

Housing is another rich topic of research in urban and social geography. Hirayama Yōsuke (2000) reported on the recovery of housing after the 1995 Kobe earthquake. Japan has innovative systems of housing supply replacement (Barlow and Ozaki, 2005). Ronald (2007, 2008) analyzed the home as consumer product and as asset. Housing stock is largely condominium homes (Ronald and Hirayama, 2006) and increasingly single-person units (Ronald and Hirayama, 2009). Housing is a story of social change (Hirayama and Ronald, 2007). Oba (2005) reported new trends in housing policies in Kansai cities. Japan's homelessness and its precarious housing of working poor are also much discussed (Obinger, 2008, 2009; Kennett and Mizuuchi, 2010).

POLITICAL GEOGRAPHY

Political geography is a rather new academic field inside Japan (Yamazaki T., 1997) and a field that has revived considerably in Western academia since the 1980s. Geopolitics, or inter-state relations, has been one subfield. Political geographers have asked about the construction of the northern limits of China and Japan along their northern borders (Edmonds, 1983, 1985).

Geographers have asked about the ideology and practice of colonial appropriations (Horiuchi, 1975; Yeh, 2011). Wartime aerial bombing of Japanese cities has been detailed (Hewitt, 1983; Karacas, 2006, 2010). Japan has unresolved contemporary territorial disputes with Russia (Eyre, 1968) and China (Suganuma, 1996, 2000). Post-Cold War changes were considered for Australia-Japan relations and geopolitics in the Asia-Pacific region (Rumley, 2001; Rumley et al., 1996).

China's interests began to drive political contests in the seas of Asia (Olson and Morgan, 1992). One contribution is a detailed study of China's irredentism and Japan's claims to the Senkaku/Diaoyu islands (Suganuma, 1996, 2000). Yamazaki (2002) saw the rise of neo-conservatism in Japan resulting from cultural and economic anxieties. Ichijō (2002) contributed comparative work on Japanese nationalism to *Geopolitics*.

Yamazaki Takashi posits that Japan's political geography is still less than sovereign while Okinawa remains under the US military (2004b, 2011). He does note active opposition movements (Yamazaki, 2004a). The internet may foster grassroots democracy in Hokkaidō and Okinawa (Rimmer and Morris-Suzuki, 1999).

Japan's soft power via aid and diplomacy has been a concomitant theme among geographers. Japan's Official Development Assistance has become among the world's largest (Ó Tuathail, 1992; Grant, 1995; Muldavin, 2000). Pritchard (2006) studied Japan's ODA to the Asian region; Tsujita (2012) found Japan's 'aidscape' in Samoa.

Energy is a geopolitical theme long-standing in the sense of security of supply, and more recently in the sense of carbon reduction and climate-change policy. Energy is Japan's 'constant anxiety' (Palmer, 1992). Voskuil (1963) saw supertankers moving West Virginia coal to Japan. Eyre (1970) studied the growth of electric power generation. Commodities moving by rail and ship within Japan are largely energy-related (Mitsuhashi 1977, 1978). Iraphne Childs (1984) researched Japan's nuclear waste in the Pacific. Parker (1990, 1997) observed Canadian coal reaching Japan. Energy security and climate security are the shared hopes for new environmental technologies upgrading Japan's power generation (Parker, 1996, 1998, 2008). Deadly disasters occurred in 1997 and 1999 at the Tokaimura nuclear-fuel facility (Cavasin, 2008), foreshadowing the 2011 damage to the Fukushima Dai-ichi nuclear-power plant.

At the level of human safety Japan's governments must let many safety functions fall to aging citizens (Maeda, 2012). Camera-based urban surveillance is increasing in Japanese cities (Murakami Wood, 2011; Murakami Wood and Abe, 2011).

ECONOMIC GEOGRAPHY

The capitalist world economy and space economy of localities are crisis-prone (Mizuoka, 1986). Geographers in Japan have long been critically engaged with institutions exploiting society and nature (Mizuoka et al., 2005). Recent decades have been years of economic challenges yet, fundamentally, Japan remains a huge economy (Cavasin, 2009). Andrew Herod (2011) recognized the immediate effect of the March 2011 earthquake and tsunami on the global economy. Economic geographers tried to explain developmentalism and the success of the Japanese economy until about 1990 then tried to explain the struggle of Japanese firms and localities against hollowing, the high yen, bubble-induced bank crises, government debt, and reregulation.

At a time when silk was Japan's old economy Richard Hough researched the decline of silk in upland regions (Hough, 1963, 1968a, 1968b). At the same time manufacturing firms moved into the Tōkyō hinterlands of Yamanashi (Takizawa, 1971). A center-periphery dichotomy was apparent in uneven regional growth (Sakai, 1972). Chauncy Harris surveyed Japan's industrialization decades after his Japan-related work in World War II (Harris, 1997), and noted already apparent limits to industrial growth (Harris, 1982).

At the International Geographical Congress in Tōkyō in 1980 world geographers recognized Japan's rapid economic growth. Publications by the hosts (Nihon Gakujutsu Kaigi [Science Council of Japan], 1980) updated Kiuchi's (1976) *Geography in Japan*. A paper at this meeting by Jean Gottman (1980), French head of geography at Oxford, searched for transformational vocabulary capturing Japan's spatial 'metamorphosis'. Gottman inspired Miyakawa's (2000) subsequent view of Japan's space economy, accepting spatial restructuring as a constant within a tolerant cultural framework and economic openness.

The lines of the successful Japanese economic 'system' were charted (Murata and Ota, 1980; Ettlinger, 1991; Humphrys, 1995a, 1995b). The manufacturing base was in small, subcontracted, and regionally linked firms (Glasmeier and Sugiura, 1991; Markusen, 1996). Lean production methods were part of this system (Kaneko and Nojiri, 2008). Industrial-location patterns of firms and cities were part of this system in Japan and Korea (Park Sang Woo, 1985).

In manufacturing, Japan's production methods, rapid product innovation, and line replacement were competitive strategies but also paths of rapid change within each firm. Even as Florida and Kenney studied Japan's high tech industries (1990) and steel industry (1992), they saw restructuring as a continuous practice. Kenney

and Florida (1993) termed the Japanese practices coming to US factories a new stage of manufacturing 'beyond mass production'. Did Japanese production signal a shift from a Fordist to a flexibly specialized post-Fordist industrial era? Peck and Miyamachi (1994) examined Japan in the framework of regulation theory.

The Institute of British Geographers' Industry and Area Development Study Group took up the theme of Japan as a world economic power in 1992. One of the members, Graham Humphrys at Swansea University, Wales, had prior research experience in northern Japan (Humphrys 1990). He and Jamie Peck reported on papers analyzing 'Japan in the Global Economy' (Humphrys and Peck, 1992). Peter Dicken at the University of Manchester noted Japan's investment in Europe and traced Japan's foreign direct investment among the drivers of 'global shift' (Dicken, 1983, 1991; Dicken et al., 1997). Japan's general trading companies also played a role in linking sectors (Dicken and Miyamachi, 1998).

What was the role of the developmental state? Baher Ghosheh (1988, 1991) weighed Japanese economic-development lessons for Arab states. The state made place for high-technology research in technopolis cities (Masser, 1990; Akimoto, 1992; Park, 1997; Cavasin, 1999). Tōkyō played a role as a capital city devoted to competing in the world economy (Takeuchi, 1998) and to fostering knowledge as a basis for innovation (Matsubara, 2007). National and regional planners built science-park infrastructure for innovative industries (Edgington 2008a, 2008b). Constraints on public finance today shift regional policy toward clusters and networks (Fujita and Hill, 2012).

Place and production are closely related in accounts of specific industries: semiconductors (Sargent, 1987), ceramics (Izushi, 1997), automobiles (Suganuma, 2001; Hayter et al., 1999), electric cars (Patchell, 1999), house production (Patchell, 2002; Patchell and Hayter, 1997), machine tools (Kalafsky, 2006a, 2006b, 2007), musical instruments (Reiffenstein, 2004, 2005, 2006), paper (Penna, 2002), domestic timber (Reiffenstein and Hayter, 2006), and multimedia and internet (Arai et al., 2004). Japanese economic geographers show Japanese manufacturers' recent locational logics and restructuring's effects on Japan's regions (Matsuhashi et al., 2013).

Industrial patterns overall, however, create regional imbalance. Tanaka Kyoko investigated regional inequality (Tanaka, 1992; Gauthier et al., 1992; Yamamoto, 2006). Sone (1993) researched municipalities' budgets. Kitajima Seiko (1994, 1998, 2000) traced industrial restructuring in Japan's rural periphery.

Labor was part of industrial success and restructuring. Labor skills within Japanese production systems in robotics and cutlery proved to be regional assets (Patchell, 1991, 1993a, 1993b; Patchell and Hayter, 1992, 1995). Shawn Banasick and Robert Hanham at West Virginia University researched labor and regional employment (Banasick, 2001, 2009; Hanham and Banasick, 1998, 2000; Banasick and Hanham, 2006, 2008). Joel Shelton (2006) stressed gender in Japan's manufacturing labor.

Heavy industries' many peripheral locations were targets for rationalizations. Labor mobility was managed within the firm in a downsizing steel plant in the Tōhoku town of Kamaishi (Wiltshire, 1991, 1992a, 1995). The outlook for the town facing plant closure was not bright (Wiltshire, 1998; Sargent and Wiltshire, 2000). The high yen was a driving force behind Japan's resiting of factories abroad, driving industrial 'hollowing' (Edgington, 1994a, 1997). Neoliberal policies interweave with developmental national and local efforts to upgrade industries in rustbelt Muroran (Edgington, 2013).

Trade has created inter-regional flows between Japan and the nations of external observers. Trade policy was relevant in the years of trade frictions (Grant, 1993). Pantulu (2002) examined the relationship between trade and foreign direct investment for countries including Japan. Alfredo Sánchez Muñoz (2006) from Chile showed Japan's economic links to the Spanish-speaking Pacific. Blain and Norcliffe (1988) at York University traced the lines of Japan-Canada trade. Edgington also studied Japan-Canada flows (1994b, 1996, 2004). Kurihara Tamiko (1986, 1993, 2000) analyzed Japanese trading companies' investments in Canada. Japan is a market for Canadian industries (Hayter and Edgington, 1997, 1999; Hayter and Barnes, 2001). British Columbia exports houses to Japan (Reiffenstein et al., 2002).

Geographers followed the growth of Japan's foreign direct investment (Sargent, 1990; Grant, 1991). Japanese auto production abroad was one dominant theme (Mair, et al., 1988; Florida and Kenney, 1991; Harvey, 1996; Reid, 1991a, 1991b; Bosman, 1999; Karan, 2001). Japanese auto factories in the USA led in environmental practices (O'Dell, 2001, 2003). Japanese auto factory location responded to the North America Free Trade Agreement (NAFTA) in Canada (Parker et al., 2000) and reached Poland (Majek and Hayter, 2008). A second sector of strong interest was electronics. Japanese semiconductor research and development functions spread to the USA (Angel and Savage, 1996). Japanese electronics production is now a global value chain (Sturgeon, 2007).

In Europe many Japanese firms locate in Düsseldorf (Flüchter, 2005). The Netherlands is another gateway for firms from Japan (Benders and Weinschenk, 1997; Loeve et al., 1985). Japan has important trade and foreign direct investment

in Nordic countries (Alvstam and Ivarsson, 1996). Schlunze researched Japanese investment linking Japan and Europe (Schlunze, 1995, 2001, 2007). Schlunze has been a leader of the SIEM academic network: Spaces of International Economy and Management. Japanese firms grew in Australia (Edgington, 1986, 1990, 1991). Godfrey Linge observed Japan's manufacturing strategies and their implications for Australia (Linge, 1991a, 1991b). His papers stimulated discussion of logistics in Japan by Nojiri and Ishikawa (1994). Japanese banking in Australia was another influential sector in the 1990s (Daly and Stimson, 1994).

Japan's growth was understood in terms of a wider Asia-Pacific region (Alvstam, 1995; Rimmer, 1997; Webber, 1998). Factory location in Asia and Japanese firms' global practices meant growing complexity of production chains (Hayter and Edgington, 2004). Recently Japanese firms have more heterarchical relationships with partners in Taiwan and China (Edgington and Hayter, 2012). Japanese subsidiary management in Southeast Asia is also decentralizing (Edgington and Hayter, 2013a, 2013b). China has become Japan's largest trade partner (Alvstam et al., 2009). The locus of thinking about globalization and the world economy has shifted to Asia (Yeung, 2000, 2007).

Yūko Aoyama moves the discussion of Japan as a bounded unit to something sustained by global networks of production (Aoyama, 1996a, 1999a, 2000b). She analyzes small- and medium-sized enterprises through policy for network-formation (Aoyama, 1996b, 1999b, 2000a; Aoyama and Teitz, 1996). Telecommunications and e-commerce are now keys to the economic space of Japan (Aoyama, 2001a, 2001b; Aoyama and Castells, 2002; Castells and Aoyama, 1994; Wheeler et al., 2000). Aoyama (2005) proposes an economic geography for the information age in which Japanese technologies and products are central. Possibilities for retail globalization come into question for the case of Japan (Aoyama and Schwartz, 2006; Aoyama, 2007). Creative industries take specific places in these networks (Aoyama and Izushi, 2003, 2004; Izushi and Aoyama, 2006; Aoyama, 2009).

Services are now the largest part of Japan's economy (Ström, 2005). Monetary policy, financial services, and real-estate practices underlay the bubble and its consequences (Kerr, 2002; Oizumi, 1994). Luo (1993) researched financial-sector investments in the USA. Seo (2004, 2012) outlined Japanese global banking. Reiffenstein (2009) described patent intermediaries' role as a producer service for industrial innovation. Japanese business and financial-service firms are keys to Japanese production around the Pacific (Edgington and Haga, 1998; Ström 2003, 2006; Ström and Yoshino, 2009). Domestic firms have advantages in the temporary staffing business; multinational entrants cannot compete well in Japan (Coe et al., 2012).

Innovation is the next policy hope for regional renewal in Japan (Kitagawa 2005, 2007; Kitagawa and Woolgar, 2008; Shapira, 2008).

Transportation

Transportation infrastructure is closely linked to Japan's construction lobby (Feldhoff, 2007, 2008). Private rail developers extended lines and housing development in Kansai (Semple, 2009) and in the Kantō area (Jacobson, 2010) and created multi-modal continuous environments in which to live, work, and shop (Aveline, 2002). Rail in the urban system creates growth advantages for certain cities (Murayama, 1994, 2000; Okamoto, 2005). The *Shinkansen* system defines Japan's fast lane (Smith, R. A. 2003; Hood, 2006a, 2006b, 2010).

Despite the advantages of rail, long commute times from the suburbs make two jobs in the city center impossible for couples with children (Okamoto, 1997). Though train commuters carry mobile devices, they cannot use them on the train due to lack of space and privacy (Ohmori and Harata, 2008). Increasing automobile use restructures society today and threatens regional transportation systems (Tanaka and Imai, 2013).

Japan's air transport and airports have been an emerging theme in the past two decades (Feldhoff, 2002, 2003). Tanaka Koichi (2008) includes airports in his review of transportation research, with a concern for Japan's competitive position in Asia. Comparing Haneda and Narita with Randstad and Frankfurt airports, Wijk (2007) finds less concentrated business development at the Japanese airports. The Global City question is examined through the lens of logistics at Japan's airports (O'Connor, 2010).

Tourism

Betty Andressen (1988) studied Japanese travellers in Canada in her dissertation at the University of Victoria in the early years of tourism geography (Murphy and Andressen, 1988). Others observed Japanese tourism in Australia (Childs, 1991a), and in Canada (Obara et al., 2005) and in comparative perspective (Hashimoto, 1996, 2000, 2007). Japanese tourism in British Columbia comes through a Japanese corporate 'tourism production system' (Yamamoto and Gill, 2002). Japanese tourist wedding firms in Hawaii reshape landscapes (McDonald, 2005).

Inside Japan tourism links agriculture, food, and place (Hashimoto and Telfer, 2008, 2010,

2011). Tourism connects people to landscape in Japan (Yasue, 2010), not least through the practice of photography (Yasue and Murakami, 2011). Tourism has been an economic hope of Japan's peripheral regions but the sector faces difficulties under conditions of recession and aging (Funck, 1999a, 1999b, 2008). Leisure industries, such as recreational coastal uses, do not take hold of new places without conflict (Funck, 2006).

SOCIAL GEOGRAPHY

Social geography of ethnicity, once pursued outside Japan, is now a lively field of analysis inside Japan (Oishi, 2008; Mori, 2009). Communities are now more diverse in terms of international newcomers (Kamiya and Lee, 2009). Warren (1994) researched Koreans in Japan. Bailey wrote on the foreign teacher in Japan (2002, 2006, 2007). Nakamura (2007, 2008, 2010) compared Ainu and First Nations of Canada. Social geography now highlights gender, too (Yoshida et al., 2013). Nishimura (2002) took up gender and work, while Kageyama (2004) produced the first book on the gendered city in Japan.

Social polarization was a question of the post-economic-miracle era. In Ōsaka's Kamagasaki district workmen have always had a rough existence (Arimura, 1991). Workers for Japan's iconic automakers in the Nagoya area feel enormous changes in their work lives (Nishimura and Okamoto, 2001). Ōsaka City University geographers study the places and people of Japan's underclass (Mizuuchi, 2006). Fielding probed socio-economic disparity across space in the Japanese city, comparing Kyōto to Edinburgh (Fielding, 2004). He mapped the occupational-class geography of the wards of Kyōto to test the 'together and equal' characterization of the Japanese city by Fujita and Hill (1997). Fielding argued that 'equal' was not entirely true for the social geography of Kyōto, based on social differentiation at a scale smaller than the *ku*, or ward. Wiltshire (2004) felt Fielding had importantly mapped the persistence of class and outcaste areas, but wondered whether Kyōto's urban continuity in recent centuries make it a distinct case. Richard Child Hill (2004) reasserted the main argument of Fujita and Hill (1997) as to the vast difference between the USA and Japan in the degree of spatial polarization of rich and poor.

Miyazawa (2013) finds recent welfare geography studies in Japan relating to aging and services for the elderly. Medical geographers revealed regional differences in strokes in Japan (Sato, 1988, 1989; Yoshino et al., 1993). Japan's 1918–19 influenza epidemic was Japan's largest disease outbreak (Palmer and Rice, 1992; Rice and Palmer, 1993).

Migration within Japan includes cases of resettlement forced by dam construction (Palmer, 1988). Vietnamese refugees are another class of migrants in Australia and Japan (Yoshida, 2011). Ishikawa (2008) reviews new population research from Japanese geographers concerning birth rates, migration, households, and distribution. At McMaster University Kao-Lee Liaw researches developments in Japan's demography and migration (Liaw, 1992, 2003; Liaw and Ishikawa, 2008; Liaw et al., 2010). Migration to Japan adds to diversity (Ishikawa and Fielding, 1998; Fielding and Ishikawa, 2003; Fielding, 2010). Migration streams are distinctly gendered (Piper, 1997, 1999, 2000, 2002; Ball and Piper, 2002, 2005; Piper and Ball, 2001).

Comparative population studies highlight many facets of changing social geographies (Coulmas, 2007; Coulmas at al., 2008; Lützeler, 1995, 2008b; Coulmas and Lützeler, 2011). Shrinking regional populations are a reality everywhere (Elis, 2008, 2011; Matanle and Rausch, 2011).

DIASPORA

Geographers have researched Japanese colonization in Argentina and Paraguay (Stewart, 1960, 1963a, 1963b, 1967), colonies of Japanese and Okinawans in the Bolivian Upper Amazon (Hiraoka, 1974, 1980; Hiraoka and Yamamoto, 1980), and migration to Latin America (White, 2003a). Japanese migration is seen in European cities (Hurdley and White, 1999; Glebe et al., 1999; Goodman et al., 2003; White, 2003b; White and Hurdley, 2003). New Asian migration reached Australia (Hugo, 2003). Rosalía Ávila Tàpies (2008a, 2008b) from Barcelona studied Japanese women living in Spain.

Japanese immigrant floriculturists and truck farmers in California were researched by Yagasaki (1982), recent president of the Association of Japanese Geographers. Immigrants' homes in Kaideima, Shiga Prefecture, and destinations in Canada were the research of Kobayashi (1983), recent president of the Association of American Geographers. All generations faced race and gender barriers in inter-cultural relations, as well as incarceration (Kobayashi, 1990, 2002; Kobayashi and Jackson, 1994; Wilson, 2011). Immigration still brings newcomers from Japan, many of them women (Chubachi, 2009). Research on Japanese-Americans has focused on the Midwest (Albert, 1980) and on Los Angeles (Toji, 1999; Smith, 2005, 2008). Cultural elements such as garden plants and food infuse the landscapes of the diaspora (Ikagawa, 1994, 1996; S. N. Tanaka 2008).

CONCLUSION

Geographers contribute ground-level studies of the places that are Japan and the processes that structure Japan. Place is a medium of social change and a continuous social product – so the spatial is the social, and the social is the spatial. In every section of this review movement has been in the direction of more transnational, inter-dependent relations between Japan and the world. From the closed book of 1850 Japan is now an open book in every way.

In human relations with Japan's environment, knowledge and values have advanced, but the triple disasters of March 2011 were deep reminders of vulnerabilities and illusions. Social movements ask about alternative futures. Almost every landscape in Japan is a human creation and more so every year. In urban geography we see the city as the focus of financial capital, constantly remade in a general sense but unevenly rebuilt and abandoned. Urban poor, homeless persons, and an aged population coexist in the polarized city. Social geography continues to see the bifurcated *kamitsu/kaso*, or over-crowded/depopulated, problem of the 1970s. Newcomers notwithstanding, population decline has hit almost every prefecture. The age of a shrinking economy has arrived in simple demographic terms.

Japan's economy is expansive globally. This is the largest sub-theme of study by geographers. Where is Japan? Everywhere. Japanese technologies and methods change the time and space of production and communications for people all over the world. Industrial restructuring subtracts jobs from places in Japan. Place and production are still closely identified but casualization of employment has suppressed incomes.

This review has also surveyed historical, cultural, and political geography, and the theme of diaspora. Geographers contribute from transnational faculties all over the globe in expansive institutional settings. This review has not included many studies from Korea or China about Japan's geography but would welcome such a survey. Flows, thoughts, and boundaries have loosened in the East Asian setting. Japanese geographers have come out to meet the world in many venues.

REFERENCES

Abe, K. (2008). The changing urban geography of Japan. *Geographical Review of Japan, Chirigaku Hyōron,* 81(5), 262–278(16–32).

Ackerman, E. A. (1949). *Japanese natural resources: A comprehensive survey.* Tokyo: General Headquarters, Supreme Commander of the Allied Powers.

Ackerman, E. A. (1953). *Japan's natural resources and their relation to Japan's economic future.* Chicago: University of Chicago Press.

Adelphi Goes Japanese. (1969). *The Delphian* (Adelphi University, Garden City, NY). Wednesday, April 16, 1969, Vol. 19, No. 19, p.3, c.5. http://contentdm. adelphi.edu/cdm/compoundobject/collection/ Delphian/id/1705/rec/1 Accessed 8 July 2014.

Adelphi Appoints New Supervisor for Japan Program. (1969). *The Adelphi Evening News* (Adelphi University, Garden City, NY). May 1969, Vol. 33 No. 1, p.3, c.5. http://contentdm.adelphi.edu/ cdm/singleitem/ collection/Evening/id/100/rec/1 Accessed 8 July 2014.

AGSG Bulletin. (2011). Volume 35, Number 1. Asian Geography Specialty Group, Association of American Geographers.

Akimoto, K. (1992). Industrial policy and industrial park development in Japan. *Asian Geographer,* 11(1–2), 1–22.

Akiyama, T. (1995). Surviving in the 21st century: The present situation of remote islands and new regional development. United Nations University and Japan's National Land Agency, International Symposium on Small Islands and Sustainable Development, 1995. www.gdrc.org/oceans/akiy-ama.html Accessed 8 July 2014.

Albert, M. D. (1980). *Japanese American communities in Chicago and the Twin Cities.* Ph.D. Dissertation. University of Minnesota.

Alcock, R. (1861). Narrative of a journey in the interior of Japan, ascent of Fusiyama (sic), and visit to the hot sulphur-baths of Atami, in 1860. *Proceedings of the Royal Geographical Society of London,* 31: 321–356.

Alvstam, C.G. (1995). Integration through trade and investment: Asian Pacific patterns. In R. LeHeron and S. O. Park (Eds.), *The Asian Pacific Rim and globalization: Enterprise, governance and territoriality* (pp. 107–128). Aldershot and Brookfield VT: Avebury.

Alvstam, C.G., and Ivarsson, I. (1996). Japan-Nordic trade and Japanese manufacturing in the Nordic countries. In J. Darby (Ed.), *Japan and the European periphery* (pp. 205–228). London: Macmillan.

Alvstam, C.G., Ström, P., and Yoshino, N. (2009) On the economic interdependence between China and Japan: Challenges and possibilities. *Asia Pacific Viewpoint,* 50(2), 198–214.

American Geographical and Statistical Society. (1859). Corresponding members. *Journal of the American Geographical and Statistical Society* 1(1), iii.

American Geographical Society of New York. (1873). Transactions of the society for 1872. *Journal of the American Geographical Society of New York,* 4, 35–56.

Andressen, B. (1988). *Travel and geographic learning: A study of perception and attitude change in a Japanese tourist segment.* Ph.D. Dissertation. University of Victoria (Canada).

Angel, D. P., and Savage, L. A. (1996). Global localization? Japanese research and development laboratories in the USA. *Environment and Planning A,* 28(5), 819–833.

Anstey, R. L. (1957). *A comparative study of the agricultural land use of the Aso Highland and the Kumamoto Lowland of Central Kyushu.* Ph.D. Dissertation. University of Maryland College Park.

Aoyagi, M., Ohshima, J., Bedford, Y., and Yuihama, S. (Eds.) (2007). *Nyuujiirando Hyakka Jiten (Japanese Encyclopedia of New Zealand).* Yokohama: Shumpūsha.

Aoyama, Y. (1996a). *From fortress Japan to global networks: Locational specificity of globalization for the Japanese electronics industry in the 1990s.* Ph.D. Dissertation. University of California, Berkeley.

Aoyama, Y. (1996b). Local economic revitalization or national industrial growth? A comparative overview of small business policy in Japan and the United States. *Review of Urban and Regional Development Studies,* 8(1), 1–14.

Aoyama, Y. (1999a). Localisation advantages for multinational firms: Views from the Japanese electronics industry in Europe. In N. Phelps and J. Alden (Eds.), *Foreign direct investment and the global economy: Corporate and institutional dynamics of global-localisation* (pp. 103–119). Regional Studies Association. London: The Stationery Office.

Aoyama, Y. (1999b). Policy interventions for industrial network formation: Contrasting historical underpinnings of the small business policy in Japan and the United States. *Small Business Economics,* 12(3), 217–231.

Aoyama, Y. (2000a). Industrial network formation and regulation: The case of Japan's SME policy. In E. Vatne and M. Taylor (Eds.), *The networked firm in a global world: Small firms in new environments* (pp. 45–63). Aldershot and Burlington VT: Ashgate.

Aoyama, Y. (2000b). Networks, keiretsu and locations of the Japanese electronics industry in Asia. *Environment and Planning A,* 32(2), 223–244.0

Aoyama, Y. (2001a). Structural foundations for e-commerce adoption: A comparative organization of retail trade between Japan and the United States. *Urban Geography,* 22(2), 130–153.

Aoyama, Y. (2001b). The information society, Japanese style: Corner stores as hubs for E-commerce access. In T. R. Leinbach and S. D. Brunn (Eds.), *Worlds of E-commerce* (pp. 109–128). Chichester and New York: John Wiley.

Aoyama, Y. (2005). Consumption and distribution in the information age: A research agenda for economic geography. *Annals of the Japan Association of Economic Geographers,* 51(1), 101–115.

Aoyama, Y. (2007). Oligopoly and the structural paradox of retail TNCs: An assessment of Carrefour and Wal-Mart in Japan. *Journal of Economic Geography*, 7(4), 471–490.

Aoyama, Y. (2009). Entrepreneurship and regional culture: The case of Hamamatsu and Kyoto, Japan. *Regional Studies*, 43(3), 495–512.

Aoyama, Y., and Castells, M. (2002). An empirical assessment of the informational society: Employment and occupational structures of G-7 countries, 1920–2000. *International Labour Review*, 141(1–2), 123–159.

Aoyama, Y., and Izushi, H. (2003). Hardware gimmick or cultural innovation? Technological, cultural, and social foundations of the Japanese video game industry. *Research Policy*, 32(3), 423–444.

Aoyama, Y., and Izushi, H. (2004). Creative resources of the Japanese video game industry. In D. Power and A. J. Scott (Eds.), *Cultural industries and the production of culture* (pp.110–129). London and New York: Routledge.

Aoyama, Y. and Schwarz, G. (2006). The myth of Wal-Martization: Retail globalization and local competition in Japan and Germany. In S. Brunn (Ed.), *Wal-Mart world* (pp. 277–292). New York: Routledge.

Aoyama, Y. and Teitz, M. B. (1996). *Small business policy in Japan and the United States: A comparative analysis of objectives and outcomes*. Policy Papers in International Affairs #44. University of California at Berkeley: Institute of International Studies.

Arai, Y., Nakamura, H., Sato, H., Nakazawa, T., Musha, T., and Sugizaki, K. (2004). Multimedia and internet business clusters in central Tokyo. *Urban Geography*, 25(5), 483–500.

Araki, H. (2002). Mechanisms of sustaining agriculture and the aging of rural communities in Takamiya-cho, Hiroshima Prefecture. *Geographical Review of Japan*, 75(5), 262–279.

Araki, H. (2003). Changes in Japan's food supply system and the spatial dynamics of agriculture in Japan. *Annals of the Japan Association of Economic Geographers*, 49(2), 159–179.

Araki, H. (2005). Transformations in geographical pattern of the fresh vegetable commodity chain: Japan-bound shipments from Asian countries. *Journal of East Asian Studies* (Yamaguchi University), 4, 1–24.

Arimura, S. (Trans. Meyerson, D. N.) (1991). The comic book diary of Kamayan: the life of a day-laborer in Kamagasaki. *Environment and Planning D, Society and Space*, 9(2), 135–149.

Association of American Geographers. (1949). Directory of Members 1949. *Professional Geographer* 1(Supplement), 7–104.

Association of American Geographers. (2011). *Guide to Geography programs in the Americas 2010–2011*. Washington DC: Association of American Geographers.

Association of Japanese Geographers (Ed.). (1980). *Geography of Japan*. Tōkyō: Teikoku Shoin.

Association of Japanese Geographers. (2011). Kokunai no chirigaku kanren houmupeeji. ajg.or.jp/link-kokunai.html Accessed 8 July, 2014.

Augerot, X. (2000). *An environmental history of the salmon management philosophies of the North Pacific: Japan, Russia, Canada, Alaska and the Pacific Northwest United States*. Ph.D. Dissertation. Oregon State University.

Aveline, N. (2002). Mobility in Japan: A model for French transportation policies? *Japan Railway and Transport Review*, 31, 42–43.

Aveline, N. (2004a). Comparison of land and real estate cycles in major Asian cities. In N. Aveline, N. and L.H. Li (Eds.), *Property markets and land policies in northeast Asia* (pp. 285–292). Tokyo and Hong Kong: Maison Franco-Japonaise and University of Hong Kong.

Aveline, N. (2004b). Property markets in Tokyo and the management of the last boom-bust cycle (1985–2002). In N. Aveline, N. and L. H. Li (Eds.), *Property markets and land policies in northeast Asia* (pp. 33–82). Tōkyō: Maison Franco-Japonaise and University of Hong Kong.

Aveline, N. (2004c). The overall context of the Asian financial crisis and its interaction with domestic property markets. In N. Aveline, N. and L. H. Li (Eds.), *Property markets and land policies in northeast Asia* (pp. 1–32). Tōkyō: Maison Franco-Japonaise and University of Hong Kong.

Aveline, N. (2008). Cooperation between France and Japan in social sciences. ISS Research Series 29: *Current and future trajectories of social science research on Japan* (pp. 105–110). Tōkyō: Maison Franco-Japonaise.

Ávila Tàpies, R. (2008a). Building friendship networks and intercultural spaces: The case of Japanese women in Spain. *Migracijske i etnicke teme*, 24(3), 341–352.

Ávila Tàpies, R. (2008b). Inmigración japonesa e interculturalidad en España: El caso de la 'Sociedad Tampopo.' *Boletín de la Real Sociedad Geográfica* (Madrid), 144, 171–186.

Azuma, R., and Wiltshire, R. J. (2001). The Japanese rural allotment. In J. Ferris, M. Morris, C. Norman and J. Sempik (Eds.) *People, land and sustainability: A global view of community gardening* (pp. 50–51). Nottingham: PLS.

Bailey, K. D. (2002). *Living in the eikaiwa wonderland: English language learning, socioeconomic transformation and gender alterities in modern Japan*. Ph.D. Dissertation. University of Kentucky.

Bailey, K. (2006). Marketing the eikaiwa wonderland: ideology, *akogare* and gender alterity in English conversation school advertising in Japan. *Environment and Planning D: Society and Space*, 24(1), 105–130.

Bailey, K. (2007). *Akogare*, ideology, and 'charisma man' mythology: Reflections on ethnographic research in English language schools in Japan. *Gender, Place and Culture*, 14(5), 585–608.

Ball, R.E. and Piper, N. (2002). Globalisation and regulation of citizenship – Filipino migrant workers in Japan. *Political Geography,* 21(8), 1013–1034.

Ball, R.E. and Piper, N. (2005). Trading labour-trading rights: the regional dynamics over rights recognition of migrant workers in the Asia-Pacific – the case of the Philippines and Japan. In K. Hewison and K. Young (Eds.), *Transnational migration and work in Asia* (pp. 213–234). London: Routledge.

Banasick, S. M. (2001). *Beyond the workplace: The uneven development of the Japanese space-economy and the role of labor, 1965–1994.* Ph.D. Dissertation. West Virginia University.

Banasick, S. (2009). GIS and spatio-temporal trends in inequality: Tracking profitability according to firm size in Japanese manufacturing, 1985–2006. In J.D. Gatrell and R.R. Jensen (Eds.), *Planning and socioeconomic applications* (pp. 87–108). *Geotechnologies and the environment, Volume 1.* Springer.

Banasick, S. and Hanham, R.Q. (2006). Time paths of uneven industrial development in Japan. *The Industrial Geographer*, 3(2), 27–45.

Banasick, S. and Hanham, R. (2008). Regional decline of manufacturing employment in Japan during an era of prolonged stagnation. *Regional Studies*, 42(4), 489–503.

Barlow, J., and Ozaki, R. (2005). Building mass customised housing through innovation in the production system: lessons from Japan. *Environment and Planning A,* 37(1), 9–20.

Barnes, T. J. (2004). Placing ideas: genius loci, heterotopia and geography's quantitative revolution. *Progress in Human Geography*, 28(5), 565–595.

Barnes, T., and Crampton, J. (2011). Mapping intelligence: American geographers and the Office of Strategic Services and GHQ/SCAP (Tokyo). In S. Kirsch and C. Flint (Eds.), *Reconstructing conflict: Integrating war and post-war geographies* (pp. 227–251). Surrey UK and Burlington VT: Ashgate.

Barrett, B., Abe, O., Harako, E., and Ichikawa, S. (2000). Oya-shima-kuni: Japan. In D. Yenken, J. Fien and H. Sykes (Eds.), *Environment, education and society in the Asia-Pacific: Local traditions and global discourses* (pp. 75–98). London: Routledge.

Beardsley, R.K., Hall, J.W., and Ward, R.E. (1959) *Village Japan.* Chicago: University of Chicago Press.

Bedford, Y.N. (1967). Senri New Town: A laboratory of modern living in Japan. *Papers of the Michigan Academy of Science, Arts, and Letters,* 52(2), 259–267.

Bedford, Y. N. (1978). Modernization of a Japanese village: Burakism and its spatial expression. Ph.D. Dissertation. University of Michigan.

Bedford, Y. N. (1980a). Research trends in Japanese studies and the modernization of Japan within the framework of area studies in America. (Amerika ni okeru earia sutaji ni yoru nihon kenkyū to nihon no kindaika.) *Jinbun Chiri/Japanese Journal of Human Geography,* 32(6), 504–517.

Bedford, Y. N. (1980b). The grass roots modernization in a Japanese village. *GeoJournal*, 4(3), 259–266.

Bedford, Y.N. (2011) Personal communication with author M. McDonald. Kyōto, Japan. 13 November.

Benders, J. and Weinschenk, V. (1997). Japanese manufacturing establishments in the Netherlands. *Tijdschrift voor economische en sociale geografie (Journal of economic and social geography)*, 8(5), 488–493.

Berque, A. (1974). La chaîne culturelle d'une colonization: Les paysans japonais à Hokkaidō. *Annales. Histoire, Sciences Sociales*, 29e Anée, No. 6, 1425–1449.

Berque, A. (1992). Identification of the self in relation to the environment. In N.R. Rosenberger (Ed.), *Japanese sense of self* (pp. 93–104). Cambridge: Cambridge University Press.

Berque, A. (Ed.). (1994). *Dictionnaire de la civilization japonais*. Paris: Éditions Hazan.

Berque, A. (1995). Conclusion: The rituals of urbanity: Temporal forms and spatial forms in Japanese and French cities. In J. van Bremen and D. P. Martinez (Eds.), *Ceremony and ritual in Japan: Religious practices in an industrialized society* (pp. 246–258). London and New York: Routledge.

Berque, A. (1996). The question of space: From Heidegger to Watsuji. *Cultural Geographies/ Ecumene*, 3(4), 373–383.

Berque, A. (1997a). *Japan: Cities and social bonds*. (Trans C. Turner). Yelvertoft Manor, Northamptonshire: Pilkington Press.

Berque, A. (1997b). *Japan: Nature, artifice and Japanese culture*. (Trans R. Schwartz). Yelvertoft Manor, Northamptonshire: Pilkington Press.

Berque, A. (1997c). Postmodern space and Japanese tradition. In G. Benko and U. Strohmayer (Eds.), *Space and social theory: Interpreting modernity and postmodernity* (pp. 336–343). Oxford and Malden MA: Blackwell.

Berque, A. (2004). Offspring of Watsuji's theory of milieu (Fūdo). *Geojournal*, 60(4), 389–396.

Berque, A. (2011). Fieldwork and hermeneutics in the case of Japan. *Cultural Geographies*, 18(1), 119–124.

Bird, I. L. (1880). *Unbeaten tracks in Japan: An account of travels in the interior including visits to the aborigines of Yezo and the shrines of Nikko and Ise.* Two volumes. London: John Murray.

Blain, R., and Norcliffe, G. (1988) Japanese investment in Canada and Canadian exports to Japan. *The Canadian Geographer*, 32(2), 141–150.

Bonnett, A. (2002). Makers of the west: National identity and occidentalism in the work of Fukuzawa Yukichi and Ziya Gökalp. *Scottish Geographical Journal*, 118(3), 165–182.

Bonnin, P., Nishida, M., and Inaga, S. (2013). *Pour un vocabulaire de la spatialité Japonaise.* Kyōto:

International Research Center for Japanese Studies.

Bosman, M. M. (1999). *Space, power and representation: The case of 'Team Toyota' and the state of Kentucky*. Ph.D. Dissertation. University of Kentucky.

Bowles, P. and Woods, L. T. (2000). Japan after the Economic Miracle: In Search of New Directions. Dordrecht: Kluwer Academic Publishers.

Bowers, N. (1950). *Problems of resettlement on Saipan, Tinian, and Rota, Mariana Islands*. Ph.D. Dissertation. University of Michigan.

Brillet, Philippe M. (2005). Ireland and Japan: The search for the tiger. *Irish Geography*, 38(2), 225–232.

Brucklacher, A.D. (1991). Facing globalization: Japanese farmers' responses to changing markets. *Japanstudien/Contemporary Japan*, 12, 229–247.

Brucklacher, A. D. (1999). *Apples and regional change: Life and economy in Tsugaru, Japan*. Ph.D. Dissertation. Louisiana State University and Agricultural and Mechanical College.

Brunton, R. H. (1991). *Building Japan, 1868–1876*. Folkestone: Japan Library.

Buhnik, S. (2011). From shrinking cities to *toshi no shukushō*: Identifying patterns of urban shrinkage in the Osaka metropolitan area. *Berkeley Planning Journal*, 23(1), 132–155.

Castells, M., and Aoyama, Y. (1994). Paths towards the informational society: Employment structure in G-7 countries, 1920–90. *International Labour Review*, 133(1), 5–33.

Cavasin, N. (1999). Science cities and technopolis in Japan: Innovative networks and regional planning. In G. Chapman, A. K. Dutt and R. W. Bradnock (Eds.), *Urban Growth and Development in Asia Vol. 2* (pp. 74–91). Brookfield VT: Ashgate.

Cavasin, N. (2008). Citizen activism and the nuclear industry in Japan: After the Tokai Village disaster. In P.P. Karan and U. Suganuma (Eds.), *Local environmental movements. A comparative study of the US and Japan* (pp. 65–74). Lexington: University Press of Kentucky.

Cavasin, N. (2009). *Le Japon, de la conquéte à l'effacement du monde*. Paris: Ellipses.

Childs, I. R. W. (1984). *Nuclear waste in the Pacific: Perceptions of the risks*. Ph.D. Dissertation. University of Hawaii.

Childs, I. (1991a). Interviewing Japanese tourists in Australia: Some observations on the difficulties. *Japanese Studies*, 11(1), 65–70. Japanese Studies Association of Australia.

Childs, I. (1991b). Japanese perception of nature in the novel Snow Country. *Journal of Cultural Geography*, 11(2), 1–19.

Childs, I. (2008). Emergence of a new volunteerism: Increasing community resilience to natural disasters in Japan. In K. Gow and D. Paton (Eds.), *The phoenix of natural disasters: Community resilience* (pp. 171–180). New York: Nova Science Publishers.

Chubachi, N. (2009). Gender and construction of the life course of Japanese immigrant women in Canada. Ph.D. Dissertation. Queen's University (Canada).

Coe, N. M., Johns, J., and Ward, K. (2012). Limits to expansion: Transnational corporations and territorial embeddedness in the Japanese temporary staffing market. *Global Networks*, 12(1), 22–47.

Coulmas, F. (2007). *Population decline and ageing in Japan – the social consequences*. London: Routledge.

Coulmas, F., and Lützeler, R. (Eds.) (2011). *Imploding populations in Japan and Germany: A comparison*. Leiden: Brill.

Coulmas, F., Conrad, H., Schad-Seifert, A., and Vogt, G. (Eds.) (2008). *The demographic challenge: A handbook about Japan*. German Institute of Japanese Studies. Tōkyō, Leiden, Boston: Brill.

Coulter, W. (1926). A dot map of the distribution of population in Japan. *Geographical Review*, 16(2), 283–284.

Cowen, A.Y. (1918). Japan: The land of silk. *Journal of Geography*, 17(2), 71–74.

Crary, D. D. (1947). *The physical geography of Iga-no-kuni, Japan*. Ph.D. Dissertation. University of Michigan.

Cushing, S. W. (1913). Coastal plains and block mountains in Japan. *Annals of the Association of American Geographers,* 3(1), 43–61.

Cusick, J. (2003). *The roles of protected areas in contemporary societies: Resident, research and recreation on the islands of Yakushima, Japan and Maui, Hawaii*. Ph.D. Dissertation. University of Hawaii.

Cybriwsky, R. (1991). *Tokyo: The changing profile of an urban giant*. London: Bellhaven Press.

Cybriwsky, R. (1998). *Tokyo: The shogun's city at the twenty-first century*. Chichester and New York: John Wiley and Sons.

Cybriwsky, R. (1999). Changing patterns of urban public space: Observations and assessments from the Tokyo and New York metropolitan areas. *Cities*, 16(4), 223–231.

Cybriwsky, R. (2005). Tokyo 's third rebuilding: New twists on old patterns. In J. Robertson (Ed.), *A companion to the anthropology of Japan* (pp. 218–30). London and Malden MA: Blackwell.

Cybriwsky, R. (2010). Alternative geographies of Tokyo. In W.-S Tang and F. Mizuoka (Eds.), *East Asia: A critical geography perspective* (Chapter 7). Tōkyō: Kokon Shoin.

Cybriwsky, R. (2011a). *Historical dictionary of Tokyo*. 2nd edition. Lanham, MD: Scarecrow Press.

Cybriwsky, R. (2011b). *Roppongi Crossing: The demise of a Tokyo nightclub district and the reshaping of a global city*. Athens GA: University of Georgia Press.

Cybriwsky, R., and Shimizu, A. (1993). Ashio. *Focus*, 43(1), 22–28.

Daly, M. T., and Stimson, R. J. (1994). Dependency in the modem global economy: Australia and the changing face of Asian finance. *Environment and Planning A,* 26(3), 415–434.

Davis, D. H. (1934a). Agricultural occupation of Hokkaido. *Economic Geography,* 10(4), 348–367.

Davis, D.H. (1934b). Present status of settlement in Hokkaido. *Geographical Review,* 24(3), 386–399.

Davis, D.H. (1934c). Type occupance patterns in Hokkaido. *Annals of the Association of American Geographers,* 24(4), 201–223.

De Bres, K. (1989). An early frost: Geography in Teachers College Columbia and Columbia University. *The Geographical Journal,* 155(3), 392–402.

Dicken, P. (1983). Japanese manufacturing investment in the UK: A flood or mere trickle? *Area,* 15(4), 273–284.

Dicken, P. (1991). The changing geography of Japanese foreign direct investment in manufacturing industry: a global perspective. In J. Morris (Ed.), *Japan and the global economy: Issues and trends in the 1990s* (pp. 14–44). London: Routledge.

Dicken, P., and Miyamachi, Y. (1998). 'From noodles to satellites': The changing geography of the Japanese sogo shosha. *Transactions of the Institute of British Geographers, New Series,* 23(1), 55–78.

Dicken, P., Tickell, A., and Yeung, H. (1997). Putting Japanese investment in Europe in its place. *Area,* 29(3), 200–212.

Dixon, T., Otsuka, N., and Abe, H. (2011). Critical success factors in urban brownfield regeneration: an analysis of 'hardcore' sites in Manchester and Osaka during the economic recession (2009–10). *Environment and Planning A,* 43(4), 961–980.

Douglass, C. M. (1993). The new Tokyo story: Restructuring space and the struggle for place in a world city. In K. Fujita and R.C. Hill (Eds.), *Japanese cities in the world economy* (pp. 83–119). Philadelphia: Temple University Press.

Edgington, D. W. (1986). *Influences upon the location and behaviour of Japanese transnational corporations in Australia.* Ph.D. Dissertation. Monash University (Australia).

Edgington, D.W. (1990). *Japanese business down under: Patterns of Japanese investment in Australia.* New York: Routledge.

Edgington, D. W. (1991). Japanese direct investment and Australian economic development. In J. Morris (Ed.), *Japan and the global economy: Issues and trends in the 1990s* (pp. 173–194). London: Routledge.

Edgington, D.W. (1994a). The geography of endaka: Industrial transformation and regional employment change in Japan 1986–1991. *Regional Studies,* 28(5), 521–535.

Edgington, D.W. (1994b). The new wave: Patterns of Japanese direct foreign investment in Canada during the 1980s. *The Canadian Geographer,* 38(1), 28–36.

Edgington, D.W. (1995). Locational preferences of Japanese real estate investors in North America. *Urban Geography,* 16(5), 373–396.

Edgington, D.W. (1996). Japanese real estate investment in Canadian cities and regions, 1985–1993. *The Canadian Geographer,* 40(4), 292–305.

Edgington, D.W. (1997). The rise of the yen, 'hollowing out', and Japan's troubled industries. In R.F. Watters, T. G. McGee and G. Sullivan (Eds.) *Asia-Pacific: New Geographies of the Pacific Rim.* Vancouver: University of British Columbia.

Edgington, D. W. (2000). New directions in Japanese urban planning: A case study of Nagoya. In P. Bowles and L.T. Woods (Eds.), *Japan after the economic miracle: In search of new directions* (pp. 145–168). Boston: Kluwer.

Edgington, D. W. (2003). Japan ponders the good life: Improving the quality of Japanese cities. In D. W. Edgington (Ed.), *Japan at the millenium: Joining past and future* (pp. 193–221). Vancouver: University of British Columbia Press.

Edgington, D. W. (2004). British Columbia's coastal forests, hemlock timber and the Japanese housing market. *Canadian Journal of Regional Science,* 27(3), 415–446.

Edgington, D. W. (2007). Urban systems, global capital and the cities of Asia-Pacific. In P. Kelley (Ed.), Geographer, Asianist, Urbanist: Celebrating the scholarship of Terry McGee. *Asia Pacific Viewpoint,* 48(2), 259–261.

Edgington, D. W. (2008a). The Japanese innovation system: University-industry linkages, small firms and regional technology clusters. *Prometheus,* 26(1), 1–19.

Edgington, D. W. (2008b). The Kyoto Research Park and innovation in Japanese cities. *Urban Geography,* 29(5), 411–454.

Edgington, D.W. (2010). *Reconstructing Kobe: The geography of crisis and opportunity.* Vancouver: University of British Columbia Press.

Edgington, D.W. (2013). Restructuring Japan's rustbelt. *Urban Affairs Review,* 49(4), 475–524.

Edgington, D.W., and Haga, H. (1998). Japanese service sector multinationals and the hierarchy of Pacific rim cities. *Asia Pacific Viewpoint,* 39(2), 161–178.

Edgington, D.W., and Hayter, R. (2012). New relationships between Japanese and Taiwanese electronics firms. *Environment and Planning A,* 44(1), 68–88.

Edgington, D.W., and Hayter, R. (2013a). 'Glocalization' and regional headquarters: Japanese electronics firms in the ASEAN region. *Annals of the Association of American Geographers,* 103(3), 647–668.

Edgington, D.W., and Hayter, R. (2013b). *In situ* dynamics of Japanese electronic subsidiaries in

ASEAN countries: Reflections from a development perspective. *Asia Pacific Viewpoint*, 54 (1), 15–32.

Edmonds, R. L. (1983). *Northern frontiers of Qing China and Tokugawa Japan: A comparative study of frontier policy*. Ph.D. Dissertation. University of Chicago.

Edmonds, R. L. (1985). *Northern frontiers of Qing China and Tokugawa Japan: A comparative study of frontier policy*. University of Chicago Geography Research Papers 213.

Elis, V. (2008). The impact of the ageing society on regional economies. In F. Coulmas, H. Conrad, A. Schad-Seifert and G. Vogt (Eds.), *The demographic challenge: A handbook about Japan (pp. 861–877)*. Leiden: Brill.

Elis, V. (2011). Rural depopulation and economic shrinkage in Japan: What can affected municipalities do about it? In F. Coulmas and R. Lützeler (Eds.), *Imploding populations in Japan and Germany* (pp. 443–460). Leiden: Brill.

Elliott, A. (2008). Ito and Isabella in the contact zone: Interpretation, mimicry and Unbeaten Tracks in Japan. *Electronic Journal of Contemporary Japanese Studies*, Article 9. Retrieved from: www.japanesestudies.org.uk/articles/2008/Elliott.html Accessed 8 July 2014.

Espenshade, A. V. (1947). *Japanese fisheries production, 1908–46: A statistical report*. Natural Resources Section Report No. 95. Tokyo: General Headquarters, Supreme Commander for the Allied Powers.

Espenshade, A. V. (1949). A program for Japanese fisheries. *Geographical Review* 39(1), 76–85.

Ettlinger, N. (1991). The roots of competitive advantage in California and Japan. *The Annals of the Association of American Geographers*, 81(3), 391–407.

Evans, N. (2001). *Community planning in Japan: The case of Mano, and its experience in the Hanshin earthquake*. Ph.D. Dissertation. School of East Asian Studies, University of Sheffield, UK.

Evans, N. (2002). *Machi-zukuri* as a new paradigm in Japanese urban planning: reality or myth? *Japan Forum*, 14:3, 443–464.

Eyre, J. D. (1950). Sea-salt production in the Inland Sea region of Japan. *Papers of the Michigan Academy of Science, Arts, and Letters* 34(3), 127–38.

Eyre, J. D. (1951). *Salt from the sea: A geographical analysis of the national and international patterns of Japanese salt production and trade*. Ph.D. Dissertation. University of Michigan.

Eyre, J. D. (1952a). Elements of instability in the current Japanese land tenure system. *Land Economics*, 28(3), 193–202.

Eyre, J. D. (1952b). Patterns of Japanese salt production and trade. In *Occasional Papers No. 3, Center for Japanese Studies* (pp. 15–46). Center for Japanese Studies Publications. University of Michigan. Accessed 8 July 2014 at http://test.

quod.lib.umich.edu/ cgi/p/pod/dod-idx/materials-for-the-study-of-local-history-in-japan-pre-meiji.pdf?c=cjs; idno=bby6909.0001.001

Eyre, J. D. (1955a). The changing role of the former Japanese landlord. *Land Economics*, 31(1), 35–46.

Eyre, J. D. (1955b). Water controls in a Japanese irrigation system. *Geographical Review*, 45(2), 197–216.

Eyre, J. D. (1956a). Japanese land development in Kojima Bay. *Economic Geography*, 32(1), 58–74.

Eyre, J. D. (1956b). Post occupation conditions in rural Japan. *Annals of the American Academy of Political and Social Science*, 308, 113–120.

Eyre, J. D. (1959). Sources of Tokyo's fresh food supply. *Geographical Review*, 49(4), 455–474.

Eyre, J. D. (1962a). Japanese inter-prefectural rice movements. *Economic Geography* 38(1), 78–86.

Eyre, J. D. (1962b). Mountain land use in Northern Japan. *Geographical Review*, 52(2), 236–252.

Eyre, J. D. (1963a). Industrial growth in the Suwa Basin, Japan. *Geographical Review* 53(4), 487–502.

Eyre, J. D. (1963b). Tokyo influences in the manufacturing geography of Saitama Prefecture. *Economic Geography*, 39(4), 283–298.

Eyre, J. D. (1964). Regional variations in Japanese internal migration. *Papers of the Michigan Academy of Science, Arts, and Letters*, 49(2), 271–284.

Eyre, J. D. (1965). Japan's electric-power supply. *Geographical Review*, 55(4), 546–562.

Eyre, J.D. (1968). Japanese-Soviet territorial issues in the Southern Kurile Islands. *The Professional Geographer,* 20(1), 11–15.

Eyre, J.D. (1970). Development trends in the Japanese electric power industry, 1963–68. *The Professional Geographer,* 22(1), 26–30.

Eyre, J. D. (1982). *Nagoya: The changing geography of a Japanese regional metropolis*. Chapel Hill, University of North Carolina. Studies in Geography No 17.

Eyre, J. D. (1994). Personal communication with author M. McDonald. Telephone interview. 30 October.

Faier, L. (2003). *On being oyomesan: Filipina migrants and their Japanese families in central Kiso*. Ph.D. Dissertation. University of California, Santa Cruz.

Faier, L. (2009). *Intimate encounters: Filipina women and the remaking of rural Japan*. Berkeley: University of California Press.

Faier, L. (2011). Fungi, trees, people, nematodes, beetles, and weather: Ecologies of vulnerability and ecologies of negotiation in matsutake commodity exchange. *Environment and Planning A*, 43(5), 1079–1097.

Faier, L. (2013). Affective investments in the Manila region: Filipina migrants in rural Japan and transnational urban development in the Philippines. *Transactions of the Institute of British Geographers*, 38(3), 376–390.

Fedman, D. (2012). Triangulating Chōsen: Maps, mapmaking, and the land survey in colonial Korea.

Cross-Currents: East Asian History and Culture Review E-Journal, (2), 1–28. Accessed 8 July 2014 at https://cross-currents.berkeley.edu/e-journal/issue-2/ triangulating-chosen-maps-mapmaking-and-land-survey-colonial-korea

Fedman, D., and Karacas, C. (2012). A cartographic fade to black: Mapping the destruction of urban Japan during World War II. *Journal of Historical Geography*, 38(3), 306–328.

Feldhoff, T. (2002). Japan's regional airports: conflicting national, regional and local interests. *Journal of Transport Geography*, 10(3), 165–175.

Feldhoff, T. (2003). Japan's capital Tōkyō and its airports: problems and prospects from subnational and supranational perspectives. *Journal of Air Transport Management*, 9(4), 241–254.

Feldhoff, T. (2007) Japan's construction lobby and the privatization of highway-related public corporations. In A. Sorensen and C. Funck (Eds.), *Living cities in Japan* (pp. 91–112). Nissan Institute/Routledge Japanese Studies. London and New York: Routledge.

Feldhoff, T. (2008). Infrastructural policy: Framework and challenges. In F. Coulmas, H. Conrad, A. Schad-Seifert and G. Vogt (Eds.), *The demographic challenge: A handbook about Japan* (pp. 781–798). Leiden: Brill.

Feldhoff, T., Flüchter, W., and Hohn, U. (Eds.) (2005). *Shaping the future of metropolitan regions in Japan and Germany: Governance, institutions and place in new context*. Proceedings of the 9th Japanese-German Geographical Conference. Duisberg: University of Duisburg-Essen.

Fielding, A. (2004). Class and space: social segregation in Japanese cities. *Transactions of the Institute of British Geographers*, 29(1), 64–84.

Fielding, A. (2010). The occupational and geographical locations of transnational immigrant minorities in Japan. In P. Kee and H. Yoshimatsu (Eds.), *Global movements in the Asia Pacific* (pp. 93–122). Singapore: World Scientific.

Fielding, A., and Ishikawa, Y. (2003). Migration and the life course in contemporary Japan. *Geographical Review of Japan*, 76(12), 882–893.

Fiévé, N. (2003) Kyoto's famous places: Collective memory and 'monuments' in the Tokugawa Period. In N. Fiévé and P. Waley (Eds.), *Japanese capitals in historical perspective: Power, memory and place in Kyoto, Edo and Tokyo* (pp. 153–171). London: RoutledgeCurzon.

Fiévé, N. and Waley, P. (Eds.) (2003). *Japanese capitals in historical perspective: Power, memory and place in Kyoto, Edo and Tokyo*. London: RoutledgeCurzon.

Fisher, C. A. and Sargent, J. (1975). Japan's ecological crisis. *The Geographical Journal*, 141(2), 165–176.

Florida R., and Kenney, M. (1990). High-technology restructuring in the USA and Japan. *Environment and Planning A*, 22(2), 233–252.

Florida R., and Kenney, M. (1991). Japanese foreign direct investment in the United States: the case of the automotive transplants. In J. Morris (Ed.), *Japan and the global economy: Issues and trends in the 1990s* (pp. 91–114). London: Routledge.

Florida, R., and Kenney, M. (1992). Restructuring in place: Japanese investment, production, organization, and the geography of steel. *Economic Geography*, 68(2), 146–173.

Flüchter, W. (Ed.) (1995). *Japan and Central Europe restructuring: Geographical aspects of socio-economic, urban and regional development*. Wiesbaden, Harrassowitz.

Flüchter, W. (2000). *German geographical research on Japan*. Duisburg Working Papers on East Asian Studies No. 33. Duisburg: Institut für Ostasienwissenschaften der Universität Duisburg.

Flüchter, W. (2003). Tokyo before the next earthquake: Agglomeration-related risks, town planning and disaster prevention. *Town Planning Review*, 74(2), 213–238.

Flüchter, W. (2005). The locational behaviour of Japanese corporations in Germany, with particular reference to Düsseldorf. In T. Feldhoff, W. Flüchter and U. Hohn (Eds.), *Shaping the future of metropolitan regions in Japan and Germany: Governance, institutions and place in context* (pp.103–116). Proceedings of the 9th Japanese-German Geographical Conference. Duisberg: University of Duisburg-Essen.

Forstall, R.L., Greene, R.P., and Pick, J.B. (2009). Which are the largest? Why lists of major urban areas vary so greatly. *Tijdschrift voor economische en sociale geografie*, 100(3), 277–297.

Friedmann, J. (1986). The world city hypothesis. *Development and Change*, 17(1), 69–83.

Friedmann, J., and Wolff, G. (1982). World city formation: an agenda for research and action. *International Journal of Urban and Regional Research*, 6(3), 309–344.

Fujita, K. (1991). A world city and flexible specialization: Restructuring of the Tokyo metropolis. *International Journal of Urban and Regional Research*, 15(2), 269–284.

Fujita, K. (2011). Financial crises, Japan's state regime shift, and Tokyo's urban policy. *Environment and Planning A*, 43(2), 307–327.

Fujita, K., and Hill, R.C. (Eds.) (1993). *Japanese cities in the world economy*. Philadelphia: Temple University Press.

Fujita, K., and Hill, R. C. (1997). Together and equal: Place stratification in Osaka. In P.P. Karan and K. Stapleton (Eds.), *The Japanese city* (pp. 106–33). Lexington: University Press of Kentucky.

Fujita, K., and Hill, R. C. (2012). Industry clusters and transnational networks: Japan's new directions in regional policy. In B.G. Park, R.C. Hill and A. Saito (Eds.), *Locating neoliberalism in East Asia: Neoliberalizing spaces in developmental states* (pp. 27–58). Malden MA, Oxford, and Chichester: Wiley-Blackwell.

Fukamachi, K., Oku, H., Kumagai, Y., and Shimomura, A. (2000). Changes in landscape planning and land management in Arashiyama National Forest in Kyoto. *Landscape and Urban Planning*, 52(2–3), 73–87.

Funck, C. (1999a). *Tourismus und Peripherie in Japan. Über das Potential touristischer Entwicklung zum Ausgleich regionaler Disparitäten*. Bonn: Dieter Born.

Funck, C. (1999b). When the bubble burst: Planning and reality in Japan's resort industry. *Current Issues in Tourism*, 2(4), 333–53.

Funck, C. (2006). Conflicts over space for marine leisure: A case study of recreational boating in Japan. *Current Issues in Tourism*, 9(4–5), 459–480.

Funck, C. (2007). Machizukuri, civil society, and the transformation of Japanese city planning: cases from Kobe. In A. Sorensen and C. Funck (Eds.), *Living cities in Japan: Citizens' movements, machizukuri and local environments* (pp.137–156). Nissan Institute/Routledge Japanese Studies Series. Oxford and New York: Routledge.

Funck, C. (2008). Ageing tourists, ageing destinations: Tourism and demographic change in Japan. In F. Coulmas, H. Conrad, A. Schad-Seifert and G. Vogt (Eds.) *The demographic challenge: A handbook about Japan*, (pp. 579–598). Leiden: Brill.

Gallacher, L. A. (2011). *The sleep of reason? On practices of reading shōnen manga*. Ph.D. Dissertation. University of Edinburgh.

Gaubatz, P. (2004). Community, modernity, and urban change in Japan and the USA: Toyokawa and Cupertino in the late twentieth century. In K. Stanilov and B. C. Scheer (Eds.) *Suburban form: An international perspective* (pp. 17–37). New York and London: Routledge.

Gauthier, H.L., Tanaka, K., and Smith, W.R. (1992). A time-series analysis of regional income inequalities and migration in Japan, 1955–1985. *Geographical Analysis*, 24(4), 283–298.

Gavin, M. (2001). *Shiga Shigetaka, 1863–1927: The forgotten enlightener*. Richmond, Surrey: Curzon.

Ghosheh, B. A. (1988). A new international economic role for the Arab world: Lessons from the Japanese experience. Ph.D. Dissertation. State University of New York at Buffalo.

Ghosheh, B. A. (1991). Spatial environment and social adaptation in Japan – A traveler's perspective. *Focus*, 41(4), 19–22.

Ginsburg, N. S. (1949a). *Japanese prewar trade and shipping in the Oriental triangle*. Ph.D. Dissertation. Department of Geography Research Paper No. 6. University of Chicago.

Ginsburg, N. S. (1949b). Manchurian railway development. *The Far Eastern Quarterly*, 8(4), 398–411.

Ginsburg, N. S. (1950). Strategic intelligence for American world policy (book review). *Annals of the Association of American Geographers*, 40(1), 89–91.

Ginsburg, N. S. (1990). Extended metropolitan regions in Asia: A new spatial paradigm. In N. S. Ginsburg (Ed.), *The urban transition: Reflections on the American and Asian experiences* (pp. 27–46). Hong Kong: The Chinese University Press.

Ginsburg, N. S. (1991) Extended metropolitan regions in Asia: a new spatial paradigm. In N.S. Ginsburg, B. Koppel and T. G. McGee (Eds.) *The extended metropolis: Settlement transition in Asia*. Honolulu: University of Hawaii Press.

Ginsburg, N. S., Koppel, B., and McGee, T. G. (Eds.) (1991). *The extended metropolis: Settlement transition in Asia*. Honolulu: University of Hawaii Press.

Glacken, C. J. (1953). *Studies of Okinawan village life*. Washington: Pacific Science Board, National Research Council.

Glacken, C. J. (1955). *The Great Loochoo: A study of Okinawan village life*. Berkeley: University of California Press.

Glasmeier, A., and Sugiura, N. (1991). Japan's manufacturing system: Small business, subcontracting, and regional complex formation. *International Journal of Urban and Regional Research*, 15(3), 395–414.

Glebe, G., Hurdley, L., Montag, B., and White, P.E. (1999). Investment-led migration and the distribution of Japanese in Germany and Great Britain. *Espace, Populations, Sociétes*, 3, 425–437.

Glickman, N. (1979). *The growth and management of the Japanese urban system*. New York: Academic Press.

Glickman, N. J., and McHone, W.W. (1977). Intercity migration and employment growth in the Japanese urban economy. *Regional Studies*, 11, 165–181.

Golledge, R., Jacobson, R.D., Kitchin, R., and Blades, M. (2000). Cognitive maps, spatial abilities and human wayfinding. *Geographical Review of Japan, Series B.* 73, 93–104.

Goodman, R., Peach, C., Takenaka, A., and White, P.E. (2003). The experience of Japan's new migrants and overseas communities in anthropological, geographical, historical and sociological perspective. In R. Goodman, C. Peach, A. Takenaka and P.E. White (Eds.), *Global Japan: The experience of Japan's new immigrants and overseas communities* (pp.1–20). London: RoutledgeCurzon.

Gottman, J. (1980). Planning and metamorphosis in Japan. *The Town Planning Review*, 51(2), 171–176.

Grant, R. J. (1991). *The political economy of international trade: A geographical perspective on the world-economy*. Ph.D. Dissertation. University of Colorado at Boulder.

Grant, R. (1993). Trading blocs or trading blows? The macroeconomic geography of US and Japanese trade policies. *Environment and Planning A*, 25(2), 273–291.

Grant, R. (1995). Reshaping Japanese foreign aid for the post-cold war era. *Tijdschrift voor economische* en sociale geografie (Journal of economic and social geography), (86)3, 235–248.

Griffis, W.E. (1878). Japan: Geographical and social. Bulletin of the American Geographical Society, 10(2), 77–92.

Grossman, M. J. (2003) Climate change, typhoons, and floods on the Ara River, central Japan. Ph.D. Dissertation. The University of Wisconsin – Madison.

Guo, N. (2009). Environmental culture and world heritage in Pacific Japan: Saving the Ogasawara Islands. The Asia Pacific Journal, 17-3-09, April 26, 2009. Electronic.

Guo, N., and McCormack, G. (2001). Coming to terms with nature: Development dilemmas on the Ogasawara Islands. Japan Forum, 13:2, 177–193.

Guo, N., Hasegawa, S., Johnson, H., Kawanishi H., Kitahara, K., and Rausch, A. (2005). Tsugaru: Regional identity on Japan's northern periphery. Dunedin, New Zealand: Otago University Press.

Hall, D. (2010). Food with a visible face: Traceability and the public promotion of private governance in the Japanese food system. Geoforum, 41(5), 826–835.

Hall, R.B. (1926). Quelpart Island and its people. Geographical Review, 16(1), 60–72.

Hall, R. B. (1930). The geography of Manchuria. Annals of the American Academy of Political and Social Science, 152(1), 278–292.

Hall, R. B. (1931). Some rural settlement forms in Japan. Geographical Review, 21(1), 93–123.

Hall, R. B. (1932). The Yamato Basin, Japan. Annals of the Association of American Geographers, 22(4), 243–292.

Hall, R. B. (1934a). Agricultural regions of Asia: Part VII, The Japanese Empire. Economic Geography, 10(4), 323–347.

Hall, R. B. (1934b). The cities of Japan: Notes on distribution and inherited forms. Annals of the Association of American Geographers, 24(4), 175–200.

Hall, R. B. (1935a). Agricultural regions of Asia: Part VII, The Japanese Empire. Economic Geography, 11(1), 33–52.

Hall, R. B. (1935b). Agricultural regions of Asia: Part VII, The Japanese Empire. Economic Geography, 11(2), 130–147.

Hall, R. B. (1937) Tokaido: Road and region. Geographical Review, 27(3), 353–377.

Hall, R. B. (1947). Area studies: With special reference to their implications for research in the social sciences. New York: Social Science Research Council.

Hall, R. B., and Watanabe, A. (1932). Landforms of Japan. Papers of the Michigan Academy of Science, Arts, and Letters, 18, 157–207.

Hall, R.B., and Noh, T. (1953). Yakihata, burned-field agriculture in Japan, with its special characteristics in Shikoku. Papers of the Michigan Academy of Science, Arts, and Letters, 38(3), 315–22.

Hall, R.B., and Noh, T. (1956). Japanese geography: A guide to Japanese reference and research materials. (Rev. ed, 1970) University of Michigan Center for Japanese Studies, Bibliographical Series No. 6. Ann Arbor: University of Michigan Press. In Romanization and kanji: www.quod.lib.umich.edu/c/cjs/bby8157.0001.001?view=toc Accessed 8 July 2014.

Hall, R. B., Jr. (1958). Hand-tractors in Japanese paddy fields. Economic Geography, 34(4), 312–320.

Hall, R. B. Jr. (1963). Japan: Industrial power of Asia. Princeton, NJ: Van Nostrand.

Hanham, R., and Banasick, S. (1998). Japanese labor and the production of the space-economy in an era of globalization. In A. Herod (Ed.), Organizing the landscape: Geographical perspectives on labor unionism (pp. 99–122). Minneapolis: University of Minnesota Press.

Hanham, R., and Banasick, S. (2000). Shift-share analysis and changes in Japanese manufacturing employment. Growth and Change, 31(1), 108–123.

Harada, T. (2000). Space, materials, and the 'social': in the aftermath of a disaster. Environment and Planning D: Society and Space, 18(2), 205–212.

Harris, C. D. (1982). The urban and industrial transformation of Japan. The Geographical Review, 72(1), 50–89.

Harris, C. D. (1997). Geographers in the US government in Washington DC during World War II. The Professional Geographer, 49(2), 245–256.

Harris, C. D. (2001). English as international language in geography: Development and limitations. Geographical Review, 91(4), 675–689.

Harvey, T. (1996). Portland, Oregon: Regional city in a global economy. Urban Geography, 17(1), 95–114.

Hashimoto, A. (1996). A cross-cultural study of attitudes toward the natural environment and tourism development: Northern Europe and East Asia. Ph.D. Dissertation. University of Surrey, UK.

Hashimoto, A. (2000). Environmental perception and the sense of responsibility of the tourism industry in Mainland China, Taiwan and Japan. Journal of Sustainable Tourism, 8(2), 131–146.

Hashimoto, A. (2007). Japanese tourism and the Japanese market. In G. Wall (Ed.), Approaching Tourism (pp. 183–210). Department of Geography Occasional Publication 21. University of Waterloo.

Hashimoto, A., and Telfer, D. (2008). From saké to sea urchin: Food and drink festivals and regional identity in Japan. In C.M. Hall and L. Sharples (Eds.), Food and wine festivals and events around the world (pp. 249–278). Oxford: Butterworth-Heinemann.

Hashimoto, A., and Telfer, D. (2010). Developing sustainable partnerships in rural tourism: the case of Oita, Japan. Journal of Policy Research in Tourism, Leisure, and Events, 2(2), 165–183.

Hashimoto, A., and Telfer, D. J. (2011). Female empowerment through agritourism in rural Japan. In R. Torres and J. Momsen (Eds.), *Tourism and agriculture: New geographies of consumption, production and rural restructuring* (pp. 72–84). Oxford and New York: Routledge.

Hayter, R., and Barnes, T. (2001). Canada's resource economy. *The Canadian Geographer*, 45(1), 36–41.

Hayter, R., and Edgington, D. (1997). Cutting against the grain: A case study of MacMillan Bloedel's Japan strategy. *Economic Geography*, 73(2), 187–213.

Hayter, R., and Edgington, D.W. (1999). Getting tough and getting smart: Politics of the North American-Japan wood products trade. *Environment and Planning C: Government and Policy*, 17(3), 319–344.

Hayter, R., and Edgington, D.W. (2004). Flying geese in Asia: The impacts of Japanese MNCs as a source of industrial learning. *Tijdschrift voor Economische en Sociale Geografie (Journal of Economic and Social Geography)*, 95(1), 3–26.

Hayter, R., Patchell, J., and Rees, K. (1999). Business segmentation and location revisited: Innovation and the terra incognita of large firms. *Regional Studies*, 33(5), 425–442.

Hebbert, M. (1994). Sen-biki amidst desakota: Urban sprawl and urban planning in Japan. In P. Shapira, I. Masser and D. Edgington (Eds.), *Planning for Cities and Regions in Japan* (pp. 70–91). Liverpool: Liverpool University Press.

Hebbert, M., and Nakai, N. (1988). Deregulation of Japanese city planning in the Nakasone era. *Town Planning Review*, 59(4), 383–396.

Hein, C. (2001). Toshikeikaku and machizukuri in Japanese urban planning - The reconstruction of inner city neighborhoods in Kobe. *Jahrbuch des DIJ* (Deutsches Institut für Japanstudien), 13: 221–52.

Hein, C. (2003). Visionary plans and planners. In N. Fiévé and P. Waley (Eds.), *Japanese capitals in historical perspective: Place, power and memory in Kyoto, Edo, and Tokyo* (pp. 309–346). Richmond, Surrey: Curzon.

Hein, C. (2008). Machi: Neighborhood and small town, the foundation for urban transformation in Japan. *Journal of Urban History*, 35(1), 75–107.

Hein, C. (2010). Shaping Tokyo: Land development and planning practice in the early modern Japanese metropolis. *Journal of Urban History*, 36(4), 447–484.

Hein, C., Diefendorf, J.M., and Ishida Y. (Eds.) (2003). *Rebuilding urban Japan after 1945*. Houndmills: Palgrave Macmillan.

Hein, C., and Pelletier, P. (2006a). Conclusion: Decentralization policies – Questioning the Japanese model. In C. Hein and P. Pelletier (Eds.), *Cities, autonomy and decentralization in Japan* (pp. 164–181). London: Routledge.

Hein, C., and Pelletier, P. (2006b). Introduction: Decentralization and the tension between global and local urban Japan. In C. Hein and P. Pelletier (Eds.), *Cities, autonomy and decentralization in Japan* (pp.1–24). London: Routledge.

Herod, A. (2011). What does the 2011 Japanese tsunami tell us about the nature of the global economy? *Social and Cultural Geography*, 12(8), 829–837.

Hewitt, K. (1983). Place annihilation: Area bombing and the fate of urban places. *Annals of the Association of American Geographers*, 73(2), 257–284.

Hill, R. C. (2004). Comment on Fielding's 'Class and space: social segregation in Japanese cities.' *Transactions of the Institute of British Geographers* 29(1), 86–87.

Hill, R. C., and Fujita, K. (2000). State restructuring and local power in Japan. *Urban Studies*, 37(4), 673–690.

Hill, R. C., and Kim, J. W. (2000). Global cities and developmental states: New York, Tokyo and Seoul. *Urban Studies*, 37(12), 2167–2195.

Himiyama, Y. (1999). Historical information bases for land use planning in Japan. *Land Use Policy*, 16(3), 145–151.

Himiyama, Y., Hwang, M., and Ichinose, T. (2002). *Land use changes in comparative perspective*. International Geographical Union Commission on Land Use and Land Cover Change. Enfield, NH: Science Publishers.

Hiraoka, M. (1974). *Pioneer settlement in Eastern Bolivia*. Ph.D. Dissertation. University of Wisconsin Milwaukee.

Hiraoka, M. (1980). *Japanese agricultural settlement in the Bolivian upper Amazon: A study in regional ecology*. Latin American Studies 1. Ibaraki, Japan: University of Tsukuba.

Hiraoka, M., and Yamamoto, S. (1980). Agricultural development in the upper Amazon of Ecuador. *The Geographical Review*, 70(4), 423–445.

Hirayama, Y. (2000). Collapse and reconstruction: Housing recovery policy in Kobe after the Hanshin Great Earthquake. *Housing Studies*, 15(1), 111–128.

Hirayama, Y., and Ronald, R. (Eds.) (2007). *Housing and social transition in Japan*. London and New York: Routledge.

Hohn, U. (1997). Townscape preservation in Japanese urban planning. *Town Planning Review*, 68(2), 213–255.

Hohn, U. (1998). Important preservation districts for groups of historic buildings. In S. Enders and N. Gutschow (Eds.), *Hozon: Architectural and urban conservation in Japan* (pp. 150–59). Stuttgart and London: Axel Menges.

Hohn, U. (2000). *Stadtplanung in Japan: Geschichte, recht, praxis, theorie*. Dortmund: Dortmunder Vertrieb für Bau- und Planungsliteratur. Dortmund, Germany.

Hones, S., and Endo, Y. (2006). History, distance and text: Narratives of the 1853–4 Perry expedition to

Japan. *Journal of Historical Geography*, 32(3), 563–78.

Hood, C. P. (2006a). From polling station to political station? Politics and the Shinkansen. *Japan Forum*, 18(1), 45–63.

Hood, C. P. (2006b). *Shinkansen: From bullet train to symbol of modern Japan*. New York: Routledge.

Hood, C.P. (2010). The Shinkansen's local impact. *Social Science Japan Journal*, 13(2), 211–225.

Horiuchi, R. N. (1975). *Chiseigaku: Japanese geopolitics*. Ph.D. Dissertation. University of Washington.

Hough, R. F. (1963). *The impact of the drastic decline in raw silk upon land use and industry in selected areas of sericultural specialization in Japan*. Ph.D. Dissertation. The University of Wisconsin-Madison.

Hough, R. F. (1968a). Impact of the decline in raw silk on the Suwa Basin of Japan. *Economic Geography*, 44(2), 95–116.

Hough, R. F. (1968b). Impact of the decline of raw silk on two major cocoon-producing regions in Japan. *Annals of the Association of American Geographers*, 58(2), 221–249.

Hugo, G. (2003). Asian migration to Australia: Changing trends and implications. *The Scottish Geographical Magazine*, 119(3), 247–264.

Humphrys, G. (1990). Population loss in Northern Japan: The experience of Hokkaido in the 1980s. *Hokkaido Chiri, Annals of the Hokkaido Geographical Society*, 64, 41–50.

Humphrys, G. (1995a). Japanese industry at home. *Geography*, 80(1), 15–22.

Humphrys, G. (1995b). Japanese integration and the geography of industry in Japan. In R. LeHeron and S. O. Park (Eds.) *The Asian Pacific Rim and globalization: Enterprise, governance and territoriality* (pp. 129–150). Aldershot and Brookfield VT: Avebury.

Humphrys, G., and Peck, J. (1992). Japan in the global economy. *Area*, 24(2), 217–218.

Hurdley, L., and White, P.E. (1999). Japanese economic activity and community growth in Great Britain. *Revue Européenne des Migrations Internationales*, 15(1), 101–120.

Ichijo, A. (2002). Scope of theories of nationalism: Comments on the Scottish and Japanese experiences. *Geopolitics*, 7(2), 53–74.

Iguchi, A., Tabayashi, A., Waldichuk, T., and Wang, P. (2007). The rejuvenation of greenhouse horticulture owing to the introduction of hydroponic cultivation on the Kujukuri plain, Chiba Prefecture, Japan. *Geographical Review of Japan/Chirigaku Hyōron*, 80(12), 732–757.

Ikagawa, T. (1993). White sand and blue pines: a nostalgic landscape of Japan. *Landscape* 32(1), 1–7.

Ikagawa, T. (1994). *Residential gardens in urban Honolulu, Hawaii: Neighborhood, ethnicity, and ornamental plants*. Ph.D. Dissertation. University of Hawaii.

Ikagawa, T. (1996). Transported landscape: traits of Japanese ornamental gardens in residential yards in Honolulu, Hawaii. *Association of Pacific Coast Geographers Yearbook*, 58, 115–137.

Ikeguchi, A., and Okamoto, K. (2008). The grassroots movement to preserve tidal flats in urban coastal regions in Japan: The case of the Fujimae tidal flats, Nagoya. In P.P. Karan and U. Suganuma (Eds.), *Local environmental movements: A comparative study of the United States and Japan* (pp. 229–243). Lexington: University Press of Kentucky.

Imazato, S. (2008). Under two globalizations: Progress in social and cultural geography of Japanese rural areas, 1996–2006. *Geographical Review of Japan, Chirigaku Hyōron*, 81(5), 323–335.

Inaba, M. G. (1959). *Japan: Some geographic aspects of industrialization and population correlates*. Ph.D. Dissertation. Columbia University.

Ishida, H. (1980). *Geographic studies of Japan presented by western observers: A retrospect*. University of Hiroshima, Research and Sources Unit for Regional Geography.

Ishida, H., Hill, R.D., and Hough, R. (Eds.) (1982). *Changing agriculture and rural development: The world and Japan*. Papers and proceedings of IGU Nagano symposium 1980. IGU Commission on Agricultural Productivity and World Food Supply. IGU Commission on Rural Development.

Ishikawa, Y. (2008). Progress in Japanese population geography: Retrospect and prospect. *Geographical Review of Japan, Chirigaku Hyōron*, 81(5), 247–261(1–15).

Ishikawa, Y., and Fielding, A. J. (1998). Explaining the recent migration trends of the Tokyo metropolitan area. *Environment and Planning A*, 30(10), 1797–1814.

Ito, Y., Nakamura, K., Kanasaka, K., and Sargent, J. (2009). *Discovering Japan: A new regional geography*. Tōkyō: Teikoku Shoin.

Iwata, O., and Oguchi, T. (2009). Factors affecting late twentieth century land use patterns in Kamakura City, Japan. *Geographical Research (Journal of the Institute of Australian Geographers)*, 47(2), 175–191.

Izushi, H. (1997). Conflict between two industrial networks: technological adaptation and interfirm relationships in the ceramics industry in Seto, Japan. *Regional Studies* 31, 117–29.

Izushi, H., and Aoyama, Y. (2006). Industry evolution and cross-sectoral skill transfers: A comparative analysis of the video game industry in Japan, the United States, and the UK. *Environment and Planning A*, 38(10), 1843–1861.

Jacobson, J. P. (2010). *Japanese transit-oriented development: The framed market and the production of alternative landscapes*. Ph.D. Dissertation. University of Minnesota.

Jefferson, M. (1916). The distribution of people in Japan in 1913. *Geographical Review*, 2(5), 368–372.

Johnston, I., and Murphy, H. (2001). The Newshot Isle Project. *The Scottish Geographical Journal*, 117(3), 207–217.

Jones, W. D. (1921). Hokkaido, the northland of Japan. *The Geographical Review*, 11(1), 16–30.

Kageyama, H. (2004). *Toshi kūkan to jendaa*. Tōkyō: Kokon Shoin.

Kakiuchi, G. H. (1958). *The rise and development of the fruit industry on the Okayama Plain*. Ph.D. Dissertation. University of Michigan.

Kakiuchi, G. H. (1960). Stone wall strawberry industry on Kuno Mountain, Japan. *Economic Geography*, 36(2), 171–84.

Kakiuchi, G. H. (1962). A study of a semiagricultural community exploiting marine resources. *Papers of the Michigan Academy of Science, Arts, and Letters*, 47(2), 507–515.

Kakiuchi, G. H., and Murakami, S. (1961). Satsuma oranges in Ocho-Mura: A study of specialized cash cropping in Southwestern Japan. *Geographical Review*, 51(4), 500–518.

Kalafsky, R. (2006a). Human capital in Japanese manufacturing: Evidence and practices from a key capital goods sector. *The Industrial Geographer*, 3(2), 13–26.

Kalafsky, R. V. (2006b). Performance and practice: Examining the machine tool industries of Japan and the United States. *Tijdschrift voor economische en sociale geografie*, 97(2), 178–194.

Kalafsky, R. V. (2007). Export dynamics, strategies and performance within Japan's machine-tool industry. *Asia Pacific Business Review*, 13(4), 481–500.

Kamiya, H., and Lee, C. W. (2009). International marriage migrants to rural areas in South Korea and Japan: A comparative analysis. *Geographical Review of Japan Series B*, 81(1), 60–67.

Kamo, T. (2000). An aftermath of globalisation? East Asian economic turmoil and Japanese cities adrift. *Urban Studies*, 37(12), 2145–2165.

Kanasaka, K., Okuno, S., Ogata N., Takayama, M., and Ikuta, M. (2006). Progress of human geography in Asia: Editorial note (Singapore, Taiwan, Korea, Vietnam). *Jinbun Chiri/Japanese Journal of Human Geography*, 58(6), 533–539.

Kaneko, J., and Nojiri, W. (2008) The logistics of just-in-time between parts suppliers and car assemblers in Japan. *Journal of Transport Geography*, 16(3), 155–173.

Kanno, M. (1977). *A comparative study of urban land use: Shizuoka, Japan, and Atlanta, USA*. Ph.D. Dissertation. University of Georgia.

Karacas, C. L. (2006). *Tokyo from the fire: War, occupation, and the remaking of a metropolis*. Ph.D. Dissertation. University of California, Berkeley.

Karacas, C. (2010). Place, public memory, and the Tokyo air raids. *Geographical Review*, 100(4), 521–537.

Karan, P. P. (Ed.). (2001). *Japan in the Bluegrass*. Lexington: University Press of Kentucky.

Karan, P. P., and Gilbreath, D. (2005). *Japan in the 21st Century: Environment, economy, and society*. Lexington: University Press of Kentucky.

Karan, P. P., and Stapleton, K. (Eds.) (1997). *The Japanese city*. Lexington, University Press of Kentucky.

Karan, P. P., and Suganuma, U. (Eds.) (2008). *Local environmental movements: A comparative study of the United States and Japan*. Lexington: The University Press of Kentucky.

Karan, P. P., and Subbiah, S.P., (Eds.) (2011). *The Indian Ocean tsunami: The global response to a natural disaster*. Lexington: University Press of Kentucky.

Kawamura, H. (1989). Kuni-ezu (provincial maps) compiled by the Tokugawa Shogunate in Japan. *Imago Mundi*, 41(1), 70–75.

Kearns, G. (2009). *Geopolitics and empire: The legacy of Halford Mackinder*. Oxford and New York: Oxford University Press.

Keen, E. A. (1965). *Some aspects of the economic geography of the Japanese skipjack-tuna fishery*. Ph.D. Dissertation, University of Washington.

Keen, E. (1988). *Ownership and productivity of marine fishery resources: an essay on the resolution of conflict in the use of the ocean pastures*. Blacksburg, Virginia: McDonald and Woodward Publishing Co.

Kennett, P., and Mizuuchi, T. (2010). Homelessness, housing insecurity and social exclusion in China, Hong Kong, and Japan. *City, Culture and Society*, 1(3), 111–118.

Kenney, M., and Florida, R., (1993). *Beyond mass production: The Japanese system and its transfer to the US* New York: Oxford University Press.

Kerr, D. (2002). The place of land in Japan's postwar development, and the dynamic of the 1980s real-estate bubble and 1990s banking crisis. *Environment and Planning D: Society and Space*, 20(3), 345–374.

Kikuchi, T. (2008). Recent progress in Japanese geographical studies on sustainable rural system: Focusing on recreating rurality in the urban fringe of the Tokyo metropolitan area. *Geographical Review of Japan, Chirigaku Hyōron*, 81(5), 336–348(90–102).

Kimura, J. C. (1966). The beginning and end of the shurin season of Japan. *Geographical Reports of Tokyo Metropolitan University*, 1, 113–138.

Kinda, A. (1997). Some traditions and methodologies of Japanese historical geography. *Journal of Historical Geography*, 23(1), 62–75.

Kinda, A. (Ed.). (2010). *A landscape history of Japan*. Kyōto: Kyōto University Press.

Kingsbury, A. J. (2012) Re-localizing Japanese wine: The grape and wine clusters of Yamanashi Prefecture, Japan. Ph.D. Dissertation. University of Hawaii.

Kingsbury, A. (2013). The historical geographies of growing and fermenting the Delaware grape in the Kōfu Basin of Yamanashi Prefecture, Japan. *Journal of Wine Research*, 24(4), 278–290.

Kingsbury, A. (2014). Constructed heritage and co-produced meaning: the rebranding of wines from the Koshu grape. *Contemporary Japan*, 26(1), 29–48.

Kingsbury, A., Maeda, Y., and Takahashi, M. (2010). Marketing the slippery local with the contrived rural: Case studies of alternative vegetable retail in the urban fringe of Nagoya, Japan. *International Journal of Sociology of Agriculture and Food*, 17(2), 89–107.

Kish, G. (1949). Some aspects of the missionary cartography of Japan during the sixteenth century. *Imago Mundi*, 6, 39–47.

Kish, G. (1951). The Japan on the 'Mural Atlas' of the Palazzo Vecchio, Florence. *Imago Mundi*, 8, 52–54.

Kish, G. (1966). Two fifteenth-century maps of 'Zipangu': Notes on the early cartography of Japan. *Yale University Library Gazette*, 40(4), 206–214.

Kiss, G. (1947). The cartography of Japan during the middle Tokugawa era: A study in cross-cultural influences. *Annals of the Association of American Geographers*, 37(2), 101–119.

Kitagawa, F. (2005). The Fukuoka silicon sea belt project: An East Asian experiment in developing transnational networks. *European Planning Studies*, 13(5), 793–799.

Kitagawa, F. (2007). Regionalisation of science and innovation governance in Japan? *Regional Studies*, 41(8), 1099–1114.

Kitagawa, F., and Woolgar, L. (2008). Regionalisation of innovation policies and new university-industry links in Japan. *Prometheus*, 26(1), 55–67.

Kitajima, S. (1994). *The state, capital and social forces: Mutsu-Ogasawara kaihatsu: The political economy of Japanese regional development*. Ph.D. Dissertation. University of Washington.

Kitajima, S. (1998). Industrial and regional restructuring and changing form of state intervention: the development of partnerships in postwar Japan. *International Journal of Urban and Regional Research*, 22(1), 26–41.

Kitajima, S. (2000). Local restructuring processes and problems of governance: A case of an old industrial city in Northern Japan. *Asian Geographer*, 19(1–2), 89–106.

Kitchin, R., and Thrift, N., eds., (2009). *International encyclopedia of human geography*. Oxford: Elsevier.

Kiuchi, S. (Ed.) (1976). *Geography in Japan*. Tōkyō: Tōkyō University Press.

Kobayashi, A. L. (1983). *Emigration from Kaideima, Japan, 1885–1950: An analysis of community and landscape change*. Ph.D. Dissertation. University of California, Los Angeles.

Kobayashi, A. (1990). Racism and law in Canada: A geographic perspective. *Urban Geography*, 11(5), 447–473.

Kobayashi, A. (2002). Migration as a negotiation of gender: recent Japanese immigrant women in Canada. In L.R. Hirabayashi, A. Kimura-Yano and J.A. Hirabayashi (Eds.), *New worlds, new lives: globalization and people of Japanese descent in the Americas and from Latin America in Japan* (pp. 205–220). Palo Alto CA: Stanford University Press.

Kobayashi, A., and Jackson, P. (1994). Japanese Canadians and the racialization of labour in the British Columbia sawmill industry. *B.C. Studies*, 103, 33–58.

Kobayashi, S. (2012). Japanese mapping of Asia-Pacific areas, 1873–1945: An overview. *Cross-Currents: East Asian History and Culture Review E-Journal*, (2), 1–38. Accessed 8 July 2014 at https://cross-currents.berkeley.edu/e-journal/issue-2/japanese-mapping-asia-pacific-areas-1873-1945-overview

Koganezawa, T. (2007). Chiiki nōgyō shinkō to shoku bunka. *Keizai Chirigaku Nenpō*, 53(1), 98–118.

Koganezawa, T. (2009). The relationship between rice production and ecosystem services. *Miyagi Kyōiku Daigaku Kiyō*, 44, 15–22.

Kornhauser, D. (1956). *The influence of geography and related factors on the rise of Japanese cities*. Ph.D. Dissertation. University of Michigan.

Kornhauser, D. (1976). *Urban Japan: Its foundations and growth*. London and New York: Longman.

Kornhauser, D. (1979). *A selected list of writings on Japan pertinent to geography in western languages, with emphasis on the work of Japan specialists*. Special Publication No. 6, Research and Sources Unit for Regional Geography, University of Hiroshima.

Kornhauser, D. H. (1982). *Japan: Geographical background to urban-industrial development*. Essex and New York: Wiley.

Kornhauser, D. (1984). *Studies of Japan in western languages of special interest to geographers*. Tōkyō: Kokon Shoin.

Kornhauser, D. H. (1989). Coefficients of urban intensification for Japanese cities: 1960–1980. In F. J. Costa, A. Dutt, L. Ma and A.G. Noble (Eds.), *Urbanization in Asia: Spatial dimensions and policy issues* (pp. 139–167). Honolulu: University of Hawaii Press.

Koto, B. (1894). The great earthquake in Japan. *The Geographical Journal*. 3(3), 213–216.

Kurihara, T. (1986). *Japanese direct foreign investment in the United States and Canada by sogo shosha since 1951*. Ph.D. Dissertation. University of British Columbia.

Kurihara, T. (1993). Direct foreign investment in Canada by *sogo shosha* since 1954. *Geographical Review of Japan, Series B*, 66(1), 52–69.

Kurihara, T. (2000). A comparative study of the economic activities of *sogo shosha* in the United

States and Canada in the early 1990s. *Geographical Review of Japan, Series B,* 73(2), 191–206.

Kurita, H., Yokohari, M., and Bolthouse, J. (2009). The potential of intra-regional supply and demand of agricultural products in an urban fringe area: A case study of the Kanto Plain, Japan. *Geografisk Tidsskrift-Danish Journal of Geography,* 109(2), 147–159.

Kusaka, H. (2008). Recent progress on urban climate study in Japan. *Geographical Review of Japan, Chirigaku Hyōron,* 81(5), 361–374(115–128).

Lacy, W. N. (1917). Coaling at Nagasaki. *Journal of Geography,* 15(5), 163–164.

Latz, G. I., (1986). *Agricultural development in Japan: The land improvement district in concept and practice.* Ph.D. Dissertation. The University of Chicago.

Latz, G. (1989). *Agricultural development in Japan: The land improvement district in concept and practice.* Geography Research Papers no. 225. Chicago: University of Chicago.

Latz, G. (1991). The persistence of agriculture in urban Japan: An analysis of the Tokyo metropolitan area. In N.S. Ginsburg, B. Koppel and T.G. McGee (Eds.), *The extended metropolis: Settlement transition in Asia* (pp. 217–238). Honolulu HI: University of Hawaii Press.

LeHeron, R. B., and Harrington, J. W. (2005). *New economic spaces: New economic geographies.* Burlington VT: Ashgate.

Liaw, K. L. (1992). Interprefectural migration and its effects on prefectural populations in Japan: An analysis based on the 1980 census. *The Canadian Geographer,* 36(4), 320–335.

Liaw, K.L. (2003). Distinctive features of the sex ratio of Japan's interprefectural migration: An explanation based on the family system and spatial economy of Japan. *International Journal of Population Geography,* 9, 199–214.

Liaw, K. L., and Ishikawa, Y. (2008). Destination choice of the 1995–2000 immigrants to Japan: salient features and multivariate explanation. *Environment and Planning A,* 40(4), 806–830.

Liaw, K. L., Ochiai, E., and Ishikawa, Y. (2010). Feminization of immigration in Japan: Marital and job opportunities. In W.S. Yang and M.C.W. Lu (Eds.), *Asian cross-border marriage migration: Demographic patterns and social issues* (pp. 49–86). Amsterdam: Amsterdam University Press.

Linge, G.J. R. (1991a). Just in time in Australia: A review. *The Australian Geographer,* 22(1), 67–74.

Linge, G. J. R. (1991b). Just-in-time: More or less flexible? *Economic Geography,* 67(4), 316–332.

Loeve, A., De Vries, J., and De Smidt, M. (1985). Japanese firms and the gateway to Europe: The Netherlands as a location for Japanese subsidiaries. *Tijdschrift voor economische en sociale geografie (Journal of economic and social geography),* 76(1), 2–8.

Luo, Y. (1993). *The spatial process of Japanese foreign direct investment in finance, insurance, and real estate in the United States, 1980–1990.* Ph.D. Dissertation. University of Georgia.

Lützeler, R. (1995). The regional structure of social problems. *Geographical Review of Japan Series B,* 68(1), 46–62.

Lützeler, R. (2008a). German geographical research on Japan: Some remarks on its current state and future prospects. In H.D. Ölschleger (Ed.), *Theories and methods in Japanese studies: Current state and future developments. Papers in honour of Josef Kreiner* (pp. 153–164). Göttingen: Bonn University Press.

Lützeler, R. (2008b). Regional demographics. In F. Coulmas, H. Conrad, A. Schad-Seifert and G. Vogt (Eds.) *The demographic challenge: A handbook about Japan* (pp. 61–79). Leiden, Boston: Brill.

Lützeler, R. (2011). Left behind in the global city: Spaces and places of ageing and shrinking in the Tokyo metropolitan area. In F. Coulmas and R. Lützeler (Eds.), *Imploding populations in Japan and Germany* (pp. 473–491). Leiden: Brill.

MacDonald, D. (1985) *A geography of modern Japan.* Woodchurch, Ashford, Kent: Paul Norbury.

Maeda, Y. (2012). Creating a diversified community: Community safety activity in Musashino City, Japan. *Geoforum,* 43(2), 342–352.

Mair, A., Florida, R., and Kenney, M. (1988). New geography of automobile production: Japanese transplants in North America. *Economic Geography,* 64(4), 352–373.

Majek, T., and Hayter, R. (2008). Hybrid branch plants: Japanese lean production in Poland's automobile industry. *Economic Geography,* 84(3), 333–358.

Manchester, C. A. (1947). *The development and distribution of sekisho in Japan.* Ph.D. Dissertation. University of Michigan.

Manchester, C. A. (1958). Igusa: A critical cash crop in the rural economy of Okayama Prefecture. *Economic Geography,* 34(1), 47–63.

Manchester, C. A. (1962). A Tokugawa map of Japan on porcelain. *Imago Mundi,* 16, 149–151.

Mansfield, B. K. (2001). *Globalizing nature: Political and cultural economy of a global seafood industry.* Ph.D. Dissertation. University of Oregon.

Mansfield, B. (2003a). Fish, factory trawlers and imitation crab: the nature of quality in the seafood industry. *Journal of Rural Studies,* 19(1), 9–21.

Mansfield, B. (2003b). Imitation crab and the material culture of commodity production. *Cultural Geographies,* 10(2), 176–195.

Mansfield, B. (2003c). Spatializing globalization: A 'geography of quality' in the seafood industry. *Economic Geography,* 79(1), 1–16.

Marchetti, B. (1993). Japan's landscape in literature. *Journal of Geography,* 92(4), 194–200.

Markusen, A. (1996). Sticky places in slippery space: A typology of industrial districts. *Economic Geography*, 72(3), 293–313.

Masai, Y. (1960). *Lansing, Michigan and Shizuoka, Japan: A comparison of areal functional organization in two different environments*. Ph.D. Dissertation. Michigan State University.

Mason, R. J. (1999). Whither Japan's environmental movement? An assessment of problems and prospects at the national level. *Pacific Affairs*, 72(2), 187–207.

Masser, I. (1990). Technology and regional development policy: A review of Japan's Technopolis programme. *Regional Studies*, 24(1), 41–53.

Matanle, P. (2013). Post-disaster recovery in ageing and declining communities: The Great East Japan disaster of 11 March 2011. *Geography*, 98(2), 68–76.

Matanle, P., and Rausch, A. (2011). *Japan's shrinking regions in the 21st century: Contemporary responses to depopulation and socioeconomic decline*. Shrinking Regions Research Group. Amherst, NY, and London: Cambria Press.

Mather, C., Karan, P. P., and Iijima, S. (1998). *Japanese landscapes: Where land and culture merge*. Lexington: University Press of Kentucky.

Matsubara, H. (2007). Spatial knowledge flows and regional innovation systems. *Komaba Studies in Human Geography*, 18, 22–43.

Matsuhashi, K., Mizuno, M., Kashima, H., and Oda, H. (2013). A review of geographical studies on manufacturing industries in Japan. *Geographical Review of Japan Series B*, 86(1), 82–91.

Matsui, K. (2008). Recent trends in the geography of religion in Japan. *Geographical Review of Japan, Chirigaku Hyōron*, 81(5), 311–322(65–76).

Matsui, K. (2014). *Geography of religion in Japan: Religious space, landscape, and behavior*. Tokyo: Springer.

Matsusaka, Y. (2012). Imagining Manmō: Mapping the Russo-Japanese boundary agreement in Manchuria and Inner Mongolia, 1907–1915. *Cross-Currents: East Asian History and Culture Review E-Journal*, (2), 1–30. Accessed 8 July 2014 at https://cross-currents.berkeley.edu/e-journal/issue-2/ imagining-manmo-mapping-russo-japanese-boundary-agreements-manchuria-and-inner-mon

McCune, S. B. B. (1939). *Climatic regions of Tyosen (Korea)*. Ph.D. Dissertation. Clark University.

McCune, S. (1941). Climatic regions of Korea and their economy. *The Geographical Review*, 31(1), 95–99.

McCune, S. (1949). Geographic regions in Korea. *The Geographical Review*, 39(4), 658–660.

McCune, S. (1950). Committee on Asian Studies. *Professional Geographer*, 2(2), 14.

McCune, S. (1956). *Korea's heritage: A regional and social geography*. Rutland, VT: Tuttle.

McCune, S. (1966). *Korea: Land of broken calm*. Princeton NJ: Van Nostrand.

McCune, S. (1970). *Ryukyu islands project, research and information papers, No. 1– No. 26*. Gainesville: University of Florida.

McCune, S. (1975a). *Geographical aspects of agricultural changes in the Ryukyu Islands*. Gainesville: University Presses of Florida.

McCune, S. (1975b). *The Ryukyu Islands*. Newton Abbot: David and Charles. Harrisburg: Stackpole Books.

McCune, S. (1984). *Islands in conflict in East Asia waters*. Hong Kong: Asian Research Service.

McCune, S. (1989). *Intelligence on the economic collapse of Japan in 1945*. Lanham MD: University Press of America.

McDonald, M. G. (1990). *Displacing rice: Factories in the fields of farm power in Tohoku, Japan*. Ph.D. Dissertation. University of California, Berkeley.

McDonald, M. G. (1996a). Farmers as workers in Japan's regional economic restructuring, 1965–1985. *Economic Geography*, 72(1), 49–72.

McDonald, M. G. (1996b). Farming out factories: Japan's law to promote the introduction of industry into agricultural village areas. *Environment and Planning A*, 28(11), 2041–2061.

McDonald, M. G. (1997). Agricultural landholding in Japan: Fifty years after land reform. *Geoforum*, 28(1), 55–78.

McDonald, M. G. (2000). Food firms and food flows in Japan 1945–98. *World Development*, 28(3), 487–512.

McDonald, M. G. (2005). Tourist weddings in Hawaii: Consuming the destination. In C. Cartier and A. A. Lew (Eds.), *Seductions of place: Geographical perspectives on globalization and touristed landscapes* (pp. 171–192). New York: Routledge.

McGee, T. G. (1991). Emergence of desakota regions in Asia. In N.S. Ginsburg, B. Koppel and T. G. McGee, Eds. *The extended metropolis: Settlement transition in Asia*. (pp. 3–25). Honolulu: University of Hawaii Press.

McGee, T. G., and Edgington, D. W. (Eds.) (2004). *Australian and Canadian approaches to Asia in an era of unstable globalization*. Centre for Australasian Research, Institute of Asian Research. Vancouver: University of British Columbia.

McMorran, C. (2005). Constructing idealized communities in Japan's countryside: Tourist place-making in Kurokawa Onsen. *Jinbun Chiri/Japanese Journal of Human Geography*, 57(5), 61–73.

McMorran, C. (2008a). *Home as performance: The reproduction and resistance of home by workers in the Japanese tourist industry*. Ph.D. Dissertation. University of Colorado at Boulder.

McMorran, C. (2008b). Understanding the heritage in heritage tourism: Ideological tool or economic tool for a Japanese hot springs resort? *Tourism Geographies*, 10(3), 334–354.

McMorran, C. (2012). Practising workplace geographies: embodied labour as method in human geography. *Area*, 44 (4), 489–495.

Millward, H. (1995). Regional variations in the development and restructuring of farming in Hokkaido, Japan. *Scottish Geographical Magazine*, 111(3), 150–158.

Millward, H. (2006). Urban containment strategies: A case-study appraisal of plans and policies in Japanese, British, and Canadian cities. *Land Use Policy*, 23(4), 473–485.

Millward, H., and Morrison, J. (1997). *Japan at century's end: Changes, challenges and choices.* Halifax, NS, Canada: Fernwood. Ninth annual conference of Japan Studies Association of Canada, October 1996.

Milne, J. (1896). The great sea-waves in Japan. *The Geographical Journal* 8(2), 157–160.

Mitsuhashi, S. (1977). *Japanese commodity flows.* Ph.D. Dissertation. University of Chicago.

Mitsuhashi, S. (1978). *Japanese commodity flows.* Research Paper No. 187. Department of Geography, University of Chicago.

Mitsuhashi, S. (1992). President Susan Hanson of the Association of American Geographers delivered a speech on the status of women in geography in the USA. *Annals of the Ochanomizu Geographical Society*, 33, 96–101.

Miyakawa, Y. (2000). The changing iconography of Japanese political geography. *GeoJournal*, 52(4), 345–352.

Miyake, Y. (2014). *The failure of agricultural policy reform in neoliberal Japan: The 2007 Multi-Product Management Stabilization Plan.* Ph.D. Dissertation. University of Hawaii.

Miyares, I., Paine, J.A., and Nishi, M. (2000). The Japanese in America. In J.O. McKee (Ed.), *Ethnicity in contemporary America: A geographical appraisal* (pp. 263–282). Second edition (1st edn. 1985). Lanham MD: Rowman and Littlefield.

Miyazawa, H. (2013). Geographical studies of welfare issues in Japan since the 1990s. *Geographical Review of Japan Series B*, 86(1), 52–61.

Mizuoka, F. (1986). *Annihilation of space: A theory of Marxist economic geography.* Ph.D. Dissertation. Clark University.

Mizuoka, F., Mizuuchi, T., Hisatake, T., Tsutsumi, K., and Fujita, T. (2005). The critical heritage of Japanese geography: Its tortured trajectory for eight decades. *Environment and Planning D: Society and Space*, 23(3), 453–473.

Mizuuchi, T. (Ed.). (2006). *Critical and radical geographies of the social, the spatial, and the political.* URP Research Paper No. 1. Ōsaka City University.

Mizuuchi, T. (2008). Editorial note: Special issue on progress of human geography in Asia (Malaysia, India, Hong Kong). *Jinbun Chiri/Japanese Journal of Human Geography*, 60(6), 1.

Mock, J. (1988). Social impact of changing domestic architecture in a neighborhood in Sapporo, Japan. *City and Society* 2(1), 41–49.

Mock, J. (1999). *Culture, community and change in a Sapporo neighborhood, 1925–1988: Hanayama.* Lewiston: Edwin Mellen Press.

Monk, J. (2011). Notes from interview with Midori Nishi in Los Angeles, 30 March 1990. Personal communication with author M. McDonald. 18 November 2011.

Morgan, J. (1978). *The tsunami hazard in the Pacific: Institutional responses in Japan and the United States.* Ph.D. Dissertation. University of Hawaii.

Morgan, J. (1979). The tsunami hazard in Tohoku and the Hawaiian Islands. *Science Reports of the Tohoku University, 7th Series, Geography*, 29(2), 149–159.

Mori, M. (2009). Country report, translation and transformation: Transactions in Japanese social and cultural geography. *Social and Cultural Geography*, 10(3), 369–397.

Muldavin, J. (2000). The geography of Japanese development aid to China, 1978–98. *Environment and Planning A*, 32(5), 925–946.

Murakami Wood, D. (2011). Cameras in context: A comparison of the place of video surveillance in Japan and Brazil. In A. Doyle, R. Lippert and D. Lyon (Eds.), *Eyes everywhere: The global spread of camera surveillance* (pp. 83–89). London and New York: Routledge.

Murakami Wood, D., and Abe, K. (2011). The aesthetics of control: Mega events and transformations in Japanese urban order. *Urban Studies*, 48(15), 3241–3257.

Murakoshi, N., and Trewartha, G.T. (1930). Land utilization maps of Manchuria. *The Geographical Review*, 20(3), 480–493.

Murata, K., and Ota, I. (Eds.) (1980). *An industrial geography of Japan.* New York: St. Martin's Press.

Murata, Y. (2005). Gender equality and progress of gender studies in Japanese geography: a critical overview. *Progress in Human Geography*, 29(3), 260–275.

Murayama, Y. (1994). The impact of railways on accessibility in the Japanese urban system. *Journal of Transport Geography*, 2(2), 87–100.

Murayama, Y. (2000). *Japanese urban system.* Dordrecht: Kluwer.

Murphy, P.E., and Andressen, B. (1988). Tourism development on Vancouver Island: An assessment of the core-periphery model. *The Professional Geographer*, 40(1), 32–42.

Nakamura, N. (2007). *Managing cultural representation: Ainu and First Nations museums in Japan and Canada.* Ph.D. Dissertation. Queen's University (Canada).

Nakamura, N. (2008). An 'effective' involvement of indigenous people in environmental impact assessment: The cultural impact assessment of the Saru

River Region, Japan. *Australian Geographer*, 39(4), 427–444.

Nakamura, N. (2010). Indigenous methodologies: Suggestions for junior researchers. *Geographical Research (Journal of the Institute of Australian Geographers)*, 48(1), 97–103.

Nakashima K. (2010). Production of forest and the green landscape: Representation and practice of the afforestation campaign in Japan, 1950s–60s. In W.-S Tang and F. Mizuoka (Eds.), *East Asia: A critical geography perspective* (Chapter 9). Tōkyō: Kokon Shoin.

Ngo, T. (2012). Mapping economic development: The South Seas government and sugar production in Japan's South Pacific mandate, 1919–1941. *Cross-Currents: East Asian History and Culture Review E-Journal*, 2, 1–23. Accessed 8 July 2014 at https://cross-currents.berkeley.edu/e-journal/issue-2/framing-economic-development-japanese-imperial-maps-south-pacific-and-their-implic

Nihon Gakujutsu Kaigi (1980). *Recent trends of geographical study in Japan*. Recent progress of natural sciences in Japan, Volume 5. Tōkyō: Science Council of Japan.

Nihon Ritō Sentaa (2004). *Shimadasu: Nihon no shima gaido*. Nihon Ritō Sentaa. 2nd edition, Heisei 16. Updates at http://www.nijinet.or.jp/publishing/shimadas/tabid/69/Default.aspx. Acessed 8 July 2014. Kagoshima University Research Center for the Pacific Islands. National Institute of Japanese Islands.

Ninomiya, K. Z. (1972). *A view of the outside world during Tokugawa Japan: An analysis of reports of travel by castaways, 1636 to 1856*. Ph.D. Dissertation. University of Washington.

Nishi, M. (1955). *Changing occupance of the Japanese in Los Angeles County, 1940–1950*. Ph.D. Dissertation. University of Washington.

Nishi, M. (1958). Japanese settlement in the Los Angeles area. *Association of Pacific Coast Geographers Yearbook*, 20, 35–48.

Nishi, M. (1962). Some aspects of Japanese postwar migration to Latin America. *The Professional Geographer*, 14(1), 47–53.

Nishi, M. (1967). Regional variations in Japanese farmhouses. *Annals of the Association of American Geographers*, 57(2), 239–266.

Nishi, M. (1968). An evaluation of Japanese agricultural and fishery developments in Micronesia during the Japanese Mandate, 1914 to 1941. *Micronesica* 4(1), 1–18.

Nishi, M., and Kim, Y.L. (1964). Recent Japanese settlement changes in the Los Angeles area. *Association of Pacific Coast Geographers Yearbook*, 24–32.

Nishimura, Y. (2002). Geography of gender in the workplace: toward a more comprehensive approach to gender studies in Japan. *Geographical Review of Japan*, 75(9), 571–590.

Nishimura, Y., and Okamoto, K. (2001). Yesterday and today: Changes in workers' lives in Toyota City, Japan. In P.P. Karan (Ed.), *Japan in the Bluegrass* (pp. 98–122). Lexington: University Press of Kentucky.

Nobuoka, J. (2010a). *Geographies of the Japanese cultural economy: Innovation and creative consumption*. Ph.D. Dissertation. Uppsala University, Sweden.

Nobuoka, J. (2010b). User innovation and creative consumption in Japanese culture industries: The case of Akihabara, Tōkyō. *Geografiska Annaler, Series B, Human Geography*, 92(3), 205–218.

Noh, T., and Gordon, D.H. (1974). *Modern Japan, land and man*. Tōkyō: Teikoku Shoin.

Noh, T., and Kimura, J. C. (1983). *Japan: A regional geography of an island nation*. Tokyo: Teikoku Shoin.

Noh, T., and Kimura, J. C. (1989). *Japan: A regional geography of an island nation, 2nd edition*. Tōkyō: Teikoku Shoin.

Nojiri, W., and Ishikawa, Y. (1994). Physical distribution studies in Japanese geography. *Progress in Human Geography*, 18(1), 40–57.

O'Connor, K. (2010). Global city regions and the location of logistics activity. *Journal of Transport Geography*, 18(3), 354–362.

O'Dell, G.A. (2001). Assessing environmental performance of Japanese industrial facilities in Kentucky. In P. P. Karan (Ed.), *Japan in the Bluegrass* (pp. 222–259). Lexington: University Press of Kentucky.

O'Dell, G. A. (2003). *Eco-efficiency and lean production: Environmental performance of Japanese transplants in the United States*. Ph.D. Dissertation. University of Kentucky.

Ó Tuathail, G. (1992). Pearl Harbor without bombs: a critical geopolitics of the US–Japan 'FSX' debate. *Environment and Planning A*, 24(7), 975–994.

Oba, S. (2005). New trends in housing policies in Japanese metropolises: Ōsaka, Kyōto, Kōbe. In T. Feldhoff and W. Flüchter (Eds.), *Shaping the future of metropolitan regions in Japan and Germany: Governance, institutions and place in new context* (pp.163–169). Proceedings of the 9th Japanese-German Geographical Conference. Duisberg: University of Duisburg-Essen.

Obara, N., Waldichuk, T., Kikuchi, T., and Tateishi, J. (2005). Diversity of Canadian images and their collaboration in Japanese tourists. *Geographical Reports of Tokyo Metropolitan University*, 40, 53–65.

Obinger, J. (2008). Homelessness in urban centers of Japan and creative strategies to escape homelessness. In H. Okano and E. Schulz (Eds.), *Managing sustainability and creativity: Urban management in Europe and Japan*. Ōsaka: Urban Research Plaza Global Center of Excellence.

Obinger, J. (2009). Working on the margins, Japan's *precariat* and working poor. *Electronic Journal of*

Contemporary Japanese Studies, Discussion Paper 1 in 2009. 25 February, 2009. www.japanesestudies.org.uk/discussionpapers/2009/Obinger.html Accessed 8 July 2014

Office of Strategic Services Personnel Files. Joint Chiefs of Staff. 6/13/1942 to 10/1/1945. Record Group 226 National Archives. Accessed 8 July 2014 at http://www.archives.gov/research/military/ww2/oss/personnel-files.html

Ogawa, Y. (2002). Challenging the traditional organization of Japanese universities. *Higher Education,* 43(1), 85–108.

Ohmori, N., and Harata, N. (2008). How different are activities while commuting by train? A case in Tokyo. *Tijdschrift voor economische en sociale geografie (Journal of Economic and Social Geography),* 99(5), 547–561.

Ohshima, G. (1991). Coastal islands on an international boundary: Dauan and Parama in the Torres Strait. In D. Rumley and J. V. Minghi (Eds.), *The geography of border landscapes* (pp. 169–188). London, Routledge.

Oishi, T. (2008). Recent trends in ethnic geography in Japan. *Geographical Review of Japan, Chirigaku Hyōron,* 81(5), 303–310 (57–64).

Oizumi, E. (1994). Property finance in Japan: expansion and collapse of the bubble economy. *Environment and Planning A* 26(2), 199–213.

Okada, T. (2009). Koji Iizuka 1906–1970. In C. Withers and H. Lorimer (Eds.), *Geographers BioBibliographical Studies,* Volume 28 (pp. 55–63). International Geographical Union 2009. London and New York: Continuum.

Okamoto, K. (1997). Suburbanization of Tokyo and the daily lives of suburban people. In P. P. Karan and K. Stapleton (Eds.), *The Japanese city* (pp.79–105). Lexington: The University Press of Kentucky.

Okamoto, K. (2005). Urban transport in an information society: some strategies for the Nagoya-Toyota Metropolitan Region and their geographic implication. In T. Feldhoff, W. Flüchter and U. Hohn, (Eds.), *Shaping the future of metropolitan regions in Japan and Germany: Governance, institutions and place in context* (pp.117–122). Proceedings of the 9th Japanese-German Geographical Conference. Duisberg: University of Duisburg-Essen.

Olson, H. F., and Morgan, J. (1992). Chinese access to the Sea of Japan and integrated economic development in Northeast Asia. *Ocean and Coastal Management,* 17(1), 57–79.

Orchard, J. E. (1928). The pressure of population in Japan. *The Geographical Review* 18(3), 374–401.

Orchard, J. E. (1929). Can Japan develop industrially? *The Geographical Review* 19(2), 177–200.

Orchard, J. E. (1960). Industrialization in Japan, China Mainland, and India – some world implications. *Annals of the Association of American Geographers* 50(3), 193–215.

Orchard, J. E., and Orchard, D. J. (1930). *Japan's economic position: The progress of industrialization.* New York: McGraw Hill.

Oro, K., and Pritchard, B. (2011). The evolution of global value chains: Displacement of captive upstream investment in the Australia-Japan beef trade. *Journal of Economic Geography,* 11(4), 709–729.

Oshiro, K. K. (1972). *Dairy policies and the development of dairying in Tohoku, Japan.* Ph.D. Dissertation. University of Washington.

Oshiro, K. K. (1984). Postwar seasonal migration from rural Japan. *The Geographical Review,* 74(2), 145–156.

Oshiro, K. K. (1985). Mechanization of rice production in Japan. *Economic Geography,* 61(4), 323–331.

Oshiro, K. K. (2003). Land price changes in Sendai and Sapporo, Japan. *Industrial Geographer,* 1(1), 35–50.

Packard, G. R. (2010). *Edwin O. Reischauer and the American discovery of Japan.* New York: Columbia University Press.

Palm, R. (1998). Urban earthquake hazards: The impacts of culture on perceived risk and response in the USA and Japan. *Applied Geography,* 18(1), 35–46.

Palmer, E. (1988). Planned relocation of severely depopulated rural settlements: a case study from Japan. *Journal of Rural Studies,* 4(1), 21–34.

Palmer, E. (1991). Land of the rising sun: Predominant east-west axis among the early Japanese. *Monumenta Nipponica,* 46(1), 69–90.

Palmer, E. (1992). The changing geography of Japan. In G. Chapman and K. M. Baker (Eds.), *The changing geography of Asia* (pp.195–219). London: Routledge.

Palmer, E. (1994). Beyond geography:The geography of the beyond in ancient Japan. *Geojournal,* 33(4), 479–485.

Palmer, E. (1996). From coastal vessel to ship of state: The transformation of Harima leaders into Yamato monarchs. *New Zealand Journal of East Asian Studies,* 4(1), 5–37.

Palmer, E. (2005). The invention and reinvention of tradition in Japan. In E. Palmer (Ed.), *Asian futures, Asian traditions* (pp. 3–22). Folkestone, Kent: Global Oriental Publishers.

Palmer, E. (2007). Out of Sunda? Provenance of the Jomon Japanese. *Japan Review (Nichibunken),* 19, 47–75.

Palmer, E., and Rice, G.W. (1992). 'Divine wind versus devil wind' popular responses to pandemic influenza in Japan, 1918–1919. *Japan Forum,* 4(2), 317–328.

Pantulu, J. K. (2002). *The effects of foreign direct investment on international trade: Empirical evidence from Germany, Japan and the United States.* Ph.D. Dissertation. State University of New York at Buffalo.

Park, S. C. (1997). *The technopolis plan in Japanese industrial policy.* Ph.D. Dissertation (Ekon. Dr.) Göteborgs Universitet (Sweden).

Park, S. W. (1985). *Agglomeration economics in manufacturing industries in Japan and Korea: A comparative analysis.* PhD. Dissertation. University of Pennsylvania.

Parker, P. (1990) Energy and environmental policies create trade opportunities: Japan and the Pacific coal flow expansion initiative. *Geoforum,* 21(3), 371–383.

Parker, P. (1996). Japan and the global environment: Leadership in environmental technology. In D. Rumley, T. Chiba, A. Takagi and Y. Fukushima (Eds.), *Global geopolitical change and the Asia Pacific: A regional perspective* (pp. 93–112). Brookfield and Aldershot: Avebury.

Parker, P. (1997). Canada-Japan coal trade: An alternative form of the staple production model. *The Canadian Geographer,* 41(3), 248–267.

Parker, P. (1998). An environmental measure of Japan's economic development: The ecological footprint. *Geographische Zeitshrift,* 86(2), 106–119.

Parker, P. (2008). Residential solar photovoltaic market simulation: Japanese and Australian lessons for Canada. *Renewable and Sustainable Energy Reviews,* 12(7), 1944–1958.

Parker, P., Rutherford, T., and Koshiba, T. (2000). New directions in Canada's Japanese owned automobile plants. In P. Bowles and L.T. Woods (Eds.), *Japan after the economic miracle: In search of new directions* (pp. 85–103). Dordrecht, Boston, London: Kluwer.

Patchell, G. R. (1991). *The creation of production systems within the social division of labour of the Japanese robot industry: The impact of the relation-specific skill.* Ph.D. Dissertation. Simon Fraser University (Canada).

Patchell, J. (1993a). Composing robot production systems: Japan as a flexible manufacturing system. *Environment and Planning A,* 25(7), 923–944.

Patchell, J. (1993b). From production systems to learning systems: Lessons from Japan. *Environment and Planning A,* 25(6), 797–815.

Patchell, J. (1999) Creating the Japanese electric vehicle industry: The challenges of uncertainty and cooperation. *Environment and Planning A,* 31(6) 997–1016.

Patchell, J. (2002). Linking production and consumption: The coevolution of interactions systems in the Japanese house industry. *Annals of the Association of American Geographers,* 92(2), 284–301.

Patchell, J., and Hayter, R. (1992). Dynamics of adjustment and the social division of labor in the Tsubame cutlery industry. *Growth and Change,* 23(2), 199–216.

Patchell, J., and Hayter, R. (1995) Skill formation and Japanese production systems. *Tijdschrift voor economische en sociale geografie (Journal of economic and social geography),* 84(4), 339–356.

Patchell, J., and Hayter, R. (1997). Japanese precious wood and the paradoxes of added value. *Geographical Review,* 87(3), 375–395.

Peck, J., and Miyamachi, Y. (1994). Regulating Japan? Regulation theory versus the Japanese experience. *Environment and Planning D: Society and Space,* 12(6), 639–674.

Pellenbarg, P. H., and Van Steen, P. J. M. (2009). Place and science in the Netherlands: A spatial perspective on Dutch universities and their knowledge output. *Tijdschrift voor economische en sociale geografie, (Journal of Economic and Social Geography),* 100(5), 686–693.

Pelletier, P. (1997). *La japonésie: Géopolitique et géographie historique de la surinsularité au Japon.* Paris: Editions du CNRS.

Pelletier, P. (2004). *Japon, crise d'une autre modernité.* Paris, Belin.

Pelletier, P. (2007). *Le Japon: Géographie, géopolitique et géohistoire.* Paris: Sedes.

Pelletier, P. (2008). *Le Japon.* Paris: Le Cavalier Bleu. (Second edition).

Pelletier, P. (2011). *L'Extrême-Orient: l'invention d'une histoire et d'une géographie.* Paris: Gallimard.

Penna, I. (2002). *The political ecology of the Japanese paper industry.* Ph.D. Dissertation. University of Melbourne.

Pezeu-Massabuau, J. (1968). *Géographie du Japon.* Presses Universitaires de France.

Pezeu-Massabuau, J. (1978). *The Japanese islands: A physical and social geography.* (Translated by Paul Blum) Rutland VT: C. E. Tuttle Co.

Piper, N. (1997). International marriage in Japan: Race and gender perspectives. *Gender, Place and Culture,* 4(3), 321–338.

Piper, N. (1999). Labor migration, trafficking and international marriage: female cross-border movements into Japan. *Asian Journal of Women's Studies,* 5(2), 69–99.

Piper, N. (2000). Globalisation, gender and migration: International marriage in Japan. In J. Roberts, G. Waylen and H. Cook (Eds.), *Towards a gendered political economy* (pp. 205–225). Basingstoke: Macmillan.

Piper, N. (2002). Global labour markets and national responses: legal regimes governing female migrant workers in Japan. In D.S. Gills and N. Piper (Eds.), *Women and work in globalising Asia* (pp. 188–208). London: Routledge.

Piper, N., and Ball, R.E. (2001). Globalisation of Asian migrant labour: The Philippine-Japan connection. *Journal of Contemporary Asia,* 31(4), 533–554.

Pitts, F. R. (1955). *Comparative land fertility and potential in the inland sea and peripheral areas of Japan.* Ph.D. Dissertation. University of Michigan.

Pitts, F. R. (1960). *Japan.* Grand Rapids: Fideler.

Pitts, F. R. (1964). Rural prosperity in Japan. In R. K. Beardsley (Ed.), *Studies on economic life in Japan* (pp.95–124). University of Michigan Center for Japanese Studies, Occasional Papers 8. Ann Arbor: University of Michigan.

Pitts, F. R. (1985). Thirty years of change in two rural areas of western Japan. *National Geographic Research Reports*, 21, 381–387.

Pitts, F. R. (1992). Personal communication with author M. McDonald. Personal interview, Santa Rosa, California. Copies of letters from Okayama fieldwork period. 24 August.

Pitts, F. R. (2002). Sliding sideways into geography. In P. Gould and F. R. Pitts (Eds.), *Geographical voices: Fourteen autobiographical essays* (pp. 269–292). Syracuse NY: Syracuse University Press.

Pitts, F. R., Lebra, W. P., and Suttles, W. P. (1955). *Post-war Okinawa*. Pacific Science Board, SIRI Series No. 8. Washington DC: National Research Council.

Potter, S. R. (2001a). Japan as a cartographic heritage without a word for 'map.' *Journal of Tsuda College*, 33, 169–200.

Potter, S. (2001b). The elusive concept of map: Semantic insights into the cartographic heritage of Japan. *Geographical Review of Japan, Series B*, 74(1), 1–14.

Potter, S. R. (2003a). Contemporary ezu on public display in Japan, continued. *Journal of Tsuda College*, 35, 77–114.

Potter, S. R. (2003b). Illustrated maps on public display in Japan: Geography and artistic tradition. *Geographical Review of Japan, Chirigaku Hyōron*, 76(12), 823–842.

Potter, S. R. (2003c). Religious sites in Japanese illustrated maps: Insights from the literature about the past, and contemporary examples from maps on public display. *Saitama Daigaku Kiyō: Kyōyōgakubu, Journal of Saitama University: Faculty of Liberal Arts*, 39(1), 51–95.

Potter, S. (2007). On the artistic heritage of Japanese cartography: Historical perceptions of maps and space. *Gengo Bunka Ronshū (Studies in Language and Culture, Nagoya University)*, 28(2), 209–225.

Powell, J. M. (1999). Environment, culture and modern historical geography: Recent Anglophone contributions. *Jinbun Chiri/Japanese Journal of Human Geography*, 51(5), 477–493.

Pritchard, B. (Ed.). (2006). *Japanese Official Development Assistance within the Asian Region*. Sydney: Research Institute for Asia and the Pacific.

Pritchard, B., and Curtis, R. (2004). The political construction of agro-food liberalization in East Asia: Lessons from the restructuring of Japanese dairy provisioning. *Economic Geography*, 80(2), 173–190.

Puppim de Oliveira, J. A. (2011). Why an air pollution achiever lags on climate policy. The case of local policy implementation in Mie, Japan. *Environment and Planning A*, 43(8), 1894–1909.

Raper, A. F. (1950). *The Japanese village in transition*. Tokyo: General Headquarters, Supreme Commander for the Allied Powers.

Rausch, A. (2006). The Heisei dai gappei: A case study for understanding the municipal mergers of the Heisei era. *Japan Forum*, 18(1), 133–156.

Reid, N. (1991a). *Japanese direct investment in the United States manufacturing sector*. Ph.D. Dissertation. Arizona State University.

Reid, N. (1991b). *Japanese direct investment in the United States manufacturing sector*. In J. Morris (Ed.), *Japan and the global economy: Issues and trends in the 1990s* (pp. 61–90). London: Routledge.

Reiffenstein, T. W. (2004). *Transectorial innovation, location dynamics and knowledge formation in the Japanese electronic musical instrument industry*. Ph.D. Dissertation. Simon Fraser University (Canada).

Reiffenstein, T. (2005). Radical innovation and the emergence of new economic spaces: The formation of knowledge in the American and Japanese electronic musical instrument industry. In R. LeHeron and J.W. Harrington (Eds.), *New economic spaces, new economic geographies* (pp.29–43). Aldershot: Ashgate.

Reiffenstein, T. (2006). Codification, patents and the geography of knowledge transfer in the electronic musical instrument industry. *The Canadian Geographer*, 50(3), 198–318.

Reiffenstein, T. (2009). Specialization, centralization and the distribution of patent intermediaries in the United States and Japan. *Regional Studies*, 43, 571–588.

Reiffenstein, T., and Hayter, R. (2006). Domestic timber auctions and flexibly specialized forestry in Japan. *The Canadian Geographer*, 50(4), 503–525.

Reiffenstein, T., Hayter, R., and Edgington, D.W. (2002). Crossing cultures, learning to export: Making houses in British Columbia for consumption in Japan. *Economic Geography*, 78(2), 195–220.

Rein, J. J. (1884). *Japan: Travels and researches undertaken at the cost of the Prussian Government*. English translation, first US edition. New York: A.C. Armstrong and Son.

Rice, G. W., and Palmer, E. (1993). Pandemic influenza in Japan, 1918–19: Mortality patterns and official responses. *Journal of Japanese Studies*, 19(2), 389–420.

Rimmer, P. J. (1986). Japan's world cities: Tokyo, Osaka, Nagoya or Tokaido Megalopolis? *Development and Change*, 17(1), 121–157.

Rimmer, P. J. (1990). The internationalisation of the Japanese construction industry: The rise and rise of Kumagai Gumi. *Environment and Planning A*, 22(3), 345–368.

Rimmer, P. J. (1992). Japan's 'resort archipelago': creating regions of fun, pleasure, relaxation, and recreation. *Environment and Planning A*, 24(11), 1599–1625.

Rimmer, P. J. (1994). Japanese investment in golf course development: Australia-Japan links. *International Journal of Urban and Regional Research*, 18(2), 234–55.

Rimmer, P. J. (1997). Japan's foreign direct investment in the Pacific Rim, 1985–1993. In R.F. Watters, T.G. McGee and G. Sullivan (Eds.), *Asia-Pacific: New geographies of the Pacific Rim* (pp. 113–132). Vancouver: UBC Press.

Rimmer, P. J., and Morris-Suzuki, T. (1999). The Japanese internet: Visionaries and virtual democracy. *Environment and Planning A*, 31(7), 1189–1206.

Robertson, R. D. (1972). *Urban water supply in Japan: A case study of Osaka*. Ph.D. Dissertation. University of Michigan.

Robertson, R.D. (1975). Regional water supply in Japan: A study of Lake Biwa. *Geographical Review*, 65(3), 311–322.

Robinson, W. I. T. (2010). *Transience and durability in Japanese urban space*. Ph.D. Dissertation. Durham University. www.etheses. dur.ac.uk Accessed 8 July 2014.

Ronald, R. (2007). The Japanese home in transition: Housing, consumption, and modernization. In Y. Hirayama and R. Ronald (Eds.), *Housing and social transition in Japan* (pp. 165–192). London and New York: Routledge.

Ronald, R. (2008). Between investment, asset and use consumption: The meanings of homeownership in Japan. *Housing Studies*, 23(2), 233–251.

Ronald, R., and Hirayama Y. (2006). Housing commodities, context and meaning: Transformations in Japan's urban condominium sector. *Urban Studies*, 43(13), 2467–2483.

Ronald, R., and Hirayama Y. (2009). Home alone: the individualization of young, urban Japanese singles. *Environment and Planning A*, (41), 2836–2854.

Rumley, D. (2001). *The geopolitics of Australia's regional relations*. Dordrecht, The Netherlands: Kluwer.

Rumley, D., Chiba, T., Takagi, A., and Fukushima, Y. (Eds.) (1996). *Global geopolitical change and the Asia-Pacific: A regional perspective*. Aldershot and Brookfield: Avebury.

Russell, J. A. (1940) The teas of Uji. *Economic Geography*, 16(2), 211–224.

Rutherford, J. (1984). *Rice dominant land settlement in Japan: A study of systems within systems*. University of Sydney, Department of Geography.

Saito, A. (2002). A global city in a developmental state: Urban planning in Tokyo. In A. Thornley and Y. Rydin (Eds.), *Planning in a global era* (pp. 27–45). Aldershot: Ashgate.

Saito, A. (2003). Global city formation in a capitalist developmental state: Tokyo and the waterfront sub-centre project. *Urban Studies*, 40(2), 283–308.

Saito, A. (2006). Tokyo: From Japanese capital to a global city. In K.C. Ho and H.H. M. Hsiao (Eds.), *Capital cities in Asia-Pacific: Primacy and diversity* (pp. 173–188). Taipei: Center for Asia-Pacific Area Studies, Academia Sinica.

Saito, A. (2012). State-space relations in transition: Urban and regional policy in Japan. In B. G. Park, R. C. Hill and A. Saito (Eds.), *Locating neoliberalism in East Asia: Neoliberalizing spaces in developmental states* (pp. 59–85). Malden MA, Oxford and Chichester: Wiley-Blackwell.

Saito, A., and Mizuoka, F. (2009). Japanese geography. In R. Kitchen and N. Thrift (Eds.), *International Encyclopedia of Human Geography*. Oxford: Elsevier.

Saito, A., and Thornley, A. (2003). Shifts in Tokyo's world city status and the urban planning response. *Urban Studies*, 40(4), 665–685.

Saito, Y. (1985). The Japanese appreciation of nature. *British Journal of Aesthetics*, 25(3), 239–251.

Saito, Y. (1992). The Japanese love of nature: A paradox. *Landscape*, 31(2), 1–8.

Saito, Y. (2002). Scenic national landscapes: Common themes in Japan and the United States. *Essays in Philosophy* 3:1, Article 5. Accessed 8 July 2014 at http://commons.pacificu.edu/cgi/viewcontent.cgi?article= 1043&context=eip

Sakai, A. (2005). *Open spaces and the modern metropolis: Evolution and preservation in London and Tokyo (c.1830-c.1930)*. PhD. Dissertation. Royal Holloway, University College London.

Sakai, A. (2011). The hybridization of ideas on public parks: Introduction of western thought and practice into nineteenth-century Japan. *Planning Perspectives*, 26(3), 347–371.

Sakai, H. (1972). *The center-periphery dichotomy in the Japanese economy: A study in distance and spatial interaction*. Ph.D. Dissertation. Columbia University.

Sánchez Muñoz, A. (2006). La globalización de Asia Pacífico, la aperatura regional, los desplazamientos de población y el desarrollo de las comunicaciones: Un desfaío para la nueva geografía. *Boletín de la Real Sociedad Geográfica* (Madrid), 142, 289–322.

Sargent, J. (1975). Regional development policy in Japan: Some aspects of the plan for remodelling the Japanese archipelago. In W. G. Beasely (Ed.), *Modern Japan: Aspects of history, literature and society* (pp. 227–243). London: George Allen and Unwin, Ltd.

Sargent, J. (1987). Industrial location in Japan with special reference to the semiconductor industry. *The Geographical Journal*, 153(1), 72–85.

Sargent, J. (1990). Japan's manufacturing investment overseas: Its implications for Britain and the European Community. *Japan Digest*, July, 32–40.

Sargent, J. (1993) The place of Japanese studies in British geography. In J. Sargent and R. Wiltshire

(Eds.), *Geographical studies and Japan* (pp. 110–120). Sandgate, Folkestone, Kent: Japan Library.

Sargent, J., and Wiltshire, R. (1989). Forging closer links with Japanese geographers. *Area*, 21(1), 104–106.

Sargent, J., and Wiltshire, R. (1993). Introduction. In J. Sargent and R. Wiltshire (Eds.), *Geographical studies and Japan* (pp. 7–13). Sandgate, Folkestone, Kent: Japan Library.

Sargent, J., and Wiltshire, R. (2000). Kamaishi: Sunset on hold. *Geography*, 85(4), 356–357.

Sasaki, H., Saito, I., Morimoto, T., and Tabayashi, A. (1996). *Geographical perspectives on sustainable rural systems*. Proceedings of the Tsukuba International Conference on the Sustainability of Rural Systems. Tōkyō: Kaisei.

Sassen, S. (1991). *The global city: New York, London, Tokyo*. Revised edition (2001). Princeton and Oxford: Princeton University Press.

Sato, T. (1988). *Socioeconomic factors associated with geographical variations in cerebrovascular disease in Miyagi Prefecture, Japan*. Ph.D. Dissertation. University of Hawaii.

Sato, T. (1989). Stroke mortality in Miyagi, Japan. *Social Science and Medicine*, 29(8), 1035–1042.

Scargill, D. I. (1976). The RGS and the foundations of geography at Oxford. *Geographical Journal*, 142(3), 438–461.

Schlunze, R.D. (1995). *Japanese investment in Germany: A spatial perspective*. Ph.D. Dissertation. Tokyo University.

Schlunze, R. D. (2001). The spatial structure of Japanese business activities in Europe. *Tijdschrift voor economische en sociale geografie, (Journal of Economic and Social Geography)*, 92(2), 217–230.

Schlunze, R.D. (2007). Spurring the Kansai economy. *Ritsumeikan International Affairs*, 5, 17–42.

Schöller, P. (1984). Urban values: A review of Japanese and German attitudes. *Urban Studies*, 5(1), 43–48.

Semple, A.-L. (2009). *The influence of Hankyu and Hanshin private railway groups on the urban development of the Hanshin region, Japan*. Ph.D. Dissertation. University of New South Wales.

Semple, E. C. (1912). Influence of geographical conditions upon Japanese agriculture. *Geographical Journal*, 40(6), 589–603.

Semple, E. C. (1913). Japanese colonial methods. *Bulletin of the American Geographical Society*, 45(4), 255–275.

Senda, M. (1992). Japan's traditional view of nature and interpretation of landscape. *GeoJournal*, 26(2), 129–134.

Seo, B. (2004). *Relational networks and geographies of global banking: Japanese city banks in global syndicated credit markets*. Ph.D. Dissertation. University of Minnesota.

Seo, B. (2012). Globalization of Japanese banks in global syndicated credit markets: A geo-relational approach. *Geographical Review of Japan Series B*, 85(1), 1–16.

Seo, K., and Taylor, J. (2003). Forest resource trade between Japan and Southeast Asia: The structure of dual decay. *Ecological Economics*, 45(1), 91–104.

Shapira, P. (2008). Putting innovation in place: Policy strategies for industrial services, regional clusters and manufacturing SMEs in Japan and the United States. *Prometheus*, 26(1), 69–87.

Shapira, P., Masser, I., and Edgington, D. (Eds.) (1994). *Planning for cities and regions in Japan*. Liverpool: Liverpool University Press.

Shelton, J. A. (2006). *Female labor in the postwar Japanese economy: A geographic perspective*. Ph.D. Dissertation. The Ohio State University.

Shibata, K. (2006). The public interest: Understanding the state and city planning in Japan. *Research Papers in Environmental and Spatial Analysis* No. 107. LSE Geography and Environment. Accessed 8 July 2014 at http://www.lse.ac.uk/geography-AndEnvironment/research/Researchpapers/107%20Shibata.pdf

Shibata, K. (2008a). Neoliberalism, risk, and spatial governance in the developmental state: Japanese planning in the global economy. *Critical Planning*, 15, 92–118.

Shibata, K. (2008b). The origins of Japanese planning culture: Building a nation-state 1868-1945. *Research Papers in Environmental and Spatial Analysis* No. 128. LSE Geography and Environment. Accessed 8 July 2014 at http://www.lse.ac.uk/geographyAnd Environment/research/Researchpapers/128%20shibata%20update%20.pdf

Shibata, Y. (2006). Saneshige Komaki's 'Japanese geopolitics' and its ideological establishment. *Jinbun Chiri/Japanese Journal of Human Geography*, 58(1), 1–19.

Shimazaki, H. (né Tanaka) (1992). Japanese gardens: Mirrors of cultural history. In S.T. Wong (Ed.), *Person, place, and thing: Interpretive and empirical essays in cultural geography* (pp. 353–378). Baton Rouge: Louisiana State University.

Shimazu T. (2004). Takeshi Kawada's geographical thought and practice. *Jinbun Chiri/Japanese Journal of Human Geography*, 56(4), 331–350.

Shrestha, N., Lewis, M., Cohen, S., and McDonald, M. (2003). Asian geography in North America. In G. L. Gaile and C. J. Willmott (Eds.), *Geography in America at the dawn of the 21st century* (pp. 618–657). Oxford and New York: Oxford University Press.

Shulman, F. J. (1970). *Japan and Korea: An annotated bibliography of doctoral dissertations in Western languages, 1877-1969*. University of Michigan. Center for Japanese Studies. American Library Association: Chicago.

Siebert, L. J. (1997). *Creating a GIS spatial history of Tokyo*. Ph.D. Dissertation. University of Washington.

Siebert, L. (2000). Urbanization transition types and zones in Tokyo and Kanagawa Prefectures. *Geographical Review of Japan, Series B*, 73(2), 207–224.

Siebert, L. (2003). Assessing rail network history in Japan's Kanto Region. In A. K. Dutt, A. Noble, G. Venugopal and S. Subbiah (Eds.), *Challenges to Asian urbanization in the 21st century* (pp. 243–254). Dordrecht, Netherlands: Kluwer.

Siebert, L. (2004). Using GIS to map rail transport history. *Journal of Transport History*, 25(1), 84–104.

Smith, G.-H., Good, D., and McCune, S. (1943). *Japan: A geographical view*. New York: American Geographical Society.

Smith, J. M. (2005). *Japanese American identities: Place and social spaces in Little Tokyo*. Ph.D. Dissertation. Kent State University.

Smith, J.M. (2008). Identities and urban social spaces in Little Tokyo, Los Angeles: Japanese Americans in two ethno-spiritual communities. *Geografiska Annaler, Series B, Human Geography*, 90(4), 409–431.

Smith, N. (2003). *American empire: Roosevelt's geographer and the prelude to globalization*. Berkeley CA: University of California Press.

Smith, R. A. (2003). The Japanese shinkansen. *Journal of Transport History*, 24(2), 222–237.

Sone, A. (1993). *An analysis of municipal government expenditures in Japan*. Ph.D. Dissertation. Syracuse University.

Sorensen, A. (2000). Conflict, consensus or consent: implications of Japanese land readjustment practice for developing countries. *Habitat International*, 24, 51–73.

Sorensen, A. (2001a). Building suburbs in Japan: continuous unplanned change on the urban fringe. *Town Planning Review*, 72(3), 247–273.

Sorensen, A. (2001b). Urban planning and civil society in Japan: Japanese urban planning development during the 'Taisho democracy' period (1905-31). *Planning Perspectives*, 16(4), 383–406.

Sorensen, A. (2002). *The making of urban Japan: Cities and planning from Edo to the 21st century*. London: Routledge.

Sorensen, A. (2005). The developmental state and the extreme narrowness of the public realm: The 20th century evolution of Japanese planning culture. In B. Sanyal (Ed.), *Comparative planning cultures* (pp. 223–258). New York: Routledge.

Sorensen, A. (2006a). Centralization, urban planning governance, and citizen participation in Japan. In C. Hein and P. Pelletier (Eds.), *Cities, autonomy, and decentralization in Japan* (pp. 101–127). London: Routledge.

Sorensen, A. (2006b). Liveable cities in Japan: Population ageing and decline as vectors of change. *International Planning Studies*, 11(3–4), 225–242.

Sorensen, A. (2007a). Changing governance of shared spaces: Machizukuri in historical institutional perspective. In A. Sorensen and C. Funck (Eds.), *Living cities in Japan: Citizens' movements, machizukuri and local environments* (pp. 56–90). London: Routledge.

Sorensen, A. (2007b). Consensus, persuasion, and opposition: Organizing land readjustment in Japan. In Y.H. Hong and B. Needham (Eds.), *Analyzing land readjustment: Economics, law, and collective action* (pp. 89–114). Cambridge MA: Lincoln Institute for Land Policy.

Sorensen, A. (2011). Uneven processes of change: Path dependence, scale and the contested regulation of urban development in Japan. *International Journal of Urban and Regional Research*, 35(4), 712–734.

Sorensen, A., and Funck, C. (Eds.) (2007). *Living cities in Japan: Citizens' movements, machizukuri and local environments*. New York: Routledge.

Sorensen, A., Marcotullio, P. J., and Grant, J. (Eds.) (2004). *Towards sustainable cities: East Asian, North American, and European perspectives on managing urban regions*. Aldershot: Ashgate.

Sorensen, A., and Okata, J. (Eds.) (2011). *Megacities: Urban form, governance, and sustainability*. New York: Springer.

Stamp, L. D. (1929). *Asia: An economic and regional geography*. London: Methuen and Company.

Statistics Bureau. (2011). *Japan statistical yearbook*. Tōkyō: Ministry of Internal Affairs and Communications. Accessed 8 July 2014 at www.stat.go.jp.

Stewart, N. R. (1960). Tea: A new agricultural industry for Argentina. *Economic Geography*, 36(3), 267–276.

Stewart, N. R. (1963a). Foreign agricultural colonization as a study in cultural geography. *The Professional Geographer*, 15(5), 1–5.

Stewart, N. R. (1963b) *Japanese colonization in Eastern Paraguay: A study in the cultural geography of pioneer agricultural settlement*. Ph.D. Dissertation. University of California, Los Angeles.

Stewart, N. R. (1967). *Japanese colonization in Eastern Paraguay*. Foreign Field Research Program Report No. 30. Washington DC: National Academy of Sciences, National Research Council.

Stradford, H. T. (1994). *Changes in the agricultural landscape of Kochi Prefecture, Japan, 1987 to 1990*. Ph.D. Dissertation. The University of Oklahoma.

Stradford, T. (2005). Jinbun Chiri 2004: A review. *Jinbun Chiri/Japanese Journal of Human Geography*, 57(5), 499–502.

Stradford, T. (2008). Citizens for saving the Kawabe: An interplay among farmers, fishermen, environmentalists, and the Ministry of Land, Infrastructure, and Transport. In P. P. Karan and U. Suganuma (Eds.), *Local environmental movements:*

A comparative study of the United States and Japan (pp. 207–218). Lexington KY: University Press of Kentucky.

Ström, P. (2003). *Internationalization of Japanese professional business service firms*. Ph.D. Dissertation. Roskilde University.

Ström, P. (2005). The Japanese service industry: An international comparison. *Social Science Japan Journal*, 8(2), 253–266.

Ström, P. (2006). Internationalization of Japanese professional business service firms: Dynamics of competitiveness through urban localization in Southeast Asia. In J. W. Harrington and P. W. Daniels, (Eds.), *Knowledge-based services: Internationalisation and regional development* (pp. 153–174). Aldershot: Ashgate.

Ström, P., and Yoshino, N. (2009). Japanese financial service firms in East and Southeast Asia: Location pattern and strategic response in changing economic conditions. *Asian Business and Management*, 8(1), 33–58.

Sturgeon, T. J. (2007). How globalization drives institutional diversity: The Japanese electronics industry's response to value chain modularity. *Journal of East Asian Studies*, 7(1), 1–34.

Suganuma, U. (1996). *Historical justification of sovereign right over territorial space of the Diaoyu/Senkaku islands: Irredentism and Sino-Japanese relations*. Ph.D. Dissertation. Syracuse University.

Suganuma, U. (2000). *Sovereign rights and territorial space in Sino-Japanese relations: Irredentism and the Diaoyu/Senkaku Islands*. Honolulu: Association for Asian Studies and University of Hawaii Press.

Suganuma, U. (2001). The geography of Toyota Motor Manufacturing Corporation. In P. P. Karan (Ed.), *Japan in the Bluegrass* (pp. 61–97). Lexington KY: University Press of Kentucky.

Sugimura, K. (1987). *Forestry and wildlife conservation on Amami Oshima, Japan: An integrated study of wildlife and human society*. Ph.D. Dissertation. University of Hawaii.

Sugimura, K. (1988). The role of government subsidies and the population decline of some unique wildlife species on Amami Oshima, Japan. *Environmental Conservation*, 15(1), 49–57.

Sugimura, K., Yamada, F., and Miyamoto, A. (2003). Population trend, habitat change and conservation of unique wildlife species on Amami Island, Japan. *Global Environmental Research*, 7(1), 79–89.

Tabayashi, A., Kikuchi, T., and Waldichuk, T. (2000). Sustainability of farm settlements in Japan after the economic miracle: A case study of Onoji hamlet in Yamanashi Prefecture. In P. Bowles and L.T. Woods (Eds.), *Japan after the economic miracle: In search of new directions* (pp. 127–144). London: Kluwer.

Tachibana, S., Daniels, S., and Watkins, C. (2004). Japanese gardens in Edwardian Britain: Landscape and transculturation. *Journal of Historical Geography*, 30(2), 364–394.

Taira, A. (2008). A critical review of recent urban social geography in Japan. *Geographical Review of Japan, Chirigaku Hyōron*, 81(5), 279–291(33–45).

Takagi, A. (1998). Japanese nationalism and geographical thought. *Geopolitics*, 3(3), 125–139.

Takahashi, M. (2001). Changing ruralities and the post-productivist countryside of Japan. In K. Kim, I. Bowler and C. Bryant (Eds.), *Developing sustainable rural systems* (pp. 163–174). Pusan: Pusan National University Press.

Takahashi, S. (1998). Social geography and disaster vulnerability in Tokyo. *Applied Geography*, 18(1), 17–24.

Takahashi, Y., and Uitto, J. I. (2004). Evolution of river management: from focus on economic benefits to a comprehensive view. *Global Environmental Change* 14(Supplement), 63–70.

Takase, Y., Kano, K., Nakaya, T., Isoda, Y., Kawasumi, T., Matsuoka, K., Seto, T. Kawahara, D., Tsukamoto, A., Inoue, M., and Kirimura, T. (2008). Virtual Kyoto: Visualization of historical city with 4D-GIS, virtual reality and web technologies. *The International Archives of the Photogrammetry, Remote Sensing and Spatial Information Sciences*, 37(B5), 975–980. Accessed 8 July 2014 at http://www.isprs.org/proceedings/XXXVII/congress/5_pdf/169.pdf

Takeuchi, A. (1998). How to sustain Tokyo's competitiveness in the 21st century. *International Journal of Urban Sciences*, 2(1), 12–23.

Takeuchi, K. (1980). Some remarks on the history of regional description and the tradition of regionalism in modern Japan. *Progress in Human Geography* 4(2), 238–248.

Takeuchi, K. (2000a). Japanese geopolitics in the 1930s and 1940s. In K. Dodds and D. Atkinson (Eds.), *Geopolitical traditions: A century of geopolitical thought* (pp. 72–92). London and New York: Routledge.

Takeuchi, K. (2000b). *Modern Japanese geography: An intellectual history*. Tōkyō: Kokon Shoin.

Takeuchi, K. (2003). Geographical thought in agronomical books of early modern Japan. *Chiiki-gaku kenkyū*, Komazawa daigaku ōyō chiri kenkyū-jo, 16, 1–8.

Takeuchi, K. (2006). Geographical societies and colonialism: Comparative considerations of Italy and Japan. Mediterranean Studies Group, Hitotsubashi University. Accessed 8 July 2014 at http://hermes-ir.lib.hit-u.ac.jp/rs/handle/10086/14912

Takizawa, B. H. (1971). *The growth of manufacturing in Yamanashi-ken, 1956-1967: A study of industrial dispersal in Japan*. Ph.D. Dissertation. University of Illinois at Urbana-Champaign.

Tanaka, H. (1975). *Pilgrim places: A study of the eighty-eight sacred precincts of the Shikoku pilgrimage, Japan*. Ph.D. Dissertation. Simon Fraser University (Canada).

Tanaka, H. (1977). Geographic expression of Buddhist pilgrim places on Shikoku Island, Japan. *The Canadian Geographer,* 21(2), 111–132.

Tanaka, H. (1981). The evolution of a pilgrimage as a spatial-symbolic system. *The Canadian Geographer,* 25(2), 240–251.

Tanaka, H. (1984). Landscape expression of the evolution of Buddhism in Japan. *The Canadian Geographer,* 28(3), 240–257.

Tanaka, K. (1992). *Dynamics of interregional migration and income in Japan during the post-World War II period.* Ph.D. Dissertation. The Ohio State University.

Tanaka, K. (2005). The impact of disaster education on public preparation and mitigation for earthquakes: a cross-country comparison between Fukui, Japan and the San Francisco Bay Area, California, USA. *Applied Geography,* 25(3), 201–225.

Tanaka, K. (2008). Recent trends and issues in geographical studies on modern transportation in Japan. *Geographical Review of Japan, Chirigaku Hyōron,* 81(5), 292–302(46–56).

Tanaka, K. and Imai, M. (2013) A review of recent transportation geography in Japan. *Geographical Review of Japan Series B,* 86(1), 92–99.

Tanaka, S. N. (2008). *Consuming the 'Oriental other,' constructing the cosmopolitan Canadian: Re-interpreting Japanese culinary culture in Toronto's Japanese restaurants.* Ph.D. Dissertation. Queen's University (Canada).

Tang, W.S., and Mizuoka, F. (2010) *East Asia: A critical geography perspective.* Tōkyō: Kokon Shoin.

Taylor, J. (1999). Japan's global environmentalism: rhetoric and reality. *Political Geography,* 18(5), 535–562.

Taylor, J. S. (2000). Okinawa on the eve of the G-8 summit. *Geographical Review,* 90(1), 123–130.

Taylor, J. S. (2001). *Environmental change in Okinawa: A geographic assessment of the role of the United States military.* Ph.D. Dissertation. University of Kentucky.

Taylor, J. (2007). Environment and security conflicts: The US military in Okinawa. *The Geographical Bulletin,* 48(1), 3–13.

Taylor, J. (2008). Antimilitary and environmental movements in Okinawa. In P. P. Karan and U. Suganuma (Eds.), *Local environmental movements: A comparative study of the United States and Japan* (pp. 271–280). Lexington KY: University Press of Kentucky.

Taylor, J. S. (2002). Grass-roots movements and environmental security and development in Okinawa. *Regional Development Dialogue (United Nations),* 23(1), 122–131.

Taylor, L. (2009). Children constructing Japan: material practices and relational learning. *Children's Geographies,* 7 (2), 173–189.

Taylor, L. (2011). Investigating change in young people's understandings of Japan: A study of learning about a distant place. *British Educational Research Journal,* 37(6), 1033–1054.

Thompson, J. H. (1957). Urban agriculture in southern Japan. *Economic Geography,* 33(3), 224–237.

Thompson, J. H. (1959). Manufacturing in the Kita Kyushu industrial zone of Japan. *Annals of the Association of American Geographers,* 49(4), 420–442.

Thompson, J. H., and Miyazaki, M. (1959). A map of Japan's manufacturing. *Geographical Review,* 49(1), 1–17.

Thomson, K. H. (2009). *Earthquakes and sea-level change in Hokkaido, north-east Japan.* Ph.D. Dissertation. Durham University.

Titiev, M. (1951). The Japanese colony in Peru. *The Far Eastern Quarterly,* 10(3), 227–247.

Tohoku Geographical Association (2011). The 2011 East Japan earthquake bulletin of the Tohoku Geographical Association. Accessed 8 July 2014 at http://tohokugeo.jp/disaster/disaster-e.html.

Toji, D. S. (1999). *Geographic bases of racial formation.* Ph.D. Dissertation. University of California, Los Angeles.

Trewartha, G. T. (1928). A geographic study in Shizuoka Prefecture, Japan. *Annals of the Association of American Geographers,* 18(3), 127–259.

Trewartha, G. T. (1929). The tea crop. *Journal of Geography,* 28(1), 1–25.

Trewartha, G. T. (1930a). The Iwaki basin: Reconnaissance field study of a specialized apple district in northern Honshiu, Japan (sic). *Annals of the Association of American Geographers,* 20(4), 196–223.

Trewartha, G. T. (1930b). The Suwa basin: A specialized sericulture district in the Japanese Alps. *Geographical Review,* 20(2), 224–244.

Trewartha, G. T. (1934a). *A reconnaissance geography of Japan.* Madison: University of Wisconsin Press.

Trewartha, G. T. (1934b). Japanese cities distribution and morphology. *Geographical Review* 24(3), 404–417.

Trewartha, G. T. (1934c). Notes on a physiographic diagram of Japan. *Geographical Review,* 24(3), 400–403.

Trewartha, G. T. (1945). *Japan: A physical, cultural, and regional geography.* Madison: University of Wisconsin Press. (5th printing 1960)

Trewartha, G. T. (1949a). Geography in Japan. *Bulletin 5, Committee on Asian Studies* (pp. 2–13). Tokyo: Supreme Commander of the Allied Powers.

Trewartha, G. T. (1949b). Utilization of upland areas in Japan. In Institute of Pacific Relations (Ed.), *The development of upland areas in the Far East, Volume 1* (pp. 59–82). New York: International Secretariat, Institute of Pacific Relations.

Trewartha, G. T. (1950). Land reform and land reclamation in Japan. *Geographical Review*, 40(3), 376–96.

Trewartha, G. T. (1952). Chinese cities: Origins and functions. *Annals of the Association of American Geographers,* 42(1), 69–93.

Trewartha, G. T. (1953). Some thoughts on the functions of the regional divisions. *The Professional Geographer*, 5(2), 35–41.

Trewartha, G. T. (1965). *Japan: A geography*. Madison: University of Wisconsin Press.

Trewartha, G.T. (1982). An interview conducted by Donna S. Taylor. Transcript of Interview 106 in 1975. University of Wisconsin Archives Oral History Project. Transcript and index courtesy of Troy Reeves, Head, Oral History Program, Steenbock Memorial Library, University of Wisconsin, 8 September 2011.

Tsujita, M. (2012). *The Samoan Aidscape: Situated knowledge and the multiple realities of Japan's foreign aid to Samoa*. Ph.D. Dissertation. University of Hawaii.

Ueda, M. (1983). *Agricultural systems efficiency: A case study of Japanese and Philippino rice farming*. Ph.D. Dissertation. Columbia University.

Uitto, J. I. (1998). The geography of disaster, vulnerability in megacities: a theoretical framework. *Applied Geography*, 18(1), 7–16.

United States Cultural Science Mission to Japan. (1949). *Report of the United States cultural science mission to Japan*. Tokyo: Civil Information and Education Section, Supreme Commander for the Allied Powers. (Members: George K. Brady, Charles E. Martin, Edwin O. Reischauer, Luther W. Stalnaker, Glenn T. Trewartha.)

University of Colorado at Boulder Library. (2009). Archives, The US Navy Japanese/Oriental Language School Archival Project. John S. Thompson, OLS 1945, Geographer. Reprinted from *The (Syracuse) Post Standard*, 23 April 1988. *The Interpreter* 140, 2. 1 October 2009. Accessed 8 July 2014 at http://ucblibraries.colorado.edu/archives/ collections/jlsp/interpreter140.pdf.

University of Michigan (2011a). Faculty history project. Robert B. Hall.www.um2017.org/faculty-history/faculty/robert-b-hall. Last accessed 8 July 2014.

University of Michigan (2011b). Center for Japanese Studies publications. www.quod.lib.umich.edu/cgi/t/text/text-idx?c=cjs;page= browse;key=author. Last accessed 8 July 2014.

University of Rochester Library. (2011). University of Rochester history, chapter 36. Part II concerning Robert B. Hall, Jr. Accessed 8 July 2014 at http://www.lib.rochester.edu/index.cfm?PAGE=2342

Unno, K. (1991). Government cartography in sixteenth century Japan. *Imago Mundi* 43(1), 86–91.

Unno, K. (1994). Cartography in Japan. In J.B. Harley and D. Woodward (Eds.), *The history of cartography, Volume 2, Book 2, Cartography in the traditional east and southeast Asian societies* (pp. 346–477). Chicago: University of Chicago Press.

Voskuil, W. H. (1963). Japan: A deep sea industrial empire. *The Professional Geographer,* 15(3), 1–3.

Waldichuk, T. (1998). A comparison of Japanese and North American attitudes towards residential landscapes in the rural-urban fringe. *The Great Lakes Geographer*, 5(1–2), 15–29.

Waldichuk, T. (2009). The satisfaction with leisure activities, facilities, and services of retirement-aged people living in a rural-urban fringe community not far from Tokyo: An examination of Ushiku City, Ibaraki Prefecture. *Geographical Review of Japan, Series B*, 82(1), 1–13.

Waldichuk, T. C. (1995). *Landscape developments on the rural-urban fringe of a commuter city near Tokyo: Residents' attitudes in Ushiku City, with Western comparisons*. Ph.D. Dissertation. York University (Canada).

Waldichuk, T., and Whitney, H. (1997). Inhabitants' attitudes toward agricultural activities and urban development in an urbanizing *Konjuka* area in the rural-urban fringe of Tokyo. *Geographical Review of Japan, Series B*, 70(1), 32–40.

Waley, P. (1994). *Symbolic space and urban change in the Japanese city: The Edo-Tokyo periphery, 1800–1930*. Ph.D. Dissertation. School of Oriental and African Studies, University of London.

Waley, P. (2000a). Following the flow of Japan's river culture. *Japan Forum*, 12(2), 199–217.

Waley, P. (2000b). Tokyo: Patterns of familiarity and partitions of difference. In P. Marcuse and R. van Kempen (Eds.), *Globalizing cities: A new spatial order?* (pp. 127–157). Oxford: Blackwell.

Waley, P. (2000c). What's a river without fish? Symbol, space and eco-system in the waterways of Japan. In C. Philo and C. Wilbert (Eds.), *Animal spaces, beastly places: New geographies of human-animal relations* (pp. 161–182). London: Routledge.

Waley, P. (2002a). Journey into another world: Tokyo's ferries and the transformation of landscape. In F. Blanchon (Ed.), *Aller et venir: Faits et perspectives* (pp. 147–73). Paris: Presses de l'Université de Paris-Sorbonne.

Waley, P. (2002b). Moving the margins of Tokyo. *Urban Studies*, 39(9), 1533–1550.

Waley, P. (2003a). Conclusion: Power, memory, and place. In P. Waley and N. Fiévé (Eds.), *Japanese capitals in historical perspective: Place, power and memory in Kyoto, Edo and Tokyo* (pp. 385–391). London: RoutledgeCurzon.

Waley, P. (2003b). A ferry to the factory: Crossing Tokyo's great river into a new world. In P. Waley and N. Fiévé (Eds.), *Japanese capitals in historical perspective: Place, power and memory in Kyoto, Edo and Tokyo* (pp. 208–232). London: Routledge Curzon.

Waley, P. (2005a). Parks and landmarks: Planning the Eastern Capital along western lines. *Journal of Historical Geography*, 31(1), 1–16.

Waley, P. (2005b). Ruining and restoring rivers: The state and civil society in Japan. *Pacific Affairs*, 78(2), 195–215.

Waley, P. (2006). Re-scripting the city: Tokyo from ugly duckling to cool cat. *Japan Forum*, 18(3), 361–381.

Waley, P. (2007). Tokyo-as-world-city: Reassessing the role of capital and the state in urban restructuring. *Urban Studies*, 44(8), 1465–1490.

Waley, P. (2009). Distinctive patterns of industrial urbanisation in modern Tokyo, c. 1880–1930. *Journal of Historical Geography*, 35(3), 405–427.

Waley, P. (2012). Japanese cities in Chinese perspective: Towards a contextual, regional approach to comparative urbanism. *Urban Geography*, 33(6), 816–828.

Waley, P. (2013). Pencilling Tokyo into the map of neoliberal urbanism. *Cities*, 32, 43–50.

Waley, P., and Fiévé, N. (2003). Kyoto and Edo-Tokyo: Urban histories in parallels and tangents. In P. Waley and N. Fiévé (Eds.), *Japanese capitals in historical perspective: Place, power and memory in Kyoto, Edo and Tokyo* (pp. 1–40). London: RoutledgeCurzon.

Waley, P., and Fiévé, N. (Eds.) (2003). *Japanese capitals in historical perspective: Place, power and memory in Kyoto, Edo and Tokyo*. London: RoutledgeCurzon.

Waley, P., and Purvis, M. (2004). Sustaining the flow: Japanese waterways and new paradigms of development. In M. Purvis and A. Grainger (Eds.), *Geographical perspectives on sustainable development* (pp. 207–229). London: Earthscan.

Waley, P., and Tinios, E. (1999). *On the margins of the city: Scenes of recreation from the periphery of the Japanese capital, 1760-1860*. Leeds: University of Leeds Press.

Walker, H. (2012). In defense of an island: Kojima's fight against the sea. *American Geographical Society's Focus on Geography*, (55)1, 11–18.

Walker, H. J. and Mossa, J. (1986). Human modification of the shoreline in Japan. *Physical Geography* 7(2), 116–39.

Warren, W. H. (1994). *Koreans in Japan: Movement, distribution, and landscape*. Ph.D. Dissertation. University of Hawaii.

Watters, R. F., McGee, T.G., and Sullivan, G. (1997). *Asia-Pacific: New geographies of the Pacific Rim*. Wellington NZ: Victoria University Press, and Vancouver: UBC Press.

Webber, M. (1998). Profitability and growth in multi-region systems: Interpreting the growth of Japan. *Environment and Planning A*, 30(3), 415–37.

Weightman, B. A. (2011). *Dragons and tigers: A geography of South, East and Southeast Asia*. Hoboken NJ: John Wiley and Sons.

Wheeler, J. O., Aoyama, Y., and Warf, B. (2000). Introduction: City space, industrial space, and cyberspace. In J.O. Wheeler, Y. Aoyama and B. Warf (Eds.), *Cities in the telecommunications age: The fracturing of geographies* (pp. 3–17). New York: Routledge.

Whitbeck, R. H. (1911). Laying the emphasis in teaching the geography of Asia. *Journal of Geography*, 10(2), 51–57.

White, P. E. (2003a). The Japanese in Latin America: on the uses of diaspora. *International Journal of Population Geography*, 9(4), 309–322.

White, P. E. (2003b). The Japanese in London: From transience to settlement? In R. Goodman, C. Peach, A. Takenaka and P.E. White (Eds.), *Global Japan: The experience of Japan's new immigrants and overseas communities* (pp. 79–97). London: RoutledgeCurzon.

White, P. E., and Hurdley, L. (2003). International migration and the housing market: Japanese corporate movers in London. *Urban Studies*, 40(4), 687–706.

Whitehand, J. W. R., and Gu, K. (2006). Research on Chinese urban form: Retrospect and prospect. *Progress in Human Geography*, 30(3), 337–355.

Wigen, K. E. (1990). *Regional inversions: The spatial contours of economic change in the southern Japanese Alps, 1750-1920*. Ph.D. Dissertation. University of California, Berkeley.

Wigen, K. (1992). The geographic imagination in early modern Japanese history: Retrospect and prospect. *Journal of Asian Studies*, 51(1), 3–29.

Wigen, K. (1995). *The making of a Japanese periphery, 1750-1920*. Berkeley: University of California Press.

Wigen, K. (2005). Discovering the Japanese Alps: Meiji mountaineering and the quest for geographical enlightenment. *The Journal of Japanese Studies* 31(1), 1–26.

Wigen, K. (2010). *A malleable map: Geographies of restoration in central Japan, 1600-1912*. Berkeley: University of California Press.

Wigen, K. (2012). Introduction to "Japanese imperial maps as sources for East Asian history: The past and future of the Gaihōzu". *Cross-Currents: East Asian History and Culture Review E-Journal*, 2, 1–5. Accessed 8 July 2014 at https://cross-currents. berkeley.edu/e-journal/issue-2/japanese-imperial-maps-sources-east-asian-history-past-and-future-gaihozu

Wijk, M. van. (2007). *Airports as cityports in the city-region*. Utrecht: Netherlands Geographical Studies 353. Accessed 8 July 2014 at http://dspace.library. uu.nl/bitstream/handle/1874/19173/index. htm?sequence =24

Wilson, R. (2011). Landscapes of promise and betrayal: Reclamation, homesteading, and Japanese American incarceration. *Annals of the Association of American Geographers* 101(2), 424–444.

Wiltshire, R. (1991). A new future for a company town: Diversification and employment in Kamaishi City. *Science Reports of the Tohoku University, 7th series, Geography*, 41(1), 1–22.

Wiltshire, R. (1992a). Inter-regional personnel transfers and structural change: The case of the Kamaishi steelworks. *Transactions of the Institute of British Geographers, New Series*, (17)1, 65–79.

Wiltshire, R. (1992b). Rural development and processes of agricultural change in Japan. In K. Hoggart (Ed.), *Agricultural change, environment, economy: Essays in honour of W.B. Morgan* (pp. 49–67). London: Mansell.

Wiltshire, R. (1993). *Geography*. In R. Bowring and P. Kornicki (Eds.), *The Cambridge Encyclopedia of Japan* (pp. 2–39). Cambridge: Cambridge University Press.

Wiltshire, R. (1995). *Relocating the Japanese worker: Geographical perspectives on personnel transfers*. Sandgate, Folkestone, Kent: Japan Library.

Wiltshire, R. (1998). Diversification and employment in Kamaishi City: A future reconsidered. *Science Reports of Tohoku University, Seventh Series (Geography)*, 48(1–2), 85–104.

Wiltshire, R. (2004). Comment on Fielding's class and space: Social segregation in Japanese cities. *Transactions of the Institute of British Geographers*, 29(1), 85–86.

Wiltshire, R., and Azuma, R. (2000). Rewriting the plot: Sustaining allotments in the UK and Japan. *Local Environment*, 5(2), 139–151.

Wiltshire, R., Crouch, D., and Azuma, R. (2002). Contesting the plot: Environmental politics and the urban allotment garden in Britain and Japan. In P. Stott and S. Sullivan (Eds.), *Political ecology: Power, myth and science* (pp. 203–217). London: Edward Arnold.

Wisner, B., and Uitto, J. (2009). Life on the edge: Urban social vulnerability and decentralized, citizen-based disaster risk reduction in four large cities of the Pacific Rim. In H. G. Brauch, U. O. Spring, J. Grin, C. Mesjasz, P. Kameri-Mbote, N. C. Behara, B. Chourou, H. Krummenacher (Eds.), *Facing global environmental change: Environmental, human, energy, food, health, and water security concepts* (pp. 215–231). Berlin: Springer.

Yagasaki, N. (1982). *Ethnic cooperativism and immigrant agriculture: A study of the Japanese floriculture and truck farming in California*. Ph.D. Dissertation. University of California, Berkeley.

Yagasaki, N. (2002). *Japan: Geographical perspectives on an island nation*. Tōkyō: Teikoku Shoin.

Yagasaki, N., and Nakamura, Y. (2008). The role of local groups in the protection of urban farming and farmland in Tokyo. In P. P. Karan and U. Suganuma (Eds.), *Local environmental movements: A comparative study of the United States and Japan* (pp. 131–144). Lexington: University Press of Kentucky

Yagasaki, N. (2013). Geography and geographers in Japan since 1980: Preface to the special issue. *Geographical Review of Japan Series B*, 86(1), 1–5.

Yamamoto, B. (2007). *A quality alternative? Quality conventions, alternative food and the politics of soybeans in Japan*. Ph.D. Dissertation. University of Washington.

Yamamoto, D. (2006). *Beyond convergence: Regional income disparities in the United States and Japan, 1955-2001*. Ph.D. Dissertation. University of Minnesota.

Yamamoto, D., and Gill, A. (2002). Issues of globalization and reflexivity in the Japanese tourism production system: The case of Whistler, British Columbia. *The Professional Geographer*, 54(1), 83–93.

Yamazaki, K., and Yamazaki, T. (2008). The grassroots movement to save the Sanbanze tidelands, Tokyo Bay. In P. P. Karan and U. Suganuma (Eds.), *Local environmental movements: A comparative study of the United States and Japan* (pp. 187–204). Lexington: University Press of Kentucky.

Yamazaki, K., and Yamazaki, T. (2011). Tsunami disasters in Seenigama Village, Sri Lanka, and Taro Town, Japan. In P. P. Karan and S. Subbiah (Eds.), *The Indian Ocean tsunami: The global response to a natural disaster* (pp. 135–159). Lexington, The University Press of Kentucky.

Yamazaki, T. (1997). Political geography in post-war Japan: Publication tendencies. *Political Geography*, 16(4), 325–344.

Yamazaki, T. (2002). Is Japan leaking? Globalization, reterritorialization and identity in the Asia-Pacific context. *Geopolitics*, 7(1), 165–192.

Yamazaki, T. (2004a). Dreaming of 'liberation' by riding on globalization: Oppositional movements in Okinawa. In J. V. O'Loughlin, L. A. Staeheli and E. S. Greenberg (Eds.), *Globalization and its outcomes* (pp. 337–360). New York: Guilford Press.

Yamazaki, T. (2004b). *Political space of Okinawa: Geographical perspectives on ethno-regional integration and protest*. Ph.D. Dissertation. University of Colorado at Boulder.

Yamazaki, T. (2011). The US militarization of a 'host' civilian society: The case of postwar Okinawa, Japan. In S. Kirsch and C. Flint (Eds.), *Reconstructing conflict: Integrating war and post-war geographies* (pp. 253–272). Surrey and Burlington, Vermont: Ashgate.

Yano, K., Nakaya, T., Isoda, Y., Brown, P., and Savas, M. (2007). *Baacharu Kyōto: Kako, genzai, mirai e no tabi*. Nakanishiya.

Yasue, E. (2010). *The practice and the reproduction of tourist landscapes in contemporary Japan*. Ph.D. Dissertation. Royal Holloway, University of London.

Yasue, E., and Murakami, K. (2011). Practicing tourist landscapes: Photographic performances and consumption of nature in Japanese domestic tourism. In C. Minca and T. Oakes (Eds.), *Real tourism: Practice, care, and politics in contemporary travel culture* (pp. 123–142). Oxford and New York: Routledge.

Yasui, E. (2007). *Community vulnerability and capacity in post disaster recovery: The cases of Mano and Mikura neighborhoods in the wake of the 1995 Kobe earthquake*. Ph.D. Dissertation (Planning). University of British Columbia.

Yeh, E.J. (2011). *Territorialising colonial environments: A comparison of colonial sciences on land demarcation in Japanese Taiwan and British Malaya*. Ph.D. Dissertation. Durham University. www.etheses.dur.ac.uk/ 3199. Accessed 8 July 2014.

Yeung, H. W.C. (2000). Organizing the firm in industrial geography 1: Networks, institutions and regional development. *Progress in Human Geography*, 24(2), 301–315.

Yeung, H.W.-C. (2007). Remaking economic geography: Insights from East Asia. *Economic Geography*, 83(4), 339–348.

Yokohari, M., and Bolthouse, J. (2011). Planning for the slow lane: The need to restore working greenspaces in maturing contexts. *Landscape and Urban Planning*, 100(4), 421–424.

Yokoyama, S. (2013). A review of the developments in nature and society studies in Japan from the 1980s onwards. *Geographical Review of Japan Series B*, 86(1), 62–74.

Yonechi, F. (1999). Description on the volcanoes of northern Japan in Shiga's "Nihon Fukei-ron": Plagiarism and its political background. *Journal of Policy Studies (Iwate University)*, 1(4), 477–488.

Yoon, H.K. (1997). The origin and decline of a Japanese temple town: Saidaiji Monzenmachi. *Urban Studies*, 18(5), 434–450.

Yoon, H.K. (2006). *The culture of fengshui in Korea: An exploration of East Asian geomancy*. Lanham MD: Lexington Books.

Yoshida, K. (2008). A recent review of vegetation science in Japanese geography. *Geographical Review of Japan, Chirigaku Hyōron*, 81(5), 375–383(129–137).

Yoshida, M. (2011). *Women, citizenship and migration: The resettlement of Vietnamese refugees in Australia*. Kyōto: Nakanishiya Shuppan.

Yoshida, Y., Murata, Y., and Kageyama, H. (2013). Toward the development of the geography of gender in Japan: Advances in research and prospects. *Geographical Review of Japan Series B*, 86(1), 33–39.

Yoshino, H., Momiyama, M., Satō, T., and Sasaki, K. (1993). Relationship between cerebrovascular disease and indoor thermal environment in two selected towns in Miyagi Prefecture, Japan. *Journal of Thermal Biology*, 18(5–6), 481–486.

7

Regionalism and the Local

Anthony Rausch

The theme 'Regionalism and the Local' is, in itself, less an academic category than a descriptive reference. In a strictly concrete sense 'regionalism' implies differences between places, processes of change among places, and policies affecting places, whereas 'the local' refers to the fundamental geographical unit of the nation-state as a concrete reality. Conceptually, 'regionalism' implies more of an ideological position, one stressing some affective loyalty to one's region in which 'the local' is an idealized notion of place as an abstract conceptualization. These two views often come together in the principle of regional autonomy, which prioritizes the regional and local at the expense of or in addition to the nation as a whole. As such, not only are there multiple dimensions inherent to the theme, but these dimensions reflect both a range of scalar variation and overlapping relationships, as well as drawing from a number of social-scientific disciplinary frames.

Regionalism and the local is, first and foremost, a project of geographical description, organized on the basis of the spatiality. This spatiality is multi-dimensional in character and scale, whether of one place (the Tohoku region of northern Honshu), of one place to another place (the Tohoku region versus the Tokyo-centered Kanto region), or of a place within a larger place (Tohoku as a distinct region within Japan as a nation-state). Regionalism and the local as a critical endeavor demands a historical component, as when tracking changing relations, and the changing perceptions about those relations, across time and through varying circumstances. The implications of such historical transitions are largely economic and political, but can also influence the social and cultural character of a society and the fates of the groups and individuals in those places. The economic implications concern the distribution of resources between places – not just natural and financial but also human, intellectual and cultural resources. The political implications concern the power relations that emerge between actors within the nation-state, whether government institutions, private enterprises, public organizations, or citizens and local residents, as the center, usually powerful and dominant, interacts with the periphery, usually weaker and more acquiescent. Understanding regionalism and the local necessitates sociological frames when considering societal structures and the societal problems that result from these continually changing economic and political relationships. Finally, regionalism and the local implies a cultural-anthropological viewpoint when considering questions of identity, the manifestations of which are largely expressed through, for example, literature, performance, or life practices.

Reflecting this complexity and element of change, the narrative of this chapter is transition and tension – the transitions of regionalism as geographical consciousness has changed, and the tensions such transitions have yielded. This narrative of regionalism and the local reveals gradual transitions from a pre-modern and powerful sense of 'local' toward modernization and a weakening of this local identity through centralization and allegiance to centralized authority, which has been followed by a gradual re-evaluation and prioritization of regionalism as a trend in academics, politics, and ordinary life. The tensions that accompany these transitions emerge not just between the competing notions of centralism versus regionalism and the realities that are manifest in them but also in the social responses and public policies that emerge as a result of these real-life tensions. This chapter begins with geography and history, and place in literature and the literature of place, all of which are tied up in the construction of place. This is followed by examination of the anthropology of identity and the sociology of depopulation and economic decline at the regional and local level. The tension of these latter two trends is seen in the local economy – in efforts toward local revitalization – and a central government response – in the policies of decentralization. The chapter then presents a brief overview of the literature of regionalism and the local in Japanese academic work, focusing on the research of relevant Japanese academic associations while also noting the value of local scholarly activity as a window onto the transitions and trends identified herein. The chapter closes by expressing a hope for a new and positive viewpoint on the value of regionalism and local area studies as an academic endeavor.

REGIONAL DIFFERENCE, LITERARY REPRESENTATION AND PRE-MODERN TRENDS: RECOGNIZING AND CONSTRUCTING PLACE

Geographically, Japan is an archipelago of four main islands (Hokkaido, Honshu, Kyushu and Shikoku) together with the Ryukyu island chain that constitutes Okinawa and the additional hundreds of populated islands that lie within its nation-state territory. Beyond this geo-physical starting point Japan is usually presented as nine major regions – Hokkaido, Tohoku, Kanto, Chubu, Kinki, Chugoku, Shikoku, Kyushu and the Nansei, or Ryukyu Islands – this on the basis of myriad physical, historical, cultural, economic, and political factors. Finally, there are 47 prefectures – although in reality these are 43 *ken* (prefectures), two *fu*, one

to and one *dō* – within which lie the *gun* (county), and the *shi, machi,* and *mura* (cities, towns and villages; more commonly referred to combinatively as *shichōson*), together with the informal and non-official notions of 'places' that make up Japan's highly complex 'local'.

In a geographically descriptive sense Japan's regionalism and its 'regional reality' are notable at the national level for differences between eastern and western Japan and between the Pacific Ocean front of Japan (*omote Nihon*) and the Sea of Japan back of Japan (*ura Nihon*) (Nakamura, 1980; Sugimoto, 1997). Broad differences reflecting historical trajectories and life practices are too many and too varied to catalog here, but range from the general – hunting and fishing historically associated with the east versus farming more important in the west and Tokyo seen as refined and aristocratic and Osaka a rough-and-tumble world of commerce and competition – to differences in food habits – saltier *soba* noodles in the east versus blander *udon* in the west – to the realities of lifestyle – higher rates of cancer in the west versus higher rates of stroke in the east (Karan, 2005). Such broadly articulated differences obscure what can be more specific and more detailed regional and sub-regional differences, a powerful example of which Yamawaki (2011) provides in a Japanese Collectivism Scale – a measure of individuals' collectivistic versus individualistic behavioral traits and tendencies. The regional patterns show a majority of collectivist prefectures are found in the Tohoku district of the north and the centrally located Chubu district; among the top 10 most collectivistic prefectures nine were from these two areas. On the other hand, while the more individualistic prefectures were spread throughout Japan, eight out of 10 were prefectures that include government-appointed major cities (*seirei shitei toshi*), ostensibly the most urbanized cities in the country. Even within regions and prefectures distinct differences exist, often in such areas as local farming practices, religious ceremonies and dialects. Taking the case of Aomori Prefecture, the northernmost of Honshu, the dialect of the western, Sea of Japan side of the prefecture, *Tsugaru ben,* is a language distinctly different from both standard Japanese and the dialect of the eastern side of the prefecture, referred to as *Nambu ben.* The explanation for such local language diversity is geographical and historical, as the western side of the prefecture, referred to as Tsugaru, was historically isolated by the north-south-running Hakkoda mountain range from the eastern side, called Nambu. While a distinct Tsugaru dialect emerged in the west, the dialect of the east was influenced through the region's association with the once powerful Fujiwara family in the late Edo period (1603–1868) as it extended its influence northward from what is now Iwate Prefecture, located just to the south of Aomori.

This power of language in its representation of place cannot be overstated – local dialects are found throughout Japan. Literature is also a site of the representation of place; this was Thunman's (2002) point in her study of translation in modern Japanese literature when she alluded to literature's tremendous power to represent place. One of the earliest examples of reference to place in modern literature was Kawabata Yasunari's (1899–1972) *Snow Country*, published in Japan in 1947 and in English in 1956, and instrumental in its author winning the Nobel Prize for Literature in 1968. While the story tells of a love affair between a Tokyo dilettante and a provincial geisha, Kawabata was writing about a 'stylized and traditional' Japan found in a place he refers to as '*yukiguni*', literally, 'snow country'. Similarly, while Osamu Dazai's (1909–1948) *Return to Tsugaru: Travels of a Purple Tramp* (2005, trans. Westerhoven) is about Dazai's journey of self-discovery through recollections of his past, the contents also portray in detail the places of Tsugaru. Westerhoven's (2009) more extended translation and contextualization of a broader range of Tsugaru literature provides ample examples of the power of literature in the image creation of both place and the lives of people living in that place: Takagi Kyozo's use of local scenes in his stories provide a vivid sense of what it feels like to live on the Tsugaru plain, in the shadow of the monolithic Mount Iwaki.

However, in addition to the use of place as setting, the connection of literature to place is also one of statement. Ann Waswo, translator of Nagatsuka's 1910 novel *Tsuchi* (The Soil) (1989), a portrait of peasant life in Ibaraki Prefecture in the Meiji Period (1868–1912), pointed out that the book has yielded numerous interpretations through its history: as a Marxist critique of exploitative social relations in the 1920s and 1930s, as a call for communal solidarity and resolve during the war years, and as a vision of a lost utopia during the late 1970s, all against the backdrop of a specific place-based narrative set in a distinct time period. Dodd (2005) took up literary representations of *furusato* (home place) in fiction published in the early twentieth century, noting how the depictions of these places connected with the broad range of discourses of the time, meaning that the *furusato* that were created were socially constructed in a mutual consensus between writer and reader. Like Westerhoven and the literature of the Tsugaru area, Bhowmik (2008) focused on a regional literature, in this case Okinawan fiction, but argued that this body of writing represents a site of resistance to the dominance of mainstream Japanese literature and a focal point for the crystallization of Okinawan identity. Long (2011) showed that

the writing of Miyazawa Kenji (1896–1933), perhaps best known as author of the classic *Night on the Milky Way Railroad* (*Gingatetsudō no Yoru*), revealed at the time it was written the hierarchies of Japan's cultural center and periphery, its networks of cultural flow and the uneven geography of its cultural production. These examples argue against the notion of a singular, monolithic Japanese literature, and rather push for an understanding of the literature of Japan as representing a more complex regionalism within Japan.

While literature as a literary endeavor thus provides portrayals of regions as well as discourses on regionalism, there is also a social-scientific literature of regionalism and the local in Japan per se. Representative of this is the work of Beardsley et al. (1959) with *Village Japan*, Fukutake (1972) with *Japanese Rural Society*, Smith (1978) with *Kurusu: The Price of Progress in a Japanese Village 1951–1975*, Bailey's (1991) *Ordinary People, Extraordinary Lives: Political and Economic Change in a Tohoku Village*, and Dore's (1994) *Shinohata: A Portrait of a Japanese Village*. These works, detailing the multitude aspects of life and social setting in rural villages on the one hand, while also describing the history of change that has taken place in postwar rural Japan on the other, provided the foundation for much of the place-based research that followed. More contemporary works with a similar theme, objective, and approach include Partner's (2004) *Toshie: A Story of Village Life in Twentieth-Century Japan*, Bernstein's (2005) *Isami's House*, Guo, et al.'s (2005) *Tsugaru: Regional Identity on Japan's Northern Periphery*, Thompson and Traphagen's (2006) *Wearing Cultural Styles*, Kalland's (2010) *Shingu: A Study of a Japanese Fishing Community*, Dusinberre's (2012) *Hard Times in the Hometown*, and Wood's (2012) *Ogata-Mura: Sowing Dissent and Reclaiming Identity in a Japanese Farming Village*. In addition to describing places these works present anthropological insights and sociological analysis of the villages and families of a particular locale and chronicle the changes regional and local Japan has undergone through its transition from a high-growth economy to responding to the forces of globalization, while also adapting to an aging and depopulating rural society. In this sense, a reading of these works gives an overview of the places that constitute much of Japan outside of Tokyo and Osaka, while also providing a detailed view of the individuals, families, groups, and communities that make up these places.

While not academic, a review of the 'travel-personal discovery' genre of writing about Japan can also contribute to the recognition and construction of place in Japan. Although penned by foreigners, each of the following books uses a different approach to take the reader to a different place (or places) within Japan. Booth's (1985) *The Roads to Sata: A 2000-Mile Walk Through Japan* walks us on the small back roads from Soya at Japan's northernmost tip to Cape Sata in the extreme south. The detail of Ritchie's (1999) *Village Japan: Everyday Life in a Rural Japanese Community* reflects his day-to-day living in a place; in it he expresses his sense that the aged inhabitants of his village home are the custodians of a fragile, barely surviving way of life, one that is informed by the cadences of the natural world under the tutelage of its ancient gods. The settings for Richie's (2002) *The Inland Sea* are the seafaring communities of the Seto Inland Sea, the south-central body of sea bounded by Honshu, Shikoku and Kyushu, where he delights in the details of local life and muses on the food, romance, work, and human foibles of the people he encounters. Moeran's (1985) *A Far Valley* depicts life, and the life of his family, in a rural Japanese village, allowing the reader to experience the thoughts of the local people as they joke, complain, gossip, and argue.

Finally, a pre-modern historical consideration of regionalism and the local within Japan is a vital point of reference for understanding what comes after, and would start with Batten's (2003) work on Japan's pre-modern frontiers, borders, and interactions, and Adolphson et al.'s (2006) edited work on center and periphery in Heian-period (794–1185) Japan. Batten's interest is in the socially and politically constructed frontiers and boundaries of pre-modern Japan, evidence not just of early place identity but also diversity of place and interaction between places. Huey noted in his review of Adolphson et al.'s work that the essays 'provide fascinating details about "central" and "peripheral" institutions and the tight connections between them' (2008: 333).

This early 'complexity of place' is contrasted by Morris-Suzuki's portrayal of the inland local in the edited volume *Multicultural Japan*, in which she asserted that the known world for most Japanese living in inland areas at the beginning of the eighteenth century stretched only as far as the nearest mountain range and then blurred in the 'realms of hearsay' (2001: 141). She argued that the word *kuni* as was used by people at that time referred to their local region or domain, as opposed to its current translation as 'country'. However, after the two centuries of self-imposed isolation that constituted the Edo period from the 1600s to the mid-1800s, this notion of identity as local fell to efforts to form a unified, national state from 280 separate feudal domains that had constituted pre-Meiji Japan. From its beginning one of the primary goals accompanying the establishment of the Meiji government in 1868 was the creation and promotion of a sense of national identity,

cultural homogeneity, and social order (Passin, 1980). However, as will be shown in the next section, the centralism of the Meiji Period and the war years that followed gave way gradually to a refocusing on the local over the postwar period and an emergent regionalism in contemporary Japan.

Thus, the descriptions so common of Japan as a monolithic, unified, and highly homogeneous nation-state of like-minded citizens belie an early history of localism, a literary tradition reflecting meaningful if not contested regionalism, and a descriptive complexity of highly diverse places, all of which portray regional complexity and underscore the importance of understanding Japan at a local level.

ANTHROPOLOGICAL VIEWS: PLACE AND IDENTITY, REAL AND IMAGINED

Identity in Japan and Japanese identity have, over Japan's modern history, reflected transitions and tensions between localism and nationalism. Thus, identity is an important mainstay in any consideration of Japanese regionalism and the local. As outlined above, the historical origins of transition and tension between centralism and regionalism precede the modern era. As described by Takeuchi (1978), the trajectory of regionalism as both reality and consciousness, as well as the establishment of local-area studies as an area of academic study, begins with the Meiji Period. This was a period when the overriding national consciousness – whether educational, political, or cultural – was to 'mobilize the Japanese people toward a national aim, the modernization of Japan, to enable her to stand on an equal footing with Western countries' (Takeuchi, 1978: 238). That said, Takeuchi hypothesized an underlying localist consciousness that worked against this strengthening centralism. This localist sentiment he defined as

> the aspirations of the residents of a region within a sovereign nation state to attain local political autonomy and to preserve and enhance a unique local culture against the centripetal force of political centralization and cultural standardization. These aspirations must stem from the local resident's sense of belonging to his own local community based on shared geopietal consciousness and historical experience with his fellow residents. (Takeuchi, 1978: 241)

Takeuchi saw this countervailing localist sentiment continuing through the pre-Second World War period. He noted that despite the national war effort necessitating policies that called for sacrifice by all of Japan there remained among some elites a powerful sense of obligation to the local areas such that they sought to protect these rural populations from the government provisions that were creating the very poverty that plagued them.

Takeuchi also saw this sentiment as providing the foundation for the early study of rural Japanese life in the work of Yanagita Kunio (1872–1962) and the terminology of *jikata kenkyū*, or 'studies of local matters' (Yanagita, 1959). Yanagita articulated the concept of *jōmin*, or 'ordinary folk', those who embodied the defining elements of a distinctive and highly place-connected, yet universal Japanese identity: ancestor worship, rice cultivation, and a fixed domicile (Harootunian, 1998). However, as meaningful and well intentioned as these depictions of early-twentieth-century Japanese rural society were (and are), some saw (and see) the work as superficial in its assumed universality, particularly in terms of the how it overlooked the diversity that even nearby areas revealed in reality. An example of this is provided in Schnell's (2005) recounting of an exchange regarding the work of Origuchi Shinobu (1887–1953), another noted early folklorist. Commenting on Origuchi's works, a local informant of Schnell's held that Origuchi indeed had a deep understanding of the places in which he worked, but that he ultimately failed to fully recognize differences to be found even in a neighboring village, differences which as referred to above – in farming, religion, and language – could be quite distinct. Others countered the idyllic depictions of such early works, portraying the reality of rural Japanese society in unflattering terms. Miyamoto Tsuneichi (1907–1981), an agricultural and forestry specialist, spent much of his career chronicling rural Japan through interviews with local residents. His major work, *Wasurerareta Nihonjin*, published in 1960 and translated as *The Forgotten Japanese* in 2010, recounts working with locals in what he describes as the chaotic negotiations necessary to reach consensus at the village level, processes that took place against a background of the materialistic deprivation, personal infidelity and economic desperation that characterized much of Japanese rural life at the time.

Wigen (2000), similarly, identified a trajectory of transition and tension between localism and centralism in both identity and local studies within Japan, showing that in pre-war Nagano, the prefecture, as one's *kyōdo*, or hometown, was viewed by some as the site of native-place identity and a place of accordingly powerful personal attachment. However, this sense of personal attachment fell into disrepute in the immediate postwar period as the romanticized term *kyōdo* gave way to the more academic *chihō*, the term widely used to refer to 'area' in both academic and general use;

and the studies that had supported exploration of native places were denigrated as sentimental, subjective, and unscientific. Turn to the latter part of the Shōwa Period (1925–1989) and many Japanese, academics and commoners alike, had begun to focus once again on the virtues of the local. Historians of local Japan also returned to the terminology of *kyōdo*, reasserting the values of personal attachment and intimate familiarity with place, and arguing that the curiosity that a scholar brings to place-based research should emerge from the essence of the place itself rather than from detached academic debates. Wigen's conclusion: pride in place had slowly regained respectability over the postwar period in Japan to the point where the level of academic reference to *chiiki* or region means that localism is now 'embedded in a distinctly progressive framework: one that weds local initiative and regional revitalization to a fluid and connective sense of place' (Wigen, 2000: 569). Hashimoto also revisited the early meaning of the term *chihō*, reframing Yanagita's use and defining it in a more academically critical sense as a 'synchronic metaphor of center and periphery', where 'things unseen in fact lived on, in the spatial margins he called *chihō*' (Hashimoto, 1998: 143).

Recognition of the power of identity and pride in one's place are perhaps the most important aspects of anthropology's contribution to the analysis of Japanese regionalism; that said, this contribution is not to be taken without caution. Criticizing an anthropology of Japan that largely functions as a 'national anthropology', one committed to identifying a 'distinct internal cultural logic', Ryang (2004: 194) argues for the denationalization of Japanese anthropology. This is to be realized in an escape from, for example, such broad anthropologic generalizations as Japan as a 'household-like society', a key theme in Nakane's (1970) *Japanese Society*, or the exclusively inward and self-absorbed view of the 'Japanese self' promoted by Doi's (1973) *Anatomy of Dependence,* and, finally, the monolithic and self-perpetuating *Nihonjinron* phenomenon that dominated Japanese studies from the 1950s to the 1970s and beyond (Mouer and Sugimoto, 1990; Sugimoto, 1999). Aside from such concerns, anthropology as a discipline rigorously applied provides useful regionalist constructs for the social-scientific exploration of modern Japanese society. Schnell (2005) takes as advantageous the flexibility of the many and varied anthropological notions as they can be applied to a regionalism in reverse: the processes of reconciliation of a highly localized past with the more modern, if not urban, present through the mediation of value-laden symbols. As an example Schnell takes up the *ie*, or stem family, noting that, while it may have passed out of dominant practice in rural life, a reflection of the challenges and changes influencing both rural society and Japanese agriculture, it survives in contemporary anthropological assessments, through being re-established in an urban-industrial context. Thus, the concept and practice of *ie* is seen as an organizational blueprint for Japanese society, reconfigured as a code for contemporary social relationships in, for example, the sense of extended family that has been common to the modern Japanese business corporation and the contemporary residential community. In response to his own question as to the value of an anthropological view of local Japan in contemporary Japanese studies, Schnell's answers range from the practical – stability and sustainability – to the ambiguous and abstract – the universality of a *furusato* (one's rural homeland, real or imagined) mentality that accompanies life in urban places. As Schnell concludes, 'whatever the actual case may be, Japan's cultural identity is *perceived* as being heavily rooted in the agrarian traditions of its rural areas. This in itself makes them important' (2005: 201; italics in original).

This notion of anthropological concepts – largely originating in localist research paradigms – serving as timeless but highly adaptable blueprints for organizing Japanese society can be seen in a range of regionalist research and often in the form of *furusato* research. Kelly's assessment of modernity in rural Japan concludes by noting that the emerging contradictions within agricultural policy and the standardizing influence of state institutions have reconfigured the employment patterns, social relationships, cultural identities and political allegiances of rural Japan to the point where '(T)here are no agrarian countrysides in contemporary Japan, except in the (senti) mental imagery of *furusato* motifs' (1990: 224). Siegenthaler (1999) assigns to domestic tourism, in the form of seeking this *furusato,* an important role in the Japanese search for national identity. He cites Graburn's (1983) assessment of Japanese domestic tourism as including both 'tourism-like' as well as 'pilgrimage-like' behaviors, the latter seen as attempts at confirmation of their Japanese identity by seeking out nostalgically meaningful local places, thereby making the *furusato* a tourism buzzword in the 1980s (Ivy, 1995; Robertson, 1998). The application of anthropological blueprints to modern society provides a basis for Robertson's (1992, 1998) exploration of *furusato-zukuri,* defined as a remaking of the past as the condition for a social transformation in the present, where the idealized characteristics and practices of the 'village of the past' are used as prescriptions for creating a similar set of traits and conventions in contemporary residential communities. Ben-Ari, in his examination of emergent communities in contemporary Japan, saw *furusato-zukuri* as 'not only a matter of how

localities are represented according to the logics of national debates about a "vanishing" tradition or a new kind of neighborhood… It is also a matter of how wider understandings are mobilized by locals in their dialogue with a variety of significant others about local identity' (1998: 84).

As for how this focus on 'the local' and local identity emerges in the contemporary reality of research on local places, examples include professional sports franchises, local media discourse and local food culture. Light and Yasaki (2002) noted that while the sponsorship of large corporations was essential for the financial establishment in 1993 of the soccer clubs that comprised the professional J League, regional and local place connections were emphasized in locating and naming the clubs in preference to any parent company. Unlike Japan's largely corporate-based world of baseball, '[P]lace was promoted in preference to institution and many clubs were set up outside the major urban centres such as Tokyo and Osaka. Built upon the foundation of community centres established in conjunction with local governments, local businesses, and parent companies, J League clubs have been explicitly designed to foster community/regional support' (Light and Yasaki, 2002: 31), and have contributed to a sense of local identity in outlying communities.

Contemporary local identity creation was examined in the discourse of local media through three separate case studies of local media in rural Japan. The first was a study of Newspaper in Education (NIE), where educational content is provided in a newspaper as part of a broad effort to cultivate newspaper reading as a practice among students, in the local newspaper of a northern, highly rural prefecture, and in the practice of local educational NIE columns which served both to educate children about their hometowns and strengthen identity associations between children and their hometowns (Rausch, 2004a). The second took up the journalistic representations of local cultural markers in local newspapers for consumption by readers, showing how these were incorporated in the newspaper not just as culture but as 'local news' (Rausch, 2004b). The third case investigated preferences for local valorization of local cultural commodities by local shops and restaurants, local cultural-commodities producers viewing the newspaper as the primary vehicle to reach the public rather than several options in industry promotional materials (Rausch, 2005). This re-evaluation of both the local and the 'content' that constitutes the local by locals is also seen in recent trends in the area of local food cultures. As Assmann (2010) points out, two current social concerns in Japan, low food self-sufficiency – 40 percent according to Assmann – and food safety, have prompted Japanese citizen action on the promotion of domestic and local food production, a trend that she argues also reflects a search for national and local identity through the (re)discovery and promotion of local foods. Similarly, Kingsbury et al. (2010) see re-embedded and re-appropriated alternative food economies as a means of combining 'locality' with 'rurality' and, in so doing, contributing to re-valorizing local products. They found the semantics of 'local' to be highly malleable, amendable to retail imperatives and subject to a number of elements in the construction and marketing of 'quality' to consumers.

Taken in total, the anthropological view of regionalism and the local has been shown to focus on a transition of local identity from Meiji-period Japan to the present. The historical trend of local identity has been shown as a transition from being officially suppressed but secretly supported, naively explored and academically questioned, artificially re-created and, finally, to being fully recognized and re-valorized as meaningful, in notions as ubiquitous and adaptable as *ie* and *furusato* and in contexts as varied and contemporary as organization and community, tourism and sports, and local media and local food culture.

SOCIOLOGICAL VIEWS: DEPOPULATION AND REGIONAL SHRINKING

Shifting from the anthropological and a viewpoint of regionalism as identity to the sociological and a social structural view, the transition of regionalism and the local reflects an evolution of outlying areas from being the sources of raw materials, food resources and semi-permanent labor, with economies sustained largely through centrally funded public-works projects in the period of high economic growth, to a contemporary reality of rural depopulation and economic decline coupled with neo-liberal decentralization as the regional policy of the central government. As described in an extensive work by Matanle and Rausch together with the Shrinking Regions Research Group (2011), titled *Japan's Shrinking Regions in the 21st Century: Contemporary Responses to Depopulation and Socioeconomic Decline*, depopulation and regional shrinking have been a process occurring across the whole of Japan throughout the post-Second World War era. As early as the 1960s regional and economic decline as a consequence of rural depopulation had been recognized on an official basis, countered by economic-revitalization initiatives such as the *jiba sangyō shinkō jygyō* (regional industry promotion projects) and the *isson ippin* (one village, one product) movements of the 1970s (Knight, 1994).

However, despite the continuance of such policy measures through the 'bubble economy' of the 1980s and the 'lost decade' of the 1990s, the trajectory of regional decline has continued (Masaki, 2006), with the terminology of decline keeping pace. As defined under the 2000 Special Law Promoting Independence in Depopulated Areas (*kaso chiiki jiritsu sokushin tokubetsu sochihō*), *kasochi* are 'depopulated rural areas that have experienced a significant population loss, whereby the area has experienced declines in its vitality and is in a lower level in terms of production function and infrastructures related to daily living, compared to other areas' (*Kaso Taisaku Kenkyūkai*, 2004: 3). *Genkai shūraku*, a term coined by Japanese rural sociologist Akira Ohno, refers to the worst of these *kaso* communities, those which have experienced large-scale depopulation and dramatic demographic ageing, which is reflected in the terminology of 'limits' (*genkai*) (Ohno, 2005). Finally, while the term *kakusa shakai*, a society of gaps, coined in the late 1990s in reference to the gradual hollowing out of Japan's middle class, can be applied across the socio-economic landscape of contemporary Japan, the term has come in the early 2000s to reflect the widening of economic profiles between the country's metropolitan and rural regions.

For a historical and highly local perspective of the phenomenon of population shift and local decline, Lewis's (2000) *Becoming Apart: National Power and Local Politics in Toyama, 1868–1945* outlined how the dynamics of national and local power relations in the mid to late nineteenth century rendered the castle town of Toyama and its surrounding agricultural base peripheral. The consequence at the local level was that agricultural workers fled their outlying villages for the castle town itself, yielding a population shift of up to one third of the villages' pre-1868 populations to the town by the 1880s. Lewis's work mirrors both Soranaka's (1997) depiction of the decline of the once powerful port town of Obama, located in rural Fukui Prefecture on the Sea of Japan coast just south of the Ishikawa Peninsula and in heart of *ura Nihon* (back of Japan), and Wigen's (1995) description of the transformation of an area of present-day Nagano Prefecture from a vital trade corridor and producer of local goods in the mid-Edo Period to a contracting economy in the mid twentieth century. These works illustrate the reality of socio-economic restructuring and population migration in Japan that will be described in what follows: population shift in contemporary Japan is a complex phenomenon of movement at both the national level, from the outlying periphery to a national-level center, and a highly local and highly devastating trajectory within the periphery itself.

Certainly, contemporary demographic transition and the implications thereof are themes not unique to Japan; however, the background and specific patterns of Japan's depopulation and the accompanying economic implications go far in describing transitions in Japan's regionalism and the state of 'the local' in rural Japan. Matanle and Rausch's (2011) work broadly outlines the origins and historical trends of depopulation and economic shrinkage for rural Japan as follows. Japan as a whole had experienced almost continuous growth in urban and industrializing regions throughout the twentieth century. This trend was matched in the pre-war period in outlying prefectures by similarly steady but slower growth, driven by levels of population reproduction that overshadowed the out-migration of labor accompanying the urban-centered industrial growth. The demographic profile shifted, however, to stability and shrinkage for rural areas after 1945 up to the period of high economic growth in the 1960s. Indeed, only Hokkaido and Okinawa grew significantly in the postwar period, a reflection of Japan's 'internal colonization' efforts to consolidate the country's territory (Weiner, 2004). Thus, while growth in metropolitan regions was commensurate with Japan's generally continuous economic expansion through and beyond the 1960s, rural populations were showing the beginnings of shrinkage from this point onward, with this rural depopulation setting the stage for regional economic and social decline as well.

National-level economic transformations such as the collapse of the 1980s investment bubble, the nature and pace of technological advance, the outward globalization of Japanese manufacturing, and changes in the domestic agricultural sector – each in their own way and in aggregate – have exacerbated the decline of Japan's regional economies. In agriculture, while trade liberalization has led to increasingly intense international competition, this has been accompanied by only modest reforms in the structure of government support for agricultural activities (Mulgan, 2006). Japan's outlying regions have been affected by national shifts in demand in the primary industries and manufacturing output, which together with adjustments in the service industry have forced associated changes in regional employment patterns (Fujita and Tabuchi, 1997; Ishiguro, 2008). Once started the trend continues. As regional employment faces downward pressure due to structural changes in global and national political economics the regional and rural areas of Japan are confronted with economic shrinkage. This in turn exacerbates the natural trends of population migration to urban areas by negating any motivation for re-located locals to return, creating long-term structural depopulation. This process is geographically multi-scalar, as this pattern of urban concentration and growth takes place on an intra-regional scale as well, with prefectural capitals and the more industrially or culturally vibrant urban cities of outlying prefectures growing at the expense of their surrounding outlying areas over the same period. In short, from the 1970s to the present Japan's contemporary economic circumstance has not been conducive to a general expansion over the full geographic extent of the country's outlying regions.

While other works have looked at the phenomenon of population decline and aging (see Coulmas, 2001; Traphagan and Knight, 2003), not only does the Matanle and Rausch book connect depopulation with economic implications in a geographically comprehensive overview across the expanse of Japan it does so on the basis of detailed case studies from specific sites from the rural regions of Japan. Population shift from periphery to center at both the national and the prefectural level is taken up in an examination of Niigata Prefecture, while the small scale dynamics of low birth rates at the village level is detailed in a case from the Kanbayashi River Valley in Kyoto Prefecture. The Niigata case revealed the multi-scalar nature of the push-pull dynamic combined with a contemporary transportation conundrum. Within the prefecture the push of limited opportunities in education, employment, and social opportunity (marriage in particular) in outlying areas of the prefecture is compounded by the pull of relatively abundant opportunities in the metropolitan areas of the prefecture. However, the same push-pull dynamic is taking place simultaneously across a regional-national divide as well, as younger people in even a relatively large urban area situated in rural Japan will opt for the larger urban areas of Tokyo or Osaka, for example, a dynamic made possible by the same efficiency component of transportation that is so important to the vitality of outlying areas (Hood, 2006). In addition to the loss of local residents the effect of depopulation in the deterioration of the village environment itself is devastating, as presented in an examination of the physical collapse and encroachment by both forest and wildlife in an example from Wakayama Prefecture.

The economics of geographic peripherality and economic transition is described in a case from Kochi Prefecture, together with case studies outlining the fragility of such extractive-based economies as forestry and mining in cases from Shiga, Kyoto, Iwate, and Hokkaido. In the case of Kochi, which is located on the southern side of Shikoku, it was clear that its geographic peripherality was exacerbated by a lack of transportation connections, showing how decisions regarding infrastructure development taken at the national level ultimately create regional 'winners and losers' irrespective of an area's independent efforts to combat or recover from peripheralization. At the opposite level the Kyoto case highlights the powerful impact that micro-level decisions, those by individuals and households, can have in determining the fate of a place. Interviews revealed that decisions to relocate at an individual or family level amounted not just to an outflow of residents and financial resources but, as importantly, created a loss of confidence about the future of the area among those who remained. These circumstances highlight another reality for the local place in terms of the downward cycle of population and economic shrinking: the fallibility of both national, i.e. central, and local responses. The case of Hokkaido's failed attempts to recover from the demise of the coal industry through tourism are detailed by Seaton (2010) as arising from a combination of market forces and 'administrative folly', a failure of both national and local government to react responsibly. Yamashita (2012a) concurs, asserting that the decline of local economies over the 1980s and 1990s must be viewed not just in terms of the management of regional industries but in decisions taken at the level of national and local government. He points to such factors as the decline of local city authority over development of their suburban areas through the Large Scale Retail Law and the demise of resort developments such as golf links, ski slopes, and spa resorts due to over-construction and questionable financing. The nature of such failures, he suggests, are hallmarks of the dysfunctional relationship between center and periphery, as the push for such approaches to local development throughout Japan often originated with the central government, whereas responsibility for the outcomes came to rest solely with the local governments. Indeed, both Culter (1999) and Matanle and Rausch et al. (2011) conclude with the notion of 'managing decline' as the final option for some communities, a task given over largely to local governments and local business and community leaders.

The sociology of regionalism and the local in Japan has thus been largely a transition of dual processes, one, the national trajectory of economic growth and accordant population expansion, overshadowing the other, the long-term and continual decline, both economically but also in population profiles, in the regions, and at most local levels. Such societal transitions can take on a life of their own, such that, despite recognition of negative trends and the initiation of policies to address them, options can dwindle and the trend continues. As will be shown in the next section, that national growth was sufficient for the state to overcome the need for local revitalization for much of the early postwar period brings into stark relief the dramatic tension that has emerged since the start of Japan's economic fall and its ripple effect through the interconnected social structure that is modern society. This tension brings us to responses: economic and political.

ECONOMIC AND POLITICAL VIEWS: REVITALIZATION AND DECENTRALIZATION

Perhaps the largest factor in the transition of local Japanese economies, as they were sustained through the 1960s and 1970s and as they have experienced gradual decline since the 1980s and 1990s, was the Iron Triangle of Japan's so-called construction state, or *doken kokka* (McCormack, 2001). As Feldhoff (2002a, 2002b) has shown, the construction state was based on an inherent contradiction between the potential for centrally supported local economic stimulus through questionable infrastructural projects and long-term locally sustainable development that emerged out of and reflected the needs of local areas. Since the 1950s comprehensive plans for national infrastructural development characterized by high levels of central government control and finance have been the standard of rural construction and a major factor in local economic stability, regional development, and social-welfare improvement, this in exchange for blocs of rural votes and political support from outlying prefectures for the ruling Liberal Democratic Party. By the 1990s the construction and public-works sector had become Japan's largest industry, with vast sums of government money poured into projects of questionable public utility, an economic transfer that was clearly proving unsustainable.

Research reflecting the dysfunctionality of such an approach to local economic stability has been multi-dimensional, focusing, for example, on the process by which the dynamic has come to be questioned, considering the environmental consequences of what was often unnecessary construction and questioning the long-term and intergenerational implications of such pork-barrel projects to the local areas themselves. Public activism has brought an increase in protest movements and referenda against the bid processes of large-scale public works (Jain, 2000; Er, 2005). An identity-ecological dimension has been outlined, as Waley highlighted; first, as public activists asserted that such centrally originating policies reflected an 'image of rurality projected from the centre, one that commodifies rural space and its attributes just as it marginalizes the inhabitants of rural areas' (Waley, 2000: 214); and second, in calls for re-landscaping Japan's rivers away from the ubiquitous concrete canals to more ecological and environmentally- friendly forms. Kajita (2001) pointed to the generational aspect of such an economy in remote and rural places where labor in the past had access to stable and high-paying work, a luxury in contemporary rural economies.

As for the potential for and the practice of rural revitalization at the local level, research and reality both yield only confusion. Providing a historical view, Phillipps (2008) showed that Japanese expansion through north-east Asia in the early 1930s provided cities along the western-Honshu, Sea of Japan coast with new hopes for local development. For local leaders in these areas Japanese imperialism was seen primarily in terms of local-development opportunities. However, in the case of Kanazawa, a coastal city in Ishikawa Prefecture, the reality of a Japan Sea era of Japanese exports was undermined by both local culture and national policy. Kanazawa merchants were largely apathetic towards the competitive practices of a modern economy, a sentiment born of generations of merchants who were patronized unquestioningly by the local samurai elites. As for national policy, central authorities were charged with designating shipping lanes and providing funds for harbor improvements, neither of which were decided in Kanazawa's favor. History repeated itself, but for different reasons. Rozman (1999) showed that the failed efforts by Sapporo, Niigata and Kanazawa (again) to capitalize on a new Sea of Japan Rim era made possible by trends toward decentralization in the 1990s were due in large part to the internally contradictory priorities that emerge when localism, regionalism, nationalism, and internationalism are thrown together in multi-level policy making.

Policy aside, coordination across the multiple levels of practice is the key that Inaba (2009) found in four case studies of local development success, each based on the concept of joint entrepreneurship put into practice. The specifics vary but the fundamental element highlighted in the research focused on inter-organizational coordination enabling diverse organizations such as for-profit enterprises, local governments, and non-profit organizations to collaborate in solving a range of business, and community, problems. Kitano (2009) also found success, as well as failure, in an examination of six declining locations in Gunma Prefecture. Each of the sites exhibited different circumstances and thus each fashioned different policies in their attempts to spur local development. The cases overall reflected a mix of such elements as agro-food businesses, urban-rural exchange programs, a rural village park project, and a quality-of-life approach based in preservation of the rural landscape and environment as a means of stabilizing area communities.

Kitano's conclusion stressed that the practice of local development must adjust both to different place characteristics as well as development trajectories, meaning that the host locales must anticipate and accept varying degrees of success, nearing the notion of 'managing decline' introduced above.

Local tourism is a prominent theme in the literature on local revitalization in Japan. Knight (1996) stressed a tension in rural tourism regarding different definitions of tourism within the industry itself, whereas Creighton (1997) and Moon (1997) both offered descriptions of the confused and contradictory nature of the marketing and consumption of rural Japan for urban Japanese. Rea (2000) noted that while resort *furusato* have been described as therapeutic remedies to the physical and mental burdens of Japan's economic miracle, urban Japanese are increasingly willing to seek such existential meaning outside of Japan, thereby undercutting domestic rural economies and highlighting a problematic disconnect between Japan's geographically separate populations. Indeed, most rural populations are familiar with and travel to urban centers, but the reverse case is not always a given. Tourism appears in several case studies among the *Japan's Shrinking Regions in the 21st Century* research group as well (Matanle and Rausch et al., 2011). The case of Yubari in Hokkaido showcases how the implementation of existing national and prefectural policy in an Industrial Heritage Tourism project provided an initial period of success, but which was followed by decline as local resort initiatives soured with the 1980s' economic downturn and the increased availability of inexpensive domestic holidays when other resort areas pushed the competitive window of success (Funck, 1999). Fragmentation and disjointed efforts characterized tourism as presented on the Oga Peninsula of Akita Prefecture. Unstable funding was just part of the problem; it was compounded by competing objectives and differing views on the essential character of tourism in terms of such elements as local versatility and flexibility versus long-term stability (Wood, 2005). Editors Genda and Nakamura (2009) offer a wealth of research on the importance of developing a common sense of 'hope' as an essential part of the historical and green tourism-development efforts by the Kamaishi region of Iwate Prefecture. Unfortunately, the March 2011 earthquake and tsunami rendered much of the existing development plans for the east coast of Tohoku meaningless. Rausch (2010a) stressed the importance of an area recognizing the conceptual parameters of its cultural potential, usually in the form of cultural tourism and cultural commodities, and then activating those by assessing the degree to which it is operationally maximizing this potential.

Such local development efforts are the essence of local governance, the contemporary process of which is described in edited work by Furukawa and Menju (2003) on *machizukuri,* literally, town-making, as emerging through citizen activism accompanied by cooperation with non-governmental organizations and community businesses. Sorenson and Funck offer an edited book on *machizukuri* that takes up, in addition to the potential of such 'town-making' to create more livable and sustainable cities, such themes as 'the changing roles of and relations between the central and local government, and between citizens and the state' (2007: 2) and the 'changing roles of civil society and local governance in Japan' (2007: 3). Their conclusion offers the sheer diversity of contemporary *machizukuri,* defined in the book as 'bottom-up and citizen-led processes of place management' that is being undertaken as evidence of its social validity and innovative potential. What is less encouraging, however, is the fact that they also admit that the efforts of so many groups continue to be ignored by central administrative authorities and private developers.

The major national political trend that relates to regionalism and the local against this background of economic decline has been decentralization and the Heisei municipal mergers (the *Heisei Dai Gappei*). Determining that the centralized political system has been one contributing cause of persistent economic problems for both local areas and the nation as a whole, Japan's political leaders began crafting a policy of neoliberalism-oriented decentralization in the early 1990s. The Comprehensive Decentralization Law came into effect in 2000 with the goal of reducing national-level spending on local-government functions by addressing the so-called trinity of local-government funding: local tax revenues, national subsidies and local allocation taxes. As noted herein, most outlying municipalities were experiencing finance hardship in the 1990s while at the same time the national government was increasingly unable to fund local infrastructure and government services, resulting in an increasing state of inequality between economically advantaged and disadvantaged areas. The Comprehensive Decentralization Law introduced changes that unified taxation and fiscal-administration powers under the control of local governments. Specifically, the law reduced local-allocation tax funds, abolished equality-based fixed-rate subsidies, and transferred revenue-raising powers to local governments. Most notable for local residents were the municipal mergers, the so-called Heisei mergers, a part of the law that encouraged the creation of larger local governmental units to create scales of economy and encourage diversity of income sources, thereby overcoming the fiscal and inequality realities that accompanied the reforms.

The tension for rural areas that the transition of decentralization highlighted ultimately reflects fundamental theories of governance. Hill and Fujita (2000) viewed Japanese local governments as having operated within a developmental state over the postwar period, where the distribution of power between central and local governments had been shaped by efforts to maximize the mobilization of scarce resources while maintaining fiscal equality and service consistency. Nakano (1998) identified a shift in governance approach in an assessment of what he saw as a concurrent rise of both nationalism and localism in the 1990s. His conclusion was that policy justifications at the time held that competitive nationalism would allow for Japan to politically integrate on an international level, while decentralization on the basis of competitive localism would ensure that the benefits of competitive localities would contribute domestically to Japan as a whole. Muramatsu (2001) also identified a contemporary nationalist-regionalist tension in Japanese governance, emerging between an integrationist model of intergovernmental relations, which stresses the benefits of building overall capacity through the sharing of staff and responsibilities among different levels of government, and a separatist model, which emphasizes the benefits of autonomy for local governments and the competition that such autonomy brings.

Theory aside, research conducted after completion of the Heisei mergers shows a decidedly mixed result. While the number of cities, towns, and villages has decreased to slightly over 1,800 – a central goal of the mergers – Rausch's conclusion questioned 'not only whether the mergers were necessary in the broadest sense of nation-state governance, but also if the objectives the merger were undertaken to achieve were, in fact, locally meaningful to the rural places of Japan that were to be impacted on the most as a result' (Rausch, 2006: 155). The conclusion emphasized that the primary questions regarding mergers for many residents in rural Aomori Prefecture concerned whether such semi-coerced autonomy was desirable for their city, town, or village, particularly given the inescapable reality of Aomori's overall geographic peripherality and depressed economic profile. Tsukamoto looked at a more complex and advantaged location, where a 'new regionalism' restructured a broader and more mixed range of local communities in the Osaka-Kansai area into a voluntary association of local governments and private-sector organizations, motivated by self-centered incentives but for joint benefits: 'an urban governance system based on both cooperation and competition' (2011: 288). However, Tsukamoto admits that this 'new regionalism' includes systemic biases and asymmetrical returns, resulting in within-region disparities. Primary to the problem are the spatial and power discrepancies that exist within any region, meaning that the smaller local governments are disadvantaged fiscally but also geographically and in terms of population concentrations, relative to the larger and more urban municipalities, even when they participate in a merger. What this has meant for the outlying municipalities that merged and their residents is loss of local identity, in the disappearance of their municipal place-name, and a general decrease in accessibility to municipal services, which post-merger are more likely to be centrally located and more distant from outlying and often transportation-burdened residents. The very real and highly complex rural tensions that the Heisei mergers have yielded lie not just in the multi-dimensional turns of fate that have emerged between the dominant municipality in a merger and the others, but have come to question the value of participation in the merger. Also problematic for regional Japan is the circumstance of those municipalities that either choose not to participate in mergers or were found to be unattractive to potential merger partners (Rausch, 2012a). A potential future tension of decentralization for rural Japan lies in the still latent plans for a further round of mergers, this time combining prefectures in the creation of 12 *dōshū*, or state, blocks. Originating in the early 2000s, the justifications for a *dōshū-sei* reorganization are, like the Heisei mergers, largely in arguments for efficiency on the basis of economies of scale, both domestic but also from an Asian-regional view. And, like the Heisei mergers, the implications are problematic, in issues such as the determination of state partners, the resulting changes in power structures both national and local, and a further hollowing out of truly local areas as larger administrative blocks are organized (Rausch, 2010b, 2012b).

The depiction of regionalism and the local that emerges with a view of the economic and political transitions that have taken place over the past twenty years in regional and local Japan concerns tensions regarding local stability and sustainability. The contemporary reality of such stability and sustainability is that it increasingly rests on the capability for areas to create economic stability and quality-of-life sustainability on their own and on their own terms. This reality, however, is often clouded by the programmed response of fiscal economization in response to a perceived need for global competitiveness that can dominate national and local policy planning. It appears that regional and local Japan faces a reality that calls into mind Tamura's (2007) caveat that the challenge of economic revitalization as a national project is to escape the influence that regional disparities, whether geographically and historically inherent or emerging as a function of policy, ultimately have in creating winners (*kachigumi*) and losers (*makegumi*). The March 2011 triple disaster adds to this tension, as Matanle (2011) highlights in his questioning of whether the catastrophe will be a watershed moment in redirecting Japan as a nation toward reconstruction of safe, sustainable, and compassionate communities throughout the country or simply a marker in the continued decline of quality of life for many rural areas. Matanle emphasizes that not only will competition for the financial, material, technical, labor, and land resources that is taking place in the devastated areas as reconstruction progresses likely extend to other regional and rural areas but that the resolution of such inter-regional controversy will bring to the fore questions regarding the approach toward governance in Japan and the state of its civil and activist society.

THE JAPANESE VIEWPOINT: RESEARCH TRENDS OF *CHIHOGAKU*

As noted earlier, the evolving terminology of regionalism and the local emerged principally in two Japanese terms, *chiiki* and *chihō*. The term *chiiki* is defined by the *Kenkyusha New Japanese English Dictionary, 4th Edition* (2000) as 'an area', 'a region', or 'a district'. By adding the suffix *–teki,* to make *chiiki-teki,* the translations provided are 'local' or 'regional'. *Chiiki* is a word that accompanies such combinative notions as community development (*chiiki kaihatsu*), area studies (*chiiki kenkyū*), regional difference (*chiiki-sa*), regional society (*chiiki shakai*), and regional organization (*chiiki dantai*). The Japanese word *chihō*, on the other hand, is translated as 'district' and, when contrasted with the center (*chūshin*), expresses such notions as 'the country', 'the provinces', or 'local' and 'provincial'. The combinative uses of *chihō*, however, far outnumber those of *chiiki*, yielding such terms as *chihōgaku*, area studies, and other specialized vocabulary, such as localization (*chihōka*) and decentralization (*chihō bunken*). Political terminology includes a local (governmental) authority (*chihō kikan*), local autonomy (*chihō jichi*), a local self-governing body (*chihō jichitai*), local tax allocations (*chihō kōfuzei*), and district court (*chihō saibansho*). Social uses include local news (*chihō kiji*), local newspaper (*chihō shimbun*), local products (*chihō sanbutsu*), and a local accent (*chihō namari*). Beyond this terminological starting point to the Japanese view of regionalism and the local is an assessment of the combinations of such terms that are used in the expansive Japanese book market. On the amazon.co.jp website, titles using the terminology of '*chiiki*' number approximately 30,000, with the most common thematic combinations being 'regional research' (*chiiki kenkyū*), 'regional welfare' (*chiiki fukushi*), 'regional health care' (*chiiki iryō*), 'regional power' (*chiiki no chikara*), and 'regional rebirth' (*chiiki saisei*). For '*chihō*' titles, the Amazon search yielded over 50,000 titles, with the most common combinations being 'local autonomy' (*chihō jichi*), and 'local civil service employment' (*chihō kōmuin*), followed by such themes as local administrative law and finance.

Looking at the mainstay of regional-studies academic associations in Japan, the Japan Association of Regional and Community Studies (*chiiki shakai gakkai*), and examining its annual journal (*Annals of Region and Community Studies*), we can discern the following trends in Japanese social-science research in the area of regional studies. The themes that dominated the years 1998 to 2004 were regional rebirth and formation of regional society. Post-2004 saw a mix of themes from theoretization through a 'social problem view' and on to grounded and pragmatic viewpoints focusing on the 'rebirth of regional society within shrinking society' and 'the reality of regional recovery'. The dominant theoretical consideration took up such issues as the Heisei municipal mergers, specifically the interaction between mergers and local development and how local government is integrated into the comprehensive nation-state system. The social-problem component looked at rural labor markets, the positive and negative implications of mobility for rural areas, the reality of social-welfare policy in rural areas under the dynamic of a shrinking society, and how local governments can address this reality. The content of the last few years, focusing on rebirth, yielded questions about whether revitalization efforts should be oriented toward system change in an efficiency paradigm versus aiming at improvements in quality of life at the individual level and assessments of various schemes to realize sustainable recovery and revitalization for rural regions. Interestingly, the 2012 journal returned to theory and methodology, taking up as its theme the subject of 'rescaling', with papers presenting the basics of rescaling against the background of new forms of local governance and new sources of local economic development in response to the influences of the economies of globalization (Tamano, 2012). Yamazaki (2012) followed this with a more in-depth analysis of the application of rescaling to Japan, noting how cases from Okinawa and Osaka reveal strategic rescaling that reflected attempts to decentralize state power in ways to revitalize local economies.

Turning to a journal of wider disciplinary focus, the *Japanese Sociological Review* (published by the Japan Sociological Society), a review of the research taking up regional and local themes highlights the following trends and themes. Watanabe (2006) found a loss of local communality in then prime minister Koizumi's neo-liberal reforms, manifest in the Heisei municipal mergers, together with confusion among both residents and leaders in the shifting context of the mergers. The mergers influence on policy focus were the focus of Morihisa's (2008) research, in conclusions that highlighted the conflicts in planning that emerged between policy crafted in the present, which was seen as functioning to consolidate political power, versus policy crafted for the future, which was viewed as functioning to preserve communities. Tomooka (2009) highlighted the tensions inherent in organizing local cultural resources for local economic and cultural revitalization against processes of economic and cultural globalization. The research pointed to the importance of protecting the diversity of cultural institutions and cultural industries in local Japan while noting that the operational mechanisms for achieving this are underdeveloped. Finally, Yamashita (2012b) and Nishimura (2012) take up themes related to social mobility and regional social structure, pointing to the increasing adaptation emerging in patterns of regional mobility. This they attribute to the influence of Japanese capitalism as a social blueprint which recalibrates the dual national structure of urban and rural to a regional cluster-hierarchy model that incorporates center and periphery within regions even at a regional level.

Turning to a handful of academic works that take up these themes, representative of the 'rebirth' genre is Shimohirao's (2006) *Jimoto no Susume* (Advancing the Local), which argues that supporting local regions is a means of providing for the stability of Japan as a nation in the future. The functioning of local society is Tanaka's (2007) focus in *Kyōdōsei no Chiiki Shakaigaku* (Cooperation as Regional Sociology), which takes up festivals, snow removal, public transportation, and disaster response as the windows on to cooperation as the operational dynamic of rural society. Yamashita, Sakumichi and Sugiyama's (2008) edited work *Tsugaru: Kindaika no Dynamism* (Tsugaru: the Dynamism of Modernization) optimistically identifies modernization as the characteristic emerging in regional and local places in Japan as the appropriate responses to the increasingly common phenomenon of migration, generational transition, and the transition from community to individualism. This modernization they see in processes of local organizational modernization, local cultural crystallization, and local social systemization. Finally, Motani's (2007) *Jissoku: Nippon no Chiikiryoku* (Surveys: Japan's Regional Power) is, as the title implies, a data-driven view of Japan's regional dynamics, outlining both current problems while also identifying potential strategies for recovery.

Finally, a resource of tremendous potential for studies of regionalism and the local are the local publications of local places, what can be termed the *chihōgaku* (regional or local studies) phenomenon, whether these are the magazines of local research groups or simply the local newspaper. There is no shortage of material: over 2,000 local *chihōgaku* publications cover the length and breadth of Japan. An assessment of the Iwata Shoin publisher webpage (undated), *Regional Historical Research Magazine Database*, reveals the trend toward *chihōgaku* as a resurgent local academic endeavor: of the 1,315 magazines that provided a founding year in their profile (excluding those from Tokyo, Osaka and Okinawa) the distribution reflected an increase from the 1960s through to the present. The number of magazines founded in the 1960s accounts for approximately 14 percent of the total, with those founded in the 1970s accounting for an additional 16 percent. For the 1980s and 1990s, the proportions rose to 25 percent and 24 percent respectively, with the 2000s accounting for 19 percent. Takada and Shimizu (2010), in *Nihon no Genba: Chihōshi de Yomu (Frontlines of Japan: Reading the Local Newspaper)*, together with Rausch (2009, 2012c, 2012d), assert that the local newspaper provides the most reliable, consistent, and accurate view of the local place, whether it be the particulars of local history and culture, the contemporary social circumstance and lifestyle, or the impact of and response to national and international trends at the local level. The paradox is that while such local *chihōgaku* phenomenon provide the perfect means for untangling the complex contributions that local studies can make both to understanding of place as well as speaking to the larger disciplinary questions in many social-science fields, they are available only to those who have both the necessary language skills and sufficient local knowledge, meaning that most of this potential goes unrealized.

CONCLUSION

This chapter opened by noting the multi-dimensionality and multi-disciplinary nature of the theme 'Regionalism and the Local' in Japan. The narrative of transition and tension has been represented and detailed on the basis of identity – real and imagined, depopulation and economic decline, and local revitalization and administrative decentralization. Japanese research has been shown to reflect both attempts to describe rural society as traditionally cooperative on the one hand and adaptively modern on the other. Regionalism and the local thus describes less an area of any established body of consolidated research than a trajectory of research themes that reveal both what regionalism constitutes as an academic endeavor and what the local offers as an object of academic focus. At the level of research in general, regionalism and the local speaks to the discovery, or re-discovery, of the significance of this 'local level' of Japan. As for the specific content of such research, regionalism and the local is about the relevance of such research to broader research and disciplinary themes. As such, it offers a highly fertile area for study within Japanese studies, one with ample opportunity to find both specific research themes, but themes that contribute to the broader theorization not just of Japan but in all social-science disciplines.

REFERENCES

Adolphson, M., Kamens, E. and Matsumoto, S. (2006). *Heian Japan: Centers and Peripheries.* Honolulu, HI: University of Hawaii Press.

Assmann, S. (2010). Food Action Nippon and Slow Food Japan: The Role of Two Citizen Movements in the Rediscovery of Local Foodways. In J. Farrar (Ed.), *Globalization, Food and Social Identities in the Asia Pacific Region.* Tokyo: Sophia University Institute of Comparative Culture. Accessed July 5 2014 at http://icc.fla.sophia.ac.jp/global%20food %20papers/

Bailey, J. (1991). *Ordinary People, Extraordinary Lives: Political and Economic Changes in a Tohoku Village.* Honolulu, HI: University of Hawaii Press.

Batten, B. L. (2003). *To the Ends of Japan: Premodern Frontiers, Boundaries, and Interactions.* Honolulu, HI: University of Hawaii Press.

Beardsley, R., Hall, J. and Ward, R. (1959). *Village Japan.* Chicago, IL: University of Chicago Press.

Ben-Ari, E. (1998). Contested Identities and Models of Action in Japanese Discourses of Place-Making: An Interpretive Study. In Hendry, J. (Ed.), *Interpreting Japanese Society: Anthropological Approaches* (pp. 68–87). London, UK: Routledge.

Bernstein, G. L. (2005). *Isami's House: Three Centuries of a Japanese Family.* Berkeley, CA: University of California Press.

Bhowmik, D. L. (2008). *Writing Okinawa: Narrative Acts of Identity and Resistance.* London, UK: Routledge.

Booth, A. (1997). *The Roads to Sata: A 2000-Mile Walk Through Japan.* New York, NY: Kodansha.

Coulmas, F. (2007). *Population Decline and Ageing in Japan: The Societal Consequences.* London, UK: Routledge.

Creighton, M. (1997). Consuming Rural Japan: The Marketing of Tradition and Nostalgia in the Japanese Travel Industry. *Ethnology*, 36, 239–254.

Culter, S. (1999). *Managing Decline: Japan's Coal Industry Restructuring and Community Response.* Honolulu, HI: University of Hawaii Press.

Dazai, O. (1995). *Return to Tsugaru: Confessions of a Purple Tramp.* Trans. J. Westerhoven. New York, NY: Kodansha.

Denoon, D., Hudson, M., McCormack, G. and Morris-Suzuki, T. (Eds.) (2001). *Multicultural Japan: Palaeolithic to Postmodern.* Cambridge, UK: Cambridge University Press.

Dodd, S. (2005). *Writing Home: Representations of the Native Place in Modern Japanese Literature.* Cambridge, MA: Harvard University Asia Center.

Doi, T. (1973). *Anatomy of Dependence.* Tokyo: Kodansha.

Dore, R. (1994). *Shinohata: A Portrait of a Japanese Village.* Berkeley, CA: University of California Press.

Dusinberre, M. (2012). *Hard Times in the Hometown: A History of Community Survival in Modern Japan.* Honolulu, HI: University of Hawaii Press.

Er, L. (2005). Local Governance: The Role of Referenda and the Rise of Independent Governors. In Hook, G. (Ed.) *Contested Governance in Japan: Sites and Issues* (pp. 71–89). London, UK: RoutledgeCurzon.

Feldhoff, T. (2002a). Japan's Construction Lobby Activities: Systematic Stability and Sustainable Regional Development. *ASIEN*, 84, 4–42.

Feldhoff, T. (2002b). Japan's Regional Airports: Conflicting National, Regional, and Local Interests. *Journal of Transport Geography*, 10(3), 165–175.

Fujita, M. and Tabuchi, T. (1997). Regional Growth in Postwar Japan. *Regional Science and Urban Economics*, 27(6), 643–670

Fukutake, T. (1972). *Japanese Rural Society.* Ithaca, NY: Cornell University Press.

Funck, C. (1999). When the Bubble Burst: Planning and Reality in Japan's Resort Industry. *Current Issues in Tourism*, 2(4), 333–353.

Furukawa, S. and Menju, T. (Eds.) (2003). *Japan's Road to Pluralism: Transforming Local Communities in the Global Era.* Tokyo, Japan: Nihon Kokusai Koryu Center.

Genda, Y. and Nakamura, N. (Eds.) (2009). *Kibōgaku [2]: Kibō no saisei: Kamaishi no rekishi to sangyō ga katarumono.* Tokyo, Japan: Tōkyō Daigaku Shuppankai.

Graburn, N. (1983). *To Pray, Pay, and Play: The Cultural Structure of Japanese Domestic Tourism.* Aix-en-Provence, France: Centre des Hautes études Touristiques.

Guo, N., Hasegawa, S., Johnson, H., Kawanishi, H., Kitahara, K. and Rausch, A. (2005). *Tsugaru: Regional Identity on Japan's Northern Periphery.* Dunedin, NZ: University of Otago Press.

Harootunian, H. D. (1998). Figuring the Folk: History, Poetics, and Representation. In S. Vlastos (Ed.)

Mirror of Modernity: Invented Traditions of Modern Japan (pp. 144–159). Berkeley, CA: University of California Press.

Hashimoto, M. (1998). Chihō: Yanagita Kunio's Japan. In S. Vlastos (Ed.) *Mirror of Modernity: Invented Traditions of Modern Japan* (pp. 133–143). Berkeley, CA: University of California Press.

Hill, R. C. and Fujita, K. (2000). State Restructuring and Local Power in Japan. *Urban Studies*, 37(4), 673–690.

Hood, C. (2006). *Shinkansen: From Bullet Train to Symbol of Modern Japan.* London, UK: Routledge.

Huey, R. N. (2008). Review of Heian Japan: Centers and Peripheries. *Japan Forum*, 21(1) (2009), 147–148.

Inaba, Y. (2009). *Japan's New Local Industry Creation: Joint Entrepreneurship, Inter-organizational Collaboration, and Regional Regeneration.* New York, NY: Alternative Views Publishing.

Ishiguro, K. (2008). Japanese Employment in Transformation: The growing number of non-regular workers. *electronic journal of contemporary japanese studies*, Article 10. Retrieved from www.japanesestudies.org.uk/articles/2008/Ishiguro.html. Accessed August 15, 2012.

Ivy, M. (1995). *Discourses of the Vanishing: Modernity, Phantasm, Japan.* Chicago, IL: University of Chicago Press.

Iwata Shoin Webpage. (undated). *Chigōshi kenkyū zasshi detabesu.* www.iwata-shoin.co.jp/ Accessed August 17, 2012.

Jain, P. (2000). Jūmin tōhyo and the Tokushima Anti-Dam Movement in Japan: The People Have Spoken. *Asian Survey*, 40(4), 551–570.

Kajita, S. (2001). Public Investment as a Social Policy in Remote Rural Areas in Japan. *Geographical Review of Japan*, 74(2), 147–158.

Kalland, A. (2010). *Shingu: A Study of a Japanese Fishing Community.* London, UK: Routledge.

Karan, P. P. (2005). *Japan in the 21st Century: Environment, Economy, and Society.* Lexington, KY: The University Press of Kentucky.

Kaso Taisaku Kenkyūkai (Ed.). (2004). *Kaso tsisaku deta bukku: Heisei 15-nendo kaso taisaku no genkyō.* Tokyo, Japan: Marui Kōbunsha.

Kelly, W. W. (1990). Regional Japan: The Price of Prosperity and the Benefits of Dependency. *Daedalus*, 119(3), 209–227.

Kingsbury, A., Maeda, Y. and Takahashi, M. (2010). Marketing the 'Slippery' Local with the Contrived 'Rural': Case Studies of Alternative Vegetable Retail in the Urban Fringe of Nagoya, Japan, *International Journal of Sociology of Agriculture and Food*, 2, 89–107.

Kitano, S. (2009). *Space, Planning, and Rurality: Uneven Rural Development in Japan.* Victoria, Canada: Trafford Publishing.

Knight, J. (1994). Rural Revitalization in Japan: Spirit of the Village and Taste of the Country. *Asian Survey*, 34(7), 634–646.

Knight, J. (1996). Competing Hospitalities in Japanese Rural Tourism. *Annals of Tourism Research*, 23(1), 165–189.

Lewis, M. (2000). *Becoming Apart: National Power and Local Politics in Toyama, 1868–1945.* Cambridge, MA: Harvard University Asia Center.

Light, R. and Yasaki, W. (2002). J League Soccer and the Rekindling of Regional Identity in Japan. *Sporting Traditions*, 18(2), 31–46.

Long, H. (2011). *On Uneven Ground: Miyazawa Kenji and the Making of Place in Modern Japan.* Stanford, CA: Stanford University Press.

Masaki, H. (2006). Japan Stares into a Demographic Abyss. The Asia Pacific Journal: Japan Focus. www.japanfocus.org/-Hisane-MASAKI/1864. Accessed August 20, 2014.

Matanle, P. (2011). The Great East Japan Earthquake, Tsunami and Nuclear Meltdown: Towards the (Re) construction of a Safe, Sustainable, and Compassionate Social in Japan's Shrinking Regions. *Local Environment: The International Journals of Justice and Sustainability*, 16(9), 823–847.

Matanle, P. and Rausch, A. (2011). *Japan's Shrinking Regions in the 21st Century: Contemporary Responses to Depopulation and Socioeconomic Decline.* Amherst, NY: Cambria Press.

McCormack, G. (2001). *The Emptiness of Japanese Affluence.* New York, NY: M. E. Sharpe.

Miyamoto, T. (2010 [1960]). *The Forgotten Japanese: Encounters with Rural Life and Folklore.* Jeffrey S. Irish, trans. Berkeley, CA: Stone Bridge Press.

Moeran, B. (1985). *A Far Valley: Four Years in a Japanese Village.* New York, NY: Kodansha International.

Moon, O. (1997). Marketing Nature in Rural Japan. In P. J. Asquith and A. Kalland (Eds.) *Japanese Images of Nature: Cultural Perspectives* (pp. 221–235). London, UK: Curzon Press.

Morihisa, S. (2008). Chiiki gyōsei ni okeru kūkan no sasshin to sonzoku (What Does the Development/Conservation of Urban Space Involve in Local Community Politics?) *Shakai-gaku hyōron*, 59(2), 349–368.

Morris-Suzuki, T. (2001). A Descent into the Past: The Frontier in the Construction of Japanese History, in D. Dennon, M. Hudson, G. McCormack and T. Morris-Suzuki (Eds.) *Multicultural Japan: Palaeolithic to Postmodern.* (pp. 81–94), Cambridge, UK: Cambridge University Press.

Motani, K. (2007). *Jissoku: Nippon no Chiikiryoku* (Surveys: Japan's Regional Power). Tokyo, Japan: Nippon Keizai Shimbun Shuppansha.

Mouer, R. and Sugimoto, Y. (1990). *Images of Japanese Society: A Study in the Social Construction of Reality.* London, UK: Kegan Paul International.

Mulgan, A. (2006). Agriculture and policy reform in Japan: The Koizumi legacy (Pacific Economic Papers No. 360, Australia-Japan Research Centre, Australian National University). Retrieved from http://www.eaber.org/node/21811 Accessed August 20, 2012.

Muramatsu, M. (2001). Intergovernmental Relations in Japan: Models and Perspectives, *The International Bank for Reconstruction and Development/The World Bank.* Stock No. 37178.

Nagatsuka, T. (1989 [1910]). *The Soil: A Portrait of Village Life in Meiji Japan.* Ann Waswo, trans. New York, NY: Routledge.

Nakamura, K. (1980). Eastern and Western Japan. In Association of Japanese Geographers (Ed.), *Geography of Japan.* Tokyo, Japan: Teiko-Shoin.

Nakane, D. (1970). *Japanese Society.* Berkeley, CA: University of California Press.

Nakano, K. (1998). Nationalism and Localism in Japan's Political Debate of the 1990s. *The Pacific Review*, 11(4), 505–524.

Nishimura, T. (2012). *Gurobaluki ni okeru chiiki kōzō no henyō to chihō toshi: chūgoku chihō no Toshi wo jirei toshite* (Changes in Regional Structure and Local Cities in the Globalization Era: A Case Study of Cities in the Chugoku Region). *Shakai-gaku hyōron*, 62(4), 459–475.

Ohno, A. (2005). *Sanson kankyo shakaigaku jyo-setsu.* Tokyo, Japan: Nōsan Ryōson Bunka Kyōkai.

Partner, S. (2004). *Toshie: A Story of Village Life in Twentieth-Century Japan.* Berkeley, CA: University of California Press.

Passin, H. (1980). *Society and Education in Japan.* Tokyo: Kodansha.

Phillipps, J. (2008). City and Empire – Local Identity and Regional Imperialism in 1930s Japan. *Urban History*, 35(1), 116–133.

Rausch, A. (2004a). 'Newspaper in Education' in Rural Japan: Education and Local Identity Creation in the Practice of Locally Scholastic NIE. *Journal of Asian Pacific Communication*, 14(2), 223–244.

Rausch, A. (2004b). Collective Identity Creation and Local Revitalization in Rural Japan: The Complex Role of the Local Newspaper. *electronic journal of contemporary japanese studies*, Article 2, 2004.

Rausch, A. (2005). Local Identity, Cultural Commodities, and Development in Rural Japan: The Potential as Viewed by Cultural Producers and Local Residents. *International Journal of Japanese Sociology*, 14(1), 122–137.

Rausch, A. (2006). The Heisei Gappei: A Case Study for Understanding the Municipal Mergers of the Heisei Era. *Japan Forum*, 18(1), 133–156.

Rausch, A. (2009). Creating Tsugaru Studies: The Paradox of Area Studies at the Local Level. *Journal of International and Area Studies*, 16(2), 35–51.

Rausch, A. (2010a). *Cultural Commodities in Japanese Rural Revitalization: Tsugaru Nuri Lacquerware and Tsugaru Shamisen.* Leiden, Netherlands: Brill Publishing.

Rausch, A. (2010b). Post Heisei Merger Japan: Potential for a New Realignment in the Dōshū

State System. *The Asia Pacific Journal of Public Administration*, 32(1), 17–33.

Rausch, A. (2012a). A Framework for Japan's New Municipal Reality: Assessing the Heisei Gappei Mergers. *Japan Forum*, 24(2), 185–204.

Rausch, A. (2012b). The Heisei Mergers in Contemporary Japan: A Step on the Road to a Dōshū-sei Realignment? In Iles, T. and Matanle, P. (Eds.). *Researching Twenty-First Century Japan: New Directions and Approaches for the Electronic Age* (pp. 97–118), Landam, MD: Lexington Books.

Rausch, A. (2012c). Tsugaru Gaku: The Contributions of Chihōgaku to Japanese Studies. *Japan Studies Review*, 16, 115–134.

Rausch, A. (2012d). *Japan's Local Newspapers: Chihōshi and Revitalization Journalism*. New York, NY: Routledge.

Rea, M. (2000). A Furusato Away From Home. *Annals of Tourism Research*, 27(3), 638–660.

Richie, D. (2002) *The Inland Sea*. Berkeley, CA: Stone Bridge Press.

Ritchie, M. (1999). *Village Japan: Everyday Life in a Rural Japanese Community*. Tokyo: Tuttle Publishing.

Robertson, J. (1992). *Native and Newcomer: Making and Remaking a Japanese City*. Berkeley, CA: University of California Press.

Robertson, J. (1998). It Takes a Village: Internationalization and Nostalgia in Postwar Japan. In S. Vlastos (Ed.), *Mirror of Modernity: Japan's Invented Traditions* (pp. 110–129). Berkeley, CA: University of California Press.

Rozman, G. (1999). Backdoor Japan: The Search for a Way Out via Regionalism and Decentralization. *Journal of Japanese Studies*, 25(1), 3–31.

Ryang, S. (2004). *Japan and National Anthropology: A Critique*. New York, NY: Routledge.

Schnell, S. (2005). The Rural Imaginary: Landscape, Village, Tradition. In J. Robertson (Ed.), *A Companion to the Anthropology of Japan* (pp. 201–217). Malden, MA: Blackwell Publishing.

Seaton, P. (2010). Depopulation and Financial Collapse in Yūbari: Market Forces, Administrative Folly, or a Warning to Others? *Social Science Japan Journal*, 13(2), 227–240.

Shimohirao, I. (2006). *Jimoto no Susume: Chiiki Saisei no ōdō wa Ashimoto ni ari* (Advancing the Region: Steps to Appropriate Regional Rebirth). Tokyo, Japan: Shinhyōron.

Siegenthaler, P. (1999). Japanese Domestic Tourism and the Search for National Identity, *CUHK Journal of Humanities*, 3, 178–195.

Smith, R. J. (1978). *Kurusu: The Price of Progress in a Japanese Village 1951–1975*. Stanford, CA: Stanford University Press.

Soranaka, I. (1997). Obama: The rise and decline of a seaport. *Monumenta Nipponica*, 52(1), 85–102.

Sorenson, A. and Funck, C. (Eds.) (2007). *Living Cities in Japan: Citizens' Movements, Machizukuri and Local Environments*. London: UK: Routledge.

Sugimoto, Y. (1997). *An Introduction to Japanese Society*. Cambridge: Cambridge University Press.

Sugimoto, Y. (1999). Making Sense of Nihonjinron. *Thesis Eleven*, 57(1), 81–96.

Takada, M. and Shimizu, M. (2010). *Nihon no Genba: Chihōshi de Yomu (Frontlines of Japan: Reading the Local Newspaper)*. Tokyo, Japan: Junposha.

Takeuchi, K. (1978). Some Remarks on the History of Regional Description and the Tradition of Regionalism in Modern Japan. *Hitotsubashi Journal of Social Studies*, 10(1), 36–44.

Tamano, K. (2012). *Nihon ni okeru resukelingu kenkyū no kanōsei wo megutte* (Possibility of Rescaling Studies Developing in Japan), *Chiiki Shakai Gakkai Nenpō*, 24, 5–19.

Tamura, S. (2007). *Jichitai kakusa ga kuni o horobosu*. Tokyo, Japan: Shūeisha Shinsho.

Thompson, C. S. and Traphagen, J. W. (Eds.) (2006). *Wearing Cultural Styles in Japan: Concepts of Tradition and Modernity in Practice*. New York, NY: State University of New York Press.

Thunman, N. (2002). Landscape in Modern Japanese Literature and the Impact of Translations. *Africa and Asia*, 2, 116–124.

Tomooka, K. (2009) *Chiiki senryaku ni dōinsareru bunkateki shigen: bunkateki gulobarizeshon no inga toshite no jichitai bunka seisaku* (Cultural Resources for City Development: Regional Cultural Policy as an Antithesis of Cultural Globalization). *Shakai-gaku hyōron*, 60(3), 379–395.

Traphagan, W. and Knight, J. (2003). *Demographic Change and the Family in Japan's Aging Society*. Albany, NY: State University of New York Press.

Tsukamoto, T. (2011). Devolution, New Regionalism and Economic Revitalization in Japan: Emerging Urban Political Economy and Politics of Scale in Osaka-Kansai. *Cities*, 28, 281–289.

Vlastos, S. (Ed.). (1998). *Mirror of Modernity: Invented Traditions of Modern Japan*. Berkeley, CA: University of California Press.

Waley, P. (2000). Following the Flow of Japan's River Culture. *Japan Forum*, 12(2), 199–217.

Watanabe, N. (2006). *Chihō kara mita 'shakai undo ron'* (Study of Social Movement from the Viewpoint of a Local Community). *Shakai-gaku hyōron*, 57(2), 348–368.

Weiner, M. (Ed.) (2004). *Race, Ethnicity and Migration in Modern Japan* (Vol. 1). London, UK: Routledge.

Westerhoven, J. (2009). *Voices from the Snow*. Hirosaki, Japan: Hirosaki University Press.

Wigen, K. (1995). *The Making of a Japanese Periphery, 1750–1920*. Berkeley, CA: University of California Press.

Wigen, K. (2000). Teaching about Home: Geography at Work in the Pre-war Nagano Classroom. *The Journal of Asian Studies*, 59(3), 550–574.

Wood, D. C. (2005). The Polder Museum of Ogata-mura: Community, Authenticity, and Sincerity in a Japanese Village. *Asian Anthropology*, 4, 29–58.

Wood, D. C. (2012). *Ogata-Mura: Sowing Diseent and Reclaiming Identity in a Japanese Farming Village*. New York, NY: Berghan Books.

Yamashita, Y. (2012a). How Does the Restoration of Tōhoku Society Begin? Center and Periphery in the Great East Japan Earthquake. *International Journal of Japanese Sociology*, 21, 6–11.

Yamashita, Y. (2012b). *Idō to seidai kara miru toshi-sonraku no henyō: sengō nihon shakai ni okeru kōiki shisutemu keisei no shiten kara* (Social Changes in Japanese Urban and Rural Community from the Perspectives of Social Mobility and Generations: Studying the Formation of a Widespread System in Japanese Society). *Shakai-gaku hyōron*, 62(4), 428–441.

Yamashita, Y., Sakumichi, S. and Sugiyama, Y. (2008). *Tsugaru: Kindaika no Dynamism*. Tokyo, Japan: Ochanomizu Shobō.

Yamawaki, N. (2011). Within-Culture Variations of Collectivism in Japan. *Journal of Cross-Cultural Psychology*, XX(X), 1–14.

Yamazaki, T. (2012). *Sukelu-Resukelingu no chirigaku to nihon ni okeru jissei kenkyū no kanōsei* (Geographies of Scale/Rescaling and Their Application to Japan), *Chiiki Shakai Gakkai Nenpō*, 24, 55–71.

Yanagita, K. (1959). Kokyo shichiji-nen. Tokyo. In Teihon Yanagita Kunio shu, volume 3 (1964), 187–88.

PART II

Society

8

Education

Robert W. Aspinall

INTRODUCTION

The study of education in Japan has only on rare occasions been undertaken without attracting controversy. The education system had a key role to play in the modernization of the first major non-Western industrial society. As such, it is and was especially subject to the competing tensions of Westernization versus the maintenance of traditional identity and tradition. From the Meiji era down to the present day debates on education reform have been highly politicized in Japan, and scholars who carry out research in this field can often find themselves being drawn in whether they choose to or not.

No section of any education system receives children who are 'blank slates': they are all products of the preceding parts of the system. The first section of this chapter will examine some significant scholarship that has been carried out on the journey made by the majority of Japanese children as they leave the embrace of the family and proceed through the various levels of the school system. This is followed by a second section that will examine research and scholarship covering efforts to reform the system from the 1980s up to the present day, and some key areas of controversy and dispute.

THE SYSTEM

The Education of the Pre-school Child

There are two main types of pre-school in Japan: *yōchien*, or kindergartens, and *hoikuen*, or nursery schools. The first *yōchien* opened in Tokyo in 1876. It was Meiji Japan's self-conscious attempt to offer Western-style pre-school education to the upper and upper-middle classes. Today *yōchien* are under the jurisdiction of the Ministry of Education and teach three to six year olds for four hours a day plus lunchtime. There are about 13,400 kindergartens in the country of which about 60% are private. Attendance at over-subscribed *yōchien* is usually decided by lottery, although an elite few have an 'exam' or interview to decide who gets in. Public *yōchien* are often located adjacent to or in the same grounds as public elementary schools.

The first *hoikuen* was opened in 1890. In marked contrast to the *yōchien*, the first *hoikuen* were built to serve the needs of poor children and working mothers. Today *hoikuen* are under the jurisdiction of the Ministry of Health, Labour and Welfare and look after babies and children up to the age of six for up to eight hours per day, allowing their mothers to work in full-time jobs. In 2011 about 2,041,000 children received nursery-school care of some description. There are currently almost 23,000 *hoikuen* in Japan, divided fairly evenly between public and private providers. The fees for public *hoikuen* are means-tested based on the income of the parents or guardian. There is an ongoing discussion about merging *yōchien* and *hoikuen* into one institution tentatively called '*kodomoen*' (literally, child garden), but there are many bureaucratic and practical problems associated with such a move.

There has long been considerable support among scholars for the notion that an analysis of how very young children are treated can give us invaluable insights into the differences between Japanese and Western society. Anthropologist Joy Hendry writes that 'it is my contention that, at least in the Japanese case, it is during that time [the pre-school years] that the foundations are laid for most of the important distinctions which will be carried through to adult life' (Hendry, 1986: 7). Tobin et al. agree with this, adding that 'Japanese pre-schools are conservative in giving children a chance to develop a traditionally Japanese sense of self difficult if not impossible for them to learn in their radically narrowed modern worlds' (Tobin, 1989: 220). In a follow-up study twenty years later Tobin found that little had changed.

> In contrast [to pre-schools in China and the United States], because many people in Japan are concerned that their society has already changed too much and become too Westernized, Japanese pre-schools do little borrowing of outside ideas. Japan looks to its pre-schools as a source of cultural continuity rather than a source of change. (Tobin et al., 2009: 241)

This perspective places the Japanese pre-school system within the context of a perceived threat to traditional values, a decline in the extended family and a general process of individualization within Japanese society as a whole. This leads inevitably to a discussion of what exactly these traditional 'Japanese' values or distinctions are, and how they are transferred from adults to young children attending pre-school. One concept which is universally acknowledged to be significant in discussions of the difference between Western and Japanese values is the concept of *amae*. This concept was made popular in the 1970s by the work of well-known psychiatrist Takeo Doi (Doi, 1971). Sociologist Yoshio Sugimoto describes Doi's notion of *amae* in the following way:

> [*amae*] refers to the allegedly unique psychological inclination among the Japanese to seek emotional satisfaction by prevailing upon and depending on their superiors. They feel no need for any explicit demonstration of individuality. Loyalty to the group

is a primary value. Giving oneself to the promotion and realization of the group's goals imbues the Japanese with a special psychological satisfaction. (Sugimoto, 2003: 3)

Most scholars who write in English on Japanese education have found it useful to retain the Japanese term *amae* and not try to translate it. This is not because they agree with Doi that the concept represents something unique to the Japanese psyche, but because of the lack of an appropriate single equivalent word in English. Words like 'dependency' or 'indulgence' are not adequate. To illustrate this point we can look at the example Lois Peak uses of a situation involving a pre-school child who demands the biggest piece of watermelon on the family dining table. Most Japanese mothers in the sample Peak questioned said they would give the child the piece he wanted. From this answer Peak draws the following inference.

> Is it fair to say that the Japanese child is indulged? The answer hinges on one's definition of indulgence. The connotations of the Western term do not fit the Japanese mother's understanding of *amae*. To an American, indulgence means overlooking commonly understood limits of behaviour to gratify excessive desires or special requests. If it occurs frequently, it is believed to have negative effects on a child's social behaviour. Japanese mothers' understanding of *amae* is somewhat different. Though *amae* also entails gratifying such desires and requests, within the Japanese family it is not an abrogation but a reaffirmation of commonly accepted rules of behaviour. By showing *amae* to family members, a Japanese child is following culturally appropriate rules for demonstrating trust and affection within intimate relationships. (Peak, 1991: 41)

Crucially, Peak found that this indulgence of selfish behaviour within the family was not extended to the *yōchien*. The parents who said that the child should be given the biggest piece of watermelon within the family setting all agreed that he certainly should not be given it in the pre-school setting. This leads to another key function of the Japanese pre-school, the teaching of appropriate behaviour *inside* the home and *outside*. In the home children can relax and express their feelings freely – even to the extent of expressing selfish desires. Outside the home children have to learn *shūdan seikatsu*, how to live in a group – a place where one must necessarily suppress one's own desires for the good of the collective. The pre-school is the first place where young children start to learn this basic rule of Japanese society.

The research of Hendry, Tobin and Peak has been criticized for extrapolating broad conclusions about a typical Japanese pre-school from a very small sample of actual observations. This is a common criticism levelled against anthropologists and other educational researchers who carry out most of their research through in-depth observation of a small number of schools located in an even more limited number of geographical locations. One way to move towards a more sophisticated analysis of the complex world of Japanese pre-schools is to divide that world up into sub-categories. This is exactly what Susan Holloway does in her study where she identifies three distinct types of pre-school (Holloway, 2000).

1 *Relationship-oriented* schools are those where the staff are focused on building the children's ability to form relationships with peers and on learning basic class routines. The teachers attempt to foster warm relationships with the children by being friendly, relaxed and non-authoritarian.
2 *Role-oriented* schools have a core curriculum consisting of group instruction in academic skills. Holloway calls these schools *role-oriented* because the aim of the schools is to nurture children to perform their role in life with diligence, confidence and competence. Directors of this type of school often show contempt for recent Ministry of Education guidelines that call for an emphasis on play rather than lessons for the pre-school child.
3 *Child-oriented* schools allow more free play for the children and teachers adopt a more individualized approach in their dealings with the children.

Comparing these types of school the *relationship-oriented* schools best fit the pattern described by Hendry, Tobin and Peak. The other two types, however, challenge some of the assumptions of that literature. *Role-oriented* schools, for example, sometimes used quite strict methods of discipline to keep children in line, while *child-oriented* schools seemed to allow staff to foster feelings of *amae* between teachers and children – something that would not be possible in the type of school described by Peak.

Elementary Schools

Elementary education from the age of six to twelve is compulsory and free in the public sector. In 2011 there were about 22,000 elementary schools in Japan. This is a decline of over 4,500 compared to the number of schools in 1960. Of the 2011 total only 213 were private, reflecting the fact that the vast majority of Japanese families still send their children to the nearest public elementary school (to which they usually walk). Recently a small minority of Boards of Education have been allowed to experiment with giving parents a limited choice of where to send their elementary-school-age children.

Scholarship in English on Japanese elementary schools is dominated by *Educating Hearts and Minds* by Catherine Lewis (Lewis, 1995) and *Primary School in Japan* by Peter Cave (Cave, 2007). The children observed by Lewis in her fieldwork carried out between 1985 and 1993 are clearly older versions of the children studied by Hendry, Peak and Tobin, adding substance to the argument that, while the model of Japanese schooling they have arrived at does not cover *every* Japanese school, it seems to be very widespread within Japan. Lewis found that the child's social and personal development was central to the elementary curriculum. Cave, whose ethnographic research covered the period 1994 to 2004, concurs with the overwhelming body of research on pre-school and elementary education in Japan that emphasizes the role of school in preparing children to fit into Japanese society when they grow up. By talking to teachers, observing classroom behaviour and reading student essays Cave concludes that the concept of *nakama* best conveys the type of group that the ideal class should be. This is a concept that not only conveys the duties one owes to others in one's class, but also the special 'warm' feeling that class members should have. The teachers see no contradiction at all in encouraging this kind of interdependence at the same time as encouraging individuality.

Secondary Schools

Secondary education in Japan is divided into junior high schools (*chūgakkō*) that teach twelve to fifteen year olds and senior high schools (*kōtōgakkō*) that teach fifteen to eighteen year olds. In 2010 there were 10,815 junior high schools in Japan of which 758 were private. In the same year there were 5,116 senior high schools of which 1,319 were private. We can see from these figures that private school provision is a major portion of the Japanese school system only in the non-compulsory sector, i.e. before six years old and after fifteen years old. This makes the Japanese system significantly different from countries like England and the USA, where a certain proportion of families opt for private education for the entire duration of their children's full-time education. Since the 1980s education reformers have proposed merging junior and senior high schools into six-year secondary schools. This has proved difficult to achieve in practice due to institutional resistance, and administrative difficulties caused by the fact that most junior high schools are administered by cities while senior high schools are administered by prefectures.

The onset of secondary education coincides with the onset of puberty for the students and the start of the most serious criticism of the education system from both domestic and foreign scholars. The 'warm feelings' of cooperation that are encouraged in the elementary-school class are supplanted by lessons that are 'intense, fact-filled and routine-based', taught by specialist-subject teachers who mostly do not have the time to develop long-term relationships with the students (Okano and Tsuchiya, 1999: 60). The hierarchical relationships between students from different year groups – the *sempai-kohai* system – become more prominent and are reinforced by the correct use of *keigo (*polite language). Children as they enter adolescence begin to learn the rules of social hierarchy and organization that they will need to follow when they become fully fledged adults. In this respect extra-curricular activities such as festivals, sports days and clubs are also of crucial importance in the process of socialization (Cave, 2004).

When children enter the secondary-school system they also find themselves inducted into Japan's notorious entrance-exam system. Although university is still a long way off, those families who want to get their children into prestigious colleges need to start preparation – at the latest – when the child is twelve (Aspinall, 2005). Since at least the 1970s the Japanese entrance-exam system has come in for a great deal of criticism from experts at home and abroad. They claim that too much pressure is put on young children, especially boys, who are forced to spend hours each day and night cramming masses of factual information into their tired heads. The stress endured by children can have severe physical as well as psychological consequences (Yoneyama, 1999: 229). Also the nature of the exams – involving the memorization of mountains of details and facts – can be pedagogically counter-productive in the case of subjects like English-language and history. The Ministry of Education's response to these criticisms was to introduce the *yutori kyōiku*, reforms which will be discussed in a later section.

Scholarship in English on junior and senior high school in Japan is dominated by studies that compare the Japanese system with that of the USA. Anthropologist Gerald LeTendre has compared the experiences of students in junior high schools in the USA and Japan and comments that in the latter the system gives young adolescents 'very few opportunities to be completely responsible for their own actions, to display self-control on their own, but organizes many group routines or "scripts" for adolescents to follow. Maturity becomes how well one follows the scripts' (LeTendre, 2000: 95). Scholarship on senior high schools in Japan is dominated by Thomas Rohlen's classic work *Japan's High Schools*, which was published in 1983 but contains insights and analysis that are still valid today. He brilliantly observed the daily routines of a variety of different senior high schools in the Kobe area and then showed how these form part of the socialization process for Japan's future workers, managers and ordinary citizens. His conclusion that the Japanese system is far better than that of the USA in generating a 'high average level of capability' (Rohlen, 1983: 322) is as valid today as when it was written.

Universities

Of all the sectors of the Japanese education system under consideration in this chapter it is the university sector that has come in for the most criticism from foreign observers. It has been accused of providing Japanese students with 'higher education' in name only and of failing to fulfil the research functions befitting an advanced industrial democracy. One of the sector's staunchest academic critics is anthropologist Brian McVeigh, who argues that it is misleading to use the English word 'university' when talking about Japan's institutions since they resemble universities in the English-speaking world in form only. He prefers to use the Japanese word *daigaku* when writing in English about this sector. This is a useful device as it constantly reminds the reader that there are fundamental differences between *daigaku* in Japan and universities in the UK, the USA Australia, New Zealand and elsewhere. McVeigh sums up his main reason for drawing this distinction in the following passage:

> What after all is 'higher education'? I will not attempt a definition here, but only state that it is an advanced schooling system that generates knowledge that previously did not exist. By this definition, Japan does not possess as much higher education as statistics, surveys and cursory examinations might indicate. What, then, does Japanese higher education do? It is for the most part best characterized as giving parents/guardians the opportunity to *purchase* diplomas for their children (ensuring entry to "middle-class" life), rather than allowing the latter to *study* for degrees as independent and full-fledged adults. (McVeigh, 2002: 238, original emphasis)

McVeigh does not deny that *some* studying goes on in Japanese *daigaku* but insists that students who do this and institutions that encourage this are in the minority. Another anthropologist, Greg

Poole, agrees that the quality of lectures and academic instruction at Japanese universities is mostly poor, but balances this judgment with the observation that many professors have different priorities: 'Guiding students in their goal of finishing the course, getting the degree and finding a job takes on greater significance than "educating" them with academic knowledge' (Poole, 2010: 140).

A point on which many experts concur is that in most cases a failure to exert oneself in a scholarly way will not get a student failed at university level. By contrast, an inability to pay the tuition fees will certainly result in failure. Given the chronic decline in the population of 18 year olds it is highly unlikely that the majority of Japan's private universities will be able to afford to introduce more stringent academic standards. Since the students know this there will be little incentive for them to study hard. Options for the managers of these universities are few. As Earl Kinmonth points out, '[c]ompared to American private colleges and universities, the most striking difference in Japanese institutions is that they essentially live a hand-to-mouth existence covering current operating expenses and capital expenditures primarily from student fees' (Kinmonth, 2005: 108). There are currently 597 private four-year universities in Japan (compared to 86 national and 95 municipal/prefectural institutions) catering for over 70 per cent of students. The number of private institutions will certainly decline in the medium term due to their dependence on student fees and the inability of all institutions to maintain minimum enrolments as the student-age population declines.

It is not only foreign experts who argue that Japanese universities are in dire need of improvement. Schoppa (1991) examined how university reform was debated firstly by the Central Council on Education in the 1970s and then by Nakasone's *Rinkyōshin* (Ad Hoc Council on Education) in the 1980s. He concluded that the lack of substantive, concrete changes to result from these councils helps to prove his 'immobilist politics' thesis: the inability of the different groups involved, in both the bureaucratic and political worlds, to come to an agreement in most areas of reform. Subsequent events have shown that the reform process was not blocked entirely, rather it was slowed down and truncated (Hood, 2001). Thirty years later substantive reform was finally achieved in the form of the privatization of national and public universities in 2004 and 2005. This reform has been described as a 'big bang' reform (Goodman, 2005) and chiefly involved transforming the national and prefectural/municipal universities into independent agencies. At one stroke 125,000 employees in public-sector universities were reassigned to the private sector (although they retained existing health and pension benefits).

One of the main purposes of the 2004 reform was to transform the job of university president from a largely formal, ceremonial role to that of an actual, top manager. One of the most important jobs for this manager would be to find new sources of income for the university since the subsidy from central government would now be cut by one per cent per year for 20 years. However, in practice the scope for independent management was highly restricted. In spite of privatization the Ministry of Education has retained a lot of control over what goes on in universities, although the means of control are now direct rather than indirect. The ministry has retained a lot of influence over how teaching and research are evaluated, and has not set up a properly independent body that would be comparable to, for example, the Higher Education Funding Council for England (HEFCE). Furthermore, it is still the ministry that is responsible for determining the medium-term goals for each university after 'taking into account' a draft prepared by each university. A limited performance-related-pay system was supposed to have been introduced for academic staff, but its application was the responsibility of each university president and in practice pay structures were retained from the pre-2004 system, i.e. pay based upon seniority. Presidents decided they did not want to anger the *kyōjukai* (the professors' council), a body which retains a lot of power and influence in former national and public universities as well as most institutions in the private sector. There is a clear lack of leadership at this level (Yokoyama, 2010: 131). After 2004 some flexibility was also allowed for the setting of tuition fees. However, by the start of the 2007 academic year only three formerly national universities (out of a total of 86) had set fees for undergraduate courses that were slightly different from the standard.

A 2009 OECD report into higher education in Japan puts forward the following explanation for the failure of the new university-president system to perform as expected:

> The President presides over a university administration which, for the system to operate effectively, rapidly needs to be transformed into a professional management team. There is a huge staff development requirement here, one which the reformers seem to have seriously underestimated. Given the traditional dependency on MEXT for even basic administrative requirements, neither the skills nor the systems are sufficiently robust or widespread to ensure the implementation of the reforms at the pace which the government intended. (OECD, 2009: 33)

The OECD report emphasizes the point that Japan simply does not have a 'pool of academic administrators with [the] extensive management and financial experience [required to] take on the strategic management of more autonomous and entrepreneurial university institutions' (OECD, 2009: 20). The same report criticizes MEXT for its failure to articulate a vision for the future for the whole tertiary system (OECD, 2009: 19–20). In the absence of such a vision and without the proper development of a new class of university managers the likelihood is that most Japanese *daigaku* will continue to 'muddle through' with efforts to resist serious (not merely rhetorical) change unless it is forced upon them either by government fiat or demographic pressure.

CONTROVERSY, CONFLICT AND CHANGE

Educational Governance: Problems with Objectivity

Some of the best research on Japanese schools is the product of hard-working ethnographers spending day after day after day observing interactions and activity in classrooms. Unfortunately, the same kind of fly-on-the-wall observational study of bureaucrats in the Ministry of Education (or in local boards of education) is simply not possible. Japanese bureaucrats prefer to work behind closed doors, forcing scholars to look elsewhere for data. This has led some scholars to rely too much on data provided by critics of the ministry, including a minority who seem to blame every problem of the education system on the bureaucrats in Tokyo, while other scholars rely too much on the formal statements of the government and its mouthpieces. The result is that some academics place themselves into one of two camps that characterize the post-war political division between teachers' unions on the left (allied with other public-sector unions and socialist and communist parties) and the Ministry of Education on the right (allied with the Liberal Democratic Party and big business). Scholarship that places itself into one or other of these two camps is not necessarily invalidated by doing so, but the reader needs to be aware of the political predisposition of the author. By way of illustration consider the following quotation from Yoneyama. After a discussion of the political conflict over education that was waged between 1945 and the late 1990s Yoneyama concludes 'there seems little doubt that the educational paradigm of Japan today is almost an antithesis to the democratic paradigm which existed in the brief ten years between 1945–54' (Yoneyama, 1999: 83). The same author also shows her opinion of the largest teachers' union's decision in 1995 to drop its policy of opposition to the Ministry of Education. When she writes about the union's stated aim to reconcile itself with the ministry she puts 'reconcile' in inverted commas, clearly showing her sympathy with those on the left who criticized the union and claimed that its policy was not one of reconciliation but 'surrender'.

Two more authors who share Yoneyama's opinions about education politics in the post-war period are Horio Teruhisa (Horio, 1988) and Brian McVeigh (McVeigh, 2002). Those who read Horio are benefitting from the insights of someone who is not only an outstanding scholar but an active participant in the progressive camp of educational politics, advising teachers' unions and taking part in their study meetings. Does the political engagement and partisanship of these scholars invalidate their writings? Not in the least – so long as the reader is aware of the political positions held by these authors before they started their research, and is able to access contrary political views (for example, publications by the Japanese government and articles by conservative publications like the *Yomiuri* newspaper).

Authors who have been more sympathetic to the government line include Chris Hood (Hood, 2001), who, in his analysis of LDP prime minister Nakasone Yasuhiro's educational policy, was more uncritical of government reports and declarations of intent than the authors quoted above. The scholar who retained the most objectivity in his study of Japanese educational politics was Leonard Schoppa in his analysis of reform in the 1970s and 80s (Schoppa, 1991). In fact, he was criticized by scholars in the progressive camp for this very objectivity, their argument being (drawing on the language of Paulo Freire, the icon of progressive education) that attempting to be neutral in the battle between the powerful and the less powerful is, effectively, to take sides with the powerful. They opposed Schoppa's insistence that he would maintain a 'formal neutrality' on the issue of whether or not the educational reforms proposed during the 1970s and 80s were desirable (Schoppa, 1991: 7), claiming that the oppressive nature of the status quo cried out for all enlightened scholars to oppose it (Platzer, 1994). The strength of Schoppa's work, however, lies in its focus on the detail of how education policy is actually made in Japan. He painstakingly guides the reader through the process of initiation, deliberation and implementation, examining closely the agenda and tactics of all the main individuals and groups involved. By distancing himself from a normative discussion of whether or not each specific reform is desirable he is able to focus on the reform *process*. The reader is able to follow Schoppa's analysis and then decide for him or herself the rights or wrongs of the policies in question.

It is to the topic of education reform that we now turn.

Education Reform in the 1980s

There can be no question that the post-war Japanese education system was successful in providing the country with the workforce that it needed to catch up economically with the West. In addition, in mathematics, literacy and science it regularly out-performed its competitors (Tsuneyoshi, 2004: 364–5). It could not be denied, however, that many of the features of the system that had brought about this success contained flaws. A consensus developed that the system was too rigid and, at times, too stressful. Calls for more flexibility and a greater allowance for the individuality and creativity of pupils grew from all educational and political quarters (Schoppa, 1991: Chapter 2). There was also pressure from many quarters for Japanese children to receive an education that would make them more internationally aware (Aspinall, 2013: Chapter 3). It soon became apparent, however, that although by the 1980s there was a clear groundswell of support for such buzzwords as 'flexibility', 'individuality' and 'internationalization', there were serious differences of opinion as to what these words actually *meant* when translated into concrete educational policy. There were also the practical as well as the ideological problems involved in getting a conservative educational bureaucracy and a large and diverse teaching force to turn new policies into reality at the 'chalkface'.

As mentioned above, Schoppa is the best guide to the process by which politicians and bureaucrats wrestled with and argued over the reform process during the 1970s and 80s. Interestingly, he throws light on the extent of the differences of opinion and ideology that exist within the 'conservative camp' of Liberal Democratic Party (LDP), bureaucracy and big business that had control of the levers of power in Japan from 1955 to 1993. Schoppa identified a 'subgovernment' in the field of education that had developed during the long period of LDP rule, wherein certain LDP politicians developed links with bureaucrats in the education ministry in order to pursue certain agendas and defend the powers of the ministry.

The major locus for the debate on education reform in the 1980s was the Ad Hoc Council on Education (AHCE) set up by prime minister Nakasone Yasuhiro, a powerful LDP politician with a long-standing interest in educational issues. Although the AHCE issued four major reports, which included about 500 different recommendations, actual tangible changes to the running of schools and universities were minimal. Scholars like Hood (2001) have argued that Schoppa, who finished his research shortly after Nakasone left office in 1987, was too quick to conclude that the reform effort had been a failure. Certain reforms proposed by the AHCE, like the privatization of national universities, were blocked at the time they were first put forward but became reality a few years later (2004 in this particular case). Other reforms that were blocked at the time have seen modest implementation in some parts of the country. One example of this is the proposal, mentioned earlier, to integrate junior high schools and senior high schools into one unified, six-year secondary school. There have also been controversial changes in the areas of patriotism and internationalization that will be dealt with in a later section of this chapter.

The main political changes that have taken place since Schoppa concluded his research have been the decline of the traditional left and the LDP's loss of its monopoly of power. Schoppa's analysis confirmed the conventional wisdom among political scientists that groups within the progressive camp were completely excluded from national-level decision making. This was as true with education policy as with any other area of national policy. However, he found that the well known ability of the Japan Teachers' Union (JTU) to disrupt or block policy implementation at the school and local-government level preyed on the mind of educational bureaucrats who were usually anxious to avoid trouble. Representatives of the union (as well as their political allies in the Japan Socialist Party) were excluded from the meetings that took place at the Ministry of Education, the CCE (Central Council on Education – the most important advisory panel for the ministry) or the AHCE. However, they were still able to wield invisible influence on the thought processes of risk-averse bureaucrats. They may have said 'Yes, Prime Minister' in an obsequious way to the demands of Nakasone but their minds were already calculating strategies for watering down reform in order to avoid disruption in schools. The split in the JTU that took place in 1989, followed by the decision in 1995 of the more moderate half to end its policy of opposition to the ministry, should have been a gift to radical reformers on the right. As we shall see below this did signal victory for the right in one particular battle – the struggle to enforce the singing of the national anthem and the hoisting of the national flag in school ceremonies – but other reform efforts were hampered by divisions within the governing conservative camp. Indeed, the removal of a 'common enemy' after 1995 meant that groups within the conservative camp that had differing agendas and interests were now more likely to bring those differences into the open (Aspinall, 2001: 187–88). During the same period the decline of the LDP as the natural 'ruling party' of Japan and the growth of the rival Democratic Party of Japan (a party that contained Diet members with direct links to the JTU), culminating in a DPJ government from 2009 to 2012, gave the union some access to the central levers of power for the first time. The experience of having a friendly party in power proved disappointing, however, with the DPJ government stumbling from crisis to crisis and unable to implement much of its agenda. In 2012 the LDP returned to power with a landslide victory in the general election.

Yutori Kyōiku: Reforms and U-turns

In 2002 a new national curriculum was introduced that aimed to offer Japanese children *yutori kyōiku*, which means a more relaxed education – an education that would allow children 'room to grow.' As part of this policy classes on Saturday mornings were ended and thirty percent of curriculum content was selectively reduced. These policies were the Ministry of Education's response to the problems of stress and rigidity in the system (Nitta, 2008: 131–2). Instead of having to cram mountains of facts into their tired heads students would now be encouraged to develop a 'zest for living' (*ikiru chikara*) and to think for themselves. A new period of 'integrated study' was introduced to the higher grades of elementary school and junior high school in order to allow more freedom and creativity for teachers as well as their pupils.

By the Ministry of Education's cautious, risk-averse standards the 2002 reforms were quite radical. Even this, however, did not prepare it for the storm of criticism it had to endure. Articles in the popular press as well as best-selling books raised the spectre of a crisis of standards, especially in the basics of reading and maths (Tsuneyoshi, 2004). Surveys showed a drastic rise in the number of parents who were considering sending their children to private elementary or junior high schools (where the new reduced curriculum did not apply). The private and unregulated cram-school, or *juku*, industry enjoyed a boom in spite of a continuing decline in the population of potential clients. The influential educational sociologist Kariya Takehiko criticized the new 'integrated learning', built around the development of a 'strong individual', as his research showed that it would widen differences between children who come from families that value educational achievement and those who do not (Kariya, 2001, 2013). Other research showed that the notorious stress related to entrance exams was in decline anyway due to declining numbers in the student population and changes to university-entrance procedures. A reduction in the official curriculum also exposed a long-standing flaw in the secondary school system: the disconnection between the national guidelines, reformed every ten years by the ministry, and the 'unofficial' curriculum that involved preparation for university-entrance exams. Starting in the 1990s the introduction

of more subject choice into university-entrance exams meant that senior high school students could now specialize in four or five subjects and more or less ignore the others. However, ministry guidelines continued to demand a minimum number of study hours for *all* major academic studies in order to graduate from high school. As a consequence some high schools concerned with getting as many of their students into top universities as possible secretly allowed students to study an exam subject during class time that was officially devoted to a subject that the students had decided not to take for an entrance exam. This practice was exposed in a sensational way by the press in 2007, forcing a series of senior high schools principals to apologize in public and swear they would discontinue this practice. Tsuneyoshi sums up this disconnection between the official and unofficial curricula in the following way:

> [I]t is not realistic to expect [pupils] and their families to sit back and enjoy the low-pressure education in public schools, if the [university entrance] exam content far exceeds the contents the child will be exposed to in the public school curriculum. This has led some to note that contrary to the popular image, the Ministry's powers are actually too weak, in the sense that it cannot control the private schools nor the universities, two institutions that greatly influence the state of public education. (Tsuneyoshi, 2004: 390)

In another sign of institutional weakness the ministry was finally forced to carry out a U-turn on its *yutori kyouiku* curriculum. The *yutori* reforms were made to take the blame for the decline in Japan's OECD PISA (Program for International Student Assessment) rankings, especially in the key subject of mathematics in which Japan was top when the first PISA was carried out in 2000, dropping to sixth place in 2003 and tenth in 2006 (recovering only a little to ninth place in 2010). The media panic that accompanied this drop in the rankings, and is now referred to as the 'PISA shock', disguised the fact – the mathematical fact – that the performance of Japanese students at mathematics between 2000 and 2003 had not declined but stayed roughly the same – and the newspapers did not mention that neither the Netherlands nor Hong Kong, two of the five nations that outperformed Japan in 2003, was included in the 2000 survey (Takayama, 2008: 397). This deliberate misrepresentation of the facts was orchestrated by those who had always disagreed with the policy of making education more relaxed (Takayama, 2008: 398–400). Their campaign succeeded and in a report issued in August 2007 the CCE recommended that time for 'integrated study' be cut and time for core subjects, like mathematics and science, be increased. This resulted in revisions to teaching guidelines implemented from April, 2011. In addition, in another U-turn, since 2010 public schools in Tokyo have been allowed to hold Saturday classes if they choose (*Daily Yomiuri*, February 8, 2014). In January 2013 a proposal was put forward for the whole country to return to Saturday classes, something which, if implemented, would mark the complete defeat of *yutori kyōiku*.

Patriotism and Internationalization: Two Sides of the Same Coin?

Reflecting changes caused by Japan's rapid economic development, educational policy-makers and ordinary teachers alike found themselves increasingly having to consider the international dimension of their work. One of the buzzwords of the educational reform debate of the 1980s was *kokusaika*, or internationalization. Some commentators have caused unnecessary confusion by treating 'internationalization' as a synonym for 'internationalism' (*kokusaishugi*). The two terms, in both English and Japanese, are quite distinct. Internationalism is an ideology that is the antithesis of nationalism: it is dedicated to the breaking down of national borders and national identities. Internationalizaion, although there are disagreements about its precise meaning, is clearly a process, not a political ideology. It increases connections of all kinds between nation states. Once this distinction is properly understood there is no logical contradiction in promoting, as Nakasone did, the development of policies for internationalization (for example, more international awareness among Japanese school children and more student exchanges) and nationalism (for example, compulsory showing of respect to the national flag and anthem).

One concrete manifestation of Japan's policy on internationalization in the field of education was the introduction of the Japan Exchange and Teaching (JET) programme in 1987. This programme recruited young foreign nationals, mostly from the economically advanced English-speaking nations, and then installed them in junior and senior high schools the length and breadth of Japan. The purpose was to improve practical English-language teaching and help 'internationalize' schools and communities by having a foreigner live and work in their midst. Twenty five years later this quite expensive programme has managed to survive, although numbers of participants have been cut from a high of almost 6,000 down to 4,370 in 2013. The number of participating countries has increased to forty but the overwhelming majority of participants still come from the USA, UK, Canada, Australia and New Zealand. The general consensus is that the programme's effect

on language teaching has been patchy at best, and certainly not a good return on the huge investment made. Its rather vague 'internationalization' goals have probably been more successfully met, both in terms of helping communities get used to hosting people from very different cultures and also in giving thousands of young non-Japanese people an opportunity to live in a culture very different to that in which they grew up. From the point of view of the Ministry of Foreign Affairs (one of the JET programme's participating ministries) this latter goal had always been the most important since it was part of a strategy to improve Japan's overseas image, especially in the USA.

The definitive study of the JET programme was written by anthropologist David McConnell (2000), and it helps to shed light on the complex and contested nature of the 'internationalization' buzzword as it applies to education policy and practice in Japan. He concludes that the JET programme's implementation refutes any notion of a monolithic Japanese response to outsiders.

> There is no single notion of internationalization in Japan, nor is there any single body that could implement such a policy. The story is rather one of competing ideologies and interests, miscommunication, and the reinterpretation of program objectives at each administrative level. In short we find an extraordinary complex picture of internal conflict and variation. Spanning three Japanese ministries, eighteen countries, dozens of consulates, forty-seven prefectures, thirteen designated cities, hundreds of municipalities, and thousands of schools and local government offices, the JET Program hangs together – but only in the most ungainly manner. (McConnell, 2000: 269)

If there is no consensus on what 'internationalization' means within Japan then the picture becomes even more confused when the opinions and perspectives of the thousands of foreign participants in the programme are brought into the picture. Many of them come from cosmopolitan communities, often located in countries that have a long history of mass immigration. McConnell describes these people as seeing 'internationalization in terms less of building bridges between people than of breaking down the walls between them' (2000: 226); frustration arose because their hosts in the Japanese secondary schools had a different conception of internationalization, which McConnell sums up as 'the development of techniques to improve understanding and communication between cultures and groups that they assumed would always be fundamentally different'. Japanese education administrators were also mostly unwilling to stretch the concept of 'internationalization' to cover ethnic minorities permanently present in

Japan. I will return to this issue in the final section of this chapter.

A nation's education system does not usually draw the attention of the citizens and politicians of other countries. An exception to this rule can arise when the issue being debated domestically is the teaching of the past. The Japanese education system has been criticized for not passing on to future generations a proper understanding of the aggression and atrocities committed in the name of Japanese imperialism during the 1930s and 40s. From time to time this criticism has escalated to the point of causing serious international incidents between Japan and its neighbours. Usually, the catalyst for such an incident has been the decision by the textbook-authorization section of the Ministry of Education either to order the correction of the controversial part of a history textbook or to approve a text that many foreign nations find offensive (Nozaki, 2008).

Western commentators on these controversies often compare the inability of Japan and its neighbours to bury the ghosts of World War II with the apparent success of Germany and the rest of Europe in coming to an agreed understanding of the past. Much of the scholarship in this area focuses on how World War II is remembered in Japan. This also involves research about shrines, especially the controversial Yasukuni Shrine, public apologies and how the war is treated in popular culture, not least movies and manga (Seaton, 2007). The highly salient nature of this controversy often obscures the fact that its impact on the day-to-day operation of the education system is minimal. History teachers at the *genba* (i.e. in the classroom) are free to use supplementary materials and to agree or disagree with whatever is in the government-approved textbook. Because of time constraints and the strictly chronological design of the curriculum many do not make it as far as the twentieth century anyway, or only have time to do a very quick overview of events (Cave, 2005: 324–5). Also, opinion surveys have shown that the revisionist views of history continue to be held only by a minority in Japanese society as a whole (Saaler, 2005: chapter 3). Finally, commentators of both left and right who are worried about mind control should contemplate those instances where students who are taught history by ideologically inspired left-wing teachers come to resent the 'masochistic' nature of the history they are being taught and, in later life, decide to support organizations that press for a more nationalistic history curriculum. In a modern complex society like Japan what is on the page of the textbook or the teacher's lesson plan is certainly not going to be transferred to young children quickly or easily. This is why the struggle over what is in the textbook, whether it is confined solely to domestic actors, or has more

international attention, is mostly a struggle about symbols. However, it can have an impact on concrete educational policy and practice, especially in tandem with other changes, like the rewriting of the Fundamental Law of Education in 2006, which placed renewed emphasis on patriotism and knowledge of traditional Japanese values.

Education of Minorities

In recent years there has been a growth in the literature on the ways in which minority communities fit into the Japanese education system, or fail to do so. Traditionally, government policy, with its emphasis on egalitarianism and uniformity, was reluctant to identify special programmes for minorities. Where they did exist they were either euphemistically titled – for example, *dōwa kyōiku* (literally 'education for social integration') for policies aimed at helping *burakumin* children, i.e. those descended from formerly outcaste communities (Gordon, 2008) – or they were explicitly designed to help children exposed to alien cultures to readjust to the norms and expectations of Japanese society; for example, policies for *kikokushijo* (returnee children from abroad) (Goodman, 1993; Kanno, 2003). The opportunity to use children with backgrounds in different cultures to improve foreign-language education has mostly not been exploited (Aspinall, 2013: 130–134).

The national census and other official statistics reject the concept of members of ethnic minorities who are also Japanese citizens (this includes the growing number of children of international marriages where one spouse is a Japanese citizen). Also, the largest ethnic minority groups living in Japan – the Koreans and Chinese – are 'visibly indistinguishable from ethnic Japanese', something that helps to explain an apparent lack of awareness among Japanese students of the ethnic diversity that surrounds them (Tsuneyoshi, 2011: 116). Research from the field, however, shows that in spite of this lack of awareness, and in spite of a lack of leadership from MEXT, local boards of education, individual schools and NGOs are striving to help an increasingly diverse set of minority communities meet their educational needs (Tsuneyoshi et al., 2010).

CONCLUSION

Researchers on education are always trying to reconcile the need to arrive at useful general theories and models with the observable fact that in a country the size of Japan containing tens of thousands of schools, hundreds of thousands of teachers and millions of pupils and students the risk is very real that the number of exceptions to any rule may be overwhelming. A certain amount of unintended assistance is provided by the centralized nature of the system, with its rules and regulations from the Ministry of Education. However, the work of anthropologists and other researchers at every level of the system has revealed that, although there is certainly a great deal of conformity to official curricula, textbooks etc., there is also scope for a considerable variety of teaching style and classroom content. A reading of the official curricula is, of course, essential, but it is worthless without an examination of how the various subjects are addressed by teachers and students at the *genba*, the classroom. Furthermore, when a major reform is announced it is the job of the researcher to sort those changes that are 'substantive' from those that are 'merely semantic' (Willis and Rappleye, 2011: 28).

One theme that runs throughout the research discussed in this chapter is the emphasis placed by Japanese educators on maintaining and defending what Tobin called 'a traditionally Japanese sense of self' (Tobin, 1989: 220). This can be seen not only in the pre-schools that Tobin studied but also the elementary schools that Cave studied, the high schools that Rohlen studied, the universities, and also in the reluctance of national education policy to recognize the ethnic diversity that exists within contemporary Japanese society. Western researchers who write about this phenomenon can find themselves accused of Orientalism and a preoccupation with Japan's uniqueness (Takayama, 2011). Japan may have had more than its fair share of foreign visitors who overemphasize the differences between Japan and the West, but that accusation cannot be made against any of the researchers discussed in this chapter (and dozens more who could not be included for reasons of space). All of them have adhered to the best principles of social-scientific research and have outlined the nature of their research, its location, duration and limits. They have paved the way for further work which can only enrich our understanding of how education works in Japan.

REFERENCES

Aspinall, R. W. (2001). *Teachers Unions and the Politics of Education in Japan*. Albany: State University of New York Press.

Aspinall, R. W. (2005). University Entrance in Japan. In J. S. Eades, Roger Goodman, and Y. Hada (Eds.) *The 'Big Bang' in Japanese Higher Education: The 2004 Reforms and the Dynamics of Change*. Melbourne: Trans Pacific Press.

Aspinall, R. W. (2013). *International Education Policy in Japan in an Age of Globalisation and Risk*. Leiden and Boston: Global Oriental.

Cave, P. (2004) Bukatsudo: The Educational Role of Japanese School Clubs. *Journal of Japanese Studies*, 30(2), 383–415.

Cave, P. (2005). Learning to Live with the Imperial Past? History Teaching, Empire, and War in Japan and England. In E. Vickers and A. Jones (Eds.) *History Education and National Identity in East Asia*. New York and Abingdon: Routledge.

Cave, P. (2007). *Primary School in Japan: Self, individuality and learning in elementary education*. London: Routledge.

Daily Yomiuri. (2014) Educational officials must find ways to make most of students, *Saturdays*. February 8th 2014.

Doi, T. (1971). *The Anatomy of Dependence*. Tokyo: Kodansha.

Goodman, R. (1993). *Japan's 'International Youth': The Emergence of a New Class of Schoolchildren*. Clarendon Press: Oxford.

Goodman, R. (2005). W(h)ither the Japanese University? An Introduction to the 2004 Higher Education Reforms in Japan. In J. S. Eades, R. Goodman, and Y. Hada (Eds.) *The 'Big Bang' in Japanese Higher Education: The 2004 Reforms and the Dynamics of Change*. Melbourne: Trans Pacific Press.

Gordon, J. A. (2008) *Japan's Outcaste Youth: Education for Liberation*. Boulder, CO: Paradigm.

Hendry, J. (1986). *Becoming Japanese: The World of the Pre-school Child*. Manchester: Manchester University Press.

Holloway, S. D. (2000). *Contested Childhood: Diversity and Change in Japanese Preschools*. London: Routledge.

Hood, C. P. (2001). *Japanese Education Reform: Nakasone's Legacy*. London: Routledge.

Horio, T. (1988). *Educational Thought and Ideology in Modern Japan*. Tokyo: University of Tokyo Press.

Kanno, Y. (2003). *Negotiating Bilingual and Bicultural Identities: Japanese Returnees Betwixt Two Worlds*. Mahwah, New Jersey and London: Lawrence Erlbaum Associates Press.

Kariya T. (2001). *Fubyôdô Seisan kara Iyoku kakusa (Insentibu Dibaido) Shakai e*. Tokyo: Yushindo.

Kariya T. (2013). *Education Reform and Social Class in Japan: The Emerging Incentive Divide*. London and New York: Routledge.

Kinmonth, E. (2005). From Selection to Seduction: The Impact of Demographic Change on Private Higher Education in Japan. In J. S. Eades, R. Goodman, and Y. Hada (Eds.) *The 'Big Bang' in Japanese Higher Education: The 2004 Reforms and the Dynamics of Change*. Melbourne: Trans Pacific Press.

LeTendre, G. (2000). *Learning to Be Adolescent: Growing up in U.S. and Japanese Middle Schools*. New Haven and London: Yale University Press.

Lewis, C. C. (1995). *Educating Hearts and Minds: Reflections on Japanese Preschool and Elementary Education.* Cambridge: Cambridge University Press.

McConnell, D. L. (2000). *Importing Diversity: Inside Japan's JET Program* Berkeley: University of California Press.

McVeigh, B. T. (2002). *Japanese Higher Education as Myth.* Armonk and London: W.E. Sharpe.

Nitta, K. A. (2008). *The Politics of Structural Education Reform.* London and New York: Routledge.

Nozaki, Y. (2008). *War, Memory, Nationalism and Education in Postwar Japan, 1945–2007.* London and New York: Routledge.

OECD (2009). *OECD Reviews of Tertiary Education: Japan.* Paris: OECD Publishing.

Okano, K. and Tsuchiya, M. (1999). *Education in Contemporary Japan: Inequality and Diversity.* Cambridge: Cambridge University Press.

Peak, L. (1991). *Learning to Go to School in Japan: The Transition from Home to Preschool Life.* Berkeley CA: University of California Press.

Platzer, S. (1994). Success by Failure. *American Journal of Education.* 103.

Poole, G. S. (2010). *The Japanese Professor: An Ethnography of a University Faculty.* Rotterdam, Boston and Taipei: Sense Publishers.

Rohlen, T. P. (1983). *Japan's High Schools.* Berkeley: University of California Press.

Saaler, S. (2005). *Politics, Memory and Public Opinion: The History Textbook Controversy and Japanese Society.* Munich: Iudicium Verlag.

Schoppa, L. J. (1991). *Education Reform in Japan: A Case of Immobilist Politics.* London and New York: Routledge.

Seaton, P. A. (2007). *Japan's Contested War Memories: The 'Memory Rifts' in Historical Consciousness of World War II.* London and New York: Routledge.

Sugimoto, Y. (2003). *An Introduction to Japanese Society.* (second edition). Cambridge: Cambridge University Press.

Takayama, K. (2008). The politics of international league tables: PISA in Japan's achievement crisis debate. *Comparative Education* 44 (4), 387–407.

Takayama, K. (2011). Reconceptualizing the Politics of Japanese Education, Reimagining Comparative Studies of Japanese Education. In D. Blake Willis and J. Rappleye (Eds.) *Reimagining Japanese Education: Borders, Transfers, Circulations, and the Comparative.* Oxford: Oxford Studies in Comparative Education.

Tobin, J. J., Wu, D. and Davidson, D. (1989). *Preschool in Three Cultures: Japan, China and the United States.* New Haven: Yale University Press.

Tobin, J. J., Hsueh, Y. and Karasawa, M. (2009). *Preschool in Three Cultures Revisited.* Chicago: University of Chicago Press.

Tsuneyoshi, R. (2004). The New Japanese Educational Reforms and the Achievement "Crisis" Debate. *Educational Policy* 18 (2), 364–394.

Tsuneyoshi, R. (2011). The "Internationalization" of Japanese Education and the Newcomers: Uncovering the Paradoxes. In D. B. Willis and J. Rappleye (Eds.) *Reimagining Japanese Education: Borders, Transfers, Circulations, and the Comparative.* Oxford: Oxford Studies in Comparative Education.

Tsuneyoshi, R., Okano, K., Boocock, S. (Eds.) (2010). *Minorities and Education in Multicultural Japan: An Interactive Perspective.* London and New York: Routledge.

Willis, D. B. and Rappleye, J. (2011). Reimagining Japanese Education in the Global Conversation: Borders, Transfers, Circulations, and the Comparative. In D. B. Willis and J. Rappleye (Eds.) *Reimagining Japanese Education: Borders, Transfers, Circulations, and the Comparative.* Oxford: Oxford Studies in Comparative Education.

Yokoyama, K. (2010). *Government, Policy and Ideology: Higher Education's Changing Boundaries in Two Island Kingdoms – Japan and England.* Lanham: University Press of America.

Yoneyama, S. (1999). *The Japanese High School: Silence and Resistance.* London: Routledge.

9

Feminism

Vera Mackie

HISTORIES OF FEMINISM

Feminism as a social movement develops in modern societies at the point where gender becomes a salient social category.[1] Once women – and sympathetic men – feel dissatisfaction with the different treatment of women and men in laws, social policies, social customs and cultural representations, they respond with political movements to seek improvement in women's situation. In the case of Japan, the machinery of a modern nation-state was created in the mid to late nineteenth century. A feudal society based on status distinctions and regional variations was transformed into a modern capitalist nation state stratified by class distinctions and a gendered division of labour. These structures were overlaid with discourses of nationalism which attempted to unify the nation. From the 1870s on there were discussions about the roles of women and men in the transformed nation state, and these discussions continue in the twenty-first century.

From the earliest days of feminist thought and action in Japan there were connections between feminists and feminist sympathisers in Japan and other countries. At first this simply took the form of Japanese thinkers reading and explicating feminist texts from European countries and in some cases translating them into Japanese. This is not to suggest that feminism developed as a derivative discourse from overseas. Rather, men and women who were trying to understand the transformations taking place in their own society found resonances in the writings of people who had grappled with similar issues in other societies.

When the government set up a new education system in the 1870s it employed teachers and educational experts from overseas. Missionaries also contributed to this process, particularly in the development of women's education. The new mass education system and the mission schools promoted women's literacy. The mission schools were also the site for the promotion of notions of companionate marriage and romantic love, and in some cases the promotion of feminist ideas. Many of the graduates of these women's schools and mission schools forged links with international women's organisations, corresponded with them in English and travelled overseas for further education. Through these connections we have a substantial English-language archive of the development of feminist thought in Japan.

Under the regime of the Constitution of the Empire of Japan (1890) and the associated legal codes, men and women were seen as subjects of the Emperor, with a limited suffrage initially only available to a small number of men who paid a certain level of property tax. (In 1925 the suffrage was extended to all adult Japanese males and male colonial subjects resident in the metropolis, but not to women.) Women and men were positioned in different ways according to the legal system and were addressed in distinctive ways according to nationalist discourse. In other words, subjecthood was *gendered* (Germer, Mackie and Wöhr, 2014a: 1–24). This consciousness of gendered difference, and a consciousness of the disadvantages suffered by women, prompted the development of feminist thought. Some women thus resisted their positioning as 'good wives and wise mothers' (*ryôsai kenbo*), who were expected to support male workers and soldiers and support the goals of the imperialist state (Koyama, 2013; 2014: 85–100).

We now have studies of the feminist movement in Japan from the late nineteenth century to the present. In 1983 Sharon Sievers published a survey of the first decades of feminist activism in Japan where she looked at women in the popular rights' movement, the Women's Christian Temperance Union (WCTU), women in the early socialist movement and the Bluestocking Society (for other surveys see Mackie, 1988: 53–76; 2003: *passim*; Buckley, 1994). We now have substantial monographs on several of the individuals, groups and themes initially surveyed by Sievers, not to mention new perspectives on the beginnings of feminism in Japan.

Marnie Anderson (2010; 2011: 38–55; 2013: 43–66) traces the exclusion of women from the political sphere in the formative years of the modern Japanese nation state and argues that public space was thus constituted as gendered space. Although women were excluded from parliamentary politics, they still found ways to be politically active – writing articles on political topics and petitioning the government on issues which concerned them. Mara Patessio takes a prosopographical approach to the period from the 1860s to the 1880s, tracing the actions and connections between groups of women who aspired to citizenship and claimed a place in the emerging public sphere (2004: 1–26; 2006: 155–182; 2011; 2013a: 93–118; 2013b: 556–581; on late-nineteenth-century debates on women's rights see also Braisted, 1976; Mackie, 1997a: 1–41; 1998a: 121–140; 2003: 15–44; Molony, 2005a: 463–492; Suzuki Mamiko, 2009; Johnson, 2013: 67–92).

The Japan chapter of the WCTU is perhaps the country's oldest women's organisation. Elizabeth Dorn Lublin traces the early history of the group, from its establishment in 1886 to 1912. She argues that although women were excluded from political organisations, political meetings and voting, members of the WCTU 'contributed to the construction of the public sphere, advanced the feminist and reform movements, and helped shape the nature of citizenship' (Lublin, 2010: 176; see also Yasutake, 2004). WCTU members worked largely within the existing nationalist and imperialist paradigm of the

late nineteenth and early twentieth centuries, but they tried to expand the possibilities for women to be active within that framework and to provide a critique of the behaviour of their male compatriots. In other public activity, women were active in the state-sponsored nationalist organisations, such as the Patriotic Women's Association from 1901, the National Women's Defence Organisation from 1932 and the amalgamated Greater Japan Women's Association from 1942 (Havens, 1975: 913–34; Garon, 1993: 5–41; Wilson, 1995: 295–314; Morita, 2005: 49–70).

Women, and some men, who were active in the socialist movement in the early twentieth century also contributed to an understanding of the 'woman question', although not always under the banner of feminism. Mikiso Hane (1993) has translated excerpts of the autobiography of Fukuda [Kageyama] Hideko (1865–1927), whose activism bridges the liberal movement of the late nineteenth century and the early decades of the socialist movement. We await a full-length English-language biography of Fukuda, but see Ushioda (1977: 9–12), Mackie (1997a: 1–69; 1997b: 126–145; 2013a: 103–114) and Loftus (1991: 73–86; 2004). Hélène Bowen Raddeker (1997; 2002; 2013: 91–102) has studied the lives and works of anarchists Kanno Suga (1881–1911), Kaneko Fumiko (1903–1926) and Itô Noe (1895–1923) (see also Miyamoto, 1975: 190–204; Large, 1977: 441–67; Kaneko, 1997; Filler 2009: 57–90; Mackie, 2013a: 103–114; Mae, 2014: 68–84). Socialist thinker Yamakawa Kikue (1890–1980) has been the subject of articles but as yet no full-length biography in English (Shapcott, 1987: 1–30; Tsurumi, 1996: 258–276; Mackie, 1997a: 95–153; 1997b: 126–145). Similarly, we have articles on Communist writer Miyamoto Yuriko (1899–1951), and some translations of her works (de Bary, 1981: 40–47; de Bary, 1984–1985: 7–28; Bowen-Struyk, 2004: 479–507) but not yet a full-length biography. (On proletarian writer, Nakamoto Takako (1903–1991), see Mackie 1997b: 126–145; 2011: 319–331). Kate Wildman Nakai has translated Yamakawa Kikue's (2001 [1943]) memoir of her samurai family in the years leading up to the Meiji restoration, while Mikiso Hane (1993) has translated excerpts from the writings of women on the left who experienced imprisonment in imperial Japan (see also Mackie, 2011: 319–331; 2013a: 103–114). Sarah Frederick has treated the leftwing feminist arts journals *Nyonin Geijutsu* (Women's Arts) and *Kagayaku* (Shine) in her research on interwar women's magazines (Frederick, 2006: 137–177; see also Coutts, 2013a: 309–312; 2013b: 362–378; Frederick 2013: 395–413).

Pioneer campaigner for family planning, Katô [Ishimoto] Shidzue (1897–2001), produced an autobiography in 1935 and has been the subject of biographical research by Helen Hopper (Ishimoto, 1992 [1935]; Hopper, 1995; 2004). Katō was a leading figure in international organisations promoting family planning and she moved from civil-society activity in the early decades of the twentieth century – until she was arrested in the late 1930s – to a long career as a parliamentarian in post-1945 Japan.[2]

BLUESTOCKINGS, NEW WOMEN AND MODERN GIRLS

The 'new woman' is a theme of several recent works. Dina Lowy (2007) traces the emergence of the figure of the new woman in Japan, beginning with the staging of such plays as Henrik Ibsen's *A Doll's House*, Hermann Sudermann's *Magda*, and the debates they engendered in the 1910s (on the development of acting as a modern profession for women see Kano, 2001). The label 'new woman' (*atarashii onna*) then became associated with the women gathered around the feminist literary journal *Seitô* (Bluestockings, 1911–1916). These women were the subject of media attention for their unconventional behaviour, which included drinking exotic liqueurs, sightseeing in the licensed prostitution district, scandalous love affairs and the espousal of feminist ideas. The appellation 'new woman', however, was transformed from a stigmatising label to a proclamation of independence through *Bluestockings* editor Hiratsuka Raichô [Haruko]'s (1886–1971) defiant manifesto: 'I am a new woman' (Hiratsuka 1987 [1913]: 41–3).

We now have several studies of the Bluestockings group (*Seitôsha*) and their journal, including biographies of several figures and translations of important works (Lippit, 1975: 155–163; Reich and Fukuda, 1976: 280–291; Sievers, 1983: 163–188; Birnbaum, 1999: 55–101; Mackie, 1997a: 70–94; Mackie, 2003: 45–72; Tomida, 2004; Bardsley, 2007; Yamazaki, 1985; Narita, 1998: 173–94; Kelley, 2011). Teruko Craig has made Hiratsuka Raichô's memoir available in a one-volume abridged English translation (Hiratsuka, 2006). Poet Yosano Akiko (1878–1942) has been the subject of several studies, focusing on her life, her writings, and her poetry (Rodd, 1991: 175–198; Rowley, 2000; Baichman, 2002). Joshua Fogel's translation of Yosano's writings on her travels in Manchuria makes an important contribution to our understanding of the cultural politics of Japanese imperialism (Yosano, 2001).

Some former members of the Bluestockings group created the New Women's Association (*Shin Fujin Kyôkai*), which was active from 1919 to 1922. One of the founders of the New Women's Association, Ichikawa Fusae (1893–1981), went on to form the Women's Suffrage League (*Fusen Kakutoku Dômei*, active under various names from 1924). Ichikawa devoted the first half of her life to the attainment of women's suffrage and became a long-serving independent member of the Japanese Diet in the post-Second World War years (Vavich, 1967: 402–436; Murray, 1975: 171–189; Molony, 2005b: 57–94; Molony, 2011: 1–27). In her study of the 'new women' Lowy also examines leftist feminist Nishikawa Fumiko's (1882–1960) 'True New Women's Society' (see also Mackie, 1997a: 84–5) and places Japan's 'new women' in the context of similar figures in other national and transnational contexts. Michiko Suzuki (2009) considers representations of new women in literature.

A related figure is the modern girl (*modan gâru*, or *moga*). While the 'new woman' is a figure of the 1910s, with something of a feminist tone, the 'modern girl' appears in the mid 1920s and is more closely associated with consumerism than feminism (Sato, 1993: 239–266; Sato, 2003; Silverberg, 1991: 239–266; Modern Girl Around the World Research Group, 2008: 240–262; 263–287; 354–361; Mackie, 2012: 53–57; 2013b: 67–82; 2013e). Miriam Silverberg (2006) analyses the figures of the modern girl, the café waitress and the modern housewife in the media, particularly in movie magazines and women's magazines. Mark Driscoll places the modern girl and modern boy in the context of Japan's imperialism, bringing together discussion of metropolitan cultural forms and representations of Japan's peripheries, such as the puppet state of Manchukuo (2010).

Modernity involved the development of gendered identities, which included a pedagogical view of desirable and undesirable forms of femininity (and masculinity, for that matter) (Mackie, 2013c: 62–91). Christine Marran considers the category of 'poison woman' (*dokufu*), a phrase used to label transgressive women from the late nineteenth century to the early post-Second World War period. She argues that 'sexuality and sexual desire came to suggestively symbolise the struggle to define women's place in society' (Marran, 2007: 171).

As Japan moved towards the total national mobilisation of the wartime period, there was increased policing of women's behaviour so that they could be seen to be supporting nationalist goals (Mackie, 2003: 99–119; Mackie, 2013b: 67–82). From the late 1930s to the 1940s the population was mobilised under the national general mobilisation system (*kokka sôdôin taisei*) (Miyake, 1991: 267–295). This made it difficult to publicly espouse feminist or other oppositional ideas. Some prominent women, however, participated in wartime government committees and general mobilisation policies, for which they would be criticised in later years.

FEMINISM AND CITIZENSHIP

After Japan's defeat in the Second World War democratic reforms meant that individuals were now positioned as citizens rather than subjects. Women gained the right to vote and stand for public office with the revision of the Electoral Law in December 1945, something which they had demanded in the suffrage movement of the early twentieth century. The Constitution of Japan (enacted 1946, effective 1947) outlawed discrimination on grounds of sex, creed, social status or family origin, and the Civil Code and other relevant legislation were revised to match the new Constitution. While the formal barriers to women's political participation were removed, gender still shaped the public sphere (Mackie, 2000a: 245–257; 2002a: 245–257; 2003: 120–143; 2007: 49–72; 2009: 139–163).

Mire Koikari revisits the history of the Allied Occupation of Japan and situates the strategic alliance between US and Japanese feminists in the context of Cold War politics. It is only relatively recently that scholars have explicitly acknowledged the *colonial* dimension of the Occupation of Japan and have thus realised that post-colonial theoretical perspectives have much to teach us about the power dynamics of the Occupation. Koikari argues that the study of gender policy in Occupied Japan cannot be abstracted from global and regional geopolitical trends. She identifies coalitions of thought where the themes of democratisation, liberalisation and gender equity were embedded in discourses of US hegemony and anti-Communism. According to this view, feminists were complicit in the establishment of the US-Japan alliance in East Asia, much as many of them had been complicit with Japanese imperialism until 1945. Koikari describes Occupation-period gender policy as 'Cold War imperial feminism in the Far East' (Koikari, 2008: 5; see also Pharr, 1987: 221–252; Gordon, 1998).

In the immediate post-war period feminist activism often involved women who spoke as 'mothers'. From this position they contributed to campaigns on pacifism, nuclear disarmament, consumer issues and environmental issues (Mackie, 2003: 120–136; Yamamoto, 2004). In some ways, speaking as a 'mother' has been revived in the aftermath of the Great Tōhoku Earthquake, tsunami and nuclear disaster of 2011 (Slater, 2011), as parents have expressed their concerns about the safety of their children. Nevertheless, as Ulrike Wöhr has noted, the most recent campaigns have involved both men and women speaking from the position of parents with concerns for their children's safety (Wöhr, 2011: 80–94).

Julia Bullock (2010) identifies an incipient feminism in literature by women in the 1950s and 1960s, a precursor of the women's liberation

movement. In Japan, as in the other advanced capitalist democracies, the 1960s and 1970s were the decades of new left and student activism, while the 1970s was the decade of women's liberation (Tanaka, K., 1974; 1994: 343–352; Tanaka, Y., 1995: 141–154; Mackie, 2003: 144–173; 2010; 2011: 319–331; 2013a: 103–114; Shigematsu, 2011: 163–179; 2012; 2014: 174–187; Loftus, 2013; Lenz, 2014: 211–229; Iijima, 2014: 290–306). On lesbian feminism see Chalmers (2002), McLelland et al. (2007: 167–223), Fujimura-Fanselow (2011: 147–196), Izumo and Maree (2000) and Maree (2007: 80–94; 2014: 230–243).

In the 1970s a group of women's liberationists set up a feminist press – Femintern – with the purpose of facilitating communication between feminists in Japan and other countries. This was a two-way process of translating important feminist works into Japanese and translating Japanese language texts into English for an international audience. An early publication was Tanaka Kazuko's *A Short History of the Women's Movement in Japan* (1974). Tanaka traced feminist thought from the liberal movement of the late nineteenth century to the women's liberation movement of the 1970s. With the translation of Japanese feminist writings into English by Femintern, a new stage of communication between feminists in Japan and other countries was inaugurated. Tanaka's essay was read by both academics and activists; it followed the protocols of academic writing but also spoke to activists in its discussion of the contemporary concerns of the Japanese women's liberation movement. Several feminist journals of the period also produced English-language editions in order to communicate with an international audience (*Feminist International*, 1980; *Asian Women's Liberation*, 1977–1995; see also *AMPO: Japan-Asia Quarterly Review*, 1969–2000; *Women's Asia: 21*, 1996–2013). In the 1970s a few articles appeared on feminism in Japan in English-language academic journals. Some were biographical studies of feminist pioneers; others translated important feminist texts into the English language (Miyamoto, 1975: 190–204; Reich and Fukuda, 1976: 280–291; Large, 1977: 441–67). Feminists have also been engaged in critiques of gendered representations in the mainstream media from the 1990s to the present (Mackie, 1992: 23–31; Shigematsu, 2005: 555–589).

The 1970s also saw the development of a more reformist strand of feminism, with activists in Japan making astute use of local and international networks in campaigns for the ratification of the United Nations (UN) Convention on the Elimination of all forms of Discrimination Against Women (CEDAW) and the creation of an Equal Employment Opportunity Law (Mackie, 2003: 174–201; Flowers, 2009: 69–112). Several collections of translations in the 1990s made the thought of these feminist thinkers and activists available to English readers (AMPO, 1996; Buckley, 1997; see also de Bary et al., 2005: 1188–1222).

We have some studies of women's political activism in the post-Second World War period, including Susan Pharr's *Political Women in Japan* (1981; see also Carlberg, 1976: 233–255; Buckley, 1997; Hastings, 1998: 271–300; 2014: 180–197; Dalton, 2008a; 2008b: 51–65; 2013: 24–42). Robin le Blanc has completed several studies of parliamentary politics, explicitly focusing on the workings of masculinity and femininity (1999; 2010; 2012: 857–871). There has been a recent explosion of interest in the radical leftist activism of the 1960s and 1970s (Steinhoff, 1996: 301–324; Igarashi, 2007: 12–128; Marotti, 2009: 97–135; Mackie, 2010: 55–62; Eckersall, 2011: 333–343), but there is room for further work which explores the gendered dynamics of the radical left.

FEMINISM, THE STATE AND THE NATION

Ichikawa Fusae's (1893–1981) life spanned most of the twentieth century, including contributions to the labour movement, pioneering activism in the suffragist movement and, like Katō [Ishimoto] Shidzue, a long post-war career as a parliamentarian (Vavich, 1967: 402–436; Murray, 1975: 171–189; Molony, 2005b: 57–94; 2011: 1–27). Figures like Ichikawa present difficult questions related to gender and militarism. In Japanese-language historiography there is criticism of those feminists who were seen to have collaborated with the wartime regime. This has focused on such women as Ichikawa, other Bluestockings such as Yosano Akiko and Hiratsuka Raichō [Haruko] (1886–1971), and feminist historian Takamure Itsue (1894–1964) (Tsurumi, 1985: 2–19; 1998: 335–57; Ryang, 1998a: 1–32).

This preoccupation has also surfaced in the English-language literature; and the translation of Ueno Chizuko's book *Gender and Nationalism* (2004 [translation of Ueno, 1998]) has been a significant contribution to this field (see also Ueno and Sand, 1999). Nevertheless, these debates would benefit from a more thoroughgoing engagement with theories of gender and citizenship and theories of the gendering of the state (Mackie, 2002a: 245–257; 2005b: 207–217; 2013d). These historical debates inform discussion about the proper relationship between feminist activists and the state in contemporary Japan.

Yoshie Kobayashi traces the development of gender policy in Japan, from the establishment of a Women's and Minors' Bureau within the Ministry of Labour in 1947 to the enactment of an Equal Employment Opportunity Act in 1986 (and subsequent revisions), and the creation of the Basic Law for a Gender Equal Society and the Office for Gender Equality in the 1990s (Kobayashi, 2004; see also Gelb, 2003). Kobayashi deploys the concept of 'state feminism' to describe the relationship between feminists and the bureaucracy. While the concept of 'state feminism' is becoming increasingly influential in the description of the development of gender-sensitive policy in Japan, it could be suggested that the concept sacrifices analytical clarity in collapsing the two terms 'state' and 'feminism' and elides the likely contradictions between state aims and the aims of the feminist movement. Furthermore, neither the state nor the feminist movement are unitary entities. The state is made up of complex formations of the legislature, the judiciary and various government departments, bureaux and agencies, while there are robust debates among various feminist groups on particular issues.

There is no doubt, however, about the importance of a particular strand of reformist feminism in influencing government policy in the 1980s and 1990s. Alongside the ratification of the UN Convention on the Elimination of all forms of Discrimination Against Women (CEDAW) in 1985, Japan overhauled discriminatory laws and practices related to the transmission of nationality and the differential treatment of boys and girls in the education system. An Equal Employment Opportunity Act was enacted in 1985, to become effective in 1986. In the 1990s, in the spirit of recommendations from the 1995 United Nations World Conference on Women (the 'Beijing Action Plan'), gender was placed at the centre of government activities with the creation of the Office for Gender Equity in the Cabinet Office, the passing of the Basic Law for a Gender-Equal Society (1999), and the promotion of the Basic Plan for a Gender-Equal Society. One measure of the importance of these initiatives is that they were met with a corresponding conservative backlash. This backlash is known as 'gender-bashing' or 'gender-free bashing' and resulted in an equally vehement 'fightback' by feminist academics and activists (these events are surveyed by Kano, 2011: 41–62).

Miriam Murase looks at the women's centres which were established in Japan in the wake of International Women's Year and the International Women's Decade, policies connected with the creation of the Office for Gender Equity, and recent policy initiatives concerning the regulation of Non-Profit Organisations (NPOs). Like several other scholars, Murase argues that through the regulation of NPOs the government is engaged in shaping civil society in Japan and that this has implications for the possibility of feminist organisations influencing government policy. Murase's study is informed by political science, and she focuses mainly on state-recognised women's groups (Murase, 2006; see also Chan-Tiberghien, 2004; Takao, 2007: 147–172). Laura Dales is also interested in women's centres. Dales deploys a combination of participant observation, ethnography and textual analysis. She provides an empathetic, theoretically informed and politically engaged account of contemporary feminist activism (Dales, 2005; 2007; 2009). Richard Calichman has included two important feminist thinkers – Ehara Yumiko and Ueno Chizuko – in his anthology *Contemporary Japanese Thought* (Calichman, 2005: 43–69, 225–262).

An important theme of feminist activism in contemporary Japan is the question of diversity. In scholarly terms, this involves theorising the intersectionality of gender, class, caste, ethnicity, sexual orientation and other dimensions of difference. In terms of activism, this involves dealing with the distinctive needs of diverse groups (Chapman, Dales and Mackie, 2008: 192–199). At times this has been expressed in terms of 'minority' groups, although this tends to leave the notion of 'majority' Japanese ethnicity unquestioned. More recent work has shifted to the language of 'diversity' (Fujimura-Fanselow, 2011: 199–256; Mackie, Okano and Rawstron, 2014: 137–161). Post-colonial feminist theory has been useful for many in theorising the relationships among diverse groups in Japan who share the history of imperialism and colonialism through their descent from colonisers and formerly colonised groups (Ryang, 1998a: 1–32; Mackie, 1998b: 599–615; 2001; 2002b: 144–148; 2002c: 181–202; 2004: 239–256; Chapman, 2006: 353–363). Such theoretical perspectives are also useful in coming to terms with the transnational dimensions of feminist activism.

FEMINISM IN A TRANSNATIONAL FRAME

As we have seen, feminism has from its earliest days been built on international links. Many of the earliest feminists in Japan were fostered through their contacts with progressive thinkers in Christian mission schools. Labour activists forged international links through the International Labour Organisation. Socialists and Communists maintained international links until the mid 1930s. The term 'international', however, can still be said to assume that the 'nation' is the basic unit of analysis and that the nation is the most relevant frame for the description of political action. More recent scholarship, however, focuses on the 'transnational': that is, it focuses on the flows and movements of people and ideas across national borders (Mackie, 2001: 180–206; 2002c: 181–202; 2004: 239–256). In the study of feminism, too, there has been a recent focus on thought and activism which crosses borders (Bullock, 2009; Germer, 2003; 2013: 92–115). Although the term 'transnational' is a relatively recent coinage, many would argue for the existence of transnational flows from the earliest days of feminism.

Tsuda Umeko (1864–1929) travelled to the USA in the 1870s and was largely educated there before returning home to set up Tsuda Juku women's college. Tsuda has herself been the subject of two biographical studies (Furuki, 1991; Rose, 1992). Rumi Yasutake (2004) has researched the links between Christian women in Japan and the West Coast of the USA in the late nineteenth century. Barbara Molony (2010: 90–109) has surveyed the transnational links forged by feminists from Japan throughout the twentieth century, in the suffrage movement and such organisations as the Women's International League for Peace and Freedom (WILPF). Fiona Paisley, in her (2009) study of the Pan-Pacific Women's Congresses, has included discussion of the participation of Japanese representatives (see also Shibahara 2011: 3–24; 2014).

As noted above, activists in the Women's Liberation movement in the 1970s were engaged in the project of making their ideas available to feminists in other countries. Other groups which produced English editions also contributed to communication across borders, as we have seen (*Feminist International*, 1980; *Asian Women's Liberation*, 1977–1991; see also *ANPO: Japan-Asia Quarterly Review*, 1969–2000; *Women's Asia: 21*, 1996–2013). The United Nations International Year for Women (1975), International Women's Decade (1975–1985) and the Beijing Women's Conference (1995) also provided opportunities for transnational communication and action. Several scholars have written about the interaction of Japan-based NGOs, international NGOs (INGOs), the Japanese government and the UN in the implementation of policies concerning gender equity (Chan-Tiberghien, 2004; Flowers, 2009).

Feminists have also focused on issues which are by their very nature transnational, including working conditions in Japanese transnational corporations, the gendered effects of the tourism industry and the gendered dimensions of labour migration (Mackie, 1998b; 2001: 180–206; 2002c: 181–202; 2004: 239–256). Journalist Matsui Yayori's (1934–2003) essays on these issues provide insight into these campaigns from an activist perspective (Matsui, 1989; 1998).

The history of colonialism, militarism and imperialism is reflected in contemporary issues, such as the campaigns for compensation for survivors of the system of enforced military prostitution/sexual slavery. This issue brings together the themes of militarism, imperialism, colonialism, nationalism, gender and sexuality. Debates on this issue raise important questions about historical evidence, as historians debate the relative weight to be given to oral testimonies and written evidence. This also has a place in the history of feminism, for it has stimulated research by feminists in activist networks. The history of enforced military prostitution/sexual slavery cannot be contained within nation-based historical narratives, for it necessarily involves individuals and experiences which cross national boundaries. Much of the initial research was devoted simply to making the experiences of the survivors accessible to an English-language audience (O'Herne, 1994; Howard, 1995; Henson, 1996; Kim, 1996: 157–160; Kim-Gibson, 1999; Schellstede, 2000; Yoshimi, 2000; Tanaka, Y., 2002). Others have reflected on the ethics of the use of traumatic narratives (Schaffer and Smith, 2004), the interpretation of these narratives (Ryang, 1998b: 3–15), the politics of memory (Ueno and Sand, 1999: 129–152; Soh, 2008) and the implications of this issue for the development of feminist theory (Mackie, 2000b: 37–59; 2005b: 207–217; Mackie and Tanji, 2014: 60–73; Wöhr, 2004: 59–90).

The academic study of feminism as a political movement, then, requires an interdisciplinary approach, drawing variously on gender and sexuality studies, literary and cultural studies, ethnography, history, political science and post-colonial theory.

NOTES

1 In this essay, I survey English-language research on feminism as a political movement in Japan. This is not a survey of women's studies, gender and sexuality studies, women's history research or research in gender and history, although it is informed by these approaches and intersects with research in these fields. On the writing of women's history, feminist history and gender history in Japan see Hayakawa (1991); Mackie (2005a: 240–248) and Takahashi (2013: 244–254); on gender and modernity in Japan see Mackie (2013c: 62–91). Readers of Japanese may wish to consult the primary document collections on the history of feminism compiled by Maruoka and Yamaguchi (1976–1980), Suzuki (1993–1998), Mizoguchi et al. (1992–1995) and Inoue et al. (2009–2011).

2 For critical views of the relationship between eugenics and feminism see Otsubo (2005: 225–256) and Robertson (2005: 329–354).

REFERENCES

AMPO: Japan-Asia Quarterly Review (Eds.) (1996). *Voices from the Japanese Women's Movement.* New York: M. E. Sharpe.

Anderson, M. S. (2010). *A Place in Public: Women's Rights in Meiji Japan.* Cambridge MA: Harvard East Asian Monographs.

Anderson, M. S. (2011). Women's Agency and the Historical Record: Reflections on Female Activists in Nineteenth-Century Japan. *Journal of Women's History*, 23 (1), Spring, 38–55.

Anderson, M. S. (2013). Women and Political Life in Early Meiji Japan: The Case of the Okayama Joshi Konshinkai (Okayama Women's Friendship Society). *US-Japan Women's Journal*, 44, September, 43–66.

Baichman, J. (2002). *Embracing the Firebird: Yosano Akiko and the Birth of the Female Voice in Modern Japanese Poetry.* Honolulu HI: University of Hawaii Press.

de Bary, B. (1981). After the War: Translations from Miyamoto Yuriko. *Bulletin of Concerned Asian Scholars*, 16 (2), 40–47.

de Bary, B. (1984–1985). Wind and Leaves: Miyamoto Yuriko's The Weathervane Plant. *The Journal of the Association of Teachers of Japanese*, 19 (1), 7–28.

de Bary, W. T., Gluck, C. and Teidemann, E. A. (Eds.) (2005). *Sources of Japanese Tradition*, second edition, volume two (pp. 1188–1222). New York: Columbia University Press.

le Blanc, R. (1999). *Bicycle Citizens: The Political World of the Japanese Housewife.* Berkeley CA: University of California Press.

le Blanc, R. (2010). *The Art of the Gut: Manhood, Power and Ethics in Japanese Politics.* Berkeley CA: University of California Press.

le Blanc, R. (2012). Lessons from the Ghost of Salaryman Past: The Global Costs of the Breadwinner Imaginary. *Journal of Asian Studies*, 71 (4), 857–871.

Bardsley, J. (2007). *The Bluestockings of Japan: New Women Essays and Fiction from Seitô, 1911–1916.* Ann Arbor MI: Center for Japanese Studies, University of Michigan.

Birnbaum, P. (1999). *Modern Girls, Shining Stars, The Skies of Tokyo: 5 Japanese Women.* New York: Columbia University Press.

Bowen-Struyk, H. (2004). Revolutionizing the Japanese Family: Miyamoto Yuriko's "The Family of Koiwai". *positions: east asia cultures critique*, 12 (2), Fall, 479–507.

Braisted, W. R. (trans. and commentary) (1976). *Meiroku Zasshi: Journal of the Japanese Enlightenment.* Cambridge MA: Harvard University Press.

Buckley, S. (1994). A Short History of the Feminist Movement in Japan. In J. Gelb and M. L. Palley (Eds.) *Women of Japan and Korea: Continuity and Change* (pp. 150–186). Philadelphia PA: Temple University Press.

Buckley, S. (1997). *Broken Silence: Voices of Japanese Feminism.* Berkeley CA: University of California Press.

Bullock, J. (2009). Fantasy as Methodology: Simone de Beauvoir and Japanese Feminism. *US-Japan Women's Journal,* 36 (October).

Bullock, J. (2010). *The Other Women's Lib: Gender and Body in Japanese Women's Fiction,* Honolulu HI: University of Hawaii Press.

Calichman, R. (ed.) (2005). Contemporary Japanese Thought. NewYork: Columbia University Press.

Carlberg, E. (1976). Women in the Political System. In J. Lebra, J. Paulson and E. Powers (Eds.) *Women in Changing Japan* (pp. 233–255). Boulder CO: Westview Press.

Chalmers, S. (2002) *Emerging Lesbian Voices from Japan.* London: RoutledgeCurzon.

Chan-Tiberghien, J. (2004). *Gender and Human Rights Politics in Japan: Global Norms and Domestic Networks.* Stanford CA: Stanford University Press.

Chapman, D. (2006). Beyond the Colonised and the Colonisers: Intellectual Discourse and the Inclusion of Korean-Japanese Women's Voices. *Japanese Studies,* 26 (3), 353–363.

Chapman, D., Dales L. and Mackie, V. (2008). 'Minority Women Will Change the World!': Perspectives on Multiple Discrimination in Japan. Women's Studies International Forum, 31 (3), 192–199.

Coutts, A. (2013a). Introduction. *Japan Forum,* 25 (3), 309–312.

Coutts, A. (2013b). How Do We Write a Revolution? Debating the Masses and the Vanguard in the Literary Reviews of *Nyonin geijutsu. Japan Forum,* 25 (3), 362–378.

Dales, L. (2005) On (not) Being Feminist: Feminist Identification and Praxis in a Kyoto Women's Group. *Graduate Journal of Asia-Pacific Studies.* 3 (1): 13–27, Retrieved on 11 July 2014 from http://www.arts.auckland.ac.nz/sites/index.cfm?P=5687

Dales, L. (2007) Connection and Collaboration: Women's Centres and NGO Women's Groups in Japan. Intersections: Gender and Sexuality in Asia and the Pacific. 17. Retrieved on 11 July from http://wwwsshe.murdoch.edu.au/ intersections/issue15/dales.htm

Dales, L. (2009). *Feminist Movements in Contemporary Japan.* London: Routledge.

Dalton, E. (2008a). A Masculinised Party Culture: Obstacles Facing Women in Japan's Liberal Democratic Party. *Proceedings of the Biennial Conference of the Asian Studies Association of Australia,* Melbourne. Retrieved on 20 May 2011 from www.arts.monash.edu.au/mai/asaa/proceedings.php#d.

Dalton, E. (2008b). The Utilization of Discourses of Femininity by Japanese Politicians: Tanaka Makiko Case Study. *Graduate Journal of Asia-Pacific Studies,* 6 (1), 51–65.

Dalton, E. (2013). More 'Ordinary Women': Gender Stereotypes in Arguments for Increased Female Representation in Japanese Politics. *US-Japan Women's Journal,* 44 (September), 24–42.

Driscoll, M. (2010). *Absolute Erotic, Absolute Grotesque: The Living, the Dead and the Undead in Japan's Imperialism, 1895–1945.* Durham NC: Duke University Press.

Eckersall, P. (2011). The Emotional Geography of Shinjuku: The Case of Chikatetsu Hiroba (Underground Plaza) 1970. *Japanese Studies,* 31 (3), 333–343.

Filler, S. (2009). Going Beyond Individualism: Romance, Personal Growth and Anarchism in the Autobiographical Writings of Itô Noe, *US-Japan Women's Journal,* 37 (April), 57–90.

Flowers, P. (2009). *Refugees, Women and Weapons: International Norm Adoption and Compliance in Japan.* Stanford CA: Stanford University Press.

Frederick, S. (2006). *Turning Pages: Reading and Writing Women's Magazines in Interwar Japan,* Honolulu HI: University of Hawaii Press.

Frederick, S. (2013). Beyond Nyonin Geijutsu, Beyond Japan: Writings by Women Travellers in Kagayaku (1933–1941). *Japan Forum,* 25 (3), 395–413.

Fujimura-Fanselow, K. (2011). *Transforming Japan: How Feminism and Diversity Are Making a Difference.* New York: Feminist Press.

Furuki, Y. (1991). *The White Plum: A Biography of Ume Tsuda: Pioneer of the Higher Education of Women in Japan.* New York: Weatherhill.

Garon, S. (1993). Women's Groups and the Japanese State: Contending Approaches to Political Integration, 1890–1945. *Journal of Japanese Studies,* 19 (1), Winter, 5–41.

Gelb, J. (2003). *Gender Policies in Japan and the United States: Comparing Women's Movements, Rights and Politics.* New York: Palgrave Macmillan.

Germer, A. (2003). Feminist History in Japan: National and International Perspectives. *Intersections: Gender, History and Culture in the Asian Context,* 9. Retrieved on 10 July 2014 from www.intersections.anu.edu.au/issue9/germer.html.

Germer, A. (2013). Japanese Feminists after Versailles: Between the State and the Ethnic Nation. *Journal of Women's History,* 25 (3), 92–115.

Germer, A., Mackie, V. and Wöhr, U. (2014a). Introduction: Gender, Nation and State in Modern Japan. In A. Germer, V. Mackie and U. Wöhr (Eds.) *Gender, Nation and State in Modern Japan* (pp. 1–24), London: Routledge.

Germer, A., Mackie, V. and Wöhr, U. (Eds.) (2014b). *Gender, Nation and State in Modern Japan.* London: Routledge.

Gordon, B. S. (1998). *The Only Woman in the Room: A Memoir.* Tokyo: Kodansha.

Hane, M. (1993). *Reflections on the Way to the Gallows: Rebel Women in Prewar Japan.* Berkeley: University of California Press.

Hastings, S. A. (1998). Women Legislators in the Postwar Diet. In A. E. Imamura (Ed.) *Re-Imaging Japanese Women* (pp. 271–300). Berkeley CA: University of California Press.

Hastings, S. A. (2014). Women's Professional Expertise and Women's Suffrage in Japan, 1868–1952. In A. Germer, V. Mackie and U. Wöhr (Eds.) *Gender, Nation and State in Modern Japan* (pp. 180–197). London: Routledge.

Havens, T. R. H. (1975). Women and War in Japan, 1937–45. American Historical Review 84 (4), 913–934.

Hayakawa, N. (1991). The Development of Women's History in Japan. In K. Offen, R. R. Pearson and J. Rendall (Eds.) *Writing Women's History: International Perspectives* (pp. 171–179). Bloomington IN: Indiana University Press.

Henson, M. R. (1996). *Comfort Woman: Slave of Destiny*. Manila: Philippine Centre for Investigative Journalism.

Hiratsuka R. (1987). Atarashii Onna [New Woman] in Kobayashi T. and Yoneda S. (Eds) *Hiratsuka Raichō Hyōronshū* [Collected Essays of Hiratsuka Raichô] (pp. 41–43). Tokyo: Iwanami, 1987 [originally published in *Chûô Kôron* [Central Review], January 1913].

Hiratsuka, R. (2006). In *the Beginning, Woman was the Sun: The Autobiography of a Japanese Feminist*. Translated with an Introduction by T. Craig. New York: Columbia University Press.

Hopper, H. M. (1995). *A New Woman of Japan: A Political Biography of Katō Shidzue*, Boulder CO: Westview Press.

Hopper, H. M. (2004). *Katō Shidzue: A Japanese Feminist*. New York: Pearson Longman.

Howard, K. (Ed.) (1995). *True Stories of the Korean Comfort Women*. London: Cassell.

Igarashi, Y. (2007). Dead Bodies and Living Guns: The United Red Army and Its Deadly Pursuit of Revolution, 1971–1972. *Japanese Studies*, 27 (2), September, 12–128.

Iijima, A. (2014). From Personal Experience to a Political Movement in the 1970s: My View of Feminism. Translated and annotated by A. Germer. In A. Germer, V. Mackie and U. Wöhr (Eds.) *Gender, Nation and State in Modern Japan* (pp. 290–306). London: Routledge.

Inoue, T., Ueno, C., Ehara, Y., Amano, M., Itô, K., Itô, R., Ôsawa, M., Kanô, M. and Saitô, M. (Eds.) (2009–2011). *Shinpen: Nihon no Feminizumu* [Japanese Feminism: New Edition], ten volumes. Tokyo: Iwanami Shoten.

Ishimoto, S. (1992) [1935]. *Facing Two Ways: The Story of My Life*. Stanford CA: Stanford University Press.

Izumo, M. and Maree, C. (2000). *Love Upon the Chopping Board*. Melbourne: Spinifex Press.

Johnson, L. L. (2013). Meiji Women's Educators as Public Intellectuals: Shimoda Utako and Tsuda Umeko. *US-Japan Women's Journal*, 44 (September): 67–92.

Kaneko, F. (1997). *The Prison Diaries of a Japanese Woman*. Translated by Jean Inglis. New York: M. E. Sharpe.

Kano, A. (2001). *Acting Like a Woman in Modern Japan: Theater, Gender and Nationalism*. New York: Palgrave Macmillan.

Kano, A. (2011). Backlash, Fightback and Back-Pedaling: Responses to State Feminism in Contemporary Japan. *International Journal of Asian Studies*, 8 (1), 41–62.

Kelley, E. (2011). Envisioning the 'New Woman': Seitō Magazine and Feminist Aesthetics in Modern Japan. *Modern Art Asia*, November, unpaginated.

Kim–Gibson, D. S. (1999). *Silence Broken: Korean Comfort Women*. Parkersburg IO: Mid–Prairie Books.

Kim, P. J. (1996). Looking at Sexual Slavery from a Zainichi Perspective. In AMPO: Japan-Asia Quarterly Review (Eds.) *Voices from the Japanese Women's Movement* (pp. 157–160). New York: M. E. Sharpe.

Kobayashi, Y. (2004). *A Path Toward Gender Equality: State Feminism in Japan*, London: Routledge.

Koikari, M. (2008). *Pedagogy of Democracy: Feminism and the Cold War in the US Occupation of Japan*. Philadelphia PA: Temple University Press.

Koyama, S. (2013). *Ryôsai Kenbo: The Educational Ideal of 'Good Wife, Wise Mother' in Modern Japan*. Leiden: Brill.

Koyama, S. (2014) Domestic Roles and the Incorporation of Women into the Nation-State: The Emergence and Development of the 'good wife, wise mother' ideology. In A. Germer, V. Mackie and U. Wöhr (Eds.) *Gender, Nation and State in Modern Japan* (pp. 85–100). London: Routledge.

Large, S. S. (1977). The Romance of Revolution in Japanese Anarchism and Communism During the Taishô Period. *Modern Asian Studies*, 11 (3), July: 441–67.

Lenz, I. (2014) From Mothers of the Nation to Embodied Citizens? Reflexive Modernisation, Women's Movements and the Nation in Japan. In A. Germer, V. Mackie and U. Wöhr (Eds.) *Gender, Nation and State in Modern Japan* (pp. 211–229). London: Routledge.

Lippit, N. M. (1975). Seitô and the Literary Roots of Japanese Feminism. *International Journal of Women's Studies*, 2 (2), 155–163.

Loftus, R. P. (1991) Is There a Woman in the Text? Fukuda Hideko's Warawa no hanseigai. in J. A. Carson and J. Rehn, (Eds.) *In the Pacific Interest: Democracy, Women and the Environment*, Willamette Journal of the Arts Supplemental Series 4: 73–86.

Loftus, R. P. (2004). *Telling Lives: Women's Self-Writing in Modern Japan*. Honolulu HI: University of Hawaii Press.

Loftus, R.P. (2013). *Changing Lives: The 'Postwar' in Japanese Women's Autobiographies and Memoirs*. Ann Arbor, MI: Association for Asian Studies.

Lowy, D. (2007). *The Japanese 'New Woman': Images of Gender and Modernity*, New Brunswick NJ: Rutgers University Press.

Lublin, E. D. (2010). *Reforming Japan: The Woman's Christian Temperance Union in the Meiji Period*. Vancouver: University of British Columbia Press.

Mackie, V. (1988). Feminist Politics in Japan. *New Left Review*, 167, 53–76.

Mackie, V. (1992). Feminism and the Media in Japan. *Japanese Studies*. 12 (2), 23–31.

Mackie, V. (1997a) *Creating Socialist Women in Japan: Gender, Labour and Activism, 1900–1937*. Cambridge: Cambridge University Press.

Mackie, V. (1997b) Narratives of Struggle: Writing and the Making of Socialist Women in Japan. In Elise K. Tipton (Ed.) *Society and State in Interwar Japan* (pp. 126–145). London: Routledge.

Mackie, V. (1998a) Freedom and the Family: Gendering Meiji Political Thought. In D. Kelly and A. Reid (Eds.) *Asian Freedoms: The Idea of Freedom in East and Southeast Asia* (pp. 121–140). Cambridge: Cambridge University Press.

Mackie, V. (1998b). Dialogue, Distance and Difference: Feminism in Contemporary Japan. *Women's Studies International Forum*, 21 (6), 599–615.

Mackie, V. (2000a). The Dimensions of Citizenship in Modern Japan: Gender, Class, Ethnicity and Sexuality. In A. Vandenberg (Ed.) *Democracy and Citizenship in a Global Era* (pp. 245–257). London: Macmillan.

Mackie, V. (2000b). Sexual Violence, Silence, and Human Rights Discourse: The Emergence of the Military Prostitution Issue. In A. M. Hilsdon, M. Macintyre, V. Mackie and M. Stivens (Eds) *Human Rights and Gender Politics: Asia–Pacific Perspectives* (pp. 37–59). London: Routledge.

Mackie, V. (2001). The Language of Globalization, Transnationality and Feminism. *International Feminist Journal of Politics*, 3 (2), 180–206.

Mackie, V. (2002a). Embodiment, Citizenship and Social Policy in Contemporary Japan. In R. Goodman (Ed.) *Family and Social Policy in Japan* (pp. 245–257). Cambridge: Cambridge University Press.

Mackie, V. (2002b). Women Questioning the Present: The Jûgoshi Nôto Collective. In J. Brown and S. Arntzen (Eds.) *Across Time and Genre: Women's Writing in Japan* (pp. 144–148). Edmonton: University of Alberta Press.

Mackie, V. (2002c). 'Asia' in Everyday Life: Dealing with Difference in Contemporary Japan. In B. S. A. Yeoh, P. Teo and S. Huang (Eds.) *Gender and Politics in the Asia Pacific: Agencies and Activisms* (pp. 181–202). London: Routledge.

Mackie, V. (2003). *Feminism in Modern Japan: Citizenship, Embodiment and Sexuality*. Cambridge: Cambridge University Press.

Mackie, V. (2004). Shifting the Axis: Feminism and the Transnational Imaginary. In B. S. A. Yeoh and K. Willis (Eds.) *State/Nation/Transnation* (pp. 239–256). London: Routledge.

Mackie, V. (2005a). Japan. In B. Caine, A. Curthoys and M. Spongberg (Eds.) *Companion to Women's Historical Writing* (pp. 240–248). London: Palgrave.

Mackie, V. (2005b). In Search of Innocence: Feminist Historians Debate the Legacy of Wartime Japan. *Australian Feminist Studies*, 20 (47), July, 207–217.

Mackie, V. (2007) The Transformation of the Gendered Discourse of Rights in Post-War Japan. In H. Scheiber and L. Mayali (Eds.) *Emerging Concepts of Rights in Japanese Law* (pp. 49–72). Berkeley: The Robbins Collection.

Mackie, V. (2009) Family Law and its Others. In H. Scheiber and L. Mayali (Eds.) *Japanese Family Law in Comparative Perspective* (pp. 139–163). Berkeley: The Robbins Collection.

Mackie, V. (2010). Gendering the 1960s: Competing Masculinities and Femininities. In F. Toshiaki and T. Hideto (Eds.) *Hanransuru Wakamonotachi: 1960 nendai Ikô no Undô, Bunka* [Young People in Revolt: Movements and Culture after the 1960s] (pp. 55–62). Nagoya: Nagoya University Research Center for Modern and Contemporary Japanese Culture.

Mackie, V. (2011). Embodied Memories, Emotional Geographies: Nakamoto Takako's Diary of the Anpo Struggle. *Japanese Studies*, 31(3), December, 319–331.

Mackie, V. (2012). The Modern Girl: Icon of Modernity. In K. H. Brown (Ed.) *Deco Japan: Shaping Art and Culture, 1920–1943* (pp. 53–57). Washington DC: Art Services International.

Mackie. V. (2013a). Four Women, Four Incidents: Gender, Activism and Martyrdom in Modern Japan. In M. Gavin and B. Middleton (Eds.) *Japan and the High Treason Incident* (pp. 103–114). London: Routledge.

Mackie, V. (2013b). Sweat, Perfume and Tobacco: The Ambivalent Labor of the Dance Hall Girl. In A. Freedman, L. Miller and C. Yano (Eds.) *Modern Girls on the Go: Gender, Mobility and Labor in Japan* (pp. 67–82). Stanford: Stanford University Press.

Mackie, V. (2013c). Gender and Modernity in Japan's 'Long Twentieth Century'. *Journal of Women's History*, 25 (3), Fall, 62–91.

Mackie, V. (2013d). Feminism and the Nation-State in Japan. *Electronic Journal of Contemporary Japanese Studies*, 12 (3). Retrieved on 10 July 2014 from www.japanesestudies.org.uk/ejcjs/vol12/iss3/mackie.html.

Mackie, V. (2013e). New Women, Modern Girls and the Shifting Semiotics of Gender in Early Twentieth Century Japan. *Intersections: Gender and Sexuality in Asia and the Pacific*, 32, July. Retrieved on 10

July 2014 from www.intersections.anu.edu.au/issue32/mackie_review_article.htm.

Mackie, V., Okano, K. and Rawstron, K. (2014) Japan: Progress towards Diversity and Equality in Employment. In A. Klarsfeld, Booysen, L.A.E, Ng, E., Roper, I. and Talti, A. (Eds.) *International Handbook on Diversity Management at Work*, second edition (pp. 137–161). Cheltenham: Edward Elgar.

Mackie, V. and Tanji, M. (2014) Militarised Sexualities in East Asia. In M. McLelland and V. Mackie (Eds.) *The Routledge Handbook of Sexuality Studies in East Asia* (pp. 60–73). London: Routledge.

Mae, M. (2014) The Nexus of Nation, Culture and Gender in Modern Japan: The Resistance of Kanno Sugako and Kaneko Fumiko. In A. Germer, V. Mackie and U. Wöhr (Eds.) *Gender, Nation and State in Modern Japan* (pp. 68–84). London: Routledge.

Maree, C. (2007). The Un/State of Lesbian Studies in Japan. *Journal of Lesbian Studies,* 11 (3–4), 291–301.

Maree, C. (2014). Queer Women's Culture and History in Japan. In M. McLelland and V. Mackie (Eds.) *The Routledge Handbook of Sexuality Studies in East Asia* (pp. 230–243). London: Routledge.

Marotti, W. (2009). Japan 1968: The Performance of Violence and the Theatre of Protest. *American Historical Review*, February, 97–135.

Marran, C. L. (2007). Poison Woman: Figuring Female Transgression in Modern Japanese Culture, Minneapolis: University of Minnesota Press.

Maruoka, H. and Yamaguchi M. (Eds.) (1976–1980) *Nihon Fujin Mondai Shiryô Shûsei* [Collection of Documents on the Woman Question in Japan], ten volumes. Tokyo: Domesu Shuppan.

Matsui, Y. (1998). *Women in the New Asia: From Pain to Power.* Translated by N. Toyokawa and C. Francis. Melbourne: Spinifex Press.

Matsui, Y. (1989) *Women's Asia*. London: Zed Books.

McLelland, M., Suganuma, K. and Welker, J. (2007). Queer Voices from Japan: Narratives from Japan's Sexual Minorities. Lanham: Rowman and Littlefield.

Miyake, Y. (1991) Doubling Expectations: Motherhood and Women's Factory Work under State Management in Japan in the 1930s and 1940s. In G. L. Bernstein (Ed.) *Recreating Japanese Women, 1600–1945* (pp. 267–295). Berkeley: University of California Press.

Miyamoto, K. (1975). Itô Noe and the Bluestockings. *Japan Interpreter*, 10 (2), Autumn, 190–204.

Mizoguchi, A., Saeki, Y. and Miki, S. (Eds.) (1992–1995). *Shiryô: Nihon Ûman Ribu Shi* [Document Collection on the History of Women's Liberation in Japan]. Kyoto: Shôkadô, three volumes.

Modern Girl Around the World Research Group (Eds.) (2008). *The Modern Girl Around the World: Consumption, Modernity and Globalization*. Durham NC: Duke University Press.

Molony, B. (2005a). The Quest for Women's Rights in Turn-of-the-Century Japan. In B. Molony and K. Uno (Eds.) *Gendering Modern Japanese History* (pp. 463–492). Cambridge MA: Harvard University Asia Center.

Molony, B. (2005b). Ichikawa Fusae and Japan's Prewar Women's Suffrage Movement. In G. Daniels and H. Tomida (Eds.) *Women in Japanese History* (pp. 57–94). London: Global Oriental Publishers.

Molony, B. (2010). Crossing Boundaries: Transnational Feminisms in Twentieth-Century Japan. In M. Roces and L. Edwards (Eds.) *Women's Movements in Asia: Feminism and Transnational Activism* (pp. 90–109). London: Routledge.

Molony, B. (2011). From "Mothers of Humanity" to "Assisting the Emperor": Gendered Belonging in the Wartime Rhetoric of Japanese Feminist Ichikawa Fusae. *Pacific Historical Review*, 80 (1) (February) 1–27.

Morita, K. (2005). Activities of the Japanese Patriotic Ladies Association. In M. Mikula (Ed.) *Women, Activism and Social Change* (pp. 49–70). London: Routledge.

Murase, M. (2006). *Cooperation over Conflict: The Women's Movement and the State in Postwar Japan*. New York: Routledge.

Murray, P. (1975). Ichikawa Fusae and the Lonely Red Carpet. *Japan Interpreter,* 10 (2), Autumn: 171–189.

Narita, R. (1998). Women in the Motherland: Oku Mumeo through Wartime and Postwar. In Y. Yamanouchi, J. V. Koschmann and R. Narita (Eds.) *Total War and "Modernization"* (pp. 173–94). Ithaca NY: East Asia Program, Cornell University.

O'Herne, J. R. (1994). *Fifty Years of Silence*. Sydney: Editions Tom Thompson.

Otsubo, S. (2005). Engendering Eugenics: Feminists and Marriage Restriction Legislation in the 1920s. In B. Molony and K. Uno (Eds.) *Gendering Modern Japanese History* (pp. 225–256). Cambridge MA: Harvard University Asia Center.

Paisley, F. (2009). *Glamour in the Pacific: Cultural Internationalism and Race Politics in the Women's Pan-Pacific.* Honolulu HI: University of Hawai'i Press.

Patessio, M. (2004). Women's Participation in the Popular Rights Movement (Jiyû Minken Undô) during the Early Meiji Period. *US-Japan Women's Journal*, 27, 1–26.

Patessio, M. (2006). The Creation of Public Spaces by Women in the Early Meiji Period and the Tokyo Fujin Kyôfûkai. *International Journal of Asian Studies*, 3 (2), 155–182.

Patessio, M. (2011). *Women and Public Life in Early Meiji Japan: The Development of the Feminist Movement*. Ann Arbor MI: Center for Japanese Studies, University of Michigan.

Patessio, M. (2013a) Opportunities and Constraints for Late Meiji Women: The Cases of Hasegawa Kitako and Hasegawa Shigure. *US-Japan Women's Journal*, 44 (September), 93–118.

Patessio, M. (2013b) Women Getting a 'University' Education in Japan: Discourses, Realities and Individual Lives. *Japan Forum*, 25 (4), 556–581.

Pharr, S. J. (1987). The Politics of Women's Rights. In R. Ward and Y. Sakamoto (Eds.) *Democratizing Japan: The Allied Occupation* (pp. 221–52). Honolulu HI: University of Hawai'i Press.

Pharr, S. J. (1981). *Political Women in Japan: The Search for a Place in Political Life*. Berkeley CA: University of California Press.

Raddeker, H. B. (1997). *Patriarchal Fictions, Patricidal Fantasies: Treacherous Women of Imperial Japan*. London: Routledge.

Raddeker, H. B. (2002). Resistance to Difference: Sexual Equality and its Law-ful and Out-law (Anarchist) Advocates in Imperial Japan. *Intersections: Gender, History and Culture in the Asian Context*, 7. Retrieved on 1 June 2011 from www.intersections. anu.edu.au/issue7/raddeker.html.

Raddeker, H. B. (2013). A Woman of Ill Fame: Reconfiguring the Historical Reputation and Legacy of Kanno Suga. In M. Gavin and B. Middleton (Eds.) *Japan and the High Treason Incident* (pp. 91–102). London: Routledge.

Reich, P. and Fukuda, A. (1976). Japan's Literary Feminists: The Seitô Group. *Signs*, 2 (1), Autumn: 280–291.

Robertson, J. (2005). Biopower: Blood, Kinship and Eugenic Marriage. In J. Robertson (Ed.) *A Companion to the Anthropology of Japan* (pp. 329–354). Oxford: Blackwell.

Rodd, L. R. (1991). Yosano Akiko and the Taishô Debate over the "New Woman". In G. L. Bernstein (Ed.) *Recreating Japanese Women* (pp. 175–198). Berkeley CA: University of California Press.

Rose, B. (1992). *Tsuda Umeko and Women's Education in Japan*. New Haven CT: Yale University Press.

Rowley, G. (2000). *Yosano Akiko and the Tale of Genji*. Ann Arbor MI: Center for Japanese Studies, University of Michigan.

Ryang, S. (1998a). Love and Colonialism in Takamure Itsue's Feminism: A Postcolonial Critique. *Feminist Review*, 60, 1–32.

Ryang, S. (1998b). Inscribed (Men's) Bodies, Silenced (Women's) Words: Rethinking Colonial Displacement of Koreans in Japan. *Bulletin of Concerned Asian Scholars*, 30 (4), 3–15.

Sato, B. H. (1993). The Moga Sensation: Perceptions of the Modan Gâru in Japanese Intellectual Circles during the 1920s. *Gender and History*, 5 (3), Autumn, 363–381.

Sato, B. (2003). *The New Japanese Woman: Modernity, Media and Women in Interwar Japan*. Durham: Duke University Press.

Schaffer, K. and Smith S. (2004). *Human Rights and Narrated Lives: The Ethics of Recognition*. New York: Palgrave Macmillan.

Schellstede, S. C. (Ed.) (2000). *Comfort Women Speak: Testimony by Sex Slaves of the Japanese Military*. New York and London: Holmes and Meier.

Shapcott, J. (1987). The Red Chrysanthemum: Yamakawa Kikue and the Socialist Women's Movement in Pre-War Japan. *Papers on Far Eastern History*, 35, 1–30.

Shibahara, T. (2011) 'The Private League of Nations': The Pan-Pacific Women's Conference and Japanese Feminists in 1928. *US-Japan Women's Journal*, 41 (December), 3–24.

Shibahara, T. (2014) *Japanese Women and the Transnational Feminist Movement Before World War II*, Philadelphia: Temple University Press.

Shigematsu, S. (2005). Feminism and the Media in the Late Twentieth Century: Reading the Limits of a Politics of Transgression. In B. Molony and K. Uno (Eds.) *Gendering Modern Japanese History* (pp. 555–589). Cambridge MA: Harvard University Asia Center.

Shigematsu, S. (2011). The Japanese Women's Movement and the United Red Army: A Radical Feminist Response to Political Violence. *Feminist Media Studies*, 12 (2), 163–179.

Shigematsu, S. (2012). *Scream from the Shadows: The Women's Liberation Movement in Japan*. Minneapolis MN: University of Minnesota Press.

Shigematsu, S. (2014). The Women's Liberation Movement and Sexuality in Japan. In M. McLelland and V. Mackie (Eds.) *The Routledge Handbook of Sexuality Studies in East Asia* (pp. 174–187). London: Routledge.

Sievers, S. (1983). *Flowers in Salt: The Beginnings of Feminist Consciousness in Meiji Japan*. Stanford CA: Stanford University Press.

Silverberg, M. (1991). The Modern Girl as Militant. In G. L. Bernstein (Ed.) *Recreating Japanese Women* (pp. 239–66). Berkeley CA: University of California Press.

Silverberg, M. (2006) *Erotic Grotesque Nonsense: The Mass Culture of Japanese Modern Times*. Berkeley: University of California Press.

Slater, D. (2011). Fukushima Women against Nuclear Power: Finding a Voice from Tohoku. *Japan Focus*. Retrieved on 13 April 2012 from www.japanfocus. org/events/view/117.

Soh, S. C. H. (2008). *The Comfort Women: Sexual Violence and Postcolonial Memory in Korea and Japan*. Chicago: University of Chicago Press.

Steinhoff, P. (1996). Three Women who Loved the Left: Radical Women Leaders in the Japanese Red Army Movement. In E. A. Imamura (Ed.) *Re-Imaging Japanese Women* (pp. 301–324). Berkeley CA: University of California Press.

Suzuki, Mamiko (2009). Between the Public Persona and the Private Narrator: The Open Space of Kishida Toshiko's Diaries. *US-Japan Women's Journal*, 35, April.

Suzuki, Michiko (2009). *Becoming Modern Women: Love and Female Identity in Prewar Japanese*

Literature and Culture. Stanford: Stanford University Press.

Suzuki Y. (Ed.) (1998). *Nihon Josei Undô Shiryô Shûsei* [Collection of Documents on the Women's Movement in Japan], ten volumes. Tokyo: Fuji Shuppan.

Takahashi, Y. (2013) Recent Collaborative Endeavours by Historians of Women and Gender in Japan. *Journal of Women's History,* 25 (4), 244–254.

Takao, Y. (2007). Japanese Women in Grassroots Politics: Building a Gender-Equal Society from the Bottom up. *The Pacific Review,* 20, 147–172.

Tanaka, K. (1974). *A Short History of the Women's Movement in Modern Japan.* Tokyo: Femintern Press.

Tanaka, K. (1994). The New Feminist Movement in Japan, 1970–1990. In K. Fujimura-Fanselow and A. Kameda (Eds.) *Japanese Women: New Feminist Perspectives on the Past, Present, and Future* (pp. 343–352). New York: The Feminist Press.

Tanaka, Yuki (2002). *Japan's Comfort Women: Sexual Slavery and Prostitution during World War II and the US Occupation.* London: Routledge.

Tanaka, Yukiko (1995). *Contemporary Portraits of Japanese Women.* Westport CT: Praeger.

Tomida, H. (2004). *Hiratsuka Raichô and Early Japanese Feminism.* Leiden: Brill.

Tsurumi, E. P. (1985). Feminism and Anarchism in Japan: Takamure Itsue, 1894–1964. *Bulletin of Concerned Asian Scholars,* 17 (2): 2–19.

Tsurumi, E. P. (1996). The Accidental Historian: Yamakawa Kikue. *Gender and History,* 8, (2), 258–276.

Tsurumi, E. P. (1998). Visions of Women and the New Society in Conflict: Yamakawa Kikue versus Takamure Itsue. In S. Minichiello (Ed.) *Japan's Competing Modernities,* (pp. 335–57), Honolulu: Hawaii University Press.

Ueno, C. (2004). *Nationalism and Gender.* Translated by B. Yamamoto. Melbourne: Trans Pacific Press.

Ueno, C. and Sand, J. (1999). The Politics of Memory: Nation, Individual and Self. *History and Memory,* 11 (2), 129–152.

Ueno, C. (1998). *Jendâ to Nashonarizumu* [Gender and Nationalism]. Tokyo: Seidosha.

Ushioda, S. C. (1977). Women and War in Meiji Japan: The Case of Fukuda Hideko. *Peace and Change,* 4 (3), October, 9–12.

Vavich, D. A. (1967). The Japanese Woman's Movement: Ichikawa Fusae, A Pioneer in Woman's Suffrage. *Monumenta Nipponica,* 22 (3/4), 402–436.

Wilson, S. (1995). Mobilizing Women in Inter-War Japan: The National Defence Women's Association and the Manchurian Crisis. *Gender and History,* 7 (2), 295–314.

Wöhr, U. (2004). A Touchstone for Transnational Feminism: Discourses on the Comfort Women in 1990s Japan. *Japanstudien,* 16, 59–90.

Wöhr, U. (2011) 'Datsu-genpatsu' no tayōsei to seijisei o kashika suru: Jendā, sekushuariti, esunishiti no shiten kara [Making Visible the Diversity and the Politics of the Movement Against Nuclear Power: From the Perspectives of Gender, Sexuality, and Ethnicity]. In K. Takao, (Ed.) *Shinsai to watashi* [The Disaster and Me] (pp. 80–94). Hiroshima: Hiroshima joseigaku kenkyūjo.

Yamakawa, K. (2001) *Women of the Mito Domain: Recollections of Samurai Family Life.* Translated by K. W. Nakai. Stanford CA: Stanford University Press.

Yamamoto, M. (2004). *Grassroots Pacifism in Postwar Japan: The Rebirth of a Nation.* London: RoutledgeCurzon.

Yamazaki, H. (1996). Military Sexual Slavery and the Women's Movement. In AMPO: Japan-Asia Quarterly Review (Eds.) *Voices from the Japanese Women's Movement* (pp. 90–100). New York: M. E. Sharpe.

Yamazaki, T. (1985). *The Story of Yamada Waka: From Prostitute to Feminist Pioneer.* Translated by W. Hironaka and A. Kostant. Tokyo: Kodansha International.

Yasutake, R. (2004). *Transnational Women's Activism: The United States, Japan and Japanese Immigrant Communities in California, 1859–1920.* New York: NYU Press.

Yosano, A. (2001). *Travels in Manchuria and Mongolia.* Translated by J. Fogel. New York: Columbia University Press.

Yoshimi, Y. (2000). *Comfort Women: Sexual Slavery in the Japanese Military during World War II.* Translated by Suzanne O'Brien. New York: Columbia University Press.

10

'How to Sex'? The Contested Nature of Sexuality in Japan

Mark McLelland

INTRODUCTION

There has been a tendency in English and other European-language reporting on Japan to stress the strangeness and otherness of Japanese values, particularly in regard to sexuality. Reports of Japanese immorality go back as far as the sixteenth century when the first Jesuit visitors to the country were appalled by open displays of cross-dressing and male-male sexual relations (Cooper, 1995). After the 'opening' of Japan in the mid nineteenth century Victorian visitors were alternately intrigued and shocked by the government-regulated prostitution that took place in Japan's many pleasure quarters. Commentators have noted how the figure of the geisha, in particular (albeit geisha do not necessarily perform sexual roles), has been much fetishised across the last century by Western observers (Allison, 2000).

It is this long-standing genre of writing that Michel Foucault drew upon when, in his *History of Sexuality* volume 1, he identified Japan, along-side China, as civilisations that had supposedly developed *ars erotica*, that is, arts of eroticism that prioritised pleasure over reproduction. Foucault notes that in this art 'pleasure is not considered in relation to an absolute law of the permitted and the forbidden, nor by reference to a criterion of utility, but first and foremost in relation to itself'

(1990: 57–58). In his *History* Foucault famously contrasts the *ars erotica* supposedly prevalent in the East with the *scientia sexualis* characteristic of the Christian West, that is, a 'science' of sexuality that attempts to unlock the 'truth' of sex through a thoroughgoing analysis of its 'nature'. In the Western tradition sex supposedly reveals itself as 'a domain susceptible to pathological processes, and hence one calling for therapeutic or normalising interventions' (Foucault, 1990: 68).

Although in later discussions Foucault was to step back from the starkness of this proposed division between Western and Eastern approaches to sexuality, in the case of Western reporting on Japan it is still very much the case that the focus is on Japanese libidinal excess, perversity and strangeness. Whether the focus is on the supposed immorality of Japanese schoolgirls engaging in 'compensated dating' (*Newsweek*, 1996; *Time*, 1999) or the all-round perversity and danger of Japan's highly sexualised manga and anime culture (McGinty, 2002) Japanese sexuality is framed as distinctly 'other' to a supposedly more rational, disciplined and 'normal' form of sexuality characteristic of the West. A classic exemplar of this genre is *Atlantic Monthly* journalist James Fallows' report, tellingly entitled 'The Japanese Are Different from You and Me', where he points to 'the prominence of pornography in everyday life', going on to make the absurd claim that '[a] director can shoot an act of sodomy or rape for a TV drama at the dinner hour with impunity' (Fallows, 1986: 38).

The problem with such reports, apart from the hyperbole, is that they homogenise 'the Japanese' and supposed 'Japanese' attitudes to sexuality which are in fact complex, diverse and highly divisive. Issues to do with sexuality play out in Japanese culture in complicated and unpredictable ways and are riven by competing truth claims and investments. As Huiyan Fu has pointed out, there exists a 'blatant contradiction between formal and informal sectors' regarding the 'understanding of sexuality and gender in Japan' (2011: 904). 'Official' discourses of sexuality in Japan are, and since the Meiji period have always been, rather moralistic. Indeed, despite sensationalistic claims in the English-language press, detailed depictions of real-person pornography are highly restricted in Japan. Due to strict adherence to censorship codes there are no images that clearly depict genitalia in any of the print or video pornography available through licensed channels (albeit such images are easily accessed via the internet). Although depictions of real-person sex acts are available in a wide range of outlets, the offending portions are always pixelated. In fact, until the early 1990s the showing of public hair even in non-sexual contexts was also censored. It is true, however, that the censorship laws are interpreted very literally and narrowly, meaning that as long as no genitalia or public hair are visible, scenarios liable to cause offense, such as violence or scatology, are permissible in both real-person and fictional pornography.

Hence although Japanese popular culture can contain many representations of potentially offensive sexual acts and scenarios that would be more tightly controlled in some Western contexts, official discourses of sexuality as promoted by government agents are much more restrictive. Indeed, since at least the middle of the Meiji period official bureaucratic pronouncements about sex have been characterised by what Foucault terms 'governmentality', and remain so today. That is, in Japan official discourse about sex has functioned in much the same manner as it has in Western contexts. In both imperial and post-war Japan sex has been 'used as a point of anchorage for a whole variety of concerns: disciplining, governing and surveying a population; securing sovereignty of a territory; [and] maintaining the productivity of the nation through the regulation of reproduction and bodily economy' (Rocha, 2011: 329). In particular, as Frühstück points out, sexuality in Japan has been constructed 'as a set of problems related to the necessity of protecting and defending girls and women from men, the populace from certain diseases, and the normal from the pathological' (2003: 16).

Yet there has also been a great deal of resistance to these forms of governmentality at the popular level. The Japanese media, in particular, have supported a wide range of sexual subcultures and representations, despite the use of national obscenity laws and a range of local ordinances aimed at reigning in this sexual expressiveness. This chapter provides a historical overview of 'official' government paradigms for shaping and understanding sexuality alongside more popular discourses that have frequently parodied, contested and undermined these top-down directives.

HISTORICAL BACKGROUND

The organisation of sexuality during Japan's period of imperial expansion dating from the beginning of the Meiji Period (1868–1912) and ending with defeat at the hands of the Allied powers in 1945 has been extensively studied by Japanese and Western researchers (Driscoll, 2010; Frühstück, 2003; Yokota-Muarakami, 1998). Prior to the re-establishment of imperial rule Japan had been divided into a number of powerful fiefdoms under the control of the Tokugawa shoguns based in Edo (present-day Tokyo). During this time there were many regional differences in the organisation of marriage and family life as well as splits between city and rural attitudes to sex.

Folk religion, strong in agricultural areas, was very much preoccupied with fertility, and peasant attitudes toward sexuality were quite distinct from the more austere Buddhist and Confucian ideals that guided the social elites. Oral histories collected by ethnologist Akamatsu Keisuke (2004) suggest that the poor rural farmers who comprised the vast majority of the population had relatively loose attitudes regarding premarital sex and monogamy. Up until the late Meiji period the practice of *yobai*, or 'night crawling', was a feature of village life in some regions where local bachelors would visit eligible young women in their homes at night, often with the knowledge and collusion of the parents. Marriage was often not contracted until pregnancy ensued. Sexual license seems to have been permissible at other times, too, including during the fertility festivals associated with the spring and autumn equinoxes when older women would initiate the young village men who had recently come of age into sexual intercourse. Akamatsu speculates that these practices may have dated back to the warring states period (mid fifteenth through the beginning of the seventeenth centuries) when young farmers were conscripted into the militia, resulting in widespread loss of life and a shortage of menfolk.

Attitudes toward sexuality were also riven with distinctions according to feudal status groups, the ruling samurai, under neo-Confucian influence, being the most constrained. Townspeople, by contrast, supported a lively popular culture that portrayed less restrained attitudes to sexuality, including celebrations of eroticism in the pleasure quarters, on stage and in literature and art. So called 'pillow books' and collections of 'spring pictures' offered instruction in sexual acts that included self-pleasure, and both male and female same-sex eroticism as well as heterosexual acts. Despite the plurality of scenarios depicted in popular culture sexuality at the time was overwhelmingly understood from a masculinist perspective, there being two contrasting 'ways' for a man to enjoy sexual pleasure: *nanshoku* (eroticism with men) and *joshoku* (eroticism with women). These two ways were not contradictory since the sexually sophisticated *iro otoko* (amorous man) was able to express his desire both with crossdressing actors associated with the kabuki theatre and female courtesans from the licensed pleasure quarters (McLelland, 2005: 16–18).

However, the fact that this erotic culture was largely produced and sustained by the merchant class (officially, the lowest rung on the Edo-period hierarchy) often led to conflict with the more austere culture of the samurai governors. It has been estimated that almost half of the woodblock prints produced in the seventeenth century featured erotica and from the 1720s on numerous injunctions came from the shogunate aimed at reining in erotic prints and other 'dubious materials' (Thompson, 2012: 56). The frequency with which these edicts had to be reissued by the authorities shows that they were never successful in stamping out the erotic-picture trade, in part because Japan's feudal political structure meant that there was no single national authority that could enforce censorship across the entire country. The final set of anti-erotica edicts promulgated by the Tokugawa shogunate were part of the Tempo reforms of the 1840s, just prior to the 1868 Meiji Restoration. The Meiji regime established a much more comprehensive and rigorous censorship system that meant that all Edo-period erotic classics went out of print or were only allowed to be reissued in bowdlerised versions (Suzuki, 2012). Indeed, as Anne Walthall has pointed out, Edo-period instruction on a range of sexual pleasures represents a 'historical dead end' as from the Meiji-period on this knowledge was largely forgotten (Walthall, 2009: 8).

Japan's opening to the West occurred at the same time as a 'science' of sexuality was being devised by European medical specialists who, building on long-standing religious prejudices encoded in law, pathologised non-marital and non-procreative sexual acts. Japan's first generation of Western-trained doctors were exposed to these new ways of thinking about sexuality and brought these perspectives back to Japan. These included Mori gai (1862–1922) whose 1909 novel *Vita Sexualis* was one of the first in the Japanese language to make the analysis of the 'sexuality' of the protagonist central to the narrative (Yokota-Murakami, 1998: 119–21).

From the late nineteenth century on a new emphasis on the regulation of the household became part of the state's attempt to manage and improve the Japanese population. The developing field of sexology was key to this attempt as it provided 'scientific' justification for the pathologisation of non-procreative sexual acts such as masturbation, prostitution and same-sex sexuality that had not been singled out under the previous regime. From the end of the Meiji period a range of press reports by a new class of sexual experts defined all expressions of non-marital sexuality as 'harmful', particularly those captured by the term *hentai seiyoku* (perverse sexual desires).

These changes occurred at a time when the Meiji state was embarking on a process of nation building, which demolished the old feudal system and attempted to centralise governance of the population. The 1872 Family Registration Law (*kōseki hō*) was a key measure that sought to organise, rationalise and control all aspects of the population from early education through to marriage and child rearing by ensuring all people were registered as belonging to a patriarchal family lineage. Part of this ongoing process was the establishment of the 1898 Civil Code, which did away with rural and class-based ways of organising marriage and family life. This new value system aimed at disciplining and controlling the sexual expression of the masses was in part rolled out through the education system and by the 1930s had been largely successful. Ethnographer Emma Wiswell, who was studying rural Japanese life at the time, noted a marked gap between conservative village youth and the more liberal attitudes of their parents. She pointed out that 'Far from denouncing the youth of the time for their loose sexual morals, their elders found them positively conservative when compared with themselves when young' (cited in Smith, 1983: 77).

Not all sexologists were on message about the deleterious effects of non-marital expressions of sexuality. One influential example was politician and biologist Yamamoto Senji (1889–1929), who was an early pioneer of sex education. Among his findings were that prostitutes made up the majority of sexual partners among the student elite, including at Tokyo University (Yamamoto, 1994: 41). Another research finding revealed the near ubiquity of masturbation among university students, suggesting that it could not be such a deleterious practice if it was so common among the future elite. Yamamoto was among the first generation of Japanese thinkers to attempt to use the status of scientific inquiry to wrest control of discourse about sexuality away from the moralists who used obscenity legislation to restrict the circulation of sexual knowledge in the pre-war period.

The prohibition of 'obscene' (*waisetsu*) publications dates back to the 1907 Criminal Code and according to Anne Allison represents the development in Japan of 'a notion of the public as a terrain that is monitored and administered by the state' (2000: 163). However, the lack of a definition of what constituted obscenity meant that any discussion about sex, particularly anything that contradicted official discourses and policies, could potentially cause trouble. As Sabine Frühstück points out, at this time 'knowledge about sex... was considered dangerous to produce, possess, and spread' (2003: 5). Frühstück notes how the authorities tended to lump sexologists in with other problem thinkers such as communists and pacifists (2003: 13). Indeed, in the 1920s Yamamoto was often pulled from the stage by the police when giving lectures in the provinces for supposedly speaking positively of masturbation and abortion (Frühstück, 2003: 14) and was eventually assassinated by a fanatic in 1929 in retribution for speaking out against escalating Japanese aggression in China. From this point onward as the power of the Japanese military over civilian affairs increased it became more difficult to speak openly about sexual issues outside of officially sanctioned paradigms of marital reproduction.

The developing discourse of sexual abstinence for the unmarried was, however, highly gendered, as it was women in particular who were expected to remain chaste (Shibuya, 2003). Ryang (2006) argues that the Japanese state, through institutionalizing the monogamous conjugal couple as reproductive unit while at the same time endorsing a wide range of extra-marital commercial sexual options for men, produced a bifurcation of love and sex – and by extension types of women. Marriage and reproduction were the exclusive provenance of 'girls from good families' whereas poor women or women from the colonies were available for recreational sex with men for a fee. Women from the middle and upper classes were considered destined to lead lives as 'good wives, wise mothers' and their sex lives were expected to be contained completely in the context of marriage. This was reinforced by the legal code, with adultery on the part of wives always being classed as a criminal act whereas for men adultery was only illegal if it involved another man's wife (Steiner, 1950).

Men, on the other hand, on account of their supposedly stronger sex drive, were still able to avail themselves of a number of sexual outlets including licensed prostitution. Indeed, the results of a survey into the sex lives of 1000 male students published in 1923 revealed that over half had their first sexual experience with a prostitute (Frühstück, 2003: 90). Other surveys into the first sexual experiences of men who came of age before or during the war indicate that it was common for them to receive sex instruction in the pleasure quarters (Dai ni ji

shin seikatsu kenkyūkai, 1982; Yamamoto, 1997). The 'hydraulic' model of male sexuality was prevalent at the time, assuming that if men were prevented from expressing themselves sexually blockages might ensue that would be deleterious to their capacity to perform as workers and soldiers. Hence, as the militarisation of Japanese society proceeded in the 1930s, poor Japanese women and women from Japan's colonies known as 'comfort women' were either recruited or coerced into providing sexual services for the increasing numbers of young men drafted into the military (Suzuki, 2001). Girls on the other hand, especially those from 'good families', had very restricted access to information about sexuality, leading to a number of misconceptions, including the idea that kissing led to pregnancy. Although there were attempts in the 1920s to translate material from European languages regarding birth control and sex techniques, these were stymied by the authorities. For instance, a 1930 Japanese translation of Dutch gynaecologist Van de Velde's best-selling sex guide, *Ideal Marriage*, despite appearing in an expurgated version, was immediately placed on the list of banned books (Akita, 1994: 86).

Despite the fact that the authorities exercised a great deal of censorship over the popular media, emphasising in particular the sanctity of the patriarchal home (Driscoll, 2010: 183), the press reported on 'unusual' sexual activities, a genre that came to be known as *ero-guro* (erotic grotesque). As Greg Pflugfelder points out, the widespread interest shown in so-called perverse sexuality thus gave 'the impression not only that "perversion" was ubiquitous but that the connotations of the term were not entirely negative' (1999: 287). Through this genre Japanese readers were 'introduced to the new kinds of pleasures, passions, anxieties, and exhaustions elicited by modern capitalism in Japan's metropolitan sites' (Driscoll, 2010: 153). But by the early 1930s, as Japanese society was increasingly placed on a war footing, this kind of reporting came under official ire and by 1933, partly due to government control of paper supplies, *ero-guro* and other 'frivolous' print genres had largely disappeared from Japan's newsstands, giving way to more 'wholesome' fare. Media interest in sex was, however, to re-emerge rapidly in the months following Japan's defeat at the hands of the Allies in 1945.

THE OCCUPATION PERIOD (1945–52)

One of the first edicts of the new Allied authorities was to dismantle the previous regime's censorship system, which had placed strict limits on what could be spoken and written about, including sex. Historian of the Occupation era, John Dower, has described the resulting emergence of 'a commercial world dominated by sexually oriented entertainments and a veritable cascade of pulp literature' (1999: 148). The widespread popularity of 'pulp literature', or *kasutori* (literally, the dregs), was just one example of post-war Japanese people's rejection of the previous regime's exhortations to frugality and sacrifice.

The Occupation authorities also embarked on ambitious social reform aimed at dismantling the 'household system' and improving the rights of women at school, at home and in the workplace. Choice of marriage partner, which in the previous period had usually been arranged by the family through a go-between, was now to be a purely individual choice, and the popular press was full of reports on the implications of this new practice of 'free love' for the post-war 'new couple' (McLelland, 2012a). The pursuit of romance, which during the long war years had been downplayed as selfish, suddenly became a means for young people to demonstrate their rejection of wartime austerity and their embrace of new 'democratic' lifestyles (Takahashi, 1969: 273). Key to this new understanding of male-female equality was the notion that women, like men, also had sexual desires and sexual needs and that sexuality was something to be discussed and negotiated between partners. However, there was very little in print that offered sex advice.

Hence, when advertisements appeared in 1946 for orders of a proposed new and unexpurgated version of Van de Velde's classic marital guide, there was overwhelming interest, resulting in an expensive full translation being published under the title *Kanzen naru kekkon* (*Perfecting Marriage*) later that year. Six months later a rival shorter and much cheaper edited version aimed at the mass market entitled *Kanzen naru fūfu* (*Perfect Coupledom*) appeared, ensuring that the book became a best-seller. Even those who did not purchase the book could read discussion of its main principles throughout the press (McLelland, 2012a; Shimokawa, 2007: 25).

In many ways Van de Velde's text confirmed the attitudes toward sexuality that had been inculcated by the previous regime. He put forward the view that it was the male partner who experienced the stronger, more 'active' sex drive and that the male should be the one to take the initiative in the sex act. He also emphasised that the ultimate role and purpose of sex was procreation. His text thus refrained from discussing contraceptive measures and his long and detailed exposition of a variety of coital postures pointed out how each aided or detracted from the aim of achieving conception. As Dower notes, what did seem 'startling' to many readers at the time (1999: 164) was Van de Velde's insistence that women, like men, had sexual needs, that the sexual satisfaction (*sei manzoku*) of both

partners was key to a successful marriage and that couples should strive for simultaneous orgasm since it was at that point that the physical and spiritual sides of matrimony were united.

This radical idea caught on and was much debated in the *kasutori* press and in a series of other sex guides aimed at tutoring couples on how best to achieve this elusive goal. The most influential of these was the magazine *Fūfu seikatsu* (*Married Life*) published between 1949 and 1955, which at its peak sold between three-hundred and four-hundred thousand copies monthly. Ronald Dore, who was researching married life in Tokyo in the early 1950s, noted that one of the couples he surveyed subscribed to the magazine. He also mentions that among his informants, '*fūfu seikatsu* – the word translated married life – is one commonly heard and has primarily sexual connotations' (1999: 178).

The editors of the magazine were able to steer clear of the censors and charges of obscenity by restricting its discussions to marital sexuality – but since there were no limits on who could purchase the title it was able to reach a much broader audience. Van de Velde's *Perfecting Marriage* was the first sex manual to be published in Japan since the Edo period and his central tenet, that sex should be satisfying for both partners, was taken up and expanded upon endlessly in *Fūfu seikatsu* and similar magazines throughout the 1950s. However, these magazines continued to support a masculinist bias since sexual knowledge was generally promoted as something that men should learn in order to improve their performance with their female partners. Although there were some editorials and reports offering a 'female perspective', there were still few women writing on sexual topics.

Despite this new emphasis on the pleasures of sex discussed in the popular press, official pronouncements and directives from Japanese government agencies continued to stress the need for 'purity education' and reinforced the connection between sexuality and reproduction (Ryang, 2006: 68). In this way the Japanese authorities carried over prewar sentiments into the post-war period, especially via the provision of sex education.

SEX EDUCATION AND THE JAPANESE STATE

Since the end of the Second World War 'official' sex-education discourses promulgated by government agencies, continuing a trend established in the Meiji period, have emphasised 'purity' and 'chastity' in materials aimed at young people. What came to be termed 'purity education' was initially conceived by the Ministry for the Interior as a response to the massive expansion in Japan's sex industry following Japan's defeat and occupation by Allied troops (Tashiro, 2000). Japan had always had, and maintained until 1958, designated areas where sex work was legal and subject to government monitoring. What concerned the post-war authorities was the sudden increase in unregulated 'private prostitutes', who blurred the previously clear distinction between the 'professional' women of the brothel world and 'women in general'. Purity education was essentially conceived as a means of promoting 'wholesome thought', providing guidance on 'correct relations between men and women' and establishing 'sexual virtue'. Establishing 'correct' attitudes toward sexuality, in particular through linking sexuality to reproduction in the context of the monogamous nuclear family, was clearly articulated by architects of the purity-education policy as a key 'nation building' initiative in response to the social instability of the early post-war years (Tashiro, 2001: 87).

From 1947 onward the provision of purity education became an official policy of the Education Ministry. This was largely in response to the imposition by the Allied administration of co-education in Japan's middle and high schools and national universities. The old Confucian maxim that 'boys and girls should not sit together after age seven' was, in the new 'democratic' environment of the Occupation period, deemed 'feudal' by the Allies and the introduction of co-education required the development of a whole new etiquette of male-female relations in classrooms and on campuses across Japan.

This policy was elaborated on in a report released by the Education Ministry in 1949 entitled *Junketsu kyōiku kihon yōkō* (*Basic points concerning purity education*). As well as promoting 'correct, scientific knowledge about sex', the report emphasised the need for developing a 'cheerful environment' that encouraged young people to engage in 'healthy recreations', such as sports, religious activities and cultural pursuits (Tashiro, 2001: 87). In this and subsequent directives from the ministry, emphasis has been placed on the role a 'correct' or 'proper' sex life plays in the context of marriage as a means of producing children. 'Uncontrolled sex' outside of marriage was represented as both physically and morally dangerous, leading to the potential for disease and estrangement from family and society. Advice has tended to stress the role of parents, particularly mothers, in instilling a 'correct' attitude toward sex, one that established a firm connection between love, monogamy and child rearing. As Sonia Ryang notes, these materials make it clear that moral standards pertaining to sex are 'not to be set randomly by individual men and women, but by the state' (2006: 68).

However, despite the official rhetoric that speaks of 'correct' relationships between the sexes, as Sabine Frühstück has pointed out, purity education has always been 'primarily, if not explicitly, directed at girls' (2003: 180). Thus post-war developments in sex education have tended to reinforce the double standard pertaining to male and female sexuality characteristic of the pre-war period. The emphasis on safeguarding the sexuality of young girls from corruption was accentuated during the New Life Movement (*Shin Seikatsu Undō*) of the late 1940s and 1950s. This movement was 'a set of loosely connected initiatives of government ministries and women's organizations' aimed at rationalising Japanese households and improving family life (Gordon, 1997: 246). This discourse was highly gendered, focusing mainly on 'proper roles for women'. As Gordon notes, 'gender issues such as sex roles, reproduction and the definition of the "housewife" were never far from the center' of these debates (1997: 247). This reflects the shift from the pre-war model of the patriarchal household to a post-war model that emphasised the nuclear family with the wife/mother as household manager. However, the particular emphasis on sexual restraint *for women* is a clear continuation of pre-war trends.

The discourse of 'purity education' carried on until 1965 when the Education Ministry began to replace this ideologically laden term with more descriptive labels such as 'guidance in sexual matters' or simply 'sex education'. However, the explicit linkage between sex, marriage and procreation has been maintained in materials developed for schools with issues such as self-pleasure, contraception and alternative sexualities receiving little attention. As Fu notes, even today the sex education curriculum of Japanese schools is primarily geared toward 'sound and healthy societal maintenance' via the management of reproduction within the context of the conventional nuclear family (Fu, 2011: 903).

Directives from the Education Ministry have been concerned with the need for instilling proper 'etiquette' between the sexes through the establishment of healthy environments and wholesome activities on school campuses. Since sex was designated as part of the 'world of adults' emphasis has been placed on maintaining the 'natural pureness' of young people and avoiding circumstances that might result in precocious interest in sexual matters (Castro-Vasquez, 2007: 34). Hence there has never been an explicit *sex* education curriculum provided by the ministry nor until 1992 were there specially designated sex-education classes – teachers were expected to follow the general guidelines provided by the ministry and address relevant aspects of sexuality in the context of other classes such as biology, the social sciences and health and fitness.

The eventual introduction of classes specifically called 'sex education' in 1992 was the result of a number of factors including an increase in teen-age pregnancy, anxieties about HIV infection and concern over declining fertility rates. The last point reinforces Fu's argument that 'the state production of sex education policy has consistently focused on the control of both the quantity and the quality of the Japanese population' (2011: 906). This can be seen in the fact that even in the more detailed post-1992 sex-education curriculum, '"unproductive" individual-oriented functions of sex such as homosexuality and pleasure are either denied or silenced' (2011: 907).

However, these 'top down' directives aimed at promoting the 'healthy development' of youth by government ministers and teams of bureaucrats should not be overestimated. As Fu notes in rela-tion to sexuality education, '[t]here are also always competing truth claims and practices, which chal-lenge the statements of the ruling elite' (2011: 908), and a range of other voices have been competing to change the course of sex education in Japan. These include representatives of sexual-minority and feminist NPOs (non-profit organisations) con-cerned with issues of women's reproductive health, sex work and HIV (Hyōdō, 2008).

One of the most long-lived of these NPOs is the Japanese Association for Sex Education (JASE), first founded in 1972, which has produced holis-tic information about sexuality in materials made available to teachers. JASE has also played an important role researching actual sexual behav-iours, including six-yearly surveys of the sexual behaviours and attitudes of high-school and tertiary students since 1974. The most recent edition is the sixth survey released in 2007 as the *Wakamomo no sei hakusho* (*White paper on young people's sexuality*; Nihon Seikyōiku Kyōkai, 2007). JASE has pointed to a number of factors when arguing that Japan's sex-education policies need to be over-hauled. These include the increasingly young age at which Japanese children are entering puberty and teens begin to engage in sexual activity. Increased sexual activity is also resulting in a gradual rise in the incidence of sexually transmitted diseases and in the teenage abortion rate. Importantly, these sur-veys also indicate that a majority of young people get their information about sex from peers and the media, not from parents or school, suggesting that the official emphasis on abstinence and the reduc-tion of sex to reproduction has had little impact on young people's attitudes and behaviours.

SEX AND THE MEDIA IN JAPAN

As noted above, the relaxation of censorship regula-tions pertaining to sexual matters during the

Occupation period enabled an entire print industry aimed at sex instruction to flourish. Despite the sexually graphic detail that many of these instruc-tions contained, they were largely protected from police intervention because they discussed marital sexuality under a 'scientific' or at least medical paradigm. The Japanese government was, however, quite prepared to use obscenity legislation to move against representations of non-marital sexuality, as can be seen in the guilty verdict in the 1951 obscen-ity trial launched against the translator and publisher of D. H. Lawrence's *Lady Chatterley's Lover*. The defence lawyers pointed to the volume of graphic sexual descriptions from the popular press to prove that such sex talk was now consistent with commu-nity values. This did not persuade the prosecution, who argued that it was the *adulterous* nature of the sex acts described that rendered them obscene. As Cather notes, 'the prosecution was attempting to stop adultery in reality via a ban in representation' (2004: 32), and this is further evidence of how on an official level at least pre-war sensitivities were carried over into the post-war period.

However, discussion of another sexual topic that had been banned during the wartime regime – contraception – was enabled in the post-war period by a number of factors. Firstly, the repatriation to Japan of over five million Japanese nationals who had been fighting overseas or living and working in Japan's colonies led to economic and social distress as there was simply insufficient food and shelter, especially in the major cities that had been ravaged by bombing. Any new increase in the population therefore needed to be carefully man-aged. With this in mind an economic distress clause was included in the 1948 Eugenic Protection Act, which permitted abortion under certain cir-cumstances. Alongside loosening restrictions on abortion, family planning was also promoted as a means of securing a more affluent lifestyle.

In 1955 an international family-planning confer-ence was held in Tokyo and reports in the media about the event ensured that *kazoku keikaku* (family planning) became a household term, women's mag-azines in particular devoting considerable space to the issue. It was about this time that condom and prophylactic-jelly manufacturer Sanshii came up with the popular catchphrase '*Sukunaku unde yutakana kurashi: ichi hime ni tarō san sanshii*', which can be translated as 'Giving birth less [leads to] an affluent lifestyle: one – a girl, two – a boy, three – *sanshii* [contraceptives]', recommending that after a couple had produced the post-war stan-dard of two children it was time to stop (Nakagawa, 2001; Ishikawa, 1977: 114). An advertisement for Sanshii jelly in the February 1955 edition of popu-lar women's magazine *Shufu no tomo* (*Housewife's friend*) shows a boy and a girl, the older girl combing the younger boy's hair (it was thought best to have a girl first so that she could help care for younger siblings) testifying to the normalcy contraceptive advice had attained by this stage.

However, despite the fact that from the early post-war period family planning was endorsed by the government and popularised via the media contraceptive choice remained limited. The Japan Medical Association prevented the contraceptive pill from being legalised until 1999, officially due to anxieties about its long-term side effects, although the Association was criticised by some feminist groups for also trying to protect the lucrative medical trade in abortion.

The idea that sexuality was something that needed to be properly 'managed' was, of course, not new. *Fūfu seikatsu* had established a strong connection between sexuality, contraception and pleasure as part of its vision of sexuality as an aspect of relationship building for the post-war 'new couple'. This trend, however, accelerated during the 1960s and was spurred on by the success of a new marital sex guide: *Sei seikatsu no chie (Sex-life Wisdom)* published in 1960 by medical professor Sha Kokuken. Whereas previous sex guides had simply described how to perform sexual acts, Sha's book used artfully posed wooden dolls to demonstrate sexual positions (Ishikawa, 1977: 114). Since the book was ostensibly about marital sexuality, and contained detailed explanations on how conception was achieved, it was able to bypass the censors despite its graphic discussion of sexual acts.

In the mid 1960s a number of factors impacted upon the scale and discussion of sex in the Japanese media. From 1964 the volume of pornographic films made in Japan shot up considerably. Known as 'pink films', these were swiftly made on low budgets by a growing number of small-scale 'eroduction' companies, who screened their wares at businessmen's retreats and at cinemas in red-light districts. Although these early 1960s efforts were of low quality, from the early 1970s some mainstream film companies who were battling with falling revenues due to the impact of television on cinema audiences moved into eroduction. One company in particular, Nikkatsu, Japan's oldest surviving studio, developed a highly successful genre known as *roman poruno* (romantic porn), which had better production values and stronger story lines.

Japan's strict censorship laws prohibiting the showing of sex organs and even pubic hair forced the eroduction directors to be creative in their approach to the filming of sex scenes, creating more interesting stories and compelling characters than was usual for pornographic movies. Thus, although these movies were much softer than those being developed in Europe or the USA at the same time, the eroduction companies were successful in bringing sex to the big screen in a new way in Japan. Many of these titles, including the

one largely credited with launching the genre, the 1971 *Danchizuma hirusagari no jōji (Apartment Wife: Affair in the Afternoon)*, featured sexually unfulfilled women in search of greater eroticism and stimulation. Although the large majority of these movies were aimed at a heterosexual audience, a few were made with homoerotic themes. The *roman poruno* genre was thus another popular media format that directly contravened official sex-education dicta, which associated sexuality with marriage, monogamy and reproduction. *Roman poruno* remained a popular Japanese film genre until the early 1980s, when the development of the VCR enabled an explosion in low-budget pornography aimed at both straight and gay audiences for the home market.

From the mid 1960s, due in large part to globalising discourses of sexual liberation, the mass media too began to discuss sexual issues with greater freedom. *Heibon panchi*, a popular weekly magazine for men dedicated to 'fashion, cars and sex', was first published in 1964 (Shimokawa, 2007: 165) and in 1965 the *11pm* show brought sexual discussion on to late night television. During the 1960s the tabloid press expanded considerably and sex and scandal was a popular way to fill its pages. These sex scandals, often involving bureaucrats and the misuse of public funds, drew attention to the growing discrepancy between 'official' discourses of sexuality and actual practice.

One important event in the development of sex-instruction literature was the publication in 1971 of the book *How to Sex* (its title was in English) by former obstetrician Narabayashi Yasushi. This was the first book in Japan to use actual couples to demonstrate positions. Widely reported on in the press, the book became a best-seller and created an entire 'how to sex' genre in tabloid (particularly sports) newspapers and magazines that henceforth included sex-instruction columns complete with raunchy line drawings. These male-oriented publications promoted the assumption characteristic of most post-war writing on sex that sexual knowledge was something that men should learn about in order to pleasure women. However, the early 1970s also saw the development of vibrant feminist and lesbian movements in Japan that channelled new ideas about the difference and autonomy of female sexuality that were being developed in Europe and the USA at that time.

A great deal of early feminist literature on women's sexuality came to Japan via translation projects, including a chapter on the myth of the vaginal orgasm, which appeared in the 1971 collection *Onna kara onna tachi e (From Women to Women)*. Other influential texts were the 1973 Japanese translation of the US women's sexual-health book entitled *Our Bodies Ourselves*, which focused on women's lived experience of sexuality, and the

1976 *Hite Report on Female Sexuality*, important for explaining the role of the clitoris and debunking the Freudian notion of the vaginal orgasm (Ishikawa, 1978: 179–80). Throughout the 70s there were also many locally produced and distributed zines associated with various women's liberation groups that addressed issues of sexuality from women's perspectives. Over the following decades a strong tradition of feminist scholarship has been established in Japan with many prominent authors launching searing critiques of the continuing patriarchal bias in Japanese society, particularly regarding the double standard in attitudes toward male and female sexuality. Many of these materials were made available in public libraries or in women's welfare centres funded by local councils. However, the distribution of feminist material that seems 'radical' and 'inappropriate' to conservative commentators has recently led to a backlash in some areas, with local women's centres being defunded or merged with broader community-focused initiatives (Kano, 2011; Women's Asia 21, 2006).

By the late 1960s the sexualisation of mainstream media outlets saw even media directed at young people beginning to deal with sexuality in a new, less restrained manner. One outlet in particular, the massively popular boys' manga magazine *Shōnen janpu* (*Boys' Jump*) pushed the envelope with its serialised comic-story *Harenchi gakuen* (*School of Shame*), about the sexual antics and frustrations of life at a co-educational high school, which began in 1968. Although very popular with young male readers, this series, which alluded to such things as the male teaching staff's sexual obsession with female students, as well as sexual tensions between students themselves, caused considerable outrage among teachers and Parent-Teacher Associations (PTAs) throughout Japan (Shimokawa, 2007: 201).

The sexualisation of media directed at young people, particularly boys, continued apace throughout the 1970s and 1980s. One genre, in particular, *rori-kon*, or Lolita-complex, manga (highly sexualised representations of school-age girls) was often singled out by parents as a bad influence on young people's sexual values. By the end of the 70s, though, girls' manga too had become increasingly sexualised. These included a genre dedicated to 'Boys Love' (BL for short) that detailed male-male love stories, containing graphic representations of the kinds of 'unproductive' sexual acts deemed inappropriate by the authorities. Indeed, such was the concern over the volume of BL materials available in public libraries that in 2007 there were unsuccessful attempts in Osaka prefecture and elsewhere to have BL titles designated 'harmful to youth' and removed from the shelves (McLelland, 2015; Ueno, 2009). Hence the sexualisation of youth media, including

some outlets directed at girls and young women, stands in stark contrast to official pronouncements on sexuality, particularly those channelled through the school system, which present 'correct' attitudes toward sexuality solely in a reproductive marital framework.

The sexualisation of youth media has been controversial in Japan and overseas. One of the most sustained calls for the reform of manga content followed on from the tragic murder of four infant girls between 1988 and 1989 by serial killer Miyazaki Tsutomu. An investigation of Miyazaki's background and lifestyle revealed that he was an isolated youth who had been an avid collector of 'Lolita'-style manga and animation as well as adult pornography. A coalition of PTA committees, feminist groups and women's organisations lobbied local and national politicians for increased surveillance and regulation of violent and sexualised imagery in manga and animation, particularly those marketed to young people. These groups also lobbied publishers, sending letters of complaint about manga that they considered particularly harmful. One result of this increased vigilance was a spike in 1990 in the number of manga designated 'harmful to youth' (Kinsella, 2000: 144–54).

The industry response to this popular movement calling for increased vigilance concerning manga content was to set up or reinforce existing systems of self-monitoring. Rather than tone down the level of fantasy sex and violence in all manga, the major publishers began to relabel manga that might be considered harmful to youth as 'adult manga'. These manga were clearly labelled on the dust jacket as 'adults only' and were often sold shrink-wrapped to stop young people reading them in-store. Some stores set up adult-manga corners to better supervise readers (Kinsella, 2000: 150).

As noted earlier Japan's obscenity legislation has been applied very specifically to rule out representations of genitalia and pubic hair, but overall sexual scenarios that can include violence, group sex and even rape are not captured by the legislation so long as the offending organs are blurred or blanked out and an appropriate age rating is published on the cover. This has caused considerable consternation overseas and lies behind the often hyperbolic denunciation of Japanese popular culture in the English-language press discussed in the introduction to this chapter. Of growing concern to some international agencies are sexual and violent representations of characters who are or 'may appear to be' underage. The manga aesthetic tends to exaggerate youthful appearance and many representations do seem to be of very young or child-like characters. This means many Japanese manga and anime that deal in sexual themes fall foul of 'child-abuse publications' legislation in some Western countries including the USA, Canada, the

UK and Australia, which have all seen successful prosecutions for possession of such material in recent years (McLelland, 2012b). In Japan, however, although the production and distribution of child pornography was outlawed in 1999, it was not until further legal reform in June 2014 that 'simple possession' of these materials was also outlawed (Ando, 2014). This delay was largely to do with arguments about what exactly constituted 'child pornography' (Nagaoka, 2009). Japan, for instance, supports a large 'junior idol' industry consisting of print and digital reproductions of Japanese and Caucasian child models in skimpy swimsuits in poses that could be deemed erotic. This material is not covered by obscenity legislation since there are no visible genitalia. Also, unlike many Western nations, Japan still does not include in its definition of child pornography purely fictional representations of young-looking characters in sexual scenarios, meaning that there are no restrictions on manga or anime depictions of under-age sexual activity so long as the no-visible-genitalia rule is followed by their creators and the more graphic titles are clearly labelled and sold as 'adults only'.

Despite lobbying by international agencies such as UNICEF (2010), there has been little movement on a national level to address concerns about fictional depictions (McLelland, 2011). However, in 2010 the Tokyo Metropolitan Government, under the leadership of conservative governor Ishihara Shintarō, used a local regulation known as the Seishōnen Hogo Ikusei Jōrei (Regulation for the Protection and Education of Young People) to introduce further restrictions on sexualised depictions in manga and increase police powers of censorship and control over their distribution (McLelland, 2015, 2011; *Japan Times*, 2010; Nogami et al., 2010). These restrictions technically only apply in the Tokyo area, but given that this is where most manga are produced and where the main distributors and markets are based the new regulations are widely expected to have a chill effect on the level of sex represented. However, in an era of convergent media where young people have unlimited access to the internet via their mobile phones it is unlikely that these measures will be effective in restricting their access to sexual content.

SEXUAL MINORITIES AND THE MEDIA

To speak of 'sexual minorities' in the early post-war years would be to read back into history a way of thinking about sexual identity and practice that was not clearly intelligible at the time. This does not mean that there was no consensus about what constituted 'normal' versus 'abnormal' sexual interests

but rather that an interest in the abnormal was not necessarily considered to be constitutive of a specific sexual identity. In the early post-war period in particular the Japanese press was much more open to discussions of 'abnormal' sexualities than were any Anglophone media.

On the whole Japanese society has not deployed legal restrictions to control sexual activities considered outside the norm: it has relied on social pressure to enforce conformity. Even during the militarist period, when homosexual men were subject to imprisonment and death under the Nazi regime as well as to a host of legal restrictions and impediments among the Allied nations, Japan never criminalised same-sex sexual behaviours. In fact, evidence from the early post-war period suggests that inter-generational same-sex relationships between senior military officials and their much younger orderlies were a visible and tolerated aspect of military life in some circles (McLelland, 2005: 45–47). The largely *moral* repugnance that has often framed Western responses to male homosexuality has not been so apparent in Japan. Indeed, as discussed earlier, the most visible representations of male-male sex and romance outside of the gay press in Japan has since the early 1970s appeared in a genre of girls' comics known collectively as 'Boys Love', a development unthinkable in the Western context (McLelland and Welker, 2015).

In the US context until the 1957 Roth decision, which limited the kinds of material that could be censored on account of their purported obscenity, the very topic of homosexuality was arguably obscene, making it hard to discuss the topic openly. However, depictions of same-sex sexualities in the Japanese press have been subject to the same obscenity codes governing heterosexual acts. This means that even at the height of the Cold War period in the 1950s, when discussion of male homosexuality in particular was highly restricted in the USA, issues to do with same-sex sexuality were widely discussed in the Japanese media, especially in relation to the entertainment world.

This does not mean however, that social elites were unconcerned with the proliferation of narratives and depictions of same-sex sexuality that were commonplace during the US Occupation. As we have seen above, official sexual discourse in the late 1940s was very much concerned with situating 'healthy', 'proper' and 'correct' sexuality in the context of a monogamous heterosexual marriage. The reason that social elites felt that they had to invest so much in 'purity education' was partly a response to the enthusiasm in the popular press for a range of sexual activities and escapades which clearly fell outside of 'normal' paradigms.

In the early post-war years, non-normative sexual interests were brought together under the rubric *ryōki*, or curiosity hunting. One of the main protagonists who emerged in the sex press of the Occupation years was the *ryōki shumi otoko,* or 'man with curiosity-hunting interests', who, rather than staying at home with his wife and engaging in nation-building acts of procreation, was out and about on the streets of Tokyo and other large cities looking for unusual sexual escapades. These sometimes included sex with the growing number of male cross-dressing prostitutes who were known to congregate in specific parts of the city. Reports in the popular press about these cross-dressers served to advertise not only their whereabouts but also their preferred sexual practices and ensure that anyone with an interest could track them down (McLelland, 2012a: 156–65).

Although an interest in male prostitution clearly ran contrary to government imperatives to develop sexual virtue, many press reports about the phenomenon were more intrigued than repulsed. Indeed, interest in *ryōki* pursuits was widespread across the media and a magazine first published in 1946, entitled *Ryōki*, self-consciously rejected the nation-building rhetoric of government officials when it announced in its editorials that the contents were aimed at those 'exhausted by the task of reconstructing the nation'. It is not surprising, then, that in January 1947, for the first time in the post-war era, the police used Japan's obscenity legislation to censure the magazine's editor and publisher for disseminating obscene materials. However, this tactic backfired since the notoriety of the case, discussed widely in the mainstream press, simply increased the cachet of the term *ryōki* with readers and led to the emergence of new titles such as *Ōru ryōki (All Curiosity Hunting)*, which carried on the tradition of reporting on the strange and unusual sexual escapades to be found in Japan's cities.

Although the *ryōki* genre had mostly run its course by 1949 when growing social stability finally meant that the police were able to rein in the largely uncensored sex press of the early Occupation period, from 1950 onwards a new genre of magazines emerged, focusing on 'perverse sexuality' (*hentai seiyoku*). Commonly referred to as *hentai* (perverse) magazines, these publications were quite different from those such as *Ryōki*, which had announced in its editorials that it had 'no intention whatsoever to enlighten' its readers. On the contrary the *hentai* magazines were edited by intellectuals who deliberately courted a readership of 'cultured persons' and included submissions from a wide range of 'experts' including sexologists, medical doctors and literary figures (McLelland, 2005: 69). Less encumbered by censorship than their wartime peers had been, this new generation of sex experts set themselves up as an alternative source of sexual knowledge and often challenged restrictive

government policies and discourses head-on in their publications. These liberal, left-leaning intellectuals provided an important counterbalance to official 'purity' discourses and disseminated their views via a variety of small-scale coterie magazines as well as in the mainstream media.

These 'sexperts' included people such as Takahashi Tetsu, a psychology graduate and Freudian counselor, whose 1953 book *Arusu Amatoria (Amorous Arts)* was a best-selling sex guide that challenged Van de Velde's emphasis on 'positions' as the key to successful sex, stressing instead the primacy of a couple's feelings. Although his sex guide was very much about the marital relationship, Takahashi's two periodicals launched in 1950, *Amatoria* and *Ningen tankyū (Human Investigation)* did much to expand the parameters of acceptable sexual expression. In contrast with clinical psychologists in Japan and the increasingly normative ends to which Freudian psychology was being put by therapists in Cold War America, Takahashi was a liberal interpreter of Freud who felt that people should be helped to come to terms with their 'abnormal' desires rather than be punished for them. Hence the focus of his magazines and other titles in the genre was very much on 'paraphilias': that is, precisely those sexual acts and interests which ran contrary to the Japanese state's formulation of 'correct' sexuality.

Despite his scientific credentials, Takahashi did, however, run foul of the censors. In 1956 he was prosecuted by the police for publishing explicit 'sexual experience' narratives solicited from readers in his members-only magazine *Seishin repōto (Life and Mind Report)*. A complete collection of reports from the magazine was later published in a two-volume set in 1987, and it is easy to see why the authorities at the time might have been wary of the publication. The reminiscences included a large number of accounts that contradicted the official 'purity' narratives of the time, including many relating to adultery as well as a range of paraphilias including group sex and bestiality. There were also a large number of accounts recalling the sexual abuse perpetrated by Japanese soldiers during the Second World War, including accounts of the 'comfort stations' set up to service the troops (Yamamoto, 1997). The comfort women issue had not been revealed in the media at the time and it is easy to see why the authorities would have been interested in restricting the circulation of these narratives.

Takahashi rejected the charge of obscenity, arguing that he published these accounts in order to analyse them using Freudian insights, but the police countered that the 'raw nature' of the reminiscences, which went into graphic detail about sexual acts, rendered them prurient. Takahashi defended the case, arguing that the 'scientific' nature of the members-only publication meant that the depiction of sex in the magazine could not be considered obscene. The court disagreed, however, and he lost the original case in a verdict handed down in 1963 as well as an appeal to the High Court handed down in 1970, just months before his death (Saitō, 1996).

Takahashi was no doubt targeted by the police because of his relatively high profile in the mainstream media and the possibility that material from his members' magazine might eventually find its way into the wider public sphere. However, the early 1950s saw a wide range of other members' clubs founded for the 'study' of sexuality, particularly non-normative sexualities, many of which produced their own members-only magazines that were not intercepted by the police. Some of these clubs emerged out of readers' requests to the editors of so-called *hentai* magazines, such as *Fūzoku kagaku* (*Sex-customs Science*) and *Fūzoku zōshi* (*Sex-customs Storybook*), to set up regular meetings for readers who wanted to take their study of perverse sexuality further. These included the FKK club that published the magazine *Rashin* (mid-1950s) and the Long Yang club, founded by the prolific author on male homosexuality Kabiya Kazuhiko, which published the members' journal *MAN* between 1954 and 1957. With names that served to obscure or subtly allude to their true interests, others clubs included the Adonisu Kai or Adonis club founded in 1952, which produced a magazine dedicated to the study of male-male love and the *Engeki Kenkyūkai*, or Theatrical Society, founded in 1955, whose members' magazine was dedicated to studying cross-dressing in the theatre and beyond (mostly beyond). These mimeographed magazines often did not contain the obligatory information concerning publication date and the names and addresses of the printer and editor required under Japanese publishing law and so were technically illegal; but as privately circulated publications, examples of which became available on and off from 1952 until their demise in the late 1960s, they largely escaped police attention even though they contained the most explicit descriptions of male same-sex activities (including full frontal nudity). Although their circulation was only ever in the hundreds, some of this early pro-homosexual writing was later republished in the 1970s' commercial gay press.

The materials discussed above were largely subcultural and not always easy to obtain, especially by readers outside major cities. Information about sexual minorities that circulated in mainstream media outlets was of a different kind altogether. Until the 1970s the majority of reporting on 'abnormal' sexual identities took place in the context of articles on deviant identities in the entertainment world. However, unlike the deeply pathologising treatment that such reports received in Western outlets the tone in Japan was rather more benign.

From the mid-1950s reports about a new style of male homosexual, the *gei bōi* (gay boy), began to circulate in tabloid journals. It was reported that early post-war *danshoku kissaten* (male-eroticism coffee shops) were being transformed into trendy nightspots where *gei bōi* hosts entertained a mainly heterosexual clientele, including many women. These trendy new *gei bā* (gay bars) were contrasted with the *homo bā* (homo bars) frequented by actual homosexuals that were smaller and usually off limits to drop-in guests. Other entertainment-oriented identities that were often discussed in the 1960s media included the *burū bōi* (blue boy), a male-to-female transgender category popular after a successful Japan tour by French transsexual cabaret Carrousel de Paris, and the female-to-male transgender identity *dansō no reijin* (male-dressing beauties), who played roles similar to the *gei bōi*, entertaining a primarily heterosexual clientele in designated clubs and cabarets.

However, media reports seemed confused as to whether these cross-dressing tendencies were symptomatic of 'abnormal' sexual tendencies or simply an expression of artistic license. This confusion was abetted by the strong division made in Japanese society between the *gei no kai* (world of entertainment) and the real world of everyday life, family and business. It was not entirely apparent whether the *gei bōi* was an example of 'abnormal' sexuality or was simply one kind of *geinōjin* (entertainer) since the Japanese term *gei* meaning entertainment is homophonous with the English loanword 'gay', meaning homosexual. Indeed, both the terms *gei* and *gei bōi* continued to be used in confusing ways and almost entirely in relation to the entertainment world by the mainstream media until the 1990s. At this time, due in part to the globalising tendency of the internet, the growing number of internationally aligned 'lesbian and gay' organisations and a 'gay boom' that saw minority sexual identities being discussed outside of an entertainment paradigm in the mainstream press for the first time, *gei* began to be recognised as a sexual-identity category both by the media and increasingly by *gei* men themselves (McLelland, 2005: 103–106).

It was due to the widespread confusion over the meaning of the term *gei* that local subcultures of same-sex-desiring men avoided the term, settling by the mid-1950s on the term *homo* as a self descriptor. However, it was not until 1970 that a commercial magazine with national distribution directly targeting *homo* men was established. The magazine's editor, Itō Bungaku, had inherited the family's publishing firm, Dai ni shobō, and their catalogue already held several sex-related publications. Itō's interest in developing a commercial magazine for homosexual men dates back to 1965, when he received a manuscript on masturbation practices by Akiyama Masami, a male writer on sexual customs. Thinking back to the sex instruction he received when a youth, which spoke of masturbation as harmful, he thought that the time had come for a book emphasising the pleasure and health benefits to be derived from masturbation. Accordingly, Dai ni shobō released the book in 1966 under the title *Hitori bottchi no sei seikatsu (A Solitary Sex Life)*.

The book was an immediate success and continued to sell well over the next decade. Itō received numerous letters relating to the book, including letters from men who confessed that they found the illustrations of naked men sexually arousing, and he began to wonder if there was a market for a book concerning male homosexuality. However, he decided that as a first venture it would be better to publish a book on lesbianism since this would appeal to a crossover market of heterosexual men as well as women with an interest in other women. He commissioned Akiyama to write a book entitled *Resubian tekunikku (Lesbian Technique)*. Contrary to appearance the book actually offers a literary, social and historical survey of lesbianism and is not particularly explicit; nevertheless, it proved popular.

Heartened by the success of *Lesbian Technique*, Itō thought the time was right for a book on male homosexuality, also written by Akiyama, which he released in 1968 under the title *Homo Technique*. Akiyama's books raised the public profile of homosexuality and led to a number of homosexual men contacting Itō requesting that he publish more similar titles. It was due to this demand that Itō conceived of *Barazoku (Rose Clan)*, the first commercial magazine targeting same-sex-desiring men. *Barazoku* was an important innovation since Itō's established connections with the book world meant he was able to ensure national distribution for the title, thus reaching a wider audience than any of the *hentai* magazines. Although Itō himself was heterosexual, he assembled a key team of same-sex-desiring men to work as contributing and commissioning editors, thus ensuring that the magazine's focus appealed to its target community. Running to 70 pages or so and originally published bi-monthly, *Barazoku* was not particularly sexually explicit, although it did include nude male photography and erotic short stories. From 1972 many of these short stories and others reprinted from the earlier *hentai*-magazine genre were gathered together and published by Dai ni shobō in a *homo poruno* (gay porn) series, helping establish same-sex-desiring men as a niche market. These texts were, however, still rather vague on the specifics of sex instruction. It was not until 1974 that Minami Teishirō, one of the original *Barazoku* editors, started his own commercial magazine, *Adon*, a much more hard-core venture than *Barazoku*, which directly addressed issues of

male-male sexuality, including sexually graphic photos as well as articles on sexual practices and sexual problems and diseases. This was followed in 1977 by the most graphic and detailed magazine of all, *Za gei (The Gay)*, published by high-profile sex-radical Tōgō Ken. Unlike the editors of other magazines, who were careful to stay within the limits of Japan's obscenity laws, Tōgō pushed the barriers in both photography and prose and was frequently in trouble with the police (Tōgō, 2002).

Actual sales figures for these and other, later, magazines is difficult to come by, but editors involved in the industry informed me that even at its peak in the mid-1990s *Barazoku* only ever sold about 40,000 copies. Yet the influence of these magazines, not only on providing sex instruction, but in helping develop what today can be described as a gay identity in Japan was extensive. Copies of the magazines have always been available to read in Japan's many gay bars, and old copies are constantly on sale throughout Japan's extensive networks of second-hand-book stores. Indeed, early copies of these magazines (and the *hentai* magazines that preceded them) have become collectors' items and are eagerly sought out by aficionados.

If we include the members' magazines circulating from the early 1950s there has been a comparatively long tradition of community-produced sex information for homosexual men; but the amount of public information available for lesbians has been considerably less. So far no evidence of members magazines aimed at a lesbian readership has come to light prior to the early 1970s. From the mid 60s the supposed activities of 'lesbians', most often reduced to the problematic term *rezu*, were often discussed in the media but this was almost exclusively in male terms and for the titillation of a male audience (Sugiura, 2006: 494). Although discussion of female same-sex love (*joshi dōseiai*) had been a staple of the early 50s' *hentai* magazines, as this genre developed into the 60s representations of 'lesbians' became increasingly pornographic and prurient, often with a sadomasochistic slant (McLelland, 2004). Indeed, it was this colonisation of lesbian sexuality by male pornography that led prominent lesbian author and critic Kakefuda Hiroko to speak of the difficulties some women experienced in identifying with the term 'lesbian' in her 1992 book *'Rezubian' de aru, to iu koto (On Being 'Lesbian')* (Suganuma, 2006).

From the early 1970s, however, small-scale lesbian groups were successful in reclaiming space for their own self-expression, achieved in part through a series of community-based publications. These self-published zines have appeared in different forms under different titles from the early 1970s, depending on available funding and community support, and today mostly exist online; but it has proven more difficult to sustain commercial publications.

The first attempt, the magazine *Phryne*, released by mainstream publisher Sanwa Shuppan in 1995, lasted only two issues. Between 1996 and 1997 seven issues of a lesbian periodical entitle *Aniise* were released by Terra Shuppan (which also released the popular gay men's magazine *Badi*), but slow sales meant the publication was put on hold. Back-number sales enabled the title's reissue in 2001 but it folded again in 2003 due to poor sales. Japan's third commercial magazine, *Carmilla*, which had a much more explicit focus on lesbian sex than the earlier, more community-oriented and political publications, was released in 2002 and saw 10 issues in all. *Carmilla* was a controversial publication for some in the lesbian community because its sexual focus also made it appealing to a readership of men, a readership that the publication's editor, Inoue Meimy, did not necessarily repudiate (Suganuma and Welker, 2006). However, despite this crossover appeal it still failed as a commercial proposition and ceased publication in 2005. The latest venture for lesbians and bisexual women was published in 2012: *Novia Novia Magazine* (with its English title) is a slick, lifestyle-oriented publication that introduces a variety of lesbian- and gay-friendly businesses and spaces around Japan. The magazine is also supported by an interactive website.

Japan's lesbian and gay magazines (and a host of publications aimed at the male-to-female transgender market that space does not allow us to discuss here) remained the key sources of information about minority sexualities for three decades until the end of the 1990s when the widespread uptake of the internet rendered them largely redundant. As Itō discovered early on, one of the main functions of these magazines was helping like-minded people contact each other through the personals columns. The ease and convenience of online interaction quickly supplanted this role, and even *Barazoku,* Japan's longest running gay publication, went out of business in 2004 after 43 years in production, although it has subsequently been revived by a different publisher.

These magazines were important as they provided a space for *tōjisha*, that is, 'those directly concerned' with the realities of gay and lesbian life in Japan, to represent themselves and establish a sense of solidarity and community (Macintosh 2009) that was very different from the misleading stereotypes prevalent in the mainstream media. However, as is the case for heterosexual sex, since the early 2000s the internet has emerged as the main conduit for information about minority sexual practices and problems and is often the first port of call for young people beginning to explore their sexual identities. This means that the market for print media aimed at sexual-minority readerships will remain limited.

CONCLUSION

As can be seen from the above account the representation of sexuality has always been the site of scrutiny and contestation in Japan with conservative factions within the ruling administration using a range of measures, including obscenity legislation, censorship, zoning laws and school curricula, to support narrow, heteronormative, pro-natalist constructions of sex. Indeed, attempts by social elites to 'manage' the sexuality of the masses have a long history in Japan. It is no surprise that those opposed to conservative Tokyo Governor Ishihara's measures to rein in depictions of sexuality in young people's media drew attention to the fact that he was displaying a paternalism characteristic of wartime leaders (Nagaoka, 2010). Ishihara's hostile attitude toward sexual minorities, too, has seen him labelled as out of touch and, rather less charitably, as an old codger (*ossan*) by some media commentators. However, conservative factions remain strong in Japanese politics and it should be noted that although obscenity prosecutions have been infrequent in the post-war period complaints are almost always upheld by the courts.

The conservative bent of Japanese politics must, however, be balanced by the wide range of sexual scenarios available in popular media. Emerging just months after Japan's defeat at the hands of the Allies, the media in Japan have always displayed an interest in things sexual. Even in the early post-war period it was possible to find rather explicit discussions of both marital sexuality (in the couples' magazines) and a range of 'paraphilias' (in the *ryōki* genre). Indeed, in the late 1940s and early 1950s in Japan it was much easier to openly discuss issues such as male and female homosexuality and cross-dressing in the media than it was in the USA or Europe. As the Cold War intensified and the USA became increasingly hostile to sexual minorities, Japanese commentators did not, on the whole, follow suit, and there remained vibrant media subcultures dedicated to the discussion of a whole range of non-marital, non-heterosexual sexualities that is only now being reconstructed by historians of sexuality.

The development of the internet, which is widely accessible in Japan on a variety of hand-held devices, has enabled the proliferation of sexual information and representation as well as people's access to them. The borderless nature of the internet has also facilitated the transmission of Japanese popular culture overseas, where certain genres, particularly those such as *rorikon* and BL, featuring sexualised depictions of characters who are or may appear to be under age, are proving problematic in jurisdictions with broad anti-child-abuse-materials legislation. International organisations have been putting pressure on Japanese legislators to further rein in sexualised media that are available to young people, and conservative lobby groups in Japan have been playing on this international concern in their calls for further restrictions on media content. The many contradictions between official restraint and media mayhem are thus likely to continue to play out in Japan in the coming years.

REFERENCES

Akamatsu K. (2004). *Yobai no minzokugaku: yobai no seiairon.* Tokyo: Chikuma shobō.

Akita M. (1994). *Sei no ryōki modan.* Tokyo: Seikyūsha.

Allison, A. (2000). *Permitted and Prohibited Desires: Mothers, Comics and Censorship in Japan.* Berkeley: University of California Press.

Ando, R. (2014) After Years of Pressure, Japan Bans Possession of Child Porn, Reuters. Online at: http://www.reuters.com/article/ 2014/06/18/us-japan-pornography-idUSK BN0ET0C520140618, 4 July 2014.

Castro-Vasquez, G. (2007). *In the Shadows: Sexuality, Pedagogy and Gender among Japanese Teenagers.* Lanham: Lexington Books.

Cather, K. (2003). *The Great Censorship Trials of Literature and Film in Postwar Japan, 1950–1983.* PhD thesis, University of California, Berkeley.

Cooper, M. (Ed.) (1995). *They Came to Japan: An Anthology of European Reports on Japan 1543–1650.* Berkeley: University of California Press.

Dai ni ji shin seikatsu kenkyūkai hensanbu (Eds.) (1982). *Nihonjin no 'hatsutaiken' ni kan suru sedai betsu ankēto chōsa, Sei seikatsu hōkoku,* August, 28–42.

Dore, R. (1958/1999). *City Life in Japan: A Study of a Tokyo Ward.* Richmond, UK: Japan Library.

Dower, J. (1999). *Embracing Defeat: Japan in the Wake of World War II.* New York: WW Norton.

Driscoll, M. (2010). *Absolute Erotic, Absolute Grotesque: The Living, Dead, and Undead in Japan's Imperialism 1895–1945.* Durham: Duke University Press.

Fallows, J. (1986). The Japanese Are Different from You and Me, *The Atlantic Monthly,* 258, September, 35–43.

Foucault, M. (1990). *History of Sexuality Vol. 1.* London: Penguin.

Frühstück, S. (2003). *Colonizing Sex: Sexology and Social Control in Modern Japan.* Berkeley: University of California Press.

Fu, H. (2011). The Bumpy Road to Socialise Nature: Sex Education in Japan, *Culture, Health and Sexuality,* 13 (8), 903–15.

Gordon, A. (1997). Managing the Japanese Household: The New Life Movement in Postwar Japan, *Social Politics,* 4 (2), 245–83.

Hyōdō C. (2008). HIV/AIDS, Gender and Backlash. In Chan, J. (Ed.) *Another Japan is Possible: New Social Movements and Global Citizenship Education.* Stanford: Stanford University Press, 198–202.

Ishikawa H. (1977). *Kanzen naru kekkon* kara *HOW TO SEX* e no sengo shi, *Kurowassan,* July, 113–15.

Ishikawa, H. (1978). Anata ni susumetai SEX no hon 16 satsu, *Kurowassan,* April, 179–181.

Japan Times (2010). Ordinance Passed against Manga 'Extreme Sex', December 16. Online: www.search.japantimes.co.jp/rss/nn 20101216a4.html. Accessed January 7, 2011.

Kano, A. (2011). Backlash, Fight Back, and Back-Pedalling: Responses to State Feminism in Contemporary Japan, *International Journal of Asian Studies,* 8 (1), 41–62.

Kinsella, S. (2000). *Adult Manga.* London: RoutledgeCurzon.

Macintosh, J. (2009). *Homosexuality and Manliness in Postwar Japan,* Oxford: Routledge.

McGinty, S. (2002). Japan's Darkest Secrets: the Dark Side of the Orient, *The Scotsman,* August 31.

McLelland, M. (2004). From Sailor-Suits to Sadists: Lesbos Love as Reflected in Japan's Postwar 'Perverse Press', *U.S.-Japan Women's Journal,* 27, 27–50.

McLelland, M. (2005). *Queer Japan from the Pacific War to the Internet Age.* Lanham: Rowman and Littlefield.

McLelland, M. (2011). Thought Policing or Protection of Youth? Debate in Japan over the 'Non-Existent Youth' Bill, *International Journal of Comic Art,* 13 (1), Spring, 348–67.

McLelland, M. (2012a). *Love Sex and Democracy in Japan during the American Occupation.* New York: Palgrave Macmillan.

McLelland, M. (2012b). Australia's Child-Abuse Materials Legislation, Internet Regulation, and the Juridification of the Imagination, *International Journal of Cultural Studies,* 15, (5), 467–83.

McLelland, M. (2015). Regulation of Manga Content in Japan: What Is the Future for BL Manga? In McLelland, M., Nagaike, K., Suganuma, K. and Welker, J. (Eds.) *Boys Love Manga and Beyond: History, Culture and Community in Japan.* Jackson: University of Mississippi Press.

McLelland, M. and Welker, J. (2015). An Introduction to 'Boys Love' in Japan. In McLelland, M., Nagaike, K., Suganuma, K. and Welker, J. (Eds.) *Boys Love Manga and Beyond: History, Culture and Community in Japan.* Jackson: University of Mississippi Press.

Nagaoka, Y. (2009). Jipohō, seishōnen jōrei nado, sei hyōgen kisei kyōka no ugoki, *Tsukuru,* 40 (1), December, 114–121.

Nagaoka, Y. (2010). Manga no sei hyōgen kisei wo nerata tōjōrei kaitei meguru kobo, *Tsukuru,* 40 (5), May, 64–71.

Nakagawa, K. (2001). Kazoku seikatsu no hendō to 21 seikino kazoku, *Kokuritsu josei kyōikukaikan kenkyūkai kyō,* 5, 3–15.

Newsweek (1996). Japan's Dirty Secret: Schoolgirls Selling Sex, 23 December, 15.

Nihon Seikyōiku Kyōkai. (2007). *Wakamono no sei hakusho: dai rokkai seishōnen seikōdō zenkoku chōsa hōkoku*. Tokyo: Shogakukan.

Nogami T., Suzuki, T. and Kanemitsu, D. (2010). *Saru de mo wakaru tō jōrei taisaku*. Tokyo: firstspear. com.

Pflugfelder, G. (1999). *Cartographies of Desire: Male-Male Sexuality in Japanese Discourse 1600–1950*. Berkeley: University of California Press.

Rocha, L. A. (2011). Scientia Sexualis versus Ars Erotica: Foucault, van Gulik, Needham, *Studies in History and Philosophy of Biological and Biomedical Sciences* 42, 328–343.

Ryang, S. (2006). *Love in Modern Japan: Its Estrangement from Self, Sex and Society*. London: Routledge.

Saitō, Y. (1996) *Sekusorojisuto Takahashi Tetsu*. Tokyo: Seikyūsha.

Shibuya, T. (2003). *Nihon no dōtei*. Tokyo: Bungei shunjū.

Shimokawa, K. (2007). *Sei fūzokushi nenpyō 1945–89*. Tokyo: Kawade shobō.

Smith, R. (1983). Making Village Women into 'Good Wives and Wise Mothers' in Prewar Japan, *Journal of Family History* 8 (1), 70–84.

Steiner, K. (1950). The Revision of the Civil Code of Japan: Provisions Affecting the Family. *The Far Eastern Quarterly* 9 (2), 169–84.

Suganuma, K. (2006). Enduring Voices: Fushimi Noriaki and Kakefuda Hiroko's Continuing Relevance to Japanese Lesbian and Gay Studies and Activism, *Intersections: Gender, History and Culture in the Asian Context*, 14, online at: www.intersections. anu.edu.au/issue14/suganuma.htm, July 4, 2014.

Suganuma, K. and Welker, J. (2006). Celebrating Lesbian Sexuality: An Interview with Inoue Meimy, Editor of Japanese Erotic Lifestyle Magazine, *Carmilla*, *Intersections: Gender, History and Culture in the Asian Context*, 12, online at: www. intersections.anu.edu.au/issue12/welker2.html, July 4, 2014.

Sugiura, I. (2006). 1970, 80 nendai no ippan zasshi ni okeru 'rezubian' hyōzō. In Yajima, M. (Ed.) *Sengo Nihon josō/dōseiai kenkyū*. Tokyo: Chūō daigaku shuppanbu, 491–518.

Suzuki, M. (2001). Senso ni okeru dansei sekushuariti (Men's sexuality during war). In Asai, H., Itō, S. and Murase, Y. (Eds.) *Nihon no otoko wa doko kara kite doko e iku?* Tokyo: Jūgatsusha, 98–119.

Suzuki, T. (2012). Introduction: History and Issues in Censorship in Japan. In Suzuki, T., Toeda, H., Hori, H. and Munakata, K. (Eds.) *Censorship, Media and Literary Culture in Japan: From Edo to Postwar*. Tokyo: Shinyosha, 7–23.

Takahashi, T. (1953). *Arusu Amatoria: Seikō taii 62 gata no bunseki, seiai funiki 86 hō no bunseki*. Tokyo: Amatoriasha.

Takahashi, T. (1969). *Kinsei kindai 150 nen sei fūzoku zushi*. Tokyo: Kubō shoten.

Tashiro, M. (2000). Sengo kaikakuki ni okeru 'junketsu kyōiku', Kagawa Nutrition University, *Kyōiku to jendā kenkyū*, 3, 26–38.

Tashiro, M. (2001). Sengo ni okeru 'junketsu kyōiku jissen no tenkai – dai ikkai zenkoku junketsu kyōiku kenkyūshūkai o chūshin ni, Kagawa Nutrition University, *Kyōiku to jendā kenkyū*, 4, 86–93.

Thompson, S. (2012). Patterns of Censorship in Ukiyo-e Prints. In Suzuki, T., Toeda, H., Hori, H. and Munakata, K. (Eds.) *Censorship, Media and Literary Culture in Japan: From Edo to Postwar*. Tokyo: Shinyosha, 54–63.

Time. (1999). 'Japan's Shame', 19 April, 60.

Tōgō, K. (2002). *Jōshiki o koete: okama no michi 70 nen*. Tokyo: Potto shuppan.

Ueno, C. (2009). 'Sakai-shi toshokan, BL hon haijo sōdō tenmatsu', *Tsukuru*, May, 106–112.

UNICEF (2010). 'Child Rights Advocates Seek to Strengthen Laws against Child Pornography in Japan.' Online at: www.unicef.org/infobycountry/ japan_53219.html, July 4, 2014.

Walthall, A. (2009). 'Masturbation and Discourse on Female Sexual Practices in Early Modern Japan', *Gender and History*, 21 (1), 1–18.

Women's Asia 21 (2006). 'Unbelievable Events Happening in Japan Motivated by Conservative Politicians', *Voices from Japan*, 17, Summer.

Yamamoto, N. (1994). *Sei no tabū ni idonda otoko-tachi: Yamamoto Senji, Kinzei, Takahashi Tetsu*. Tokyo: Kamogawa bukkuretto.

Yamamoto, N. (1997). Senjō de no heishi no 'sekushuariti': Takahashi Tetsu no 'Seishin repōto' yori, *Sensō sekinin kenkyū*, 18, Tokyo: Nihon no sensō sekinin shiryō sentā, 18–27.

Yokota-Murakami, T. (1998). *Don Juan East/West: On the Problematic of Comparative Literature*. Albany: SUNY Press.

11

Gender Equity in Japan

Joyce Gelb

The concept of gender equity in Japan may be analyzed from several different perspectives. While the term gender equity is open to interpretation, agreed definitions include the following: equal access to education and educational attainment; equal participation in the work force, including hiring, promotion and salary; and access to political and governmental positions, including ministerial, legislative and possibly judicial roles that involve policy making. Additional meanings may challenge biased treatment of women in school texts and other relevant publications, extend equality to local and prefectural as well as national government and seek to redefine relations between men and women in other significant ways.

This chapter focuses on selected policies related to gender equity, specifically education, gender equality and employment. At the outset, and to provide a context for the analysis, it should be noted that on international indices which compare gender equality, such as the Gender Empowerment Index compiled to evaluate women's international standing related to educational attainment and participation in economic and political life and decision making (elected and administrative), Japan ranks 57 out of 100 nations (Social Watch, 2012, a survey compiled by a consortium of 60 international NGOs committed to ending gender discrimination and poverty). The Global Gender Gap index finds women in Japan at 105 out of 136 nations in 2010, reflecting disparities in economic, political, educational and health fields. (World Economic Forum, 2013; *Nikkei Online*, 2011). Women in Japan occupy only a small percentage of managerial posts (12 percent in 2012, 10 percent in 2005, up from 8.9 percent in 1995; this is less than half the OECD average) (Gender Equality Report, 2006; Kingston, 2013). They occupy only 1.7 percent of senior public management positions (as of 2009, they made up just 4.1 percent of managers in private companies) (Reuters, 2010b). Over two thirds of women retire from the labor force after having children (Gender Equality Bureau, 2009), and just 45 percent of women are regular labor-force employees (42 percent work part-time without benefits, pensions or job security), a huge decline from the 1980s when the figure was 68 percent (Women and Men in Japan, 2007), though they comprise the bulk of part-time workers. However, some recent data shows that younger women are now earning more than men, though this may reflect the serious decline in male earning power rather than real increases for women (Reuters, 2010a). In 2009 women still earned salaries that were 30 percent lower than men's, one of the widest disparities in the developed world (Kitiyama, 2010). Women's options are still constrained by traditional values upholding the male-breadwinner model in which women stay at home (Gender Equality in Japan, 2007). As of 2013 this number has declined to a third, though far more men say they would like to see their wives work (*Japan Today*, 2013).

Women are poorly represented in elected positions as well. In the more powerful lower house of the Japanese parliament 10.9 of the members are women; the figure for the upper house is 18.6 percent. This is a considerable recent improvement and places Japan at place 101 out of 187 nations included in an International Parliamentary Union survey (2012). Women have achieved greater equality as members of government advisory committees, with numbers approaching 30 per cent, a goal of gender-equality policy.

This chapter will show the considerable progress made in educational attainment in terms of increased gender equity; however, there have been far fewer positive gains in employment opportunities. The record on gender-equality policy is a mixed one.

EDUCATION

For most of the post-war period higher education was overwhelmingly gender-segregated. One of the major causes of this inequality was the two-tiered system of higher education consisting of two-year junior colleges and four-year universities. These distinctive educational institutions segregated largely along gender lines, women going to the former and men to the latter. Many junior colleges were for women only and considered inferior to four-year universities. Even in the 1990s women made up the bulk of students at two-year junior colleges, while men remained in the ascendancy at four-year universities. Thus, even though men and women had almost equal rates of participation in higher education, gender inequality remained a distinctive feature of the system, with adverse consequences for women in the labor market (Curtin, 2003: 42).

The junior-college system was generally associated with a second-class education, primarily for women. In the 1990s some aspects of the gender imbalance in higher education finally began to recede. From the mid-1990s onwards record numbers of women started to enter four-year universities, while the numbers going to two-year junior colleges began to drop drastically. By 2002 there were less than half the numbers at junior colleges than a decade earlier, while women more than doubled their numbers in universities. The data clearly illustrate that the two-year junior-college system is in a state of serious decline and may be extinct within a few decades. The divide between male and female education has clearly narrowed significantly in the last decade and the trend has continued. However, actual gender equity in four-year

institutions has not been achieved. In 2009 38 percent of undergraduates were women, while over 50 percent of men were enrolled at this level. Only half the number of women attended graduate school as men (Gender Equality Bureau, 2009).

GENDER EQUALITY POLICY

The Japanese government was motivated in part by external pressure in adopting and implementing a gender-equality law in 1999. The Fourth World Conference on Women was held in Beijing for the first time in Asia in September 1995, and the Beijing Declaration and Platform for Action were adopted. Among the twelve tenets of the Platform for Action adopted by the forum were the expansion of women's rights in the following areas: women and poverty; the education and training of women; women and health; violence against women; women in power and decision-making; institutional mechanisms for the advancement of women; human rights of women; and women and the media.

Measures to create formal structural change were undertaken by the Japanese government, partially in response to the Platform for Action recommendations and also because the Japanese government reports along with other nations to the UN Commission on the Status of Women, with an annual review of progress (at which Japan has always been found to fall short of the stated goals). Among these were measures to strengthen the national machinery for the advancement of women.

In 1994 the Headquarters for the Promotion of Gender Equality was set up within the Cabinet, with the prime minister as its president and a membership made up of every Cabinet minister. In addition, the Office for Gender Equality and the Council for Gender Equality were established in the Prime Minister's Office. As part of a 2001 governmental reorganization a Cabinet Office headed by the Prime Minister was established in the Cabinet, and a Council for Gender Equality and a Gender Equality Bureau were established within this Cabinet Office. The Gender Equality Bureau, comprising 25 members appointed by the prime minister (with no more than 50 percent of each gender) was mandated to formulate and coordinate plans for promoting the formation of a gender-equal society, as well as promoting the Basic Plan for Gender Equality and formulating and implementing plans for matters not falling under the jurisdiction of any particular ministry. A 1995 revision of the Gender Equality Law, the Second Basic Plan, included goals related to equal participation in policy and decision-making processes, increased support for women, and efforts to promote work-life balance and prevent domestic violence (Gender

Equality Report, 2006). A further revision of the Basic Law for Gender Equal Society was passed in 2005. At that time 74 percent of men and women polled by the Cabinet Office (2004) indicated that they felt that men were still treated more favorably in all aspects of Japanese society (Gender Equality Report, 2004).

One of the chief stated objectives of the Headquarters for the Promotion of Gender Equality has been to boost representation of women in the policy-making process. The Government, based on a resolution made by the Headquarters for the Promotion of Gender Equality in May 1996, pushed ahead with measures 'to achieve a 20% participation rate as early as possible before the end of FY 2000'.

The Basic Law for a Gender Equal Society went into effect in June 1999 to clarify basic concepts pertaining to formation of a gender-equal society and indicate the direction these should take, and to comprehensively and systematically promote the state's, local governments' and citizens' measures pertaining to formation of a gender-equal society.

THE BASIC LAW FOR GENDER EQUAL SOCIETY

The Basic Law on Gender Equal Society (also known as the Law for Cooperative Participation of Men and Women in Society) was passed in June 1999. Basic Laws are intended to address fundamental issues of the state system and are presumed to take priority in relation to other laws in the same policy area. The Basic Law system creates a framework to enact other legal measures and laws by the national and local governments, providing a basic guideline within which bureaucrats and Diet members may formulate new policies and laws and judges are asked to hand down decisions. In the analysis to follow the significance of a largely symbolic law on gender-equality policies will be considered.

The term 'gender equality' was first used in Japan when the former Prime Minister's Office for Women was redefined as the Office for Gender Equality as part of a reorganization in 1994, although its origins date back to the early 1990s in public discourse and even earlier in response to international women's meetings which inspired efforts at change within Japan. The Japanese government in the mid-1990s began to realize that greater gender equality could have a positive impact on the moribund economy and the declining birth rate, even if such recognition was always balanced by competing discourses of traditional values and business as usual (Osawa, 2000). In 1997 then Prime Minister Hashimoto Ryutaro included gender equality in a

speech outlining six areas for reform. This led to the submission to the prime minister of A Vision of Gender Equality (the Vision Statement), a report by the Advisory Council for Gender Equality of the Prime Minister's Office.

The passage of the Basic Law appears to have been motivated in large measure by international pressure, as well as internal feminist efforts to prod the Japanese government (Osawa, 2000; Gelb, 2003). In this instance the 1995 Fourth World Conference on Women in Beijing was a major catalyst; and feminist groups, and some Diet members, petitioned to create 'national machinery' for women: a Ministry for Women's Affairs and Women's Headquarters. Impetus provided by the Beijing + Five meeting in 2000 in New York City also helped to galvanize support from bureaucrats for new legislation (Osawa, 2000). The Basic Law 'incorporated the results of the Special Session of the UN General Assembly, Women 2000' (Women in Japan Today, 2001: 2; Osawa Mari, 2000).

The preamble to the Basic Law (Law 78, 1999) stresses 'human rights' and calls for genuine equality between men and women, emphasizing the ability of each citizen to exercise individuality and ability regardless of gender, in language reminiscent of international documents. Among the law's provisions are efforts to secure 'non-discriminatory treatment' of women including positive action to harmonize work and family life (and the sharing of home-related activities between men and women), to secure equal employment and to eliminate violence against women (the latter two were added in a Basic Plan for Gender Equality subsequent to passage of the law) (Women in Japan Today, January 2001: 3–4; Basic Law for Gender Equal Society, 2000). The Basic Law does not contain any responsibilities for companies and lacks provisions for a monitoring system, such as an ombudsperson, as initially recommended (Working Women's International Network (WWIN), 2003). It was generally agreed that this legislation was vague and would require active enforcement to become meaningful. While some view the law as useless and inadequate, others see it as a resource for changing future policy. It has been praised as creating the basis for 'national machinery' intended to further the role and status of women in Japan through the institutionalization of a government agency (Asakura interview; 2001; Osaw interview 2002; Stetson and Mazur, 1995: 2–3).

The Significance of the Basic Law

The Basic Law was a government initiative driven by bureaucrats primarily from the Prime Minster's Office, although NGOs played a role in the deliberations, as has now become more common practice in

Japan with regard to gender-based legislation. The coalition government then in power under the leadership of the (somewhat) reformist Hashimoto Ryutaro (1996–1998) included the female-led Socialist and New Sakigake parties. The latter stipulated the creation of gender-quality 'national machinery' and the passage of a basic law on gender equality as the price for their support for the coalition Cabinet (Osawa, 2000: 5). The Democratic Party of Japan (DPJ) also prepared an alternative version of the legislation. A series of six town meetings to include public comments were held after the preparation of an interim report; it is estimated that about 2,000 people participated in these (Osawa, 2000). Women's voices influenced the preamble and gained recognition of women's rights as human rights, but they were not able to influence the bill's content to the same extent. Observers noted a disjunction between the more progressive language embodied in the initial Vision Statement and the far weaker language of the actual legislation with regard to issues of indirect discrimination, surname change and the like. (Yamashita interview, 2003). There was much controversy over the naming of the law, whether it should be called the *Danjo Kyodo Sankaku Shakai Kihon-Ho* (gender-equal society) or *Danjo Byodo* (gender equality). 'Gender Equal Society' was adopted (modifying the original), meaning joint participation by men and women, rather than 'Gender Equality', which was favored by most feminists. The revised name as a frame for the policy may have been more appealing to conservative politicians, who feared the idea of equality of outcomes rather than equality of opportunity, as the law presently suggests, given their opposition to affirmative action, feminism, positive discrimination, etc. (Osawa, 2000: 6).

The bill has had at least two significant results. The administrative structure to implement the new Basic Law was given impetus by the reorganization of government ministries and agencies, made operational in 2001. One result was the strengthening of the Bureau (which replaced the former Office) of Gender Equality, and Council for Gender Equality, established in the newly created Cabinet Office in January 2001 in the aftermath of national administrative reorganization, aimed at enhancing the functions of the Cabinet and Prime Minister's Office. Among its four consultative organs is the Council for Gender Equality. Headed by the Chief Cabinet Secretary, the Council is intended to serve as a force for 'mainstreaming' gender policy, in line with efforts to institutionalize such policy systemically in other nations. Its goal was to provide this agency with more power than individual ministries and to act as policy coordinator, providing opinions to other ministries and agencies through review and advisement, monitoring and investigation, in addition to disseminating surveys to assess the effectiveness of specific policies (Osawa, 2000: 13). The Gender Equality Bureau, the administrative arm and secretariat of the Council, may act to formulate plans 'not falling within the jurisdiction of any particular ministry' (Women in Japan Today, 2001: 2). A Liaison Conference for the Promotion of Gender Equality links the work of these bodies with NGOs and local governments (Osawa, 2000: 7). Nonetheless, since its creation, the role of the Bureau as policy advocate has been relatively weak (Yamashita, 1993).

This set of presumably enhanced powers for the equality Council and Bureau are referred to in official documents (for example, the Basic Law) and by some feminists as having created 'state feminist national machinery' to advance women's rights in Japan in line with the directives of the Fourth World Conference on Women in Beijing. Some female intellectuals associated with the women's movement were incorporated into the new bureaucratic structure; but this co-opting of movement activists may bring feminists closer to policy-making roles and provide them with new access to power without meeting their demands.

The Basic Law is to be made operational by prefectural and local governments in order to become more than a symbolic document (the promotion, or *shorei suru*, of gender equality). This is stated as an expectation, not an obligation (*doryoko gimu*), which involves prefectural and local governments developing basic plans for gender equality and then passing appropriate ordinances to follow them up (Ueno and Osawa, 2001). Ultimately, the Basic Law requires prefectural and local, rather than national, implementation.

Some observers contend that the Basic Law has already created a foundation which makes other legislation possible. Recent proposals that emanate in part from the Council for Gender Equality include tax and pension reform, currently under review. Others feel that the provision of the Basic Law related to indirect discrimination, part-time work and positive action may bear fruit as resources for women plaintiffs fighting sex discrimination. (Ueno and Osawa, 2001). Critics argue that the new law failed to adequately address the issue of indirect discrimination, on which the government argued there was no consensus (WWIN, 2003).

The Adoption of the Basic Law

As early as 1985, after the Third World Women's UN Conference in Nairobi, Japanese women's groups demanded the establishment of 'national machinery' for women's policy. The law's specific origins date back to a Research Group in 1992 which sent members to seven developed nations to investigate their approaches to 'national machinery' (Furuhashi interview, 2000). The process of policy adoption was in part a political tug of war between the Ministry of Labor Women's Bureau (MOL WB) and the Prime Minister's Office over responsibility for women's issues. Conflict, which involved women's groups, related to the marginalization and structural weakness of the MOL WB and the ability of the Section of Gender Equality, as it was then known, to coordinate comprehensive policies and gain support of a strong ministry, the Prime Minister's Office (Kobayashi, 2002: 214). Arguing that the MOL was too narrow in its focus solely on labor-related issues, and with its ability to co-opt a wide range of women's groups into its advisory council, the Prime Minister's Office ultimately won and the first Council for Gender Equality was established (Furuhashi interview, 2000; *Asahi Shimbun*, 1994).

The initial report of the Research Group had few concrete outcomes other than the appointment of gender-equality officers in each ministry. In 1994 a *shingikai* (advisory council) on Gender Equality was established. Members included Furuhashi Genrokuro, a veteran bureaucrat, and Nuita Yoko, its head and a long-time advocate of reforms for women. The advisory group, whose members included prominent women's advocates, met over 60 times between 1991 and 1997. The group's Vision Statement, which formed the basis for the later legislation, was adopted in 1996. Although at that time legislation was not contemplated, ultimately public opinion supported it and the bureaucracy acquiesced (Furuhashi interview, 2000). The Vision Statement was initially intended as a protest by feminists on the then Council for Gender Equality against a proposed draft of a report written by a low-ranking bureaucrat at the Prime Minister's Office which they deemed unacceptable. Instead, the Vision Statement stressed a far-reaching conception of a gender-equal society embodying drastic social and economic reforms (Osawa, 2000: 7–11). It included specific proposals including reform of the Civil Code to permit retention of maiden names after marriage and correction of gender bias in pensions and other benefit programs aimed at challenging the dominant 'male breadwinner' model prevalent in Japan.

In June 1997 a new Gender Equal Society *shingikai* was established (Furuhashi interview, 2000). The moderate reformism of Hashimoto Ryutaro, the LDP prime minister from 1996 to 1998, helped to promote the new law's passage during this period when much of the groundwork was laid. Hashimoto's receptivity may have been attributable to his three daughters' insistence on the need for new legislation (Osawa, 2000: 4). In his administration, gender-equality-related 'machinery' was strengthened in a restructured central bureaucracy (Osawa, 2000). The political environment at that time, which involved a coalition of the LDP,

New Sakigake and the Social Democratic Party of Japan, also facilitated consideration of the policy; the bill was one of the fruits of coalition government, similar to other legislation discussed here (anti-pornography, anti-stalking, domestic violence (DV)). At the time the leaders of two of the coalition parties were women: Domoto Akiko of New Sakigake and Doi Takako of the Socialist Party of Japan. Domoto, though the head of a minor party with just five Diet seats, was particularly forceful in pressing Prime Minister Hashimoto for gender reform (Osawa, 2000). The opposition parties and women's groups pressed for a strong preamble; their language was not incorporated during the bureaucratic negotiations but was added in the Diet deliberations (Furuhashi interview, 2000). It is possible that agreement to pass the Basic Law was a trade-off for the government's failure to create an independent Ministry for Women's Problems, which would have had a more direct approach to the creation of 'national machinery' (Ueno and Osawa, 2001: 10–92).

In February 1999 the Cabinet passed a bill proposing the Basic Law and it was introduced to the Diet. Its sponsors feared that opposition amendments unacceptable to the LDP might kill it but women's groups negotiated with them to accept this version (Furuhashi, 2000). The UN Women's Conference (Beijing + Five) in 2000 in New York City helped to galvanize bureaucrats in support of the Basic Law (Osawa, 2000). The bill passed unanimously in both houses reflecting its government sponsorship, and perhaps also because it lacked concrete provisions. There was a provision for public comment; the Council for Gender Equality received over 3,600 comments, the first time that more than 1,000 had been received in a similar process. Poll data at the time revealed that only 10 to 15 percent of Japanese people had any familiarity with the new law (Osawa, 2000).

The Basic Law that was passed was heavily influenced by recommendations of the Council for Gender Equality. Article 8 states that the State is responsible for the comprehensive formulation and implementation of policies, including positive action (Gender Equality Bureau, 2002). Article 17 specifies grievance procedures, although no independent mechanism for complaint resolution was designated. Articles 8 and 9 state that prefectural and local governments are responsible for taking positive steps to implement the law (Hashimoto, 2002a). As a way of following up on this policy, the National Personnel Authority in May 2001 published guidelines for hiring and appointing women to the national civil service; at that time, as now, only 1.2 percent of the highest positions were held by women. It suggested that each ministry should set goals and consider the ratio of women to total employees at the time of examination for the service. A major effort of the Gender Equality 'machinery' has been to increase women's participation in advisory councils and committees, which rose from 2.4 percent in 1977 to 24.7 percent in 2001, close to the goal of 30% (Hashimoto, 2002a; Women in Japan Today, 2009).

Local Enforcement

Perhaps the most significant impact of the Basic Law to date has been at the local level. Articles 8 and 9 of the Basic Law specify that prefectural and local governments are responsible for making efforts to take positive measures to promote a gender equal society (*doryoku gimu*). As of April 2008 all prefectures and close to a thousand municipalities have considered gender policy; most have also established liaison conferences to coordinate departmental policies (Women in Japan Today, 2009). Proposals for policies related to Gender Equality emanated from administrative leadership, citizen groups or assemblies and assembly members, and the presence of women in government can make a difference to the outcomes.

Some observers contend that a clear legacy emanating from local-government support for delegates to UN meetings (such as the Fourth World Conference on Women) exists with regard to those local governments which have succeeded in passing progressive gender-related ordinances – another example of the significance of transnational feminism. In this view feminists have brought back the lessons learned at international conferences to create local networks and continued to pressure for policy change (Yamashita interview, 2003). They have built upon an infrastructure of local women's centers and female assembly members to create structures of support.

Many governments have held public hearings, although they were not mandated, in order to develop equality plans and then ordinances to implement them. While the policies adopted are not binding, but rather require a good-faith effort, numerous towns and prefectures have taken these initiatives seriously. Some local governments have developed ordinances which involve ombuds systems (in particular, Saitama prefecture and Kawasaki City) in order to resolve human-rights complaints. In Okayama and Hiroshima private companies were asked to submit records (*joetsu*) related to gender-equality measures (Hashimoto, 2002a). Other governments have established an independent compliance system to monitor compliance efforts and mediate complaints. Although quotas per se are prohibited by the Japanese constitution, ratios have been employed in some localities and prefectures (including Tottori and Saitama prefectures) – either a 50/50 or a 60/40 ratio of female-to-male

representation on local advisory committees In Fukuoka a 30 percent target for women in office has already been achieved (Hashimoto, 2002a). Ordinances have also addressed other gender-related issues, including sex-segregated public high schools and the Japanese custom of calling boys' names first when the daily school register is read. Policies adopted vary with each locality: Saitama and Hokkaido prohibit indirect discrimination. In Tottori, Okayama and Fukuoka prefectures Councils for Gender Equality handle complaints, while the Governor may have a dispute resolution role as well. In Tokyo the governor may ask companies to report to the Metropolitan Assembly regarding their revised practices, with the possibility of publicizing the names of companies who do not comply (the latter sanction has not been invoked to date). No ordinances stipulate punishment for violation of these new initiatives at any level.

Despite these apparently positive efforts, in other instances local and prefectural governments have opposed the adoption of gender policies. In Tokyo, for example, under the conservative leadership of Governor Ishihara, the Tokyo Jyosei Women's Foundation was abolished; it ceased to exist at the end of 2002 and prefectural leadership was put in control of the remaining services. Budgets for many women's centers have been cut. In Osaka right-wing assembly members who alleged that gender-equality efforts would destroy the family, as well as Japanese culture and society, prevailed in the policy process. Consequently, Osaka passed a weak ordinance recognizing differences between men and women. In both of Japan's leading urban areas, then, the policy outcomes have been disappointing to feminists – and in Okayama City the final version of the ordinance excluded a specific quota for women in managerial positions.

Many in Japan speak of a 'backlash' against even those modest policies adopted to date. In Chiba prefecture Governor Domoto Akiko's efforts to adopt a more proactive policy involving affirmative action for companies bidding for prefectural contracts have thus far been ineffective. Right-wingers, including housewives led by a male former Diet member (Murakami) who maintains that gender equality is as radical as 'communism', appear to be winning the struggle to develop prefectural policy (Hashimoto, 2002b). A group called the *Nihon Kaigi* (Japan Conference) and its women's branch, *Nihon Josei Kaigi*, has attacked the concept of gender-equal society as denying the differences between men and women, demanding that such differences (women's traditional role as homemakers, for example) be acknowledged in the provisions of the regulations being drafted (WWIN, 2003; Yamashita interview, 2003). In Yamagata prefecture a vice-governor who sought progressive policies and had good connections to women's groups was ousted by the more conservative governor (Hashimoto, 2002a). Women intellectuals who have served on the Council of Gender Equality have been vilified in the conservative press (for example, *Nihon Jiji Hyoron,* or *Japan Current Events Critique*) as radical feminists who are challenging 'family values' and introducing 'communist' ideas in the guise of 'gender equality' (*Nihon Jiji Hyoron,* 2002). This newspaper has also attacked the notion of gender-free education proposed by Ministry of Education bureaucrats. Other national newspapers, including the *Yomiuri Shimbun* and *Sankei Shimbun,* have engaged in unremitting, front-page publicity for anti-gender-equality interests. The hostility has spilled over to other policy issues, including education reform, adoption of local ordinances on gender equality and the proposal for Civil Code reform relating to women's surnames. Ten years after the law's passage there has been limited positive change affecting the role and status of women in Japan (Hashimoto, 2009).

Specific Policy Outcomes

While it is difficult to document a precise relationship between the Basic Law for Gender Equal Society and specific policy outcomes, several new policy initiatives which may be linked in part to the passage of the Basic Law include the DV (domestic violence) law; efforts to amend the Civil Code to permit retention of the wife's surname (selective surnames); and analysis and revision of gender-related inequities in taxation, retirement and pensions, and insurance and corporate allowances (Osawa, 2000). A special committee for the balance between work and life, chaired by well known academic feminist Higuchi Keiko, proposed the elimination of waiting lists for day-care centers and increased childcare and long-term care-leave policies. The latter two policies have become law via the Revised Childcare and Nursing Care Leave in 2005.

Selective Surnames: An Emerging Policy Area?

The issue of amending the Civil Code to permit dual surnames, allowing married women to retain their maiden names, has gained momentum on the systemic agenda in Japan although it has failed to achieve policy acceptance in the decision making process. While this reform has been a long-standing demand of Japanese feminists, the revision of Code 750 (husband and wife can choose surname) has been actively resisted by the Japanese government for years, despite its promise of 'revision in the future' in a report to CEDAW in 1988 (Yamashita, 1993: 82). In the century-old

patriarchal-household system the bride loses her identity when she becomes part of her husband's family. Wives are required to use their married names on drivers' licenses, health-insurance cards and other official documents. Official change was first proposed in 1991; in 1996 the Judicial Advisory Council (*hosei shingikai*), a conservative advisory body to the Justice Ministry, proposed a draft bill to revise the Code. It is most unusual for a favorable proposal by a strong council such as this to fail to pass (Kobayashi, 2002). However, this effort, as well as many others, failed to achieve consensus due to reluctance of Diet members challenge established traditional practices. As in the case of DV, a survey of public attitudes toward this reform was undertaken by the Cabinet office, under the aegis of Justice Minister Moriyama Mayumi, in an effort to garner widespread support (*Japan Times,* July 2002). The Cabinet Office survey showed that 68.1 percent of women and 61.8 percent of men supported the use of two surnames, an increase of 10 percent from the previous survey a decade before (*Japan Times,* April 2002). The Council for Gender Equality recommended a Civil Code revision, via a 12-person panel, in October 2001. In 2001 the LDP agreed, after years of opposition, to consider the issue. The combined efforts of the Justice Minister, the positive poll numbers, the record number of female lawmakers (74 in that year) and the exit of a primary opponent due to a scandal seemed to augur well for change (Magnier, 2002). However, due to opposition within the LDP and other parties, from women as well as men, none of these efforts proved successful.

Women advocates of change hoped for a positive outcome to this policy initiative as long as Moriyama Mayumi retained her position as Justice Minister in the Koizumi cabinet (Yamaguchi interview, 2001–02). However, Moriyama judged that opposition, both within her own LDP party and from opposition-party members, particularly from two right-wing *Minshuto* (DPJ) women, was too great and abandoned plans to introduce a government sponsored bill (Yamaguchi interview, 2001–02). She asked Noda Seiko, who had been involved in the Anti Child Pornography and Prostitution Law, to help sponsor the change from within the Diet (Moriyama interview, 2001; Noda interview, 2001). Chairing a project team similar to the one in the DV law reform process, Noda, a Diet member who is in a common-law marriage, made efforts to gain support from LDP members and opposition-party women. (Yamamoto, 2001; *Japan Times,* 2002; Noda interview, 2001). Her efforts were opposed by conservative women's groups, who argued that this policy change would trigger the collapse of the family. Conservative LDP members also feared that it would foster too much 'individualism' in society (*Asahi Shimbun,*

November 2001; *Japan Times*, 2002). To date this policy has proven more resistant to *giin rippo* (or collective action by female Diet members across party lines) than other, largely victim-related, policies directed at the role of women and children in Japan. The proposed reform may more directly challenge the patriarchal system which lies at the core of Japanese society. As suggested above, it is viewed with hostility by numerous Diet members (including perhaps up to half of the LDP's female Diet members) (Moriyama, 2001), while others avidly support the change. If the bill were passed it would require a specially designated court to allow for selective surnames as an 'exception' rather than providing for a general opting-out of the system which requires a single surname for married women. However, even this limited approach has not succeeded in gaining support (Moriyama interview, 2001; Noda interview, 2001). There has, though, been some incremental change related to surname retention. Central government offices, many local governments, 16 prefectures and some private companies have already institutionalized such policies (Yamamoto, 2001). In the then ruling party, the DPJ, endorsed the dual-name policy but it did not gain support in the Diet.

EQUAL EMPLOYMENT POLICY

The final policy area to be examined relates to gender equality in the workplace, specifically the Equal Employment Opportunity Law (EEOL), initially passed in 1985.

Among developed nations Japan is an outlier regarding women's labor-force participation. Despite women's high levels of education and experience, Japan has the highest gender wage gap in the developed world. According to the International Labor Organization, women in Japan earned, on average, 65.3 percent of men's salaries in 2001, up from 63.1 percent in 1997 (Kinetz, 2004). Japan, effectively, has a two-tiered labor market. Over 85 percent of male workers in Japan are so-called regular employees, who have a long-term relationship with their employer; in contrast, so-called casual or non-regular employees, the vast majority of whom are female, frequently work part-time, receive less pay and have few, if any, opportunities for training and promotion.

The Japanese government ratified the ILO Convention on Equal Remuneration for Men and Women Workers for Equal Value (100) in 1967 and the CEDAW in 1985. Japan's decision to participate formally in the newly developing international norms related to gender equality may have been at least partially due to a desire to be considered a 'modern' nation, worthy of prestige and acceptance. The activism of Japanese feminist groups also may have 'embarrassed' the Japanese government into signing the treaty, as they sought to prod the government into action through expanding norms of gender equity. The Japanese government began to review its statutes in terms of the Convention to reconcile its demands for gender equality, seeking a balance with national customs and law. After protracted negotiations in the consultative committee, or *shingikai*, the tripartite group essentially accepted the views of employers, who insisted on a weak law, with provisions merely to 'endeavor' to attain gender equality, as the price for acquiescing to any law. The Equal Employment Opportunity Law (EEOL), passed in 1985, became effective the following year, meeting the UN deadline.

Nonetheless, signing the treaty and the subsequent passage of the EEOL did produce some changes in Japanese society including some that were unforeseen. Among these was an increase in women attending four-year colleges, and an increase in the hiring of female college graduates during the period of the 'bubble economy' in the late 1980s. The law has certainly helped to increase the number of qualified women who can fulfill managerial and professional responsibilities. Some women, albeit few, were able to gain access to the managerial or career track (*sogo shoku*), which involves transfers and more responsibility as well as higher wages, promotion and benefits. However, many large companies introduced a 'two-track system' after the law's adoption to limit women to clerical tasks (*ippan shoku*) as opposed to managerial roles. The combination of increased education and aspirations that resulted from the law's passage led to more women applying for full-time employment. However, an 'M' shaped curve still characterizes the labor-force participation of women in Japan: work after graduation from college or other school, then 'retirement' after marriage and/or children; and having left the lifetime-employment, seniority-led system it is not possible to go back to jobs and careers. According to 2006 data 90.8 percent of disputes related to retirement and dismissal under the EEOL pertained to pregnancy and childbirth (Nakakubo, 2003).

It is clear that in large measure the non-coercive weak law that was adopted left unchallenged the male-dominated, seniority-based system, replete with gender distinctions. Ambitious women are forced to seek employment in foreign companies or outside of the Japanese corporate structure and its norms. As of 2004 women earned only 57.7 percent of male salaries on average and women held only 9 percent of managerial positions, many of which may be only token titles (Women in Japan Today, 2005), suggesting that the concept of equal pay for work of equal value, although accepted through treaty ratification, is a long way off in reality. By 2008 the number in managerial positions had risen only to 10 percent (*New York Times*, 2008); and the percentage of women in the highest directorial positions (*bucho*) remained a dismal 2.7 percent in 2004 (Weathers, 2005). It has been suggested that the wage gap is widening rather than decreasing: to 32.9 percent in 2006 (*Asahi Shimbun*, 2008). Although a large percentage of women are employed, a disproportionately large percentage of women work part-time (90 percent) – and yet their hours may be longer than those of so-called regular employees, while their average annual wage is 44 percent of their male counterparts' salaries. (*Asahi Shimbun*, 2008; Faiola, 2007). Such workers, who are non-regular, often contract-based *paato* (part-timers), also lack secure wages and access to benefits. The percentage of part-time workers has almost doubled from 1994 to 2007 (now 34%). (*Asahi Shimbun*, 2008; Faiola, 2007). They are not protected by the EEOL.

Increased attention to such data, as well as concern about the declining birth rate in Japan and the possibility of labor shortages (Weathers, 2005), may have helped pressure the Japanese government into revising the EEOL through amendments, effective April 1999, that mandated equal opportunity in recruitment, hiring, assignments, training and promotion (excluding on-the-job training). The 1997 amendments also introduced new provisions concerning employers' obligation to devote due care to prevent sexual harassment as well as positive action for the promotion of equal opportunity between men and women.

The new amendments changed the scope of the Equal Employment Opportunity Law from discrimination against women to gender-based discrimination, thus prohibiting discrimination against men as well. In addition, the areas where discriminatory treatment is prohibited are now provided in more detail, including assignment of tasks, provision of powers, kinds of occupation, change of employment status and renewal of labor contracts. A special provision on sexual harassment was also addressed in the EEOL, barring 'quid pro quo' and 'hostile environment' practices.

In June 2006, twenty years after the enactment of the EEOL, further revisions were made to the law. They moved from prohibiting discrimination against women to 'prohibiting discrimination on the basis of sex'. New provisions were added to protect female workers from pregnancy-related discrimination and to prohibit 'indirect discrimination' (Nakakubo, 2003).

The concept of discrimination includes allocation of duties and grant of authority (Nakakubo, 2003). Provisions against sexual harassment were

strengthened by obligating employers to take 'necessary measures' to deal with this issue. There are also efforts included to revise the ineffective prefectural dispute procedures related to sex discrimination, although it is feared that lawsuits may still be the major recourse, as the administrative remedies often do not work. Positive action remained a recommended rather than mandated action. The amendments also permit mediation to go forward through a request from only one side (in the past both sides had to agree, making the process very difficult to implement), and names of recalcitrant employers are to be publicized. In 2006, the revised EEOL was used as the basis for a successful lawsuit against Nomura securities, after nine years of litigation. The court granted lump-sum settlements but only from the time the revised EEOL took effect, in April 1999 (Nakakubo, 2003).

Furthermore, the concept of indirect discrimination was introduced as a form of prohibited discriminatory measures. Indirect discrimination means that if any measures bring about discriminatory consequences for either men or women they will be regarded as discrimination even if they do not constitute an explicit distinction between men and women. Such measures are permitted only when there are reasonable grounds, such as those necessary for the performance of specific tasks. It has been pointed out that the two-track employment-management system, which began to be introduced widely when the original Equal Employment Opportunity Law was enforced, amounts to this form of discrimination because workers are, effectively, segregated by gender in different career courses under the system. In view of this and other situations the international Commission on the Elimination of Discrimination Against Women recommended awareness-raising and measures to decrease wage disparities and non-discriminatory employment (CEACR, 2007, ILO).

When, prior to the adoption of the 2006 amendments to the EEOL, the Labor Policy Council of the Ministry of Labor considered the introduction of the concept of indirect discrimination, employers expressed strong opposition, stating that the concept was not yet well recognized. Consequently, prohibition of indirect discrimination in general was not provided for in the amended law. Instead, the following three forms of indirect discrimination are prohibited in statutory orders: (a) providing for weight and height requirements in recruitment and hiring; (b) requiring applicants for managerial positions to accept transfer to any places in the country; and (c) requiring candidates for promotion to have experience of being transferred to other places.

Other new provisions included the prohibition of dismissal and other unfavorable treatment of female workers on the basis of pregnancy, childbirth and maternity leave. Dismissal of women was made invalid during pregnancy and the first year following childbirth. Also, sexual harassment against men was now in the scope of the law: employers are required not only to devote due care to its prevention but also to make specific arrangements for dealing with complaints, including setting up focal points. Provisions for 'positive action' were included.

In June 2006, twenty years after the enactment of the EEOL, further revisions were made to the law. They moved from prohibiting discrimination against women to 'prohibiting discrimination on the basis of sex'. New provisions were added to protect female workers from pregnancy-related discrimination and to prohibit 'indirect discrimination'.

The 2006 amendments to the EEOL (and Labor Standards Law) prohibit discrimination based on sex in assignment of tasks and responsibilities as well as changes in the terms of occupation and contract. However, pay discrimination itself is not outlawed and there is no reference to equal pay for work of equal value (Working Women's International Network, 2007). The definition of indirect discrimination in the law's revisions is still insufficient to deal with pay discrimination, temporary and full-time employment and the tracking systems. It applies to body height, weight or physical capacity when recruiting or hiring workers; if there is a two-career ladder, permitting transfers; requiring workers to 'have experiences of job relocation' when requesting promotion (Working Women's International Network, 2007). Companies must provide 'legitimate reasons' for job distinctions or evaluate them on a case by case basis The goal was to permit female workers to be able to engage in full working lives 'with respect to maternity' (Working Women's Network, 2007).

UTILIZING THE LEGAL ARENA

At least some of the incremental change related to the EEOL may be attributed to the filing of law suits challenging sex-based workplace discrimination by working women's groups and their labor-lawyer allies and advocates (now the Working Women's International Network [WWIN]). Although Japan is often referred to as a non-litigious culture, women's and other change-oriented groups have sought to use the courts as an alternative means of putting pressure on the political system in order to change established norms. After years of limited success, during which the courts suggested that discrimination was not 'contrary to public order' in Japan (Sumitomo Electric case, 2000), the tide has begun to change in recent years. The Sumitomo Electric case was reversed in the Sumitomo

Metals case in 2003. Successive efforts at litigation began with the Kyoto Gas case in 1998 and have progressed through the Kanematsu and other suits challenging discriminatory labor practices. In 2000 the Tokyo High Court ruled in favor of female plaintiffs in the Shiba Shinyo Credit case, ordering promotions and damages for lost wages and attorney fees. In 2002 the Tokyo District Court ruled in the Nomura Securities case that the two-track system based on gender was illegal and ordered compensatory payments to the affected women. In the Kanematsu case, ruled on in January 2008, Kanematsu Corporation was ordered to pay compensatory wages to four of six employees, though the pleas of two employees were denied (*Asahi Shimbun*, 2008). In 2008 a challenge to the two-track system was finally accepted by the Tokyo High Court in a ruling that found a gender-based wage system was illegal (*Japan Times*, 2008). This case had initially been filed in 1995, and it took efforts by working women's groups who persisted throughout this period to get a favorable ruling.

However, it should be cautioned that specific legal decisions in Japan are not precedent-setting – and the EEOL is considered a 'guideline' rather than binding in terms of company policy. The government and the courts still tend to favor private concerns in practices related to hiring and promotion, given the strong link between the LDP and the corporate sector. In this regard even the positive changes in the EEOL in recent years will need to be carefully monitored to assess successful adoption and implementation.

LITERATURE REVIEW

There are a number of resources that are helpful in analyzing gender-equality policy in Japan.

The Gender Equality Bureau in the Cabinet Office in Japan publishes data with some frequency in addition to providing a copy of the Basic Law on Gender Equality and a description of the government processes established to oversee and implement the law.

The Gender Equality Bureau also issues annual reports on women's equality. Other Gender Equality Bureau resources include:

Women and Men in Japan, 3 February 2010 (pamphlet, issued annually).

Kick-off Seminar towards 2010 APEC WLN Meeting in Japan (24 March 2010), 7 April 7 2010.

The Active Participation of Women and Revitalization of Economy and Society, 29 September 2010 (from the 'White Paper on Gender Equality 2010' Summary).

What's a Gender-Equal Society?

Activities of the Government for Realizing a Gender-equal Society.
The Organizational Structure of the National Machinery in Japan.
The Basic Law for a Gender-Equal Society (Law No. 78 of 1999).

Additional resources include:

The Equal Employment Children and Families Bureau issues some data on equality related issues from time to time.

The Japanese government sources provide an important record of policy enactments from a textual perspective, tracing the path from adoption to implementation in most instances. They also provide information on the policy structures were created. The annual reports on Women in Japan are particularly helpful in evaluating trends related to gender equality over time.

The Ichikawa Fusae Memorial Association publishes a quarterly newsletter, *Japanese Women*, which reviews policies relevant to women's status in Japan. These factual reports, which deal with policy changes and events, provide an important resource for scholars of feminism, primarily at the policy level.

Joyce Gelb's *Gender Policies in Japan and the United States* (2003) and Vera Mackie's *Feminism in Japan* (Cambridge, 2003) deal with aspects of gender-equality policy. Gelb's work is primarily comparative, assessing differences between the USA and Japan with regard to policy adoption and implementation. Mackie's focus is primarily on the history of Japanese feminism, with less emphasis on gender-equality policy.

Ueno, Chizuko's *The Modern Family in Japan* (2009) and numerous other writings in her prolific output deal with aspects of gender equity. Ueno has been a strong critic of the role of the Japanese government, which she views as militaristic and nationalistic even today, in repressing women's aspirations.

Japanese resources include the following.

Yoshida Hiroshi's *Nihon ni okeru danjo byoudou shihyou no kaihatsu – Norway toukei-kyoku no danjobyoudou shihyou wo sankou ni* (*Development of Gender Equality Index in Japan with Reference to the Gender Equality Index in Norway*) applies the Norwegian Gender Equality Index to the reality in Japan to demonstrate local discrepancies in the achievement of gender equality in Japan, finding the Japanese case wanting in effective change.

Kuniko Funabashi, Nihon no *'Danjo kyoudou sankaku seisaku deha naze seisabetukaishou ha susumanainoka,'* ('Why Has Gender Equality Made Only Little Progress in Japan?'), People's Plan Study Group, No. 51, Summer 2010. Page number unavailable. The main argument, which is unusual, is that the policy of Gender Equality in Japan sought not the participation of women in workplace but mobilization of women in workplace

Miyoko Tsujimura, Kenpou to Gender: *Danjo Kyoudou Sankaku to Tabunka Kyousei heno Tenbou* (The Japanese Constitution and Gender: Gender Equality and the Prospect for Multiculturalism), Tokyo: Yuhikaku, 2009. This is an analysis of the Japanese constitution from the perspective of gender equality. It finds the constitution's promise to have been unfulfilled.

Momoko Nakamura, Kotoba to Gender (Language and Gender), Tokyo: Keisou Shobou, 2001. The author demonstrates how gendered language in Japan, e.g., some expressions only male or female can use, worked as an ideology for the consolidation of gender distinction between men and women in Japanese society, adding to the difficulty in creating meaningful gender equality.

CONCLUSION

The comparative analysis of policy related to gender equity in Japan demonstrates that the most progress has been made with regard to educational opportunity, although even in this area there continue to be clear differences between patterns of male and female education and resulting opportunities. With regards to gender-equality policy, initial progress was followed by a significant backlash, with few recent examples of positive momentum either at the national, prefectural or municipal level. Finally, in the area of equal employment policy the EEOL has undergone three revisions. Aspects of gender inequity in the workplace have been addressed but the data cited in this article suggests how much further anti-gender-discrimination policy in Japan needs to go.

After the Democratic Party of Japan gained electoral dominance in summer 2009 a government panel in April 2010 proposed a menu of measures tailored to promote gender equality, including a call to revise the Civil Code to allow a dual-surname system. These efforts were met with fierce opposition from then Financial Affairs Minister Shizuka Kamei, who threatened to retract his own People's New Party from the DPJ-led coalition if a bill was submitted to parliament (Sanchanta and Koh, 2011), and hopes that progessive policy would be enacted were dashed. As of 2014 efforts at recognizing fundamental demands for gender equality in Japan have yet to be realized.

REFERENCES

Asahi Shimbun (2001). Surname debate heats up. 6 November 2001.

Asahi Shimbun (2008). ILO: Japan Needs to Correct Gender Wage Gap. 12 May 2008.

Asakura Mitsuko, interview October 2001.

CEACR, ILO (2007). Individual Observation concerning Equal Opportunity Convention, 1951 (No. 100), Japan (Ratification: 1967).

Chizuko, U. (2009). *The Modern Family in Japan*. Melbourne: Transpacific Press.

Curtin, S. (2003). Gender Equality in Japanese Education: Part One – Male and Female Participation Rates in Higher Education. *Social Trends*, 42, June.

Curtin, S. (2003). Gender Equality in Japanese Education: Part Two – The Development of the Two Year Women's Junior College System. *Social Trends*, 43, June.

Faiola, A. (2007). Japanese Working Women Still Serve the Tea. *Washington Post*, 2 March.

Furuhashi, G. (2000) Interview, (Retired bureaucrat, President, Salt Science Research Foundation.

Gelb, J. (2003). *Gender Policies in Japan and the United States*. New York: Palgrave Macmillan.

Gender Equality Bureau, Cabinet Office, Government of Japan (2001–12). *Gender Equality in Japan*.

Gender Equality Bureau, Cabinet Office, Government of Japan. (2001–12). *Women in Japan Today*. 2010 pamphlet (February 3).

Gender Equality Bureau, Cabinet Office, Government of Japan. (2001–12). *Women and Men in Japan*.

Hashimoto, H. (2002a). Danjo Kyodo Sankakau Shakai Kihonho to Jichitai Jyorei. Unpublished paper.

Hashimoto, H. (2002b). Personal email, 30 December.

Hashimoto, H. (2009). Personal email, June.

International Parliamentary Union. (2012). www. ipu. org.

Japan Times. (2002). Interview July 2002, House of Representatives, Tokyo, Japan.

Japan Times. (2008). Kanematsu Loses Gender Suit in Appeal Reversal, February 2. Tokyo, Japan.

Japan Today (2013). Heenali Patel, Who's Afraid of Japanese Women?, October 29, 2013.

Kinetz, E. (2004). Wages of Equality: A World of Unfinished Business. *International Herald Tribune*, 21 February.

Kingston, J. (2013). Japan and Korea Slide Down Gender Index Ranking, *Japan Times*, November 2, 2013.

Kitayama, A. (2010). Japan Lags Behind in Labor Equality. *New York Times*, March 7, 2010.

Kobayashi, Y. (2002). Personal email, 9 August.

Mackie, V. (2003). *Feminism in Modern Japan: Citizenship, Embodiment and Sexuality*. Cambridge: Cambridge University Press.

Magnier, M. (2002). In Japan, Women Fight for the Last Word on Last Names. *LA Times,* 10 March.

Moriyama Mayumi, interview, 2001.

Nakakubo, H. (2003). Canadian Embassy. Gender Equality and the Role of Law. *Asia Foundation*, 24 June.

New York Times. (2008). Rusell Shorto 'No Babies in Europe', June 29.

Nikkei Online. (2011). www.nikkei.com.

Noda, interview, 2001.

Osawa, M. (2000). Government Approaches to Gender Equality in the mid-1990s. *Social Science Japan Journal*, 3 (1), 3–19.

Sanchanta, M. and Koh, Y. (2011). Japan Ponders quotas for Women in Politics, *Wall Street Journal*, January 7, 2011.

Social Watch (2012). Measuring Inequity: The 2012 Gender Equity Index. Retrieved on 17 July, 2014, www.socialwatch.org.

Stetson, D. and Mazur, A. (1995). *Comparative State Feminism*. Thousand Oaks CA: Sage Publications.

Ueno, C. and Osawa, M. (2001). Danjo Byodo Sankaku Shakai kihon ho Osawa no mezasu mon. In C. Ueno (Ed.) *Radikaru ni katareba taidan sho* (pp. 19–92). Tokyo: Hiebon Sha Publishing.

Weathers, C. (2005). Equal Opportunity for Japanese Women: What Progress? *Znet*, 5 October.

Working Women's International Network (2003). Counter Report to the Japanese Government's Fourth and Fifth Report on the Implementation of CEDAW. Unpublished letter, February.

Working Women's International Network. (2003). Report on the Situation of Working Women in Japan. Letter to Director General ILO, 23 May.

Working Women's International Network. (2007). Report on the Situation of Working Women in Japan.

World Economic Forum. (2013). Global Gender Gap. Retrieved on October 6, 2014, http://www.weforum.org/issues/global-gender-gap.

Yamashita, Y. (1993). The International Movement toward Gender Equality and Its Impact on Japan. *US-Japan Women's Journal. English Supplement*, 5, 69–86.

Yamashita, Y. Interview, 2003.

Yamamoto, T. (2001). LDP Divorced Over Dual Surname System. *Nikkei Weekly,* 24 December.

12

Policing in Japan

David T. Johnson

INTRODUCTION

The essence of the police role is the general right to use coercive force within a state's domestic territory (Bittner, 1980; Klockars, 1985). For this reason it is sometimes said that police are to government as the edge is to a knife (Chevigny, 1995: vii). In Japan police may be the state's most powerful agency – and certainly one of the most powerful (Johnson, 2004c). One might suppose, therefore, that there must be much research about policing in Japan. But one would be wrong. Empirical research about Japanese police is surprisingly sparse, leaving students of the subject tempted to weave large swatches of narrative from little rags of data.

The point of departure for this survey of policing in contemporary Japan is the recognition of two basic truths: that police are an extremely important institution in Japanese society and that hardly anyone studies them in a serious way. As one Japanese reporter has observed:

> If a prominent sociologist from the West…came here to research the Japanese police, that scholar undoubtedly would conclude that this country is 'a strange land.' First he would run into the police wall of secrecy, and he would be unable to investigate actual police practices and conditions. Next he would

be informed that there is no investigative reporting about the police by newspaper or other mainstream journalists, and that there are very few free-lance journalists who follow police issues. Then he would learn that in Japanese colleges and universities there are no courses about the police (as there are in the West) and no scholars who seriously study them. In the end, our friend the sociologist would discover that citizens and taxpayers (who have entrusted their safety to the police) have an extremely weak consciousness to try to check the police. Such a scholar, I think, would be seized by this question: Is Japan really a democratic country? (Kobayashi, 1998: vi)

Fifteen years after this passage was published Japan remains a 'strange land' with respect to police research. Naoko Yoshida of Meiji University has studied some aspects of Japanese policing, but her fine work leaves large lacunae in the field, including in such fundamental subjects as the police role in crime control and the problem of police misconduct (Yoshida, 1999, 2008, 2010; Yoshida and Leishman, 2006). Besides Yoshida there is little serious research activity in Japanese police studies at the time of writing in 2013. In fact, much of the best research about Japanese policing is based on fieldwork that was finished decades ago – and much of that was done by foreigners (Bayley, 1976, 1991; Ames, 1981; Parker,

1984, 2001; Murayama, 1990; Miyazawa, 1992). In this sense Japanese police studies today is behind where it was twenty years ago. This is unfortunate not only for scholars and students who want to know about policing in Japan but also for the Japanese police themselves, who could benefit from scholarly scrutiny (as their American counterparts have), and for residents of Japan, who have a personal stake in how policing is done.[1]

Police studies in Japan are moribund for two main reasons. First, empirical criminology is not well developed in Japan, and the dearth of studies about police also applies to other institutions of Japanese criminal justice, from prosecutors and prisons to parole and capital punishment. But a more fundamental obstacle to doing empirical research about the police is the closed and secretive nature of Japan's police organizations. It is much easier to gain access to police research sites in the USA than in Japan, as several researchers have described and lamented (Ames, 1981; Bayley, 1991; Miyazawa, 1992; Ochiai, 2000; Parker, 2001) – and as I can attest from personal experience.[2] More than two decades ago one analyst observed that 'American police are one of the country's most studied institutions' while the Japanese police 'are one of the most closed' (Bayley, 1991: 77). There might be an irony in this contrast, for the propriety of police behavior in America may be worse than in Japan, yet the Japanese police, who have less to hide, are more closed to outside scrutiny (Bayley, 1991: 78). Police behavior in Japan is not perfect or even 'astonishingly good', as some scholars have maintained (Bayley, 1991: 4). As will be described later in this chapter, there are some serious problems of police misconduct in Japan. But information limitations do mean that it is hard to say much about many aspects of policing in Japan and harder still to hold Japanese police accountable for their behavior.

This chapter proceeds in six parts. Section one briefly summarizes the history of policing in Japan, concentrating especially on how police changed during and after World War II. Section two describes the dualistic structure of the Japanese police, with duties divided between the national and local levels, and with most critical functions concentrated in the elite National Police Agency. Section three identifies two critical contexts of policing – authority and danger – and explores how they shape the 'working personality' of the Japanese police. Section four examines the police role in crime control. It posits that Japan is a safe society in some but not all senses; it describes several significant difficulties in assessing how much police contribute to public order in Japan; and it identifies several mechanisms by which police in Japan seem to make a positive crime-control difference. Section five examines four problems of police misconduct in Japan: the construction of misleading crime statistics, especially as related to clearance rates; corruption, especially at the elite levels of the organization, where the use of slush funds has been endemic for at least thirty years; deception and coercion in the interrogation room, where an all-important confession is extracted from the large majority of criminal suspects; and a striking lack of accountability of the Japanese police. Finally, section six suggests reforms that could improve the quality of policing in Japan.

POLICE HISTORY

Before 1600 formal social control in Japan was performed largely by the military and by local groups organized for mutual defense. During the Tokugawa period (1600–1867) a more elaborate system of policing was developed. In most cities and towns magistrates (*machi bugyo*) with samurai status served as police chiefs, prosecutors, and judges. They were assisted by inspectors (*metsuke*) who paid special attention to people or groups that posed a threat to government. In turn, the magistrates delegated authority to mounted police sergeants (*yoriki*) and police officers (*doshin*), both of whom were sword-carrying samurai. Detectives (*meakashi*) were low class or outcaste in origin, and some were ex-offenders who offered to help the government as a way of avoiding their own execution (Botsman, 2005: 69).[3]

Japan's modern system of policing began taking shape in the Meiji period (1868–1912) after a former samurai from Kagoshima named Toshiyoshi Kawaji returned from a study trip to Europe. Kawaji recommended a series of reforms based on his observations in France and Prussia, and the result was the establishment of Japan's Home Ministry (*Naimusho*) in 1873, which controlled police at the prefectural level through its own police bureau. This new police system had a range of responsibilities that went well beyond the core duties of crime control, the protection of life and property, and the maintenance of social order. Now police also regulated public health, construction work, factories, and businesses of various kinds (Westney, 1987).

During the Pacific War (1931–1945) police duties expanded even further, as the Home Ministry mobilized labor for the war effort, controlled transportation, and regulated speech and publications. As the scope of police activities increased the Home Ministry became Japan's most powerful governmental agency, even trying to 'purify politics' in the inter-war period (in cooperation with conservative allies in the procuracy and other parts of Japan's central government). The Special Higher Police (*tokko*) were established in 1928 to control thought and political activity (Mitchell, 1976; Steinhoff, 1991), and after the Manchurian Incident of 1931 the Military Police (*kempei*) assumed a wide range of control functions (Deacon, 1990), leading some analysts to call the Japan of this period a 'police state' (Tipton, 1990; Mitchell, 1992 and 1996).

After Japan surrendered to the Allied Powers in 1945 its police went through three stages of change: reform, reversion, and reinvention (Aldous and Leishman, 1997). During the reform stage the Home Ministry was abolished and police were relieved of various duties, from fire protection to public health. Japan's police system was also decentralized, resulting in some 1600 independent police forces at the municipal level, and public safety commissions (*koan iinkai*) were established to control and supervise the police. Members of these commissions were appointed by the prime minister, prefectural governors, and local mayors.

But the effort to decentralize the Japanese police 'ran into immediate problems' (Ames, 1981: 11). Many municipalities did not have sufficient funds to support their own police force, and there were widespread complaints of inappropriate influence on the police by local political bosses and *yakuza* (gangsters). In 1951 the Police Law was amended to permit small communities to merge their police forces with the National Rural Police, and soon thereafter the vast majority of local forces surrendered their independent status.

Japan's Police Law was revised again in 1954, despite strong opposition from leftists who feared a return to the pre-war problems of the police state. This revision recentralized police administration in some of the same ways that prevailed in the pre-war period (Aldous, 1997: 180). Over the next two decades, as Japan's economy grew and its international prestige increased, the Japanese police were reinvented (at least in public perception), and the predominant policing paradigm shifted 'from one of firm centralized control to one of softer community-centered service' (Aldous and Leishman, 1997: 144). The police also cultivated this new image, both to promote their domestic legitimacy and to enhance their international regard. The positive opinions of the Japanese police in many Western minds (Bayley, 1976; Vogel, 1979: 204–222) coincided with a deepening concern about rising crime rates and other 'law and order' problems in Western nations (Garland, 2001).

POLICE STRUCTURE

Japan's present police system is based on a structural dualism between 47 prefectural police units,[4] on the one hand, and the National Police Agency (*keisatsucho*), on the other. At the prefectural level many day-to-day police operations – from the allocation of police resources to criminal investigation – are autonomous, while the NPA performs most central functions. It supervises police education and training. It compiles criminal statistics. It provides criminal-identification services. It procures police equipment. It coordinates inter-prefectural and international police activities. It supervises security police (*koan keisatsu*). And, crucially, it provides the top management staff for all of the prefectural police departments. The concentration of these critical functions in the NPA – from communications and training to command and security – not only ensures some consistency across police operations in different parts of the country it is also 'a skillful method of retaining all the key and potentially problematic police duties in the hands of the [elite] National Police Agency' (Ames, 1981: 218).

As of 2010 there were only 7709 personnel in the NPA: 1969 police officers (just one quarter of that total), 901 Imperial guards, and 4839 civilians. By contrast, the total number of prefectural police personnel (283,766) was 36 times greater, with 255,156 police officers and 28,610 civilians serving in the 47 prefectural police units.

Japan's police force is overwhelmingly male. There were 14,900 female police officers in Japan in 2010, or less than 6 percent of the total. The comparable figure for the USA was 13 percent (Sklansky, 2008: 142).

Measured by police per unit of population, Japan's police force is smaller than those in comparable developed democracies (Kyo, 2007: 179). As of 2005 the country had 520 citizens per police officer – about 50 percent more citizens per police than in the USA (353) and nearly twice as many as France (275). Some analysts believe the perception of Japanese police efficiency is largely a product of their light workload and of 'the high degree of law abidingness of the [Japanese] people' (Miyazawa, 1992: 15).

Japan's prefectural public-safety commissions are composed of five members in large prefectures and three members in small ones, while the National Public Safety Commission has six members including the chairperson, who is also a minister with portfolio in the prime minister's cabinet. The main mission of all these commissions is to supervise the police under their jurisdiction and to assure democratic control. The continued existence of the commissions is the main remnant of the post-war period of police decentralization, but their effectiveness is questionable. Commission members are mainly old and conservative men who 'almost always defer to police decisions' (Ames, 1981: 13; Ochiai, 2000; Johnson, 2004a, 2004b, 2004c, 2004d; Terasawa, 2009). If the question is who controls the Japanese police the answer is that they are 'totally autonomous' in the structural sense (Ames, 1981: 219). Ultimately, the police control themselves and are formally responsible only to the head of the NPA. Some analysts have argued that the media and public opinion sometimes function as effective informal controls on police in Japan (Bayley, 1991: 80; Katzenstein and Tsujinaka, 1991: 84; Katzenstein, 1996), but there is considerable evidence that the Japanese media often turn a blind eye to problematic police behavior and thereby narrow the range of societal inquiry into important police practices (Araki, 1988; Miyazawa, 1992: 227; Steinhoff, 1993; Ochiai, 1998; Otani, 2000; Terasawa, 1998, 2009).

AUTHORITY, DANGER, AND WORKING PERSONALITY

Policing is shaped by its environment, and Japan has been called 'heaven for a cop' (Bayley, 1991: 1) for some of the same reasons it is considered 'paradise for a prosecutor' (Johnson, 2002: 21). Crime rates are low, case loads are light, the Code of Criminal Procedure is highly enabling of law enforcement's interests in solving crimes and 'making cases' (Miyazawa, 1992), the quiescent politics of crime and punishment give police considerable autonomy to do as they like[5] (though 'the politics of law and order' has become more active in Japan in recent years), and there are few significant external checks on police behavior. Japan is also an orderly country (Miller and Kanazawa, 2000) with a culture of conformity so intense that some insiders have called it a 'straitjacket society' (Field, 1991; Honda, 1993; Miyamoto, 1994).

The police 'working personality' is shaped by the interaction of certain outstanding elements in the police milieu – especially authority and danger (Skolnick, 1994). In Japan, as elsewhere, *authority* is the first defining dimension of the police role because, unlike other occupations, the police possess authority to use coercive force in a wide variety of situations – situations where 'something-ought-not-to-be-happening-about-which-something-ought-to-be-done-NOW!' (Klockars, 1985: 16). In this respect the capacity to use coercive force distinguishes police from other professions, and how police use this power – including their perceptions of its consequences – is largely what distinguishes good police from bad (Klockars, 1985: 122).

Compared to their counterparts in the USA and other rich democracies police in Japan have broad legal authority to detain, arrest, investigate, and interrogate suspects and defendants (Miyazawa, 1992; Foote, 1993; Foote, 2010). At the same time, however, Japanese police have limited legal authority to use investigative powers that are taken for granted in nations such as the USA and Italy, including the powers to wiretap, conduct undercover operations, offer immunity in exchange for testimony and cooperation, and plea bargain (which is illegal in Japan – though it does still occur (Johnson, 2002: 245)).[6] This combination of authority and incapacity calls to mind what Anglo-Irish satirist Jonathan Swift said in the eighteenth century, that 'laws are like cobwebs, which may catch small flies, but let wasps and hornets break through'. Japan's laws of criminal procedure enable police and prosecutors to make cases against many ordinary street criminals who steal, rob, and assault (Miyazawa, 1992), but political, white-collar, and corporate offenders often violate the law with impunity because police and prosecutors cannot use those investigative methods that are most likely to make cases against these high-status offenders (Johnson, 1999).

The second major influence on the police working personality is *danger*. Policing in Japan is a relatively safe occupation – and far safer than policing in the USA. Guns play a small part in Japanese crime, with only a few hundred crimes each year involving the use of handguns – and only a handful of homicides. In 2008, for example, the USA had over 12,000 firearms-related homicides (about 33 per day), while Japan, with less than half the population, had only 11 (and this was a bad year for Japan). In 2006 there were only two gun-related homicides in Japan, and when the number surged to 22 in 2007 'it became a national scandal' (Fisher, 2012).

Japan's low crime and homicide rates and its tiny supply of guns make the unexpected eruption of violence much less threatening to police work than it is in the USA.[7] Japanese police are not haunted by the fear of armed motorists or panicky criminals like their American counterparts are. The safety of Japanese police is reflected in mortality statistics, too. From 2004 to 2010 only 6 Japanese police were feloniously killed in the line of duty, while another 17 were killed accidentally (mostly in auto accidents), for a death toll total of 23 in seven years – about 3.3 per year.[8] By contrast, 133 American police were killed in the line of duty in 2008 and 125 more fell in 2009 – the lowest American total since 1959 (*Honolulu Advertiser*, 2010). Controlling for population differences, American police are about 20 times more likely to die in the line of duty than Japanese police are. This is more than double the difference in the two countries' homicide rates.

Given the different contexts of authority and danger in the USA and Japan, one would expect to see differences in the typical police officer's *working personality* – and one does, along with some similarities. In the USA *police culture* tends to include these characteristics: conservative political views, machismo, risk aversion, mistrust, cynicism, loyalty, an us-versus-them mentality, a strong code of silence, and a sense of mission that police are 'the thin blue line' between order and anarchy as well as soldiers in an all-out 'war on crime' (Skolnick and Fyfe, 1993: 89–112). In Japan, too, police tend to be macho (especially with respect to drinking and womanizing), politically conservative, risk averse, strongly inclined to remain loyal to their organization, and strongly disinclined to violate the organization's code of silence. The available evidence also suggests that Japanese police culture is distinctive in several respects. For example, police in Japan seem less cynical and mistrustful of the citizens they encounter and more inclined to believe in the human potential for positive change. They spend more time listening to citizens than many American police do, and they are more willing to show sympathy towards the citizens and suspects they encounter.[9] They acknowledge more openly their huge discretionary powers. They are less likely to verbally disparage the people they meet – even offenders who are caught red-handed. They are more inclined to give small sermons and little lectures about morality and duty, as preachers and teachers do.[10] They are less quick to resort to arrest than American police are. Their orientation to law enforcement is less categorical and more individualized than that of most American police. And their relations with the rest of the criminal-justice system tend to be more collegial and less antagonistic (Ames, 1981; Parker, 1984; Murayama, 1990; Bayley, 1991; Miyazawa, 1992; Yoshida, 2010; Johnson et al., 2012). In all of these ways the modal working personality of the Japanese police differs from that of their counterparts in the USA.

POLICE AND CRIME CONTROL

How safe is Japanese society? And what roles do Japanese police play in controlling crime and maintaining public order? This section explores these important questions about police effectiveness.

Is Japan a Safe Society?

In some respects crime rates in Japan are much lower than crime rates in the developed democracies of the West. One scholar has even observed that the differences are so large they require 'a different statistical scale' (Zimring, 2012: 47). Large differences also are evident when we compare Tokyo and New York City, the largest cities in their respective countries and two of the most influential urban areas in the world.

In the 1960s and 1970s people of all classes in New York City lived in fear that they might be mugged or assaulted – or worse. But in the last 20 years the city's crime rates have fallen to their lowest levels in half a century. In 2012 the typical New Yorker is safer than he or she has been at any time since 1960. A quarter century ago nobody predicted that crime in a major American city would drop by 80 percent, but New York City has done what most people thought was impossible (Zimring, 2012).

New York City's homicide rate has dropped more than 80 percent since 1990 but, as Table 1 shows, its homicide rate remains 12 times higher than Tokyo's. Similarly, the rape rate in New York City has fallen by two thirds in 20 years yet remains six times higher than the rape rate in Tokyo. New York City's robbery rate has fallen 84 percent but it is still 56 times higher than that in Tokyo. New York City's burglary rate has fallen 86 percent yet it remains twice as high as the burglary rate in Tokyo. And New York City's auto theft rate has fallen an astounding 94 percent but is still 13 times higher than the auto theft rate in Tokyo.

In short, New York City today is a much safer place than it used to be with respect to most kinds of street crime, but in comparison with Tokyo it remains a very dangerous place.[11] A broader comparison of Japan and the USA would reach similar conclusions: big crime declines throughout America for the past two decades or so, and a large and persistent gap in public safety between the USA and Japan. It appears the only cities that can rival Tokyo in their capacity to control crime are other municipalities in Japan and the Asian metropolises of Hong Kong and Singapore (though both of those cities have higher robbery rates than Tokyo). Seoul, by contrast, has 2 to 11 times more crime than Tokyo for the offenses of homicide, rape, robbery, and burglary (see Table 1).

Three Qualifications

One critical question is *how* Japan has managed to achieve such a safe society. But before offering an answer the premise of the question needs to be qualified. Japan's low crime rates cannot be explained away as a statistical chimera, for cross-national victimization surveys show that official crime figures in Japan reflect about the same level of 'underreporting' as do official crime figures in the USA and other developed democracies. In this sense Japan's low rates of street crime are not a statistical illusion.

But two kinds of crime do not receive the attention they deserve in most discussions of public safety in Japan. The first is *domestic violence*. The Law for the Prevention of Spousal Violence and the Protection of Victims was implemented in 2001, which helped stimulate some increases in

Table 12.1 Crime rates in seven cities in 2007 (per 100,000 population)

	Homicide	Rape	Robbery	Burglary	Auto Theft
New York City	6.0	10.6	265.0	254.0	161.0
London	2.2	30.7	610.0	1290.0	501.0
Sydney	1.5	51.4	159.0	1008.0	461.0
Seoul	2.1	20.0	10.3	287.5	n/a
Hong Kong	0.3	1.6	17.6	65.2	20.2
Singapore	0.4	1.6	22.3	20.1	n/a
Tokyo	0.5	1.8	4.7	137.0	12.0
Tokyo as % of NYC	8.3%	17.0%	1.8%	53.9%	7.5%

Sources: Zimring, 2012, p.45; Hong Kong Police Web Site (www.police.gov.hk); Singapore Police Web Site (www.spf.gov.sg); Korean National Police Agency (www.police.go.kr/KNPA/main.jsp).

reporting, yet many observers believe this kind of crime (which disproportionately victimizes women) remains severely underreported. The first national survey on violence against women (conducted in 2000) found that nearly 1 in 20 wives had been subjected to 'life-threatening violence' (Leonardsen, 2010: 102), while a more recent survey (in 2006) revealed that one third of married women had experienced physical and mental abuse (with 13 percent of wives saying they had feared for their lives). But only 3 percent of those women consulted the police or a hospital (Leonardsen, 2010: 103). If a large proportion of violent crime remains hidden in Japan's domestic sphere, as these observations suggest, then the country's much celebrated crime-control achievements must be taken with a large grain of salt.[12]

The second significant form of underreporting concerns *white-collar crime*. Some scholars have argued that the same social facts that help explain why Japan has little street crime also help explain why it has a serious problem with white-collar offending (which can be defined as crimes committed by 'respectable people' in the course of performing their occupations). In this view, Japan's high levels of order on the street are an unintended consequence of institutionalized group conformity, small group dynamics, and informal norms. In a phrase, Japan has achieved 'order by accident' (Miller and Kanazawa, 2000). But if white-collar crime is significantly under-reported, as the same study claims, then Japan surely has a serious crime problem, for research in other countries suggests that white-collar offending causes far more damage to society – in injuries, loss of life, financial terms, and damage to the social fabric – than do the street crimes which tend to preoccupy criminologists, politicians, and criminal-justice professionals (Coleman, 2006).

White-collar crime and domestic violence share three characteristics that help explain why they are underreported: (1) they take place behind closed doors; (2) the offender is 'legitimately present' at the scene of the crime; and (3) there are strong incentives

for victims not to report the crime because complaining about the behavior of members of one's in-group can have negative consequences for the complainant (Leonardsen, 2010: 100).

Evaluating Japan's crime-control achievements becomes even more complicated when one expands the scope of analysis beyond the usual field of vision. In many respects 'crime' is a social phenomenon – by definition and in its causes and consequences. One may reasonably wonder, therefore, about its relationship with other social facts – even those that analysts often ignore because they are not 'crime' per se. One such social fact is suicide.

Japan has one of the lowest homicide rates in the world (see Table 2).[13] But homicide – the killing of another person – is neither the only kind of killing nor the only kind that matters. People kill themselves, too, and acts of self-destruction are no less violent for being self-inflicted. In the late 1990s the number of suicides in Japan surged and remained above 30,000 per year until 2012. On average 30 Japanese children lose a parent to suicide every day, and some analysts regard suicide as the single biggest healthcare issue in the country (Zielenziger, 2006). Yet the responses of Japan's government and media have been characterized by 'active denial' of the scope and seriousness of the problem (Leonardsen, 2010: 159). At present a Japanese person is 4.5 times more likely to kill him or herself than to die in a traffic accident, and 40 times more likely to die by his or her own hand than by someone else's (the analogous figures for the USA, the UK, and France are 2, 8, and 20, respectively). Nonetheless, government officials and reporters in Japan devote only a fraction of their attention and resources to suicide that they concentrate on issues of 'criminal' violence.

The third column of Table 2 shows that at the turn of the millennium suicide had become so common in Japan that the country's overall rate of 'lethal violence' (homicide plus suicide) exceeded that for every other industrialized nation for which decent data exist. Japan's lethal violence rate was

Table 12.2   Lethal violence in 36 nations (homicide and suicide per 100,000 population)

Nation	(H) Homicide Rate	(S) Suicide Rate	(H+S) Lethal Violence Rate	(S/(H + S)) Suicide Homicide Ratio
Industrialized				
Kuwait (1999)	2.2	1.5	3.7	.41
Greece (1998)	1.2	3.1	4.3	.72
Portugal (1999)	1.1	4.0	5.1	.78
Spain (1998)	0.8	6.5	7.3	.89
Italy (1997)	1.1	6.2	7.3	.85
UK (1999)	0.8	6.8	7.6	.89
Holland (1999)	1.3	8.3	9.6	.86
Germany (1999)	0.9	10.6	11.5	.92
Norway (1997)	0.9	10.9	11.8	.92
Hong Kong (1996)	1.0	11.2	12.2	.92
Canada (1997)	1.4	11.3	12.7	.89
Sweden (1996)	1.2	11.8	13.0	.91
Singapore (1998)	1.3	11.7	13.0	.90
Ireland (1997)	0.8	12.5	13.3	.94
Denmark (1996)	1.1	13.6	14.7	.93
South Korea (1997)	2.0	12.8	14.8	.86
Australia (1998)	1.6	13.3	14.9	.89
France (1998)	0.7	14.8	15.5	.95
Austria (1999)	0.8	15.5	16.3	.95
USA (2000)	6.0	10.4	16.4	.63
New Zealand (1998)	1.5	15.0	16.5	.91
Switzerland (1996)	1.1	16.7	17.8	.94
Belgium (1995)	1.6	17.9	19.5	.92
Finland (1998)	2.2	21.1	23.3	.91
Japan (2000)	0.6	24.1	24.7	.98
Industrializing				
Thailand (1994)	7.5	5.2	12.7	.41
China (1999)	1.8	13.7	15.5	.88
Philippines (1993)	14.2	1.5	15.7	.96
Mexico (1997)	15.9	3.9	19.8	.20
Cuba (1997)	6.2	17.1	23.3	.73
Brazil (1995)	23.0	4.7	27.7	.17
Puerto Rico (1998)	20.6	8.1	28.7	.28
Hungary (1999)	2.6	26.9	29.5	.91
Russia (1998)	21.6	38.4	60.0	.64
Columbia (1995)	61.6	3.4	65.0	.05
South Africa (1995)	75.3	—	75.3+	—

Sources: Johnson, 2006; World Health Organization statistics, at http://www.who.int/en (various years).

also about twice the average for all industrialized nations (Johnson, 2008) – and for a decade or so after that analysis was completed Japan continued to have one of the highest rates of lethal violence in the developed world.

For the past two decades or so Japanese policy-makers have become increasingly punitive toward crime (Miyazawa, 2008), and police in Japan and Japanese officials more generally have a 'sensitive stethoscope' with respect to some kinds of disorderly behavior (Bayley, 1991: 188; Leonardsen, 2010: 69). But until quite recently policy-makers in Japan largely shied away from investing in suicide-prevention programs. The preoccupation with crime and disregard of suicide is not been a prudent approach to public health or public safety.[14]

One may also ask how crime and suicide are related. This is a difficult question, but some analysts argue that many of the same forces which account for Japan's low crime rates – such as the high salience of shame (*haji*) in Japanese society, the subordination of the individual to the group (*shudanshugi*), the cultural imperative not to cause 'trouble' (*meiwaku*) to other people, and the emphases on perseverance and endurance (*gaman*) in difficult times – also help explain why suicide is so prevalent (Leonardsen, 2010: 155–170).[15] On this view, Japanese who encounter adversity are culturally encouraged to 'suffer in silence'. When they cannot or will not suffer silently any longer they tend to 'strike in' at themselves through suicide and other forms of self-reproach more often than they 'strike out' at others in acts of protest or violence. To put it in plain English, Japanese culture might prefer and promote 'damn me' responses more than those of the 'damn you' kind.[16]

If the same features of Japanese culture and society that account for the country's low rates of street crime also help explain its high suicide rate then evaluating Japan's crime-control accomplishments is a complicated task, for one must assess the country's total package of values and their consequences as an 'interconnected totality' (Leonardsen, 2010: 11). Suicide is often considered the manifestation of mental illness or the product of social forces over which the 'victim' has little control. It is both of these, of course, but frequently it is also a subversive act that expresses dissatisfaction with the present order and hopelessness for the future (Lieberman, 2003). What does it say about a society when its members choose, in very large numbers, to die by their own hand?

Three Methodological Difficulties

As for the role of the Japanese police in producing these crime and violence patterns, there are at least three methodological difficulties that inhibit the formation of confident conclusions. First, criminologists have made great gains in explaining why certain individuals are more likely to commit crimes than others are, but they have made meager gains in understanding what lies behind differences in cross-national crime rates. Thus, the first and most fundamental difficulty in trying to explain the Japanese patterns is the undeveloped state of comparative criminology (Wilson, 2002).

Second, few scholars have tried to engage questions about crime control in Japan with rigorous research methods. For an evaluation study to be deemed 'sound' and a crime-control program to be judged 'effective' the program must meet the following criteria: a good research design (ideally, random assignment into treatment and control groups); evidence of significant effects; replication of the program across multiple sites; and a positive crime-control benefit that lasts for at least one year after the program ends (Greenwood 2002: 98; Wilson 2002: 553). In Japan hardly any studies of crime-control programs satisfy these criteria. Indeed, even when the evaluation criteria are relaxed considerably, few empirical studies rise to the level of 'decent' (Miyazawa, 1990; Johnson, 2011a).

The third difficulty in explaining Japanese crime and violence patterns is that in the absence of sound evaluation studies of what works to control crime there are so many plausible causal candidates that it is impossible to say with confidence which ones make a significant difference. Some studies stress structural factors, such as the standard of living (Park, 2006), the unemployment rate (Kanayama, 2010a), or the levels of stress in the economy (Roberts and LaFree, 2004).[17] Other studies stress cultural factors, such as social norms (Bayley, 1991; Komiya, 1999; Leonardsen, 2004, 2010) and small-group dynamics (Braithwaite, 1989; Thornton and Endo, 1992; Miller and Kanazawa, 2000). At present, however, most of these 'explanations' remain mere hypotheses: plausible hunches about what makes Japan a safe place, but in their failure to meet the evaluation criteria outlined above, and in the presence of so many competing explanations, little more than educated guesses. As one high-level police official told me in 2010, 'our system for assessing crime-control effectiveness is like a hospital patient who takes 100 medicines simultaneously. If the patient gets better it is impossible to tell which of the drugs cured him, and if the patient gets worse we are unable to say why'.[18] In this sense, Japan illustrates what criminologist Mark Kleiman warned against in the American context: 'lots of activities with "crime control" as part of their nominal justification, but with no one actually accountable for whether those activities generate crime control benefits' (Kleiman 2009: 171).[19]

How Police (Might) Matter

On the available evidence, we cannot be sure what role police have played in producing Japan's crime and violence patterns. But informed speculation is possible, and I will base mine mainly on the work of David Bayley and Walter Ames, two of the most astute observers of policing in Japan.

Ames opens his book *Police and Community in Japan* by stating that 'The Japanese police pride themselves on being the world's best. Their confidence is apparently well founded, for Japan has the lowest crime rate in the industrialized world, and its crime totals have actually followed a downward curve since 1955' (Ames, 1981: 1). Ames closes his book by concluding that citizen cooperation with the police is the key to crime control in Japan, and that 'Japanese society, in effect, polices itself' (Ames, 1981: 228). In between he cautions that citizen cooperation with the police is declining – and this observation was made more than 30 years ago (Ames, 1981: 62). Concerns about cooperation have been repeated many times since (often by the police), but my own view is that there remains something special about the relationship between the police and the public in Japan – and it is not well captured by surveys which suggest that citizen trust in the police is significantly lower in Japan than in the USA (Cao et al., 1998; Cao and Stack, 2005).

Research on 'what works in policing' shows that police *can* make a significant difference in crime control. For example, about half of the huge crime decline in New York City can be attributed to changes in policing – from increasing the number of officers on the beat, to more aggressive patrol strategies, to new systems of accountability (Zimring, 2012). That police do matter is a fresh finding, for the orthodox view not long ago was that 'police do not prevent crime' (Bayley, 1996: 3). In recent years evidence has accumulated to show that police can make a difference, especially by focusing on high-risk places, times, situations, and people. In the USA over the past two decades or so there has been much experimentation and reform in policing, and the 'innovations' that work do so mainly because they focus on these high-risk factors (Weisburd and Braga, 2006).[20]

Japan has substantially fewer police per capita than do comparable democracies in the West (Kyo, 2007). In this sense, the country illustrates the truth that the number of police cannot by itself explain crime levels or patterns. But Japanese police probably do contribute to their country's crime control success in at least two ways.

First, it is helpful to think of the Japanese police not as one organization among many in the country's crime-control field but rather as the central node of a large and interconnected policing network that includes a wide array of individual and corporate actors: employees and institutions in the country's massive private security industry (Yoshida, 1999); 40,000 or so volunteer crime-control groups and their 2.5 million participants; two million 'safe houses' where children receive help and protection; 200,000 school-guard volunteers; a safety-education curriculum for children that has been implemented in schools nationwide; safe building guidelines for public facilities and apartments; a certification system for crime-proof locks and other forms

of crime-control hardware; and crime-prevention standards for convenience stores, supermarkets, and other businesses (Kanayama, 2010a).[21] In these ways, policing in Japan extends far beyond the 'law enforcement' and 'peacekeeping' activities that constitute the core police duties in many academic accounts of what police do. To make progress in understanding why Japan is (in some respects) a low-crime society one must stop thinking about the police as merely or mostly a law-enforcement agency and reconceive them as the central node in a far-flung crime-control web (Brodeur, 2010). To change metaphors, it is instructive to regard the Japanese police as like a film director (think Itami Juzo, who directed *Minbo no Onna, Ososhiki* and other fine films) who plays a central role but whose most crucial activities involve planning, instruction, coordination, facilitation, motivation, and mobilization.[22]

If my first point is to show how to conceptualize the *position* of the police in Japan's crime-control field, my second is to identify the specific *mechanisms* by which Japanese police may prevent and control crime. Here, the framework provided by David Bayley in *Forces of Order* describes several ways in which the Japanese police matter. According to Bayley (1991: 183), 'the primary function of the Japanese police is not deterrence; it is crime prevention through enhancing the capacity of the society to discipline itself'.[23] And Bayley believes police do this in three overlapping ways, by prodding, guiding, and alerting the public about crime problems and challenges.

Prodding refers to the activities of the Japanese police in continuously urging and encouraging the public to report suspicious activities, buy security hardware, learn crime-avoidance techniques, join crime-prevention groups, and read and circulate crime-prevention material. One key aspect of this prodding is stressing that 'the situation is worse' than most people imagine, which heightens public sensitivity to crime issues and thereby enables police to intervene early and aggressively, before the problems become unmanageable (Bayley, 1991: 184).

The second mechanism by which Japanese police prevent crime is *guidance* of the kind that the founder of the Tokyo Metropolitan Police Department (Toshiyoshi Kawaji) stressed in the 1870s when he called police 'nurses of the people'. A similar function is evoked by commentators who call Japan a 'Nanny State' or a system of 'Friendly Authoritarianism' (Leonardsen, 2010: 23). Japanese police enlist thousands of citizens to monitor behavior in their neighborhoods. For example, the Japanese police provide guidance to a mind-boggling array of juvenile counselors – teachers, parents, juvenile probation officers, and the like – who watch and warn youth in a wide variety of ways. The result is 'thousands of respectable "busybodies"... [who] work hand in glove with the police to extend the boundaries of family and school discipline into public places' (Bayley, 1991: 186). This level of control would probably be resented as unduly intrusive in many parts of America and other democratic societies, but there has not been much pushback by the Japanese public.[24] Schools are also central to this social control mission, and their power to 'guide' and 'nurse' children in their charge is broad in scope. Indeed, compared with the periods when Bayley did his research (the 1970s and 1980s), the 'guidance' of juveniles by police and schools probably has intensified (Leonardsen, 2010: 57, 91).

The third crime-control mechanism – *alerting* – refers to the police focus on 'anticipating emerging problems of order' and then working with other actors and agencies to 'take preventive action' (Bayley, 1991: 188). Police in Japan usually do not wait until a crisis has emerged in order to respond. Instead they aim to address crime and disorder problems before they become severe. This not only helps prevent serious problems from emerging, it also helps explain why police in Japan sometimes exaggerate the severity of crime (Kawai, 2004).

Deterrence and Human Nature

Bayley's account of how police matter must be modified in at least one way, for he seems to discount the significance of deterrence when he argues that the 'primary function of the Japanese police is not deterrence; it is crime prevention through enhancing the capacity of the society to discipline itself' (Bayley 1991: 183). This contrast rests on a false distinction between 'deterrence' and 'crime prevention'. In the USA, Japan, and many other nations, deterrence lies 'at the heart of the preventive aspiration of criminal justice' (Kennedy, 2009: 1). Hence, rather than contrasting deterrence and prevention, a better approach is to ask how (and how well) deterrence works to prevent crime in different contexts. Here, too, there is little systematic evidence about Japan, but the available information does seem to suggest that Japan does deterrence differently – and perhaps more effectively – than some American jurisdictions.

Deterrence rests on the premise that the *costs* attached to an action will reduce its frequency. But in thinking about how to design and implement 'costs' so as to reduce criminal conduct, criminal-justice policymakers frequently forget that what matters most is what matters to *offenders themselves*. The practical implication is that people who design deterrence regimes must provide sanctions that matter to offenders – and that may well differ from sanctions that are easy to administer or that appeal to the sensibilities of experts and professionals (Kennedy, 2009). Policing in Japan – and Japanese criminal justice more generally – takes this teaching seriously in three ways.

First, for many if not most offenders, formal sanctions matter less than informal sanctions do. The police in Japan and other institutions of Japanese criminal justice often rely on informal controls, which may well be more effective than reliance on formal and legal ones (Foote, 1992a). Reliance on informal controls also reflects the fact that Japanese criminal-justice officials are more inclined than their American counterparts to treat formal arrest and punishment as human and social costs, not benefits (Kleiman, 2009: 175). For people who believe that there should be limits to the criminal sanction, this parsimony about employing criminal sanctions is a good thing (Packer, 1968).

Second, paying attention to what matters to offenders means recognizing that the dynamics within groups, networks, and communities may have an especially strong deterrent influence on the perceptions and behavior of offenders. Particular people – parents, friends, employers, teachers – and particular beliefs – that one should not cause 'trouble' (*meiwaku*) to people one cares about, or that one should 'reflect' (*hansei*) on one's own shortcomings – often have a strong influence on individual behavior. In Japan, police and other institutions of criminal justice often try to intervene through key people and around key ideas. The crime-control effects of recognizing that humans are deeply 'social animals' may be salutary (Kennedy, 2009).

Third, humans are also 'moral animals' in the Durkheimian sense that their behavior is shaped by social norms that are internalized while at the same time being 'external to and coercive on' the individual (Garland, 1990: 25). It is, therefore, a mistake to treat people as value-free 'rational calculators' of the costs and benefits of different courses of conduct (Kahneman, 2011; Haidt, 2012). Even serious criminal offenders can be influenced by deliberate moral engagement (Kennedy, 2009), and this is frequently tried and sometimes accomplished in Japanese criminal justice (Bayley, 1991: 126; Foote, 1992; Foljanty-Jost, 2003: 5; Leonardsen, 2004).

The premise that humans are both moral and social animals seems to be taken more seriously by police and other criminal-justice professionals in Japan than in the USA (Leonardsen, 2008: 19). As Bayley observes, 'Japanese police officers are not viewed by the community simply as agents of law. They possess enormous moral authority... [The Japanese police officer] acts with the aura of a teacher shaping conduct to conform to community standards' (Bayley, 1991: 142). But, as we shall now see, the Japanese police sometimes have difficulty making their own behavior conform to the standards of law and community morality.

POLICE MISCONDUCT

Bayley is instructive about how police might help to control crime in Japan, but he also seems mistaken about the propriety of Japanese police behavior. He argues that

> if generality of agreement among people in a country is the mark of truth, then Japanese police behavior is astonishingly good. The incidence of misconduct is slight and the faults trivial by American standards. Though a cynical American may always wonder if enough is known about the conduct of individual officers – whether by himself or by insiders – he must begin to consider the possibility that police conduct need not inevitably, recurrently, require substantial improvement. (1991: 4)

If there was ever a time when this position seemed tenable it no longer is today. So many disconcerting truths about the Japanese police have been revealed in recent years that one must conclude that their behavior does in fact 'require substantial improvement'. My own view is that police behavior in Japan was never all that good to begin with, a position that is shared by some other observers (Miyazawa, 1992; Ochiai, 2000; Terasawa, 2009). This section summarizes problems of police misconduct in four areas: the construction of crime statistics and clearance rates, corruption, criminal interrogations, and accountability.

Crime Statistics and Clearance Rates

The 'clearance rate' – the percentage of cases known to the police that they have solved – is widely regarded as one of the most important measures of police effectiveness (Skolnick, 1994). One obvious indicator of problematic police performance in Japan is this rate, which plummeted from 40 percent in 1997 to 20 percent in 2001 – a 50 percent decline. For serious crimes such as homicide and robbery, the clearance rate declined over the same period of time from 80 percent to 48.6 percent – a 40 percent decline. There are several causes of these declines, including increases in some crime categories, but one major force is the fact that the police cannot 'cook the clearance-rate books' (by failing to report crimes that have been reported and by other forms of fibbing) like they used to.[25] It seems Japan's impressive clearance rates of the past were built on a foundation of police prevarication (Kuroki, 2000; Kawai, 2004; Johnson, 2004c, 2004d).

In some ways, the lower clearance rates of the present reflect and reinforce public distrust of the Japanese police. Some previous scholars wrongly concluded that Japanese police enjoy more trust from the public than do police in the USA (Ames, 1981; Bayley, 1991; Parker, 2001). In fact, however, the best available evidence demonstrates that Japanese citizens have significantly lower levels of confidence in police than Americans do (Cao et al., 1998). In one poll taken during a wave of police scandals some 60 percent of Japanese adults said their trust in police has declined, and 45 percent said they do not trust the police at all. As one elderly Japanese man put it, 'Today the police are a shame and an embarrassment for all of Japan' (Sims, 2000). By contrast, in a poll taken at about the same time as the Japanese survey, only 15 percent of American city residents said they were dissatisfied with their local police, and even among African-Americans only 24 percent expressed discontent (Johnson, 2004c).

Corruption

Japanese police have had serious problems with corruption for several decades. In 1984 Matsuhashi Tadamitsu, a former high-level official in the National Police Agency, published a 400-page mea culpa with a title taken from the 51st Psalm: *My Sin is Ever Before Me (Wagatsumi wa Sude ni Wagamae ni Ari)*. His book meticulously detailed how police agencies throughout Japan embezzled money from their budgets in order to create slush funds that would cover under-the-table payments to senior police officials, pay for gifts and entertainment for police and their friends and supporters, and buy silence from people whose complaints could cause them trouble. Since this book's publication its revelations have been confirmed and elaborated by many other sources, including former police, former prosecutors, and journalists (Johnson, 2004c). This kind of police corruption is pervasive in Japan – and it only one part of the picture. Numerous cases of bribe-taking have also been exposed, though the Japanese police invariably (and implausibly) insist that such misconduct is limited to 'a few bad apples' (Ochiai, 2000). Other forms of corruption stem from police control over Japan's enormous pachinko industry and from police regulation of organized crime (Szymkowiak, 2002; Hill, 2003a, 2003b; Kaplan and Dubro, 2003; Johnson, 2004a; Adelstein, 2009).[26] These problems of police corruption are harmful in two interacting ways: they reinforce a culture of secrecy and deceit that is itself the breeding ground for other abuses of authority, and they prevent police from properly enforcing laws against criminal offenders. We do not know as much about police corruption in Japan as we do about the same subject in the USA or Mexico, but we do know enough to conclude that the problem is more severe than many previous analysts believed.

Interrogation

Japanese police misuse their authority in other ways as well, through acts of brutality, perjury, and coercion and deception in the interrogation room – just to name three. What happens in the interrogation room is especially critical because criminal justice in Japan remains deeply reliant on confessions. This may well be the most important issue of all in Japanese criminal justice, for confessions are the heart of Japan's criminal process – the pump that keeps cases circulating in the system (Miyazawa, 1992; Foote, 1992b; Johnson, 2002). Confessions are single-mindedly pursued by police and prosecutors, they are practically required by judges and lay judges in order to convict, and they are deemed by virtually everyone involved to be the 'king of evidence'. Confessions are also the precondition for many of the real achievements in Japanese criminal justice. Indeed, here is the primary postulate of Japan's criminal process and the premise that animates much of its criminal justice system: no confession, no truth, no consistency, no corrections, no convictions, and no justice (Johnson, 2002: chapter 8).

But confessions can be difficult to obtain, and some of the biggest problems in Japanese criminal justice occur when a case is serious, the level of suspicion is high, and the suspect refuses to confess. In these circumstances dropping the case is not considered an acceptable option, and the system's extreme reliance on confessions leads to extreme efforts to obtain them. As one Japanese detective confessed during a murder investigation, 'We go after [the suspect] relentlessly until 11 or 12 at night. We give him as little sleep as possible. We exhaust him physically and mentally. It's rough, but it's the only option remaining to us [because the suspect refuses to confess]' (Johnson, 2004c). Another Japanese detective said, 'There aren't any confessions that are really voluntary. They're told that if they don't talk they won't eat, won't smoke, won't meet with their families' (Miyazawa, 1992: 161). And an executive police officer in Japan's National Police Agency admitted this about interrogation tactics: '[N]o real statements will be made by the suspect unless he feels compelled to do so. Hence, the aim of interrogation is to bring this about *by any means possible*' (Johnson, 2004c, emphasis added). All of these statements suggest that Japanese police are willing to overbear the will of some criminal suspects. This attitude is not only widespread, it is inconsistent with the interrogation ideal of 'storytelling without fear' (Johnson, 2002: 264).

In Japan much of the most disturbing police behavior stems from two connected facts: the system's overwhelming dependence on admissions of guilt, and the absence of checks on police power in the interrogation room. The conditions of interrogation – the duration and intensity of questioning, the duty to endure questioning even after the right to silence has been invoked, and the unavailability of defense lawyers – mean that an overborne will is more than merely an occasional problem. Japanese courts have been reluctant to acknowledge this problem, but the United Nations is not. It has repeatedly rebuked the Japanese state for violating international protocols about the length, location, and methods of interrogation; for excessive reliance on confessions for evidence; and for inadequate disclosure of evidence to the defense. In the view of one of Japan's preeminent legal scholars, the country 'cannot go on forever ignoring the UN's counsel' (Hirano, 1989: 4).

Some observers believe that the solution to Japan's interrogation problem is to relax the reliance on confessions, but this is easier said than done. Norms as deeply embedded as this one are difficult to change, and whatever evolution does occur will take time. A related proposal is to institute alternatives such as plea bargaining and immunity to the standard practice of confession through interrogation (Ukawa, 1997), but this fix also faces formidable obstacles. Many Japanese resist the notion that justice can be 'bargained' (Johnson, 2002: 271). In addition, giving investigators more legal levers would exacerbate the already extreme imbalance of power between the state and the defense in Japan's criminal process.

The most viable solution to the most serious problem in Japanese criminal justice is to require the electronic recording of all custodial interrogations. In my view, there is no good reason to oppose a recording requirement. Since it is a medium for preserving the *truth* of interrogations and confessions, recording helps achieve the 'cardinal objective' of Japanese criminal justice – uncovering and clarifying the truth (Johnson, 2002: 98). Recording also serves the interests of all the parties in the criminal process. It benefits suspects and defense attorneys by deterring impermissible interrogation techniques and thereby affording protection against false confessions and wrongful convictions. Police also benefit, for recording protects them against false accusations by creating a record that they can use to demonstrate the propriety of their interrogation methods. Most importantly, recording helps prosecutors, judges, and lay judges by giving them information they can use to assess the voluntariness and veracity of confessions. In these ways, electronically recorded interrogations promote the goals of accuracy in fact-finding, due process, transparency, accountability, and public respect for the justice system. These are compelling objectives, and the American experience shows that the vast majority of police departments that record believe it has led to improvements in police practice (Johnson, 2010).

The Japanese expression for 'let them talk' (*iwaseru*) is the same as the one for 'make them talk'. Inside the interrogation room, however, the difference between these two realities must be maintained (Johnson, 2002: 275). In the mid-2000s Japanese police and prosecutors started to record some parts of some interrogations in a small percentage of cases (Sasakura, 2012). By recording more comprehensively, the conduct of interrogations and the quality of Japanese criminal justice could be much improved. Many police and prosecutors are resisting reform that would require more comprehensive recording, but sooner or later such reform will probably occur. The international movement towards recording seems unstoppable, and, in the words of Bob Dylan, 'you don't need a weather man to know which way the wind blows'.[27]

Accountability

Japanese police are largely unaccountable to legitimate organs of authority. This final problem of police misconduct is also the most fundamental because research shows that (with few exceptions) government agents act according to law only when they must (Maravall and Przeworski, 2003).

The question of accountability raises the issue of accountability for what. In Japan, as in other democracies, one critical concern is the accountability of police officers' discretionary decisions. Discretion consists of the *choices* that legal officials make in the criminal process: where there is choice there is discretion. In the aggregate the quality of discretionary decisions of a criminal-justice system largely determines the content and the quality of the justice that is delivered (Walker, 1993). Discretion is also complicated because it is both necessary and dangerous. It is necessary because resources are limited and because case dispositions should be individualized. It is dangerous because the freedom to choose implies the capacity to choose badly. In these ways, discretion is like an axe: it can be a useful tool for achieving important ends, but it also can be a weapon that, if misused, causes mischief or mayhem. The challenge is to eliminate unnecessary discretion and to control, channel, and check that, which remains.

In the USA it is widely believed that more than half of all discretion in the criminal justice-system is exercised by the police (Davis, 1969). Whatever the exact percentage, 'who gets what' in American criminal justice is significantly shaped by police decisions. In this respect, American criminal justice is largely 'justice without trial', and practitioners, reformers, and consumers of criminal justice are rightly concerned about what the police do outside the court room (Skolnick, 1994).

In Japan criminal justice may be even more a matter of 'justice without trial' than it is in America. Even after the advent of lay-judge trials in 2009 (lay judges are used to try only a small percentage of criminal cases) the vast majority of Japanese criminal trials are little more than rituals for ratifying police and prosecutor decisions (Johnson, 2011b). The 'real substance of criminal procedure' and the 'truly distinctive character' of Japan's criminal process are found in the investigative stages that are dominated by the police (Hirano, 1989). For this reason Hirano Ryuichi (1989), a former president of Tokyo University and the dean of criminal-justice studies in Japan, concluded that Japanese criminal justice is 'abnormal', 'diseased', and 'really quite hopeless' (see also Ishimatsu, 1989).

In some respects, police in Japan also wield more power than their American counterparts, especially when it comes to criminal interrogation (Miyazawa, 1992). Many labels have been used to characterize criminal justice in Japan. 'Precise justice' and 'prosecutor justice' are two of the most familiar, but 'police justice' – perhaps the most telling label of all – may be the least appreciated (Johnson, 2004c). The immense power of the Japanese police produces problems that need to be checked, but in the present system of criminal justice there are precious few mechanisms of accountability or transparency that perform the requisite function. As the rest of this section describes, police in Japan are largely unaccountable to prosecutors, courts, politicians, the public, the Board of Audit, and the media.

For starters, Japanese prosecutors are notoriously lenient (*amai*) toward police wrongdoers, in part because they depend on police for the information they need to charge and try cases. Former Prosecutor General Itoh Shigeki's 'parable' about the illegal police wiretapping of the Japan Communist Party makes precisely this point (Itoh, 1992: 137). In Itoh's view, if prosecutors had pushed any harder for police accountability the police would have pushed back, and the police would have prevailed in the resulting confrontation (Miyazawa, 1989).

As for judges, the Japanese police perceive 'no significant threat in judicial control' of their behavior (Miyazawa, 1992: 225; Foote, 1993) because judicial decisions that are unfavorable to the police are exceptionally rare in Japan. One result is that judicial scrutiny functions mainly to legitimate police behavior not to restrain it. And one illustration of the permissive nature of Japanese courts concerns 'duty questioning' (*shokumu shitsumon*) – the informal questioning of citizens on the street by the police (Miyazawa, 1992: 114). Japanese court decisions permit police to restrain and question citizens in ways that would clearly constitute illegal arrest in the American context. In one case I observed at the Tokyo District Court on

14 March 2013 a defendant on trial for using meth-amphetamines was physically prevented by several police from boarding a train at Ikebukuro station for more than an hour, and when he was finally allowed to move he was followed on to the same train car by no fewer than nine police officers, who then proceeded to restrain his movements after he arrived at his destination. The police even told taxi drivers (who had been telephoned by the man being duty questioned and by his friend) to drive away without letting the man into their cabs. The man eventually succeeded in getting a ride, whereupon he was followed for many kilometers by police in several patrol cars. After several hours of this duty questioning – which is supposed to be voluntary – the police finally obtained an arrest warrant and formally arrested a person they had actually arrested long before they put him in handcuffs. According to lawyer Shinomiya Satoru, who was defending this case, his client will almost certainly be convicted, either because the court finds that the police did nothing illegal or because the court reaches the Kafkaesque conclusion (as Japanese courts sometimes do when it comes to duty questioning) that the police behavior was 'illegal but not unacceptable'.[28]

Similarly, for more than 60 years Japan's Board of Audit has conducted spot inspections of all of the nation's prefectural police headquarters. Despite clear evidence of systemic embezzlement (the slush-fund problem described above), the Board has exposed no cases of spurious accounting. Where police are involved 'this watchdog trembles' (Ochiai, 2000: 55). Politicians dissemble too, often because they fear that if they attempt to disclose police misconduct their own corruption will be exposed by the police, who possess an abundance of sensitive and potentially damning information. As one Japanese reporter has said, 'everyone fears the police but the police fear no one' (Johnson, 2004c).

As for citizen oversight of the police, Japan's national and prefectural Public Safety Commissions are silent watchdogs. As described in the section on police structure, their members tend to be elderly, conservative men from the community – business owners, doctors, ex-bureaucrats, and the like – who have neither police experience nor expertise and who have no staff or office with which to conduct meaningful investigations. In reality, the Public Safety Commissions are controlled by the police themselves, and their deliberations are, for the most part, 'empty rituals' (Kubo, 2001: 147). In the wake of a wave of police scandals that started in 1999 Japan's Police Law was amended, purportedly to enable commissioners to exercise greater supervision over the police, but the changes were cosmetic and have not stimulated significant reform. More ambitious reform was avoided at least partly because conservative politicians claimed that 'policing the police would be bizarre' (Iitake, 2000). But,

of course, 'policing the police' is not bizarre, it is a democratic imperative, and there are many examples of successful citizen oversight of the police in other countries (Walker, 2005).

Finally, the weak formal controls on Japanese police are little supplemented by journalistic, scholarly, or other outside scrutiny – as stressed at the start of this chapter. If the question is who controls the Japanese police the answer is that they are almost totally autonomous (Ames, 1981: 219). Ultimately, the police in Japan control themselves – except when they do not.

CONCLUSION

In many societies police are the most visible face of government, and one that almost all people recognize and many encounter with frequency. Police also have awesome powers, including the authority to use coercive force in a wide variety of circumstances. In democracies what police do is shaped by two expectations: to deal with crime and disorder by preventing them when possible and by bringing to account people who break the law; and to produce justice through the fair and impartial exercise of authority. In the USA this dual mandate of effectiveness and fairness has been the subject of much empirical research. The same two imperatives exist in Japan and they may be related to each other in much the same way as they are in the USA, where studies show that fairness and effectiveness in policing are not mutually exclusive but rather mutually reinforcing (National Research Council, 2004: 2). If this finding holds true in Japan – and there are reasons to believe it does – then addressing the problems of police misconduct discussed in the previous section will also bolster the ability of the Japanese police to prevent and control crime.

I hope that in the years to come more research will be done to discover how fairness and effectiveness are related in Japanese policing. One big step toward that end would be greater openness of Japanese police institutions to researchers and journalists. It is sometimes said that information is the currency of democracy. I conclude this review by stressing that, in many respects, the Japanese public lacks a key to the treasury of truths concerning some of their most important officials.

NOTES

1   Japan is hardly the only country where police are under-researched. In Germany more than 80 scholars and police officials signed a petition

lamenting the lack of importance attached to police research and calling for improvements in police studies (www.empirische-polizeiforschung.de/resolution.php, retrieved 18 December 2012). And in China and India there is little serious study of police behavior despite the size and importance of their police forces and serious problems in their performance. Still, I believe police studies in China and India are more advanced than police studies in Japan. See, for example, Wong, 2009, and Verma and Subramanian, 2009.

2 From July to October 2010 I was a visiting scholar at the Police Policy Research Center in Japan's National Police Academy. I was invited by a high-level official in the National Police Agency and assured that I could do field research in and around the *koban* (police box) in the redlight district of Kabukicho in the Tokyo ward of Shinjuku. But the access I was promised never materialized, and access to other police sites was extremely limited too (wherever I went I was followed by two or more handlers). The individual Japanese police officers I met were (on the whole) serious, open, and generous, but Japan's police institutions were rigidly bureaucratic and antediluvian in their orientation to outsiders and their commitment to empirical research.

3 This paragraph and section rely on Ames, 1981: 9–12.

4 More precisely, Japan has 43 prefectural police forces, two urban prefectural (*fu*) police forces (in Osaka and Kyoto), one district (*do*) police force in Hokkaido, and the Tokyo Metropolitan (*to*) Police Department.

5 Note, though, that 'the politics of law and order' in Japan has become more active in recent years (Miyazawa, 2008).

6 Japan's Act on Wiretapping for Criminal Investigation took effect in 2000, but its provisions tightly circumscribe the circumstances in which wiretapping is permitted. In 2010 a record total of 47 people were arrested in investigations using authorized wiretaps, and in the same year Japanese investigators wiretapped a total of 7475 communications in eight drug-smuggling cases, one gang-related murder, and one case of gun possession (*Japan Times*, 2011a). Many Japanese resist the expansion of wiretapping and other undercover police powers out of concern that police might misuse their authority, as their predecessors often did in the pre-war and wartime years (Mitchell, 1976, 1992, 1996; Tipton, 1990). In Italy, which has a similar history of political authoritarianism and police abuse of power, wiretaps are routinely used to obtain criminal evidence (Levy, 2011).

7 Guns were first brought to Japan by Europeans in 1543 and for a century or so thereafter they were widely used. But then guns were gradually abandoned. For a colorful but controversial account of how this occurred see Perrin, 1979. In my view, Perrin's explanation barely hints at the main reason Japan gave up the gun: the Tokugawa shogunate established hegemony over the country and made people (samurai especially) stop using guns in an effort to maintain peace and prevent reversion to the bloody disorder of the Warring States period of 1467–1573.

8 Data on police deaths are not published in Japan; these data were provided to the author by a Japanese police official in 2011.

9 Police around the world are pretty much the same with respect to what citizens want and expect from them – and they are unlike prosecutors, for whom expectations vary significantly across countries and cultures (Tonry, 2012: 2).

10 Walter Ames has described the role of the Japanese police as 'humbling machines', which aim to 'teach deference to moral order' (quoted in Bayley, 1991: 149). See also Ames (1981: 82) on how police use 'street guidance' (*gaito hodo*) to control the conduct of juveniles, and Leheny (2006: 48–113) on how police have responded to the problem of 'compensated dating' (*enjo kosai*) by juvenile girls.

11 The crime contrasts between New York City and Tokyo have also been noticed by previous observers. For example, when American lawyer John Henry Wigmore visited Japan in the 1930s he said: 'One can see in New York in one night such exhibitions of violence, brawling, and abandoned lawlessness as one would not see in an entire year in Tokyo' (quoted in Johnson, 2011a). For similar contrasts see Vogel, 1979; Ames, 1981; Bayley, 1991; Miyazawa, 1992; and Johnson, 2008.

12 Of course, much domestic violence goes unreported by victims and unrecorded in official crime statistics in most (if not all) societies, but these problems seem especially severe in Japan (Leonardsen, 2010). Research in the USA shows that women who live in communities that invest in social services are less at risk of intimate-partner violence, and so are women who live where police respond sensitively to domestic-violence complaints. In contrast, mandatory-arrest policies appear to have no effect on domestic-violence victimization in the USA (Xie et al., 2012).

13 Because of defects in Japan's system for conducting autopsies the country's homicide rate may well be higher than it appears. In 2009, for example, the police dealt with about 160,000 'suspicious corpses', but autopsies were carried out on only 10.1 percent of them (a 'suspicious corpse' is a corpse for which the cause of death is unclear). Based on this figure, one newspaper estimates that 'the police every year mistake some 1700 crime-related deaths for deaths not caused by crime' (*Japan Times*, 2010). If this

estimate is accurate then Japan's true homicide rate might be double its reported rate, though it would still be a lot lower than America's homicide rate.

14 Suicide also exacts a heavy economic toll. A report by Japan's Labor Ministry concluded that the Japanese economy lost 2.7 trillion yen ($32 billion) in 2009 because of 'suicides and loss of employment due to depression' (*Metropolis*, 2010: 4).

15 Scholars tend to treat homicide and suicide as separate events, but the 'stream analogy' of lethal violence depicts them as two currents in a single river. Analysts in this tradition aim to explain two main variables: the 'forces of production' (the total amount of lethal violence, expressed as the sum of the homicide and suicide rates) and the 'forces of direction' (the proportion of lethal violence expressed as homicide or suicide). The stream analogy may be a useful device for exploring the links between homicide and suicide in Japan and other nations (Johnson, 2008).

16 That Japanese culture prefers 'silent suffering' over resistance – "exit" rather than "voice" – is also apparent in the high and apparently increasing rates of 'social withdrawal' (*hikikomori*). One of the most widely cited experts on this subject estimates that between 500,000 and 1 million people in Japan have completely withdrawn from social interaction for at least six months, with men comprising 70 to 80 percent of the total (Leonardsen, 2010: 146).

17 In explaining Japan's low rates of crime, Roberts and LaFree (2004) emphasized the relatively low levels of economic stress that prevailed in the post-war period, but they did not consider the large increases in poverty and inequality that have occurred since 1990. As of 2010 nearly one in six Japanese live below the poverty line, and there is widespread 'hidden poverty' as well (Kojima, 2013).

18 This interview was conducted on 29 July 2010 at the National Police Academy in Fuchu. One illustration of the primitive nature of many evaluation studies in Japan concerns the crime-control effectiveness of the 160 closed-circuit television cameras (*bohan kamera*) that were used in 2010 by the Tokyo police in the Kabukicho district of Shinjuku (55 cameras), the Udagawa district of Shibuya (20), Ikebukuro (35), Ueno 2-chome (15), and Roppongi (35). On 25 August 25 2010 police in the Tokyo Metropolitan Police Department presented me with information about 'the effects of the CCTV system', and they concluded that the cameras have powerful crime-prevention consequences. But their methodology was seriously flawed because they simply compared the number of crimes reported to the police in these five jurisdictions one year

before and one year after the installation of the cameras (which showed crime declines of 22 percent, 68 percent, 53 percent, 1 percent, and 26 percent, respectively). This methodology fails to take into account two important facts: that crime has declined all over Japan in recent years (not just in the areas where surveillance cameras were installed) and that many aspects of Japanese society changed during the period considered in this 'study' (Kanayama, 2010a).

19 Some analysts believe that agnosticism about Japanese police effectiveness is unwarranted, arguing that 'Japan is peaceful, safe and regimented not because of, but despite, the frequently disgraceful performance of its [police] guardians'. On this view, many individual Japanese police officers are honest and dedicated, but 'as an institution, the force they serve is arrogant, complacent and incompetent' (Parry, 2012). For evidence from high-profile murder investigations that supports an 'incompetent' verdict see also Parry, 2011.

20 In the last two decades there has been far less innovation and experimentation in policing in Japan than there has been in America (Weisburd and Braga, 2006). Moreover, the Japanese police reforms that did occur through the revisions of the Police Act in 2000 and 2004 were not primarily directed at making the police more attentive to high-risk crime situations, people, or places; they were aimed at making the police more transparent and responsive to citizens' requests for service. Observers disagree about the effectiveness of those reforms (Kyo, 2007; Kanayama, 2010b).

21 In his classic analysis of why Swiss cities are safe Marshall Clinard also stressed the central importance of citizens' sense of responsibility for crime control (Clinard, 1978).

22 The Japanese police see themselves as occupying the center of the country's crime-control network. In the National Police Agency's official account of the 'eight strengths' of Japanese policing the first strength is deemed to be 'the tradition of extracting community power', which involves close connection, cooperation, and collaboration with other actors – citizens, schools, and organizations – in Japan's crime-control field. The seven other police strengths are said to be: high-level working conditions to sustain the 'good quality and prestige of police officials'; a stress on conducting 'close and careful investigations'; maximum utilization of the 'information system'; the maintenance of 'comprehensive authority for traffic control'; high expectations for 'cooperation of the public, including criminal suspects'; a police organization with the dual sense that it is both 'part of the local community' and also 'nationally unified'; and a system of Public Safety Commissions that permits 'no command and no intervention from politicians' (Tamura, 2010).

23 Bayley's stress on the police's role in enhancing the capacity of society to control itself was later echoed and elaborated by Walter Ames (1981: 228) and Dag Leonardsen (2004: 159).

24 In 2010 I was permitted to 'walk along' with police and citizen volunteers engaged in this kind of 'guidance' of young people in the Shinjuku district of Tokyo, and I was surprised at how arbitrary and intrusive the adults' encounters with juveniles seemed. Sometimes the adults (who wore arm bands identifying themselves as part of a 'citizen patrol' team) simply walked up to kids and asked them to show the contents of their handbags and backpacks. At other times the adults carded young people who were smoking and, if the smokers were deemed underage, made the kids tear up their cigarettes and provide contact information for their parents. At other times the adults entered video arcades to ask game-playing children where they were from and how much money they had. My first (unspoken) reaction to these encounters was a vulgar English phrase that can be abbreviated 'WTF', but this eventually evolved into puzzlement as to why the kids did not tell the adults, who had no reasonable suspicion to examine bags or ask for identification, to 'mind your own business'. For an insightful account of how the Japanese police try to control the sexual behavior of youth see Leheny, 2006: 48-113.

25 It became more difficult for Japanese police to 'cook the books' largely because a series of police scandals generated increased attention to their behavior from the Japanese public and media (Hamai and Ellis, 2006; Hamai and Serizawa, 2006; Kawai, 2004).

26 In some respects the Japanese police have had limited success controlling organized crime (for the best evaluations see Hill, 2003a, 2003b). In other respects the Japanese police have been more effective, as in reducing the amount of corporate extortion by *sokaiya* (Szymkowiak, 2002) and in crushing the biker gangs known as *bosozoku* (Osaki, 2013).

27 These lyrics are from Dylan's 'Subterranean Homesick Blues' (1965). A survey of 1042 prosecutors by Japan's Ministry of Justice found that 86 per cent were reluctant to introduce total recording and 58 per cent opposed a partial recording requirement (*Japan Times*, 2011b). On the international movement toward recording interrogations see Johnson, 2010.

28 Japanese journalist Mori Tatsuya has written insightfully (and humorously) about his own encounter with 'duty questioning' police. Mori, who frequently writes about Japanese criminal justice, told the policeman who stopped him at the Kita-Senju train station in Tokyo that he would not open his backpack, as the policeman had asked him to. But when the policeman persisted Mori struck a deal: he would reveal the contents of his backpack if the officer let Mori take a face photograph. The officer agreed and Mori published the photo in his article on this case, though he obscured part of the officer's face so that it would be harder to identify who it was (Mori, 2008). This case suggests how difficult it can be to refuse to cooperate with the police, even for someone with high levels of knowledge and experience, and even when that cooperation is supposed to be 'voluntary'. Mori's documentary films about Aum Shinrikyo (*A* and *A2*) make a similar point.

FURTHER READING

Abe, K. (2004). Everyday Policing in Japan: Surveillance, Media, Government, and Public Opinion. *International Sociology*, 19 (2), 215–231.

Adelstein, J. (2012a). Japan's 'Life-Less' Anti-Stalking Laws Are Costing Lives To Be Lost. *Japan Times*, December 2.

Adelstein, J. (2012b). The Yakuza Lobby: How Gangsters Run Japanese Politics. *Foreign Policy*, December 13. Retrieved December 14, 2012, from www.foreignpolicy.com/ articles/2012/12/13/the_yakuza_lobby

Haley, J. O. (1991). *Authority without Power: Law and the Japanese Paradox*. New York: Oxford University Press.

Johnson, D. T. (2003). Above the Law? Police Integrity in Japan. *Social Science Japan Journal*, 6 (1), April, 19–37.

Johnson, D. T. (2007a). Crime and Punishment in Contemporary Japan. In Tonry, M. (Ed.) *Crime, Punishment, and Politics in Comparative Perspective*. Volume 36 of *Crime and Justice: A Review of Research*. Chicago: The University of Chicago Press, 371–423.

Johnson, David T. (2007b). Changes and Challenges in Japanese Criminal Justice. In Foote, D. H. (Ed.) *Law in Japan: Into the Twenty-First Century*. Seattle: University of Washington Press, 343–383.

Kanayama, Taisuke. (2010c). What Type of Crime Is Affected by Unemployment in Japan? Unpublished paper (May), Police Policy Research Center, National Police Agency of Japan, 1–13.

Matsuhashi, T. (1984). *Wagatsumi Wa Sude ni Wagamae ni Ari: Kitai Sareru Shinkeisatsucho Chokan e no Tegami*. Tokyo: Shakai Shisosha.

Miyazawa, S. (2001). The Politics of Judicial Reform in Japan: The Rule of Law at Last? *Asian-Pacific Law & Policy Journal*, 2, 89–121.

Nakabo, K. (2002). Judicial Reform Must Pursue Public Interest. *International Herald Tribune*, July 18.

Nakada, K, Hiroto, S. and Nagasawa, C. (2001). Shijo saiaku: 'Hanzai kenkyoritsu 24.2%' ga imi suru mono. *Spa*, January 31, 20–23.

Nakada, N. (1988). Keisatsu Shiho. *Ho to Minshushugi*. September.

Nihon Bengoshi Rengokai (Ed.) (2003). *Daijobu? Nihon no Keisatsu: Kensho Keisatsu Kaikaku*. Tokyo: Nihon Hyoronsha.

Ouchi, A. (2002). *Keishicho Uragane Tanto*. Tokyo: Kodansha.

Putnam, R. (1993). *Making Democracy Work: Civic Traditions in Modern Italy*. Princeton: Princeton University Press.

Reid, T. R. (1999). *Confucius Lives Next Door: What Living in the East Teaches Us About Living in the West*. New York: Random House.

Saga, J. (1991). *Confessions of a Yakuza*. Tokyo: Kodansha.

Sato, I. (2002). Judicial Reform in Japan in the 1990s: Increase of the Legal Profession, Reinforcement of Judicial Functions and Expansion of the Rule of Law. *Social Science Japan Journal*, 5 (1), 71–83.

Sato, M. (1999). *Fushoji Zokushutsu Keisatsu ni Tsugu*. Tokyo: Shogakkan.

Seymour, C. (1996). *Yakuza Diary: Doing Time in the Japanese Underworld*. New York: Atlantic Monthly Press.

Shipper, A. W. (2008). *Fighting for Foreigners: Immigration and Its Impact on Japanese Democracy*. Ithaca: Cornell University Press.

Simon, D. (2012). *In Doubt: The Psychology of the Criminal Justice Process*. Cambridge: Harvard University Press.

Siniawer, E. M. (2008). *Ruffians, Yakuza, Nationalists: The Violent Politics of Modern Japan, 1860–1960*. Ithaca: Cornell University Press.

Siniawer, E. M. (2012). Befitting Bedfellows: Yakuza and the State in Modern Japan. *Journal of Social History*, 45 (3), 623–641.

Steinhoff, P. G. (1989). Protest and Democracy. In Ishida, T. and Kraus, E. S. (Eds.) *Democracy in Japan*. Pittsburgh: University of Pittsburgh Press, 171–198.

Tendo, S. (2008). *Yakuza Moon: Memoirs of a Gangster's Daughter*. Heal, L. (Trans.) Tokyo: Kodansha.

Wilson, J. Q. (1968). *Varieties of Police Behavior: The Management of Law & Order in Eight Communities*. Cambridge: Harvard University Press.

Wood, D. M. (2009). The 'Surveillance Society': Questions of History, Place, and Culture. *European Journal of Criminology*, 6 (2), No.2: 179–194.

Wood, D. M. (2012). Cameras in Context: A Comparison of the Place of Video Surveillance in Japan and Brazil. In Doyle, A., Lippert, R. and Wood, D. (Eds.) *Eyes Everywhere: The Global Growth of Camera Surveillance*. New York: Routledge, 83–99.

Yomiuri Shimbun. (2002). Juribo ni Keibi na Nusumi Shirusazu: Kenkyo Appu no Ura Waza? July 8, 1.

Yomiuri Shimbun. (2003). Keishicho Keibu Wairo 1000 Man. October 29, 14.

Yomiuri Shimbun Osaka Shakaibu. (1992). *Keisatsukan Nekobaba Jiken: Onaka no Akachan ga Tasukete Kureta*. Tokyo: Kodansha.

REFERENCES

Adelestein, J. (2009). *Tokyo Vice: An American Reporter on the Police Beat in Japan*. New York: Pantheon Books.

Aldous, C. (1997). *The Police in Occupation Japan: Control, Corruption, and Resistance to Reform*. London: Routledge.

Aldous, C. and Leishman, F. (1997). Policing in Post-War Japan: Reform, Reversion, and Reinvention. *International Journal of the Sociology of Law*, 25, 135–154.

Ames, W. L. (1981). *Police and Community in Japan*. Berkeley: University of California Press.

Araki, N. (1988). The Role of the Police in Japanese Society. *Law & Society Review*, 22 (5), 1033–1036.

Bayley, D. H. (1976). *Forces of Order: Police Behavior in Japan and the USA*. Berkeley: University of California Press.

Bayley, D. H. (1991). *Forces of Order: Policing Modern Japan*. Berkeley: University of California Press.

Bayley. D. H. (1996). *Police for the Future*. New York: Oxford University Press.

Bittner, E. (1980). *The Functions of Police in Modern Society*. Cambridge: Oelgeschlager, Gunn, & Hain.

Botsman, D. V. (2005). *Punishment and Power in the Making of Modern Japan*. Oxford: Princeton University Press.

Braithwaite, J. (1989). *Crime, Shame, and Reintegration*. Cambridge: Cambridge University Press.

Brodeur, J-P. (2010). *The Policing Web*. New York: Oxford University Press.

Cao, L. and Stack, S. (2005). Confidence in the Police between America and Japan: Results from Two Waves of Surveys. *Policing: An International Journal of Police Strategies and Management*, 8 (1), 139–151.

Cao, Liqun, Stack, S. and Sun Y. (1998). Public Attitudes Toward the Police: A Comparative Study Between Japan and America. *Journal of Criminal Justice*, 26 (4), 279–289.

Chevigny, P. (1995). *Edge of the Knife: Police Violence in the Americas*. New York: The New Press.

Clifford, W. (1976). *Crime Control in Japan*. Lexington: Lexington Books.

Clinard, M. (1978). *Cities with Little Crime: The Case of Switzerland*. Cambridge: Cambridge University Press.

Coleman, J. W. (2006). *The Criminal Elite: Understanding White-Collar Crime* (sixth edition). New York: Worth Publishers.

Davis, K. C. (1969). *Discretionary Justice: A Preliminary Inquiry*. Urbana and Chicago: University of Illinois Press.

Deacon, R. (1990). *Kempei Tai: The Japanese Secret Service Then and Now*. Tokyo: Tuttle.

Field, N. (1991). *In the Realm of a Dying Emperor: A Portrait of Japan at Century's End*. New York: Pantheon Books.

Fisher, M. (2012). A Land Without Guns: How Japan Has Virtually Eliminated Shooting Deaths. *The Atlantic*, July 23. Retrieved 17 December 2012, from www.theatlantic.com/international/archive/2012/07/a-land-without-guns-how-japan-has-virtually-eliminated-shooting-deaths/260189

Foljanty-Jost, G. (2003). *Juvenile Delinquency in Japan: Reconsidering the 'Crisis'*. Leiden and Boston: Brill.

Foote, D. H. (1992a). The Benevolent Paternalism of Japanese Criminal Justice. *University of California Law Review*, 80 (2), 317–390.

Foote, D. H. (1992b). Confessions and the Right to Silence in Japan. *Georgia Journal of International and Comparative Law*, 21, 415–488.

Foote, D. H. (1993). Policing Japan. *The Journal of Criminal Law & Criminology*, 84 (2), 410–427.

Foote, D. H. (2010). Policymaking by the Japanese Judiciary in the Criminal Justice Field, *Hoshakaigaku*, 72, 1–21.

Garland, D. (1990). *Punishment and Modern Society: A Study in Social Theory*. Chicago: University of Chicago Press.

Garland, D. (2001). *The Culture of Control: Crime and Social Order in Contemporary Society*. Chicago: University of Chicago Press.

Greenwood, P. W. (2002). Juvenile Crime and Juvenile Justice. In Wilson, J. Q., and Peterselia, J. (Eds.) (2002). *Crime: Public Policies for Crime Control*. Oakland: Institute for Contemporary Studies, 75–108.

Haidt, J. (2012). *The Righteous Mind: Why Good People Are Divided by Politics and Religion*. New York: Pantheon Books.

Hamai, K. (2004). Nihon no Chian Akka Shinwa wa Ika ni Tsukurareta. *Japanese Journal of Sociological Criminology*, 29, 10–26.

Hamai, K. and Ellis, T. (2006). Crime and Criminal Justice in Modern Japan: From Re-integrative Shaming to Popular Punitivism. *International Journal of the Sociology of Law*, 34, 157–178.

Hamai, K. and Serizawa, K. (2006). *Hanzai Fuan Shakai*. Tokyo: Kobunsha.

Herbert, W. (1996). *Foreign Workers and Law Enforcement in Japan*. London: Kegan Paul International.

Hill, P. B. E. (2003a). *The Japanese Mafia: Yakuza, Law, and the State*. New York: Oxford University Press.

Hill, P. B. E. (2003b). Heisei Yakuza: Burst Bubble and Botaiho. *Social Science Japan Journal*, 6 (1), 1–18.

Hirano, R. (1989). Diagnosis of the Current Code of Criminal Procedure. Foote, D. H. (Trans.) *Law in Japan*, 22, 129–142.

Honda, K. (1993). *The Impoverished Spirit in Contemporary Japan: Selected Essays of Honda Katsuichi*. Lie, J. (Ed.) New York: Monthly Review Press.

Honolulu Advertiser. (2010). Law Enforcement Fatalities Fall to 125. January 2, 3.

Iitake, K. (2000). Accord Made on Police Reforms. *Asahi Evening News*, March 17.

Ishimatsu, T. (1989). Are Criminal Defendants in Japan Truly Receiving Trials By Judges. Foote, D. H. (Trans.) *Law in Japan*, 22, 143–153.

Itoh, Shigeki. (1992). *Kenji Socho no Kaiso*. Tokyo: Asahi Shimbunsha.

Japan Times. (2010). Rising Unnatural Death Toll. September 29, 12.

Japan Times. (2011a). Record 47 Wiretap Arrests Made. February 5, 2.

Japan Times. (2011b). Report on Interrogation Recording. August 23, available at www.japantimes.co.jp/opinion/2011/08/23/editorials/report-on-interrogation-recording/#.UXBol spLGIQ (last accessed 18 April 2013).

Johnson, D. T. (1999). Kumo no Su ni Shocho Sareru Nihonho no Tokushoku. *Jurisuto*, 1148 (January 1–15), 185–189.

Johnson, D. T. (2002). *The Japanese Way of Justice: Prosecuting Crime in Japan*. New York: Oxford University Press.

Johnson, D. T. (2004a). Police Integrity in Japan. In Klockars, C. B., Ivkovic, S. K. and Haberfeld, M. R. (Eds.) *The Contours of Police Integrity*. Thousand Oaks: Sage, 130–160.

Johnson, D. T. (2004b). Police Misconduct in the United States and Japan. In Amir, M. and Einstein, S. (Eds.). *Police Corruption: Challenges for Developed Countries – Comparative Issues and Commissions of Inquiry*. Huntsville, TX: Office of International Criminal Justice of Sam Houston State University.

Johnson, D. T. (2004c). Nihon ni okeru Shiho Seido Kaikaku: Keisatsu no Shozai to Sono Juyosei [Justice System Reform in Japan: Where Are the Police and Why Does It Matter?]. *Horitsu Jiho*, 76 (2), 8–15.

Johnson, D. T. (2004d). Chohoki teki Sonzai: Nihon no Keisatsu ga Shiho Seido Kaikaku kara Hazusareta Riyu. *Causa*, March, 39–44.

Johnson, David T. (2008). The Homicide Drop in Postwar Japan. *Homicide Studies*, 12 (1), 146–160.

Johnson, D. T. (2010). Kazemuki o Shiru no ni Otenki Kyasta wa Iranai: Nihon ni okeru Torishirabe Rokuon-Rokuga ni tsuite Gasshukoku to Kankoku kara Manabu koto. In Ibusuki, M. (Ed.) *Higisha Torishirabe to Rokuga Seido: Torishirabe no Rokuga ga Nihon no Keiji Shiho o Kaeru*. Tokyo: Shojihomu, 185–238.

Johnson, D. T. (2011a). Nihon no Hanzai Boshi Seisaku: Seika, Kyokun, Kadai. *Keisatsu Seisaku Kenkyu*, 15, 75–82.

Johnson, D. T. (2011b). War in a Season of Slow Revolution: Defense Lawyers and Lay Judges in Japanese Criminal Justice. *Asia Pacific Journal*, 9, 26 (2), available at www.japanfocus.org/-David_T_-Johnson/3554 (last accessed on 23 April 2013).

Johnson, D. T., Kanayama, T. and Tamura, M. (2012). Nichibei Keisatsu no taihō kenkōshi ni kasuru gensoku ni tuite no hikaku kenkyū – Okinawa ni okeru keiji kahōsei no ikō wo chushin ni. Tokyo: Shakai Anzen Kenkyu Zaidan, 1–29.

Kahneman, D. (2011). *Thinking, Fast and Slow*. New York: Farrar, Straus and Giroux.

Kanayama, T. (2010a). Rising Crime and Crime Reduction Strategies in 21st Century Japan. Unpublished paper (January), Police Policy Research Center, National Police Agency of Japan, 1–39.

Kanayama, T. (2010b). A Decade of Police Reforms in Japan: Has a Police for the People Been Realized? Unpublished paper (February), Police Policy Research Center, National Police Agency of Japan, 1–12.

Kaplan, D. E. and Dubro, A. (2003). *Yakuza: Japan's Criminal Underworld*. Berkeley: University of California Press.

Katzenstein, P. J. (1996). *Cultural Norms and National Security: Police and Military in Postwar Japan*. Ithaca: Cornell University Press.

Katzenstein, P. J, and Tsujinaka, Y. (1991). *Defending the Japanese State: Structures, Norms and the Political Responses to Terrorism and Violent Social Protest in the 1970s and 1980s*. Ithaca: Cornell University East Asia Program.

Kawai, M. (2004). *Anzen Shinwa Hokai no Paradokkusu*. Tokyo: Iwanami Shoten.

Kennedy, D. M. (2009). *Deterrence and Crime Prevention: Reconsidering the Prospect of Sanction*. London and New York: Routledge.

Kleiman, M. A. R. (2009). *When Brute Force Fails: How to Have Less Crime and Less Punishment*. Princeton and Oxford: Princeton University Press.

Klockars, C. B. (1985). *The Idea of Police*. Thousand Oaks: Sage.

Kobayashi, M. (1998). *Nihon Keisatsu no Genzai*. Tokyo: Iwanami Shoten.

Kojima, S. (2013). Japanese Temp Workers: The Culture and Politics of Precarious Employment. PhD dissertation, Department of Sociology, University of Hawaii at Manoa, July.

Komiya, N. (1999). A Cultural Study of the Low Crime Rate in Japan. *British Journal of Criminology*, 39, Summer, 369–390.

Kubo, H. (2001). *Do Sureba 'Keisatsu' wa Shimin no Mono ni Naru no ka*. Tokyo: Shogakukan.

Kuroki, A. (2000). *Keisatsu Fuhai: Keishicho Keisatsukan no Kokuhatsu*. Tokyo: Kodansha.

Kyo, A. (2007). Policing and the Police in Japan: An Overview. *Corrections and Rehabilitation Research Center (CRRC) Journal*, 4, September, 175–180.

Leheny, D. (2006). *Think Global, Fear Local: Sex, Violence, and Anxiety in Contemporary Japan*. Ithaca: Cornell University Press.

Leonardsen, D. (2004). *Japan as a Low-Crime Nation*. Basingstoke: Palgrave Macmillan.

Leonardsen, D. (2010). *Crime in Japan: Paradise Lost?* New York: Palgrave Macmillan.

Levy, A. (2011). Bunga, Bunga, Bunga. *The New Yorker*, June 6. Retrieved 18 December 2012, from www.newyorker.com/reporting/ 2011/06/06/110606fa_fact_levy

Lieberman, L. (2003). *Leaving You: The Cultural Meaning of Suicide*. Chicago: Ivan R. Dee.

Maravall, J. M. and Przeworski, A. (2003). *Democracy and the Rule of Law*. Cambridge: Cambridge University Press.

Metropolis. (2010). Here & There. September 24, 4.

Mikami, T. and Morishita, H. (1996). *Sabakareru Keisatsu: Hanshin Fan Boko Keikan to Fushinpan Jiken*. Tokyo: Nihon Hyoronsha.

Miller, A. S., and Kanazawa, S. (2000). *Order by Accident: The Origins and Consequences of Conformity in Contemporary Japan*. Boulder: Westview Press.

Mitchell, R. H. (1976). *Thought Control in Prewar Japan*. Ithaca: Cornell University Press.

Mitchell, R. H. (1992). *Janus-Faced Justice: Political Criminal in Imperial Japan*. Honolulu: University of Hawaii Press.

Mitchell, R. H. (1996). *Political Bribery in Japan*. Honolulu: University of Hawaii Press.

Mitsui, T. (2003). *Kokuhatsu! Kensatsu 'Uraganezukuri.'* Tokyo: Kobunsha.

Miyamoto, M. (1994). *Straitjacket Society: An Insider's Irreverent View of Bureaucratic Japan*. Tokyo: Kodansha International.

Miyazawa, S. (1989). Scandal and Hard Reform: Implications of a Wiretapping Case to the Control of Organizational Police Crimes in Japan. *Kobe University Law Review*, 23, 13–27.

Miyazawa, S. (1990). Learning Lessons from Japanese Experience in Policing and Crime: Challenges for Japanese Criminologists. *Kobe University Law Review*, 24, 29–61.

Miyazawa, S. (1992). *Policing in Japan: A Study on Making Crime*. Bennett, F. G. Jr., with Haley, J. O. (Trans.) Albany: State University of New York Press.

Miyazawa, S. (2008). The Politics of Increasing Punitiveness and the Rising Populism in Japanese Criminal Justice Policy. *Punishment & Society*, 10, 47–77.

Mori, T. (2008). Kitasenju de no Shokumu Shitsumon. *Tsukuru*, August, 184–189.

Murayama, M. (1990). *Keira Keisatsu no Kenkyu*. Tokyo: Seibundo.

National Research Council. (2004). *Fairness and Effectiveness in Policing*. Washington, D.C.: The National Academies Press.

National Research Council, Skogan, W. and Kathleen Frydl, K. (Eds.). (2004). *Fairness and Effectiveness in Policing: The Evidence*. Washington, D.C.: The National Academies Press.

Ochiai, H. (1998). *'Ura Chobo' 'Naibu Kokuhatsu' 'Taisaku Manyuaru' no San-Ten Setto de Semero*. In Teraswa, Y. (Ed.) *Omawari San wa Zeikin Dorobo*. Tokyo: Mediaworks, 128–161.

Ochiai, H. (2000). Corruption: Who Polices the Police? *Japan Quarterly*, April-June, 50–57.

Ono, M. (2007). *Keisatsu Seisakuron*. Tokyo: Tachibana Shobo.

Osaki, T. (2013). Documentary Chronicles Disappearing World of 'Bosozoku'. *Japan Times*, April 18, available at www.japantimes.co.jp/news/2013/04/18/national/documentary-chronicles-disappearing-world-of-bosozoku/#.UXb7UcpLGIQ (last accessed 23 April 2013).

Otani, A. (2000). *Nihon Keisatsu no Shotai: Jiken no Inpei, Sosa Misu, Fushoji wa Naze Okoru?* Tokyo: Nihon Bungeisha.

Packer, H. (1968). *The Limits of the Criminal Sanction*. Palo Alto: Stanford University Press.

Park, W-K. (2006). *Trends in Crime Rates in Postwar Japan: A Structural Perspective*. Morioka City, Iwate Prefecture: Shinzansha.

Parker, L. C. Jr. (1984). *The Japanese Police System Today: An American Perspective*. Tokyo and New York: Kodansha International.

Parker, L. C. Jr. (2001). *The Japanese Police System Today: A Comparative Study*. Armonk: M. E. Sharpe.

Parry, R. L. (2011). *People Who Eat Darkness: The Fate of Lucie Blackman*. London: Jonathan Cape.

Parry, R. L. (2012). Japan's Inept Guardians. *New York Times*, June 24. Retrieved 11 December 2012, from www.nytimes.com/2012/06/25/opinion/japans-inept-guardians.html

Perrin, N. (1979). *Giving Up the Gun: Japan's Reversion to the Sword, 1543–1879*. Boston: David R. Godine.

Roberts, A and LaFree, G. (2004). Explaining Japan's Postwar Violent Crime Trends. *Criminology*, 42, 179–210.

Sasakura, K. (2012). False Confessions as Major Cause of Wrongful Convictions in Japan. The Wrongful Convictions Blog, June 28, available at www.wrongfulconvictionsblog.org/2012/06/28/false-confessions-as-major-cause-of-wrongful-convictions-in-japan (last accessed on 17 April 2013).

Sims, C. (2000). Misdeeds By Once-Honored Police Dismay the Japanese. *New York Times*, March 7.

Sklansky, D. A. (2008). *Democracy and the Police*. Stanford: Stanford University Press.

Skolnick, J. H. (1994). *Justice without Trial: Law Enforcement in a Democratic Society* (3rd edition). New York: MacMillan.

Skolnick, J. H., and Fyfe, J. J. (1993). *Above the Law: Police and the Excessive Use of Force*. New York: The Free Press.

Steinhoff, P. G. (1991). *Ideology and Societal Integration in Prewar Japan*. New York: Garland.

Steinhoff, P. G. (1993). 'Pursuing the Japanese Police.' *Law & Society Review*, 27 (4), 827–850.

Szymkowiak, K. (2002). *Sokaiya: Extortion, Protection, and the Japanese Corporation*. Armonk: M. E. Sharpe.

Tamura, M. (2010). Characteristics of the Japanese Police: Eight Strengths. National Police Agency of Japan, 1–7.

Terasawa, Y. (1998). *Omawarisan wa Zeikin Dorobo*. Tokyo: Mediaworks.

Terasawa, Y. (2009). *Hodo Sarenai Keisatsu to Masukomi no Fuhai: Eiga 'Pochi no Kokuhaku' ga Abaita Mono*. Tokyo: Inshidentsu.

Thornton, R. Y., with Endo, K. (1992). *Preventing Crime in America and Japan: A Comparative Study*. Armonk: M. E. Sharpe.

Tipton, E. K. (1990). *The Japanese Police State: The Tokko in Interwar Japan*. Honolulu: University of Hawaii Press.

Tonry, M. (Ed.) (2012). *Prosecutors and Politics: A Comparative Perspective*. In *Crime and Justice: A Review of Research*, 41. Chicago and London: The University of Chicago Press.

Ukawa, H. (1997). Shiho Torihiki o Kangaeru. *Hanrei Jiho*, 1583, 31–47.

Verma, A. and Subramanian, K. S. (2009). *Understanding the Police in India*. Delhi: LexisNexis Butterworths Wadhwa.

Vogel, E. (1979). *Japan as Number One*. New York: Harper.

Walker, S. (1993). *Taming the System: The Control of Discretion in Criminal Justice, 1950–1990*. New York: Oxford University Press.

Walker, S. E. (2005). *The New World of Police Accountability*. Thousand Oaks: Sage.

Weisburd, D. and Braga, A. A. (Eds.) (2006). *Police Innovation: Contrasting Perspectives*. New York: Cambridge University Press.

Westney, D. E. (1987). *Imitation and Innovation: The Transfer of Western Organizational Patterns to Meiji Japan*. Cambridge: Harvard University Press.

Whiting, R. (1999). *Tokyo Underworld: The Fast Times and Hard Life of an American Gangster in Japan*. New York: Pantheon Books.

Wilson, J. Q. (2002). Crime and Public Policy. In Wilson, J. Q., and Peterselia, J. (Eds.) (2002). *Crime: Public Policies for Crime Control*. Oakland: Institute for Contemporary Studies, 537–557.

Wilson, J. Q., and Peterselia, J. (Eds.) (2002). *Crime: Public Policies for Crime Control*. Oakland: Institute for Contemporary Studies.

Wong, K. C. (2009). *Chinese Policing*. New York: Peter Lang.

Xie, M., Lauritsen, J. L. and Heimer, K. (2012). Intimate Partner Violence in U.S. Metropolitan Areas: The Contextual Influences of Police and Social Services. *Criminology*, 50 (4), 961–992.

Yoshida, N. (1999). The Taming of the Japanese Private Security Industry. *Policing and Society*, 9, 241–261.

Yoshida, N. (2008). Keisatsu no Seitosei Tsuikyu to Keisatsu no Katsudo no Teika: Koban ni okeru Kansatsu Kenkyu ni yotte. *Hoshakaigaku*, 69, 183–208.

Yoshida, N. (2010). Nihon ni okeru Keisatsukan Shokugyo Bunka: Chosahyo Chosa ni yotte. *Hoshakaigaku*, 72, 250–283.

Yoshida, N., and Leishman, F. (2006). Japan. In Jones, T. and Newburn, T. (Eds.) *Plural Policing: A Comparative Perspective*. London: Routledge, 222–238.

Zielenziger, M. (2006). *Shutting Out the Sun: How Japan Created Its Own Lost Generation*. New York: Doubleday.

Zimring, F. E. (2012). *The City That Became Safe: New York's Lessons for Urban Crime and Its Control*. New York: Oxford University Press.

13

Organised Crime

Peter Hill

INTRODUCTION

The yakuza occupy an ambiguous space within Japanese popular consciousness. Their traditional role in *matsuri* (festivals), itself a celebration of *Nihonrashisa* (Japanese-ness), links them firmly with something dear to most Japanese hearts. Their mythologised history, immortalised in countless films, honours a value system of loyalty, duty, self-sacrifice, superhuman endurance and physical courage in the face of overwhelming odds. An aesthetic combining exaggerated native attire, lurid shell-suit gangster chic and self-mutilation rituals simultaneously excludes and accommodates them. Whatever the myths, in reality they inspire fear and revulsion as well as a morbid fascination. With the rise of cool Japan, Tarantino's *Kill Bill* and Sega's Playstation game *Yakuza 2*, organised crime Japan-style has impinged itself on global culture as well.

Is Japanese organised crime of interest to students of Japan purely as an item of prurient cultural consumption, or do the yakuza in some way inform our understanding of the Japanese social matrix? The once oft-used phrase *hitsuyō aku* (necessary evil) displays clear ambivalence about their existence and raises questions: necessary to whom and why? Is the phrase's declining currency a reflection of its diminishing relevance or an increasing sensitivity to uncomfortable truths?

Despite the considerable interest that the yakuza generate, this has not translated into corresponding levels of research, and the quantity of available literature in this field is meagre in comparison with the other topics in this volume. The necessarily clandestine nature of much criminal activity, combined with the yakuza's reputation for violence, present obvious methodological hurdles to those wishing to engage in primary research of yakuza groups. Reflecting these difficulties, there has been a general perception amongst Japanese academics, with some notable exceptions, that first-hand data collection in this field is best left to the authorities. Analyses of those activities that the police have uncovered present a useful but partial picture of the totality of organised-crime operations.

This chapter provides an empirical primer on the evolution of organised crime in Japan. In doing so it touches upon some of the familiar battlegrounds and issues in mainstream Japanese studies: cynics v. optimists; convergence v. uniqueness; rationalists v. culturalists; globalisation; dynamism and stagnation; systemic corruption. The chapter will conclude with a literature review providing a new generation of researchers with a springboard into this under-researched sub-discipline.

THE YAKUZA

In its annual report on the state of *bōryokudan* (literally, violent groups) for 2010[1] the National Police Agency identified 78,600 active gang members. This figure comprises 36,000 fully initiated members (*kōsei-in*) and a further 42,600 trainees and associate members who, whilst actively benefiting from their close links to a particular gang, remained formally uninitiated (*jun-kōsei-in*). Whilst the overall number of identified *bōryokudan* has remained reasonably stable over the last two decades, there has been a noticeable decline in initiated members and a corresponding increase in the number of associate members. We can be reasonably confident that the *kōsei-in* data is accurate for a number of reasons: membership of a yakuza gang is not in itself a crime; gangs maintain membership records; the police regularly visit or raid gang offices and can check; gangs have an obvious interest in informing the police when a member has been expelled. The number of informal members is much more nebulous and is ultimately a question of police intelligence and classification criteria. The police do, of course, keep close tabs on *bōryokudan* groups and maintain detailed records of members and known associates. It should be noted that one explanation for the shift in the ratio of full members to associates is that gangs are taking greater steps to conceal their activities from the authorities.

Members of these organisations can be found throughout Japan, frequently in offices that are easily identifiable; until recently gang crests would adorn entrances, now a plethora of CCTV cameras is a good indicator. Increasingly the yakuza world is dominated by three large syndicates: the Inagawa-kai, the Sumiyoshi-kai and the Yamaguchi-gumi boasting 4,800, 6,100 and 20,300 *kōsei-in* respectively. These three groups maintain a presence in nearly every area of Japan and together comprise just under three quarters of total yakuza strength (73 per cent), though this apparently relentless process of oligopolisation seems to have peaked in 2005 (*Keisatsu Hakusho*, 2008: 107). Of the remaining 22 associations designated by the police as *bōryokudan* groups only two others, the Matsuba-kai and the Kyokutō-kai (both Tokyo-based), have memberships exceeding a thousand.

The large syndicates are based on a quasi-feudal structure: the members of the head 'family' are bosses of their own second-tier organisations, the senior members of which will be bosses of third-tier gangs and so on and so forth. This hierarchy is cemented through the creation of fictive father-son (*oyabun-kobun*) bonds by ceremonially exchanging sake cups (*sakazuki*). Leadership of gangs is also transferred from one boss to the next through *sakazuki* ceremonies. These are, of course, enormously important events attended by the group's members

and senior executives of allied organisations, some of whom may be asked to act as official guarantors or sponsors of the transition. Videos are made which reveal these events to be similar to Japanese weddings, from the Shintō ritual and traditional *hakama-haori* dress to the boring speeches. Similarly, brotherhood bonds exist linking yakuza both within and between groups; friendly inter-gang relations are often cemented in this way (Aizukotetsu-kai, Yamaguchi-gumi and Kyōdō-kai succession-ceremony videos, private collection).

Stark (1981: 62–70) points out that these organic social bonds reinforce a parallel rational organisational hierarchy comprising executives, advisors and committees. Since Stark's classic study this bureaucratic imperative has increased at least as far as the big syndicates go. Within the large syndicates there is now as system of regional blocks to control and co-ordinate the activities of subgroups (this is a formalised version of the local *shinkon-kai* (friendly associations), which had existed as local intra-syndicate conflict-resolution clubs). The Sumiyoshi-kai streamlined its formerly loose federal structure to a more tightly controlled pyramid in the early 1990s and modernised its managerial structure yet further when Fukuda Hareaki became the new overall syndicate leader in 1998 (Yamadaira, 2001: 92–4; Shinoda, 2002: 34, 39). The Sumiyoshi-kai seems particularly keen on managerial reorganisation, though this is not universally welcomed; 'Kashimoto', a middle-ranking boss based in Kabuki-chō, Tokyo, complained to me during my fieldwork in 2000 about self-important windbags and the endless meetings they called: that wasn't why he had become a yakuza.

Once a month the head family summons its members for a meeting at which key information is relayed from the senior executive committee and instructions given about how members are to behave. A common misconception arising from this bureaucratic hierarchy is that these syndicates are structurally similar to large business corporations. Whilst the leadership may prohibit members from certain types of business, yakuza income-generating activities are conducted on an individual or subgroup basis. Although individuals are expected to support their boss's business schemes, they need to earn on their own account. Rather than receiving a salary from the gang, members generally pay for the privilege of membership. This is not a hard and fast rule; an individual who can provide the physical capital to protect or enforce the interests of smarter colleagues without having the entrepreneurial skills to develop his own sources of income obviously has a place in such organisations. Young, newly initiated members may also be financially dependent on their bosses, 'big brothers' or girlfriends.

However, one of the key factors determining how quickly an individual yakuza rises up the gang's ranks is how effectively he can rustle up money-making opportunities and pass on this wealth to his boss. The higher up the hierarchy one ascends the higher the expected level of monthly payments (known as *jōnōkin* by the police; the yakuza prefer *kaihi*). The 67 ordinary members (*wakashu*) of the Yamaguchi-gumi head family were reportedly paying 800,000 yen per month in membership dues; the 25 executives (*kanbu*) were paying one million. There are additional payments of 300,000 yen to a contingency reserve (Mizoguchi, 2007: 100). The headquarters, therefore, derives an annual income of roughly one billion yen to cover administration, legal costs, jail-release money and maintenance for families of members incarcerated for crimes committed on behalf of the gang as a whole. These funds are held by several front companies. The police have, of course, investigated these firms but 'they seem to be scrupulously administered. At the moment we can not identify the slightest law being broken' (Mizoguchi, 2007).

The source of this money is the various economic activities, or, as the yakuza themselves refer to it, *shinogi*, of the syndicate's members. An understanding of their business activities is absolutely indispensible to comprehending the yakuza. Yakuza business activities have evolved at least as fast as the rest of the Japanese economy over the last century and in many cases have proved more dynamic.

The business of the earliest recognisable yakuza can be split neatly into *bakuto* (gamblers) and *tekiya* (peddlers). This lineage consciousness is still retained by both yakuza themselves and the police, though these activities are now of only marginal economic importance to these groups. Gambling dens grew up in labourers' quarters and fire-stations (fire-fighting, then as now, combines intense bursts of excitement with long periods of inactivity). Some bosses of *bakuto* gangs not only organised gambling sessions but served as labour brokers, thus exercising an influence with the construction industry that continues to this day.[2]

What gambling and peddling share is that they lack access to the normal protections afforded to mainstream legitimate businesses; they must develop extra-legal protective mechanisms. To shield gambling sessions from the risk of theft and rival suppliers they inevitably came under the control of those capable of judiciously deploying violence. Conflicts amongst *tekiya* over rights to the most lucrative pitches for their stalls at festivals and markets were, similarly, resolved by the gang bosses with the muscle to enforce their will. Bosses were, and are, violent entrepreneurs.

This ability to deploy organised violence provides the potential to exert influence over other areas of economic activity; Iwai states that by the end of the Meiji period yakuza groups were also involved in protecting sexual services and other *water trades* (1963: 45–6). It is not clear just how diversified yakuza were in the early twentieth century. Ichiji Sozo, an elderly gambler, recalls that whilst 'today's yakuza are mixed up in the construction business, in loan-sharking, and all kinds of things... before the war we made all our money by running gambling rackets' (Saga, 1991: 44). This is not to suggest a romanticised past; Ichiji goes on to lament his wasted, violent life.

What is clear is that yakuza diversification really took off following Japan's surrender in 1945. The ensuing period of chaos contained all the necessary conditions for mafia efflorescence: the absence of effective law-enforcement; a large market requiring regulation; and a ready supply of violent men, in the form of demobilised soldiers, capable of providing that extra-legal protection. As wartime shortages grew worse a black market developed to meet the shortfall. This mushroomed after the surrender as military stockpiles were plundered and the authority of the state disintegrated. By 1946 the government formally legitimised *tekiya* control of Tokyo's open-air markets and some bosses were even 'officially designated collectors of Tokyo mercantile taxes' (Wildes, 1948: 1157–8). Whilst regulating informal markets is the *tekiya* raison d'etre, *bakuto* also became involved, their core business having been squeezed by the establishment of state-run gambling. *Bakuto* gangs that didn't diversify tended to fold or be taken over by more proactive groups (De Vos and Mizushima, 1973: 295).

The Iwato and Jinmu booms of the 1950s saw a massive expansion in construction projects and shipping. Consequently the entertainment and hospitality industries recovered too. All of these became important sources of yakuza revenue and encouraged a dramatic rise in gang membership from the late 1950s on, peaking in 1963 at 184,091. This period was also characterised by intense inter-gang conflict over control of the most lucrative industries.

Despite various legal changes and increased penalties, gang conflict continued. In response to growing public discontent with rampant gang violence and concern for Japan's image at the forthcoming Tokyo Olympics the authorities were finally spurred into taking what purported to be concerted action against yakuza bosses and executives. This was done by changing the laws concerning gambling so that convictions could be obtained purely on the basis of two witness statements. This had some effect: gang membership started to fall and a number of gangs disbanded. The unintended consequence of this strategy was, however, to encourage yakuza diversification and oligopolisation: the gangs which were hit hardest were the more traditional *bakuto* groups whilst sophisticated larger syndicates managed to survive, even if their leadership cadres were temporarily incarcerated. In particular the Yamaguchi-gumi in Kansai, and the Sumiyoshi-kai and the Kinsei-kai (later the Inagawa-kai) in Kantō, started to dominate the yakuza map. These syndicates restructured, introducing the *jōnōkin* system, effectively insulating high-level bosses from the authorities under the existing legal regime.

In the 1970s, when victims of the summit strategy were released from prison, many of them identified stimulant drugs as a way to quickly regenerate their gangs. An epidemic of amphetamine abuse resulted (Tamura, 1992: 102–3). Drugs have remained a significant component of the unambiguously criminal source of yakuza income. Illegal income, however, came to be overshadowed by activities in a legal grey zone.

MINJI KAINYŪ BŌRYOKU

Both increased police pressure and the impact of the 1973 oil shock hurt yakuza finances, further stimulating diversification. In particular there was a significant growth in *minji kainyū bōryoku* (violent intervention in civil affairs) or *minbō* for short. In *minbō* activities yakuza exploit the *implicit* threat of their gang membership to gain some sort of negotiating advantage in a whole range of disputes. Because no explicit threat has been made, and yakuza trademarks are widely recognised, no criminal laws have been violated, although the victim clearly understands the likely consequences of opposition.

Many *minbō* disputes fall under the purview of civil law, but due to the high costs and delays involved in litigation those involved may find it advantageous to seek alternative informal dispute-resolution mechanisms. Yakuza bosses, as local 'men of influence', have historically played a role as mediators (Siniawer, 2008: 22). This is problematic for several reasons: impartiality is questionable as, usually, one side will gain yakuza backing in order to force his preferred outcome on the other party; the process of appealing unsatisfactory decisions is severely limited; it opens the door for yakuza to engineer disputes in a purely exploitative fashion; and it has facilitated and normalised the penetration of criminal organisations into the fabric of mainstream Japan.

The official categorisation of *minbō* includes debt-collection; *sōkaiya* corporate extortion; bankruptcy management; real-estate dispute-management such as land-sharking (*jiage*) and auction obstruction; out of court settlement of traffic disputes; and pre-text racketeering. It is instructive to examine some of these in more detail.

SŌKAIYA

Sōkaiya refers to the practice of threatening to disrupt shareholders' annual general meetings unless payments are made. Its existence is initially puzzling; surely it is appropriate for a company's owners to hold the managers to account with questions. This fails to take into account crucial institutional differences between Japan and those countries where contentious AGMs are considered healthy. West (1999) and Milhaupt and West (2004) demonstrate that limited disclosure requirements expand the range of sensitive information which Japanese companies have to hide. Those in possession of such information have traditionally lacked means to exploit them available to US shareholders such as short-selling or class-action suits. *Sōkaiya* prevalence has developed a logic of its own; a disrupted AGM is taken as a barometer of a company's health and can, in itself, affect share prices.

Disruption ranged from simple loudmouths who would just shout down the managers to sophisticated researchers with genuinely relevant information to disclose. Initially *sōkaiya* were distinct from yakuza, who entered this sector from the 1970s onwards. *Sōkaiya* specialists came under the protection of yakuza, some of whom then served apprenticeships in this niche business. To deal with this threat companies sought yakuza protection from extortionists leading to a bifurcation of the industry into insider and outsider *sōkaiya*. By 1982 police judged *sōkaiya* numbers to be 6,783, of whom about one third were yakuza members (Szymkowiak, 1996: 70).

In response to this problem, the commercial code was amended to criminalise payments to racketeers. The law also imposed a stockholding threshold below which the right to attend AGMs was removed. Though *sōkaiya* numbers plummeted, there was a corresponding rise in other types of extortionists. Payments continued but were better disguised, as evinced by a succession of revelations in the 1990s involving blue-chip companies (at least one of whom had previously stated they had rid themselves of any *sōkaiya* connection). Koike Ryūichi, a yakuza-protected *sōkaiya*, received 26 billion yen from Dai'ichi Kangyō Bank in 'loans', some of which was used to invest in financial institutions enabling him to extract 320 million yen from Nomura Securities and undisclosed sums from other securities operations.

BANKRUPTCY MANAGEMENT

Until reform of the relevant laws in 2000, bankruptcy management (*tōsan seiri*) was a specialised niche *shinogi* exploiting the cumbersome, costly and time-consuming legal machinery for disposing of a bankrupt company's liquidated assets amongst its creditors. Due to the law's inefficiency 85 per cent of bankruptcies were settled outside of the formal procedures. Skilled yakuza could profit in either case. Firstly, because of the problems in recovering assets creditors were often happy to sell their claims at a substantial discount, especially once they realised that yakuza were already involved. Yakuza can also get involved as a firm starts to flounder; deprived of regular sources of finance a struggling firm may resort to yakuza loans. Ideally, the bankruptcy manager will become the largest creditor thereby chairing the creditors' committee, from which position he can manage the liquidation to his advantage. Yakuza can be brought in by managers seeking protection from their creditors. The annual number of bankruptcies in Japan in the early 1980s was about 18,000 with liabilities between 2 to 3.5 trillion yen. Survey data suggests that 23 per cent of such liquidations involved yakuza (see Alexander 1999, 2000).

LAND SHARKING (JIAGE)

'By judicial interpretation, almost all leases in Japan… give the tenant an interest close to a life estate' (Ramseyer and Nakazato, 1998: 38). This is problematic for property developers as they not only have to pay for the land but need to negotiate with tenants who still retain rights to it. Tenants, aware of this, can effectively hold a projected development to ransom. Land with such residual rights is known as *teichi* (low land). *Jiage* (land raising) refers to the process of persuading tenants to relinquish their rights. Frequently yakuza were the persuaders (for which service they would typically receive a 3 per cent commission). Whilst, initially at least, trying to remain within the law, they would make an increasing nuisance of themselves until the tenants' resistance crumbled. During the real-estate speculative boom of the 1980s this became the main earner for yakuza in the Kantō and Kansai regions (Mizoguchi, 1997: 66). Having entered this business at the behest of developers, smarter yakuza, such as the Inagawa-kai's Ishii Susumu, started their own businesses.

A significant proportion of the wealth generated by *jiage* was ploughed into real-estate and stock-market speculation. These initial investments were used as collateral to build highly leveraged portfolios. They were, of course, not alone in adopting aggressive investment strategies. What made them different was their attitude towards falling prices. Often they will demand reimbursement, but not necessarily: in 1985 a Nomura branch manager was beaten to death after one of his inside tips turned

sour for some of his yakuza clients (Alletzhauser, 1990: 205–6). The extent of this problem would only become apparent following the bursting of the economic bubble.

FAKE SOCIAL MOVEMENTS

Although, as Sinawer (2008) points out, there is nothing new about ruffians acting under the guise of political activism as a pretext for extortion, this technique expanded rapidly in response to the revision of the commercial code in 1982 aimed at eradicating *sōkaiya* (Takagi, 1988: 152–3). The two main types are *buraku* (descendants of Japan's outcast communities who have historically suffered from discrimination) liberation (*ese-dōwa*) and right-wing (*ese-uyoku*). A classic approach is for an *ese-dōwa* group to sell expensive 'educational literature' to companies. Those that refuse are subjected to threatening and disruptive denunciations. *Ese-dōwa* activists have engaged in other yakuza activities, such as debt-collection and intervening in traffic disputes, and, in so doing, employ more violence than conventional yakuza (Mizoguchi, 1986: 196).

Perhaps the biggest *ese-dōwa* scam was the systematic abuse of the 1969 special-measures law to help *burakumin* communities. Some opportunities have dried up in recent years as this law expired in 2002. Whilst there has been a shift to fake environmental, disaster-relief or civil-rights movements, *ese-dōwa* has by no means disappeared. It has expanded into areas, such as Okinawa and Hokkaidō, devoid of *burakumin* communities. It has also shifted emphasis; in targeting authorities rather than private business it seeks access to public-work subcontracting and exploit lax policing of government regulations (Tawara, 2005: 117). The issue of *burakumin* remains extraordinarily sensitive in Japan: this confuses victims and police as to how to respond to activism.

Not all extreme right-wing groups are yakuza fronts. Ōsato (2005: 14), writing in the police-related *Jian Fōrumu*, estimates that 400 of Japan's 900-odd extreme right-wing organisations are yakuza outfits. But the number is increasing. Armoured *sendensha* (trucks and cars equipped with public address systems on the roof) blaring out *gunka* or abusive rhetoric can be seriously disruptive to businesses, which has proved profitable to real and *ese-uyoku* alike.

Japanese political history has a strong thread of violent extremism which continues to this day; this still engenders widespread fear of offending extreme right-wing and *dōwa* groups. In 2007 the left-wing *Nikyōso* teachers union booked 190 rooms and a large hall for a 2008 conference at the Grand Prince Hotel in Tokyo. Later, fearing that the meeting would attract right-wing activists, the hotel cancelled the bookings. The hotel then ignored orders from the Tokyo District and High Courts demanding that the hotel honour its booking. Ultimately, the hotel was ordered to pay 290 million yen and issue a public apology. It is telling that the hotel was more concerned about offending right-wing extremists than complying with court orders.

THE BŌTAIHŌ

As mentioned above, the whole point of *minbō* is that the implicit threat of yakuza trademarks means explicit, actionable intimidation is not necessary. In addition to the *minbō* activities outlined above a wide range of injuries or wrongs have been exploited as grounds for compensation or refund. Ordinary members of the public as well as businesses were victimised. These scams were extremely difficult or impossible for the police to deal with under the existing law.

By the end of the 1980s a combination of factors made it politically necessary to close this apparent loophole: popular anxiety, already high after a protracted succession war between rival factions of the Yamaguchi-gumi, came to a head when a schoolboy was killed accidentally during an unrelated conflict in Okinawa; a succession of corruption scandals within the ruling Liberal Democratic Party (LDP) required the government to show that it was cleaning up its act; and in the 'new world order' following the cold war the War on Drugs and international organised crime became the new crusade for US hawks, and Japan was patently not pulling its weight.

In 1991 the *Bōryokudan-in ni Yoru Futō na Kōi no Bōshi nado ni kan suru Hōritsu* (law regarding the prevention of unjust acts by *bōryokudan* members) was passed unanimously. This law was a landmark: it provided a legal definition of *bōryokudan* and applied special controls to members of such groups. In particular it addressed the loophole of *minbō*. Under the provisions of the *bōtaihō* the local Public Safety Commissions (PSCs) are empowered to designate a yakuza group as a *bōryokudan*. Once designated, *bōryokudan* groups became susceptible to injunctions if they were found to be engaging *minbō* activities or upsetting members of the public by displaying gang emblems. Violating injunctions incurred a fine (of up to one million yen) or imprisonment (maximum one year). PSC were also empowered to close gang offices during periods of inter-gang conflict and establish special centres promoting *bōryokudan* eradication.

Whilst this law has had some modest impact in providing remedies to victims of *minbō* demands,

its main impact was to make yakuza disguise such extortion; *ese-dōwa* and *ese-uyoku* groups increased whilst other gang members formally left their gang to become 'business brothers' (*kigyō shatei*). Gang offices removed their crests and name-plates. Members removed their gang lapel badges and had another set of *meishi* printed; yakuza *meishi* for insiders and front-company *meishi* for outsiders.[3] The Yamaguchi-gumi executive committee also instructed subgroups to establish legitimate corporate identities.

THE BUBBLE BURSTS

Measuring the full effect of the *bōtaihō* is difficult as its introduction coincided with the collapse of the bubble. Whilst this had massive consequences for construction, *jiage* and the ability of companies to pay off yakuza, it also presented significant opportunities to yakuza. These revolved around the swathe of bad debt that enmired Japan: some banks made use of yakuza syndicates to collect debts, including those held by other gangs, and debtors sought yakuza protection from creditors (Hill, 2003: 184–190).

In particular two techniques stand out: auction obstruction (*kyōbai bōgai*) and loss-cutting (*songiri*). The main way in which a real-estate auction was obstructed was for a yakuza to get leaseholder's rights to a property due to be auctioned and then make this fact apparent by displaying recognisable but legal trademarks (such as an *uyoku sendensha* outside) to deter possible purchasers and thus depress the price. Associates could then buy the property at an artificially low price and sell it on at a healthy profit. If done carefully such a scam could be hard to prosecute. By the end of the 1990s, however, civil courts started interpreting the law in a more robust fashion and evictions were taking place (Konishi, 1997: 99–109).

Loss-cutting refers to yakuza intermediaries who negotiated between creditors and debtors, arranging for a repayment that both sides could live with. For example, a five billion-yen loan might be reduced to three and the loss-cutter would get a 3 per cent commission of 90 million yen (Hinago, 1998: 166).

The bursting of the bubble made clear that yakuza had borrowed massively. If we look at just one aspect of Japan's bad-debt problem, MOF officials estimated that yakuza borrowed five trillion yen from the *jūsen* (housing and loans) companies. At the end of the 1990s the scale of total bad debt held by Japanese banks and non-bank financial institutions was put at 35 trillion. One informed estimate of how much of this was yakuza-linked was 10 per cent directly and 30 per cent indirectly.

As much of this has been shuffled through various front companies, recovery has proved difficult.

YAKUZA FINANCE

The turmoil in Japanese financial institutions in the 1990s also resulted in a lack of available credit for consumers and small businesses. One yakuza business that flourished, therefore, was money-lending. Historically, the banking sector in Japan has not provided loans to individual consumers or small businesses. This has created a market niche for specialist lenders known as *sarakin*. About 10,000 licensed businesses exist with a total $100 billion in outstanding loans (70 per cent of which is in the hands of the biggest seven companies). One tenth of the Japanese population has at some time borrowed money from such companies. Whilst *sarakin* are not illegal, their aggressive collection methods have brought them into disrepute in the past. Money lending in Japan is governed by a number of laws; most recently a law introduced in 2006 provides for tighter control of collection practices and a maximum interest rate of 20 per cent.

Whilst yakuza have traditionally had links with *sarakin*, for example, taking over hard to recover debt, they also are involved in illegal money lending to those who are unable to access legal finance (either because they are considered bad credit risks or they need immediate help with a short-term cash-flow problem such as covering gambling or bar debts). Such loan sharking is known as *yamikin* (dark money). Interest rates vary but typically work on a system known as *tō-ichi* in which every ten days an interest payment of one tenth must be paid. Yakuza may engage in this business themselves or provide protection to non-yakuza *yamikin* lenders.

The scale of direct yakuza involvement in this sector can be seen from the uncovering of the Goryō-kai's *yamikin* operations. In 2002 Takagi Yasuo succeeded to the leadership of the Shizuoka-based Mio-gumi, a subgroup of the Yamaguchi-gumi. To flatter Watanabe he renamed his group the Goryō-kai (five-diamond association).[4] Takagi had a background in bankruptcy management but had expanded into *yamikin* activities to rapidly expand his power base following his recruitment to the Mio-gumi. The 'system finance' operations that he set up initially lent small amounts of money (up to 100,000 yen) to housewives and employees of the soapland sexual-services industry. Takagi expanded this system by buying lists of multiple debtors and then contacting these individuals with offers of personal finance. At its peak this operation comprised

1,000 loan sharks bringing in 100 billion yen annually under the direction of Kajiyama Susumu, a member of the Yamaguchi-gumi subgroup formerly led by Takagi. Ten debtors resorted to suicide as a result of the group's violent collection methods (Mizoguchi, 2003: 56).

For his part in this operation Kajiyama was sentenced to two and a half years in prison and fined 30 million yen. In addition the courts ruled that nine billion yen should be seized from him and two of his close associates. This has been difficult as the money was transferred to unnamed accounts in Switzerland. The Swiss authorities confiscated 5.8 billion yen and eventually agreed to return half of that to Japan. A further $600,000 was seized from Kajiyama's accounts in the USA (and put into a US government fund to help fight organised crime).

A class-action suit has been launched on behalf of some of the Goryō-kai's victims and, in an interesting ruling by the Supreme Court, the plaintiffs can seek return not only of the extortionate interest they were forced to pay but the principal they borrowed in the first place. Compensating all such victims will, however, be difficult; the sort of multiple debtors typically targeted by Kajiyama's operation are unlikely, five years on, to have a clear record (or even recollection) of how much they have borrowed from whom. Moreover, because of the large number of names under which the gang traded many victims may not actually be aware that they are eligible for compensation.

Not all illegal money lenders are themselves yakuza. Such businessmen, operating outside of the law, require a mechanism which will ensure that customers, many of whom will be poor credit risks, keep their agreements. The threat of yakuza intervention in the case of default provides that. By the same token, when money lenders are operating outside of the law they are vulnerable to yakuza predation. As such, they may actively seek a yakuza protector to shield them from other yakuza.

A quote from a loan shark operating in the Tokyo area makes this clear:

> The way in which I came to get a gang behind me was, of course, because I was intimidated by yakuza. Yakuza will do anything to earn a crust. Therefore, illegal dealers like me that can't make use of the law make a good target. I was introduced to someone… I won't say the name but it is a branch of a well-known group. He said he could become my protector if I paid ¥300,000/month. Because that amount of money didn't matter, I agreed. That 30,000 is the lowest amount I pay; whenever I make a request, I pay them money. Even so, it is much better than being eaten away. The other lenders I know, nearly are all attached to someone or other. (Natsuhara, 2003: 56)

This loan shark recognises that protection *from* yakuza is his main priority. He does not, however, pay off the predatory yakuza targeting him but actively seeks out personal recommendations as to who can best protect his business interests. He does not seem to consider his monthly payments as particularly onerous.

CONTINUED STOCK MARKET PENETRATION

It might be thought that with the Japanese economy in the doldrums yakuza involvement in the stock market might wither away. This is not the case.

S, one of my informants, works for a large securities operation in Tokyo, where he polices his firm's clients for possible yakuza involvement. Whilst he believes that he successfully screens out undesirable business partners, his competitors are less cautious or scrupulous. He appraises the situation in this way:

> I'm not much for conspiracy theories and like to keep things in context, but Yakuza involvement at the high-end of the financial world where [my firm] operates is breath-taking ... Part of the problem here is that there is no real venture capital. Thus, start up companies have to turn to the Yakuza in many cases... We've come across a handful of securities companies that are effectively Yamaguchi operations. (private correspondence, 1 September 2008)

Yakuza involvement in the stock market, and particularly in the volatile IT venture-capital market, is not confined to an elite but involves quite low-level gangsters, too. In many cases these individuals scrape together their proceeds from criminal activity to create investing associations (*tōshi jigyō kumiai*) where it has been comparatively easy to conceal the identity of those who have invested in these associations.

In 2006, Horie Takafumi was arrested on suspicion that he had ramped the value of a Livedoor subsidiary, which had derived much of its financing from associations of this type. Shortly afterwards Noguchi Hideaki, who had been closely involved in Livedoor's financial engineering, was found dead in a hotel room with four severed arteries and his body mutilated. It is widely speculated but not confirmed in the press that Livedoor was yakuza-financed. 'Horie/Livedoor was heavily involved with yakuza and one more properly regards the whole affair as a yakuza shaped effort' (S, personal communication, 14 August 2009).

Since Horie's arrest the police and Tokyo Stock Exchange (TSE) have co-operated in attempts to identify and eradicate yakuza from financial markets. To combat this some yakuza have provided homeless people with a new economic identity, which can then be used to set up an internet trading account (NHK, 2008: 39–40). There are, however, plenty of established professional traders, including graduates of elite universities both in Japan and abroad, who are quite willing to collaborate with criminal groups in order to make money. With financial firms laying off staff the recruiting pool has grown. Some yakuza groups have managed to gain influence with auditing firms, which can legitimise the accounts of gang-related companies. These firms give every appearance of probity; not only are they fully certified public accountants they often boast retired prosecutors or police bureaucrats on their boards 'to keep the authorities at bay' (S, personal communication, 14 August 2009).

Should we be concerned about yakuza involvement in the financial markets? Arguably, if money is being diverted from illegal to legal activities that is a good thing. Moreover, given that there is a shortage of clean capital to fund new start-ups, yakuza finance can play a useful role in stimulating development in cutting-edge new industries. It is, of course, not that simple. Not only should we be concerned not to provide a financial safe haven to the proceeds of crime, the yakuza introduce worrying market distortions. Their violent potential, good information networks and willingness to cut corners give them an enhanced ability to violate normal trading practices; those who might object can be intimidated. Whilst investors generally try to beat the market, yakuza try to cheat it.

A case study of just how is provided by the Ryōzenpaku group, the boss of which, Toyotomi Harukuni, was a Yamaguchi-gumi *kigyō-shatei*. Toyotomi co-ordinated the systematic ramping of shares in an IT firm called P-map by having 20 yakuza executives sell them back and forth before assigning them to unsuspecting investors. Ryōzenpaku also took over ICF, an internet firm listed on the TSE Mothers market. Various dud Ryōzenpaku subsidiaries were then sold off to ICF. Having boosted the value of ICF stock by falsifying ICF's financial records with the connivance of certified accountants, Ryōzenpaku then sold it off. These various complicated transactions generated an estimated 4 billion yen. Toyotomi and several associates were arrested in February 2008 and what was left of ICF was delisted the following month (Arimori and Group, 2008).

Japanese investors are not the only victims of these scams. In 2008 it became apparent that Lehman Brothers and various hedge funds had been fallen prey to a 37.1 billion yen fraud fronted by a Marubeni employee, Yamaura Shingo. Yamaura later received a three-year sentence for his part in the crime. This was, in fact, a Yamaguchi-gumi operation. A number of other similar scams are coming to light as the global economic crunch forces companies to investigate their balance sheets more carefully. Many have 'clear links' to yakuza syndicates.

KASHIMOTO: ONE YAKUZA'S PORTFOLIO OF INTERESTS

The description of *shinogi* above gives some idea of the diversity of yakuza economic activity. It is important to realise that successful yakuza will have many different sources of income. Not only do such individuals tend to be opportunistic risk-takers but many of their businesses are precarious and subject to fluctuations. Kashimoto illustrates the multi-income streams of a contemporary gang boss. Kashimoto was a mid-level boss in the Sumiyoshi-kai syndicate whom I got to know during my fieldwork in the Kabuki-chō entertainment district in 2000. The title Kashimoto refers to the gambling origins of his gang, and he did run gambling sessions from time to time, but this was not a major part of his business.

In addition to his Kabuki-chō-specific interests of protecting illegal traders, money-lending and debt-collecting Kashimoto had a web of interlocking interests. He was closely associated with Y, a popular enka singer whose career he had helped get under way; he had connections with other musical troupes. His patronage helped when negotiating concerts, appearance fees and contracts. Another of Kashimoto's associates was C, the owner of a group of chemicals companies based in a large provincial city.

I was invited along with Kashimoto and his wife to one of C's corporate junkets, which enabled me to gain some insight to their relationship. Kashimoto's group assists with the disposal of C's industrial waste. From the way in which Kashimoto was on display but separate from the other recipients of C's largesse, various suppliers and customers, it was evident that Kashimoto's presence was meant to remind them that C was a man to be reckoned with. At the end of the trip C took me to one side and, after praising Kashimoto, told me that chivalry was all about crushing the strong and helping the weak. He was emphatically grateful for the help Kashimoto provided him.

Kashimoto exploited his musical and business interests by arranging parties and golf competitions. Rich businessmen like C would pay to spend time socialising with famous artists. This is, of course, also a good way of concealing and/or sweetening protection payments.

CONSTRUCTION

Construction companies require licences according to the scale of work they can carry out. These are supposed to be screened for links to organised crime and there are cases where this happens (see *Keisatsu-gaku Ronshū*, 2005 for a special issue on eradication efforts). How successful are they at eradicating yakuza from construction?

The police conduct surveys of the construction industry to try and assess the scale of *bōryokudan* involvement. The data they yield must be treated with caution; not only do they have a low response rate, the companies polled with something to hide can be expected to exercise a degree of censorship. In a 2007 NPA survey one third of respondents had received 'unfair demands'. These were overwhelmingly from fake social movements, particularly *ese-dōwa*, groups rather than *bōryokudan*.[5] It is very hard from such sources to get any idea of the scale of yakuza penetration of this industry.

Construction remains a core component of the yakuza economy. The ascendancy of the Kōdō-kai within the Yamaguchi-gumi was in no small part due to the increased wealth they derived from construction work on Chubu International Airport, which opened in 2005. One Nagoya-based construction company involved in this project and with ties to the gang reportedly charged a five per cent fee for allowing subcontractors to work. Other Yamaguchi-gumi subgroups tried to negotiate with the Kōdō-kai on behalf of their affiliated construction companies, who had pleaded that the *pinhane* (commission) was too high for them to make a profit. Ultimately. Watanabe Yoshinori, the then fifth-generation boss, resolved the dispute. Whilst he forced the other groups to back down, he insisted that a construction group owned by one of his own protectees be given some of the work (Mizoguchi, 2007: 60–1).

The extent to which yakuza inflate construction costs is hard to estimate. One former Ichiwa-kai interviewee suggested a standard protection rate of 3 per cent in the construction industry in the Kansai region (Hill, 2003: 97). In many cases the construction companies have close yakuza links so that the protection is effectively internalised. One Yamaguchi-gumi front company skimmed off 30 percent then subcontracted out the work to other companies. S, who has closely tracked yakuza involvement in financial markets over the last ten years, believes that as much as 10 per cent to 20 per cent of Japan's public-works budget ends up in yakuza hands, which presumably refers to the quantity of work carried out by yakuza-related subcontractors.

KOKUSAIKA NO YAKUZA: GLOBALISATION

The yakuza have long had an international dimension. Guns and drugs are more readily available abroad than in Japan and importing them has typically required links with foreign criminals. Similarly, recruitment of foreign women, often but not always forcible, for the Japanese sexual-services industry has forged links between yakuza and brokers in the various countries of origin. This business has required a criminal infrastructure providing fake marriages, forged documents, employment broking and so on. Yakuza have been closely involved. In recent decades the numbers of foreigners living and visiting Japan, as well as that of Japanese going abroad, has mushroomed. How has this affected the yakuza?

In 2000, Tokyo governor Ishihara Shintar⁻o expressed the view that 'crimes by illegal immigrants are rising rapidly.... Japanese people can no longer walk the streets of the Ikebukuro and Shinjuku districts at night. Those places are like other countries. Even the yakuza don't dare to go in' (*The Guardian*, 2000). This reflected widespread anxiety about foreign criminality in both the press and amongst ordinary Japanese. Whilst the issue of foreign criminality is dealt with elsewhere in this volume, we must address here the relationship between the yakuza and foreign crime gangs in Japan.

A 2008 police report on the state of organised crime in Japan analyses foreign criminal organisations by nationality. Chinese (excluding Taiwan and Hong Kong) organisations are by far the biggest category comprising 35 per cent of all foreign arrestees. There are two distinct themes to Chinese gang criminality. At the unsophisticated end we see property crimes, sometimes violent, involving breaking and entering ordinary homes. The police made arrests for 604 such cases in 2008. At the other end of the spectrum Chinese gangs make and distribute fake credit cards, exploiting data skimmed from real cards (NPA, 2009: 10).

Other ethnically based groups are involved in organised raids on homes. The most conspicuous are Korean nationals, who come over for short intensive crime sprees then return home to avoid arrest, and Colombians (NPA, 2009).

The second biggest category by volume is Brazilian. Brazilian gangs are primarily engaged in car theft (either of whole vehicles or parts), though they feature in the amphetamine arrest statistics. These groups are small and fissiparous based on acquaintances within the Brazilian community. There are a number of Pakistani businessmen active in the second-hand-car export trade serving the Middle East and Africa. Some of these businesses have been found to make use of stolen vehicles (NPA, 2009).

Vietnamese groups tend to specialise in shoplifting, systematically targeting goods for which there is a strong market demand. These gangs are often armed and violently resist arrest. Vietnamese groups also focus on motorbikes, which can readily be resold in Vietnam (NPA, 2009). Iranians, comprising a comparatively small 1.7 per cent of total foreign arrestees, are primarily involved in street-level drug dealing (NPA, 2009).

Socially disruptive and unpleasant though such criminal groups may be, the activities of criminal gangs as portrayed by the arrest data do not represent a significant threat to the yakuza economy. In the case of property crime they do not really affect the yakuza at all. In the case of drug dealing and credit card scams it appears that they are plugged in to the yakuza criminal infrastructure: with drugs, yakuza are farming out the riskiest end of the trade to outsiders; with credit-card fraud, yakuza are customers of Chinese gangs (author's interview data, 2000).

Kabuki-chō has been the focus of anxiety about foreign criminal gangs running amok. There have indeed been conflicts between yakuza groups and Chinese gangs, such as the widely-publicised shooting of Sumiyoshi-kai subgroup members in Parisienne, a popular Kabuki-chō yakuza hangout, in September 2002. It has also been suggested that some yakuza groups have sought to borrow the strength of Chinese gangs to bolster their own standing vis-à-vis other yakuza groups (Natsuhara, 2003: 81). One yakuza interviewee pointed out that there are considerable trust issues, which limit the usefulness of such a strategy. Whilst the quality of data in this area is poor, it suggests that foreigners in Kabuki-chō have generally been working within the yakuza economy rather than trying to take it over. Whilst some Chinese-run businesses were paying protection money to Chinese gangs, some of these were also paying yakuza, and protection of other businesses remains firmly a yakuza affair. The main shift in the balance of power has been due to an incursion of Yamaguchi-gumi subgroups at the expense of the various Tokyo gangs that had hitherto established a generally peaceful co-existence in this entertainment district (Natsuhara, 2003).

The position of foreign groups in Kabuki-chō is more precarious than that of the yakuza. Following a widely publicised shooting incident involving Sumiyoshi-kai and Chinese criminals in September 2002 the police and immigration officials increased pressure on illegal foreigners in Kabuki-chō and many of them have relocated to other parts of Tokyo and outlying areas.

Since the period of post-war chaos ethnic Koreans have featured in Japanese organised criminality.

One Yamaken-gumi subgroup I visited during fieldwork in 1998 and 2003 was overwhelmingly Korean. Members of other ethnic groups have been employed by yakuza, including Westerners. One told me how he had been lured away from his job as an English teacher by lavish hospitality to become the front man for a yakuza-owned night club; a member of my karate *dōjō* in the 1980s performed unspecified tasks for a Tokyo gang; and at least one 'white-man' has been formally initiated into a Sumiyoshi-kai subgroup (author's interview data 2000).[6] It is not clear to what extent this represents a growing phenomenon, or whether it is in the long-term interests of the yakuza as a whole.

The other side of internationalisation has been Japanese visiting abroad. Yakuza have served as touts introducing Japanese tourists to particular places of entertainment and in some cases have invested in such businesses themselves. There does not seem to be evidence that yakuza have however managed to supplant indigenous criminal gangs as governors of the domestic criminal infrastructure. Yakuza protection/extortion exists abroad but is limited to targeting Japanese firms. Given the considerable barriers to entry for this type of organised criminality, this is what we would expect. There is, however, a dearth of first-hand empirical research in this area.

At the top end they have invested in real estate throughout Asia, in Canada, the west coast of the USA and Hawaii. In terms of the globalisation of yakuza capital S reports:

> The yakuza operate on a global scale – though are hiding it much better than during the 'bubble era.' We've tracked their financial operations to Hong Kong, Singapore (especially popular), Korea, Vietnam, UAE, Israel, UK, the Caribbean, and the United States. Business opportunities, ease of incorporation, and tax advantages drive Yakuza overseas expansion the same way they do for legitimate firms.

Yakuza seem to have little problem moving around Asia. It has, however, become much harder for those with criminal records to enter the USA. Guam, with its pistol ranges, karaoke bars and massage parlours catering specifically for Japanese tourists, is much easier to get to; Kashimoto was a regular visitor to its golf courses. Cage-fight promoters there have established links with Yamaguchi-gumi executives who have brought local fighters to participate in Japan's K1 (Japanese Mixed Martial Arts slugfests).

Gotō Tadamasa, at the time the boss of one of the most successful subgroups in the Yamaguchi-gumi, became an exception to the USA travel ban in 2001 when he went to Los Angeles for a liver transplant. His visa application had been facilitated by the FBI in exchange for information concerning yakuza money-laundering operations in the USA. Gotō, it seems, provided information of negligible value. This story generated considerable anger within the Yamaguchi-gumi. When Gotō later attracted further negative publicity by having famous Japanese singers perform at one of his parties he was expelled.[7]

Between 1985 and 2006 the number of registered resident aliens rose from 850,000 to 2,084,919, an increase of 145 per cent (*Nihon Tōkei Nenkan*, 2009). In addition as of 2007 there were an estimated 24,000 who had entered Japan illegally, just under 150,000 of whom had overstayed their visa or short-stay permission and a varying number of short-stay visitors (*Nyūkoku Hakusho*, 2008). Over the same period the number of foreigners arrested for criminal- or special-law violations (excluding traffic offences) rose from 13,779 to 28,135 (an increase of 104 per cent) (*Hanzai Hakusho*, passim). If we break down these violations by type the biggest single category is for immigration-related offences. In 2008, 39 per cent of all sentences handed down to foreigners were for immigration offenses.

EMPLOYER RESPONSIBILITY

Employer responsibility (*shiyōsha sekinin*) is the most innovative legal countermeasure to be deployed against yakuza bosses since the introduction of the *bōtaihō*. This makes use of civil-law provisions for accountability of managers of legitimate enterprises who cause, through the actions of their employees, harm to third parties. Because of the very different nature of the structure and operations of yakuza gangs and legitimate businesses it has not been easy to prove liability. Plaintiffs must establish the following: the yakuza group is itself a business enterprise; the inuries for which litigants seek compensation were committed by gang members in the course of executing gang business; and that there is a clear managerial chain linking the perpetrators to the boss being sued. This has, historically, been difficult; before the landmark suit against Watanabe there had only been a very few cases of successful employer-responsibility litigation.

The litigants against Watanabe were the relatives of Fujitaka Tsuyoshi, a police officer who had been mistaken for an Aizu Kotetsu gang member, and fatally shot whilst he had been staking out a gang headquarters during a period of conflict between that gang and a subgroup of the Yamaguchi-gumi in 1995. The deceased man's family received immense support: from the police in terms of technical evidence concerning the nature of the Yamaguchi-gumi's organisational structure; financially from the *Bōryokudan* Harm Relief Fund. This enabled them to assemble a team of 72 lawyers which, in 1998, finally filed their suit against Watanabe and the sub-boss of the Yamashita-gumi, the group directly responsible for the killing (Asada and Sugahara, 2005: 156–8).

Four years later the District Court ruled in favour of Watanabe: the Yamaguchi-gumi had formally maintained amicable relations with the Aizu Kotetsu; the subgroup involved in the conflict was ordered to disband by the Yamaguchi-gumi headquarters the day after the incident took place. The head of the Yamashita-gumi was, however, found liable and ordered to pay 80 million yen to the plaintiffs. This he was clearly unable to do.

The litigants appealed this decision and, one year later, the Osaka High Court overturned the decision finding that the core enterprise of the Yamaguchi-gumi leadership was to maintain the prestige of the syndicate (based on its reputation for violence) in order to facilitate the money-making operations of subgroups. To ensure the credibility of this reputation gang members will inevitably have to deploy violent force against rival groups and those who defy them. Inter-gang conflict is therefore an essential part of yakuza enterprise. Given the clear chain of command from Watanabe down through the various subgroup bosses to the lowest members, he was clearly responsible for the violent activities of all syndicate members (Asada and Sugahara, 2005: 167–9).

Watanabe, in turn, appealed this decision but in 2004 the Supreme Court upheld the ruling of the Osaka High Court and ordered the defendants to pay more than 117 million yen. This was a crucial precedent as it established the responsibility of syndicate bosses for the actions of low-ranking members of subordinate gangs even though they are not acting under the top boss's direction or with his approval. This interpretation has been given a firm legal status with revision of the *bōtaihō* clearly establishing employer responsibility.

In September 2007 the top leadership of the Sumiyoshi-kai syndicate and that of a subordinate group were ordered by the Tokyo High Court to pay a total of 88 million yen to relatives of one of the three men mistakenly identified as a members of the Inagawa-kai and shot dead in a bar in Maebashi in 2003. It is encouraging to see how this more recent case took only four years from victimisation to judgement, whilst Watanabe v. Fujitaka took nine.

Whilst this is clearly a positive development in providing disincentives to violent yakuza activity, and some sort of compensation to those who suffer from it, it must be pointed out that these remedies are civil and do not carry any criminal penalties. Therefore, in addition to the civil provisions for employer responsibility which can be brought to bear upon yakuza bosses the *bōryokudan taisaku hō* has once more been revised to provide for gang bosses' criminal responsibility for the actions of their subordinates. The first instance of this sanction being implemented came in 2007 when Yano Osamu, a Sumiyoshi-kai sub-boss, was sentenced to death for organising two separate shootings including the 2003 attack on the bar in Maebashi in which three non-yakuza were killed. This clearly provides the Japanese criminal-justice system with a powerful weapon with which to tackle organised criminality.

REGIME CHANGE

The effect of the Watanabe decision was far-reaching. In November 2004 it was announced that Watanabe was taking a break from directly running the syndicate's activities. This was a ploy to protect him from further employer-responsibility suits. This distance provided his many enemies with the chance to move against him. Watanabe was unpopular for a number of reasons: he was widely suspected to have acquiesced to the murder of Takumi Masaru, the highly able, dynamic and popular *wakagashira* (deputy head) in 1997; he had consistently shown favouritism to members of the Yamaken-gumi, his old subgroup; he had provided weak, cautious leadership; and he had squeezed his underlings with increasing demands for cash. Even members of the Yamaken-gumi were dissatisfied with him.

The following May Tsukasa Shinobu (real name Shinoda Ken'ichi), boss of the Nagoya-based Kōdō-kai, was named as *wakagashira*. Two months later Tsukasa and his supporters effectively dismissed Watanabe.

Alongside Tsukasa's promotion there has been a raft of personnel changes at the top of the Yamaguchi-gumi. The executive council (*shikō-bu*) has been reformed and strengthened with Tsukasa's allies given key posts (*Keisatsu-chō*, 2006: 4). The new *wakagashira* is Takayama Seiji, formerly Tsukasa's *wakagashira* at the Kōdō-kai. This is the first time in the history of the Yamaguchi-gumi that the *wakagashira* has been chosen from the serving boss's subgroup. Equally significantly, following the coup Tsukasa has split up the Yamaken-gumi, promoting several of its senior executives to membership of the first-level group.

Tsukasa is a more aggressive and proactive personality than his predecessor. This reputation was first established in 1969 by his activities during a gang war between the expanding Hirota-gumi and local rivals belonging to the Dai Nippon Heiwa-Kai, culminating in his murder of the boss of a Dai

Nippon Heiwa-kai subgroup in the traditional way, using a Japanese sword. Tsukasa served 13 years in prison for this attack (Shinoda, 2004: 15–16). Tsukasa has not rested on his reputation: his group has been one of the Yamaguchi-gumi subgroups most aggressively expanding into eastern Japan. During 2003 the Kōdō-kai was engaged in a number of running disputes with the Sumiyoshi-kai as it tried to expand into the latter's territory.

Tsukasa, alongside two other senior Yamaguchi-gumi executives, was indicted for violations of the Sword and Firearms Control Law (*jūtōhō*) (in 1997 their bodyguards were found to be armed in their presence). In March 2001 Tsukasa had been found not guilty by the district court. The prosecutors then appealed to the Osaka High Court, which in February 2004 overturned this ruling and sentenced him to six years' imprisonment. Tsukasa, in turn, appealed to the Supreme Court, which on the 29 November 2005 upheld the High Court's verdict. Until Tsukasa's release in April 2011 his highly capable *wakagashira* led the syndicate.

Yamaguchi-gumi interests in Tokyo took a significant turn in September 2005 when one of the members of the Kantō Hatsuka-kai federation, the Kokusui-kai, unexpectedly left the federation, and its boss, Kudō Kazuyoshi, joined the Yamaguchi-gumi, sealing a brotherhood relationship with Tsukasa the next day. The Kokusui-kai, with only 350 members, is not the largest gang in Tokyo by any means, but its heartland, the swanky Ginza entertainment area, gives it a disproportionate significance. For some years the gang had allowed the Sumiyoshi-kai to operate in its territory in some niche markets, but following this change it may want to reclaim these for itself. Kudō's defection finally destroys the polite fiction that the Yamaguchi-gumi has no formal presence in Tokyo.

Whilst one likely effect of this more aggressive leadership, will be increased conflict with Tokyo-based groups, it should be noted that some subgroups of the Tokyo gangs have good relations with some Yamaguchi-gumi subgroups (Mizoguchi, interview, 2006). On a national level, too, many of the smaller designated *bōryokudan* have links with the Yamaguchi-gumi: Tsukasa has a brother relationship with Zukoshi Toshitsugu, boss of the fifth-generation Aizu Kotetsu-kai and acted as guardian (*kōken-nin*) in the leadership-succession ceremonies of the bosses of the Kyōsei-kai, the Sōai-kai and the Fukuhaku-kai. Takayama, his *wakagashira*, has done the same for the Sakaume-gumi and the Gōda-ikka. The Yamaguchi-gumi has a near monopoly on organised crime in Japan; only the Sumiyoshi-kai and the Kyokutō-kai exist as significant independent groups. Monopolisation will have implications for the ways in which the yakuza operate.

FURTHER LEGAL TIGHTENING

Since the introduction of the *bōtaihō* there have been further legal changes targeting the yakuza. In particular, three organised-crime countermeasure laws were introduced in 1999. The first key provision was the clarification of the rules surrounding intercepting communications. This was now clearly permitted for investigating a limited number of serious organised crimes. Secondly, punishment of certain offences is increased if they are committed repeatedly in a group comprising at least two members with defined roles. In line with organised-crime countermeasures in the USA and Europe, provisions for the seizure of the proceeds of crime and imposition of supplementary charges were enhanced. Similarly, money-laundering provisions were expanded considerably. Finally, further protections were put in place for witnesses and their families. With the exception of the lengthening of sentences it is not clear how much effect these changes have had.

In 2007 the Firearms and Swords Control Law was revised to provide for harsher penalties against members of designated *bōryokudan* groups, or those operating on their behalf, who discharge firearms in order to further the interests of the group. In addition to the extension of the minimum prison sentence for such a crime from three to five years a fine of up to 30 million yen will also be applied. Similarly, the minimum penalty for gun ownership is increased if the weapon in question is linked to a *bōryokudan* group. This raises interesting legal questions as it applies different levels of punishments to offenders purely on the basis of their connection to a *bōryokudan* group (not in itself a crime under Japanese law).

Other legal changes have also had an impact on yakuza business. In the field of bankruptcy management two laws have cleaned up the messy system which favoured yakuza resolution. The first of these is the 1999 Civil Rehabilitation Law (implemented in April 2000), which provides for protection of bankrupt companies from asset seizing by creditors and removes some of the bottlenecks of the old regime. Additionally, the law requires greater disclosure of information, thereby increasing the chances of a takeover. Secondly, the 2004 Bankruptcy Law speeds up resolution of large-firm bankruptcies by directing them to the Tokyo or Osaka courts, which have superior resources and expertise than courts in other areas. This law also provides for injunctions to protect the firm from premature seizure of assets and prioritises employees' and pensioners' renumeration. Whilst these changes by no means guarantee the end of yakuza involvement in bankruptcy management, they do make such operations considerably harder (Alexander, 2000).

HITSUYŌAKU: WHY DO YAKUZA STILL EXIST?

The cynical interpretation as to the yakuza's continued existence is that they are, in some way, 'servants of the system' (van Wolferen, 1990: 100; in addition to van Wolferen the popular exposition provided by Kaplan and Dubro (2003) best illustrates this). There are four key constituencies that the yakuza have been seen to provide services for: legitimate businesses, the public at large, the police and politicians. There is considerable historical evidence to back up the cynics' view with respect to each of these interest groups, but can this argument still be sustained in twenty-first-century Japan?

YAKUZA AND LEGITIMATE BUSINESS

A key protective role yakuza have traditionally offered to businesses has been as strike-breakers, most famously in the Miike coal miners' strike of 1960 in which yakuza armed with iron bars and clubs fought with strikers with the police watching on the sidelines. One striker was even killed with a sword (Siniawer, 2008: 162–3). Companies also bought private protection when faced with protestors disrupting annual general meetings. Yakuza support for the Chisso corporation, responsible for mercury poisoning at Minamata, and Mitsubishi Heavy Industries, which was profiting from the Vietnam war, were particularly important as they stimulated a big expansion in predatory *sōkaiya*. This, in turn, generated demand for protective yakuza/*sōkaiya* (Szymkowiak, 1996: 98–104).

In response to the horrific consequences of pollution caused in Minamata and elsewhere during Japan's rapid industrial growth environmental-protection laws and regulations have been introduced. These impose additional costs on those firms that observe them thereby conferring a comparative advantage on those that do not. Polluters such as Kashimoto's protectee require yakuza. If they try and pollute without protection, yakuza, activists or affected parties will inevitably find out and cause trouble. Industrial-waste-disposal firms that operate outside of the law similarly require a yakuza shield. One company in Tochigi paid up to 900 million yen between 2002 and 2004 to a Sumiyoshi-kai subgroup.

Within various industries bid-rigging and illegal cartel collusion exists. In such cases there is always the temptation for an individual company to cheat on the collusive agreement, profiting in the short-run but at the expense of the viability of the cartel. To prevent this all participants can benefit by having a yakuza on board to police the agreement and

punish renegades. Of course, if yakuza get wind of an unpoliced bid-rigging agreement they may try to exploit this, which is an additional reason to bring in protection from the start.

In some cases a company might wish to impose a bid-rigging agreement on unwilling competitors or simply deter competitors from bidding. It is in such cases that collusion is most likely to be discovered. In 2004 the Katsumura construction company employed a Sumiyoshi-kai subgroup to persuade competitors to submit inflated bids for water-supply projects to the Tokyo government. The co-operating firms were each to receive kickbacks of 2 per cent of the winning bid or promises that they would be allowed to win future contracts at similarly inflated prices. The plot was uncovered when one firm managed to switch their forcibly extracted bid for their initial tender at the last minute. Katsumura executives and yakuza were arrested.

The construction industry is in a similar position: yakuza prevalence creates the conditions for yakuza protection. As one police specialist in this field admits, 'in order to have business flow smoothly, many people think they have no option but to pay greeting fees' (Namba, 2005: 15). In addition to negative protection (i.e. protection from disruption by other yakuza, *ese-dōwa* or *ese-uyoku*) yakuza may help contractors by deterring competition, policing cartels, negotiating with other firms in the subcontracting chain and helping with the cost-effective disposal of building waste. The yakuza-dominated day labourers' markets, which provided the workers at the bottom of the subcontracting chain, have largely withered away. It seems plausible to assume that yakuza exercise a degree of control over the supply of illegal foreign workers but this is an area meriting further research.

As mentioned above with respect to techniques such as *jiage*, the yakuza also provide companies with para-legal dispute-resolution services. In an important contribution to this field Milhaupt and West (2004) have used regression analysis to demonstrate the significance of this role. Rather than rely on formal legal mechanisms for resolving bad debt or evicting intransigent tenants it is expedient to contract yakuza. It should be noted that some features which facilitate this role are institutional. At the same time firms might feel the need to employ yakuza because their disputants are similarly protected.

Finally, in the financial markets, we have seen that yakuza can assist fledgling businesses with start-up capital. This often proves to be a mixed blessing. Yakuza investors do not always have the long-term interests of their companies at heart. Organised-crime involvement in the stock market provides serious distortions, undermines investor confidence and retards the development of dynamic new firms which should be at the forefront of Japan's technical and economic innovation.

With respect to yakuza relations with legal business there are, therefore, ways in which genuine services are provided. On closer inspection some of the demand for yakuza protection is generated by the existence of yakuza themselves. This demonstrates the importance of path-dependency: once you have deep penetration of organised crime it develops a logic of its own. In other ways yakuza benefit business interests but to the detriment of society at large. Institutional factors are more problematic. It is, however, encouraging to see that Japan's institutional landscape is changing in ways which might be expected to reduce the scope for yakuza dispute resolution. This is something which merits further research.

YAKUZA AND THE PEOPLE

Popular tolerance of organised crime is facilitated if its main activities are perceived as victimless crimes and violence is limited to the gangland. Of course, organised crime does not exist in a vacuum; its traditional role in Japan and elsewhere is to provide goods and services that the state has either banned or sought to monopolise but that at least some of the population desires. The demand for sexual services, recreational drugs and gambling (arguably, none of them victimless crimes) all remain part of the underground economy and subject to yakuza influence. To the extent that we accept the inevitability of these markets, but feel unable to legalise them, the yakuza or a similar system of underworld governance can be considered a necessary evil *within those limited markets*. Their activities are not, however, confined to this niche.

Historically, yakuza violence has adversely affected some segments of the population, especially day labourers and other marginal figures. However, as shown above, police countermeasures against their least problematic crimes, especially gambling, has progressively pushed them into *minbō* activities that directly impinge on the lives of greater numbers of ordinary members of the public. Whatever the reality, the perception of the yakuza as increasingly sociopathic has grown. Public tolerance has, in turn, declined; this is evinced by the growing number of cases in which local residents have successfully sought court orders forcing gang offices to move out. There were more than 50 such cases ongoing in 2008. Most significantly, in April 2009 the people of Akasaka won their legal battle to prevent the Inagawa-kai from relocating their headquarters to their neighbourhood.

Despite this, a number of people make use of yakuza and not just as consumers of drugs,

gambling or sex. One example is provided by the reaction of a victim of the Super-Free Circle, a club arranging parties for students at prestigious universities in Tokyo. The organisers, themselves students or recent drop-outs, were able to earn up to 700,000 yen a month each. The money was not, however, the only attraction; at the parties the most attractive women would be herded into a VIP room, plied with alcohol and then gang-raped. Photographs were taken to shame the victims into silence. One woman sought justice and asked a yakuza group to extract 10 million-yen compensation from the club. Wada, the leader of the circle, was himself a yakuza protectee. The upshot of this was that a compromise settlement was reached. Wada paid 5 million, though it is not clear how much the woman received. Private protection is an imperfect good. Another victim of the club sought public protection and went to the police in 2003; subsequently other women came forward and the following year Wada and 13 other organisers were given sentences ranging from 28 months to 14 years.

Stark, in his superb ethnography of a yakuza group in Okayama prefecture in the late 1970s, gives another illustration of the limitations to private justice. He observed a case in which a businessman approached the local boss to seek his help in discreetly dealing with his violently abusive, drunken brother-in-law. The boss wisely refused telling his supplicant that a family dispute, especially with an unstable character, would inevitably cause trouble for everyone (Stark, 1981: 215–220).

YAKUZA AND THE POLICE

In a telling phrase van Wolferen referred to the relationship between the police and the yakuza as 'the ultimate symbiosis' (1990: 101). Similar arguments are put forward by Kaplan and Dubro (1986) and, in a slightly more nuanced form, Ames (1981). Under this analysis, the police benefit from the existence of yakuza in a number of ways: intelligence; control of disorganised crime; and self-restraint and co-operation. Yakuza, not least through their close links to the *mizushōbai* world of flowing drinks and loose tongues, have well developed information-gathering networks. Historically, police would visit gang offices periodically to chat informally over coffee and cigarettes about what was happening on the streets and within the yakuza world. Information disclosure can, of course, be useful to yakuza groups themselves if it helps get rid of competitors or expelled yakuza who might cause trouble.

With respect to controlling disorganised crime there are two main mechanisms by which this might operate: policing and recruitment. Yakuza are businessmen. In their traditional role of gamblers and protectors of *mizushōbai* operations they have a vested interest in preventing street crime from deterring the customers on whom they depend. As protectors they also have a vested interest in maintaining their monopoly on extra-legal violence. On a more basic level, the argument goes, by providing structured employment to young toughs it prevents them from engaging in random acts of violent criminality.

Finally, in this schema, gangs exercise self-restraint. Because gang bosses want to remain in business they do not go out of their way to antagonise the police. Not only do they prevent others from causing trouble on their patch they refrain from activities that the public and police might find unacceptable. They also co-operate with police investigations. Gang members turn themselves in after a gang crime. In some cases the surrendering gangster is not guilty but is taking the rap for a superior (a practice known as *migawari*) for which he will be rewarded on his release. Similarly, a gang might be asked to provide a few guns for the police to 'seize'. In return they will be rewarded with lax policing and tip-offs before their operations are to be 'raided'. In short, the van Wolferen perception is of a very Japanese affair predicated on notions of harmony, face, *ura* and *omote* (hidden reality and the surface pretense of things). How accurate is it?

There is considerable empirical evidence and theoretical models to support this thesis. It is, however, but one facet of a complex and dynamic reality. Whilst Ames commented on the 'remarkable cordiality' between the police and yakuza, he was subtle enough to see that this was strained and based on the recognition that a 'complete rupture in the relationship would be counterproductive for both sides' (1981: 107). Stark, writing about the gang he closely observed for a year, observed that the 'limited amount of co-operation with law-enforcement personnel is all behind the scenes, marked by mutual contempt, and necessitated only by their respective self-interests' (1981: 17).

As a crude generalisation, yakuza in Tokyo have tended to adopt a more docile co-operative stance vis-à-vis the authorities than their counterparts in the Kansai region (especially the Yamaguchi-gumi). The Kantō Hatsuka-kai is a loose association comprising the prominent Tokyo gangs. The purpose of this is to resolve conflict quickly and without raising the ire of the local police. Similar friendly associations exist in other cities. Within Kansai the Sakaume-gumi, a small gambling gang, traditionally enjoyed good relations with the Osaka police. Discussions with Yamaguchi-gumi members about their violent treatment in police custody suggests that their relationship was not nearly as cosy (author's interviews, 1998).

Historically, the authorities have tended to adopt a pragmatic relationship with the yakuza when the latter were weak and to repress them when they were strong. In the aftermath of the Second World War there was a period when impotent, underfunded local Japanese police forces were partially bankrolled and overseen by yakuza (Wildes, 1954: 188; Aldous and Leishman, 1997: 138). Since then the police have steadily grown in power with consequences for their relationship with the yakuza.

Starting with the first summit strategy, they have put pressure on traditional yakuza businesses, encouraging a process of diversification into less socially acceptable activities, such as drugs and *minbō* activities, which victimise ordinary members of the public. With the introduction of the *bōtaihō* the willingness of the yakuza to co-operate with the police noticeably declined and they further adapted to conceal their activities from the authorities. The increased punishments meted out to yakuza have made it much harder for bosses to tell gang members to hand themselves in for some crimes (Mizoguchi, 2007: 242). Though it still happens now, it usually follows a botched killing, in which the wrong people were targeted. One can imagine what would have happened to the Yamaguchi-gumi members who had killed the Kōbe policeman if they had not given themselves up. Under the system of employer responsibility bosses are keen to save their own skins (and this must have implications for group solidarity).

At the same time as squeezing the yakuza with increased regulation the police have started competing with them over lucrative *shinogi*. This is most noticeable with respect to the vast pachinko industry, the prize-exchange business, which was formerly a big yakuza earner. Through the regulatory powers endowed by the Public Morals Law the police have enormous power over pachinko and they have effectively forced yakuza out of this business, replacing it with public-welfare bodies managed by retired police officers.

A more basic consideration as to why the police tolerate the yakuza is the prospect of financial reward. Kaplan and Dubro (2003: 144–152) catalogue the many incidents of police corruption to have hit the headlines over recent decades. My own interviewees suggest that, at a street level, this continues. S's observation of the existence of retired NPA bureaucrats filling *amakudari* posts in yakuza-related auditing firms is more worrying. Corruption is encouraged when the existence of organised crime has become normalised as a fact of life too big to deal with. This fatalistic view was evinced in a briefing to journalists by Suganama Mitsuhiro, a retired Public Security Intelligence Agency officer. He informed them that Chubu International Airport and the Aichi Expo could never have been realised without yakuza approval and cooperation.

On the balance of evidence, the cosy equilibrium of van Wolferen's analysis has lost what relevance it once had. The police-yakuza relationship is now broadly antagonistic. And yet the yakuza survive. A slightly different argument as to why the police at an organisational level are not interested in eradicating the yakuza is that their existence justifies the current levels of police funding and manning (author's interviews with Mizoguchi, 2000, Yamaken-gumi sub-boss, 1998). Evil is necessary for the forces of good to battle with and almost triumph over (if only they were slightly better funded).

The legal changes of the last two decades have been significant, but the resulting laws are still weak by international standards and do not pose an existential threat to the yakuza. To get really serious about tackling organised crime the criminal-justice system would need plea-bargaining, credible protection for supergrasses, sustained undercover and sting operations, and laws similar to America's RICO statutes. Alternatively, one could simply criminalise yakuza membership. These are all, of course, political decisions.

YAKUZA AND POLITICIANS

This is the holy grail of yakuza studies. The historical links between yakuza and politicians are well documented and little effort was made to conceal them. Siniawer's (2008) study of violence in Japanese politics from 1860 to 1960 is essential reading here. Two things stand out. Looking back from the early twenty-first century it is hard to understand the level of paranoia amongst the political elite for much of the twentieth century about the red menace. Secondly, violence has been a consistent theme in Japanese politics, democratic or otherwise; yakuza have supplied some of it.

In 1952, faced with strident opposition to the passage of the Subversive Activities Bill, ministers in the Liberal administration arranged for *tekiya* to protect the Diet building from left-wing students and parliamentarians (Iwai, 1963: 693). The previous year the justice minister had attempted to organise a force of 200,000 yakuza and right-wingers to combat an anticipated communist revolution (Hori, 1983: 137–8; Ino, 1993: 254–7). In the 1960 Anpo riots, yakuza played a role in combating left-wing protestors and it is 'widely believed' that then prime minister Kishi asked Kodama to organise yakuza and rightists into a protective force to ensure the safety of Eisenhower on his visit (Ino, 1992: 269; Siniawer, 2008: 166–7). As it happened, Eisenhower cancelled.

In addition to their role as violent suppressors of dissent, how might yakuza be a necessary evil for politicians? Stark, observing at a local level,

describes a clique comprising, in addition to the gang boss, political, business and bureaucratic elites who exploit clique membership for their own personal advantage. Gang participation enhances the effectiveness of the clique and its illegal transactions:

> The regulation, application of sanctions, enforcement, and adjudication of these transactions are provided for by the gang. The gang has the organization, the coercive forces, and expertise in illegal dealings to make the clique self-regulating. (1981: 197–8)

Yakuza participation also helps enforce secrecy surrounding the clique's activities. As public perceptions have changed, especially following the Lockheed scandal, visible proximity to yakuza has ceased to be an electoral asset. Politicians no longer regularly turn up at the weddings and funerals of prominent bosses. The Sagawa Kyūbin scandal, now more than two decades old, was the last time direct links between yakuza and senior LDP figures were laid bare. Do they still exist?

Given the age of many senior LDP politicians, entrenched LDP rule and the hereditary nature of the Japanese political system, many members of the political elite derive their position, either directly or indirectly, from support networks established at a time when yakuza support was normal and unconcealed; it would be surprising if such links did not remain in at least vestigial forms. The continued importance of the construction industry to the finances of both yakuza and politicians reinforces this expectation. Early in 2004 the Mainichi Shimbun, examining the annual financial reports of local chapters of the LDP in the Osaka area, reported that over 20 had received money from companies managed by yakuza or their relations in 2001. When this was made public the overall chief of the Osaka chapters said that if the allegations were true the money would be returned. His comments seemed to imply that the LDP would never have accepted the money in the first place if they had known the tainted nature of its provenance.

During my fieldwork in 2000 I was informed by the underground accountant of a prominent Inagawa-kai business associate of the financial support he provided to an LDP faction leader. Sometimes both the businessman and his yakuza associate would attend fund-raising parties with this politician who, of course, knew exactly what these men did for a living. On another occasion in 2000 whilst interviewing a mid-level boss in the Yamaguchi-gumi in his office the secretary of an LDP politician dropped in to discuss a land deal. My interviewee had supported this politician for many years, though now, to avoid embarrassing him, his financial contributions are given in smaller, less detectable amounts.

Are such links currently common? The crony-packed anti-reform Abe cabinet (2006–7) may be a particularly egregious case, but newspaper reports linked Agriculture Minister Matsuoka Toshikatsu (who committed suicide after several money scandals came to light) and Defence Agency Chief Kyūma Fumio with gangs. Financial intelligence expert S suggests at least six members of this cabinet had yakuza connections of some sort (author's interview 2008).

The widespread popular discontent with the LDP culminating in their decisive electoral defeat on 30 September 2009 was, apparently, shared in unexpected places. Prior to the 2007 upper house election the Yamaguchi-gumi sent directives to its subgroups telling them to support the Democratic Party of Japan (DPJ). One direct boss recalls the telephone call:

> The current LDP is doing nothing but producing laws that will crush the yakuza. Under the LDP-CGP government we will end being crushed at some stage. In order to stop the LDP movement this time, we would like the DPJ to win. Please do your best for us. (Mizoguchi, 2007: 247–8)

A cynical interpretation of this might be that the story was leaked to bolster LDP support. The Kōdō-kai does, however, have a history of supporting the DPJ due to its links with the Toyota union. If it is true this story does suggest that such yakuza-politician links as exist are not generating blanket immunity from prosecution; anti-yakuza bills are passed unanimously into law (but then who would be the one to oppose them?). What they are more likely to be getting is influence in the allocation of public work and the erosion of any clear political will to confront the yakuza head-on with US-style organised-crime countermeasures.

Writing in the immediate aftermath of the DPJ's landslide victory of August 2009, one interesting question is what the implications of this development will be for the yakuza. The LDP are, of course, not the only party to have benefited from yakuza links in the past but, as the party of government for the last half century, it has been inevitably the one worth talking to. A cadre of old LDP renegades in the new administration tempers excessive expectations. We shall see.

Should a future Japanese government attempt to eradicate yakuza, how would they react? In 2002 Ishii Kōki, a DPJ parliamentarian, was stabbed to death by Itō Hakusui, a right-wing extremist. Itō surrendered himself to the police the next day. The ostensible reason for this murder was that Ishii had refused to buy Itō's publications. Ishii was a prominent corruption buster in the construction and finance industries and his death is generally accepted by S's underworld sources as a yakuza murder. As the Italian state found when they finally went to war with the Mafia after decades of inaction, mafias fight back.

MAFIA-KA NO YAKUZA?

It is a common theme amongst watchers of Japan's underworld that the yakuza is becoming more like the mafia. What is meant by this is that those aspects of Japanese organised crime which are peculiar to the yakuza will progressively disappear; the yakuza will increasingly resemble organised-crime groups elsewhere (the default comparator being the USA). This homogenisation thesis is one that will be familiar to all scholars of Japanese studies. The aspects of the yakuza that are generally considered to be peculiar to them are their open existence, their preparedness to co-operate with the authorities and their symbiotic relationship with key power holders.

As this chapter has demonstrated, some of these supposed peculiarities have already been seriously eroded. In response to a harsher legal environment gangs are concealing more of their activities and co-operating with the authorities less. The expansion of employer-responsibility provisions will accelerate this process. It is ironic that at a time when Japan is slowly becoming more transparent their gangsters are becoming less so.

Employer responsibility may also encourage a reduction in the number of gang members as bosses offload the loose cannons and peripheral members whose activities will come back to haunt them. At the same time they will retain their real earners, the 'business brothers' and protectees in the financial sector, who operate without visible yakuza links but can call on extra-legal enforcement when necessary.

A conceptually flawed subtext of the mafia-isation thesis contrasts a romanticised view of the friendly rough-diamond neighbourhood yakuza of old with a cold-blooded sociopathic mafia. The yakuza have always had this dual aspect. They exist at the interface of the upper and under worlds; good social intelligence remains an important asset in bridging the two. Many of the yakuza I have met, murderers included, are literally charming. At the same time a credible potential for violence has always been crucial to yakuza. Without it they are irrelevant.

A more important criticism of the mafia-isation is that many of the supposedly unique aspects of the yakuza are not so special on closer inspection. There is a wide body of literature, both theoretical and empirical, relating to organised crime in other jurisdictions which is highly relevant to the Japanese case.

For example, the pragmatic relationship between organised crime and the authorities in which good behaviour is rewarded by partial policing has been theoretically modeled by Celantini et al. (1995). Schelling (1984: 172) points out that criminal organisations partially internalise the costs (in terms of increased policing) generated by individual criminal acts. Organised crime groups therefore have a greater incentive to minimise police aggravation than individual criminals do. Empirically, the observation that mafias provide informal policing within their territories has been made often (for example, Gambetta (1993: 166)).

Yakuza involvement in cartel management has corollaries elsewhere. Gambetta and Reuter (1995) analyse the mafia's role in policing collusive agreements in Italy and the USA. They conclude, significantly, that the bulk of monopoly profits is retained by colluding firms, not the mafia. Mafia involvement in collusive business arrangements in the USA is studied in greater detail by Jacobs (1999). From a policy perspective his work is important as it shows that, despite widespread perceptions that the problem was too big to handle, something can be done about deeply entrenched mafias given a clear political will and the right set of legal tools.

The idea that organised crime is a 'servant of the system' is not unique to Japan. Booth (1999) examines the links between political and criminal elites in China in the early twentieth century. The Marxist writer Pearce (1976) discusses gangster efforts to break strikes and suppress radicalism in the USA. If we extend our scope to democracies in areas including the Caribbean, the former Soviet Union, South and Central America, we might wonder whether the participation of organised criminals in the political process is not, in fact, the norm.

In terms of theoretical contributions to our understanding of organised crime, Fiorentini and Peltzman's edited volume *The Economics of Organised Crime* (1995) is highly instructive. Other classic theoretical analyses include: Dixit (2004), with his contribution to the economic modelling of extra-legal governance; Tilly (1985), with his disturbing comparison of the state and organised crime; and Schelling (1984), who in two short chapters laid the groundwork for subsequent conceptualisations of organised crime.

The single text which this author found most useful in making sense of the yakuza is Gambetta's study of the Sicilian Mafia (1993). Gambetta's central argument is that the core competence of the mafia is the provision of private protection. As this chapter has demonstrated, yakuza protection exists as a genuine product too. This should not be interpreted as arguing that the yakuza are either necessary or desirable. As Gambetta points out forcibly, mafias are 'protecting the wrong people'

(1993: 32). Gambetta's analysis has been applied to other contexts: Russia (Varese, 2001), China (Chu, 2000) and Japan (Hill, 2003). We must, of course, be aware that the key factor which has generated so much demand for yakuza protection is their own existence.

FURTHER READING

There is very little primary scholarship in English available in this field. Stark's 1981 unpublished PhD thesis, an ethnography of yakuza in Okayama, is still essential reading. Ames (1981), in his study of community policing also provides useful insights. Siniawer (2008) provides a thorough historical analysis of the role of yakuza in Japanese politics from the fall of the Tokugawa through to 1960. Szymkowiak (1996) analyses *sōkaiya* extortion. Milhaupt and West (2004) and Haley (1991) examine yakuza involvement in extra-legal fixing. Hill (2003) surveys Japanese organised crime in the last decades of the twentieth century in light of legal, economic and institutional change.

In addition to the academic literature available in English, there are a number of journalists who have made contributions in this field. Understandably, they do not adopt academic conventions and display variable standards of rigour. Kaplan and Dubro (1986, 2003) is the most well known and comprehensive of these. Wildes (1954), as an experienced Japan hand on site during the occupation period, paints a fascinating picture of the turbulent post-war era. This period is also ably treated by Whiting (1999). Adelstein (2010), the only American to be granted membership of the Tokyo Metropolitan Police Press Club, gives insights into the complex relationships police, criminals and journalists foster in pursuit of their respective ends. Adelstein writes extensively on yakuza-related matters on his website and this provides good background material on contemporary developments in this field (www.japansubculture. com). Seymour (1996), an unashamedly subjective celebration of the author's derring-do, represents the extreme end of this genre.

Some autobiographical material has been translated into English, providing a more personal, subjective take on yakuza life. These include the reminiscences of an elderly gambling boss (Saga, 1987, 1991), a gangster's deviant drug-addict daughter (Tendo, 2007) and *Toppamono*, a fascinating account of a gangster, radical activist and businessman, which graphically illustrates the seat-of-the-pants corporate governance of small-medium firms operating at the margins of legality (Miyazawa, 2005).

Looking at the Japanese literature, Iwai (1963) remains the standard reference for yakuza up to the mid-twentieth century, whilst Tamura (1964) covers earlier yakuza history. For contemporary issues the monthly *Keisatsu-gaku Ronshū*, produced by elite police bureaucrats and legal scholars, is useful, whilst the NPA website provides up to date statistics on yakuza numbers, arrests and crime trends (www.npa.go.jp). The National Research Institute for Police Science published useful research on the yakuza in the late twentieth century but has since moved out of this field. Most Japanese scholarship in this field is drawn largely from these sources and tends to be worthy, dry and uncontroversial as a result.

There is, however, a wealth of popular journalistic literature dealing with organised crime and the underworld economy. Whilst these works are of wildly varying quality and disparaged by the academic community, they are widely read by police and, in some cases, by yakuza themselves. The work of Mizoguchi Atsushi, for instance, was recommended to me by yakuza and police specialists alike. More recently, a specialist investigative team known as Group K, sometimes working in co-operation with Arimori Takashi, has been producing good work on yakuza involvement in the legitimate corporate world (and this too is recommended by individuals working in this field). Because these works make use of sources within and peripheral to the underworld they provide potentially rich pickings to qualitative researchers. The problem of veracity remains a very real one. In my own research I made use of sources which were personally recommended by people familiar with the illegal world or which corresponded with my own fieldwork-research findings. I realise that this rule of thumb will not be of much use to researchers who lack the time or inclination to conduct hands-on research.

For those seeking a comparative angle or further grounding in theoretical developments in this field Abadinsky's encyclopaedic *Organized Crime* (currently in its ninth edition) is a useful starting point; it serves as a clearinghouse for scholarship and recent empirical data on all aspects of the subject (though with an American bias). My own theoretical preferences have been signposted clearly above.

NOTES

1 www.npa.go.jp/sosikihanzai/bouryokudan/boutai/h22_bouryokudan.pdf

2 The early history of the yakuza is outside the remit of this chapter. Interested readers are directed to Siniawer (2008), Tamura (1964) and Iwai (1963).

3 *Meishi* etiquette is sensitive; when meeting yakuza for the first time they would frequently look at the person introducing me to see if it was safe to hand over their gang card.

4 Watanabe was the fifth generation Yamaguchi-gumi boss and the gang's crest is in the shape of a diamond (*hishi* is a commonly used shorthand for the syndicate).

5 See www.npa.go.jp/sosikihanzai/kikakubunseki/bunseki3/kensetsugyo.pdf

6 During the course of my fieldwork I was invited to join two different organisations; obviously, selection criteria are not too high.

7 Since then, in a move interpreted as a protective measure, Gotō has entered a Buddhist temple.

REFERENCES

Adelstein, J. (2010) *Tokyo Vice: An American Reporter on Japan's Police Beat*. Tokyo: Kōdansha International.

Aldous, C. and Leishman, F. (1997). Policing in Post-War Japan:Reform, Reversion and Reinvention, *in International Journal of the Sociology of Law*, 25.

Alexander, A. (1999). Managing Financial Distress in Japan's Business World. *Japan Economic Institute: JEI Report*, 25, 2 July.

Alexander, A. (2000). Business Failures Rising in Japan as New Bankruptcy Law Takes Effect. *Japan Economic Institute: JEI Report*, 22, 9 June.

Alletzhauser, A. (1990). *The House of Nomura*. London: Bloomsbury.

Ames, W. (1981). *Police and Community in Japan*. Berkeley CA: University of California Press.

Arimori, T. and Group K. (2008). *Jituroku Angura Manee: Nihon Keizai wo Kuichigiru Yami Seiryoku-sha*. Tokyo: Kōdansha.

Asada, T. and Sugahara, H. (2005). Bōryokudan Kumi-chō ni Taisuru Songai Baishō Sekinin Tsuikyū Oyobi Kisō to Yamaguchi-gumi Kumi-chō no Shiyōsha Sekinin wo Mitometa Saikōsai Hanketsu ni Tsuite (Chū). *Keisatsu-gaku Ronshū*, 58(7): 156–182. Tokyo: Tachibana Shobō.

Booth, M. (1999). *The Dragon Syndicates: The Global Phenomenon of the Triads*. London: Doubleday.

Celantini, M., Marrelli, M. and Martina, R. (1995). Regulating the Organised Crime Sector. In G. Fiorentini and S. Peltzman (Eds.) *The Economics of Organised Crime*. Cambridge: Cambridge University Press.

Chu, K. (2000). *The Triads as Business*. London: Routledge.

De Vos, G. and Mizushima, K. (1973). Organization and Social Function of Japanese Gangs: Historical Development and Modern Parallels. In G. De Vos (Ed.) *Socialization for Achievement: Essays on the*

Cultural Psychology of the Japanese. Berkeley CA: University of California Press.

Dixit, A. (2004). *Lawlessness and Economics: Alternative Modes of Governance*. Princeton: Princeton University Press.

Fiorentini, G. and Peltzman, S. (Eds.) (1995). *The Economics of Organised Crime*. Cambridge: Cambridge University Press.

Gambetta, D. (1993). *The Sicilian Mafia: The Business of Private Protection*. Cambridge MA: Harvard University Press.

Gambetta, D. and Reuter, P. (1995). Conspiracy among the Many: The Mafia in Legitimate Industries. In G. Fiorentini and S. Peltzman (Eds.) *The Economics of Organised Crime*. Cambridge: Cambridge University Press.

Haley, J. (1991). *Authority Without Power: Law and the Japanese Paradox*. Oxford: Oxford University Press.

Hanzai Hakusho. White Paper on Crime. Annual Reports from the Ministry of Justice. http://www.moj.go.jp/housouken/houso_hakusho2.html

Hill, P. (2003). *The Japanese Mafia: Yakuza, Law and the State*. Oxford: Oxford University Press.

Hori, Y. (1983). Sengo no Uyoku Seiryoku. Tokyo: Keiso Shobo.

Ino, K. (1992). *Kenryoku to Yakuza no Rekishi* in *Yakuza to Iu Ikikata: Kore ga Shinogiya!* Tokyo: Takarajima.

Ino, K. (1993). *Yakuza to Nihonjin*. Tokyo: Gendai Shokan.

Iwai, H. (1963). *Byōri-shūdan no Kōzō*. Tokyo: Seishin Shobō.

Jacobs, J. (1999). *Gotham Unbound: How New York City was Liberated from the Grip of Organized Crime*. New York: New York University Press.

Kaplan, A. and Dubro, A. (1986). *Yakuza*. London: Addison-Wesley Publishing.

Kaplan, D. and Dubro, A. (2003). *Yakuza: Japan's Criminal Underworld*. Berkeley CA: University of California Press.

Keisatsu-gaku Ronshu. (2005). *The Journal of Police Science*. Vol. 58 No. 10. Published by Tachibana-Shobo in Tokyo.

Keisatsuchō Soshikihanzai Taisakubu (2007). Kensetsu-gyō ni Okeru Futō Yōkyū Nado ni Kan suru Jittai Chōsa. Retrieved from www.npa.go.jp/sosikihanzai/kikakubunseki/bunseki3/kensetsugyo.pdf

Konishi, Y. (1997). *Boryokudan Ni Yoru Shikko Bogai in T Fujimoto (ed) Boryokudan Taisaku Ho Shikko Go-nen no Boryokudan Taisaku*. Tokyo: Hitosei.

Millhaupt, C. and West, M. (2004). *Economic Organizations and Corporate Governance in Japan: the Impact of Formal and Informal Rules*. Oxford: Oxford University Press.

Miyazawa, M. (2005). *Toppamono*. Tokyo: Kotan Publishing.

Mizoguchi, A. (1986). 'Urashakai no Seiji-kezaigaku' in Bessatsu Takarajima (Ed.) Yakuza to iu Ikikata: Kore ga Shinogiya! Tokyo: Takarajima.

Mizoguchi, A. (1997). *Gendai Yakuza no Ura-chishiki*. Tokyo: Takarajima.

Mizoguchi, A. (2003) *Yamikin Teiō to Yamaguchi-gumi no Kankei* in *Tsukuru*, October 2003.

Mizoguchi, A. (2007) *Tsukasa Shinobu to Takayama Seiji no Roku-Daime Yamaguchi-gumi* (The Sixth-generation Yamaguchi-gumi of Tsukasa Shinobu and Takayama Seiji). Tokyo: Take Shobō.

Namba, Masaki (2005) *Kōkyō Kōji kara no Bōryokudan Haijo ni Tsuite* (concerning the exclusion of *bōryokudan* from public construction work) in *Keisatsugaku Ronshū*, Vol. 58, No. 10.

National Police Agency (Japan). Organised Crime Countermeasures Bureau (2009). *Heisei 20 nen no Soshiki Hanzai no Jōsei*. Retrieved from www.npa.go.jp.

Natsuhara, T. (2003). Yamikin wa Nemuranai. In T. Natsuhara (Ed.) *Kabuki-chō Autorō Sensō*. Tokyo: Bessatsu Takarajima.

NHK (Nippon Hoso Kyokai) (2008). www3.nhk.or.jp/nhkworld/

Nihon Tokei Nenkan. (2009). Japan Statistical Yearbook. Produced by the Japanese Government's Statistics Bureau http://www.stat.go.jp/index.htm

Nyukoku Hakusho. (2008). White Paper on Immigration. Annual Reports from the Japanese Ministry of Justice Immigration Control Office. http://www.moj.go.jp/nyuukokukanri/kouhou/nyukan_nyukan42.html

Ōsato, K. (2005). Bōryokudan-kei Uyoku no Shinchō to sono Akusjitu-sei. *Jian Fōramu*, August.

Pearce, F. (1976). *Crimes of the Powerful: Marxism, Crime and Deviance*. London: Pluto Press.

Ramseyer, J. M. and Nakazato, M. (1998) *Japanese Law: An Economic Approach*. Chicago IL: University of Chicago Press.

Saga, J. (1991). *Confessions of a Yakuza*. Tokyo: Kodansha International.

Saga, J. (1987) *Memories of Silk and Straw*. Tokyo: Kodansha International.

Schelling, T. (1984). *Choice and Consequence*. Cambridge MA: Harvard University Press.

Seymour, C. (1996). *Yakuza Diary: Doing Time in the Japanese Underworld*. New York: Atlantic Monthly Press.

Shinoda, K. (2002). *Nihon Yakuza Chizu*. Tokyo: Take Shobo.

Siniawer, E. M. (2008). *Ruffians, Yakuza, Natonalists: The Violent Politics of Modern Japan, 1860–1960*. New York: Cornell University Press.

Stark, H. (1981). The Yakuza: Japanese Crime Incorporated. Unpublished PhD thesis, University of Michigan.

Szymkowiak, K. (1996). Necessary Evil: Extortion, Organized Crime and Japanese Corporations. PhD thesis, University of Hawaii.

Takagi, M. (1988). *Shin-Dowa Mondai to Dowa Dantai*. Tokyo: Doyo Bijutsu.

Tawara, S. (2005). *Heisei Nippon Taboo Taizen*. Tokyo: Bessatsu Takarajima.

Tamura, E. (1964). *Yakuza no Seikatsu*. Tokyo: Yuzankaku.

Tamura, M. (1992). *The Yakuza and amphetamine abuse in Japan* in H. Traver and M. Gaylord (eds) Drugs, Law and the State. Hong Kong: Hong Kong University Press.

Tendo, S. (2007). *Yakuza Moon: Memoirs of a Gangster's Daughter*. Tokyo: Kōdansha International.

Tilly, C. (1985). War Making and State Making as Organized Crime. In P. Evans, D. Rueschemeyer and T. Skocpol (Eds.) *Bringing the State Back In*. Cambridge: Cambridge University Press.

Van Wolferen, K. (1990). *The Enigma of Japanese Power*. London: Macmillan.

Varese, F. (2001). *The Russian Mafia: Private Protection in a New Market Economy*. Oxford: Oxford University Press.

West, M. (1999) Information, Institutions, and Extortion in Japan and the United States: Making Sense of *Sōkaiya* Racketeers. *Northwestern University Law Review*, 93 (3).

Whiting, R. (1999). *Tokyo Underworld: The Fast Times and Life of an American Gangster in Japan*. New York: Vintage.

Wildes, H. (1948). Underground Politics in Post-War Japan. *The American Political Science Review*, 42 (6), December.

Wildes, H. (1954). *Typhon in Tokyo: The Occupation and its Aftermath*. London: George Allen and Unwin.

Yamadaira, S. (2001). *21 Seiki no Yakuza Kiso Chishiki*. Tokyo: Tokuma Shoten.

Interviews

Interview with Mizoguchi, A. in 2000.

Interview with Mizoguchi, A. in 2006.

PART III

Medicine and Health Care

14

A Brief History of Japanese Medicine

Izumi Yokoyama and Michael D. Fetters

OVERVIEW

Medicine in Japan today can best be understood by placing it in the context of its historical roots. In Table 14.1, we trace Japan's story of a healing tradition that is attributed to mythical practices and beliefs. Medical practice transformed gradually in Japan following the introduction of Chinese medical practices and theory. We provide pivotal events in history to illustrate the rich influences on medicine during different eras from the Chinese, Portuguese, Dutch, Germans, and Americans. A comprehensive history of medicine in Japan would require many more volumes. Although there are many other interesting stories and portraits that could have been added, we have chosen select events and individuals to illustrate the origins of Japanese medicine that continue to influence views and practices in Japan today.

HEALING IN ANTIQUITY

Mythical Era (Antiquity to 96 BC)

Relatively little literature addresses Japan's healing traditions in ancient times. Its native medicine is only partially described in very important chronicles that include the *Kojiki* (Chronicles of Ancient Times), the *Nihon Shoki (also known as Nihongi)* (Chronicle of Japan), and the *Fudoki* (Descriptions of the Provinces). The *Kojiki* (Chronicles of Ancient Times), the oldest existing chronicle in Japan, dates from the early eighth century (711–712) and was written by Ōno Yasumaro[1]. This work covers the origins of Japan and its mythology, as well as events in Yamato, historical Japan (Frederic & Roth, 1987). The *Nihon Shoki* (Chronicle of Japan) covers much of the same period as the *Kojiki,* but focuses much more on the day-to-day activities of emperors and empresses. It also provides versions of many myths, legends, and stories (McCormick & White, 2010). The *Fudoki* (Descriptions of the Provinces) focuses on a specific geographical area and reports on the local topography, etymology of place names, natural resources, local legends, folktales, deities, and folk beliefs. Approximately 60 *Fudoki* were compiled in the eighth century by order of the emperor (McCormick & White, 2010).

These writings provide descriptions of two gods, *Ōnamuji-no-Mikoto* and *Sukunahikona-no-Mikoto,* who could control disease. These gods, by uniting their strength, offered power for curing disease. Charms were used to exorcise evil influences of beasts, birds, and insects (Okuma & Huish, 1970; Shinmura, 2006). During this time, people believed that diseases could be from the deeds of gods, the

Table 14.1   Historical highlights of medicine in Japan

Year	Major Historical Events
414	Kon Mu, a Korean physician, visits Japan bringing the first formally recorded introduction of Chinese-style medicine to Japan
562	Zhi Cong, a Chinese monk, visits via Korea and brings books that introduce acupuncture to Japan
1549	Francisco de Xavier, Roman Catholic missionary supported by the Portuguese, visits Japan to teach Christianity for the first recorded contact with Westerners
1555	Luis De Almeida, a Portuguese surgeon, visits Japan and introduces the full scope of European medicine
1641	Tokugawa government of early Edo Period officially adopts a national isolation policy and strictly forbids foreign book importation
1720	Edo government relaxes restrictions on importing Western books
1771	Sugita Genpaku and Maeno Ryōtaku observe the dissection of the body of an executed female criminal, nicknamed *Aocha Baba* (Green Tea Granny)
1774	Sugita Genpaku publishes *Kaitai-Shinsho*, the first Western anatomic work translated into Japanese
1853	Late Edo government opens its doors to trade with the United States and other Western countries
1861	Pompe van Meerdervoort, a Dutch military surgeon, opens *Nagasaki Yōjōsho*, the first Western-style hospital with a modern medical school
1869	Meiji period government officially adopts German medicine
1883	Meiji period Diet establishes new regulations that require all medical providers, including Kanpō practitioners, to pass a licensure examination, ultimately leading to demise of the legal practice of Kanpō in 1895
1877	University of Tokyo Medical School formally established as one of the first faculties of the University of Tokyo
1945	American occupation of Japan begins
1961	Japan establishes a universal health insurance (*kokumin kenkō hoken*) system
2000	Japan establishes the long-term care insurance (*kaigo hoken*) system

---

Box 14.1 Key points

- Mythical medicine in antiquity is related to the spirits associated with the Shinto tradition and practices that continue to pervade modern Japan
- An East Asian medicine paradigm strongly influenced by China formed the foundation of the first organized practice of medicine that lasted over a thousand years before being overshadowed by a Western medicine paradigm that began establishing a foothold in the mid-19th century in Japan
- Western influences from the Portuguese, Dutch, Germans, and Americans in subsequent eras all helped shape modern Japanese medicine
- The introduction of national health care insurance *(kokumin kenkō hoken)* in 1961 was pivotal for ensuring universal access to health care for the Japanese population
- The adoption of public long-term care insurance *(kaigo hoken)* in 2000 dramatically enhanced access to services for the activities of daily living needs for the frail and disabled aged 40 or over who need long-term care, particularly for the rapidly growing population of people who suffer from the problems of aging
- Japan's ability to control health care costs and the advances in medical research, especially by pharmaceutical and medical device manufacturers, has propelled Japan to become a global player in medicine

---

work of malign spirits, or brought about by the spirit of a dead person. Preventing such disease-making influences involved such actions as sacrifices, prayers, exorcisms, and magical incantations rather than medicines. In these ancient communities, diseases could threaten not only a person's life but also the subsistence of the community. The chief of a community was required to manage diseases and

prevent disaster through such means (Shinmura, 2006). Evidence of the continued influence of these historically rooted practices and places, Shintō[2] shrines are frequented regularly by Japanese to this day. In Shintō shrines, individuals worship and pray for good health and fortune and can purchase charms and talismans against a variety of unfavorable things, including ill health (Print 14.1).

Print 14.1 Gojōten Shrine (五條天神社), Ueno, Tokyo. The Japanese gods of medicine, Ōnamuji-no-Mikoto and Sukunahikona-no-Mikoto, are enshrined here

Source: Yokoyama Izumi.

Sake (rice wine) appears much later as one of the first medicaments, and its use continues today as a component in home remedies, for example in the treatment of the common cold. Surgery appears to have been no more than a very rudimentary practice involving scattering sawdust upon wounds and treating burns by 'painting them with the juice of venous muscle' (Fujikawa, 1978). Bloodletting appears to have been known at this time. Mineral baths and water douches were also utilized (Fujikawa, 1978).

EAST ASIAN MEDICINE (Toyō Iqaku)

Era of Chinese Influence on Medicine (Fifth Century to 1542)

The introducution of the systematized approach of Chinese healing practices initiated the tradition of Toyō Igaku, East Asian Medicine, that continues into the present. Germinated in China, these practices traveled and were influenced by their application and development in Korea and Japan. Ancient Chinese medicine was recorded in two medical texts, the *Huangdi Neijing* and the *Shang Han Lun* (Print 14.2), during the Han Dynasty (202 BC to 220 AD). Medicines were transmitted from China to Japan via the Korean Peninsula from the fourth to the sixth century AD (Nishimura, Plotnikoff, & Watanabe, 2009). During this period, Japan adopted the Chinese writing system to learn from China about topics such as Buddhism and Confucianism. This process accelerated the study of Chinese medicine in Japan (Wynn & Fougere, 2006). The *Kojiki* (Chronicles of Ancient Times) and the *Nihon Shoki* (Chronicle of Japan) record that a physician, Kon Mu, was invited from Silla, a kingdom in southeast Korea, to serve as physician to the Emperor of Japan in 414 AD. Although it is believed that acupuncture was introduced into Japan in the fifth century from the Korean Peninsula, the first formally recorded introduction of acupuncture in Japan occurred in 562 AD (Yasui, 2010) when a Chinese monk, Zhi Cong, brought 164 volumes on medicine from China via Korea (Birch & Felt, 1999; Dharmananda, 2001). Later, in 602 AD, a Buddhist priest, Kwan Roku, came to Japan from Paekche, another kingdom in southern Korea, and taught Chinese medicine to 34 young men selected by the Imperial Court (Bowers, 1965). In direct exchanges starting during the seventh century, Buddhist monks played a major part in the introduction and diffusion of Chinese medicine (Shibata & Wu, 1997).

Schools of Kanpō Medicine

In these times, the healing practices from China were the primary source of systematic medical knowledge and served as the basis of training for many years to come. Chinese medical theories began to take root in the fifteenth century, and in the

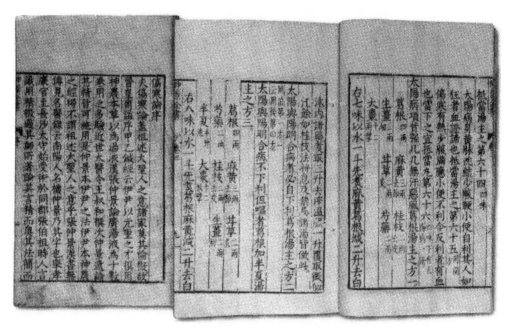

Print 14.2 *The Shang Han Lun* (傷寒論). **Ancient medical text of Chinese medicine**

Source: Hal Pharmacy

sixteenth century Kanpō and acupuncture theories started to develop in Japan. It wasn't until the mid-sixteenth century that the term Kanpō[3] came into use as a term to refer to medical practices based on the healing tradition from China and to distinguish it from Western approaches to medicine. Kanpō literally means 'Han method' and refers to its roots in China during the Han period, 206 BC to 220 AD. From the beginning of the seventeenth century, the practice of Kanpō took on a particular Japanese flavor with a reduction in the number of formulations used – beginning with thousands in traditional Chinese medicine and dropping to only about 300. Kanpō practice also became distanced from its Chinese origins that involved theoretical considerations such as the influences of *yin* and *yang*, and, beyond a small elite group, became more focused on pragmatic findings from the examination of the patient (Watanabe et al., 2011). The two major schools of Kanpō in Japan include the Goseiha school (the school of latter-days) and the Kohōha school (the school of classicism in medicine). Goseiha school of medicine refers to the Chin–Yuan medicine of China because the Chin and Yuan dynasties were much later than the Han dynasty when the *Shang Han Lun* was produced. Tashiro Sanki (1465–1537) studied a branch of Chinese medicine in China in 1487 for 12 years, then brought this knowledge back to Japan and pioneered the Goseiha school development. One of his pupils in Japan, Manase Dōsan, played a central role in the

Goseiha school and contributed to the development of Kanpō into a comprehensive system of diagnosis and treatment based on disease pattern identification (Shibata & Wu, 1997). He contributed significantly to the diffusion of Kanpō in Japan through teaching of students in a private school, Keiteki-in in Kyoto, and is credited with teaching nearly 800 students. Tashiro and Manase are credited as significant contributors to the diffusion of Kanpō theories among the Japanese people (Shibata & Wu, 1997).

The Kohōha School (Classical School) emerged about 150 years later. It stood in contrast to Chin–Yuan medicine and advocated a return to the *Shang Han Lun* (Lock, 1980; Nishimura, et al., 2009; Otsuka, 1977). Shibata and Wu credit the Kohōha School with shaping Kanpō into a distinctly Japanese endeavor, while the Goseiha school's most significant contribution was the diffusion of Kanpō. The latter continues as an important theme in Kanpō today (Shibata & Wu, 1997). For more details about education in East Asian medicine, please see Chapter 16. Suffice it to say, East Asian healing practices dominated, albeit with considerable variation across Japan, unopposed as 'medicine' until the mid-sixteenth century when Western medicine was introduced to Japan. In the mid-nineteenth century, the Western paradigm began to overshadow the East Asian tradition. For example, the Japanese Diet[4] in 1895 restricted the practice of medicine to those with medical training, an act that severely limited Kanpō trained practitioners (Izumi & Isozumi, 2001). A handful of practitioners kept the tradition alive, however, and in the early twentieth century, researchers at Japanese universities began to see Kanpō as a potential source of modern drugs and rediscovered the potential utility of Kanpō for treating a broad range of medical conditions. An example of the fruits of such research was the isolation of ephedrine from the Ephedra herb by a Japanese organic chemist and pharmacologist, Nagai Nagayoshi (1844–1929) (Shibata & Wu, 1997). Furthermore, in 1910, one of the pioneers of the revival movement of Kanpō, Wada Keijuro (1872–1916), published a book titled *Ikai no Tettsui* (The Iron Hammer of the Medical World) that depicted Kanpō medicine as a form of clinical medicine. In 1927, Yumoto Kyūshin (1876–1941), influenced by this book, published another book on Kanpō, titled *Kōkan Igaku* (Japanese–Chinese Medicine).

East Asian medicine continues to thrive among the Japanese. Walking the streets in Japanese cities, one readily spots clinics for acupuncture and moxibustion, chiropractors (*seitai*) and Kanpō shops. Many hotels aggressively market therapeutic massage with services available in the guest's room or in a designated area of the hotel, often connected with a gender-segregated bathing facility. In establishments that offer hot spring (*onsen*) bathing, an extremely popular custom among Japanese, one routinely finds placards posted by the bath announcing ten or so ailments that the naturally occurring minerals in the water of that particular *onsen* are effective for treating. These treatments clearly fill a niche in the tools employed by Japanese for supporting their sense of health and well-being.

In the present daily life of the Japanese people, some degree of integration between East Asian medicine and Western approaches does occur. In 1976, the Ministry of Health and Welfare approved 82 prescriptions of Kanpō formulas for coverage by the national health insurance and the number grew to 148 (Dharmananda, 2001; Shibata & Wu, 1997). But this integration largely occurs on Western medicine terms because the prescriptions are provided much like a prescription for an antibiotic, laxative, or painkiller without requirement to consider East Asian medical theory. The following section highlights the fascinating story of the emergence and domination of Western medicine after a thousand years of domination by East Asian medicine.

WESTERN MEDICINE INFLUENCES ON JAPAN

Western influences on medicine in Japan can generally be traced to four eras, the Portuguese,

Dutch, German, and American. While these were the dominant Western influences in these eras, pioneers of other nationalities made contributions as well. For example, in the Dutch era during Japan's isolation (*Sakoku*), the first physician to work on the tiny artificial island of Dejima was Casper Schamberger, a German. During the German influence after the Meiji restoration, notable researchers such as Takamine and Noguchi studied in other countries. We will provide an overview of these other world influences to offer an understanding of the development and practice of modern medicine in Japan. It is unclear how quickly and diffusively Western practices became, although it is certain that they developed in parallel and interacted with the predominant East Asian paradigm (see, for example, the later discussion of Hanaoka Seishū).

Era of Portuguese Influence (1542–1641)

From the middle of the fifteenth century to the middle of the sixteenth century, the Portuguese introduced Western medicine to Japan as part of their missionary work. After a brief contact in 1543, direct cultural exchange between Europe and Japan began in 1549 when Francisco de Xavier (1506–1552), a Jesuit missionary from Portugal, came to Japan to teach Christianity. Xavier provided nursing level skills and cared for sick people as well. He successfully employed different kinds of Western-made medical materials, and this success attracted interest in Western medicine. The new style of Western medicine introduced by the Portuguese as part of their missionary work contrasted significantly with the Japanese treatment approaches previously introduced from China. To distinguish this new style of medicine introduced by the so-called 'southern barbarians' (the people of the Iberian peninsula), the term *Nanban-igaku* emerged.

Luis de Almeida (1525–1583) figured prominently in this era. A merchant licensed in medicine, Almeida later became a Jesuit. He came to Japan in 1555 and provided medical treatment to local people to encourage their conversion to Christianity. He propagated Christianity under the cover of medical treatment. He was the first person to offer the full scope of European medicine. Two years after arriving, he founded the first Western hospital in Oita with the assistance of *Ōtomo Sōrin* (1530–1587), the feudal lord of Bungo. Almeida directed the hospital with the help of several Japanese assistants. His surgical operations earned him a very good reputation, and he also instructed his assistants in external treatment techniques, as well as in certain practices of internal medicine.

Almeida and other foreigners were forced to leave shortly after the hospital was constructed due to opposition to Christian missionary work and a rumor that the Spaniards and Portuguese intended to occupy Japan (Fodstad, Hariz, Hirabayashi, & Ohye, 2002; Izumi & Isozumi, 2001; Otori, 1964). While the influence of Portuguese medicine thus waned due to anti-Christian sentiments, a physician who had learned Portuguese medicine and the Dutch language and medicine, Nishi Kichibei, founded the Nishi school, which used Dutch-style surgery, and he served the public as a surgeon. According to existing literature, he practiced only Western medicine. He later became physician to the Shogunate (general) of Japan (Boscaro, Gatti, & Raveri, 1990).

Era of Dutch Influence: Medicine During Japan's Isolation From Foreign Countries (1641–1870)

Fearing foreign influence on domestic matters, in 1641 the Edo government officially adopted a national isolation policy *(Sakoku)* that lasted more than 200 years. As it was counter to the Edo government interests to completely sever ties with the West, it permitted a lone exception to the strict isolation policy – a single trading post to operate on the small island of Dejima in Nagasaki. Amazingly, the only source of information about Western medicine for two centuries came through this island trading post. The *Sakoku* isolation period triggered a shift in Western medical influence from the Portuguese medical missionaries to doctors of the Dutch merchant's office and their Dutch medical books. To distinguish the medicine from the Portuguese, a new name for Dutch medicine emerged. At the time, Japanese people referred to the Dutch as the 'red hair people *(Kōmō-jin)*' because many of them were distinguished by the red color of their hair. This reference spilled over into the rubric of medical practice and spawned the term 'red hair style surgery *(Kōmō-ryū-geka)*' (Fodstad et al., 2002; Izumi & Isozumi, 2001). While Dutch studies in Japan progressed during this period, as described later, Western medicine and surgery still never established a foothold until the end of the isolation policy, when American Admiral Matthew Perry forced Japan to open its doors in 1853 (Fujikawa, 1978; Izumi & Isozumi, 2001).

Despite the prohibition on importing medical books under the isolation policy, many Japanese doctors remained eager to learn European medicine. They learned through oral teachings, instruction, and demonstrations by Western practitioners: Casper Schambergen (1623–1706), who founded a school of surgery in Japan; Willem ten Rhijne (1647–1700), who taught medicine in Japan and introduced the Japanese version of traditional Chinese medicine to the West; and Engelbert Kaempfer (1651–1716), who taught Western medicine in Japan and introduced Japanese culture to Europe. Japanese pupils, who in turn composed their own medical and surgical works, soon reflected such Western teachings. One of these pupils, Hoan Arashiyama (1633–1693), who learned surgery from the Dutch, wrote the Dutch clinical lectures in his works entitled *Bankoku chihō ruiju* and *Kōmō-gekka sōden* (Izumi & Isozumi, 2001; Mestler, 1957).

Liberalization of Western Knowledge – Rangaku

In 1720, Shogun Tokugawa Yoshimune (1684–1751) relaxed the rule prohibiting the importation of Western books and this permitted the introduction of Dutch books and manuscripts into Japan. This body of knowledge, developed in Japan through contact with the Dutch enclave of Dejima, became known as '*Rangaku*,' a term that literally means 'Dutch Studies.' While learning medicine from other countries was still restricted, the lifting of the embargo on the importation of Dutch books contributed to the rapid development of Dutch Studies in Japan.

The story leading to the translation of the first Western anatomic work into Japanese is one of the most interesting and pivotal of the period. The story actually begins with the first anatomical dissection in Japan by Yamawaki Tōyō (1705–1762) in 1754. A renaissance man, Yamawaki moved in circles beyond the average physician of his era. A member of the Kohoha School (also known as Koiho School) of Chinese Medicine, he sought objective, factual information in the study of medicine. By virtue of connections with a *daimyō* (feudal lord), who was a director of police activities, Yamawaki obtained permission to have a body dissected by an *eta* (the most severely stigmatized people in the feudal caste system, usually, executioners, undertakers, and butchers). Yamawaki recorded his observations in a publication entitled *Anatomical Record* (Zōshi). He ran the risk of harsh criticism for ignoring the religious taboo and governmental edict against dissection – Yamawaki's work could have been interpreted as an insult to the dead and could have threatened traditional *Shintō* views of death and religion. Nevertheless, through his bold actions, Yamawaki established himself as a pioneer who contributed greatly to the advancement of Japanese medicine (Sugimoto, 1987).

In 1771, two Japanese doctors (both students of Dutch Studies), Sugita Genpaku (1733–1817) and Maeno Ryōtaku (1723–1803), were struck by the differences between the anatomical charts of the internal structure of the body depicted in a Dutch version of the German *Anatomische*

Tabellen (1722) by Johann Adam Kulmus and the illustrations available at the time based on East Asian medical theory and anatomical representations. The differences in the drawings in the books imported from Europe roused the two physicians' curiosity and were compelling enough for them to pursue the unthinkable – a dissection. The pair observed an *eta* (outcast class) elderly butcher dissect the beheaded body of an executed criminal, a woman of about 50 years nicknamed *Aocha Baba* (Green Tea Granny, author's translation[5]). As the butcher carried out the dissection, Sugita and Maeno were impressed by how closely the anatomical depictions found in the Dutch version of *Anatomische Tabellen* correlated with the structure of the women's body. Equally important, Sugita and Maeno found the actual anatomy to be very different from writings and illustrations according to existing East Asian medical theory and anatomical depictions. Scholars believe that extant Chinese and Japanese anatomical books were incorrect due to taboo against opening the body in East Asia (Ravitsky, Fiester & Caplan, 2009). Their observations and excitement compelled Maeno and Sugita to translate the Dutch version of *Anatomische Tabellen* into Japanese under the title *New Book on Anatomy* (*Kaitai Shinsho*) (Itasaka, 1983; Jansen, 1989), a painstaking task given the lack of substantive dictionaries.

As Maeno, the better of the two in Dutch, made a vow to become fluent in Dutch before getting credit, he was not included as a co-author of the book. Published in 1774 by Sugita Genpaku (1733–1817) (Print 14.3), this publication marked a pivotal event in the history of the introduction of Western medicine.

Hanaoka Seishū and Development of General Anesthesia

While often omitted in Western accounts of the discovery of general anesthesia, the credit for the first documented surgery under anesthesia belongs to the medical pioneer Hanaoka Seishū (1760–1835) (Portrait 14.1). Hanaoka was a widely respected surgeon who integrated the study of both *Rangaku* surgical techniques and traditional Chinese medicine. Hanaoka successfully performed surgery under general anesthesia for breast cancer on a 60-year-old woman, Aiya Kan, on October 13, 1804 using a combination of herb extracts he called *tsūsensan* (also known as *mafutsusan*). This first successful surgery under general anesthesia occurred 38 years before Crawford Long administered diethyl ether by inhalation in order to remove a neck tumor from a man in Jefferson, Georgia on March 30, 1842. Hanaoka's first case of surgery under general

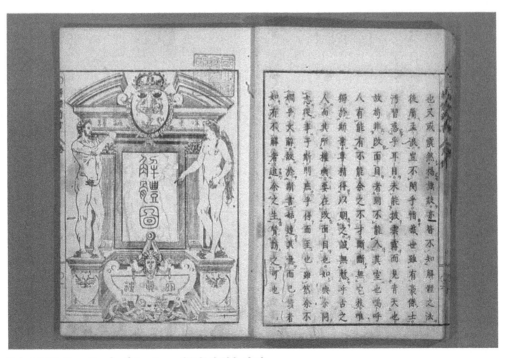

Print 14.3 *New Book of Anatomy* (Kaitai Shinsho)

Source: National Diet Library, Japan

anesthesia occurred almost 42 years before William Green Morton demonstrated publicly the use of diethyl ether as a general anesthetic for a dental extraction at Massachusetts General Hospital on September 30, 1846.

Hanaoka's *tsūsensan* preparation was inspired by a report from 1,600 years earlier of the Chinese physician Hua Tuo (also known as Kada in Japan), who used a five-herb formula; however, it was of obscure formulation and not effective for major surgery anesthesia. After extensive experimentation that included use on his wife and the tragic loss of her vision due to toxic side effects, Hanaoka successfully developed an effective formula. *Tsūsensan* involved an expanded number of ingredients from the five-herb formula, but required careful attention to the proper proportions of the herb extracts. The main component of the formulation, Datura tatura (also known as Korean morning glory), contains alkaloids such as scopolamine, hyoscyamine, and atropine. According to his medical records, Hanaoka treated 165 cases of breast cancer, 150 of which used *tsūsensan,* during his lifetime. In addition to breast cancer surgery, he also performed surgery for tongue cancer, various kinds of tumors, harelip, anal fistula, gangrene, extremity amputations, among others (Okuma & Huish, 1970; Shinmura, 2006). The legacy of his integration of traditional Chinese medicine with Western surgical technique remains ever-present in Japan because Datura tatura is featured in the symbol of the Japan Society of Anesthesiology (Hyodo, 1992). Ariyoshi Sawako composed a historical novel regarding this saga, *The Doctor's Wife,* published in 1966 (Ariyoshi, 1966).

Portrait 14.1 Japanese medical pioneer, Hanaoka Seishū

Source: Website of Wakayama prefecture

Innovations in Infectious Disease

Several events mark the initial milestones in infectious disease prevention in Japan. In 1848, Dutch doctor, Otto Mohnike (1814–1887) implemented the first successful nationwide smallpox vaccination in Japan. This program was remarkable because previous attempts at immunizing en masse had failed due to vaccines losing their effectiveness while being transported on long sea journeys. In the same year, Ogata Kōan (1810–1863) established *Jotō-kan*, a smallpox clinic, in Osaka (Itasaka, 1983). Subsequently, in 1858 the *Shutōjo*, the Institute for Vaccination, was established in Tokyo with funds donated by *Rangaku* scholars. This was the first governmental institute of Western medicine and it became the predecessor of the University of Tokyo Medical School.

Era of Modern Western Influence with German Pre-eminence (1870–1945)

As access to Western anatomical texts and knowledge improved, it became obvious that Western medicine, especially surgery and anatomical expertise, was superior to East Asian medicine approaches. Depictions of anatomy and evolving medical theory and research were more compelling than the theoretical constructs and approaches of Chinese medicine. After Japan opened its doors to trade with the United States and other Western countries in 1853, Western medicine was rapidly promulgated. By 1869, the Japanese government decided to adopt German medicine, especially its educational approach, rather than English medicine. Thus, German medicine became the next wave of Western influence on medicine in Japan, an influence that lasted until the end of World War II. In an act symbolizing this dramatic change in focus, Kanpō was effectively prohibited in 1895 by the National Diet when the practice of medicine required training credential in Western-style medical education (Izumi & Isozumi, 2001).

During the era of German influence, Japanese medicine made great advances, especially in the fields of research and education. In Germany, medicine was treated as an experimental science, and the study of bacteria and access to well-equipped laboratories were key components of medical education. Japan selectively imported and adapted the German model, German medical books were translated into Japanese, and Japanese scholars traveled to Germany to study. In 1870, the University of Tokyo hired German doctors to set up a model of medical training, an approach to medical education that became institutionalized as the approved Japanese method by the early 1880s (Smith, 2005). The structure of

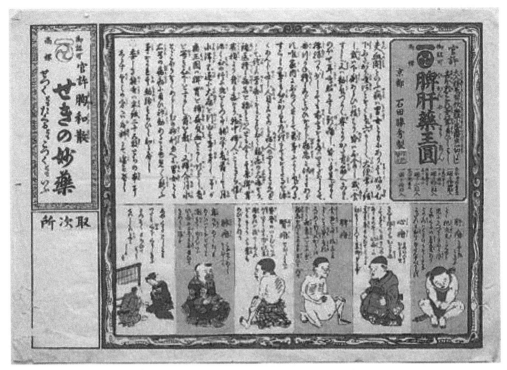

Print 14.4 Woodblock advertisement for medicines – Hikanyakuōen, Kyōwasan, Seki no Myōyaku

Source: Naito Museum of Pharmaceutical Science and Industry

the *ikyoku*-clinical departments, *kōza*-academic departments (see Chapter 16) and approaches of departments and research labs in medical institutions today can be traced to these roots.

In 1877, the University of Tokyo formally established the medical school that would become, and continues as, the most dominant and prestigious in Japan. It later became an Imperial University in 1886 and was renamed the Tokyo Imperial University (*Tōkyō Teikoku Daigaku*) in 1897 when the imperial University system was created. Remarkably, in 1879, just two years after its establishment, the University of Tokyo Medical School sent the best students from its first graduating class to Germany to study medicine. Upon their return, they took over from all the foreign professors at the University of Tokyo Medical School and established Japan's independent medical educational system. The second imperial university, featuring a medical department, was established in Kyoto in 1897, and about 10 years later, the third and the fourth imperial universities were established with medical departments in Tohoku and Kyushu. These imperial universities (Tokyo Imperial University, Kyoto Imperial University, Tohoku Imperial University, and Kyushu Imperial University) were Japan's original four imperial universities with medical departments.

A reminder of this historic period can be seen in Print 14.4 showing a woodblock print advertising medicines. During the Meiji era (1868–1912), multi-colored woodblock printings were frequently used for marketing medicines. This particular woodblock print (Print 14.4) was crafted by Ishida Katsuhide during the Meiji era, and promotes two medicines, *Kyōwasan: Seki no Myōyaku (cough medicine)* and *Hikanyakuōen*. The descriptions are statements about the virtues of *Hikanyakuōen*, and the pictures portray its effects on symptoms of the liver, spleen, kidneys, heart, and lungs (Naito Museum of Pharmaceutical Science and Industry, n.d.).

Kitasato Shibasaburō

Several Japanese scientists stand out as pioneers in medical research and helped establish the scientific method in Japan. Kitasato Shibasaburō (1853–1931) was the first medical researcher to travel to Germany where he studied, conducted research, and acquired skills in bacteriology (Portrait 14.2). After graduating eighth in his class from the University of Tokyo School of Medicine in 1883, Kitasato was sent to Germany where he studied at the University of Berlin under Robert Koch from 1885 to 1891. Kitasato conducted research on the typhus bacillus, cholera vibirio, and blackleg in

Portrait 14.2 Kitasato Shibasaburō

Source: National Diet Library, Japan

Portrait 14.3 Shiga Kiyoshi

Source: The Kitasato Institute

cattle. In 1889, Kitasato became the first to grow tetanus bacillus in pure culture and he discovered the tetanus toxin. In the following year (1890), he and Emil von Behring (1854–1917) used this pure culture to develop a serum therapy for tetanus (Fujikawa, 1978; Izumi & Isozumi, 2001). The paper about their work, written in German, which listed Kitasato as the second author, established the foundation for the development of serum therapy and the initial step toward the establishment of humoral immunology. While Emil von Behring later won the Nobel Prize for this work, arguably, Kitasato should at least have shared the prize (Bartholomew, 1998).

Kitasato's accomplishments earned him the stature of an eminent scientist of his time. During an outbreak of the bubonic plague in Hong Kong in 1894, the Japanese government sent Kitasato to conduct research about the outbreak. Kitasato also served as Director of the Institute for Infectious Disease (1893–1914). When the Institute for Infectious Diseases was incorporated into Tokyo Imperial University in 1914, he founded the Kitasato Institute (1915–1918), the forerunner of the current Kitasato University. He served as Professor and first Dean at the Keio University Medical School (established 1917), one of the three most famous private medical schools collectively called the *Shiritsu Idai Gosanke* (see Chapter 16) (Bartholomew, 1971, 1998). Like many true pioneers, Kitasato also inspired others to greatness.

Shiga Kiyoshi

Shiga Kiyoshi (1871–1957) (Portrait 14.3) became one of Kitasato's most famous mentees. While a medical student at Tokyo Imperial University, Shiga heard a lecture by Kitasato and

was inspired to work with him. After graduating in 1896, Shiga became a research assistant in Kitasato's Institute where Kitasato assigned him research on the topic of dysentery. At the time, dysentery was a general term for severe diarrhea and Shiga was assigned to work specifically on *sekiri*, or bloody diarrhea. Based on his work with 36 patients, Shiga meticulously applied Koch's postulates and successfully isolated and described the bacillus that causes dysentery, now known as *Shigella dysenteriae*. He further identified toxic substances from the bacteria now known to be Shiga toxin. In 1901, he went to Germany after graduating from the University of Tokyo School of Medicine and worked as a research assistant under German bacteriologist, Paul Ehrlich, at the Institut für Experimental Therapie in Frankfurt until 1905. Under Ehrlich, Shiga worked on various projects, including early studies of chemotherapy for trypanosomiasis. He returned to Japan to resume work in Kitasato's laboratory in 1905. There he continued his research of infectious diseases with Dr. Kitasato and became a professor at Keio University in 1920 (Fujikawa, 1978; Trofa, Ueno-Olsen, Oiwa, & Yoshikawa, 1999).

Yamagiwa Katsusaburō

Another Japanese medical pioneer also influenced by German medicine around that time was Yamagiwa Katsusabur̄o (1863–1930) (Portrait 14.4). Yamagiwa graduated from University of Tokyo's Faculty of Medicine in 1889. In just two years, he advanced from an assistantship to Assistant Professor in the pathology graduate program. In 1892, he began working at the Rudolph Virchow's Institute in Berlin where he immersed himself in general pathology and the study of cell

Portrait 14.4 Yamagiwa Katsusaburō

Source: Courtesy of Miyazono-Laboratory, Department of Molecular Pathology, Graduate School of Medicine, University of Tokyo

morphology. After 16 months, Yamagiwa returned to Tokyo where he ultimately became Director of the Department of Pathology at Tokyo Imperial University Medical School. Yamagiwa researched illnesses common at the time such as plague, beri-beri, pulmonary distomiasis, and Japanese blood fluke disease; however, his major contribution to medicine was in carcinogenesis. Yamagiwa tragically contracted tuberculosis in 1899, and for unknown reasons, he thereafter became intent on proving Virchow's contention that cancer can be caused by chronic, repetitive, external stimulus. In the ensuing years, his tuberculosis was debilitating, and to implement his research ideas he relied heavily on collaborators, especially Ichikawa Koichi, who assisted Yamagiwa. In a series of experiments, their research demonstrated that coal tar applied to the skin of rabbits produced cancerous tumors. Thus, Yamagiwa proved Virchow's theory that chronic irritation can cause cancer (Bartholomew, 1998; CA Cancer J Clin, 1977). While nominated to receive the Nobel Prize four times for this work, Yamagiwa never received it and credit for the proof of Virchow's theory went, undeservingly, to Johannes Fibiger (Bartholomew, 1998).

Other Contemporary Influences

Though not directly influenced by German medicine, because their training abroad occurred in other Western countries, two additional medical pioneers of this time, Takamine Jōkichi and Noguchi Hideyo, made notable contributions to modern medicine.

Takamine Jōkichi

Takamine Jōkichi (1854–1922) (Portrait 14.5) was a Japanese chemist who isolated and purified the hormone adrenaline from animal adrenal glands. He was the first researcher to extract a glandular hormone (Fujikawa, 1978; Izumi & Isozumi, 2001). After graduating from the University of Tokyo School of Medicine in 1879, he was selected by the Japanese government to conduct postgraduate work at the University of Glasgow and Anderson College in Scotland. He studied the Industrial Revolution and fertilizer manufacturing. After a brief return to Japan, he was sent to serve as co-commissioner of the Cotton Exposition held in New Orleans in 1884. While there, he met his future wife, Caroline Field Hitch, whom he married in 1887. With his new bride, Takamine returned to Japan and started a successful super-phosphate fertilizer plant, but his wife was unhappy and they subsequently moved back to the United States. Rather than work in the competitive fertilizer business there, Takamine's strategy was to introduce from Japan to the United States an efficient fermentation process involving an amylase, then called diastase. An initially successful venture in the distillery business using this process failed disastrously after a fire, thought possibly due to racially motivated arson. Not to be discouraged, Takamine applied for a patent in 1894 entitled, 'Process of making diastatic enzyme' (US Patent No. 525,823). His method involved growing mold on bran and using aqueous alcohol to extract the amylase. This method has significance as the first patent on a microbial enzyme in the United States (Bennett & Yamomoto, 2004). Takamine licensed the product to Parke, Davis & Company in Detroit, Michigan who successfully marketed it as a medical product 'Taka-diastase' for use as a digestive aid

Portrait 14.5 Takamine Jōkichi

Source: Daiichi Sanyko Co., LTD

for the treatment of dyspepsia. Based on revenue under the licensure and from consulting for Parke, Davis & Company, he was able to establish a research laboratory in New York City. Working with a young chemist, Uenaka Keizo, he adapted procedures to extract substances from the adrenals. The resulting crystalline powder, that he called adrenaline, is a substance with multiple uses in medicine. His work ultimately led to five patents (Bennett, 2001; Bennett & Yamomoto, 2004; Fujikawa, 1978).

Noguchi Hideyo

Like Kitasato and Shiga, Noguchi Hideyo (1876–1928) became a famous medical pioneer for his work in infectious disease when he discovered the agent of syphilis, *Treponema pallidum*, the cause of a progressive paralytic disease, while working at the Rockefeller Institute of Medical Research in 1911 (Portrait 14.6). When only one-and-a-half-years old, Noguchi sustained a serious burn injury to his left hand when he fell into a fire pit. This accident resulted in the loss of his left fingers but he was inspired by surgical care he received after entering elementary school 7 years later. With the support of his family, he excelled academically and successfully achieved entrance into medical school. As his impaired left hand hindered the performance of clinical activities, he specialized in microbiology. When he was 23 years old, he traveled to the United States to pursue research. In part, his move was motivated by difficulties in obtaining a medical position in Japan because employers were concerned that his disability would be a barrier to patient care. In the United States, his handicap was

Portrait 14.6 Noguchi Hideyo

Source: National Diet Library, Japan

more accepted and he worked diligently as a research assistant at the University of Pennsylvania. Later at the Rockefeller Institute of Medical Research, he successfully demonstrated the existence of syphilis spirochetes in the cerebral tissue of a neurosyphilis patient. This achievement brought him hero status in Japan. Noguchi was awarded the Imperial Prize from the Japan Academy in 1915, and he became a member of the Japan Imperial Academy in 1923. Passionate to do work in infectious disease, Noguchi traveled in South and Central America to conduct yellow fever and Oroya fever research. The death of many American soldiers from yellow fever in the US war with Spain fought in Cuba weighed heavily on Noguchi, and apparently motivated him to conduct research for a yellow fever vaccine. As part of this work, he traveled to Accra (modern-day Ghana) in Africa where the disease was highly prevalent. There, he tragically contracted yellow fever and died in 1928 when only 53 years old (Fujikawa, 1978; Gustav, 1931). As one reflection of the reverence for Noguchi in Japan, the Japanese government replaced the image of the famous literary giant Natsume Sōseki on the ¥1,000 bill with Noguchi Hideyo's image in 2004.

Era of American Influence (1945–1987)

The most recent era of significant Western influence on medicine in Japan can be called the American era. After the Japanese surrender in World War II, the United States Armed Forces acquired overall administrative authority in Japan. The Japanese Imperial Army and Navy were decommissioned and all military bases taken over. Under the control of MacArthur's General Headquarters (GHQ), many aspects of Japanese society began to be 'Americanized' and this similarly affected medicine. This point in time marked a transition from a strong German influence to an American influence upon medical education and research in Japan.

During the American occupation after World War II, the Public Health and Welfare section (PHW) was established to control medical welfare in Japan. The head of the PHW, Crawford F. Sams, led public health policies in Japan for the 5 years and 8 months during the American occupation until he retired in May 1951. When Sams arrived in Japan in 1945, Japan faced serious problems such as epidemics and food shortages. In the aftermath of World War II, addressing these problems was a priority, and the PHW took various preventive measures against epidemics and ensured that, at minimum, a supply of food sufficient for survival was supplied. However, as these problems settled and Japanese society became more stable, Sams shifted his attention to policy reforms on medical care in Japan.

In 1946, the PHW ordered structural reorganization of the Ministry of Health, Labour and Welfare. Subsequently, three bureaus – the *Public Health Bureau (Kōshū Eisei Kyoku)*, *Medical Affairs Bureau (Imu Kyoku)*, and *Prevention Bureau (Yobō Kyoku)* – were established. The most notable point about this restructuring was that the PHW assigned a doctor to head each bureau. This reflects the fact that Sams was a doctor and sought to have in place an administration strong in science and technology. The PHW also sought to improve the quality of local public health by forming a network of health centers (*hokenjo*). To achieve this, the PHW first established a model health center in Tokyo, and then tried to encourage the practice of 'ideal' service to health centers in other areas by giving lectures to the staff in local health centers. These *hokenjo* continue to play a prominent role in public health today.

During the American occupation, various laws and acts concerning health care and welfare were revised and established. Article 25 of the current Japanese Constitution, written in 1946 and adopted in 1947, guarantees the right to the maintenance of minimum standards of welfare. This affected the administration of health care in Japan and contributed indelibly to the development of Japanese medicine after World War II. Subsequently, various laws and acts such as the Medical Care Law; Law for Public Health Nurses, Midwives, and Nurses; the Livelihood Protection Act; the Child Welfare Act; the Act on Welfare of Physically Disabled Persons and the Welfare Act for the Elderly were established one after another. The establishment of these laws contributed to the current structure of the Japanese health care system (Shinmura, 2006).

Other contributors to the shift to American influence included the direct power of General Douglas MacArthur as Supreme Commander for the Allied Powers (SCAP), the controlling entity of Japan's four major islands of Honshu, Hokkaido, Shikoku and Kyushu, as well as the immediately surrounding islands; the decline of Germany internationally after World War II; and a growing positive reputation of US medicine. Evidence of the shift to an American influence included a gradual change in charting from German[6] to English in the medical record and study abroad destinations other than Germany.

EMERGENCE AND ESTABLISHMENT OF NATIONAL HEALTH INSURANCE DURING THE PERIOD OF RAPID ECONOMIC GROWTH

In parallel with the rapid economic growth that started in the mid-1950s until the collapse of the economic bubble in 1991, the most notable accomplishment in Japanese medicine was the emergence and refinement of a national health insurance plan. In 1922, the first health insurance law was established to protect workers, and it took effect in 1927; however, the coverage of the law was very limited, and farmers, who comprised the majority of workers in Japan at the time, were not covered. In 1938, when the Ministry of Health, Labour and Welfare was established, coverage was extended to farmers by the introduction of the National Health Insurance Law. In the following year, the Employees Health Insurance Law and Seamen's Health Insurance Law were enacted, and these laws also contributed to the expansion of the number of people eligible for health insurance. However, even after World War II, there was no health insurance that covered self-employed workers in commerce and industry and those working for them. In 1956, the Social Security System Committee issued its 'Recommendations concerning Medical Insurance', which revealed the fact that there were 30 million people who were not covered by any health insurance at that time leading to the realization of the need for national health insurance (Fukawa, 2002; Japan International Cooperation Agency, 2005; Shinmura, 2006).

During this period of rapid economic growth, many large companies succeeded in boosting productivity through innovations in technology, and the gap between large companies and small companies widened. At the same time, self-employed workers and people working for them also suffered under a highly competitive economy. Given these circumstances, a new National Health Insurance Law was enacted in 1958, and the universal public health insurance coverage was finally realized in 1961. Driven by concern for an unhealthy workforce, it provided support to those people who suffered financially under the period of rapid economic growth. Although the insurance system still had problems such as limited benefits and heavy insurance premium burdens, it is undeniable that this new national health insurance act helped to form the foundation for the current medical care system in Japan (Shinmura, 2006).

An expansion of hospitals was also a notable trend during this period, but there was uneven geographic distribution, such that hospitals were more likely to be constructed in large cities. One of the reasons for this trend was an increase in the number of private medical facilities, hospitals, and clinics with a small number of beds. Before the period of rapid economic growth, the Medical Care Law established the foundation for hospitals to operate as organizations that provided a minimum level of medical care to the nation. However, the procedures laid out in the Medical Care Law were too strict to be realized due to budgetary pressures. This hampered the establishment of public facilities. The Japanese government then tried to find a way to establish hospitals with a limited budget, and revised the Medical Care Law in 1950. This revision made it easier for general practitioners to establish and operate hospitals by pooling their resources. The number of private facilities started increasing dramatically in 1951, leading to a boom of the founding of hospitals during this time of rapid economic growth.

Medical insurance for the whole nation improved access to health care services and the average life expectancy became significantly higher. By 1985, life expectancy had increased from approximately 50 years for both genders to 75 years for men and 80 years for women. Questions loom about the extent that medicine contributed to the dramatic increase in longevity during this time because there were certainly other important contributors in public health, such as sanitation, improved availability of nutritional foods, the healthy nature of the Japanese diet, and exercise, the latter due at least in part to the mass public transportation system and the associated walking to access services. Regardless of medicine's actual contribution – quantifying it is difficult – Japanese physicians do have a great sense of pride and ownership for advances made (Itasaka, 1983; Shinmura, 2006).

GLOBAL JAPANESE MEDICINE (1987 TO THE PRESENT)

Overview

As Japan emerged as a world economy, Japanese medicine became much more global as well. Through economists' eyes, the 1990s are often referred to as 'the lost decade' due to a significant decrease in the valuing of Japanese assets that occurred in the aftermath of the bursting of the economic bubble in 1991. After this collapse in Japan, there was a growing realization and awareness of limits of financial resources in the face of a rapidly aging population. Nevertheless, during this time Japanese medicine began to draw the attention of the international community. For example, Ikegami and Campbell's report on medical care in Japan in *The New England Journal of Medicine* in 1995 emphasized Japan's egalitarian approach to medicine with limited health care expenditures through manipulation of a single national fee schedule (Ikegami & Campbell, 1995). A comprehensive volume on medicine in Japan followed this work by the same authors in their subsequent book, *The Art of Balance in Health Policy* (Campbell & Ikegami, 1998). More recently, the journalist T.R. Reid took up the significant differences in the practices of health globally for a general readership, and the Japanese model of medicine served as a key case in the book (Reid, 2009).

While defining a specific point in Japan's emergence into the global limelight is arbitrary, the mid-1980s seems a fitting point. In part, it correlates with Japan's emergence as a dominant global player. Japanese technological innovations increasingly became prized for their high quality. Medical researchers had growing success in publication. Clinicians increasingly wrote in the medical records using Japanese rather than English. A key event harkening the transition was the awarding of a Nobel Prize.

Tonegawa Susumu and the Nobel Prize

In 1987, Tonegawa Susumu (Portrait 14.7) became the first Japanese person to receive the Nobel Prize for Physiology or Medicine. The Nobel Committee awarded the prize to Tonegawa for his discovery of the genetic mechanism that produces antibody diversity. Though he won the Nobel Prize for his work in immunology, he trained as a molecular biologist. Tonegawa attended Kyoto University during tumultuous times when radical, leftist-minded students opposed the renewal of a 10-year defense treaty between Japan and the United States. Thus, the social upheaval from the debate about renewal of the treaty steered Tonegawa to academic life and the newly emerging field of molecular biology. Interestingly, it was the pending expiration of his visa during graduate studies in the United States that led him to leave the United States for Switzerland to focus on immunological research at the Basel Institute for Immunology in Basel.

Portrait 14.7 Tonegawa Susumu

Source: Tonegawa Susumu.

There, in a series of ingenious experiments in the 1970s, he unlocked the secret of how a limited amount of genetic material is able to rearrange itself to generate an array of proteins that recombine in a multitude of ways to form a wide variety of antibodies. He discovered that antibody diversity is generated by somatic recombination of the inherited gene segments and by somatic mutation. More simply stated, he showed that several genes work together to produce proteins that combine in numerous ways to form the antibodies needed to fight infections. The wide variety of ways that the proteins recombine to form antibodies allow the body to not only stave off current infections, but also prepare against micro-organisms that invade the body in the future (Wigzell, 1987).

Japanese Medical Industry

Japanese medicine's global place can be illustrated further by medical industry development. For example, Japanese medical device manufacturers have become active players in the global market (Medical Product Outsourcing, 2011). According to a 2011 Medical Products Outsourcing report, three Japanese companies ranked in the top 25 device companies in the world. Toshiba specializes in imaging devices such as computed tomography (CT) and magnetic resonance (MR) scanners and was ranked 15th in the world. Olympus Medical specializes in endoscopes and emerged 20th in the

rankings, and Terumo, with expertise in cardiovascular medical devices, rounded out the top 25 rankings. In a report 5 years prior by the same group, only Terumo was ranked in the top 25.

Japanese Pharma Achieves Global Status

Penetration in the world pharmaceutical market provides another example of Japan's presence in the global scene. According to a 2006 report in *Pharmaceutical Executive,* six Japanese companies made the top 30 for pharmaceutical sales in the world (Gray, 2006). While driven by domestic sales, their stature in the global rankings were impressive: Takeda (15th), Astellas (16th), Eisai (22nd), Sankyo (25th), Otsuka (26th), and Daiichi (28th), and nearly half-a-dozen more made the top 50 list (Gray, 2006). In addition, a Japanese medical school, University of Tokyo, has been ranked as a world-class university, rated by Thomson Reuter as the 37th best in the world (Times Higher Education, 2010). Japan's success in longevity and health care access became a point of global interest, particularly in light of excellent health care indices and a relatively low proportion of gross domestic product (GDP) spent on health care.

The success in limiting GDP spending on health care is particularly remarkable given the radical changes in the population pyramid (Figure 14.1), that is much like a pillar with an increasing expansion

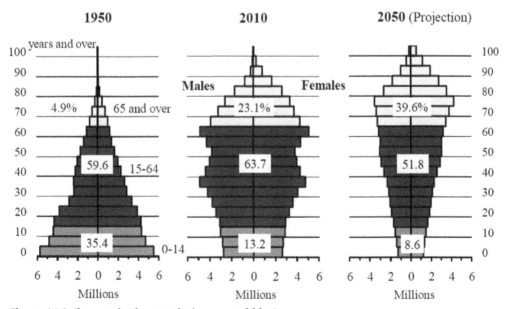

Figure 14.1 Changes in the population pyramid in Japan

Source: Courtesy of Statistical Handbook of Japan 2011 by Statistics Bureau, Japan (Statistics Bureau)

of individuals in the upper age levels with an ever-narrowing younger population base. This changing demographic has led to the widespread use of the term *shōshi-kōrei shakai*, a society with few children and many older people. Perhaps the most significant event amongst all this angst was the calculated development of a comprehensive long-term care insurance program.

The Long-term Care Insurance System

In response to the aging of Japanese society and an increase in the number of nuclear families, Long-term Care Insurance (LTCI) was introduced in 2000 to facilitate a system in which the society as a whole supports those who require long-term care. The LTCI objectives include socialization of care, expansion of local government responsibility for social policy, enhancement of consumer choice and competition, sharing of costs by elders via insurance premiums and co-payments, and integration of social services with some medical services (Campbell & Ikegami, 2003). The LTCI also aims to reduce the costs to the National Health Insurance system because it encourages homecare and reduces cases of 'social hospitalization,' that is, hospitalizations for social issues, often respite for family members, rather than medical illness (Ikegami, Yamauchi, & Yamada, 2003). Half of the expenditure is covered by the insurance premium payments and the other half is paid with public funds (25 percent of the total expenditure is incurred by the national government, 12.5 percent by prefecture, and 12.5 percent by local municipality). The average premium incurred by each insured person is approximately 4,000 yen (roughly US$40) per month (General Affairs Division, 2002).

Persons aged 40 or over are eligible for the insurance and they are divided into two groups: Category 1 consisting of persons aged 65 and over, and Category 2 consisting of persons aged 40 to 64 who are covered by health care insurance. The levels of support vary based on the mental and physical conditions of the insured person and are categorized into seven levels: 'Support Required: Level 1 or 2' and 'Long-term Care Required: Level 1–5.' The long-term care approval board investigates the mental and physical condition of the insured person and makes a screening judgment on whether or not they should be certified as requiring long-term care or support, and at which level they should be categorized, based on the opinions of a regular doctor. Then, based on the results of the screening judgment by the long-term care approval board, municipalities provide long-term care requirement certification and support requirement certification.

If the insured person is certified as requiring long-term care, he/she will be provided with various services for both in-home and in-facility care. Those individuals certified as requiring support are provided with various in-home services to prevent the condition from worsening and requiring long-term care (General Affairs Division, 2002). According to April 2011 statistics, the number of people who belonged to Category 1 was approximately 29 million, and 17.5 percent of them were certified as requiring long-term care or support. According to one estimate, the number of insured people who received in-home services was about 3 million, while the number of those who received in-facility care was about 0.8 million (Long-term Care, 2011).

Physician Scientists in Japan

One daunting issue given the emerging challenges to medicine in Japan is the shrinking interest and lack of growth in the number of physician scientists in Japan (Koike et al., 2012). Koike and colleagues examined the number of physician scientists in Japan between 1996 and 2008. Their assessment shows that the number of physician–scientists during this period hovered around 5,000, with a low of 4,893 and a high of 5,325. The authors found two striking points. First, the number of junior physician–scientists (those registered 0–4 years at the time of the surveys) declined from 828 in 1996 to 253 in 2008. Second, while the absolute number of female physician–scientists increased modestly from 528 in 1996 to 746 in 2008, their percentage of all physician scientists decreased slightly from 1.6 to 1.4 percent, even though the number of female physicians grew from 13.4 to 18.1 percent. These problems speak to the need for policy to balance the age and gender of physician scientists in Japan (Koike et al., 2012).

CONCLUSION

In this chapter, we have explored ancient practices of Japanese medicine, considered the long history of East Asian medicine in Japan, addressed the prominent influences of Western countries upon medicine in Japan, marveled at the magnificent contributions of Japanese researchers, and witnessed Japan's emergence into the realm of global medicine. We have touched also upon the challenges that medicine in Japan faces in the light of unprecedented demographic changes. We hope this overview has given the reader a sense of many pivotal events and inspirational individuals that have influenced the development of medicine in Japan.

NOTES

1 Scholarly work in English has generally adopted the convention of family name (last name) first for Japanese who do not publish regularly in Japanese. Unless noted otherwise, we have followed this convention for historical Asians cited in the text, including historical Chinese and Korean individuals. In addition, we use upper bar on long vowels in Japanese terms. This is not the case for city names and names of some institutions that have established their English names without this convention.

2 We have utilized phonetic spelling to be consistent with the actual Japanese, though in other English contexts the reader may also find this spelled as Shinto.

3 We have utilized phonetic spelling to be consistent with the actual Japanese, though in other English contexts, including the references, the reader may also find this spelled as Kampo, Kanpou, or Kanpo.

4 The National Diet of Japan is a two-chamber legislature with a lower house, the House of Representatives, and an upper house, the House of Councilors.

5 Green Tea Hag has been propogated by many, perhaps as a derogatory way of depicting a female criminal. But "Baba" is often used as a term of endearment, and the authors believe "Granny" to be a more close approximation of the actual Japanese.

6 Gradually, really gradually. One of us (MF) observed some physicians were still charting all or some portions of medical records as recently as the mid-1980s.

REFERENCES

Ariyoshi, S. (1966). *The doctor's wife*. Tokyo: Kodansha International.

Bartholomew, J.R. (1971). *The acculturation of science in Japan: Kitasato Shibasaburo and the Japanese bacteriological community, 1885–1920*. Palo Alto, CA: Stanford University Press.

Bartholomew, J.R. (1998). Japanese nobel candidates in the first half of the twentieth century. *Beyond Joseph Needham: Science, Technology, and Medicine in East and Southeast Asia* (2nd Series, Vol. 13, pp. 238–284). Chicago, IL: University of Chicago Press.

Bennett, J.W. (2001). Adrenalin and cherry trees. *The Timeline*, Retrieved June 2, 2012, from http://www.pubs.acs.org/subscribe/journals/mdd/v04/i12/html/12timeline.html

Bennett, J.W., & Yamomoto, Y. (2004). *Dr Jokichi Takamine: Japanese father of American biotechnology-the 150th anniversary of his birth*. Retrieved January 3, 2012, from http://home.kpn.nl/b1beukema/JokichiTakamine.pdf

Birch, S.J., & Felt, R.L. (1999). *Understanding acupuncture*. Edinburgh; New York: Churchill Livingstone.

Boscaro, A., Gatti, F., & Raveri, M. (Eds.). (1990). *Rethinking Japan: social sciences, ideology & thought* (Vol. II). London: Japan Library Ltd.

Bowers, J.Z. (1965). *Medical education in Japan; from Chinese medicine to Western medicine*. New York, NY: Hoeber Medical Division, Harper & Row.

CA Cancer J Clin. (1977). Katsusaburo Yamagiwa (1863–1930). *A Cancer Journal for Clinicians*, 27(3), 172–173.

Campbell, J.C., & Ikegami, N. (1998). *The art of balance in health policy: Maintaining Japan's low-cost, egalitarian system*. Cambridge, UK: Cambridge University Press.

Campbell, J.C., & Ikegami, N. (2003). Japan's radical reform of long-term care. *Social Policy and Administration*, 37(1), 21–34.

Dharmananda, S. (2001). *Kampo medicine: the practice of Chinese herbal medicine in Japan*. Portland, OR: START Manuscripts, ITM.

Fodstad, H., Hariz, M.I., Hirabayashi, H., & Ohye, C. (2002). Barbarian medicine in feudal Japan. *Neurosurgery*, 51(4), 1015–1024, discussion.

Frederic, L., & Roth, K. (1987) *Japan Encyclopedia*. Boston, MA: Harvard University Press.

Fujikawa, Y. (1978). *Japanese medicine* (1st AMS ed.). New York, NY: AMS Press.

Fukawa, T. (2002). Public health insurance in Japan. Retrieved June 2, 2012, from http://wwwwds.worldbank.org/external/default/WDSContentServer/WDSP/IB/2005/07/25/000011823_20050725163501/Rendered/PDF/330560JP0wbi37201.pdf

General Affairs Division, Health and Welfare Bureau For the Elderly. (2002). *Long-term care insurance in Japan*. Retrieved September 10, 2011, from http://www.mhlw.go.jp/english/topics/elderly/care/index.html

Gray, N. (2006). *Changing landscapes: a special report on the world's top 50 pharma companies* (7th Annual Report of the Pharmaceutical Executive, 78–101). Retrieved on August 6, 2014, from http://www.pharmexec.com/pharmexec/data/article-standard/pharmexec/182006/323799/article.pdf

Gustav, E. (1931). *Noguchi*. New York, NY: Harper & Brothers.

Hyodo, M. (1992). *Doctor S. Hanaoka, the world's first success in providing general anesthesia*. Paper presented at the The Pain Clinic IV: Proceedings of the Fourth International Symposium, Utrecht, the Netherlands.

Ikegami, N., & Campbell, J.C. (1995). Medical care in Japan. *New England Journal of Medicine*, 333(19), 1295–1299.

Ikegami, N., Yamauchi, K., & Yamada, Y. (2003). The long term care insurance law in Japan: impact on institutional care facilities. *International Journal of Geriatric Psychiatry*, 18, 217–221.

Itasaka, G. (1983). *Kodansha Encyclopedia of Japan* (pp. 942). Tokyo: Kodansha.

Izumi, Y., & Isozumi, K. (2001). Modern Japanese medical history and the European influence. *Keio J Med*, 50(2), 91–99.

Jansen, M.B. (1989). *The Cambridge history of Japan: the nineteenth century* (Vol. 5). Cambridge, UK: Cambridge University Press.

Japan International Cooperation Agency. (2005). *Japan's experiences in public health and medical systems* (chapter 11, pp. 245–259). Retrieved August 6, 2014, from http://jica-ri.jica.go.jp/IFIC_and_JBICI-Studies/english/publications/reports/study/topical/health/pdf/health_01.pdf

Koike, S., Ide, H., Kodama, T., Matsumoto, S., Yasunaga, H., & Imamura, T. (2012). Physician–scientists in Japan: attrition, retention, and implications for the future. *Academic Medicine*, 87(5), 662–667.

Lock, M.M. (1980). *East Asian medicine in urban Japan: varieties of medical experience.* (Vol. 4). Berkeley, CA: University of California Press.

Long-term Care. (2011). 介護保険事業状況報告 (平成23年4月分) (*Long-term care insurance report April 2011* [author's translation]). Retrieved September 10, 2011, from http://www.mhlw.go.jp/topics/kaigo/osirase/jigyo/m11/1104.html

McCormick, C.T., & White, K.K. (2010). *An encyclopedia of beliefs, customs, tales, music, and art.* Santa Barbara, CA: ABC-CLIO, Inc.

Medical Product Outsourcing. (2011). *Top 30 Medical Device Company Report.* Retrieved September 27, 2014, from http://www.mpo-mag.com/heaps/view/497/8

Mestler, G.E. (1957). Introduction to Western influences in pre-Meiji Japanese medicine. *Proceedings of the Royal Society of Medicine*, 50(12), 1005–1013.

Naito Museum of Pharmaceutical Science and Industry (n.d.). くすりの博物館 (Museum of Medicines [author's translation]). *Website of Eisai Co.* Retrieved August 6, 2014, from http://search.eisai.co.jp/cgi-bin/historyphot.cgi?historyid=E00051

Nishimura, K., Plotnikoff, G.A., & Watanabe, K. (2009). Kampo medicine as an integrative medicine in Japan. *Japan Medical Association Journal*, 52(3), 147–149.

Okuma, S., & Huish, M.B. (1970). *Fifty years of New Japan (Kaikoku Gojunen Shi).* (Kraus reprint ed.). New York, NY: General Books.

Otori, R. (1964). The acceptance of Western medicine in Japan. *Monumenta Nipponica*, 19(3/4), 254–274.

Otsuka, Y. (1977). Chinese traditional medicine in Japan. In C. Leslie (Ed.), *Asian medical systems* (pp. 322–339). Berkeley, CA: University of California Press.

Ravitsky, V., Fiester, A., & Caplan, A.L. (2009). *The Penn Center guide to bioethics.* New York, NY: Springer.

Reid, T.R. (2009). *The healing of America: a global quest for better, cheaper, and fairer health care.* New York, NY: Penguin Press.

Shibata, Y., & Wu, J. (1997). *Kampo treatment for climacteric disorders: a handbook for practitioners.* Brookline, MA: Paradigm Publications.

Shinmura, T.. (2006). *Nihon iryoshi* 日本医療史 (*The history of Japanese medicine*). Tokyo: Yoshikawa Kobunkan 吉川弘.

Smith, S.L. (2005). *Japanese American midwives: culture, community, and health politics, 1880–1950 (Asian American experience).* Urbana, IL: University of Illinois Press.

Sugimoto, T. (1987). 解体新書の時代: 江戸の翻訳文化をさぐる (*The period of the New Book on Anatomy* [author's translation]). Tokyo: Waseda University.

Times Higher Education. (2010). *Top 50 clinical, preclinical and health universities. The world university rankings 2010–11.* Retrieved December 8, 2011, from http://www.times highereducation.co.uk/world-university-rankings/2010-2011/clinical-pre-clinical-health.html

Trofa, A.F., Ueno-Olsen, H., Oiwa, R., & Yoshikawa, M. (1999). Dr Kiyoshi Shiga: discoverer of the dysentery bacillus. *Clinical Infectious Diseases*, 29(5), 1303–1306. doi: CID990042 [pii] 10.1086/313437

Watanabe, K., Matsuura, K., Gao, P., Hottenbacher, L., Tokunaga, H., Nishimura, K., & Witt, C.M. (2011). Traditional Japanese Kampo medicine: clinical research between modernity and traditional medicine-the state of research and methodological suggestions for the future. *Evidence-Based Complementary and Alternative Medicine*, 2011, 1–19.

Wigzell, H. (1987). *The Nobel Prize in physiology or medicine 1987: Susumu Tonegawa.* Retrieved December 22, 2011, from http://www.nobelprize.org/nobel_prizes/medicine/laureates/1987/presentation-speech.html

Wynn, S.G., & Fougere, B. (2006). *Veterinary herbal medicine* (Part I, pp. 36). Amsterdam: Mosby Inc.

Yasui, H. (2010). History of Japanese acupuncture and moxibustion. *The Journal of Kampo, Acupuncture and Integrative Medicine*, 1, 2–9.

15

Health Care in Japan: Excellent Population Health, Low Medical Expenditures, yet Ambiguous Place of Primary Care

Jonathan E. Rodnick, Izumi Yokoyama and
Michael D. Fetters

OVERVIEW

The Japanese experience one the longest life expectancies of any country in the world, yet spend modestly on medical care – in 2011, only 10.0 percent of Japan's gross domestic product. They use high technology imaging intensively and surgical procedures less intensively.

We believe one key to this paradox is easy access to medical care. The Japanese see physicians almost twice as frequently as any other people. Universal health coverage makes care financially accessible. Japanese private solo practitioners work long hours, providing time-accessible care. Japan's high population density makes care geographically accessible for the majority of the population living in urban areas. Ironically, Japan's highly subspecialty-trained, private practitioners act as default primary care physicians. A lack of admitting privileges and limited emergency care hours reinforce outpatient management of medical problems. Access to care in Japan stands out as the most important lesson Japan has to offer.

INTRODUCTION

With outstanding health indices, but moderate medical expenditures, the Japanese health care system merits scrutiny for lessons that could help inform the health crises in many other countries. The purpose of this chapter is to examine an apparent Japanese paradox of outstanding health indices and modest health care expenditures, all in the context of virtually unrestricted access to subspecialists and high technology. Specific comparisons include patients' morbidity and mortality and the components and costs of the medical systems of Japan, the United States, and select other countries. By describing key characteristics of the Japanese medical care system, we provide insights about why the Japanese may get a 'bigger bang' for their medical care expenditures than many countries. Of note, international comparisons of multiple indices are a challenge as data about all areas of interest are published over time. Hence, the focus of this chapter is on Japan in the first decade of the twenty first century. The chapter tends to focus on Japan and United States comparisons as these are the systems best known to us.

POPULATION HEALTH

The Japanese are among the world's healthiest people. In 2011, they had the second longest life expectancy of any country in the world (82.7 years, second to Switzerland, tied with Italy) (OECD, 2014b), yet spent a modest amount on medical care – 10.0 percent of its GDP. (The World Bank, 2014). To many observers, the reason for this longevity is obvious – it's the Japanese lifestyle. And it is true that compared to United States and many European citizens, the Japanese are much thinner and have a diet lower in fat. They live in a less violent society, but there are less desirable aspects of their lifestyle behaviors. For example, per capita alcohol consumption has been found to be only marginally lower than that in the United States (OECD, 2011). According to OECD data published in 2011, Japanese men's smoking prevalence is one of the highest in the world, over two times that of the United States (OECD, 2011).

Table 15.1 compares morbidity and mortality statistics of the populations of Japan and the United States using statistical data from the first decade of the twenty-first century. In addition to the Japanese, the Australians, Austrians, Belgians, Canadians, Finns, French, Germans, Greeks, Icelanders, Israelites, Italians, Koreans, Luxembourgers, Dutch, New Zealanders, Norwegians, Spaniards, Swedes, Swiss, and British were also long-lived, averaging over 80 years (OECD, 2011). In this timeframe, Americans had an average life expectancy at birth of 78.2 years, similar to the Portuguese and Danish. White Americans had a life expectancy of 78.0

years in 2003, 4 years less than the Japanese average. Japanese women also had the world's longest life expectancy at birth, as well as at age 65, and had the second lowest potential years of life lost before age 70 (OECD, 2011). Some of the reasons for this longevity are an extraordinary low infant mortality rate (Japan Center for Economic Research, 1993), less than 50 percent than that of the United States; a low cancer mortality, ranking fourth among developed countries and 88 percent that of the United States (with a particularly low mortality rate from breast and prostate cancer (OECD, 2009); and low mortality from ischemic heart disease (IHD). Japanese men had one-quarter the mortality rate of men in the United States and less than half the mortality rate from IHD of men in the Mediterranean countries of Greece and Italy (OECD, 2009). However, Japanese mortality rates from suicide, stroke, and stomach cancer exceeded those of the United States. Specifically, stroke mortality was double that of the United States.

INTERPLAY OF MULTIPLE FACTORS AND THE HEALTH CARE SYSTEM ON JAPANESE HEALTH INDICES

The population statistics in Table 15.1 are influenced by personal, family and community, environmental,

Table 15.1 Population health indicators in Japan and the United States

Parameter	Japan	United States
Population in millions (OECD Factbook, 2010)	127.6 (2008)	304.2 (2008)
Life expectancy at birth (OECD Publications, 2011)	83.0* (2009)	78.2 (2009)
Female life expectancy at age 65 (OECD Publications, 2011)	24.0* (2009)	20.0 (2009)
Male life expectancy at age 65 (OECD Publications, 2011)	18.9 (2009)	17.3 (2009)
Female potential years of life lost before age 70 (per 100,000) (OECD Publications, 2011)	1,762.7 (2009)	3,554.7 (2007)
Male potential years of life lost before age 70 (per 100,000) (OECD Publications, 2011)	3,287.1 (2009)	6,132.8 (2007)
All-cancer mortality rate (per 100,000) (OECD Publications, 2011)	138.4 (2007)	157.9 (2005)
Male ischemic heart disease mortality rate (per 100,000 males) (Organization for Economic Cooperation and Development, 2009)	41.4* (2006)	144.6 (2006)
Male suicide death rate (per 100,000 males) (Organization for Economic Cooperation and Development, 2009)	28.1 (2006)	16.6 (2006)
Violence-related mortality rate (per 100,000) (World Health Organization (WHO), 2004)	0.6 (2002)	5.4 (2002)
Infant mortality rate (per 1,000 live births) (OECD Publications, 2011)	2.6 (2007)	6.7 (2006)
Low birth weight infants (% weighing <2500g. at birth) (OECD Publications, 2011)	9.7% (2007)	8.3% (2007)
Male % of deaths attributed to smoking, ages 35–69 (Peto et al., 2006)	15.8% (2000)	29.1% (2000)
Female % of deaths that are smoking attributed, ages 35–69 (Peto et al., 2006)	4.9% (2000)	27.2% (2000)

*Leads developed world in this category

genetic, and socioeconomic as well as medical factors (Raphael, Curry-Stevens, & Bryant, 2008). Consequently, it is difficult to tease out just how much a medical system contributes to longevity. For example, some of the factors that determine infant mortality include teenage pregnancy rate, socioeconomic status, nutrition, smoking habits, and the availability of good prenatal care and well-staffed neonatal intensive care units. IHD mortality depends primarily on the incidence and severity of risk factors, including diet, smoking, high blood pressure, and exercise. IHD natural history is also influenced by the medical treatment of hypertension and high cholesterol, as well as by coronary bypass and other vascular surgery. IHD and stroke mortality rates are declining throughout the developed world, but declining less in Japan than in many other countries (OECD, 2009). Cancer incidence and mortality has genetic, nutritional, and environmental associations; however, early diagnosis and aggressive treatment can influence mortality. Despite having high smoking rates in Japan, Peto, et. al. found the percentage of deaths attributed to smoking much lower than in the United States (Peto et al., 2006), partially due to the lower baseline incidence of diseases associated with smoking and the lower rate of smoking in females.

Lifestyle and Health in Japan

The 'lifestyle' statistics of Table 15.2 illustrate that the Japanese have two key cardiovascular and cancer risk factors that are at the opposite ends of the spectrum. The Japanese lay claim to the developed world's lowest rate of obesity (especially remarkable compared to the United States – the world's highest) and, as noted, one of the world's highest rates of adult cigarette smoking (particularly in males) (OECD, 2011). Although the authors are not aware of population-based comparison data for other IHD risk factors, data from those diagnosed with IHD suggest a higher rate of hypertension and hypercholesterolemia in North Americans. However, patients with elevated risks appear to be less aggressively treated in Japan (Bhatt et al., 2006). The Japanese live in a less violent society, with a mortality rate from homicide that is about 10 percent that of Americans, although the difference in nonviolent crime is not as dramatic (OECD, 2009; World Health Organization (WHO), 2004). Furthermore, personal income inequity between the rich and the poor is much less in Japan. In the United States, increasing income inequity is correlated with worse population health statistics (Lynch, Smith, Harper, & Hillemeier, 2004). Although still narrow compared to many countries, the growing social inequality in Japan highlights the importance of equal access to health care under the national insurance system.

In summary, Japanese longevity is heavily related to economic, lifestyle, genetic, and societal factors. Still, some of their longevity may have to do with medical care – they have universal health care, adequate numbers of physicians and access to hospitals, and a penchant for going to the doctor. Although an accurate division of the determinants of population health between

Table 15.2   Life styles and demographics: Japan–United States comparison

Parameter	Japan	United States
Percentage of those 15 and older who smoke daily (OECD Publications, 2011)	23.9% (2010)	16.1% (2009)
Percentage of men 15 and older who smoke daily (OECD Publications, 2011)	36.6% (2010)	17.9 % (2009)
Alcohol consumption (liters per adult per year) (OECD Publications, 2011)	7.4 (2009)	8.8 (2008)
Percentage of those 15 and older with BMI > 30 (OECD Publications, 2011)	3.9% (2009)	33.8%^ (2008)
Percentage of females age 15 and older with BMI > 30 (OECD Publications, 2011)	3.5%* (2009)	35.5%^ (2008)
Percentage of population age 65 and older (OECD Publications, 2011)	23.1%* (2010)	13.0% (2010)
Percentage of population age 80 and older (Population Division of the Department of Economic and Social Affairs of the United Nations Secretariat, 2010)	6.3%* (2010)	3.8% (2010)
Percentage of population victimized by crime in 2004–2005 (OECD Publications, 2011)	9.9% (2005)	17.5% (2005)
Road fatalities (per million) (OECD Publications, 2011)	47 (2008)	123 (2008)
Estimated fertility rate (number of children born to each woman in her reproductive years) (OECD Publications, 2011)	1.37 (2008)	2.12 (2007)
Gini index of income inequality (0=no inequality, 100=maximum inequality) (OECD Publications, 2011)	32.1 (2005)	38.1 (2005)

Leads developed world in this category

^ *Worst in the world in this category*

primary factors and factors related to medical care is impossible, modeling for IHD suggests risk factor control is responsible for about 50–80 percent of the reduction in mortality, and modern treatments for patients with known IHD is responsible for 20–50 percent (Unal, Critchley, & Capewell, 2005). The medical system does matter.

THE JAPANESE MEDICAL INSURANCE SYSTEM

All Japanese have comprehensive health insurance through three major categories of health insurance, namely Society-Managed Health Insurance (Kumiai Hoken, also known as *Kenpo*) that covers employees of large companies; Government-Managed Health Insurance[1] (*Seifu Kanshou* or *Seikan*) that covers employees of small companies; and Citizens Health Insurance (*Kokumin Hoken* or *Kokuho*) that covers non-employees and retirees (Ikegami, 2007). None of these insurance schemes cover pregnancy because the government does not consider it an illness. Instead, the government provides cash payments to expectant mothers to alleviate the costs of pregnancy (Ministry of Health, Labour and Welfare, n.d.). Moreover, the public health system plays an important niche for support of pregnant and new mothers. Although those employed and their dependents are insured through a different entity than those who are governmental employees, unemployed, disabled, or retired, all programs use a standard, unified fee schedule for physicians and hospitals. These plans are each supported by a combination of taxes, premiums, and co-payments. Premiums increase with income (for those with nongovernmental jobs, the respective employer and employee contributions average about 4 percent). Co-payments are charged for all services. Though in flux under socioeconomic pressures, during this timeframe, co-pays were generally 30 percent for most, with 20 percent for pre-elementary children and 10 percent for those 70 years and older (except for high-income elderly who pay 30 percent) (Kanto, n.d.). This compares, for example, to 20 percent for Medicare in the United States, and is at maximum about $350/month (Ikegami, 2007). Recently, long-term care insurance for the elderly has been added (see Chapter 14). The overall system has low administrative costs, less than half that of the United States (Lynch et al., 2004).

Health Expenditures

In the beginning of the twenty-first century, overall health expenditures per capita in Japan were substantively lower than the United States, but were increasing, a trend similar to many other OECD countries. Data from 2011 illustrate Japan consumed 10.0 percent of its GDP, the same amount as New Zealand (OECD 2014a; The World Bank, 2014). Other OECD developed countries spending less than 10 percent of GDP devoted to health care in 2011 included Australia, Finland, Ireland, Italy, South Korea, Norway, Spain, Sweden and the United Kingdom (OECD 2014a). Some OECD countries spending more than Japan in 2011 included Austria, Canada, Belgium, Denmark, France, Germany, Netherlands, Switzerland, but none came close to the US where 16.9 percent of the GDP was spent on healthcare (OECD, 2014b). Table 15.3 displays medical expenditures by various categories. Percentages of total expenditures, but not the per capita amount going to long-term care, physicians, and pharmaceuticals, was higher in Japan than in the United States (OECD, 2011) during the years compared, and the percentage of out-of-pocket payments was also higher in Japan than the United States (OECD, 2011). The percentage going to other areas, especially administration and research and development, was higher in the United States.

Pharmaceutical Expenditures

Compared to other developed countries during this time, the Japanese were spending about an average amount on pharmaceuticals – $558 in Japan versus $919 annually per person in the United States. Per capita, the Japanese were consuming about 50 percent less pharmaceuticals than Americans (Danzon & Furukawa, 2008), though the reasons for this are unclear. It could be attributed to higher pricing in Japan, or just more sick people with chronic illness, and more severe illnesses in the United States. The spectrum of pharmaceutical use is different in Japan compared to the United States. In Japan, there is higher use of gastrointestinal medicines, anti-hypertensives (such as calcium channel blockers), and anti-anxiety agents, and historically lower use of antidepressants[2] and birth control pills (Okkes et al., 2002). Thus, Japanese longevity and population health cannot be attributed to an unusually high use of pharmaceuticals.

Practicing Physicians

Entering the twenty-first century, Japan had slightly fewer practicing physicians (2.2 versus 2.4 per 1,000 population), slightly fewer nurses, and many more hospital beds per capita than the United States (Bhatt et al., 2006; OECD, 2011). Medical resources and personnel of both countries are presented in Table 15.4. A striking aspect of the Japanese system is the very high number of

Table 15.3   Medical expenditures, comparison of Japan to United States

Parameter	Japan	United States
Health expenditure per capita (USD) (OECD Publications, 2011)	$2,878 (2008)	$7,960^ (2009)
Health expenditure per capita (USD) (Adjusted for differences in cost of living) (Anderson & Squires, 2010; Anderson & Markovich, 2010)	$2,474 (2005)	$7,538^ (2008)
Health expenditure as % of Gross Domestic Product (GDP) (OECD Publications, 2011)	8.5% (2008)	17.4%^ (2009)
Hospital spending per discharge (USD) (Adjusted for differences in cost of living) (Anderson & Squires, 2010; Anderson & Markovich, 2010)	$11,181 (2005)	$16,708^ (2006)
Inpatient care as % of health expenditure (Anderson & Markovich, 2010; Organization for Economic Cooperation and Development, 2009)	24.0% (2006)	25.9% (2006)
Cost per bed-day at tertiary care hospital, excluding drugs and tests (USD) (World Health Organization, 2005)	$264.45 (2005)	$1944.77 (2005)
Public funding as a % of total health care expenditure (OECD Publications, 2011)	80.8% (2008)	47.7% (2009)
Out-of-pocket payments as % of total health expenditure (OECD Publications, 2011)	15.8% (2008)	12.3% (2009)
Physician services as % of health expenditures (Cylus & Anderson, 2007; Frogner, Bishop, & Anderson, 2007)	25.0% (2003)	22.2% (2005)
Public health expenditures as % of Gross Domestic Product (GDP) (OECD Publications, 2011)	6.6% (2007)	7.3% (2007)
Long-term care and home care as % of health expenditures (Anderson & Frogner, 2008; Organization for Economic Cooperation and Development, 2009)	15.7% (2006)	6.2% (2006)
Pharmaceutical expenditure per capita (USD) (OECD Publications, 2011)	$558.3 (2008)	$919.1 (2008)
Pharmaceutical expenditures as % of total health expenditure (OECD Publications, 2011)	19.4% (2008)	11.9% (2008)
Rank of 191 countries in overall health system performance (World Health Organization, 2000)	10 (2000)	37 (2000)

^ *Worst in the world in this category*

imaging machines. Magnetic resonance imaging (MRIs) and computed tomography scans (CTs) are frequently ordered, but are reimbursed at a much lower rate than in the United States – about 25 percent of the Medicare rate (Ikegami, 2007; Ikegami & Campbell, 1995). Furthermore, billing for interpretation fees is limited.

Specialists, Generalists or Both?

There is a perception that virtually all Japanese doctors are sub-specialists, but it is only partly true. While virtually all experience subspecialty training, many have spent time, sometimes months, sometimes years, training in more than one discipline. Through the first decade of the twenty first century, a physician's indication of specialty was self-proclaimed. Most belonged to subspecialty societies, often more than one, and often medical societies had no prerequisite of training for membership other than paying the membership fee. Continuing medical education requirements were loose, if present, and there were no skill-based criteria for continued

membership. In addition to outlining many of these problems, the 2013 Report of the Committee on the Status Medical Specialists provided planning for new, stricter standards that are expected to examine qualifications much more carefully to increase the quality of health care in Japan (Organization of the New Specialist, 2013).

Incongruence in Specialty Training and Practice

While few physicians in Japan identify themselves as primary care physicians, over half of current physicians were trained as internists or pediatricians, primarily in nongeneralist specialties (Takemura, 2003). A few have trained as general internists or family physicians (Aoyama, 2003; Takemura, 2003). Most physicians work in solo private practice in Japan and are self-employed. In contrast to the United States where specialists are paid significantly more, private practitioners, earn considerably more, about 1.7 times as much, than hospital-based specialists (Bodenheimer, Berenson, & Rudolf, 2007;

Table 15.4 Medical care resources, comparison of Japan to the United States

Parameter	Japan	United States
Practicing physicians (per 1,000 population) (OECD Publications, 2011)	2.2 (2008)	2.4 (2009)
Percentage of female physicians (American Medical Association, 2008; Ministry of Health Labour and Welfare, 2008a)	18.1% (2008)	27.8% (2006)
Percentage of physicians in 'primary care' (Government Accountability Office (GAO), 2008; Ministry of Health Labour and Welfare, 2008a)	34.1%+ (2008)	32.3% (2005)
Population per 'primary care' physician (Government Accountability Office (GAO), 2008; Ministry of Health Labour and Welfare, 2008a)	1307.19 (2008)	1111.1 (2005)
Annual physician visits per capita (Anderson & Squires, 2010; Anderson & Markovich, 2010)	13.7* (2005)	4.0 (2007)
Primary care/specialists income (Bodenheimer, 2006; Ministry of Health Labor and Welfare, 2009)	1.71++ (2009)	0.54 (2004)
Practicing nurses (per 1,000) (OECD Publications, 2011)	9.5 (2008)	10.8 (2009)
Acute care hospital beds (per 1,000) (OECD Publications, 2011)	8.1 (2009)	2.7 (2007)
Inpatient days of care/person/year (Anderson & Frogner, 2008; Anderson & Markovich, 2010)	2.1 (2005)	0.6 (2006)
Average hospital length of stay for acute care (OECD Publications, 2011)	18.5* (2009)	5.4 (2009)
Average length of stay for normal delivery (days) (Ministry of Health Labour and Welfare, 2008b; OECD Publications, 2011)	8.0 (2008)	2.1 (2008)
Hospital discharges (per 1,000) (OECD Publications, 2011)	107.09 (2008)	130.86 (2008)
MRI units (per 1,000,000 population) (OECD Publications, 2011)	43.1* (2008)	25.9 (2007)
CT scanners (per 1,000,000) (OECD Publications, 2011)	97.3* (2008)	34.3 (2007)

+Active medical doctors working for clinics (medical institutions with less than 20 inpatient beds), were recognized as primary care physicians for Japanese data. (Matsumoto et al., 2010)

*Leads developed world in this category

++In the Japanese data, this is calculated as a gap in average annual incomes between private practice physicians and physicians employed by hospitals

Ministry of Health, Labour and Welfare, 2009). Unlike the United States, there is no difference in the fee paid for a similar service between doctors of different specialties or between private and public facilities.

Scope of Practice in Primary Care

While private practice physicians maintain the persona and aura of a subspecialist, they enter into a second career as a 'default primary care practitioner' when they open a private clinic. Functionally, they provide accessible, first-contact care, relatively comprehensive care (except women's health care), and continuity of care. Though lacking in training in the care of children, many provide some pediatric services. While some have billboards proclaiming their specialty expertise, a substantial component of their practice income comes from the treatment of common primary care problems. Most do electrocardiograms (ECGs) and simple X-rays; many do ultrasounds or upper gastrointestinal (UGI) endoscopy (Aoyama, 2003), and a growing number have CT or

MRI imaging on site (OECD, 2011). Most forego the invasive specialty skills they learned during residency training, particularly procedures that require support of a hospital environment. Large hospitals have closed staffing (*kinmui*) for the most part, and do not allow community physicians to access facilities needed to practice and maintain subspecialty skills. Under the national fee schedule system that does not distinguish between a facility fee and professional fee, experimentation with open access in Japan largely failed due to low reimbursement from the hospital for physician work. Hence, the bulk of Japan's private practice physicians are characterized as subspecialty trained, but practicing limited specialty care and a lot of primary care by default.

Visits to the Doctor

Japanese see their physicians very frequently, an average of 14 visits per patient per year, the highest rate of any country! This rate of physician visits is much more than that of the next highest country Denmark, which has a rate of 8.9 annual physician visits per capita) (Anderson & Squires, 2010). In part, this trend is likely due to the payment system (relatively low and fixed payments per visit), and partially due to historical factors (patients in the past could only get two weeks of medications at each visit). However, access to physicians of any type is quick and inexpensive. Most offices do not use appointment systems; patients show up to be seen that day (a type of open access). Although there are co-payments, they are capped according to income. To generate a good income, physicians work long hours, six days a week, and see 60 to 100 patients a day. These visits are very narrowly focused, and many are for simple medication refills.

Health Promotion and Disease Prevention

Public health, prevention, and patient education are seen as a nursing, community, or governmental responsibility. Patients often receive preventive care, predominantly screening care using medical testing, through workplace, school, or local government programs. Frequently, these are conducted as group health checkups in the school or work place. Japanese children have higher rates of many childhood immunizations than in the United States (OECD, 2009).

Acute and Long-term Care in Japanese Hospitals

While the situation has improved dramatically with the introduction of the Long-term Care Insurance (LTCI) system, Japanese hospitals are often part acute and part long-term care facilities. Since development of the LTCI system, there are growing numbers of stand-alone, skilled nursing facilities. Japan has a lot of hospital beds per population, three times as many as the United States (OECD, 2011). Lengths of stays are extraordinarily long by international standards, but the number of admissions or discharges per capita is less than in the United States (OECD, 2011). The long length of stay leads to a greater percentage of overall health expenses going to the hospital sector in Japan, but reimbursement per day is much lower. Hospitals in Japan can be privately owned (80 percent) or owned by universities or municipalities (20 percent). Private clinics are also allowed to run small, loosely regulated hospitals (up to 19 beds), but the number of these facilities is decreasing as doctors are faced with increasingly prohibitive regulations.

Surgery in Japan

The number of surgical operations per capita is only one-third of that in the United States. Again, this is probably related to low reimbursement, few anesthesiologists, and a cultural aversion to invasive procedures (Ikegami & Campbell, 1995). The emergency medical system is not as well developed and hospitals typically minimize the emergency services available on nights and weekends. Although there are few 24/7 emergency centers, their numbers are rising. There are fewer nursing home beds per population in Japan than in the United States because hospitals often provide care for less acute conditions. Home visits by physicians are still common and actively encouraged by the Japanese government.

CHALLENGES TO THE SYSTEM

Health Care in Aging Japan

Though access has been a building block for the 'good health' of the Japanese, a significant challenge is the increasing number of older patients and the budgetary difficulties the government faces. Noticeably, this challenge has begun to result in limiting access to patients in need in certain situations, such as stroke patients that have restricted periods of treatment, for example 'recovery-period rehabilitation' ('*kaifukuki rihabiri*') services. In the face of a rapidly aging population, so-called 'social hospitalization' is highly prevalent in Japan. For example, more than 500,000 people aged 65 years and older currently live in hospitals. To deal with the problem, in 1989 the Japanese government instituted the Ten Year Strategy for Health and Welfare of the Elderly (so-called Gold Plan). This policy aimed to double the number of beds in hospitals and triple home services and community-based services for older people over 10 years. (Tamiya et al., 2011) Since 1989, the government actively encouraged home care to help reduce cases of 'social hospitalization.' The most important example of this movement is the LTCI system that was introduced in 2000 (General Affairs Division, 2002) (see also Chapter 14). The LTCI system could also raise new tax revenue and premiums to help pay for institutional long-term care rather than medical insurance.

In summary, the Japanese medical system has 50 years of experience with universal coverage and offers easy access to physicians, though training has not necessarily focused on the primary needs of the population (Ban and Fetters, 2011). Physicians see high numbers of outpatients daily and use extensive imaging and testing. Hospitals provide fewer but longer stays with less intense care. Overall costs are truly low compared to most other developed countries. With changing health parameters due to a growing population of aging people and changes in dietary and exercise patterns, the system will need to evolve to keep Japan in an enviable paradox of having excellent health outcomes with modest health expenditures.

Challenges to Health Care in Japan

However, there are many concerns on the horizon. First, Japan is a rapidly aging society. In 2010, 23.1 percent of the population was 65 or older (Statistics Bureau, 2010), and this is projected to increase to 26.3 percent by 2015, 29.3 percent by 2025 and 35.6 percent by 2050 (Population Division of the Department of Economic and Social Affairs of the United Nations Secretariat, 2010). Second, there is widespread concern about the plummeting birth rate, now about 65 percent of that in the United States (OECD, 2011). Third, Japan's system is not 'patient-centered' and short consultation times (Wooldridge et al., 2010) mean patients are not always well informed about their problems, coordination of care can suffer, and patient education and preventive care may not be done. Fourth, the details and quality of hospital and office medical records are of surprising variability (Ikegami & Campbell, 2004). In a 2009 report, it was estimated that only about 10 percent of primary care practices had an electronic health record (EHR) with penetration in hospitals being a little higher except for large hospitals. Castro estimated it to be nearly one-third (Castro, 2009). Fifth, postgraduate medical education in ambulatory or primary care is limited. Although a required two-year rotating internship with a community rotation has recently been implemented for most medical school graduates, this may be more akin to the clinical clerkships of the fourth year of medical school and first year of residency in the United States (see Chapter 16).

DISCUSSION

Considering these parameters, it is reasonable to ask if the Japanese medical system helps or hinders the good health statistics and long life expectancy of the Japanese. A number of possible attributes stand out: lots of imaging and testing; low financial barriers to care; fewer invasive procedures; and long but less intense hospitalizations. While a number of medical system attributes may contribute to the good health of the Japanese, excellent access seems to be the most important.

Access to Health Care

Access to care has many components. First is financial access. There are few financial barriers to care, with co-pays capped for those with low income. Indeed, physicians have incentives to see patients because all care is fee-for-service (FFS). For non-procedural services, reimbursement is set by the visit, regardless of length or complexity. This incentivizes frequent contact and visits when patient symptoms are minor and easiest to treat, and illustrates that capitation does not always encourage access. Low payments per visit encourage repeat visits and continuity. Second is timely access. Access to physicians is related to their availability. Japanese private practice physicians typically start work late in the morning and extend into the evening. They take few vacations. As most are in solo practice, access is usually to the same physician, though it can be fragmented for patients who see multiple doctors. As most doctors do not significantly utilize appointment systems, for most people, physicians' offices are open access. Third is geographic access. Because Japan has a high population density with the majority of people living in urban areas with good public transportation, the distances and travel times for those lving in densely populated areas to see a physician are short. Fourth, there is virtually unrestricted access to low-cost technology, especially ultrasound, CT, and MRI imaging.

It is important to note that large community, university, and government hospitals are not open access – community physicians do not admit to them – and emergency care (especially after hours) is less available, and so default primary care physicians try to maximize outpatient management in the outpatient setting that is accessible to patients. As hospital-based clinics frequently have long waits, quick access is an important distinguishing factor for physicians in private practice.

Critical constructs of effective primary care include access, first contact care, comprehensive care, coordination of care, continuity of care, and community-based care. One cannot overlook access to health care as a factor critical to success of the Japanese medical system. Universal coverage emerges as the first and foremost financial factor facilitating access, and its importance cannot be overestimated. The Japanese medical system features additional attributes supporting primary care – continuity and physicians practicing in the context of the community. Coordination of care and comprehensiveness of care could be enhanced through improved primary care training (Ban and Fetters, 2011).

WHY DOES THE MEDICAL SYSTEM PERFORM BETTER THAN IT LOOKS ON PAPER?

Using criteria developed by Barbara Starfield, a leading researcher on the role of primary care in achievement of excellent health care outcomes, Japan's primary care system only scores 7.5 (out of 20 possible points for a perfect primary care system), while the United States scores 3, and the United Kingdom scores 19 (Macinko et al., 2003). In other words, Japan scores low, but 'paradoxically' has good health care outcomes. A strong primary care system in a country-by-country analysis (or county-by-county in the United States) is associated with lower all-cause mortality, less premature mortality, and lower cardiovascular disease mortality (Macinko et al., 2003). Shi and colleagues found that United States counties with higher availability of primary care experienced 2 to 3 percent lower mortality (Shi et al., 2005).

We feel that the Starfield scoring underrates Japan. As noted, Japan's physicians, while virtually all categorized as specialists, function predominantly as primary care doctors. Japanese physicians see their patients frequently (for example, every few days for someone with bronchitis and every two weeks for someone with hypertension), and can do tests or change therapy when needed. Despite shorter visits, there are much more frequent visits; total face-to-face time with the physician-per-illness episode may be similar in both countries (Wooldridge et al., 2010). Last, there are a reasonable number of patients (about 1,000) per 'primary care' physician in Japan, many fewer patients per physician than in the United States. Although access does not ensure quality of care (Hussey et al., 2004), seeing patients frequently allows quick adjustments of treatment so that acute and chronic conditions can be managed and complications can be recognized early.

Success in Keeping Patients in the Outpatient Setting

Another important contributing factor may be the less intense use of hospitals. Wennberg and colleagues have shown that for American patients with chronic conditions, the more resources used (more hospitalizations), the worse the outcomes (either in functional status, survival, or satisfaction (Wennberg et al., 2005). The United States' penchant for short, intense hospitalizations and surgical and procedural interventions (especially towards the end of life) occasionally gives dramatic results, but sometimes is futile and may contribute to iatrogenic illness and increased costs without benefiting population health.

Keeping Prices Low Keeps Costs Low

A separate issue is the low overall costs of the Japanese medical system. As Anderson and colleagues note in their article, *It's The Prices, Stupid,* costs are low for one key reason – low prices (Anderson, Reinhardt, Hussey, & Petrosyan, 2003). Japans' physicians and hospitals, like most of those in the United States, live in an FFS environment. Japan has nationally fixed prices for each service, including procedures and pharmaceuticals (not too different than Medicare in the United States). But in Japan, bills for each service are more efficiently handled than in the United States; they are bundled together and submitted monthly. Prices are revised individually (not across the board, as with the annual adjustment of Medicare physician payments). In particular, prices of procedures that have large volume increases are often decreased. For example, when the number of head MRIs was noted to go up, the fee for a head MRI in Japan was reduced from about $151 to $104 USD (Ikegami & Campbell, 2004). This approach of periodically revising the reimbursement for high volume tests and procedures could be used, for example, in the United States.

Challenges on the Horizon

Despite the many exemplary outcomes of Japan's health care system, especially access and cost containment, emerging social challenges are causing unprecedented change in the system (Ministry of Internal Affairs and Communications, 2011). Japan stands as the most aged and rapidly aging population in the world. The fertility rate has been dropping as well to a level of 1.37 in 2009 (Ministry of Internal Affairs and Communications, 2011). The major causes of morbidity include malignancy, cerebrovascular disease, and cardiovascular disease. The costs associated with treating these chronic diseases pose a significant challenge for any system.

Resolving the Riddle

The reasons for the apparent paradox of outstanding population health with low expenditures in Japan are multifactorial, and there are important lifestyle and environmental factors. But universal insurance coverage, less intense hospital care, and excellent access to default primary care physicians stand out as three medical system factors that are helping to keep the Japanese healthy. As health care policymakers around the world look for ways to improve their systems and lower costs, they should not ignore the remarkable, though not utopian, results in Japan. The critical ingredient we feel that has not been appreciated is access.

Concerns with the Solution

Unfortunately, most of the physicians providing this access – default primary care physicians – have not been trained for their role. The Japanese government is attempting to address the public perception that medical school graduates lack the comprehensive skills expected of physicians by experimenting with the new required two years of postgraduate training (Ikai, 2000). Japan could best serve its aging society and rapidly growing population of patients with chronic medical conditions through systematic training programs in primary care specialties, such as family medicine, general medicine, and pediatrics. The rapidly aging society and economic downturn that started in 2010 will dramatically influence future directions of medical care in Japan. Given Japan's long history, as well as the resilience and adaptability of the Japanese people, the response will undoubtedly be remarkable.

NOTES

1   In October 2008, the operation of the Government-Managed Health Insurance was taken over by the Japan Health Insurance Association from the Social Insurance Agency.
2   While detailed data escaped our searches, every indication from conversations with clinicians from Japan, and from management of Japanese patients arriving from Japan, is that anti-depressant use is on the increase in Japan.

REFERENCES

Anderson, G.F., Reinhardt, U.E., Hussey, P.S., & Petrosyan, V. (2003). It's the prices, stupid: why the United States is so different from other countries. *Health Affairs (Millwood)*, 22(3), 67–74.

Anderson, G.F., & Squires, D.A. (2010). Measuring the US health care system: a cross-national comparison. *Issue Brief (Commonw. Fund)*, 90, 1–10.

Aoyama, M. (2003). The concept of primary care in Japan: turning point for the 21st century. *Primary Care Japan*, 1(1), 1–13.

Ban N and Fetters, MD. (2011). Education for health professionals in Japan–time to change. *The Lancet*, 378(9798): 1206–7.

Bhatt, D.L., Steg, P.G., Ohman, E.M., Hirsch, A.T., Ikeda, Y., Mas, J.L., ... Reach Registry Investigators. (2006). International prevalence, recognition, and treatment of cardiovascular risk factors in outpatients with atherothrombosis. *Journal of the American Medical Association*, 295(2), 180–189.

Bodenheimer, T., Berenson, R.A., & Rudolf, P. (2007). The primary care-specialty income gap: why it matters. *Annals of Internal Medicine*, 146(4), 301–306.

Castro, D. (2009). *Explaining international IT application leadership: health IT.* Retrieved April 29, 2012, from http://www.itif.org/files/2009-leadership-healthit.pdf

Danzon, P.M., & Furukawa, M.F. (2008). International prices and availability of pharmaceuticals in 2005. *Health Affairs (Millwood)*, 27(1), 221–233.

General Affairs Division, Health and Welfare Bureau For the Elderly. (2002). *Long-term care insurance in Japan.* Retrieved September 10, 2011, from http://www.mhlw.go.jp/ english/topics/elderly/care/index.html

Hussey, P.S., Anderson, G.F., Osborn, R., Feek, C., McLaughlin, V., Millar, J., & Epstein, A. (2004). How does quality of care compare in five countries? *Health Affairs (Millwood)*, 23(3), 89–99.

Ikai, S. (2000). 日本における医師のキャリア-医局制度における日本の医師卒後教育の構造分析 (The career of Japan's medical profession: an analysis of the informal medical graduate education system). 季刊社会保障研究 (*Quarterly of Social Security Research*), 36, 269–278.

Ikegami, N. (2007). The Japanese health care system: achieving equity and containing costs through a single payment system. *American Heart Hospital Journal*, 5(1), 27–31.

Ikegami, N., & Campbell, J.C. (1995). Medical care in Japan. *New England Journal of Medicine*, 333(19), 1295–1299.

Ikegami, N., & Campbell, J.C. (2004). Japan's health care system: containing costs and attempting reform. *Health Affairs (Millwood)*, 23(3), 26–36.

Japan Center for Economic Research. (1993). 日米医療システムの比較研究 (*US–Japan comparative health care systems-econometric analysis of US and Japanese health care systems*). Vols. 1 & 2. Retrieved June 2, 2012, from http://www.nira.or.jp/past/pubj/output/dat/2807.html

Kanto. (n.d.). 関東ITソフトウェア健康保険組合 (Kanto IT Software Health Insurance Society). Retrieved August 6, 2014, from http://www.its-kenpo.or.jp/index.html

Lynch, J., Smith, G.D., Harper, S., & Hillemeier, M. (2004). Is income inequality a determinant of population health? Part 2. US National and regional trends in income inequality and age-and cause-specific mortality. *Milbank Quarterly*, 82(2), 355–400.

Macinko, J., Starfield, B., & Shi, L. (2003). The contribution of primary care systems to health outcomes within organization for economic cooperation and development (OECD) countries, 1970–1998. *Health Services Research*, 38(3), 831–865.

Ministry of Health Labour and Welfare. (2009). 「勤務医の給料」と「開業医の収支差額」について *(Survey on economic conditions in health care)*. Retrieved August 6, 2014, from http://www.mhlw.go.jp/bunya/iryouhoken/iryouhoken12/iryouhoushu.html

Ministry of Health, Labour and Welfare. (n.d.). About the Birth and Childrearing single payment system after April 23, 2006. 平成23年4月以降の出産育児一時金制度について *[author's translation]*. Retrieved August 6, 2014, from http://www.mhlw.go.jp/seisaku/2011/05/01.html

Ministry of Health, Labour and Welfare. (n.d.). Response to a Society with a Decreasing Birth Rate–Focusing on Childrearing Support Measures. Retrieved August 6, 2014, from http://www.mhlw.go.jp/english/wp/wp-hw4/dl/honbun/2_2_4.pdf

Ministry of Health, Labour and Welfare. (n.d.). About the 'Prenatal care and Delivery financial burden will decrease' Government Report 政府広報「妊婦健診や出産の経済的負担が軽減されます！」について *[author's translation]*. Retrieved August 6, 2014,from http://www.mhlw.go.jp/topics/2009/03/tp0327-1.html

Ministry of Internal Affairs and Communications. (2011). *The Statistical Handbook of Japan 2013*. Retrieved August 6, 2014, from http://www.stat.go.jp/english/data/handbook/index.htm

Organization for Economic Cooperation and Development (OECD). (2009). *Society at a glance 2009 – OECD Social Indicators*. Retrieved October 1, 2014, from doi: 10.1787/soc-glance-2008-en

Organization for Economic Cooperation and Development (OECD). (2011). *OECH health data 2011*. Retrieved October 1, 2014, from doi: 10.1787/soc-glance-2008-en

OECD (2014a). OECD Health Data: Health expenditure and financing: Health expenditure indicators, *OECD Health Statistics* (database).

OECD (2014b). Society at a Glance 2014: OECD Social Indicators, OECD Publishing.

Okabe, Y. (岡部陽二). (2001–2003). 医療システムの日米比較 *(Comparison of the health care systems of Japan and the United States)* (pp. 88–96). Retrieved August 6, 2014, from http://www.y-okabe.org/medical/post 144.html

Okkes, I. M., Polderman, G. O., Fryer, G. E., Yamada, T., Bujak, M., Oskam, S. K., ... Lamberts, H. (2002). The role of family practice in different health care systems: a comparison of reasons for encounter, diagnoses, and interventions in primary care populations in the Netherlands, Japan, Poland, and the United States. *Journal of Family Practice*, 51(1), 72–73.

Peto, R., Lopez, A.D., Boreham, J., & Thurn, M. (Eds.). (2006). *Mortality from smoking in developed countries 1950–2000* (2nd ed.). New York: Oxford University Press.

Raphael, D., Curry-Stevens, A., & Bryant, T. (2008). Barriers to addressing the social determinants of health: insights from the Canadian experience. *Health Policy*, 88(2–3), 222–235.

Shi, L., Macinko, J., Starfield, B., Politzer, R., Wulu, J., & Xu, J. (2005). Primary care, social inequalities and all-cause, heart disease, and cancer mortality in US counties: a comparison between urban and non-urban areas. *Public Health*, 119(8), 699–710.

Statistics Bureau, Ministry of Internal Affairs and Communications. (2010). 総合統計データ月報 (Japan monthly statistics). *Journal of the American Medical Association*, 295(2), 180–189.

Takemura, Y. (2003). Family medicine: what does it mean in Japan? *Asia Pacific Family Medicine*, 2, 188–192.

Tamiya, N., Noguchi, H., Nishi, A., Reich, M.R., Ikegami, N., Hashimoto, H., ... Campbell, J.C. (2011). Population ageing and wellbeing: lessons from Japan's long-term care insurance policy. *Lancet*, 378(9797), 1183–1192.

The Organization of the New Specialist (2013) 新たな専門医に関する仕組みについて (authors' translation). Retrieved August 11, 2014 from http://www.mhlw.go.jp/stf/shingi/2r985200000300ju-att/2r985200000300lb.pdf

The World Bank (2014) Health Expenditure, total (% of GDP) Retrieved August 11, 2014, from http://data.worldbank.org/indicator/SH.XPD.TOTL.ZS

Unal, B., Critchley, J.A., & Capewell, S. (2005). Modelling the decline in coronary heart disease deaths in England and Wales, 1981–2000: comparing contributions from primary prevention and secondary prevention. *British Medical Journal*, 331(75/7), 614.

United Nations, Department of Economic and Social Affairs, (2010). *World Population Prospects: The 2012 Revision*. Retrieved August 6, 2014, from http://esa.un.org/wpp/unpp/panel_population.htm

Wennberg, J.E., Fisher, E.S., Baker, L., Sharp, S.M., & Bronner, K.K. (2005). Evaluating the efficiency of California providers in caring for patients with chronic illness. *Health Affairs (Millwood)*, W5-526–43.

Wooldridge, A.N., Arato, N., Sen, A., Amenomori, M., Fetters M.D. (2010) Truth or fallacy? Three hour wait for three minutes with the doctor: Findings from a private clinic in rural Japan. *Asia Pacific Family Medicine* 9(1), 11.

World Health Organization (WHO). (2004). *Causes of death*. Retrieved August 6, 2014, from http://www.who.int/healthinfo/statistics/ bodgbddeath-dalyestimates.xls

16

Medical Education in Japan

Michael D. Fetters and Izumi Yokoyama

OVERVIEW

In this chapter, we provide a concise overview ranging from the historical to the modern era about the medical education system in Japan. Though shorter than the fascinating overview of John Z. Bowers (Bowers, 1965), the current synopsis seeks to include historical events and their consequences, as well as an updated in-depth view based on the literature and extensive professional experience held by one of us (MF) in teaching and lecturing in Japanese medical schools and hospitals. An understanding of that evolution requires some retracing of historic events introduced in Chapter 14 with a focus on educational features.

HISTORICAL ROOTS OF JAPAN'S MODERN MEDICAL EDUCATION SYSTEM

As illustrated in Chapter 14, Japan's long medical history includes two strong influences, East Asian medicine (*Tōyō igaku*) and Western medicine. *Tōyō igaku* is an umbrella term that includes Kanpō, acupuncture, and moxibustion[1] in Japan. Kanpō includes herbal, animal, and mineral combinations. The current practice of East Asian medicine developed in a historical context involving interaction and learning in China, Japan, and Korea. While the Western tradition has overshadowed the East Asian tradition since the end of the nineteenth century, use of East Asian medicine occurs extensively in Japan (Lock, 1980, 1984), though mostly outside the mainstream medicine except for national health insurance approved Kanpō treatments, and typically for conditions less effectively treated by Western medicine, as for example chronic pain. Western and East Asian medicine co-exist and the majority of Japanese physicians prescribe Kanpō, at least to a limited extent, for common ailments, such as colds, constipation, and other chronic diseases, from a formulary approved under the national health insurance scheme. In this chapter, we provide an overview of historical developments of the two educational systems through current times and acknowledge the mutual influences and continued practice of both. We have sought to seek a balance in presentation of the historical and current importance of both systems, though we would emphasize that since the twentieth century, Japanese medical education shifted its emphasis onto Western medicine (actually just 'medicine' in contexts not making a comparison to East Asian medicine), and the same Western medicine paradigm dominates in Japanese medical education institutions with Kanpō having only minor status secondary to the dominant

---

Box 16.1 Key points

- Organized instruction of healing first emerged In 414, under East Asian medicine (*Tōyō igaku*) and the tradition dominated in Japan until the end of the nineteenth century
- Tashiro Sanki, who studied medicine in China for 12 years, began teaching Kanpō at the Ashikaga School at the end of the fifteenth century
- Since 2004, Kanpō education assumed a place in the curriculum in all medical schools
- In 2007, 85 acupuncture schools provided education for the sighted, and 69 schools provided education for the visually impaired
- From the time the Japanese government adopted the German medicine model to guide its modernization in 1869, it continued to dominate the organization of medical education approach until the end of World War II
- In the 1970s, the number of medical schools grew from 46 to 80
- Reforms beginning in the 1990s and spanning two decades resulted in significant changes in undergraduate medical education including problem-based learning, medical simulation and standardized patients, and the common achievement test
- Medical education predominantly involves lectures and students observing more senior physicians as they care for patients, though recent reforms have introduced, on a limited basis, an expectation for a basic level of clinical skills
- Teaching faculty: student ratios are significantly lower in number in Japan than many Western countries
- Passing the written national licensure examination remains the foremost focus in Japanese undergraduate medical education; graduating clinicians receive substantively less focus
- 2004 witnessed the implementation of a 2-year preliminary postgraduate internship training and matching program that has changed the Japanese postgraduate medical education structure

---

model. As we will show, there are a number of institutions dedicated to teaching *Toyo igaku*.

EDUCATION IN EAST ASIAN MEDICINE

Although it is believed that there were Chinese influences in Japanese medicine as early as 200 BC, the oldest event found in Japanese historical records speaks to the visit of Kon Mu from China in 414 (Table 16.1). At the beginning of the eighth century, medical studies modeled on the Tang Dynasty (618–907) in China were promulgated in Japan, although it never became effective because of incessant civil war (Bowers, 1970). The first general university in Japan was the Ashikaga School (fifteenth century–1872), and its academic repertoire included medical courses. Tashiro Sanki (1465–1537), who studied a branch of Chinese medicine in China for 12 years, brought this knowledge back to Japan and started teaching Kanpō at the Ashikaga School at the end of the fifteenth century. One of his pupils, Manase Dōsan (1507–1594), developed his own medical approach that better integrated theory, diagnosis, and therapy (Yasui, 2007). He built a private medical school, *Keiteki-in*, in Kyoto in the mid-sixteenth century (Leslie, 1977) where he taught his medical theory of Kanpō to approximately 800 students.

During the Edo period (1603–1867), many private medical schools were established. Training

in medicine was based exclusively on the study of Kanpō with practical instruction through anatomical models and clinical demonstrations (Bowers, 1970). A blind Japanese acupuncturist named Sugiyama Waichi (1610–1694) contributed substantively to the advancement of acupuncture in Japan. He developed many acupuncture techniques and established 45 acupuncture schools for the blind. Hence, providing acupuncture and moxibustion became – and continues to be – a common occupation among the blind (Izumi & Isozumi, 2001; Yasui, 2010). Until the mid-nineteenth century, Kanpō on the one hand and acupuncture and moxibustion on the other were the two main modes of medicine in Japan.

As discussed in Chapter 14, after Japan opened its doors to trade with the US and other Western countries in 1853, German medicine became the main influence on medicine in Japan as Western surgical techniques and anatomical depictions were more advanced and more accurate. The perception of German medicine's superiority was so strong that the practice of medicine was restricted in 1895 by the National Diet of Japan to individuals with Western-style training, and the practice of Kanpō medicine drastically declined (Izumi & Isozumi, 2001). Although Kanpō doctors virtually disappeared from the medical scene by the end of the nineteenth century, some continued to practice privately, and the tradition was kept alive primarily among pharmacists and sellers of Kanpō formulations.

Table 16.1   Selected East Asian medicine education and development events

Year	Major Historical Events
414	Visit of Kon Mu from China, the oldest documented evidence of Chinese influence on Japanese medicine
681	Emperor Monbu initiates the establishment of the Taihō Code, the first penal and administration code
701	Government enacts the Taihō Code, and the first official medical education system in Japan is formed under a section of the Taihō Code. Acupuncture and moxibustion are set up as specialties in Japanese medical education
1487	Tashiro Sanki visits China to learn medicine
1545	Manase Dōsan, Tashiro's pupil, builds a private medical school in Kyoto and teaches Chinese medicine
1603–1867 (Edo period)	Many private medical schools are established. Acupuncture and moxibustion dominate medical practice and the terms distinguishing Kanpō (Chinese medicine) and Ranpō (Dutch medicine) emerge
1885	Nagai Nagayoshi isolates ephedrine from Ephedra herb
1895	Despite petitions by Kanpō practitioners following strict licensure requirements enacted in 1863, the legal practice of Kanpō becomes impossible due to a ruling by the Japanese government
1910	Wada Keijūrō publishes a book addressing Kanpō, *Ikai no Tettsui* (The Iron Hammer of the Medical World)
1927	Yumoto Kyūshin publishes another book on Kanpō, *Kōkan Igaku* (Japanese-Chinese Medicine)
1937	A course on Kanpō medicine is set up at Takushoku University
1938	The Association of East-Asian Medicine is established
1950	The Japan Society for Oriental Medicine, now the central organization for research on East Asian Medicine, is established
1976	Ministry of Health and Welfare approves 82 prescriptions of the Kanpō formulas for coverage by the national health insurance
1998	The Government obliges acupuncture and moxibustion practitioners to pass a national qualifying examination to obtain a license to practice these treatments
2001	The Japanese government proposes a model core curriculum for medical schools that includes teaching about East Asian Medicine

Since 1938, a number of organizations have been established to promote East Asian medicine. The Association of East Asian Medicine was established in 1938; the Japan Society for Oriental Medicine, now the primary organization for research on East Asian Medicine, was established in 1950; and the Institute of Natural Medicine, the first full-scale institute for Chinese and Japanese drugs, was established at the University of Toyama in 1963 (Leslie, 1977). At the same time, the foundations for modern East Asian medical education were laid. In 1937, a course on Kanpō medicine was set up at Takushoku University. Later, Toyama Medical and Pharmaceutical University (established in 1975 and merged into University of Toyama in 2005) and some other universities also started Kanpō courses (Dharmananda, 2001; Shibata & Wu, 1997).

The last several decades witnessed the emergence of Kanpō into the medical classroom. According to a national survey conducted in 1998, only about 20 percent of medical schools had a curriculum on Kanpō medicine (Nishimura, Plotnikoff, & Watanabe, 2009; Tsuruoka, Tsuruoka, & Kajii, 2001). However, in 2001, the Ministry of

Education, Culture, Sports, Science and Technology announced the Medical Education Model Core Curriculum, that included education about Kanpō, and it became a topic integrated into the core curriculum of medical schools. By 2004, Japanese Kanpō education had assumed a place in the curriculum in all medical schools (Ministry of Education, Culture, Sports, Science and Technology, 2011).

Today, acupuncture and moxibustion are widely accepted and used in many settings. By the end of 2000, there were 94 colleges and vocational schools in Japan for seeing, as well as blind, students to learn acupuncture and moxibustion. Three-year programs in vocational schools are most common. The first national qualifying examination was given in 1993, and passing the examination is necessary to obtain a license from the Minister of Health, Labour and Welfare (Japan Society of Acupuncture and Moxibustion, 2005; Yamada, 2005). According to the Japan Society of Acupuncture and Moxibustion website, in 2012 there were 85 acupuncture schools for sighted, non-visually impaired students, and 69 acupuncture schools for the visually impaired (Japan Society of Acupuncture and Moxibustion, 2012).

EDUCATION IN WESTERN MEDICINE

As discussed in detail in 'A Brief History of Japanese Medicine' Chapter 14, Western medicine was introduced in the mid-sixteenth century. Direct cultural exchange between Europe and Japan began in 1549, when Francisco de Xavier (1506–1552), a Jesuit missionary, came to Japan to teach Christianity. From the middle of the fifteenth century to the middle of the sixteenth century, the Portuguese introduced Western medicine to Japan as part of their missionary work. However, in 1641, the Japanese government, fearing foreign influence, officially adopted a national isolation policy (*Sakoku* policy) that closed all ports in Japan except for one called Dejima, in Nagasaki. This national isolation lasted until 1853, when the American Admiral Matthew Perry forced Japan to open its doors to trade. During these 200+ years of isolation, only Dutch and Chinese merchants were permitted to trade at Dejima in Nagasaki. The body of knowledge developed by Japan through its contacts with the Dutch enclave of Dejima was called '*Rangaku*,' which literally means 'Dutch Studies'. Medical training during this period could be acquired by attending a private medical school, or a cram school (*juku*), or by taking an apprenticeship with a medical practitioner. For example, Philipp von Siebold (1796–1866) established the famous Narutaki Cram School (Narutaki-Juku), during this time. Many pupils studied Dutch there and observed Siebold's clinical work (Izumi &

Isozumi, 2001) (Print 16.1). As there were no academic medical institutions during this time, the transmission of medical knowledge in Japan occurred almost entirely as a private matter through apprenticeship (Jannetta, 2007).

After Japan opened its doors to trade with the US and other Western countries in 1853, Japan rapidly introduced Western medicine (Table 16.2). The Japanese government chose to adopt German medicine as a model in 1869, and it became the primary influence on mainstream medical education in Japan until the end of World War II. Not surprisingly, the government's decision resulted in medical education within universities and colleges during the 1870s and 1880s resembling the German medical education system. Medical education was structured as a 3-year, pre-medical period followed by 5 years of clinical training. At this time, the most common approach to medical training was via an apprenticeship or vocational training program in a government or other-approved hospital. For some time, doctors who were licensed to practice in this manner were in the majority, but their status was held to be inferior to that of graduates of the universities and colleges, even though the latter were fewer in number (Powell & Anesaki, 2010).

In 1857, one year before establishment of the *Shutōjo* (the Institute for Vaccination), a Dutch military surgeon, Pompe van Meerdervoort (1829–1908), was invited to teach at the Naval Training Institute in Nagasaki, an educational facility established in the

Table 16.2   Selected Western medicine education and development events

Year	Major Historical Events
1549	Francisco de Xavier, the first European to visit Japan, introduces Christianity and Western medicine concepts
1641	Japanese government officially adopts a national isolation policy, and strictly forbids foreign book importation
1853	Japan government rescinds isolation policy and open its doors to trade with the US and other Western countries
1869	Japanese government adopts German medicine as official model of medical education
1886–1911	Japan's original four imperial universities with medical departments are established: Imperial University (Tokyo Imperial University), 1886; Kyoto Imperial University, 1897; Tohoku Imperial University, 1907; Kyushu Imperial University, 1911
1918–1939	Three more Imperial medical schools are established in the Japan homeland: Hokkaido Imperial University (1918), Osaka Imperial University (1931), and Nagoya Imperial University (1939). Two additional Imperial medical schools are established overseas in line with conquests in Korea: Keijo Imperial University in 1924 (merged with 9 other colleges to form Seoul National University after World War II), and in Formosa, Taihoku Imperial University in 1928 (renamed National Taiwan University in 1945)
1939–1945	Rapid increase in number of medical technical colleges for the training of clinicians during World War II
1946–1950	Medical technical colleges that satisfy the requirements to become universities do so, while other medical technical colleges are abolished
1970–1979	34 medical schools are newly established, the so-called *Shinsetsu Ika Daigaku* (Newly Established Medical Universities)
2004	National medical schools become independent organizations under the National University Corporation Law

Print 16.1 Narutaki Cram School (Narutaki Juku)

Souce: Nagasaki University Library

latter part of the Edo period (1603–1867). In 1861, he opened the first Western style hospital affiliated with a modern medical school in Nagasaki. This hospital, *Nagasaki Yōjōsho*, was renamed *Seitokukan* in 1865, and became the predecessor of the Nagasaki Medical School (*Nagasaki Igakkō*). Because of its stature as the first Imperial university, it is sometimes mistakenly assumed University of Tokyo is the oldest Western-style medical school in Japan. Actually, it wasn't until 1877, 16 years after the establishment of the medical school at Nagasaki, that the University of Tokyo Medical School was first established. When Emperor Meiji moved the Imperial Court from Kyoto to Tokyo, the center of medical education also shifted from Nagasaki to Tokyo (Bowers, 1965).

ORIGINS OF JAPANESE MEDICAL SCHOOLS

There are 80 medical schools in Japan[2] (Table 16.3). Based on their origins, they can be organized into five groups: (1) original imperial universities (*Kyū-Teikoku Daigaku*); (2) original three private universities (*Shiritsu Idai Gosanke*); (3) original medical universities (*Kyūsei Ika Daigaku*) established in the early 1920s; (4) original medical technical colleges (*Kyū Igaku Semmon Gakkō*); and (5) 'new medical schools' (*Shinsetsu-Ika-Daigaku*) established in the 1970s. Table 16.3 lists the current 80 medical schools with their historic

roots. The significance of these groupings lies with prestige and the current scope of influence, with the oldest generally having the greatest scope of influence and the more recent a lesser scope of influence within academic medicine.

The Reign of Imperial Universities

At the end of the nineteenth century, the Japanese government sought to construct a new educational system by placing imperial universities on the top of its hierarchical structure. Tokyo Imperial University, Kyoto Imperial University, Tohoku Imperial University, and Kyushu Imperial University were Japan's original four Imperial universities with medical departments. In accordance with the Medical Practitioner Law of 1906, the licensing of medical practitioners was restricted to graduates of universities or colleges subject to regulation by the education authorities.

Following the outbreak of World War I and prior to World War II, three more Imperial Medical Schools were created (Hokkaido Imperial University, Osaka Imperial University, and Nagoya Imperial University) bringing the total number to seven (Bowers, 1965). The order of the schools' establishment was Imperial University (Tokyo Imperial University) in 1886, Kyoto Imperial University in 1897, Tohoku Imperial University in 1907, Kyushu Imperial University in 1911, Hokkaido Imperial University

Table 16.3   Medical schools in Japan

National universities (N=43)	Prefectural medical schools (N=8)	Private medical schools (N=29)
• Akita University[e]	• Fukushima Medical University[d]	• Aichi Medical University[e]
• Asahikawa Medical University[e]	• Kyoto Prefectural University of	• Dokkyo Medical University[e]
• Chiba University[c]	Medicine[c]	• Fujita Health University[e]
• Ehime University[e]	• Nagoya City University[d]	• Fukuoka University[e]
• Fukui University[e]	• Nara Medical University[d]	• Hyogo College of Medicine[e]
• Gifu University[d]	• Osaka City University[d]	• Iwate Medical University[d]
• Gunma University[d]	• Sapporo Medical University[d]	• Jichi Medical School[e]
• Hamamatsu University School of	• Wakayama Medical University[d]	• Jikei University School of Medicine[b]
Medicine[e]	• Yokohama City University[d]	• Juntendo University[d]
• Hirosaki University[d]		• Kanazawa Medical University[e]
• Hiroshima University[d]		• Kansai Medical University[d]
• Hokkaido University[a]		• Kawasaki Medical School[e]
• Kagawa University[e]		• Keio University[b]
• Kagoshima University[d]		• Kinki University[e]
• Kanazawa University[c]		• Kitasato University[e]
• Kobe University[d]		• Kurume University[d]
• Kochi University[e]		• Kyorin University[e]
• Kumamoto University[c]		• Nihon University[b]
• Kyoto University[a]		• Nippon Medical School[b]
• Kyushu University[a]		• Osaka Medical College[d]
• Mie University[d]		• Saitama Medical School[e]
• Nagasaki University[c]		• Showa University[d]
• Nagoya University[a]		• St. Marianna University School of
• National Defense Medical College[e]		Medicine[e]
• Niigata University[c]		• Teikyo University[e]
• Oita University[e]		• Toho University[d]
• Okayama University[c]		• Tokai University[e]
• Osaka University[a]		• Tokyo Medical University[d]
• Saga University[e]		• Tokyo Women's Medical University[d]
• Shiga University of Medical Science[e]		• University of Occupational and
• Shimane University[e]		Environmental Health[e]
• Shinshu University[d]		
• Tohoku University[a]		
• Tokyo Medical and Dental University[d]		
• Tottori University[d]		
• University of Miyazaki[e]		
• University of the Ryukyus[e]		
• University of Tokushima[d]		
• University of Tokyo[a]		
• University of Toyama[e]		
• University of Tsukuba[e]		
• University of Yamanashi[e]		
• Yamagata University[e]		
• Yamaguchi University[d]		

a-Original system Imperial university (*Kyū Teikoku Daigaku*)

b-Original private medical university (*Shiritsu Kyūsei Ika Daigaku*): another term *Shiritsu Idai Gosanke* (three houses of private medical universities), referring to Keio, Jikei, and Nippon medical universities, describes the three private schools established before the addition of the Nihon University that introduced a medical department during World War II

c-Original system medical university (*Kyūsei Ika Daigaku*)

d-Original medical technical university (*Kyu Igaku Semmon Gakkō*)

e-Newly established medical school established in 1970s (*Shinsetsu Ika Daigaku*) in 1918, Osaka Imperial University in 1931, and Nagoya Imperial University in 1939. Furthermore, two Imperial schools were established overseas in line with conquests in Korea and Taiwan. Keijo Imperial University was established in Seoul in 1924 and Taihoku Imperial University in Taiwan in 1928.

Imperial universities placed priority on research and education and led the field of medical education in Japan by sending faculty to other medical schools. In contrast, three large private medical schools – Keio University, Jikei University School of Medicine, and Nippon Medical School – were established to train clinicians. These schools were called 'the big three of private medical schools' *(Shiritsu Idai Gosanke)* because they were the only medical schools that were permitted to be universities during the Taisho Era (1912–1926).

World War II Period Changes in Training

During World War II, the Japanese government faced a shortage of clinical doctors, leading to a rapid increase in the number of medical technical colleges that trained clinicians. The bolus of practitioners trained in the technical colleges formed a significant component of the Japanese practitioner workforce for many decades. After the end of World War II in 1945, some technical colleges that satisfied the requirements to become universities did so, while other medical technical colleges were abolished. The oversight of medical training and affairs was divided. The Ministry of Education would address educational policy and the Ministry of Health, Labour and Welfare would address health care policy. The transition from medical students as medical school-based learners to residents in hospitals reflects a change in the controlling ministry from the former to the latter. While one would hope for seamless transitions and collaborations, this has not always been the case.

Economic Growth and Rural-urban Physician Distribution

During the period of rapid economic growth from the mid-1950s to early 1990s, medical facilities were more likely to be constructed in large cities. This increasingly led to uneven distribution of health care services, with a concentration in the cities at the expense of rural areas. The poor distribution of physicians became socially problematic. With the intent to solve the rural–urban discrepancy and meet the increasing demand for health care services, the government increased the number of medical schools, aiming for 'one

university with a medical department for each prefecture.' From the mid-1960s to the 1980s, the number of national medical schools expanded from 24 to 43, and the number of private schools expanded from 13 to 29, while the number of prefectural schools remained constant. This increase was particularly notable during the 1970s, when 34 medical schools were newly established. The total number of medical schools had now expanded from 46 to 80 (Orie, 2003; Suzuki, Gibbs, & Fujisaki, 2008). Many of these medical colleges are independent colleges without other degree granting programs, though others may have additional degree programs in health sciences. For example, the Shiga University of Medical Science includes medical education and nursing education programs. Of the 80 medical schools in Japan in 2012, 43 are national (including the National Defense Medical College), 8 are public (founded by a local government), and 29 are private (Kozu, 2006; Suzuki et al., 2008) (Table 16.3).

Public Universities

Public universities (particularly national universities) rather than private universities are generally the most prestigious and competitive institutions. The former imperial universities, in particular, are very competitive. These institutions tend to attract the most academically talented individuals and their faculty compete successfully for research grants from the government.

Private Universities

Private universities, especially the most recently established, generally have more lenient admission criteria, but tuition tends to be much more expensive than the national universities. These schools tend to have a higher percentage of students who are the children of physicians who can afford the expensive tuition. Student scores in the national licensing examination – a criterion often used for national rankings and institutional prestige – tend to be lower for these universities.

One unique private university, Jichi Medical School, was formed through an alliance of the 47 prefectures, the so-called *todōfuken*. The mission of Jichi Medical School is to train physicians for care in rural areas (Inoue, Hirayama, & Igarashi, 1997). Each of the contributing governments of the prefectures sends two students per year. Jichi Medical School exempts students from paying tuition as long as they return to their home region and work for 9 years in a shortage area chosen by the sponsoring government entity. Within the first 24 years of its establishment, 792 (42 percent) graduates had practiced in a rural area (Inoue et al., 1997).

IKYOKU-KŌZA AND JITTSU SYSTEM IN JAPAN

Discussion about medical education in Japan would be incomplete without an introduction of the *ikyoku-kōza* and *jittsu* system (Onishi & Yoshida, 2004; Teo, 2007; Yoshida, 2011). The *ikyoku*, that is clinical departments, in each medical school have influence over a clinical content area, related undergraduate and graduate education, as well as research. The *jittsu* (derived from the German word *sitz* and reflecting persistent German influences on medicine in Japan), are often compared to the hierarchical structure of feudal times. Under this system the *ikyokuchō*, i.e. head of the *ikyoku*, dictates matters relative to clinical care, education, and research within the clinical department in the hospital. Based on personal connections and historical relationships, the *ikyokuchō* dictates where *ikyoku*-trained physicians will work. Affiliated hospitals, the *jittsu*, must maintain a good relation with the *ikyokuchō* because they depend upon a regular flow of clinicians to the affiliated hospitals. Given the lack of a specialty matching system (see later discussion of the matching system for preliminary postgraduate training), young physicians depend on the *ikyokuchō* for placement for advanced residency training and clinical appointments in affiliated hospitals. They entrust, though not always enthusiastically, the *ikyokuchō* with their overall professional development and understand their placement in affiliated hospitals will be determined by overall needs, as viewed by the *ikyokuchō*, as well as their individual needs. Affiliated *jittsu* hospitals are eager for, and often depend upon, these connections because a powerful *ikyokuchō* can serve as a consistent source of physician manpower. Without an *ikyokuchō* connection, hospitals, especially rural ones or those located in less socially desirable areas, face great difficulty finding physicians to staff their hospitals.

Academic departments are referred to by the name *kōza* and have the distinction of being able to award the doctoral degree, *igakuhakase*, doctorate of medicine to students who favorably complete requirements of the *kōza*. Obtaining the stature bestowed by *igakuhakase* is essentially a prerequisite for a career in academic medicine, and earning this degree provides prestige. Each medical school therefore has a series of *ikyoku-kōza*. These tend to be organized by specialty, but not exclusively so. For example, the internal medicine-related departments would typically have three departments – the first, second, and third departments of internal medicine. There will be some variation by institution but, for example, the first department of internal medicine may represent cardiology and renal; the second,

pulmonary and endocrine; and the third, gastroenterology and hematology. Within these 'fiefdoms,' a hierarchical structure exists. Onishi highlights three issues that arise under the *ikyoku-kōza* system: (1) the clinical service, education, and research are all provided by the same group of people; (2) members of an *ikyoku-kōza* work together like a family; and (3) conflicts with other departments about any matter such as academic appointments, educational duty, budgets, etc. become political issues (Onishi & Yoshida, 2004). Even individuals who opt out of climbing the academic ladder any further, or those who cannot because of bad timing relative to the hierarchy of age and therefore leave the university, still remain part of the *ikyoku*. Typically, such individuals transition into private practitioners. Frequently, they open their practices in geographical proximity to the *ikyoku*, retain patients they have met through the *ikyoku*, and use the *ikyoku* for inpatient services. This arrangement provides a buffer for maintaining the integrity of the *ikyoku* system among those who are its members. Going into private practice provides an alternative work option that is also much more lucrative when progressing up the hierarchical ladder in the *ikyoku* is not possible (Yoshida, 2011).

Because Japanese medical departments are much smaller than many other countries, there is usually only one professor per department, and this person functions fully as a department chair, or division chief in the U.S. The professor of each department typically moves upwards internally based on a combination of excellent skills in research, such as grant funding and publication record, as well as luck relative to the timing of mandatory retirement of senior leadership. When a suitable candidate does not develop, or is not present, then external candidates may be hired. Mid-level faculty who mature, but fail to meet the criteria for promotion can create dilemmas for medical schools if the person's clinical skills are essential, but the other credentials lag. The ability to transition well from a successful researcher to *ikyokuchō* requires astute political and administrative skills. An incoming *ikyokuchō*'s success in this transition will determine the overall success of the *ikyoku* and all its members. Moreover, the *ikyokuchō* provides the leadership for introductions of faculty for the clinical needs of the *jittsu* hospitals (Yoshida, 2011).

GOVERNMENTAL AND ACADEMIC STAKEHOLDERS IN MEDICAL EDUCATION

External to the *ikyokuchō*, medical school dean, and patient groups, there are a number of stakeholders in medical education in Japan. From a regulatory perspective, the Ministry of Education, Culture, Sports, Science and Technology (MEXT) bears responsibility for all aspects of undergraduate medical examination except for the national licensure examination. Starting with the national licensure examination, the Ministry of Health, Labour and Welfare bears responsibility for all postgraduate aspects of medical education. There are a series of academic stakeholders as well. Founded in 1967, the Association of Japan Medical Colleges (AJMC) represents the deans and presidents of university hospitals. The Japan Society of Medical Education (JSME) was founded a short time later in 1969, and the Japan Medical Education Foundation (JMEF) followed 10 years after in 1979. JMEF founders sought to develop research and research instruments addressing common problems to all medical schools. Finally, the Foundation for Promotion of Medical Training (PMET), formed in 1995, focused on training in faculty development. PMET holds a workshop about training for clinician-educators every year under the leadership of the Ministry of Health, Labour and Welfare. PMET also constructed a system that provides/collects information about medical training via the Internet that contributes to efficient distribution of information (Foundation For Promotion of Medical Training, 2011).

ACHIEVING ENTRANCE INTO MEDICAL SCHOOL

The story of medical education would be incomplete without a discussion about the requirement of the pre-admission educational system. Generally, applicants seek matriculation directly out of high school. Ninety percent of medical students are accepted directly from secondary schools, while 10 percent have other college experience (Suzuki et al., 2008). Most students take the common national entrance examination (National Center for University Entrance Examinations, 2011). Though it is an independent administrative institution, the National Center for University Entrance Exams (*Dokuritsu Gyōsei Hōjin Daigaku Nyūshi Center*, DNC) operates under control of MEXT. All of the medical schools rely on a written entrance examination and some combination of essays, high school grade point average, and letter of recommendation from the high school principal (Kozu, 2006). Entrance examinations weigh most heavily in the admissions process, and the system selects students who excel at test taking.

Nearly half of Japanese medical colleges accept for entry applicants who have completed college education elsewhere, although depending on the school, these so-called *hennyū* entrants will still be required to take 4 or 5 years of the 6-year curriculum. These positions are limited to only 10 percent of students per class. It remains unusual, but some medical colleges accept students who have completed education in other fields or who have work experience. Even if a student has completed relevant coursework at another university, for example in biology, functionally there is no or very little 'transfer credit.' Officially, medical schools state that students need exposure to the same subjects as their classmates. One might speculate that accepting students into an upper level class without the requirement to take the first 1–2 years would result in lost revenue for the medical school. Tuition is a source of funding, and the medical school would lose money if transfer students could opt out of 1 or 2 years of tuition when they transfer. Consequently, the student composition in Japanese medical schools remains remarkably homogeneous. The student body as a whole will have less diversity in life experiences or breadth of study than one finds in alternative systems that encourage a broad spectrum of experiences prior to matriculation to medical school. The one major demographic shift has been the growing number of female medical students within the student body, nearly half in some medical schools. In 2006, nearly one-third of all medical students were female (Kozu, 2006). The number of female medical students in 2013–14 academic year was 8,936 corresponding to 30.9 percent of all medical students. If students from Dentistry, Pharmacy and other health-related departments are included, the percent of female students is 49.7 percent of health professions students and 50 percent for national universities (Government Statistics for Japan, 2014).

MEDICAL SCHOOL CURRICULUM

Medical education lasts 6 years, with a general structure of 2 years general curriculum, 2 years of basic science, and then 2 years of clinical education. Many equate the first 2 years to a truncated undergraduate education (possible in part due to the rigors of secondary school in Japan) and the final 4 years as equivalent to a graduate medical course. The 6-year course is quite similar to that of many European countries, though fundamentally, all who matriculate in Japan are expected to graduate. Upon graduation, medical students receive their degree as a physician. The curriculum was rather static through the 1980s (Table 16.4), but many changes have occurred in Japan since the 1990s, including the introduction of problem-based learning, the common achievement test, medical simulation, and clinical teaching and learning (Table 16.5).

Table 16.4   Key events in Japanese medical education since World War II

Year	Major Historical Events
1946	The first postgraduate training system is established and a one-year internship mandated
1962	Japanese Society of Anesthesiologists becomes established as first specialty system in Japan
1968	The first postgraduate training system is eliminated and replaced by a non-compulsory two-year postgraduate clinical training system
1970s	Establishment of medical specialties systems accelerates
1981	An organization, later becoming the current Japanese Board of Medical Specialties, is founded with the aim to redress the gaps among professional associations
1987	Japan Medical Association establishes a continuing medical education system and encourages lifelong learning among physicians
1995	The Science and Technology Basic Law is enacted, and the government increases the budget for research and development in the fields of science and technology
2002	Ministry of Health, Labour and Welfare allows physicians qualified as specialists by the relevant professional associations to announce their official qualifications as medical specialists
2004	Ministry of Health, Labour and Welfare introduces a compulsory two-year postgraduate clinical training system and an internship-matching system

Table 16.5   Two decades of change in undergraduate Japanese medical education

Change	Explanation	Comment
Problem-based learning (PBL) (Onishi & Yoshida, 2004; Suzuki, et al., 2008; Teo, 2007)	First introduced in 1990, used by most medical schools to some extent today	The limited number of faculty required for teaching persists as a barrier to integration, and problem-based learning remains relatively minor
Common Achievement Test (Kozu, 2006; Onishi & Yoshida, 2004; Suzuki, et al., 2008)	Introduced in 2005 and utilized by all medical schools at the end of the 6th (last) year of medical school, involves a computer-based test and an Objective Structured Clinical Examination (OSCE)	Assures a minimal level of knowledge and competence in basic clinical examination skills
Medical simulation and standardized patient training	Most medical schools have incorporated to some level	Standardized patients focus mostly on communications skills and some very basic clinical examination skills
Two-year mandatory internship for post-graduate training (*shoki kenshu*) (Kozu, 2006; Onishi & Yoshida, 2004; Teo, 2007)	Implemented in April 2004, all medical graduates who want to practice clinical medicine must complete a two-year structured training program	This two-year program is most like the US fourth year of medical school and first-year internship in terms of content and expectations; quality of clinical experiences and development as a clinician varies significantly
Matching system for two-year mandatory internship for post-graduate training (Teo, 2007; Kozu, 2006; Onishi & Yoshida, 2004)	Medical students use the matching system to choose their two-year mandatory internship for post-graduate training	Match results are released prior to students taking the national licensure examination; matching does not guarantee a preliminary two-year clinical training position until successful passing of the national licensure examination in March

The General Education Years

As medicine remains a popular career choice, applicants must prove themselves highly competitive on the entrance examination to gain admission to medical school. The curriculum for newly matriculated students in the first 2 years focuses on subjects such as biology, chemistry, physics, mathematics, English, and some other liberal arts topics, although the bulk of their education focuses on science. Starting in the second year and continuing into the third year, students begin taking courses in basic medical sciences, for example anatomy, immunology, pathology, pharmacology, and physiology. The curriculum, as set by the school, offers few opportunities for students to take interdisciplinary courses or with other health professions students. As medical schools tend to focus on providing skills required for research or clinical care, other than intense studies in high school and general education in the first 2 years of medical school, there is minimal exposure to the liberal arts in the creation of the physician work force. A critique of this approach is that medical graduates will have less connection with the arts and humanities, and may be less able to relate at a humanistic level to the general population.

Matriculating medical students generally start around the age of 18 or 19, usually directly out of high school or a 1-year cram school, and the first 2 years are similar to the first 2 years of college, with the associated newfound freedom and independence. Undergraduate students often take part-time jobs or participate in clubs *(bukatsu)* and frequently compete with clubs from other medical schools in sporting events or competitions. Anecdotally, course work during these years, much like the course work of their age-matched cohorts in other universities in Japan, requires relatively little effort (Teo, 2007).

Basic Medical Science Years

Third and fourth year medical students principally take courses organized by clinical specialties, for example cardiology, gastroenterology, infectious disease, neurology, obstetrics and gynecology, and others. The duration of rotation in each specialty is usually two weeks, the same for major and minor specialties. In addition to the basic sciences in the third year, and clinical sciences in the fourth year, students take some coursework designed to introduce them to the skills necessary for interacting with patients, such as interviewing and examination skills. Topics are taught mainly along specialty lines and it seems that there are few, if any, institutions pursuing an integrated systems-based view of teaching rather than the traditional organ-based view.[3] Many schools have integrated some level of problem-based learning, but the large number of teaching staff required is prohibitive for extensive adoption due to the relatively few number of instructors (see later under Medical Education Departments). As a rule, students are expected to be able to demonstrate a set minimum of clinical skills. Successfully passing an OSCE (Objective Structured Clinical Examination) evaluation is required for advancement in the curriculum and for participation in clinical rotations. Notable gaps in the medical curricula of most Japanese medical schools includes family planning/contraception and physical examination skills for male and female genitalia. The curriculum has consistently included introductory material on East Asian medicine since 2004 (Ministry of Education, Culture, Sports, Science and Technology, 2011).

The Clinical Years of Medical School During the Fifth and Sixth Years

Due to greater public expectation for clinical competency and student desire for greater skills in clinical medicine, there were significant efforts by Japanese medical schools to improve clinical training in the first decade of the twenty-first century (Table 16.5).

Undergraduate Clinical Education

At the time of writing, the clinical rotations, *rinshō jishū*, span a period of about 46 weeks, substantively fewer months than many medical education systems in the world. The bulk of this training occurs during the fifth year. The fifth year of education parallels that of the third-year system in the US because students are on the wards, but it differs dramatically in terms of content and, particularly, responsibility. Rotations in many schools tend to be set for exactly the same duration in each department, for example 2 weeks, resulting in students getting a sampling of all medical specialties rather than an immersion in clinical care. Briefly, clinical learning during rotations in Japan is passive, and has been called 'osmotic learning' (Inada, Mitsunami, Motohara, & Fetters, 2010) in the sense that students passively watch senior physicians and are expected to absorb the knowledge of the faculty attending. Known in Japan as *minarai* (literally, see–learn), students have little opportunity for hands-on experience and virtually no responsibility for patient care. Another downside of the 2-week rotation system is that it takes students a week to become oriented to new departments and develop rapport with supervising physicians. By the end of the second week, when students have just become comfortable with the environment and styles of supervising physicians, their rotations are over. For faculty, there are few rewards other than personal gratification, to supervising physicians for teaching excellence. Medical students may be considered as a burden, and may be relegated into the position of observers where they receive little opportunity for hands-on learning or direct teaching.

Many observers compare the Japanese fifth year to the third year in US medical schools because this is a time when medical students have their first systematic exposure to clinical medicine in a setting with patients. On the whole, one would expect that over the course of a year, students' clinical skills would gradually grow. In short, they would transition from being 'book smart' to 'clinically smart.' The reality is that clinical rotations for medical students in Japan involve relatively little patient interaction and virtually no responsibility. While students may be 'assigned' to one or two patients, it is not unusual for a pair of students to be assigned to a single patient. Students are expected to observe on clinical rounds, form study groups, and talk about the patients seen, but they primarily observe (Teo, 2007). Activities like conducting clinically relevant literature reviews or guidelines, writing patient progress notes, or making case presentations seldom occur. Students might spend an entire week preparing a case presentation of one patient who had already been discharged or whose clinical work-up had been completed. Students typically do not have responsibility for real-time work-ups of newly admitted patients or discussing medical decision making or differential diagnosis development in a way that contributes to patient care. They are not permitted to participate in even basic clinical activities, such as blood drawing, as this is considered medical care that requires a medical license. While efforts are underway for changes, Japanese medical students do not seem to be considered as a member of the medical team or contributors to patient care or team education (Pesch, 2011).

Japanese Sixth and Final year – The Clinical Educational Content

Medical education observers also often compare the sixth year of medical school in Japan to the fourth year of medical school in the US. While this appears logical, the content of the final year of training differs dramatically. Medical students in the US can take Step 2 of the three-step United States Medical Licensing Examination (USMLE) during their fifth year, while Japanese medical students take their board examination in the last month of their sixth year. Consequently, the fifth year of medical school for students in Japan serves as the bulk of their limited clinical education. A typical Japanese sixth-year student has clinical rotations for only 2–3 months, including elective time. During these set blocks at the beginning of the academic year, students often schedule rotations in one or more hospitals that they are considering for residency training. Eager to show prospective candidates the opportunities for clinical training, supervising physicians (i.e., other residents and faculty) on community rotations often provide more opportunity for hands-on clinical care than the university-based hospital rotations. During set window of time, some senior medical students take a month or two for an international rotation, although finding destinations for students abroad is a challenge for medical institutions. Most activities are self-pay, and there are few scholarships for study abroad. Remarkably, there is a very brief period of active involvement in clinical care in the final year of medical school.

Senior Student Seclusion to Study for the Licensure Examination

Despite recent literature examining the state of medical education and its reform in Japan, relatively little discussion addresses what we term 'senior student seclusion.' (Teo, 2007; Suzuki, Gibbs & Fujisaki, 2008; Terasaki, 2011) During the final 8–9 months of the sixth and final year of medical school, students are excused from most college-based activities, including patient care, in order to study for the national licensure exam. The only exception might be a single weekly lecture or forum for announcements. As the national medical licensure examination is offered only once a year, failure to pass the examination will paralyze advancement of one's career for at least another year until there is an opportunity to retake the examination. In contrast to the US where students take the licensure examination in steps that cover material appropriate to the stage of learning, the Japanese licensure examination, a single test, includes many basic science questions about material covered early in the medical school curriculum, though this has gradually improved. Students often complain that the most difficult questions address esoteric, basic science material with little relevance to clinical care, the clinical knowledge and skills that the students will need in their next phase of professional life as residents. Ironically, participating in clinical care would actually be a hindrance to achieving an excellent score on the licensure examination and hence a barrier to passing the national board examination.[4]

The Cost of Senior Student Seclusion

In contrast, a widely held premise of medical education in the US is that the learner should have incrementally increasing experience and responsibility relative to the next stage of development. For example, during their fourth (senior) year of medical school, US students have ever-increasing responsibilities, albeit under close supervision of an experienced physician. Clinical functions include taking an appropriate history and documenting it for a sick patient, draft order writing, performing necessary medical procedures, discharge planning, teaching third year medical students, etc. Medical schools require students to participate in an 'acting internship' in a critical care specialty rotation, for example in an intensive care unit (ICU) or cardiac care unit (CCU). During this time, the students work in nearly the same fashion as the first year graduates, namely interns. While US students also use time in their last year for interviewing for residency, the senior year is considered critical for the transition to becoming a clinician.

Apathy to Change of the Senior Student Seclusion Status Quo

There seems to be little concern among medical educators about the prolonged period of senior student seclusion in Japan. First, the medical schools want students to study intensively and achieve the highest possible marks on the national licensure examination because a primary criteria for medical school rankings in Japan is student scores and passage percentage on the exam; second, while obvious, but seldom mentioned, medical schools collect senior year tuition with virtually no teaching costs; third, students are practically minded and realize that passing the examination is a critical next step in their career trajectories. Failure will place them in the unenviable position of being *rōnin*, namely, a 'master-less samurai' for a year while they prepare to take the examination over again a year later. Hence, students are reluctant to demand more clinical time if it comes at the cost of their precious study time. The sixth year student seclusion, the most critical year of education, illustrates that the emphasis in Japanese medical schools is passage of the national licensure examination rather than producing graduates equipped with applied clinical skills.

The Educational Commission for Foreign Medical Graduates (ECFMG®) in September, 2010, announced new international standards that are projected to take effect in 2023 and will require students who wish to be eligible to have postgraduate clinical training in the US to have substantively more clinical experience than in Japan.

Based on conversations with a number of deans in various Japanese medical schools, most medical schools anticipate expanding the fifth year, rather than intrude on the intensive study period of the sixth year that is deemed critical for study time to pass the National Medical Examination.

CHANGES IN JAPANESE MEDICAL EDUCATION

Though historically very conservative, a particularly large number of reforms have occurred in medical education in the last two decades (Table 16.5). Most medical schools have experimented with and implemented some level of integrated curricula, problem-based learning, and pre-clerkship clinical skills teaching. During the early-to mid-2000s, the Japanese government also implemented changes to postgraduate medical education, including a new postgraduate residency program that requires 2 years of postgraduate training and a 2-year preliminary postgraduate training matching system. Medical schools throughout the country are now observing and incorporating modern medical education and faculty development (Kozu, 2006; Smith, 2005; Suzuki et al., 2008; Teo, 2007). In 2004, all national schools became independent organizations under the National University Corporation, although the corporation itself remains under governmental control. This change required the universities to take responsibility for their own finances and financial management. To cope with this change, seven of the 12 stand-alone national medical schools had merged with their neighboring national universities by 2006 (Kozu, 2006; Suzuki et al., 2008).

Medical Teachers Working in Medical Schools

Many studies have discussed Japan's shortage of doctors. A lesser-known issue regards the shortage of teaching physicians (Ito et al., 2007). According to the *School Fundamentals Survey, 2011* of the Ministry of Education, Culture, Sports, Science and Technology, the total number of staff in medical departments in Japan, including professors, associate professors, lecturers, assistant professors and instructors, is 21,999. In contrast, the number of students in medical departments is 50,235 (School Fundamentals Survey, 2011). A simple calculation of dividing the number of students by that of staff yields a ratio of 2.3 students to one teaching staff member on average. Citing an example of Tohoku University and several representative universities in the US and the UK, Ito and colleagues demonstrate that the number of faculty at that particular medical school in Japan is only one-third to one-fifth of that in the US and UK (Ito et al., 2007).[5] A daunting issue not clear from this calculation is an even greater difference during clinical education years. The reduced numbers of teaching staff in the preclinical years render small group teaching much more difficult to accomplish. But the real eye-opener is in clinical departments. For example, while family medicine remains a relatively new specialty in the US, the University of Michigan's Department of Family Medicine (UMDFM) – the home institution of one of us (MF) – has approximately 70 faculty members. About 80 percent of this group primarily work as clinical educators, while approximately 20 percent are primarily researchers, although most also provide clinical care. All faculty are involved in medical education, for example resident and/or student education. While most third-year medical students rotate internally, the department also relies extensively on community preceptors (i.e. private practitioners) to help with teaching. This further expands the number of teaching physicians. In contrast, a department of general medicine (sōgōshinryōbu) in Japan might have about four full-time faculty and one or two research fellows or graduate students. The use of community preceptors in Japan occurs, but remains very limited. Consequently, the number of clinical teaching staff is roughly one-tenth of a large university system in US. Although general medicine remains a younger specialty in Japan than family medicine in the US, the ratio remains roughly the same for traditional departments, such as surgery or internal medicine.

There are more competing demands on the time of teaching physicians in Japan – virtually all the department faculty in Japan are expected to contribute to clinical care, education, and research activities. Moreover, faculty salaries are so low compared to general practitioners that many academic faculty moonlight in other hospitals.[6] While previous work highlights the staffing shortages in Japanese medical settings, this analysis illustrates that staffing shortage is particularly pronounced during clinical education years. With such profound differences in capacity and competing demands for the time of teaching faculty, the perilous implications for the quality and quantity of teaching becomes much more transparent.

National Licensure Examination

The physician national licensure examination (ishi kokka shiken) occurs once each year for 3 days in mid-February. Administered by the Ministry of Health, Labour and Welfare, the examination is offered in 12 sites across Japan. To sit for the examination, applicants must provide a certificate of completion of medical training in undergraduate medical education (usually from Japan, but those from selected foreign countries are also accepted). For a foreign medical graduate, the pathway for licensure in Japan remains extremely challenging and occurs on a diminishingly small frequency. Students who have already graduated in a previous year, are from a foreign school, or are eligible to graduate at the end of the academic year, March 31, can sit for the examination that year.

At the time of writing this chapter, the examination included 500 questions, 100 required items, 200 general questions and 200 clinical vignettes. To pass, one must answer correctly 80 percent of these. Since 2001, faculty of medical schools and teaching hospitals, as well as representatives from the Japan Medical Association, compose the test questions. In recent years, the passing rate of the exam has been about 90 percent. Students who pass receive a National Licensure for physicians and become eligible to then engage in the preliminary postgraduate internship training (shoki kenshū).[7]

UNDERGRADUATE MEDICAL EDUCATION REFORM

Japanese society is demanding more competence in clinical skills and general medical care. In addition, a growing number of medical students are demanding more from their medical education. In particular, students are hungry for more hands-on opportunities for learning. Medical education in Japan has been responsive on a number of fronts (see Table 16.5).

New Clinical Resident Training System

The first compulsory postgraduate training in Japan, a 1-year internship, began in 1946. Although this original internship system lasted for 22 years, it eventually collapsed and was eliminated in 1968 due to problems with inconsistent curricula and lack of financial support for interns. The lack of payment for the 1-year internship was the spark setting aflame student protests in 1968 at the University of Tokyo and across the nation. The 1-year compulsory system was replaced by a non-compulsory 2-year postgraduate clinical training system. Under this internship system, graduates were only advised to pursue at least 2 years of postgraduate training before setting up an independent practice. Thus, between 1968 and 2004, there was no postgraduate internship requirement, so it was possible, and became the norm, for graduates to move directly into specialty training (Kozu, 2006; Suzuki et al., 2008; Teo, 2007).

Challenges of the New System

There were multiple problems in this non-compulsory system. First, because training was likely to put an almost exclusive weight on a specialty, there were not many residents who were trained to be physicians with general competencies. This was particularly problematic due to the passive, osmotic learning approach during medical school (Inada et al., 2010). Young physicians in this era had very little systematic exposure to all fields of medicine. The public became increasingly dissatisfied and criticized that 'Japanese doctors look at the disease and not at the person.' The young doctors themselves were not really to be blamed. The system actually only prepared them to look at diseases, and most could competently care for only a very narrow spectrum of disease. Second, the financial support available to newly graduated residents was insufficient, and many of them found their training distracted by moonlighting because even working a few days a month could profoundly increase their personal income. Third, the training itself received poor evaluations and was ineffective in producing skilled clinicians. Fourth, residents and medical students had to negotiate directly with specific departments for a position, and consequently, residents tended to match within the academic institutions where they had trained because they had little opportunity to see other systems and were not encouraged to look because faculties preferred to hoard manpower. This dilemma resulted in 'in-breeding' as residents would not be exposed to other clinical approaches for similar clinical problems. For example, surgical residents might only be exposed to a limited number of surgical approaches, whilst there might be additional approaches less familiar to the surgeons in their particular institution.

As an acknowledgment of these problems, a new compulsory two-year postgraduate clinical training system was introduced in 2004. Under this system, all graduates are required to spend two years rotating through the seven main specialties (internal medicine, surgery, emergency medicine or anesthesiology, pediatrics, psychiatry, community-based medicine, and obstetrics and gynecology) in approved teaching and community hospitals. While the government anticipated this procedure would provide a solid grounding and effective training in primary care and foster general skills among Japanese physicians, we believe this is a misguided notion, because the required rotations are almost exclusively inpatient-based with no emphasis on outpatient practice where primary care occurs. This misperception – the belief that broad exposure to medical problems in the inpatient setting is appropriate to prepare physicians for primary care outpatient practice – is a pervasive problem in Japan, although Yoshida has recently recognized this system as inefficient (Yoshida, 2011). Under the new system, 'moonlighting' for these residents has been prohibited and residents are paid reasonably well (about four million yen, roughly \$40,000 USD, per year) so they can concentrate on their training. Following the pivotal case of a resident who died from excessive work *(karōshi)* (Kozu, 2006), in the new system, work hours are restricted to 40 hours per week during the first 2 years (although working well beyond this limit appears to be widespread) in order to protect new residents as laborers with reasonable hours and wages, while also allowing them to focus on their education.

Introduction of a Match System

At the same time in 2004, the Council for Matching, a non-governmental organization, introduced the first internship-matching system. The matching system enabled graduates to freely apply for the hospital of their interest for the internship. Unlike the previous system where the power to choose initial training primarily resided with the *ikyoku*, students could now rank their preferred location for clinical training. Prior to the matching system, there was a steady stream of new graduates, eager and possibly desperate, to secure a position within their own academic institutions because leaving the academic center would jeopardize, or was at least perceived to jeopardize, their future career planning. The results of the first match astonished many academic hospitals (Table 16.6). In the first matching year (2004), only 34.5 percent matched to the medical student's own university hospital, 18.2 percent matched to another university hospital, while a plurality, 47.3 percent, went to other teaching hospitals, mostly community-based hospitals approved by the Ministry of Health, Labour and Welfare (MHLW) (Kozu, 2006). Many observers believe that the passive nature of training in academic settings led to the exodus from academic institutions and into community setting. Flabbergasted, the academic hospitals suddenly found themselves in dire straits due to the lack of laborers.

This mass exodus to other hospitals highlighted the problems that beleaguered residency training in academic centers at the time. Case mixes in academic institutions tended to have unusual cases rather than general cases. Patients were often admitted with known diagnoses so admission work for many cases was perfunctory and did not require the resident to use clinical reasoning to work-up and treat them. Finally, the pecking order from senior to junior status, with the bottom rung scrambling for clinical scraps that landed on the floor, was obvious to medical students as they rotated on the wards.

Table 16.6   Distribution of medical student selection of residency institution in the 3-Year period surrounding the implementation of matching system in 2004

	2003		2004		2005	
	Number of students matched	%	Number of students matched	%	Number of students matched	%
Matched to the medical student's own university hospital	3,235	41.7	2,760	34.5	2,496	30.8
Matched to another university hospital	1,328	17.1	1,456	18.2	1,420	17.5
Went to other teaching hospitals that were approved by the MHLW	3,193	41.2	3,784	47.3	4,184	51.7
Total	7,756	100.0	8,000	100.0	8,100	100.0

Source: Japan Residency Matching Program (ND)

Suddenly and painfully, academic institutions realized they needed to compete for medical school graduates and offer them better quality experiences for broad medical training. This enormous shock to the system focused attention to heretofore threadbare educational approaches and policies, and became an important catalyst for initiatives to improve clinical education in academic settings. Time will tell if such initiatives will be sufficient to win back trainees to university hospital settings.

After completing the preliminary 2-year postgraduate training internship, trainees can proceed on one of three paths: (1) advanced clinical training as a specialist; (2) entering graduate school; or (3) serving as a general physician in the community, though few choose the latter option (Kozu, 2006).

ADVANCED POSTGRADUATE TRAINING – *KŌKI KENSHŪ*

After completion of the compulsory two-year clinical experience, a common pathway is the pursuit of advanced training as a medical specialist. Such training can be found in both the clinical departments of medical schools and teaching hospitals. The duration of advanced training depends on the program but takes generally 4–6 years. There has never been a matching program for such specialty training, and finding a program often requires the introduction of an esteemed professor or senior physician.

Certification Procedures

Trainees can sit for their specialty board examination as approved by respective academic societies after 5 years of training (including the first 2 years of preliminary clinical training, *shoki kenshū*).

Trainees who successfully complete these requirements earn the title of Board-Certified Medical Specialist. This requirement for new graduates to pass a board examination is a relatively recent phenomenon, and in the not-too-distant past, physicians could become a member of many specialty societies just by paying the annual dues. This history must be considered when making international comparisons on the numbers of specialists in Japan, particularly if one considers members to be active in the core activities of the specialty. As illustrated next, specialists who become private practitioners must often forego performing procedures defining their specialization because the specialty-defining procedures require hospital infrastructure, yet Japan lacks effective, open-access hospital systems (Asai & Fetters, 2010). In fact, most private physicians become hybrid primary care/specialists (Saigal, Takemura, Nishiue, & Fetters, 2007) with an ever-increasing proportion of their practice becoming primary care-oriented as their years in practice increase.

GRADUATE EDUCATION

Both medical and non-medical graduate courses are offered in all medical schools. Generally, master's degree coursework requires two years, and the doctor of medicine *igakuhakase* track is variable and often will be conferred upon completion of research of adequate quality. Many students in graduate courses are also working, and so it is not unusual for courses to be offered during non-traditional work hours. Many universities allow graduate students to pay tuition while independently conducting the research. Productivity in research is expected by Japanese medical institutions, and all graduate students actively pursue original research. Completion of the requirements results in the *igakuhakase*, Doctor of Philosophy of Medicine degree. This process contrasts to some European institutions where the Doctor of Philosophy is awarded from the college and in the US where one earns a Doctor of Philosophy in a particular field, for example pathology. Due to the structure of medical institutions, the vast majority of physicians who earn *igakuhakase,* do so by conducting basic research. Many Japanese medical researchers excel in their basic science research endeavors and are major players in contributing to global knowledge through their publications in the world's top ranking journals.

The quality of training in graduate coursework is varied. Curricula in graduate schools, based on an apprenticeship mode, are not well structured. Graduate students are dependent on the infrastructure of the labs where they work, and grants or fellowship funding for graduate students are sparse. The agreement of the *ikyokuchō*, chair (professor) is required for earning the *igakuhakase*. The criteria for awarding of the degree often hinges upon completion of the doctoral dissertation – publication of an original research article in an English-language journal may suffice[8]. The 'completion' of training will be determined by the professor, in as much by the needs of the *ikyoku* as by the research skills and independence of the graduate student.

MEDICAL SPECIALTIES SYSTEMS

Medical specialties systems in Japan have a history of about 50 years. In 1962, the Japanese Society of Anesthesiologists established the first specialty system in Japan. Four years later, two other professional associations, the Japan Radiological Society and the Japan Neurosurgical Society, established medical specialties systems. During the 1970s, the establishment of medical specialties systems accelerated, and many other professional associations started their own systems; however, each association created and followed its own qualification process and training guidelines. In some societies, membership required little more than paying the membership fee with no proof of qualification. As a result, the skills and knowledge of 'specialists' has varied greatly among the professional associations. The lack of uniformity among professional associations has been an issue for a long time in Japan (Arai, 2009; Terasaki, 2011).

While changes are in the making, physicians are allowed to declare their particular specialties freely as long as they have a physician's license. Medical specialists are not approved and recognized on the basis of 'standardized' public qualifications (Terasaki, 2011). These characteristics of

the medical specialties systems in Japan have led some patients to question the specialty care quality provided by 'specialist' physicians in Japan. In response to these criticisms, in 1981 an organization was founded that went through several name evolutions before becoming the current Japanese Board of Medical Specialties in 2008 (Arai, 2009; Terasaki, 2011). It aims to address the discrepancies between professional associations in certifying procedures. Since the early 2000s, this board has enabled physicians qualified to be specialists by the relevant professional associations to announce their qualification as a medical specialist if their professional association (i.e., the provider of the qualifications) satisfies certain criteria (Sakai, 2003). Expectations are high for the Japanese medical specialties system to become more rigorous consequent to these changes.

PRIMARY CARE TRAINING IN JAPAN

For many years, the Japan Medical Association opined that all doctors were family doctors regardless of their training background because they served family members in their community. In fact, most private practitioners were functioning as hybrid specialist/primary care physicians (Saigal et al., 2007) by default. Since Japanese hospitals do not have an effective privileging system, most procedure-based specialists cannot continue the procedures (after they become private practitioners) that they studied so diligently during residency training. By default, they must learn to practice medicine for common problems. Unfortunately, a lack of emphasis on clinical epidemiology in medical schools and consequently, a lack of understanding among physicians about the epidemiology of illness, and excessive reliance on extensive laboratory and radiological testing, results in primary care with many idiosyncrasies.

Indeed, it surprises many that despite excellent health care indices, Japan lacks a strong primary care system (Ban & Fetters, 2011). Fortunately, change is in the making. In 2004, the Japanese Academy of Family Medicine introduced a 3-year training program for family medicine specialists, even though the Japanese government did not consider family medicine a specialty. But there is evidence of growing momentum for recognition of generalists also as specialists. The Japan Primary Care Association (JPCA) formed in 2010 through a merger of the Japanese Academy of Primary Care Physicians, the Japanese Academy of Family Medicine, and the Japanese Society of General Medicine. The JPCA is now the largest academic association of primary care physicians and provides the board certification of family physicians for residents who complete the requirements laid out by the Academy. The Japanese government has announced intention to recognize a general medicine specialty, *Sōgōi*, effective in 2017. This will help Japan catch up with most countries of the world given the recognition that a well-trained workforce based on primary care physicians is the most efficient.

MEDICAL EDUCATION DEPARTMENTS

The establishment of departments of medical education is still a relatively new phenomenon in Japan. In 2008, Suzuki et al reported 50 Departments of Medical Education had been established in Japanese medical schools over the previous decade. (Suzuki et al., 2008). No fewer than three organizations address medical education in Japan. The Medical Education Development Center, established at Gifu University, focuses on faculty development and teaching skills. Specifically, the Center specializes in the training of medical educators and development of teaching materials with emphasis on tutorial systems, medical interviewing skills, and computer-assisted learning. The Tokyo Center for Education Research in Medicine and Dentistry primarily addresses student assessment, and the Tokyo International Research Center for Medical Education facilitates international collaborations.

LIFELONG EDUCATION AND LEARNING

The Japan Medical Association Continuing Medical Education (CME) system was established in 1987 to encourage continuing medical education among physicians. The system is designed with the expectation that physicians should maintain the quality of health care they provide by continuing their education after obtaining a physician's license and, by doing so, earn their patients' trust. A CME certificate of completion is awarded to a physician who has earned the required credits through CME courses. There are various ways to obtain credits: (1) utilizing medical journals; (2) e-learning; (3) attending seminars, lectures, study meetings, workshops, and conferences; (4) writing a question for the National Medical Practitioners Qualifying Examination; (5) teaching clinical training sessions; (6) on-the-job training; and (7) writing academic medical papers. The CME system had been revised several times since 1987 to improve its quality. However, prior to 2010, only about 35 percent of physicians had completed CME courses. Therefore, in 2010 the CME system was again revised to further encourage physicians to acquire CME certification. The changes included: (1) the introduction of an evaluation system for earning credits through the utilization of medical journals and e-learning; (2) the issuing of a Japan Medical Association CME certificate to those whose credits met certain criteria; and (3) the establishment of a 3-year period for which the certificate is valid (The Japan Society for Medical Education, 2010). Data demonstrating that such a system works to ensure high quality care is difficult to come by, but the efforts are certainly well intended.

MEDICAL RESEARCH

Japan has experienced a rapid growth of inputs in research and development (R&D). The expenditure for R&D by the government, private companies, and universities increased from 1.3 trillion yen in 1970 to 16.8 trillion yen in 2003 (Hirota, 2006). The *ikyoku* system that encourages research and the apprenticeship model of research, contribute to the high research output in Japan. This growth of R&D is remarkable, particularly in the fields of science and technology. The enactment of the Science and Technology Basic Law (Law No. 130 of 1995: effective Nov. 15, 1995) was intended to achieve a higher standard of science and technology. Accordingly, the Japanese government began a Science and Technology Basic Plan: a multi-year, government-wide plan coordinated at Prime Minister level through the Council for Science and Technology Policy. Increasing its R&D budget in these fields under the Basic Plan, the government invested 17 trillion yen in science and technology during the first period of the Basic Plan (1996–2000) and 24 trillion yen during the second period (2001–2005). (Government of Japan, 2011). The government anticipated spending 25 trillion yen in the field during the third period (2006–2011), though spending fell short of this amount. On 19 August, 2011 the Japanese government launched the 4th Science and Technology Basic Plan that laid five mid-to-long-term objectives aimed at making Japan: (1) Achieve sustainable growth and societal development, particularly the recovery and restoration of earthquake damaged areas; (2) Realize a safe and secure, high quality of life for its people; (3) Take the initiative in solving global issues, including large scale natural disasters; (4)Possess a quality of science and technology that undergirds national sustainability; (5) Continue to create 'knowledge' assets and foster science and technology as culture. (Government of Japan, 2011).

A central element for achieving a competitive system of science and technology is having competitive research funding. According to Hirota (2006), the budget for competitive funds going to the Ministry of Health, Labour and Welfare was almost 12 percent of the total budget of the government in 2004. Furthermore, 80 percent of the total competitive funds went to universities, 15 percent to public institutions, and 5 percent to private companies (Hirota, 2006).

Collaborations between universities and industries, particularly pharmaceutical companies, occur commonly in Japan. Through collaboration, industries can seek academic advice from universities. Universities can also develop their ideas through their alliance with industry. Success can therefore attract further industry funds for partnerships, prompting patenting and licensing of university inventions (Odagiri, 2006). For example, collaboration between Kagawa Medical University and Fuso Pharmaceutical Industries yielded anti-cancer drugs, and a significant business venture. An alliance between Osaka University and the pharmaceutical company Daiichi Seiyaku resulted in the development and retailing of gene-therapy medication (Pradyumna, Gilbreath, & Gilbreath, 2005). Although private companies and industries might be key for boosting Japan's technological levels, the share of private companies among the total central fund is only 5 percent (Hirota, 2006). Approaches for developing collaborations between universities and private companies and industries, and extracting the advantages of such collaborations continues to be a challenge for Japanese medicine.

limited clinical experiences in their fifth-year clinical rotations, and then spend almost the entirety of their last year of medical school sequestered with books and lecture notes, to have substantive clinical skills at the time of their graduation and start of internship.

5 US medical schools often include not only full-time faculty, but also volunteer physicians who teach, and receive in return an affiliation as a clinical faculty member or community preceptor with the host institution. In our opinion, such an approach, adapted to Japan through the 'old boys' alumni network, could expand the teaching capacity in Japan.

6 One of us (MF) vividly recalls teaching rounds during an invited professorship in a prestigious national university teaching hospital where he advised discharging a patient and was told by the residents that it would have to wait because the attending physician was moonlighting that day.

7 Literally, *shoki kenshū* means 'early period/preliminary residency.' Functionally, the two-year period serves as an internship (in US parlance), and we have adopted this terminology as the most meaningful cultural equivalent, even though one could argue for a more literal translation.

8 One of the authors (MF) has served as a mentor for two individuals who earned their *igaku-hakase* in this manner.

NOTES

1 The practice of acupuncture includes acupressure. Moxibustion is the process of attaching cured mugwort to an acupuncture needle and burning the mugwort to influence the patient's internal *ki* (or *chi* in Chinese and as assimilated into English).

2 Some authors present Japan as having 79 medical schools because they do not include the National Defense Medical College in the total. We prefer to include the National Defense Medical College in the total because, functionally, its graduates are indistinguishable in their practice of medicine from other medical graduates. As this article went to press, an additional medical college was approved for establishment in Miyagi Prefecture.

3 In the opinion of one of us (MF), the lack of an integrated approach to clinical education stems from the lack of strong family medicine or general medicine departments – the specialties that provide integrated and comprehensive care.

4 In the view of one of us (MF), even an experienced clinician can easily lose valuable clinical skills and knowledge in a short time. It is unreasonable to expect Japanese medical graduates who received

REFERENCES

Arai, H. (2009). An ideal system of medical specialties requested by the Japanese Board of Medical Specialties (日本専門医制評価・認定機構の求める専門医制度). About the Foundation For Promotion of Medical Training. *Japanese Journal of Neurosurgery* (Tokyo) 18, 12–14.

Asai, H., & Fetters, M.D. (2010). Creating e-learning modules using the Internet and its possibilities: from the experience of contraception module. *Journal of Integrated Medicine*, 20(10), 798–800.

Ban, N., & Fetters, M.D. (2011). Education for health professionals in Japan: time to change. *Lancet*, 12–13.

Bowers, J.Z. (1965). *Medical education in Japan: from Chinese medicine to Western medicine*. New York, NY: Hoeber Medical Division, Harper & Row.

Bowers, J.Z. (1970). The history of medical education in Japan: the rise of Western medical education. In C.D. O'Malley (Ed.), *The history of medical education* (Vol. 673, pp. 391–416). Los Angeles, CA: University of California Press.

Dharmananda, S. (2001). *Kampo medicine: the practice of Chinese herbal medicine in Japan*. Portland, OR: START Manuscripts, ITM.

Foundation For Promotion of Medical Training (PMET). (2011). Retrieved September 12, 2011, from http://www.pmet.or.jp

Government of Japan. (2011). *Science and technology basic plan*. Retrieved August 17, 2011, from http://www8.cao.go.jp/cstp/ english/basic/index.html

Government Statistics for Japan(政府統計の総合窓口). (2014). Main Statistics Search, Basic School Survey, College/Graduate School, Table 2. College Student Counts by Affiliated School in Universities (主要な統計から探す, http://www.e-stat.go.jp/SG1/estat/GL02100104.do?tocd=00400001, 学校基本調査, http://www.e-stat.go.jp/SG1/estat/GL08020103.do?_toGL08020103_&tclassID=000001054431&cycleCode=0&requestSender=dsearch, 大学・大学院、表2. 大学の関係学科別学部学生数, (author's translation). Retrieved October 2, 2014 from http://www.e-stat.go.jp/SG1/estat/html/GL02100101.html.

Hirota, H. (2006). *Function of competitive fund institution at promotion of science & technology: the central institution to design competitive circumstances for successful research & development and its subjects for reform*. Retrieved October 1, 2014, from http://www.nagaokauniv.ac.jp/m-edu/pdf/04paper3.pdf

Inada, H., Mitsunami, K., Motohara, S., & Fetters, M.D. (2010). 参加型臨床実習は医学生のモチベーションを高める―「浸透学習」からの脱却のための事例報告 (Increasing motivation of medical students through a participatory style of learning: a case study demonstrating how to get away from 'osmotic learning'). *Medical Education (Japan)*, 41(5), 347–352.

Inoue, K., Hirayama, Y., & Igarashi, M. (1997). A medical school for rural areas. *Medical Education*, 31(6), 430–434.

Ito, T., Hongo, M., Mizoguchi, J., Kanemura, M., Kimura, H. & Ogasawara, H. (2007). 日本の医師不足を放置できるか―日本の医療制度を荒廃・崩壊させないために―(Can we leave shortage of doctors as it is? Thoughts on preventing Japanese medical system from being ruined/damaged [author's translation]). Retrieved August 9, 2014, from http://www.zck.or.jp/info/190613/0706PDF.pdf

Izumi, Y., & Isozumi, K. (2001). Modern Japanese medical history and the European influence. *Keio Journal of Medicine*, 50(2), 91–99.

Jannetta, A.B. (2007). *The vaccinators smallpox, medical knowledge, and the 'Opening' of Japan*. Stanford, CA: Stanford University Press.

Japan Society of Acupuncture and Moxibustion. (2005). *Japanese Acupuncture-Legislation and Education*. Retrieved August 9, 2014, from http://en.jsam.jp/contents.php/ 020000RNSXjD/

Japan Society of Acupuncture and Moxibustion. (2012). *History of Japanese Acupuncture*. Retrieved August 9, 2014, from http://en.jsam.jp/contents.php/020000RNSXjD/

Kozu, T. (2006). Medical education in Japan. *Academic Medicine*, 81(12), 1069–1075.

Leslie, C. (1977). *Asian medical systems*. Berkeley, CA: University of California Press.

Lock, M.M. (1980). *East Asian medicine in urban Japan: varieties of medical experience* (Vol. 4). Berkeley, CA: University of California Press.

Lock, M.M. (1984). East Asian medicine and health care for the Japanese elderly. *Pacific Affairs*, 57(1), 65–73.

Ministry of Education, Culture, Sports, Science and Technology. (2011). *Medical education model core curriculum*. Retrieved August 26, 2011, from http://www.mext.go.jp/b_menu/shingi/chousa/koutou/032/index.htm

National Center for University Entrance Examinations. (2011). (大学入学者選抜大学入試センター試験 *(University candidate selection – university admissions center test)*. Retrieved August 9, 2014, from http://www.dnc.ac.jp

Nishimura, K., Plotnikoff, G.A., & Watanabe, K. (2009). Kampo medicine as an integrative medicine in Japan. *Japan Medical Association Journal*, 52(3), 147–149.

Odagiri, H. (2006). National innovation system: reforms to promote science-based industries. In T. Shibata (Ed.), *Japan, moving toward a more advanced knowledge economy* (Vol. I: Assessment and Lessons, pp. 127–146). Washington, DC: World Bank.

Onishi, H., & Yoshida, I. (2004). Rapid change in Japanese medical education. *Medical Teacher*, 26(5), 403–408.

Orie, R. (2003). 患者が決めた!いい病院―患者9万人アンケート関東版 *(Good hospitals selected by patients* [author's translation]). Tokyo: Oricon Medical.

Pesch, M. (2011). Medical education in Japan: a threat to the Japanese health care system. *The New Physician*, 60(6), 1111.

Powell, M., & Anesaki, M. (Eds.). (2010). *Health care in Japan* (Vol. 79). London: Routledge.

Pradyumna, P., Gilbreath, K., & Gilbreath, D. (2005). *Japan in the 21st century: environment, economy, and society*. Lexington, KY: University Press of Kentucky.

Saigal, P., Takemura, Y., Nishiue, T., & Fetters, M.D. (2007). Factors considered by medical students when formulating their specialty preferences in Japan: findings from a qualitative study. *BMC Medical Education*, 7(1), 31.

Sakai, O. (2003, January 6). 日本の専門医制度を再考する (Reconsideration about medical specialties systems in Japan [author's translation]). 週刊医学界新聞 *(Medical Community Weekly Newspaper)*, 医学書院 (Igakushoin). Retrieved August 9, 2014, from http://www.igaku-shoin.co.jp/nwsppr/n2003dir/n2517dir/n2517_04.htm

Shibata, Y., & Wu, J. (1997). *Kampo treatment for climacteric disorders: a handbook for practitioners*. Brookline, MA: Paradigm Publications.

Smith, S.L. (2005). *Japanese American midwives: culture, community, and health politics, 1880–1950 (Asian American experience)*. Urbana, IL: University of Illinois Press.

Suzuki, Y., Gibbs, T., & Fujisaki, K. (2008). Medical education in Japan: a challenge to the healthcare system. *Medical Teacher*, 30(9–10), 846–850.

Teo, A. (2007). The current state of medical education in Japan: a system under reform. *Medical Education*, 41(3), 302–308.

Terasaki, F. (2011). The medical specialties system past and present: toward appropriate medical specialists. *The Journal of Kyoto-Furitsu Medical School*, 120(6), 419–428.

The Japan Society for Medical Education. (2010, August 30). Minutes of The Japan Society for Medical Education. '社会に求められる医学教育とは' (The need for medical education in society [author's translation]). 週刊医学界新聞 (*Medical Community Weekly Newspaper*), 医学書院 (Igakushoin). Retrieved August 9, 2014, from http://www.igaku-shoin.co.jp/paperDetail.do?id= PA02893_04

Tsuruoka, K., Tsuruoka, Y., & Kajii, E. (2001). Complementary medicine education in Japanese medical schools: a survey. *Complementary Therapies in Medicine*, 9(1), 28–33.

Yamada, H. (2005). *WHO global atlas of traditional, complementary and alternative medicine: text volume*. Geneva: World Health Organization.

Yasui, H. (2007). Medical history in Japan: Dosan Manase and his medicine. *The Journal of Kampo, Acupuncture and Integrative Medicine*, 2(1), 30–33.

Yasui, H. (2010). History of Japanese acupuncture and moxibustion. *The Journal of Kampo, Acupuncture and Integrative Medicine*, 1, 2–9.

Yoshida, A. (2011). Physicians' career building and their shortage in some specialties. *Japan Labor Review*, 8(4), 5–21.

17

Bioethics and Medico-legal Issues in Japan

Michael D. Fetters

OVERVIEW

Ascension into the world's spotlight for its excellent health care outcomes and highly advanced technology also aroused attention to Japan in the realm of biomedical ethics because of very different cultural values. Furthermore, different legal systems and social institutions, particularly in the multidisciplinary field of biomedical ethics, make for rich comparisons, discussions, and inquiries. Though not a unanimous position among scholars, Japan's long history of feudalism appears to have influenced the physician paternalism and views about professionalism that dominated for the bulk of the twentieth century (Nishigori, Harrison, Busari & Dornan, 2014). The early emergence in the modern bioethics movement in North America of the four principles approach to medical ethics – respect for autonomy, non-maleficence, beneficence, and justice as popularized by Beauchamp and Childress (Beauchamp & Childress, 1994), was awkward and difficult to embrace in Japan (Hoshino, 1997). One early observer in the modern bioethics era described the status quo in the 1980s as being dominated by values of harmony and consensus, and avoidance of conflict or controversy (Feldman, 1985). Initially more reactive to the precepts of the North American paradigm of medical ethics (Hoshino, 1997), biomedical ethics

in Japan has emerged increasingly to challenge North American and absolutist notions about biomedical ethics, and help shape global thinking in non-Western cultures about the most ethical approaches (Akabayashi, Slingsby & Kai, 2003). Given the interdisciplinary nature of medical ethics, the following discussion draws from various fields – anthropology, law, and medicine – to highlight several issues and events that have shaped medical ethics in Japan. The reader will get a flavor for this difference by looking at the principles of medical ethics espoused by the Japan Medical Association (Table 17.1). While making no claim as to being systematic, this chapter does cover many key issues and discussions that have emerged as central to biomedical ethics in Japan. The reader will notice a predominance of discussion and debate about end-of-life issues with relatively little emphasis on beginning-of-life issues that to this observer reflects proportionately ethics discussions in Japan.

Many medical ethicists consider an ethical choice, 'the right thing to do, "all things" considered.' When tensions emerge between North American views and the views from Japan about ethically charged issues, to this observer, these often arise from differences regarding how 'all things' should be considered and what constitutes 'all things?'

Box 17.1 Key points

- Wada *Jurō* conducts the world's second heart transplant in Japan in 1968 under highly ethically suspect circumstances and sets the stage for a protracted social debate about brain death and organ transplantation in Japan
- Under the leadership of Ōta Tenrei in 1976, the Japan Euthanasia Society (renamed the Japan Society for Dying with Dignity in 1983) is established and convenes an international meeting of national right-to-die societies
- In 1990, the Japan Medical Association convenes the Second Bioethics meeting and releases a report entitled, '*Setsumei to dōī* literally, 'Explanation and agreement' to respond to Western notions of 'informed consent'
- In 1991, a physician at Tokai University hospital administers potassium chloride to a terminally ill patient and was subsequently found guilty of murder in 1995 at the Yokohama District Court. In the 'Tokai University Euthanasia Judgment,' the Court provides conditions under which active euthanasia might be permitted
- In 1992, the Declaration on the Establishment of Patient Rights, the Japan Federation of Bar Associations proclaims and takes a legal position that informed consent is central to the patient's right to self-determination
- In 1994, the Japanese Society of Legal Medicine (*Nihon Hōi Gakkai*), promulgates new guidelines that broaden the interpretation of notifiable 'unnatural deaths' to include unexpected deaths related to the course of medical treatment
- The Japanese government passes legislation in 1997 that legalizes brain death and organ transplantation from brain dead donors under very strict criteria – the ruling fails to clarify medically, ethically, or legally whether brain death constitutes a human death in Japan
- In 1998, a physician injected a muscle relaxant into an unconscious male who had suffered severe hypoxemia causing brain damage, and was in a coma. Known as the Kawasaki-Kyodo case, the Yokohama District Court ruled the physician guilty of murder in 2005. Upon appeal to the Tokyo High Court, the decision was upheld in 2007 and, upon further review by the Supreme Court in 2009, the charge again was upheld with no change or clarification of the conditions set forth in the 1995 Yokohama District Court ruling
- Passage in 2003 of the Act on the Protection of Personal Information gives patients the legal right to access their own medical charts
- The humiliating arrest and handcuffing of an obstetrician from Ōno Hospital in rural Fukushima, Japan, broadcast on national television in February 2006 for the death of a patient after a difficult Caesarean section, raises alarm about the over-intrusion of criminal law into the practice of medicine
- In October 2006, the Tokyo High Court overruled a local Tokyo Ward decision and recognized the donor mother as the legitimate mother of twins born from the embryos created by the eggs and sperm of a Japanese couple, but born to a surrogate mother in the United States

---

Table 17.1   Principles of medical ethics, Japan Medical Association

The mission of medical science and health care is to cure diseases, to maintain and promote the health of the people; and based on an awareness of the importance of this mission, the physician should serve society with a basic love for humanity.

1   The physician should strive to achieve a lifelong dedication to continuing education, to keep abreast of medical knowledge and technology, and to support its progress and development.
2   The physician should be aware of the dignity and responsibility of his/her occupation and strive to enhance his/her cultural refinement, education, and integrity.
3   The physician should respect the individuality of his/her patients, treat them with compassion, provide full explanations of all medical treatment, and endeavor to earn the trust of the patient.
4   The physician should maintain respect for his/her fellow physician, cooperate with medical care personnel and serve the cause of medical care to the best of his/her abilities.
5   The physician should respect the spirit of public service that characterizes health care, contribute to the development of society while abiding by legal standards and establishing legal order.
6   The physician will not engage in medical activities for profit-making motives.

ETHICS AND END-OF-LIFE ISSUES

Brain Death and Organ Transplantation

A prominent area that has dominated biomedical ethics discourse emerged following the second heart transplant in the world in 1968 by Wada Jurō amidst a host of suspect circumstances. Although the recipient lived 83 days – 65 days more than the first heart transplant in South Africa – serious questions emerged, such as whether the donor was actually dead, whether the recipient needed an artificial heart valve more than a transplant, whether records might have been altered or embellished, and why the problematic heart valve was missing from the recipient's diseased heart (Feldman, 2000). One keen observer, Eric Feldman proclaims, 'This single operation is regularly credited with fomenting the entire debate over brain death and organ transplantation in Japan' (Feldman, 2000, p. 133). Transplantation law in Japan can be traced back to the 'Cornea Transplant Act of 1958.' Amid expectations for segue to acceptance of organ transplantation on a greater scale, the law was revised subsequently in 1979 as the 'Cornea and Kidney Transplantation Act.' Hoshino Kazumasa, a senior scholar of modern medical ethics in Japan, discussed his own first reaction to the new law as 'emotional uneasiness' and brought Western observers' attention to aspects of the law that would be surprising: the law restricted transplantation to dead donors and transplantation was only possible with the consent of the surviving family, even if the deceased had expressed in advance the desire to donate (Hoshino, 1997). Seemingly incoherent from a North American perspective of patient autonomy, the revised law was only another milestone during a long and contentious debate about brain death and organ transplantation in Japan.

Only after substantive social and legal maneuvering did organ transplantation from non-living donors ultimately receive passage by the Japanese Parliament in 1997, but only under prohibitively strict circumstances (Akabayashi, 1997). Potential donors must not only indicate a willingness to donate their organs, but also consent to being diagnosed as brain dead – and their consent can still be revoked by family members. While the law made organ transplantation possible, the criteria were so strict that a diminishingly small number of organ transplants from brain dead donors occurred (Feldman, 2000; Terayama, 2010). Moreover, organ transplantations from children under the age of 15 were not permitted. Hospitals and clinicians found the law nearly impracticable. For example, Yokota noted the heavy burden on

the donor hospital, and estimated a time of more than 45 hours from the diagnosis of brain death to time of organ harvesting (Yokota, 2010a, 2010b). The first case of organ transplantation conducted from a brain-dead donor as outlined in the law did not occur until 1999. The organ transplant law was revised in 2009, and Japan decided to adopt the opt-out system. Transplants from children became possible, although the law still required family consent (Aita, 2011; Akabayashi, 2009). The amended law also allowed individuals to prioritize family members to receive their donated organs after death, a twist that has raised concern about fairness in organ allocation (Aita, 2011). Passage of the Istanbul Declaration in 2008 calling against organ traffic for self-sufficiency in organ transplantation highlighted the persistent low rate of organ transplantation in Japan, including the rather stark point that all heart transplants for children had been done outside of Japan. This renewed the call for self-sufficiency in organ transplantation, further research on understanding why Japanese society does not accept organ transplantation, and research on alternative treatments and technology not requiring transplantation (Kobayashi, 2010).

From a Western perspective, the brain death and organ transplantation debate highlights cultural influences and views about patient rights (Feldman, 2000). Surprisingly, brain death criteria developed largely behind closed doors in the United States and became promulgated with relatively little debate. The very different views of brain death, and hence the feasibility of organ transplantation in Japan, stirred much debate in perhaps a much more 'healthy' way because there was greater opportunity for social discourse (Akabayashi, 2009). Medical anthropologist Margaret Lock's articulation of Japanese perspectives provided considerable points for reflection by the North American Bioethics movement (Lock, 2002). Interestingly, recent survey research suggests a low level of content among the Japanese public with the process of policymaking about charged ethical issues, such as brain death for organ transplantation (Sato, Akabayashi, & Kai, 2005). As Feldman asserted in 2000 and many years later, the degree that brain death is medically, ethically, or legally human death in Japan remains cloudy (Feldman, 2000).

Cancer Non-disclosure Versus Truth-telling

The complexity of whether to tell patients a cancer diagnosis and the intricacies of physician communication about cancer was a topic of social interest in Japan well before North American biomedical ethics made an entrée into Japan, as illustrated by the classic 1952 movie by Akira Kurosawa called '*Ikiru*' (i.e. 'To Live') (Kurosawa, 1952). Though led to believe he had a bleeding ulcer by his doctor, the protagonist, a Japanese bureaucrat, ultimately surmises he has cancer and sets out to find meaning in his life (Kurosawa, 1952). The movie leaves doubt in the viewer's mind as to whether patients should or shouldn't know about cancer. The Japanese approach to cancer patients began capturing the attention of the Western community in the 1980s (Long & Long, 1982). Framed as a 'truth telling about cancer' in the West and '*gan kokuchi*' (cancer disclosure) in Japan, discussions about this issue in Japan were awkward. If Japanese doctors were not 'truth tellers,' were they just liars?

Hence, debates about cancer disclosure illustrated challenges for framing the biomedical ethics movement in Japan (Akabayashi, 1995, 2009). At the ethical heart of the truth-telling versus non-disclosure of cancer debate, was the opportunity, or lack thereof, for a patient to exercise a right to self-determination through an informed consent discussion and decision, and the physician to exercise 'therapeutic privilege' to avoid harm. Rather than a conclusion for an overarching, unassailable need to respect patient autonomy and self-determination, debates in Japan centered on the potential harms of disclosure and the inherent conflict physicians encountered when considering respect for patient wishes, weighing of beneficence and non-maleficence by the physician, and inclusive views about the role of the family in medical decision making (Fetters, 1998). Describing the impasse, Norio Higuchi described the situation as thus, 'Americans criticize Japanese for their paternalism, and Japanese counterattack Americans for too much autonomy without professional responsibility' (Higuchi, 1992).

CAN KNOWLEDGE HURT?

Key to professional responsibility was the fear of harming the patient. In numerous discussions, Japanese physicians asserted that disclosing cancer was dangerous, though the proof always seemed to be from unverifiable rumors. The prevailing judgment about cancer was that many patients would lose all hope, give up fighting, and die much faster if told they had cancer. Physicians exercised judgment whether to disclose on a 'case-by-case' basis, frequently with consultation with a family member, typically an eldest son or other male family member. Patients might be especially prone to commit suicide because it is viewed as both tragic, and honorable (e.g., tradition of *hara-kiri*) or even romantic (e.g., lover's suicide). In order to avoid caustic discussions, elaborate language used to veil the diagnosis led to a conspiracy of silence with everyone knowing the underlying cause except the patient, or the patient vaguely knowing and collaborating with the illusion.

Would Japanese Patients Do Worse if They Knew They had Cancer?

Like many Westerners in the 1980s who dismissed Japanese clinicians' concerns that patients would give up hope as overstated and paternalistic, as a resident physician on family medicine elective rotations in Japan in the early 1990s, I was also quite skeptical. Although I had heard such rumors or anecdotal reports from multiple physicians, those physicians he met always responded that it happened, but they could not describe any specific cases or if they had heard it from someone else. Then, at an informal dinner, I had a chance meeting with a US-trained Japanese breast cancer surgeon who shared a gut-wrenching experience. It occurred shortly after his return to become a faculty member in Japan. While in the United States, the surgeon trained under and practiced a US model of informed consent. He returned to Japan uneasy with Japan's status quo, feeling that informed consent was the ethically right approach. He felt determined to implement this Western model in his own practice, against the prevailing wisdom. He thought it best to begin with a patient with an excellent prognosis. When he identified a patient who had a breast cancer tumor, in his own words, 'smaller than the tip of my pinky', which was 100 percent curable, he felt she would be a good candidate for 'truth telling.' Holding the tip of his pinky with his opposite hand to show his emphasis on the size and curability, he explained how he disclosed to her the diagnosis and excellent prognosis and scheduled her for the surgery one week later. As he was going against social norms, he discussed his extraordinary efforts to ensure informed consent, to convey his confidence of a total cure with surgery, and to reassure her. One week later, she 'no-showed' for the surgery. When he attempted to contact the patient by phone, her family told him that she had committed suicide by going into a rice paddy, pouring kerosene on herself and setting it on fire. So much for rumors. The reality was further demonstrated empirically in a 2004 study of 140 cancer patients – suicidal ideation was subthreshold in 37 patients (26.4 percent) and present in 12 (8.6 percent) (Akechi et al., 2004).

Although in stark contrast to another contemporaneous story of breast cancer not disclosed to the patient with bad outcomes from non-disclosure (Leflar, 1996) and the author's own bias as to the centrality of informed consent to the trusting doctor–patient relationship, the inescapable point is that Japanese physician reluctance and concerns about potential harms of cancer disclosure – at the time of the initial push for a North American bioethics model of cancer disclosure and informed consent in Japan – were perceived by physicians and family members as extremely real.

Cancer Disclosure, Informed Consent and Patient Rights

The debate about the preferred approach to cancer disclosure in Japan had broader implications. Discussions about cancer and informed consent have and continue to be strongly intertwined in Japan. As articulated by Leflar, aversion to the concept of informed consent has been most pronounced in the treatment of cancer (Leflar, 1996). Moreover, cancer disclosure and informed consent also emerge as central to discussions about the status of patient rights in Japan and challenges to realizing cancer disclosure and informed consent as routine practice (Feldman, 2000; Leflar, 1996).

Development of a Japanese Informed Consent: Explanation, Agreement and Informed Consent in Japan

In 1990, under the lead of the scholar Kato Ichiro, the Japan Medical Association convened the Second Bioethics Roundtable to address the idea of informed consent. The resulting report, '*Setsumei to dōi*,' was a first step for introducing informed consent to Japan (Zasshi, 1990). Literally, *setsumei* means explanation and *dōi* means agreement.[1] The report argues the need for developing a model that considers Japan's cultural background, national character, public sentiment, and avoiding collusion while having a heart to heart relationship. Critics were quick to point out problematic nuances. A physician's explanation does not equal the patient being informed, and agreement has a passive tone lacking the more active or volitional connotation of consent. Thus, a physician's explanation and the patient's agreement would not necessarily equal informed consent according to North American standards.

Two years later, in November 1992, in the Declaration on the Establishment of Patient Rights, the Japan Federation of Bar Associations proclaimed that the right to self-determination is a fundamental human right recognized in international human rights law. At the core of this right is informed consent, namely that the patient can receive an accurate explanation and understanding of the nature of the disease, the purpose of the treatment, the nature of the intervention, the risks, alternative treatments,

and then voluntarily choose to agree or decline. This proclamation makes informed consent essential to the right to receive appropriate health care (Japan Federation of Bar Associations, 1992).

A second report emerged in 1995 from the Commission for the Study of Informed Consent. The authors of this report decided to 'pull the plug' on the Japanese adaptation, *Setsumei to dōi*, and advised using the cognate for informed consent, that is *infōmudo konsento* (Hisashi, 1995). As summarized by Leflar, this new report advocated for a full-bodied informed consent to be central to the trusting doctor–patient relationship and for full diffusion into medical practice (Leflar, 1996).

Cancer Disclosure and Informed Consent Update

Over the next two decades, a consensus slowly began emerging about disclosing cancer (Long, 2000), although physicians still continued modulating their decisions on a case-by-case basis on factors such as patient age, prognosis, social status, and, to a limited degree, religion (Elwyn, Fetters, Sasaki, & Tsuda, 2002). Despite reports from physician colleagues that cancer disclosure has increasingly become the modus operandi, the author's own recent direct observations in a rural hospital's general and cancer wards[2] suggests some, but not all, patients are being informed of their cancer diagnosis. Moreover, participation in decision making about treatment and candid discussion among those informed, at least for those cases the author has observed and as reported by Akabayashi (2009), remains limited at this time. While the practices in one hospital cannot be construed to reflect the practices across all of Japan, this experience does confirm that cancer disclosure sometimes occurs, sometimes not, and that a model of informed consent, as described in the 1992 Declaration on the Establishment of Patient Rights (Japan Federation of Bar Associations, 1992), cannot be assumed to be completely pervasive. The 2003 Act on the Protection of Personal Information now gives patients the legal right to access their own medical charts. It is possible to secure full information through a medical record request, but the procedure for obtaining a copy of the medical record is prohibitively expensive for everyday use and mostly utilized in medical malpractice suits.

OTHER ETHICAL ISSUES AT THE END OF LIFE

Starting in the 1970s, shortly after Wada's first heart transplant in 1968, a growing interest and spirited discussions about medical care at the end of life developed (Akabayashi, 2009). A death-with-dignity movement that included the development of living wills, increasing interest about quality at the end of life, and growing recognition of the elimination of wasteful life-extending care also emerged. Naturally, interest in palliative care and hospice care increased. A momentous case in 1991 occurred when it was discovered a physician had administered potassium chloride to a terminally ill patient in the first known case of active euthanasia. Details about these end-of-life issues follow.

Potential Utility of Advance Directives in End-of-life Decision Making

In debates about the preferred approach for allowing patients who become incapacitated due to illness or injury to have an influence on decisions regarding use of cardiopulmonary resuscitation, intubation, and other heroic measures to prolong their life, a mechanism referred to as an 'advance directive' emerged. In spirit, an advance directive allows an individual to convey in advance, verbally or in writing, his or her preferences for how clinical decisions should be made at some time in the future should the individual lack the ability to do so due to profound injury or illness. Amidst substantive international interest in this movement, Japanese scholars participated in the transcultural and interdisciplinary rhetoric on how to empower patients through advance directives (Sass, Veatch, & Kimura, 1998). Advocates for advance directives believe such initiatives can help clarify the often murky and painstaking decisions that must occur when an individual reaches such an incapacitated state.

Regarding specifics in Japan, advance directives are not legally recognized, and this contrasts with the specific legal recognition of advance directives in the United States through the Patient Self-Determination Act (Omnibus Budget Reconciliation Act of 1990 (OBRA-90), 2002). In 1991, the passage of the Patient Self-Determination Act (PSDA) required all healthcare institutions to inform patients about their right to complete an advance directive, including their right to refuse life-sustaining interventions such as cardiopulmonary resuscitation (Omnibus Budget Reconciliation Act of 1990 (OBRA-90), 2002). Despite the lack of legal footing for advance directives, bioethicists have sought to utilize advance discussions in patient care as the ethically right thing to do, but interpreting the meaning of advance discussions when they occur still raises uncertainty about actual interpretation and implementation (Akabayashi, Fetters, & Elwyn, 1999).

The *Songenshi Kyōkai* (Japan Society for Death with Dignity), with roots tracing back to 1976,[3] is the most active advocacy group for death with dignity and advance directives in Japan. Data collected from 1993 to 1996 amongst members who had completed a living will demonstrated the challenges of using such an advance directive in Japan. Amongst individuals who had completed a living will, the contents of the living will were often not known about. For example of 1626 survey respondents, 36 percent never presented the living will, while 96 percent of the remaining 1040 respondents said they presented the living will and it was respected (Masuda et al., 2001). However, in a follow-up survey of 459 responding physicians to whom family members stated that they had presented the living will, only 301 responded and 69 percent said the living will did not change the course of the patient's treatment (Masuda et al., 2003). Results from a survey of the general public in the Tokyo area suggests many patients want advance discussions to address specifics of medical treatment; are comfortable expressing preferences verbally with family members and/or their physician; have low interest in legal measures for setting up an advance directive; feel proxies should have leeway in decision making; and find family members, relatives, and spouse as the most suitable proxies (Akabayashi & Slingsby, 2003). Although one would like to be optimistic about the potential for advance directives in Japan, the substantive problems that plague advance directives in the United States, even with the legal basis of the PSDA and its passage 20 years ago (Yuen, Reid, & Fetters, 2011), suggests that widespread adoption in Japan may remain an upstream paddle. Unclear legal standing of advance directives, physician and family reluctance to respect the contents, and lack of accessibility to the advance directive at the point of care persist as problems with execution of advance directives. Furthermore, growing mistrust of the medical profession by patients, unclear legal standing, and lack of knowledge about availability may persist as barriers to patients completing advance directives.

Euthanasia and Death with Dignity

Two events have framed the death-with-dignity debate in Japan: the Tokai University Hospital Euthanasia Case and Kawasaki Kyodo Hospital Case (Kai, 2009).

Tokai University Hospital Case

In 1991, a young physician at Tokai University Hospital was caring for a critically ill and unconscious 58-year-old man. The son of the patient requested the intravenous drip, etc. to be removed from his father to relieve his suffering. The physician responded by removing the intravenous line and the patient's breathing tube. The patient developed loud snoring and agonizing difficulty in breathing, to which the son demanded the physician to act. An hour after the physician injected twice the dose of a sedative, there was no improvement and, responding again to the son's request, he injected twice the dose of a psychotropic drug, but still an hour later there was no improvement. The son vehemently complained and the physician injected twice the dose of an antiarrythmic, but to no avail. The doctor then resorted to injecting undiluted potassium chloride and subsequently the patient died. In 1995, the Yokohama District court found the physician guilty of homicide and sentenced him to 2-years imprisonment with hard labor, but with suspension of the sentence of 2 years. The resulting Tokai University Euthanasia Judgment provided four conditions under which active euthanasia might be permitted: (1) the patient is suffering from unbearable physical pain; (2) the patient's death is unavoidable and the time of death is imminent; (3) the doctor tries everything to remove or relieve the patient's physical pain, and there is no alternative measure; and (4) there is an explicit expression of the patient's will to consent to shorten his life. Controversy persisted as to whether these criteria were sufficiently clear to justify euthanasia (Kai, 2009).

Kawasaki-Kyodo Hospital Case

In November 1998, a 58-year-old man suffered a severe asthma attack that caused brain damage from hypoxemia (Kai, 2009). His condition deteriorated and the treating physician told the family that the patient was 99 percent in a coma and she removed the breathing tube from the patient's airway with reported intent to avoid infection. When the patient developed uncontrollable coughing, she injected first a tranquilizer to no avail, and then a muscle relaxant that led to the patient's demise. Prior to acting, she did not test to confirm brain death, nor did she obtain a second opinion. In March 2005, the Yokohama District Court ruled that the physician was guilty of murder and provided a detailed rationale. The physician appealed and the Tokyo High Court upheld the guilty charge in February 2007 and commented on the grounds for the rejection. The High Court said that legislation or a guideline was needed to fundamentally clarify interpretation of death with dignity. The accused physician appealed again to the Supreme Court, that upheld the conviction in September 2009, and dismissed her appeal stating the grounds for rejection of the appeal, but not clarifying conditions that would be excusable ('Top court dismisses euthanasia appeal', 2009). The significance of this case is that despite criteria laid out in the Tokai University Hospital Euthanasia

judgment in 1995, ambiguity persists about the legality of active euthanasia in Japan and a definition of death with dignity remains elusive.

Contextualizing the Death-with-dignity and Euthanasia Debate

Susan Long, an erudite observer and scholar of Japanese studies, articulates the essence of such difficult debates. People encounter conflicts between their deeply held values, for example life versus pain, self versus other, and burden versus self-reliance, that renders rational decision making difficult. In clinical situations, patients, families, and healthcare workers must sort through ambivalent feelings and conflicting values as applied to the situation at hand. In contrast, at the societal level, policymakers, lawyers, and bioethicists must grapple with developing policies and regulations about practices for which there are deeply held beliefs and that can cover a variety of situations (Long, 2001, 2002).

Withholding and Withdrawing Life-sustaining Treatment

To this clinician observer, one of the most challenging issues relative to end-of-life care in contemporary Japan relates to withholding and withdrawing life-sustaining treatment. To illustrate the issue, the North American approach can be informative. When benefits of life-sustaining treatments are unclear for an acutely ill patient, providing aggressive care to the patient to assess for the benefit and then withholding the treatment in the event that it does not produce the anticipated effect, has become widely accepted. In short, when aggressive life-sustaining treatment, such as using a breathing machine as a temporizing measure to determine if the patient can breathe independently and recover, does not work, it can be withdrawn if agreement among the treatment team and family (and patient if applicable) has been sought. In contrast, Japanese physicians who employ life-sustaining treatment with a patient feel compelled to continue using the treatment until the patient's death, even if the probability of recovery is very low. Withholding treatment that a patient has become dependent upon as a life-sustaining treatment is regarded as the same as intentionally causing the patient's death. The unfortunate outcomes are (1) patients who are dependent on life-sustaining treatments and who have no hope of recovery, and (2) patients who are older or have a particularly difficult underlying issue for whom aggressive life-sustaining treatment is not provided due to the fear that the patient would become dependent on the life-sustaining treatment (e.g. breathing machine).

The status quo prolongs the life of patients with no hope of recovery, and deprives from patients treatments that might be effective but are withheld due to concerns that the patient would not recover. The physician could not withhold this treatment because it would be considered as killing the patient.

ETHICS AND BEGINNING-OF-LIFE ISSUES

Overview

While beginning-of-life issues are less predominant, though no less passionate, than end-of-life issues in global ethics discourse, these issues had initially stirred even less debate in Japan. Despite abortion being a lightning rod of debate in the West, and particularly North America, abortion received less attention in Japan, where there is profoundly different access, views, and approaches to family planning. Furthermore, ethical issues in assisted reproductive technology began percolating in the 1990s and 2000s to boiling point and merit further discussion.

Induced Abortion as Minor Topic of Ethical Debate

That women request and obstetricians routinely provide abortions in Japan as a medical procedure generates little ethical debate. In a nutshell, abortion is practiced over family planning (Coleman, 1992; Norgren, 2001). The practice of induced abortion can be traced at least to the beginning of the twelfth century, and was utilized for family planning, especially among the poor, to survive 35 famines and excessive taxation that occurred in the Edo period (1603–1867). After restriction of abortion by the Meiji government in 1868 due to the anticipated need for healthy soldiers (Obayashi, 1982), the post World War War II government later legalized induced abortion in 1948 (Norgren, 2001). A fascinating and multifaceted modern history followed in Japan that was characterized by a progressive view towards abortion and a conservative view about contraception, with oral contraceptives still infrequently used (Norgren, 2001). While the Western discussion remains polarized almost entirely along religious lines, the relative lack of controversy and absolutist discourse in Japan is remarkable. LaFleur (1994) explores reasons for the minimal degree of controversy regarding the ethics of induced abortion. He illustrates that families are not emotionally indifferent and that induced abortion touches their hearts and minds. His analysis suggests that historical context, views about life and Buddhist rituals for the aborted (*mizuko kuyō*) have contributed to a context where induced abortion is accepted (LaFleur, 1994).

Assisted Reproductive Technology

While artificial insemination by donor first occurred in Japan in 1949, assisted reproductive technology didn't emerge significantly into the bioethics spotlight until much later. In 1987, Bai and colleagues provided a systematic overview of and highlighted the lack of consensus about reproductive technologies in Japan (Bai et al., 1987). Nevertheless, Japan took the lead in assisted reproductive technology use and development in Asia. In 1999, Schenker and Shushan reported on the number of assisted reproductive technology centers in the 40 countries of Asia – only 20 countries had such facilities and half were found to be in Japan (Schenker and Shushan, 1996).

In Vitro Fertilization in Japan

Infertility treatments are widely available, and although not covered by the national health insurance scheme, costs are much less than in many other developed countries, so much so that many Japanese patients of mine have chosen to return to Japan for infertility treatment. The combined costs of the international flight and treatment in Japan are less than treatment alone in the United States. Chambers and colleagues reported on the economics of assisted reproduction in multiple developed countries – United States, Canada, United Kingdom, Japan, and Australia, and Scandinavian countries – and noted that a standard *in vitro* fertilization (IVF) cycle cost nearly three times less in Japan than in the United States ($12,513 in the United States compared to $3,956 in Japan based on 2006 US dollars), although cost per birth was closer to half (Chambers et al., 2009). IVF is relatively common, with over 10,000 cases occurring each year (Tsuge, 2010). Although physician clinical management of embryos developed for IVF interventions is perceived as detached, Kato and Sleeboom-Faulkner articulate a much greater sociocultural meaning to women, based on their investigation of 58 women who underwent IVF, and also the need for greater national dialogue about the status of embryos in Japan (Kato and Sleeboom-Faulkner, 2011).

Surrogate Motherhood

Although the Japan Society of Obstetrics and Gynecology, a powerful body with over 15,000 members, has banned surrogate motherhood, the procedure does occur in Japan, albeit infrequently, in private clinics. For example, a Japanese physician made the news for his report of a birth from the oldest surrogate mother, aged 61 at time of the birth. As the pregnancy resulted from a fertilized egg donated by her daughter who lacked a uterus, the surrogate mother gave birth to her own grandchild (MSNBC, 2008; Fujioka, 2008). Given the lack of surrogate parenting options in Japan, some couples have resorted to medical tourism to address their infertility.

Surrogate Motherhood and Medical Tourism

Two cases have exposed the need for clarity regarding surrogate motherhood occurring through medical tourism. In the first case, Mukai Aki, a television personality who had a hysterectomy due to uterine cancer, and her husband Takada Nobuhiko, a wrestler, found a surrogate mother in Nevada, United States, who successfully delivered twins from embryos using Mukai's eggs and Takada's sperm. Based on a surrogacy contract, the twins were awarded to the contracting couple, but their local Ward Office in Japan refused registration of Mukai as the mother of the twins, favoring recognition of the parent mother instead. The couple sued and the Tokyo High Court October 2006 recognized Mukai as the twin's mother (Franco-Malone, 2007).

In the second case, the ban on surrogate motherhood and pursuit of medical tourism abroad resulted in confusion regarding the nationality of the resulting child, Baby Manji. In brief, a Japanese couple travelled to India in 2007 to hire a surrogate mother to bear a child for them under contract. An Indian fertility specialist created an embryo from the sperm of the father and an egg harvested from an anonymous women that he then implanted into yet a different Indian woman. The Japanese couple divorced in June 2008, a month before Baby Manji's birth to the surrogate mother. When born, Baby Manji had three mothers, namely the intended Japanese mother who contracted the surrogate pregnancy, the woman who donated the egg, and the gestational surrogate who carried the pregnancy, but legally Baby Manji did not have a mother. While the contracting Japanese father wanted the baby, under Indian Law, a single man cannot adopt and the contract didn't anticipate the possibility of divorce. This created a diplomatic crisis, although the father was ultimately able to take Baby Manji home. The case highlights the complex issues that have evolved under assisted reproductive technology (Pasayat, 2008). Semba and colleagues consider Japan's lack of legal rules on surrogacy using a multinational comparison with the United States, the United Kingdom, Taiwan, South Korea, and France. They question policies distinguishing between commercial and non-commercial surrogacy and identify areas needing clarification about surrogacy in Japan

(Semba et al., 2011). For the interested reader, Tsuge also provides further exploration of assisted reproduction issues in Japan (Tsuge, 2010).

INTERFACE OF LAW, MEDICINE, AND ETHICS

Ethical issues often become intertwined with legal issues. Several issues that have generated particular interest are addressed below.

Self-regulation and Accountability in Japanese Medicine

Given the strong paternalistic pattern of Japanese medicine and hierarchical structure in many facets of Japanese society, it seemed medicine was virtually immune to legal influences late into the twentieth century. Compared to the United States and many Western countries, there were low rates of litigation over medical injury. Ironically, this seeming invincibility and thus failure of Japanese medicine to promote self-regulation and accountability through peer-review, hospital accreditation, specialty certification, licensure and discipline, death inquests, and civil liability arguably led to a sub-optimal, possibly detrimental approach[4] of regulation of medical malpractice through criminal law (Leflar, 2009b).

Medical Malpractice

On the surface, the substantive content of Japanese law affecting claims for medical malpractice, that is, patients and family members seeking monetary compensation for harms alleged to have occurred due to failure to meet standards of professional care, appears quite similar to other countries (Leflar, 2009b). What emerges as unique in Japan is not how standards are applied, but how particular aspects of the legal system works (few private attorneys working in the field, relatively low rates of litigation, delays in case resolution, structured and predictable damage awards, cheap malpractice insurance for physicians), notably the unusual emphasis on criminal law to regulate poor-quality health care (Leflar, 2009a, 2009b).

Criminal Law in the Regulation of Medical Practice

Criminal prosecutions for severe medical care misjudgments are few in Japan, just like many Western countries, such as United States, United Kingdom, Canada, New Zealand, and France

(Leflar, 2009b). However, when these events do occur, they attract intense media attention in Japan, as in the following cases: (1) in 1999, the wrong surgical procedures were carried out on patients with similar names – heart surgery was performed on the patient with a lung condition and lung surgery performed on the patient with a heart condition; (2) also in 1999, a fatal injection with a disinfectant thought to be heparin was administered; (3) in 2002, mechanical failure of a heart–lung machine occurred during pediatric cardiac surgery; and (4) in 2002, the incredulous, botched, 13-hour-long laparoscopic prostatectomy by neophyte surgeons conducted while they read a manual and consulted with a device manufacturer's representative (Leflar, 2009b). In these cases, police arrested medical personnel or filed papers with prosecutors that resulted in criminal charges (Leflar, 2009b). These cases prompted public attention to the need for safeguards in medicine, but investigations revealed a total lack of self-policing of its ranks by the medical profession. As mentioned earlier, public astonishment achieved a new height of incredulousness at the humiliating arrest and handcuffing that was broadcast on national television in February 2006 of an obstetrician from Ōno Hospital in rural Fukushima for the death two years prior of a woman after a difficult Caesarean section, complicated by massive hemorrhage. Although eventually acquitted, his arrest, detention, and prosecution were denounced by physician groups across Japan (Leflar, 2009b).

Legal Grounds for Criminal Prosecution and 'Unnatural Deaths'

The legal grounds for criminal prosecutions in Japan are threefold: (1) professional negligence; (2) concealment or destruction of evidence; and (3) failure to notify police in timely fashion of 'unnatural deaths.' Leflar, an expert on medical law in Japan, opines that although even the first point is stringent, because mere negligence and not gross negligence is the standard, it is the third point that has elicited significant controversy. The notification requirement, found in Article 21 of the Medical Practitioners' Law, was intended originally to cover public safety and public health-related events, such as non-medical criminal activity, sudden accidents, violent deaths, suicides, epidemics, and other unusual circumstances. In 1994, the Japanese Society of Legal Medicine (*Nihon Hōi Gakkai*), an association of forensic medical specialists who collaborate with police on crime investigations, set forth new guidelines broadening the interpretation of notifiable 'unnatural deaths' to include those possibly caused by medical mismanagement – 'unexpected deaths related to the course of medical treatment

and deaths suspected of being so related' (Leflar, 2009a). The pivotal case after the new interpretation of the law occurred following a mistaken injection case. A patient died at the prestigious Tokyo Metropolitan Hiroo hospital when a nurse injected a disinfectant into a patient from a syringe she mistakenly believed to contain a heparin solution. The hospital CEO ordered the death certificate falsified and delayed reporting the death for 11 days. Convicted under the 'unnatural death' clause and upheld in 2004 by the Supreme Court, the CEO's conviction sent shockwaves through the medical community. Although a number of stakeholder medical societies have weighed in with various guidelines, confusion reigned among doctors, hospital administrators, and legal advisors (Leflar, 2009a). In September 2005, the Ministry of Health, Labour and Welfare launched the 'Model Project for the Investigation and Analysis of Medical Practice-Associated Deaths' that would pilot a new process to include reviewing possible iatrogenic deaths, informing affected parties, and developing preventive measures. Although off to a rocky start, iterations of the program provided optimism for amelioration (Leflar, 2009a).

Self-regulation Vacuum in Medical Research

Slingsby et al. illustrated the overarching lack of self-regulation in Japanese medicine occurred not just in clinical medicine, but also in scientific research (Slingsby, Kodama, & Akabayashi, 2006). Exposed behaviors included manipulating the analysis of data to achieve more compelling results for publication in prestigious international journals, outright fabrication of data, lack of reproducibility of data, and fabrication of article citations in the application for a prestigious grant. While such activities affect researchers at the highest level in Western societies as well[5] (Altman, 1996), the lack of systematic structures in Japan for investigating such events is noteworthy. Perceived barriers to resolving the lack of oversight include: (1) whistle-blowing, which is socially discouraged; (2) uncertainty regarding whether academic societies would be willing to cooperate; and (3) the lack of precedent for a central independent agency to regulate such matters in research (Slingsby, Nagao & Akabayashi, 2006).

Administrative Legislation and Guidelines on Scientific and Ethical Standards

The 1990s witnessed a rapid series of guidelines and legislation relevant to biomedical research and medical treatment. Slingsby and colleagues provide a comprehensive overview and relation of regulatory bodies affecting this work, as well as an explanation of the different kinds of (1) statutory orders, for example, ministerial ordinances and government ordinances, and (2) administrative regulations, such as circulars, orders, notifications, and guidelines (Slingsby et al., 2004). Relative to clinical and practice ethical conduct, it is worth noting two types of committees. The *chiken shinsa iinkai,* namely review and monitoring committee (RMC) is akin to a data safety and monitoring board in the United States. But RMCs only review pharmaceutical clinical trials, which are regulated by the Ministry of Health, Labour and Welfare and function according to the ICH (International Conference on Harmonisation of Technical Requirements for Registration of Pharmaceuticals for Human Use) Good Clinical Practice. The *rinri iinkai*, an ethics committee, is a self-governing body established by each institution without oversight of a governmental ministry. Ethics committee tasks include reviewing research protocols from medical schools and general hospitals, setting hospital policies, and providing clinical ethics consultations (Slingsby et al., 2004).

The Second Phase of Biomedical Ethics in Japan

Akabayashi and colleagues, prolific writers and observers of the biomedical ethics movement in Japan, assert that since the turn of the century, biomedical ethics has moved from an importation phase into a second development phase (Akabayashi, Slingsby, & Kai, 2003; Akabayashi, 2009). They characterize the field as now moving away from the expectation for wholesale importation of ethical principles from North American models towards greater diffusion across health institutions through interdisciplinary efforts and savvy consideration of ethical problems and development of valid positions in a Japanese manner. The more recent emerging bioethical issues address technologically spawned topics similarly found across highly technologically developed societies, for example reproductive technology, human gene research, and other research related to embryonic states of life. In terms of issues yet to come, Akabayashi opines next steps will have to balance further concerns about individual rights and self-determination through a public health ethics given the emerging infectious diseases, such as pandemic influenza, tuberculosis, SARS, AIDS, etc. Akabayashi also forecasts ethical dilemmas that can arise from maldistribution in the physician workforce (e.g., dropping interest in pediatrics, obstetrics and gynecology, general surgery, and growing numbers of citizens, particularly the

elderly, who cannot afford their healthcare premiums) and emerging issues in neuroethics and enhancements (Akabayashi, 2009). Assisted reproductive technology will undoubtedly also spawn further dilemmas as demand is likely to increase given declining fertility.

Admittedly terse, this brief, but broad-strokes overview has sought to highlight major concerns and key issues that have influenced biomedical ethics and medico-legal practices in Japan, as well as the way that Japanese views have been influencing discussions in Western biomedical ethics. Though further details are beyond the scope of this chapter, the reader may wish to explore many additional areas of fascinating inquiry in biomedical ethics and comparative research in Japan about topics, such as medical mistakes (Miyasaka, Kiyota, & Fetters, 2006); quality of care at the end of life (Fetters & Danis, 2002; Long, 2005); contemptible decision making by government officials that caused hemophilia patients to be transfused with a clotting factor contaminated with HIV (Hoshino, 1995; Feldman, 2000); industrial diseases (Walker, 2010); and conflict of interest in medicine (Akabayashi, Slingsby, & Takimoto, 2005; Rodwin, 2011) to mention a few.

CONCLUSIONS

As an observer of the evolution of biomedical ethics and medico-legal influences on them, it strikes the author that North American bioethicists and universalist ethics advocates are sometimes chagrinned by Japanese medicine's resistance to embrace choices that seem logical and philosophically correct to the critic. Japanese medical ethics discourse at the Japanese pace involves the weighing of different cultural and historical viewpoints through a complex process, just as occurs in North America and in other contexts. Ongoing Japanese bioethical discourse is contributing to global discussions and shaping its course. Given a particular North American penchant for absolutes, quick and bold answers, winners and losers, something can be said for having, or at least tolerating, a more involved process. Perhaps the take-home message for biomedical ethics from the Japanese experience is that the most ethical choice is the right thing to do, 'all things' considered, cultural context included, with the understanding that such consideration occurs *at a particular moment* in time.

Challenges to Medicine in Japan

Despite Japan's increasing success in the global environment, Japanese medicine at home experiences stressors. Japan prides itself for the top spot in longevity in the world, although recently there has been slippage in the average life expectancy among the male population. At the same time, the aging of the Japanese society has triggered rising costs of medical care, especially for the treatment of diseases (such as cancer, high blood pressure, and diabetes) that affect older patients, a major topic of concern (Itasaka, 1983; Shinmura, 2006). Despite the recent fiftieth anniversary milestone of the National Health Insurance system (Ikegami et al., 2011), the system is under financial strain that will continue given Japan's low natality. There are many hybrid, specialty-trained, primary care practitioners whose scope of care is restricted to ambulatory practice due to the lack of financial models that would support an open access system in hospitals where their particular specialty procedural skills could be supported. With the ever-increasing complexity of ambulatory primary care practice and demographic changes, ongoing efforts to develop a sytic primary care training system need governmental and academic center support. To the extent that high scores on the national licensure examination persist as the implicit top priority in medical student education, further advances in clinical training will continue to be difficult. The aging of the population and low birth rate in Japan will likely further intensify discussion of many of the major topics of ethical debate. In the absence of regulatory change or ingenious changes to the current regulation of medical practical under criminal law, promoting a culture of safety in medicine in Japan will remain difficult. Japan's technical experience in assisted reproductive technology and new possibilities for pregnancy will continue to encounter uncharted territory needing careful contemplation.

NOTES

1   Others have chosen to translate *dōi* as 'consent' and this translation can be found, among other choices, in Japanese–English dictionaries. Still, the characters for '*dō*' and '*i*' mean 'same' and 'thought.' This seems much more akin to agreement. It particularly seems to lack a volitional nuance found in consent. If *dōi* was equivalent to consent in meaning, perhaps the choice to use the informed consent cognate, *infomudo konsento* would have been avoided. So perhaps it is a moot point since *setsumei to dōi* was abandoned.

2   In one recent experience while teaching on the wards in a rural hospital, the author observed a patient who was told he had cancer, eventually. Interestingly, nearly a week passed between the diagnosis and the ultimate disclosure in a family meeting. In the time between diagnosis and

disclosure, the resident physician who the author precepted on the case appropriately identified the patient's suicidal ideation (thoughts of jumping out the third floor hospital window). These resident's concerns were summarily dismissed by the attending who admonished the patient not to have such thoughts. The family meeting went satisfactorily and treatment was pursued.

3   Established originally in 1976 as the Japan Society for Euthanasia, the society changed its name to the Japan Society for Death with Dignity (JSDD) in 1983. On its website, the JSDD claims a membership of over 125,000 people.

4   Rob Leflar articulates six arguments against the use of criminal law to discipline health professionals for unintentional medical acts: (1) failure as an effective deterrent; (2) severity of punishment seems disproportionate to evil of the act; (3) law enforcement has a poor understanding of medicine's subtleties; (4) criminal prosecutions are protracted; (5) fear of criminal liability may prevent physicians from developing innovative approaches or selecting fields of high risk, for example obstetrics; and (6) a focus on blame deflects attention away from important underlying systemic causes (Leflar, 2009a).

5   Prior to his appointment as Director of National Institutes of Health, Francis S. Collins was operating his own laboratory at the University of Michigan when a graduate student working in his lab was discovered to have systematically fabricated data. Five published articles based on the fabricated data had to be retracted.

REFERENCES

Aita, K. (2011). New organ transplant policies in Japan, including the family-oriented priority donation clause [Article in Japanese]. *Transplantation*, 91(5), 489–491.

Akabayashi, A. (1995). An introductory report on the 'Clinical Ethics' movement in the US and its implication to Japan. *Journal of the Japan Association for Bioethics*, 5(1), 55–59.

Akabayashi, A. (1997). Japan's parliament passes brain-death law. *The Lancet*, 349, 1895.

Akabayashi, A. (2009). Bioethics in Japan (1980–2009): importation, development, and the future. *Asian Bioethics Review*, 1(3), 267–278.

Akabayashi, A., & Slingsby, B.T. (2003). Biomedical ethics in Japan: the second stage. *Cambridge Quarterly of Healthcare Ethics*, 12(3), 261–264.

Akabayashi, A., Fetters, M.D., & Elwyn, T.S. (1999). Family consent, communication, and advance directives for cancer disclosure: a Japanese case and discussion. *Journal of Medical Ethics*, 25(4), 296–301.

Akabayashi, A., Slingsby, B.T., & Kai, I. (2003). Perspectives on advance directives in Japanese society: a population-based questionnaire survey. *BMC Medical Ethics*, 4, E5.

Akabayashi, A., Slingsby, B.T., & Takimoto, Y. (2005). Conflict of interest: a Japanese perspective. *Cambridge Quarterly of Healthcare Ethics*, 14(3), 277–280.

Akechi, T., Okuyama, T., Sugawara, Y., Nakano, T., Shima, Y., & Uchitomi, Y. (2004). Suicidality in terminally ill Japanese patients with cancer. *Cancer*, 100(1), 183–191.

Altman, L.K. (1996, October 30). Falsified data found in gene studies. *New York Times*. Retrieved September 14, 2014 from http://www.nytimes.com/1996/10/30/us/falsified-data-found-in-gene-studies.html?pagewanted=all&src=pm

Bai K., Shirai Y., and Ishii M. 1987. Consensus Has Limits. *The Hastings Center Report*. Vol. 17, No. 3, pp. 18–20.

Beauchamp, T.L. & Childress, J.F. (Eds.). (1994). Beneficence. In *Principles of biomedical ethics* (pp. 259–325). Oxford, UK: Oxford University Press.

Chambers G.M., Sullivan E.A., Ishihara O., Chapman M.G. & Adamson G.D. 2009. The economic impact of assisted reproductive technology: a review of selected developed countries. Fertility and Sterility, 91 (6), 2281–2294.

Coleman, S. (1992). Family Planning in Japanese Society. Princeton, NJ: Princeton University Press, 288.

Elwyn, T.S., Fetters, M.D., Sasaki, H., & Tsuda, T. (2002). Responsibility and cancer disclosure in Japan. *Social Science & Medicine*, 54(2), 281–293.

Feldman, E.A. (1985). Medical ethics the Japanese way. *Hastings Center Report*, 15(5), 21–24.

Feldman, E.A. (2000). *The ritual of rights in Japan: law, society, and health policy*. Cambridge, UK; New York, NY: Cambridge University Press.

Fetters, M.D. (1998). The family in medical decision making: Japanese perspectives [Abstracted version in the *Philosopher's Index*, 32(4), 164]. *Journal of Clinical Ethics*, 9(2), 132–146.

Fetters, M.D., & Danis, M. (2002). Death with dignity: cardiopulmonary resuscitation in the United States and Japan. *Philosophy and Medicine*, 74, 145–163.

Franco-Malone, D. (2007). Forging family ties through full surrogacy: An argument in favor of recognizing non-traditional parents in Japan. *Pacific Rim Law and Policy Journal Association*, October, 1–25.

Fujioka, C. (2008). Japan's surrogate mothers emerge from the shadows. *Reuters*. Retrieved June 2, 2102, from http://www.reuters.com/article/2008/03/13/us-japan-surrogate-idUST3565520080313

Higuchi, N. (1992). The patient's right to know of a cancer diagnosis: a comparison of Japanese paternalism and American self-determination. *Washburn Law Journal*, 31(3), 455–473.

Hisashi K, 1995. インフォームド・コンセント (Informed consent). Retrieved August 10, 2014 from www.lap.jp/lap1/nlback/nl11/nl11kusa.html

Hoshino, K. (1995). HIV+/ Aids related bioethical issues in Japan. *Bioethics*, 9(3/4), 303–308.

Hoshino, K. (1997). Bioethics in the light of Japanese sentiments. In K. Hoshino (Ed.), *Japanese and Western bioethics: studies in moral diversity* (Vol. 54, pp. 13–23). Dordrecht, Netherlands: Kluwer Academic Publishers.

Ikegami, N., Yoo, B.K., Hashimoto, H., Matsumoto, M., Ogata, H., Babazono, A., … Kobayashi, Y. (2011). Japanese universal health coverage: evolution, achievements, and challenges. *Lancet*, 378(9796), 1106–1115.

Itasaka, G. (1983). *Kodansha Encyclopedia of Japan* (pp. 942). Tokyo: Kodansha.

Japan Federation of Bar Associations. (1992). *Declaration on the establishment of patient rights*. Retrieved June 2, 2012, from http://www.nichiben-ren.or.jp/activity/document/civil_liberties/year/1992/1992_3.html

Kai, K. (2009). Euthanasia and death with dignity in Japanese law. *Waseda Bulletin of Comparative Law*, 27, 1–13.

Kato, M., & Sleeboom-Faulkner, M. (2011). Meanings of the embryo in Japan: narratives of IVF experience and embryo ownership. *Sociology of Health & Illness*, 33(3), 434–447.

Kobayashi, E. (2010). Post Istanbul Declaration [Article in Japanese]. *Nihon Rinsho*, 68(12), 2229–2233.

Kurosawa, A. [Writer]. (1952). *Ikiru* (To Live) [Film].

LaFleur, W.R. (1994). *Liquid life: abortion and Buddhism in Japan*. Princeton, NJ: Princeton University Press.

Leflar, R.B. (1996). Informed consent and patients' rights in Japan. *Houston Law Review*, 33(1), 1–112.

Leflar, R.B. (2009a). 'Unnatural deaths,' criminal sanctions, and medical quality improvement in Japan. *Yale Journal of Health Policy Law Ethics*, 9(1), 1–51.

Leflar, R.B. (2009b). The regulation of medical malpractice in Japan. *Clinical Orthopaedics and Related Research*, 467(2), 443–449.

Lock, M.M. (2002). *Twice dead: organ transplants and the reinvention of death*. Berkeley, CA: University of California Press.

Long, S.O. (2000). Public passages, personal passages, and reluctant passages: notes on investigating cancer disclosure practices in Japan. *Journal of Medical Humanities*, 21(1), 3–13.

Long, S.O. (2001). Ancestors, computers, and other mixed messages: ambiguity and euthanasia in Japan. *Cambridge Quarterly of Healthcare Ethics*, 10(1), 62–71.

Long, S.O. (2002). Life is more than a survey: understanding attitudes toward euthanasia in Japan. *Theoretical Medicine and Bioethics*, 23(4–5), 305–319.

Long, S.O. (2005). *Final days: Japanese culture and choice at the end of life.* Honolulu, HI: University of Hawaii Press.

Long, S.O., & Long, B.D. (1982). Curable cancers and fatal ulcers, attitudes toward cancer in Japan. *Social Science & Medicine*, 16(24), 2101–2108.

Masuda, Y., Fetters, M.D., Hattori, A., Mogi, N., Naito, M., Iguchi, A., & Uemura, K. (2003). Physicians's reports on the impact of living wills at the end of life in Japan. *Journal of Medical Ethics*, 29(4), 248–252.

Masuda, Y., Fetters, M.D., Shimokata, H., Muto, E., Mogi, N., Iguchi, A., & Uemura, K. (2001). Outcomes of written living wills in Japan: a survey of the deceased one's families. *Bioethics Forum*, 17(1), 41–52.

Miyasaka, E., Kiyota, A., & Fetters, M.D. (2006). Japanese primary care physicians' errors and perceived causes: a comparison with the United States. *Japan Medical Association Journal*, 49(9 & 10), 286–295.

MSNBC. (2008). *Surrogate mom, 61, gives birth to own grandkid: clinic implants Japanese woman with egg donated by daughter.* Retrieved June 2, 2012, from http://www.msnbc.msn.com/id/26326998/ns/health-pregnancy/t/surrogate-mom-gives-birth-own-grandkid/

Nishigori H., Harrison R., Busari J. & Dornan T. (2014). Bushido and medical professionalism in Japan. Acad Med. 2014 Apr;89(4), 560–3.

Norgren, T. (2001). *Abortion before birth control: the politics of reproduction in postwar Japan.* Princeton, NJ: Princeton University Press.

Obayashi, M. (1982). Historical background of the acceptance of induced abortion. *Josanpu Zasshi*, 36(12), 1011–1016.

Omnibus Budget Reconciliation Act of 1990 (OBRA-90) (2002).

Pasayat A. (2008). Baby Manji Yamada vs Union Of India & Anr (Supreme Court of India Bench: Arijit Pasayat, Mukundakam Sharma). Retrieved August 10, 2014 from http://indiankanoon.org/doc/854968/

Rodwin, M.A. (2011). *Conflicts of interest and the future of medicine.* New York, NY: Oxford University Press.

Sass, J.M., Veatch, R.M., & Kimura, R. (Eds.). (1998). *Advance directives and surrogate decisionmaking in health care.* Baltimore, MD: Johns Hopkins University Press.

Sato, H., Akabayashi, A., & Kai, I. (2005). Public appraisal of government efforts and participation intent in medico-ethical policymaking in Japan: A large scale national survey concerning brain death and organ transplant. *BMC Medical Ethics*, 6, E1.

Schenker J.G., and Shushan A. 1996. Ethical and legal aspects of assisted reproduction practice in Asia *Human Reproduction*, 11 (4), 908–911.

Semba Y., Chang C., Hong H., Kamisato A., Kokado M. & Muto K. (2011). Surrogacy: Donor Conception Regulation in Japan. Bioethics, 24(7), 348–357.

Shinmura, T. 新村拓. (2006). *Nihon iryoshi* 日本医療史 *(The history of Japanese medicine).* Tokyo: Yoshikawa Kobunkan 吉川弘文館.

Slingsby, B.T., Nagao, N., Akabayashi, A. (2004) Administrative legislation in Japan: guidelines on scientific and ethical standards. Cambridge Quarterly of Healthcare Ethics. 13, 245–253.

Slingsby, B.T., Kodama, S., & Akabayashi, A. (2006). Scientific misconduct in Japan: the present paucity of oversight policy. *Cambridge Quarterly of Healthcare Ethics*, 15(3), 294–297.

Terayama, Y. (2010). Revised act on organ transplantation from the neurological viewpoint [Article in Japanese]. *Brain Nerve*, 62(6), 583–586.

Top court dismisses euthanasia appeal. (2009). *Kyodo News.* Retrieved on August 10, 2014 from http://www.japantimes.co.jp/news/2009/ 12/10/national/top-court-dismisses-euthanasia-appeal/

Tsuge, A. (2010). How society responds to desires of childless couples: Japan's position on donor conception. Retrieved on August 10, 2014, from http://soc.meijigakuin.ac.jp/fuzoku/wp-content/uploads/2010/04/35tuge.pdf

Walker, B.L. (2010). *Toxic archipelago: a history of industrial disease in Japan.* Seattle, WA: University of Washington Press.

Yokota, H. (2010a). Problems of the revised organ transplantation law for organ donation from child [Article in Japanese]. *Nihon Rinsho*, 68(12), 2322–2326.

Yokota, H. (2010b). Revised organ transplantation act in Japan from the view of emergency doctors [Article in Japanese]. *Brain Nerve,* 62(6), 565–573.

Yuen, J.K., Reid, M.C., & Fetters, M.D. (2011). Hospital do-not-resuscitate orders: why they have failed and how to fix them. *Journal of General Internal Medicine*, 27(7), 791–797.

Zasshi N.I. (1990). Setsumei to Doi nituiteno Houkokusho (Report on Explanation and Consent). Japan Medical Association, 103, 515–535.

18

Mental Health in Japan

Denise St Arnault

The investigation of culture, society, and mental health always involves a broad investigation of norms, values, interpersonal behaviors, self-development, and theories about personality. All of this must be contextualized within the historical, political, and economic frameworks within which mental health care is financed and delivered. Understanding mental health requires examining the experiences of symptoms, the social contexts that constrain or support the communication of those, as well as community level forces such as stigma and labeling. In addition, understanding mental health care requires an examination of the larger political and economic aspects of Japanese culture and society such as gendered expectations of the ideal Japanese citizen, the importation of Western or American psychiatry, and the governmental regulation of medical and mental health services.

American psychology and psychiatry have held a particular fascination about the differences between the Japanese and American personality and social organization, and there is an extensive library of materials on this topic, making a synopsis a daunting challenge. Therefore, I will focus on providing an overview of efforts to understand 'the Japanese personality' from both inside and outside of Japan as a starting point. Next, research about Japanese social behavior and self-organization can help the

reader understand Japanese expectations about mental health and social functioning. This brings us to indigenous psychologies and psychotherapeutics, as well as 'Japanese-specific' mental health problems. Finally, a brief history of legislation and funding for mental health services and medications will be offered, leading us to the awareness of the impact of a rapidly Westernizing culture on the mental health for the Japanese.

THE MYTH OF JAPANESE UNIQUENESS

The aim of this brief introduction is to help the reader retain a critical stance about the seeming 'uniqueness' of the Japanese personality, mental health problems, and therapeutic solutions. It is very difficult for the student of Japanese culture to avoid the plethora of material that was generated around the world about the Japanese; however, it is important to understand that material within its historical development and context.

Japanese society developed their modern political and economic policies within a historical context of a people who had remained in relative cultural isolation for more than 700 years (1185–1853). During that time, Japan had a feudal agricultural economy, which was characterized by a patrilineal kinship system organized around the household, or *ie* (Befu, 1980, 1993). Within this system, the eldest son inherited the family property and the responsibilities as the househead, and the other sons established stem families. Stem families were essentially equivalent to nuclear families because they were established outside the *ie* or household structure. Because these stem families had a marginal role in the economics of the village, these families were free to move to the cities with the coming of urbanization and industrialization in the mid to late 1800s. Vogel has attributed the social organization of the stem families as a primary factor that allowed for the massive urbanization of Japan, but until then, this familial organization shaped the political organization of the village, and was legally upheld by the Imperial government (Vogel, 1967). The Meiji restoration in 1873 abolished this class-based economic system.

Some authors believe that this political isolation and economic organization allowed a cultural, aesthetic, and psychological fascination with what was deemed Japanese uniqueness, or *Japanese-ness*. Engagement with the West was held at bay until the late 1800s, but at the advent of this encounter with the West, the concept of *Japanese-ness* became a study in the contrast between 'the East' and 'the West' (Befu, 1993; Dale, 1986; Mouer & Sugimoto, 1986). *Nihonjinron*, or the study of *Japanese-ness*, has been described as a form of cultural nationalism that occurred in the humanities, the sciences, and within political circles. Initially arising in Japan, and later propagated within academic circles worldwide, these studies became the prominent models the world used to understand Japan, and to compare the Japanese with people in the West.

Nihonjinron aimed to articulate, and sometimes to scientifically prove, the essential, homogeneous, and unique character of the Japanese. In Japan, these writings and studies generally took the tone of a 'racial' superiority of the Japanese people (Morris-Suzuki, 1995; Weiner, 1997). In the West, theories about Japanese personality development provided a sort of looking glass with which to contrast and therefore clarify and articulate Western ways of being.

There have been two primary critiques about these waves of academic and political writings. One critique was that *Nihonjinron* studies received wide support and dissemination by the Japanese Ministry of Education, major Japanese philanthropic groups, and other grant-making bodies (Mouer & Sugimoto, 1986). This critique emphasizes that, whether these studies were accurate or not, this was the way the West came to know the Japanese because they were extensively available to the academic and popular readerships. This dissemination of *Nihonjinron* literature by the Japanese government enforced cultural ideologies

about in-group and outsider boundaries and group harmony (which we review later) at the political level.

Another critique has taken the form of efforts to discredit the reliability of the *Nihonjinron* writings by challenging the methods used, or challenging the validity of the conclusions drawn (Befu, 1993; Dale, 1986; MacDonald, 1995; Morris-Suzuki, 1995; Smith, 1961; Yoshino, 1992). These authors have generally posited that group orientation, hierarchy, conflict, dissension, resistance, and diversity exist in all societies, including Japan. They give examples of conflict and resistance in Japan even when the political pressures enforced the dominant ideology of conformity and homogeneity. These studies have sought to demonstrate the fallacies of *Nihonjinron* research by displaying that economic divisions exist despite the popularly held and politically useful idea that Japan is a middle-class society.

Maintaining this critical stance is essential when evaluating how the Japanese understand themselves, and how the Western reader should attempt to understand them. Despite these critiques, it is also true that cultural frames *do* define preferred social behaviors, and that socialization *will* shape styles of self-perception and interacting. In order to understand mental health and health care in Japan, therefore, we examine literature about the Japanese styles of relating, and how these styles might manifest into personality organization, symptom experience, and communication of need.

JAPANESE SELF AND SOCIAL ORGANIZATION

Despite the previously mentioned caveats about the overgeneralizations about the uniqueness and homogeneity in Japanese culture in the 1800 through the early 1900s, understanding the concepts of group boundaries, as well as hierarchical organization, is important (Clark, 1996; Lebra, 1974; Nakane, 1970; Smith, 1961). The concept of group-ness involves the perception of interpersonal boundaries, as well as recognition of the separation between the inside and the outside. In Japan, the idea of the inside, or *uchi*, suggests emotionality, familiarity, intimacy and group solidarity. However, within any group there are also differences in age, social status and social roles. These differences create another important dimension of Japanese social life, referred to as hierarchy or the vertical principle. Nakane and Reischauer have written about vertical relationships within organizations, relating roots of this type of social organization to the historical formation of the traditional family and village (Nakane, 1970; Reischauer, 1981).

Several factors determine one's relative social status. Variables that decrease intimacy includes social differences, including regionality, education, age, gender, occupation, and race. Variables that increase intimacy include similarities in age, social status, occupational affiliation, interdependence and familiarity. These factors exist in dynamic tension, so that these variables may shift to the foreground or background in any given situation. It is also possible for the person of higher social status to either emphasize or de-emphasize this status, allowing for decreased or increased intimacy in a given situation. Other factors that are central to hierarchical organization include both the levels of education as well as the relative prestige of the institution with which one is affiliated (Goodman, 1992; Rohlen, 1983; Smith, 1961). Finally, there are more subtle factors within a given social scene that influence hierarchy and social behavior. These social variables include regionality, dialects, and the status held by one's family.

Because of these important social dynamics, Japanese social behavior involves astute and accurate perceptions about the relative closeness or distance between the other and oneself (Bachnik, 1994; Hendry, 1992; St Arnault, 2002). Bachnik describes Japanese social relationships in terms of the level of intimacy between the parties interacting (Bachnik, 1994). The closest or most intimate level is referred to by the Japanese as *uchi*. The people within the *uchi* include one's closest friends and one's family, especially those with whom one lives. Relations among members of the *uchi* are characterized by relatively free expression of emotions and needs, referred to as *honne*. Interactions between the members of the *uchi* are also characterized by interdependency, referred to as *amae*. The next level of closeness in Japanese social relationships includes those within the community, school affiliations, and relationships with extended kin. These are semi-intimate relationships with members of this social circle, in which flexible and careful attention to shifting levels of status are required.

The final level of social distance in Japanese society includes all those who are outside of the other two social circles. This level includes the mass society and international relations. Relationships with outsiders are characterized by polite, ritualized interactions, or *tatamae*. The importance of this interpersonal formality is so great that Japanese culture is referred to as *wrapped* (Ben-Ari, Moeran, & Valentine, 2011). *Tatemae*, or wrapping, means that 'the self' is packaged or presented for public viewing, as opposed to the freedom and private behavior shown only to intimates. The members of this outer social sphere are referred to by the Japanese as soto-they are strangers-suspect and unknown. Relationships with strangers are characterized by distrust, avoidance, and ritualized

public performance. The *soto* is to be avoided and protected against. Japanese culture values engagement with one's own intimate and semi-intimate members, and therefore discourages out-group or multiple group affiliations.

Members within any group rely on each other for assistance, and the exchange of favors referred to as reciprocity (Befu, 1980; Lebra, 1974; Lebra, 1983; St Arnault, 2002, 2004). However, seeking help varies depending on the type of social circle. Help seeking from within the semi-intimate social circle involves drawing on the obligation each member feels toward the welfare of the group. This type of exchange of assistance is referred to as *gimu*. *Gimu* or reciprocal exchange is an important feature of Japanese life because for every favor one draws upon, an exchange is owed. Therefore, careless or repeated use of favors leads one into some situations whereby one is indebted to many people.

Because of the complexities of social organization within and between groups, and reciprocity rules for the exchange of help, Japanese culture places high value on self-reliance. Self-reliance allows one to live relatively free from interpersonal indebtedness. Since everyone has an intimate social network, within which one is interdependent, seeking help for personal needs within the *uchi* is the preferred choice.

THE SELF IN JAPANESE CULTURE

As we have seen, the ideology of the group is based on consensus and solidarity of the group as a whole, while the vertical principle is a force that emphasizes differences among members within the group. These complementary social factors affect the way a person defines his or her self in any given situation. The combination of the level of intimacy and the social position within the group provides the guidelines for behavior. Bachnik (1994) refers to the self in Japanese society as *situated* – that is, the meaning of the situation and the self within it are derived from a multitude of situational factors. Therefore, understanding Japanese personality, and mental health, must begin with these contrasting and complementary notions of *uchi, soto,* conformity, harmony and the vertical principle or hierarchy. The abilities to understand these subtleties, and oneself within them, are considered by the Japanese to be marks of social and psychological maturity (Bachnik, 1994; Hendry, 1992; Kamitani, 1993; Markus, Kitayama, & Heiman, 1996).

Markus and Kitayama have referred to Japan and other Asian cultures as sociocentric (Markus & Kitayama, 1991). This is in contrast to individualistic cultures that socialize people to define and focus on individual needs. The self in sociocentric cultures, such as the Japanese, has been difficult to understand using the individualistic model as the standard. The self in a sociocentric culture is defined in relation to the group rather than separate from it. The sociocentric self is better understood as relational, situated within a given context, or shifting. Roland has suggested that the self in Japanese society is so embedded within the group that individuals struggle to access it consciously (Roland, 1988). This analysis is challenged by authors such as Keiichi and Kamitani, who assert that not only do the Japanese have a stable sense of self, but also that the recognitions of *both* group and individual needs allow for mature interpersonal relationships (Kamitani, 1993; Keiichi, 1978).

Japanese socialization within the inner circle of intimate relationships, while emphasizing group solidarity, does not overlook each individual's unique nature (Hendry, 1992; Mouer, 1984). However, the recognition of individual temperament and talents is not the same as self-assertion. Self-assertion is frowned upon in Japanese culture because it is seen as crudely pushing forth one's personal needs without adequate recognition of the context or the needs of the group. The cultural ideal of 'autonomy apart from others' is not a part of the sociocentric socialization. The recognition of interdependency with others is the primary cultural training. The inability of an individual to recognize this interdependency is considered by the Japanese to be immature. Pushing forth one's needs in groups, as if one were autonomous from the support of that group, is seen as a threat to the harmony of that group. Because the individual has an essential interdependency on the group for meeting basic and social need, self-assertion is also seen as self-destructive to the individual (Keiichi, 1978).

Within the Japanese cultural frame, people learn to determine the values that are important to them, and create social and life situations that are in line with them. Keiichi refers to this as value constancy. The idea of value constancy is an interpersonal strategy in which one keeps his or her awareness of themselves intact despite the group focus in social relationships. This formulation of value constancy in Japanese social relationships allows an understanding of a stable consistent sense of self alongside a keen awareness of context and others. Thus, people with socially embedded selves are aware of their personal needs, their socially prescribed roles, the roles and relative rank of others, and the social demands of the context (Johnson, 1995; Kondo, 1990).

The concept of value constancy in social relationships formulation also allows an understanding of the Japanese self as active in decision making. The individual with a socially embedded self will examine the social situation and decide the action that maximizes overall satisfaction (Keiichi, 1978). The Japanese person remains mindful of his or her individual differences, personal needs, and the Japanese community as a whole. This complex view of interdependency allows for a culturally specific definition of emotional and psychological maturity for the Japanese (Doi, 1973; Johnson, 1995; Kamitani, 1993; Kondo, 1990), and allows us to avoid the generalizations about the Japanese as *only* group-oriented. The Japanese person learns to focus on the interpersonal variables within a given social sphere. Kamitani (1996) has defined the concept of interdependency as the expression of independence while understanding and acting according to the principle of that interdependence. She calls this idea integrated dependence, socially sensitive independence, or *jiritsu*. Kamitani defines *jiritsu* as 'a refined, mature state capable of being independent and responsible and at the same time interdependent, mutually reliant, and sympathetic' (Kamitani, 1996: 1355). She defines independence as free decision-making, mutual non-interference, self-confidence, and self-assertion and concludes that it is a mark of psychological maturity.

EMOTIONAL EXPERIENCE AND EXPRESSION WITHIN A GROUP ORIENTED SOCIETY

Maintaining Harmony

As indicated earlier, the group is a central feature in Japanese cultural ideology. Smooth functioning within the group requires a person to sensitively assess each interpersonal situation and one's role within it. Carefully enacting the expected behavior in each situation proves that one seeks to maintain harmonious relations with others; however, role fulfillment includes personal sacrifices. Each individual understands these sacrifices as part of the membership within an interdependent social network, with the needs of the group taking precedence over their personal hardships. Each member of the Japanese family experiences these sacrifices; therefore, part of maintaining harmony within the family and the broader society requires perseverance in suffering, referred to as *gaman*. This quality of inner strength is an important feature of social life and involves many other areas of life (Johnson, 1995; Keiichi, 1978; Mouer, 1984; Mouer & Sugimoto, 1986).

As we have seen, self-understanding and self-confidence are important aspects of maturity; however, the expression of these personal characteristics must be done judiciously to preserve harmony. Japanese culture values and nurtures the ability for people to sensitively measure or discriminate the relative distance within the social situation. This discrimination of key variables in a social situation is referred to *kejime* (Doi, 1973; Johnson, 1995; Lebra, 1974, 1976). The ability to discriminate is essential because the relative intimacy of the parties involved in a situation determines the appropriate level of formality required in the situation. Actual situations may vary from case to case, but the cultural principle governing cross-situational interaction is simple and clear – one situation should not be mixed with another.

Conformity and Social Sanctions for Deviance

Japanese socialization also emphasizes the cultural ideal of harmony. Behaviors that foster conflict or indicate deviance are frowned upon (Bestor, 1996; Johnson, 1995; Lebra, 1983; St Arnault, 2004; St Arnault & Roels, 2012; Smith, 1961). The Japanese have a cultural edict that states 'a tall tree catches the wind.' This edict is also related to the ritualized public performance indicated previously. People behave in a culturally defined way in public. Although Japanese culture may have been modified somewhat with urbanization, Bestor and St. Arnault have documented that urban Japanese communities may use gossip and the threat of ostracism to ensure conformity and socially appropriate behavior. Social control behaviors draw on the distinctions between the inside and the outside, the importance of group harmony, and the values placed on the individual to remain self-reliant and strong (Bestor, 1996; St. Arnault, 2003; St. Arnault and Roels, 2012). In this cultural milieu, the presence of any deviance, especially mental illness, is considered at least a personal failure, and at most, an example of the failure of the family to care for its own. Therefore, expressions of mental suffering are often avoided in order to prevent these perceptions within the individual, within the family, and of others about the family.

The Importance of the Body in a Group Oriented Society

Culture directs how to communicate needs, what feelings can be expressed, and how these should be expressed (Ellsworth, 1994; Fiske et al., 1998; Jenkins and Karno, 1992; Mesquita & Frijda, 1992; St Arnault, 2002). Cultural expectations or cultural models can be described as predominately interdependent or independent. Interdependent cultural models, in general, consider personal needs less important than the overall needs of the group. Most non-Western and indigenous cultural models are believed to be oriented toward interdependence. People in an interdependent cultural environment tend to behave in ways that foster harmonious group interaction, tend to seek the approval of others within the social environment, and respect rules of social conformity as a means of minimizing the potentially disruptive quality of personal needs. These people may be socialized to downplay expression of both positive and negative emotions in the interest of meeting the needs of others. Independent cultural models, in contrast, value personal needs as more salient and important than the needs of the group. People in an independent cultural environment tend to emphasize their personal needs and characteristics. They tend to value agency, environmental control and mastery, individuality, and tend to emphasize personal strengths. They are socialized to verbally articulate personal needs and feelings, and to distinguish these from physical sensations (Cross & Markus, 1991; Fiske et al., 1998; Kitayama, Markus, & Kurokawa, 2000; Markus, Mullally, & Kitayama, 1997).

In the Japanese cultural system, experiences of health are understood to be the result of respectful and appropriate relationships with spirits and with others, especially those in one's family, and are seen in people whose thoughts and emotions are balanced and harmonious. In the Japanese cultural system, physical sensations are closely monitored because they are understood as signs of emerging disharmony in one of more of these areas. For the Japanese, attending to physical, emotional, and social disharmony is an important focus, and restoration of harmony or balance is the key to health; therefore, attention to subtle physical sensations, diet patterns, sleep patterns, social rules, and spiritual activities are attended to daily (Kirmayer, 2001; Kleinman, 1982, 1983, 1988; Lin, 1996; Lock, 1987a; Ohnuki-Tierney, 1984).

Somatization has been defined as 'both the expression of physical complaints in the absence of defined organic pathology and the amplification of symptoms resulting from established physical pathology (e.g. chronic disease)' (Kleinman, 1982: 129). However, somatic expression of distress depends on cultural influences related to the illness. Some researchers have speculated that for the Japanese, reporting somatic symptoms is culturally more acceptable compared with reporting emotional symptoms. In this formulation, we can see that somatic symptoms may be understood as a culturally accepted and normative way to express stress, resistance to perceived oppression, and general social discontent, rather than an indication of pathology (Kirmayer, 1989, 1991; Kirmayer, Dao, & Smith, 1998; Kitayama, Markus, & Matsumoto, 1995). In a culture where direct expression of discontent is seen as deviant or disruptive, somatization can be understood as a non-confrontational interpersonal communication that is adaptive.

JAPANESE THEORIES AND THERAPIES

Cultural, folk, or indigenous theories about mental health explain expectations about what is normative, preferred, acceptable, typical, or ideal. They refer to expectations about perceptions, emotions, and social behaviors that are within the realm or acceptable, and they define when deviations from these have reached a threshold that indicates 'illness.' These theories further define causation for those deviations, as well as the remedies for them. In Japanese psychiatry, there have been three major efforts to define mental illness deviations prior to the massive import of Western psychiatric categories. These are the theories and therapies defined by Morita, the Buddhist therapy known as Naikan therapy, and the Japanese psychoanalytic theories espoused by Doi.

The Morita School of Japanese psychology was developed by Japanese psychiatrist Shoma Morita beginning in 1919, and was influenced by the principles of Zen Buddhism. His theory of anxiety was based on the philosophy that negative human emotions are natural and acceptable human responses. The aim of Morita therapy is to relieve conditions of *shinkeishitsu* or nervosity, which are characterized by hypochondriasis, self-preoccupation and introversion, perfectionism, egocentricity, and high achievement motivation. Similar to Eastern traditions in Buddhist meditation, Morita believed that efforts to control negative emotion was wasted energy, and that it is better for the person to accept these feelings as natural and take responsibility for them. Morita therapy is a structured approach that removes the patient from their physical environment and teaches them to practice techniques that create positive meanings for their nervous and anxious nature, and how to use this natural inclination for practical purposes. Patients are directed to engage in meaningful activities as they learn to accept themselves as productive and healthy people. This method was originally an inpatient treatment; however, applications of Morita therapy have expanded to outpatient, and are now used in both Japan and North America (Ishiyama, 1986). One such application is the Acceptance and Commitment therapy (ACT) (Hofmann, 2008).

Naikan refers to inward-looking, and is a therapy developed in the 1940s by Ishin Yashimoto, a devout Buddhist of the Pure Land sect (Murase, 1982). In the 1960s, he translated the Buddhist practice of *mishirabe*, which is a method of meditation and self-reflection, into a therapeutic modality.

The aim of the therapy is to answer three essential life questions: (1) 'What did this person give to me?'; (2) 'What did I return to this person?'; and (3) 'What trouble did I cause this person?'. This is accomplished by facilitating the patient to reflect on their past, which is divided into 3-year segments. The patient is confronted with their obligations to their parents, teachers, peers, siblings, and society as a whole. Studies have indicated that *Naikan* is an effective therapeutic treatment for disorders such as addiction, psychosomatic disorders, anxiety disorders, and criminal behavior (Ozawa-de Silva & Ozawa-de Silva, 2010).

The introduction of psychoanalysis in Japan in the 1920s and 1930s prompted Takeo Doi to introduce the concept of *amae* to the world. *Amae* is a concept in Japanese culture that refers to the need to be in good favor with, and to be able to depend upon, the people within one's close inner circle (Doi, 1992). In Doi's theoretical analysis, this is a uniquely Japanese phenomenon; however, the importance of attachment in the parent–child to healthy self-development is widely understood. Doi's early work links the idea of *amae* to other Japanese concepts such as *enryo* (restraint) and *giri* (social obligation). Doi and others have examined the importance of *amae* throughout life in varieties of social bonding – teacher–student, supervisor–subordinate, or husband–wife – and hypothesized that these relationships are patterned after the primary mother–child experience. Doi argued that Japanese culture encourages individuals to use *amae* throughout their lives, whereas Western culture encourages people to outgrow the desire to use *amae* as quickly as possible – the end result being an emphasis on the group in Japanese society and on the individual in the West.

These three examples provide the reader with a framework for understanding the ways that the Japanese have developed treatment for their own mental illness that is consistent with their views about health. In these examples, one can see the emphasis on social interaction between a person and his social world, both in the causal formulations as well as the therapeutic modalities. In Morita therapy, it is the obsessive preoccupation with the inner world that creates symptoms, and the remedy is removal from the social world while one develops an awareness that their fears about fears others perceptions are normal and natural. In *Naikan* therapy, the emphasis is on the recognition that one is always fundamentally indebted to others and to engage in gratitude in order to live within the social world. Finally, for Doi, the intimate interdependency of people with others is a core developmental task in Japanese life. As we shall see, the illnesses that are specific to Japanese culture are also variations of these fundamental conceptions of mental health in Japan.

MENTAL ILLNESSES IN JAPAN

Western Diagnoses: The Problem of Equivalence

Examining mental disorders across cultures requires recognition of the problem without the uncritical importation of Western diagnostic labels. Using the term 'idioms of distress,' we can understand and describe culturally specific experiences of psychosocial and physical suffering, understanding them from within a cultural frame. In this way, we can document and explain diversities in idioms of distress for the Japanese, rather than incidence of mental illness, allowing us to recognize culturally distinct patterns and avoiding the premature or possibly erroneous conclusion that mental illness is experienced the same way across cultures. Distress experiences in the Japanese can therefore be understood as conditions that may signify the presence of physical diseases or disorders, may indicate mental illnesses, may symbolically represent interpersonal and intrapsychic conflicts, or may be culturally coded ways of expressing social discontent (Kirmayer, et al., 1998).

For example, what is labeled as 'depression' in Western culture is primarily an affective phenomenon that may not be experienced by the Japanese in the same way. Unfortunately, these caveats have largely been ignored in global psychiatry; very few studies have used culturally sensitive, systematic methods to examine mental illness in Japanese samples. While many studies have confirmed the reliability of the use of Western-developed depression instruments in cross-cultural studies (Barrera & Garrison-Jones, 1988; Beck, Steer, & Garbin, 1988; Kojima et al., 2002; Yeung et al., 2002), from a *construct validity* point of view, investigators have found that the East Asian and Japanese beliefs and practices around the experience and expression of positive emotions may falsely inflate the depression scores on a variety of self-report depression screening instruments (Cho & Kim, 1998; Cho, Nam, & Suh, 1998; Iwata & Buka, 2002; Iwata & Roberts, 1996; Iwata, Roberts, & Norito, 1995; Iwata, Saito, & Roberts, 1994; Iwata et al., 1998; Noh, Kasper, & Chen, 1998). In addition, reliance on somatic indicators such as sleep, appetite, and fatigue (as with Western depression instruments) may be based on the idioms of distress for Western samples, thereby systematically overlooking important symptoms for members of other groups – symptoms such as headache, neurological symptoms, pain, and abdominal distress.

Another important issue in the importing of Western concepts into Japanese psychiatry is the Western focus on mood symptoms with the relative exclusion of somatic ones. As we have seen, somatic distress may be common in Japanese and other East Asian cultures (Draguns, Phillips, Broverman, & Caudill, 1970; Gureje et al., 1997; Hinton & Hinton, 2002; Hong, Lee, & Lorenzo, 1995; Iwata & Roberts, 1996; Kanno, 1981; Kawanishi, 1992; Kirmayer et al., 1998; Kirmayer & Groleau, 2001; Lock, 1987b; Maeno, Kizawa, Ueno, Nakata, & Sato, 2002; Pang, 1998; Parsons & Wakeley, 1991; Simon et al., 1999). For example, in Japanese clinics, 13–15 percent of patients had both depression and co-occurring physical symptoms (Maeno et al., 2002; Mino, Aoyama, & Froom, 1994). Lock's ethnographic research on somatic distress in middle-aged women found that *futeishūso* (non-specific physical complaints) included symptoms such as coldness, shoulder pain, palpitations, and nervousness (Lock, 1987b). Both the physicians and patients in her study related these symptoms with social discontent, problems with the autonomic nervous system, pelvic inflammatory disease, and general personality sensitivity (Lock, 1987b). Like Lock, transcultural psychiatry has examined how somatic symptoms in depression in may be partly the result of the socially and cultural understanding that emotions are symbolically and holistically interrelated with somatic sensations and interpersonal disharmony.

PREDOMINANT PSYCHIATRIC DIAGNOSES IN JAPAN

Consistent with the importance of social context – and functioning within it – in Japanese culture, Japanese psychiatry has articulated anxiety and social-relatedness disorders most thoroughly. This tendency is exemplified in this section, where the reader will find several similar but distinct anxiety-like disorders. Next, we will look at the relatively newer phenomenon of depression-like disorders, as well as the dramatic increase in suicide in Japanese culture. In the interest of a complete analysis of mental disorders in Japan, I will also address the concerns about labeling schizophrenia, and changes in rates and types of substance use in Japan.

Anxiety-like Conditions

Neurasthenia was hypothesized by Beard as early as 1829 to be a functional disorder produced by modern civilization. The label originally referred to a 'weakness of the nerves' in a person, and sometimes was referred to as a constitutional weakness that made a person unable to tolerate or manage the stresses of modern civilization. The term for neurasthenia in Japanese loosely translates as 'nervous breakdown,' and is a condition with symptoms of fatigue, anxiety, headache, nerve pain, and depressed mood. Neurasthenia remains a diagnosis in the World Health Organization's International Classification of Diseases (World Health Organization, 1992). Beard's concept was accepted widely in the early twentieth century, not only in Japanese psychiatry, but throughout the East and in Europe (Kitanishi & Kondo, 1994). Morita recognized neurasthenia, but developed the concept of *shinkeishitsu,* or constitutional neurasthenia. For Morita, the overwhelming anxiety components became his clinical focus. S*hinkeishitsu* describes a person who is overly sensitive to the social environment, and who worries about what others will think of them, has fears and worries about somatic symptoms, and worries about their appearance. They are also easily agitated and sensitive to noises, the cold, or are either fearful or sensitive to dirt. Morita developed the therapy described earlier to help these people accept these sensitivities and regain their ability to function in the world (Russell, 1989).

Taijinkyofusho (also called TKS) is an indigenous diagnostic label and can be understood as a subcategory of *shinkeishitsu.* It can be loosely translated to be social phobia, phobia of people, or fear of interpersonal relationships or situations. The symptoms of this disorder are varied, but include an intense fear that one's body will displease or offend others. The person can experience anxiety, as well as shame and embarrassment in social circumstances. People with TKS find it extremely difficult to engage in interpersonal situations. It is typically diagnosed in adolescence or early adulthood, affects 10–20 percent of the Japanese population, and is more common in males than females. This condition also has diagnostic subcategories that include fear of blushing, fear that the body is disfigured, and fear that one has a foul odor. This condition is treated with cognitive behavioral therapy, mild medications, as well as Morita therapy (Russell, 1989).

Hikikomori (meaning to pull in and close up) is a protracted social withdrawal among adolescent males in which the inflicted person will remain in their house for at least 6 months or more, and who strictly limit communication with others (Koyama et al., 2010). Interestingly, people will be described as having the condition, but the people themselves might also use the label to refer to themselves ('I am *Hikkikomori*'). There has been research examining whether these young adults have other existing disorders, and one study found that 54.5 percent had also experienced a lifetime psychiatric disorder (including mood, anxiety, or substance abuse), and that these people had a 6.1-times higher risk of having had a mood disorder (Nagata et al., 2013). The remaining did not to meet any other diagnostic criteria (Watts, 2002). There is also interest in

the cause of this disorder, including research on the correlates in the family environment (Umeda & Kawakami, 2012), whether this disorder is a reaction to the stress of being a member of Japanese society, or whether it is a new form of depression experienced by youth in a modern era in many rapidly developing countries (Kato et al., 2012).

Depression-like Conditions, Overwork, and Suicide

Examining depression in Japanese culture presents an interesting set of problems. As is evident in the illnesses listed earlier, Japanese conceptions of mental health problems have emphasized anxiety rather that depression. Depression was generally considered a 'rare disease,' but it is now referred to as a health crisis in Japan in the last 10–15 years. According to recent literature, although there has been an increase in awareness and diagnosis of depression recently, the Japanese may not have wholly subscribed to the idea that depression is primarily due to neurotransmitter dysregulation (Kitanaka, 2011). Other new concepts have also been introduced, such as 'Japanese-style fatigue-induced depression,' or 'Modern Type Depression (MTD)' (Kato et al., 2011). MTD is seen in those born after 1970, and is characterized by (1) limited loyalty for social structures; (2) negativity about rules and order; (3) vague sense of omnipotence; and (4) rejection of the social mandate to be hard working (Kato et al., 2011). People with MTD may experience fatigue, self-reproach, blame others, and engage in avoidance and impulsivity.

Other depression-like concepts have made the news in the last 20 years. *Kar̄oshi* (death from overwork), *kar̄o utsubȳo* (overwork depression), and *kar̄o jisatsu* (overwork suicide) have become public conditions in the 1990s (Kitanaka, 2011; Targum & Kitanaka, 2012). These are health crises among men. In contrast to the people with MTD, men who have these conditions strongly embrace the Japanese work ethic to their detriment. Rapidly increasing suicide rates and deaths and suicide by overwork have forced Japan to begin to take depression seriously. International headlines are alarming, with over 100 suicide deaths a day and 30,000 annually for 12 consecutive years. In men, these deaths are at rates of 3 to 1 compared to women. For men under 44 and women 15–34, suicide is the most frequent cause of death. Among the G8 developed countries, the suicide rate is highest in Russia, then Japan, France, Germany, Canada, United States, Italy, and the United Kingdom (World Health Organization, 2013).

The rise in depression and suicide rates have become the rallying cry for mental health advocates who have acknowledged the collective crises in Japanese culture and have facilitated expansion of mental health services and mental health system reform.

> Socially aware psychiatrists, in particular, turn depression into not only a symbolic token for the anguish of workers living in a recession but also a practical means of obtaining long-term sick leave and economic compensation. Thus, for those involved in workers' movements, the psychiatric diagnosis of depression has become an indispensable tool. What is notable is that these psychiatrists have opened up the etiology of depression to legal, public debates, turning it into a political battleground for disputing whether the responsibility of an individual's breakdown lies in their biological vulnerability or in the social environment (Kitanaka, 2011: 10).

Understanding how mental health, suicide, sociopolitical and economic realities, and culturally based gender norms intersect is a challenge that has moved to the forefront of psychiatry in Japan. For example, since there was a dramatic increase in suicide in 1998, as well as an economic recession, some speculate that these forces are deeply connected. However, as we have seen, the incidence of anxiety-like disorders and MTD are also on the rise. Finally, suicide is the leading cause of death among women 15–34, which argues against purely economic reasons for these rates (Kaga, Takeshima, & Matsumoto, 2009). Many commentators have therefore focused on how rapid culture change and rigid cultural rules and norms might be a central factor shaping the mental health of the modern Japanese, rather that economics and urbanization as we often see in other countries.

Schizophrenia

People with schizophrenia had a complicated and difficult treatment in Japan in the early twentiethth century, marked by special legislation that mandated that families take custody of these patients (*Seishin Byo Sha Kango Ho*) (Sato, 2006). This law was replaced in 1950 by a Mental Hygiene Law; however, at least two-thirds of the inpatients in mental institutions in Japan are still diagnosed with schizophrenia (Sato, 2006). The Japanese term for schizophrenia is *bunretsubyo*, meaning a mind-split disease. The stigma experienced by individuals with schizophrenia prompted the National Federation of Families of Mentally Ill Individuals in Japan to fight for a more neutral term. In 1993, a Japanese Committee on Concept and Terminology changed the term to '*togo shitcho sho*' meaning 'dysfunction of integration' (Tsuchiya & Takei, 2004). This new term for schizophrenia emphasizes vulnerability to stress, and thereby suggests

that the illness is treatable through humane measures and psychosocial rehabilitation, which is consistent with a movement in mental health in Japan to move people out of hospitals (see later).

Substance Misuse Disorders

An epidemiologic survey conducted by the National Research Institute in Japan indicates that substance abuse is still very low compared with other countries. Among inpatients in psychiatric hospitals in Japan, only 5 percent had a diagnosis of alcoholism, 0.2 percent were diagnosed with methamphetamine-induced psychosis, and 0.5 percent had other substance-related disorders (Tsuchiya & Takei, 2004). According to a national survey, solvent abuse is the most common substance of abuse, and some link this with subsequent methamphetamine abuse (Wada, 2011). About one-third of mental hospital outpatients and inpatients hospitalized because of drug-induced psychiatric disorders had abused solvents before abusing methamphetamines. New data also indicates that the abuse of drugs such as MDMA (ecstasy) and cannabis are also on the rise.

JAPANESE MENTAL HEALTH CARE SYSTEM

Japanese psychiatry was developed from German neuropsychiatry in the early 1900s and has generally been neurologically or biologically oriented. Some examples of this conceptualization mentioned earlier are the hypotheses about weakness in the nervous system in neurasthenia, psychosomatic disorders, and *futeishuso*. In theory, therefore, Japanese psychiatrists do not object to the use of medications, but have historically preferred low dose antipsychotics or antianxiety medications. Antidepressants were not generally used in Japan until around 2000–2001, when Paxil was introduced to the Japanese psychiatric community (Kirmayer, 2002).

Japanese citizens are covered comprehensively by the universal medical care insurance system and the cost of services is relatively low. Out-of-pocket expenses for people with insured persons is about 30 percent, but people with persistent mental illness, such as schizophrenia, dementias, and chronic conditions, only pay 10 percent or no out-of-pocket costs. Most mental health treatment was carried out in the hospital until very recently. This is because the 1950 Mental Hygiene Law increased the total number of beds that were reserved for psychiatric patients – still, the number of psychiatric beds in Japan is one of the highest in the world (Tsuchiya & Takei, 2004). In 1999, the largest total number of patients in hospitals per 100,000 were tied between mental illnesses and circulatory diseases (259 each) (Health Statistics Division, 1999). In addition, hospitalization tends to be reserved for chronic mental health conditions, and only 5 percent of inpatients have mood disorders or substance misuse disorders.

Mental illnesses rank second to the lowest number of patients using outpatient services (at 124 per 100,000) compared with digestive disorders, at 1198 per 100,000. The Mental Hygiene Law was revised in 1965, reformed in 1988, and again in 1995. These reforms aimed at decreasing inpatient hospitalization and improving community-based access to outpatient care. As of April 2013, the Japanese government will make mental health reform its fifth top national priority (Frank, 2013). Despite existing and planned efforts to reform, Japan has a very difficult road ahead. The Japanese tend not to use outpatient mental health services because of historical patterns, increased costs for the family, stigmatization of mental illness in communities, and the disorganization or lack of availability of services. Community-based outpatient and psychiatric rehabilitation programs are not available in many prefectures, and those that are available are not well coordinated with inpatient services. Because inpatient services for chronic conditions are nearly fully covered by the national health care program, moving a family member into outpatient services may incur costs for the patients that would otherwise be covered in an inpatient setting. These services are often voluntary and are sometimes organized and run by volunteer patient family groups. The Ministry of Health and Welfare carried out an evaluation of the issue of deinstitutionalization in 1983 and found that more than 30 percent of current inpatients could move into community-based outpatient settings, but 60 percent of the families of those patients said they could not care for them. Finally, specialty services are also not available in adequate numbers (Asai, 1995). For example, child and adolescent psychiatry is not well developed, with only about 100 child and adolescent psychiatrists in Japan as late as the 1990s (Tsuchiya & Takei, 2004).

The rise in suicide rates has prompted the Basic Act on Suicide Countermeasures legislation in 2006. Interestingly, this legislation includes explicit statements about the nature of suicide – that people are driven to it rather than choosing it. This philosophical stance has compelled national and local governments to take action to protect the citizenry. One such effort is the Comprehensive Suicide Prevention Initiative (CSPI) enacted in 2007, which has as its charge 'Creating a Society Where Life is Easier.' This initiative includes the explicit philosophies that suicide prevention will require consideration of social factors, education, care for survivors, and long-range planning (Kaga et al., 2009).

Attitudinal Barriers to Use of Mental Health Services

In Japan, the proportion of access to mental health services was lower among those who had anxiety, mood, and substance disorders and was almost half of other high-income countries (Wang et al., 2007). However, internalized and public attitudinal barriers to accessing the care are very high in Japan. Because of this, the Japanese government has launched several programs. These include changing the names of illnesses, deinstitutionalization efforts, and public education campaigns (Kido & Kawakami, 2013).

The study of Japanese mental health provides an excellent example of how roles, rules, and values become translated into psychiatric diagnoses and mental health care. The social expectations of a citizen within a culture are the set of expectations against which normalcy and deviancy are evaluated. Deviance is marked and society then defines what causes it and what should be done about it. In a rapidly modernizing and Westernizing country such as Japan, these internal forces are at interplay with external forces such as education, global pharmaceutical distribution, and the globalization of Western biomedical psychiatry.

REFERENCES

Asai, K. (1995). Psychiatric diagnosis and mental health services in Japan. In J.E. Mezzich, Y. Honda, & M.C. Kastrup (Eds.), *Psychiatric diagnosis: a world perspective* (pp. 228–240). New York, NY: Springer Verlag.

Bachnik, J. (1994). Introduction: Uchi/Soto: challenging our concept of self, social order and language. In J.M. Bachnik & C. Quinn (Eds.), *Situated meaning: inside and outside in Japanese self, society and language.* (pp. 3–37). Princeton, NJ: Princeton University Press.

Barrera, M. & Garrison-Jones, C. V. (1988). Properties of the Beck Depression Inventory as a screening instrument for adolescent depression. *Journal of Abnormal Child Psychology*, 16, 263–273.

Beck, A.T., Steer, R.A. & Garbin, M.G. (1988). Psychometric properties of the Beck Depression Inventory: twenty-five years of evaluation. *Clinical Psychology Review*, 8, 77–100.

Befu, H. (1980). The group model of Japanese society and its alternative. *Rice University Studies, 66*(1), 169–187.

Befu, H. (1993). Cultural nationalism in East Asia: Representation and identity Berkeley, CA: University of California.

Ben-Ari, E., Moeran, B. & Valentine, J. (2011). *Unwrapping Japan: society and culture in anthropological perspective* (Vol. 71). New York, NY: Routledge.

Bestor, T. (1996). Forging tradition: social life and identity in a Tokyo neighborhood. In G. Gmelch & W.P. Zenner (Eds.), *Urban life: reading in urban anthropology* (2nd ed., pp. 524–547). Prospect Heights, NY: Waveland Press.

Cho, M. & Kim, K. (1998). Use of the Center for Epidemiologic Studies Depression (CES-D) Scale in Korea. *Journal of Nervous and Mental Disease*, 186(5), 304–310.

Cho, M., Nam, J. & Suh, G. (1998). Prevalence of symptoms of depression in a nationwide sample of Korean adults. *Psychiatry Research*, 81(3), 341–352.

Clark, S. (1996). Maintaining Yoshino traditional hierarchy: the roles of gender and race in Japanese management. *Journal of Organizational Change Management.*, 9(3), 6ff.

Cross, S. & Markus, H. (1991). Possible selves across the life span. *Human Development*, 34(4), 230–255.

Dale, P. (1986). *The myth of Japanese uniqueness*. New York, NY: St Martin's Press.

Doi, T. (1973). *The anatomy of dependence*. Tokyo: Kodansha.

Doi, T. (1992). On the concept of amae. *Infant Mental Health Journal*, 13(1), 7–11.

Draguns, J.G., Phillips, L., Broverman, I.K., & Caudill, W. (1970). Social competence and psychiatric symptomatology in Japan: a cross-cultural extension of earlier American findings. *Journal of Abnormal Psychology*, 75(1), 68–73.

Ellsworth, P. C. (1994). Sense, culture, and sensibility. Emotion and culture: empirical studies of mutual influence (pp. 23–50). Washington, DC, American Psychological Association.

Fiske, A.P., Kitayama, S., Markus, H.R. & Nisbett, R.E. (1998). The cultural matrix of social psychology. In D.T. Gilbert, S.T. Fiske, & G. Lindzey (Eds.), *The handbook of social psychology* (Vol. 2, 4th ed., pp. 915–981). Boston, MA: McGraw-Hill.

Frank, R. (2013). *Lessons for Japan from the US rebalancing of Mental Health Care*. Washington, DC: Center for Strategic and International Studies.

Goodman, R. (1992). Ideology and practice in Japan: toward a theoretical approach. In R. Goodman & K. Refsing (Eds.), *Ideology and practice in modern Japan* (pp. 1–25). NY: Routledge.

Gureje, O., Simon, G.E., Ustun, T.B. & Goldberg, D.P. (1997). Somatization in cross-cultural perspective: a World Health Organization study in primary care. *American Journal of Psychiatry*, 154(7), 989–995.

Health Statistics Division. (1999). *Patients and medical institutions in Japan: graphical review of health statistics.* Tokyo: Health and Welfare Statistics Association.

Hendry, J. (1992). Individualism and individuation: entry into a social world. In R. Goodman & K. Refsing (Eds.), *Ideology and practice in modern Japan* (pp. 55–71). NY: Routledge.

Hinton, D. & Hinton, S. (2002). Panic disorder, somatization, and the new cross-cultural psychiatry: the seven bodies of a medical anthropology of panic [comment]. *Culture, Medicine & Psychiatry*, 26(2), 155–178.

Hofmann, S.G. (2008). Acceptance and commitment therapy: new wave or Morita Therapy? *Clinical Psychology: Science and Practice*, 15(4), 280–285.

Hong, G.K., Lee, B.S. & Lorenzo, M.K. (1995). Somatization in Chinese American clients: implications for psychotherapeutic services. *Journal of Contemporary Psychotherapy*, 25(2), 105–118.

Ishiyama, F.I. (1986). Morita therapy: its basic features and cognitive intervention for anxiety treatment. *Psychotherapy: Theory, Research, Practice, Training*, 23(3), 375–381.

Iwata, N. & Buka, S. (2002). Race/ethnicity and depressive symptoms: a cross-cultural/ethnic comparison among university students in East Asia, North and South America. *Social Science & Medicine*, 55(12), 2243–2252.

Iwata, N. & Roberts, R. (1996). Age differences among Japanese on the Center for Epidiologic Studies Depression scale: an ethnocultural perspective on somatization. *Socail Science and Medicine*, 43(6), 967–974.

Iwata, N., Roberts, C. & Norito, K. (1995). Japan–US comparison of responses to depression scale items among adult workers. *Psychiatry Research*, 58, 237–245.

Iwata, N., Saito, K. & Roberts, R.E. (1994). Responses to a self-administered depression scale among younger adolescents in Japan. *Psychiatry Research*, 53(3), 275–287.

Iwata, N., Umesue, M., Egashima, K., Hiro, H., Mizoue, T., Mishima, N. & Nagata, S. (1998). Can positive affect items be used to assess depression disorders in the Japanese population? *Psychological Medicine*, 28, 153–158.

Jenkins, J. H. & M. Karno (1992). The meaning of expressed emotion: theoretical issues raised by cross-cultural research. *Am J Psychiatry* 149: 9–21.

Johnson, T. (1995). *Dependency and Japanese socialization*. New York, NY: New York University Press.

Kaga, M., Takeshima, T. & Matsumoto, T. (2009). Suicide and its prevention in Japan. *Legal Medicine*, 11, S18–S21.

Kamitani, K. (1993). The structure of Jiritsu (socially sensitive independence) in young Japanese women. *Psychological Reports*, 72, 855–866.

Kamitani, Y. (1996). The structure of Jiritsu (socially sensitive independence) in middle-aged Japanese women. *Psychological Reports*, 78(3, part 2), 1355–1362.

Kanno, S. (1981). On the somatization of symptom in psychosomatic disease: consideration of Rorschach score [author's translation]. *Shinrigaku kenkyu [The Japanese Journal of Psychology]*, 52(1), 30–37.

Kato, T.A., Shinfuku, N., Fujisawa, D., Tateno, M., Ishida, T., Akiyama, T., ... Kanba, S. (2011). Introducing the concept of modern depression in Japan; an international case vignette survey. *Journal of Affective Disorders*, 135(1), 66–76.

Kato, T.A., Tateno, M., Shinfuku, N., Fujisawa, D., Teo, A. R., Sartorius, N., ... Kanba, S. (2012). Does the 'hikikomori' syndrome of social withdrawal exist outside Japan? A preliminary international investigation. *Social psychiatry and psychiatric epidemiology*, 47(7), 1061–1075.

Kawanishi, Y. (1992). Somatization of Asians: an artifact of Western medicalization. *Transcultural Psychiatric Research Review*, 29, 5–36.

Keiichi, S. (1978). Controversy over community and autonomy. In V. Koschmann (Ed.), *Authority and the individual in Japan* (pp. 220–249). Tokyo: University of Tokyo Press.

Kido, Y. & Kawakami, N. (2013). Sociodemographic determinants of attitudinal barriers in the use of mental health services in Japan: findings from the World Mental Health Japan Survey 2002–2006. *Psychiatry and Clinical Neurosciences*, 67(2), 101–109.

Kirmayer, L.J. (1989). Cultural variations in the response to psychiatric disorders and emotional distress. *Social Science & Medicine*, 29(3), 327–339.

Kirmayer, L.J. (1991). The place of culture in psychiatric nosology: Taijin kyofusho and DSM-III–R. *Journal of Nervous & Mental Disease*, 179(1), 19–28.

Kirmayer, L.J. (2001). Cultural variations in the clinical presentation of depression and anxiety: implications for diagnosis and treatment. *Journal of Clinical Psychiatry*, 62(Suppl 13), 22–28.

Kirmayer, L.J. (2002). Psychopharmacology in a globalizing world: the use of antidepressants in Japan. *Transcultural Psychiatry*, 39(3), 295–322.

Kirmayer, L.J., Dao, T.H.T., & Smith, A. (1998). Somatization and psychologization: understanding cultural idioms of distress. In S.O. Okpaku (Ed.), *Clinical methods in transcultural psychiatry* (pp. 233–265). Washington, DC: American Psychiatric Press.

Kirmayer, L.J. & Groleau, D. (2001). Affective disorders in cultural context. *Psychiatric Clinics of North America Special Issue: Cultural psychiatry: International Perspectives*, 24(3), 465–478.

Kitanaka, J. (2011). *Depression in Japan: psychiatric cures for a society in distress* Princeton, NJ: Princeton University Press.

Kitanishi, K. & Kondo, K. (1994). The rise and fall of neurasthenia in Japanese psychiatry. *Transcultural Psychiatry*, 31(2), 137–152.

Kitayama, S., Markus, H.R. & Kurokawa, M. (2000). Culture, emotion, and well-being: good feelings in Japan and the United States. *Cognition & Emotion*, 14(1), 93– 124.

Kitayama, S., Markus, H.R. & Matsumoto, H. (1995). Culture, self, and emotion: a cultural perspective on 'self-conscious' emotions. In J.P. Tangney & K.W. Fischer (Eds.), *Self-conscious emotions: the psychology of shame, guilt, embarrassment, and pride* (pp. 439–464). New York, NY: Guilford Press.

Kleinman, A. (1982). Neurasthenia and depression: a study of somatization and culture in China. *Culture, Medicine & Psychiatry*, 6(2), 117–190.

Kleinman, A. (1983). The cultural meanings and social uses of illness: a role for medical anthropology and clinically oriented social science in the development of primary care theory and research. *Journal of Family Practice*, 16(3), 539–545.

Kleinman, A. (1988). *Rethinking psychiatry: from cultural category to personal experience*. New York, NY: Free Press.

Kojima, M., Furukawa, T.A., Takahashi, H., Kawai, M., Nagaya, T. & Tokudome, S. (2002). Cross-cultural validation of the Beck Depression Inventory-II in Japan. *Psychiatry Research*, 110(3), 291–299.

Kondo, D.K. (1990). *Crafting selves: power, gender, and discourses of identity in a Japanese workplace*. Chicago, IL: University of Chicago Press.

Koyama, A., Miyake, Y., Kawakami, N., Tsuchiya, M., Tachimori, H. & Takeshima, T. (2010). Lifetime prevalence, psychiatric comorbidity and demographic correlates of 'hikikomori' in a community population in Japan. *Psychiatry Research*, 176, 69–74.

Lebra, T.S. (1974). Reciprocity and the asymmetrical principle: an analytic reappraisal of the Japanese concept of On. In T.S. Lebra and W.P. Lebra (Eds.), *Japanese culture and behavior: selected readings* (pp. 192–207). Honolulu, HI: University of Hawaii Press.

Lebra, T.S. (1976). *Japanese pattern of behavior*. Honolulu, HI: University of Hawaii Press.

Lebra, T.S. (1983). Shame and guilt: a psychocultural view of the Japanese self. *Ethos*, 11(3), 192–209.

Lin, K.-M. (1996). Asian American perspectives. In J.E. Mezzich & A. Kleinman (Eds.), *Culture and psychiatric diagnosis: a DSM-IV perspective* (pp. 35–38). Washington, DC: American Psychiatric Association.

Lock, M. (1987a). Introduction: health and medical care as cultural and social phenomena. In E. Norbeck & M. Lock (Eds.), *Health, illness, and medical care in Japan: cultural and social dimensions* (pp. 1–23). Honolulu, HI: University of Hawaii Press.

Lock, M. (1987b). Protests of a good wife and wise mother: the medicalization of distress in Japan. In E. Norbeck & M. Lock (Eds.), *Health, illness, and medical care in Japan: cultural and social dimensions* (pp. 130–157). Honolulu, HI: University of Hawaii Press.

MacDonald, G. (1995). The politics of diversity in the nation-state. In J.C. Maher & G. MacDonald (Eds.), *Diversity in Japanese culture and language* (pp. 291–316). New York, NY: Kegan Paul.

Maeno, T., Kizawa, Y., Ueno, Y., Nakata, Y. & Sato, T. (2002). Depression among primary care patients with complaints of headache and general fatigue. *Primary Care Psychiatry*, 8(2), 69–72.

Markus, H. R. & S. Kitayama (1991). Culture and the self: implications for cognition, emotion and motivation. *Psychological Review*, 98(2), 224–253.

Markus, H.R., Kitayama, S. & Heiman, R.J. (1996). Culture and 'basic' psychological principles. In E.T. Higgins & A.W. Kruglanski (Eds.), *Social psychology: handbook of basic principles* (pp. 857–913). New York, NY: The Guilford Press.

Markus, H.R., Mullally, P.R. & Kitayama, S. (1997). Selfways: diversity in modes of cultural participation. In U. Neisser & D.A. Jopling (Eds.), *The conceptual self in context: culture, experience, self-understanding. Part of Emory Symposia in Cognition* (pp. 13–61). New York, NY: Cambridge University Press.

Mesquita, B. & N. H. Frijda (1992). 'Cultural variations in emotions: A review.' *Psychological Bulletin* 112(2): 179–204.

Mino, Y., Aoyama, H. & Froom, J. (1994). Depressive disorders in Japanese primary care patients. *Family Practice*, 11(4), 363–367.

Morris-Suzuki, T. (1995). The invention and re-invention of Japanese culture. *The Journal of Asian Studies.*, 54(3), 759–780.

Mouer, R. (1984). Individual, group and seishin: Japan's culture debate. *Man*, 19 (252–266).

Mouer, R. & Sugimoto, Y. (1986). *Images of Japanese society*. New York, NY: Routledge and Kegan Paul.

Murase, T. (1982). Sunao: a central value in Japanese psychotherapy. In A.J. Marsella & G. White (Eds.), *Cultural conceptions of mental health and therapy* (pp. 317–329). Netherlands: Springer.

Nagata, T., Yamada, H., Teo, A.R., Yoshimura, C., Nakajima, T. & van Vliet, I. (2013). Comorbid social withdrawal (hikikomori) in outpatients with social anxiety disorder: clinical characteristics and treatment response in a case series. *International Journal of Social Psychiatry*, 59(1), 73–78.

Nakane, C. (1970). *Japanese society*. Berkeley, CA: University of California Press.

Noh, S., Kasper, V. & Chen, X. (1998). Measuring depression in Korean immigrants: assessing validity of the translated Korean version of the CES-D scale. *Cross-Cultural Research: The Journal of Comparative Social Science*, 32(4), 358–377.

Ohnuki-Tierney, E. (1984). *Illness and culture in contemporary Japan: an anthropological view*. Cambridge, UK: Cambridge University Press.

Ozawa-de Silva, C. & Ozawa-de Silva, B. (2010). Secularizing religious practices: a study of subjectivity and existential transformation in Naikan therapy. *Journal for the Scientific Study of Religion*, 49(1), 147–161.

Pang, K.Y.C. (1998). Symptoms of depression in elderly Korean immigrants: narration and the healing process. *Culture, Medicine & Psychiatry*, 22(1), 93–122.

Parsons, C.D. & Wakeley, P. (1991). Idioms of distress: somatic responses to distress in everyday life. *Culture, Medicine & Psychiatry*, 15(1), 111–132.

Reischauer, E.O. (1981). *The Japanese*. Cambridge, MA: Harvard University Press.

Rohlen, T.P. (1983). *Japan's high schools*. Berkeley, CA: University of California Press.

Roland, A. (1988). *In search of the self in India and Japan: toward a cross-cultural psychology.* Princeton, NJ: Princeton University Press.

Russell, J.G. (1989). Anxiety disorders in Japan: a review of the Japanese literature on Shinkeishitsu and taijinkyōfushī. *Culture, medicine and psychiatry*, 13(4), 391–403.

St Arnault, D.M. (2002). Help-seeking and social support in Japan sojourners. *Western Journal of Nursing Research*, 24(3), 295–306.

St Arnault, D.M. (2004). The Japanese. In C.R. Ember & M. Ember (Eds.), *Encyclopedia of medical anthropology* (Vol. 1, pp. 765–776). New Haven, CT: Yale University Press.

St Arnault, D.M. & Roels, D.J. (2012). Social networks and the maintenance of conformity: Japanese sojourner women. *International Journal of Culture and Mental Health*, 5(2), 77–93.

Sato, M. (2006). Renaming schizophrenia: a Japanese perspective. *World Psychiatry*, 5(1), 53.

Simon, G.E., VonKorff, M., Piccinelli, M., Fullerton, C. & Ormel, J. (1999). An international study of the relation between somatic symptoms and depression. *New England Journal of Medicine*, 341(18), 1329–1335.

Smith, R. (1961). The Japanese rural community: norms, sanctions and ostracism. *American Anthropologist*, 61, 522–533.

Targum, S.D. & Kitanaka, J. (2012). Overwork suicide in Japan: a national crisis. *Innovations in Clinical Neuroscience*, 9(2), 35–38.

Tsuchiya, K.J. & Takei, N. (2004). Focus on psychiatry in Japan. *British Journal of Psychiatry*, 184, 88–92.

Umeda, M. & Kawakami, N. (2012). World Mental Health Japan Survey G: association of childhood family environments with the risk of social withdrawal ('hikikomori') in the community population in Japan. *Psychiatry and Clinical Neurosciences*, 66(2), 121–129.

Vogel, E. (1967). Kinship structure, migration to the city and modernization. In R.P. Dore (Ed.), *Aspects of social change in modern Japan.* (pp. 91–111). Princeton, NJ: Princeton University Press.

Wada, K. (2011). The history and current state of drug abuse in Japan. *Annals of the New York Academy of Sciences*, 1216(1), 62–72.

Wang, P.S., Aguilar-Gaxiola, S., Alonso, J., Angermeyer, M.C., Borges, G., Bromet, E.J., ... Wells, J.E. (2007). Use of mental health services for anxiety, mood, and substance disorders in 17 countries in the WHO world mental health surveys. *Lancet* 370, 841–850.

Watts, J. (2002). Public health experts concerned about 'hikikomori'. *Lancet* 359, 1131.

Weiner, M. (Ed.). (1997). *Japan's minorities: the illusion of homogenity*. New York, NY: Routledge.

World Health Organization. (1992). *The ICD-10 classification of mental and behavioural disorders*. Geneva: World Health Organization.

World Health Organization. (2013). *Suicide prevention (SUPRE)*. Retrieved May 20, 2013, from http://www.who.int/mental_health/prevention/suicide/suicideprevent/en/index.html

Yeung, A., Howarth, S., Chan, R., Sonawalla, S., Nierenberg, A.A. & Fava, M. (2002). Use of the Chinese version of the Beck Depression Inventory for screening depression in primary care. *Journal of Nervous & Mental Disease*, 190(2), 94–99.

Yoshino, K. (1992). *Cultural nationalism in contemporary Japan: a sociological inquiry*. New York, NY: Routledge.

PART IV

Politics and Foreign Relations

19

Political 'Science' and the Study of Japanese Politics

James Babb

As with much of modernity, the Japanese were present at the early stages of the development of the study of politics. This might not always have been obvious because before the war, Japan largely followed the German model of political studies and since the war there has been a shift to the Anglo–Saxon (mostly the US) model of political 'science.' Nonetheless, the legacy of both approaches is significant even today. Within the United States, three major approaches have had the most systematic and sustained impact on the study of Japanese politics – structural–functionalism, historical institutionalism, and rational choice. This chapter will examine key trends in the study of Japanese politics, both inside Japan and outside, to demonstrate how the reintegration of aspects of political thought with so-called political science enables us to better understand the history of the study of Japanese politics and also the problems when this unity of thought and empirical research is ignored.

THE ORIGINS OF POLITICAL RESEARCH ON JAPAN

The Initial German Influence

For many years the study of Japanese politics in Japanese universities was located in the Law Departments of the major state universities. This was because the study of politics initially followed the pattern of German *Staatswissenschaft*, literally state science. This was due to the fact that Itō Hirobumi, as part of the Iwakura Mission, went to Europe in order to study Western institutions and practices and established a relationship with Lorenz von Stein and his student Albert Mossee, who were key figures in the *Staatswissenschaft* school (Takii, 2010: 205). When he returned to Japan, Itō was instrumental in having *Staatswissenschaft* or *kokkagaku* adopted by the first Imperial universities established in 1886 and helped to found the Kokkagakkai or 'Society for Staatswissenschaft' (Takii, 2010: 208). Not surprisingly, Germans played a major role in the formation of the Meiji state and writing of the Meiji Constitution (Siemes, 1964, 1969). Subsequent debates in Japan influenced or paralleled in German debates historically, and the conceptual framework is still used significantly as a basis for Japanese scholarship and academic debates today (see, for example, Shibata, 2005; Makino, 2008; Kimura, 2010; Tanaka, 2010).

Before the Japanese are dismissed as backward in their political studies, we have to remember that late nineteenth century political scholarship in the United States was similarly legal formal (Wilson, 1898). In recent years, the field of politics has returned to a focus on institutions and the state, as we will see later. There was also less of an attempt in prewar political studies around the world to separate empirical political research from thought. The separation of political thought from political 'science' is largely a postwar phenomenon in the United States. In fact, if we turn to political thought, we can also see that legal philosophy is core to political debates in ways not unrecognizable from a *kokkagaku* point of view. It is significant that even Rawls, who is often credited with saving political philosophy from the onslaught of empiricism, focuses on justice, as much in a legal context as a political one, and this legalistic tendency of political thought is clear in diverse figures such as Carl Schmitt, H.L. Hart, and Dworkin (Forsyth & Keens-Soper, 1996). In Japan, the conservative political theorist Sakamoto Takao (2001) certainly follows this tendency and ties it nicely to *kokkagaku*. In any case, the focus on legal and conceptual issues, such as the state, sovereignty, rights, freedom, justice, is preferable to the alternative, which has tended to plague political research on Japan: culture.

Culture versus Politics

One might argue that most of the problems arising in the study of postwar Japanese politics are due to an inadequate treatment of what is often called the cultural aspect of Japanese politics. This term is somewhat misleading because it includes, amongst other things, superficial similarities to the past, practices with a link to the past although substantially modified over time, and traditional political ideas that continue to have resonance in Japan. For most non-specialists, culture is constituted by norms and practices that seem different from other countries.

One of the problems with the use of culture in the study of Japanese politics is that it is often reified. It is often seen as fixed and eternal, as in the notion of traditional culture; however, the elements that constitute culture do change. They are reinterpreted anew by each generation and in response to historical events. Older elements might be revived and those considered outdated abandoned. We notice culture the most where it is contested. In a sense, culture is an outcome of a political process itself, both politics with a small 'p', as in gender politics, and with a big 'P' in terms of national political debates.

The main problem with a static notion of culture as a determinant of politics is that it tends to disengage those who study Japan and their readers from a dynamic understanding of Japanese politics. Work influenced by culture also has a patronizing relativistic tendency. One need only contrast prewar work on Japanese politics with the immediate postwar studies to gauge the difference. Prewar writers such as Robert Karl Reischauer (1939) and Hugh Byas (1942), for all their faults, were engaged with their subjects and seemed to care about the political consequences of the events they recorded. They were critical, but engaged and contemporary.

During World War II, however, independent information on Japanese politics was limited and so the US government relied on an anthropologist, Ruth Benedict, who had never visited Japan but used her knowledge of comparative cultures to make sense of the information she was given about Japan during the war. The result was *The Chrysanthemum and the Sword: Patterns of Japanese Culture* (Benedict, 1946) that created or reinforced cultural stereotypes about Japan. This was adopted as a definitive statement of Japanese culture both in the West and also in Japan, where her book was widely read long after it had been placed aside in Western academic circles.

This is not to utterly condemn Benedict. Her theories had plausibility, often rooted in fact, but the notion of culture used was too monolithic and static. The problem was that this type of cultural approach limited understanding of Japanese politics by attributing too much to culture and not enough to political dynamics. This is also manifest in the popular textbooks by Edwin O. Reischauer, such as *The Japanese* (1977) – a standard supplemental reading for politics courses in the last decades of the twentieth century – based on historical generalization and reflecting the cultural biases of immediate postwar Japanese studies, not the rough-and-tumble of politics in works by his elder brother, Robert.

Early Postwar Political Science

The issue of culture is raised at the outset of this chapter on political science and Japan because it is a recurring problem in various guises, as we shall see later; however, it would be a mistake to dismiss all of the early work of scholars of Japanese politics in the immediate postwar period. Within Japan itself, the Japanese Political Science Association published its annual *Nenpō Seijigaku* from 1950, which discussed and applied many cutting edge theories of political science over the years. Scholars such as Masumi Junnosuke did impressive work (for example, Masumi, 1966), sometimes in collaboration with Western scholars such as Nobutaka Ike and Robert Scalapino (Kyogoku & Ike, 1959; Scapalino & Masumi, 1962).

There are a few important characteristics of this immediate postwar generation. In the United States, and to a lesser degree in the United Kingdom, many of these scholars had initially been mobilized and trained during the war against Japan and/or during the Allied Occupation of Japan. A good example is Robert Ward who later played a leading role in the study of Japanese politics. Others, similarly trained, populated numerous academic posts in politics across the United States. Many of the top scholars, however, such as Robert Scalapino or Chalmers Johnson, came from an East Asian studies background where they were familiar with both Chinese and Japanese languages. This was particularly true in the United Kingdom, given the organization of teaching of the subjects in universities in Faculties or Schools of Oriental Studies. In Japan itself, however, research into politics was initially limited to academics in the Law Faculty, as noted earlier, or literature departments. None of the early scholars of politics in Japan had formal training in politics or political science. In short, political science was secondary or incidental to this generation of scholars of Japanese politics. Even so, these early works were focused on voting behavior and political parties informed by advances in political research on these subjects in the United States in the 1950s.

Once trained political specialists approached the study of Japan, the field began to transform. One of the seminal works at the end of the immediate postwar period was Gerald Curtis's *Election Campaigning Japanese Style* (1971). It is still widely read because it combined field work with an anthropological dimension and provides useful empirical generalizations informed by comparative political studies, such as Maurice Duverger's *Political Parties* (1951, 1954). The problem was that Curtis was a rare example. Travel to Japan was much more difficult in the early post-War periods and few scholars had the linguistic ability, the access, and inclination to probe the depths of the grassroots reality of Japanese politics. Subsequent developments in political science theory moved scholars even further from Japanese political reality, although in recent years, there has been a return to the subjects and approaches of early postwar political science research on Japan.

The Impact of the Behavioral Revolution

Japan was one of the key countries to be the subject of the behavioral revolution in political science (Dahl, 1961). Armed with the social science tools of survey research and statistical analysis, behavioralism attempted to make political science more scientific by collecting empirical data from surveys and subjecting the data to rigorous hypothesis testing. Originally used in studies of US electoral behavior, the data was used to identify the beliefs and values behind turnout or party choice. Of course, the questions asked were based on American understanding of key political beliefs and values as if they were universal to all political systems. Early postwar studies of voting behavior in Japan (Rōyama, 1949; Rōyama et al., 1955) did not reflect these categories, but as electoral studies developed in Japan the sociological and political theories behind the behavioral revolution were increasingly applied to Japan (Watanuki, 1962; Miyake, Kinoshita &Aiba, 1965).

One of the most influential political science approaches of the period was the political culture theory of Almond and Verba. Using evidence from survey research in five nations (Germany, Great Britain, Italy, Mexico, and the United States) examining mass attitudes and values, Almond and Verba's *Civic Culture* (1963) identified three types of political culture: (1) parochial, where political relations are based on personal subjective relationships; (2) subject, where political involvement is minimal and citizen passively accept authority; and (3) participant, where there is active citizen involvement and interaction with authority. This approach has been criticized as too dependent on the recent political history of the nations studied. That is, parochial or subject orientations were caused by the lack of opportunities for political participation and not due to an inherent political culture. Once greater opportunities for participation arose, the culture changed. Thus, culture does not by itself determine modes of political participation; rather the institutional structure of opportunities for participation heavily influences culture. The fatal flaw of cultural approaches to politics is that they often play into stereotyping and essentialist arguments.

This approach had a big impact on the study of Japan in the 1970s and into the 1980s. First of all, the Almond and Verba approach was directly applied to Japan by Bradley Richardson in his *Political Culture of Japan* (Richardson 1974) using surveys and analysis with the same problematic assumptions of Almond and Verba. Almond's subsequent development of a comparative culture approach using structural functionalist theory (Almond and Powell, 1966) was also applied to Japan through the Little, Brown & Company series of textbooks on politics in individual countries. Whereas in some volumes the theory was loosely applied, in Japan the categories were used relatively rigidly by Richardson and Flanagan in their version of *Politics in Japan* (Richardson & Flanagan, 1984). The driving force in the functional differentiation in Japan was culture. This approach was continued later in Richardson's Japanese politics textbook entitled *Japanese democracy* (1997).

The problems of the cultural approach to politics are well demonstrated by *The Japanese Voter* (Flanagan, Kohei, Miyake, Richardson & Watanuki, 1991). The problems are not entirely due to the analysis of voting in Japan being too focused on concepts and categories drawn from early postwar US political science. Studies of American electoral behavior, such as *The American Voter* (Campbell, Converse, Miller & Stokes, 1960), were pioneering work and it seemed only natural to use the questions developed in these studies as the basis for comparative studies of voting behavior. The field of voting behavior in the United States and other countries continues to explore some of the larger issues of values, such as trust, civic duty, and interpersonal context. The problem was that the focus of *The Japanese Voter* tended to be attitudes and values that were seen as peculiar to the Japanese context.

The categories used made the Japanese appear to be as 'particularistic' and undeveloped, as the theories of Almond and Verba implied. The differences also legitimated the view that the Japanese were somehow unique in terms of social structure or values that could not be captured by comparative analysis. It would have been better if more appropriate and nuanced definitions and categories had been used. More effort might have been put into examining the basis for a Japanese attitude rather than assuming it was peculiar to Japan or demonstrated Japanese backwardness.

A classic example was the assumption that Japanese focused on candidate personality or local ties rather than a political party, and this was proof of some backward personalistic and parochial tendency in Japan. The problem was that the Japanese electoral system was a multicandidate electoral system so more than one candidate might run from the same party. Often the easiest way to differentiate one candidate from the other was personal or local ties. When the number of candidates was controlled for, the tendency to vote based on personality rather than party disappeared (Rochon, 1981). It was not culture; it was institutional structure that largely influenced this seemingly personality-focused behavior.

This should not be a complete surprise. This political culture thesis was widely critiqued. Philip Converse demonstrated that the differences in the countries studied by Almond and Verba were largely due to differences in the number of years the countries had been democratic rather than the cultural attributes of the population (Converse, 1969). Similarly, Przeworski and Teune showed that the differences in feelings of relative freedom to discuss politics in various countries studied by Almond and Verba made some nations, such as the United States, look freer, and others, such as Mexico, look less free, but when the relative freedom was adjusted by educational attainment differences between countries, the differences disappeared or were reversed (Przeworski & Tuene, 1970: 28–29). Almond and Verba appeared to be measuring differences in educational attainment and not cultural differences in political attitudes. This suggests that political culture is the result of historical and socio-political processes of which culture and other beliefs are simply the outcome. It is not an independent variable because it is not the cause – it is the dependent variable if a discrete variable at all (Elkins & Simeon, 1979).

This focus on culture, attitudes, and personality was understandable, nonetheless. The behavioralist/cultural school was following a similar trend in the Japanese literature that was even less comparative. For example, it was common for political science reading lists in the 1970s and the early 1980s to include the work of writers such as Doi Takeo (1973) and Nakane Chie (1967). The problem with this literature is that it followed the logic of the so-called *Nihonjinron* (literally, 'theories of the Japanese'), which argued that the Japanese have unique cultural and even physical differences with other nations that make the Japanese unique. Writers in this genre did not ask if there were specific social or political conditions that fostered and sustained this behavior – they simply assumed these characteristics to be an enduring and essential part of the Japanese social system and psyche. By the mid-1980s, this approach was widely criticized (Dale, 1986; Befu, 1987), but its influence continued to linger in studies of Japanese politics.

The cultural approach of Almond and Verba also continued in more sophisticated forms in mainstream US political science in the work of scholars such as Ronald Inglehart who argued that change in advanced industrial societies was shifting younger generations to 'post-modern' values (Inglehart, 1977, 1990). This struck a chord with one of Gabriel Almond's students, Scott Flanagan, who was an early adopter of the approach in his application of the conceptual framework to Japan (Flanagan, 1979); however, the problem is that it is based on a similar type of logical fallacy about the static notion of the relationship between ideas or beliefs and political behavior, as is inherent in the political culture literature (Seligson, 2002).

We can therefore see the limitations to a focus on culture and attitudes in political research. Cultural attributes vary within a nation and over time, and are often the outcome of political processes. This focus suggests that detailed and multilayered political history is more useful in teasing out the relationship between political ideas and political outcomes than the traditional political culture approach.

COMPARATIVE HISTORY, HISTORICAL INSTITUTIONALISM AND THE STATE

Modernization and Development Theory

Parallel to the cultural–behavioral school, the study of politics in Japan was also caught up theoretically with modernization theory and the US Social Science Research Council initiative on political development. These approaches had significant problems that were relevant to the study of Japan. Many of the leaders of the initiative were the same individuals who supported the political culture approach (Holt & Turner, 1975: 979; Almond & Coleman, 1960, Almond & Powell, 1966; Almond, 1970). It has been criticized on the one hand for failing to build a coherent theory of political development despite the time, money, and effort allocated to the project (Holt & Turner, 1975: 994) and, on the other, has also been seen as an extension of American ideology of the period (Latham, 2000). These views are slightly at odds with each other. It is true that there was considerable eclecticism in the approaches taken by the authors of chapters in the volumes, with some more empirical and others theoretical (and not always complementary theories). Still, there was a general sense that social science could tease out a model of political development that the West (the United States and the United Kingdom in particular) had successfully pioneered. Developing countries, which appropriately or not included Japan, were still works in progress and if they did not fit the model then it was a problem with the country and not the model itself.

Japan was one of the key countries covered in this initiative. Two volumes in particular were notable. One was purely dedicated to Japan and focused on political modernization (Ward & Burks, 1968). It contained primarily empirical chapters, with the notable exception of the chapter by Bernard Silberman on 'Structural and functional differentiation in the political modernization of Japan' (Ward & Burks 1968: 337–386) with a heavy dose of structural–functionalist theory. There was also the earlier volume edited by Ward and Rustow (1964) on *Political Modernization in Japan and Turkey*, two of the 'success stories' of non-Western modernization. The seminar event in postwar social science research on Japan was the Hakone Conference in 1960, which brought together Japanese and American social scientists to discuss a range of subjects in the development of modern Japan. It resulted in several volumes that became the standard background reading on Japan for two decades at least and influenced scholarship for long afterward.

The problem with the US Social Science Research Council was not only that there was a lack of consensus on theory, but also that the focus was on static cultural sources of backwardness. It was only when analysis of political development became more historical and institutional that the results were far more intriguing. This was especially clear when the political development of the West was given similar treatment. Significantly, the volumes in this series ended on Western history with a focus on the state (Tilly, 1975; Grew, 1978). This shift from culture to the state and institutions was significant for Japan, although it took many years before it had an impact on politics specialists focusing purely on Japan.

In stark contrast to the ahistorical US social science bias of most immediate postwar scholarship on Japan, one of the most important works in this period is Barrington Moore Jr.'s *Social Origins of Dictatorship and Democracy: Lord and Peasant in the Making of the Modern World* (1966) in which the case of Japan was given a prominent place. Moore's grasp of the details of Japanese history can easily be criticized but his ability to tease out patterns and trends from large swathes of the history of major states is impressive. His work was comparative and demonstrated an ability to see underlying dynamics in seemingly unique cases. His definitions of concepts of class and institutions, as well as political orientations of collective actors, might be questioned but the attempt demonstrated the flaws in narrow national historical studies as the basis for political analysis. Most significant was his skillful treatment of culture, which he termed 'tradition,' particularly in the Japanese context. He admits it is important,

> but one must explain why the tradition continued. Human sentiments do not persist simply of their own momentum. They have to be drilled into each generation anew and be kept alive through social structures that make them seem more or less sensible and appropriate (Moore, 1966: 291).

This is a quotation that a Japan specialist should have written but would not in this period of scholarship. Once again, this shift to historical and institutional analysis was significant.

Another standard political science text of the 1970s and 1980s was Samuel Huntington's *Political Order in Changing Societies* (1968), which put an explicit emphasis on institutions and the balance between the level of political mobilization in a society and the ability of its institutional framework to cope. It used a comparative framework that avoided an excessive focus on culture and its particularistic manifestations. Japan was simply one of a number of cases used to illustrate a universal set of political dynamics. Huntington's work came at the beginning of a period in which the concept of institutions was to play a major role and the study of Japanese politics in comparative perspective would be swept up in the manifestations of institutionalism that followed.

The New Institutionalism and Japan

The focus on institutions and the subsequent development of schools of 'institutionalism' in political science led political studies into a morass from which it never emerged. It was particularly a problem in the Japanese context because of the poor translation of the concept as *seidoshugi*. The term *seido* in Japanese literally means system and it was initially confused with the very different functionalist systems theory of David Easton (1959, 1979) which was translated as *seidoron* in Japanese. However, this confusing translation of the term institutionalism merely reflected a general confusion in political science between types of institutionalism.

Scholars have tended to identify at least three types of new institutionalism, which are usually grouped into historical institutionalism, sociological institutionalism (an extension of the field of organizational behavior), and rational choice (see Hall & Taylor, 1996; Koelble, 1995). Historical institutionalism seemed the natural focus for scholars of Japanese politics, particularly following from Barrington Moore Jr. and Samuel Huntington. Moreover, historical institutionalism provided a deeper set of theoretical assumptions to challenge structural–functional–culturalist logic because institutions and their development could be seen as an alternative to explaining how political behavior was structured rather than seen as functional responses based on culture. This focus on institutions, in turn, led to an examination of the state. The state was not a neutral institutional broker as in structural–functionalism but 'a complex of institutions capable of structuring the character of outcomes of group conflict' (Hall & Taylor, 1996: 938).

One problem was that historical institutionalists developed too loose a conception of institutions, including 'formal or informal procedures, routines, norms and conventions embedded in the organizational structure of a polity' and led them to focus on organization and the rules and conventions of organizations (Hall & Taylor 1996: 938). This looseness of definition of institution and organization, as well as the inclusion of norms and conventions, allowed all sorts of analysis to be considered historical institutionalism.

The biggest flaw in the application of institutionalism to the study of Japanese politics was

that it became entangled with the notion of the state, which in most cases when applied to Japan was defined rather narrowly as the bureaucracy. The seminal account of Japanese state power was Chalmers Johnson's *MITI and the Japanese Miracle* (1982). Challenging or refining Johnson's account of Japanese state power became something of a growth industry for several years after its publication, with Richard Samuels' study (1987) of the Japanese energy industry as perhaps the best counterargument. It is true that both Johnson and Samuels were not really historical institutionalists because both predated the rise of historical institutionalism as an approach, and Japan's higher civil servants had been a focus for research for many years (for example, Kubota, 1969; Koh & Kim, 1982). This meant that historical institutionalist theory was ignored and the old emphasis on bureaucracy was merely reinforced. Even later comparative work emphasizes the bureaucracy. One example is Bernard Silberman (1993), who focused on the origins of the Meiji state in terms of constitutional and legal frameworks, but ends his analysis of the Japanese case with an emphasis on the bureaucracy rather than the socio-political impact of institutional arrangements as historical institutionalist theory would suggest.

One other trend in the analysis of Japanese institutional arrangements was the focus on interest intermediation in Japan. Japanese scholarship tended to rely on the old terminology of 'pressure groups' from V. O. Key (1962) and others in immediate postwar scholarship on interest groups. The classic debate between pluralism and elite theory did not have a major impact on scholarship in Japan. There was one 'community power' study – an example of elite political theory analysis – but it was by a foreign-trained Japanese political scientist (Kuroda, 1986). This relative silence on the pluralism/elitism debate was somewhat understandable because the organization of interests in Japan was not the same as in the United States.

Scholars of Japanese politics struggled to characterize Japanese interest organization. Michio Muramatsu and Ellis S. Krauss (1987) described it as 'patterned pluralism' but it was unclear how it was patterned and how pluralistic it was. Following on from Johnson, others tried to argue that Japanese interest organization was statist, primarily due to international pressures (Katzenstein, 1985). This statism was meant to be distinct from the liberalism of the United States and Britain or the corporatism of smaller European states. In contrast, some tried to argue that Japan was corporatist, although they did point out that this corporatism did not include labor (Pempel & Tsunekawa, 1979). However, because corporatism is a system of interest intermediation based on key segments of the economy organized into peak associations and coordinated by the state, the absence of labor would be fatal to any notion of corporatism in Japan. Research into Japanese interest groups declined slightly after the 1980s and then became seen less as pluralist interests as they were caught up in the notion of civil society as we see later.

Political economy has been another significant area of political research on Japan with an institutionalist or statist focus. A lot of discussion of Japanese political economy, including the state, interest groups, and economy policy, was driven by the fact that Japan was a strong economic power and looked to be getting stronger. As the Japanese economy declined, however, the myth of the all-powerful Japanese state lost its appeal. Attempts were made to explain this decline using an historical institutionalist approach, for example Gao (2001) who, significantly, is a sociologist and not a political scientist. When political scientists did look at the Japanese political economy, the bureaucracy still loomed large. Amyx (2004), for example, focused specifically on the Japanese Financial Crisis and identified diffuse responsibility, lack of regulatory oversight or transparency, and resistance to change as the main factors in Japan's inability to cope with its prolonged financial crisis since the economic bubble burst in the early 1990s. Nonetheless, political economy was becoming less popular as a topic of research because the main focus of political studies started shifting to political parties.

REVIVAL OF THE STUDY OF PARTIES AND ELECTIONS

Rise and Fall of Rational Choice

The shift away from the state and public policy toward elections and political parties was anticipated to some degree by the rise of the rational choice approach to politics. As noted earlier, rational choice has also been put forward as a form of 'institutional' approach, and this makes sense if one looks at how rational choice can be used to clarify the dynamics of specific behaviors in institutional context with fixed rules, such as voting. It was natural that such an approach would lead to a shift in interests in elections and party politics rather than focus on historical institutionalism and the state.

The game theoretical approach as the basis of rational choice has been part of political studies since at least the 1950s and was applied with varying degrees of rigor to Japan over the following decades (Leiserson, 1970; Ike, 1982). What was new in the 1990s was the large number of American politics specialists who were trained in the rational choice approach and sought to expand its application to all fields because they believed in its universal truth. Professors in US political science departments began to encourage those who used the rational choice to apply it to new areas, such as Japan.

There has been tension between the rational choice approach and the area studies, particularly country-specific studies such as those focusing on a country like Japan. Rational choice assumes that actors have a fixed set of preferences (Hall & Taylor, 1996: 944) and rational choice theorists are not very interested in the content of these preferences. Moreover, they believe that institutions are formed by voluntary agreement of the relevant actors in terms of gains from cooperation and that institutions survive through competitive selection because it provides more benefits than alternatives (Hall & Taylor, 1996: 946). Rational choice is less interested in the historical process by which preferences are formed or institutions are created because the assumptions that their theories are valid regardless of how actors and institutions came into being.

The first attempt at applying rational choice systematically to Japanese politics was Ramseyer and Rosenbluth's *Japan's Political Marketplace* (1993), which used a relatively simple principal-agent approach to explain the relationship between ruling Japanese politicians and the bureaucracy. It was extremely useful for challenging the notion that bureaucrats in Japan were all-powerful, but there was considerable doubt, based on previous work that demonstrated the power of the Japanese bureaucracy, that politicians were really stronger than bureaucrats. Even so, the idea that the politicians might be delegating authority to the bureaucracy and patrolling to make sure their preferences were respected had some plausibility. One unfortunate characteristic of the book was that it was based on the notion that the Liberal Democracy Party (LDP) was permanently in power, as they had been from 1955, but when the LDP soon fell from power and new parties, coalitions, and political arrangements took center stage, it made the argument look obsolete.

There were other drawbacks to the rational choice approach to Japanese politics. One of the limitations was that the scholars of Japan did not have the technical background to provide sophisticated applications of rational choice. The early work of Ramseyer and Rosenbluth, as well as others who adopted the approach, such as Kohno (1997), was fairly simple and non-technical. Those scholars proficient at rational choice theories and methods, however, were sometimes lacking in a deep understanding of the Japanese political system and political history, and consequently made basic mistakes and even seemed to show contempt for country-specific knowledge as if it did not matter (Clemons, 1994; Johnson & Keehn, 1994; Johnson, 1997a). Moreover, one of the main criticisms of rational choice overall is that the approach is poor in testing theories rigorously with empirical research (Green & Shapiro, 1994). There was an inherent tension between the highly abstract rational choice theories and the messy detail of politics in a real political system, such as that of Japan.

Even so, Japan attracted interest from rational choice theorists who paired up with experts on Japanese politics and this contributed much to our understanding of Japan as well as electoral dynamics in general. The field developed scholars who formed teams of knowledgeable experts in both substantive knowledge and theoretical expertise (McCubbins & Thies, 1997; Cox & Thies, 1998; Cox, Rosenbluth & Thies, 1998; Baker & Scheiner, 2004). There is still a soft strain of rational choice (for example, Margarita Estevez-Abe 2008), and the field of Japanese political studies is less split on the issue as a new generation of political scientists with a variety of approaches, some quantitative and some not, have emerged. The potential for mindless rational choice hegemony over the studies of Japanese politics seems less threatening for the time being at least.

Revival of the Study of Voting Behavior and Party Politics

One important change that the rational choice work signaled was the re-emergence of party politics and voting behavior as a central concern of political studies of Japan. Of course, the subject had not been ignored previously, but there was a revival of interest in parties and voters due to the dramatic changes that Japan experienced after 1992. As noted earlier, in 1993 the LDP fell after nearly 40 continuous years in power. Within a few short years, the Japanese Socialist Party, the LDP's main rivals had effectively collapsed and a plethora of new parties emerged. Japan was also thrown into a situation where government was unstable and depended on fragile coalitions and interparty agreements. Moreover, the electoral system was reformed and transformed beyond recognition. All these developments provided political scientists with an abundance of new information and phenomena to explore (Christensen, 2000).

Beyond rational choice theorists, there have been a number of important studies of voting behavior in Japan, including a significant number of monographs and studies by Japanese scholars. The journal 'The Annals of the Japanese Election Studies Association' (*Senkyo Kenkyū*)

was established in 1986 and contains the contemporary analysis of electoral behavior, as well as historical work on elections in Japan. Miyake Ichirō has been a long-time and prolific scholar focused on voting in Japan (1989, 1990, 1995, 1998). He also collaborated in the *Japanese Voter* volume discussed earlier (1965). Other notable works on Japanese elections are Horie and Uemura (1986), Araki (1994), and Kobayashi (1997, 2000) Such works by Japanese scholars tend not to be discussed or even cited in English literature. In contrast, some Japanese scholars (for example, Kabashima, 1998; Kabashima, Marshall & Uekami, 2000; Kabashima & Steel, 2010) do publish in both Japanese and English and so bring a broader and more nuanced perspective to the field. Steven Reed based at Chuo University in Japan has done excellent work on the impact of electoral rule changes in Japan, which is comparative and has potential to contribute to a cumulative understanding of Japanese electoral system dynamics (Reed, 1990, 1996, 2003, 2007, 2009).

Parties have been the focus of research over the years. There have been overviews of the postwar Japanese party system, for example those edited by Ronald Hrebenar and colleagues (Hrebenar, Fukui, Berton & Nakamura, 1992; Hrebenar, 2000) but the pace of change in the Japanese party system has been fierce and it is difficult for published research to keep up with all the changes, especially the frequent emergence and mergers of small parties. The fragmentation of the Japanese party system has been covered by Cox and Rosenbluth (1995), Kato (1998), and Reed and Scheiner (2003). At the same time, the ideological fissures that might be behind some of these party splits are ignored. It is almost always assumed that the motives are strategic rather than ideological.

In terms of research on political parties, the LDP, which was dominant in Japanese politics from 1955–2009, has naturally attracted the lion's share of interest. This interest goes back to the empirical work of Thayer (1969), but also includes the debate over why one party government has been so dominant in Japan compared to the small number of similar cases in democratic states (Pempel, 1990). Thayer's and others' early work in the field tended to imply that LDP rule was stable and benign if not good for Japan, but the later work tended to question the nature of democracy in Japan if one party was continually in power, regardless of the apparent fairness of Japanese elections and party competition itself. Structural corruption and clientelism tended to lead some to believe that party competition was inherently unfair and that the opposition stood little chance of winning elections (Scheiner, 2005).

To be fair, Prime Minister Koizumi's successive destruction or disruption of his own LDP's clientelistic networks when he was in power from 2000 to 2005 did set the stage for the fall of the LDP in 2009. The background to this shift in conservative politics is still unclear. Indeed, it is curious that despite the LDP being avowedly a conservative party, there are few studies of its conservative ideology. Even discussions of the Koizumi phenomenon are more about leadership style than ideology, despite the fact the he and his allies appeared to be pursuing a clear neo-liberal agenda.

Ideological issues figured more prominently in the studies of the LDP's main rival, the Japanese Socialist Party (JSP). There was relatively little written on the JSP in English – the best is by Cole, Totten & Uyehara (1967) – and in Japanese the works were mostly potted histories or polemics against the party, usually from critics on the left. One of the last and perhaps the best in this genre was Uezumi (1992), an articulate insider in the JSP in its final days as a major party. What has been more remarkable is the number of academic studies of the decline and collapse of the party that has appeared in recent years (Shinkawa, 1999; Hara, 2000; Mori, 2002; Yamaguchi & Ishikawa, 2003; Okuda, 2005; Matsushita & Eguchi, 2006). There have been no serious full length studies of the fall of the JSP or the rise of the Democratic Party of Japan, which effectively replaced the JSP as the main alternative to the LDP, except Hyde (2009), and so in this respect English language research is far behind that of Japan.

The Japanese Communist Party seemed to benefit temporarily from the demise of the JSP in the 1990s but is looking increasingly to be a spent force in Japanese politics. At the height of the Cold War, it often seemed to attract more attention than the JSP because it was clearly more interesting to those studying comparative communism (Swearington & Langer, 1952; Scalapino, 1967; Langer, 1972). After the mid-1970s, however, the threat of Japanese communism seemed to wane. Within Japan, there has been some studies of the JCP but these tend to be journalistic (for example, Tachibana, 1983) or exposés by former members (for a recent example, Hyōmoto (2008)), and so there is very little serious academic work on the party. It is difficult for Japanese scholars to pursue given that there are political tendencies and affiliations within academia that makes such research difficult. The JCP is still active, although its activists continue to age and its policy revisions in recent years have made it a moderate if dwindling remnant of a declining left. It no longer attracts much attention from scholars, although it may be more important in what is left of the political left than ever before.

The Komeito, in contrast, has been involved in the highest level of government in recent years; yet there has been very little on Komeito in recent years, despite its increasing importance for a time. An early work by Palmer (1971) was the main source until an article by Merteaux (1999) brought the discussion more up-to-date. However, it was not until 2012 that another full-length study, by Fisker-Nielsen (2012), considered the issue again, this time focusing on the important tensions between the youth sections of Sokagakkai and the Komeito political leadership. In contrast, there is a massive literature on the Komeito and its parent organization Sokagakki in Japanese, including its complex relationships with other parties, such as the JCP and the LDP (a review essay by George Ehrhardt in 2008 of several Japanese language books in this genre discusses a small recent selection of what is a much larger body of work). It is true that this literature is generally not academic or very rigorous in its research or criticisms, but it indicates the profound interest in the party in Japan. The absence of research in political science, however, would seem to reflect an inability to deal with ideas and beliefs.

There is a lot of focus in political science on parties and voters for the obvious reason that voting generates a lot of data that is useful for quantitative research and model building. However, other related areas of research are often poorly analyzed because there is too much emphasis on electoral rules. One aspect that is missing is institutional constitutional context, that is, the importance of the structure of Japanese parliamentary institutions. There were the works of Hans Baerwald, updated over the years (Baerwald, 1974, 1987, 2010) and also the work of Mike Mochizuki (1982), which was an influential unpublished PhD thesis on the Japanese parliament and parliamentary committee rules, but it is surprising that there is not more work on this subject given that the limits of parliamentary structures in Japan have been tested severely in recent years. Parliamentary rules and norms should seem more relevant now in the period of coalition governments of the past few years. Constitutional issues such as a divided government also have implications from both a political and an institutional point of view. Indeed, one should not take a static view of institutions any more than one should accept a static view of culture. There are debates over the nature and appropriateness of Japanese institutions within Japan. These seem to be missed because the focus on institutions is usually the focus on the outcomes shaped by historicaly or existing institutions. Debates on institutional change are strangely ignored. Again, the problem might be that debates on possible changes to institutions often focus on ideas and beliefs. Recent studies by political scientists focusing on Japan seem unwilling or unable to cope with ideas.

DO OR SHOULD IDEAS MATTER?

Culture and Politics Again

The shift to political research more informed by political science theory came at the same time as the revival of cultural issues. By the 1980s, works were published aimed at a popular audience that had a profound influence on the field of Japanese studies and raised questions about how Japanese politics in particular was studied.

The two classic examples are Ezra Vogel's *Japan as Number 1* (1979) and Karel Van Wolferen's *The Enigma of Japanese Power* (1990). It may seem strange in a review of the scholarly literature to discuss these two popular works. Even so, both had an impact on the study of Japanese politics. Vogel is a manifestation of the interest in and fear of Japan in the late 1970s and early 1980s, some of which looks silly in light of subsequent developments, but at least Vogel's book was informed and well-presented if a bit too positive about Japanese society and politics. In contrast, Van Wolferen's logic was appalling and appealed to the worse type of essentialist, static and conspiratorial notions of culture, but he raised a lot of the taboo subjects that scholars of Japan, for a variety of reasons, had avoided, such as the collusion of the media with those in power.

Chalmers Johnson also attacked what he called the 'Chrysanthemum Club' (Johnson, 1997b), which he argued was centered on the old guard of Japan specialists and academics in the Edwin O. Reischauer Institute at Harvard University, but also included lobbyists and pro-Japanese politicians and officials in Washington and beyond. These scholars were accused of whitewashing the negative aspect of Japan. There was even an implication that anyone who took Japanese funding was suspect. This was a position that was shown to be misleading by the rapid expansion in the number of scholars, funded not only by the Japan Foundation and other Japanese sources, but also US government-supported scholarships, such as the Foreign Language Area Scholarships (FLAS), Fulbright awards, and Social Science Research Council (SSRC) funding. Even with the advent of the massive expansion of the Japan Teaching English (JET) program and the funding for scholars from the Foundation for Global Partnership, the Sasagawa Foundation, and Japanese Society for the Promotion of Science, it would be hard to argue that the scholars who have benefited are uniformly or even mainly sympathetic to the Japanese government point of view. Johnson may be right that the most prestigious institutions in the world are careful not to offend the Japanese, but that just reflects the conservatism of the academic establishment. Most, if not all, scholars of Japanese politics

are independent minded and not mindlessly pro-Japanese even if they have a deep understanding of and even sympathy for some Japanese views.

In the end, it became clear that much of the so-called 'revisionism' of Johnson and others had more to do with internal debates over the direction of US policy than anything to do with Japan. Johnson's final major works were pointing in that direction. It is also implicit in the analysis of current US policy toward Japan, particularly the analysis of economic policy and military policy. This is a parochial dead end from the point of view of Japanese political studies. Yet, despite Johnson's parochialism and Van Wolferen's lack of analytical skill, they prompted a new generation of scholars to raise questions about aspects of Japanese politics that had been ignored.

Subsequent research on the media or the nature of Japanese democracy, for example, has been no less critical of the Japanese political system but pursued key issues in a more rigorous and scholarly manner (see chapter 4 on the media and chapter 21 on democracy in this Handbook for an overview of this literature.) The fundamental critique of Van Wolferen – that Japan was a spiderless web – was presumably based on an inscrutable culture inaccessible to foreigners. This conspiratorial and essentialist approach had to be rejected but what could be put in its place? It is almost as if political science has decided to ignore culture in preference to empirical research and 'political science,' but is that viable in the long-run?

Political Anthropology, Political History and Political Science

If we want to take ideas or even 'culture' seriously, and there is an argument that it cannot be ignored, then how does one do it well? Most scholars of Japan would reject a static essentialist view of culture. Even anthropologists, who focus on culture, have adopted critical approaches that attempt to 'describe, analyze, and open to scrutiny otherwise hidden agendas, power centers, and assumptions that inhibit, repress, and constrain' (Thomas, 1993: 2–3) in ways that are not dissimilar to the efforts of political science. Anthropologists focusing on Japan have been good at maintaining a malleable notion of culture unlike that used in mainstream political science, for example, Bestor's work on a Tokyo neighborhood (1985, 1989) or recent work by Le Blanc (1999, 2009). The work of Le Blanc is particularly important. It harks back to the initial scholarship of Curtis (1971), but raises more sophisticated conceptual issues. It may be that political anthropology is particularly suited to many issues in political science. Nonetheless, there is the problem that anthropological categories and concerns do not always translate into the theoretical issues of political research.

Historians have also undertaken important research focused on ideas and their historical manifestations. A good example is Tessa Morris-Suzuki, who explicitly avoids the slippery notion of 'culture' (Boey, 2002), but engages the intellectual and conceptual context of Japanese modern history to tease out important tensions (see, for example, Morris-Suzuki (1997)). Some Japanese historians have also written important work that is relevant to the analysis of contemporary politics in Japan. For example, Oguma has written two books, one on the origins of the notion of Japaneseness (1995) and the other on patriotism and democracy in Japan (2002), both of which include subtle and wide-ranging analysis of trends and texts well into the postwar period. In English, however, intellectual history seems to stop at World War II. There are, of course, exceptions (for example, Hein (2004)), but there is none of the wide-reading intellectual critique in Japanese scholarship. If political scientists want to understand politics, they need to understand the intellectual foundations of postwar Japan as much as the studies of prewar thought and praxis provide insights into prewar Japanese history.

Research into civil society in Japan is a good case study of the problems of separating political research from political ideas and political history, including comparative political history and thought. Research on Japanese civil society seems as if it has been approached in such a way that ignores past discussion and sets up an implicit ideal drawn from US concepts. It also ignores the political dimension in that the implicit politics of the use of the concept is rarely, if ever, revealed. Instead, static notion of Japanese culture or tradition is seen as the basis for civil society in Japan. As the *kokkagaku* discussion at the outset of this chapter suggests, Japan confronted these issues at least 100 years earlier, and premodern traditions have been thoroughly transformed in the process of institutional change over the years or simply cultural artifacts if they still exist as an influence at all.

It is more important to first understand the ideological origins of the civil society debate in the West and then examine how the aspirations of scholars of Japanese politics have been grafted onto these debates. The premise for recent discussions of civil society is Neo-Tocquevillean, which means that it is based on contemporary American readings of Alexis De Toqueville's thesis that the United States, from its early days, has been particularly prone to produce independent associations. The assumption is one of American exceptionalism so that it lacks an appreciation of the alternative modes of interaction and association in other countries and even in the history of United States

itself. (Edwards, Foley & Diani, 2001). Much of the discussion of Japan is therefore similarly ahistorical and fails to explore the hidden complex of ideas in which the debate is embedded.

If civil society is defined purely as Non-governmental Organizations (NGOs) and NGOs as charitiable organizations then there would appear to be few NGOs in Japan on the American model. This leads to an implicit assumption that the origins of charitable giving are Western and Christian. It would also seem to suggest that Japan has no tradition of charity or civil society. Buddhism has a concept of charity, even if it did not develop in the same way, due partly to the modern organization of Japanese Buddhist temples on proprietorial lines. Non-religious forms of charitable activity and philanthropy have existed in Japan, particularly in Meiji and most of prewar Japan, but for a variety of reasons, there was a decline in this activity after the war. It is true that Christians in Japan were important in many forms of charitable organization (schools, etc.) especially after the war, but so was the left, albeit often including Christian socialists. In Japan, NGOs were inhibited by the involvement of the state in society and conservative patronage using the state since the war (Calder, 1991). The Japanese have tended to see the government, the powerful, and the wealthy as a source of assistance, as in the phrase 'our patron Japan' (*'oyakata hino maru'* – see Kyogoku, 1983), so that voluntary organization often seemed unnecessary. The lack of organizations or professional staff in NGOs merely reflects the fact that individuals and groups could express grievances and solicit compensation through political and bureaucratic channels, which were adequate for the time. Those groups that were not successful would have been just as unsuccessful if they had more trained staff. In short, the outcomes would have been the same because the organization of civil society was different.

One might ask why is there handwringing over lack of a certain type of civil society in Japan? It is easy to forget that the more recent roots of the push towards the 'ideal' type of civil society are to be found in conservative neoliberalism, particularly that of US President Ronald Reagan and more recently manifest in the British Prime Minister David Cameron's notion of the 'Big Society,' that is, the state does less and society does more. The assumption is that the state is bad and voluntary society is good. The counterarguments in favor of the state are ignored, such as the fact that society will pick and choose whom to help, and is therefore less universal and may be less fair than the state, which must follow impartial rules. Instead, the focus is on the bureaucratic nature and inefficiency of the state. This is not to say that the notion of civil society is conservative in Japan.

Many on the left have embraced the notion to foster groups that advocate progressive ideals. There is a left-wing/progressive tone to the handwringing, especially in Japan but also in Western literature; however, this misses the nuances of the origins and uses of the type of civil society being advocated. The politics of academic research and how it is used by different groups, including scholars, is overlooked and so Japan is once again made to look peculiar rather then just different for understandable reasons.

CONCLUSIONS

This chapter has examined the shifts in theoretical orientation of political studies of Japan over a large number of years. What should be clear from this discussion is that there is no neutral 'political science' because choices of topics and approaches include inherent assumptions. There are political issues and debates involved, which should not be surprising to scholars of politics. This is not to advocate that scholars should become partisan, but there is a need for a healthy dose of reflexivity on the part of scholars, Japanese or foreign, to situate their research in relation to others. In additional to theory and empirical evidence, the ideological basis of political research also needs to be examined.

The big dominant approaches over the years, such as political culture, structural–functionalism, historical institutionalism, and rational choice, were primarily imports from the United States and included biases and tendencies toward a false universalism, which is now obvious in retrospect. What is also striking is the relatively weak role of Japanese scholars in political studies as a result of the dominance of US political science and the lack of development of the field in Japan. It is always surprising that there are so many US-trained specialists in Japanese politics, but that is because US political science is so strong due to the percentage of school leavers going onto higher education (although other countries are gaining). There is also a captive audience of students for compulsory introduction to US politics courses in undergraduate general education that enables politics departments in the United States to employ more members of staff than elsewhere and subsidize other areas of the field, such as Japanese politics.

The level of theoretical sophistication and abilities of non-Japanese scholars focused on Japan, including language skills, has improved dramatically over the years but one would still expect Japanese to have a better command of the language and understanding of contextual nuance to pursue quality research. There is danger if one is too immersed in a society to become purely empiricist or focusing only on the peculiar or unique; however, this is a problem for all social scientists everywhere. Moreover, knowledge of a country's history and wider social context is invaluable. Some might sneer that such knowledge focuses on 'path dependency,' but history does matter. It influences the patterns and possibilities of political life. Similarly, ideas matter. Analysis of ideas requires a sophistication and depth of knowledge that is sometimes overlooked by crude, but more theoretically elegant and methodologically simple approaches. It is not a matter of rejecting deep country-specific knowledge, but a question of putting this knowledge to use to further develop theory rather than make it impossible to develop. Empirical research and theory development should be based on methodological rigor and attempts to extend and refine the research of others rather than always searching for innovation.

One positive development in recent years is the diversity of approaches to and centers of scholarship. The hubris of early postwar social science and rational choice has been replaced by 'soft' universality, empiricism, and small-scale theory based on eclectic foundations and approaches. It is true that this carries the danger of a lack of theory refinement and cumulative theory development. The only way to overcome these problems of theory development is more dialogue and interaction between groups engaged in different approaches and methods. There is certainly still opportunity for dialogue over what constitutes good political research, and an open-minded attitude prevails at the moment. This means there is plenty of room for innovative and conceptually sophisticated research into Japanese politics. Reflexivity and dialogue will be key to an open and vibrant scholarly community focused on Japanese politics.

REFERENCES

Almond, G. (1970). *Political development: essays in heuristic theory*. Boston, MA: Little, Brown & Company.

Almond, G. and Coleman, J. (Eds.). (1960). *The politics of the developing areas*. Princeton, NJ: Princeton University Press.

Almond, G. and Powell Jr., G. B. (1966). *Comparative politics: a developmental approach*. Boston, MA: Little, Brown & Company.

Almond, G. and Verba, S. (1963). *The civic culture: political attitudes and democracy in five nations*. Princeton, NJ: Princeton University Press.

Amyx, J. (2004). *Japan's Financial Crisis: Institutional Rigidity and Reluctant Change*. Princeton, NJ: Princeton University Press.

Araki, T. (1994). *Tōhyō Kōdō no Seijigaku – Hoshuka to Kakushin Seitō*. Sapporo: Hokkaido Daigaku Zusho Kankōkai.

Baerwald, H. (1974, 1987, 2010). *Japan's parliament: an introduction*. Cambridge, UK: Cambridge University Press.

Baker, A. and Scheiner, E. (2004). Adaptive parties: party strategic capacity under Japanese SNTV. *Electoral Studies*, 23, 251–278.

Befu, H. (1987). *Ideorogī toshite no nihonbunkaron*. Tokyo: Shisō no Kagaku Sha.

Benedict, R. (1946, 1954). *The chrysanthemum and the sword: patterns of Japanese culture*. Rutland, VT: Charles E. Tuttle Co.

Bestor, T. C. (1985). Tradition and Japanese social organization: institutional development in a Tokyo neighborhood. *Ethnology*, 24(2), 121–135.

Bestor, T. C. (1989). *Neighborhood Tokyo*. Stanford, CA: Stanford University Press.

Boey, K. C. (2002, November 24). Giving culture a hearing. *New Straits Times*.

Byas, H. (1942). *Government by assassination*. New York, NY: A. A. Knopf.

Calder, K. (1991). *Crisis and compensation: public policy and political stability in Japan*. Princeton, NJ: Princeton University Press.

Campbell, A., Converse, P. E., Miller, W. E., and Stokes, D. E. (1960). *The American voter*. Chicago, IL: University of Chicago Press.

Christensen, R. (2000). *Ending the LDP hegemony in Japan*. Honolulu, HI: University of Hawaii Press.

Clemons, S. C. (1994). Japan studies under attack: how rational choice theory is undermining America's understanding of the world. *JPRI Working Paper*, No. 1 (August).

Cole, A. B., Totten, G. O. and Uyehara, C. H. (1967). *Socialist parties in postwar Japan*. New Haven, CT: Yale University Press.

Converse, P. (1969). Of time and partisan stability. *Comparative Political Studies*, 2(2), 139–171.

Cox, G. W. and Rosenbluth, F. M. (1995). The anatomy of a split: the liberal democrats of Japan. *Electoral Studies*, 14(4), 355–376.

Cox, G. W., Rosenbluth, F. M., and Thies, M. F. (1998). Mobilization, social networks, and turnout: evidence from Japan. *World Politics*, 50(3), 447–474.

Cox, G. W. and Thies, M. F. (1998). The cost of intra-party competition: the single, non-transferable vote and money politics in Japan. *Comparative Political Studies*, 31(3), 267–291.

Curtis, G. (1971). *Election campaigning Japanese style*. New York, NY: Columbia University Press.

Dahl, R. (1961). The behavioral approach in political science. *American Political Science Review*, 55(4), 763–773.

Dale, P. N. (1986). *The myth of Japanese uniqueness*. London: Croom Helm.

Doi, T. (1973). *The anatomy of dependence: the key analysis of Japanese behavior* (J. Bester, Trans.). Tokyo: Kodansha International.

Duverger, M. (1951). *Les partis politiques*. Paris: Librairie, Armand Collin.

Duverger, M. (1954). *Political parties: their organisation and activity in the modern state*. New York, NY: Wiley.

Easton, D. (1959). *The political system: an inquiry into the state of political science*. New York, NY: Alfred A. Knopf.

Easton, D. (1979). *A systems analysis of political life*. Chicago, IL: University of Chicago Press.

Edwards, B., Foley, M. W. and Diani, M. (2001). *Beyond Tocqueville: civil society and the social capital debate in comparative perspective*. Hanover, NH: Tufts University Press.

Ehrhardt, G. (2008). Review essay on Komeitō. *Politics and Religion*, 1(1), 137–148.

Elkins, D. J. and Simeon, R. E. B. (1979). A cause in search of its effect, or what does political culture explain? *Comparative Politics*, 11(2), 127–145.

Estevez-Abe, M. (2008). *Welfare and capitalism in postwar Japan: party, bureaucracy, and business*. Cambridge, UK: Cambridge University Press.

Fisker-Nielsen, A. M. (2012). *Religion and politics in contemporary Japan: Soka Gakkai youth and Komeito*. London: Routledge.

Flanagan, S. C. (1979). Value change and partisan change in Japan: the silent revolution revisited. *Comparative Politics*, 11(3), 253–278.

Flanagan, S. C., Kohei, S., Miyake, I., Richardson, B. M., and Watanuki, J. (1991). *The Japanese voter*. New Haven, CT: Yale University Press.

Forsyth, M. and Keens-Soper, M. (1996). *The political classics: Green to Dworkin*. Oxford, UK: Oxford University Press.

Gao, B. (2001). *Japan's economic dilemma: the institutional origins of prosperity and stagnation*. Cambridge, UK: University of Cambridge Press.

Green, D. P. and Shapiro, I. (1994). *Pathologies of rational choice theory: a critique of applications in political science*. New Haven, CT: Yale University Press.

Grew, R. (Ed.). (1978). *Crises of political development in Europe and the United States*. Princeton, NJ: Princeton University Press.

Hall, P. A. and Taylor, R. C. R. (1996). Political science and the three new institutionalisms. *Political Studies*, 44, 936–957.

Hara Y. (2000). *Sengo no naka no Nihon Shakaitō – Sono Risoshugi to wa nan de atta ka?* Tokyo: Chuo Koron Sha.

Hein, L. (2004). *Reasonable men, powerful words: political culture and expertise in twentieth century Japan*. Berkeley, CA: University of California Press.

Holt, R. T. and Turner, J. E. (1975). Crisis and sequence in collective theory development. *American Political Science Review*. 69, 979–994.

Horie, F. and Uemura, M. (1986). *Tōhyō Kōdō to Seiji Ishiki*. Tokyo: Keio Tsushin.

Hrebenar, R. J. (Ed.). (2000). *Japan's new party system*. Boulder, CO: Westview Press.

Hrebenar, R. J., Fukui, H., Berton, P. and Nakamura, A. (1992). *The Japanese party system*. Boulder, CO: Westview Press.

Huntington, S. (1968) *Political order in changing societies*. New Haven: Yale University Press.

Hyde, S. (2009). *The transformation of the Japanese left: from old socialists to new democrats*. London: Routledge.

Hyōmoto, T. (2008). *Nihon Kyōsantō no Sengo Hisshi*. Tokyo: Shinshio Sha.

Ike, N. (1982). *A theory of Japanese democracy*. Boulder, CO: Westview Press.

Inglehart, R. (1977). *The silent revolution*. Princeton, NJ: Princeton University Press.

Inglehart, R. (1990). *Culture shift in advanced industrial society*. Princeton, NJ: Princeton University Press.

Johnson, C. (1997a). Preconception vs. observation, or the contributions of rational choice theory and area studies to contemporary political science. *PS: Political Science and Politics*, 30(2), 170–174.

Johnson, C. (1997b). The Chrysanthemum Club seizes the American Embassy, Tokyo. *JPRI Critique*, 4 (9). Retrieved from http://www.jpri.org/publications/critiques/critique_IV_9.html on 12 December 2012.

Johnson, C. (1982). *MITI and the Japanese miracle: the growth of industrial policy, 1925–1975*. Stanford, CA: Stanford University Press.

Johnson, C. and Keehn, E. B. (1994). A disaster in the making: rational choice and Asian studies. *The National Interest*. 36, Summer, 14–22.

Kabashima, I. (1998). The instability of party identification among eligible Japanese voters. *Party Politics*, 4(1), 151–176.

Kabashima, I., Marshall, J. and Uekami, T. (2000). Casual cynics or disillusioned democrats? Political alienation in Japan. *Political Psychology*, 21(4), 779–804.

Kabashima, I. and Steel, G. (2010). *Changing politics in Japan*. Ithaca, NY: Cornell University Press.

Kato, J. (1998). When the party breaks up: exit and voice among Japanese legislators. *The American Political Science Review*, 92(4), 857–870.

Katzenstein, P. J. (1985). *Small states in world markets: industrial policy in Europe*. Cornell, NY: Cornell University Press.

Key Jr., V. O. (1962). *Politics, parties, and pressure groups*. New York, NY: Crowell.

Kimura, S. (2010). Kindai Genri no Keishisei to Doitsu Kokkagaku no Jishitsusei. *Seiseki Daigaku Keizai Kenkyū*, 190, 130–83.

Kobayashi, Y. (1997). *Nihon no Tōhyō Kōdō to Seiji Ishiki: Hendō suru Nihonjin no Senkyo*. Tokyo: Bokutaku Sha.

Kobayashi, Y. (2000). *Senkyo/Tōhyō Kōdō*. Tokyo: Tokyo Daigaku Shuppankai.

Koelble, T. A. 1995. The new institutionalism in political science and sociology. *Comparative Politics*, 27(2), 231–43.

Koh, B. C. and Kim, J. (1982). Paths to advancement in the Japanese bureaucracy. *Comparative Political Studies*, 15(3), 289–313.

Kohno, M. (1997). *Japan's postwar party politics*. Princeton, NJ: Princeton University Press.

Kubota, A. (1969). *Higher civil servants in postwar Japan: their social origins, educational backgrounds, and career patterns*. Princeton, NJ: Princeton University Press.

Kuroda, Y. (1986). *Reed town Japan: study in community power structure and political change*. Honolulu, HI: University of Hawaii Press.

Kyogoku, J. (1983). *Nihon no Seiji*. Tokyo: Tokyo Daigaku Shupppankai.

Kyogoku, J. and Ike, N. (1959). *Urban–rural voting differences in postwar Japan. Political Science Series No. 66*. Stanford, CA: Stanford University.

Langer, P. F. (1972). *Communism in Japan; a case of political naturalization*. Stanford, CA: Hoover Institution Press.

Latham, M. (2000). *Modernization as ideology: American social science and 'nation building' in the Kennedy era*. Durham, NC: University of North Carolina Press.

Le Blanc, R. M. (1999). *Bicycle citizens: the political world of the Japanese housewife*. Berkeley, CA: University of California Press.

Le Blanc, R. M. (2009). *The art of the gut: manhood, power, and ethics in Japanese politics*. Berkeley, CA: University of California Press.

Leiserson, M. (1970). Coalition government in Japan. In S. Groennings, E. W. Kelley and M. Leiserson (Eds.), *The study of coalition behavior: theoretical perspectives and cases from four continents* (pp. 80–102). New York, NY: Holt, Rinehart and Winston.

Makino, M. (2008). *Kokkagaku no Saiken: Ierineku to Wēbā*. Nagoya: Nagoya Daigaku Shuppankai.

Masumi, J. (1966). *Nihon seito shiron, 7 vols*. Tokyo: Tokyo Daigaku Shuppankai.

Matsushita, N. and Eguchi, M. (2006). *Shakaitō no Tōkai – Uchigawa kara Mita Shakaitō/Shamintō 15 nen*. Ōmuta, Japan: Minato Kōgei Sha.

McCubbins, M. D., and Thies, M. F. (1997). As a matter of factions: the budgetary implications of shifting factional control in Japan's LDP. *Legislative Studies Quarterly*, 22(3), 293–328.

Metraux, D. A. (1999). Japan's search for political stability: the LDP-New Komeito alliance. *Asian Survey*, 39(6), 926–939.

Miyake, I. (1989). *Senkyo Seido to Tōhyō Kōdō*. Tokyo: Bokutaku Sha.

Miyake, I. (1990). *Seiji Sanka to Tōhyō Kōdō – Daitoshi Jūmin no Seiji Seikatsu*. Tokyo: Mineruba Shobō.

Miyake, I. (1995). *Nihon no Seiji to Senkyo*. Tokyo: Tokyo Daigaku Shuppankai.

Miyake, I. (1998). *Seito Shiji no Kōzō: Hendō suru Nihon no Senkyo Kōdō*. Tokyo: Bokutakusha.

Miyake I., Kinoshita, T. & Aiba, J. (1965). Seiji Ishiki Kōzōron no Tameshi. In Nihon Seiji Gakkai (Ed.), *Nenpō Seijigaku: Seiji Ishiki no Riron to Chōsa*, pp. 1–104. Tokyo: Iwanami Shoten.

Miyake, I., Kinoshita, T. and Aiba, J. (1967). *Kotonaru Reberu no Senkyo in okeru Tōhyō Kōdō no Kenkyū*. Tokyo: Sōbun Sha.

Mochizuki, M. M. (1982). *Managing and influencing the Japanese legislative process: the role of parties and the national Diet* (PhD thesis). Harvard University, MA.

Moore Jr., B. (1966). *Social origins of dictatorship and democracy: lord and peasant in the making of the modern world*. Boston, MA: Beacon Press.

Mori, H. (2002). *Nihon Shakaitō no Kenkyū – Rōsen Tenkan no Seiji Katei*. Tokyo: Bokutaku Sha.

Morris-Suzuki, T. (1997). *Re-inventing Japan: nation, culture, identity*. Armonk, NY: M. E. Sharpe.

Muramatsu, M. and Krauss, E. S. (1987). The conservative policy line and the development of patterned pluralism. In K. Yamamura and Y. Yasuba (Eds.), *The political economy of Japan* (Vol. I, pp. 516–54). Stanford, CA: Stanford University Press.

Nakane, C. (1967). *Tate Shakai no Nigen Kankei – Tanitsu Shakai no Riron*. Tokyo: Kodansha.

Oguma, E. (1995). *Tantsu no Minzoku no Kigen: 'Nihonjin' no Jikazō no Keifu*. Tokyo: Shinyo Sha.

Oguma, E. (2002). *'Minshu' to 'Aikoku': Sengo Nihon no Kokyosei*. Tokyo: Shinyo Sha.

Okuda I. (2005). *Nihon Shakaitō – Sono Sōshiki to Taibō no Rekishi*. Tokyo: Shin Jindai Sha.

Palmer, A. (1971). *Buddhist politics: Japan's clean government party*. New York, NY: Springer-Verlag.

Pempel, T. J. (Ed.). (1990). *Uncommon democracies: the one party dominant regimes*. Ithaca, NY: Cornell University Press.

Pempel, T. J. and Tsunekawa, K. (1979). Corporatism without labor? The Japanese anomaly. In C. P. Schinitter and C. Lembruch (Eds.), *Trends toward corporatist intermediation* (pp. 231–270). Beverly Hills, CA: Sage Publications.

Przeworski, A, and Teune, H. The Logic of Comparative Social Inquiry. New York: Wiley-Interscience, 1970.

Ramseyer, J. M. and Rosenbluth, F. M. (1993). *Japan's political marketplace*. Cambridge, MA: Harvard University Press.

Reed, S. R. (1990) Structure and behaviour: extending Duverger's law to the Japanese case. *British Journal of Political Science*, 20(3), 335–356.

Reed, S. R. (1996). Seats and votes: testing Taagepera in Japan. *Electoral Studies*, 15(1), 71–81.

Reed, S. R. (2003). What mechanism causes the M + 1 rule? A simple simulation. *Japanese Journal of Political Science*, 4, 41–60.

Reed, S. R. (2007). Duverger's law is working in Japan. *Senkyo Kenkyu*, 22, 96–106.

Reed, S. R. (2009). Party strategy or candidate strategy: how does the LDP run the right number of candidates in Japan's multi-member districts? *Party Politics*, 15(3), 295–314.

Reed, S. R. and Scheiner, E. (2003). Electoral incentives and policy preferences: mixed motives behind party defections in Japan. *British Journal of Political Science*, 33, 469–490.

Reischauer, E. O. (1977). *The Japanese*. Cambridge, MA: Harvard University Press.

Reischauer, R. K. (1939). *Japan: government-politics*. New York, NY: Thomas Nelson.

Richardson, B. M. (1974). *Political Culture of Japan*. Berkeley, CA: University of California Press.

Richardson, B. M. (1997). *Japanese democracy: power, coordination, and performance*. New Haven, CT: Yale University Press.

Richardson, B. M. and Flanagan, S. C. (1984). *Politics in Japan*. Boston, MA: Little, Brown & Company.

Rochon, T. R. (1981). Electoral systems and the basis of the vote. In J. C. Campbell (Ed.), *Parties, candidates and voters in Japan: six quantitative studies. Michigan papers in Japanese Studies, No. 2*. (pp. 1–28). Center for Japanese Studies, University of Michigan.

Rōyama, M. (1949). *Seiji Ishiki no Kaibō*. Tokyo: Asahi Shinbun Sha.

Rōyama, M., Ukai, Tsuji, Kawahara, & Nakamura, (1955). *Sōsenkyo no Jittai*. Tokyo: Iwanami Shoten.

Sakamoto, T. (2001). *Kokkagaku no Susume*. Tokyo: Chikuma Shoten.

Samuels, R. J. (1987). *The business of the Japanese state: energy markets in comparative and historical perspective*. Cornell, NY: Cornell University Press.

Scalapino, R. A. (1967). *The Japanese communist movement, 1920–1966*. Berkeley, CA: University of California Press.

Scapalino, R. A. and Masumi, J. (1962). *Parties and politics in contemporary Japan*. Berkeley, CA: University of California Press.

Scheiner, E. (2005). *Democracy without competition in Japan: opposition failure in a one-party dominant state*. Cambridge, UK: Cambridge University Press.

Seligson, M. A. (2002). The renaissance of political culture or the renaissance of the ecological fallacy? *Comparative Politics*, 34(3), 273–292.

Shibata, T. (2005). Zenki Shutain no Kokkagaku in okeru Kokusai Kankei Riron to Jichi Riron. *Tōyō Daigaku Shakaigakubu Kiyō*, 43(2), 25–35.

Shinkawa, T. (1999). *Sengo Nihon Seiji to Shakai Minshushugi – Shakaitō/Sōhyō burokku no Kyōbō*. Tokyo; Hōritsu Bunka Sha.

Siemes, J. (1964). Hermann Roesler's commentaries on the Meiji constitution. *Monumenta Nipponica*, 19(1–2), 37–65.

Siemes, J. (1969). *Hermann Roesler – The making of Meiji state*. Tokyo: Charles E. Tuttle Co.

Silberman, B. (1993). *Cages of reason: the rise of the rational state in France, Japan, the United States, and Great Britain*. Chicago, IL: University of Chicago Press.

Swearington, R. and Langer, P. (1952). *Red flag over Japan: international communism in action*. Westport, CT: Greenwood.

Tachibana, T. (1983). *Nihon Kyōsantō no Kenkyū*, 3 vols. Tokyo: Kodansha.

Takii, K. (2010). Itō Hirobumi wa Nihon no Bisumaruku ka? *Yūroppa Kenkyū*, 9, March, 203–210.

Tanaka, S. (2010), Shūkenron wo meguru 'Nihonteki Keifu' no Kanosei ni tsuite. *Journal of International Cooperation Studies*, 18(1), 21–35.

Thayer, N. B. (1969). *How the Conservatives rule Japan*. Princeton. NJ: Princeton University Press.

Thomas, J. (1993). *Doing critical ethnography*. Newbury Park, CA: Sage Publications.

Tilly, C. (Ed.). (1975). *The formation of nation states in Western Europe*. Princeton, NJ: Princeton University Press.

Uezumi, S. (1992). *Nihon Shakaitō Kyōbō Shi*. Tokyo: Jiyū Sha,

Van Wolferen, K. (1990). *The enigma of Japanese power: people and politics in a stateless nation*. New York, NY: Vintage Books.

Vogel, E. (1979). *Japan as Number 1: lessons for America*. Cambridge, MA: Harvard University Press.

Ward, R. and Burks, A. W. (1968). *Political development in modern Japan*. Princeton, NJ, Princeton University Press.

Ward, R. and Rustow, D. (Eds.), (1964). *Political modernization in Japan and Turkey*. Princeton, N J: Princeton. University Press,.

Watanuki, J. (1962). *Gendai Seiji to Shakai Hendō*. Tokyo: Tokyo University Press.

Wilson, W. (1898). *The state: elements of historical and practical politics*. Boston, MA: D. C. Heath & Co.

Yamaguchi, J. and Ishikawa, M. (Eds.), (2003). *Nihon Shakaitō – Sengo Kakushi no Shisō to Kōdō*. Tokyo: Nihon Keizai Hyōron Sha.

20

Parties and Elections in Japan

Kenneth Mori McElwain

INTRODUCTION

The central meme of postwar Japanese politics is the Liberal Democratic Party's (LDP) electoral dominance. Following its formation in 1955, the LDP held a majority in the House of Representatives for 38 consecutive years. Every prime minister came from its ranks, and through its control of the government policy apparatus, the LDP established deep formal and informal networks with other elite actors, particularly the bureaucracy and major business conglomerates. However, this '1955 system' came crashing down in the watershed 1993 election, when the LDP lost its majority and was replaced by an eight-party coalition of opposition parties. The new coalition government fulfilled its popular mandate to change the electoral system, but fell apart shortly thereafter due to disagreements on most other issues. The LDP returned to power in 1994, albeit in a partnership with its long-time rival, the Japan Socialist Party (JSP). The LDP once again held the reins of Japanese politics, although it had to rely on coalitions with a variety of conservative and centrist minor parties to do so. Its second stint was shorter than its first: the LDP was soundly defeated in 2009 by the Democratic Party of Japan (DPJ), which became the first non-LDP party with a parliamentary majority since 1955. But Japanese politics had

been in turmoil even before that election, as evinced by the near-annual rotation of prime ministers. In fact, even the DPJ's victory was short-lived: it replaced its leader three times in 3 years, before falling once again to the LDP in the 2012 Lower House election.

What factors explain the LDP's dominance, given much higher rates of government turnover in other democracies? Existing accounts point to conservative voter attitudes, the success of the postwar economy, and institutional factors that produced entrenched incumbents. If these accepted wisdoms are true, then we should observe alternations in power – or at least a substantially weakened LDP – when these underlying factors change. This chapter describes a number of important shifts since the 1990s: voter partisanship has been declining, the economy has been mired in a prolonged slump, and the electoral system was altered to encourage more robust two-party competition. Do these changes explain the LDP's ouster by the DPJ in 2009? How does the LDP's quick rebound to electoral success in 2012 fit into this picture? More generally, has there actually been a paradigm shift in Japanese democracy since the 1990s?

This essay explores these issues by reviewing the trajectory of postwar electoral politics and examining the core explanations for LDP dominance. The literature is broken down into analyses of three time periods, which correspond to variations in the level of LDP power: single-party dominance (1955–1993), LDP defeat and electoral reform (1993–1994), and coalitional politics (1994–present). In addition to explaining the causes of LDP dominance and its eventual fall, I will also discuss some of the *effects* of the party's tenure, such as the redistributive nature of public policy and the relative salience of ideology versus clientelism in voter–politician relationships. I will conclude with some thoughts about the future prospects of government stability in Japan, focusing on the growing salience of independent voters in the last two decades.

HISTORICAL BACKGROUND: BEFORE AND AFTER WORLD WAR II

Prewar Party Politics

Party politics in Japan dates back to the early twentieth century. The Meiji Constitution of 1889 established a political framework with an elected Lower House (House of Representatives) and a peerage-based Upper House (House of Peers). However, the Meiji oligarchs, who held the extra-constitutional status of *genro* or elder statesmen, jealously guarded their power over cabinet appointments and major policy issues (Duus, 1998). While all Prime Ministers until 1901 were oligarchs, popular criticism of clique or factional governments increased confrontations between the Cabinet and the elected Lower House. Faced with intractable political conflicts, the Meiji oligarchs eventually conceded the utility of electoral participation and established parties of their own. The most prominent, *Rikken Seiyukai* (or Seiyukai for short), formed in 1900 under the leadership of Ito Hirobumi, one of the main architects of the Meiji Constitution. Because the right to vote was restricted by tax qualifications, the Seiyukai served as an electoral coalition of large landlords, prosperous farmers, and business leaders. A number of alternative elite parties, such as the *Kenseikai* and *Doshikai* (each led by other Meiji oligarchs), challenged the Seiyukai's rule, but the party retained its pre-eminent status until the 1920s.

In 1925, suffrage was expanded to all males over the age of 25. As Duus (1998) notes, calls for greater popular participation in democracy had been growing for over a decade, catalyzed by the rice riots of 1918 and labor unrests in the 1920s. In 1927, the Kenseikai merged with splinter factions of the Seiyukai to form the second major party of prewar Japan, the *Rikken Minseito* (or Minseito for short). The Seiyukai and Minseito had roughly even parliamentary representation, and their alternations in power ushered in a period of party government that is frequently referred to as 'Taisho Democracy' (McElwain, 2014).[1]

As the country descended into militarism in the 1930s, however, the power and independence of political parties began to wane (Yamanouchi, Koschmann & Narita, 1998). A series of political assassinations by military cliques robbed parties of their leaders, and by the 1930s, both the Minseito and Seiyukai began to splinter internally over whether to confront or accommodate the military. Under Prime Minister Konoe Fumimaro's initiative to establish a single-party totalitarian state, both parties disbanded in 1940 and joined the *Taisei Yokusankai*, or Imperial Rule Assistance Association. For the remainder of the Pacific War, competitive multi-party elections were abolished and the prime ministership came under the control of the military.

The Postwar Decade

The end of World War II and the enactment of the 1947 Constitution brought about fundamental changes in democratic competition. The Diet, not the Emperor or Meiji *genro*, would select the Prime Minister, and members of both houses of parliament – the House of Representatives, or Lower House, and House of Councillors, or Upper House – would be directly elected by voters.[2] In addition, the establishment of universal suffrage and freedom of assembly gave voice to new socio-economic groups and progressive ideologies.[3] Amidst postwar food shortages and escalating unemployment, labor unions mobilized against the formerly privileged *zaibatsu* (business conglomerates) and major landowners. Socialists and communists – many of who were imprisoned during the war – quickly established political parties with deep organizational ties to public and private sector unions.

By the late 1940s, there was a three-way split in the Diet between the conservative Liberal Party, the centrist Democratic Party, and the left-leaning Socialist Party. The Liberals and Democrats were natural allies, as both espoused a strong security alliance with the United States – one of the main ideological issues of the day – despite disagreements about the wisdom of demilitarization. The two parties were comprised largely of conservative politicians from the prewar *Seiyukai* and *Minseito*, but rivalry between the two party leaders, Yoshida Shigeru (Liberals) and Hatoyama Ichiro (Democrats), made a permanent partnership elusive. The left-wing also experienced intra-party disputes over accepting the San Francisco Peace Treaty and the continued presence of US military bases. The Socialist Party temporarily split into the 'Left Socialists' and 'Right Socialists' – each with its own headquarters and electoral strategy – over confrontational versus accommodationist stances vis-à-vis the United States–Japan alliance.

A number of factors led to the 1955 consolidation of the conservatives into the LDP and the progressives into the unified JSP. In the 1953 and 1955 elections, the Democrats – the political centrists – won a plurality (but not a majority) of the votes. They had the option of forming a coalition with either the Right Socialists or the Liberals, but chose to rule as a minority government. This came with legislative consequences: without majority support in the Diet, the Hatoyama Cabinet faced significant hurdles to passing the fiscal budget. Labor union leaders, fearing a disorganized progressive camp and seeing the opportunity for greater political influence, urged the two wings of the JSP to reunite. The Left Socialists had its own concerns: should the Right Socialists be enticed to form a coalition with the Democrats, they could be locked out of power altogether (Kohno, 1997). Instead, it proposed a joint party, which the Right Socialists accepted in October 1955.

On the conservative end of the spectrum, business leaders were pressuring the Liberals and Democrats to form a joint party in opposition to the reunified JSP (Masumi, 1985). Competing campaign donation demands from the conservative parties were straining the coffers of business associations and led to a number of embarrassing bribery scandals. The Democrats, with a plurality in the Diet, were in a stronger bargaining position, and their leader, Hatoyama, refused to amalgamate with the Liberals unless he could be the new party's president. Personal rivalry between Hatoyama and the Liberals' senior politician, Yoshida Shigeru, made compromise difficult. However, when the JSP reunited, the Liberals and Democrats agreed to put aside their differences and form a joint front against the Socialists. In November 1955, the Liberals and Democrats formally created the Liberal Democratic Party, with Hatoyama as the leader.

THE 1955 SYSTEM

With the consolidation of the conservative and progressive camps into two distinct parties, the political landscape was poised for the classic 'Left versus Right' partisan divide that one finds in other advanced industrialized democracies. Despite the early size advantage of the LDP, there were no *ex ante* reasons to expect the Socialists to be in permanent opposition. Given the enmity between Hatoyama (Democrats) and Yoshida (Liberals), the LDP 'marriage of convenience' could have

collapsed had the party failed to win decisive majorities, returning the electoral landscape to three-party competition. Some of this conflict dissipated with the untimely death of Hatoyama, but more puzzling was the inability of the Socialists to win over the electorate. Instead of robust competition between the two ideological poles, electoral margins widened and the LDP continued to win parliamentary majorities. Indeed, the JSP became even weaker as the progressive base splintered with the founding of the Democratic Socialist Party (DSP) in 1960 and the Komeito (also known as the Clean Government Party, or CGP) in 1964.

Figure 20.1 displays the vote share of the five principal parties between 1955 and 1993. One notable factor is that new political parties were durable: once formed, they survived over the entire time period. The exception is the New Liberal Club (not listed in Figure 20.1), a small splinter party of the LDP that later rejoined its co-partisans. This issue of durability is important to understanding divisions within the Japanese electorate because it signifies that parties represented deep-rooted socioeconomic cleavages, regional interests, or personalistic allegiances to specific politicians, not flash-in-the-pan ideologies.

A second interesting factor is the relative vote ratio between the LDP and the JSP. Although their vote shares converged at certain points, there was a longstanding 2:1 split between the two principal parties, prompting Japan's description as a '1.5 party system'. As Figure 20.2 demonstrates, this ratio is much larger than one finds in almost any other advanced democracy. Both Norway and Sweden come close, but in neither country does one party routinely win a majority of the seats. This gap is puzzling, insofar as opposition parties should have incentives to merge to become a viable competitor to the dominant party (Cox, 1997). The question here, therefore, is why the LDP was so successful and why the opposition remained fractured.

The following subsections will explore two issues. First, I will describe the party system between 1955 and 1993, focusing on the emergence and salience of new political parties. Importantly, I will analyze institutional and structural explanations for *why* Japan had multiple opposition parties. Second, I will look at the determinants of LDP electoral success, focusing on voter attitudes, the relative salience of ideological versus clientelistic competition, and institutional hurdles to the opposition.

The Party System: Ideology and Institutions

Political scientists distinguish between individual political parties and collective party *systems*

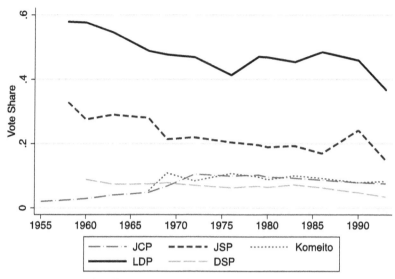

Figure 20.1 Vote shares of political parties (1955–1993)

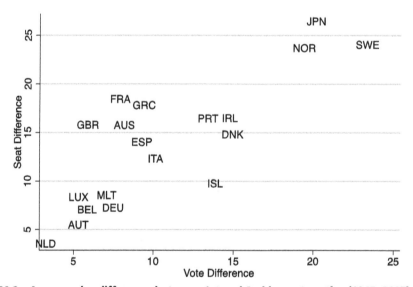

Figure 20.2 Average size difference between 1st and 2nd largest parties (1945–2005)

(Mair, 1997). Over the course of history, different political parties may form, merge, or dissolve, even though many descend from related ideological and structural lineages. In the immediate postwar period, for example, the Democratic Party succeeded the Progressive Party, which in turn was formed out of the remnants of the prewar *Minseito*. These parties shared members and ideological trajectories, although one would be accurate in calling them distinct political parties. However, the party *system* over the postwar decade was fairly constant. The Liberal Party was more conservative,

the Progressives/Democrats tended to be centrist, while the Socialists and Communists held the left flank. In other words, Japan in the late 1940s–early 1950s could be described as a three-party or three-bloc system, even though the electoral salience of individual parties fluctuated.

In a similar way, we can examine the *party system* after the formation of the LDP. The defining characteristics of a party system are (1) the number of parties, which is strongly influenced by the electoral system, and (2) the social or ideological cleavages, which determine the types of policy disagreements that divide parties. In other words, the dimensions are: how many parties compete, and what issues do they compete over?

Domestic and International Cleavages

Let me begin with ideological differentiation. Political ideology is a consistent set of ideas and attitudes that reflect how we prioritize and evaluate social, economic, and political affairs. The typical differentiation in advanced democracies is on economic policies, ranging from greater government activism and redistribution on the Left to smaller governments with strict adherence to market principles on the Right. Of course, most societies are divided on more than one issue. In Japan, we can identify three prominent cleavages: *class conflict*, *regional divisions* between urban and rural areas, and *foreign policy* vis-à-vis the United States. As Kabashima (1999) points out, however, political parties' policy differences on these dimensions can be arrayed along a single spectrum from progressive (*kakushin*) to conservative (*hoshu*).[4] In Japan, conservatives tend to be pro-business and rural and pro-US alliance, while progressives tend to be pro-worker and urban and pro-international neutrality (if not anti-US alliance). Here, I will explore the three core issue areas in greater detail.

As discussed earlier, various socioeconomic actors mobilized on different fronts after the end of World War II. In one corner, the conservatives – dating back to the prewar *Seiyukai* and *Minseito* – received strong support from major business conglomerates, small business owners, and farmers. In the other corner, the progressives represented labor unions and Marxist intellectuals.

Following the formation of the LDP, the 'Yoshida School' of politics, advocating neo-mercantilism and export-driven economic growth, seized the party's reins. Yoshida Shigeru brought in many economic and foreign policy technocrats into the LDP, and ex-bureaucrats monopolized the premiership (Pempel, 1998). Much like its prewar counterparts, the LDP received significant backing from business conglomerates. The party advocated private property, low taxes, weaker unions, and market competition, albeit under the direction and coordination of the government (Johnson, 1982).[5] Prime Minister Ikeda Hayato's 'income-doubling plan' in the 1960s called for the rationalization of heavy industry, investment in education and science research, and infrastructural expenditures.

The pursuit of economic growth is not inherently confrontational, in that few politicians or voters are *anti*-growth. However, economic goals create political cleavages when the fruits of prosperity are distributed unequally. For example, business owners may generate capital gains from corporate profits by keeping workers' wages low,

or urban regions may benefit from industrialization while farming in rural areas decline. The relative strength of political parties, therefore, is a reflection of the size of these economic constituencies and the ability of parties to capture their support.

Bradley Richardson (1997) attributes LDP dominance to the inability of progressives to corner labor union support in the way that the LDP encapsulated farmers and small business owners. While 70–80 percent of farmers and 55–65 percent of small-business owners supported the LDP over time, the JSP could only corral about 15–30 percent of manual workers and salaried employees (Richardson, 1997, Table 2.2). Blue-collar ambivalence to the JSP was due in part to the economic system's co-optation of labor interests. In a movement called *shunto*, or 'spring wage offensive,' unions would annually renegotiate wages with employers. This produced a continuous and incremental adjustment of compensation, which redistributed economic growth to workers and contributed to socioeconomic stability (Fukatsu, 1995).

More important, however, was fracture within the progressive ranks. In the 1960s, the unions split between *Sohyo* (General Council of Trade Unions) and *Domei* (Japan Federation of Labor). Sohyo represented public sector employees, such as teachers and hospital workers, while Domei was comprised of private sector workers (Pempel, 1998). Because public sector workers were restricted from industrial action (strikes, sit-ins, etc.), they advocated confrontational politics against the LDP; private sector unions, who enjoyed greater rights over collective bargaining, favored accommodationist tactics (Kohno, 1997).[6] Making matters worse, union membership began to fall in the 1960s. Given that most labor activism occurred at the firm level, the collective impact of coordinated union-wide bargaining diminished.

The second cleavage, between rural and urban voters, also maps onto the conservative versus progressive spectrum. In many countries, left-wing movements and socialist parties tend to cluster around urban centers, while right-wing movements are located in rural areas. This is a reflection of each side's electoral base: cities often emerge out of industrialization and the development of factories, while farmers and large landowners tend to be based outside population centers. This differentiation can be seen in Figure 20.3, which shows election-by-election differences in the relative performance of LDP and JSP candidates.

To create this graph, I first estimated the proportion of each party's candidates that were victorious by election (WIN=# winning candidates / # total candidates), and then took the difference in those ratios between the LDP and JSP (WIN$_{LDP}$ – WIN$_{JSP}$). The vertical axis denotes this difference: a positive value indicates that a greater share of

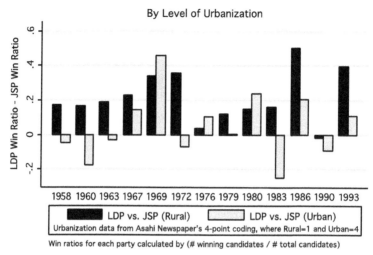

Figure 20.3   LDP vs. JSP candidate victory ratios

LDP candidates won, while a negative value indicates that more JSP candidates were successful. I calculated these values separately for urban and rural regions: the dark bars denote the most rural districts, as calculated by the Asahi Newspaper's four-point scale, and the light bar denotes the most urban districts.[7] While there is year-on-year difference in the performance of the LDP and JSP, we can see that the LDP almost always did better than the JSP in rural regions, while there were greater swings in urban regions.

One reason for strong rural support of the LDP is the government's redistribution of income from the richer (urban) regions to the poorer (rural) regions. Economic development narrowed inequality in the long run, but the initial concentration of industrialization in urban areas worsened regional income stratification. As Kabashima (1984) argues, however, higher levels of political participation in rural regions encouraged the LDP to solidify their support among farmers by equalizing income through budgetary redistribution. I will save a lengthier discussion of the LDP's redistributive policies to later sections on the determinants of LDP dominance.

In addition to these distributive cleavages based on urbanization and class conflict, the Japanese party system was also divided by non-structural, *ideational* cleavages. The most salient dimension was foreign policy, specifically over the United States–Japan Security Treaty and Article 9 of the Japanese Constitution. For most of the postwar period, the Yoshida School, which espoused low military spending and a close alliance with the United States, dominated LDP politics (Pyle, 1996; Samuels, 2007).[8] Although the US Occupation had originally pushed for the Article 9 'Peace Clause' to limit future remilitarization, the Korean and

Vietnam Wars prompted a *volte-face* as the United States increased pressures on Japan to strengthen its defense capacity. The LDP gradually warmed to overturning Article 9, although its ability to do so was limited because of the high hurdles to constitutional amendments.[9]

Progressives, on the other hand, defended the importance of Article 9 as a national commitment to pacifism. Domestically, left-wing supporters, particularly the teachers' union, drew a hard line on constitutional reform. Pacifist sentiment among the electorate made increased military spending unpopular, and opinion surveys consistently showed support for preserving Article 9 and opposition to remilitarization (Katzenstein, 1996; Samuels, 2007).

In terms of votes and seats, however, Japanese remilitarization and Article 9 were low-salience electoral issues, especially after the 1960 reaffirmation of the United States–Japan Security Treaty. The Socialist and Communist parties managed to corner some popular support for their firm defense of the status quo, and these positions paid off as electoral gains when exogenous shocks – Nixon's visit to China, China joining the United Nations, and the Vietnam War – created popular backlash against the United States. However, Miyake, Nishizawa, and Kohno's (2001) analysis of public opinion data demonstrates that most voters retained stable and warm sentiments towards the United States, favoring alignment with the US/liberal coalition over an alliance with the USSR/communist sphere. Although foreign policy attitudes developed into a consistent ideological cleavage between supporters of the LDP and the JSP, the disparity in numbers meant that foreign policy was a losing electoral basket for the JSP's eggs.

Electoral Institutions and the Number of Political Parties

This analysis of ideological differentiation helps us understand what issues political parties *could* compete over; however, they do not necessarily explain which issues *will* become electorally salient. For example, while there are measurable differences in the electorate over rural versus urban, employer versus worker, or pro- and anti-US issues, these do not necessarily translate into distinct political parties. This leaves us with the question, 'Why were there *five* stable parties in Japan, with the LDP on the right, the JSP and the JCP on the left, and the DSP and Komeito in the center?' Why didn't Japan have a two-party system resembling the United States or the United Kingdom, or even *more* parties as in the Netherlands or Sweden? And given the proliferation of parties, how did the LDP manage to maintain a single-party majority instead of fragmenting, as did the progressives?

There is an extensive political science literature on the relationship between electoral institutions and the party system.[10] The underlying logic is strategic behavior by voters and politicians: rational actors will not invest resources (votes, time, money) on lost causes. If there is only one seat per district, then a winning candidate needs 50 percent of the votes to guarantee a victory. Fringe candidates should opt out of elections they cannot win, but even if they decide to compete, strategic voters should choose to support candidates with greater viability, resulting in a decline in the number of competitive candidates to two. In electoral systems with multiple seats per district, by contrast, pressures to converge around a few candidates is weakened.

Although a number of eminent scholars have examined electoral and party systems, some of the most innovative work has been done by Japan scholars. In his seminal study, Steven Reed (1991) posits the 'M+1' rule: where the number of seats in a given district equals M, we should expect to see M+1 competitive candidates. The logic is straightforward: a candidate needs to win $1/(M+1)$ share of the total electorate to guarantee a victory. In a one-seat district, 50 percent of the votes will win a seat, while in a two-seat district, 33 percent of the votes will do the job. To the extent that strategic behavior or simple market forces will weed weaker parties, we should see a convergence towards M+1 'competitive candidates'.[11]

From 1947 to 1994, Japan used a multi-member district, single non-transferable vote system (MMD-SNTV), where the country was divided into approximately 130 electoral districts with three to five seats each.[12] This system impacted a variety of political outcomes, such as factionalism within the LDP and the nature of electoral campaigning, but its most salient effect was on the number of political parties in the Diet. Because the average district magnitude (M) in Japan under MMD-SNTV was four, it was theoretically possible for an average of five candidates or parties (M+1=5) to be competitive in each electoral district. Prior to 1955, these five parties were the Liberals, Democrats, the left- and right-wing Socialists, and the Communists. Indeed, we can postulate that had Japan employed a single-member plurality (SMP) system, the LDP would have formed earlier and the JSP would never have split. The flipside, however, is that the two-party landscape of 1955 – the LDP representing the conservatives and the JSP representing the progressives – was unsustainable.

This institutional perspective allows us to better understand opposition fragmentation from 1955 to 1993. The first party to emerge after 1955 was the Democratic Socialist Party (DSP), which formed in 1960 as an offshoot of the JSP's right-wing faction. The DSP was backed by *Domei*, the private sector workers union, and advocated greater political compromise with conservative parties and labor moderation with corporations. The second new party was the Komeito, which formed in 1964. The Komeito (which remains in operation today) is unique in Japan because its primary support group is a lay Buddhist organization, the *Soka Gakkai*. Komeito is a largely urban party with a centrist policy platform, drawing support from nonunionized workers and small business owners. The final new actor, the New Liberal Club, was established in 1976 when an LDP faction split off to protest Prime Minister Tanaka's corruption scandals, although it later rejoined the LDP in 1986. For the most part, the NLC maintained a strong partnership with the LDP and joined forces in the Diet when the latter fell short of a parliamentary majority.

The question here is why these particular parties emerged after 1955, and what effect it had on parliamentary competition. Kohno (1997) argues that the success of new political parties is a function of the MMD-SNTV system. As evidence, he demonstrates that new parties did better in districts where M=5, because the vote share needed to win a seat is smaller [$(1/(M+1)$=16.7 percent]. In other words, the quasi-two party system in 1955 was unsustainable because there were insufficient centripetal pressures to overcome ideological disagreements or personal rivalries within the LDP or JSP.

While the institutional backdrop is crucial, socioeconomic and structural transformations underlay the emergence of these particular parties. To put it differently, a larger district magnitude will support more candidates, but it is not clear whether we should see more conservative, centrist, or socialist parties. In the Japanese context, most of the 'new' votes up for grabs were in metropolitan areas, where urbanization and industrialization unmoored voters from traditional allegiances in their home districts. Scheiner (1999) makes these points in critiquing Kohno's finding, arguing that although institutional structure mattered, new parties cared about electoral viability more than institutional benefits. He demonstrates that parties tended to run candidates in urban districts where voters had weaker identification with the larger parties, not where district magnitude equaled five (although the two factors overlap). This did not greatly harm the LDP, whose support base was in rural areas, the proliferation of floating voters diluted the JSP's urban support base, leading to the emergence of new parties like the DSP that fragmented the progressive vote.

Explaining LDP Single-party Dominance: Voter Assessments and Institutional Advantages

Although the preceding section reviewed the literature on the Japanese party system, focusing on the number and type of political parties, these arguments cannot explain the overriding phenomenon of postwar Japan: *how* did the LDP dominate parliamentary politics for so long? There are three principal arguments for the LDP's longevity. First, the LDP kept on winning because most voters approved of the LDP's performance and/or its ideological platform. Second, the LDP won not because voters liked them, but because the opposition failed to provide an effective alternative to the LDP. Third, the institutional environment had built-in advantages for the LDP that allowed it to create an 'artificial majority.' The first two arguments hinge on voter attitudes, while the third focuses on the electoral system.

Voter Attitudes and LDP Success

A commonsensical observation about elections is that candidates and parties who are more popular tend to win. However, it is not so obvious *which* factors affect voter preferences because popularity is a joint function of party identification and performance assessment. Party identification is a durable psychological attachment that voters develop towards a party, based on culture, social environment, or agreement with a party platform. Some voters will always support the LDP or the JSP because they like the overall ideological goals of the party, regardless of short-term disagreements over policy priority. Performance assessment, on the other hand, is an empirical judgment that voters form about a party or candidate at a given point in time. Voters without partisan allegiances may cast their ballot based on their approval of a government's recent performance or an opposition party's alternative policy pledges.

The party identification argument hinges on structural factors – demographic or socioeconomic identities, such as income distribution, region, or occupation – which determine (or proxy for) electoral preference. As Richardson (1997) argues, however, there is weak correlation between economic class and party attachment in Japan, especially among salaried middle-class workers. Regional divisions are somewhat stickier, especially in rural areas where the LDP has dominated the vote (see Figure 20.3). However, rapid urbanization inhibited the development of durable party attachments because voters faced different policy appeals or candidate choices as they moved to different parts of the country. Moreover, given the steady decline in the agricultural sector and the rural population, regional voter biases are insufficient to explain the continuing electoral success of the LDP.

If anything, more voters are becoming *non-partisan*, which Richardson (1997) attributes to disillusionment with repeated bribery and corruption scandals. Figure 20.4 plots data from the *Jiji Tsushin*'s monthly opinion polls, which asks respondents which political party they support. I focus on three primary options: LDP, JSP, and Independents.[13] We can see that the JSP's support has been declining since the early 1960s. By the mid-1970s, only 10 percent of voters claim to support the party. Although the LDP has remained stagnant, it has routinely outpaced the JSP by about 20 percent. By contrast, the fastest growing segment of voters is political independents.

In some ways, this is a rational response to the fickle policy stances of Japanese political parties. Kobayashi (1997) reviews the pre-election policy promises of political parties and finds that campaign platforms lack consistency and tend to be very malleable. In other words, there is very little substance or permanent ideological anchor for voters to hold on to. This raises a crucial question about political preference: if voters are not motivated by deep-rooted party identification, based on adherence to a particular party's policy platform, then what determines how they vote?

Here, we can turn to the second factor influencing voter preference: performance assessment. If voters have no allegiance to a political party, then they are more likely to make electoral choices based on perceptions about *policy competence*.[14] For example, if economic growth is strong and unemployment is low, then voters are more likely to support the incumbent government; should the economy collapse, however, then voters may prefer to turn over the reins to the opposition. Miyake and colleagues (2001) present one of the most thoroughly tested arguments about performance-based voting (sometimes called retrospective voting). Relying on monthly opinion polls of party identification, cabinet approval, and sentiments towards foreign nations, they argue that LDP dominance was built upon overwhelming *relative* support for the LDP. 'Relative' is the key term here: although LDP support fluctuated over time, opposition parties suffered even greater drop-offs.

An illustrative turning point came in the 1970s. The LDP had benefited from double-digit GDP growth in the 1960s, when 35–40 percent of voters expressed strong preference for the party (Miyake et al., 2001). However, three events jolted voter sentiment. First, the two oil shocks in the 1970s slowed the rate of economic growth. Second, the Vietnam War and Nixon Shocks[15] raised anti-US sentiment in the country and decreased voter identification with the LDP. Third, voters came face-to-face with the negative externalities of the growth-at-all-cost policies of the LDP. New issues, such as urban overcrowding and environmental degradation, prompted questions about the tradeoff between money and quality of life. This general trend is not unique to Japan, as evinced by similar changes in voter priority in Western Europe (Inglehart, 1987).

These transformations in the social, economic, and international environment should have provided the opposition parties with ample opportunity to bring new voters into their fold. Miyake and colleagues' (2001) surprising finding, however, is that the greatest growth was in the ranks of *independent* voters, that is the opposition failed to capture dissatisfied voters. They go so far as to argue that the 1.5 party system, with dueling LDP versus JSP competition, really only existed until the late 1960s and since then, the LDP's main competitor has been independent voters,

whose allegiance was up for grabs. This finding is bolstered by Figure 20.4, which shows an inverse relationship between LDP support and independents. In fact, the correlation between the two variables (1960–94) is –0.74. By contrast, LDP and JSP support is *positively* correlated at 0.43 (JSP and independents are correlated at –0.65), indicating that both parties are primarily losing votes to independents, not to one another.

The LDP'S Co-optation of Opposition Issues

The greatest failure of the opposition was the inability to attract voters who were increasingly concerned with the negative externalities of industrialization, such as rising real estate prices and environmental hazards in the major cities. Instead, the JSP continued to define themselves by foreign policy and the United States–Japan security alliance, which had low electoral salience (Miyake et al., 2001).

The flipside of the argument is that the opposition was out-maneuvered by the LDP, which co-opted emergent issues and redistributed income to protect sectors that were falling behind. Dan Okimoto (1989) argues that the LDP's laissez-faire attitude towards industrial and financial policy was in stark contrast to its activist intervention in fiscal programs that benefited their core constituents. One notable beneficiary was agriculture. In return for votes, the LDP granted subsidies for production and placed price controls – particularly on rice – to insulate farmers from international competition (Pempel, 1998; Mulgan, 2000). The main industrial group, *Nokyo* (Japan Agricultural Cooperatives), worked closely with the LDP and developed individual ties to rural legislators through campaign donations and

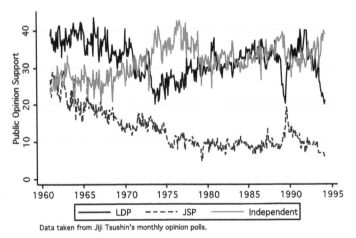

Data taken from Jiji Tsushin's monthly opinion polls.

Figure 20.4   Public support of political parties (1960–1994)

votes. Similarly, when the LDP was pressured by foreign governments to reduce trade barriers in the 1980s, the Japanese government fought to keep quotas that protected small and medium-sized enterprises (Calder, 1988). Looking at election data, Anderson and Ishii (1997) found that increased exposure to international trade hurt the LDP's vote share because its core base in farming and construction tended to be less efficient than foreign competitors.

Indeed, research on LDP pork-barrel politics abound. Brian Woodall's (1996) definitive book on the LDP-construction industry nexus shows that the party doled out expensive public works projects and trade protectionism in exchange for votes and financial contributions. This strategy was part of the LDP's exploitation of the urban–rural cleavage, seen most effectively under Tanaka Kakuei, who served as prime minister between 1972 and 1974. Tanaka made his original fortune as a construction magnate, and as a native son of Niigata prefecture, he appealed to voters in the poorer, Northeastern regions (*Tohoku, Hokuriku*) along the Sea of Japan. Although farming had been the largest sector in these regions, urban migration had decimated local industry. Arguing that Japan needed to help those who had been left behind, Tanaka penned *Rebuilding a New Japan* (1972), an action plan calling for infrastructural developments to physically connect rural areas to urban centers, reverse migration flows, and industrialize the rural economy. Tanaka's strident rhetoric was a big hit with the public, although his manuscript caused a huge spike in real estate prices, particularly in areas he had identified for redevelopment. During and after

his tenure, the LDP used the disbursement of rail and road construction as political pork. Kohno and Nishizawa (1990) employed statistical tests to demonstrate that the LDP increased construction projects immediately prior to elections to fill the coffers of construction companies, which in turn donated campaign funds and mobilized votes for the party.

Due to the government's redistributive policies, income stratification was fairly limited in postwar Japan. One common measure is the Gini coefficient, which calculates the distribution of income inequality across households. Figure 20.5 plots the Gini coefficient in Japan between 1960 and 2000 in two ways: first, using household income directly, and second, using household income adjusted for social insurance benefits and costs. Keeping in mind that high values of the Gini coefficient denote more unequal income distribution, Japan has had relatively mild income disparities despite a rapid growth in per capita GDP.[16] This is particularly apparent when examining the adjusted Gini coefficient, which incorporates the value of the government's income redistribution policies. Historically, Japan has had one of the lowest Gini coefficients around the world, on par with Denmark and Sweden and significantly lower than the United States or Great Britain.

Institutional Advantages to the LDP

Even if we stipulate that the LDP enjoyed greater popular support than the opposition parties due to positive performance assessment of its economic management and the co-optation of opposition issues, we still need to explain the *degree* of LDP

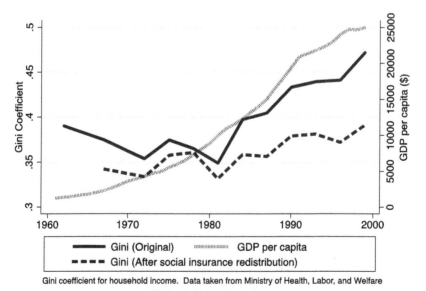

Gini coefficient for household income. Data taken from Ministry of Health, Labor, and Welfare

Figure 20.5 Gini coefficient in Japan (1960–2000)

electoral dominance. Foremost is the disjuncture between the LDP's popularity ratings and its seat share in parliament. Even during its heyday in the 1960s, most surveys indicate that popular support for the LDP averaged 40 percent, while Cabinet approval ratings – a proxy for LDP leadership – was about 5 percent higher. As Figure 20.4 shows, LDP popularity has been in the low-30s to high-20s since the 1970s. Although these are sizable numbers, they are far from clear-cut majorities. How did the LDP muster a parliamentary majority in the Diet despite lower public approval ratings?

The key factor here is the postwar electoral system, which gave a seat boost to the largest political party. The magnitude of this boost is a function of the district magnitude (M), or the number of seats per district (Taagepera & Shugart, 1989; Gallagher, 1991). If there is only one seat per district, a candidate or party can win 100 percent of the seats (in this case, one) with 50 percent+1 votes, generating a seat:vote ratio of 1/0.5 or 2:1. If M=2, then a candidate/party can win both seats with 66.7 percent of the votes, generating a seat:vote ratio of 1/0.67 or 3:2. As M increases, the proportionality between votes and seats approaches 1:1. In effect, this means that a plurality party can win a majority of the seats without a majority of the votes *if* the electoral system is sufficient disproportionate.

How proportional was the MMD-SNTV system? Given an average district magnitude of four, a candidate needs to win 20 percent+1 votes to *guarantee* himself a victory; in practice, a candidate can win with less if a sufficiently large number of candidates split the vote. Empirically, the average winning vote share between 1952 and 1993 was 23.7 percent in three-member districts, 18.3 percent in four-member districts, and 15.2 percent in five-member districts. This means that the LDP could theoretically win two out of four seats (50 percent) with less than 40 percent of the district's votes, yielding a seat:vote ratio (the 'bonus ratio') of 0.5:0.4, or 1.25. This prediction is in line with the party's *actual* bonus ratio between 1955 and 1993, which ranged between 1.25 and 1.06, with a mean of 1.15.

To achieve this seat bump from disproportionality, the party needed to avoid the over-concentration of votes in one candidate. To do so, the LDP divvied up conservative support in the district by nominating candidates from different geographical hometowns (Hirano, 2006) and with varying policy expertise (Ramseyer & Rosenbluth, 1993). At the same time, the LDP tried to reduce electoral uncertainty by pressuring conservative independent candidates to stay out of the election (Baker & Scheiner, 2004).[17]

Strategic nomination coordination is only one factor that affects the translation of votes to seats. Another element is the degree of *malapportionment*, or cross-district differences in the number of voters per seat. In a perfectly apportioned world, the electorate-to-M ratio would be constant across districts. For example, each district would have exactly 100,000 voters. In Japan, however, gradual urbanization led to distorted malapportionment favoring rural districts (Ohmiya, 1992). The implication of malapportionment is that the electoral cost of a rural seat is smaller than an urban one because 40 percent in a given rural district is a smaller absolute number of votes than 40 percent in urban areas. In the 1986 election, for example, the population ratio between the most sparsely populated district (Hyogo 5) and the most crowded one (Chiba 4) was 1:5 (*Shuugiin Chousakyoku* 2002). In effect, the LDP could continue to win a majority by catering to a pro-LDP electoral minority in rural areas because each rural vote was more valuable than an urban vote.

An important point here is that the LDP purposely fostered and took advantage of malapportionment. While Japanese law mandates redistricting every five years, the LDP ignored this stipulation except when the Supreme Court threatened to void election results. The informal standard of the Supreme Court has been to accept population disparities of less than three, i.e., the most populous district could have up to three times more voters than the least populous one (Ohmiya, 1992; McElwain, 2008). This is still a sizable boon to the LDP because urban regions – where the opposition parties are more competitive – are serially undercounted in elections.

In addition to its effects on proportionality, malapportionment produced second-order effects on the clientelistic nature of voter–politician relations. The fiscal structure of the Japanese government is highly centralized: local governments collect one-third of all taxes but spend two-thirds of it. In other words, local governments are dependent on central transfers to fund most social and infrastructural projects. This fiscal centralization produced two effects. First, it helped the LDP redistribute income from urban areas (where it was less popular) to its rural bailiwicks (DeWit & Steinmo, 2002). Thies (1998) finds that despite gradual urbanization, agricultural spending increased as the percentage of rural electoral districts increased. Similarly, Horiuchi and Saito (2003) demonstrate that the level of fiscal transfers from central to local governments increased with the level of malapportionment in votes. The postwar economic boom made this redistributive, pork-barrel oriented strategy more effective, as urbanization left rural areas impoverished and dependent on LDP largesse to survive.

Second, fiscal centralization put pressure on local government officials to affiliate with the LDP in order to gain access to the central government budget. Scheiner (2006) argues that this significantly strengthened the LDP's competitiveness in *national* elections because ex-local politicians tend to make the best candidates for the Diet. Indeed, Scheiner suggests that this was the long-term factor reinforcing LDP dominance in the Diet: candidate quality matters, especially in systems where voters care more about individual candidates than parties, and the LDP could stay in power as long as it continued to dominate candidate recruitment.

A final institutional cause of LDP dominance is Japan's restrictive framework of *campaign regulations*. *Ceteris paribus*, incumbent candidates tend to have greater name recognition than challengers. As such, challengers need more time and resources to sell their image and ideas to voters. Japan's 'Public Office Election Law,' however, is extremely proscriptive: it prohibits door-to-door campaigning, limits the amount of money that candidates can spend, and regulates the number and type of newspaper ads, posters, and flyers that can be posted during the campaign period. Of note is the limitation on the number of days that candidates are permitted to campaign. In 1950, electioneering was allowed from 30 days prior to the election date, but by the early 1990s, this window was reduced to 12 days. Crucially, the LDP made these regulations more restrictive as its popularity waned. The party's strategy was to go 'defensive': the LDP insulated itself from declining popularity by making it difficult for voters to identify viable alternative candidates (McElwain, 2008). This is consistent with Scheiner's argument that ex-local politicians make the best national candidates. Local politicians with established support bases can tap their electoral networks quickly, even in an abbreviated campaign period. The end result of this strategic electoral rule manipulation was the extension of LDP single-party majorities beyond what their overall popularity warranted.

LDP DEFEAT AND ELECTORAL REFORM

To reiterate, the LDP's parliamentary majority from 1955 to 1993 rested on three factors. First, it was more popular relative to opposition parties due to positive performance assessments during the high-growth era and the successful cooptation of opposition issues after the economy cooled off. Second, the electoral system magnified LDP popularity by promoting opposition fragmentation and overvaluing rural votes. Third, the LDP could draw from a pool of better candidates and, once elected, these incumbents were protected by restrictive electioneering rules.

Nonetheless, the LDP *did* fall from grace in 1993 when the party lost its Lower House majority for the first time since its founding in 1955. There had been early warning signs of the LDP's demise. In 1976, 1979, and 1983, the LDP fell short of a single-party majority and had to entice conservative independents and the New Liberal Club to join the party *after* the election. In 1989 and 1992, the LDP lost its Upper House majority outright, conceding some parliamentary control to the opposition parties. However, its moment of reckoning was ultimately caused by intra-party fissures as key factions chose to defect from the LDP. In other words, the story of the LDP's first defeat hinges on percolating voter dissatisfaction *and* the short-term strategic behavior of LDP politicians.

Voter Dissatisfaction and Intra-LDP Fissures

A number of factors contributed to the LDP's growing unpopularity. Beginning with long-term trends, gradual economic slowdown soured voter perceptions about LDP competence. As Miyake and colleagues (2001) discuss, a hefty portion of the LDP's popularity hinged on positive performance assessment, based on the rapid economic growth of the 1950s and 1960s. The inverse, of course, is that when the economy plateaued – compounded by the Oil Shocks of the 1970s – voter enthusiasm also faded. Postwar industrialization diminished the labor market share of agriculture, shrinking the LDP's support base. The gradual reduction of trade barriers, forced under foreign criticism of Japan's huge trade surpluses, also disproportionately harmed the LDP's core constituency.

At the same time, earlier policy choices came back to haunt the LDP. Reckless spending on pork-barrel politics had ballooned government deficits, and the LDP was compelled to institute a 3 percent consumption tax in 1989. The opposition parties, especially the JSP and JCP, heavily opposed the regressive tax, and the LDP was soundly defeated in the 1989 Upper House election. At the same time, the bursting of the asset bubble in the 1990s led to conspicuous drops in business investment and household consumption, which slowed GDP growth and raised unemployment.

Although the eventual magnitude of the ensuing economic 'Lost Decade' was not known in 1993, the illumination of high profile scandals illustrated the level of cronyism, corruption, and clientelism that underlay the 1955 system. Two salient cases include the Recruit Cosmos Scandal (1988–1989), which forced Prime Minister Noboru Takeshita and other senior cabinet members to resign, and the Sagawa Kyuubin Scandal (1993) that implicated

LDP Deputy President Shin Kanemaru. In both examples, LDP bosses – mainly from the pork-barrel oriented Tanaka faction – accepted bribes or kickbacks in return for preferential government regulation (Schlesinger, 1997). Anger at corruption was evident even among allied interest groups: Keidanren (Japan Business Federation) halted automatic campaign donations to the LDP in 1993 to protest the high business costs of bribes and corruption. Although voters and interest groups may have tolerated the inefficiencies of pork-barrel politics as long as the economic pie was growing, their willingness to countenance LDP clientelism disappeared once the pie began to shrink.

Although voter disenchantment was a significant problem, a more proximate concern was the effect of corruption scandals on internal fissures within the LDP. The LDP had faced temporary spikes in unpopularity in the past, but given greater voter emphasis on individual candidates and high levels of electoral incumbency, the party had managed to hold onto its parliamentary majority. Under MMD-SNTV, voters emphasized the personal qualities of the candidates over their party affiliation. Because each district had 3–4 seats but voters could only pick one candidate, co-partisans from major parties were forced to compete against one another, as well as against the opposition party. Same-party candidates have a harder time distinguishing themselves based on ideology because they must appeal to the same pool of conservative or liberal voters. As such, candidates from the LDP, and to some extent the JSP, campaigned based on their personal competence at extracting pork-barrel projects or patronage from the central government's coffers (Curtis, 1971; Ramseyer &, Rosenbluth 1993; Kohno, 1997).

To incorporate voters into a stable base, politicians built up *koenkai*, or personal support networks, in their districts. Koenkai linked Diet members to local political elites and community organizations, and different LDP candidates wooed distinct geographical and socioeconomic segments of the district (Iwai, 1990; Krauss & Pekkanen, 2011). In exchange for votes and campaign contributions, politicians would subsidize local baseball teams, cooking classes, and chorus groups, and attend numerous funerals and weddings in their district. By contrast, LDP politicians had weaker incentives to encourage supporters to become dues-paying members of the party organization itself because those voters could end up supporting a different LDP candidate in their district. In sum, the LDP was structured as a collection of individual legislators with overlapping but not identical support bases, rather than a coalition of like-minded individuals united by ideological goals.

Theoretically, political parties are viable insofar as the benefits to legislators of membership outweigh its costs. In Japan, belonging to a majority party – the LDP – conferred (1) the ability to control fiscal redistribution and generate bribes and kickbacks, and (2) the brand reputation of the party as an effective economic manager. These benefits became less salient, however, with the emergence of high profile scandals and the bursting of the economic bubble. Given stronger voter allegiance to the candidate over the party, LDP politicians could reasonably gamble that their *koenkai* would continue to support them even if they left the party, at least in the short-run. For the LDP to remain united, therefore, it had to maintain a positive brand; it could not afford to be seen as defending political clientelism and corruption.

Electoral Reform as Political Reform

Reforming the status quo could be achieved in a number of ways. The LDP, under pressure from voters and opposition parties over its scandals, had been increasing penalties for electoral corruption for over 30 years (McElwain, 2008). At the same time, the party went through a parade of prime ministers as successive leaders were accused of various misdeeds.

By the early 1990s, however, political reform had become synonymous with electoral system change. Many reformists advocated a switch from MMD-SNTV to a Westminster-style, single-member district (SMD) system. Their logic was that MMD-SNTV necessitated intra-party competition in elections, which prioritized pork-barrel politics and raised campaigning costs, which in turn created incentives and opportunities for corruption. Much of this is borne by empirical studies: greater intra-party competition is correlated with higher campaign expenditures (Cox & Thies, 1998) and corruption cases (Nyblade & Reed 2008). Prime Minister Kaifu Toshiki, who had been selected in 1989 because of his 'clean' image, linked the survival of his administration to successful electoral reform (Woodall, 1999). Ozawa Ichiro, a top lieutenant in the dominant Tanaka faction, also pushed for electoral reform, arguing that an SMD system would promote two-party competition, which would (1) increase government accountability because small swings in vote share can produce large swings in seat shares,[18] and (2) foster ideological competition because voters would have an easier time differentiating the political views of two parties than of five.

Opposition to electoral reform came from a number of fronts. The non-LDP parties supported electoral system change but were opposed to SMD, which tends to benefit larger parties over smaller ones because they require successful candidates to win close to 50 percent of the vote.

Instead, they pushed for a mixed-electoral system that would combine some single-member districts with a proportional representation tier, wherein seats would be distributed across a broader geographical region (Christensen, 1994; Reed & Thies, 2001a).

The strongest opposition came, however, from *within* the LDP. Many incumbent LDP members, especially those with established koenkai, did not want their geographical bases of support uprooted by major electoral reform (Christensen, 1994). Indeed, electoral reform had been suggested by LDP leaders in the past, dating back to the Hatoyama Cabinet in 1955, but these bills were blocked due to intra-party pushback against anything that would harm the re-election prospects of incumbents (McElwain, 2008). Ultimately, Kaifu's proposal for electoral reform was shelved because of defection threats from within the party.

Recalcitrance to reform began to melt away, however, with the Sagawa Kyuubin Scandal of 1993. As voter dissatisfaction mounted, the immediate costs of opposing electoral reform began to dwarf longer-term concerns about how those votes would be translated into LDP seats. Reed and Thies (2001a) reference a number of polls of Diet members, showing that support for keeping SNTV versus switching to a mixed electoral system flipped from 51 percent versus 20 percent, respectively, in 1984 to 12 percent versus 55 percent in April 1993. The LDP proposed a 500-seat single-member district system in March 1993, but this was rejected not only by the opposition party, but also by the Hata faction (which included Ozawa Ichiro) for being heavy-handed and unrealistic. Miyazawa, capitulating to pressure from other LDP bosses, announced that he would postpone electoral reform to future Diet sessions.

Given the weakening ties binding the LDP, however, this recalcitrance towards reform led to a series of factional defections. When the Socialist Party filed a no confidence motion against the Miyazawa Cabinet in June, the Hata–Ozawa faction of the LDP broke ranks and sided with the opposition, forcing Miyazawa to resign. The Takemura faction soon split off and created a new political party, *Sakigake*, or 'New Party Harbinger,' and the Hata–Ozawa faction followed suit and established *Shinseito*, or 'Renewal Party.' Reed and Scheiner (2003) found that these defectors shared a common profile: they were either junior LDP politicians who did not have strong koenkai and therefore needed to reach out to skeptical independents, or senior LDP politicians who were ideologically committed to reform and were sufficiently well-known that they could afford to run in a new district.[19]

The 1993 election was a watershed moment in Japanese politics because it led to the first ouster of the LDP from majority status in the Lower House. While the remaining LDP candidates did fairly well – the party actually increased its seats from 222 to 223 – the defections of the Takemura and Hata–Ozawa factions meant that the party was starting from a losing position. In some ways, the 1993 election was a transformational moment for all established parties. Kabashima and Reed (2001) found that both the LDP and JSP lost votes in districts where they had to compete against the new reformist parties, such as Sakigake, Shinseito, and Nihon Shinto (Japan New Party).

Despite the LDP's losses, however, no opposition party had enough seats to form a majority government unilaterally. Instead, all non-LDP parties (except for the Communists) joined together to form an eight-party coalition government, headed by Hosokawa Morihiro of the Japan New Party. The clear – and perhaps only – mandate of this coalition was to legislate electoral reform, but there was still internal disagreement over what system to adopt.[20] Following compromise with the LDP, the coalition government adopted a 'mixed-member majoritarian' (MMM) electoral system. Under this new rule, the country was divided into 300 single-member districts and 11 regional blocks, which would select 200 proportional representation candidates (soon reduced to 180). Voters would have two ballots: one to pick a candidate for their smaller single-member district, and another to pick a party in the larger regional block. While the plurality winner would obtain the SMD seat, the PR seats would be divided within the regional block among parties based on their vote share.[21]

This coalition government quickly collapsed after electoral reform was adopted. The JSP and Sakigake left the coalition first, and from April to June 1994, Hata and his Renewal Party formed a minority cabinet purely to pass the annual government budget. On June 30, the LDP and JSP passed a no confidence motion, ushering an end to the 9-month rule of the first non-LDP government since 1955.

The new Cabinet was a surprising coalition of the two major parties of postwar Japan: the LDP and JSP. Between June 1994 and January 1996, these two parties and the smaller Sakigake partnered to form a coalition government under Murayama Tomiichi, the first Socialist prime minister since 1948. The remaining opposition struggled to come up with a viable competitor to the LDP. For the 1996 election, the centrist groups – Renewal, Democratic Socialists, Japan New Party, and Komeito – coalesced into the New Frontier Party (NFP or *Shinshinto*) under Ozawa Ichiro's leadership. Some center-left opposition parties, including JSP and Sakigake dissidents, formed the Democratic Party of Japan (DPJ). The 1996 election, which was the first under the new MMM electoral system, strengthened the LDP's hold on power. It increased its seats from 223 to 239, while the JSP fell from 70 to 15. The NFP and the DPJ fared better, but they were unable to overcome the combined majority of the LDP–JSP–Sakigake partnership.

The failure of Ozawa's New Frontier Party to oust the LDP led to a new round of party formation. Komeito split off in 1998 to compete in that year's Upper House election independently, and many of the remaining progressive parties decided to join the DPJ. Ozawa himself created a smaller Liberal Party and joined the LDP's coalition with Komeito between 1998 and 2000. The LDP–Komeito–Liberal coalition remained intact until 2003, when Ozawa once against switched affiliations, joining the opposition DPJ.

As a result of significant party switching (much of it by Ozawa), the party system landscape had realigned significantly over 10 years. The JSP – now rebranded as the Social Democratic Party (SDP) – had become a minor opposition party. The NFP, once seen as the main opposition challenger to the LDP, folded after 2 years. Left standing are the LDP and DPJ – the two major players in Japanese electoral politics today.

POLITICS AFTER ELECTORAL REFORM

The stated purpose of electoral reform was to create a two-party system that would strengthen ideological competition, party-centric politics, and government accountability. For the most part, the proximate goal – two-party competition – has

been realized. However, it is unclear whether two-party politics has produced the other desired-for outcomes of electoral reform. The most obvious sign of business-as-usual is that the LDP remained in power again from 1994 to 2009, albeit in a series of coalition governments.

In analyzing the current, post-1994 state of Japanese politics, there are two pressing questions. First, is the emergent two-party system between the LDP and DPJ stable? Second, has the nature of political transactions shifted from clientelism to ideological competition?

Two-party Competition in Japan

Figure 20.6 depicts the combined Lower House vote and seat shares of the two largest political parties since 1955, that is, the LDP for the entire period plus the JSP (to 1993), NFP (1996), or DPJ (2000 to present). The seat and vote sizes of the two main parties began to fall in the 1960s, as the progressive camp was split by the emergence of minor centrist parties. However, the seat ratio in particular recovered after electoral reform in 1994 as the smaller parties gradually withdrew from competition in the single-member districts. In 2009, the LDP and DPJ combined controlled approximately 90 percent of the Lower House seats, a ratio not seen since the mid-1960s, although the ratio fell to 73 percent in 2012 (more on the 2012 election later.)

The flipside, of course, is the remarkable fall in the representation of minor parties. The Social Democratic Party – comprised of remnants of the

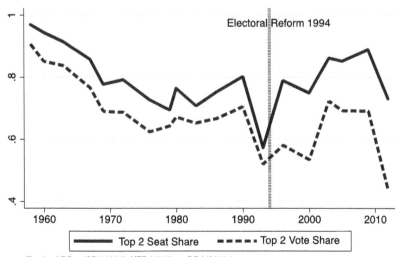

Top 2 = LDP + JSP (-1994), NFP (1996), or DPJ (2000-)
Vote share after 1994 is based on proportional representation tier results

Figure 20.6   The resurgence of the Top 2 parties

JSP – is now a tertiary player in the Diet. Over the six elections between 1993 and 2012, they have captured, on average, 5.4 percent of the vote and 1.9 percent of the seats. The Communist Party is in a similar situation, with 8.6 percent of the vote and 2.8 percent of the seats. The lone exception is the Komeito, which has been in coalition with the LDP since 1999. Komeito is in a unique position because its primary support base is the *Soka Gakkai*, a religious organization whose membership has risen over the last two decades. The Komeito's vote share has stayed stable at about 12.8 percent, making it the fourth largest party today.

These smaller parties survive as independent entities because of the proportional representation (PR) tier of the new electoral system. One hundred and eighty seats (200 in the 1996 election) are allocated across 11 regional blocks, which means that on average, each block contains slightly more than 16 seats. Mathematically, a party would need to capture $1/(16+1)=5.9$ percent of the regional votes to win one seat. This is a fairly low threshold for even minor parties insofar as they are willing to compete without any real hope of capturing a parliamentary majority.

An important caveat is that the *stability* of two-party competition depends on the frequency of party switching by legislators, which was rampant in the mid-1990s. It is difficult for elections to revolve around two ideologically coherent parties if there are frequent changes to the identity and membership of those parties. Since 1993, there have been over 100 party-switches involving LDP members, whereby a politician leaves, is kicked out, and/or later rejoins the LDP (often *en masse* with his faction). The reasons for party switching vary by case and includes generational conflicts within the LDP hierarchy (Kato, 1998), ideological disagreements about electoral reform (Reed & Scheiner, 2003), and the need to tap government funds for pork-barrel projects (Saito, 2009). Whole-scale party dissolutions and mergers have been even more pronounced within the opposition camp as the NFP briefly took up the opposition leader's mantle in 1996, only to give way to the Democratic Party after one election. In fact, none of the new parties that emerged in the 1993 election – Shinseito, Nihon Shinto, or Sakigake – currently exist. Of the pre-1993 parties, Komeito agreed to join the NFP in 1996, only to break off in 1998 and ultimately join a coalition with the LDP. The Democratic Socialists no longer exist, while the JSP has become a rump party.

A common theme of these party switches and mergers is that they involve strategic realignment by parliamentarians, rather than the bottom–up emergence of new grassroots organizations. This top–down pattern of party system change suggests that the impetus for realignment is not clear-cut

ideological differentiation between the LDP and DPJ, but rather elite-level bargaining and positioning. On the one hand, electoral reform created the strongest pressure for realignment because the new mixed-member electoral system penalizes smaller parties that cannot win a plurality of seats in the SMDs. On the other, party switching continued for over a decade because of uncertainty about voter priorities and ideological cleavages. Given voter dissatisfaction with the LDP and the inability of new opposition parties to capture an electoral majority, office-seeking politicians lacked clarity about which camp to align with. This, in turn, has produced lurches towards two-party competition rather than a smooth pattern of realignment.

The ¥64,000 question, of course, is what this augers for the future. Importantly, the stability of the party system is not the same as a stable *electoral* arena. As Scheiner (2006) demonstrates, Japanese elections have traditionally hinged on the quality of candidates. Until recently, the strongest predictor of individual electoral races was candidate-level characteristics, not which party that candidate belonged to. However, Reed, Scheiner, and Thies (2009) found that in the 2005 and 2009 elections, the calculus had flipped, with weak candidates from a popular party capable of defeating strong candidates from unpopular ones. McElwain (2012) similarly noted the 'nationalization' of Japanese elections: constituency-level election outcomes are increasingly correlated, suggesting that voters are responding to similar national cues rather than focusing on idiosyncratic local factors. One manifestation of this is a rapid decline in incumbency advantage. Figure 20.7 depicts diachronic changes in the proportion of incumbent candidates who were successfully re-elected. The solid line shows this rate for all incumbents, while the hashed line does so for the LDP and the dotted line for the main opposition (JSP until 1994, NFP in 1996, DPJ after 2000). We can observe a stable 80 percent rate during the earlier SNTV system, and a temporary drop after electoral reform as voters and parties alike adjusted to new institutional incentives. In 2009, however, 45 percent of seats turned over, with 158 freshmen legislators (143 from the DPJ) entering the Lower House. By contrast, only 75 of 133 'hereditary' candidates, typically the strongest in postwar elections, won. This pattern was repeated in the 2012 election, when 174 DPJ legislators lost their seats and the LDP gained 176. In fact, the DPJ picked up only one new seat that year, demonstrating the devastating effect of swings in national public opinion.

This type of electoral uncertainty may strengthen incentives for party switching because incumbents, no longer invincible, will think twice about staying on a sinking ship. One of the effects of party switching is that neither the LDP nor the DPJ has internally coherent ideological principles.

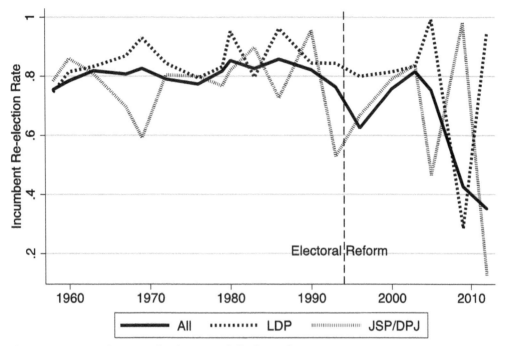

Figure 20.7   Incumbent re-election rates fall after reform

Overall, the DPJ can be characterized as center-left and the LDP as center-right, but each party contains members who, based on policy preferences, would be a natural fit in the other party. No one epitomizes this phenomenon as much as Ozawa Ichiro, who was considered hawkish within the LDP when he left in 1993, and after a series of transfers, ended up as leader of the progressive DPJ between 2006 and 2009. At the same time, many new parties act as temporary homes for candidates who want to leave their old homes but are not yet committed to joining the main opposition party. Not coincidentally, such new parties typically start with about five legislators, which is the threshold at which parties can qualify for state subsidies.

But this party system instability poses a new puzzle. If candidate quality no longer matters *and* parties do not offer consistent party platforms, then what has been driving electoral volatility since 2005? I shall now argue that the key culprit is the increasing salience of *party leaders*.

The Nature of Party Competition: Leaders Trump Parties

Reformers in the early 1990s pursued a two-party system in order to emphasize ideological, policy-based competition over clientelistic, pork-barrel politics. While these concepts are intrinsically

difficult to operationalize or interpret using existing data, there are mixed signs that the old artifices of clientelism are on the decline.

First, the *koenkai*, or personal support network, of individual politicians have become less salient. While koenkai played a prominent role in the first MMM election in 1996 (Christensen, 1998), electoral reform – which involved massive redistricting to transform 130 multi-member districts into 300 single-member districts – severed geographical linkages between the pre-reform koenkai and the post-reform SMD boundaries. Taniguchi (2004) reports weaker ties between candidates and other interest groups – firms, unions, neighborhood associations – in 1996 than in 1993. At the same time, Reed and Thies (2001b) argue that public financing for political parties has enhanced the resources controlled by the party organizations versus individual candidates. The decline in koenkai appears to be particularly pronounced for new, younger politicians (Carlson, 2007).

On the other hand, it is still too early to ring the koenkai's death knell. The new MMM system includes a provision for dual candidacy, wherein a candidate can be nominated in both the SMD *and* the PR list. If the candidate wins his SMD seat, then he is taken out of the PR pool. Should the candidate lose, he can be 'resurrected' based on his *sekihairitsu*, or losing ratio, which is that candidate's ratio of votes relative to the SMD winner. While PR candidates should theoretically have incentives to appeal to their broader regional bloc, their electoral focus is actually much narrower because victory is tied to their performance in the smaller SMDs (McKean & Scheiner, 2000). The value of securing 'core votes' has also increased with the recent rise in electoral uncertainty due to the unpredictability of how swing voters will cast their ballots (Krauss & Pekkanen, 2011). At the same time, because each party only nominates one candidate per district, a party's district headquarters no longer has to divide its allegiance across multiple candidates. This allows politicians to colonize the party's headquarters, transforming it into his koenkai in all but name.

Second, factions are no longer the predominant players or cleavages within the LDP. Prior to electoral reform, each faction boss would give his supporters campaign funds and election endorsements in exchange for their support in LDP presidential elections. Single-member districts simplify candidate endorsements, however, because there is only one party slot per district. The introduction of public campaign funds also shifted the locus of money from factions to the party boss (Cox, Rosenbluth, & Thies, 1999). Factions are still important for managing career advancement in the party and allocating Cabinet positions, but their organizational cohesion has weakened (Krauss & Pekkanen, 2004, 2011).

Perhaps the most consequential change in the nature of party competition is the growing importance of party leaders. Traditionally, LDP leaders were selected based on their proficiency at factional bargaining and negotiations. This flowed from the LDP's method of selecting its president by a vote of all parliamentarians from the Upper and Lower Houses of the Diet. This system produced a straightforward incentive structure for presidential aspirants: craft majority coalitions among factions by doling out cabinet or party portfolio and allocating pork-barrel projects to key allies. At the same time, because election outcomes depended on the popularity of individual candidates, not the party label, the identity of party leaders was downplayed in election campaigns.

Two changes since the 1980s have transformed the influence of party leaders. First, media coverage of parliamentary leaders has grown rapidly, not just in Japan but also around the world. Globally, party leaders receive more news coverage, especially on television, and it has become commonplace to see telegenic leaders featured prominently in campaign advertisements (Poguntke & Webb, 2005). In Japan, Krauss and Nyblade (2005) note steady increases in the number of newspaper articles on the prime minister and the proportion of votes that rely on TV news.

Second, the LDP's leader selection rule has switched from a parliamentary vote to an electoral primary framework. Following Mori Yoshiro's resignation in 2001, the LDP decided to give more voice to grassroots members, hoping to drum up voter enthusiasm in the wake of Mori's highly unpopular tenure. Under the new format, LDP legislators kept their votes, but the party's prefectural branches were also given three votes each. This mix of elite and grassroots influence had a real effect in the 2001 LDP presidential election. While Hashimoto Ryutaro was the heavy favorite among legislators, the prefectural branches overwhelmingly voted for Koizumi Junichiro, who went on to become the next prime minister (Lin, 2009).

When voters pay greater attention to party leaders, the *electoral* value of leader popularity also increases. A leader elected in a primary is more likely to be popular among voters, simply because he *has* to be popular to win a primary. A leader selected by his peers, on the other hand, does not *need* the electorate's backing as long as he is supported by other legislators. A popular leader is valuable to his party because he can generate electoral coattails: his speeches, campaign visits, and other public actions may convince independent voters to cast a ballot for the party's candidate, even if they are indifferent to that candidate personally (Kabashima & Imai 2002; McElwain, 2009). McElwain and Umeda (2011) show that media coverage of party leader selection rises significantly when it involves an electoral primary, thereby conferring greater brand recognition to the party overall.

Importantly, party leaders can leverage their electoral coattails to obtain policy concessions from co-partisans with conflicting preferences. A leader who is selected in a primary is similar to a national president: his constituency spans all electoral districts, regardless of whether that district has an LDP incumbent. A leader selected by other legislators, on the other hand, only has to cater to the interests of that party's incumbents (McElwain & Umeda, 2011). Given the LDP's rural base, the traditional goal of LDP leader–aspirants has been to keep rural voters happy. Under the new system, however, party leaders need national appeal because his selection is contingent on votes from LDP members in urban regions as well. Accordingly, we can expect a shift in the distributive focus of LDP policies away from clientelistic quid pro quos towards programmatic public goods. Noble (2010) notes, for example, a rapid decline in the budgetary share of construction and agriculture since the late 1990s, offset by commensurate increases in social welfare and education.

One example of this reversal in policy priorities is Prime Minister Koizumi's attempts to privatize the postal system in 2005. Since postal savings have been used to fund infrastructural projects, Koizumi's proposal generated backlash from within the party.[22] Unpredictably, Koizumi fought back: he kicked out LDP members who had voted against postal privatization and called for snap elections. Despite widespread dissatisfaction with Koizumi's threats, many LDP politicians who opposed postal privatization decided to support his reform bill nonetheless. Koizumi's leverage derived from his electoral coattails: while postal privatization would weaken the government's pork-barreling powers, many politicians gambled that the reflected glory of Koizumi's popularity would make up for that loss. Indeed, campaign stops by Koizumi during the 2005 election yielded an additional 2–3 percent of the vote to LDP legislators who were running in those districts (McElwain, 2009).

There are good reasons to believe that both the LDP and DPJ are committed to running presidential primaries. First, presidential elections provide an effective campaigning venue and capture the attention of the media. When Abe Shinzo resigned abruptly in 2007, the LDP could have chosen the next leader through a parliamentary vote, but instead held a primary, ultimately electing Fukuda Yasuo.[23] The party similarly used primaries to select Fukuda's successor, Aso Taro. Second, neither party can afford to look less democratic than the other. When the DPJ went against form and used a parliamentary vote to select Ozawa Ichiro's replacement in May 2009, media and intra-party criticism over the 'anti-democratic process' was swift. Given that party leaders are increasingly visible in the media, the value of leaders who look and sound good on the evening news can be a huge electoral asset. As voter criticism of pork-barrel politics and (perceived) corruption mounts, the

electoral coattails of leaders may become the most valuable asset of political parties.

The shift in leader selection method should produce a greater electoral emphasis of party labels than candidate qualities as confirmed by Reed and colleagues (2009). However, this is not synonymous with the growing salience of ideology over clientelism because the increased visibility of charismatic leaders is not identical to the emergence of ideologically coherent parties. As mentioned earlier, we can link party switching among legislators to the fickleness of voters. Politicians will leave their current home only if they think that they can win under a different label. This logic holds if party affiliation matters more (otherwise candidates wouldn't bother changing teams) *and* most voters are independents or have weak partisan attachments (otherwise they would punish defecting legislators for abandoning core ideological beliefs). McElwain (2012) confirms that elections are 'nationalizing': vote trends in one region are increasingly correlated with swings in other areas, suggesting that more voters are willing to switch their ballot to a different party from election to election. This is a relatively new phenomenon, given that vote swings themselves used to be small and regional factors (including candidate quality) trumped national issues.

If the relative attraction and qualifications of party leaders are driving this nationalization, then the key task for each party is to cultivate and market popular leaders. As of now, this doesn't seem to have been achieved, as shown by two trends. First, Figure 20.8 displays the relative proportion of the electorate that claims no attachment to a party (solid line) or Cabinet (hashed line); the

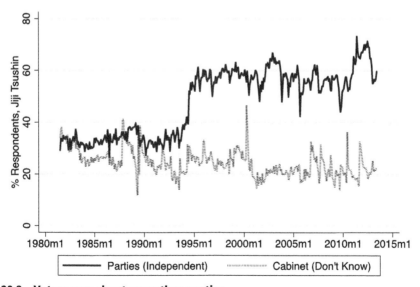

Figure 20.8   Voters care about more than parties

latter is a rough proxy of the popularity of the leader of the government party. Since electoral reform, an average of 50 percent of voters have no partisan attachments, while only 20 percent have no opinion on the Cabinet. This suggests that most voters do care about the identity and performance of the head of government, even if they do not necessarily care for a particular party.

Figure 20.9 depicts the shifting popularity of actual Cabinets since 2005. Here, the solid line shows the proportion of voters saying they approve of the Cabinet, while the hashed line displays the proportion that disapproves. While Prime Minister Koizumi managed to retain a 50 percent approval rating, successive leaders have experienced boom-and-bust cycles. The prime minister's approval generally spikes right after his selection, reflecting either faith in a new administration or utter disillusionment with the preceding one. However, this popularity does not last: within the space of one year, approval falls to around 20 percent with a corresponding increase in disapproval. To a large extent, this precipitous fall explains the high rate of Cabinet turnover. Because voters increasingly cast their ballots based on the image of the party leader, Diet members cannot afford to run for re-election under an unpopular leader's banner. This is a worrisome long-term trend because rapid Cabinet turnover can, itself, produce ineffectual governments and progressively lower party support. It can also reduce incentives for the Cabinet to propose structural reforms that produce long-term gains but require short-term sacrifices because there is no guarantee that the Cabinet will survive long enough to reap the electoral benefits.

DISCUSSION: PROSPECTS FOR POLITICAL STABILITY

Over the last two decades, we have observed numerous changes to Japanese party politics. The postwar multi-party system is consolidating into two-party competition, although the DPJ's setback in the December 2012 election casts doubts as to if and when it can rebound as the chief center-left counterpart to the LDP. Although some of the artifices of the 1955 system such as factionalism and koenkai persist, their salience has diminished. Instead, the importance of party leaders has skyrocketed, which in turn has shifted electoral attention from candidates to parties (but not necessarily ideologies).

Despite these changes in Japanese politics – some superficial and some substantial – the most intriguing question of all is whether a return to single-party dominance by the LDP is likely. For parties to consistently win elections, their popularity must be anchored by deep-rooted, affective factors that insulate their candidates from adverse shocks caused by unforeseen scandals, foreign crises, and the like. Historically, LDP dominance depended on high degrees of personalism, which reduced volatility by making individual re-election independent of broader national trends. I do not believe that a return to candidate-centered elections is likely, but it is uncertain whether a replacement anchor exists today. As news consumption habits have changed, more voters now care about party leaders than candidates, but these attachments are far from stable, as seen in Figures 20.8 and 20.9. This fickleness suggests that government turnover is more likely than not

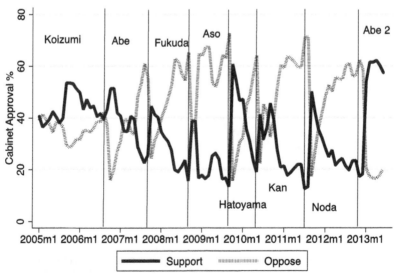

Figure 20.9 New PM gets boost, but not for long

because large groups of voters appear willing to change their ballot from one election to the next. Put differently, there is a good chance that uncompetitive districts today will become competitive districts tomorrow. Nothing signifies this trend as does the DPJ's enormous success in 2009 and its quick collapse in 2012. Indeed, the emergence of new local parties, such as Hashimoto Toru's Japan Restoration Party (JRP), suggests that voters are dissatisfied with *all* established parties. In Asahi's 2012 exit poll, more independents supported the JRP (28 percent) in the proportional representation tier (where voters pick preferred parties, not candidates) than they did the LDP (19 percent) or the DPJ (14 percent).[24]

With more independent votes up for grabs, party leaders have strong incentives to advocate policies that attract a broad cross-section of the electorate. Indeed, all parties now publish campaign 'manifestos,' which outline their policy goals and legislative priorities. Over time, this trend may manifest as stable partisan attachments and coherent ideological competition, but these remain elusive today. One important manifestation is the renewal of legislative party switching before the 2012 Lower House election. Ozawa Ichiro, who led the DPJ in 2007–2009, left the party in 2012, criticizing the leadership's handling of the 3/11 Great East Japan Earthquake and the Cabinet's proposal to raise the consumption tax. In the span of 6 months, he created or joined three parties – the People's Life First Party (July), Tomorrow Party of Japan (November), and People's Life Party (December).

The common thread tying recent political instability is the behavior of independents, whose ballot choices are swayed by perceptions of leader competence as much as (if not more than) the content of policy programs. One obvious sign of political competence is a party's ability to control its own caucus, but frequent party splits connote significant internal disagreement about policy and divided support for the leadership. What we are seeing, therefore, is a downward spiral of leaders stepping down when the party's popularity sinks, which makes voters mistrust the party even more, which spurs legislators to leave the party altogether, which fosters even more mistrust. According to the Jiji Tsushin, the proportion of independents climbed to 70 percent before the 2012 election, prompting 12 political parties and over 1500 candidates to try their luck. While the LDP's seat haul of 61 percent could be seen as a sign of resurgent conservatism, it is worthwhile to note that the party lost 2 million absolute votes compared to 2009, when its vote share was a paltry 25 percent. The LDP nevertheless emerged victorious because the DPJ lost *20 million* absolute votes from 2009 to 2012. Many of these former-DPJ voters decided to stay at home – turnout was a postwar-low 59 percent – or

voted for one of the new political parties. According to the Asahi's exit poll for the SMD ballot (where voters pick a specific candidate), 58 percent of independents voted for the DPJ in 2009, but only 23 percent did so in 2012.

There is no reason to believe that the party system is stable now, especially after the DPJ's spectacular loss in 2012. The electoral system creates strong incentives for parties to consolidate, but it is not clear if the DPJ has the right mix of policy platforms and strong leadership to build a stable core of partisan voters. Indeed, the fickleness of leadership approval makes it difficult for *any* party – including the LDP – to hold on to the support of independents long-term. The next decade of Japanese politics is most likely to be one of continuing instability as we wait to see if a new party system equilibrium can take hold.

NOTES

1 'Taisho' refers to the period between 1912 and 1926 – the reign of the Taisho Emperor.
2 The hereditary House of Peers was replaced with the elected House of Councillors.
3 More specifically, the 1947 Constitution expanded suffrage to women and lowered the voting age from 25 to 20. Univeral male suffrage had been granted in 1925.
4 The collapsing of multidimensional cleavages into one dimension is not unique in Japan. Kabashima argues that it is a reflection of a broader worldwide conflict between capitalism and communism.
5 A detailed examination of the government's role in the postwar economic miracle is beyond the scope of this paper, but for more detail, see Johnson (1982), Okimoto (1989), Katz (1998), Pempel (1998).
6 Because private sector unions had more bargaining leverage in the economic sphere, they did not need to resort to confrontation in the Diet. Public sector unions, by contrast, fought harder for legislative concessions in the political sphere because their power in the marketplace was less.
7 Thanks to Steve Reed for the Asahi's urbanization data.
8 This is not to say that the LDP was united internally on foreign policy. A sizable minority, tied to Hatoyama and the pre-merger Democratic Party, wanted a more muscular defense posture with greater foreign policy autonomy.
9 The Japanese Constitution requires amendments to be approved by a 2/3 supermajority in the Diet and a majority in a national referendum.
10 One of the most cited works in political science is Maurice Duverger's (1954) argument that

single-member districts (one seat per district) tend to have two effective or competitive candidates, while multi-member districts (more than one seat per district) result in multi-candidate competition. Other prominent scholars who have examined the relationship between electoral and party systems include Cox (1997), Rae (1967), Sartori (1976), and Taagepera and Shugart (1989).

11 What made the Reed study innovative was his usage of district-by-district data in a country with a distinctive electoral system. Most countries have electoral systems with very little internal variation in 'M' (e.g. every district has one seat, as in the United States or United Kingdom) or votes are aggregated at the national level, instead of by district (as in the Netherlands). Japan, however, used a multi-member district system where the number of seats varied between three to five per district.

12 The SNTV system had been used – with some brief exceptions – since 1900, although district sizes varied over time. For example, following universal male suffrage in 1925, each district had between one and thirteen seats.

13 Independent voters are comprised of survey respondents who reported that they do not have an affinity towards any party.

14 For more on economic voting generally, see Hibbs (1977), Lewis-Beck and Stegmaier (2000), and Powell and Whitten (1993).

15 Nixon Shock refers to two events in the early 1970s: (1) President Richard Nixon's decision to pull the United States out of the Bretton Woods gold standard system, and (2) Nixon's surprising visit and subsequent official recognition of the People's Republic of China.

16 Data on Gini coefficients taken from the Ministry of Health, Labor, and Welfare. Retrieved from http://www.e-stat.go.jp/SG1/estat/NewList.do?tid=000001024668

17 There is an expansive, technical literature on candidate nomination strategy. In a hypothetical four-seat district, the LDP can win two seats with 40 percent of the vote if each LDP candidate splits the vote equally at 20 percent. This is easier said than done, however, because some politicians may be more popular than others, and voters cannot be coerced (legally) to follow voting orders from the party. At the same time, the LDP must avoid *over*-nominations (e.g. nominate three candidates who win 13.3 percent each) or *under*-nominations (e.g. nominate one candidate who wins all 40 percent) to win more seats with the same share of votes. The technical difficulty in judging nomination errors is that neither the LDP nor the opposition is making choices in a vacuum. They have to deal with some uncertainty about how voters will cast their ballots, rendering *ex post* judgments about strategic error problematic. At the same time, one side will be penalized

for nomination errors only if the other side makes fewer mistakes; in essence, this is a strategic game based not only on one's own decision, but how the opposition counters its moves. Baker and Scheiner (2004) make the most nuanced analysis, based on the ability of parties to coordinate beforehand and minimize uncertainty. When the LDP pressured conservative independents to stay out of the election, it tended to have fewer nomination errors. In districts where the opposition parties made informal pacts to avoid nominating too many candidates, on the other hand, the LDP tended to do worse. For some differing perspectives about nomination errors and their causes, see Christensen and Johnson (1995), Cox (1996), and Browne and Patterson (1999).

18 Hypothetically, Party A could win 100 percent of the seats if it won 51 percent of the votes in every district. In the next contest, should Party A's vote share drop to 49 percent versus Party B's 51 percent, it could lose all of its seats.

19 For more analysis of the politics behind LDP defection, see Christensen (1994), Kato (1998), Woodall (1999), Kawato (2000), and McElwain (2008).

20 For more on the partisan debate regarding electoral reform, see Christensen (1994), Narita (1996), Hrebenar (2000), Reed and Thies (2001a), and McElwain (2008).

21 Parties must also rank-order candidates on their PR lists in order to determine *which* candidates would be allocated seats from each party.

22 In Japan, the postal system provides banking and insurance services, as well as mail delivery. Due to favorable interest rates and an explicit government deposit guarantee, postal savings is a popular financial instrument for consumers. Postal deposits are managed by the Ministry of Finance, which invests this money in a variety of public projects, under the Fiscal Investment and Loans Program (FILP). While the government is nominally tasked with allocating deposits to underprovided but profitable services, LDP politicians effectively colonized this program to fund pet infrastructure projects for electoral gain (Park, 2011). Koizumi argued that postal privatization would force the Ministry of Finance to pay greater attention to the profitability of their investments, rather than the priorities of LDP politicians (Maclachlan, 2006).

23 Although the LDP's party constitution requires electoral primaries after each presidential term, it also permits parliamentarians to pick the party president when the leader resigns mid-term. Faction bosses can also negotiate around the primary process by strong-arming challengers from running against a consensus candidate. The same can be said for the DPJ, which also only mandates party primaries after a leader's term in office expires.

24 http://www.asahi.com/senkyo/sousenkyo46/news/TKY201212160215.html

REFERENCES

Anderson, Christopher J. and Jun Ishii, 1997. The political economy of election outcomes in Japan. *British Journal of Political Science*, 27 (4), 619–30.

Baker, Andy and Ethan Scheiner, 2004. Adaptive parties: party strategic capacity under Japanese SNTV. *Electoral Studies*, 23, 251–78.

Browne, Eric C. and Dennis Patterson, 1999. An empirical theory of rational nominating behavior applied to Japanese district elections. *British Journal of Political Science*, 29, 259–89.

Calder, Kent E., 1988. *Crisis and compensation: public policy and political stability in Japan, 1949–1986*. Princeton, NJ: Princeton University Press.

Carlson, Matthew, 2007. *Money politics in Japan: new rules, old practices*. Boulder, CO: Lynne Rienner Publishers.

Christensen, Raymond, 1994. Electoral reform in Japan: how it was enacted and changes it may bring. *Asian Survey*, 34 (7), 589–605.

Christensen, Raymond, 1998. The effect of electoral reforms on campaign practices in Japan: putting new wine into old bottles. *Asian Survey*, 38 (October), 986–1004.

Christensen, Raymond and Paul E. Johnson, 1995. Toward a context-rich analysis of electoral systems: the Japanese example. *American Journal of Political Science*, 39 (3), 575–98.

Cox, Gary W., 1996. Is the single nontransferable vote superproportional? Evidence from Japan and Taiwan. *American Journal of Political Science*, 40 (3), 740–55.

Cox, Gary W., 1997. *Making votes count: strategic coordination in the worlds electoral systems*. Cambridge, UK: Cambridge University Press.

Cox, Gary W. and Michael F. Thies, 1998. The cost of intraparty competition: the single, nontransferable vote and money politics in Japan. *Comparative Political Studies*, 31 (3), 267–91.

Cox, Gary W., Frances McCall Rosenbluth and Michael F. Thies, 1999. Electoral reform and the fate of factions: the case of Japan's Liberal Democratic Party. *British Journal of Political Science*, 29, 33–56.

Curtis, Gerald L., 1971. *Election campaigning Japanese style*. Tokyo: Kodansha International Ltd.

DeWit, Andrew and Sven Steinmo, 2002. The political economy of taxes and redistribution in Japan. *Social Science Japan Journal*, 5 (2), 159–78.

Duus, Peter, 1998. *Modern Japan*. 2nd ed. New York, NY: Houghton Mifflin Company.

Duverger, Maurice, 1954. *Political parties: their organization and activity in the modern state*. New York, NY: Wiley.

Fukatsu, Masami, 1995. Whither goes the 1955 system? *Japan Quarterly*, 42 (2), 163–69.

Gallagher, Michael, 1991. Proportionality, disproportionality, and electoral systems. *Electoral Studies*, 10 (1), 33–51.

Hibbs, Douglas, 1977. Political parties and macroeconomic policy. *American Political Science Review*, 71, 1467–87.

Hirano, Shigeo, 2006. Electoral institutions, hometowns, and favored minorities: evidence from Japanese electoral reforms. *World Politics*, 58 (October), 51–82.

Horiuchi, Yusaku and Jun Saito, 2003. Reapportionment and redistribution: consequences of electoral reform in Japan. *American Journal of Political Science*, 47 (4), 669–82(14).

Hrebenar, Ronald J., 2000. *Japan's new party system*. Boulder, CO: Westview Press.

Inglehart, Ronald, 1987. Value change in industrial societies. *American Political Science Review*, 81 (4), 1289–303.

Iwai, Tomoaki, 1990. *Seiji Shikin no Kenkyuu*. Tokyo: Nihon Keizai Shimbunsha.

Johnson, Chalmers, 1982. *MITI and the Japanese miracle: the growth of industrial policy, 1925–1975*. Stanford, CA: Stanford University Press.

Kabashima, Ikuo, 1984. Supportive participation with economic growth: the case of Japan. *World Politics*, 36 (3), 309–38.

Kabashima, Ikuo, 1999. An ideological survey of Japan's national legislators. *Japan Echo*, (August).

Kabashima, Ikuo and Ryosuke Imai, 2002. Evaluation of party leaders and voting behavior: an analysis of the 2000 general election. *Social Science Japan Journal*, 5 (1), 85–96.

Kabashima, Ikuo and Steven R. Reed, 2001. The effect of the choices available on voting behaviour: the two Japanese elections of 1993. *Electoral Studies*, 20, 627–40.

Kato, Junko, 1998. When the party breaks up: exit and voice among Japanese legislators. *American Political Science Review*, 92 (4), 857–70.

Katz, Richard, 1998. *Japan: the system that soured*. Armonk, NY: M.E. Sharpe.

Katzenstein, Peter J., ed., 1996. *Cultural norms and national security: police and military in postwar Japan*. Ithaca, NY: Cornell University Press.

Kawato, Sadafumi, 2000. Strategic contexts of the vote on political reform bills. *Japanese Journal of Political Science*, 1 (1), 23–51.

Kobayashi, Yoshiaki, 1997. *Politics in Japan, 1955–1993*. Tokyo: University of Tokyo Press.

Kohno, Masaru, 1997. *Japan's postwar party politics*. Princeton, NY: Princeton University Press.

Kohno, Masaru and Yoshitaka Nishizawa, 1990. A study of the electoral business cycle in Japan: elections and government spending on public construction. *Comparative Politics*, 22 (2), 151–66.

Krauss, Ellis S. and Benjamin Nyblade, 2005. Presidentialization in Japan? The prime minister, media, and elections in Japan. *British Journal of Political Science,* 35, 357–68.

Krauss, Ellis S. and Robert J. Pekkanen, 2004. Explaining party adaptation to electoral reform: the discreet charm of the LDP? *Journal of Japanese Studies,* 30 (1), 1–34.

Krauss, Ellis S. and Robert J. Pekkanen, 2011. *The rise and fall of Japan's LDP: political party organizations as historical institutions.* Ithaca, NY: Cornell University Press.

Lewis-Beck, Michael and Mary Stegmaier, 2000. Economic determinants of electoral outcomes. *Annual Review of Political Science,* 3, 183–219.

Lin, Chao-Chi, 2009. How Koizumi won. In S. R. Reed, K. M. McElwain and K. Shimizu, eds. *Political change in Japan: electoral behavior, party realignment, and the Koizumi reforms.* Palo Alto, CA: Walter H. Shorenstein Asia-Pacific Research Center, 109–32.

Maclachlan, Patricia L., 2006. Storming the castle: the battle for postal reform in Japan. *Social Science Japan Journal,* 9 (1), 1–18.

Mair, Peter, 1997. *Party system change.* Oxford, UK: Oxford University Press.

Masumi, Junnosuke, 1985. *Postwar politics in Japan, 1945–1955.* Translated by L. E. Carlile. Berkeley, CA: Institute of East Asian Studies, UC Berkeley.

McElwain, Kenneth Mori, 2008. Manipulating electoral rules to manufacture single party dominance. *American Journal of Political Science,* 52 (1), 32–47.

McElwain, Kenneth Mori, 2009. How long Are Koizumis coattails? Party-leader visits in the 2005 election. In S. R. Reed, K. M. McElwain and K. Shimizu, eds. *Political change in Japan: electoral behavior, party realignment, and the Koizumi reforms.* Palo Alto, CA: Walter H. Shorenstein Asia-Pacific Research Center, 133–56

McElwain, Kenneth Mori, 2012. The nationalization of Japanese elections. *Journal of East Asian Studies,* 12 (3), 323–50.

McElwain, Kenneth Mori, 2014. Party system institutionalization in Japan. In A. Hicken and E. Kuhonta, eds. *Re-examining party system institutionalization through Asian lenses.* Cambridge, UK: Cambridge University Press, 74–107.

McElwain, Kenneth Mori and Michio Umeda, 2011. Party democratization and the salience of party leaders. *Social Science Japan Journal,* 62 (1), 173–93.

McKean, Margaret and Ethan Scheiner, 2000. Japan's new electoral system: La plus ça change … *Electoral Studies,* 19, 447–77.

Miyake, Ichiro, Yoshitaka Nishizawa and Masaru Kohno, 2001. *55-Nen Taisei-ka no Seiji to Keizai: Jiji Yoron-chousa Data no Bunseki.* Tokyo: Bokutaku-sha.

Mulgan, Aurelia George, 2000. *The politics of agriculture in Japan.* New York, NY: Routledge.

Narita, Norihiko, 1996. Seiji Kaikaku Houan no Seiritsu Katei: Kantei to Yotou no Ugoki wo

Chuushin to shite. *Hokudai Rippo-Katei Kenkyukai Shiryou,* 46 (6), 405–86.

Noble, Gregory, 2010. The decline of particularism in Japanese politics. *Journal of East Asian Studies,* 10 (2), 239–73.

Nyblade, Benjamin and Steven R. Reed, 2008. Who cheats? Who loots? Political competition and corruption in Japan. *American Journal of Political Science,* 52 (4), 926–41.

Ohmiya, Takeo, 1992. *Senkyo-Seido to Giin-Teisuu no Zesei.* 3rd ed. Tokyo: *Hokuju Shuppan.*

Okimoto, Daniel I., 1989. *Between MITI and the market: Japanese industrial policy for high technology.* Stanford, CA: Stanford University Press.

Park, Gene, 2011. *Spending without taxation: FILP and the politics of public finance in Japan.* Stanford, CA: Stanford University Press.

Pempel, T. J., 1998. *Regime shift: comparative dynamics of the Japanese political economy.* Ithaca, NY: Cornell University Press.

Poguntke, Thomas, and Paul Webb, eds., 2005. *The presidentialization of politics: a comparative study of modern democracies.* Oxford, UK: Oxford University Press.

Powell, G. Bingham, and Guy D. Whitten, 1993. A cross-national analysis of economic voting: taking account of the political context. *American Journal of Political Science,* 37 (2), 391–414.

Pyle, Kenneth B., 1996. *The Japanese question: power and purpose in a new era.* 2nd ed. Washington, DC: AEI Press.

Rae, Douglas, 1967. *The political consequences of electoral laws.* New Haven, CT: Yale University Press.

Ramseyer, J. Mark and Frances McCall Rosenbluth, 1993. *Japan's political marketplace.* Cambridge, MA: Harvard University Press.

Reed, Steven R., 1991. Structure and behavior: extending Duverger's Law to the Japanese case. *British Journal of Political Science,* 29 (1), 335–56.

Reed, Steven R. and Ethan Scheiner, 2003. Electoral incentives and policy preferences: mixed motives behind party defections in Japan. *British Journal of Political Science,* 33, 469–90.

Reed, Steven R., Ethan Scheiner and Michael F. Thies, 2009. Party-centered, more volatile: new ballgame in politics. *The Oriental Economist,* 8–9.

Reed, Steven R. and Michael F. Thies, 2001a. The causes of electoral reform in Japan. In M. S. Shugart and M. P. Wattenberg, eds. *Mixed-member electoral systems: the best of both worlds?* New York, NY: Oxford University Press, 152–72.

Reed, Steven R. and Michael F. Thies, 2001b. The consequences of electoral reform in Japan. In M. S. Shugart and M. P. Wattenberg, eds. *Mixed-member electoral systems: the best of both worlds?* New York, NY: Oxford University Press, 380–403.

Richardson, Bradley M., 1997. *Japanese democracy: power, coordination, and performance.* New Haven, CT: Yale University Press.

Saito, Jun, 2009. Pork barrel and partisan realignment in Japan. In S. R. Reed, K. M. McElwain and K. Shimizu, eds. *Political change in Japan: electoral behavior, party realignment, and the Koizumi reforms*. Palo Alto, CA: Walter H. Shorenstein Asia-Pacific Research Center, 67–86.

Samuels, Richard J., 2007. *Securing Japan: Tokyo's grand strategy and the future of East Asia*. Ithaca, NY: Cornell University Press.

Sartori, Giovanni, 1976. *Parties and party systems: a framework for analysis*. Cambridge, UK: Cambridge University Press.

Scheiner, Ethan, 1999. Urban outfitters: city-based strategies and success in post-war Japanese politics. *Electoral Studies*, 18, 179–98.

Scheiner, Ethan. 2006. *Democracy without competition in Japan: opposition failure in a one-party dominant state*. Cambridge, UK: Cambridge University Press.

Schlesinger, Jacob M., 1997. *Shadow shoguns: the rise and fall of Japan's postwar political machine*. New York, NY: Simon and Schuster.

Shuugiin Chousa-kyoku, Dai-Ni Tokubetsu Chousa-shitsu, 2002. *Senkyo-seido Kankei Shiryou-shu*. Tokyo.

Taagepera, Rein and Matthew Soberg Shugart, 1989. *Seats and votes: the effects and determinants of electoral systems*. New Haven, CT: Yale University Press.

Tanaka, Kakuei, 1972. *Building a new Japan: a plan for remodeling the Japanese archipelago*. Tokyo: The Simul Press.

Taniguchi, Masaki, 2004. *Electoral reform in Japan*. Tokyo: University of Tokyo Press.

Thies, Michael, 1998. When will pork leave the farm? Institutional bias in Japan and the United States. *Legislative Studies Quarterly*, XXIII (4), 467–92.

Woodall, Brian, 1996. *Japan under construction: corruption, politics, and public works*. Berkeley, CA: University of California Press.

Woodall, Brian, 1999. The politics of reform in Japan's Lower House electoral system. In B. Grofman, S. C. Lee, E. A. Winckler and B. Woodall, eds. *Elections in Japan, Korea, and Taiwan under the single non-transferable vote: the comparative study of an embedded institution*. Ann Arbor, MI: The University of Michigan Press, 23–50.

Yamanouchi, Yasushi, J. Victor Koschmann and Ryuichi Narita, eds., 1998. *Total war and modernization*. Ithaca, NY: Cornell University Press.

21

Postwar Democracy

Sherry Martin Murphy[1]

'I feel as though all of our choices are losing ones.'
(Japanese focus group participant, Tokyo, Fall 2000)

Democracy enables citizens to participate in making the decisions that govern their lives. Elections structure competition between opposing political parties that offer voters choices between alternative visions for government and society. Elections aggregate mass preferences that are translated into political outputs by the winning party or coalition. Democratic performance, how closely elections and the policies enacted by the winners reflect voters' preferences, hinges upon meaningful electoral choices. Choice, the ability to replace one alternative with another, is the mechanism that enables voters to control elected politicians and enforce transparency, accountability, and responsiveness. Japanese voters commonly complain, however, that national elections do not serve as a forum for competing views, the electoral choices offered are not meaningful, and the policies implemented by the winning team do not reflect the views of everyday citizens. In short, nationally elected politicians are out of touch with the people, and the distance between citizens and their representatives raises concerns about the quality of Japanese democracy.

Long-term dominance by one party, the Liberal Democratic Party (LDP), has produced a rich scholarly literature examining the development and quality of Japanese democracy (Ishida and Krauss, 1989; Richardson, 1998; Scheiner, 2005; Martin and Steel, 2008).[2] The consensus throughout the 1980s was that Japan was a democracy in both form and practice. The economic crisis of the early 1990s and the decade-long recession that followed raised concerns about the capability of the LDP to adapt and lead in new domestic and global contexts. Yet, there were no other parties that the public deemed capable of replacing the LDP, and this meant that the party's power was unchecked. Economic crisis underscored the institutional barriers that new and old opposition parties – such as they were – faced in dislodging the LDP from power. The LDP had become so entrenched that it was insulated from electoral pressures and voters watched the electoral process from the sidelines as 'spectators' (Hrebenar, 2000: 28). Politicians, policymakers, and political researchers across the ideological spectrum renewed initiatives for electoral reform to produce an alteration in power between two programmatic, catchall parties. Proponents of the electoral reform package enacted in 1994 predicted new electoral choices for voters and, through choice, government power would again reside in everyday citizens.

Two decades after reform and a three-year interlude under a Democratic Party of Japan (DPJ) administration, the LDP in coalition with New

Komeito still retains control over the more powerful House of Representatives where the majority party or coalition selects the prime minister, approves the Cabinet, sets the budget, and can override vetoes by the House of Councilors Election after election. Japanese politics has verged on alteration in power between the LDP–New Komeito coalition and the DPJ, a centrist party formed in 1998, for a decade. The continuation of LDP dominance into the post-electoral reform period, despite trends in public opinion showing voters' preferences for an altera-tion in power, suggests that citizens have less say in making the decisions that govern their lives in the post-reform period than under the 1955 System.[3]

The DPJ gained control over the House of Councilors in 2007 and finally succeeded in gain-ing control over the government in the August 2009 election. Though political observers use outcomes of House of Councilors elections, Local Unified elec-tions, gubernatorial and mayoral elections, and ref-erenda and recall elections as barometers of national level change as frequently in the post-reform period as in the pre-reform period, electoral reforms con-tinue to receive the lion's share of attention as the key mechanism facilitating national level change.

In evaluating Japanese democracy from the top–down, we lose sight of a broader electoral connection that extends from the grassroots, underestimate the breadth and depth of citizen engagement, and run the risk of concluding that one-party dominance is a failure of democracy. The number of meaningful choices that voters face in Lower House elections has expanded and contracted across the pre- and post-reform period. The independence of meaningful electoral choices and electoral reform suggests a need to examine other institutional features of the Japanese politi-cal system that influence the number of mean-ingful electoral choices available, engage voters, and safeguard Japanese democracy. This chapter argues for closer examination of the full array of elections – national, prefectural and local, and ref-erenda and recall – as interlocking mechanisms that deepen democracy in the aggregate in post-war Japan. When choices in national elections lose meaning, elections for the House of Councilors and regional elections become important venues for voters to regain power over the legislative decision-making process from the bottom–up. A vibrant grassroots democracy is an enduring norm in Japanese politics.

I begin this chapter with an overview of politi-cal participation literature that establishes the rela-tionship between electoral choice and the nature of individual and aggregate level political partici-pation, and its implications for how democracy works at the systemic level cross-nationally and in Japan. Next, I examine what electoral rules, spe-cifically the multimember district system (MMD) and single non-transferable vote (SNTV) that were used to elect the Lower House until 1993, can and cannot explain about the expansion and contraction of electoral choice in national Japanese politics. I extend this analysis to the current electoral system – a mixed single member district (SMD) and proportional representation (PR) system enacted in 1994 – to examine how closely changing electoral choices in the aftermath of reform conform to pre-dictions rooted in widely accepted propositions about how electoral rules shape party and voter behavior. This chapter then compares and contrasts trends in electoral choices in the Lower and Upper Houses over time, and discusses trends in electoral participation in subnational politics. Bicameralism and multiple elections are important safety valves for democracy; both institutional features provide important outlets for voters to re-establish control over representatives, from the ground up, when national politics grows stagnant.

CONSENSUAL INSTITUTIONS, MEANINGFUL CHOICES, AND VIRTUOUS CYCLES OF POLITICAL ENGAGEMENT

Electoral Choice and Political Engagement in Advanced Industrialized Democracies

I define electoral choice(s) as 'meaningful' when the parties and/or candidates represented on the ballot enable a voter to identify at least one party that (a) best represents her substantive preferences and (b) has a real chance of winning enough seats to influence the decision-making process. Whether choices are meaningful cannot be captured solely by the number of parties in the system; there may be many parties, but few that offer substantive platforms and none that are viewed as capable of governing. Conversely, two parties (or even one) might offer more substantive choices (Anderson, 2009). Even if these conditions are met, the vote cannot be meaningful if it is not weighted equally with all other votes, that is, one person, one vote (see Pempel, 1989).

Fewer meaningful electoral choices promote political cynicism. When choice is limited, citizens cannot legitimately threaten to kick unaccount-able, unresponsive, and non-performing rascals out of office. Without a threat of being removed from office, elites have little incentive to represent the views of the median voter. Without public input, legislative decision-making produces outcomes that are less representative. Consequently, citizens are more likely to say that political elites are self-interested, do not follow the rules, do not keep campaign promises, cannot be trusted to 'do the right thing,' and listen to a narrow range of powerful interests at a cost to everyday voters (Cappella and Jamieson, 1996: 72).[4] These attitudes correlate with a decline in voter turnout and publics are demobilized as more voters state that participation in politics makes no difference to electoral outcomes. When participation declines, citizens' voices are not aired and democracy is compromised. Persistent high levels of cynicism are viewed as potentially problematic in democracies because, over the long term, the legitimacy of the system is weakened (Easton, 1965). 'Corrosive cynicism' can promote legislative gridlock, threaten the legitimacy of legislative decision-making, and unravel civil society groups, associations, and networks (Capella and Jamieson, 1996: 71).

We can draw a parallel between the effects of no meaningful choices and the experience of voting for the losing team on democracy. Similar to voters who support parties that lose elections, voters who support a winning party that does not represent a 'meaningful' choice do not have their preferences reflected in legislative decision-making processes and the policies that are produced. Existing research shows that voters who support losing parties are less likely than those supporting winning parties to trust politics (Anderson et al, 2005). Losing increases dissatisfaction with politics – a sentiment that is ameliorated by functioning consensual decision-making mechanisms that facilitate losers' representation in decision-making processes.

Limited choices and perpetual losers both tell us something about the electoral context. Specifically, electoral contexts may, by design and/or strategic adaptation by parties and candidates, insulate parties from the vagaries of the ballot box. Consequently, the same remedies are applied to both: change the electoral rules to deliver better choices and/or give voters more control over translating votes into seats. While national electoral rules exert significant influence on the range and quality of electoral choices, their impact is mediated by other mechanisms for aggregating public interests that are operative elsewhere in the system, and how these mechanisms are institutionally linked to national government.

Consensual institutions such as federalism, bicameralism, separation of powers, checks and balances, and elections across different administrative levels (local to national) provide other participatory outlets for voters to (in)directly influence the number and range of national electoral choices (Anderson 2009, Young 2002, MacDougall 1989). Importantly, these institutions guard against majority tyranny and protect minority rights. When alternative viewpoints are aired, members of under-represented groups are more likely to feel that their opinions were heard and are more likely to accept policies that emerge from legislative processes as legitimate (Young, 2002). When these mechanisms work, voting for the losing team is still a meaningful choice because losers attain some level of representation. If these mechanisms fail, then voting for the losing team loses utility. In Japan, long-term one-party dominance means that choices are limited and there is a pool of perpetual, electoral losers (Weiner 2008). As discussed later, this has not always meant that support for the opposition party was an entirely 'wasted' vote.

Electoral Choice and Political Engagement in Japan

Multiple factors correlate with cynicism, all of which are present in the Japanese case: public expectations exceed government performance and capacity (Mishler and Rose, 2001); voters see their choices as severely limited when none of the major parties offer appealing policy alternatives (Miller, 1974); voters disapprove of the incumbents (Citrin, 1974); negative press coverage exacerbates mass cynicism (Cappella and Jamieson, 1996; Pharr, 1997); and corruption scandals are ongoing. I focus on the quality of the 'electoral supply,' or the choices that Japanese voters have at elections, which renew the democratic contract between citizens and representatives. Evidence suggests that citizens increasingly view national elections as producing an 'unequal treaty.' Pempel (1989) found that Japanese voters had 'a reasonably wide choice of candidates, if not in all town and village elections … at least in most large city, prefectural, and national elections,' and 'a wide range of choices among candidates, parties, and approaches to governance.' The Japanese party system and elections provided voters a range of choice 'close to, if not greater than, that of almost any other democracy' (Pempel, 1989: 29). Yet, more and more voters, such as the one quoted at the beginning of this chapter, express that all of their choices are losing ones.

Japanese voters characterize politicians as unresponsive and, consequently, find the system unrepresentative (Richardson and Flanagan, 1984). Majorities have agreed that politics is too complicated to understand, everyday people have no say in the political process, and voters are limited in their ability to influence local or national politics (Martin and Stronach, 1992). Japanese voters at the turn of the century were less likely than voters in other democracies to view national House of Representatives elections as fair (Anderson et al., 2005: 39). Voters who supported opposition parties (and were therefore losers) were less dissatisfied with democracy and less likely to rate the system as responsive, producing a gap between themselves and LDP supporters that was among the largest cross-nationally (Miyake, 1991; Kabashima, Marshall, Uekami, and Hyun 2000; Martin, 2004; Anderson et al., 2005: 43). Still, Japanese voters were more likely than voters in other democracies to agree that voting makes a difference (Anderson et al., 2005: 39). Why?

Japanese voters have long used 'low stakes' elections as a referendum on and to protest national LDP leadership. The LDP is attentive to losses to opposition parties in the less powerful House of Councilors and on prefectural and local assemblies because these outcomes foreshadow House of Representatives elections and, if the proportion of opposition-held seats reaches a tipping point, the opposition can check LDP power. In this chapter, I propose that (a) voters use other electoral venues to exercise voice and (b) participation in one venue spills over to impact outcomes in another.

Electoral Rules and Meaningful Choice

Electoral rules determine how meaningful choices are made in three ways. First, rules impact the number of parties in the system. Second, electoral rules produce stable choices, which, in turn, make voting meaningful across elections. Third, rules produce meaning by converting votes into seats so that the preferences that underlie choice are expressed in decision-making processes and policy outcomes. Consequently, electoral reform is a common prescriptive measure for improving the quality of electoral choices and democratic performance.

Proportional representation systems (PR) award parties seats in relative proportion to percentage of votes won, which delivers incentives for small parties to compete and voters to support them because they will win representation with a small percentage of the vote. Conversely, single member district systems (SMDs) are strongly correlated with two-party dominant systems because they are majoritarian systems that award seats to the party that gains the most votes; citizens have no incentive to support minor parties because they will not gain representation. A consequence is that PR systems are seen as more broadly representative and consensual because minority perspectives achieve voice. Anderson (2009) delivers a cautionary note that holds for the Japanese case – it is not the number of party choices that makes a difference, but the diversity of choices. Three ideologically similar parties offer fewer, distinct choices to voters than three ideologically dissimilar parties. Although PR typically produces multi-party

systems and SMD systems produce two-party dominant systems, the increase in the number of parties from one system to the next does not automatically produce an increase in meaningful choices.

The age of the party system is also an indicator of, though not necessarily a prerequisite for, whether voters have meaningful electoral choices (see Anderson, 2009). Institutionalized party systems offer stable choices in that the same parties persist from one election period to the next. Traditional parties, pragmatic or programmatic, repeatedly present voters with the same choices. This repetition reduces the information costs for voters by making it easier to vote on past performance (retrospectively) and predicted performance (prospectively) (Miller and Wattenberg, 1985). Established parties have solid voter support bases that they represent in the political process, making it easier for voters to hold parties and candidates accountable to campaign promises. Further, supporters develop stronger psychological ties to parties that endure – and that they have voted for – over time. Voters trust that parties and candidates are worth voting for because they will be around for the next election when voters will have another opportunity to reward or punish them at the ballot box.

Finally, electoral rules produce meaning by converting choice into seats. Voters can choose from a large number of parties that also present substantively different choices. Even so, their choice can be pre-empted by rules that do not convert votes into seats, effectively robbing voters of the opportunity to have their preferences represented in the legislative decision-making process and the policies that it produces. Efficient conversion of votes into seats allows voters to exercise greater control over elected parties and politicians because they are able to replace them with greater ease when political outputs do not reflect citizens' preferences.

By 1993, the electoral system in Japan was no longer producing meaningful choices for voters. Though there were between three and seven parties challenging elections throughout the postwar period, the LDP was the only party to govern. The party's monopoly over government resources increased incentives for 'rational' voters to support the party for continued access to 'pork,' even if they did not think the party best represented their interests. The LDP was unable to adapt to demographic shifts such as rapid urbanization, but the movement of voters to urban districts intensified rural malapportionment, which enabled the party to return to power with a shrinking base of conservative rural voters (Tanaka, 2004). All parties were unable to reinvent themselves to reflect the changing geopolitical environment. The proportion of voters who did not support any party in the system increased to 50 percent of the electorate by the end of the decade. A common reason for not supporting any parties in the system was 'no party represents my preferences.'

Electoral reforms can take a number of forms, from strengthening campaign finance laws and instituting term limits to create a wider and more diverse candidate pool by lowering the barriers to entry, to changing district magnitude and balloting procedures to offer greater or lesser choice between parties and candidates, to lowering the costs of voter registration to increase turnout. Directly or indirectly, electoral reforms influence the number and quality of choices that confront voters in the ballot box. More choice can restore voters' confidence that elections are a vehicle for steering national politics in alternative directions.

THE 1994 ELECTORAL REFORMS: EXPECTED VS. OBSERVED OUTCOMES

Prior to 1994, Japanese voters cast a single non-transferable ballot (SNTV) in multimember districts (MMD) that ranged in size from two to six seats in House of Representatives elections. Voters chose from among 5 to 14 candidates (depending on district size) representing three to seven parties (see Pempel, 1989). To have any chance of winning a majority of Lower House seats, parties had to run more than one candidate in the same district. SNTV meant that votes had to be carefully distributed among candidates to ensure that parties could secure the maximum number of seats. One LDP candidate could win with over 50 percent of the vote, or several candidates could win with as little as 15 percent of the vote (Reed and Thies, 2001). The LDP's long-term monopoly over government provided resources to solve these coordination problems and ensure the re-election of its candidates (see Ramseyer and Rosenbluth 1993; Scheiner, 2005). Through policy specialization and constituency service (i.e. pork-barrel politics) and personal candidate support organizations (*koenkai*), LDP politicians organized votes to efficiently split them across candidates running in the same district. This helped them to secure their individual (re)election and helped the party win the maximum number of seats in the district, and in the House of Representatives. Strategic coordination meant that candidates only needed to be responsive to a narrow set of voter interests to be (re)elected.

Electoral reforms, enacted in 1994 by a grand coalition that included all parties with the exception of the LDP and the JCP, replaced MMD-SNTV with a mixed system wherein 300 seats are elected in SMDs and 180 seats (reduced from 200) are elected by PR with closed-party lists in 11 regional blocs. Reforms to the rules for electing the politicians to the House of Representatives were treated as a master key for unlocking a host of changes that would improve the quality of Japanese democracy. Electoral reform would restore meaning to vote choice because the new rules delivered incentives for two large programmatic parties to form and compete on the basis of clear policy alternatives. SMDs would make the lines of accountability clearer, thereby reducing the costs of replacing members of parliament (MPs) belonging to the governing party or coalition, making an alteration in power more likely. Voters as principals would have more control over their agents through the ballot box.

Expected Outcomes

Larger, single member districts required candidates to win a majority of votes and to do so, MPs had to speak to a much broader segment of voters in their district than under MMD – the winner needed to win a plurality if competing against multiple candidates or over 50 percent with one challenger. Consequently, the new system would deliver incentives for candidates to reach out to the median voter (Duverger, 1954). Under MMD and LDP dominance, the balance of policies favored the LDP's solid base of organized support: corporate interests, small and medium-sized business owners, and farmers. The new system would force the LDP and challengers to broaden their appeal through policies that favored 'the white-collar middle class, youth, and urban housewives, the left wing of value politics in the ideological conflict over defense – [who] found themselves without a party to defend their occupational and local interests' (Otake, 2000: 130) under the 1955 System. Strategic efforts to appeal to the old base would not disappear, but incentives to speak to a broader voter base would result in more inclusive politics (Ramseyer and Rosenbluth, 1993).

The winner-take-all SMDs would also deliver incentives for traditional opposition parties to merge into one large party to effectively challenge the LDP, but the PR seats would enable small parties to survive. Small parties could no longer capture district level seats by coming in second, third, or fourth. Ideologically, proximate opposition parties were expected to merge to increase their base of support and their chance of defeating the LDP in the larger SMDs. But, smaller opposition parties were not expected to disappear because PR seats continued to award small parties. Consequently, PR would operate as a consensual mechanism that ensured opposition party supporters achieved some representation.

Finally, voters' accountability over elected politicians would be enforced because competition in the new system would revolve around substantive issues. Prior to reform, Ramseyer and Rosenbluth predicted that 'without a need to divide the vote among several candidates in most districts, the LDP would be free to compete electorally with other parties on the basis of a party platform' (Ramseyer and Rosenbluth, 1993: 197).

Observed Outcomes

In the 1990s, Japanese parties continued to violate conditions for meaningful choice in national elections. As an indication of traditional parties' inability to reinvent themselves to speak to a rapidly changing social, economic, and political context at home and abroad, parties began splintering, merging, and dissolving. This process began immediately before electoral reform and continues. Rapid changes in the party system and politicians' movement between parties not only reduced incentives for voters to support parties they did not think would survive over the long-term, but muddied the lines of accountability because parties that did not exist could not be punished in the next cycle. Voters who enthusiastically supported new parties in one election cycle found that their choice of party no longer existed in the very next cycle, and the candidate representing their district had moved to another party.

The actions of parties and leaders throughout the 1990s degraded the meanings of party label despite predictions that electoral reforms, especially PR, would make party labels more important (Steel, 2008). First, the LDP regained power in 1994 in a 'strange bedfellows' coalition with the Socialists, its former enemy which had renamed itself the Social Democratic Party of Japan (SDPJ) in 1996 to reflect adaptation to the post-Cold War context. This move discredited the SDPJ and the evidence that parties were willing to compromise their principles to maintain power deepened voter cynicism. Voters were further frustrated because this new legislative governing coalition was forged between elections.

The electoral instability of the 1990s was in large part due to the fact that, electoral reforms aside, the Japanese system required a more wide-ranging set of administrative and fiscal reforms to fix structural problems that undermined state capacity to implement policies to surmount economic problems. The Democratic Party of Japan (DPJ), which grew to become the largest, stable opposition party, was formed in 1998 by a group of reform-minded politicians from across the ideological spectrum. The result of this diversity was that the party struggled to develop an ideologically cohesive policy agenda and a substantive alternative to the LDP.

Japan throughout the 1990s demonstrated that voters can have many choices, but few that are meaningful. Small parties that splintered from the LDP, such as the now defunct Japan New Party, Sakigake, the New Frontier Party and Shinseito, struggled to craft ideologically distinct identities. Innovative policy proposals, however, may not have constituted a viable choice for many voters because the small size of these parties meant that their chances of winning enough seats to control government were low; they would either have to form a coalition with a larger, less popular party that they were running against (the LDP) or cobble together an unstable minority coalition (e.g. the Hosokawa Government, 1993–1994). Small parties do not run in all districts, and so voters have to rely on the PR round to actively choose minor parties and their candidates. Further, the short lifespan of many small, new parties makes it difficult for voters to hold parties responsible for their actions when they dissolve between elections.

Perhaps the biggest blow to meaningful electoral choices has been the demise of the traditional opposition parties of the left. While many former leftist politicians joined the DPJ, the new party is more moderate than the parties it supplanted. Some might argue that the traditional opposition parties were not 'meaningful' choices because their ideological differences forestalled strategic cooperation to unseat the LDP in the pre-reform period. But, the ideologically fragmented left, comprised of the Japan Communist Party (JSP), the Japan Socialist Party (JSP), and the Democratic Socialist Party (DSP), offered distinct choices. The JSP, the largest opposition party, was also capable of winning one-third of Lower House seats and effectively using minority status to challenge LDP dominant decision-making processes and extract concessions for its supporters. Voters' range of progressive choices began to narrow even prior to electoral reform. Parties of the left were unable to successfully revamp their images after the collapse of the USSR and the Cold War world order. Further, a decline in labor union membership eroded their traditional support bases. The JCP and the SDPJ now hold a combined 10 seats in the House of Representatives; the DSP has disappeared from the scene. Consequently, voters who would have supported the traditional parties of the left and found the DPJ too moderate, have fewer electoral choices today than under the 1955 System.

Rural malapportionment, a prominent feature of the 1955 System, 'does not accord well with more common presumptions about "one citizen, one vote" and the ability to depose officials with facility once they lose favor' (Pempel, 1989: 30), and remains a problem after electoral reform. The organizational advantages that the LDP enjoys in rural districts continue to amplify the electoral voice of rural voters relative to urban voters. The LDP won with approximately the same absolute number of votes in 2000 as in 1979, approximately 21 million votes, even though the absolute number of voters in the electorate increased by 20 million (from 80 to 100 million eligible voters) during this same period (Tanaka and Martin, 2003: 32–33).

Convergence to a two-party system in national politics after electoral reform has been a slow process that is often attributed to the fact that the PR seats in the House of Representatives keep small parties alive, as does the operation of a mixed MMD and PR system for House of Councilors elections and more proportional systems in subnational elections. The electoral rules for selecting the Upper House provide legislative access points to minority perspectives. Further, voters are more likely to take a chance on outsider parties in the Upper House elections because it has been traditionally viewed as less powerful than the Lower House – they cast a 'sincere' vote because less is at stake when the LDP loses of control in the Upper House. In tipping the balance toward the opposition in the Upper House, opposition parties gain the power to delay LDP legislation and negotiate for the inclusion of a broader range of perspectives. Voting against the LDP is seen as a warning for the party to increase its responsiveness to voters in advance of the next Lower House Election. In short, while choices are narrowing in national elections to the Lower House, voters continue to face a wider range of meaningful choices in elections in different parts of the system and these elections serve as important access points that (a) create pressures on national parties to align more closely with everyday voters, and (b) facilitate consensual decision-making by giving voice to outsider perspectives. Multiple access points help voters to influence politics and, in the aggregate, make democracy work in Japan.

MANUFACTURING MEANINGFUL CHOICE IN JAPAN: ELECTIONS AS CONSENSUAL MECHANISMS

Bicameralism: Checking Majority Tyranny

When the LDP government and public opinion diverge, voters protest at the grassroots and reward opposition parties and outsider candidates in local

elections and House of Councilors elections. Citizen engagement with these other electoral venues speaks to the strength and resilience of Japanese democracy in terms of the multiple access points for citizen participation. In this section, I examine the relationship between the number of parties that voters have had to choose from in elections for the House of Representatives and the House of Councilors, and the disparity between votes and seats, to draw some general conclusions about the degree of control that elections give voters over their representatives.

I use the 'least squares index,' a common measure of disproportionality as an indicator of how much collective control voters exercise in converting votes into seats (see Gallagher and Mitchell, 2005). When the least squares index is close to '1', parties receive seats in direct proportion to the percentage of votes cast in its favor. The value of the index is high when parties receive a number of seats that is out of proportion relative to the percentage of votes cast. Disproportionality is typically lower in PR systems than in SMD systems because smaller parties, once they have passed a minimum threshold, are able to win a number of seats that reflect the percentage of votes won. In contrast, the winner takes all in SMD systems, frequently with a plurality rather than a majority of votes. Multi-member districts fall between these two extremes with district magnitude (the number of seats elected in a district) as a significant determining factor.

Systems that fail to translate vote shares into seat shares do not directly translate preferences into representation, leading to a decline in voter turnout and greater dissatisfaction with government performance (Gallagher and Mitchell, 2005). Even if choices are 'meaningful' in every other regard, voter intention is undermined by electoral rules that fail to translate votes to accurately reflect the underlying distribution of mass preferences. This evidence suggests that it is a condition particularly acute in the Japanese case – the barriers to unseating the LDP in House of Representatives are exceedingly high and increase the importance of other elections in giving voters a say.

I also calculate the effective number of parties that Japanese voters have had to choose from for each Lower House and Upper House election under the 1955 System. The effective number of parties is a measure of electoral fragmentation (developed by Laasko and Taagepera, 1979); it reflects how concentrated or dispersed the choices voters have are, and the effective number of legislative parties tells us about the concentration of legislative decision-making power. I examine the effective number of parties alongside the measure of disproportionality because I am interested in drawing inferences about how much control voters have at the ballot box; seemingly small shifts in the effective number of parties in the electorate and legislature can hide large swings in disproportionality.

I predict disproportionality to be relatively low for seats elected by proportional representation in the Upper House and after 1994 in the Lower House. Conversely, I expect high disproportionality for constituency seats in the Upper House, the MMD seats in the Lower House (pre-1994), and the SMD seats in the Lower House to reflect the over-representation of rural districts that are the LDP's stronghold. Further, I expect an increase in disproportionality over time to reflect voters' complaints that voting does not matter. Figures 21.1, 21.2, and 21.3 illustrate the effective number of parties that voters faced in elections for both national parliamentary houses between 1955 and 2005, alongside the corresponding least squares index score for disproportionality, the disparity between the distribution of votes and the allocation of seats following each election.

Between 1955 and 1993, the effective number of parties that voters had to chose from in Lower House elections ranged from 2 to 5, with an average of 3.5. In the two decades elections after reform, voters had to choose between an average of 3.3 parties for the SMD seats and 4.1 for the PR seats in the Lower House. The effective number of parties for the SMD seats has, in line with predictions, converged toward two large parties – the effective number of parties in 2005 was 2.73 for the SMD seats and 3.22 for the Lower House overall. Voters enjoy a larger effective number of parties in Upper House elections – 4.2 for the PR seats and 3.8 for the constituency seats.

Over time the effective number of parties that voters have to choose from remained relatively stable across the different electoral sytems operative in both Diet chambers, but disproportionality increased. Between 1993 and 2005, there was a general trend of increase in the level of disproportionality for MMD seats in the Upper House and in the Lower House pre-reform. As expected with

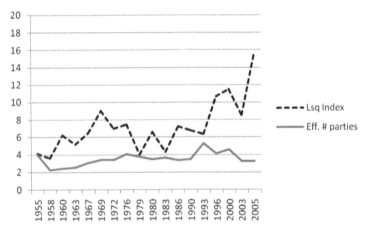

Figure 21.1 Electoral supply and disproportionality in House of Representatives Elections, 1955–2005

Notes: Values for the least squares index (Lsq) and effective number of parties (Eff. # parties) were generated by a calculator constructed by Michael Gallagher and Paul Mitchell (2005), available from http://www.tcd.ie/Political_Science/staff/michael_gallagher/ElSystems/index.php

The values from 1996 onward are composite scores that merge data from the SMD and PR seats, reported by Gallager and Mitchell (2005). I computed separate values (not reported here) for the SMD and PR seats and found that the Lsq index for the PR seats was much lower (2.5–4.6) than for the SMD seats (10.6–23); the SMD seats account for the dramatic increase in disporportionality after electoral reform.

Sources: Ministry of Internal Affairs and Communications, Statistics Bureau. 2008. Persons Elected and Votes Polled by Political Parties of the Elections for the House of Representatives (1958-1993). Historical Statistics of Japan. Retrieved July 12, 2009 from http://www.stat.go.jp/english/data/chouki/27.htm

Ministry of Internal Affairs and Communications, Statistics Bureau. 2008. Persons Elected and Votes Polled by Political Parties of the Elections for the House of Representatives (1996–2005). Historical Statistics of Japan. Retrieved July 12, 2009 from http://www.stat.go.jp/english/data/chouki/27.htm

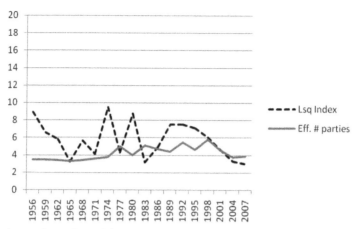

Figure 21.2   Electoral supply and disproportionality in House of Councillors Elections, PR seats, 1956–2007

Sources: Ministry of Internal Affairs and Communications, Statistics Bureau. 2008. Persons Elected and Votes Polled by Political Parties – Ordinary Elections for the House of Councillrs (1947–2004). Historical Statistics of Japan. Retrieved July 12, 2009 from http://www.stat.go.jp/english/data/chouki/27.htm

Alvarez-Rivera, Manuel. 2007, July 27. Japan's 2007 House of Councillors election. Global Economy Matters. Retrieved July 12, 2009 from http://www.globaleconomydoesmatter.blogspot.com/2007/07/japans-2007-house-of-councillors.html

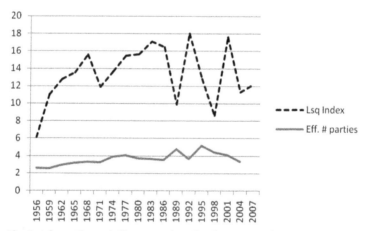

Figure 21.3   Electoral supply and disproportionality in House of Councillors Elections, Constituency seats, 1956–2007

Sources: Ministry of Internal Affairs and Communications, Statistics Bureau. 2008. Persons Elected and Votes Polled by Political Parties – Ordinary Elections for the House of Councillors (1947–2004). Historical Statistics of Japan. Retrieved July 12, 2009 from http://www.stat.go.jp/english/data/chouki/27.htm

Alvarez-Rivera, Manuel. 2007, July 27. Japan's 2007 House of Councillors election. Global Economy Matters. Retrieved July 12, 2009 from http://www.globaleconomydoesmatter.blogspot.com/2007/07/japans-2007-house-of-councillors.html

the move from MMDs to a side-by-side system, there is a marked increase in disproportionality in the post-reform Lower House due to the introduction of SMDs, which is only slightly offset by the 37.5 percent of seats elected under PR. In the case of the Lower House, voters' assessment that they have less choice is partly accurate. Although there

has been small variation in the effective number of parties that voters have to choose from, the introduction of SMDs has made it increasingly difficult for opposition party supporters to translate votes into seats. The choices that voters have and make might be meaningful at the time votes are cast, but the end results are manifest in the translation of votes to seats, which undermine the initial choice. Upper House seats are almost evenly divided between MMD and PR seats, which are elected from larger population bases than Lower House seats, with the effect that it is on average easier for opposition party supporters to translate votes into seats in Upper House elections.

The pattern of fluctuation in disproportionality in the district elections relative to PR elections warrants attention because these seats are central to the Upper House's long-term function as a consensual mechanism that represents minority views and alleviates potential tyranny under one-party dominance. First, disproportionality for the constituency seats in the Upper House was lowest whenever the LDP suffered a significant loss – as in the 1971, 1989, and 1998 Upper House elections. LDP loses and a decline in disproportionality corresponds to periods when an LDP-led government has gone against the tide of public opinion. In 1989, the LDP lost control of the Upper House for the first time in postwar history when voters awarded the JSP after the LDP passed an unpopular consumption tax and was suffering the aftershocks of the Recruit Scandal. In 1998, voters dissatisfied with the government's economic management turned out the LDP again. In 2004, the DPJ won more votes and seats than the LDP, but the latter retained control of the Upper House in coalition with the New Komeito. In 2007, voters turned their 2004 setback for the LDP into a definitive loss, and the DPJ took control and immediately began to call for an early House of Representatives election.

Whereas the conventional wisdom holds that the Upper House is a safe place for risk-adverse voters to penalize the LDP, this view downplays the fact that it is here that voters are able to make meaningful choices in the sense that the translation of votes to seats results in a physical, and often substantive, representation of the distribution of preferences in the electorate. Voting against the LDP in the Upper House is a warning to the LDP that its policies and practices have deviated too far from mainstream public opinion, and is a measure of how much the party will need to compensate voters to avoid a commensurate loss in the Lower House. The Upper House grants opposition party occupants enough power to intervene in the legislative process to articulate their constituents' preferences, providing access to citizens who would otherwise be perpetual losers.

Local Elections: Changing Politics from the Ground Up

In this section, I briefly overview critical junctures in Japanese politics in the the 1970s and 2000s when local elections precipitated national change.

The changing character of the connection between local and national elections is masked by researchers' focus on national elections to the Diet where there has been more continuity than change. The privileging of national elections has been furthered by the traditional weakness of local party organizations in a centralized state. The emphasis on national elections has inhibited researchers from redirecting attention to other parts of the Japanese system where there have been marked changes in political engagement over time. Patterns of civic and political engagement at the grassroots tell a very different story about national politics. Everyday citizens are trying to shorten the distance between the center and the periphery by bringing national democratic practices into closer alignment with popular democracy at the grassroots. Common efforts to promote direct participation in democracy – referenda and recall movements, citizens' and antiestablishment parties, and the election of independent executives – are increasing in frequency across Japan.

Local opposition politics in the 1970s are often invoked as evidence of the importance of electoral pressures at the grassroots in checking national politics when it grows stagnant and distant from voters. Patterns of urban–rural migration and demographic change began to undermine the strength of the LDP's support base in the 1970s (Ramseyer and Rosenbluth, 1993). The LDP's pro-business policies and rapid industrialization caused environmental degradation and extensive pollution in urban areas that resulted in grassroots environmental movements and opposition party victories in local elections (see McKean 1981). The shift from extended to nuclear families and the graying of the population gave rise to pressures for a more comprehensive social welfare state. Over the course of the 1970s, the proportion of prefectural assembly seats held by the LDP declined and those held by opposition parties increased (Ramseyer and Rosenbluth, 1993: 46–48). Opposition-led local governments in urban areas innovated and instituted environmental and social welfare policies with popular support. To prevent the opposition from converting local electoral success into national success, the LDP co-opted opposition party policies enacted in local governments and implemented them at the national level. The LDP's co-optation of local social programs at the national level helped it to recover in local elections in the 1980s (Ramseyer and Rosenbluth, 1993; see also Steiner, 1965, Steiner et al., 1980). The effectiveness of grassroots citizen participation in pressuring the LDP to respond to changing voter interests nationally speaks to the importance of multiple access points generally, and to the specific role that subnational elections play in forging a new national consensus.

Turnout has decreased at all administrative levels, but participation in local politics has not experienced a drop as pronounced as that in national elections.[5] Higher percentages of voters continue to participate in deciding contests for local office – turnout for the 2007 Local Unified Elections ranged from 50 to 75 percent.[6] Higher turnout in local elections, especially town and village elections, is opposite to what one finds in other democracies, where turnout is higher for high salience national elections and declines for elections held at lower administrative units. Yusaku Horiuchi (2005) has dubbed this a 'turnout twist,' which can be explained by voters' calculations about how much their votes will matter. Everyday Japanese correctly conclude that their vote has a higher chance of mattering – and if votes are equivalent to voice – their voices have a greater chance of being heard in local elections. Voters are using citizen's parties, independent and antiestablishment candidates, and information disclosure, referenda, and recall movements to further increase the likelihood that their voices will be heard (Le Blanc, 2008).

Local citizens' parties and independent candidates for local executive offices appeal directly to the growing numbers of voters who feel disconnected from national politics and parties. The 1995 Law to Promote Decentalization altered the relationship between the national and local governments. The latter assumed increased fiscal and administrative social welfare responsibilities that precipitated a wave of municipal mergers as small towns and villages were encouraged to pursue economies of scale to assume new roles. Administrative decentralization has provided both incentives and opportunities for voters to intensify use of successful pressure tactics adopted in the 1970s to change national politics from the ground up. These strategies from the 1970s period of opposition politics, which are being redeployed with renewed vigor in recent years, is evidence that the gap between voters and national elites has once again grown too large. Participation in local elections can directly impact citizens' immediate environment while sending a clear message to national officials by disrupting the 'electoral connection' between local and national government (Le Blanc, 2008). When citizens shake up local assemblies to protest national politics, assembly members no longer function as 'reliable grassroots activists' and 'significant voter-gathering machines' for the LDP in national, prefectural, and municipal elections (Kohara, 2007: 10).

CONCLUSION

In this chapter, I have argued that electoral choices are less meaningful if they do not allow voters to effectively exercise control over their nationally elected representatives – their voice in politics. Even if there are a relatively large number of parties that offer substantively different choices, and citizens vote for the party that most closely reflects their preferences, elections fail to reproduce the distribution of public preferences when the allocation of seats in elected assemblies does not accurately reflect the distribution of votes.

Two decades after reform, voters continue to complain that their choices are losing ones. This outcome is not inevitable, as evidenced by the efforts of political outsiders to gain traction in elections in other parts of the system in an effort to bring about national political change. Other features of the political context interact with the electoral system and must be brought into focus to understand the dynamic relationship between choice and democracy. Japan demonstrates how important it is to look at subnational politics as another level in a multi-level game.

Falling turnout, the loosening of partisanship, and the decrease in public confidence in national politics does not mean that Japanese voters have abandoned politics or party organizations altogether. Japanese voters reinvest their political resources into local politics where the impact of their efforts is most immediately felt. Some voters are engaging in local action that is crafted to send a direct message to national politicians and effect change from the bottom–up.

NOTES

1   The views expressed in this chapter are those of the author, and do not necessarily reflect those of the U.S. Department of State or the U.S. Government.

2   Meaningful electoral choice has been undermined by long-term, one-party dominance by the Liberal Democratic Party (LDP) that, with the exception of brief interludes between 1993–1994 and 2009–2012, has controlled government since 1955. During the LDP's first ten months in opposition, an eight-party coalition government comprised of every party with the exception of the LDP, and the Japan Communist Party (JCP) passed an electoral reform package that changed voting procedures for the House of Representatives. The LDP seized power when it formed a legislative coalition with New Party Sakigake and the long-time rival Social Democratic Party of Japan (SDPJ, previously the Japan Socialist Party) in 1994. The LDP has ruled in coalition with New Komeito since 1999.

3   The '1955 System' summarizes political dynamics under one-party dominance. The 1955 merger of the Liberal Party and Japan Democratic Party to form the Liberal Democratic Party (LDP) marks the

beginning of this period. The 1993 Lower House elections, which produced a coalition government, comprised of all parties except the LDP and the Communists and passed an electoral reform package that ushered in a new era in Japanese politics.

4   Political cynicism, also referred to as political alienation and political distrust, has been commonly measured through a battery of national election studies items that originate in the US context and have been replicated cross-nationally and over time. American National Election Studies survey respondents are asked (a) How much of the time do you think you can trust the government in Washington to do what is right?, (b) Do you think that people in government waste a lot of the money we pay in taxes, waste some of it, or don't waste very much of it?, (c) Would you say the government is pretty much run by a few big interests looking out for themselves or that it is run for the benefit of all people?, and (d) Do you think that quite a few of the people running the government are crooked, or many are, or hardly any of them are crooked? (see Koch (2003) for a representative piece). In Japan, these same attitudes are measured by (a) To what extend do you feel you can trust national politics?, (b) What do you think of the people who were elected to the National Diet? Generally speaking, do you think they stop thinking about the public's interest immediately after taking office? Or do you think this is false? (c) Do you think this country's politics are largely run in order to benefit the interests of a few big organizations like large companies and big unions? Or do you think this country's politics are largely run on behalf of the people as a whole?, (d) Do you think the people who manage our national politics are dishonest, somewhat dishonest, or honest?, and (e) Do you think that Japanese politicians and political parties are neglecting the interests of the people because of factional competition and corruption problems? Kabashima and colleagues (2000) in recognition of the multiple dimensions that constitute this contested concept – political alienation or cynicism – also seek to understand how this manifests in attitudes about individual participation (respondents' level of interest in politics, assessment of the importance of voting and how much an individual vote makes, and ability to understand politics).

5   Voter turnout has fallen cross-nationally in established democracies. Japan, however, is not an outlier; its trends are no more or less pronounced than elsewhere. In fact, voter turnout in Japan for parliamentary elections during the period covered in this chapter is higher on average. Turnout for Diet elections – at 59 percent in 2000 and 2003, and 66.6 percent in 2005 – was higher than turnout for midterm Congressional elections – 35 percent in 2002 and 37.3 percent in 2006. Voter turnout for national elections in Japan is on par with US presidential elections in 2004 when 56.6 percent of eligible American voters cast a ballot). See International IDEA at http://www.idea.int/

6   There was tremendous variation across administrative units. Turnout tended to be on the lower end in population-dense urban areas but on the higher end in rural towns and villages.

REFERENCES

Anderson, Christopher J. 2009. The interaction of structures and voter behavior. In Russell Dalton and Hans-Dieter Klingemann, eds. *The Oxford handbook of political behavior*. Oxford, UK: Oxford University Press, 589–609.

Anderson, Christopher J., André Blais, Shaun Bowler, Todd Donovan, and Ola Listhaug. 2005. *Losers' Consent: Elections and Democratic Legitimacy*. New York: Oxford University Press.

Cappella, Joseph N. and Kathleen Hall Jamieson. 1996. News frames, political cynicism, and media cynicism. *Annals of the American Academy of Political and Social Science*. 546, 71–84.

Citrin, J. 1974. Comment: the political relevance of trust in government. *American Political Science Review*, 68, 973–988.

Duverger, Maurice. 1954. *Political parties: their organization and activity in the modern state*. London, John Wiley and Sons.

Easton, David. 1965. *A systems analysis of political life*. New York, NY: Wiley.

Gallagher, Michael and Paul Mitchell, eds. 2005. *The politics of electoral systems*. Oxford, UK: Oxford University Press.

Horiuchi, Yusaku. 2005. *Institutions, incentives and electoral participation in Japan: Cross-level and cross-national perspectives*. London and New York: RoutledgeCurzon.

Hrebenar, Ronald J. 2000. *Japan's New Party System*. Boulder, CO: Westview Press.

Ishida, Takeshi and Ellis S. Krauss, eds. 1989. *Democracy in Japan*. Pittsburg, PA: University of Pittsburg Press.

Kabashima, Ikuo, Jonathan Marshall, Takayoshi Uekami and Sae-Song Hyun. 2000. Causal cynics of disillusioned democrats? Political alienation in Japan. *Political Psychology*, 21 (4), 779–804.

Koch, Jeffrey W. 2003. Political cynicism and third party support in American presidential elections. *American Politics Research*, (31) 1, 48–65.

Kohara, Takaharu. 2007. The great Heisei consolidation: a critical review. *Social Science Japan Newsletter*, 37, 7–11.

Laasko, Markku and Rein Taagepera. 1979. 'Effective' number of parties: a measure with application to

West Europe. *Comparative Political Studies,* 12 (1), 3–27.

Le Blanc, Robin. 2008. The potential limits of antiparty electoral movements in local politics. In Sherry L. Martin and Gill Steel, eds. *Democratic reform in Japan: assessing the impact.* Boulder, CO: Lynne Rienner Publishers, 81–100.

MacDougall, Terry E. 1989. Democracy and local government in postwar Japan. In Takeshi Ishida and Ellis S. Krauss, eds. *Democracy in Japan.* Pittsburg, PA: University of Pittsburg Press, 139–169.

Martin, Curtis H. and Bruce Stronach. 1992. Politics east and west: A comparison of Japanese and British political culture. Armonk, NY: M.E. Sharpe.

Martin, Sherry. 2004. Alienated, independent, and female: Lessons from the Japanese electorate. *Social Science Japan Journal,* 7, 1–19.

Martin, Sherry L. and Gill Steel, eds. 2008. *Democratic reform in Japan: Assessing the impact.* Boulder, CO: Lynne Rienner Publishers.

McKean, Margaret A. 1981. *Environmental politics and citizen politics in Japan.* Berkeley and Los Angeles, CA: University of California Press.

Miller, Arthur H. 1974. Political issues and trust in government: 1964–1970. *American Political Science Review.* 68, 951–972.

Miller, Arthur H. and Wattenberg, Martin P. 1985. Throwing the rascals out: Policy and performance evaluations of presidential candidates, 1952–1980. *American Political Science Review.* 79 (2), 359–372.

Mishler, William and Richard Rose. 2001. What are the origins of political trust? *Comparative Political Studies,* 34, 30–62.

Miyake, Ichiro. 1991. Types of partisanship, partisan attitudes, and voting choices. In Scott C. Flanagan, Shinsaku Kohei, Ichiro Miyake, and Bradley M. Richardson, eds. *The Japanese voter.* New Haven: Yale University Press, 226–264.

Otake, Hideo. 2000. Political realignment and policy conflict. In Hideo Otake, ed. *Policy shuffles and policy processes: coalition government in Japan in the 1990s.* Tokyo: Japan Center for International Exchange, 125–151.

Pempel, T. J. 1989. Prerequisites for democracy: political and social institutions. In Takeshi Ishida and Ellis S. Krauss, eds. *Democracy in Japan.* Pittsburg, PA: University of Pittsburg Press, 17–37.

Pharr, Susan J. 1997. Public trust and democracy in Japan. In J. S. Nye Jr., P. D. Zelikow and D. C. King, eds. *Why people don't trust government.* Cambridge, MA: Harvard University Press, 237–252.

Ramseyer, J. Mark and Frances McCall Rosenbluth. 1993. *Japan's political marketplace.* Cambridge, MA: Harvard University Press.

Reed, Steven R. and Michael F. Thies. 2001. The causes of electoral reform in Japan. In Matthew Soberg Shugart and Martin P. Wattenberg, eds. *Mixed-member electoral systems: the best of both worlds?* Oxford and New York: Oxford University Press, 152–172.

Richardson, Bradley M. 1998. *Japanese democracy: power, coordination, and performance.* New Haven, CT: Yale University Press.

Richardson, Bradley M. and Scott C. Flanagan. 1984. *Politics in Japan.* Boston: Little Brown.

Scheiner, Ethan. 2005. *Democracy Without Opposition in Japan.* Cambridge, Cambridge University Press.

Steel, Gill. 2008. Policy preferences and party platforms: what voters want vs. what voters get. In Sherry L. Martin and Gill Steel, eds. *Democratic reform in Japan: assessing the impact.* Boulder, CO: Lynne Rienner Publishers, 81–100.

Steiner, K. (1965). *Local government in Japan.* Stanford, CA: Stanford University Press.

Steiner, Kurt, Ellis S. Krauss, Scott C. Flanagan, eds. 1980. *Political opposition and local politics in Japan.* Princeton, NJ: Princeton University Press.

Tanaka, Aiji. 2004. Changes in Japanese electoral politics, 2003–2004: the impact of pension reform or the Koizumi effect? *Social Science Japan,* (29):3–5.

Tanaka, Aiji and Sherry Martin. 2003. The new independent voter and the evolving Japanese party system. *Asian Perspective,* 27 (3), 21–51.

Weiner, Robert J. 2008. Prefectural politics: party and electoral stagnation. In Sherry L. Martin and Gill Steel, eds. *Democratic reform in Japan: assessing the impact.* Boulder, CO: Lynne Rienner Publishers, 151–174.

Young, Iris Marion. 2002. *Inclusion and democracy.* Oxford, UK: Oxford University Press.

22

Civil Society in Japan

Yuko Kawato, Robert J. Pekkanen,
and Hidehiro Yamamoto

Civil society is the non-state, non-market sector that exists above the family and individual. This chapter presents an overview of Japan's civil society, which includes neighborhood associations, environmental groups, and organizations representing the interests of consumers, religions, women, minorities, and foreigners in Japan. The Japanese nonprofit sector considerably overlaps but does not exactly correspond with civil society because it includes some social welfare organizations that are virtually quasi-public organizations, and some market sector organizations such as agricultural cooperatives, labor, and business associations. This chapter, however, includes these organizations in recognition of debates over their roles in civil society. We also highlight the media as a sphere of discourse and participation of civil society actors in protest movements.

The number of civil society organizations in Japan has increased steadily in the post-World War II era (Tsujinaka, 2003). This reflects a growing popular interest in participating in social and political activities through civil society organizations. It is also driven in Japan, as elsewhere around the world, by advances in technology cutting the cost of communications, and rising education and income levels. Along with waxing popular attention, scholars have also renewed their interest in research on Japanese civil society. After some discussion about definitions of civil society, we will present the historical development of the Japanese civil society. We will then discuss the characteristics and roles of civil society organizations today, and review recent research on various organizations to provide a sense of the diversity and actual practices of Japanese civil society groups. We will conclude with suggestions for future research.

DEFINITION OF CIVIL SOCIETY

The most common definition of civil society is that it is the non-state, non-market sector that exists above the family and individual. Schwartz, for example, offers the 'median' definition of civil society: the 'sphere intermediate between family and state in which social actors pursue neither profit within the market nor power within the state' (Schwartz, 2003: 23).

Civil society is difficult to define, however, and scholars have used the term differently. A common perspective defines civil society as a set of organizations. Of course, just which organizations should be counted is a matter of debate. Some scholars include economic actors, such as business organizations, trade associations, employer associations, labor unions, and consumer groups, in their study of civil society. For example, Tsujinaka (2002a, 2003) and Diamond (1994) include economic organizations in their analyses. Some scholars also argue that analyses of civil society can include non-market activity of economic actors (Pharr, 2003: xiv; Schwartz, 2003: 32), although recognizing that it could be difficult to distinguish market and non-market activities of economic actors. Many scholars avoid the inclusion of economic actors in their analyses to maintain definitional consistency. Pekkanen, for example, defines civil society as the 'organized, nonstate, nonmarket sector,' which does not include 'labor unions, companies, or other profit-oriented groups' (Pekkanen, 2003: 118). Another fault line in the study of Japan's civil society is the inclusion of religious groups, which is the norm for scholars in the United States, while inclusion of media corporations, such as newspapers, is debated everywhere.

A second conceptualization of civil society sees it not as a collection of organizations but as a sphere of discourse – and thus raises a question as to what extent civil society has to be organized. In this conception, economic organizations might move into civil society as they engage in non-economic activity or public sphere debate, but then move out as they don their economic guise. Overall, the emphasis is not on being counted once and for all as civil society, but doing civil society. Thus, the 'space' of civil society can wax and wane over time even as the number of organizations may remain constant. This different conceptualization naturally leads to the use of different methodologies. Some scholars study organizational dimensions of civil society (number, size, structure, and function of organizations), while others study modes of communication and development of public opinion. However, these conceptualizations of civil society are not mutually exclusive. Acknowledging their different explanatory focuses, some scholars include both in their definition of civil society (Hardacre, 2004: 391).

Finally, some scholars incorporate public interest to the definition of civil society, suggesting that civil society actors seek to contribute to the public good (Anheier, 2004: 22; Hardacre, 2004: 391). What constitutes public good is contested (Schwartz, 2003: 35). Some civil society organizations also engage in activities that hurt the public interest, although when discovered they could be rejected as part of civil society (Hardacre, 2003).

OVERVIEW OF JAPANESE CIVIL SOCIETY

Development of Japanese Civil Society

The idea of civil society is specific to time and place (Garon, 2003; Mouer and Sugimoto, 2003;

Yamaguchi, 2005). While European and North American thinkers often wrote of 'civil society' between the late eighteenth and early nineteenth centuries, the Japanese did not use the corresponding term – *shimin shakai* – until after World War II because the notion of 'citizens' governing society that existed autonomously from the state directly challenged shogunal and imperial authority (Garon, 2003: 42–45; Barshay, 2003: 65; Avenell, 2010: passim). Nevertheless, non-state and non-market entities engaging in nonprofit activities existed as early as the late sixth century, when Buddhist temples started to engage in charitable relief and development of infrastructure like bridges and irrigation systems (Yamaoka, 1998: 19–20). In addition, there were merchants' organizations (*za*), protest movements (*ikki*), and religious organizations (*monto*) during the Middle Ages (Fukuda, 2006).

Associational life developed further in the Tokugawa era (1600–1868), including samurai's academies for learning and martial arts that diffused political knowledge, merchants' philanthropic and learned societies that proposed various reforms, wealthy farmers and rural entrepreneurs' networks, and publishing firms (Garon, 2003: 45; Fukuda, 2006). Furthermore, there were mutual aid and mutual loan associations to provide relief to farmers, although the farmers revolted approximately 2800 times during the Tokugawa period against heavy taxation and corrupt government (White, 1995; Yamaoka, 1998: 22–23; Iokibe, 1999: 54–56).

Several changes with implications to associational life happened after the Meiji Restoration of 1868. The status system's abolishment facilitated association and discussion of public issues between samurai, merchants, and peasants. Associational life beyond one's local area also became possible when freedom of physical mobility and better transportation became available. Western liberalism, which valued a freer society outside of government, also influenced people's thinking. Many privately owned newspapers and associations (including popular rights groups and professional associations) emerged, through which people debated political and public issues (Iokibe, 1999: 69–70; Garon, 2003: 46–47). The popular rights movement (*jiyū minken undō*) emerged in this context, calling for a constitutional government and a national legislature. The state, however, responded to these challenges to its authority by restricting freedom of speech and assembly with the 1880 Public Assembly Ordinance (Iokibe, 1999: 70). The Civil Code of 1896 also allowed the state to mould civil society by encouraging the growth of organizations that served the 'public interest' as defined by the state (Pekkanen, 2006).

At the turn of the century, state ministries reorganized various private associations into bureaucratically administered national federations and associations. Associations' incorporations into the state's hierarchical organization facilitated implementation of official policies. The state also controlled radicalism and collective labor activity with the Police Law of 1900 that outlawed instigation to strike, joining unions, or engaging in collective bargaining (Garon, 2003: 49–50). Barshay explains the context:

> By the 1890s, 'society' *(shakai)* emerged on the scene, but as a problem, the seedbed of conflict and strife and division *among* the emperor's subjects. With urbanization and industrialization…'society' came all too soon to be captured by that most polarizing notion of 'class' (Barshay, 2003: 64).

Even in this context of increasing state control over associational life, groups still had the capacity to oppose state policies. In the early decades of the twentieth century, trade associations were successful in pressuring the state to enact favorable laws, and young men's associations espoused radical politics. Labor unions also organized in record numbers, and in alliance with intellectuals, liberal politicians, and tenant-farmer unions, created socialist parties to demand labor and social legislation, as well as the workers' right to vote. In response, the state enacted universal manhood suffrage in 1925 (Garon, 2003: 50–51). Although the state also enacted the Peace Preservation Law in 1925 to further restrict people's freedom of speech and assembly, and generally resisted institutionalization of social organizations' participation in political processes, diverse organizations existed and they increased in number in the 1920s (Iokibe, 1999: 75). For this, Tsujinaka characterizes the Taisho era 'the formative period of Japan's civil society' (2003: 97).

While many associations criticized state policy in various issue areas, they also worked with the state to achieve some of their objectives. According to Garon (1997), many associations' objectives complemented the state's goal in social management, or transforming how Japanese people thought and behaved so that the state could mobilize them for its various projects. Bureaucrats and private associations like women's and religious groups engaged in moral suasion to mould people's minds and succeeded in enlisting their active participation in modernization, industrialization, wartime mobilization, welfare provision, and other projects. This cooperative relationship between the state and many of the private associations originated in the Meiji era and has continued after World War II.

Japan's total war required mobilization in the home front, and this involved extensive control of associational life. Most associations became incorporated into the Imperial Rule Assistance Association (IRAA) founded in 1940 as patriotic associations. The Home Ministry bureaucrats also mobilized neighborhood associations (which existed since the Meiji period with earlier precursors). Kasza (1995) refers to the prewar and wartime civil society organizations as the Administered Mass Organizations (AMOs) that officials controlled, in order to create a 'conscription society' in the image of a conscript army. Kasza argues that the purpose of AMOs was to implement official policy, such as curbing political opposition, mobilizing for war, and effecting socioeconomic changes. These associations facilitated wartime mobilization through participation in civil defense, mutual surveillance, distribution of rations, collection of metal goods, saving drives and other activities (Havens, 1986). Religious and labor associations were two of the most repressed groups in this period.

After Japan's defeat, the Allied Occupation authorities introduced reforms to promote civil society's activities and independence from the state. The new constitution guaranteed the freedoms of assembly, association, speech, press, and religion. The occupation dissolved the Home Ministry that controlled much of the wartime associational life, as well as the IRAA and patriotic associations. The postwar reforms led to a dramatic increase in the number of civil society organizations. Indeed, according to Tsujinaka, the period between 1946 and 1950 was a 'peak-formation period' of Japanese civil society organizations (Tsujinaka and Choe, 2002; Tsujinaka, 2003: 105; Tsujinaka, Choe, Yamamoto, Miwa, and Otomo, 2007). Tsujinaka attributes this to the postwar regime change, which encouraged the formation of new association and pressurized old associations to 'restructure and realign' (Tsujinaka, 2003: 105). Kage (2007) argues that people's organizational experience and informational network from before and during World War II contributed to the postwar increase in civil society participation.

In the 1950s and the 1960s, leftist parties, labor unions, and other organizations engaged in various protests, including those against the United States–Japan security treaty, rearmament, and the Vietnam War. The term 'civil society' or 'civic society' had a leftist, progressive connotation at this time (Yamamoto, T., 1998; Tsujinaka, 2002b). In the 1960s and the 1970s, thousands of local organizations formed 'citizens' movements *(shimin undō)*' to demand improvements in pollution and quality-of-life problems. These organizations' activities contributed to the election of many progressive local governments in urban areas in the 1970s, which pressured the state to improve environmental and welfare policies.

In the aftermath of the Hanshin–Awaji earthquake, energetic volunteer activities by 1.3 million people made some in the media to declare 1995 'Year One of Volunteerism.' Ogawa (2004, 2009) argues that since then the Japanese government at different levels has cultivated 'volunteer subjectivity' among citizens, with the ultimate aim of shaping civil society organizations that augment and replace the government's provision of services. Cusick (2007), however, argues that most volunteers (college students in his study) have more personal motivations (self-discovery, creating diverse friendships), instead of motivations oftentimes encouraged by the state and civil society actors (strengthening communities or alleviating social problems). In addition, Haddad (2007) has developed the Community Volunteerism Model to explain why local communities have different types and rates of volunteering. The model predicts that the types of volunteer organizations in a community depends on citizens' attitude about governmental and individual responsibility for dealing with social problems, and the rates of volunteer participation depend on the extent to which communities legitimize, organize, and fund volunteers. According to Haddad, in Japan, where citizens think that the government should take responsibility for dealing with social problems, there is more participation in organizations that have close, embedded relationships with the government.

In 1998, the Special Nonprofit Organization Law (NPO Law) was established to promote the development of independent NPOs by liberalizing conditions under which they could form and operate. The law significantly expanded the scope of groups that qualify for legal status, and curtailed bureaucratic supervision (Pekkanen, 2000). Civil society organizations participated actively in the lawmaking process in the early 1990s. The Hanshin–Awaji earthquake in 1995 accelerated the lawmaking process in acknowledgment of volunteer groups without legal status (and thus without work insurance) that mobilized quickly to deliver relief. Also important were the coalition politics at the time and the electoral reforms of 1994, which increased political parties' interest in NPOs as a vote coordination mechanism (Pekkanen, 2000: 139–140; Sato, 2006: 114).

By helping more groups obtain legal status, the NPO Law has given legitimacy to the NPO sector as having a socially valued purpose. The number of NPOs with legal status has steadily increased, from 1,176 NPOs in December 1999 to 47,123 in January 2013 (Cabinet Office NPO Homepage). However, the NPO Law has not led to a fundamental change in the Japanese civil society or the state-civil society relationship. There are several factors that have limited the transforming effect of the NPO Law. First, for many lawmakers, the main purpose of the law was to increase the number of NPOs that would support the state's provision of services at the local level instead of increasing professional advocacy groups that operate nationally. Therefore, many small local groups and few large professional advocacy groups continue to make up the civil society, and NPOs' impact on policymaking and implementation remains more at the local level than at the national level (Pekkanen, 2000).

The second factor that has limited the transformative effect of the NPO Law is the inadequate financial support for NPOs. Although the NPO Law allows groups with legal status to receive tax breaks and grants, many NPOs remain short of funds. Third, although the NPO Law made group formation and operation easier in many ways, some disincentives to obtaining legal status remain and many organizations continue to operate as voluntary groups. Many organizations do not apply for legal status because they consider the accounting and finance reporting requirements too onerous, and they fear that bureaucrats might still control the objectives or activities of the NPOs (Noumi, 1997; Pekkanen, 2004a: 227). However, the increasing number of NPOs and new channels of interest articulation also show that the NPO Law has had some positive effects on the development of the Japanese civil society (Kawato and Pekkanen, 2008).

Characteristics of Japan's Civil Society Organizations

The Cabinet Office's surveys on NPOs identify 19 fields of interest for NPOs. NPOs are able to name multiple fields in their mission statements. The percentage of NPO participation in each field in 2012 was as follows: health/medical/social welfare (53.1 percent), local infrastructure development (37.6 percent), child development (36.7 percent), social education (34.0 percent), academics/culture/art/sports (28.6 percent), environmental protection (25.2 percent), NPO support (20.6 percent), employment (18.5 percent), aiding economic activities (12.7 percent), human rights and peace (12.2 percent), local safety (12.1 percent), international cooperation (11.7 percent), information society (9.6 percent), development of tourism (9.0 percent), gender equality (8.4 percent), disaster aid (7.9 percent), development of agricultural areas and fishing villages (7.8 percent), science and technology (5.6 percent), and consumer protection (5.1 percent) (Cabinet Office, 2012). This statistics reveals that more than half of the NPOs are interested in working in the fields of health, medicine, and social welfare. A substantial portion of the NPOs are also interested in local infrastructure development, child development, and social education.

Most NPOs engage in local activities. Only 7.0 percent of the NPOs in the Cabinet Office's survey in 2010 participated in activities abroad. Almost 40 percent (39.7 percent) of the NPOs engaged in activities in one city, town, or village, and 40.7 percent of the NPOs engaged in activities in multiple cities, towns, or villages within one prefecture. Only 11.8 percent worked in multiple prefectures, and 7.8 percent worked nationwide (Cabinet Office, 2011: 3–4; on NGO's international activities, see Osa, 2003).

Most NPOs have small number of paid staffs and members. In the aforementioned survey, 50.1 percent of the NPOs had less than 20 paid staffs, and only 10.2 percent had more than 100 paid staffs. As for the number of members (excluding paid staff), 67.3 percent had less than 20 members, and 21.7 percent had between 20 and 99 members. Only 11.0 percent of the NPOs had more than 100 members (Cabinet Office, 2011: 5).

Roles of Civil Society Organizations

There are several roles that Japanese civil society organizations play. First, they can support state provision of social services. For many in the conservative Liberal Democratic Party (LDP), the main purpose of the NPO Law was to increase the number of organizations that support the state's provision of social services, such as health, medical, and welfare services (D moto, 2000: 166–167; Sato, 2006: 115). Organizations such as the social welfare associations serve this role through contract projects (*itaku jigyō*), with the majority of the funding coming from the state. Neighborhood organizations also participate in the local provision of social services. The government has encouraged civil society's growth so that it would take on more tasks while the government implements administrative reform to become more streamlined and efficient (Ota, 1999; Sato, 2006: 109–112). Ogawa argues that volunteer activities not only augment but also replace the government's provision of social services. He attributes this policy to cost cutting in public administration (Ogawa, 2004: 73, 2009).

The second role that civil society organizations play is in creation of social capital (Putnam, 1993, 2000; Skocpol, 1998). Scholars have pointed out that in Japan, many join civil society organizations and there is a high level of social capital (Inoguchi, 2000, 2002; Pekkanen, 2004a, 2006). The Cabinet Office sponsored a study by leading Japanese civil society scholars (2003), which concludes that civil society organizations can create new social capital

and influence preexisting social capital (similar findings in the Cabinet Office, 2005; Yamauchi and Ibuki, 2005; Nihon Sōgō Kenkyūsho, 2008). When, for example, organizations realize that their region lacks a service that it needs, they look for people in the region who can help them achieve their goal. They can seek cooperation from preexisting groups like neighborhood associations and Parent–Teacher Associations and, as they work together, a new network for communication and cooperation emerges. This process creates new social capital and also transforms the preexisting social capital from being 'bonding' (internal to the preexisting groups) to 'bridging' (bringing together various groups). The increase in social capital in turn positively influences future civil society activities.

The third role for civil society organizations is improving representation through increasing citizens' access to political parties and politicians. In the civil society organizations' effort to have the NPO Law passed and even after the Law's passage, new channels of communication between the public and politicians emerged, and preexisting channels became stronger. For example, political parties have established NPO committees and study groups, and this has institutionalized civil society organizations' access to politicians. NPO *Giin Renmei*, a league of Diet members that gives legislative support for NPO activities, was established in 1999 with 204 starting members from various parties (C's, 1999).

Finally, civil society organizations can participate in policymaking and implementation through advocacy and monitoring. Many local governments have promotion offices for civil society activities, and organizations and local governments cooperate in policymaking and implementation. Organizations submit policy proposals and petitions to various levels of government, and send representatives to deliberative councils. Organizations also organize symposiums and create publications.

Despite the growing number and influence of civil society organizations, the Johns Hopkins Global Civil Society Index, which measured the robustness of civil societies around the world based on their capacity, sustainability, and impact, ranks Japan nineteenth out of thirty-four countries. This is the second lowest rank of all developed nations (Salamon and Sokolowski, 2004: Yamauchi, 2005: 58). It suggests that civil society organizations' role in advocacy and monitoring is more limited in Japan than in other countries. One of the most important reasons for this is the Japanese state's tendency to limit access to policymaking at the national level and grant unilateral concessions to social groups (Pharr, 1990). Civil society organizations' weak financial foundation and receipt of government funds also limit their advocacy and monitoring roles. Organizations' efforts in advocacy and monitoring remains mostly at local levels, although there have been some important exceptions (Reimann, 2001, 2010; Maclachlan, 2004).

RESEARCH ON JAPANESE CIVIL SOCIETY

Neighborhood Associations

Neighborhood associations (NHAs) are 'voluntary groups whose membership is drawn from a small, geographically delimited, and exclusive residential area (a neighborhood) and whose activities are multiple and are centered on that same area' (Pekkanen, 2006: 87). There are about 300,000 NHAs, and nearly all Japanese belong to a NHA; the average membership rate is 92.2 percent. NHAs are the most common form of civil society organization in Japan. Dore (1958) and Bestor (1989) discuss them in their monographs on Japanese society.

NHAs' activities provide various social services and offer socializing opportunities to residents. Tsujinaka, Pekkanen, and Yamamoto (2009; also, Pekkanen, Tsujinaka, and Yamamoto, 2014) conducted a nationwide survey (N=18,404) and found that NHAs typically organize cleaning (88.0 percent), maintain roads (87.3 percent), organize local festivals (74.7 percent), support elderly groups (70.9 percent), organize garbage collection (69.6 percent), participate in celebrations and funerals (68.7 percent), organize sports and cultural events (65.0 percent), support school education (63.9 percent), maintain buildings where residents meet (63.7 percent), and engage in fire prevention (60.1 percent).

Residents living in a neighborhood share various concerns and interests, and need to cooperate to deal with them. Therefore, it is ideal for all households in a neighborhood to join a NHA. Iwasaki et al. (1985) express this with the concept of '*jyūen* (relation by residence) association.' Nakata (1993) proposes the concept of '*chiiki kyōdō kanri* (local and joint maintenance),' as residents themselves deal with local issues and maintain the shared resources.

Through participation in NHA activities (especially socializing activities), residents build a stronger network and foster mutual trust and norm of reciprocity. This is how NHAs contribute to the formation of social capital in local communities Pekkanen, 2004a, 2006). Moreover, strong social capital prevents free riding and promotes local residents' participation to NHA activities (Tsujinaka, Pekkanen, and Yamamoto, 2009; Pekkanen, Tsujinaka, and Yamamoto, 2014).

NHAs have a close relationship with local governments. Local governments give NHAs some

subsidies and grants, and fees for NHAs to undertake contract work. Tsujinaka, Pekkanen, and Yamamoto (2009; also, Pekkanen, Tsujinaka, and Yamamoto, 2014) show that 94.9 percent of NHAs help disseminate administrative information through *kairanban* (circulating message boards), 91.9 percent help distribute government publications, and 90.3 percent cooperate in collecting donations for charity. NHAs also help build consensus for public works among residents through prior consultation (Pekkanen, 2006: 112–115).

Furthermore, NHAs communicate residents' needs to local governments. Tsujinaka, Pekkanen, and Yamamoto (2009) show that 84.4 percent of NHAs maintain contact with local government officials responsible for NHAs, and 68.4 percent attend periodically organized meetings with local governments. Local governments take NHAs' requests seriously and their response is often favorable (Pekkanen, 2006: 121). In sum, NHAs maintain a close relationship with local governments in both policymaking and implementation, and thus are 'straddling civil society' (Pekkanen and Read, 2003; Read with Pekkanen, 2009; Tsujinaka, Pekkanen, and Yamamoto, 2009; Pekkanen, Tsujinaka, and Yamamoto, 2014). However, NHA leaders very rarely protest local governments' decisions or engage in policy debates through advocacy. NHAs, with their role in fostering social capital and lack of involvement in advocacy, therefore support Pekkanen's characterization of Japanese civil society as 'members without advocates' (2006).

NHAs became crucial in responding to the Tōhoku Earthquake of March 11, 2011. The high level of social capital is likely to have maintained general order. Media reports also suggest that NHAs' efforts to improve disaster preparedness and response had some positive impact. (The national survey by Tsujinaka, Pekkanen, and Yamamoto (2009; Pekkanen, Tsujinaka, and Yamamoto, 2014) shows that 55.6 percent of NHAs engage in activities to improve disaster preparedness and response.) For example, Sendai City has encouraged NHAs to organize disaster prevention and response groups (*jishu bōsai soshiki*) since the earthquake off the coast of Miyagi in 1978. According to the city's website, 95 percent of the NHAs in the city had organized such groups by January 2010. One NHA in Kesennuma City had prepared a list of elderly who would need special assistance in case of disaster, and the list (and local residents' memory of who were on this list) helped organize visits to these people by doctors, nurses, and care managers after the disaster.

In addition, many residents continued to rely on NHAs as a mechanism to facilitate coordinated action and to maintain social networks. NHA-like self-governing groups emerged in evacuation centers to organize and carry out various tasks. Residents in some NHAs evacuated to other towns or prefectures together as a unit in order to maintain their social network and facilitate communication during recovery efforts. Furthermore, NHAs continued to serve as a bridge between residents and local governments. In Urayasu City in Chiba prefecture, where liquefaction due to the earthquake damaged roads and homes, NHA members held discussion sessions and decided to submit a list of requests to local government, including stabilizing the ground and restoring infrastructure (Kawato, Pekkanen, and Tsujinaka, 2012: 83–85).

Volunteer firefighters played a central part in many NHAs' disaster response, but some of them lost their lives while helping others (Kawato et al., 2012: 85–86). We do not claim that NHAs functioned without cost and, although NHAs facilitated coordination in many communities as they responded to the disasters, we also recognize the possibility that the strength of these groups may have made local communities more resistant to working with outsiders in relief efforts (cf Yamagishi (2003) on trust).

There are various arguments for NHAs' origin. In old cities like Kyoto and Nara, it might be traced back to *chō* (a self-governing urban area) in the Muromachi period. In Tokyo, *chō* or *machigumi* in the Tokugawa period might have been the forerunners of NHAs. In rural areas, villages and settlements might have been NHAs' predecessors. NHAs in today's form were established in the Meiji period. There was a wide-scale incorporation in 1888, unifying smaller towns and villages into larger cities, towns, and villages. As local governments did not have enough funds, and as former towns and villages continued to be the locale of residents' daily life, former towns and villages provided funds and labor for infrastructure and school constructions, hygiene, and cleaning activities (Torigoe, 1994; Yamaoka, 1998: 34–35). Division of roles between local governments and original towns and villages therefore remained unclear, and the original entities were maintained as *gyōseiku* (administrative area) supplementary to the local governments. This administrative area became the prototype of the NHAs in rural areas (Akimoto, 1971; Torigoe, 1994).

In cities, migration in the Meiji era complicated local elites' effort to maintain control. This contributed to the creation of NHAs. In the 1920s, the state played a crucial role in the spread of NHAs throughout Japan, when it introduced sanitary associations to which all households joined. Sanitary associations came to deal with various problems of daily life (Tanaka, 1990). Pekkanen (2006) argues that this spread of NHAs shows how government policy shapes civil society by encouraging a particular type of civil society organization

to develop. Current NHAs' prototypes were thus formed in the Meiji and Taisho periods.

Leading up to World War II, the state incorporated NHAs into local governments in order to strengthen social control. In 1940, the Home Ministry unified all NHAs as either *chōnaikai* or *burakukai* (organizations of households in a neighborhood of *chō* or *buraku*), and placed *tonarigumi* (units of 10–15 households) under them. In 1941, NHAs became subordinate organizations of the IRAA and served in wartime mobilization. Residents' participation in NHAs was compulsory, and NHAs took part in rationing, civil defense, fire fighting, and other tasks.

In 1947, the allied occupation forces (GHQ) abolished the NHAs for their role in war mobilization. GHQ considered that NHAs with compulsory membership would prevent the development of a free and democratic society with voluntary associations (Nakagawa, 1980). Similar criticisms about NHAs – that they were terminal organizations within the government to serve state interests – emerged in the postwar era, and observers argued that modernization and democratization will help create a society that would function without NHAs (Matsushita, 1971; Akimoto, 1971). However, NHAs had emerged not only to serve state interests, but also to serve residents' needs. After Japan regained its independence in 1952, the government reversed the ban on NHAs – they were allowed to form as voluntary and independent organizations.

Since then, increase in population has led to more NHAs' establishment; however, development of individualism and urban sprawl reduced residents' involvement in local community, generating some concern about the weakening role of NHAs. In addition, the close relationship between NHAs and local governments has, at times, produced tension between NHAs and residents' movements in the 1970s. NHAs no longer seemed to represent the interests of all residents (Nakata, 1993). In this context, the state implemented a policy for community revitalization around 1970. It encouraged residents' participation in social activities and discussions to resolve local problems in newly designated 'community areas' and newly built community facilities (Kikuchi and Egami, 1998). This policy aimed at creating some distance between the state and the NHAs by encouraging the establishment of community groups that would replace the NHAs as a mechanism to organize local residents (Yoshihara, 1993, 1997). For this, the policy created tension and conflicts between the state and the NHAs, and failed to achieve its objective to revitalize communities.

Since the 1990s, the state has supported local improvement activities while it implemented decentralization and incorporation of cities, towns, and villages. The public's interest in civil society and governance has increased, adding importance to local self-government, civil society groups' local activities, and cooperation between local government and residents. There are some examples among newly incorporated cities, towns, and villages of establishing *chiiki jichiku* (local self-government areas) and *chiiki kyōgikai* (local councils) as new ways of engaging in local self-governance. In this context, NHAs in various forms are expected to serve a central role. But the decline in residents' participation to NHA activities has worsened since the 1970s, and whether and how NHAs will play a central role in revitalization of local communities remains to be seen.

Social Welfare

Garon (1997) traces the development of Japanese welfare policy since the Tokugawa era and argues that the state has avoided costly social programs for the poor by organizing private social work. The state subsidized private charity and relief organizations, and relied on family members, neighbors, municipalities, businesses, and other volunteers to provide care and advice on savings, employment, and self-help to the poor. The authorities granted relief only to those who could not work and did not have anyone to rely on. Although such a system helped minimize the state's welfare expenditure, private efforts were often insufficient to cope with poverty. Except during the years of economic prosperity coinciding with the wars of 1895, 1904–1905, and 1915–1920, private organizations were short of funds (Anderson, 1993: 44).

According to Margarita Estevez-Abe (2003), for most of the postwar period the state continued to economize by relying on societal partners, including welfare commissioners, social welfare corporations, regionally organized social welfare councils, and seniors' clubs. Most social welfare corporations, however, are heavily dependent on public support: on average, between 80 and 90 percent of their total income comes from the state (Amenomori and Yamamoto, 1998: 5). Welfare provision through the hierarchically arranged system has gone through changes in recent years. In the early 1990s, it became compulsory for local governments to draft a long-term plan for meeting increasing public demands for elderly care. Most local governments turned to social welfare councils, but where the traditional system was ineffective, they established new relationships with residents and citizens' groups.

Other scholars explore causes of welfare expansion and retrenchment. Kasza (2002) focuses on the period between 1937 and 1945 to argue that the state expanded welfare in order to strengthen the nation's human resources for war. Lambert (2007) examines postwar family policy up to the

1990s to demonstrate that economic imperatives (labor shortages and demand for female labor) and electoral incentives (challenges to LDP dominance) led to the expansion of publicly funded childcare, as well as maternity and childcare leave legislations. Economic recessions and LDP electoral successes, on the other hand, led to welfare retrenchment. In the early 1980s, for example, civil society groups' protestations against welfare cuts did not have much impact due to lack of economic and electoral incentives.

The 1990s witnessed several reforms with focus on the elderly (long-term care insurance) and children (increased public childcare, child allowance, childcare leave, and flexible working hours for parents). Peng (2004) explains that the policy changes are due to the interaction between postindustrial pressures (economic globalization that made enterprise welfare systems too costly, demographic shifts, and changing family and gender relations) and political factors (political realignment following the end of LDP's one-party dominance in 1993, as well as increasing role for NPOs).

More child-related reforms took place in the 2000s in response to the falling birthrate (prohibition of overtime work, additional childcare leave to employees with preschool children). In 2003, a special minister was appointed to counter the falling birthrate. Suzuki Kenji (2008) argues that the LDP has shown relative lack of interest in child-related policies, but Komeito has encouraged development of child allowance since it joined the LDP in the coalition government in 1999. Suzuki argues that Komeito's pressure on the LDP to improve child-related welfare is selective and strategic, and its influence is constrained due to its position as a minor partner in the coalition government.

Another research area is on changes in care giving in an aging society. Webb (2002, 2003) discusses changing perspectives on care giving among the elderly and women (who constitute 85 percent of family care givers). Although the state continues to regard home-based care services as supplementing rather than substituting for family care, there is an increasing public demand for augmented public services. Distribution of cash allowance for family care was also rejected at the time of the Long-Term Care Insurance Law's enactment in 1997, partly due to Japanese feminists' opposition that it would lead to fixation of women as care givers and to retardation of public service development. Long and Harris (2000) explore how the aging population, the decreasing number of three-generational households, and women's labor force participation have created an increased demand for men to care for elderly parents and spouses. Hotta (2007) reviews issues regarding homehelpers under the Long-Term Care Insurance system.

Pension reform is another research area. Campbell (1992) focuses on the bureaucracy's role in the pension reform of 1985. Estevez-Abe (2002) examines the interaction among interest groups, bureaucrats, and scholars that have shaped pension reform. Yoshida, Guo, and Cheng (2006) explain the stream-rolled passage of the pension legislation in 2004 with the increase of non-payers and the competition between the LDP and DPJ.

There is also research on organizations serving disabled persons. Nakamura (2002) argues that the Japanese Federation for the Deaf, one of the most powerful disability groups in Japan, has shown organizational flexibility to reap the benefits of cooperating with the state while limiting the loss of their independence. The federation achieves this by splitting its organizational structure between politically independent national organization and prefectural associations with corporate status that allows them to receive government funds for various projects.

Yoda (2002) explores the movement for the rights of people with disabilities, which started in the late 1960s. The movement aimed to liberate disabled persons from institutions and support their rights to independent life. The welfare system for disabled persons also assumes that public assistance is supplementary to care by family members, and therefore the movement has tried to make mothers' burdens lighter in caring for their disabled children. Neary (2000) also writes about the limits of institutions and families in providing quality care to psychiatric patients. Also notable is Stevens's (2007) work on accessibility, which is important for people to exercise full citizenship through participation in political, social, and economic activities. Hasegawa (2007) examines the Japanese employment policy for the disabled, based on the employment quota approach.

Women's Organizations

During the interwar years, growing numbers of women entered professions such as teaching, medicine, nursing, journalism, and social work. They formed women's professional associations to lobby the government to further their interests. Hiratsuka Raichō, Ichikawa Fusae, and others created the *Shin Fujin Kyōkai* (New Women's Association) in 1919 to improve women's political and social freedoms and rights. According to Garon (1997), the state and women's organizations cooperated in various projects, furthering the state's agenda of social work, savings promotion, improving public hygiene, and moral reform. As women assumed more responsibility for war mobilization, leaders in women's associations hoped to receive state support for suffrage and a

larger public role for women (Garon, 1997, 2003; Tomie, 2005).

Women found new rights in the postwar constitution, including suffrage and equality of the sexes. The largely cooperative relationship between the state and women's organizations continued, as they worked together to dissuade women from using the black market and engaged in various social education programs. In recent years, women's organizations have worked with the state to promote recycling and economizing on water and energy. These campaigns have helped serve state goals of reducing dependency on foreign energy sources and encouraging savings (Garon, 2003: 61).

However, the state and women's organizations were divided on prostitution in the prewar period. Women's and Christian organizations participated in the abolitionist movement, advocating human rights, equality of the sexes, and sexual relations only in marriage. The state defended licensed prostitution to manage the economy, military development, social hygiene, sexuality, and gender roles. The state and brothel owners successfully blocked the abolitionists' efforts in the prewar period (Garon, 1997).

After World War II, many women's organizations supported the American occupation and the Japanese state's regulation of prostitution, which included arrests and detainment of prostitutes and other women who the police thought were prostitutes, for medical examination and treatment. Many women's organizations, considering prostitutes as women with a shameful occupation who needed proper moral guidance, worked with the state to enact the 1956 Prostitution Prohibition Law, which primarily focused on criminalizing the selling of sex. This law differed in focus from a United Nations convention in 1949, which prohibited 'exploitation of prostitution' and focused on brothel owners and pimps (Fujime, 2006).

While many scholars highlight the cooperative relationship between women's organizations and the state, there are others that argue that many women are reluctant to cooperate with the state, or reject politics as ineffective in addressing issues that are important to them. LeBlanc (1999), for example, explores the relationship between Japanese housewives and politics. She argues that their role as caretakers restricts them from participating in traditional politics (running in elections), and housewives also perceive that politics seldom touch issues that are close to home. Housewives, with their distinct identity and the 'caring, personalistic, egalitarian ethic,' see the political world as 'stagnant, corrupt, and dominated by men,' and separate politics from 'socially concerned public behavior' in which they engage. Housewives' public participation is therefore characterized by its 'rejection of political routes to social change,' and includes community activities through volunteer groups that focus on person-to-person ties. Martin (2004) also writes that female voters' perception that the political system is unresponsive to the issues that they care about could be why an increasing number of women are independent voters with deepening alienation from politics.

Shin (2004), in her study of the *fufubessei* movement (a family law reform movement to allow women to keep their maiden names in marriage), also finds that participants gather in local, apolitical support groups and wish to 'preserve their space out of reach of the opponents and authorities.' Instead of confronting the state directly, they mostly engage in 'everyday form of resistance,' including not registering their marriage to the state, using their maiden names in daily life, and practicing 'paper divorce.'

While many women reject political routes to change, other women actively engage in politics and seek to increase women's participation in politics. Pharr (1981) specifies the process of 'role redefinition' for women who join political groups: a 'permissive' family environment that enables role experimentation, mothers' often indirect support for role change, and people (usually males) who serve as models for behavior associated with political roles. Pharr also illustrates how women reduce 'role strain' that accompanies their political involvement.

Bochel and Bochel (2005) credit NGO efforts in encouraging and educating women about involvement in politics, for the increasing number of women in local government since the 1980s. They also note the influence of attitudinal changes (falling trust in established male politicians, improving perception of women's political involvement) and greater prominence of issues that concern women (aging population, education, violence against women). Takao (2007) studies the women's grassroots groups' nationwide campaign to elect more women to local assemblies in 1999. His case study suggests that newly elected representatives have served as intermediaries between the nonprofit sector, the local administration, and the business sector in improving the community life and revitalizing the local economy. Gelb and Estevez-Abe (1998) present a case study of the Seikatsusha Network movement, and show that the movement has been successful in recruiting and mobilizing women for local electoral politics. Seikatsu-elected representatives have influenced policy on various issues, and movement groups have become service providers and policy implementers.

Takeda (2006), however, cautions women against emphasizing their maternal role in their movements, as in her three case studies on birth control, anti-nuclear power, and groundwater protection movements. Takeda argues that such an emphasis obscures other lifestyles of women and preserves the current differentiation of political space by gender. Steel (2003, 2004) also questions the effectiveness of organizations' focus on 'women's issues' in mobilizing women's votes. She demonstrates that no significant gender gap exists in the votes for main parties in Lower House elections, because 'women's issues' have no special relevance to women in their voting choice, and membership in community networks does not influence the voting preferences of women.

There is also research on gender equality in employment. Japanese companies are often reluctant to hire women for management or career-track positions. Companies often treat men and women differently in work assignment, training, promotion, evaluation, compensation, and retirement. Moreover, the majority of temporary and part-time workers are women. They often work the same hours as regular workers and stay with the same employers indefinitely, although companies could dismiss them in economic downturns. These factors contribute to women's generally lower status, wage, and benefits than men in their workplace (Upham, 1987; Brinton, 1993; Shire, 2000; Broadbent, 2001; Weathers, 2001a). Upham (1987) argues that 'bureaucratic informalism,' which emphasizes dispute resolution through a bureaucratically controlled mediation system, helps prevent the development of litigation as an effective dispute resolution method. The Ministry of Labor (the Ministry of Health, Labour and Welfare since 2001) took a lead on equal employment opportunity, and created (and appointed members to) the Equal Opportunity Mediation Commission. Fighting employment discrimination in court is difficult. Courts set difficult standards for proving discrimination, and Weathers (2005) reports that there is lack of support for plaintiffs and activists fighting in court. He also argues that women's rights activists lack 'strategic partners'; their relationship with national labor bureaucrats is distant, and enterprise unions remain reluctant to support equal opportunity.

Huen (2007) addresses sexual harassment, another issue related to female workers. She reviews the process that led to the Revised Equal Employment Opportunity Law (EEOL) in 1997 that included a provision on sexual harassment. The Ministry of Labor also issued guidelines for companies to remedy the problem; however, the EEOL leaves implementation to companies and lacks strong sanctions for companies that fail to act. Huen argues that such a soft approach will contribute little in fighting sexual harassment unless social beliefs (gender stereotypes and discrimination) change. Mclean and L'Heureux

(2007) conducted research on NGOs supporting survivors of sexual violence. Despite the recent improvement in relations between the police and NGOs, the Japanese criminal law is traditionally more focused on punishment of offenders than victim care. The authors also write that state support given to the organizations, in funding and other resources, is insufficient.

On gender equality, Osawa (2000) writes that government awareness of gender issues increased in the mid-1990s, as more LDP politicians (pushed by their Social Democratic and Sakigake partners) perceived that gender equality might help improve the economy and counter the falling birth rate. The newly established Council for Gender Equality's vision of creating a gender free society (going beyond gender equality defined as women's rights) was reflected in reform proposals for nursing care, child-rearing, and pensions. However, discourse on traditional values and lack of fiscal commitment have stymied the efforts.

Finally, scholars note the increasingly international orientation of women's movements. Chan-Tiberghien (2004) argues that Japanese women's and children's organizations had a significant impact on legal changes in Japan in the 1990s, with their ability to (1) mobilize around international norms against violence against women and children, (2) educate the public and the government about the norms, and (3) ally with target domestic politicians. Lenz (2006) also identifies women's organizations' international orientation in the 1990s as one of the factors that transformed the women's movements. Other factors include the turn from 'women's issues' to gender concepts, engagement in knowledge politics (creation and distribution of knowledge in the information society), and advocacy for political and legal changes.

Religious Organizations

According to Hardacre (2004), there is no clear consensus on the question whether religious organizations are civil society organizations, due to some of their qualities that distinguish them from other kinds of associations. First, religion and religious practices are perceived as largely private matters without public significance. Second, while membership to other associations is through adults' voluntary decisions, most people affiliate with religious organizations while they are young, through socialization by their parents. Third, religious organizations often have leaders with concentrated authority and power, which may not be the case in other types of associations. Hardacre proposes that religious organizations can be inside or outside of the civil society, depending on their focus at a particular time. On one hand,

when they serve their members' private spiritual needs, they lie outside of the civil society; on the other hand, when they engage in public policy debates and participate in social works, disaster relief, and other activities, they are a part of civil society. Hardacre's research (2005) on religious organizations' participation in the process of constitutional revision is an example of the latter.

Garon (1997) has examined the relationship between religious organizations and the state since the Meiji era. He found that the state enlisted religious organizations' support in providing relief to the poor and orphans, as well as 'reforming' wayward youths and released offenders. Established religious organizations also advocated a strict state regulation of new sects that emerged after World War I. Starting in 1935, the state crushed these charismatic sects with encouragement from established religions and progressive intellectuals. The Religious Organizations Law of 1940 labeled all religious organizations, except Buddhism, *Shintō* sects, and Christianity, as 'pseudo-religions' (Hardacre, 2003: 137).

Garon (1997) also found that once the war against China started, the state relied on religious associations to provide certain services such as collecting donations for the war effort and consoling families of the dead. The authorities also persecuted several Christian groups for their anti-war and anti-military sentiments, rationalized religious associations through mergers of denominations, and urged religious organizations to reconcile the differences between their teachings and State *Shintō*.

The postwar constitution included freedom of religion, and new religions increased in number. The Religious Corporations Law of 1951 gave religious organizations a legal right to own property and businesses, and a special tax status. Religious organizations in the postwar era have resisted attempts to increase state monitoring over them and have enjoyed freedom from state interference as long as they serve the public good (Garon, 1997, 2003: 57–58; Hardacre, 2003: 138).

Hardacre (2003: 138–144) describes the three main sectors that are the Japanese religious world today – the 'established religions' (temple Buddhism, shrine *Shintō*, and Christianity), 'new religions' (including *Sōka Gakkai, Risshō Kōseikai, Reiyūkai Kyōdan, Tenrikyō,* among others), and 'new-new religions' that emerged since the mid-1970s. Distinguishing the three sectors is important because they differ in their history, worldviews, and relationship with society. The public, however, may not always make a clear distinction between them when considering the religious world. Hardacre writes that the religious organizations' position in civil society has been 'significantly undermined' since *Aum Shinrikyō's* attacks in the early 1990s. After the *Aum* incident,

Hardacre (2003: 150–153) observes that there was a shift in public policy preference from safeguarding religious organizations' freedoms to protecting the society (including potential converts) from religious organizations' abuses (see also Shimazono, 1998). Hardacre (2003: 142–144) also writes about the limited and often negative coverage of religion in the media, attributing this to journalists' antagonism towards religion and religious organizations' generally passive reactions to the media attack.

Another area of research is on the state's effort to strengthen regulation of religious organizations after the *Aum* incident. Hardacre reviews *Aum's* development, activities and crimes, and writes that *Aum's* status as a religious corporation, 'which carried the presumption that *Aum* was working for the public good and won it the privileges of autonomous operation, undoubtedly retarded impartial investigation by the police, media, and scholars' (2003: 144–146). Following the *Aum* attacks, the Religious Corporations Law was revised. The revision included state certification of organizations active in more than one prefecture and the opening of financial records for public inspection. Although *Shintō* shrines supported the revision, Catholic and Protestant churches and the United Church of Christ opposed the revision. Oppositions to the strengthened state control reflected concerns about reduction in freedom of religion and separation of church and state. Those opposed also suspected that the state wished to increase control over *Sōka Gakkai* and politically active new religions (Kisala, 1997: 60–74; Hardacre, 2003: 146–150).

Hardacre (2004) has also studied many religious organizations' involvement in peace activism against the New Guidelines Bill in 1999 and the war in Iraq in 2003. She reports that new religions are working with secular civil society organizations, and ties among religious organizations are strengthening. Hardacre argues that although there are limits to religious organizations' engagement in peace activism – the centrality of the priesthood, the difficulties of whole sects adopting political positions, and the dependence on external stimulus – peace activism presents religious organizations with an opportunity to assert their leadership in civil society because peace is a value that unites religion and society.

Ainu

Since the mid-fifteenth century, the Japanese sought control over trade ports and routes in Ainu Mosir (*Ezochi*), and the Meiji state annexed the territory in 1873. The state pursued an aggressive assimilation policy, which included forcible relocation, banning nearly all aspects of Ainu culture and imposition of Japanese names (Lie, 2001; Howell, 2004). After World War II, many Ainu people remained poor with low educational attainment. Although *Ainu Kyōkai* (Ainu Association, later renamed Utari Association) formed in 1930, a Japanese headed it and it operated as an extension of the Hokkaidō government, emphasizing assimilation to Japanese society (Stevens, 2001). External events in the 1960s, such as the rise of the student movement, Burakumin activism, and the global movement of indigenous people, inspired some Ainu people to create new groups and engage in political and cultural activities (Lie, 2001). Furthermore, Ainu activists strengthened their advocacy efforts after the Japanese government denied the existence of the Ainu in its reports to the Human Rights Committee under the International Covenant on Civil and Political Rights in 1980 and 1987 (Neary, 2003). In 1981, an Ainu representative attended the NGO-led World Conference of Indigenous People for the first time, signaling the Ainu people's increasing self-definition as an indigenous people and making them more visible at the international level (Chan-Tiberghien, 2004). The Japanese government included the Ainu people for the first time as a minority in its International Covenant on Civil and Political Rights (ICCPR) report in 1991.

In 1997, the Sapporo District Court found that expropriation of Ainu land and submersion of important religious, cultural, and archeological sites for a dam construction project were illegal under the ICCPR and the Japanese Constitution (Stevens, 2001). The Act for the Promotion of Ainu Culture was also enacted in 1997, and the Hokkaidō Aborigine Protection Act of 1889 was overturned. The latter had forbidden the Ainu people to fish, cut trees, and speak their native language, among other restrictions on their traditional way of living. Despite these events and the state's admission in the 1997 Act that the Ainu's indigenous status 'could not be denied,' the state continues to resist that the indigenous status would form a basis for compensation and articulation of rights (Stevens, 2001; Siddle, 2002; Neary, 2003). Siddle (2002) also argues that the 1997 Act has many shortcomings and has not significantly changed general attitudes about Japanese homogeneity.

Burakumin

The Burakumin are descendents of a former outcaste group. The Burakumin were originally assigned the outcaste status due to their occupation as butchers, tanners, leatherworkers, and executioners, who were ill-regarded in a Buddhist society

(Upham, 1987; Pharr, 1990; Amos, 2007). The Meiji state abolished status distinctions with the Emancipation Edict of 1871, but as a consequence the Burakumin lost their monopoly over occupations, incurring great economic losses. The state neglected services to Burakumin villages, in education, transportation, communications, housing, and other areas. Discrimination in social life and employment continued.

In order to end discrimination and improve their living conditions, young Burakumin formed *Suiheisha* (Leveling Society) in 1922. *Suiheisha* turned away from supplication of the past and adopted *kyūdan* (denunciation) as a strategy. Although the police and courts were unsympathetic to the *Suiheisha's* alliance with the leftist movement, *Suiheisha* achieved some success in institutional change in the 1930s (Upham, 1987: 81–83). In 1946, left-leaning *Suiheisha* and more moderate Burakumin formed what later came to be known as the *Buraku Kaihō Dōmei* (Buraku Liberation League, BLL). In response to the BLL's efforts, the state acknowledged persisting discrimination against the Burakumin in its 1965 Cabinet Dōwa Policy and passed the Special Measures Law for Assimilation Projects in 1969 to improve Buraku residences and neighborhoods (Lie, 2001). The state extended the program several times until its termination in 2002 (Neary, 2003).

Upham (1987) studied the Osaka District Court's acquittal of two BLL defendants in 1969, accused of unlawful imprisonment of three teachers for denunciation. The court affirmed the right of denunciation within acceptable bounds. Denunciation has been effective in fighting discrimination and improving services to the Burakumin, and the Burakumin consider private and public legal redress as unavailable. Upham says, however, that the state endorsement of denunciation over law as the preferred way to fight discrimination is problematic. Upham argues that the state has tried to prevent the development of litigation as an effective means for social change, and reliance on denunciation keeps the question of equality out of the courts despite its relevance to other social groups.

Pharr (1990) researched another case, in which some BLL's student members who wanted a study group on Burakumin problems at school clashed with their teachers in Hyogo in 1974. Pharr's research illuminates the complex political environment in which the BLL operated. The BLL had links with the Japan Socialist Party (JSP), and the teachers were connected to a union allied with the Japan Communist Party (JCP). The two parties had different views on the content of education on Burakumin problems, and competed for leadership in distributing government funding for the Burakumin.

The BLL has also engaged in international activities. It began to attend meetings of the United Nations Commission on Human Rights in 1983, and has networked with international NGOs, such as the Minority Rights Group. In 1988, the BLL also supported the creation of the International Movement against Discrimination and Racism (Neary, 2003; Chan-Tiberghien, 2004).

Resident Koreans

Japan made Korea a protectorate in 1905, and colonized it from 1910 to 1945. During this period, tens of thousands of Koreans migrated to work in Japan. Japan also took thousands of Korean men forcibly to mines, construction sites, and factories in Japan and elsewhere, to work under severe and discriminatory conditions. The consensus among historians is that Japan also forced Korean women into military prostitution, although this is contested by some Japanese scholars and politicians. After World War II, many Koreans repatriated but others stayed in Japan (Kang and Fletcher, 2006). The state denied them Japanese nationality and various rights and opportunities attached to it, making the Koreans in Japan stateless (Morris-Suzuki, 2004, 2006a). In 1965, normalization of diplomatic relations between Japan and South Korea enabled Koreans in Japan to obtain the right of permanent residence in Japan on condition that they apply for South Korean nationality. Those who chose not to acquire the South Korean nationality, approximately 250,000 out of 640,000 in 1974, remained without civil status or overseas travel document until the early 1980s, when international human rights conventions forced the Japanese government to grant permanent residence and re-entry permits without the requirement to obtain South Korean nationality (Ryang, 2000). In 1982, Korean residents also became entitled to national pension and welfare plans as a result of Japan's ratification of the UN Convention Relating to the Status of Refugees, which prohibited discrimination based on nationality.

Two opposing Korean organizations in Japan, *Sōren* (Chongryun) supporting North Korea and *Mindan* supporting South-Korea, dominated the politics of the first generation Korean residents, but they no longer form part of public opinion among Korean residents (Ryang, 2000). According to Chapman (2004), increased integration of later generations into the Japanese society and changing location of identity ('hybridity,' instead of being either Korean or Japanese) explain this shift in power and politics away from the *Sōren* and *Mindan*. Today, the vast majority of resident Koreans are Japan-born, and 90 percent of Korean children attend Japanese schools. Intermarriage and naturalization have increased.

Resident Koreans seek to retain ethnic identity and cultural heritage while securing rights and opportunity as residents in Japan (Kashiwazaki, 2000).

Despite their increased integration into the Japanese society, resident Koreans continue to face social, economic, and political discrimination. Because of their status as foreigners, many are barred from governmental and corporate jobs (Lie, 2001). They are also unable to vote (except in local plebiscite voting in three cities; Chapman, 2004), and often experience discrimination in employment, housing, and marriage. One of the strategies to fight discrimination has been to bring their cases to court. In the Hitachi employment discrimination lawsuit in 1974, the court ruled against Hitachi, which had retracted an employment offer after learning that the prospectus employee was a resident Korean. In 1995, the Supreme Court also ruled that resident Koreans were not entitled to vote in local elections, but suggested that a law that would allow them to vote would not be unconstitutional (Neary, 2003). Resident Koreans have also brought cases on public housing discrimination, lack of eligibility for government jobs, and discriminatory access to higher education (Takao, 2003).

Another key effort was the anti-fingerprinting movement in the 1980s, which led to the repeal of fingerprinting requirement for permanent residents in 1992. An umbrella organization of resident Korean civil rights groups, *Mintōren* (the League to Fight Ethnic/National Discrimination) played a central role in this movement, although individual refusals to fingerprint at the local level were important (Wender, 2000). Many grassroots groups and local governments also supported the movement. Strausz (2006) argues, however, that the success of this movement and Japan's policy responses that improved the lot of resident Koreans have made it more difficult for resident Koreans to organize social movements.

Organizations representing the Ainu, Burakumin, and resident Koreans have worked together to fight discrimination. With Okinawan, migrant, and women's groups, they formed a NGO coalition Durban 2001 Japan, to pursue common goals for mobilization at the World Conference against Racism. The coalition's three goals were the enactment of an anti-discrimination law in Japan, the creation of an independent national human rights protection machinery, and the development of an individual complaint procedure for the International Convention on the Elimination of All Forms of Racial Discrimination (ICERD) (Chan-Tiberghien, 2004).

Foreigners in Japan

There have been several waves of postwar foreign migration to Japan. Morris-Suzuki (2006b)

examines illegal migration from Korea between 1946 and 1970s. In the late 1940s and 1950s, most immigrants were former Korean residents in Japan who reentered after repatriation, or Koreans escaping the disruptions of the Korean War. Starting in the late 1950s, Korean migrants came for better-paid employment opportunities. Morris-Suzuki (2006b) argues that the official responses to the illegal migrants in the early postwar era, which consisted of highly restrictive controls and great administrative discretion, had a lasting impact on Japan's migration and border control policies.

Since then, people from other states have arrived. First, women from South East and East Asia, who mostly worked (or were forced to work) in the entertainment and sex industries, dominated migration between the late 1970s to mid-1980s. Next, between the mid-1980s to 1990, male workers from Iran, Pakistan, Bangladesh, the Philippines, China, Malaysia, Thailand, and South Korea arrived and took low-skilled jobs. Finally, South Americans of Japanese descent arrived after the revision of the Immigration Control Act in 1990, which made it legal for them to live and work in Japan (Chan-Tiberghien, 2004).

Takao argues that Japanese local governments have played an important role in promoting foreigners' rights because 'the state's inability to manage international migration leaves it up to local communities to deal with the increasing presence of foreigners' needs' (Takao, 2003: 531). Despite the state's opposition, many local governments have extended insurance and medical services to all foreigners, and eliminated the nationality clause for hiring city employees.

Many civil society organizations have also offered support to foreigners. According to Shipper (2006), Christian NGOs were the first to organize support groups for foreign migrant workers in the mid-1980s. Since then, other civil society groups have joined the effort (community workers' unions, women's support groups, medical NGOs, lawyers' NGOs, and concerned citizens groups). The NPO Law of 1998 encouraged groups that provide social welfare services to the foreigners (womens' support groups and medical NGOs) to obtain NPO status and deepen their cooperation with local governments.

Civil society organizations have also worked internationally. For example, they have mobilized around the 1990 Convention on the Rights of Migrants, although Japan has not ratified it. The National Network in Solidarity with Migrant Workers, formed in 1997 with more than 89 Japanese and international NGOs, became part of the Migration and Refugees NGO Caucus in the 2001 World Conference against Racism (Chan-Tiberghien, 2004).

In several cities and prefectures, representative foreigners serve on foreigners' assemblies to discuss the various challenges that they face in Japan, including discriminatory practices related to employment, medical care, housing, and education. Foreigners' assemblies are advisory panels to local governments and prefectures, and their decisions are not legally binding. Han (2004) writes that the establishment of these assemblies was through bureaucratic initiatives. Advocates appealed not directly to international human rights norms but to the ideal of the territorially based local community that encompassed all residents within its boundary. This ideal served to counter the concept of the ethnically based community. Han also writes that some foreigners' assemblies have debated local voting rights, but could not reach a consensus.

Since the mid-1990s, several foreign residents have also fought discrimination in courts. In November 1999 and November 2000, foreign residents won cases against private businesses that refused them entry because they were foreigners.

There is some research on education for foreign children. Aoki (2000) points out that Japanese school textbooks tend to emphasize 'our' (*watashitachino*), as in 'our national language,' 'our nation-state,' and 'our history.' Such emphasis ignores the fact that there are non-Japanese children in the classroom. Burgess (2007) writes that 80 percent of schools with four or fewer students who need Japanese instruction do not qualify for state assistance, such as dispatch of special teachers. In non-urban areas, where the concentration of foreign students is lower, support for them tends to come from volunteer groups.

Several scholars have studied issues related to illegal foreigners in Japan. Shipper (2005) argues that some politicians and police officials construct negative images of illegal foreigners as criminals and potentially dangerous, while taking crime statistics out of their social and demographic contexts. In contrast, activists in foreigner support groups portray illegal foreigners as victims by disseminating information about maltreatment of illegal foreigners by Japanese officials, employers, and husbands, as well as lack of access to medical treatment. Shipper writes that this contest over the image of illegal foreigners in the media and other publications has produced a mixed public opinion in the 1990s, which shows an increasing association of illegal foreigners and criminality, as well as a rise in the perception of illegal foreigners as victims without basic rights.

Stevens, Lee, and Sawada (2000) write that undocumented migrant mothers and children underutilize health and welfare services available to them because they fear that their illegal status would be discovered. The authors argue that volunteer groups serve as important mediators between the undocumented mothers and public service providers.

Liu-Farrer (2008) examines the problem of student visa overstay among the Fujian Chinese in Japan, and argues that social capital that facilitates migration and secures the livelihood for immigrants can prohibit their upward mobility in Japan. According to Liu-Farrer, the debts that the students incur in the migration process make continuing education difficult due to forgone working hours. Furthermore, there is a norm that positively sanctions undocumented immigrants among the Fujian Chinese social network. Families in China may expect remittances, and being undocumented is not considered shameful. Liu-Farrer (2008) shows that those who are not undocumented tend to have alternative resources and social support from family and churches that make them more detached from the typical Fujian immigrant networks.

Finally, Flowers (2008) examines Japan's refugee policy. She argues that despite some positive changes (for example, a Japanese UN High Commissioner for Refugees, the growth of civil society, and reduced structural constraints for NGOs to influence state policy), NGOs have not had a significant impact on the reform of refugee policies toward greater compliance with international norms of protection. Flowers writes that this is due to NGOs' lack of legitimacy and authority, as well as the Ministry of Justice's conservative organizational culture, that hinder NGO access to policymaking.

Consumer Organizations

According to Maclachlan, the consumer movement has pressured and worked with the state and business to better guarantee 'consumer's rights to product safety and choice, access to consumer information, representation in governmental decision making, and, more recently, redress for consumer-related damages' (Maclachlan, 2003: 226).

In the immediate postwar period, the consumer movement – with a structural overlap with the women's movement – focused on improving people's material well-being, including food, clothing, and shelter. The movement fought against price gouging and other negative effects of the black market, and taught women about household accounting and child-rearing methods (Maclachlan, 2003: 217–222). Maclachlan writes that a holistic consumer identity emerged in this period, which was simultaneously:

(1) a human being in pursuit of survival and well-being, (2) a worker or small producer (or the spouse or dependent of a worker or producer), (3) a

consumer who purchases and consumes goods and services in the marketplace, (4) a citizen of a particular country (*kokumin*), or 'nationalist,' and, (5) a citizen (*shimin*) of civil society (Maclachlan 2003: 219–220; see also Maclachlan, 2004; Vogel, 1999).

This holistic consumer identity permitted the consumer movement's combination of protest against the state and market actors on one hand and selective cooperation with those actors on the other. The movement gained legitimacy and financial resources through cooperation with the state and business, when possible (Machlachlan, 2003: 221–223).

Consumer groups proliferated in the 1960s and 1970s, but consumer protection was 'approached primarily as an obligation of a paternalistic government' (Maclachlan, 2003: 226). However, the state tended to prioritize producers' interests over those of consumers in the high economic growth period. Business also had stronger ties with the state, and had more influence on policymaking. The 1968 Consumer Protection Basic Law, therefore, makes no mention of consumer rights. Consumer policies also shield producers from negative effects of consumer protection (Maclachlan, 2003: 227–228). The 1994 Products Liability Law, for example, expanded a network of low-cost alternative dispute resolution facilities that are situated within the bureaucracy and the business sector, and are closed to public scrutiny. This deflects products liability cases away from the courts, leaving consumer protection up to pro-producer interests (Maclachlan, 1999, 2003: 228).

Despite the laws' shortcomings, the consumer movement without many resources and with a limited access to policymaking was still instrumental in strengthening Japan's antitrust regulations and in enacting stringent food safety standards and a product liability law. Maclachlan (2002a) argues that consumer representatives, faced with obstacles at the national level, focused on forging alternative channels of interest articulation at the local level, where there are more institutional opportunities for political participation. The rise of progressive local governments following the spread of environmental activism in the 1960s was important in creating the channels. Many local officials and politicians have embraced consumer rights and helped enact local ordinances. Prefectures often consult consumer representatives on consumer-related policies and accept them as equal participants in local advisory councils (Maclachlan, 2003: 228–229). Consumer representatives activated these local channels and mobilized public opinion behind specific policy options to pressure national policymakers. When the alliance of conservative politicians, bureaucrats, and business representatives is disorganized (with conflict and indecision) and the

decision-making process among them is diffuse, the movement-activated public opinion was able to influence policy. When there is consensus in the pro-producer alliance, however, the consumer movement and public opinion have had little impact on policy (Maclachlan, 2002a).

Since the end of LDP dominance in 1993, the government-business relationship has weakened and the state has become more attentive to consumer needs. Consumer organizations are thus devoting more time to lobbying politicians (Maclachlan, 2002a: 242–247). In addition, the Consumer Agency (*Shōhisha Chō*) started its operations in October 2009. Consumer organizations are also establishing new networks. For example, consumer and environmental organizations are working together to encourage consumers to become 'environment friendly' (Yamaoka, 1998: 52–53). Consumer and other citizen groups also pressured the government for the enactment of the Information Disclosure Law in 1999. Maclachlan (2002a) notes that the consumer organizations' participation in the campaign suggests that they are increasingly working towards attaining good governance and enhanced citizen participation in national politics. However, consumer organizations also continue to face challenges, such as curtailment in national budget for consumer centers in response to economic recession and regulatory and administrative reforms (Maclachlan, 2002a: 249; Maclachlan, 2002b).

One example of consumer organizations is Seikatsu Club Consumers' Cooperative and its political wing the *Nettowaku* (Netto). Seikatsu founder Iwane Kunio started the club as a milk buying cooperative in 1965, with the ultimate aim of mobilizing greater suburban support for his progressive policy concerns (LeBlanc, 1999: 127–128; Bouissou, 2000). Over time, the club evolved into the full co-op with over 240,000 members nationwide, who support the club's vision of consuming safe, environmentally friendly and mostly domestically produced goods.

Gelb and Estevez-Abe (1998) argue that the Seikatsu movement has been successful in recruiting and mobilizing women for local electoral politics. LeBlanc points out that their candidacy as ordinary housewives highlights their criticism of traditional politics:

> Their association with housewifery is simultaneously a criticism of hierarchy, of large, impersonal organizations, of the pursuit of a politics of interest over a politics of compassion, of the absence of communal values, and of a lack of willingness to work hard for one's achievements (LeBlanc, 1999: 150).

Seikatsu-elected representatives have influenced policy on various issues, and movement groups have become service providers and policy implementers. However, scholars point to some potential challenges for the Netto's growth. LeBlanc (1999) says that as the Netto movement grows, it would need a larger organizational structure to support it. However, women who participate in the movement 'often see that sort of growth as a challenge to their housewife identities and to the anti-elite, anti-organizational ethic bound up with those identities' (LeBlanc, 1999; 151). Gelb and Estevez-Abe (1998) also write that the Netto's commitment to electoral rotation (representatives must resign their seats after two mandates) and income sharing may limit the growth of female professional politicians arising from the movement.

In the aftermath of the Tōhoku Earthquake of March 2011, the Japanese Consumers' Cooperative Union delivered relief materials swiftly. The co-op has agreements with 46 prefectures and 310 local governments to help provide relief in case of natural disasters. These agreements allowed the co-op to react quickly to the disaster in Tōhoku (Kawato et al., 2012: 88).

Environmental Organizations

In Europe and the United States, organizations that engage in nature conservation and wildlife preservation compose most of the environmental organizations (Dunlap and Mertig, 1992). However, in Japan, organizations representing pollution victims and engaging in anti-development movements mainly compose environmental organizations, despite the increasing diversity of organizations in recent years (Iijima, 2000). Although there are organizations like the Wild Bird Society of Japan that engage in nature conservation, and national trust movements to protect Shiretoko and Shirakami Sanchi, they are not the most typical Japanese environmental organizations (Yamaoka, 1998: 50–52).

In prewar Japan, mines that discharged polluted water and chemicals caused the most important environmental problems (Iijima, 2000). The most famous case is the *Ashio Dōzan* incident in the late 1800s in which a copper mine released poisonous waste water and smoke, causing health problems, deforestation, floods, and damages to crops. In the postwar period, the state continued to prioritize economic development over environmental protection. Rapid urbanization, industrialization, and infrastructure development caused environmental destruction. The state imposed virtually no restrictions on pollution until the mid-1960s (Broadbent, 2002: 295), and Japan became the world's most polluted country in the 1950s (Schreurs, 2002: 36). Serious pollution problems emerged, including the 'four big pollution diseases' of Minamata mercury

poisoning in Kumamoto (publicly acknowledged in 1954), Niigata mercury poisoning (1965), 'Itai-itai' cadmium poisoning in Toyama (1968), and Yokkaichi asthma in Mie (1973).

In these four cases, victims faced denial of corporate responsibility by the polluting companies, local politicians, and state bureaucrats. Many people in their communities were also unsympathetic, partly due to the perceived importance of the companies as employers. Victims and their supporters were discredited as left-wing radicals (Ui, 1968; Iijima, 1970; McKean, 1981; Upham, 1987; Schreurs, 2002). However, the media shaped the broader public's perception of pollution as a severe social problem by disseminating information about these cases and images of disabled victims (Broadbent, 2002: 306, Schreurs, 2002: 42). Small, local protest movements against industrial pollution and pollution-related health problems emerged throughout Japan in the 1960s (Ui, 1968; Miyamoto, 1970; Schreurs, 2002). These movements, however, mostly took a 'not in my backyard' stance, paying little attention to problems in other communities or to protection of the environment for its own sake (Krauss and Simcock, 1980: 198; Broadbent, 2002: 302–303, 307). Avenell (2006) argues that the movements' emphasis on achieving local autonomy produced this 'strategy of residential activism,' which was an autonomous, non-aligned activism willing to use any useful resource regardless of the conservative-progressive political divide.

Media reports about pollution and its negative health effects contributed to the rise of some movements against new industrial development (Krauss and Simcock, 1980: 194–195). Residents of Numazu city, Mishima city, and Shimizu *chō* in Shizuoka prevented an establishment of a petrochemical complex by organizing movements in 1963-1964 (Lewis, 1980). In the midst of high economic growth, these residents prioritized the protection of living and natural environment over the potential economic benefits. In addition, various sectors of the population, including those engaging in agriculture and fishing, housewives, professionals, and laborers participated in the movement (Iijima, 2000). This type of movement against large-scale industrial development took place also in Tomakomai city in Hokkaidō (Motojima and Shoji, 1980), Oita (Broadbent, 1998), and Rokkasho village in Aomori (Funabashi, Hasegawa, and Iijima, 1998). Furthermore, pollution victims and their supporters organized lawsuits in the late 1960s. In 1967, victims of Niigata Minamata disease started a lawsuit against the polluting company. Cases brought by victims of Itai-itai disease, Yokkaichi asthma, and Minamata disease followed, and they all won their cases with large damage settlements in the early 1970s.

The state was ill equipped to deal with pollution issues (Schreurs, 2002: 42), but responded to large protests with various measures between the mid-1960s and the mid-1970s. In 1965, the Ministry of International Trade and Industry (MITI) began to use its administrative guidance to encourage industries to install tall smokestacks, use low-sulfur fuels, and build greenbelts between new industrial zones and residential areas (Broadbent, 2002: 309). From 1965, prefectures under state guidance also started to enter into informal pollution control agreements with local factories, at times creating more stringent pollution control standards than existed at the national level (Schreurs, 2002: 72–73). In 1967, the Basic Law for Pollution Control was established.

The state wished to defuse protests with the Basic Law, but the mostly symbolic law legitimized citizen concerns and triggered even more protests (Broadbent, 2002: 311). Local environmental movements elected many opposition-party affiliated candidates on pollution control platforms in mayoral and gubernatorial elections. The LDP began to fear a similar electoral defeat in national elections (Schreurs, 2002: 41). In response, business compromised to assure the LDP's hegemony (Broadbent, 1998). The 'Pollution Diet' (*kōgai kokkai*) established 14 laws related to pollution towards the end of 1970, including measures for polluters' compensation to victims and mediated dispute resolution (Upham, 1987). In 1971, the Environmental Agency (current Ministry of the Environment) was established, although it had little regulatory power and funding. Its proposals, including mandatory environmental impact assessment based on local citizen participation for all large-scale public and private projects, also met opposition from the MITI, LDP, and industries (Broadbent, 2002: 314–317). Nevertheless, the state subsidized industry's acquisition of pollution technology and equipment, significantly improving air and water pollution. Protests subsided after 1973, without leaving behind strong, national, institutionalized environmental NGOs (Broadbent, 2002: 321; Schreurs, 2002: 70–71, 89; Pekkanen, 2006). With the decline of protests and the number of progressive local officials, the Environmental Agency's effectiveness and the new laws' enforcement also declined (Broadbent, 1998: 341–342, Schreurs, 2002: 75–76).

State responses up to the early 1970s dealt with the most visible air, water, and other pollution that threatened public health and electoral defeats for the LDP. The state did little for invisible and long-term pollutants, such as toxic waste, or problems associated with parks, noise, and crowding, which had not gathered enough public attention to cause large protests (Broadbent, 2002: 323). However, protest movements against high-speed transportation, including *shinkansen* (bullet trains) and airplanes – sources of noise and vibrations – emerged in the 1970s (Funabashi et al., 1985; Groth, 1996). Lawsuits were organized in these movements, although they illustrated the limits of legal remedy (Hasegawa, 2003; see also Upham, 1987; Stevens, 2001). While contending parties in industrial pollution cases were pollution victims and polluting companies, in high-speed transportation cases the defendants were public administrations and the focus was on defining what consists *kōkyōsei* (public interest). Defendants emphasized the social necessity of high-speed transportation. Plaintiffs argued that they must be a part of the decision-making process and that their basic human rights and preferences on projects must be taken into account (Funabashi et al., 1985; Hasegawa, 2003).

In the 1980s, new types of environmental activism emerged, such as conservation of architecture and other unique characteristics of neighborhoods (*machinami hozon*) and conservation of views (*keikan hozen*) (Yamaoka, 1998: 49–50; Katagiri, 2000). Groups also engaged 'life pollution (*seikatsu kōgai*)' and consumer pollution problems. These problems involve polluting products, such as synthetic detergents and studded tires, which make consumers both causes and victims of environmental problems (Hasegawa, 2003). In general, environmental activism's focus shifted from organizing protests, to 'everyday environmentalism,' such as recycling, organic farming, and educational activities (Reimann, 2001: 70).

In 1993, opposition parties won control of the Lower House and the coalition government started new environmental initiatives. The Basic Environmental Law was revised in 1993 and the Basic Environmental Plan was established in 1994, calling for joint efforts of government, citizens, NGOs, and business. More environmental NGOs were established in this period and they gained more legitimacy. More international NGOs also entered Japan. NGOs have built stronger links with government and business-based environmental organizations (Broadbent, 2002: 333–336; Schreurs, 2002: 221). Some environmental organizations have also worked with the state to promote conservation and restrain mass consumption. Such campaigns help serve state goals of reducing dependency on foreign energy sources and encouraging savings (Garon, 2003: 61).

Since the mid-1990s, public concerns about toxic chemicals (dioxin, PCBs) and accidents at several nuclear plants have triggered some environmental protests. The state established new laws for waste disposal and business associations announced measures for environmental protection, including a voluntary plan to reduce greenhouse gas and to acquire ISO 14001 certification (Broadbent, 2002: 337–338; Schreurs, 2002: 222–223). In recent years, communication between NGOs and industry has also increased, through environmental seminars, employees in major corporations becoming members of environmental networks, and funding to NGOs from corporations and foundations (Schreurs, 2002: 222–225).

Finally, attention on the global environment has increased since the late 1980s. Environmental protection emerged as an important international issue leading up to the 1992 Earth Summit. Environmental NPOs and NGOs became active, and an environmental NGOs' coalition Kiko Forum played a key part in the Kyoto conference on climate change in 1997 (Takeuchi, 1998; Schreurs, 2002: 220). The coalition lobbied governments for higher greenhouse gas emission reduction targets, monitored the negotiation processes and agreements, and provided information to the media and the public. Reimann (2001) shows how international processes (international opportunities, transnational diffusion of ideas and tactics, and international socialization of state actors) provided new external resources for Kiko Forum activists to overcome domestic barriers. Japanese environmental NGOs may be less integrated into the policymaking process than in some other states (Foljanty-Jost, 2005), but they have more access to the process than ever before.

NGOs have worked on other international environmental issues. For example, NGOs stopped Mitsubishi's plan to build a salt plant in a Mexican bay, which gray whales use as a nursery. NGOs also lobbied the Japanese government to withdraw its support for World Bank funding for a dam in India (Broadbent, 2002: 336). NGOs working abroad have also received funding and training from the Ministry of Foreign Affairs (Schreurs, 2002: 225).

Agricultural Cooperatives and Business Associations

Agricultural cooperatives (*nōkyō*) and business associations are market actors that many scholars do not recognize as civil society organizations. Some scholars argue otherwise for two reasons. First, these economic interest groups can also participate in social and political activities. For example, Bullock writes that *nōkyō* (one of the largest mass-membership organizations in Japan with 99 percent of farmers as members) and small retail (largest and most politically active subcategory of small business) are 'central to local community life in Japan, helping to organize festivals, sponsor youth groups and culture circles, settle disputes, implement state policy, and direct political action' (Bullock, 2003: 176). Bullock also says that these organizations are capable of independent action and have resisted *amakudari* appointments (on *amakudari*; Colignon and Usui, 2001). Second, scholars argue that it is important to study economic interest groups as a subset of civil society organizations in order to highlight their differences from other groups. Tsujinaka and Pekkanen (2007) demonstrate that economic interest groups (industry associations, professional groups, labor unions, and agricultural cooperatives) have more resources (budget and staff) and more access to policymaking (especially through bureaucracies) than other civil society organizations. In this section, we will review the literature on *nōkyō* and business associations. The next section reviews labor unions.

Nōkyō has served as one of the main social bases of conservative rule since the 1950s. Farmers, however, had not always supported political conservatives. In the interwar period, farmers engaged in large protests to demand rent reductions for the land they tilled and improvements in other conditions. Their protests peaked around 1920. Furthermore, according to Babb (2005), farmers originally supported the Japan Socialist Party in the postwar era; however, the socialist grip on farmers weakened due to fragmentation among the socialists and competition for power with the communists and conservatives. Once back in power after a period of socialist rule, conservatives offered helpful policy to *nōkyō*, including loans and subsidies. This happened as a part of reorganizing the agricultural cooperatives to form a more centralized and dependent system, leading to the conservative capture of the farmers. Since then, *nōkyō* has been the LDP's valuable support base for elections due to its numbers, high turnout, stable conservative support over time, organizational strength, and bloc-like voting behavior (Bullock, 2003: 175).

However, *nōkyō's* support for the LDP remains conditional on the provision of subsidies and market protection (Bullock, 2003: 182). Given the state's recent cuts in subsidies and shift from protectionist agricultural policies towards an agricultural export promotion policy, *nōkyō's* continued support for the LDP is in question. Sasada (2008) argues that the electoral reform of 1994 – which moderated malapportionment and made receiving support from a broader constituency more important than serving particularistic interests – changed legislators' incentives and led to the export promotion policy. The export promotion policy is more likely to win support from the general public than a protectionist policy because it encourages farmers' self-sufficiency and competitiveness, and aims to stimulate rural economy and reduce the income gap between cities and the countryside.

According to Mulgan (2005: 264), *nōkyō's* organizational power is diminishing due to the general decline in the number of farmers and increasing number of farmers going outside *nōkyō* to sell their products and purchase farm inputs. Goudo (2006) also argues that *nōkyō's* political power has declined due to liberalization in finance and circulation of agricultural products, decline in the number of farming population, and public opinion that is critical of public works. However, *nōkyō* still maintains strong ties with the LDP and relevant ministries to influence policy. Mulgan also writes that *nōkyō* has networked with foreign agricultural groups that share its policy preference against trade liberalization. In addition, *Nōkyō* has engaged in public relations efforts in Japan, pointing out common interests with consumers (food safety, food self-sufficiency, conservation of natural resources and traditional cultures) in order to gather public support (Mulgan, 2005: 293–296).

After the nuclear accident of March 2011, the Central Union of Agricultural Cooperatives collected information from *nōkyō* in different prefectures about damages caused by the accident, and represented them in negotiations over compensation from the Tokyo Electric Power company and the government. *Nōkyō* sought compensation for reduced sales due to bans on selling nuclear-contaminated products and rumors of contamination, as well as for restrictions preventing many farmers from planting crops (Kawato et al., 2012: 88–89).

Business associations also supported the LDP in the post-World War II period, laying the foundation for Japan's evolution as the developmental state. Today, business associations constitute a plurality (about 40 percent) of all associational establishments and have more than 40 percent of all associational income (Tsujinaka, 2003: 114). Businesses are organized under a peak association, the Federation of Economic Organizations (*keidanren*). Under the *keidanren* are numerous industrial-sector associations that represent the sectors' interests. *Keidanren's* membership consists of about 1300 leading enterprises and 130 industrial associations (Yoshimatsu, 2005: 259). *Keidanren* has enabled business to coordinate action in relation to both the state and civil society. Yoshimatsu (2005) demonstrates that *keidanren* played an important part in defining the scope and content of Japan's free trade agreements with Singapore, Mexico, and South Korea by coordinating business's interests and communicating them to government officials. Although *keidanren* and the state have often collaborated to secure producers' interests when faced with challenges from the civil society (Broadbent, 1998: Maclachlan, 1999), *keidanren* has recently established the '1 percent Club,' inviting member companies to pledge a donation of at least 1 percent of their pretax profit for charitable purposes (Amenomori and Yamamoto, 1998: 1).

Next, while policy cooperation between business, conservative politicians, and the bureaucracy have resulted in many protectionist measures for uncompetitive industries, Saadia Pekkanen (2001) argues that the bureaucracy is increasingly relying on international legal rules through the World Trade Organization (WTO) to reject industries' demands for protection. Pekkanen demonstrates that bureaucrats have stressed the importance of upholding international legal obligations and the inevitability of WTO-authorized retaliation to legitimate their claims against protectionist measures for some domestic industries like textiles and *shōchū*. Meanwhile, politically influential sectoral interests, such as automobiles and steel, have successfully lobbied the bureaucracy to initiate WTO complaints on their behalf (Pekkanen, 2003).

Unlike larger businesses and industries, small business associations are not organized under a peak association. Bullock (2003: 183) estimates that there are 'hundreds, even thousands,' of small business organizations. In his study of coalition formation and change, Bullock focuses on small retailers. According to Bullock, the coalition of big business, the bureaucracy and the conservative politicians relied on urban small businesses as a mass base since the 1950s (Bullock, 2003: 179). However, small retailers were 'squeezed out of the coalition' in the 1990s, as small-business protection through the Large Stores Law – which imposed barriers to entry on large retail operations – became too costly for big-business interests (Bullock, 2003: 176, 189–192). As junior members to the conservative coalition, small retail lost to big business when they had zero-sum interests. As a result, small businesspeople have been turning away from the LDP towards opposition parties, especially the JCP (Bullock, 2003: 193).

Labor Unions

Due to labor unions' primary objective of defending workers' economic interests, some question if they are part of the 'non-market' civil society organizations; however, labor unions participate in political debates – their opposition to the United States–Japan security treaty in 1960 is an example. They also organize social events for their members. Indeed, Suzuki (2003: 195) notes that unions 'can offer a rich associational life for their members by performing political and social as well as purely economic functions,' although in Japan they have failed to become important civil society actors because their associational life has become 'dominated by and incorporated into corporate society' (Suzuki, 2003: 195).

In 2007, there were 27,226 labor unions and over ten million union members in Japan. Rate of unionization was 18.1 percent (Ministry of Health, Labour and Welfare, 2007). However, the numbers of unions and union members have continued to decline. Most Japanese unions are enterprise unions, with autonomy to negotiate with employers on wages and working conditions. Enterprise unions from the same industry come together in federations, and industry federations form national confederations. The enterprise union structure makes Japanese labor organization different from those in Europe and the United States (Olson, 1982; Igarashi, 1998). The strength of enterprise unions also tends to make labor cooperative to management, with an assumption that improvement in companies' productivity would benefit labor (Kume, 2005).

Although enterprise unions have considerable amount of autonomy, industry and national-level labor organizations are active. An important example is the annual Spring Labor Offensive (*shuntō*), in which industry and national-level organizations coordinate wage negotiations among their member unions. Since the 1980s, national-level confederations have also made efforts to influence political decision-making. The Japanese Trade Union Confederation (*Rengō*), a comprehensive labor organization, was established with this aim in 1989.

The first national confederation, the Japan General Federation of Labor (*Sōdōmei*, former *Yūaikai*) was established in 1921, following over 100 labor disputes between 1900 and 1920 (Gordon, 1991). A fierce dispute over the movement's direction divided labor between social democratic line of labor-management cooperation and communist emphasis on revolutionary militancy. Although the state did not legally recognize unions, it tacitly acknowledged moderate unions as a means of managing social unrest, and severely repressed radical unions with the Maintenance of the Public Order Act and other laws (Garon, 1987; Suzuki, 2003: 196). The authorities dissolved trade unions after 1938 and established the Greater Japan Industrial Patriotic Association to coordinate wartime production.

In the postwar era, the Labor Union Law of 1945 and return of socialist and communist activists led to many unions' establishment (Gordon, 1998). Unionization rate peaked at 55.8 percent in 1949 (Suzuki, 2003: 196). The communist-dominated Japan Council of Industrial Labor Unions (*Sanbetsu*) played a central part in the labor movement, but repression of the '2–1 general strike' and the Red Purge in 1950 weakened the leftist labor movement. Since then, labor activities continued mostly at the industry level, until the anti-communist General Council of Trade Unions of Japan (*Sōhyō*) was established in

1951 and led the labor movement. Socialists soon dominated *Sōhyō*, however. *Sōhyō* became the Socialist Party's strong support base, and secured political access through the party (Shinkawa, 1999). *Sōhyō's* capture by the socialists triggered conservative union leaders to establish the Japanese Trade Union Congress (*Zenrō*) in 1954. *Sōhyō* advocated class-based militancy and *Zenrō* advocated cooperative labor-management relations (Suzuki, 2003: 196).

In the early 1950s, labor movement became active in opposition to the intensified production for the Korean War. A prolonged labor dispute against the Mitsui Miike mine in 1959, and the struggle against the United States–Japan security treaty in 1960 were also significant, but these struggles ended in labor's defeat (Hirai, 2000). Since Mitsui Miike's union was a key member of *Sōhyō*, the defeat greatly undermined *Sōhyō's* influence. Nevertheless, some argue that the labor organizations in this period formed a social movement and thus functioned as civil society organizations (Shinoda, 2005).

In the high economic growth period, labor movement shifted its emphasis from political and ideological struggles towards struggles to improve workers' standard of living. The Spring Labor Offensive was introduced in 1955. In this period, the Japanese Confederation of Labor (*Dōmei*, successor of *Zenrō*), *Shin Sanbetsu* (New *Sanbetsu*), and *Chūritsu Rōren* were also established in competition with *Sōhyō*, ushering in the 'Four Labor Union Period' (Igarashi, 1998).

During the 1960s, militant political unionism gave way to cooperative economic unionism (neo-corporatism) (Suzuki, 2000). *Sōhyō's* influence declined, and after a move to unify labor by uniting *Sōhyō* and *Dōmei*, *Rengō* was established in 1989. Since then, labor organizations developed close relations and contacts, not only with progressive parties like the Socialist and Communist Parties, but also with the LDP and bureaucrats (Igarashi, 1998). Kume (1998) argues that this was partly due to the ruling LDP's labor union strategy, which improved the political opportunity structure for unions.

In comparative politics, Japan was characterized as 'corporatism without labor' in the late 1970s, highlighting the weakness of labor unions' influence in the policymaking process (Pempel and Tsunekawa, 1979). However, since the 1980s labor organizations have participated in the policymaking process through policy deliberation councils (*shingikai*) (Tsujinaka, 1987), signaling a move towards neo-corporatism (Inagami et al., 1994). However, some argue that 'limited corporatism' better describes the situation due to labor's limited political influence (Inagami et al., 1994; Igarashi, 1998).

Rengō has continued labor's engagement in the policy processes; however, by participating in the establishment of the non-LDP coalition government in 1993, it shifted its strategy towards 'political democracy' through political reorganization (Shinoda, 1996). Then, following the change in government, it has shifted the strategy towards 'industrial democracy' through lobbying the LDP and bureaucrats. *Rengō* has moved back and forth between these two strategies since then (Igarashi, 1998).

Although labor organizations have increased its involvement in the political decision-making process since the 1980s, their influence remains limited. Since the economic recession of the 1990s, the unions have failed to protect jobs and real incomes (Weathers, 2001b). Moreover, following the political reorganization and reforms in the 1990s, the policymaking process's character shifted from encouraging consensus building to majority rule, and from focus on policy deliberation councils to political parties. With this change, labor organizations' political influence declined (Miura, 2007; Nakakita, 2009). Union membership continues to fall and some argue that the existence of labor organizations is at risk. In addition, neoliberal economic policy has increased wage disparity as well as part-time and temporary workers, making union members more diverse in terms of employment status, gender, and age (Suzuki, 2003: 212). Some argue that unions, which have mostly represented full-time, permanent, and male workers at the enterprise level, are not suited to represent a more diverse labor force (Shinoda, 2005). Labor organizations have emerged outside enterprises to serve the interests of certain categories of workers such as women and middle managers (Suzuki, 2003: 213; Broadbent, 2005; Nakakita, 2009).

Protests and Citizen Movements

Between the establishment of the 1955 system and the 1960 United States–Japan security treaty, there were many 'popular disturbances' and 'mass movements' (Takabatake, 1977; Sugimoto, 1981; on prewar protests see Lewis, 1990). Mostly in support of progressive political parties, they were anti-war and peace movements supporting the 'Peace Constitution' and opposing the reverse course on postwar reforms. They also opposed nuclear and expansion of an American military base in Sunagawa (current Tachikawa-shi). Furthermore, protests against the government's attempt to strengthen the Police Duties Execution Law (which was perceived as the state's effort to increase its control over labor and other movement organizations) forced the state to cancel the plan.

In 1960, massive protests tried to block the revision of the United States–Japan security treaty, marking the peak of the progressive movement. Takabatake (1977) writes, however, that the explosive protest was not due to the revision of the treaty per se, but due to the public's perception that Prime Minister Kishi Nobusuke had violated the democratic process by expelling opposition party members from the parliament to forcibly ratify the treaty. Takabatake argues that the Socialist Party and *Sōhyō* led this 'mass movement' made up of various organizations. The Communist Alliance (Bund) also actively participated in the protests (Otake, 2007). Sasaki-Uemura (2001), however, writes that most protesters did not adhere to Marxist ideology, and grassroots groups emphasized their independent participation in the protests.

In the high economic growth period, protest groups' focus shifted from organizing mass political protests to achieving improvements in standard of living through non-ideological protest. The anti-Vietnam War movement in the late 1960s was thus mostly organized independent of the progressive political parties or labor unions (Takabatake, 1977). According to Havens (1987: 55), the Citizens' Federation for Peace in Vietnam (*Beheiren*), a key federation composed of about 400 groups, had 'policy goals but no political affiliations, and a commitment to individual action but no collective ideology'.

University students were a significant part of the protest movements in the 1950s, 1960s, and 1970s. At first, student organizations protested against various problems internal to their universities. As they faced police interventions to control and suppress their protest activities, however, groups in various universities started to coordinate action to engage in a broader movement against the state (*Zen Kyōtō Undō*). The movement became further radicalized in the early 1970s and this, together with some violent incidents associated with the movement, alienated many students, leading to the movement's decline.

In the late 1960s and the 1970s, 'citizen movements' or 'residents' movements' emerged in response to various social problems related to high economic growth. The living environment in cities worsened as pollution became a serious problem and improvement in infrastructure (roads, water system, garbage disposal facilities, nurseries, etc.) could not catch up with the increase in population. Many residents' movements emerged to protest against these and other problems (Matsubara and Nitagai, 1976, take up protests on nuclear plants, bypasses, bullet trains, and shopping malls; Krauss and Simcock, 1980; Apter and Sawa, 1984). Nishio (1977) reports that there were more movements to prevent and deal with (mostly pollution) problems, than movements to attract new facilities (that would bring new benefits to communities but also create pollution). Yamamoto and Nishikido (2004) argue, however, that the citizens' movements arose not only because of the problems associated with the rapid economic development, but also because of the political opportunity structure in which LDP politicians occupied a smaller number of seats in the Upper House and members of progressive parties occupied a larger number of seats in local assemblies. Citizens' movements were distinguished from labor movements because citizens' movements were not based on pre-existing organizations or ideology (Matsubara, 1974; Takabatake, 1977).

In the 1970s, governors and mayors with support from socialist and communist parties emerged in Tokyo, Kyoto City, Kanagawa Prefecture, and other places, promising to deal with social problems with citizen inputs (Matsushita, 1971; Shinohara, 1977). This led to creation of various routes through which residents could directly discuss with local administrations, such as public meetings with mayors and governors, and participation in policy deliberation councils. Some scholars have conceptualized this relationship as 'oppositional division of labor (taikōteki bungyō, Funabashi and Funabashi, 1976), or 'oppositional complementality (taikōteki sōhosei, Kajita, 1988). These concepts describe a process that starts when residents' movements protest local governments about some problems. The two parties go through conflicts and debates to eventually find mutually agreeable solutions. Such a relationship between citizens and government – in which citizens demand changes and participate in policy debates to find new solutions instead of leaving everything up to the local governments – can also be found in collaborative projects between civil society organizations and local administrations (kyōdō) and in the concept of 'governance', which are attracting attention today (Ushiyama, 2006). This change in the relationship between citizens and local administrations signaled the development of participatory democracy. Some argue, however, that progressive chiefs needed to cultivate support from citizens' organizations as they faced conservative opposition parties in local assemblies and the central government (Muramatsu, 1974; Nishio, 1977).

Progressive local administrations focused on working with residents and at times resisted the central government's initiatives, moving away from the traditional practice of strengthening their ties with the central government to win subsidies for industrial infrastructure and development. In addition, progressive local administrations prioritized improvements in living conditions and welfare over industrial development, improving social infrastructure and welfare (Nishio, 1977). Behind these policies was the concept of 'civil minimum,' which is the minimum standard of living (including social security, infrastructure, and health) that local administrations sought to guarantee their residents (Matsushita, 1971).

However, progressive local administrations and residents' movements declined in the low economic growth period following the oil shocks. Movements became more difficult to organize because pollution and other problems in cities had been generally resolved. Progressive administrations experienced financial difficulties due to their focus on residents' standard of life and welfare. Replacing the progressive administrations were the 'technocrats' with bureaucratic experience who focused on maintaining local administrations' financial discipline. Candidates supported by both conservatives and progressives also increased, making local administrations generally less sympathetic to residents' movements (Higuchi, Nakazawa, and Mizusawa, 1998). Some movements maintained their access to the policymaking process, but otherwise the 1980s is considered as the 'winter period' for residents' movements (Nitagai, 1991; Higuchi et al., 1998).

There were some new developments in citizens' movements in the 1990s. First is the emergence of volunteerism. Energetic volunteer activities in the aftermath of the Hanshin–Awaji earthquake led to increased citizen participation in NPO and other civil society activities (Iwasaki et al., 1999; Yamashita and Suga, 2002; Nitagai, 2008). Second, organizations have emerged to support people with newly recognized problems, such as social withdrawal (hikikomori) and NEET (Not in Employment, Education or Training) (Tatsushi, 2006).

Third, residents mobilized for local referenda in the 1990s as a means to deal with local problems. As residents' movements emerged regarding controversial facilities such as nuclear energy plants and industrial waste disposal facilities, local administrations created ordinances to enable local referenda. A local referendum without legally binding power was held in Okinawa in August 1996, regarding revision of the United States–Japan Status of Forces Agreement and military base reduction (Kamimura, 2001). Another one was held in 1997 in Maki (current Niigata City) over nuclear plant construction (Lesbirel, 1998). There were referenda in Mitake (Gifu) in 1997 over the establishment of an industrial waste disposal facility; in Nago (Okinawa) in 1997 on construction of an offshore American military heliport; in Tokushima (Tokushima) over weir construction in Yoshino River; and in Iwakuni (Yamaguchi) in 2006 over accepting an American military aircraft carrier. There have also been many referenda regarding incorporation of cities, towns and villages.

The emergence of local referendum movements in Maki and Tokushima surprised some people because the LDP was strong in those places. The minister of construction at the time of Tokushima's vote said that local referenda were 'democracy malfunctioning (*minshushugi no gosadō*).' Mobilizations for local referenda triggered a debate about how democracy should be: indirect democracy through representative assemblies or direct democracy through citizen participation (Nakazawa, 2004; Ito et al., 2005; Kubota et al., 2008). Based on the case in Maki, Nakazawa (2004) argues for the possibility of 'radical democracy' that fully adheres to the democratic process. Kubota and colleagues (2008) study the Tokushima case and argue that local referendum movements signal a formation of new social cleavages in Japan. Nakatani (2005) also writes that these movements represent a new political culture.

Direct democracy, however, has limits. State authorities may seek to prevent protests and exercise of direct democracy. Aldrich (2008) demonstrates in his research on divisive facilities (nuclear power plants, dams, and airports) that state authorities first try to avoid costly local resistance by identifying potential sites in communities that have weaker civil society. Typical sites are thus 'likely to be relatively unpopulated and rural and to have low or diminishing community solidarity and diffuse civil society' (Aldrich, 2008: x). When authorities nevertheless face long and intense opposition, they use incentives (side payments) and soft social control (persuasion) to win compliance. According to Aldrich, even when strong opposition arises, state authorities rarely back away from their energy and infrastructure goals.

Other scholars have also found that state authorities seek to contain protests by marginalizing protesters and keeping them outside the policymaking process, while giving some pre-emptive concessions to prevent future protests. Pharr (1990) argues that this pattern of state response to protests emerged in the Tokugawa era, and she observes such responses in social status conflicts involving the Burakumin and female workers. Broadbent (2002) also argues that environmental protests and threats of electoral defeats pushed the LDP, relevant ministries, and business leadership to deal with the worst pollution on the one hand and impose 'soft social control' to curb future protests on the other. Strausz's (2006) research on the anti-fingerprinting movement among resident Koreans also supports this pattern of state response to protests by highlighting state policies to pre-empt the movement and reassert control over the pace of social change. Upham (1987) also writes that the state seeks to manage conflict by channeling cases away from the courts into bureaucratically controlled mediation mechanisms. This allows the state to control the pace, process, and substance of policy change in response to social conflicts.

Despite the difficulty of protests attaining specific goals, Steinhoff (1989: 191) argues that they have served to 'temper the ambitions of conservative politicians and thus helped to keep the country on a moderate course'. Furthermore, the nuclear accident of March 2011 reinvigorated anti-nuclear activism in Japan. Many civil society organizations and ordinary citizens have engaged in mass protests, petition drives and other activities to voice their opposition and concerns (Aldrich, 2012; Kawato et al., 2012: 80–83). The extent to which these protest activities have influenced Japan's nuclear energy policy, and whether civil society will have more significant advocacy and monitoring roles in the future, will be an important topic of research.

The Media

According to Freeman (2000: 4), the media in Japan is dominated by information cartels, which are 'institutionalized rules and relationships guiding press relations with their sources and with each other that serve to limit the types of news that get reported and the number and makeup of those who do the reporting'. Three institutions form the information cartels: press clubs, newspaper industry associations, and intermedia business groups. Press clubs have an exclusive membership of journalists from major news organizations, which helps monopolize the news sources (politicians, bureaucrats, business leaders, and the police). Press clubs also have strict and enforced rules that govern the members' activities, discouraging independent and investigative reporting. Industry associations manage the club system, and intermedia business groups help the press club members control the news reported by their family enterprises (Freeman, 2000: 15–16).

Freeman argues that there are five consequences of information cartels. First is an overreliance on credentialed facts. The media mostly communicates the narrowly controlled official information to the public (for example, Krauss (1996) shows that a large percentage of the stories and the time in NHK's evening news is on the state and its bureaucracies). Freeman points out that this reduces political choice and thus affects the quality of politics. Second, the close relationship between the journalists and their sources limits monitoring against dishonesty and corruption. Third, the media has mostly responded to the state's agendas and does not play a significant role in agenda setting. Fourth, the press clubs' exclusive membership has marginalized alternative media. The fifth consequence is the homogenization of the news and opinion (Nanri, 2005; Seaton, 2006; and Shinoda, 2007 see less homogenization of the news). As information cartels limit the flow of information to the public, Freeman argues that the media serves as 'collaborators' or 'coconspirator' with the state in social management, 'capturing, subverting, misleading, or alternatively ignoring the political periphery represented by the public sphere' (2000: 162–169; 2003: 236).

The first Japanese-language newspaper was published during the Tokugawa era, and the Meiji state made the 'first real attempt' to use it as a tool to modernize the country and 'civilize and enlighten' the public (Freeman, 2000: 23–25). The state nurtured the newspapers' development by providing financial support to the industry, employing legal constraints and informal incentives to discourage opposing viewpoints, and cultivating close ties between state elites and journalists (Freeman, 2000: 26–34).

These measures led to the creation of apolitical 'patronage press,' but 'political press' with openly partisan perspectives emerged to challenge them. Many of the 'political press' eventually became the organs of Japan's first political parties, and played an important role in the movement to demand a constitution and a representative assembly. However, in response to the 'political press,' the state enacted several strict press ordinances starting in 1875. The papers began to avoid partisan political debate, and published materials that appealed to a broader audience (Freeman, 2000: 35–39).

Press clubs were established in the early 1890s. When the war in the Pacific began, the state established formal measures to control the press, making the press clubs important in disseminating wartime propaganda. The state and the newspaper industry collaborated to provide the public with a 'standardized, homogenized, and sanitized version of the news, leaving little room for the expression of alternative interpretations of the war' (Freeman, 2000: 52–55). The postwar Occupation authorities removed formal press controls but 'ignored informal mechanisms of informational control such as the exclusionary, cartelized practices of the press clubs and the considerable power that sources still maintained over them,' which remain today (Freeman, 2000: 56).

Although the close relationship between the state and mainstream media may limit independent news reporting, it is also important to note that the media has at times influenced politics in a way that undermines state elites' interests. Pharr (1996) characterizes the media as 'trickster,' which can serve or undermine state interests in different contexts. For example, Farley (1996) examines the media's role in four postwar political scandals and demonstrates that the media (widely defined, including 'outside' media without access to press clubs, such as popular magazines, sports papers, freelancers, Japan Communist Party's *Akahata*, and foreign press) was instrumental in forcing some state officials to step down. In each scandal, the outside press with more distance from state officials broke the news, and then the mainstream media followed up with investigative journalism. Farley notes, however, that these scandals did not result in real reforms. Altman (1996) also argues that some television news programs, namely *News Station* and the *Sunday Project,* which confronted politicians directly and aired political debate, influenced voters' decisions in the 1993 election, leading to the LDP's historical defeat. Campbell (1996) also credits the media as a cause of change in elderly care and pension benefit increase in the early 1970s, in a way that the state did not intend. In all of these studies, the media influenced public opinion.

According to Kabashima and Broadbent (1986) and Kabashima (1990), the media has become a new and powerful political resource for social groups that seek to influence state policy. The media distributes 'emotionally meaningful symbols and events' to shape public opinion and generate social movements, to which the state must respond (Kabashima and Broadbent, 1986: 351). Kabashima and Broadbent propose the concept of 'referent pluralism' – the media redistributes power to social groups and strengthens political pluralism. In addition, Flanagan (1996: 278) writes: 'the media appear to have played a positive transforming role in improving the quality of mass political participation over the postwar period'. According to Flanagan, the media increases the citizen's political knowledge and influences their electoral choices. Media exposure also increases people's interest in politics, and this leads to higher levels of political involvement and participation.

Politicians seem well aware of the media's potential in shaping the public opinion, and are increasingly media-savvy. Public reliance on television for political news has increased since the 1980s, and changes in style and content of news programs have made politics and political analysis more accessible to the public. As a result, politicians were forced to adjust to 'image politics,' in which their image on television influences their electoral prospects and power in their parties (Altman, 1996; Taniguchi, 2007). Kabashima and Steel (2007) argue that Junichiro Koizumi took advantage of these changes in television news to win the LDP presidential election in 2001, and his media-driven popularity had a significant impact in the 2001 Upper House election. Television shows could also influence the policymaking process, serving as 'another Diet' (Taniguchi, 2007). Bureaucrats are also well aware of the media's role in shaping the public opinion. According to Potter and Van Belle (2004: 122), bureaucracies use the news media as one indicator of issue salience, and allocate foreign aid accordingly 'in an anticipatory effort to remain in sync with public opinion'.

Some scholars argue, however, that the media today falls short as a truly representative and democratic public sphere. Iwabuchi (2000) writes that minority groups are seldom represented on Japanese television because the Buraku Liberation League's use of denunciation strategy has led to the media's excessive self-censorship to avoid criticism. Farley (1996: 138) also reports what *Asahi Shimbun's* former editorial chairman told her that 'nobody likes to read' stories about burakumin and other issues of discrimination. Iwabuchi (2000) criticizes that the media has chosen to avoid the minority issues rather than search for an alternative, more democratic representation.

Iwabuchi (2005) also criticizes the television's representation of foreign residents in Japan. He believes it reproduces and reinforces the association of foreigners with crime and danger by highlighting the increase and viciousness of crimes committed by foreigners, when crimes by foreigners are an insignificant proportion of total crime in Japan. Shipper (2005) also says that the media tends to use police reports on crimes by illegal foreigners without critical assessment. Media reports on the increase in number of crimes by illegal foreigners do not consider demographic factors or the separate types of crimes, which would challenge the foreigners' image as dangerous criminals. Shipper also writes that media reports associate particular crimes with particular national groups. As Iwabuchi (2005: 108) argues, television shows tend to use foreigners to highlight Japan's uniqueness to 'discursively construct an exclusive Japanese imagined community,' focusing on multinationalism instead of multicultural and multiracial Japan.

Barnard (2000) points out another potential problem with the media, which is self-censorship. Comparing articles on the Tokaimura nuclear accident in *Newsweek* and its Japanese version, Barnard argues that the Japanese version downplayed officials' irresponsibility and incompetence, muted the citizens' voices of protest, and minimized the seriousness of the incident as well as the Japanese nuclear power industry's structural problems.

Finally, Freeman (2003: 237) examines the Internet's political potential as 'an alternative or parallel public sphere' to the mainstream media that maintains a close relationship with the state. She says there are three ways in which the Internet might empower the political public sphere. First, it allows grassroots activists and volunteers to spread information about their causes, increase memberships, and gain financial support. Second, the Internet may facilitate the communication between the public and the government. The state can use it to inform the public about its activities and policies, and the public may communicate their preferences through email and other means. Third, the Internet may facilitate exchanges of information and opinions between individuals, groups, and candidates during election periods (Freeman, 2003: 245–255).

CONCLUSION

This research shows that Japan's civil society organizations play multiple roles and engage in various activities. They contribute to the creation of social capital, provide various services, increase citizens' access to policymaking, and engage in protests, advocacy, and monitoring. Given their various roles and activities, their relationship with the state has many facets. First, as Pekkanen (2006) demonstrates, the state has moulded civil society with its regulatory power, encouraging the growth of certain organizations (like the neighborhood organizations that facilitate governance and organizations that help provide social services) and discouraging the growth of others (e.g. protest organizations). Second, the state has cooperated with some civil society actors to achieve its objectives. Garon (1997) argues that the state has relied on women's and religious organizations for social management. The state has also worked closely with agricultural cooperatives, business associations, and social welfare corporations. The state also promotes volunteering to curtail and replace state provision of services (Ogawa, 2004, 2009; Haddad, 2007). Third, the state–civil society relationship can be more oppositional when organizations engage in protests and advocacy. Some civil society actors, however, wish to avoid any interaction with the state (LeBlanc, 1999; Shin, 2004). Finally, the state–civil society relationship differs at different levels of government – local governments have had more opportunities to interact and cooperate with civil society organizations. In some policy areas, such as the environment and on foreigners, there has been more extensive policy change at the local level than at the state level.

The research thus far has significantly contributed to our understanding of Japan's civil society and its relationship with the state, but many exciting avenues for research remain. We conclude with some agendas for future research.

The steady growth in the number of civil society organizations raises several questions. First, organizations with similar aims seem to have proliferated, and research on the extent of this proliferation and reasons behind it could be interesting. What are the costs and benefits of creating similar organizations? To what extent and how do they compete and cooperate with each other? Second and a related issue is the role of umbrella organizations and the division of labor between local and national associations. Although local organizations are the most numerous in Japanese civil society, examining national and regional organizations is also important. Nakamura (2002) engages this topic and reports that the Japanese Federation of the Deaf, a national organization with prefectural associations, has a two-tiered strategy in interacting with the state. The federation has maintained political independence at the national level, while prefectural associations have received state funding for projects at the local level. More research on organizations working at various levels would be welcome.

Third, there is currently much focus on organizations' establishment and activities as scholars continue to examine the 'development' of Japanese civil society. Scholars should also be concerned if the organizations that have been established remain active, and if not, why that is. An examination of organizations' life cycle – birth, growth, inactivity, decline, and death – would teach us much about the opportunities and challenges that organizations face in their operations.

Another set of potential research topics concerns organizations' activities in the international arena. First, the activities of organizations that take place abroad are few in comparison to those within Japan. What are the factors contributing to this? What are the implications of this as the Japanese government seeks greater international leadership in various issues? We invite scholars to follow Reimann's groundbreaking work in this area (Reimann, 2003). Second, Tsujinaka and Pekkanen's work (2007) shows that foreign policy and national security policy are among the least popular policy issues among the civil society organizations. Why is this? The change from civil society's active involvement in these issues in the 1960s and 1970s (through anti-security treaty, anti-nuclear, and anti-Vietnam War protests) to the current situation needs to be explained.

Finally, we should continue to examine civil society as a cultural and political construction. What are the imagined boundaries for Japanese civil society? Who qualifies as being a part of it and who are excluded? Who decides? What are the imagined functions for civil society organizations? Public and academic discourse on Japanese civil society has focused on its positive functions, such as civil society's contributions to democracy and communal life. Does the assumption that civil society organizations aim to contribute to the public good exclude from analyses some organizations that influence people's social, political, and economic life? Gangs, for example, are not legally eligible to become NPOs. Extreme right organizations also organize political events and obstruct protests by the left, but they do not seem to fit the public or academic image of civil society organizations. *Aum Shinrikyō* had a legal status as a religious incorporation before its criminal activities were discovered, but its status was subsequently revoked; it seems to have moved beyond the imagined boundary of civil society.

These and many other questions continue to make Japanese civil society an exciting area for research.

REFERENCES

Akimoto, Ritsuo. 1971. *Gendai Toshi No Kenryoku Kōzō*. Tokyo: Aoki Shoten.

Aldrich, Daniel P. 2008. *Site Fights: Divisive Facilities and Civil Society in Japan and the West*. Ithaca, NY: Cornell University Press.

Aldrich, Daniel P. 2012. Civil Society Rising. *Bulletin of the Atomic Scientists*, March 9.

Altman, Kristin Kyoko. 1996. Television and Political Turmoil: Japan's Summer of 1993. In Susan J. Pharr and Ellis S. Krauss, eds. *Media and Politics in Japan*. Honolulu, HI: University of Hawaii Press, 165–186.

Amenomori, Takayoshi, and Tadashi Yamamoto. 1998. Introduction. In Tadashi Yamamoto, ed. *The Nonprofit Sector in Japan*. Manchester, UK: Manchester University Press, 1–18.

Amos, Timothy. 2007. Binding Burakumin: Marxist Historiography and the Narration of Difference in Japan. *Japanese Studies* 27 (2), 155–171.

Anderson, Stephen. 1993. *Welfare Policy and Politics in Japan: Beyond the Developmental State*. New York, NY: Paragon House.

Anheier, Helmut K. 2004. *Civil Society: Measurement, Evaluation, Policy*. London: CIVICUS, Earthscan.

Aoki, Eriko. 2000. Korean Children, Textbooks, and Educational Practices in Japanese Primary Schools. In Sonia Ryang, ed. *Koreans in Japan: Critical Voices from the Margin*. Abingdon, UK: Routledge, 157–174.

Apter, David E., and Nagayo Sawa. 1984. *Against the State: Politics and Social Protest in Japan*. Cambridge, MA: Harvard University Press.

Avenell, Simon. 2006. Regional Egoism as the Public Good: Residents' Movements in Japan During the 1960s and 1970s. *Japan Forum*, 18 (1), 89–113.

Avenell, Simon. 2010. *Making Japanese Citizens: Civil Society and the Mythology of the Shimin in Postwar Japan*. Berkeley, CA: University of California Press.

Babb, James. 2005. Making Farmers Conservative: Japanese Farmers, Land Reform and Socialism. *Social Science Japan Journal*, 8 (2), 175–195.

Barnard, Christopher. 2000. The Tokaimura Nuclear Accident in Japanese Newsweek: Translation or Censorship? *Japanese Studies*, 20 (3), 281–294.

Barshay, Andrew. 2003. Capitalism and Civil Society in Postwar Japan: Perspectives from Intellectual History. In Frank J. Schwartz and Susan J. Pharr, eds. *The State of Civil Society in Japan*. Cambridge, UK: Cambridge University Press, 63–80.

Bestor, Theodore. 1989. *Neighborhood Tokyo*. Stanford, CA: Stanford University Press.

Bochel, Catherine, and Hugh Bochel. 2005. Exploring the Low Levels of Women's Representation in Japanese Local Government. *Japanese Journal of Political Science*, 6 (3), 375–392.

Bouissou, Jean-Marie. 2000. Ambiguous Revival: A Study of Some 'New Civic Movements' in Japan. *The Pacific Review*, 13 (3), 335–366.

Brinton, Mary C. 1993. *Women and the Economic Miracle: Gender and Work in Postwar Japan*. Berkeley, CA: University of California Press.

Broadbent, Jeffrey. 1998. *Environmental Politics in Japan: Networks of Power and Protest*. Cambridge, UK: Cambridge University Press.

Broadbent, Jeffrey. 2002. Japan's Environmental Regime: The Political Dynamics of Change. In Uday Desai, ed. *Environmental Politics and Policy in Industrialized Countries*. Cambridge, MA: MIT Press, 295–355.

Broadbent, Kaye. 2001. Shortchanged? Part-Time Workers in Japan. *Japanese Studies*, 21 (3), 293–304.

Broadbent, Kaye. 2005. 'For Women, By Women': Women-Only Unions in Japan. *Japan Forum*, 17 (2), 213–230.

Bullock, Robert. 2003. Redefining the Conservative Coalition: Agriculture and Small Business in 1990s Japan. In Frank J. Schwartz and Susan J. Pharr, eds. *The State of Civil Society in Japan*. Cambridge, UK: Cambridge University Press, 175–194.

Burgess, Chris. 2007. 'Newcomer' Children in Non-Metropolitan Public Schools: The Lack of State-Sponsored Support for Children Whose First Language Is Not Japanese. *Japan Forum*, 19 (1), 1–21.

C's. 1999. NPO Giin Renmei Hassoku. Retrieved September 19, 2014 from: http://www.npoweb.jp/modules/news1/article.php?storyid=680

Cabinet Office. 2003. Sōsharu Kyapitaru: Yutaka Na Ningen Kankei to Shimin Katsudō No Kōjyunkan Wo Motomete. Retrieved September 19, 2014 from: https://www.npo-homepage.go.jp/data/report9_1.html

Cabinet Office. 2005. Keizai Shakai Sōgō Kenkyū Sho. Komyunitii Kinō Saisei To Sōsharu Kyapitaru Ni Kansuru Kenkyū Chōsa Hōkokusho.

Cabinet Office. 2011. Heisei 22-nendo Tokutei Hieiri Katsudō Hōjin No Jittai Oyobi Nintei Tokutei Hieiri Katsudō Hōjin Seido No Riyōjyō Ni Kansuru Chōsa.

Cabinet Office. 2012. 'Heisei 23-nendo Tokutei Hieiri Katsudō Hōjin No Jittai Oyobi Nintei Tokutei Hieiri Katsudō Hōjin Seido No Riyōjyō Ni Kansuru Chōsa.'

Cabinet Office NPO Homepage. 'Number of applications for NPO legal status, and number of approved NPOs'. Available at: https://www.npo-homepage.go.jp/portalsite/syokatsutyobetsu_ninshou.html

Campbell, John Creighton. 1992. *How Policies Change: The Japanese Government and the Aging Society*. Princeton, NJ: Princeton University Press.

Campbell, John Creighton. 1996. Media and Policy Change in Japan. In Susan J. Pharr and Ellis S. Krauss, eds. *Media and Politics in Japan*. Honolulu, HI: University of Hawaii Press, 187–212.

Chan-Tiberghien, Jennifer. 2004. *Gender and Human Rights Politics in Japan: Global Norms and Domestic Networks*. Stanford, CA: Stanford University Press.

Chapman, David. 2004. The Third Way and Beyond: Zainichi Korean Identity and the Politics of Belonging. *Japanese Studies*, 24 (1), 29–44.

Colignon, Richard, and Chikako Usui. 2001. The Resilience of Japan's Iron Triangle: Amakudari. *Asian Survey*, 41 (5), 865–895.

Cusick, Brady. 2007. The Conflicted Individualism of Japanese College Student Volunteers. *Japan Forum*, 19 (1), 49–68.

Diamond, Larry. 1994. *Rethinking Civil Society: Comparative Politics*. Orlando, FL: Harcourt Brace College Publishers.

Dōmoto, Akiko. 2000. NPO Hō No Rippō Katei. In Hiroyuki Torigoe, ed. *Kankyō Borantia: NPO No Shakaigaku*. Tokyo: Shinyōsha, 164–174.

Dore, Ronald. 1958. *City Life in Japan*. Berkeley, CA: University of California Press.

Dunlap, Riley E., and Angela G. Mertig. 1992. *American Environmentalism: The US Environmental Movement, 1970–1990*. Philadelphia, PA: Taylor & Francis.

Estevez-Abe, Margarita. 2002. Negotiating Welfare Reforms: Actors and Institutions in the Japanese Welfare State. In Bo Rothstein and Sven Steinmo eds. *Restructuring the Welfare State*. New York, NY: Palgrave Macmillan, 157–182.

Estevez-Abe, Margarita. 2003. State–Society Partnerships in the Japanese Welfare State. In Frank J. Schwartz and Susan J. Pharr, eds. *The State of Civil Society in Japan*. Cambridge, UK: Cambridge University Press, 154–172.

Farley, Maggie. 1996. Japan's Press and the Politics of Scandal. In Susan J. Pharr and Ellis S. Krauss, eds. *Media and Politics in Japan*. Honolulu, HI: University of Hawaii Press, 133–163.

Flanagan, Scott C. 1996. Media Exposure and the Quality of Political Participation in Japan. In Susan J. Pharr and Ellis S. Krauss, eds. *Media and Politics in Japan*. Honolulu, HI: University of Hawaii Press, 277–312.

Flowers, Petrice R. 2008. Failure to Protect Refugees? Domestic Institutions, International Organizations, and Civil Society in Japan. *Journal of Japanese Studies*, 34 (2), 333–361.

Foljanty-Jost, Gesine. 2005. NGOs in Environmental Networks in Germany and Japan: The Question of Power and Influence. *Social Science Japan Journal*, 8 (1), 103–117.

Freeman, Laurie Anne. 2000. *Closing the Shop: Information Cartels and Japan's Mass Media*. Princeton, NJ: Princeton University Press.

Freeman, Laurie Anne. 2003. Mobilizing and Demobilizing the Japanese Public Sphere: Mass Media and the Internet in Japan. In Frank J. Schwartz and Susan J. Pharr, eds. *The State of Civil Society in Japan*. Cambridge, UK: Cambridge University Press, 235–256.

Fujime, Yuki. 2006. Japanese Feminism and Commercialized Sex: The Union of Militarism and Prohibitionism. *Social Science Japan Journal*, 9 (1), 33–50.

Fukuda, Ajio. 2006. *Kesshū, Kessha No Nihonshi*. Tokyo: Yamakawa Shuppansha.

Funabashi, Harutoshi, and Keiko Funabashi. 1976. Taikōteki Bungyō No Riron. *Gendai Shakaigaku*, 3 (2), 114–129.

Funabashi, Harutoshi, Koichi Hasegawa, Munekazu Hatanaka, and Harumi Katsuta. 1985. *Shinkansen Kōgai: Kōsoku Bunmei No Shakai Mondai*. Tokyo: Yuhikaku.

Funabashi, Harutoshi, Koichi Hasegawa, and Nobuko Iijima. 1998. *Kyodai Kaihatsu No Kōsō to Kiketsu: Mutsu Ogawara Kaihatsu to Kaku Nenryō Saikuru Shisetsu*. Tokyo: Tokyo Daigaku Shuppan Kai.

Garon, Sheldon. 1987. *The State and Labor in Modern Japan*. Berkeley, CA: University of California Press.

Garon, Sheldon. 1997. *Molding Japanese Minds: The State in Everyday Life*. Princeton, NJ: Princeton University Press.

Garon, Sheldon. 2003. From Meiji to Heisei: The State and Civil Society in Japan. In Frank J. Schwartz and Susan J. Pharr, eds. *The State of Civil Society in Japan*. Cambridge, UK: Cambridge University Press, 42–62.

Gelb, Joyce, and Margarita Estevez-Abe. 1998. Political Women in Japan: A Case Study of the Seikatsusha Network Movement. *Social Science Japan Journal*, 1 (2), 263–279.

Gordon, Andrew. 1991. *Labor and Imperial Democracy in Prewar Japan*. Berkeley, CA: University of California Press.

Gordon, Andrew. 1998. *The Wages of Affluence: Labor and Management in Postwar Japan*. Cambridge, MA: Harvard University Press.

Goudo, Yoshihisa. 2006. *Nihon No Shoku To Nou: Kiki No Honshitsu*. Tokyo: NTT Shuppan.

Groth, David Earl. 1996. Media and Political Protest: The Bullet Train Movements. In Susan J. Pharr and Ellis S. Krauss, eds. *Media and Politics in Japan*. Honolulu, HI: University of Hawaii Press, 213–241.

Haddad, Mary Alice. 2007. *Politics and Volunteering in Japan: A Global Perspective*. Cambridge, UK: Cambridge University Press.

Han, Seung-Mi. 2004. From the Communitarian Ideal to the Public Sphere: The Making of Foreigners' Assemblies in Kawasaki City and Kanagawa Prefecture. *Social Science Japan Journal*, 7 (1), 41–60.

Hardacre, Helen. 2003. After Aum: Religion and Civil Society in Japan. In Frank J. Schwartz and Susan J. Pharr, eds. *The State of Civil Society in Japan*. Cambridge, UK: Cambridge University Press, 135–153.

Hardacre, Helen. 2004. Religion and Civil Society in Contemporary Japan. *Japanese Journal of Religious Studies*, 31 (2), 389–415.

Hardacre, Helen. 2005. Constitutional Revision and Japanese Religions. *Japanese Studies*, 25 (3), 235–247.

Hasegawa, Koichi. 2003. *Environmental Movements and the New Public Sphere: The Perspective of Environmental Sociology*. Tokyo: Yuhikaku.

Hasegawa, Tamako. 2007. Equality of Opportunity or Employment Quotas? A Comparison of Japanese and American Employment Policies for the Disabled. *Social Science Japan Journal*, 10 (1), 41–57.

Havens, Thomas R. H. 1986. *Valley of Darkness: The Japanese People and World War Two*. Lanham, MD: University Press of America.

Havens, Thomas R. H. 1987. *Fire across the Sea: The Vietnam War and Japan 1965–1975*. Princeton, NJ: Princeton University Press.

Higuchi, Naoto, Hideo Nakazawa, and Hiromitsu Mizusawa. 1998. Organizational Strategies of Japanese Resident's Movements: How the Dynamics of Local Politics Change Social Movement Organizations. *Japanese Sociological Review*, 49 (4), 498–512.

Hirai, Youichi. 2000. *Miike Sōgi: Sengo Rōdō Undō No Bunsuirei*. Tokyo: Minerva Shobō.

Hotta, Satoko. 2007. Toward Maintaining and Improving the Quality of Long-Term Care: The Current State and Issues Regarding Home Helpers in Japan under the Long-Term Care Insurance System. *Social Science Japan Journal*, 10 (2), 265–279.

Howell, David. 2004. Making 'Useful Citizens' of Ainu Subjects in Early Twentieth-Century Japan. *The Journal of Asian Studies*, 63 (1), 5–29.

Huen, Yuki W. P. 2007. Workplace Sexual Harassment in Japan: A Review of Combating Measures Taken. *Asian Survey*, 47 (5), 811–827.

Igarashi, Jin. 1998. *Seitō Seiji to Rōdō Kumiai Undō: Sengo Nihon No Tōtatsuten to 21 Seiki Heno Kadai*. Tokyo: Ochanomizu Shobou.

Iijima, Nobuko. 1970. Kogai and the Community Resident's Movement: The Case of the Minamata Disease. *Japanese Sociological Review,* 21 (1), 25–45.

Iijima, Nobuko. 2000. *Kankyō Mondai No Shakaishi.* Tokyo: Yuhikaku.

Inagami, Tsuyoshi, H. Whittaker, Naohito Oumi, Toru Shinoda, Yoshihiro Shimodaira, and Yutaka Tsujinaka. 1994. *Neo-Kōporatyizumu No Kokusai Hikaku.* Tokyo: Nihon Rōdō Kenkyū Kikō.

Inoguchi, Takashi. 2000. Social Capital in Japan. *Japanese Journal of Political Science,* 1 (1), 72–112.

Inoguchi, Takashi. 2002. Broadening the Basis of Social Capital in Japan. In Robert Putnam, ed. *Democracies in Flux: The Evolution of Social Capital in Contemporary Society.* Oxford, UK: Oxford University Press, 359–392.

Iokibe, Makoto. 1999. Japan's Civil Society: An Historical Overview. In Tadashi Yamamoto, ed. *Deciding the Public Good: Governance and Civil Society in Japan.* Tokyo: Japan Center for International Exchange, 51–96.

Ito, Mamoru, Noboru Watanabe, Katsuhiro Matsui, and Nahoko Sugihara. 2005. *Democrasii Rifurekushon: Makichō Jyūmin Tōhyō No Shakaigaku.* Tokyo: Liberta Shuppan.

Iwabuchi, Koichi. 2000. Political Correctness, Postcoloniality and the Self-Representation of 'Koreanness' in Japan. In Sonia Ryang, ed. *Koreans in Japan: Critical Voices from the Margin.* Abingdon, UK: Routledge, 55–73.

Iwabuchi, Koichi. 2005. Multinationalizing the Multicultural: The Commodification of 'Ordinary Foreign Residents' in a Japanese TV Talk Show. *Japanese Studies,* 25 (2), 103–118.

Iwasaki, Nobuhiko, Manabu Ajisaka, Korekazu Ueda, Masao Takagi, Moriaki Hirohara, and Naoki Yoshihara, eds. 1985. *Chōnaikai No Kenkyū.* Tokyo: Ochanomizu Shobō.

Iwasaki, Nobuhiko, Masaki Urano, Kamon Nitagai, Takeo Yamamoto, Kōzō Ukai, Katsuji Tsuji, and Takashi Noda. 1999. *Hanshin-Awaji Daishinsai No Shakaigaku, 1–3.* Nagasaki: Shōwadō.

Kabashima, Ikuo. 1990. Masu Media to Seiji. *Leviathan,* 7, 7–29.

Kabashima, Ikuo, and Jeffrey Broadbent. 1986. Referent Pluralism: Mass Media and Politics in Japan. *Journal of Japanese Studies,* 12 (2), 329–361.

Kabashima, Ikuo, and Gill Steel. 2007. How Junichiro Koizumi Seized the Leadership of Japan's Liberal Democratic Party. *Japanese Journal of Political Science,* 8 (1), 95–114.

Kage, Rieko. 2007. Civic Engagement in Japan: War, Mobilization, and Path Dependency. *Leviathan,* 41, 45–73.

Kajita, Takamichi. 1988. *Tekunokurāto to Shakai Undō: Taikōteki Sōhosei No Shakaigaku.* Tokyo: Tokyo Daigaku Shuppankai.

Kamimura, Naoki. 2001. Japanese Civil Society, Local Government, and United States–Japan Security Relations in the 1990s: A Preliminary Survey. In Chieko Kitagawa Otsuru and Edward Rhodes, ed. *Nationalism and Citizenship Iii.* Osaka: Japan Center for Asia Studies, 1–16.

Kang, Sangjung, and Robin Fletcher. 2006. Memories of a Zainichi Korean Childhood. *Japanese Studies,* 26 (3), 268–281.

Kashiwazaki, Chikako. 2000. The Politics of Legal Status: The Equation of Nationality with Ethnonational Identity. In Sonia Ryang, ed. *Koreans in Japan: Critical Voices from the Margin.* Abingdon, UK: Routledge, 13–31.

Kasza, Gregory J. 1995. *The Conscription Society: Administered Mass Organizations.* New Haven, CT: Yale University Press.

Kasza, Gregory J. 2002. War and Welfare Policy in Japan. *The Journal of Asian Studies,* 61 (2), 417–435.

Katagiri, Shinji. 2000. *Rekishiteki Kankyō No Shakaigaku.* Tokyo: Shinyosha.

Kawato, Yuko, and Robert Pekkanen. 2008. Civil Society and Democracy: Reforming Nonprofit Organization Law. In Sherry L. Martin and Gill Steel, eds. *Democratic Reform in Japan: Assessing the Impact.* Boulder, CO: Lynne Rienner Publishers, 193–210.

Kawato, Yuko, Robert Pekkanen, and Hidehiro Yamamoto. 2011. State and Civil Society in Japan. In Alisa Gaunder, ed. *The Routledge Handbook of Japanese Politics.* Abingdon, UK: Routledge, 117–129.

Kawato, Yuko, Robert Pekkanen, and Yutaka Tsujinaka. 2012. Civil Society and the Triple Disasters: Revealed Strengths and Weaknesses. In Jeff Kingston, ed. *Natural Disaster and Nuclear Crisis in Japan: Response and Recovery after Japan's 3/11.* Abingdon, UK: Routledge, 78–93.

Kikuchi, Miyoshi, and Wataru Egami. 1998. *Komyunitii No Soshiki To Shisetsu.* Tokyo: Taga Shuppan.

Kisala, Robert J. 1997. Reactions to Aum: The Revision of the Religious Corporations Law. *Japanese Religions,* 22 (1), 60–74.

Krauss, Ellis S. 1996. Portraying the State: NHK Television News and Politics. In Susan J. Pharr and Ellis S. Krauss, eds. *Media and Politics in Japan.* Honolulu, HI: University of Hawaii Press, 89–129.

Krauss, Ellis S., and Bradford L. Simcock. 1980. Citizens' Movements: The Growth and Impact of Environmental Protest in Japan. In Kurt Steiner, Ellis S. Krauss and Scott C. Flanagan, eds. *Political Opposition and Local Politics in Japan.* Princeton, NJ: Princeton University Press, 187–227.

Kubota, Shigeru, Naoto Higuchi, Takuya Yabe, and Ryosuke Takaki. 2008. *Saikiteki Kindai No Seijishakai Gaku: Yoshinogawa Kadōseki Mondai* to *Minshushugi No Jikken*. Tokyo: Minerva Shobō.

Kume, Ikuo. 1998. *Disparaged Success: Labor Politics in Postwar Japan*. Ithaca, NY: Cornell University Press.

Kume, Ikuo. 2005. *Rōdō Seiji: Sengo Seiji No Naka No Rōdō Kumiai*. Tokyo: Chuko Shinsho.

Lambert, Priscilla A. 2007. The Political Economy of Postwar Family Policy in Japan: Economic Imperatives and Electoral Incentives. *Journal of Japanese Studies*, 33 (1), 1–28.

LeBlanc, Robin M. 1999. *Bicycle Citizens: The Political World of the Japanese Housewife*. Berkeley, CA: University of California Press.

Lenz, Ilse. 2006. From Mothers of the Nation to Global Civil Society: The Changing Role of the Japanese Women's Movement in Globalization. *Social Science Japan Journal*, 9 (1), 91–102.

Lesbirel, S. Hayden. 1998. *NIMBY Politics in Japan: Energy Siting and the Management of Environmental Conflict*. Ithaca, NY: Cornell University Press.

Lewis, Jack G. 1980. Civic Protest in Mishima: Citizens' Movements and the Politics of the Environment in Contemporary Japan. In Kurt Steiner, Ellis S. Krauss and Scott C. Flanagan, eds. *Political Opposition and Local Politics in Japan*. Princeton, NJ: Princeton University Press, 274–313.

Lewis, Michael. 1990. *Rioters and Citizens: Mass Protest in Imperial Japan*. Berkeley, CA: University of California Press.

Lie, John. 2001. *Multiethnic Japan*. Cambridge, MA: Harvard University Press.

Liu-Farrer, Gracia. 2008. The Burden of Social Capital: Visa Overstaying among Fujian Chinese Students in Japan. *Social Science Japan Journal*, 11 (2), 241–257.

Long, Susan Orpett, and Phyllis Braudy Harris. 2000. Gender and Elder Care: Social Change and the Role of the Caregiver in Japan. *Social Science Japan Journal*, 3 (1), 21–36.

Maclachlan, Patricia. 1999. Protecting Producers from Consumer Protection: The Politics of Products Liability Reform in Japan. *Social Science Japan Journal*, 2 (2), 249–266.

Maclachlan, Patricia. 2002a. *Consumer Politics in Postwar Japan: The Institutional Boundaries of Citizen Activism*. New York, NY: Columbia University Press.

Maclachlan, Patricia. 2002b. Japanese Civil Society in the Age of Deregulation: The Case of Consumers. *Japanese Journal of Political Science*, 3 (2), 217–242.

Maclachlan, Patricia. 2003. The Struggle for an Independent Consumer Society: Consumer Activism and the State's Response in Postwar Japan. In Frank J. Schwartz and Susan J. Pharr, eds. *The State of Civil Society in Japan*. Cambridge, UK: Cambridge University Press, 214–232.

Maclachlan, Patricia. 2004. From Subjects to Citizens: Japan's Evolving Consumer Identity. *Japanese Studies*, 24 (1), 115–134.

Martin, Sherry L. 2004. Alienated, Independent and Female: Lessons from the Japanese Electorate. *Social Science Japan Journal*, 7 (1), 1–19.

Matsubara, Jiro. 1974. Chihō Jichi No Hensitsu to Jyūmin Undō. In Jiro Matsubara, ed. *Jyūmin Sanka to Jichi No Kakushin*. Tokyo: Gakuyō Shobō, 12–28.

Matsubara, Jiro, and Kamon Nitagai. 1976. *Jyūmin Undō No Ronri: Undō No Tenkai Katei, Kadai to Tenbō*. Tokyo: Gakuyō Shobō.

Matsushita, Keiichi. 1971. *Shibiru Minimam No Shisō*. Tokyo: Tokyo Daigaku Shuppankai.

McKean, Margaret. 1981. *Environmental Protest and Citizen Politics in Japan*. Berkeley, CA: University of California Press.

Mclean, Iain, and Stephan L'Heureux. 2007. Sexual Assault Aftercare Services in Japan and the UK. *Japan Forum*, 19 (2), 239–256.

Ministry of Health, Labour and Welfare. 2007. Rōdō Kumiai Kiso Chōsa. Tokyo.

Miura, Mari. 2007. Koizumi Seiken to Rōdō Seiji No Henyō. *Nenpō Gyōsei Kenkyū* 42, 100–122.

Miyamoto, Kenichi. 1970. *Kōgai to Jyūmin Undō*. Tokyo: Jichitai Kenkyūsha.

Morris-Suzuki, Tessa. 2004. An Act Prejudicial to the Occupation Forces: Migration Controls and Korean Residents in Post-Surrender Japan. *Japanese Studies*, 24 (1), 5–28.

Morris-Suzuki, Tessa. 2006a. Defining the Boundaries of the Cold War Nation: 1950s Japan and the Other Within. *Japanese Studies*, 26 (3), 303–316.

Morris-Suzuki, Tessa. 2006b. Invisible Immigrants: Undocumented Migration and Border Controls in Early Postwar Japan. *Journal of Japanese Studies*, 32 (1), 119–153.

Motojima, Kunio, and Kokichi Shoji. 1980. *Chiiki Kaihatsu to Shakai Kōzō: Tomakomai Tōbu Daikibo Kōgyō Kaihatsu Wo Megutte*. Tokyo: Tokyo Daigaku Shuppankai.

Mouer, Ross E, and Yoshio Sugimoto. 2003. Civil Society in Japan. In David S. Schak and Wayne Hudson, eds. *Civil Society in Asia*. Farnham, UK: Ashgate Publishing, 209–224.

Mulgan, Aurelia George. 2005. Where Tradition Meets Change: Japan's Agricultural Politics in Transition. *Journal of Japanese Studies*, 31 (2), 261–298.

Muramatsu, Michio. 1974. Political Participation and Administrative Process in Contemporary Japan. In *The Annuals of the Japanese Political Science Association*. Tokyo: Iwanami Shoten, 41–68.

Nakagawa, Gou. 1980. *Chōnaikai: Nihonjin No Jichi Kankaku*. Tokyo: Chūōkōronsha.

Nakakita, Koji. 2009. Nihon No Rōdō Seiji: Minshushugi No Taisei No Henyō to Rengō. In Toshimitsu Arakawa and Toru Shinoda, eds. *Rōdō*

To Fukushi Kokka No Kanōsei: Rōdō Undō Saisei No Kokusai Hikaku. Tokyo: Minerva Shobō.

Nakamura, Karen. 2002. Resistance and Co-Optation: The Japanese Federation of the Deaf and Its Relations with State Power. *Social Science Japan Journal,* 5 (1), 17–35.

Nakata, Minoru. 1993. *Chiiki Kyōdō Kanri No Shakaigaku.* Tokyo: Tōshindō.

Nakatani, Miho. 2005. *Niihon Ni Okeru Atarashii Shimin Ishiki: Nyū Porityikaru Karuchā No Taitō.* Tokyo: Keio Gijyuku Daigaku Shuppankai.

Nakazawa, Hideo. 2004. *Jyūmin Tōhyō Undō to Rōkaru Rejiimu: Niigata Ken Makichō to Kongenteki Minshushugi No Hosomichi, 1994–2004.* Tokyo: Hābesto Sha.

Nanri, Keizo. 2005. The Conundrum of Japanese Editorials: Polarized, Diversified and Homogeneous. *Japanese Studies,* 25 (2), 169–185.

Neary, Ian. 2000. Rights and Psychiatric Patients in East Asia. *Japan Forum,* 12 (2), 157–168.

Neary, Ian. 2003. Japan's Human Security Agenda and Its Domestic Human Rights Policies. *Japan Forum,* 15 (2), 267–285.

Nihon Sōgō Kenkyūsho. 2008. *Nihon No Sōsharu Kyapitaru To Seisaku: Nihon Sōken 2007 Nen Zenkoku Ankēto Chōsa Kekka Hōkokusho.* Tokyo: Nihon Sōgō Kenkyūsho.

Nishio, Masaru. 1977. Political and Administrative Process of Urbanization. In *The Annals of the Japanese Political Science Association.* Tokyo: Iwanami Shoten, 193–258.

Nitagai, Kamon. 1991. Gendai Shakai No Chiiki Shūdan. In Kazuo Aoi, ed. *Chiiki Shakaigaku.* Tokyo: Saiensu Sha.

Nitagai, Kamon. ed. 2008. *Jiritsu shien no jissenchi: Hanshin-Awaji daishinsai to kyōdō, shimin shakai.* Tōshindō.

Noumi, Yasushi. 1997. Kōekiteki Dantai Ni Okeru Kōekisei to Hieirisei. *Juristo,* 1105, 50–55.

Ogawa, Akihiro. 2004. Invited by the State: Institutionalizing Volunteer Subjectivity in Contemporary Japan. *Asian Anthropology,* 3, 71–96.

Ogawa, Akihiro. 2009. *The Failure of Civil Society? The Third Sector and the State in Contemporary Japan.* Albany, NY: State University of New York Press.

Olson, Mancur. 1982. *The Rise and Declines of Nations.* New Haven, CT: Yale University Press.

Osa, Yukie. 2003. The Role of Japanese NGOs in the Pursuit of Human Security: Limits and Possibilities in the Field of Refugees. *Japan Forum,* 15 (2), 251–265.

Osawa, Mari. 2000. Government Approaches to Gender Equality in the Mid-1990s. *Social Science Japan Journal,* 3 (1), 3–19.

Ota, Hiroko. 1999. Sharing Governance: Changing Functions of Government, Business, and NPOs. In Tadashi Yamamoto, ed. *Deciding the Public Good: Governance and Civil Society in Japan.* Tokyo: Japan Center for International Exchange, 125–126.

Otake, Hideo. 2007. *Shin Sayoku No Isan: Nyū Refuto Kara Posto Modan He.* Tokyo: Tokyo Daigaku Shuppankai.

Pekkanen, Robert. 2000. Japan's New Politics: The Case of the NPO Law. *Journal of Japanese Studies,* 26 (1), 111–148.

Pekkanen, Robert. 2003. Molding Japanese Civil Society: State-Structured Incentives and the Patterning of Civil Society. In Frank J. Schwartz and Susan J. Pharr, eds. *The State of Civil Society in Japan.* New York, NY: Cambridge University Press, 116–134.

Pekkanen, Robert. 2004a. Japan: Social Capital without Advocacy. In Muthiah Alagappa, ed. *Civil Society and Political Change in Asia.* Stanford, CA: Stanford University Press, 223–255.

Pekkanen, Robert. 2004b. After the Developmental State: Civil Society in Japan. *Journal of East Asian Studies,* 4, 363–388.

Pekkanen, Robert. 2006. *Japan's Dual Civil Society: Members without Advocates.* Stanford, CA: Stanford University Press.

Pekkanen, Robert J., Yutaka Tsujinaka, and Hidehiro Yamamoto. 2014. *Neighborhood Associations and local Governance in Japan.* Routledge: London and New York.

Pekkanen, Robert, and Benjamin Read. 2003. *Explaining Cross-National Patterns in State-Fostered Local Associations.* Paper presented at the American Political Association Annual Meeting, Philadelphia, PA.

Pekkanen, Saadia M. 2001. International Law, the WTO, and the Japanese State: Assessment and Implications of the New Legalized Trade Politics. *Journal of Japanese Studies,* 27 (1), 41–79.

Pekkanen, Saadia M. 2003. International Law, Industry and the State: Explaining Japan's Complainant Activities at the WTO. *Pacific Review,* 16 (3), 285–306.

Pempel, T.J., and Keiichi Tsunekawa. 1979. Corporatism without Labor? In Philippe C. Schmitter and Gerhard Lehnbruch, eds. *Trends Towards Corporatism Intermediation.* London: Sage Publications, 231–237.

Peng, Ito. 2004. Postindustrial Pressures, Political Regime Shifts, and Social Policy Reform in Japan and South Korea. *Journal of East Asian Studies,* 4, 389–425.

Pharr, Susan J. 1981. *Political Women in Japan: The Search for a Place in Political Life.* Berkeley, CA: University of California Press.

Pharr, Susan J. 1990. *Losing Face: Status Politics in Japan.* Berkeley, CA: University of California Press.

Pharr, Susan J. 1996. Media as Trickster in Japan: A Comparative Perspective. In Susan J. Pharr and

Ellis S. Krauss, eds. *Media and Politics in Japan*. Honolulu, HI: University of Hawaii Press, 19–43.

Pharr, Susan J. 2003. Preface. In Frank J. Schwartz and Susan J. Pharr, eds. *The State of Civil Society in Japan*. Cambridge, UK: Cambridge University Press, xiii–xviii.

Potter, David M., and Douglas Van Belle. 2004. News Media Coverage Influence on Japan's Foreign Aid Allocations. *Japanese Journal of Political Science*, 5 (1), 113–135.

Putnam, Robert. 1993. *Making Democracy Work*. Princeton, NJ: Princeton University Press.

Putnam, Robert. 2000. *Bowling Alone: The Collapse and Revival of American Community*. New York, NY: Simon and Schuster.

Read, Benjamin, with Robert Pekkanen. 2009. *Local Organizations and Urban Governance in East and Southeast Asia: Straddling State and Society*. London: Routledge.

Reimann, Kim. 2001. Building Networks from the Outside. In International Movements, Japanese NGOs, and the Kyoto Climate Change Conference. *Mobilization*, 6 (1), 69–82.

Reimann, Kim. 2003. Building Global Civil Society from the Outside In? Japanese International Development NGOs, the State, and International Norms. In Frank J. Schwartz and Susan J. Pharr, eds. *The State of Civil Society in Japan*. Cambridge, UK: Cambridge University Press, 298–315.

Reimann, Kim. 2010. *The Rise of Japanese NGOs: Activism from Above*. London: Routledge.

Ryang, Sonia. 2000. *Koreans in Japan: Critical Voices from the Margin*. Abingdon, UK: Routledge.

Salamon, Lester M., and S. Wojciech Sokolowski. 2004. Global Civil Society: An Overview. In Lester M. Salamon, Helmut K. Anheier, Regina List, Stefan Toepler and S. Wojciech Sokolwski, eds. *Global Civil Society: Dimensions of the Nonprofit Sector*. Bloomfield, CT: Kumarian Press, 1–64.

Sasada, Hironori. 2008. Japan's New Agricultural Trade Policy and Electoral Reform: 'Agricultural Policy in an Offensive Posture [Seme No Nosei]'. *Japanese Journal of Political Science*, 9 (2), 121–144.

Sasaki-Uemura, Wesley. 2001. *Organizing the Spontaneous: Citizen Protest in Postwar Japan*. Honolulu, HI: University of Hawaii Press.

Sato, Iwao. 2006. Kokka Shakai Kankei: Shimin Sekutā No Hatten to Minkan Hieiri Hōsei. In Institute of Social Science University of Tokyo, ed. *Ushinawareta 10-Nen Wo Koete*. Tokyo: University of Tokyo Press.

Schreurs, Miranda A. 2002. *Environmental Politics in Japan, Germany, and the United States*. Cambridge, UK: Cambridge University Press.

Schwartz, Frank J. 2003. What Is Civil Society? In Frank J. Schwartz and Susan J. Pharr, eds. *The State of Civil Society in Japan*. Cambridge, UK: Cambridge University Press, 23–41.

Schwartz, Frank J., and Susan J. Pharr. 2003. *The State of Civil Society in Japan*. Cambridge, UK: Cambridge University Press.

Seaton, Philip. 2006. Reporting the 'Comfort Women' Issue, 1991–1992: Japan's Contested War Memories in the National Press. *Japanese Studies*, 26 (1), 99–112.

Shimazono, Susumu. 1998. The Commercialization of the Sacred: The Structural Evolution of Religious Communities in Japan. *Social Science Japan Journal*, 1 (2), 181–198.

Shin, Ki-young. 2004. Fufubessei Movement in Japan: Thinking About Women's Resistance and Subjectivity. *F-GENS Journal*, 2, 107–114.

Shinkawa, Toshimitsu. 1999. *Sengo Nihon Seiji to Shakai Minshushugi: Shakaitō, Sōhyō Burokku No Kōbō*. Tokyo: Hōritsu Bunka Sha.

Shinoda, Tomohito. 2007. Becoming More Realistic in the Post-Cold War: Japan's Changing Media and Public Opinion on National Security. *Japanese Journal of Political Science*, 8 (2), 171–190.

Shinoda, Toru. 1996. 'From Chicken to Duck' Again?: The Collapse of the 1955 System and Rengo. In *The Annuals of the Japanese Political Science Association*. Tokyo: Iwanami Shoten, 129–149.

Shinoda, Toru. 2005. Shimin Shakai No Shakai Undō He: Rōdō Undō No Furukute Atarashii Pāsupekutibu. In Jirou Yamaguchi, Taro Miyamoto and Minoru Tsubogou, eds. *Posuto Fukushi Kokka to Sōsharu Gabanansu*. Tokyo: Minerva Shobō, 243–272.

Shinohara, Hajime. 1977. *Shimin Sanka*. Tokyo: Iwanami Shoten.

Shipper, Apichai W. 2005. Criminals or Victims? The Politics of Illegal Foreigners in Japan. *Journal of Japanese Studies*, 31 (2), 299–327.

Shipper, Apichai W. 2006. Foreigners and Civil Society in Japan. *Pacific Affairs*, 79 (2), 269–289.

Shire, Karen A. 2000. Gendered Organization and Workplace Culture in Japanese Customer Services. *Social Science Japan Journal*, 3 (1), 37–58.

Siddle, Richard. 2002. An Epoch-Making Event? The 1997 Ainu Cultural Promotion Act and Its Impact. *Japan Forum*, 14 (3), 405–423.

Skocpol, Theda. 1998. Advocates without Members: The Recent Transformation of American Civic Life. In Theda Skocpol and Morris P. Fiorina, eds. *Civic Engagement in American Democracy*. Washington, DC: Brookings Institution Press, 461–509.

Steel, Gill. 2003. Gender and Voting Preferences in Japanese Lower House Elections. *Japanese Journal of Political Science*, 4 (1), 1–39.

Steel, Gill. 2004. Gender and Political Behaviour in Japan. *Social Science Japan Journal*, 7 (2), 223–244.

Steinhoff, Patricia G. 1989. Protest and Democracy. In Takeshi Ishida and Ellis S. Krauss, eds. *Democracy in Japan*. Pittsburgh, PA: University of Pittsburgh Press, 171–196.

Stevens, Carolyn S. 2007. Living with Disability in Urban Japan. *Japanese Studies,* 27 (3), 263–278.

Stevens, Carolyn S., Setsuko Lee, and Takashi Sawada. 2000. Undocumented Migrant Maternal and Child Health Care in Yokohama. *Japanese Studies,* 20 (1), 49–65.

Stevens, Georgina. 2001. The Ainu and Human Rights: Domestic and International Legal Protections. *Japanese Studies,* 21 (2), 181–198.

Strausz, Michael. 2006. Minorities and Protest in Japan: The Politics of the Fingerprinting Refusal Movement. *Pacific Affairs,* 79 (4), 641–656.

Sugimoto, Yoshio. 1981. *Popular Disturbance in Postwar Japan.* Hong Kong: Asian Research Service.

Suzuki, Akira. 2000. The Transformation of the Vision of Labor Unionism: Internal Union Politics in the Japanese Steel Industry in the 1960s. *Social Science Japan Journal,* 3 (1), 77–93.

Suzuki, Akira. 2003. The Death of Unions' Associational Life? Political and Cultural Aspects of Enterprise Unions. In Frank J. Schwartz and Susan J. Pharr, eds. *The State of Civil Society in Japan.* Cambridge, UK: Cambridge University Press, 195–213.

Suzuki, Kenji. 2008. Politics of the Falling Birthrate in Japan. *Japanese Journal of Political Science,* 9 (2), 161–182.

Takabatake, Michitoshi. 1977. Mass Movements: Changes and Diversities. In *The Annuals of the Japanese Political Science Association.* Tokyo: Iwanami Shoten, 323–359.

Takao, Yasuo. 2003. Foreigners' Rights in Japan: Beneficiaries to Participants. *Asian Survey,* 43 (3), 527–552.

Takao, Yasuo. 2007. Japanese Women in Grassroots Politics: Building a Gender-Equal Society from the Bottom Up. *The Pacific Review,* 20 (2), 147–172.

Takeda, Hiroko. 2006. Gendering the Japanese Political System: The Gender-Specific Pattern of Political Activity and Women's Political Participation. *Japanese Studies,* 26 (2), 185–198.

Takeuchi, Keiji. 1998. Chikyū ondanka no seiji-gaku. Tokyo: Asahi Sensho.

Tanaka, Shigeyoshi. 1990. Chōnaikai No Rekishi to Bunseki Shikaku. In Susumu Kurasawa and Ritsuo Aikimoto, eds. *Chōnaikai to Chiiki Shūdan.* Tokyo: Minerva Shobō, 27–60.

Taniguchi, Masaki. 2007. Changing Media, Changing Politics in Japan. *Japanese Journal of Political Science,* 8 (1), 147–166.

Tatsushi, Ogino. 2006. New Social Problems and Social Movements: Private Activities for School Refusal, Social Withdrawal (Hikikomori), and NEET. *Japanese Sociological Review,* 57 (2), 311–329.

Tomie, Naoko. 2005. The Political Process of Establishing the Mother–Child Protection Law in Prewar Japan. *Social Science Japan Journal,* 8 (2), 239–251.

Torigoe, Hiroyuki. 1994. *Chiiki Jichikai No Kenkyū: Burakukai, Chōnaikai, Jichikai No Tenkai Katei.* Tokyo: Minerva Shobō.

Tsujinaka, Yutaka. 1987. Rōdōkai No Saihen to 86 Nen Taisei No Imi. *Leviathan,* 1, 47–150.

Tsujinaka, Yutaka. 2002a. *Gendai Nihon No Shiminshakai: Rieki Dantai.* Tokyo: Bokutakusha, 255–286.

Tsujinaka, Yutaka. 2002b. Sekai Seijigaku No Bunmyaku Ni Okeru Shimin Shakai, NGO Kenkyū. *Leviathan,* 31, 8–25.

Tsujinaka, Yutaka. 2003. From Development to Maturity: Japan's Civil Society Organizations in Comparative Perspective. In Frank J. Schwartz and Susan J. Pharr, eds. *The State of Civil Society in Japan.* New York, NY: Cambridge University Press, 83–115.

Tsujinaka, Yutaka, and Jae-Young Choe. 2002. Rekishiteki Keisei. In Yutaka Tsujinaka, ed. *Gendai Nihon No Shimin Shakai: Rieki Dantai.* Tokyo: Bokutakusha.

Tsujinaka, Yutaka, Jae-Young Choe, Hidehiro Yamamoto, Hiroki Miwa, and Takafumi Otomo. 2007. Nihon No Shimin Shakai Kōzō to Seiji Sanka: Jichikai, Shakai Dantai, NPO No Zentai Zō to Sono Seiji Kanyo. *Leviathan,* 41, 7–44.

Tsujinaka, Yutaka, and Robert Pekkanen. 2007. Civil Society and Interest Groups in Contemporary Japan. *Pacific Affairs,* 80 (3), 419–437.

Tsujinaka, Yutaka, Robert Pekkanen, and Hidehiro Yamamoto. 2009. *Jichikai Ni Okeru Rōcaru Gabanansu: Jichikai Zenkokuchōsa No Bunseki.* Tokyo: Bokutakusha.

Ui, Jyun. 1968. *Kōgai No Seijigaku:* Sanseidou.

Upham, Frank K. 1987. *Law and Social Change in Postwar Japan.* Cambridge: Harvard University Press, MA.

Ushiyama, Kunihiko. 2006. Social Movement and Public Policy. *Japanese Sociological Review,* 57 (2), 259–274.

Vogel, Steven K. 1999. When Interests Are Not Preferences: The Cautionary Tale of Japanese Consumers. *Comparative Politics,* 31 (2), 187–207.

Weathers, Charles. 2001a. Changing White-Collar Workplaces and Female Temporary Workers in Japan. *Social Science Japan Journal,* 4 (2), 201–218.

Weathers, Charles. 2001b. The Last Gasp of Labor's Dual Strategy? Japan's 1997 Wage-Setting Round. *Japan Forum,* 13 (2), 215–232.

Weathers, Charles. 2005. In Search of Strategic Partners: Japan's Campaign for Equal Opportunity. *Social Science Japan Journal,* 8 (1), 69–89.

Webb, Philippa. 2002. Time to Share the Burden: Long Term Care Insurance and the Japanese Family. *Japanese Studies,* 22 (2), 113–129.

Webb, Philippa. 2003. Legislating for Care: A Comparative Analysis of Long-Term Care Insurance

Laws in Japan and Germany. *Social Science Japan Journal*, 6 (1), 39–56.

Wender, Melissa. 2000. Mothers Write Ikaino. In Sonia Ryang, eds. *Koreans in Japan: Critical Voices from the Margin*. Abingdon, UK: Routledge, 74–102.

White, James W. 1995. *Ikki: Social Conflict and Political Protest in Early Modern Japan*. Ithaca, NY: Cornell University Press.

Yamagishi, Toshio. 2003. Trust and Social Intelligence in Japan. In Frank J. Schwartz and Susan J. Pharr, eds. *The State of Civil Society in Japan*. Cambridge, UK: Cambridge University Press, 281–297.

Yamaguchi, Yasushi. 2005. *Shimin Shakai Ron: Rekishiteki Isan to Shintenkai*. Tokyo: Yuhikaku.

Yamamoto, Hidehiro, and Makoto Nishikido. 2004. Ibento Bunseki No Tenkai: Seijiteki Kikai Kōzōron Tono Kanren Wo Chūshin Ni. In Seiji Soranaka, ed. *Shakai Undō to Iu Kōkyō Kūkan: Riron to Hōhō No Furontia*. Tokyo: Seibundō.

Yamamoto, Tadashi. 1998. Nihon No Shibiru Sosaetii No Hatten To Gabanansu He No Eikyou. In Makoto Iokibe, Akira Irie, Hiroko Ota, Tadashi Yamamoto, Shinichi Yoshida and Jyun Wada, eds. *Kan Kara Min He No Pawā shifto: Darenotame No Kōeki Ka*. Tokyo: Hankyu Communication.

Yamaoka, Yoshinori. 1998. On the History of the Nonprofit Sector in Japan. In Tadashi Yamamoto, ed. *The Nonprofit Sector in Japan*. Manchester, UK: Manchester University Press, 19–58.

Yamashita, Yusuke, and Mashiho Suga. 2002. *Shinsai Borantyia No Shakaigaku: 'Borantyia = NPO' Shakai No Kanōsei*. Tokyo: Minerva Shobō.

Yamauchi, Naoto. 2005. Shibirusosaetii O Sokuteisuru. *Kōkyō Seisaku Kenkyū*, 5, 53–67.

Yamauchi, Naoto, and Eiko Ibuki. 2005. *Nihon No Sōsharu Kyapitaru*. Osaka: Osaka Daigaku NPO Kenkyū Jyōhō Sentā.

Yoda, Hiroe. 2002. New Views on Disabilities and the Challenge to Social Welfare in Japan. *Social Science Japan Journal*, 5 (1), 1–15.

Yoshida, Kenzo, Yung-Hsing Guo, and Li-Hsuan Cheng. 2006. The Japanese Pension Reform of 2004: A New Mode of Legislative Process. *Asian Survey*, 46 (3), 381–400.

Yoshihara, Naoki. 1993. Komyunitii Seisaku to Chiiki Jyūmin Soshiki. In Kamon Nitagai, Otohiko Hasumi and Sumiko Yazawa, ed. *Toshi Seisaku To Shimin Katsudō*. Tokyo: Tokyo Daigaku Shuppankai.

Yoshihara, Naoki. 1997. Tenkanki No Komyunitii Seisaku In Kamon Nitagai, Otohiko Hasumi and Sumiko Yazawa, eds. *Gendai Toshi To Chiiki Keisei: Tenkanki To Sono Shakai Keitai*. Tokyo: Tokyo Daigaku Shuppankai, 101–120.

Yoshimatsu, Hidetaka. 2005. Japan's Keidanren and Free Trade Agreements: Societal Interests and Trade Policy. *Asian Survey*, 45 (2), 258–278.

23

Japan's International Relations

Christopher W. Hughes

JAPAN'S INTERNATIONAL RELATIONS: A GROWING AND DYNAMIC FIELD OF STUDY

Japan's international relations has moved from being a minor and rather marginalised field of study during the Cold War period to becoming increasingly mainstream and vibrant in the past two decades, and capable of attracting considerable attention from both Japan and non-Japan specialists alike. Indeed, it is even arguable that Japan's international relations, and the related sub-fields of security policy and international political economy, have now shifted to become the dominant arenas for debate on Japanese politics and economics. Japan's perceived domestic political and economic stultification has inevitably engendered a move towards concentrating on the comparatively fresh dynamism of its international relations; although, of course, Japan's domestic and international politics and economics continue to be inextricably linked and influence each other, and thus need to be studied in tandem.

The objective of this chapter is to outline the different ways in which Japan's international relations have been understood in the postwar period, but especially how they have been revisited in the post-Cold War period and ascribed a new importance. The chapter demonstrates how there has been a vigorous and increasingly rigorous debate on the motivations, means, arenas and patterns of Japan's engagement with the external world, and, despite the fact that no overall new consensus has been reached, all sides are agreed that Japan has only become more important to study as an international player capable of maintaining or even challenging the evolving international system.

THE STUDY OF JAPAN'S INTERNATIONAL RELATIONS UNTIL THE END OF THE COLD WAR

Japan's international relations up until the latter stages of the Cold War were relatively understudied in a number of ways due to a combination of factors. Japan's own concentration of national efforts upon the rebuilding of its economy in the postwar era, and low profile role in international security through reliance on the United States–Japan security treaty (encapsulated in the so-called 'Yoshida Doctrine), and its subsequent record of spectacular economic growth, meant that it was the Japanese economic model which attracted the major attention of Japan specialists and social scientists. Consequently, the quantity of studies focused on Japan's international relations, either in English or Japanese, was limited in comparison with the near avalanche of studies on the Japanese economy. Amongst this limited number of studies there were some fine and pioneering evaluations of Japan's security policy by primarily Japan specialists written in English (Mendel 1961; Weinstein 1971; Endicott 1975; Chapman, Drifte and Gow 1982; Holland 1988; Welfield 1988) and a few in Japanese (Ōtake 1983; Chūma 1985). Nevertheless, continuing societal taboos meant that, despite the centrality of security issues to Japan's international relations, their discussion still failed to reach the mainstream of social science debate amongst Japanese scholars, and the discussion of military and security affairs (particularly the role of nuclear weapons) was left more to the critical and Marxist-influenced tradition of Japan Peace Studies (Sakamoto 1982). Moreover, there were only a few studies that purported to provide a more general overview of Japan's international relations with regard to a variety of states and regions (Scalapino 1977; Ozaki and Arnold 1985; Inoguchi and Okimoto 1988), and even these tended to lack an integrated framework to help explain Japan's key international objectives and behaviour. Furthermore, there were virtually no systematic attempts to interpret Japan's international relations embedded within wider theories of International Relations (IR) as a discipline.

Japan's anonymity within mainstream IR was no doubt a reflection of its perceived lack of actual international influence, and its heavy reliance internationally on the shield of US economic and military hegemony, which seemed to provide a ready overall explanation of the limited ambitions of its international relations. In fact, one of the most dominant characterisations and explanations for Japan's international relations, which grew out of this context of Japanese reliance on the United States and which has proved influential to the current day, is the 'Reactive State' thesis (Calder 1988). This thesis posits that the Japanese state's fragmented domestic policymaking means it finds it difficult to convert its economic resources into proactive international leverage and strategies, thus rendering it passive and reactively pliant to external international pressures, particularly from the United States.

JAPAN RE-EMERGES AS AN INTERNATIONAL ACTOR POST-COLD WAR

However, both Japan specialists and the discipline of IR began to look again at Japan's international relations with a new sense of importance and depth in the late 1980s and early 1990s. In the first instance, this strengthened interest, driven by Japan's ascent to economic superpower status, was even thought at one stage to rival that of the United States, and the concomitant expectations that Japan would look to convert its economic might into political and military power. Japan watchers began to sense a new potential for proactivity or even leadership in its external relations. Japan was touted as the new 'Number One' in the international system, and even a rising hegemonic power in East Asia (Vogel 1979, 1986; Nester 1990). Other observers were less sanguine about the potential benefits of a rising Japan for the international system. Japan was viewed as a 'problem' because of its believed mercantilistic free-riding on the liberal international order, with no strategy other than the pursuit of market share and crushing of economic rivals (van Wolferen 1990). The so-called 'Japan Revisionists' viewed the Japanese economic model as a direct threat to continued US economic and political dominance (Prestowitz 1988; Fallows 1994; Johnson 1995) and argued that the United States could only counter Japan's rise through adopting a similar style of industrial policy.

These predictions of Japanese attempts to exert hegemony over the international system and to displace US dominance were soon shown to be overplayed though by the events of the first Gulf War of 1990–1991 and by the bursting of the Japanese 'bubble economy' at the turn of the decade and onset of the Heisei recession. Japan's inability due to constitutional prohibitions to respond to US and international expectations to provide a 'human contribution' to the military coalition through the despatch of the Japan Self Defence Forces (JSDF), and its resort instead to providing US$13 billion to underwrite the war effort, often derided as 'chequebook diplomacy', highlighted its limitations as a political and security power. Moreover, the domestic gridlock that ensued in the wake of attempts by the Japanese government to articulate an effective response to the international crisis, and its desperation to try to conform to US requests to support the war effort, seemed to confirm the Reactive State thesis, and that Japan was essentially a follower of US hegemony. Added to this, although the impact of the bursting of the bubble on economic dynamism was only to be slowly and fully revealed by mid-decade, Japan's prospects for dominating the international economic and political system already looked limited by the early 1990s.

Nonetheless, even though the experience of the Gulf War and onset of the Heisei recession thwarted expectations for Japan to establish a more proactive and dominant international role, and thus might have seemed to call into question the initial basis for new scholarly interest in Japan in the post-Cold War period, these events were actually to form a new point of departure for an even deeper and more sophisticated scholarly investigation of Japan's international relations. The reasons for interest in Japan actually deepening after the Gulf War were related to the fact that in revealing its inadequacies as an international actor it had nevertheless begun to reveal new ambitions for an expanded international role in response to its changing external environment, as well as presenting new puzzles concerning the formulation of its international strategy. All of these issues were of central interest to traditional Japan specialists as well as the broader field of IR.

In particular, Japan's demonstration of new attempts to strengthen its international security profile by enacting an International Peace Cooperation Law in June 1992 to enable the first despatches of the JSDF overseas on UN peacekeeping missions was seen as one indication of potential new proactivity growing out the initial diplomatic rout of the Gulf War. In turn, Japan's facing of new security challenges from a more militant North Korea in the postwar period, manifested in ongoing nuclear crises since the mid-1990s, and then the looming issue of the impact of the rise of China on Japan's regional position, have been seen to force Japan into taking steps to strengthen the United States–Japan alliance relationship and its own military options, all of which have attracted scholarly and policy attention. Similarly, rapid change in Japan's wider regional environment, taking the form of greater economic interdependence, but also problems of economic crises, have pushed Japan towards greater efforts in region-building, and raised interesting questions about the possibilities for Japanese regional leadership and the impact of a more integrated East Asia region on global politics as a whole. Finally, Japan in searching for a new international role has often failed to conform to existing models of its international behaviour. Japan has actually been seen to increasingly defy the reactive state thesis, not simply because it has often shown more regular proactivity, but also because it has shown itself to be less predictably pliant to US and international pressures. Indeed, the fact that the Japanese government in the end did not succumb to US expectations in the Gulf War, and instead domestic politics momentarily trumped these external pressures, has presented Japan and IR specialists with the need to reassess previous standard explanations of Japan's international relations as purely shaped by dependence on the United States.

Japan's international profile and interest in its international relations was then further elevated by its reaction under the premiership of Koizumi Junichirō to the 11 September attacks. Japan's comparatively rapid despatch of the JSDF to support the US 'war on terror' in Afghanistan and Iraq, albeit on non-combat missions, again seemed to challenge the image of Japanese reactivity. Koizumi's generally assertive stance on international affairs, the rising antagonism between Japan and China during his administration, and his high-profile diplomacy towards North Korea, again further raised Japan's international notoriety. Koizumi's successors, Abe Shinzō, Fukuda Yasuo and Asō Tarō, have proved less successful in pursuing a proactive international policy, but again Japan's reversion to a more cautious international strategy has only contributed to its intrigue and attraction as an object of academic investigation.

KEY ISSUES AND DEBATES IN JAPAN'S INTERNATIONAL RELATIONS

Japan now presents a compelling set of reasons in the post-Cold War period for being studied, if not as a hegemonic power, then as an increasingly proactive actor of growing importance regionally and globally, and of central theoretical and empirical significance to mainstream IR. In turn, the evolving study of Japan's international relations can perhaps be divided into four central questions that preoccupied scholars and policymakers (Hook, Gilson, Hughes and Dobson 2005: 21–23), although clearly many of these questions and studies overlap and feed off each other. The first main question has been to try to explain the fundamental roots of *why* Japan behaves the way it does in the international system, and to focus in particular on questions of whether Japan is driven mainly by external forces or by internal political constraints when devising its security policy. The second main question devotes attention to examining the principal means of *how* Japan pursues its international relations, often involving detailed studies of its willingness to deploy various types of military, economic and 'soft' power. The third main question and set of studies fix upon the various arenas for *where* Japan has pursued its international relations, in both the geographical sense of particular relations with a range of other states and regions, and in the sense of interaction with international frameworks, and institutions. The fourth main question, strongly informed by the other three, therefore revolves around exactly *what* type of behaviour and actor Japan has and will assume in the international system. This question often involves attempts to handily encapsulate Japan as a particular type of state in order to capture the essence of its international behaviour, and attempts to estimate how far the impact of Japan's behaviour is beneficial or detrimental to its own international standing and the strength of the international system as a whole.

EXPLAINING MOTIVATIONS FOR JAPAN'S INTERNATIONAL RELATIONS

The first school of IR theory, which has attempted to grapple with explaining the motivations and drivers of Japan's international stance, has been that of Realism and its subvarieties. Japan appeared virtually off the radar of the Classical Realist and English School examinations of great power politics in the interwar, postwar and periods (Suganami 1984; Suzuki 2005), but with the resurgence of Realism in the shape of Neo-Realism from the late 1970s onwards, coinciding with Japan's own international resurgence, Japan began to appear in the mainstream of Realist analysis, even if still viewed as a marginal actor or apparent exception to Realist assumptions regarding state behaviour. Neorealists – in line with their theoretical assumptions about the anarchical, self-help international system, characterised by states' search for security determined by the distribution of material capabilities – asserted that Japan would be eventually pushed by the less stable post-Cold War international structure to convert its economic power into military power, to build a supporting regional bloc and to aspire great power status. Japan, it was argued, at the end of the Cold War stood as 'structural anomaly', because it had not yet emerged from the shadow of US hegemony, but that it would inevitably be obliged to give up this status and fend more for its own security and even to acquire nuclear weapons (Layne 1993; Waltz 1993: 55–70).

Other, more recent, Neo-Realist analysis since the 1990s has reinforced this type of analysis, although working more from the assumption that Japan is a relatively declining power. 'Offensive Realists' view international security as in short supply, and thus argue that states are compelled to take assertive or even aggressive steps to ensure their national interests, and this tendency is particularly pronounced in an increasingly fluid and multi-polar international environment. Hence, Japan, in line with this analysis and encountering conditions of weakening US hegemony, the rise of China as a possible new hegemon, and the weakening of its own economic power, would be tempted to strengthen alliance ties with the United States, but also to convert itself into a formidable independent military power (Mearsheimer 2001: 372–377, 396–400). Indeed, 'Offensive Realism' would argue that the only reason Japan has not yet sought to convert its economic power into truly significant military power is because of its ability to 'free ride' or 'buck pass' on security through reliance on the US security guarantee (Lind 2004).

'Defensive Realists' take a different tack, viewing the dangers of the international system as mitigated somewhat by the superiority of defensive weapons systems, geographical distance between rival states, and an aversion to unnecessary conflict built up in response to past costly wars. In accordance with this interpretation, Japan is set to concentrate on simply augmenting its defensive military capabilities, seeking to avoid conflict with a rising China, and to make only the minimal necessary commitments to the United States–Japan alliance so as to function as a 'circumscribed balancer' against China (Twomey 2000). Other 'Defensive Realist' analysis argues that Japan is certainly wary of the dangers of the international system but seeks to ameliorate tensions that might lead to conflict through a strategy of reassuring its neighbours about its purely defensive intent (Midford 2002). Similarly, other Realist-style interpretations of Japan have pointed to these highly defensive and cautious motivations behind its foreign and security policy (Pharr 1993), and a tendency to hedge against over-reliance on the alliance with the United States in order to avoid the dilemmas of 'entrapment' (becoming drawn into a conflict on the side of the United States) and 'abandonment' (becoming distanced from the United States if not seen to be a reliable ally) (Heginbotham and Samuels 2002). These 'Defensive Realist' analyses have been further refined through definitions of Japan as a 'mercantile realist' state which seeks to navigate its way through the hazards of the international system relying principally on economic power (Heginbotham and Samuels 1998; Samuels 2007a); and as a state undergoing a conversion to 'reluctant realism' (Green 2001) or 'transitional realism' (Kliman 2006), whereby Japan is gradually cajoled by new security challenges to undertake enhanced alliance and international commitments. Meanwhile, other analysts, even if not explicitly using the language of Realist theory, share in the view that Japan is being pushed by the transforming international system to revisit some of its prewar assumptions about how to secure its national interests (Pyle 2007).

The second school of IR theory, less mainstream in recent years but still offering potentially useful insights into Japan's international motivations, is Marxism and its Critical Theory derivatives. These theories are driven by different assumptions from Realism concerning the purpose of theory, the key actors in the international system and the possibility for escape from an endless historical cycle of international conflict. Nevertheless, Marxism and Critical Theory converge somewhat with Realism in emphasising the inherently conflictual nature of international politics, especially around economic issues, the material motivations driving state behaviour and the propensity of states to aspire to hegemonic and even imperialistic power designs. Analyses of Japan in an overt classical Marxist framework are relatively rare, especially in the post-Cold War period, and tend to emphasise Japanese ambitions to assert a form of neo-imperialism over East Asia and other regions. Japan is seen to do this by locking developing states into a relationship of direct economic subordination and into new regional frameworks geared to reinforcing its dominance (Stevens 1990). Critical Theory has viewed Japan as asserting its potential hegemony not only through economic ties but also more subtly through setting ideological agendas and international institutions (Cox 1989). The influence of Marxist and Critical Theory can also be seen to have filtered through into other critical analyses of Japan's foreign relations, even if they are not explicitly termed in line with these theories. For instance, Japanese perceived subservience to the United States in political and security affairs as an example of the Japanese ruling elites' complicity with and the Japanese population's victimisation by a form of near US neo-imperialism, and Japanese remilitarisation is seen to be driven by narrow military–industrial commercial interests in Japan (McCormack 2007). Indeed, much of the later work of the members of the 'Japan Revisionist' school, as mentioned earlier, appears to have shades of Marxist interpretations in regard to Japan's supposedly relentless drive for material domination over other societies.

The third IR theory school to tackle Japan, and which, in contrast to Marxism, is strongly opposed to Realist assumptions and predictions, is Liberalism and its subvarieties of Idealism, Liberal Internationalism and Neoliberal Institutionalism. Liberalism's emphasis on the role of democracy, institutions and economic interdependence in governing the international system has meant that Japan is seen to have powerful incentives to pursue international cooperation. Japan has been examined as a new form of 'civilian power' (Maull 1990–1991; Funabashi 1991–1992) or 'trading state' (Rosecrance 1986), seeking to pursue its interests in the post-Cold War period, not through military power, but through economic ties and international institutions.

However, it is fair to say that Liberalism, despite its mainstream position in IR theory, has proved less prevalent as a form of analysis of Japan's international relations and as a counter to Realist interpretations of Japan. This is due largely to Japan's own behaviour, which, whilst it has been seen to not always conform to Realist assumptions of the pursuit of great power military status, has also not always conformed to Liberal assumptions either, due to the apparent prioritisation of economic interests to the detriment of other states and the reticence to provide leadership as an advanced democracy in international institutions. Instead, in recent years, a fourth school of IR theory, Constructivism, has provided the main counterpoint to Realism. Constructivism rejects the

Realist proposition that the condition of anarchy is inherently conflictual and instead posits that states through a process of socialisation construct identities and norms that may allow for more cooperative outcomes. In addition, other varieties of Constructivism stress that domestic norms constitute and regulate state interests and behaviour, and in many cases these domestic norms may prove more dominant than international structural pressures in shaping a state's international orientation. In the case of Japan, Constructivists' analysis has been particularly innovative in relation to the role of domestic norms, and argued that deeply vested societal norms of anti-militarism account for why Japan has been so resistant to moving towards becoming a major military power, despite its economic size and growing international pressures (Katzenstein and Okawara 1993; Katzenstein 1996, 2008; Berger 1993, 1998; Hook 1996; Dobson 2003; Leheny 2006; Oros 2008). Constructivist analyses have also been used to demonstrate why Japan adheres to particular environmental and economic policies, apparently at times even against its own rational interests in the international system, due to the contestation between its domestic and international norms (Miyaoka 2003; Sato and Hirata 2008). Many of these Constructivist approaches have tended to fix upon more 'progressive' norms such as anti-militarism, pacifism and internationalism, and thus come to similar conclusions to Liberalism about Japan's military-averse and cooperative international stance (Berger 2004).

Constructivism and Liberalism's focus on more domestic-oriented explanations of Japan's international behaviour have also been increasingly complemented and reinforced by foreign policy analysis (FPA) studies. These FPA studies help to open up the proverbial 'black-box' of Japanese internal decision-making and to create a bridge between theoretical explanations located at the international systemic level and developments in domestic politics that readily impact on external policy. Japan's foreign policy has thus been analysed from the perspective of interactions between the international and domestic levels in the form of 'two-level games' in trade negotiations, whereby effective trade negotiations between Japan and the United States can only be pursued if the conditions satisfy both national governments and domestic constituencies (Schoppa 1997). More recent analyses have demonstrated the increasing pluralism and expanding range of actors involved in the formation of Japanese foreign policy (Hashimoto 1999; Shinoda 2006). Recent studies, for instance, have focused on the growing role of the prime minister, especially during the tenure of Koizumi, in leading Japanese foreign policy (Ijima 2007; Shinoda 2007), the role of the National Diet (Nakano 2000), of local government actors in international affairs (Jain 2005), and also the role of public opinion in continuing to restrain political leaders' international ambitions (Eldridge and Midford 2008).

Constructivism's and FPA recent success as a theoretical approach can largely be accounted for by its apparent ability to explain the motivations in Japan's international behaviour that are supposedly inexplicable to Realism. Consequently, Realist and Constructivist approaches spent much of the 1990s butting heads and claiming to definitively refute each other. However, by the end of the decade it became clear that both schools had over-caricatured and over-simplified each others' key assumptions and that they actually shared a degree of common ground and explanatory leverage on Japan's international relations. Despite the fact that both Classical Realist and Neo-Realism had never neglected the role of 'second image' domestic variables in shaping states' foreign policy, Realists felt the need to respond to the challenge of Constructivism and Liberalism through articulating a new form of 'Neoclassical Realism'. This variety of Realism looks to demonstrate how, whilst international anarchy sets the general parameters for state behaviour, the actual form of responses selected by states will be heavily conditioned by domestic variables such as norms (Rose 1998). At the same time, Constructivist analysts also began to acknowledge the need to break down often artificial barriers with other paradigms and to combine the best of insights of Realism, Liberalism, Constructivism and even Critical approaches, and especially to combine domestic and international level approaches, in order to produce a new 'analytical eclecticism' to explain Japan's international behaviour (Berger 1996; Katzenstein and Okawara 2001; Hook, Gilson, Hughes and Dobson 2005). This move to integrate different IR theoretical approaches promises to provide a rich area for future analysis of Japan's external relations, in regard to the interaction between international systemic change, multiple domestic actors and a variety of norms, including less progressive norms connected with historical memory and nationalism (Berger 2003).

JAPAN'S INSTRUMENTALISATION OF ITS INTERNATIONAL RELATIONS

Japan's choice of means to pursue its international relations has been scrutinised from an ever-widening series of perspectives as its own range of international activities has increased. In turn, there has been a widening series of perspectives on how effective these means have been for Japan to achieve its international ends.

In line with Japan's traditional image as a major economic power, but enjoying lesser political and military capabilities, many early studies focused on the Japanese advancement of interests through economic means. In the 1980s, as Japan climbed to achieve the position as the larger provider of Official Development Assistance (ODA) in East Asia and globally, so there was a mini-plethora of studies on the Japanese strategic use of aid to augment its international economic and political influence, and to compensate for its relative lack of military power (Orr 1990; Igarashi 1990; Islam 1991; Rix 1993; Arase 1995; Soderberg 1996; Yasutomo 1986; Hughes 2004a).

However, as Japan's relative economic power declined in the 1990s, and as Japan began to undertake enhanced international security responsibilities, an increasing number of studies began to emerge relating to the evolution of its security policy and growing military power (Tanaka 1997; Sadō 2003a, 2003b; Asahi Shimbun Jieitai 50nen Shuzaiha, 2005; Nakajima 2006). The first of these studies examined the linkages between Japanese economic and technological prowess (or 'techno-nationalism'), defence production, and national security objectives (Green 1995; Samuels 1996). More recent studies have examined the Japan Self Defence Forces (JSDF) new found societal confidence (Frühstück 2007), and its expanding military capabilities and international role (Maeda 1993, 2007; Hughes 2004b, 2004c), in areas such as maritime security (Woolley 1999; Graham 2006), UN peacekeeping operations (Dobson 2003) and the response to the 'war on terror' (Hughes 2004a, 2009a). The Japan Coast Guard has also been examined as a form of 'second navy', augmenting Japan's military capabilities (Samuels 2008). Japan's interest in acquiring a nuclear weapons option to guarantee its own security has also been a subject of study in line with fluctuations in Japan's security ties with North Korea and China and its confidence in the US 'nuclear umbrella' (Self and Thompson 2003; Hughes, L. 2007).

Even more recent studies have fixed upon new Japanese approaches to furthering international influence, such as using 'aggressive legalism' and turning international rules against the United States and other states in order to pursue its interests in international trade negotiations (Pekkanen 2008); and 'soft power' in the form of Japanese high and popular culture (Drifte 1998; McGray 2002; Watanabe and McConnell 2008).

JAPANESE ARENAS FOR THE EXERCISE OF ITS INTERNATIONAL RELATIONS

Japan, in addition to employing new forms of power to pursue its international relations, has been seen in the post-Cold War period to have widened the range of arenas for where it has pursued it international relations. These arenas encompass traditional and new bilateral relationships, and a new-found interest in regional and global multilateralism.

Despite the fact that Japan's international relations continue to be so heavily influenced by bilateral ties with the United States, it is perhaps surprising that there are still few major comprehensive studies of United States–Japan relations which take in political, economic and security ties. The most prolific types of United States–Japan studies tend to be those focusing on security relations. These studies have highlighted the efforts Japan and the United States have made to upgrade the alliance in response to emergent threats from North Korea and China, and to the issues of transnational terrorism and weapons of mass destruction post-11 September. Hence, studies have covered issues such as the revision of the United States–Japan Guidelines for Defence Cooperation in the late-1990s (Funabashi 1999); US force realignments with regard to Okinawa; Ballistic Missile Defence; cooperation in defence production; and general alliance management (Muroyama 1992; Mochizuki 1997; Green and Cronin 1999; Sotooka, Honda and Miura 2001; Ikenberry and Inoguchi 2003; Samuels 2003; Hughes 2004a, 2009a; Calder 2007, 2009). However, set alongside the United States–Japan military alliance studies, there are a smaller number of prominent edited collections and co-authored collections that examine the full gamut of bilateral relations, including security, trade, finance, technology and societal interchange (Schaller 1997; Iriye and Wampler 2001; Vogel 2002; Krauss and Pempel 2004; Hook et al. 2005: 87–176).

Japan's key bilateral ties with other states in its own immediate East Asia region have seen a very strong expansion in recent years. Japan's ties with South Korea and North Korea with regard to the issues of history, economic ties and security have been explored and debated as sources for cooperation but also continuing tensions (Bridges 1993; Cha 1999; Hughes 2009b; Hyon 2006; Hagstrom and Soderberg 2006a; 2006b). Academic analysis of Japan's relations with China has also expanded as a result of China's rise relative to Japan and a host of interconnected policy issues often leading to bilateral tensions. Some forms of analysis have focused on Sino–Japanese ties as characterised by increasing competition and even the potential for conflict, as seen in frictions over history, trade, energy resources, the shaping of the East Asian regional order, territorial disputes and military security (Whiting 1989; Green and Self 1996; Rose 1998, 2005; Austin and Harris 2001; Drifte 2003; Hagstrom 2005; Wan 2006; Iechika, Matsuda

and Dan 2007; Heazle and Knight 2007; Hughes 2009c). For other perspectives, the relationship, whilst full of potential tensions, has been viewed in more cooperative terms as economic interdependency and political pragmatism take hold (Zhao 1993; Howe 1996; Kokubun and Wang 2004).

Japan's other key sets of bilateral relationships in the East Asia region are with individual Association of South East Asia Nations (ASEAN) states and with ASEAN as a collective whole. More recent studies have sought to demonstrate how Japan has attempted to build a special relationship in this subregion in order to bolster its overall economic and political regional influence vis-à-vis the United States and a rising China (Mendl 2001; Sudo 2002; Seekins 2007). Japan's wider region-building efforts, and the place of these in its wider international strategy, have also garnered considerable attention in the last two decades.

Japan has been seen as buttressing its overall international position by variously seeking to integrate the East Asian region in line with its own developmental state model (Hatch and Yamamura 1996; Lee 2008), and to forge more effective multilateral frameworks for economic cooperation through the Asia–Pacific Economic Cooperation (APEC) (Funabashi 1995; Terada 2001; Krauss 2003), the Asian Development Bank (ADB) (Wan 2001), and the ASEAN Plus Three (APT) and East Asian Community (EAC) (Satō and Tanaka 2005). Japan has been viewed increasingly as contributing to regional integration not only through economic engagement, but also through new political and security ties in the ASEAN Regional Forum (ARF) (Yuzawa 2007), and working through informal, non-state business actors, and soft forms of power (Katzenstein and Shiraishi 1997, 2006; Miyashita and Sato 2001; Pempel 2005; Rozman, Togo and Ferguson 2007). Japan is regarded as having been particularly active in pushing forward its leadership in regional monetary cooperation in the wake of the East Asian financial crisis of the late 1990s – as seen in its abortive proposals for an Asian Monetary Fund and subsequent support for ASEAN's Chiang Mai Initiative regional liquidity fund – in order to insulate the region from further shocks of globalisation (Hughes 2000; Katada 2001; Hayashi 2006; Grimes 2009); and to promote bilateral free trade agreements (Urata 2002; Watanabe 2007), with one objective being to counterbalance the rise of China.

Japan's new proactivity has been further detected on the margins of the East Asia region and in developing new sets of relations in regions much further away. Japanese policymakers have been seen to seek stronger ties with Australia (Beeson 1999; Terada 2006; Bisley 2008) and India (Jain 1996; Emmott 2008) as potential new partners in diluting and counterbalancing the rising influence of China in the East Asia region. Japan's troubled relationship with the Soviet Union and Russia over the disputed sovereignty of the Northern Territories has long been chronicled (Wada 1999; Williams 2007; Kimura 2008). However, more recent studies are also beginning to examine Japan's attempts to construct a more comprehensive relationship with Russia in the fields of energy, industrial cooperation and wider diplomacy, again as a means to soft balance against the rise of China (Kuhrt 2007). Finally, Japan's expanding diplomatic horizons have been seen to take in the Middle East (Sugihara and Allan 1993; Miyagi 2008), Africa (Ampiah 1997) and the European Union (Gilson 2000; Davies 2003), as it seeks new partners to tackle questions of energy and resource security, international trade, economic integration, and reform of international institutions.

Japan has been further analysed as an increasingly effective actor within a range of international institutions. The degree to which Japan's international relations have been influenced by the United Nations have been examined (Pan 2005; Hook et al. 2005: 367–388), and in turn the degree to which it has attempted to reform the United Nations in order to gain for itself a permanent Security Council seat (Drifte 2000). Similarly, Japan has been revealed to be a much more adept actor in supplying norms and ideas to other UN family organisations, such as the World Bank and World Health Organization (Tadakoro and Shiroyama 2004), and the G-8 and G-20 processes (Dobson 2004).

CONCLUSION

The Character of Japan as an International Actor

This overview of the motivations, methods and arenas now brings forward consideration of the final main question relating to Japan's international relations, which concerns itself with the character and direction of the international role that Japan is capable of fulfilling. It is safe to say that most analysts of Japan view it as an increasingly proactive, assertive and even efficacious actor, regardless of their particular theoretical stance, or focus on types of power or areas of international interaction (Iokibe 2000; Hook et al. 2005; Berger, Mochizuki and Tsuchiyama 2007). However, where analysts diverge is over how far Japan is diverging from its traditional low posture international role and the overall impact on the international system of a more assertive, rising or even declining Japan.

For some analysts, Japan is demonstrating more proactivity in responding to a changing international system, and especially in response to the rise of China and United States relative hegemonic decline. However, these analysts see the deviation in Japan's international line as marginal. Even though Japan may continue to add military capacity to compensate for its reduced economic power, nevertheless its intention is not to make a dash for new autonomy, but to continue to support the US-inspired international system and preserve its cautious foreign policy posture (Samuels 2006, 2007a, 2007b). Other analysts echo this line by insisting that Japan will remain nearly immovable in terms of its adherence to an anti-militaristic culture (Friman, Katzenstein, Leheny and Okawara 2006), or an attachment to related liberal institutions and values (Berger 2004).

Other analysts take an alternative line and see Japan as acquiescing in its decline, but attempting to manage this process by maintaining good ties with the United States, whilst playing a fuller part in constructing more cooperative relations in East Asia, and functioning as a 'middle power' (Soeya 2005) rather than great power.

However, other analysts take yet another tack and see Japan as struggling to cope with the possible eclipsing of itself and the United Staes by a new hegemonic China. In this instance, a Japan, feeling itself on the defensive with frustrated great power ambitions, may become more proactive and assertive, but also less predictable and more erratic as an international partner (Funabashi 2007; Hughes and Krauss 2007; Hughes 2009a). In this instance, Japan could actually become a destabilising influence in the international system.

Arguably, at the end of the first decade of the twenty-first century, all these scenarios and characterisations of Japan remain open possibilities. However, one point is indisputable at this juncture concerning Japan's international relations, and that is that Japan only promises to become ever more fascinating as a subject of study in the future. Japan remains of ever-more interest to mainstream IR as the key to understanding much of the trajectory of the dynamic East Asia region and as a central actor in determining the future of US hegemony and the maintenance of the international system. Japan has moved far from the model of the Reactive State. Any student of IR, or any policymaker, would be mistaken to not take more seriously this dynamic and challenging Japan.

REFERENCES

Ampiah, Kweku. (1997). *The dynamics of Japan's relations with Africa: South Africa, Tanzania and Nigeria*. London: Routledge

Arase, David. (1995). *Buying power: the political economy of Japanese foreign aid*. Boulder, CO: Lynne Rienner Publishers.

Asahi Shimbun Jieitai 50nen Shuzaiha. (2005). *Jieitai shirarezaru henyō*. Tokyo: Asahi Shimbunsha.

Austin, Greg and Harris, Stuart. (2001). *Japan and greater China: political economy and military power in the Asian century*. London: Hurst and Company.

Beeson, Mark. (1999). *Competing capitalisms: Australia, Japan and economic competition in the Asia Pacific*. Basingstoke, UK: Macmillan.

Berger, Thomas U. (1993) From sword to chrysanthemum: Japan's culture of anti-militarism. *International Security*, 17 (4), 119–150.

Berger, Thomas U. (1996) Norms, identity and national security in Germany and Japan. In Peter J. Katzenstein (Ed.), *The culture of national security: norms and identity in world politics* (pp. 317–356). New York, NY: Columbia University Press.

Berger, Thomas U. (1998). *Cultures of antimilitarism: national security in Germany and Japan*. Baltimore, MA: Johns Hopkins University Press.

Berger, Thomas U. (2003). Power and purpose in Pacific East Asia: a constructivist interpretation. In G. John Ikenberry and Michael Mastanduno (Eds.), *International relations theory and the Asia–Pacific* (pp. 387–420). New York, NY: Columbia University Press.

Berger, Thomas U. (2004). Japan's international relations: the political and security dimensions. In Samuel S. Kim (Ed.), *The International relations of Northeast Asia* (pp. 101–134). New York, NY: Rowman and Littlefield.

Berger, Thomas U., Mochizuki, Mike M. and Tsuchiyama, Jitsuo. (2007). *Japan in international politics: the foreign policies of an adaptive state*. Boulder, CO: Lynne Rienner Publishers.

Bisley, Nick. (2008) The Japan–Australia security declaration and the changing regional security setting: wheels, webs and beyond? *Australian Journal of International Affairs*, 61 (1), 38–52.

Bridges, Brian. (1993). *Japan and Korea in the 1990s: from antagonism to adjustment*. Aldershot, UK: Edward Elgar.

Calder, Kent A. (1988). Japanese foreign economic policy: explaining the reactive state. *World Politics*, 40 (4), 517–541.

Calder, Kent A. (2007). *Embattled garrisons: comparative base politics and American globalism*. Princeton, NJ: Princeton University Press.

Calder, Kent A. (2009). *Pacific alliance: reviving US–Japan Relations*. Yale, CT: Yale University Press.

Cha, Victor D. (1999). *Alignment despite antagonism: the US–Korea–Japan security triangle*. Stanford, CA: Stanford University Press.

Chapman J. M. W., Drifte, Reinhard, and Gow, I. T. M. (1982). *Japan's quest for Comprehensive Security: defence, diplomacy and dependence*. New York, NY: St. Martin's Press.

Chūma, Kiyofuku. (1985). *Saigunbi no seijigaku*. Tokyo: Chishikisha.

Cox, Robert. (1989). Middlepowermanship, Japan, and the future world order. *International Journal*, 44 (4), 823–862.

Davies, Christina L. (2003). *Food fights over free trade: how international institutions promote agricultural trade liberalisation*. Princeton, NJ: Princeton University Press.

Dobson, Hugo. (2003). *Japan and United Nations peacekeeping: new pressures, new responses*. London: Routledge.

Dobson, Hugo. (2004). *Japan and the G7/8, 1975–2002*. London: Routledge.

Drifte, Reinhard. (1998). *Japan's foreign policy for the twenty-first century: from economic superpower to what power?* London: Macmillan.

Drifte, Reinhard. (2000). *Japan's quest for a permanent security council seat: a matter of pride or justice?*. Basingstoke, UK: Macmillan.

Drifte, Reinhard. (2003). *Japan's security relations with China since 1989: from balancing to bandwagoning?* London: Routledge.

Eldridge, Robert D. and Paul Midford (Eds.). (2008). *Japanese public opinion and the war on terrorism*. New York, NY: Palgrave Macmillan.

Emmott, Bill. (2008). *Rivals: how the power struggle between China, India and Japan will shape our next decade*. London: Routledge.

Endicott, John. (1975). *Japan's nuclear option: political, technical and strategic factors*. New York, NY: Praeger.

Fallows, James. (1994). *Looking at the sun: the rise of the new East Asian economic and political system*. New York, NY: Vintage Books.

Friman, Richard H., Katzenstein, Peter J., Leheny, David, Okawara, Nobuo. (2006) Japan's national security: structures, norms and policies. In Peter J. Katzenstein and Takashi Shiraishi (Eds.). *Beyond Japan: the dynamics of East Asian regionalism* (pp. 85–107), Ithaca, NY: Cornell University Press.

Früstück, Sabine. (2007). *Uneasy warriors: gender, memory, and popular culture in the Japanese army*. Berkeley and Los Angeles, CA: University of California Press.

Funabashi, Yōichi. (1991–1992). Japan and the new world order. *Foreign Affairs*, 70 (5), 58–74.

Funabashi, Yōichi. (1995). *Asia Pacific fusion: Japan's role in APEC*. Washington, DC: Institute for International Economics.

Funabashi, Yōichi. (1999). *Alliance Adrift*. New York, NY: Council on Foreign Relations.

Funabashi, Yōichi. (2007). *Nihon koritsu*. Tokyo: Iwanami Shoten.

Gilson, Julie. (2000). *Japan and the European Union. A new partnership for the twenty first century?* Basingstoke, UK: Macmillan.

Graham, Euan. (2006). *Japan's sealane security, 1940–2004: a matter of life and death?*. London: Routledge.

Green, Michael J. (1995). *Arming Japan: defense production, alliance politics, and the postwar search for autonomy*. New York, NY: Columbia University Press.

Green, Michael J. (2001). *Japan's reluctant realism: foreign policy challenges in an era of uncertain power*. New York, NY: Palgrave Macmillan.

Green, Michael J. and Patrick M. Cronin. (1999). *The US–Japan alliance: past, present and future*. New York, NY: Council on Foreign Relations Press.

Green, Michael J. and Self, Benjamin L. (1996). Japan's changing China policy, *Survival*, 38 (2), 35–58.

Grimes, William W. (2009). *Currency and contest in East Asia: the great power politics of financial regionalism*. Ithaca, NY: Cornell University Press.

Hagstrom, Linus. (2005). *Japan's China policy: a relational power analysis*. London: Routledge.

Hagstrom, Linus and Soderberg, Marie (Eds.). (2006a). Special issue. The other binary: why Japan–North Korea relations matter. *Pacific Affairs*, 79 (3), 373–508.

Hagstrom, Linus and Soderberg, Marie (Eds.). (2006b). *North Korea policy: Japan and the great powers*. London: Routledge.

Hashimoto, Kōhei (Ed.). (1999). *Nihon no Gaikō seisaku kettei yōin*. Tokyo: PHP Kenkyūjo.

Hatch, Walter and Yamamura, Kozo. (1996). *Asia in Japan's embrace: building a regional production alliance*. Cambridge, UK: Cambridge University Press.

Hayashi, Shigeko. (2006). *Japan and East Asian monetary regionalism*. London: Routledge.

Heazle, Michael and Knight, Nick (Eds.). (2007). *China–Japan relations in the twenty-first century: creating a future past?* Cheltenham, UK: Edward Elgar.

Heginbotham, Eric and Samuels, Richard J. (1998). Mercantile realism and Japanese foreign policy. *International Security*, 22 (4), 171–203.

Heginbotham, Eric and Samuels, Richard J. (2002) Japan's dual hedge. *Foreign Affairs*, 81 (5), 110–121.

Holland, Harrison M. (1988). *Managing Defense: Japan's Dilemma*. New York, NY: University Press of America.

Hook, Glenn D. (1996). *Demilitarization and remilitarization in contemporary Japan*. London: Routledge.

Hook, Glenn D., Gilson, Julie, Hughes, Christopher W., and Dobson, Hugo. (2005). *Japan's international relations: politics, economics and security*. London: Routledge.

Howe, Christopher (Ed.). (1996). *China and Japan: history, trends and prospects*. Oxford, UK: Clarendon Press.

Hughes, Christopher W. (2000). Japanese policy and the East Asian currency crisis: abject defeat or quiet victory?. *Review of International Political Economy*, 7 (2), 219–53.

Hughes, Christopher W. (2004a). *Japan's security agenda: military, economic and environmental dimensions*. Boulder, CO: Lynne Rienner Publishers.

Hughes, Christopher W. (2004b) *Japan's reemergence as a 'normal' military power*. Oxford, UK: Oxford University Press.

Hughes, Christopher W. (2004c) Japan: military modernization in search of a 'normal' security role. In Ashley J. Tellis and Michael Wills (Eds.), *Strategic Asia 2005–06: military modernization in an era of uncertainty* (pp. 105–134). Seattle, WA: National Bureau of Asian Research.

Hughes, Christopher W. (2009a). *Japan's remilitarisation*. London: Routledge.

Hughes, Christopher W. (2009b). Supersizing the DPRK threat: Japan's evolving military posture and North Korea. *Asian Survey*, 49 (2), 291–311.

Hughes, Christopher W. (2009c) Japan's response to China's rise: regional engagement, global containment, dangers of collision. *International Affairs*, 85 (4), 837–854.

Hughes, Christopher W. and Krauss, Ellis S. (2007). Japan's new security agenda. *Survival: The IISS Quarterly*, 49 (2), 157–176.

Hughes, Llewelyn. (2007). Why Japan will not go nuclear (yet), international and domestic constraints on the nuclearization of Japan. *International Security*, 31 (4), 67–96.

Hyon, Deson. (2006). *Ryōdo nashonarizumu no tanjō: Tokdo/Takeshima no seijigaku*. Tokyo: Minerva Shobo.

Iechika, Ryōko, Matsuda, Yasuhiro, and Dan, Zuisō. (2007). *Kiro ni tatsu Nicchū kankei*. Tokyo: Shōyō Shobō.

Igarashi, Takeshi (Ed.). (1990). *Nihon no ODA to kokusai chitsujo*. Tokyo: Nihon Kokusai Mondai Kenkyūsho.

Ijima, Isao. (2007). *Jitsuroku: Koizumi gaikō*. Tokyo: Nihon Keizai Shimbunsha Shuppan.

Ikenberry, G. John and Inoguchi, Takashi (Eds.). (2003). *Reinventing the alliance: US-Japan security partnership in an era of change*. New York, NY: Palgrave Macmillan.

Inoguchi, Takashi and Okimoto, Daniel I. (Eds.). (1988). *The political economy of Japan, volume 2: the changing international context*. Stanford, CA: Stanford University Press.

Iokibe, Makoto. (2000). *Sengo Nihon no gaikōshi*. Tokyo: Yūhikaku Maruma.

Iriye, Akira and Wampler, Robert A. (Eds.). (2001). *Partnership: the United States and Japan, 1951–2001*. New York, NY: Kodansha International.

Islam, Shafiqul (Ed.). (1991) *Yen for development: Japanese foreign aid and the politics of burdensharing*. New York, NY: Council on Foreign Relations.

Jain, Purnendra. (1996). *Distant Asian neighbours: Japan and South Asia*. New Dehli: Sterling Pub Private Ltd.

Jain, Purnendra. (2005). *Japan's subnational governments in international affairs*. London: Routledge.

Johnson, Chalmers. (1995). *Japan: who governs? The rise of the developmental state*. New York, NY: W. W. Norton and Company.

Katada, Saori. (2001). *Banking on stability: Japan and the cross-Pacific dynamics of international financial crisis management*. Ann Arbor, MI: University of Michigan Press.

Katzenstein, Peter J. (1996). *Cultural norms and national security: police and military in postwar Japan*. Ithaca, NY: Cornell University Press.

Katzenstein, Peter J. (2008). Japanese security in perspective. In Peter J. Katzenstein (Ed.), *Rethinking Japanese security: internal and external dimensions* (pp. 1–31). London: Routledge.

Katzenstein, Peter J. and Okawara, Nobuo. (1993). Japan's national security: structures, norms, and policies. *International Security*, 17 (4), 84–118.

Katzenstein, Peter J. and Okawara, Nobuo. (2001). Japan, Asia–Pacific security, and the case for analytical eclecticism. *International Security*, 26 (3), 153–185.

Katzenstein, Peter J. and Shiraishi, Takashi (Eds.). (1997). *Network power: Japan and East Asia*. Ithaca, NY: Cornell University Press.

Katzenstein, Peter J. and Shiraishi, Takashi (Eds.). (2006). *Beyond Japan. The dynamics of East Asian regionalism*. Ithaca, NY: Cornell University Press.

Kimura, Hiroshi. (2008). *The Kurillian knot: a history of Japanese–Russian border negotiations*. Stanford, CA: Stanford University Press.

Kliman, Daniel M. (2006). *Japan's security strategy in the post-9/11 world: embracing a new realpolitik*. New York, NY: Praeger.

Kokubun, Ryosei and Wang, Jisi (Eds.). (2004). *The rise of China and a changing East Asian order*. Tokyo: Japan Center for International Exchange.

Krauss, Ellis S. (2003). The US, Japan, and trade liberalization: from bilateralism to regional multilateralism to regionalism. *The Pacific Review*, 16 (3), 307–329.

Krauss, Ellis S. and Pempel, T. J. (2004). *Beyond bilateralism: US–Japan relations in the new Asia–Pacific*. Stanford, CA: Stanford University Press.

Kurht, Natasha. (2007). *Russian policy towards China and Japan: the El'tsin and Putin periods*. London: Routledge.

Layne, Christopher. (1993). The unipolar illusion: why new great powers will rise. *International Security*, 17 (4), 5–51.

Lee, Yong Wook. (2008) *The Japanese challenge to the American neoliberal world order*. Stanford, CA: Stanford University Press.

Leheny, David. (2006). *Think global, fear local: sex, violence and anxiety in contemporary Japan*. Ithaca, New York, NY: Cornell University Press.

Lind, Jennifer. (2004). Pacifism or passing the buck? Testing theories of Japanese security policy. *International Security*, 29 (1), 92–121.

Maeda, Tetsuo. (1993). *Jieitai wa, nani o shite kita no ka?*. Tokyo: Sakuma Shoten.

Maeda, Testuo. (2007). *Jieitai: henyō no yukie*. Tokyo: Iwanami Shinsho.

Maull, Hans W. (1990–1991). Germany and Japan: the new civilian powers. *Foreign Affairs*, 69 (5), 91–106.

McCormack, Gavan. (2007). *Client state: Japan in the American embrace*. London: Verso.

McGray, Douglas. (2002). Japan's gross national cool. *Foreign Policy*, 130, 44–54.

Mearsheimer, John J. (2001). *The tragedy of great power politics*. New York, NY: W. W. Norton and Company.

Mendel, Douglas H. (1961). *The Japanese people and foreign policy: a study of public opinion in post-treaty Japan*. Westport, CT: Greenwood Press.

Mendl, Wolf (Ed.). (2001). *Japan and South East Asia. Volume II: the Cold War era 1947–1989 and issues at the end of the twentieth century*. London: Routledge.

Midford, Paul. (2002). The logic of reassurance and Japan's grand strategy. *Security Studies*, 11 (3), 1–43.

Miyagi, Yukiko. (2008). *Japan's Middle East policy: theory and cases*. London: Routledge.

Miyaoka, Isao. (2003). *Legitimacy in international society: Japan's reaction to global wildlife preservation*. Basingstoke, UK: Palgrave Macmillan.

Miyashita, Akitoshi and Sato, Yoichiro. (2001). *Japanese foreign policy in Asia and the Pacific: domestic interests, American pressure, and regional integration*. New York, NY: Palgrave Macmillan.

Mochizuki, Mike M. (Ed.). (1997). *Toward a true alliance: restructuring US–Japan security relations*. Washington, DC: Brookings Institution Press.

Muroyama, Yoshimasa. (1992). *Nichibei anpōtaisei*. Tokyo: Yūhikakusha.

Nakajima, Shingo. (2006). *Sengo Nihon no bōei seisaku: 'Yoshida rosen' o meguru seiji, gaikō, gunji*. Tokyo: Keio Gijuku Daigaku Shuppankai.

Nakano, Kunimi (Ed.). (2000). *Kokkai to gaikō*. Tokyo: Shinoyamasha.

Nester, William. (1990). *The foundations of Japanese power: continuities, changes, challenges*. Armonk, NY: M. E. Sharpe.

Oros, Andrew L. (2008). *Normalizing Japan: politics, identity and the evolution of security practice*. Stanford, CA: Stanford University Press.

Orr, Robert, M. (1990). *The emergence of Japan's foreign aid power*. New York, NY: Columbia University Press.

Ōtake, Hideo. (1983). *Nihon no bōei to kokunai seiji*. Tokyo: Sanichi Shobō.

Ozaki, Robert S. and Arnold, Walter. (1985). *Japan's foreign relations. A global search for economic security*. Boulder, CO: Westview Press.

Pan, Liang. (2005). *The United Nations in Japan's foreign and security policymaking, 1945–1992*. Cambridge, MA: Harvard University Press.

Pekkanen, Saadia M. (2008). *Japan's aggressive legalism: law and foreign trade politics beyond the WTO*. Stanford, CA: Stanford University Press.

Pempel, T. J. (2005). *Remapping East Asia: the construction of a region*. Ithaca, NY: Cornell University Press.

Pharr, Susan J. (1993). Japan's defensive foreign policy and the politics of burden sharing. In Gerald L. Curtis (Ed.), *Japan's foreign policy after the Cold War: coping with change* (pp. 235–262). Armonk, NY: M.E. Sharpe.

Prestowitz, Clyde V. (1988). *Trading places: how we allowed Japan to take the lead*. New York, NY: Basic Books.

Pyle, Kenneth B. (2007). *Japan rising. The resurgence of Japanese power and purpose*. New York, NY: Public Affairs.

Rix, Alan. (1993). *Japan's foreign aid challenge: policy reform and aid leadership*. London: Routledge.

Rose, Caroline. (1998). *Interpreting history in Sino–Japanese relations*. London: Routledge.

Rose, Caroline. (2005). *Sino–Japanese relations: facing the past, looking to the future?*. London: Routledge.

Rose, Gideon. (1998). Neoclassical Realism and theories of foreign policy. *World Politics*, 51 (1), 144–172.

Rosecrance, Richard. (1986). *The rise of the trading state*. New York, NY: Basic Books.

Rozman, Gilbert, Togo Kazuhiko and Ferguson, Joseph P. (2007). *Japanese strategic thought toward Asia*. New York, NY: Palgrave Macmillan.

Sadō, Akihiro. (2003). *Sengo Nihon no bōei seisaku to seiji*. Tokyo: Kikkawa Hirobumikan.

Sadō, Akihiro. (2003). *Sengo seiji to Jieitai*. Tokyo: Kikkawa Hirobumikan.

Sakamoto, Yoshikazu. (1982). *Kakujidai no kokusai seiji*. Tokyo: Iwanami Shoten.

Samuels, Richard J. (1996). *Rich nation, strong army: national security and the technological transformation of Japan*. Ithaca, NY: Cornell University Press.

Samuels, Richard J. (2003). *Machiavelli's children: leaders and their legacies in Italy and Japan*. Ithaca, NY: Cornell University Press.

Samuels, Richard J. (2006). Japan's Goldilocks strategy. *Washington Quarterly*, 29 (4), 111–127.

Samuels, Richard J. (2007a). *Securing Japan: Tokyo's grand strategy and the future of East Asia*. Ithaca, NY: Cornell University Press.

Samuels, Richard J. (2007b). Securing Japan: the current discourse. *Journal of Japanese Studies*, 33 (1), 125–151.

Samuels, Richard J. (2008). 'New fighting power!' Japan's growing maritime capabilities and East Asian security. *International Security*, 32 (3), 84–112.

Satō, Kenichi and Tanaka, Akihiko. (2005). *Higashi Ajia Kyōdōtia to Nihon no shinro*. Tokyo: NHK Shuppan.

Sato, Yoichiro and Hirata, Keiko. (2008). *Norms, interests and power in Japanese foreign policy*. Basingstoke, UK: Palgrave Macmillan.

Scalapino, Robert A. (1977). *Foreign policy of modern Japan*. Berkeley, CA: University of California Press.

Schaller, Michael. (1997). *Altered states: the United States and Japan since the Occupation*. New York, NY: Oxford University Press.

Schoppa, Leonard J. (1997). *Bargaining with Japan: what American pressure can and cannot do*. New York, NY: Columbia University Press.

Seekins, Donald M. (2007). *Burma and Japan since 1940: from 'co-prosperity' to 'quiet dialogue'*. Copenhagen: NIAS Press.

Self, Benjamin L. and Thompson, Jeffrey W. (Eds.). (2003). *Japan's nuclear option: security, politics and policy in the 21st century*. Washington, DC: Henry L. Stimson Center.

Shinoda, Tomohito. (2006). *Reisengo no Nihon gaikō*. Tokyo: Minerva.

Shinoda, Tomohito. (2007). *Koizumi diplomacy: Japan's Kantei approach to foreign and defense affairs*. Seattle, WA: University of Washington Press.

Soderberg, Marie (Ed.). (1996). *The business of Japanese aid: five cases from Asia*. London: Routledge.

Soeya, Yoshihide. (2005). *Nihon no 'midoru pawā' gaikō: sengo Nihon no sentaku to kōsō*. Tokyo: Chikuma Shinsho.

Sotooka, Hidetoshi, Honda Masaru and Miura, Toshiaki. (2001). *Nichibei dōmei hanseiki: anpo to mitsuyaku*. Tokyo: Asahi Shimbunsha.

Steven, Rob. (1990). *Japan's new imperialism*. Basingstoke, UK: Palgrave Macmillan.

Sudo, Sueo. (2002). *The international relations of Japan and Southeast Asia: forging a new regionalism*. London: Routledge.

Suganami, Hidemi. (1984). Japan's entry into International Society. In Hedley Bull and Adam Watson (Eds.), *The Expansion of International Society* (pp. 185–99). Oxford, UK: Clarendon Press.

Sugihara, Kaoru and Allan, J. A. (1993). *Japan in the contemporary Middle East*. London: Routledge.

Suzuki, Shogo. (2005). Japan's socialization into Janus-faced European International Society. *European Journal of International Relations*, 11 (1), 137–164.

Tadakoro, Masyuki and Shiroyama, Hideaki. (2004). *Kokusaikikan to Nihon: katsudō bunseki to hyōka*. Tokyo: Nihon Keizai Hyōronsha.

Tanaka, Akihiko. (1997). *Anzen hoshō: sengo 50-nen no mosaku*. Tokyo: Yomiuri Shimbunsha.

Terada, Takashi. (2001). Directional leadership in institution-building: Japan's approaches to ASEAN in the establishment of PECC and APEC. *The Pacific Review*. 14 (2), 195–220.

Terada, Takashi. (2006). Thirty years of the Australia–Japan partnership in Asian regionalism: evolution and future directions. *Australian Journal of International Affairs*, 60 (4), 536–551.

Twomey, Christopher P. (2000). Japan, a circumscribed balancer: building on defensive realism to make predictions about East Asian security. *Security Studies*, 9 (4), 167–205.

Urata, Shūjirō (Ed.). (2002). *Nihon no FTA senryaku*. Tokyo: Nihon Keizai Shimbunsha.

Van Wolferen, Karel G. (1990). *The enigma of Japanese power*. New York, NY: Albert A. Knopf.

Vogel, Ezra. (1979). *Japan as number one: lessons for America*. New York, NY: Harper Row.

Vogel, Ezra. (1986). Pax Nipponica? *Foreign Affairs*, 64 (4), 752–767.

Vogel, Steven K. (Ed.). (2002). *US–Japan relations in a changing world*. Washington, DC: Brookings Institution Press.

Wada, Haruki. (1999). *Hoppō Ryōdo mondai: rekishi to mirai*. Tokyo: Asahi Shimbunsha.

Waltz, Kenneth A. (1993). The emerging structure of international politics. *International Security*, 18 (2), 44–79.

Wan, Ming. (2001). *Japan between Asia and the West: economic power and strategic balance*. Armonk, NY: M. E. Sharpe.

Wan, Ming. (2006). *Sino-Japanese relations: interaction, logic and transformation*. Stanford, CA: Stanford University Press.

Watanabe, Yorizumi (Ed.). (2007). *FTA-EPA kōshō*. Tokyo: Nihon Keizai Hyōronsha.

Watanabe, Yasushi and David L. McConnell. (2008) (Eds.). *Soft power superpowers: cultural and national assets of Japan and the US*. Armonk, NY: M. E. Sharpe.

Weinstein, Martin E. (1971). *Japan's postwar defense policy, 1947–1968*. New York, NY: Columbia University Press.

Welfield, John. (1988). *An empire in eclipse: Japan in the postwar American alliance system*. London: Athlone Press.

Whiting, Allen S. (1989). *China eyes Japan*. Berkeley, CA: University of California Press.

Williams, Brad. (2007). *Resolving the Russo–Japanese territorial dispute: Hokkaido–Sakhalin relations*. London: Routledge.

Woolley, Peter J. (1999). *Japan's navy: politics and paradox*. Boulder, CO: Lynne Rienner Publishers.

Yasutomo, Dennis T. (1986). *The manner of giving: strategic aid and Japanese foreign policy*. Lexington, KY: Lexington Books.

Yuzawa, Takeshi. (2007). *Japan's security policy and the ASEAN Regional Forum: the search for multilateral security in the Asia-Pacific*. London: Routledge.

Zhao, Quansheng. (1993). *Japanese policymaking: the politics behind politics, informal mechanisms and the making of China policy*. Oxford, UK: Oxford University Press.

24

Japan and Globalization

Hugo Dobson

INTRODUCTION

Whereas Bernard Crick once famously described democracy as one of the most promiscuous words in the world of public affairs, today this honour could arguably go to globalization. Not only has it been described as promiscuous, it has also been seen as fuzzy and, in the case of one discipline, international relations (IR) theory, the 'trendiest craze ... at the turn of the century' (Weber 2001: 104). A number of other IR scholars have reaffirmed this point and as Higgott and Reich (1998: 2) have written: '"Globalisation" is rapidly replacing the "Cold War" as the most overused and under-specified explanation for a variety of events in international relations'.

For some, it describes 'the benevolent spread of liberal economic, political, and cultural processes, institutions, and practices throughout the world' (Weber 2001: 105). In an official and oft-quoted definition, the World Bank, one of the touted engines of globalization, has termed globalization as the 'freedom and ability of individuals and firms to initiate voluntary economic transactions with residents of other countries'. Another usual suspect in the line-up of globalizing agents, the Group of 7/8 summit process, has acted as a sensitive weathervane for the *zeitgeist* and first mentioned globalization in its Communiqué

for the 1994 Naples Summit. Two years later, the Preamble to the Lyon Summit's Economic Communiqué built on this by attempting to provide a balanced view:

Economic growth and progress in today's interdependent world is bound up with the process of globalization. Globalization provides great opportunities for the future, not only for our countries, but for all others too. Its many positive aspects include an unprecedented expansion of investment and trade; the opening up to international trade of the world's most populous regions and opportunities for more developing countries to improve their standards of living; the increasingly rapid dissemination of information, technological innovation and the proliferation of skilled jobs. These characteristics of globalization have led to a considerable expansion of wealth and prosperity in the world. Hence, we are convinced that the process of globalization is a source of hope for the future. History shows that rising living standards depend crucially on reaping the gains from trade, international investment and technical progress.

Globalization also poses challenges to societies and economies. Its benefits will not materialize unless countries adjust to increased competition.

In the poorer countries, it may accentuate inequality and certain parts of the world could become marginalized. The adjustment needed is, however, imposing rapid and sometimes painful restructuring, whose effects, in some of our countries, can temporarily exacerbate the employment situation. Globalization of the financial markets can generate new risks of instability, which requires all countries to pursue sound economic policies and structural reform (G7 1996).

As pointed to in the latter half of this statement, for others globalization creates fear and insecurity of an unbridled, Western model of capitalism that threatens to subsume all local distinctions. Hasegawa and Hook (2006: 1) have likened globalization to 'some giant, ongoing experiment [that] has seemed to envelop the world'.

In short, there is little agreement over the scale, impact, nature or origins of globalization. Most discussions of globalization (this one being no exception) begin by stating and exploring the wide confusion surrounding its meaning, impact and whether it is new or old. However, there does seem to be agreement on how relevant and important it is, although we might not agree what it is. Whilst arguing for a fair distribution of the benefits of globalization, former United Nations Secretary-General Kofi Annan famously said that 'arguing against globalization is like arguing against the laws of gravity', and in an address to the World Economic Forum in Davos that 'globalization is a fact of life. But I believe we have underestimated its fragility' (United Nations 1999). Furthermore, there is a consensus that technology has allowed it to accelerate over recent years, although its impact is uneven across the globe.

A number of synonyms have been mooted to capture the nature of globalization, including internationalization, universalization, Westernization, Americanization, liberalization, to mention but a few. In the first characterization, globalization is regarded as little more than an updated version of internationalization. In other words, having emerged from the Cold War and now living in an increasingly crossborder, transnational, interconnected and interdependent world that will eventually undermine the building block of the previous international order, the nation-state. Under this definition, globalization could be seen as little more than a historical period. In the second characterization, globalization is seen as a process that works to disseminate certain goods, practices or understandings onto a global scale. Related to this is the characterization of globalization as either a form of Westernization or, more specifically, Americanization whereby the goods, practices or understandings that are spread across the globe ignore local cultures in favour of a Western or American model. Finally, equating globalization with liberalization stresses the removal of barriers, controls and obstacles to the creation of a global economy (Scholte 2000: 15–16).

More interestingly, and possibly making globalization distinct, is its characterization as deterritorialization by which space is radically rethought beyond the distinctions of borders that have previously existed. In discussing globalization, Giddens points to

the intensification of worldwide social relations which link distant localities in such a way that local happenings are shaped by events occurring many miles away and vice versa ... Local transformation is as much a part of globalization as the lateral extension of social connections across time and space (Giddens 1990: 64).

This leads us to focus on the distinct and defining aspects of time and space. Hughes suggests that '[g]lobalization represents a qualitatively different process because of its essential deterritorialization – or, stated in reverse, supra-territorialization – of social interaction' (Hughes 2001: 408). In other words, a range of different activities – political, economic, security, cultural – can now take place without regard for geographical distance or physical boundaries and it is advances in information technology and communications (ITC) that have provided the drivers behind these processes. As Hughes stresses, none of the extant definitions are entirely divorced from these territorial considerations and are thus different from globalization, although they may result in it.

So, scale, speed and cognition are often identified as the key processes related to globalization. In other words, how far globalization reaches, how it compresses time and space and the sense that we live in a much smaller world (Kinnvall 2002: 5–7). These processes extend across a range of academic disciplines and social activities from the exchange of goods, capital, culture or the provision of security, and in so doing raise a number of corollary questions: is globalization a one-way process or have recent events demonstrated that it can be reversed? Are regionalist projects, like the European Union, responses to globalization, or a stage in globalization? One of the most commonly raised questions, however, regards reactions to globalization and, in particular, the anti-globalization movement that has sought to harness, resist or reverse many of these process and in turn has led to the creation of a global civil society.

When thinking about Japan, a number of further questions emerge. In response to globalization, has the Japanese state withered away, or has it changed in form? How has Japan's leading technological position fostered globalization?

If globalization is the same as Americanization, is Japan playing the role of an engine of globalization as a result of its core bilateral relationship with the United States? Or, is it seeking to supplement this role by fostering new mechanisms of global governance?

These questions could be asked of any nation-state in the world today. Globalization and Japan are particularly worthy of joint consideration because discussion of the two inevitably collides with discussions of *Nihonjinron* and Japanese exceptionalism (discussed elsewhere in this Handbook). Prior to the current ubiquity of the term 'globalization', this discourse was framed within the language of 'internationalization' and, within various Japanese circles, the term *kokusaika* was the buzzword of the 1980s and 1990s in various walks of life. The introduction to the book-length treatment of Japan and internationalization edited by Glenn Hook and Michael Weiner explore its usage in similar ways to which globalization has been written about:

> Analytically, internationalization can be understood to involve a multi-dimensional process – of one nation penetrating another; of a nation being penetrated; of policy adjustment on the national level in response to international pressures; and of substantial actors influencing the international system (Hook and Weiner 1992: 1).

Thus, internationalization worked in two directions, both inward and outward. As regards inward internationalization, former Prime Minister Nakasone Yasuhiro was outspoken in his desire during the 1980s to make Japan an international state – *kokusai kokka*. Fuelled by Japan's position in the world and internal and external demands and pressures, Nakasone's objectives were built on a belief that:

> ...the creation of a *kokusai kokka Nihon* was necessary in that Japan's peace and prosperity could not exist without world peace and prosperity in today's deeply interdependent international society (Itoh 1998: 6).

The three underlying principles were that 'Japan would no longer be a follower nation; Japan would be prepared for global leadership by being remade into "international state"; and Japan would assume an active role in global strategic affairs' (Moon and Park 2000: 73). This role was symbolized at the 1983 G7 Williamsburg Summit when Nakasone stood at the centre of and shoulder-to-shoulder with the leaders of the great powers of the day but was set back by the 1991 Gulf War and hindered by a decade of soul-searching known as the 'lost decade'.

As regards outward internationalization, in contrast to Americanization, a note should be made of the idea of Japanization. During the 1980s, a cottage industry developed that sought to extract and implement the 'secrets' of Japan's economic miracle for a Western audience. The most prominent of these treatments was Ezra Vogel's *Japan as Number One: Lessons for America*. Richard Falk commented on these trends:

> ...even Japanese foreign investment in the United States is sometimes perceived as the equivalent of a benign occupation, a way to bring the Japanese miracle home to America... Even Japanese culture is studied with unquestioning admiration, envied especially for its relative success in sustaining civil life and domestic stability despite the many years of steady economic growth, and more recently, of affluence. More and more Americans envy Japan, and believe sincerely that Japanese culture is superior in its formation of character and citizen behaviour (Falk 1992: 47–8).

By the turn of the millennium, except in the case of Japanese culture (as explored later), these claims would be met with justified scepticism and possibly a dose of *schadenfruede*.

Today, internationalization and *kokusaika* no longer have the ubiquity that they once did, and instead globalization or *gurobarizeshon* or *gurobaruka* have taken their place although differences have been noted. For example, '[i]nternationalization implies a relationship between two or more nations: a minimum of two nations can engage in "international relations". "Globalization", on the other hand, implies simultaneous extension and expansion in all directions' (Befu 2001: 3). However, it is not just a matter of scale or the number of partners – we return to the point that technology plays a crucial role in the defining characteristic of globalization:

> The word 'globalization' carries a specific emphasis on the nature of the dismantling of barriers to the flows of information, goods, services, capital, technology, values and cultures. The emergence of a 'borderless world' has become possible because of scientific revolutions in the fields of information and telecommunications. Globalization is thus different from internationalization, because the latter term carries no emphasis on the disappearance of national barriers (Chittiwatanapong 1999: 71).

So, for most of the discussion that follows in the areas of politics, economics, security and culture, globalization will be used in place of internationalization, although the alternative ways in which the two have been defined and understood will be acknowledged and discussed.

POLITICS

Japan appears to have spent most of its recent history attempting to ignore or resist the forces of internationalization and globalization. As a result of its particular position in the international system, Japan developed a unique, and often misunderstood, role in the world. Yet, ironically, this may well place it in a particularly good position to cope with the challenges of globalization. In this context, the impact of globalization upon Japan's political behaviour and the reaction to it can be seen both domestically and internationally in terms of the constraints it places on the Japanese state and its people and the opportunities it offers.

For long periods of history the Japanese state was able to regulate its own territorial space relatively effectively from the seventeenth century through to the Cold War. The Japanese political system that prevailed during the Cold War has been characterized as one-party dominance by the Liberal Democratic Party (LDP) and policy-making dominated by an iron triangle of the LDP, bureaucracy and big business. With the end of the Cold War, a shift from the cocoon it provided and the buffeting of the Japanese domestic political landscape by the winds of globalization can be seen. This insularity that characterized previous historical periods is an impossibility today and the traditional structures that dominated Japanese domestic politics began to unfurl with the fall of the LDP from power in 1993. Although it soon returned to power the following year, it was part of a coalition until 2009 when it lost power again in a landslide election. It won its own landslide election in 2012 but was still forced to form a coalition government. In short, globalization, seen as the compression of time and space, undermines the monolithic position of the state and challenges its legitimacy and acceptance.

For example, in Japan's domestic politics, Takahashi demonstrates how one political leader – former Prime Minister Hashimoto Ryutaro – attempted to highlight his response to globalization in the following statements:

...the great change of the international environment such as the end of the Cold War, the borderless world economy and the rising status of Japan in world society forces Japan, whether it likes or not, to accomplish big reforms in every policy field...

...globalization was not only a challenge for Japan but also the chance of reforming Japan. We should try to react to globalization for the purpose of gaining more flexibility for the Japanese economy and society (cited in Takahashi 2006: 40–41).

In this case, the emphasis was placed on the need for Japan to react to and exploit globalization. To this end, Hashimoto's 'big bang' reforms were the main response of his administration to attempt to liberalize Japan's financial system and force it to meet global standards. However, ironically, the outcomes of these reforms demonstrated the flipside to the panacea of globalization and led to the exposure and meltdown of Japan's financial markets, ultimately impacting on Hashimoto's popularity, leadership and electability so that he eventually fell in mid-1998.

Thus, globalization is seen to undermine the position and authority of the state, and in its place provide opportunities for other actors to exert an influence. One of the most-focused upon of these actors is Japanese civil society, which is seen to have grown dramatically in qualitative and quantitative terms since the end of the Cold War and especially since the non-profit organizations (NPO) Law of 1998 came into effect, which recognized twelve areas of civil society activity. Many of the NPOs and non-governmental organizations (NGO) that were given legal status by this law have been concerned with issues around which the sense of global citizenship is created and developed around issues such as trade liberalization, militarization and human rights to name but a few that have gained attention (Chan 2008). However, the iron triangle has continued to express residual resistance. This can be seen most clearly in the opposition that existed in more conservative sections of the Japanese state to the participation of the Japanese NGO Peace Winds in the Conference on Afghan Reconstruction that was held in Tokyo in January 2002.

Internationally, Japan's role in the world has been dominated traditionally by the state; however, globalization has challenged this dominant, monolithic position by allowing non-state actors, from Japan's famous business corporations to NGOs and CSOs (civil society organization), the opportunity to play a role not only domestically but also internationally. What has emerged since the end of the Cold War is a pluralist and multifaceted policymaking process whereby the Japanese state now operates alongside a range of other actors, at times making use of their expertise (Hook, Gilson, Hughes and Dobson 2005).

At the same time, in an international system predicated on the state as the building blocks, globalization appears to be challenging the territorialization at the heart of any definition of the state. Thus, as the process of deterritorialization continues, it is likely that the state will become more porous in its ability to exert sovereignty and eventually wither away.

In its place, the processes of globalization have allowed a greater role for global institutions, often seen as the engines of globalization, such as the United Nations, G8, G20, World Trade Organization, World Bank and International Monetary Fund. Several of these institutions were paralysed by the bipolarity of the Cold War, but with its collapse experienced a new lease of life. In response, the Japanese state and its people have embraced the opportunities presented to consolidate its core bilateral alliance with the United States, but also move beyond it and supplement this relationship with new avenues of activity, particularly multilateral. To this end, they have attempted to shape globalization through the contribution of funds, ideas and personnel to support the creation and shaping of these global institutions.

In addition, Japan's role in the world since the end of the Second World War has been driven by a number of behavioural norms, several of them domestically located, such as anti-militarism (that military force should not be used in resolving disputes) and economism (where possible economic solutions should be sought to international problems). Globalization has challenged the peculiarity of these norms by promoting more universal and global (although some would argue Western/American) norms. On the one hand, the Japanese state and its people have reacted to these challenges by projecting these domestic norms onto the international level. On the other hand, they have sought to undermine traditional norms and promote norms that render Japan a more 'normal' state. Japan's international behaviour has previously been dubbed 'quiet diplomacy' and proved to be successful for the most part during the Cold War period. 'Quiet diplomacy' consisted of a multi-channel foreign policy where a mélange of formal, informal and proxy channels of interaction with the outside world existed; a multilevel approach whereby the bilateral, regional, multilateral levels were all utilized; a more long-term approach to the resolution of issues that avoids the idea of a quick fix; and the use of a range of actors, such as NGOs, within Japan in the pursuit of its national interest (Hook et al. 2005).

In responding to globalization, Japan may find it difficult to separate issues and areas of foreign policy and find instead that the degree of overlap is considerable. For example, the East Asian economic crisis of the late-1990s demonstrated the confluence of Japan's relationship with the United States, the East Asian region and a number of global institutions across a range of issues areas from economics to politics to security (Hook, Gilson, Hughes and Dobson 2002). However, Japan's position as a 'quiet diplomat' with its comprehensive approach and instrumentalization of available policy tools might well place it in a positive position as regards its ability to weather the winds of globalization.

Seen from a different perspective, it could be argued that what we have witnessed since the end of the Cold War and after the events of 9/11 is not globalization at all but Americanization. In terms of foreign policy, especially during the overlapping Koizumi and Bush administrations, Japan's willingness to assume a more active role could be interpreted through the prism of the United States attempting to garner support for its ideological project of democratization. In either case, it would appear that isolationism is no longer a viable option for any state in the world today. Although Japan's domestic politics have been regarded as a barrier to globalization, or at best unable to effectively handle the demands and pressures, prime ministers like Nakasone, Hashimoto and Koizumi have sought to reform them as part of a neo-liberal response to the pressures of globalization.

ECONOMICS

A historical approach to globalization and the idea of Japan being exposed to intense periods of globalization – the Meiji period after the *sakoku* (closed country) era, the US Occupation of 1945 to 1952, and then the end of the Cold War and the progress of globalization – can be seen across the literature (Itoh 1998; Befu 2000; Funabashi 2002). The accumulated impact of this history is apparent in Itoh's assertion (1998) that the *sakoku* mentality of the Tokugawa period has continued to undermine efforts of globalization. According to Itoh, 'this mindset is not only ubiquitous in the business sector but is also prevalent in Japan's cultural, educational and social systems' (1998: 13). During the Cold War period, it was the opening of Japan's markets that provided the focus of this intense pressure and, in particular, the Structural Impediments Initiative to remove structural barriers to trade between Japan and the United States, but this could also be seen in actions taken within General Agreement on Tariffs and Trade (GATT) against Japan.

Today, globalization is closely associated with developments in the world economy, such as the mobility of labour, movement of capital and accelerated movement of trade resulting in the porous nature of national boundaries and the withering of the state. As in the political sphere, the impact of globalization in the economic sphere has been driven by technological developments and has resulted in the compression of time and space and ultimately the reduction of barriers to interaction. On the one hand, this impact of globalization could be seen as Westernization/Americanization of global economic activity in line with the neo-liberal agenda as expressed by the Washington

Consensus and embedded in the global institutions that fuel globalization, such as the World Bank and International Monetary Fund (IMF). On the other hand, this could be seen as creating a global playing field on which Japanese corporations can operate. However, in light of the global recession at the end of the first decade of the twenty-first century, globalization should not be viewed as a unidirectional process that can be both resisted and reversed.

Another distinction to add to the mix is 'spontaneous globalization' and 'governed globalization'. The former being 'the process of economic interdependence and integration through market forces that have resulted from the development of technology and world capitalism' and the latter being 'coping strategies [that] can take several forms. Countries can defy, adapt, and accommodate forces of spontaneous globalization on the one hand or, on the other, restructure them' (Moon and Park 2000: 66–7). In other words, how the Japanese state and its people have attempted to manage and mediate the pressures of globalization.

Each differing interpretation of globalization results in a different response from the Japanese state and its people. Are we witnessing Japanese corporations taking over the world as was the fear at the end of the 1980s? Is Japan promoting its own economic model globally? Its support for the World Bank's report on the East Asian economic miracle could be regarded as evidence of this (Wade 1996). Will Japan have to restructure domestically in order to retain its global competitiveness? Will it revert to protectionism as a rational choice in the face of a recession or will it support the global institutions, such as the G8 and G20, which have sought to resist such reactions.

As regards the domestic impact of globalization, the 'iron triangle' was the dominant characterization not only of Japan's political processes but also economic activity, with the three poles providing mutual support and ensuring that big business had an important influence to the extent that Japan was seen as an economic animal overseas. Note that when UK Prime Minister Tony Blair first visited Japan in 1998, his first visit was to the CEO of Toyota. Before the end of the Cold War, the processes of globalization were discussed in terms of the language of internationalization and the external pressure that needed to be applied to Japan in order for trade barriers to be reduced or Japanese aggressive exporting practices to be curtailed. This discourse continued with the end of the Cold War but was framed within the language of globalization. As an example of the Japanese state responding to the challenge of globalization and attempting to become leaner and more competitive, the reforms of Hashimoto and Koizumi mentioned earlier provide evidence. These neo-liberalist reforms go

back to the 1980s with Nakasone's promotion of Reagan–Thatcherite neo-liberal reforms, through the collapse of the bubble economy and into the lost decade of the 1990s and up to Koizumi. Reforms have included commercial law, anti-monopoly law, financial big bang, foreign exchange control law (including the reorganization of big business in banking, chemical, car, electricals, steel industries) and employment reforms (Hasegawa 2006).

Schaede and Grimes have argued that:

> Japan's response to the global and domestic challenges of the 1990s [and beyond, one can presume] is neither one of retreat and denial, nor one of full acceptance of global standards and practices. Instead the basic thrust is one of pragmatic utilization of new rules and circumstances to continue industry policies of promotion or protection in a new, post-developmental, paradigm (Schaede and Grimes 2003a: 8).

The term they coin to capture this response to managing globalization is 'permeable insulation':

> 'Insulation' is the outcome of a set of policies that have at their core an attempt at continued protection of domestic interests – for example, by allowing restrictive practices in the distribution system that fall outside the scope of international agreements. However, in contrast to previous instances of industrial policy, this new insulation is 'permeable' in that it allows those sectors in need of more freedom in corporate strategy to break free from the fetters of domestic production.
>
> Permeable insulation is Japan's attempt to manage the forces of globalization by affecting both the speed and reach with which global rules and markets affect domestic players. It is Japan's attempt to structure a process that is potentially upsetting and disruptive. It is the outcome of a mix of active and passive measures by both governments and firms taken in response to world changes in the twenty-first century (Schaede and Grimes 2003b: xi)

Thus, the Japanese state, society and businesses have not simply caved in to the pressures of globalization. In fact, Hasegawa (2006: 155) has claimed that the influence of Keidanren and Nikkeiren 'has increased in tandem with globalization and low growth'. Rather, they have strategically sought to protect and maintain the status quo where possible and also concede and adjust in certain areas. The result is that there may no longer appear to be a solid consistency to Japan's economic policy and differentiation is more accurate.

Internationally, Japan has been more active in the regional and global institutions of economic globalization, such as the World Trade Organization

(WTO). In this context, Japanese policymaking agents have been skilled and active in responding to the new set of foreign policy tools and resources available, which is all the more salient when contrasted with its low-profile role in GATT. Regionally, it proposed an Asian Monetary Fund in the 1990s, thereafter, in reaction to its failure, the New Miyazawa Initiative, and has played a hand in the birth of other fora like the Asia Pacific Economic Cooperation (APEC), whilst managing its core relationship with the United States. On the global level, it has promoted an internationalist and regionalist agenda within the G8. The 1998 G8 Birmingham Summit provides a particularly pertinent example with Japan seeking to place the East Asian economic crisis on the agenda when it might have otherwise been overlooked by a Western-dominated mechanism of global governance. In the WTO, it has campaigned for an East Asian voice to be heard through the support for Thai national Supachai Panitchpakdi to become the WTO's Secretary-General. In addition, the Japanese state and businesses have skilfully and effectively learned and adapted to the new mechanisms of the WTO by adopting a much more active and legalist approach to defending itself and promoting its interests through instrumentalization of WTO rules as a sword and shield (Pekkanen 2008). In the World Bank, as mentioned earlier, the East Asian Economic Miracle report demonstrated Japan's willingness to develop and disseminate its own model of economic development, but in addition Japan has sought to increase its funding and representation at the World Bank and IMF, which in the wake of the G20 London Summit has been imbued with greater responsibility, suggesting that Japan will continue to pursue its own interests with increasing activity.

If globalization is seen as something to be resisted as a result of its unfair impacts that result in greater disparities between rich and poor, then once again (but on the international level) a variety of actors can be pointed to as having emerged in reaction to, and under conditions of, globalization. Previously during the Cold War period, the norms that shaped Japan's economic activity were an effective marriage of economism (privileging economic development) and developmentalism (catching-up with the early starter economies) that resulted in a series of domestic environmental disasters that earned the Japanese state the title of 'environmental bogeyman'. Japanese NGOs and CSOs, which previously addressed these issues on a domestic level, have begun to operate on a more global level within Japan and across the region in addressing environmental issues that have been caused by Japanese economic activity (the environmental damage caused by the creation of golf courses providing one pertinent example).

The 2000 Kyushu–Okinawa Summit saw local protestors against US bases and global protestors, such as Greenpeace, come together in campaigning towards their respective goals. The same happened at the 2008 Hokkaido–Toyako Summit, where hosting this global summit provided the engine for the extension of the status and rights of indigenous people to the Ainu minority, giving international exposure to the issue and providing a domestic and global impact. It also brought Japanese domestic civil society and global civil society together. Here one can also see the argument that the language of globalization and its portrayal as an external threat to which Japan must respond has been used to justify reductions, restructuring and reforms – similar to the language of globalization in security terms as will be seen in the next section.

SECURITY

Adding to the definitional confusion and controversy surrounding the term 'globalization' is the fuzziness of the term 'security'. As Hughes (2001: 407) suggests: '[t]hat both issues are so often poorly conceptualized, therefore, only gives further grounds for concern when attempting to examine the two in conjunction'.

Nevertheless, the impact of globalization can be seen in the acceleration of processes that were already occurring before the end of the Cold War, including the expansion of actors that provide or threaten security from the traditional emphasis on the state, to a range of domestic and internationally located actors from ethnic groups, to women and so on. No longer is the emphasis on 'state security' but a range of different actors. In fact, not only is the state no longer regarded as one amongst other actors in providing security, but it is also even seen to be the source of insecurity, thereby infringing upon its legitimacy and compounding the processes that undermine the ability of the state to provide for the security of citizens within its territorial boundaries. Another relevant trend is the expansion in the range of issues that has now become securitized, from traditional 'guns-and-bombs' definitions of security to the environment and gender, operating either on the domestic or transnational levels.

Japan's management of its security has been dominated by the bilateral relationship with the United States throughout the postwar period. Famously described as 'the most important bilateral relationship in the world, bar none' by former Ambassador Mike Mansfield, it served during the Cold War period as a useful umbrella that allowed Japan to concentrate on its economic development, whilst also providing a cocoon by which the Japanese state deferred to the United States in all security matters. Admittedly some prime ministers, like Nakasone, sought to pursue a more active, equal or 'normal' security relationship with the United States, but were constrained by the anti-militarist sentiment that pervaded Japan. With the end of the Cold War, however, external pressure continued to accrue, but the ability of anti-militarism to act as a bulwark began to wane. This pressure peaked during the 1990–1991 Gulf War when Japan's traditional approach of bankrolling the multilateral effort was roundly criticized as lacking a human dimension in the concrete form of dispatching personnel to the combat zone.

Thus, the reaction of the Japanese state and its people, on the one hand, was to begin a process of dismantling many of the postwar taboos that had curtailed a military role for Japan. This could be seen in a number of fields, such as the dispatch of Japanese SDF (Self-Defence Forces) personnel on UN-sponsored peacekeeping operations and other missions across the globe from East Timor to Iraq, the technological development of the SDF and the upgrading of the Defence Agency to Ministry status in 2007. However, the events of 9/11 and subsequent invasions of Afghanistan and Iraq could be seen as a watershed when the reaction of the Japanese state and its people is contrasted with that of the 1990–1991 Gulf War. A much speedier and active response was demonstrated both in the immediate and mid-term. Thus, the Japanese state and its people appear to be responding both to its international commitments in a globalized world as well as reinforcing its ability to protect its national interests in a traditional, military sense. In the case of the region in which Japan is located, state building is often a work-in-progress and this could compound the problems that more established states encounter in attempting to navigate the storms of globalization. In this context, one reaction has been nationalism as a last-stand effort to deny their loss of sovereignty as a result of the globalization process, and Japan is not immune from this. Opinion polls demonstrate that attitudes to constitutional revision have modified in favour of revision, the image of the SDF is higher than it has ever been, support for a permanent seat on the UN Security Council is solid and, as a result, Japan's traditional guiding norm of behaviour in security matters, anti-militarism, has waned. Education reform and the teaching of a more nationalist agenda in terms of ethics, as well as history, could be seen as a nationalist response to reinforce the idea of 'being Japanese' (McVeigh 2000).

On the one hand, Japan's growing role in UN peacekeeping operations and humanitarian efforts serves as a case study of the Japanese government and society's initial wariness of assuming an active role in the world and the inability to comprehend the end of the Cold War and the forces of globalization. As Itoh has argued:

> The Murayama cabinet's reluctance to send the SDF to the Golan Heights and the Diet's futile debate concerning Japan's participation in UNDOF demonstrated the parochial mind-set and the lack of 'international awareness' (the recognition of one country's roles and responsibilities in the international community commensurate with its global standing) on the part of the Japanese government and its people (Itoh 1998: 2).

However, by the time of 9/11 and after a number of successfully completed operations, participation in peacekeeping operations was accepted by the Japanese public and a role outside the cocoon of UN-sponsored missions could be undertaken by supporting US-led efforts in Afghanistan and Iraq, although this dilemma could be highlighted by the Japanese reaction to casualties in Cambodia and kidnappings in Iraq. Shetler-Jones (2010) demonstrated how the Japanese government has used the challenges and buzzword of globalization in official reports and reviews, such as the New Defence Programme Outline, in order to justify and promote significant changes to its security profile in an attempt to render it a more 'normal' state.

On the other hand, the Japanese state and its people also responded by promoting broadly defined concepts such as 'human security' that seek to expand the definition of security to embrace the humanitarian and environmental. This can be seen in both the expanding range of actors and areas that have now become securitized and regarded as security issues: peacekeeping and humanitarian assistance, terrorism, the environment, piracy. In turn, these processes of globalization have again impacted upon the range of actors that are involved in the process. The once monolithic dominance of the Japanese state and the emphasis of the US alliance have broken down to the extent that, once again, civil society has a role to play, especially in any definition of human security that stresses non-military aspects.

CULTURE

Traditionally, the process of cultural globalization has been understood to be a one-way street emanating from the West, whether in the form of Harry Potter movies, McDonald's hamburgers or Ikea furniture. However, the globalization of culture is not simply monolithic Westernization,

Americanization or homogenization and, instead, elements of localization in the adoption and consumption of these global brands is very much in evidence (Condry 2006: 2). Thus, in relation to culture, globalization has been discussed in terms of 'the global diffusion and "creolization" of cultural forms and meanings' (Eades 2000: 5). It may sound odd to our ears at the end of the first decade of the twenty-first century, but a decade previously, Japan watchers had opined that in cultural terms, Japan did not have the global presence or impact to match its position in economic globalization (Allen and Sakamoto 2006: 1–2). At the time of writing, it appears that the reverse is more accurate. With a global economic recession impacting upon Japan's export-led developmental model coming on the heels of the 'lost decade' of the 1990s, it is Japan's economic presence that appears to offer little and, in contrast, its popular culture that remains recession-proof in its solid appeal across the globe. Examples can be seen in other cultural areas. Kerr (2002) has argued that Japanese cinema is past its 'golden age', which seems to be defined in terms of internationally popular directors like Kurosawa Akira or Ozu Yasujiro. However, Japanese cinema is making great impact in terms of Western remakes or Western distributors, particularly in the genre of horror and anime, picking up Oscar nominations and awards along the way.

Linking the cultural to the political, the soft power thesis of Joseph Nye (2004) articulates a positive and rose-tinted view of the power of persuasion rather than coercion. In the case of Japanese popular culture in the immediate East Asian region, the accusation of cultural imperialism is never very far away, but under the soft power thesis, the resonance of Japan's popular culture may well serve to assuage wartime memories and postwar divisions that have served to distance Japan from its East Asian neighbours. Possibly with this end in mind, the Japanese government recognized the global impact of its popular culture with the appointment of a number of 'ambassadors' to promote Japan regionally and globally. It also created an annual International Manga Award in 2007 (Ministry of Foreign Affairs of Japan 2007). In contrast, however, it could be questioned as to how this popularity translates into concrete power and influence, and can it not equally be a cause of protest and repulsion as much as adoption and attraction. Iwabuchi (2006) explores the extent of Japanese popular culture's penetration into the East Asian region and argues that although Japanese popular culture has been localized and hybridized within the region, it still demonstrates unequal power relations between Japan and the rest of the region that reinforces attitudes of Japan's cultural superiority and are redolent of Japan's previous attempts to assert leadership over East Asia, although they may be presented to the region as a shared cultural heritage (Iwabuchi 2006).

The penetration of Japanese popular culture into the East Asian region can be seen on a country-by-country basis. In the case of South Korea, it was only in April 1998 that President Kim Dae-Jung announced that the boundaries to the import of Japanese popular culture would be removed, explaining that 'Koreans as mature citizens have enough power to digest Japanese culture' (cited in Han 2001: 203), presumably without becoming brainwashed by their former colonial master. In return, the 'Korean wave' hit Japan in the shape of TV soap operas. However, this rather simplistic characterization fails to acknowledge, on the one hand, the anti-Korean reaction in Japan to the 'Korean wave', as seen in the 'Hating the Korean wave' *Kenkanryu* series of manga (Sakamoto and Allen 2007) and, on the other hand, the distinction that is maintained in South Korean minds between love of contemporary Japanese culture and continued disgust at the events of the colonial period (Iwabuchi 2006: 27). Thus, once again, Nye's concept of soft power is open to criticism.

Similarly, in the case of China, whilst Japanese popular culture has made in-roads, this took place at a time when political relations soured over textbook revisions, prime ministerial visits to Yasukuni Shrine and perceived Japanese militarization. Again, this suggests that the link between the consumption of a country's popular culture and more positive views of that country is only superficial at best. However, in the case of Taiwan, the adoption and consumption of Japanese popular culture has been portrayed in the media as a much more uncomplicated process because the history issue is not seen to be as sensitive, at least among conservative circles in Japan (Iwabuchi 2006: 27–28).

In Hong Kong, the import and popularity of Japanese comics has been seen as dialectic process between the two countries' respective comic cultures and societies, and not simply a one-way process that resulted in a new form mediated by local circumstances (Lai and Wong 2001). A similar conclusion is hinted at in a different context of research into Japanese popular music in Hong Kong, where although initially no mediation and no hybridization resulting from the dialectic process has taken place, the potential is beginning to be realized (Ogawa 2001).

Sports are another area in which processes of globalization can be seen. On the one hand, once 'traditional' Japanese sports have been impacted upon and become more global, for example in the case of sumo wrestling, the recent top-flight of wrestlers now come from Hawaii, Mongolia and Russia. The Sumo Wrestling Association has both embraced this trend (as seen in the hosting of foreign tournaments (*basho*) to spread the sport across the world) and has experienced a number of problems adapting to the new environment (as seen in the exposure of a number of doping scandals). The case of Japanese baseball also demonstrates the dual flow of globalizing trends. Although the sport put down early roots in Japan, US Major League players originally came to Japan to 'entertain, instruct and compete' (Holden 2006: 121). However, by the turn of the twentieth century, Japanese players, such as Nomo Hideo, Suzuki Ichiro and Matsui Hideki to name but three of the most high profile, represented highly successful exports from Japan to the United States. Thus, the market in Japanese sportsmen can also be seen as responding to and accommodating neoliberal economic principles that underpin globalization's processes.

The co-hosting of the 2002 Football World Cup in Japan provided an opportunity for the global promotion of the sport in Japan (and the region), only a decade after the establishment of the first professional Japanese football league. Conversely, Japan's profile in world football has grown, with the Japanese team not only winning their first game in a World Cup final but also qualifying for the knock-out stage of the tournament. Added to this, the number of foreigners who have coached the Japanese national team (as well as at club-level), the influx of foreign players to Japan, the outflux of Japanese players to European football teams and the broadcasting of related games all demonstrate that the processes of globalization are ever present. Although football in general, and the World Cup specifically, could be seen as reviving nationalism in Japan, rather than a globalizing force, the reaction of Japanese supporters during the World Cup was to adopt and support fervently foreign teams, in particular England, which was also not only surprising but demonstrative of the borderless world of international sport (Ebihara and Yamashita 2006: 128–129, 133).

Linking back to the introduction to this chapter, for some, globalization is not simply Americanization, convergence or homogenization. Rather, what is celebrated as the Japanese 'local' or 'diverse' has become global. Does this amount to globalization on a Japanese cultural model, as opposed to the Western model? In other words, Japanization, as opposed to the Americanization definition of globalization? According to Allen and Sakamoto, this is not the case: '...there is no doubt that multiple and often unpredictable interconnections are creating new situations and cultural hybrids rather than reducing human experiences to a monolithic whole' (Allen and Sakamoto 2006: 3). This also results in the issue of ownership – is it a national, uniquely Japanese culture? Would this not just be a recasting of the Nihonjinron thesis of

Japanese uniqueness? How has Japanese popular culture been adopted in other contexts and localized? Is the result that 'differentiating the local and the global is not always possible or useful' (Allen and Sakamoto 2006: 6).

One particular pertinent case that builds on this phenomenon is that of rap music. Condry (2006) demonstrates how rap music was neither simply the adoption of US-centred styles and fashions, nor its adoption with Japanese elements attached. Without being driven by the previously mentioned global corporations, hip-hop and rap music has become a global phenomenon, including Japan, with its own hybrid version that eventually became mainstream, but was reinterpreted and renegotiated repeatedly to create a new entity that challenges traditional understandings of the genre, in addition to Japan. Only once established in the immediate spaces where hip-hop was performed did it move into the commercial realm. This reaches the point at which Japanese hip-hop, a musical form originating in New York, was used in the aftermath of 9/11 against US anti-terrorist policies, in contrast to what proponents of soft power would argue (Condry 2006). In short, the adoption and enduring popularity of hip-hop in Japan is not driven by global corporations, but by the spaces in which this new form is created through interaction so that

> ...we see a deepening and quickening connection between hip-hop scenes worldwide, at the same time that a wider diversity of styles appears in Japan and globally. In other words, the opposition between globalizing and localizing turns out to be a false dichotomy' (Condry 2006: 19).

Rather, the ironic contradiction is that increasing interconnectedness and diversity are both in evidence simultaneously.

CONCLUSION

To summarise briefly, globalization clearly means different things to different people – from an updated version of internationalization, to universalization via the more sinister Westernization/Americanization, or liberalization of the global economy, through to more distinguishing deterritorialization driven by ITC. However, it does become clear that whatever globalization may be, its impact is uneven and it can neither be characterized by monolithic homogenization nor by local consumption of global trends. Rather, it is concerned with the multi-levelled and transboundary connections that undermine the nation-state and allow for new forms of politics, economics, security and culture to emerge, and then be repeatedly renegotiated. In addition, it empowers new actors – civil society or the global corporation – as well as providing challenges for older actors, chiefly the nation-states. Clearly, there are other areas in which the impact of globalization can be explored – migration, labour, gender and education to name but a few – but in these cases as well, the words of Shue (2002: 210) ring true, '[g]lobalization may give us our daily new hybridities, but it leads us not into homogenization'.

REFERENCES

Allen, Matthew and Sakamoto, Rumi. (2006). Inside-out Japan? Popular culture and globalization in the context of Japan. In Matthew Allen and Rumi Sakamoto (Eds.), *Popular culture, globalization and Japan* (pp. 1–12). London: Routledge.

Befu, Harumi. (2000). Globalization as human dispersal: from the perspective of Japan. In Jerry S. Eades, Tom Gill and Harumi Befu (Eds.), *Globalization and social change in contemporary Japan* (pp. 17–40). Melbourne: Trans-Pacific Press.

Befu, Harumi. (2001). The global context of Japan outside Japan. In Harumi Befu and Sylvie Guichard-Anguis (Eds.), *Globalizing Japan: ethnography of the Japanese presence in Asia, Europe and America* (pp. 3–22). London: Routledge.

Chan, Jennifer (Ed.). (2008). *Another Japan is possible: new social movements and global citizenship education.* Stanford, CA: Stanford University Press.

Chittiwatanapong, Prasert. (1999). Challenges of and responses to globalization: the case of Southeast Asia. In Yoshinobu Yamamoto (Ed.), *Globalism, regionalism and nationalism: Asia in search of its role in the 21st century* (pp. 70–92). Oxford, UK: Blackwell.

Condry, Ian. (2006). *Hip-hop Japan: rap and the paths of cultural globalization.* Durham, NC: Duke University Press.

Eades, Jerry S. (2000). Introduction: globalization and social change in contemporary Japan. In Jerry S. Eades, Tom Gill and Harumi Befu (Eds.), *Globalization and social change in contemporary Japan* (pp. 1–16). Melbourne: Trans-Pacific Press.

Ebihara, Hitoshi and Yamashita, Rieko. (2006). FIFA 2002 World Cup in Japan: the Japanese football phenomenon in cultural context. In Joseph Maguire and Masayoshi Nakamura (Eds.), *Japan, sport and society: tradition and change in a globalizing world* (pp. 125–39). London: Routledge.

Falk, Richard. (1992). American hegemony and the Japanese challenge. In Glenn D. Hook and Michael A. Weiner (Eds.), *The internationalization of Japan* (pp. 32–60). London: Routledge.

Funabashi, Yoichi. (2002). *Gurobarizeshon Torikku.* Tokyo: Iwanami Shoten.

G7. (1996). *Economic communiqué: making a success of globalization for the benefit of all.* Lyon Summit Document, Lyon, 28 June 1996. Retrieved 6 June 2009 from: http://www.g8.utoronto.ca/summit/1996lyon/ communique.html

Giddens, Anthony. (1990). *The consequences of modernity.* Cambridge, UK: Polity Press.

Han, Seung-Mi. (2001). Consuming the modern: globalization, things Japanese, and the politics of cultural identity in Korea. In Harumi Befu and Sylvie Guichard-Anguis (Eds.), *Globalizing Japan: ethnography of the Japanese presence in Asia, Europe and America* (pp. 194–208). London: Routledge.

Hasegawa, Harukiyo. (2006). Japanese corporate response to globalization: the state's role in economic development. In Glenn D. Hook and Harukiyo Hasegawa (Eds.), *Japanese responses to globalization: politics, security, economics and business* (pp. 151–183). Basingstoke, UK: Palgrave Macmillan.

Hasegawa, Harukiyo and Hook, Glenn D. (2006). Introduction: the dialectics of globalization. In Glenn D. Hook and Harukiyo Hasegawa (Eds.), *Japanese responses to globalization: politics, security, economics and business* (pp. 1–15). Basingstoke, UK: Palgrave Macmillan.

Higgot, Richard and Reich, Simon. (1998). *Globalization and sites of conflict: towards definition and taxonomy.* CSGR Working Paper 01/98, March. Retrieved 5 August 2009 from: http://www2.warwick.ac.uk/fac/soc/csgr/research/workingpapers/1998/wp0198.pdf

Holden, T. J. M. (2006). 'Sportsports': cultural exports and imports in Japan's contemporary globalization career. In Matthew Allen and Rumi Sakamoto (Eds.), *Popular culture, globalization and Japan* (pp. 118–36). London: Routledge.

Hook, Glenn D. and Weiner, Michael A. (1992). Introduction. In Glenn D. Hook and Michael A. Weiner (Eds.), *The internationalization of Japan* (pp. 1–12). London: Routledge.

Hook, Glenn D., Gilson, Julie, Hughes, Christopher W. and Dobson, Hugo. (2002). Japan and the East Asian financial crisis: patterns, motivations and instrumentalisation of Japanese regional economic diplomacy. *European Journal of East Asian Studies,* 1 (2), 177–197.

Hook, Glenn D., Gilson, Julie, Hughes, Christopher W. and Dobson, Hugo. (2005). *Japan's international relations: politics, economics and security.* London: Routledge.

Hughes, Christopher. (2001). Conceptualising the globalisation-security nexus in the Asia–Pacific. *Security Dialogue,* 32 (4), 407–421.

Itoh, Mayumi. (1998). *Globalization of Japan: Japanese Sakoku mentality and US efforts to open Japan.* Basingstoke, UK: Macmillan.

Iwabuchi, Koichi. (2006). Japanese popular culture and postcolonial desire for 'Asia'. In Matthew Allen and Rumi Sakamoto (Eds.), *Popular culture, globalization and Japan* (pp. 15–35). London: Routledge.

Kerr, Alex. (2002). *Dogs and demons: tales from the dark side of Japan*. London: Penguin.

Kinnvall, Catarina. (2002). Analyzing the global–local nexus. In Catrina Kinnvall and Kristina Jönsson (Eds.), *Globalization and democratization in Asia: the construction of identity* (pp. 3–18). London: Routledge.

Lai, Cherry Sze-Ling and Wong, Dixon Heung Wah. (2001). Japanese comics coming to Hong Kong. In Harumi Befu and Sylvie Guichard-Anguis (Eds.), *Globalizing Japan: ethnography of the Japanese presence in Asia, Europe and America* (pp. 111–120). London: Routledge.

McVeigh, Brian. (2000). Education reform in Japan: fixing education or fostering economic nation-statism? In Jerry S. Eades, Tom Gill and Harumi Befu (Eds.), *Globalization and social change in contemporary Japan* (pp. 76–92). Melbourne: Trans-Pacific Press.

Ministry of Foreign Affairs of Japan (MOFA). (2007). International manga award, 2 July. Retrieved 3 August 2014 from http://www.mofa.go.jp/announce/announce/2007/6/1174276_828.html

Ministry of Foreign Affairs of Japan (MOFA). (2014). International manga award, 31 March. Retrieved 3 July 2014 from www.mofa.go.jp/policy/culture/exchange/pop/manga/index.html

Moon, Chung-In and Park, Han-Kyu. (2000). Globalization and regionalization. In Inoguchi Takashi and Purnendra Jain (Eds.), *Japanese foreign policy today: a reader* (pp. 65–82). Basingstoke, UK: Palgrave Macmillan.

Nye, Joseph S. (2004). *Soft power: the means to success in world politics*. New York: PublicAffairs.

Ogawa, Masashi. (2001). Japanese popular music in Hong Kong: analysis of global/local cultural relations. In Harumi Befu and Sylvie Guichard-Anguis (Eds.), *Globalizing Japan: ethnography of the Japanese presence in Asia, Europe and America* (pp. 121–130). London: Routledge.

Pekkanen, Saadia M. (2008). *Japan's aggressive legalism: law and foreign trade politics beyond the WTO*. Stanford, CA: Stanford University Press.

Sakamoto, Rumi and Allen, Matthew. (2007, 4 October). Hating 'The Korean Wave' comic books: a sign of new nationalism in Japan?. *The Asia–Pacific Focus: Japan Focus*. Retrieved 5 August 2009 from http://www.japanfocus.org/-Rumi-SAKAMOTO/2535

Schaede, Ulrike and Grimes, William. (2003a). Preface. In Ulrike Schaede and William Grimes (Eds.), *Japan's managed globalization: adapting to the twenty-first century* (pp. xi–xiii). London: M. E. Sharpe.

Schaede, Ulrike and Grimes, William. (2003b). Introduction: the emergence of permeable insulation. In Ulrike Schaede and William Grimes (Eds.), *Japan's managed globalization: adapting to the twenty-first century* (pp. 3–16). London: M. E. Sharpe.

Scholte, Aart Jan. (2000). *Globalization: a critical introduction*. Basingstoke, UK: Macmillan.

Shetler-Jones, Philip. (2010). *The effects of contemporary globalization on Japan's defence and national security policy* (unpublished PhD thesis). University of Sheffield, UK.

Shue, Vivienne. (2002). Global imaginings, the state's quest for hegemony, and the pursuit of phantom freedom in China. In Catarina Kinnvall and Kristina Jönsson (Eds.), *Globalization and democratization in Asia: the construction of identity* (pp. 210–229). London: Routledge.

Takahashi, Susumu. (2006). The impact of globalization on domestic politics in Japan. In Glenn D. Hook and Harukiyo Hasegawa (Eds.), *Japanese responses to globalization: politics, security, economics and business* (pp. 35–54). Basingstoke, UK: Palgrave Macmillan.

United Nations. (1999). *Secretary-General proposes global compact on human rights, labour, environment, in address to World Economic Forum in Davos* [Press release, 1 February 1999]. Retrieved 3 August 2009 from http://www.un.org/News/Press/docs/ 1999/19990201.sgsm6881.html

Vogel, E. (1979). *Japan as Number 1: Lessons for America*. Cambridge, MA: Harvard University Press.

Wade, Robert. (1996). Japan, the World Bank, and the art of paradigm maintenance: the East Asian miracle in political perspective. *New Left Review*, 17, 3–36.

Weber, Cynthia. (2001). *International relations theory: a critical introduction*. London: Routledge.

25

Japan–United States Relations

Paul Midford

Seen from the broadest historical perspective, Japan–United States relations have traced several full circles: from hostility to friendship to war to ally. And seen from the perspective of the early twenty-first century, it stands as a supreme irony that the relationship was launched in the early 1850s in no small measure as a by-product of American whaling. The United States was the world's leading whaling power at that time, and beyond ordinary trade, it wanted humane treatment for the crews of its shipwrecked whaling vessels at a minimum, and at maximum ports where these ships could resupply (Gibney 1992: 53–54; La Feber 1998: 3, 8; Cohen 2000: 261–262).[1]

By the late twentieth century, Japan and the United States would switch places, with Japan becoming the world's leading whaling power while the United States emerged as a leading opponent of whaling.[2] The tensions that have periodically emerged in recent years as a result of this conflict are but one element of a very complex and wide-ranging relationship, one that, at least until the last decade or so, was frequently heralded by leaders of both countries as being, in the words of former US ambassador to Japan, Mike Mansfield, 'the most important bilateral relationship in the world, bar none' (cited in Mastanduno 2003: 22).

Although the contemporary relationship is defined by the formal alignment of these two

nations as consummated in the 1960 mutual security treaty, and the earlier 1951 security treaty,[3] the whaling example demonstrates the far greater historical depth and wider scope of Japan–United States relations, a depth and scope that ranges beyond the current definition of the relationship as an 'alliance.' As we will see later, this broader historical context continues to subtly influence the relationship. The balance of this chapter focuses, nevertheless, on Japan–United States relations as defined by the hegemonic definition of the relationship for the last 60 years: alliance.

The United States–Japan alliance has spawned a vast academic and policy literature. A search of books on the alliance relationship per se on Amazon.com between 1976 and 2010 turned up 22 books (monographs and edited volumes) focused on the alliance itself (Destler et al. 1976; Tokinoya 1986; Kataoka and Myers 1989; Holland 1992; Fukuyama 1993; Sasae 1994; Buckley 1995; Cossa 1997; Mochizuki 1997; Green and Mochizuki 1998; Funabashi 1999; Green and Cronin 1999; Nishihara 2001; Berger 2004; Ikenberry and Inoguchi 2003; Swenson-Wright 2005; Ota 2006; McCormack 2007; Wakabayashi 2008; Calder 2009; Arase and Akaha 2010).[4] There were also 12 books on bilateral relations (Frost 1988; Lauren and Wylie 1989; Makin and Hellmann 1989; Lewis 1991; Armacost 1996; Maga 1997; La Feber 1998;

Curtis 2001; Vogel 2002; Krauss and Pempel 2003; Yamamoto, Iriye, and Makoto 2006), not including books focusing on the relationship between Japan and the United States and third countries, such as China or Korea, or books focused more narrowly on particular areas of the relationship, such as economic ties. A vast literature to be sure, although one that has expanded at a rate of just under one book a year on average, with slower growth from the mid-1970s to the mid-1980s, but faster growth from the end of the 1980s (with the end of the Cold War), in the late 1990s when the alliance was redefined, and during the first decade of the twentieth century when the relationship was effectively redefined again by the war on terror.

This chapter focuses on six key questions that have been widely debated regarding the nature of the alliance. First, and most fundamentally, why does this alliance exist and persist, even after the Cold War? Second, is the alliance characterized by one-sided dependence, or is there a high degree of mutual interdependence? Third, is the alliance fundamentally an alliance of equals or is it more like a client–patron relationship? Fourth, what is the role of democracy in the alliance? Fifth, can Japan's limited and restricted defense be understood as an attempt to free-ride off the US provision of defense, or as an attempt to avoid entrapment in US conflicts, which are not in its interest, or neither? Sixth, is the alliance a help or hindrance to Japan's relations with its East Asian neighbors?

WHY ARE JAPAN AND THE UNITED STATES IN ALLIANCE?

During the Cold War, explaining the existence and persistence of the United States–Japan alliance was comparatively easy. It was an alliance of two non-communist, capitalist liberal democracies allied against the threat of communism posed by China, North Korea, and ultimately the Soviet Union, which was the other great military power in the bipolar distribution of power that defined the Cold War. It could be easily understood in terms of balancing against threat, defined principally as the combination of military capabilities plus perceived aggressiveness (Walt 1987). It could also be understood in terms of balance of power, or balancing against a strong military threat. However, since the Soviet Union was the weaker of the two superpowers, especially in the Pacific where US naval and air dominance was decisive and the Soviet Union's comparative advantage in land power was of less importance, pure balance of power logic would more plausibly have led Japan to neutrality, if not to bandwagon with the weaker Soviet side against the stronger

United States.[5] Despite what Stephen Walt calls a fundamental 'imbalance' of power during the Cold War, (Walt 1987: 273–276), Japan nonetheless decided to align and remain aligned with the United States, a fact that returns us to the greater explanatory power of balance of threat theory. Given the ease of explaining Japan's alignment with the United States using balance of threat logic, the reason for the existence of the alliance was usually not questioned during the Cold War.[6]

There were those who predicted that Japan would become a great power, if not a superpower in its own right (Kahn 1971), and therefore would have no need for alliance with the United States. Others wondered whether the Japanese Socialist Party's (JSP) quest for neutrality, if they were able to win power, could lead to the end of the alliance (Curtis 2000: 30, 255 note 7; and on JSP neutrality in general, see Stockwin 1968). The late Harvard academic and US ambassador to Japan, Edwin O. Reischauer, writing for *Foreign Affairs* in the Fall of 1960, thought the prospects for the Socialists and other alliance opponents taking power seemed 'not just possible but probable' (Reischauer 1960: 13). Similarly, prominent Liberal Democratic Party (LDP) politician Hirohide Ishida, writing in the mid-1960s, saw the Socialists coming to power within a decade (Ishida 1963). These doubts about the durability of the alliance during the Cold War were the exception rather than the rule, however. This situation changed when the Soviet Union collapsed at the end of 1991, removing the threat that the alliance had ostensibly been targeting. Following the Soviet collapse, the question of why the United States–Japan alliance should continue became more pressing, as did questions about NATO and other US alliances.

From a longer-term balance of power perspective, the alliance still made sense for the United States because Washington could use its alliance with Japan, and indeed NATO, to prevent the emergence of a Eurasian hegemon that could threaten the United States. As far back as 1942, Nicholas Spykman had identified this as America's most fundamental strategic interest (Spykman 1942). Seen from this perspective, the Soviet Union was less a singular threat than a type of threat, less a proper noun than a generic. Although Japan might share such an objective, especially as long as Japan itself was not a candidate to dominate Eurasia, its security interests were more localized in East Asia, and hence, not perfectly overlapping with the United States in this respect. Also, since the Soviet Union had been sold in Japan, the United States, and Europe as a singular rather than a generic threat, Spykman's argument and underlying long-term US strategic interests notwithstanding, the Japan–United States alliance, like NATO, came into question following Soviet collapse.

On the Japanese side as well, the alliance continued in the eyes of many analysts to serve the national interest. Posing the question of alliance or autonomy, Green argues in *Reluctant Realism*: 'in the end there is no better option for Japan than alliance with the United States. ...Strategically, Japan has no place else to go' (Green 2001: 22). Writing a decade after the Cold War, Green sees Japan as no longer being a candidate to dominate East Asia, thereby rendering a continuation of alliance as the only palatable option: 'If a Pax Nipponica is not likely, then Tokyo clearly will prefer a Pax Americana to a Pax Sinica in Asia' (Green 2001: 10). Underlying Green's argument here is the assumption that Japan, at most, has the choice of whether to dominate or be dominated, and if the later, by whom to be dominated, a point to which we will return in the following pages.

With wording less suggestive of the inevitability of domination, Calder (2009) essentially agrees with Green that changes in the balance of power increase Japan's stake in continuing the alliance. According to Calder, for Japan

> ongoing changes in the global political economy generate important new rationales for the transpacific alliance. Japan, after all, is a middle-range power, lacking strategic depth, which finds benefit with a larger power in world affairs ... alignment with a preeminent global naval power has particular attraction... (Calder 2009: 5).

Like Green, Calder is thus indicating that Japan is no longer a candidate great power or potential rival of the United States, as had been discussed in the 1980s and early 1990s.[7] For Green, writing in 2001, this conclusion was based upon the relative decline of Japan in relation to the rest of Asia and the United States, whereas for Calder, writing in 2009, it was based increasingly on the rise of China in relation to not only Japan, but also the United States. Neither seem willing to consider the possibility that Japan might find it in its interest to bandwagon with China, although some observers consider this a realistic possibility given, in Reinhard Drifte's view, Japan's 'historical inclination to join the regionally preponderant state' (Drifte 2003; see also Inoguchi 1999; Parker 2000). It is also striking that neither Green nor Calder, although clearly using bandwagoning-like logic, are willing to describe Japan's decision to align with the United States as bandwagoning.[8]

Adopting an entirely contrary position, Rajan Menon, in his book *The End of Alliances* (2007), argues that the United States–Japan alliance, like America's other major alliances, is anachronistic and now more harmful than beneficial. 'What is the logic,' he asks, 'for deploying troops and retaining a network of bases in countries that are now wealthy enough to protect themselves and that face no threat comparable to the Soviet Union?' (Menon 2007: 128). 'None,' is essentially Menon's answer. Regarding the United States–Japan alliance, he claims the lack of such viable logic makes it unsustainable:

> The continued positioning of 46,000 [US] troops and substantial air, ground, and naval assets on and around the Japanese archipelago will become infeasible, imprudent, and unnecessary – not only because the challenges we face are new but also because of the imbalance of obligations within the U.S.–Japan alliance...the codification of an anachronistic and iniquitous allocation of burdens, benefits, and hazards (Menon 2007: 128–130).

Although writing from a structural realist perspective, Menon in this regard echoes the views of revisionists who see the traditional alliance deal of US bases and troops in Japan in exchange for Japanese access to US markets as a bad deal for both countries (Johnson 2000; Millard 2000). Unlike these revisionists, or Gavan McCormack who sees an 'East Asian community' as a viable alternative to the United States–Japan alliance (McCormick 2007), Menon emphasizes that Japan has to be able to defend itself independently, but sees that as easily within Japan's reach. Although not necessarily agreeing with Waltz's neo-realist view of Japan as a candidate superpower (Waltz 1993; Waltz 2000; see also Layne 1992; Layne 1993), Menon's analysis largely dovetails with that of Jennifer M. Lind (2004), who emphasizes Japan's great military prowess and ability to defend itself and, like Menon, views the alliance as a case of Japanese buckpassing, if not free-riding, on the United States.[9] Menon and Lind thus see an option between Pax Nipponica on the one hand and domination by either the United States or China on the other, namely strategically autonomous defense.

Menon also frontally challenges the views of Calder, Green, and what he himself describes as virtually everyone 'in American official and foreign policy circles,' who view the prospect of the dissolution of the alliance 'as wholly negative', (Menon 2007: 140) and believe that United States–Japan cooperation, including military cooperation, is dependent upon the continuation of a formal alliance. Instead, Menon calls for redefining United States–Japan relations as a more equal partnership, 'shorn of asymmetric benefits and burdens,' claiming that 'this is the best way to ensure that Japan and the United Sates work in harmony well into the future' (Menon 2007: 143).

In place of alliance, Menon argues that Japan needs 'to cultivate a coalition of states that share Japan's assessment of what the threats are and who poses them,' including the United States (Menon 2007: 140–141). 'An unallied Japan will thus not stand alone…the threats it faces…will be other states' problems as well'. Consequently, Menon insists that 'Japan and the United States will have ample room and occasion to cooperate even though they are not bound by a formal military pact'. This would amount to relying on 'coalitions of the willing' and alignment over alliance: 'pooling of military resources based on convergent interests amount to an alignment, not a formal military pact…' (Menon 2007: 142). Indeed, one could argue that Japan is already taking steps in this direction by engaging in alliance or alignment 'diversification' as it builds strategic alignments with India and Australia, precisely the sort of policy Menon recommends.[10] Developments during the George W. Bush administration appeared to reinforce the logic of Menon's argument, as the United States itself started to deemphasize traditional alliances in favor of coalitions of the willing, a concept very similar to Menon's. Indeed, as Ikenberry and Inoguchi (2003) observe, 'no one talks about the U.S.–Japan alliance in terms of Mike Mansfield, who called it the most important alliance bar none. The U.S. government has ceased to use the phrase special relationship' (Ikenberry and Inoguchi 2003: 13).

Nonetheless, the questioning of the alliance's rationale in the wake of Soviet collapse was, at a policy level at least, resolved by the mid-1990s, with the decision to revitalize the alliance and redefine it from focusing on the Soviet threat to Japanese security to an alliance that deals 'with the latent, unspecified sources of instability' in East Asia (Kamiya 2003: 93). This shift was spelled out in the Pentagon's February 1995 East Asian Strategic Review (EASR), also known as the 'Nye Report,' and fourteen months later in the Clinton–Hashimoto joint statement: 'U.S.–Japan Join Declaration on the Security Alliance for the 21st Century' (Kamiya 2003: 93, 114; see also Cronin and Green 1994; Satake 2011: 92–96). This new definition of the alliance implied military cooperation beyond Japanese territory, and led to the negotiation of a revised set of defense guidelines specifying military cooperation between the two allies.

The Revised US–Japan Defense Guidelines issued in September 1997 updated the first set of guidelines concluded between the two countries in 1978. The 1978 Defense Guidelines specified forms of military cooperation between the two sides for repelling an armed attack against Japan. They were largely silent on the issue of military cooperation in situations and regions surrounding Japan. The new September 1997 Guidelines specified expanded defense cooperation for crisis situations in 'areas surrounding Japan,' with this concept being situational rather than geographic

(Japanese Defense Agency 2002: 388–394). This step was taken largely to avoid specifically including or excluding Taiwan in the ambit of the agreement, and hence to avoid specifically threatening China (Midford 2004a: 124–125). The Self Defense Forces (SDF) was to offer logistical support 'on the high seas and international airspace around Japan which are distinguished from areas where combat operations are being conducted' (Midford 2004a: 124–125; see also Green and Mochizuki 1998: 55–72). The Guidelines listed 40 examples of such support, including sea transportation of personnel and materials (including weapons and ammunition) to US ships on the high seas, and cooperation in noncombatant evacuation operations. The agreement also mandated cooperation in surveillance, minesweeping, search and rescue, and sea and airspace management. To these ends, the revised Guidelines authorized joint operational planning between the two militaries (Midford 2004a: 124–125).

AN ALLIANCE OF INTERDEPENDENCE OR ONE-SIDED DEPENDENCE?

How do the United States and Japan matter to each other? And is this an alliance of interdependence or one-way dependence? If the relationship is fundamentally one-way dependence, then presumably Japan is the dependent partner. Consequently, this section will consider the question of whether Japan is dependent on the United States.

First, however, it is worth considering the extent, economically and socially, despite the growing importance of China for both Japan and the United States, that the world's number one and number three economies still matter to each other. It can be argued that they continue to matter a great deal to each other in several areas beyond military security. The United States is the largest source of foreign direct investment (FDI) in Japan, with invested stock valued at $75 billion in 2009, although FDI in Japan remains very low in absolute and relative terms.[11] Japan is the leading East Asian destination for US visitors and serves as a gateway to Asia, accounting for 25 percent of all US passenger traffic to Asia. More US passengers fly to the land of the rising sun than to the next five top destinations combined (South Korea, Taiwan, Hong Kong, China, and Australia). Two-way passenger traffic between the two countries totaled 11.3 million in 2008, an increase of 20 percent since 1990. Japanese comprised 51 percent of all visitors from East Asia to the United States, and is the second largest source of foreign visitors to the United States.[12] The United States has more sister-city relationships with Japan than with any other country.[13] In short, despite the rise of China, economically, socially, and culturally, Japan and the United States continue to matter a great deal to each other.

Nonetheless, in other areas, most notably trade, Japan and the United States are of declining importance to each other, with China surpassing Japan as America's leading Asian trade partner in 2004, and China passing the United States as Japan's leading trade partner in 2007. These changes are also occurring in a context of not only Japanese relative decline but also relative American decline. As Calder notes, 'today U.S.–Japan trade is the most anemic link of what for most of the past half century was an America-centric economic triangle among Japan, China, and the United States.'[14]

Consequently, how the alliance has mattered to the two partners has changed over time, both in degree and qualitatively, and also in terms of symmetry. Calder observes,

> for Japan, the compelling part of the alliance was once the economic dimension, with the military aspect being more important to America; since the 1980s, with the rise of Japanese capital outflows and the parallel expansion of deficit-enabled U.S. military power, the incentive structure has arguably been reversed (Calder 2009: 7).

He concludes that the alliance 'is decidedly a hybrid political-economic creature,' and essentially always has been (Calder 2009, 7). In short, today Japan primarily depends on the United States for military security while the United States depends on Japan economically, especially for financial support.

Overall, however, how symmetrical is the level of dependence in this openly asymmetrical alliance? Starting with the financial leg of the two-legged asymmetrical alliance: how much does Japanese financial support matter for the United States? Japan currently contributes approximately $2 billion annually to fund US military deployments in Japan, and has supplied more than half the total host nation support received by US military forces from allies worldwide.[15] More important is Japan's consistent support for maintaining the US dollar as the pre-eminent global reserve currency. For example, according the *Asahi Shimbun*, in 2003 and 2004 Japan pumped over 30 trillion Yen or around $250 billion into US Treasuries and other US financial markets in an attempt to shore up the position of the dollar and moderate US borrowing costs while simultaneously helping Japanese exporters with a cheap Yen.[16] According to Taggart Murphy, a long-time observer of United States–Japan financial ties, 'Japan continues to play the central role it has for 25 years now in

supporting the global value of the dollar – and by extension, US hegemony.'(Murphy 2006: 43) Or as McCormack puts it, 'Japanese support has become the sine qua non of Washington's global, superpower strategy and status' (McCormack 2007: 82).

To be sure, China has been catching up with Japan as a leading global creditor that contributes to bankrolling US debt.[17] At the end of the first decade of the twenty-first century, China overtook Japan as the leading overseas holder of US currency reserves. Nonetheless, this fact in many ways appeared more threatening than reassuring for the United States because it potentially gives China financial leverage over what Calder aptly calls the 'deficit-enabled US military,' thereby reemphasizing Japan's role as the second, leading, external funder of US debt, and presumably a funder to which the United States could turn in case the leading funder, China, applied financial pressure on the United States for political reasons.

On the other hand, Japan (and indeed China), are also highly dependent upon the United States financially. In view of Tokyo's massive dollar holdings, a significant portion of its national wealth is tied up in maintaining the stability and value of the dollar, a fact that tends to mitigate US financial dependence upon Japan. Calder thus partially contradicts his point, presented earlier, about how the United States depends upon Japan financially: 'The US–Japan alliance is thus highly important for Japan, as NATO is for Europe, in reinforcing the stability and credibility of delicate, often asymmetrical economic relationships' (Calder 2009: 6).

In the wake of the great recession of 2008–2009, however, it is reasonable to ask whether these asymmetries are either sustainable or desirable economically, or even whether they, and by extension the alliance, helped to contribute to the great recession. Writing with prescience a year before the start of the great recession, McCormack claims

> the paradox of the global financial structure is that it is precariously poised atop 'twin peaks' of Japanese and American debt – each of similar height….[Japan] takes every possible step to prop up the equally ailing US economy, pouring Japanese savings into the black hole of American illiquidity in order to subsidize the US global empire, fund its debt, and finance its over-consumption…US fiscal irresponsibility is in the long term unsustainable, but nowhere is confidence in it higher, and readiness to support it stronger, than in Tokyo (McCormack 2007: 82–83).

Japan's financial support may have just delayed an inevitable economic reckoning for the United States, and made that eventual reckoning more difficult as a result.

Turning to military dependence, the orthodox view states that it is entirely one-way: Japan depends on the United States while the United States does not depend on Japan. Bipolarity, according to Waltz, by definition means that neither of the superpowers depend on allies; yet, they continue to value allies because they overreact to inconsequential shifts in the balance of power on the periphery (Waltz 1979). Similarly, William Wohlforth (1999) argues that under unipolarity, the unipole does not depend on allies. Notably, however, Wohlforth did not consider the extent to which America's 'deficit-enabled military' depends on America's massive overseas borrowing, approximately $2.5 trillion dollars in 2006. This massive annual infusion in turn depends not only on large and continued infusions of Japanese capital, which totaled $1.2 trillion in 2007, but also upon Japan's role in maintaining the dollar as the key international currency, which encourages China and others to lend to the United States, as discussed earlier. As Calder emphasizes, 'the global key currency allows the United States an autonomy from fiscal constraints in its military deployments available to no other nation' (Calder 2009: 4–5).

The United States depends on Japan militarily in other ways as well. Japan plays a key role by providing the United States access to an extensive array of bases for the nearly 50,000 troops stationed in Japan.[18] These bases are crucial to the US ability to maintain its forward military presence in East Asia (Green 2001: 10). By the end of the first decade of the twenty-first century, American bases in Japan were arguably becoming even more important given China's growing anti-area access capabilities, such as its growing fleet of sophisticated submarines and a new anti-ship ballistic missile, which can target aircraft carriers, even as some of these capabilities (e.g. its force of more than 1000 land-to-land missiles) render US bases increasingly vulnerable to Chinese offensive strikes (Blumenthal 2010; Chinese Missiles 2010).

The US depends on Japan militarily in two ways that are often underappreciated if not unacknowledged: by being an important source of military technology to the United States, and by denying such technologies to others. Regarding the first point, Green observed in his 1995 book, *Arming Japan*, that Japan has retreated from *kokusanka*, or domestic production, in weapons procurement, especially in aerospace. In its place, Japan began promoting US technological dependence on Tokyo, thereby transforming a dependent relationship into an interdependent relationship. The debut of this strategy in the alliance began with the contentious development of Japan's follow-on ship and ground attack aircraft (replacing the indigenously developed but low performing F-1) – the FSX (later known as the F-2) – at the beginning of the

1990s. Japan brought technologies to the table where the United States was lagging, most notably phased-array radar and composite wing technology. Japan's offer to make these technologies available to the United States in the process of negotiating over joint development of the FSX, based upon the American designed F-16, arguably enhanced Japan's bargaining position (Green 1995).[19] More recently, Japan has contributed important technologies to the development of missile defense, most notably sensors and nose cone guidance systems, second and third stage boosters and steering systems (Umemoto 2003: 187–188; Kyodo 2005, 2009; Calder 2009: 145; Hughes 2009: 108–110; Pekkanen and Kallender-Umezu 2010: 180–193 Grønning 2011). Beyond missile defense, Japan also has cutting-edge technology in space robotics, a key to developing advanced anti-satellite weapons (Pekkanen and Kallender-Umezu, 2010: chapter 6).

However, America's most important military dependency upon its ally comes in the form of technological denial: denying Japan's cutting-edge militarily-relevant technology to America's strategic rivals, most importantly, China. Japan possesses great technological prowess in areas of strategic significance: space robotics and anti-satellite (ASAT) weapons, rocket and missile technology, especially second and third stage control systems, missile nose cones and sensors, nuclear technology, including most phases of the fuel cycle, radar technology, microelectronic circuitry, and precision manufacturing and machine tools, among others. In some of these areas, such as satellite robotics, nose cone technology, second or third stage rocket control, aspects of the nuclear fuel cycle, and precision-manufacturing, Japanese technology exceeds, in some respects, that of its ally and the global hegemon – the United States. In all of these areas, however, Japanese technology is , if not leading, at least a close follower behind the United States and well ahead of Chinese technological capabilities. Given China's very dynamic and rapidly developing economy, if Japan were to end its alliance with the United States and bandwagon with China, and thereby give China access to these militarily significant technologies, it would be a hegemony ending event for the US.[20]

The United States also relies on Japanese technology to help it develop its next generation of intermediate range missile defense interceptor, the SM-3-IIA. A Japanese withdrawal would undoubtedly slow US development, although it would be unlikely to stop it. However, if Japan were to make its technology in these areas available to China's fledging missile defense development program, it would undoubtedly greatly accelerate its development. Japanese technology would similarly accelerate China's development of ASAT weapons, short, intermediate, and long-range missiles, and precision-guided munitions (PGMs), among others.[21] Access to Japanese technology would, in short, offer China the potential to quickly close the military gap with the United States in many areas, perhaps assume technological leadership in a few areas, and dramatically narrow the gap in almost every area. Given China's numerical advantage in the size of its military, this would quickly allow China to potentially almost match US military power globally, and clearly overshadow it in East Asia. The technological impact of Japanese bandwagoning with China would be compounded by the US loss of military bases in Japan, its loss of host nation support, Japan's purchases of US weapons, particularly missile defense systems, which helps to drive down the costs of these weapons for the United States, and not least of all, the loss of Japan's crucial financial support for the US budget deficit and the US dollar. A US shorn of its Japanese ally in such a scenario would thus face a rapidly strengthening Chinese military, just at a time when its own ability to spend on defense would become seriously impaired.

To be sure, a Japanese decision to end the alliance and bandwagon with China would be a radical decision that can only be judged as highly unlikely at present. However, as noted earlier, some analysts do see this as a real possibility. Moreover, no responsible US military planner, whose job it is to engage in worst-case scenario planning, could fail to seriously consider this possibility and its implications for US security. The very possibility of this scenario, as unlikely as it may be, is therefore an additional source of latent Japanese influence or power over the United States, and indicates that the United States has a great and largely unrecognized latent military dependency on Japan. This reality also suggests that Japanese fears about US abandonment of Japan are simply unrealistic.US security and its continued hegemony depend on defending Japan. Although Japan is not a major military power, it has the sinews of a great military power, and holds the global military balance in its hands.

A RELATIONSHIP OF EQUALS OR CLIENT-PATRON?

There is essentially no disagreement that the United States–Japan alliance began as a profoundly unequal alliance.[22] There is less agreement on the causes or extent to which this inequality has persisted due to the original alliance structures. This inequality may have even deeper roots in the bilateral relationship, as Calder claims 'there has been a faint hierarchical tinge to U.S.–Japan

relations…from the very inception' (Calder 2009: 32), in other words, even in the pre-alliance period of the first 90+ years.

Regarding the post-war United States–Japan relationship, McCormack claims the relationship is characterized by Japan's 'submission and exploitation by the US' (McCormack 2007: 5). McCormack traces this back to the US policy of creating a structural dependence during the occupation: '…such dependence upon the US, giving it such priority over the relationship with the rest of Asia, is…a natural extension of a dependency deeply structured in Japan's postwar and occupation settlement' (McCormack 2007: 6–7).

Calder agrees that the origins of the alliance were highly asymmetric. Indeed, the security alliance was a de facto condition for Japan regaining its independence. 'The peace and mutual security treaties were really a package: the peace treaty had no separate existence of its own, but rather was contingent upon Japan's agreeing to a military alliance with America' (Calder 2009: 32–33). This package deal was, according to John Dower, 'magnanimity under lock and key' (Dower 1969: 24).

Yet Calder disagrees with McCormack's claim that this asymmetry was because of US design instead of being the result of the force of circumstances. Rather, he sees the 'highly asymmetric agreements crafted by Dulles' as 'almost preordained' by 'similarly unbalanced economic and political conditions' (Calder 2009: 32–33). Menon also sees the origins of the alliance in this way: The US occupation reflected an asymmetry of power that 'allowed Washington to craft the institutions and agreements that transformed the erstwhile enemy into a dependent, even subservient ally' (Menon 2007: 105). Calder and Menon are credible here in that it would be hard to imagine a truly equal alliance emerging between the United States and Japan in the 1950s, or between the United States and any power for that matter.

McCormack sees the structure of dependence built into the early alliance as still governing the relationship even today, and claims on this basis that Japan lacks influence on the global stage commensurate with its national power. According to him, Japan 'is the most durable, generous and unquestioning ally of the United States, and one of the world's largest donors of international aid, yet it casts a pale diplomatic shadow' (McCormack 2007: 39–54). In the 1990s, with the end of the Cold War, things did not get any better in his view as Japan 'experienced humiliation by being forced to yield to the United States on one policy matter after another while being sidelined on major issues of regional or global concern' (McCormack 2007: 39–54).

To what extent does Japan subjugate its policies to those of Washington? Clearly there is a significant degree of coordination regarding foreign aid, especially regarding some of the top recipients, coordination that an observer like McCormack could easily characterize as subjugation. Among the 25 top Official Development Assistance (ODA) recipients of both Japan and the United States, seven countries were shared in common. Iraq was the number one recipient of both Japanese and US aid in 2008 (receiving a combined total of $4.5 billion), a case that would be especially easy to fit into a subjugation narrative, as would Afghanistan, which received a combined total of $2.3 billion from the two allies. On the other hand, it is hard to view the other top recipients of Japanese and American aid as necessarily reflecting Japan's subjugation to American policy demands: Sudan ($958 million), Ethiopia ($858 million), Uganda ($410 million), Tanzania ($318 million), and Democratic Republic of the Congo ($248 million).[23] Moreover, Japan has clearly demonstrated independence over the years in giving economic assistance to countries that the United States does not, or cannot, give to due to domestic legal or political restraints – Burma, Cambodia, China (the leading recipient of Japanese ODA for many years), and Vietnam, being notable examples.

How does the subjugation of Japan hypothesis look in terms of behavior at the United Nations? In UN General Assembly voting, Japan votes with the US 58 percent of the time. This is significantly higher than the UN General Assembly average of 39 percent, yet hardly represents overwhelming support for the US position, with Japan diverging from the US position more than four times out of ten. Moreover, in greater East Asia, there are several states that vote more often with the United States: the Marshall Islands, Micronesia, New Zealand, Palau, and Australia.[24] Of course, in at least some cases it might be the United States that is supporting Japan's position rather than the reverse, but even ignoring this possibility, Japan's UN voting behavior hardly offers strong support for the subjugation hypothesis, and shows that Japan can and often does openly disagree with the United States in international politics.

Moreover, McCormack (2007) has examples undermining his claim that Japan exercises little influence internationally. He observes that Japan, under Chief Cabinet Secretary Abe Shinzō's leadership, 'played a key role in securing UN Security Council Resolution 1695 denouncing North Korea's threats to peace after the July 2006 missile launches' (McCormack 2007: 197). However, McCormack does not credit this as an example of Japan exercising international leadership and influence, suggesting that McCormack simply ignores examples of Japanese leadership that he does not support or areas that he is not interested in, such as Japan's long-term leadership role in Southeast Asia, a point that will be explored later.

If Japan is truly a client state, as McCormack claims, has this given the United States a large influence over Japan's domestic economy? Not surprisingly, McCormack answers in the affirmative, offering the novel interpretation that Koizumi Jun'ichirō's quest to privatize Japan's postal savings and insurance systems was in no small part motivated by US pressure, instead of primarily resulting from Koizumi's personal and political obsessions and interests. He also discounts the role of ideology in Koizumi's neo-liberal market oriented reforms (McCormack 2007: 39–54). Relying on the simplicity of neo-realist theory, Menon also sees American *gaiatsu* on Japan's domestic economic as a forgone conclusion: 'Japan's dependence on the United States for so basic a necessity as safety also gave Washington leverage in the economic realm' (Menon 2007: 110). However, Leonard Schoppa (1997) concludes his careful study of US leverage in relation to Japan's domestic economy with the finding that Washington's ability to use pressure tactics 'are constrained.' US *gaiatsu*, he concludes, will not work without domestic allies inside Japan: 'Participant expansion will not work when U.S. demands lack domestic support inside Japan. Alternative specification will not work when there is no recognized domestic "problem"...' (Schoppa 1997: 305–306). As for the most direct and blunt instrument, 'threats – even when coming from a more "powerful" nation will not work if they are perceived to be illegitimate...' (Schoppa 1997: 305–306).

While for McCormack the alliance is one of Japanese subordination to US demands and interests, for Calder mutual accommodation has been the defining dynamic of the alliance: 'Historically, fear of future disruption – of radical departure from a fragile yet vital status quo – has been the force driving mutual accommodation between Washington and Tokyo as well as policy innovation...' (Calder 2009: 12). Surprisingly, even a scholar and former policymaker as closely associated with championing the bilateral alliance as Michael Green often appears closer to McCormack than Calder in acknowledging the unequal nature of the alliance. Green does try to consign this inequality to the past tense, however, when he admonishes that 'U.S. policy-makers can no longer assume Japan's automatic compliance with U.S. diplomacy – and certainly cannot assume Japanese passivity' (Green 2001: 6).[25] He is thus essentially agreeing with McCormack that, up to the beginning of the twenty-first century at least, Japan 'however close it has become to Washington, its opinion is rarely sought or expected' (McCormack 2007: 1), even while warning that this situation cannot continue. Green sees the continuation of excessive hierarchy as threatening US interests: 'In order to sustain its own position in Asia, the United States will have to do more to demonstrate reciprocal support for Japanese diplomatic initiatives...so that

Japan is more forthcoming when its help becomes essential' (Green 2001: 9). Kamiya Matake, a professor at Japan's National Defense University is even more blunt, claiming

> despite the rhetoric used by Washington, many Japanese feel that their country is still treated as a junior partner by the United States...if Japan continues to be treated as a second-class political power...the Japanese might be forced to consider ending its military dependence on the United States' (Kamiya 2003: 111).

Yet the solution Green proposes is little more than a modest mitigation of the great inequality of the bilateral alliance, as he suggests, at best, a limited independence for Japan defined by the United States and one that, seemingly grudgingly, gives Japan little more than independence regarding tactics, but not strategy or principles:

> The United States will have to frame its policy toward East Asia and multilateral organizations in terms that give Japan responsibilities at all stages of diplomacy – from conceptualization, to funding, to implementation on the ground. And at each stage, the United States will have to raise the bar of expectations on Japan – giving more responsibility, but insisting on more sharing of the risk.... There is no question that the partnership must begin with clear strategic principles from the United States... (Green 2001: 9–10).

In essence, the deal Green proposes is more autonomy for Japan regarding tactics in exchange for more risk sharing (Green 2001: 192).[26] Risk sharing clearly points to the US demand for greater Japanese military support of US policies beyond Japanese shores. The outlines of this proposed deal are remarkably well echoed in the so-called first and second 'Armitage' reports. In the first report of October 2000, Armitage and Japan-hands, such as Green, argued that the two allies were now moving toward a 'mature partnership,' presumably a change from the hierarchy of the past, and that the Revised Defense Guidelines of three years earlier 'should be regarded as the floor – not the ceiling – for an expanded Japanese role in the transpacific alliance' (Armitage et al. 2000).The second 'Armitage' report issued in February 2007 by the same group appealed to Japanese hawks with great power aspirations, claiming that deployments to the Indian Ocean, Iraq, and other areas of the Middle East'in support of US policy goals have 'accelerated' Japan's emergence as a global power. They also claimed that these deployments had 'helped to diminish the security hierarchy that typified the U.S.-Japan relationship in the past (Armitage and Nye 2007).[27]

Yet, the picture drawn looks contradictory: Japan's emergence as a global power while under the tutelage and ultimate control of its US ally. McCormack captures the contradiction of this proposal when he claims that Koizumi and Abe, by supporting this agenda, sought to recast 'the constitutionally pacifist, diplomatically reticent, Cold War-dependent relationship with the US...into a full subordinate, global alliance..."the Britain of the Far East"...Could Japan be simultaneously dependent and assertive?' (McCormack 2007: 4).

The 2009–2010 bilateral dispute over the relocation of the US Marine airbase from Futenma Okinawa offers an important case study for considering the degree of equality versus inequality in the Japan–United States alliance. When the Democratic Party of Japan (DPJ) swept the LDP out of power in the August 2009 Lower House election, it came to power having promised to review the 2006 decision by the Bush and Koizumi administrations to relocate the Futenma airbase to Henoko off the northeast coast of Okinawa island, effectively extending Camp Schwab into offshore waters. As Axel Berkovsky and Linus Hagström note, this was 'the first time that a Japanese government made the reduction of US military presence the central item of an election and policy agenda' (Berkovsky and Hagström 2010: 8).[28]

As newly elected Prime Minister Hatoyama Yukio set about considering either relocation outside of Okinawa, or even outside of Japan, US Secretary of Defense Robert Gates, during a visit to Japan a few weeks after the Hatoyama administration took office, declared the 2006 agreement 'non-negotiable,' and warned that the United States would not relocate 8000 Marines from Okinawa as promised unless Japan implemented the 2006 plan to relocate Futenma airbase (Okinawa Hovers, 2009; Hongo 2009). In May 2010, in the face of strong US pressure, Hatoyama gave up his attempts to renegotiate the relocation of the Futenma airbase to Nago and decided to largely stick with the 2006 agreement. Consequently, he resigned soon after. Indeed, the Obama administration has been criticized even in the United States for essentially deposing Hatoyama (Sneider 2010).

According to Berkovsky and Hagström (2010), Hatoyama's retreat may have only 'confirmed the ingrained view in much research on Japanese foreign and security policies,' including by authors like McCormack, that 'tends to take Japanese reactivity to and dependency on the USA more or less for granted.' Moreover, Japan's eventual caving to US pressure could 'support the interpretation that the junior–senior alliance structure survived Hatoyama's attempts to make the alliance more 'equal'....it might be argued in retrospect that Tokyo's attempt to re-negotiate the base relocation did more harm than good to its ambitions to make the alliance with the US less asymmetrical' (Berkovsky and Hagström 2010: 9).

Yet, Berkovsky and Hagström, based on interviews with various DPJ Diet members, suggest the opposite outcome could be more likely in the medium to long-term:

> Japan requesting to review an existing base relocation agreement and not instantly yielding to US pressure, could have created an important precedence of how and to what extent Tokyo might in the future be prepared to protect its interests in the context of the bilateral security alliance (Berkovsky and Hagström 2010: 9).

Many DPJ Diet members, according to Berkovsky and Hagström, 'want Japan to have the same kind of "equality" which exists in the alliance relationships that the US maintains with other countries' (Berkovsky and Hagström 2010: 10). This view tracks remarkably well with advice Green (2001) directed toward US policymakers that

> Tokyo will insist on a level of consultations on security issues comparable with NATO, for example, as well as more say in U.S. decisions on force structure in Japan. Mismanagement of these expectations could accelerate calls for reduced U.S. military presence in Japan (Green 2001: 273).

Nonetheless, this advice stands in marked contrast to Green's hardline position against Hatoyama's attempts to renegotiate the Futenma deal, when he asserted that accepting Hatoyama's demands would have 'a devastating effect' on the alliance (Tokyo Accepts Defeat 2010).

Based on several interviews, Berkovsky and Hagström (2010: 10) found 'some DPJ Diet members even question if the USA really needs regular presence in Japan in order to defend the country in line with the Japan-US security treaty.'[29] They further note that some Japanese policymakers and scholars argue that Guam or even Hawaii is '"close enough" to intervene in a regional crisis contingency' (Berkovsky and Hagström 2010: 11). Similarly, a few weeks before becoming prime minister, Hatoyama reportedly stated 'I truly wonder if it is appropriate that a military of another country will continue to station in this country forever' (Yasumoto 2009).

On the other hand, pressure to abandon Hatoyama's intention to revise the Futenma airbase relocation plan came not just from Washington, but also from the Japanese press (Berkovsky and Hagström 2010; Seeking Deep Analysis 2010). Similarly, when Ichirō Ozawa suggested in February 2009 that retaining the US Navy's 7th Fleet base in Yokosuka would be 'enough for the U.S. presence in the Far East,' and for maintaining Japan's security, he was roundly criticized in the Japanese press for making an irresponsible statement and lacking any knowledge of foreign affairs, even though this is well within the range of what security experts have been debating (Hanai 2009; Berkovsky and Hagström 2010; Seeking Deep Analysis 2010). For example, Ozawa's proposal is conservative compared with Menon's proposal for abolishing the alliance and all US bases in Japan. Ironically, conservative media outlets, such as *Yomiuri Shimbun* who champion Japan becoming a normal nation, are the very media voices who most oppose the start of serious domestic debate about Japan's strategic options. When it comes to ending or reforming the United States–Japan alliance, these media voices fit Menon's characterization of '...the Japanese, who are reticent to contemplate that prospect and seem to believe that by not discussing it, they will keep it at bay' (Menon 2007: 101).

Overall, there is a very wide consensus that the Japan–United States alliance has been highly hierarchical from the beginning with Japan as the junior partner, and with almost as wide a consensus that it retains this hierarchy to a significant degree up to today. On the other hand, claims that Japan has essentially no room for policy independence are significantly exaggerated as Japan often shows independence at the United Nations and in its foreign aid policy. Moreover, as discussed in greater detail later, Japan has often shown its independence in East Asia itself, where Japan has pursued policies toward nations such as Cambodia, Burma, and to a lesser extent Indonesia, that have clashed with American policy, and has acted to promote regional security cooperation, even against US wishes. On the other hand, the degree of inequality also varies over time. In the 1990s, after the end of the Cold War, there was a push for greater equality and closer relations with East Asia, a push that was somewhat undermined by the 'Taepodong shock' of August 1998 when North Korea test fired a missile over Northern Honshu (Green 2001: 33). The rise of Chinese military power has had a similar impact. Changes in Japanese administrations have also mattered, with many administrations in the mid-1990s, most notably those of Hosokawa, Hashimoto, and Obuchi, seeking greater equality, while the Koizumi administration prioritized strengthening the alliance over equalizing it. Since the emergence of a Sino-Japanese confrontation over control of the Senkaku (Diaoyu in Chinese) islands in the East China from late 2010 Japan has again tended to de-emphasize equaling the alliance in favor of strengthening it.

THE ROLE OF DEMOCRACY IN THE ALLIANCE?

Is the Japan–United States alliance based primarily upon realist balance-of-power or balance-of-threat logic, or is it fundamentally an alliance based upon shared liberal democratic values? Is it an alliance predicated on defending and promoting liberal democracy?

Calder argues that the bilateral alliance fits 'a pattern of sustained alliance persistence in the face of waning military threats, and that this "contrasts strikingly" to "the earlier history of alliances" and "to the assumptions of realist theory"' (Calder 2009: 83). Indeed, it is precisely based on such realist theory that Menon (2007) argues in *The End of Alliances* that, regardless of democracy or regime type, the Japan–United States alliance, like NATO and America's other alliances, is bound to end now that the Soviet threat is gone. On the other hand, Democratic Peace theory contains no theoretical basis for predicting the persistence of alliances among democracies without an external threat.

By contrast, Peter Woolley claims that the United States–Japan alliance stands 'against anti-liberal governments' and argues that the two countries share a common interest with European NATO members in 'the defeat of anti-liberal ideologies' (Wooley 2000: 11–12). Yet, this view is rare in the Japan–United States alliance literature. Green, a strong supporter of the alliance, does not make this argument in *Reluctant Realism*. On the contrary, he outlines a pattern of diplomatic conflict between the two allies over Japan's assistance to the military junta in Burma, and support for less than democratic regimes in Cambodia and Suharto's Indonesia (Green 2001: 188–190).

Seemingly supporting Woolley's claim is Japan's 1991 ODA Charter, whose fourth point is 'give full consideration to the recipient's advancement of democracy, efforts at introducing a market-style economy, and protection of basic human rights and freedom'[30] – language that is repeated in the 2003 ODA Charter (Japanese Ministry of Foreign Affairs 2003). Yet, this priority comes well after the first priority, which is promoting sustainable development. Under the first principle of supporting self-help efforts by developing countries, the 2003 Charter states 'Japan will give priority to assisting developing countries that make active efforts to pursue peace, democratization, and the protection of human rights...',[31] language and placement that imply this concern is subsidiary to promoting development itself. Thus, Japan has traditionally adhered to developmentalism rather than a focus on democracy promotion as the way to enhance peace and security as well as prosperity, a clear contrast with the US focus on democracy promotion.

On the other hand, Japan moved away from developmentalism and toward a clear embrace of democracy promotion in 2006–2007 during the first Abe Cabinet, when Foreign Minister Asō Tarō proclaimed that Japan would promote an 'arc of freedom' in Asia. This new policy appeared to be more narrowly aimed at containing an authoritarian China than it did at promoting democracy more broadly.[32] This new concept did not noticeably interfere with Japanese relations with authoritarian regimes in Burma or Central Asia. More decisively, however, this concept was short-lived, as Prime Minister Fukuda Yasuō replaced it in 2008 in favor of returning to a focus on economic development as the best way to promote peace and prosperity. Conceptually, the arc of freedom was replaced with 'strengthened Asian diplomacy' (Jiyū to hanei 2008). This return to developmentalism suggests its durability and Japan's long-term desire not to define its alliance with the United States as one targeting non-democratic regimes.

More fundamentally, the very inequality of the alliance itself calls into question the role of democracy within the alliance. Notwithstanding McCormack's claim that the US occupation's decision to retain the emperor 'balanced and restrained' the development of Japanese democracy (McCormack 2007: 8), Dower (2000) is surely correct that the 'revolution from above' of imposing democracy through undemocratic means (force of arms of a victory rather than a national referendum) surely influenced not only the development of democracy in Japan, but also the future relationship between these two allies. As he observed, 'the contradictions of the democratic revolution were clear for all to see: while the victors preached democracy they ruled by fiat' (Dower 2000: 211, 69–73).

From the time of the occupation, the United States dealt with democratically elected Japanese politicians, mostly conservatives from the LDP and its antecedent parties, the Democrats and Liberals, politicians who followed the orders of the occupation and their postwar successors who did not often forcefully challenge US policy, especially US bases and deployments in Japan. Clearly, the US side became used to an essentially unbroken line of reasonably pliable conservative politicians in Japan, which from 1955 took the form of the LDP. Indeed, the United States played a role behind the scenes in promoting the formation of the LDP. This arguably created what could be called "ruling-partyism," or *yotōshugi*. American disdain for the idea that popular sovereignty ruled in Japan can be seen in a remark by the US Ambassador to Tokyo to an American public opinion researcher: 'forget about what the mass public tells you in your opinion polls, because the men in Japan who really count are all on our side.'[33] In short, the United States became used to dealing with only one party in a one-party-dominant democracy, and largely ignored opposition parties, most notably the largest of these, which was the Japan Socialist Party.[34]

Given the long dominance of the LDP, this tendency on the part of the United States is not surprising. Nonetheless, ignoring opposition parties does not accord with interdemocratic norms or smart policy because in a democracy today's opposition party can be expected to become tomorrow's ruling party. More surprising, given the fairly regular rotations in power by the two-major US parties, is the gradual growth of a reciprocal belief in Japan, and especially in the LDP, namely that Republicans are better for Japan than Democrats. Japanese observers making this point focus on President Carter's plan to withdraw US troops from South Korea (a policy idea that was withdrawn after his first year in office, but one that appeared to ignore Japan's security interests) versus the very close 'Ron–Yasu' relationship in the 1980s between US President Ronald Reagan and Japanese Prime Minister Nakasone Yasuhirō. This discourse also focuses on Clinton's heavy pressure on Japan to adopt numerical import targets for US products, his prioritization of China and even criticism of Japan while visiting China, in contrast to the perceived priority George W. Bush put on the bilateral alliance with Japan over relations with China. Evidence tending to falsify this view, such as the 'Nixon Shocks' of the early 1970s (including his abandonment of the Bretton Woods System of fixed exchange rates that led to undesired Yen appreciation, Nixon's secret opening to China while Japan was kept in the dark, and his protectionist measures against Japanese textile imports); the very close Carter–Ohira relationship; George H. W. Bush's very loud criticism of Japanese economic policies during his visit in January 1992 and the *gaiatsu* (foreign pressure) he applied on Japan during the Structural Impediment Talks; the reaffirmation of the Japan–United States alliance under Clinton (see the earlier discussion of the Clinton–Hashimoto Declaration); and George W. Bush's decision to ignore Japanese objections when pursuing a nuclear deal with North Korea in 2007 and 2008 are usually ignored.

While a fuller look at the record might thus lead one to conclude that Democratic and Republican parties are nearly equal in their treatment of Japan, the belief, especially in the LDP, that Republicans are better for Japan, had taken a firm hold by the first decade of the twenty-first century. Consequently, during the first 6 years of the George W. Bush administration, Japan essentially ignored the Democratic Party. Koizumi pursued a Bush policy rather than an American policy, focusing on cementing a personal, as opposed to a nation-to-nation, relationship. This partly explains why Koizumi decided in 2003 to dispatch the SDF to Iraq instead of Afghanistan, a decision that would have bought him less credit with the US president but more credit with the broader US public and elites.[35] Also indicative was Koizumi's public statement on the eve of the

2004 US Presidential election that he hoped Bush would be re-elected. Similarly, when Democrats won back control of the US Senate and House in November 2006, Japanese embassy staffers were said to be reluctant to meet with the leadership of the new majority and preferred meeting with the minority Republicans. The lack of communication between the Embassy and Tokyo on the one hand and Congressional Democrats on the other hand was undoubtedly one factor contributing to a resolution that the new majority passed in the House of Representatives in 2007 calling on Japan to apologize for its treatment of the so-called comfort women forced to provide sexual services for the Imperial Japanese army during World War II (Kyodo 2007).

Reciprocally, the Bush administration was wary of, and made little effort to communicate with the opposition DPJ. Notably, US Ambassador Schieffer did not try to meet with DPJ leader Ozawa before August 2007, just after the DPJ won control of the Upper House (Ozawa Tells U.S. Envoy 2007). Overall, the two sides displayed a tendency to focus on ruling party ties and ignore opposition parties, ignoring interdemocratic norms that recognize that today's (especially leading) opposition party may well be tomorrow's governing party.

The evident trepidation with which the LDP Asō administration greeted the inauguration of the Barack Obama administration in January 2009 was only exceeded by the discomfort with which this Democratic President's administration greeted the coming to power of Democrats in Japan nine months later. This discomfort, as discussed earlier, was almost immediately evident in the hardline position the Obama administration took regarding the new DPJ government's intention to revisit the Futenma airbase relocation plan. For Berkovsky and Hagström (2010), Gates' position that the relocation plan was 'non-negotiable' could 'be interpreted as US 'interference' in Japan's political decision-making process and its democratic practices. ...That is not only highly unusual in international diplomacy between alliance partners, but must indeed also be interpreted as almost complete disregard for the fact that a DPJ-led government's alliance policies may not be identical with the previous LDP alliance policies' (Berkovsky and Hagström 2010: 8). Claiming that Obama administration officials 'quietly encouraged talk of replacing' the Prime Minister, Daniel Sneider (2010) accuses Washington of engineering the downfall of the democratically elected Hatoyama government: '...eventually, if not immediately, the Japanese public is likely to notice that the nation's principal ally, the United States, was intimately involved in, if not directly responsible for, the downfall of the Japanese prime minister. ...the Japanese people will turn their eyes toward Washington and wonder whether this is how allies should treat each other. It is a good question' (Sneider 2010: 1, 5). An even more pressing question is whether this is the way democracies should treat each other? 'The high level of "alarmism" amongst US policymakers and many scholars' that Berkovsky and Hagström (2010: 9) observe concerning the danger of escalating DPJ demands for reconfiguring the status of US forces and bases in Japan may more generally reflect a fear of the unknown, namely dealing with a left-of-center government not directly descendant from the pliable conservative politicians Washington had largely been dealing with since the occupation. The long-term prevalence of *yotōshugi* in the bilateral relationship, and its replacement by an open US disregard for Japan's democratic politics in the context of the Futenma base issue, suggests the weakness, if not broad absence, of interdemocratic norms within the bilateral relationship. This may also account for the high degree of mistrust Japanese hold toward the United States generally, and even toward America's democratic institutions. According to *Yomiuri Shimbun*'s annual December poll, after 2003, a plurality (and often a majority) of Japanese consistently expressed distrust of the United States over several years. Similarly, research by Global Market Insite in 2004 showed that although Japanese overwhelmingly have positive views of Americans, 60.5 percent of Japanese have a negative view of the US system of government versus a mere 29.3 percent who have a positive view (Midford 2011: 45, 47, Figure 3.2, Table 3.13). Given the origins and history of the alliance, it is safe to conclude that to-date democratic norms have not played a significant role in the bilateral alliance.

FREE-RIDING OR AVOIDING ENTRAPMENT?

Has Japan's comparatively minimalist defensive defense military strategy been a strategy of free-riding, or an attempt to avoid entrapment? Certainly, a number of American critics, especially during the period of high economic tensions, claimed that Japan was free-riding off US defense efforts, supposedly gaining unfair trade advantages in relation to US manufacturers as a result.[36] Representative of this claim is Menon's observation that Japan 'is content to entrust its security to the United States – and why not? It has been a long, inexpensive, and comfortable ride' (Menon 2007: 103). Similarly, Richard J. Samuels & Eric Heginbotham argue Japan has been enjoying a 'cheap ride,' if not a free-ride in defense spending,

largely ignoring regional military threats, and concentrating its efforts on balancing a primary technoeconomic foe, the United States: 'decisions in the military realm have been driven as much by economic considerations as by strictly military calculations' (Heginbotham and Samuels 1998: 171–203, esp. 188–189 and 197–198).

A major problem with this debate is that it usually unquestioningly assumes that the United States is producing collective goods that Japan benefits from.[37] The free-riding literature largely leaves unexplored alternative possibilities, especially the possibility that the United States is primarily producing private goods for US consumption only.[38] DPJ leader Ozawa's refusal in August 2007 to agree to an extension of the Maritime Self-Defense Force (MSDF) refueling mission in the Indian Ocean in support of US combat operations in Afghanistan was essentially based upon the argument that the US war in Afghanistan was for the production of private goods, or at least public goods that Japan could not enjoy. As Ozawa told US Ambassador Thomas Schieffer, 'We cannot send (Self-Defense Force) troops to an area that does not directly affect the peace and security of Japan to participate in joint operations with the United States and others' (Ozawa Tells U.S. Envoy 2007).[39]

Another major possibility that has also generally been ignored, at least by the free-riding literature, is that the United States is producing private or public bads – the former only hurt the United States while the later hurt everybody. The late Chalmers Johnson, beginning with his book *Blowback*, has been a leading proponent of this view (Johnson 2000; Johnson 2004; Johnson 2008; Johnson 2010). Indeed, Johnson's use of the concept of 'blowback' can be considered a partial synonym for public and private bads. He defines 'blowback' as 'unintended consequences of policies that were kept secret from the American people' (Johnson 2000: 8–12), where unintended consequences appears to be synonymous with bad outcomes. Public and private bads do not have to be secret by definition, although it should come as no surprise that those knowingly producing them would seek to keep them secret. In any case, Johnson argues that overseas US military operations are primarily producing public and private bads.

Like Johnson, many other critics of the war on terrorism, for example, make essentially the same point, arguing that the US military operations in predominantly Islamic countries, such as Afghanistan and Iraq, are breeding Islamic extremists, anti-Western nationalists, and terrorists faster than it is killing them. If so, then supporting US military operations related to the war on terror might make Japan more rather than less vulnerable to terrorist attacks for two reasons: first, by encouraging (and reducing the cost) of counter-productive US policies; and second, and more directly, by associating Japan with policies that are seen as an attack on Islam or national independence. More generally, Johnson quotes members of the US Defense Science Board, who in a 1997 report to the undersecretary of defense for acquisition and technology, observed 'Historical data show a strong correlation between U.S. involvement in international situations and an increase in terrorist attacks against the United States' (Johnson 2000: 9, quoting Eland 1998: 3). Based on the same dynamic, Japan's support for US involvement in overseas conflicts, such as the war on terrorism, by contributing to the overproduction of public bads and blowback relative to public goods could thus be expected to lead to an increase in terrorist attacks against Japan.

Of course, the United States can, and undoubtedly usually does, produce a mixture of public and private goods and bads. Even the most ardent advocates of US global military power and the United States–Japan alliance acknowledge at least occasional 'collateral damage' from the exercise of US military power, which is an obvious synonym for a private if not public bad. If the mix is weighted toward producing private goods or bads and public bads, and away from producing public goods, then Japan's refusal, or that of any other ally, to support US military operations overseas and other foreign policies are not cases of free-riding, but cases of escaping entrapment in wars that are not in Japan's national interest. If, on the other hand, the mix is weighted toward producing public goods, then the refusal of Japan or other allies to participate constitutes free-riding. To be sure, calculating the balance in the mix of public goods versus private goods and public bads is not easy and, to this author's knowledge, no one has attempted in a systematic and balanced way to do so. Rather, different authors assume one or the other to be the case. Thus, Johnson and McCormack assume US policy to be producing mostly public bads and perhaps some private goods, while Calder, Green, and Wooley assume US policy is mostly producing public goods. We cannot expect a consensus on this issue until one or more systematic and balanced study is carried out, and even then, given the policy stakes, differences in worldview and ideology, and the potential for political polarization, it is unlikely that a consensus will be reached. Nonetheless, the point to emphasize here is that claims about Japan free-riding off US defense efforts in general, or more crucially in the case of a specific conflict, are based upon the assumption that these efforts (or conflicts) serve Japan's national interests. By contrast, claims that Japanese policy is more motivated by a desire to avoid 'entrapment' in American military conflicts are based upon the assumption that these conflicts are not in Japan's national interest.[40] Entrapment, of course, is the opposite of abandonment by an ally in the face of a threat, as discussed earlier.

THE ALLIANCE AS A HELP OR HINDRANCE IN JAPAN'S RELATIONS WITH EAST ASIA?

Finally, this chapter considers whether the Japan–United States alliance has been a help or hindrance in Japan's relationship with East Asia. Observers disagree on this point, with two major schools of thought on this question: one sees the United States trying to keep Japan apart from Asia by encouraging Japanese nationalist myths of national uniqueness, while another sees the US alliance as reassuring East Asian nations that Japan will not become a threat again, thereby allowing East Asian countries to trust Japan as an economic and even political partner, although not as a military partner.

McCormack in particular asserts that the United States seeks to divide Japan from East Asia as a way of keeping the former dependent, arguing that 'US insistence on Japan's national uniqueness and fundamental difference from Asia, and its implacable opposition to any moves towards Japanese involvement in an East Asian community, have been fundamental to US policy since the very outset of the occupation' (2007: 2). It is because of the designs of US policy, in his view, that Japan 'is at odds with all its neighbors over issues of history, accountability, resources and territory' (2007: 1). He argues that American psychological war fighters sought to subjugate Japan by promoting 'the idea of a deep "pattern" of Japanese culture as ineffable, emperor-centered, and above all non-Asian. ... [It] suited the US occupation forces to encourage the persistence in Japan of these myths' so Japan '...would therefore remain dependently tied to the US'. McCormack even cites a wartime comment by Reischauer arguing for turning Japan into America's puppet by making Hirohito America's Pu Yi (McCormack 2007: 1–2).[41] McCormack therefore offers a very different view of the occupation than Dower, who sees the United States as intent on 'denaturing' Japan through Westernization and Americanization, rather than reinforcing a traditionalist emperor-centric definition of Japanese identity (Dower 2000: 80).

Calder agrees with McCormack that Japan became divorced from Asia after the end of the war, although Calder does not ascribe this to US policy, but to postwar conditions. He traces this out in trade: before the war Asia, especially Korea,

Taiwan, and Manchuria accounted for 53 percent of Japanese imports and 64 percent of exports. However, by 1947, trade with Japan's former possessions had fallen to a mere 6 percent of imports and 4 percent of Japan's exports. 'Japan, in short, was effectively divorced from the Asian continent and consequently dependent on the United States for both markets and economic assistance' (Calder 2009: 33, 35). Calder makes clear that the United States gave largely unfettered trade access to Japan in exchange for a highly asymmetrical security relationship and isolation from China. In many ways, US market access was therefore a substitute for the denial of China market access (Calder 2009: 33, 35). In this sense, Calder's analysis coincides with McCormack regarding Communist China, but not regarding the non-communist nations of East Asia, with whom the United States actively encouraged Japanese rapprochement. Moreover, although opposed, the United States did not have the power to prevent the reestablishment of diplomatic and trade relations between Japan and the Soviet Union in 1956.

One issue that emerges is the competing conception of what East Asia really stands for. For example, when discussing Japan's toughness in response to the North Korean nuclear test of October 2006, McCormack claims this 'opened a gap between Japan and its Asian neighbours, who were anxious not to push Pyongyang into a corner' (McCormack 2007: 197). McCormack seems to be equating 'Asian neighbours' with China and, perhaps to a lesser extent, South Korea, revealing a major weakness in his argument about Japan's isolation from 'Asia' (McCormack 2007: 197). Indeed, McCormack's book is almost entirely silent on that other half of East Asia, namely Southeast Asia. These countries and the Association of Southeast Asian Nations (ASEAN) do not receive much discussion in *Client State* (McCormack 2007), nor are they even referenced in the index. Therefore, his claim that 'for much of the Cold War, Japan stood with its back turned to Asia,' might have some validity in the case of communist China (although Japan was China's largest source of economic assistance from the 1980s), and even more validity in regards to North Korea, but it has little relation to the empirical reality of Japan's deep engagement with other East Asian nations, especially those in Southeast Asia (McCormack 2007: 9).

The claim that the United States tried to isolate Japan from Asia does not track well with actual US policy. For example, the United States tried to integrate Japan militarily with the other non-communist countries of East Asia through its proposal for a NATO-like Pacific Pact in the early 1950s. Later, the United States supported Japan's attempts to build a special relationship with

ASEAN, even going so far as allowing Japan to exclude the United States from any involvement with the 1976 ASEAN Summit in Bali, leaving the field to Japan so it could give 'the impression of an exclusive role for Japan' (Sudo 1992: 83). After the end of the Vietnam War and before Vietnam's invasion of Cambodia, Japan assumed a leadership role as part of its Fukuda Doctrine in trying to promote reconciliation between ASEAN and the communist states of Indochina, beginning with Vietnam (Sudo 1992: chapter 6). Later, Japan got out ahead of the United States on regional security and promoted the establishment of a regional multilateral forum, playing a leadership role along with ASEAN in establishing the ASEAN Regional Forum in 1993–1994 (Midford 2000: 367–397).

Although McCormack notes that the United States gave 'a clear thumbs-down' to the East Asian Summit proposal in 2005 (McCormack 2007: 119), his account of Japan as submissive is contradicted here because even the pro-American Koizumi cabinet ignored US objections and forged ahead with the East Asian Summit. His account of US policy is also inaccurate because the United States did not object to the establishment of ASEAN Plus Three (China, Japan, and South Korea), a multilateral forum that excludes the United States.

An alternative view argues that the Japan–United States alliance, far from isolating Japan from Asia, has been indispensible for promoting Japanese integration and even leadership in East Asia. As Menon explains,

> the alliance has also enabled Japan to play an extensive political and economic role in East Asia because, by containing Japan in the course of protecting it, the United States allays fears in the region...policy-makers and observers in Japan and neighboring countries are united in the belief that the best Japan is a militarily weak Japan that pursues its ends through economic and political means...a Japan that is cut adrift from, or that abandons, the U.S. alliance would destabilize Northeast Asia, a region pivotal to the world's prosperity and stability. Even Japan's traditional adversaries – China, North Korea, and Russia – prefer a Japan tethered... (Menon 2007: 101, 111, 113).

Menon here is essentially restating the well known 1990 claim of Henry C. Stackpole III, then commander of US Marines in Japan, that the US alliance was a cap-in-the-bottle containing a resurgence of Japanese militarism (Hiatt 1990).[42] Although he offended Tokyo with this statement, in fact Japanese leaders routinely endorse a perceptual cap-in-the-bottle theory as a means for reassuring Asian nations. In September 1995, then Socialist Prime Minister Murayama Tomoiichi affirmed the reassurance value of the alliance for Asian states:

> Some countries in Asia fear that Japan may turn into a military power, but as long as we have the security treaty and take the position that we will not become a military power, they need not worry. In that sense (the treaty) has a role.[43]

In 1992, former Prime Minister Nakasone claimed that the US alliance is seen in Asia as an important barrier 'preventing the resurgence of Japanese militarism.'(Nakasone says 1992) In September 2000, then Prime Minister Mori Yoshirō told visiting US Defense Secretary William Cohen that 'Asian countries worry about Japan again becoming a great military power. Therefore, the U.S. military in Japan has become a reassuring fact for neighboring countries.'[44]

The reassurance value of the Japan–United States alliance for Asian nations, including China (Midford 2004a), points to a broader reality, namely that Japanese integration into an East Asian community need not be inconsistent with the continuation of the Japan–United States alliance. In the early 1990s, Kuriyama Takakazu, a senior Japanese diplomat claimed that 'the [U.S.–Japan alliance] security system makes it easy for neighboring countries to accept a large political and economic role from Japan' (Kuriyama 1990: 20). Although McCormack pointed to US opposition to an East Asian Summit that excluded the United States, it is not clear why Japan's support for US inclusion should undermine its ties with other East Asian states, and indeed the other members agreed in 2010 to include the United States. At the same time, he is undoubtedly correct in claiming that 'Japan's subordination undermines its credibility and helps isolate it from its neighbours' (McCormack 2007: 119).

Of course, subordination is in the eye of the beholder. Yet, surely some elites in Tokyo have been promoting US relations to such an extent that they do in fact endanger Japan's independent Asian diplomacy. The clearest example of this, and one that offers a diametrically opposed view to McCormack's, is Prime Minister Koizumi's claim that 'there is no such thing as the US–Japan relationship being too close....It is easier to have better relations with South Korea and China if we have better relations with the US' (Johnston 2005). Several months later, reacting to criticism that his diplomacy was too US-centric, thus damaging relations with Asia, Koizumi replied, 'It is extremely important for Japan and the U.S. to be close in developing strategic diplomacy toward Asia' (Kajimoto 2006). More recently, Tokyo University Professor Tanaka Akihiko echoed this view in more pessimistic terms, arguing that Japan cannot enjoy good relations with East Asian

nations when its relations with the United States are bad: 'I think we've seen in the past 1.5 years what happens when Japan–U.S. relations are not on good terms – Japan's relations with other countries also deteriorate,' Tanaka said. 'What Japan needs to do is strengthen ties with the U.S. and then form good relations with other countries such as China' (Kan's foreign policy 2011). Yet, on balance, the evidence suggests that Japan can and should continue to engage Asia directly, on its own terms, rather than via the United States. Indeed, Japan ceases to be taken seriously as an independent actor when it is seen as becoming too close and dependent upon the United States[45].

CONCLUSIONS

The picture that emerges from this examination of the United States–Japan alliance is an alliance that has been transformed from the narrow mission of defending Japan during the Cold War from the Soviet threat to a broader alliance that, although still centered on the defense of Japan, now also promotes regional stability and responds to regional conflicts. Although often seen as an alliance of one-sided dependence, in fact the alliance is much better characterized by deep interdependence, even in the military realm. Japan, with its possession of the sinews of a great military power, even while abstaining from becoming a military power, is simply too valuable strategically, especially in terms of denial to China, for the United States to ignore Japanese security needs or to abandon Japan. Strikingly, many Japanese appear to consistently underestimate their nation's strategic heft and to define alliance management in interpersonal terms such as American pride or self-esteem.[46] At the same time, the alliance retains a significant degree of its founding inequality, an inequality that is inconsistent with the highdegree of interdependence that, as opposed to one-way dependence, characterizes the alliance today. This inequality in turn has contributed to a notable weakness in the role of interdemocratic norms in relations between the two allies.

Finally, the Japan–United States alliance has played a valuable role in reassuring East Asian nations that they can accept a large economic and even political role from Japan without having to worry about Japan becoming a potential military threat again. Although McCormack claims that East Asia is attempting to create a 'European-type' regional community (McCormack 2007: 120), and that this offers Japan a viable alternative to the US alliance, it ignores the fact that European integration was limited to liberal democracies, and there is no such community in East Asia. Consequently, a Japan independent of the US alliance would have to build up its own military capabilities for national defense, a prospect China and Japan's other neighbors prefer less than the status quo. At the same time, overdependence and excessive closeness to the United States undermines perceptions of Tokyo as an independent actor, and hence the nation's influence in the region.

Calder identifies a 'quiet crisis' in the alliance as bilateral popular, cultural, and elite networks fray, and due to the rising importance of China, 'China and a dynamic growing Asia are attractive new magnets pulling Washington and Tokyo away from their traditional focus on one another' (Calder 2009: 12, 117–118). Given that both Japan and the United States are democracies, the mutual difficulties they experience with changes of government, especially those stemming from the DPJ's replacement of the LDP as the governing party in Japan during 2009–2012, are an ironic and not so quiet crisis. The ability of the two allies to strengthen democratic norms in their relationship will be another key test of the alliance's durability and its ability to evolve into a more equal alliance. However, as various DPJ leaders and Menon (2007) rightly point out, even if the Japan–United States alliance does not continue in its present form, with a large (or any) US military presence in Japan, or even if the alliance itself does not continue (a very unlikely scenario for now), the prospects for continued Japan–US security cooperation, even if on an ad hoc basis, remain excellent.

NOTES

1 La Feber's work offers a comprehensive and highly readable historical account of the bilateral relationship from the 1850s to the 1990s.

2 Out of a total of more than 5400 US diplomatic cables originating from the Tokyo Embassy that Wikileaks obtained, it is striking that the first three, released on January 1, 2011, all concerned the whaling controversy between these two allies (Wikileaks 2011).

3 For the complete text of the 1960 'Treaty of Mutual Cooperation and Security Between Japan and the United States of America,' see Japanese Ministry of Foreign Affairs (undated). Regarding the 1951 'Security Treaty Between the United States and Japan,' see United States Department of State (1957).

4 This list, and the one that follows, excludes working papers and institute reports.

5 Regarding the balance-of-power prediction that 'states, if they are free to choose, flock to the weaker side,' see Waltz (1979: 127; 1993: 190).

6 Although balance of threat theory was not formally developed by Walt until the 1980s, many of its basic propositions have been around for far longer.

7 The first and most noted work in this literature is Vogel (1979). Perhaps the final, and less than convincing, contribution to this genre is Fingleton (1995).

8 It should be noted that Parker and Drifte's arguments about bandwagoning, and the similar logic that Green and Calder use, must be seen within the context of balance of power theory – bandwagoning with the strongest power – not balance of threat theory, which would imply bandwagoning with the most threatening power. For an analysis of this distinction and an argument that balance of power theory is indeterminant about whether Japan should bandwagon with the United States or align with China to balance the United States, see Midford (2004a: 113–145). For a view that Japan may end up subordinated to, if not bandwagoning with, a threatening China, see Hiramatsu (2009).

9 However, Lind appears to exaggerate Japan's military capabilities in some respects, especially her claim that Japan has some offensive capabilities in relation to China, a result that appears to reflect her comparison of late 1990s and early 2000s Chinese capabilities with post 2005 Japanese capabilities (e.g. Japan's deployment of in-air-refueling capabilities in 2008).

10 On alliance diversification, see Wilkins (2011).

11 East–West Center (2010: 14), which in turn cites *Toyo Keizai* as its source. US investment in Japan equals the investment total for the entire European Union (EU), meaning that if the EU is considered to be a single entity, then the United States is tied for first place with the EU. FDI composes only 2.2 percent of Japanese gross domestic product (GDP), and the absolute value of FDI stock in Japan is a mere one-third of that in China (Calder 2009: 37, 244, who cites UNCTAD, *World Investment Report 2006*).

12 East–West Center (2010: 16), which cites the US Department of Transportation. However, this picture may soon change as China is projected to become the world's largest outbound tourist market by 2015 Alan Wheatley (2010, December 21). "Preparing for China's Tourism Boom," *International Herald Tribune*, p. 18.

13 Calder (2009: 32), who cites the US State Department.

14 Calder (2009: 15), who cites the US Department of Commerce and Jetro's website, www.jetro.go.jp for this trade data.

15 Committee on Armed Services (2013: 39, 41). Calder (2009: 4, 239), cites a higher estimate of $4.5 billion in annual contributions based on the US Department of Defense's annual report: *Report on Allied Contributions*. The Senate

Armed Services report notes a gradual decline in Japan's host-nation support, but puts the peak of Japanese contributions at under $3 billion in the late 1990s, suggesting a difference in methodology between the Senate Committee and the Pentagon.

16 Kawawe kainyu 3 cho 3420 oku en – 2 gatsu, *Asahi Shimbun*, February 28, 2004, as cited by McCormack (2007: 85).

17 Total Chinese holdings of all foreign exchange reserves, at the end of 2010, were $2.85 trillion dollars, compared with $1.04 trillion for Japan, the second largest holder. Overall, China held roughly one-third of total global foreign exchange reserves (see Schneider 2011).

18 Committee on Armed Services 2013: 39.

19 For more on the FSX controversy, see also Samuels (1994: 231–244) and Lorell (1996).

20 Even a small leakage of Japanese precision machine-tool technology from Toshiba to an economically ailing Soviet Union in the mid-1980s significantly damaged US naval dominance by making Soviet submarines much quieter and harder to detect (see Yamamoto 2006: 185–188; and more generally Mastanduno 1992).

21 Regarding Japan's prowess in military relevant technology, see Pekkanen and Kallender-Umezu (2010), and Grønning (2011).

22 For a partial exception, see Swenson-Wright (2005).

23 McCormack (2007: 38), citing US State Department and the OECD. All figures represent combined Japan and US aid totals.

24 McCormack (2007: 38), citing US State Department and the OECD.

25 Other US policymakers saw the same pattern in the late 1990s. Former US Ambassador Michael H. Armacost for example, argued '...powerful forces of change are visible, and both domestic and international pressures are propelling Japan toward...a less US-centered foreign policy' (Armacost 1996: 196).

26 'Over the long term a carefully coordinated Japanese role in regional diplomacy will sustain broader U.S. leadership in the region – even if Tokyo and Washington adopt different tactics' (Green 2001: 192).

27 Although the Japanese press presented this as a 'new Armitage report,' it could also be seen as a 'new Nye report,' or more accurately as a new bipartisan 'Armitage–Nye' report. Similarly, 2 years later, at his last press conference as US Ambassador to Tokyo, J. Thomas Schieffer said, 'I think the interpretation of collective defense [limiting Japanese military support for US forces] needs to be looked at as a prerequisite to the equal bilateral partnership desired' (Hanai 2009).

28 Regarding this pledge in the 2009 DPJ general election manifesto, see Democratic Party of Japan (2009: 46).

29 Berkovsky and Hagström (2010: 10), who cite interviews with Yukio Hachiro and Masaki Nakajima in late 2009. For a media report on DPJ plans for reducing the US military presence in Japan, see Yasumoto (2009).

30 The 1992 ODA Charter language appears in Japanese Ministry of Foreign Affairs (2003).

31 The 1992 Charter language on promoting democracy also appears in the 2003 Charter under 'Principle of ODA Implementation' (2003: 8).

32 This arc of freedom is highlighted in chapter 1 of the 2007 Diplomatic Bluebook; indeed it is even featured in the title of the Bluebook (Japanese Ministry of Foreign Affairs 2007).

33 Douglas H. Mendel, Jr., was that researcher, and he reported this quote in Mendel Jr. (1967). Thomas Havens kindly provided a copy of this paper.

34 Wada (2010: 405–431), who cites Kawakami (1994: 124–128).

35 See the discussion on this point in Midford (2004a, 2004b).

36 Representative examples of the free-rider literature include Prestowitz 1988; Hellmann 1989; Encarnation 1993. The free-riding claim provoked a significant literature focused on exploring the relationship between defense spending and economic performance in the two countries. See Dekle (1989); Wong (1989); Ward, Davis and Lofdahl (1995).

37 Regarding the theory of collective goods from which the concept of 'free-riding' derives, see Olson (1971). A variant of the free or cheap riding literature is buckpassing see Lind (2004). Additionally, Lind questions whether Japan really is under-producing military security, a claim that would negate the free-rider claim. Regarding buck passing, see Mearsheimer (2001: 158–159, 391, 392, 531, n. 75).

38 Another possibility is that the US inadvertently or intentionally produces private goods (or bads) for Japan (and other allies) – goods these allies can consume, but which the US cannot. While this is a theoretical and empirical possibility, this chapter does not explore this and assumes, for the sake of simplicity, that all private goods (or bads) related to the alliance are for US consumption only.

39 Ozawa was paraphrased elsewhere in the press as having told the Ambassador that 'Japan should not keep providing logistic support to the NATO-led counterterrorism operations in Afghanistan because he believes they are U.S.-centered' (Ozawa rejects Schieffer 2007). See also Tero tokuso hō (2007: 4) and Seiken tantō nōryoku (2007: 3).

40 For an analysis of Japanese fears of entrapment by the United States in a conflict in East Asia, see Hughes (2009).

41 Pu Yi was the last emperor of China, deposed in 1911, whom Japan installed as the figurehead monarch of the Japanese puppet state of Manchukuo in the 1930s.

42 Regarding this function of an alliance, referred to as a pacta de contrahendo by Paul Schroeder see Schroeder 1976: 227–262; Weitsman 1997: 156–192.

43 Japan Digest, October 19, 1995. A former diplomat and advisor to Murayama confirmed in an interview with the author that Murayama's Diet statement represented his Cabinet's official position, and was not just a personal opinion (interview of 1 February 1996). Murayama has since reiterated this position in his memoirs (see Murayama, 1998: 113). For a similar statement by a top Japanese diplomat, see Kuriyama (1990: 20).

44 On Mori, see *Asahi Shimbun*, 22 September 2000, 1.

45 A number of Southeast Asian elites interviewed by the author during 2010–2011 said that if they wanted to know Japan's policy there was no reason to go to Tokyo, rather they needed to go to Washington.

46 One typical media story suggested that Hatoyama's handling of the Futenma issue, by damaging Americans' self-esteem, thereby threatened the alliance (Japan could pay 2010).

REFERENCES

Arase, D. and Akaha, T. (Eds.). (2010). *The US–Japan alliance: balancing soft and hard power in East Asia*. Abingdon, UK: Routledge.

Armacost, M. H. (1996). *Friends or rivals? The insider's account of U.S.–Japan relations*. New York, NY: Columbia University Press.

Armitage, R. L. (2000). The United States and Japan: advancing toward a mature partnership. *INSS Special Report, October 11*. Washington, DC: National Defense University.

Armitage, R. L. and Nye, J. S. (2007). *The U.S.–Japan alliance: getting Asia right through 2020*. Washington, DC: Center for Strategic and International Studies. Retrieved July 17, 2014 from http://www.csis.org/component/option,com_csis_pubs/task,view/id,3729/type,1/

Asahi Shimbun 2000. (22 September, p. 1).

Berger, T. U. (2004). *Redefining Japan and the U.S.–Japan alliance*. New York, NY: Japan Society.

Berkovsky, A. and Hagström, L. (2010). *Futenma and the mobilisation of bias: an alternative perspective on the Japan–US alliance*. Istituto Per Gli Studi Di Politica Internazionale Working Paper #38.

Blumenthal, D. (2010) Sino–U.S. competition and U.S. security: how do we assess the military balance? *NBR Analysis, December*. Seattle, WA: National Bureau of Asian Research.

Buckley, R. (1995). *US–Japan alliance diplomacy 1945–1990*. New York, NY: Cambridge University Press.

Calder, K. E. (2009). *Pacific alliance: reviving U.S.–Japan relations*. New Haven, CT: Yale University Press.

Chinese missiles could disable U.S. bases in Asia. *Chosun Ilbo*, November 13, 2010. Retrieved January 9, 2011 from http://english.chosun.com/site/data/html_dir/2010/11/13/2010111300370.html

Cohen, W. I. (2000). *East Asia at the center: four thousand years of engagement with the world*. New York, NY: Columbia University Press.

Committee on Armed Services, United States Senate (2013). *Inquiry into US Costs and Allied Contributions to Support the US Military Presence Overseas*. (April 15).

Cossa, R. A. (Ed.). (1997). *Restructuring the U.S.–Japan alliance: toward a more equal partnership*. Washington, DC: Center for Strategic and International Studies.

Cronin, P. and Green, M. J. (1994). *Redefining the U.S.–Japan alliance: Tokyo's national defense program*. Washington, DC: Institute for National Strategic Studies, National Defense University.

Curtis, G. L. (2000). *The logic of Japanese politics: leaders, institutions, and the limits of change*. New York, NY: Columbia University Press.

Curtis, G. L. (Ed.). (2001). *New perspectives on U.S.–Japan relations*. Tokyo: Japan Center for International Exchange.

Dekle, R. (1989). The relationship between defense spending and economic performance in Japan. In J. H. Makin and D. C. Hellmann (Eds.). *Sharing world leadership? A new era for America and Japan* (pp. 127–152). Washington, DC: American Enterprise Institute.

Democratic Party of Japan. (2009). *The Democratic Party of Japan's platform for government: putting people's lives first*. Retrieved January 8, 2010 from http://www.dpj.or.jp/english/manifesto/manifesto2009.pdf [in Japanese, Minshutō *Seiken seisaku manifesto*. Retrieved September 26, 2014 from http://www.dpj.or.jp/special/manifesto2009/pdf/manifesto_2009.pdf, 12].

Destler, I. M. (1976). *Managing an alliance: Politics of U.S.–Japanese relations*. Washington, DC: Brookings Institution.

Dower, J. W. (1969). The eye of the beholder: background notes on the U.S.–Japan military relationship. *Bulletin of Concerned Asian Scholars*, 2 (1), 15–31.

Dower, J. W. (2000). *Embracing defeat: Japan in the wake of World War II*. New York, NY: W. W. Norton & Company.

Drifte, R. (2003). *Japan's security relations with China since 1989: from balancing to bandwagoning?* London: RoutledgeCurzon.

East–West Center. (2010). *America matters for Japan, Japan matters for America*. Honolulu, HI: East–West Center.

Eland, I. (1998). Protecting the Homeland: the best defense is to give no offense. *Policy Analysis* (Cato Institute), No. 306, May 5.

Encarnation, D. J. (1993). *Rivals beyond trade: America versus Japan in GLOBAL Competition*. Ithaca, NY: Cornell University Press.

Fingleton, E. (1995). *Blindside: why Japan is still on track to overtake the U.S. by the year 2000*. New York, NY: Houghton Mifflin.

Frost, E. L. (1988). *For richer, for poorer: the new US–Japan relationship*. New York, NY: Council on Foreign Relations.

Fukuyama, F. (1993). *The U.S.–Japan security relationship after the Cold War*. Santa Monica, CA: RAND Corporation.

Funabashi, Y. (1999). *Alliance adrift*. New York, NY: Council on Foreign Relations.

Gibney, F. (1992). *The Pacific century: America and Asia in a changing world*. New York, NY: Charles Scribner's Sons.

Green, M. J. (1995). *Arming Japan: defense production, alliance politics, and the postwar search for autonomy*. New York, NY: Columbia University Press.

Green, M. J. (2001). *Japan's reluctant realism: foreign policy challenges in an era of uncertain power*. New York, NY: Palgrave Macmillan.

Green M. J. and Mochizuki, M. (1998). *The U.S.–Japan security alliance in the 21st century: prospects for incremental change*. New York, NY: Council on Foreign Relations.

Green, M. J. and Patrick M. Cronin, P. M. (Eds.). (1999). *The U.S.–Japan alliance: past, present, and future*. New York, NY: Council on Foreign Relations Press.

Grønning, B.E.M. (2011) *An assessment of Japan's impact on U.S. Ballistic Missile Defense (BMD) capabilities*. MA thesis, Department of Political Science, University of Oslo (October).

Hanai, K. (2009, March 23). Costly transfer to Guam. *Japan Times*.

Heginbotham, E. and Samuels, R. J. (1998). Mercantile realism and Japanese foreign policy. *International Security*, 22 (4), 171–203.

Hellmann, D. C. (1989). The imperatives for reciprocity and symmetry in U.S.–Japanese economic and defense relations. In J. H. Makin and D. C. Hellmann (Eds.), *Sharing world leadership? A new era for America and Japan* (pp. 237–267). Washington, DC: American Enterprise Institute.

Hiatt, F. (1990, March 27). Marine General: U.S. troops must stay in Japan. *Washington Post*.

Hiramatsu, S. (2009). *Nihon ha chugoku no zokkukoku ni naru*. Tokyo: Kairyūsha.

Holland, H. M. (1992). *Japan challenges America: managing an alliance in crisis*. Boulder, CO: Westview Press.

Hongo, J. (2009, October 22). Guam move depends on Futenma: Gates. *Japan Times*.

Ikenberry, G. J. and Inoguchi, T. (Eds.). 2003. *Reinventing the alliance: U.S.–Japan security partnership in an era of change*. New York, NY: Palgrave Macmillan.

Inoguchi, T. (1999, September 15). Nichi-Bei-Chu 3 koku kara mita sekai. *Nihon Kenkyū Senta Kaihō*.

Ishida, H. (1963). Hoshuseitō no bijon. *Chūō Kōron*, 98 (1), 88–97.

Japan could pay a big price for hurting American pride. (2010, January 25). *Japan Times*.

Japanese Defense Agency. (2002). *Defense of Japan 2002*. Tokyo: Urban Connections.

Japanese Ministry of Foreign Affairs. (2007). *Diplomatic Bluebook 2007: arc of freedom and prosperity: Japan's expanding diplomatic horizon*. Retrieved May 16, 2008 from http://www.mofa.go.jp/policy/other/bluebook/2007/html/index.html

Japanese Ministry of Foreign Affairs. (undated) *The 1960 Treaty of Mutual Cooperation and Security Between Japan and the United States of America*. Retrieved January 8, 2011 from www.mofa.go.jp/region/n-america/us/q&a/ref/1.html

Japanese Ministry of Foreign Affairs, Economic Cooperation Bureau. (2003). *Review of Japan's Official Development Assistance Charter*, March 14. Retrieved July 17, 2014 from www.mofa.go.jp/policy/oda/reform/review0303.html

Jiyū to hanei no yumi' kie "Ajia gaikō kyōka" e gaikō seisho' (April 1).

Johnson, C. (2000). *Blowback: the costs and consequences of American empire*. New York, NY: Metropolitan Books.

Johnson, C. (2004). *The sorrows of empire: militarism, secrecy, and the end of the Republic*. New York, NY: Metropolitan Books.

Johnson, C. (2008). *Nemesis: the last days of the American Republic*. New York, NY: Metropolitan Books.

Johnson, C. (2010). *Dismantling the Empire: America's last best hope*. New York, NY: Metropolitan Books.

Johnston, E. (2005, November 17). Koizumi, Bush stress strong ties. *Japan Times*. Retrieved December 1, 2005 from http://www.search.japantimes.co.jp/cgi-bin/nn20051117a1.html

Kahn, H. (1971). *The emerging Japanese superstate: challenge and response*. New York, NY: Prentice-Hall.

Kajimoto, T. (2006, November 17). Koizumi is not backing down on Yasukuni. *Japan Times*. Retrieved November 29, 2006 from www.search.japantimes.co.jp/cgi-bin/nn20060126a1.hmtl

Kamiya, M. (2003). Reforming the U.S.–Japan alliance: what should be done? In G. J. and Inoguchi, T. (Eds.). *Reinventing the alliance: U.S.–Japan security partnership in an era of change*. New York, NY: Palgrave Macmillan.

Kan's foreign policy plate full, waiting to be attacked. (2011, January 1). *Japan Times*. Retrieved January 7, 2011 from http://www.search.japantimes.co.jp/cgi-bin/nn20110101f3.html

Kataoka, T. and Myers, R. H. (1989). *Defending an economic superpower: reassessing the U.S.–Japan security alliance*. Boulder CO: Westview Press.

Kawakami, T. (1994). *Shakai-tō no Gaikō: Atarashii Jidai-tzukuri no tame ni*. Tokyo: Simul Press.

Krauss, E. and Pempel, T. J. (Eds.). (2003). *Beyond bilateralism: U.S.–Japan relations in the new Asia–Pacific*. Stanford, CA: Stanford University Press.

Kuriyama, T. (1990). Gekido no 90 nendai to Nihon gaikō no shintenkai: Atarashii kokusai chitsujyō kenchiku e no sekkyokuteki kōken no tame ni. *Gaikō Forum* (May).

Kyodo. (2005, September 23). Interceptor nose cone to be Japanese. *Japan Times*.

Kyodo. (2007, March 2). Sex slaves coerced, U.S. Rep. Honda says in Abe rebuttal. *Japan Times*.

Kyodo. (2009, October 25). U.S. urges Japan to export SM3. *Japan Times*.

La Feber, W. (1998). *The Clash: U.S.–Japanese relations throughout history*. New York, NY: W. W. Norton & Company.

Lauren, P. G. and Wylie, R. F. (Eds.). (1989). *Destinies shared: U.S.–Japanese relations*. Boulder, CO: Westview.

Layne, C. (1992, January 6). The challenge from a rising Japan is inevitable. *International Herald Tribune*.

Layne, C. (1993). The unipolar illusion: why new great powers will rise. *International Security*, 17 (4), 5–51.

Lewis, M. (1991). *Pacific rift:*. Knoxville: Whittle Direct Books.

Lind, J. M. (2004). Pacifism or passing the buck? Testing theories of Japanese security policy. *International Security*, 29 (1), 92–121.

Lorell, M. (1996). *Troubled partnership: a history of US–Japan collaboration on the FS-X Fighter*. Santa Monica, CA: RAND Corp.

Maga, T. P. (1997). *Hands across sea: US–Japan relations 1961–1981*. Athens, OH: Ohio University Press.

Makin, J. H. and Hellmann, D. C. (Eds.). (1989). *Sharing world leadership? A new era for America and Japan*. Washington, DC: American Enterprise Institute.

Mastanduno, M. (1992). *Economic containment: COCOM and the politics of East-West Trade*. Ithaca, NY: Cornell University Press.

Mastanduno, M. (2003). The U.S.–Japan alliance and models of regional security order. In G. J. Ikenberry and T. Inoguchi, (Eds.). *Reinventing the alliance: U.S.–Japan security partnership in an era of change*. New York, NY: Palgrave Macmillan.

McCormack, G. (2007). *Client state: Japan in the American embrace*. London: Verso.

Mearsheimer, J. J. (2001). *The tragedy of great power politics*. New York, NY: Norton.

Mendel Jr., D. H. (1967). *Japan, Okinawa, and Vietnam*. Paper presented to the Annual Meeting of the Association for Asian Studies, Chicago, March 20–22.

Menon, R. (2007). *The end of alliances*. New York, NY: Oxford.

Midford, P. (2000). Japan's leadership role in East Asian security multilateralism: the Nakayama proposal and the logic of reassurance. *The Pacific Review*, 13 (3), 367–397.

Midford, P. (2004a). China views the revised US–Japan defense guidelines: popping the cork? *International Relations of the Asia–Pacific*, 4, 113–145.

Midford, P. (2004b). A war in the Gulf and a Bush in the White House: déjà vu for Japan? In Y. Sugita (Ed.). *Evaluation of the Bush Administration*. Musashino, Japan: Smallworld Libraries. Retrieved December 17, 2004 from www.smallworld.co.jp

Midford, P. (2004c). Busshyu ni 'No-' to ieru Nihon. In Y. Sugita (Ed.). *Busshyu wo saiten suru: Naisei to gaikō no seisaku hyōka* (pp. 175–206). Tokyo: Akishobo.

Midford, P. (2011). *Rethinking Japanese public opinion and security: from pacifism to realism?* Stanford, CA: Stanford University Press.

Millard, M. (2000). *Leaving Japan: observations on the dysfunctional U.S.–Japan relationship*. New York, NY: M. E. Sharpe.

Mochizuki, M. M. (Ed.). (1997). *Toward a True Alliance: Restructuring U.S.–Japan Security Relations*. Washington, DC: Brookings Institution Press.

Murayama, T. 1998. *Sō jyanō...* Tokyo: Daisanshyokan.

Murphy, T. (2006). East Asia's dollars. *New Left Review*, 40, 39–64.

Nakasone says security treaty helps keep Japanese militarism in check. (1992). *Japan Digest*, 3 (33), February.

Nishihara, M. (Ed.). (2001). *The Japan–U.S. alliance: new challenges for the 21st century*. Tokyo: Japan Center for International Exchange.

Okinawa hovers at the negotiating table. (2009, November 12). *Financial Times*, Retrieved from www.ft.com/cms/6df59cd4-cf2b-11de-8a4b-00144feabdc0.html

Olson, M. (1971). *The logic of collective action: public goods and the theory of groups*. Cambridge, MA: Harvard University Press.

Ota, F. (2006). *The US–Japan alliance in the 21st century: a view of the history and a rationale for its survival*. Folkestone, UK: Global Oriental.

Ozawa rejects Schieffer antiterror overture. (2007, August 9). *Japan Times*.

Ozawa tells U.S. Envoy he won't budge. (2007, August 9). *Asahi.com*. Retrieved August 12, 2007, from www.asahi.com/english/Herald-asahi/TKY200708080383.html

Parker, J. M. (2000). Japan at century's end: climbing on China's bandwagon? *Pacific Focus*, XV (1), 5–33.

Pekkanen S. and Kallender-Umezu, P. (2010). *In defense of Japan: from the market to the military in space policy*. Stanford, CA: Stanford University Press.

Prestowitz Jr., C. V. (1988). *Trading places: how we allowed Japan to take the lead*. New York, NY: Basic Books.

Reischauer, E. O. (1960). The broken dialogue with Japan. *Foreign Affairs*, 39 (1), October, 11–26.

Samuels, R. J. (1994). *Rich nation, strong army: national security and the technological transformation of Japan*. Ithaca, NY: Cornell University Press, 1994.

Sasae, K. (1994). *Rethinking Japan–US relations: an analysis of the relationship between Japan and US and implications for the future of their security alliance* (Adelphi Paper 292). London: Brassey's for the Institute of Stategic Studies.

Satake, T. (2011). The origin of trialateralism? The US–Japan–Australia security relations in the 1990s. *International Relations of the Asia–Pacific*, 11, 92–96.

Schneider, H. (2011, January 11). China's exchange reserves hit record level. *Washington Post*.

Schoppa, L. (1997). *Bargaining with Japan: what American Pressure Can And Cannot Do*. New York, NY: Columbia University Press.

Schroeder, P. (1976). Alliances, 1815–1945: weapons of power and tools of management. In K. Knorr (Ed.). *Historical dimensions of national security problems* (pp. 227–262). Lawrence, KS: University Press of Kansas.

Seeking Deep Analysis. (2010). *The Oriental Economist*, 78 (7), 10–11.

Seiken tantō nōryoku ni gimonfu ga tsuita. (2007, August 9). *Yomiuri Shimbun* (morning edition).

Sneider, D. (2010, June 3). Did Washington bring down the Japanese Prime Minister? It'll be even harder for the next leader to meet U.S. demands. *Slate*. Retrieved June 6, 2010, from http://www.slate.com/formatdynamics/CleanPrintProxy.aspx?1275982975405

Spykman, N. J. (1942). *American's strategy in world politics*. New York, NY: Harcourt, Brace & Company.

Stockwin, J. A. A. (1968). *The Japanese socialist party and neutralism*. Melbourne: Melbourne University Press.

Sudo, S. (1992). *The Fukuda Doctrine and ASEAN: new dimensions in Japanese foreign policy*. Singapore: Institute of Southeast Asian Studies.

Swenson-Wright, J. (2005). *Unequal allies? United States security and alliance policy toward Japan, 1945–1960*. Stanford, CA: Stanford University Press.

Tero tokuso hō hantai tsutaeru. (2007, August 9). *Asahi Shimbun* (morning edition), 4.

Tokinoya, A. (1986). *The Japan–US alliance: a Japanese perspective*. Adelphi Paper No. 212. London: International Institute for Strategic Studies.

Tokyo accepts defeat over Okinawa Marine Base. (2010, May 5). *Financial Times*. Retrieved January 7, 2011, from http://www.ft.com/cms/s/0/2955eab6-a3a7-11de-9fed-00144feabdc0.html

Umemoto, T. (2003). Ballistic missile defense and the U.S.–Japan alliance. In Ikenberry, G. J. and Inoguchi, T. (Eds.). *Reinventing the alliance: U.S.–Japan security partnership in an era of change* (pp. 187–212). New York, NY: Palgrave Macmillan.

United States Department of State. (1957). Security Treaty Between the United States and Japan. American Foreign Policy 1950–1955 Basic Documents Volumes I and II. *Department of State Publication 6446, General Foreign Policy Series 117*. Washington, DC: US Government Printing Office. Retrieved January 9, 2010, from http://www.avalon.law.yale.edu/20th_century/japan001.asp#b1

Vogel, E. F. (1979). *Japan as number one: lessons for America*. Tokyo: Charles E. Tuttle Co.

Vogel, S. K. (2002). *U.S.–Japan relations in a changing world*. Washington, DC: Brookings Institution Press.

Wada, S. (2010). Article Nine of the Japanese Constitution and security policy: realism versus idealism in Japan since the Second World War. *Japan Forum*, 22 (3–4), 405–431.

Wakabayashi, H. (2008). *The U.S.–Japan alliance: a new framework for enhanced global security*. Washington, DC: Center for Strategic and International Studies.

Walt, S. M. (1987). *The origins of alliances*. Ithaca, NY: Cornell University Press.

Waltz, K. (1979). *Theory of International Politics*. New York, NY: Random House.

Waltz, K. (1993). The emerging structure of international politics. *International Security*, 18 (2), 44–79.

Waltz, K. (2000). Structural realism after the Cold War. *International Security*, 25 (1), 5–41.

Ward, M. D., Davis, D. R. and Lofdahl, C. L. (1995). A century of tradeoffs: defense and growth in Japan and the United States. *International Studies Quarterly*, 39 (1), March, 27–50.

Weitsman, P. A. (1997). Intimate enemies: the politics of peacetime alliances. *Security Studies*, 7 (1), 156–192.

Wikileaks. (2011). *Japan receptive to further engagement on whaling*. Retrieved January 1, 2011 from http://www.wikileaks.ch/cable/2009/11/09TOKYO2588.html

Wilkins, T. S. (2011). Japan's alliance diversification: a comparative analysis of the Indian and Australian strategic partnerships. *International Relations of the Asia-Pacific*, 11, 115–155.

Wohlforth, W. (1999). The stability of a unipolar world. *International Security*, 24 (1), 5–41.

Wong, K. (1989). National defense and foreign trade: the sweet and sour relationship between the United States and Japan. In J. H. Makin and D. C. Hellmann, (Eds.). *Sharing world leadership* (pp. 90–98). Washington, DC: American Enterprise Institute.

Woolley, P. J. (2000). *Japan's navy: politics and paradox, 1971–2000*. Boulder, CO: Lynne Reiner Publishers.

Yamamoto T., Iriye A., and Iokibe M. (Eds.). (2006). *Philanthropy and reconciliation: rebuilding postwar U.S.–Japan relations*. Tokyo: Japan Center for International Exchange.

Yamamoto, T. (2006). A regional export control regime in East Asia: from no regime to a soft regime. In D. Joyner (Ed.). *Non-proliferation export controls: origins, challenges, and proposals for strengthening*. Aldershot, UK: Ashgate.

Yasumoto, M. (2009, December 6). DPJ plan to cut U.S. forces said behind Futenma delay. *Japan Times*.

26

Foreign Relations with China

Caroline Rose

Japan's relationship with its near neighbour China is its most important bilateral relationship after the United States. Indeed, given increasing economic ties, in addition to a nascent move towards cooperation in East Asian regional affairs, the Sino–Japanese relationship may well overtake the United States–Japan relationship as Japan's paramount partnership in the next thirty years or so. The early twenty-first century represents the first period in history when both China and Japan have been politically, militarily and economically strong, dealing with each other from a (more or less) equal position. China's rise since the 1980s has prompted a great deal of interest in Japan's management of the situation, and the implications of China's rise for regional politics, and in particular regional leadership, are profound. As a result, the China–Japan relationship has attracted considerable academic, and indeed popular, attention in the last two decades. The study of Sino–Japanese relations is enjoying a boom which, when combined with the extant literature on the subject, provides readers with rich pickings and an increasingly nuanced understanding of this enduring, if sometimes troubled, relationship. Given the vicissitudes of the political, economic and security relations between the two countries since the late nineteenth century, the relationship is often described dichotomously: competition versus cooperation, rivalry versus collaboration, hot economics versus cold politics are terms frequently used to describe the duality of this bilateral relationship.

The aim of this chapter is to provide an overview of the main developments in Sino–Japanese relations, looking briefly at pre-modern relations before focusing on the history of the relationship since the late nineteenth century (that is, Meiji Japan/late Qing China) and moving on to consider the main issues facing China and Japan at the start of the twenty-first century. In the first instance, the chapter adopts a chronological approach, outlining major events and periods, before moving to a thematic approach to describe the trends in the relationship (and its academic study) since diplomatic normalisation in 1972.[1]

It is useful first to map out very broadly the main periods of China–Japan relations. To adopt the terminology often used by Chinese and Japanese academics and politicians, China and Japan enjoyed over two thousand years of friendly relations (as 'two neighbours separated by a narrow strip of water'), which were then overshadowed by fifty years of conflict and tension, starting with the first Sino–Japanese war (1894–1895) and leading to the second, devastating, war between China and Japan (1937–1945). In the post-World War II period, the rebuilding of relations between Japan and mainland China commenced in the late 1940s after the conclusion of the Chinese civil war, albeit informally until diplomatic normalisation in 1972. The signing of the Peace and Friendship Treaty in 1978 signalled the full recommencement of relations between the two countries and all facets of the relationship developed apace. However, problems emerged in the early 1980s and continued intermittently throughout the decade relating to different interpretations of history and commemoration of the past (most notably with the textbook controversy in 1982 and former Prime Minister Nakasone Yasuhiro's visit to the controversial Yasukuni Shrine in 1985). The late 1980s ushered in a number of major changes in global and domestic affairs, which had a long-lasting influence on the relationship between China and Japan. The end of the Cold War, the Tiananmen Square massacre, economic modernisation in China, and the bursting of Japan's bubble economy all combined to prompt adjustments in each country's policy vis-à-vis the other. As problems intermittently (re-)appeared on the diplomatic and political front in the 1990s and 2000s, economic relations flourished, giving rise to the 'cool politics, hot economics' epithet. After a particularly low period in diplomatic relations during former Prime Minister Koizumi Junichiro's time in office between 2001 and 2006, the relationship nonetheless recovered. Prime Minister Abe Shinzō's visit to China in October 2006 succeeded in 'breaking the ice' and culminated in a joint press statement in which both sides agreed to build a 'mutually beneficial relationship based on common strategic interests'.

The upgrading of the relationship to encompass strategic interests symbolised the adoption of a more mature and pragmatic approach by both sides, which continued under Liberal Democratic Party (LDP) Prime Ministers Fukuda Yasuo and Aso Taro. When political power was transferred to the Democratic Party of Japan (DPJ) in the 2009 elections, one aim of the new government's foreign policy was to improve relations with China further, and create an East Asian Community. However, Prime Minister Hatoyama Yukio's preoccupation with the Futenma base issue meant that Japan's China policy took somewhat of a back seat. The vulnerability of the relationship to the intermittent flare up of the territorial dispute over the Diaoyu/Senkaku Islands was highlighted in September 2010 with the collision between a Chinese fishing boat and the Japanese Coast Guard. Prime Minister Kan Naoto's poor handling of the incident, which coincided with the DPJ leadership election, revealed weaknesses in the DPJ's decision-making structures, and the incident once again cast a shadow over the China–Japan relationship. China's sympathetic response

to Japan's triple disaster of March 2011 helped to mend fences to a certain extent, and the fortieth anniversary celebrations of diplomatic normalisation in 2012 produced standard reassurances by both sides of the importance of the relationship to the peace and security of East Asia. However, by 2012 the relationship was coming under strain once again over Japan's 'nationalisation' of three of the Senkaku islands, and power transitions in both countries in the form of the return to power of the LDP under Prime Minister Abe Shinzō and the emergence of Xi Jinping as President of the PRC.[2]

TWO THOUSAND YEARS OF FRIENDSHIP?

Relations between China and Japan are generally agreed to have commenced in the third century BC, with Chinese cultural influence reaching Japan directly or indirectly in various periods since that time. Formal relations were sporadic, but Chinese artisans and craftsmen brought their knowledge and skills to Japan, and cultural and economic exchange was often maintained in the absence of official relations between the respective courts. Japan's cultural borrowing from China reached a peak during the Sui and Tang dynasties (sixth to tenth centuries), the most significant and long-lasting influences being the introduction of the writing system, Confucian and Buddhist thought, arts and crafts, and economic and political thought. Trade flourished during the Song dynasty (tenth to thirteenth centuries), but relations were strained during the Yuan dynasty (thirteenth to fourteenth centuries) due to problems arising from (Japanese) piracy on China's east coast. Japan was not fully part of the Ming (1368–1644) tribute system, tending to drift in and out of the hierarchical structure, and ultimately falling out of favour by the late sixteenth century. Conflict between Japanese and Ming troops broke out in the 1590s as a result of Japan's attempts to expand into Korea, and Japan's formal links with the Qing dynasty were minimal, reinforced by Tokugawa Japan's *sakoku* policy, which although initially allowing Chinese trading ships into Nagasaki and Hirado, later became more stringent in its regulations. Nonetheless, private trade continued, and cultural and intellectual exchange again flourished during this period, enjoying a renaissance marked by a keen interest on the part of the Japanese elite in Chinese literature, art, law and administration, religion and music.[3]

The periods of cultural adoption and adaptation from China clearly contributed to the development of Japanese society and culture at different times, and have given rise to the generally accepted belief that the two countries share a certain cultural affinity. However, the two thousand years of friendly exchange to which politicians are apt to refer overstates a relationship marked by periods of tension, and also, at times, a complete lack of interest in each other. Attitudes at court changed considerably according to domestic circumstances. Japan was never as closely incorporated into the Chinese world order as, for example, Korea and Vietnam, nor did it fall under Chinese control. For centuries, China had little interest in Japan (it being off world trade routes). For Japan's part, a desire not always to be subordinated to China's hierarchical world structure, and a belief in its own superior position as the 'place where the sun rises' is revealed in early (Chinese) records. At other times, however, Japanese rulers acknowledged Chinese supremacy and cultural position in the region.[4]

FIFTY YEARS THAT OVERSHADOW TWO THOUSAND

The threat of Western imperialist incursion in the mid-nineteenth century was dealt with very differently by China and Japan, and this in turn impacted upon the nature of their bilateral relationship from the 1890s. By the end of the Tokugawa period, China's economic and intellectual importance to Japan had declined as China's weak response to Western imperialism highlighted the state's inability to transform itself and modernise its creaking political, economic and social systems. By contrast, Japan responded to the threat of the West by a programme of rapid modernisation under the direction of the new Meiji government. In 1894, after more than two decades of growing friction, war broke out between China and Japan over Korea. Overwhelmed by Japan's superior army and navy with its modern ships and equipment and highly trained soldiers, the Chinese were quickly defeated and the war represented a turning point in Sino–Japanese relations.[5] Chinese resentment of Japan was mixed with admiration and Chinese reformers were keen to learn the secrets of Japan's success. Chinese students were sent to Japan from 1898, many of whom would become leading lights in China's subsequent transformation.[6]

Japan's imperialist aspirations grew further after the Sino–Japanese war, so that by 1931 the Japanese empire encompassed the Ryukyu Islands, Taiwan, Korea, the Kwantung Leased Territory (Liaodong) and South Manchuria, Sakhalin (Karafuto) and the Micronesian islands. In China, its influence had grown to the extent that it now enjoyed the same rights and privileges as the Western powers and had established itself as China's major trading partner with a vast commercial and financial infrastructure comprising its 'informal' empire.[7] Part of Japan's perceived 'mission' in China, as expressed by pan-Asianists, was to assist China in its modernisation. Without a programme of reform, it was feared that a collapse of the Qing dynasty would lead to a partition of China by Western powers bent on a racial war in Asia. Such anxieties produced a sense of commitment amongst Japanese thinkers and politicians to an 'Asian cause' based on ideas of kinship.[8] Such ideas, however, were not shared by Chinese, who suspected that Japan's pan-Asianist claims masked less than altruistic ambitions as Japan's empire building continued apace. Japan's massive economic presence in China would lead, it was feared, to a military presence. Indeed, during the 1910s, Japan's China policy adopted a more aggressive position, for example taking advantage of Germany's preoccupation with war in Europe to add Qingdao and other German territories to her formal empire in 1914. The notorious Twenty One Demands of 1915 were regarded by some Chinese as a plan to take advantage of a 'helpless neighbour' (Jansen 1975: 214). The Chinese backlash to Japan's manoeuvres came in the form of growing anti-Japanese nationalism manifested in demonstrations and boycotts, most notably in the May Fourth Movement of 1919. During the 1920s, Japan's China policy fluctuated between soft and hard-line approaches, reflecting the internal divisions in Japan's government, military and bureaucracy over the so-called 'China problem'.

Increasingly, however, elements of the Japanese military, in particular the Kwantung Army, gained sway in their quest for an autonomous Japan – that is, a Japan looking to retain markets, gain access to raw materials and create space for a growing population in the midst of worldwide economic depression. One answer to the problem, at least for Kwantung Army officers, was to grasp the 'lifeline' that Manchuria represented. The 1931 Manchurian Incident (or September 18 Incident) – the conspiracy carried out by the Kwantung army to blow up part of the railway at Mukden (Shenyang) and lay the blame on Chinese forces with the purpose of invading and taking control in Manchuria – saw the start of decline into war. Presenting a fait accompli to the civilian government, which was unable to prevent an escalation, the Kwantung Army proceeded over the ensuing months with its plans to seize Manchuria, leading to the establishment of Manchukuo in 1932.

War broke out in 1937. Although the Japanese military and government had expected the 'China incident' to be quickly resolved, they had not anticipated the fierce resistance of Chinese troops, and the Japanese army found itself bogged down in what has been termed the China 'quag-mire' (Coox 1988). The ideological rationale for Japan's action in the invasion of China shifted as the war progressed and the international environment became more hostile: from discussions of a Japan–Manchukuo–China bloc in the early 1930s, the concept of pan-Asianism developed to incorporate larger amounts of territory in Southeast Asian and the Pacific under the title of the Greater East Asia Co-Prosperity Sphere.

The atrocities perpetrated against the Chinese population by the Japanese army are increasingly well documented, but nonetheless continue to be the focus of controversy and debate at the beginning of the twenty-first century. Millions of Chinese military personnel and civilians died or were wounded during the conflict, and the material damage incurred was also devastating. The Nanjing Massacre of December 1937 perhaps stands out as one of the most serious atrocities carried out by the Japanese army, with an estimated (and disputed) 300,000 casualties, but countless other atrocities were also committed during the war. Thousands of Chinese were mobilised to work at the front or shipped to Japan where they were forced to work in mines and factories; Chinese girls and women were forced into prostitution in Japanese 'comfort stations'; and unknown numbers of Chinese underwent horrific human experimentation under the Japanese chemical and biological warfare programme. The impact of the Sino–Japanese war continues to be felt by Japanese and Chinese alike to this day, largely due to the failure to fully settle the past, despite attempts to reconcile through formal mechanisms such as war crimes trials and peace treaties. The reasons for this failure can be found both in immediate postwar developments in each country, and the continued divergence of opinion within Japanese popular and intellectual circles on the justification for the war and behaviour of the Japanese troops.

The literature on the Sino–Japanese war is substantial, and continues to grow. Major studies focusing both on the events of the war years themselves and the way in which the events have since been remembered, re-interpreted and commemorated have provided fresh insight into the multi-faceted and complex nature of the war and its legacy. In addition to solid general histories of the war (for example, Morley 1983; Iriye 1987; Mitter 2013), there has been a surge of interest in recent years in particular dimensions of the war, such as collaboration, the social impact of war, local war histories, and in particular the horrors of war.[9] In addition, studies of policymakers and the many different agencies involved in the war have demonstrated the pluralistic nature of decision making in both countries, and highlighted the complexities of an extremely fluid and uncertain situation China

in the run up to war (see, for example, Brooks 2000; Dryburgh 2000). The Nanjing Massacre has become a powerful symbol of the atrocities of war (referred to by some as the Chinese Holocaust), and has spawned considerable research, particularly since the publication of the controversial book by Iris Chang in 1997. To do full justice to the scholarship in this area would require a separate chapter, but Fogel (2002), Wakabayashi (2007), Yoshida (2006) and Yang (1999) provide lucid explanations of the anatomy of the Nanjing Massacre debate. Other important aspects of the war overlooked until the 1980s are studies of Japan's biological and chemical warfare (see, for example, Williams and Wallace 1989; Harris 1994), the 'comfort women' system (Yoshimi 2000; Tanaka 2002), and forced labour (see William Underwood's numerous articles posted on *Japan Focus*, available from www.japanfocus.org).

PRE-NORMALISATION

The postwar Sino–Japanese relationship has been characterised by periods of relaxation followed by tension. The cyclical nature of the relationship has reflected changes in the domestic and international environments, in addition to specific problems relating to perceptions and misperceptions (for example, threat debates), poor planning and communication (for example, the Baoshan shock), different views of war history and inflammatory statements and behaviour on the part of Japanese politicians and revisionist academics.

Attempts at Reconciliation and Informal Diplomacy 1945–1972

In the immediate aftermath of the war, both Japan and China were preoccupied with domestic issues – the former under Allied Occupation, the latter embroiled in civil war until 1949. The business of reconciliation was, however, partially undertaken during this early period in the form of war crimes trials and a fledgling (later to be aborted) reparations programme. In addition to the Tokyo war crimes, which dealt with Japan's Class A war crimes (crimes against peace) and found 23 of the defendants guilty of waging war against China, military tribunals were also held across Asia to try Class B and C criminals (those accused of war crimes and crimes against humanity). Trials were also held across China and Taiwan between 1946 and 1949 by the Guomindang and later in Shenyang in 1956 by the Communists (see Cathcart and Nash 2008; Chen 2009; Kushner 2010). A reparations programme was drawn up by the US/Supreme Commander of the

Allied Powers (SCAP) with a view to transferring Japanese machinery and equipment to China (and other victors) but was scrapped by the late 1940s as US policymakers felt that the programme would be detrimental to Japan's economic recovery (Holman 1947; Scheiber 2002).

Although the resumption of diplomatic relations between Japan and mainland China did not take place until 1972, this did not preclude interaction between the two sides. To be sure, in the early 1950s, amidst the rising tensions of the Cold War and now a member of the Western bloc, Japan was somewhat constrained in its dealings with China. However, a number of pro-China politicians and big business interests were keen to rekindle links with the mainland and, under the rubric of separation of politics and economics, pursued the re-opening of trade and some cultural exchange. For China's side, after the initial hostility displayed by the newly established People's Republic of China (PRC), policy towards Japan shifted towards a more friendly approach using 'people's diplomacy' as a means of attempting to sway public and political opinion in Japan in favour of normalisation with the PRC.[10] Private trade agreements signed between 1952 and 1958 are a measure of the enthusiasm of both sides to keep exchange going, and Soeya argues that the volume of China–Japan trade when viewed as a percentage of Japan's total North East Asian trade was 'substantial and constant', reaching almost 30 per cent in 1956, 26.6 per cent in 1966 and 25.9 per cent in 1975 (Soeya 1998: 1).

Given the lack of official contacts between the two countries, it is not surprising that they were vulnerable to changes in the regional and international environments and domestic political trends. With the emergence of Prime Minister Kishi Nobusuke in 1957, for example, Japan's relations with China entered a rocky period as Kishi's pro-US and pro-Taiwan government sought to strengthen relations with the United States. At the same time, within China, a more radical leadership emerged, introducing a set of policies stressing self-reliance (most notably in the form of the disastrous Great Leap Forward). In 1958, using the pretext of the Nagasaki flag incident, the PRC cancelled the freshly signed fourth trade agreement and suspended all business and cultural agreements with Japan. The situation gradually improved, although Japan was constrained by the 'three principles' set out by Zhou Enlai, which stipulated that Japan should stop treating China as an enemy, stop attempting to create 'two Chinas' and stop obstructing normalisation of relations with the PRC (Rose 1998: 46). Anti-Kishi press campaigns in China and accusations that Japan was (or rather 'a small handful of Japanese' were) attempting to revive militarism in the late 1950s would continue (for example, against Prime Minister Sato Eisaku) in the 1960s, representing a theme in the Chinese media which re-emerged from time to time, even after diplomatic normalisation. Trade revived in the 1960s (with some disruption due to the Cultural Revolution) under the rubric of Friendship Trade, whereby only Japanese firms deemed friendly towards the PRC were allowed to trade, and later LT/Memorandum Trade.[11]

POST-NORMALISATION: 1972–PRESENT

Economic Relations

The signing of the Joint Statement in 1972, in which the PRC waived demands for reparations and Japan expressed deep reproach for the damage caused to the Chinese people through war, heralded a new stage in Sino–Japanese relations. Between 1972 and 1978, a series of commercial agreements were signed, culminating in 1978 with the Long Term Trade Agreement and the Treaty of Peace and Friendship (TPF). While by no means free of problems (for example, the aviation agreement was slowed down by disagreements over the continuation of Taiwanese flights between Tokyo and Taipei, and the TPF negotiations stalled over the inclusion of an anti-hegemony clause), the various agreements facilitated a boom in China–Japan relations marked by 'China fever' in Japan.

Teething problems emerged in the economic side of the relationship however, most prominently over plant and technology transfer, which led in 1979 to the unilateral cancellation of contracts by the Chinese government due to a readjustment of its economic policy. The 'Baoshan shock' (named after the postponement of contracts to develop, amongst other things, the Baoshan steel complex near Shanghai), left Japanese business and government circles disenchanted with China and reluctant to invest in what was perceived as an unstable environment. Nonetheless, two-way trade was relatively unaffected and increased year-on-year, representing the strongest aspect of the bilateral relationship. In 2000, two-way trade amounted to $85.8 billion compared to United States–China trade of $116.4 billion; by 2008, China–Japan trade exceeded $230 billion, with China overtaking the United States as Japan's largest trading partner; and by 2012 the figure amounted to $340 billion.

A major element of China–Japan economic relations has been Japan's 'economic cooperation' (or Official Development Assistance, ODA), which has undoubtedly contributed to China's modernisation and economic development. Beginning in 1979 under former Prime Minister Ohira Masayoshi, Japan's ODA to China comprised a series of long-term, low-interest loans plus grant and technical assistance. The loan element is of particular note, amounting to over 3.3 trillion yen between 1979 and 2007 and making Japan China's top ranking donor until the early 2000s. Aid was used largely to help develop China's infrastructure, with projects including the construction of railway lines, air and sea ports, roads and power stations. Environmental projects were prioritised from the late 1990s as Japanese anxiety grew over degradation of the environment (and transboundary pollution) as a result of China's rapid industrialisation. Japan's ODA to China has also been seen as an important foreign policy tool, a means of gaining leverage over the general direction of China's economic and political development and socialising China into international norms (Drifte 2006). The threat of cancellation or postponement of loans also offered the opportunity to leverage China on certain sensitive issues, such as in the aftermath of the Tiananmen Square massacre, during China's nuclear testing in 1994–1995, and in response to unnotified incursions of Chinese survey ships into Japan's exclusive economic zone (EEZ) in the late 1990s/early 2000s. The effectiveness of Japan's politicisation of aid in the 1990s, however, was a mixed bag (see Katada 2001 and Takamine 2003). Japan's decision to end the yen loan programme as of 2008 came about as a result of China's own rapid economic development (in contrast to Japan's decade-long economic stagnation and dependence on China trade) and a lengthy internal debate in Japan in the mid-2000s touching on issues such as concern over increases in Chinese military expenditure and a lack of transparency, anti-Japanese education in China and a perceived lack of Chinese awareness of, and gratitude for, Japan's considerable aid provision since 1979.

Japan's foreign direct investment (FDI) represents the third element of Japan's economic relations with China. Beginning in the late 1970s and early 1980s, after the implementation of China's open door policy, the joint venture law, and the creation of Special Economic Zones, Japan's FDI grew very gradually. In the 1990s, however, there was a surge of FDI into China's manufacturing industries (encouraged partly by Deng Xiaoping's 'southern tour', which facilitated greater access to foreign firms). This reached a peak in 1994–1995 when approximately 35 per cent of Japan's annual FDI flows went to China. In the latter half of the 1990s, FDI declined as a result of the Asian financial crisis and economic stagnation in Japan, but recovered again in the early 2000s, reaching a record high of over 40 per cent of total Japanese FDI in Asia (Xing 2008).

The complementarity of the two economies, facilitated by other factors such as geographical proximity and historical and cultural factors are frequently stressed in the literature, as well as by policymakers and business interests alike,

to affirm that cooperation not competition best describes the economic relationship. Also noteworthy is the perceived resilience of the economic aspect of the relationship in the face of political tensions. A number of studies demonstrate how deepening economic interdependence has helped to offset political tensions or crises. Xing (2008: 1) argues, for example, that economic integration has 'been immune to the political disputes'. Austin and Harris (2001: 269) also argue that the high level of interdependence provides a sound basis for the relationship as a whole, and Taylor (1996: 9) views the interlinking of the Japanese and Greater Chinese economies in terms of an Asian supply network that provides mutual benefits for all. Koo's (2009: 205) study of the impact of the Senkaku/Diaoyu territorial dispute on political–economic relations argues that economic interdependence has 'repeatedly fostered the de-escalation of Sino–Japanese conflict over territorial and maritime rights'. In other areas of interaction between Japan and China, political tensions appear to have little impact. Jain's (2006: 140) enlightening study of subnational governmental (SNG) links (such as sister city arrangements, trade promotion offices and technical cooperation) concludes, for example, that 'the relationship at the sub-national level apparently does not suffer from the kinds of tensions and conflict that arise from time to time between the two national governments.'

On the other hand, Yahuda (2006: 165) argues that despite the rapid increase in social and economic ties, 'these have led neither to noticeable improvements in political relations between the two sets of leaders nor to better perceptions of each other by Chinese and Japanese'. Similarly Calder (2006) considers that mutually beneficial economic ties are not sufficient to quell tensions arising from increasing popular involvement in politics and resurgent nationalism. Furthermore, with China's rapid growth since the 1990s contrasted to Japan's economic downturn and the 'hollowing out' of Japan's manufacturing base, the debate has often turned to the question of rising competition between the two, and the risk of Japanese dependence on China. For example, Hattori (2003: 53) argues that the cooperation model that characterised the relationship during the ODA years will be accompanied by competition in the early twenty-first century. Indeed, problems emerged in the form of trade friction, violation of Japanese intellectual property rights and problems with faulty Japanese goods in the Chinese market (Hattori 2003: 54; see also Hilpert and Haak 2002; Ohashi 2004). These negative factors contributed to the economic element of the 'China threat' rhetoric in Japan, but there is nonetheless widespread agreement that China has contributed to economic

recovery in Japan. Research on Japanese multinationals in China points to the need for them to
develop more flexible business practices in order
to cope with the challenges presented by China's
continued economic rise (Cross and Horn 2009).
Other observers consider that Japan and China
are still at significantly different levels of industrialisation and that complementarity should be
pursued in order for Japan to enjoy a win–win
situation (Kwan 2003).

Political/Diplomatic relations

The dual structure of Sino–Japanese relations is
most evident in diplomatic sphere with periods of
friendship and relaxation interspersed with periods
of tension, often relating to issues 'left over' from
history, territorial spats or the status of Taiwan. The
history problem, in particular, has placed constraints on the relationship, despite the efforts of
some Chinese and Japanese leaders since the 1990s
to adopt a more pragmatic and moderate response,[12]
and the lack, as yet, of a permanent political solution to the problem suggests that it is more than
likely to re-emerge in the future.

The origins of the history problem can be traced
to the first major dispute in 1982 between the two
governments on the issue of how Japanese school
history textbooks depicted Japan's behaviour in
China during the war. This remains an ongoing
issue in the twenty-first century, and contributed
to the outbreak of anti-Japanese demonstrations in
Chinese cities in 2005 (when protesters also vented
their anger at Japan's attempts to lobby for a permanent seat on the UN Security Council). The history problem also includes other recurring issues,
such as Japanese prime ministerial or ministerial
visits to the Yasukuni Shrine, dubious statements
about the war made by high-ranking (usually, but
not exclusively) LDP politicians and ministers,
denials of culpability for (and even occurrence of)
the Nanking Massacre and the military sexual slavery system, disputes over the wording of Japanese
apologies, and (the lack of) compensation for former forced labourers and victims of Japan atrocities. The literature on each of these aspects of the
history problem has expanded rapidly since the
1990s, offering explanations for its longevity.[13]
Clearly, historical revisionism in Japan (in particular a resurgent neo-conservative movement in the
1990s) and a perceived reluctance on the part of
some Japanese to accept war responsibility lie at
the heart of the problem, but China is also accused
of instrumentalising the history problem (playing
the history card) for purposes of boosting patriotic sentiment and reinforcing the legitimacy of
the Chinese Communist Party (CCP, for a discussion of this phenomenon, see Yang 2002). Work

on reconciliation has been undertaken since the
1990s both at governmental and non-governmental
levels, and its success and failures have been discussed in a number of studies.[14] The agreement of
both governments to embark on a joint history project from 2006 was an acknowledgement of the need
to 'squarely face the past', but the outcome perhaps
fell short of expectations.[15]

The failure to resolve the history problem, and
the mistrust this has produced, has impacted more
broadly on the relationship, influencing popular
nationalist sentiment in both countries, contributing
in part to the China and Japan threat debates, and
also adversely affecting attempts to develop a North
East Asian regional community. Clearly, other factors are at play too, not least the rise of China and
Japan's attempts to manage a changing regional
and global environment.

Starting in the early 1990s in Japan, China's
rapid modernisation programme and increasing
economic, political and military power were increasingly viewed with some caution (even alarm in some
circles). By the same token, Japan's shift towards a
more assertive foreign policy and the strengthening
of United States–Japan relations was perceived in
some Chinese circles as a move towards a remili-
tarised Japan, and therefore something to be wary
of, particularly combined with the refusal of some
Japanese to 'adopt a correct view of history'. The
rise of popular nationalist sentiment in both countries since the 1990s has also been viewed with
concern, along with the deterioration of friendly
feelings towards each other as recorded in public
opinion polls.[16]

The lack of robust regional institutions in North
East Asia is partly due to the vestiges of Cold
War politics, the sometimes-strained relationship
between China and Japan and an aversion (until
recently) to multilateralism on the Chinese side.
China and Japan are members of all the major track
one and track two organisations in the region, which
provides greater scope for the expansion of dialogue between them.[17] There is also convergence in
terms of their stated aims for regional development
(peace, stability, security, a healthy trading environment and concerns over transnational issues
such as terrorism, energy and the environment).
Since the late 1990s, there have been attempts to
cooperate on regional initiatives, for example in
the financial sphere in the wake of the Asian crisis (Katada 2004) and in the establishment of the
East Asia Summit (EAS). However, while leaders in both China and Japan talk about the need to
cooperate in the interests of economic stability and
prosperity, there are major differences in the conceptualisation of a regional community, its membership and function. This was clearly highlighted
in the EAS of December 2005, which, in Malik's
(2006: 211) view, 'may well have intensified

China's rivalry with Japan as both sought to use the EAS to undercut the other'. For Wesley (2007: 208), this sort of competitive regionalism represents 'a fatal retardant to the process of regional consolidation'. While former Prime Minister Hatoyama's concept of an East Asian Community based on the European model had no time to develop during his brief term in office, the now regular trilateral summits between China, Japan and South Korea may offer a foundation for greater regional institutional developments in future.

Security Relations

For some observers, it is the nature of the strategic rivalry between China and Japan that raises concerns. While kept at arms' length during the Cold War, the set of conditions that has prevailed since the late 1980s has forced each to reconsider the other's military capabilities and intent and has, inevitably, been attended by much academic attention. Here the main arguments revolve around the conflict versus cooperation axis. Those who argue for rivalry point to historical precedents and the continued antagonism over the history problem, the contest for regional leadership, Chinese concerns over a revival of militarism in Japan versus Japanese anxieties over China's military modernisation and lack of transparency, and the brewing tensions over energy sources. These factors, it is argued, will lead China and Japan into a security dilemma, and enmity, rather than friendship, will characterise future relations. In such a scenario, the strength of economic bonds would not be sufficient to prevent the pursuit of national interests and an escalation of tension and rivalry would seriously hamper the ability of leaders on both sides to manage the relationship.[18] In his comprehensive study of China–Japan security relations since the end of the Cold War, for example, Bush (2010: 258) argues that the nature of the decision-making structures in China and Japan, the role of domestic interest groups and the limitations of Chinese and Japanese crisis management systems mean that in situations of stress 'the prospect of limiting the possibility of escalation ... is not good'.

The counter-argument to the 'strategic rivalry descending to conflict' view maintains that although problems and tension will continue to present themselves, both governments have, in the past, displayed the ability to manage issues in such a way that suggests they could maintain a strategic stability in the future. Manicom and O'Neill (2009), for example, argue that the handling of the East China Sea dispute (over maritime boundaries and the rights to explore for oil and gas) demonstrate a certain pragmatism through the, albeit slow but persistent, attempts at negotiation, which

bodes well. A number of major studies of Japan's security policy on China have tended to describe variations on a general theme of engagement (for example, friendship diplomacy, constructive engagement, commercial liberalism, etc.), hedged by the development of Japan's own military force in addition to the security alliance with the United States (Drifte 2003: 84). Since the end of the Cold War, it is argued that this policy has shifted in a more assertive direction as evidenced in the various National Defence Programme Outlines, the Hashimoto–Clinton Joint Statement of 1996 and joint United States–Japan cooperation on theatre missile defence (TMD). This 'reluctant Realism' (Green 2001), or 'military and political power balancing' combined with 'political and economic enmeshment' (Drifte 2003), or 'positive engagement and realistic balancing' (Mochizuki 2007), has thus far been viewed as a successful means of managing China's rising military power and balancing against perceived threats.

The role of the United States is, of course, integral to any study of Sino–Japanese security relations and forms a substantial literature of its own. Strategically, the United States–Japan security alliance has brought benefits to the China–Japan relationship, acting as balancer or moderator, and was at times welcomed by the Chinese as a means of keeping the 'cap in the bottle' of Japanese militarism. However, it has also introduced negative dynamics to Sino–Japanese relations, seen in particular in the mid-1990s with the strengthening of the United States–Japan security relationship, seen by some Chinese as a means of containing China. The United States–Japan–China 'strategic triangle' is considered vital to the maintenance of peace and stability in the region for the foreseeable future, and much consideration is given to the role of the United States between China and Japan.[19]

In terms of specific security problems facing China and Japan, the Taiwan problem, territorial disputes and, increasingly, resource rivalry are generally agreed to be the most likely flashpoints. The status of Taiwan and the PRC's frequent criticisms of the nature of Japan's relationship with Taipei were a common refrain prior to diplomatic normalisation as the PRC sought to persuade Tokyo to accept Beijing as the sole legal government of China. Even after this goal was achieved, however, the Taiwan problem has continued to be a thorn in the side of Sino–Japanese relations on a number of levels. The relatively friendly relationship between Japan and Taiwan, hailing from the pro-Japan sentiment of a generation of Taiwanese who have some nostalgia for the colonial period and reinforced by the early postwar re-establishment of business and cultural ties, continued even after the Taiwan–Japan Peace Treaty was rescinded, and has arguably improved in the last decade or so

(Sun 2007). A high level of trade has been maintained, and the pro-Taiwan lobby in the Japanese government has been keen to maintain links, albeit on a non-official basis, with counterparts in Taipei. This has sometimes caused problems in China–Japan relations when the PRC has felt that relations have become a little too close. Taiwan's status in the United States–Japan alliance has also been the cause of tension between China and Japan, most notably in the mid-1990s when the revision of the United States–Japan Defense Guidelines made somewhat ambiguous reference to Japan's actions in the case of an emergency in areas surrounding Japan – a reference which Beijing took to mean the Taiwan Strait (Hughes 2001).

The dispute over the contested Senkaku/Diaoyu Islands concerns a group of rocks and uninhabited islands within 200 nautical miles of Japan, China and Taiwan, all of whom claim ownership. China's claims originate on the basis of historical records, Japan's from its active use of the islands from the late nineteenth century to the 1940s. A UN survey suggested the potential for oil and gas reserves in the area in 1968, and Beijing staked its claim for the first time in 1970. But the dispute was a relatively minor irritant until the 1990s, due to the pragmatic stance taken by both the Chinese and Japanese. Deng Xiaoping famously announced in 1978, for example, that the issue should be left to future generations to decide, and apart from a standoff in the areas surrounding the islands in 1978 (viewed as a move by the Chinese to get the stalled Peace and Friendship Treaty negotiations moving again), the issue was indeed shelved. A number of developments in the 1990s, for example the introduction in 1992 of the Law of the PRC on its Territorial Waters and their Contiguous Areas (which specifically included the Diaoyu Islands) and Japan's declaration of an exclusive economic zone (EEZ) of 200 miles around the islands in 1996, in addition to differences of opinion on the interpretation of the UN Convention on the Law of the Sea, signalled changes in the politico-strategic view of the islands in both China and Japan.

The dispute also escalated at a popular level in the mid-1990s, becoming more entwined in the politics of nationalist groups in China, Taiwan and Japan.[20] In the late 1990s, the nature of the dispute changed again when activities of Chinese survey ships in the vicinity of the islands started to raise concerns in Tokyo about China's intentions in terms of oil and gas exploration in the East China Sea (ECS). The Senkaku/Diaoyu dispute therefore developed from an issue concerning sovereignty and national identity to become part of a growing concern in Japanese political circles about China's overall strategic direction and energy security, while the Chinese also harboured their own suspicions about Japan's pursuit of its own energy needs. The main sticking point in the ECS has been the designation of the ownership of the continental shelf and the rights to explore and produce oil and gas deposits. After many rounds of negotiations on the possibility of cooperation, an agreement was reached in June 2008 that referred to joint development in a defined area, and 'cooperative' development of the Chunxiao oil and gas field. To date, however, the 2008 agreement has not been implemented and negotiations have been, at best, sporadic (Drifte 2008; Valencia 2007). The territorial dispute took a slightly different turn in 2012 when the Noda government 'nationalised' three of the island(s) in response to Tokyo Governor Ishihara Shintarō's attempt to raise funds to purchase them. The Chinese government's response was robust and led to a stand-off on both sides, with Japan insisting that no territorial dispute exists, and China linking the issue closely to the wartime history of China–Japan relations.

In addition to the ECS dispute, the potential for energy rivalry between China and Japan has manifested itself in other areas, such as the competition for Russian oil pipelines in the early 2000s, and concerns over the safety of sea lines of communication (SLOCs) (Liao 2007). Furthermore, in September 2010, the furore over the collision of a Chinese fishing boat with the Japanese Coast Guard vessels in Japanese waters coincided (or was presented as coinciding) with a temporary halt in Chinese exports to Japan of rare earth minerals (REM) (Japan relies on China for approximately 90 per cent of its REM imports), highlighting Japan's resource vulnerability in this area. In fact, China had announced a considerable reduction in its export quota earlier in the year (in an attempt to address the problem of environmental degradation associated with the mining of REMs). But the impact and timing of the REM issue, according to one analyst, 'transformed Sino–Japanese economic relations from a mutually prosperous rivalry to one with an undertone of mistrust' (Nakano 2011: 65). Yet there is also a case to be made for the potential cooperation, not just on the issue of resource security but in other aspects of Sino–Japanese non-traditional security relations – notably environmental protection, food safety, and nuclear power technology (see, for example, Hirono 2007, Itoh 2007, Liao 2007 and Wishnick 2009).

EMERGING TRENDS

The study of Sino–Japanese relations continues apace, and virtually all periods and aspects of the relationship remain the focus of serious academic study. While the more contemporary issues relating to security concerns, regional leadership issues, the history problem and economic interactions attract most attention, historical and cultural aspects are by no means neglected. The field has certainly benefited from the opening of archives and the release of hitherto restricted material, greater scholarly exchange, inter-disciplinarity and a general zeal to understand more fully the dynamics of the relationship between these two Asian powers.

In the short to medium term, it appears that themes relating to energy and environmental issues, the evolution of a Northeast Asian regional community (and the role therein of China and Japan) and Sino–Japanese strategic rivalry will continue to be closely monitored by observers of Sino–Japanese relations. Chinese and Japanese activities beyond the Asia–Pacific are also drawing attention, often within the context of an extended rivalry for power, but also from the point of view of (the potential for) converging strategies, for example in Africa.[21]

The effects of generational change in both countries, regime change (from the LDP to DPJ and back to the LDP), and succession management (PRC) are also of interest, and studies undertaken thus far seem to indicate that we can expect more of the same in terms of pragmatic and moderate stances from both governments, although this optimistic view is tempered in the knowledge that there are now fewer leaders who have first-hand knowledge and experience of the other country, and a younger generation of Chinese and Japanese who have negative mutual images.[22]

Finally, the field would benefit from further study of subgovernmental activities and initiatives, the effects of the boom in cultural exchange (tourism, foreign students, pop culture, etc.) and the role of soft power and cultural diplomacy[23] – all of which provide evidence of the multifaceted and complex nature of the relationship, which is perhaps too often overshadowed by developments at the elite level.

NOTES

1   Due to space limitations, the emphasis here is on English-language literature. There is, of course, a plethora of Chinese and Japanese studies of Sino–Japanese relations. Leading scholars in China are Jin Xide, Liu Jiangyong, Bu Ping, Zhu Jianrong to name but a few, while in Japan Kokubun Ryosei, Soeya Yoshihide, Tanaka Akihiko, Okabe Tatsumi and many others have steered the discussion of Sino–Japanese relations. For a useful review of the Chinese and Japanese academic literature on Sino–Japanese relations since 1990, see Xu (2007).

2   The most up-to-date textbook on China–Japan relations is Yahuda (2013), which focuses on

post-Cold War developments but also provides an overview of relations from the Mao period.

3   The best account of pre-modern relations between China and Japan is the introductory chapter in Fogel (2009). Wang (2005) is a detailed account of official relations between Japan and China from the second century BC to the tenth century AD. Chinese views of Japan in the Ming and Qing dynasties are considered in a collection of essays edited by Fogel (2002), while Fogel's single-authored volume on cultural dimensions of Sino–Japanese relations contains essays spanning interaction in the nineteenth and twentieth centuries (1995). For Japan's relations with China during the Tokugawa period see Jansen (1992).

4   See De Bary, Keene, Tanabe and Varley (2001) for accounts of Japan in the Chinese dynastic histories, and descriptions of the adoption of Chinese thought and institutions. Kang (2005) offers a fresh view of the Asian international system from 1300–1900 and China's and Japan's role in it.

5   Excellent book-length accounts of the first Sino–Japanese war are provided by Lone (1994) and Paine (2003).

6   There are some substantial studies of the experiences and impact of Chinese foreign students in Japan – see, for example, Jansen (1954), Harrell (1992), Reynolds (1993) and Lu (2004).

7   For a comprehensive study of the extent of Japan's interests in China in the early twentieth century, see Duus, Myers and Peattie (1989).

8   Pan-Asianism is dealt with extensively by Hotta (2007) and Saaler and Koschmann (2007).

9   It is impossible to narrow down this vast field to just a few sources, though the edited volume by Peattie, Drea and Van De Ven (2010) should be essential reading.

10 For coverage of this period and the role of informal diplomacy in China–Japan relations, see Passin (1963), Mendl (1978), Johnson (1987), Radtke (1990) and Zhao (1993).

11 LT trade was so-called after its architects Liao Chengzhi and Takasaki Tatsunosuke, and was renamed Memorandum Trade during the Cultural Revolution. See Radtke (1990), Soeya (1998) and Lee (1976) for a full account of this period, and the individuals and business organisations involved in maintaining important channels of communication.

12 See Hughes (2008) and Reilly (2009).

13 The sources on each aspect of the history problem are too many to mention here, but a sample includes: on the textbook issue and interpretations of history, Dirlik (1996), Rose (1998), and Hein and Selden (2000) and Reilly (2004); on the Yasukuni Shrine issue, Wan (2006), Breen (2007), Deans (2007) and Lai (2013); Yamazaki (2005), Lind (2008), and Suzuki (2008) cover the apology issue well; and the redress movement is discussed

by Schmidt (2000), Rose (2005), Underwood (2005), Wan (2006) and Xu and Pu (2010).

14 He (2009) is a comprehensive study of Sino–Japanese reconciliation. There are also a number of important university-run projects. For example, the project run by Peter van Ness at Australia's National University (ANU) on Reconciliation between China and Japan was published as a special issue of *Asian Perspective 31*(1), and further information is posted at www.China-Japan-reconciliation.blogspot.com; the George Washington University project on Memory and Reconciliation can be found at www.gwu.edu/~memory, and the ANU programme on Asia Beyond Conflict can be found at http://asiapacific.anu.edu.au/blogs/asiabeyondconflict/

15 Reflections on the joint history project from some of its participants are provided in Bu (2007), Kawashima (2010) and Kitaoka (2010). On joint history more generally, see Yang, Lui, Mitani and Gordon (2012).

16 Li, R. (2008) considers China's discourse on Japan's security role in the region, while Sato (1998) provides a comprehensive and sober overview of Japan's China perceptions at the height of the China threat debate in Japan. For a sample of the literature dealing with the effects of the rise of nationalism in both countries, see He (2007), Zhang (2007) and Sakamoto (2007).

17 For an interesting account of China and Japan in the Asian Development Bank, see Rathus (2008).

18 For a sample of these sorts of views, see Calder (2006), Wan (2006) and He (2007).

19 For a sample of strategic triangle studies, see Zhang and Montaperto (1998), and Abramowitz, Funabashi and Wang (1998). US think-tanks and research institutes produce regular analyses of the US role in Sino–Japanese relations. See, for example, publications produced by the Brookings Institution, the National Bureau of Asian Research (NBR) and Pacific Forum CSIS, etc.

20 There are some excellent studies of the politics of the Senkaku/Diaoyu dispute. See, for example, Downs and Saunders (1998), Deans (2000), Suganuma (2000), Hagstrom (2005) and Valencia (2007).

21 See, for example, Cornellisen and Taylor (2000), Ampiah (2008) and Raposo and Potter (2010).

22 On leadership change, see Boyd and Samuels (2008) and Li (2008), and on public opinion see Reilly (2012).

23 See Reilly (2009), Heng (2010), Vyas (2011) and Sun (2013) on soft power and public diplomacy; see Jain (2006) and Takahara (2006) for SNG activities.

REFERENCES

Abramowitz, Morton I., Funabashi Yoichi and Wang Jisi. (1998). *China–Japan–US managing the trilateral relationship.* Tokyo: JCIE.

Ampiah, K. (2008). The ideological, political and economic imperatives in China and Japan's relations with Africa. In K. Ampiah and S. Naidu (Eds.), *Crouching Tiger, Hidden Dragon?: Africa and China* (294–313. Scottsville: University of KwaZulu-Natal Press.

Austin, Greg and Harris, Stuart. (2001). *Japan and Greater China: political economy and military power in the Asian century.* London: Hurst.

Boyd, J. Patrick and Samuels, Richard J. (2008). Prosperity's children: generational change and Japan's future leadership. *Asia Policy,* 6, 15–51. Retrieved from http://www.nbr.org/publications/element.aspx?id=93, Access date 1 August 2014.

Breen, John (Ed.). (2007). *Yasukuni, the war dead and the struggle for Japan's past.* London: Hurst.

Brooks, Barbara J. (2000). *Japan's imperial diplomacy: consuls, treaty ports, and war in China 1895–1938.* Honolulu, HI: University of Hawaii Press.

Bu, Ping. (2007). Guanyu ZhongRi gongtong lishi de sikao (Thoughts on the Sino–Japanese Joint History Project). *KangRi Zhanzheng Yanjiu,* 1, 197–210.

Bush, Richard C. (2010). *The perils of proximity: China–Japan security relations.* Washington, DC: The Brookings Institution.

Calder, Kent. (2006). China and Japan's simmering rivalry. *Foreign Affairs,* 85(2), 129–139.

Cathcart, Adam and Nash, Patricia. (2008). War criminals and the road to Sino–Japanese normalization: Zhou Enlai and the Shenyang Trials, 1954–1956. *Twentieth Century China,* 34(2), 89–111.

Chang, Iris. (1997). The Rape of Nanking: The Forgotten Holocaust of World War II. New York: Penguin Putnam.

Chen, Jing. (2009). The trial of Japanese war criminals in China: the paradox of leniency. *China Information,* 23(3), 447–472.

Coox, Alvin D. (1988). The Pacific War. In Peter Duus (Ed.). *The Cambridge history of Japan, volume 6.* Cambridge, UK: Cambridge University Press.

Cornellisen, Scarlett and Taylor, Ian. (2000). The political economy of China and Japan's relationship with Africa: a comparative perspective. *The Pacific Review,* 13(4), 615–633.

Cross, Adam and Horn, Sierk. (2009). Japanese management at a crossroads? The changing role of China in the transformation of corporate Japan. *Asia Pacific Business Review,* 15(3), 285–308.

Deans, Phil. (2000). Contending nationalisms and the Diaoyutai/Senkaku Dispute. *Security Dialogue,* 31(1), 119–131.

Deans, Phil. (2007). Diminishing returns? Prime Minister Koizumi's visits to the Yasukuni Shrine in the context of East Asian nationalisms. *East Asia,* 24, 269–294.

De Bary, William T., Keene, Donald, Tanabe, George and Varley, Paul (Eds.). (2001). *Sources of Japanese tradition, volume one: from earliest times to 1600* (2nd ed.). New York, NY: Columbia University Press.

Dirlik, Arif. (1996). Past experience if not forgotten is a guide to the future. In Masao Miyoshi and Harootunian, Harry D. (Eds.), *Japan in the world* (pp. 49–78). Durham, NC: Duke University Press.

Downs, Erica S. and Saunders, Phillip C. (1998). Legitimacy and the limits of nationalism. *International Security*, 23(3), 114–146.

Drifte, Reinhard (2003). *Japan's security relations with China since 1989*. New York, NY: Nissan Institute/Routledge.

Drifte, Reinhard. (2006). The ending of Japan's ODA loan programme to China – all's well that ends well? *Asia–Pacific Review*, 13(1), 94–117.

Drifte, Reinhard. (2008). Japanese–Chinese territorial disputes in the East China Sea – between military confrontation and economic cooperation. *LSE Asia Research Centre Working Paper 24*. Retrieved from http://www.lse.ac.uk/asiaResearchCentre/_files/ARCWP24-Drifte.pdf, access date 1 August 2014.

Dryburgh, Marjorie. (2000). *North China and Japanese expansion 1933–37: regional power and the national interest*. Richmond, UK: Curzon.

Duus, Peter, Myers, Ramon H., and Peattie, Mark R. (Eds). (1989). *The Japanese informal empire in China, 1895–1937*. Princeton, NJ: Princeton University Press.

Fogel, Joshua A. (1995). *The cultural dimension of Sino–Japanese relations: essays on the nineteenth and twentieth centuries*. Armonk, NY: M. E. Sharpe.

Fogel, Joshua A. (Ed.). (2002). *Sagacious monks and bloodthirsty warriors: Chinese views of Japan in the Ming-Qing Period*. Norwalk, CT: Eastbridge.

Fogel, Joshua A. (2009). *Articulating the Sinosphere: Sino–Japanese relations in space and time*. Cambridge, MA: Harvard University Press.

Green, Michael J. (2001). *Japan's reluctant realism*. Basingstoke, UK: Macmillan.

Hagstrom, Linus. (2005). *Japan's China policy: a relational power analysis*. London: Routledge.

Harrell, Paula. (1992). *Sowing the seeds of change: Chinese students, Japanese teachers, 1895–1905*. Stanford, CA: Stanford University Press.

Harris, Sheldon H. (1994). *Factories of death: Japanese biological warfare 1932–45 and the American cover-up*. London: Routledge.

Hattori, Kenji. (2003). Sino–Japanese economic relations: problems and prospects. *The Japanese Economy*, 31(3–4), 51–59.

He, Yinan. (2007). History, Chinese nationalism and the emerging Sino–Japanese conflict. *Journal of Contemporary China*, 16(50), 1–24.

He, Yinan. (2009). *The search for reconciliation: Sino–Japanese and German–Polish relations since World War Two*. New York, NY: Cambridge University Press.

Hein, Laura and Selden, Mark (Eds.). (2000). *Censoring history: citizenship and memory in Japan, Germany and the United States*. Armonk, NY: M. E Sharpe.

Heng, Yee-Kuang. (2010). Mirror, mirror on the wall, who is the softest of them all? Evaluating Japanese and Chinese strategies in the 'soft' power competition era. *International Relations of the Asia Pacific*, 10, 275–304.

Hilpert, Hans Gunther and Haak, Rene (Eds.). (2002). *Japan and China: cooperation, competition and conflict*. Basingstoke, UK: Palgrave.

Hirono, Ryokichi. (2007). Japan's environmental cooperation with China during the last two decades. *Asia–Pacific Review*, 14(2), 1–16.

Holman, D. S. (1947). Japan's position in the economy of the Far East. *Pacific Affairs*, 20(4), 371–380.

Hotta, Eri. (2007). *Pan-Asianism and Japan's War 1931–1945*. Basingstoke, UK: Palgrave Macmillan.

Hughes, Christopher R. (2008). Japan in the politics of Chinese leadership legitimacy: recent developments in historical perspective. *Japan Forum*, 20(2), 245–266.

Hughes, Christopher W. (2001). Sino–Japanese relations and ballistic missile defense. *CSGR Working Paper No 64* (1). Retrieved from http://www2.warwick.ac.uk/fac/soc/csgr/research/workingpapers/2001/wp6401.pdf, access date 1 August 2014.

Iriye, Akira. (1987). *The origins of the Second World War in Asia and the Pacific*. New York, NY: Longman.

Itoh, Shoichi. (2007). China's surging energy demand: trigger for conflict or cooperation with Japan? *East Asia*, 25(1), 79–98.

Jain, Purnendra. (2006). Forging new bilateral relations: Japan's sub-national governments in China. In Peng Er Lam (Ed.). *Japan's relations with China: facing a rising power* (pp. 128–148). London and New York: Routledge.

Jansen, Marius B. (1954). *The Japanese and Sun Yatsen*. Cambridge, MA: Harvard University Press.

Jansen, Marius B. (1975). *Japan and China: from war to peace, 1894–1972*. Chicago, IL: Rand McNally.

Jansen, Marius B. (1992). *China in the Tokugawa World*. Cambridge, MA: Harvard University Press.

Johnson, Chalmers. (1987). The patterns of Japanese relations with China, 1952–1982. *Pacific Affairs*, 59, 402–428.

Kang, David C. (2005). Hierarchy in Asian international relations: 1300–1900. *Asian Security*, 1(1), 53–79.

Katada, Saori. (2001). Why did Japan suspend foreign aid to China? *Social Science Journal Japan*, 4(1), 39–58.

Katada, Saori. (2004). Constructing regional interests in Japan and China. *The Japanese Economy*, 31(3–4), 126–150.

Kawashima, Shin. (2010). The three phases of Japan–China joint-history research: what was the challenge? *Asian Perspective*, 34(4), 19–43.

Kitaoka, Shinichi. (2010). A look back on the work of the joint Japanese–Chinese History Research Committee. *Asia–Pacific Review*, 17(1), 6–20.

Koo, Min Gyo. (2009). The Senkaku/Diaoyu dispute and Sino–Japanese political-economic relations: cold politics and hot economics? *The Pacific Review,* 22(2), 205–232.

Kushner, Barak. (2010). Pawns of empire: postwar Taiwan, Japan and the dilemma of war crimes. *Japanese Studies,* 30(1), 111–133.

Kwan, C. H. (2003). Complementarity in Sino–Japanese relations: toward a win–win game. *The Japanese Economy,* 31(3–4), 60–66.

Lai, Yew Meng. (2013). *Nationalism and power politics in Japan's relations with China: a neoclassical realist interpretation.* London and New York: Routledge.

Lee, Chae-Jin. (1976). *Japan faces China: political and economic relations in the postwar era.* Baltimore, MD: Johns Hopkins University Press.

Li, Cheng. (2008). China's fifth generation: is diversity a source of strength or weakness? *Asia Policy,* 6, 53–93. Retrieved from http://www.nbr.org/publications/element.aspx? id=147, access date 1 August 2014.

Li, Rex. (2008). A regional partner or a threatening other? Chinese discourse of Japan's changing security role in East Asia. In Christopher M. Dent (Ed.). *China, Japan and regional leadership in East Asia.* Cheltenham, UK: Edward Elgar.

Liao, Xuanli. (2007). The petroleum factor in Sino–Japanese relations: beyond energy cooperation. *International Relations of the Asia Pacific,* 7, 23–46.

Lind, Jennifer. (2008). *Sorry states: apologies in international politics.* Ithaca, NY: Cornell University Press.

Lone, Stewart. (1994). *Japan's first modern war: army and society in the conflict with China, 1894–5.* New York, NY: St Martin's Press.

Lu, Yan. (2004). *Re-understanding Japan: Chinese perspectives, 1895–1945.* Honolulu, HI: Association for Asian Studies and University of Hawai'i Press.

Malik, Mohan. (2006). The East Asia Summit. *Australian Journal of International Affairs,* 60(2), 207–211.

Manicom, James and Andrew O'Neil. (2009). Sino–Japanese strategic relations: will rivalry lead to confrontation? *Australian Journal of International Affairs,* 63(2), 213–232.

Mendl, Wolf. (1978). *Issues in Japan's China policy.* Basingstoke, UK: Macmillan.

Mitter, Rana. (2013). *China's war with Japan, 1937–1945: the struggle for survival.* London: Allen Lane.

Mochizuki, Mike. (2007). Japan's shifting strategy towards the rise of China. *Journal of Strategic Studies,* 30(4), 739–776.

Morley, James William (Ed.). (1983). *The China Quagmire: Japan's expansion on the Asian continent 1933–1941.* New York, NY: Columbia University Press.

Nakano, Jane. (2011). Rare earth trade challenges and Sino–Japanese Relations: a rise of resource nationalism? In Gabe Collins, Andrew S. Erickson, Yufan Hao, Mikkal E. Herberg, Llewelyn Hughes, Weihua Liu and Jane Nakano (Eds.). *Asia's rising energy and resource nationalism: implications for the United States, China, and the Asia–Pacific Region.* NBR Special Report, 31, 53–65.

Ohashi, Hideo. (2004). The Impact of China's rise on Sino–Japanese economic relations. In Kokubun Ryosei and Wang Jisi (Eds.). *The rise of China and a changing East Asian order* (pp. 175–193). Tokyo: Japan Centre for International Exchange.

Paine, S. C. M. (2003). *The Sino–Japanese War of 1894–5: perceptions, power, and primacy.* Cambridge, UK: Cambridge University Press.

Passin, Herbert. (1963). *China's cultural diplomacy.* New York, NY: Praeger.

Peattie, Mark R., Drea, Edward. J., and Van De Ven, Hans J. (Eds.). (2010). *The battle for China: essays on the military history of the Sino–Japanese War of 1937–1945.* Stanford, CA: Stanford University Press.

Radtke, Kurt W. (1990). *China's relations with Japan, 1945–83: the role of Liao Chengzhi.* Manchester, UK: Manchester University Press.

Raposo, Pedro Amakasu and Potter, David M. (2010). Chinese and Japanese development co-operation: South–South, North–South, or what? *Journal of Contemporary African Studies,* 28(2), 177–202.

Rathus, Joel. (2008). China, Japan and regional organisations: the case of the Asian Development Bank. *Japanese Studies,* 28(1), 87–99.

Reilly, James. (2004). China's history activists and the war of resistance against Japan: history in the making. *Asian Survey,* 44(2), 276–294.

Reilly, James. (2009). The rebirth of Minjian Waijiao: China's popular diplomacy toward Japan. *Japan Policy Research Institute Working Paper 115.* Retrieved from http://www.jpri.org/publications/workingapers/wp115.html, access date 1 August 2014.

Reilly, James. (2012). *Strong society, smart state: the rise of public opinion in China's Japan policy.* New York, NY: Columbia University Press.

Reynolds, Douglas R. (1993). *China 1898–1912: the Xinzheng revolution and Japan.* Cambridge, MA: Harvard University Press.

Rose, Caroline. (1998). *Interpreting history in Sino–Japanese Relations.* London: Routledge.

Rose, Caroline. (2005). *Sino–Japanese relations: facing the past, looking to the future.* London: Routledge.

Saaler, Sven and Koschmann, Victor J. (Eds.). (2007). *Pan-Asianism in modern Japanese history: colonialism, regionalism and borders.* London: Routledge.

Sakamoto, Rumi. (2007). 'Will you go to war? Or will you stop being Japanese?' Nationalism and history in Kobayashi Yoshinori's *Sensoron.* In Michael Heazle and Nick Knight (Eds.). *China–Japan relations in the twenty-first century: creating a future past?* Cheltenham, UK: Edward Elgar.

Sato, Hideo. (1998). *Japan's China perceptions and its policies in the alliance with the United States*. Stanford University, APARC. Retrieved from http://fsi.stanford.edu/publications/japans_china_perceptions_and_its_policies_in_the_alliance_with_the_united_states/, access date 1 August 2014.

Scheiber, Harry N. (2002). Taking responsibility: moral and historical perspectives on the Japanese war-reparations issues. *Berkeley Journal of International Law*, 20, 233–249.

Schmidt, Petra. (2000). Japan's wartime compensation: forced labour. *Asia–Pacific Journal on Human Rights and the Law*, 2, 1–54.

Soeya, Yoshihide. (1998). *Japan's Economic Diplomacy with China 1945–78*. Oxford, UK: Oxford University Press.

Suganuma, Unryu. (2000). *Sovereign rights and territorial space in Sino–Japanese relations: irredentism and the Diaoyu/Senkaku Islands*. Honolulu, HI: University of Hawaii Press.

Sun, Jing. (2007). Japan–Taiwan relations: unofficial in name only. *Asian Survey*, 47(5), 790–810.

Sun, Jing. (2013). *Japan and China as charm rivals: soft power in regional diplomacy*. Ann Arbor, MI: University of Michigan.

Suzuki, Shogo. (2008). Can apology serve as a security policy? Responsible scholarship and breaking the chains of negative history in Sino–Japanese relations. *Korean Journal of Defense Analysis*, 20(4), 319–333.

Takahara, Akio. (2006). Japanese NGOs in China. In Peng Er Lam (Ed.). *Japan's relations with China: facing a rising power* (pp. 166–179). London: Routledge.

Takamine, Tsukasa. (2003). Domestic determinants of Japan's China aid policy. *Japanese Studies*, 22(2), 191–206.

Tanaka, Yuki. (2002) *Japan's comfort women*. London: Routledge.

Taylor, Robert. (1996) *Greater China and Japan: prospects for an economic partnership in East Asia*. London: Routledge.

Underwood, William. (2005, July 8). Chinese forced labor, the Japanese government and the prospects for redress. *Japan Focus*. Retrieved from http://www.japanfocus.org

Valencia, Mark J. (2007). The East China Sea dispute: context, claims, issues and possible solutions. *Asian Perspective*, 31(1), 127–167.

Vyas, Utpal. (2011). *Soft power in Japan China relations: state, sub-state and non-state relations*. London: Routledge.

Wakabayashi, Bob T. (Ed.). (2007). *The Nanking Atrocity 1937-8: complicating the picture*. New York, NY: Berghahn Books.

Wan, Ming. (2006). *Sino–Japanese relations: interaction, logic, and transformation*. Stanford, CA: Stanford University Press.

Wang, Zhenping. (2005) *Ambassadors from the Islands of the Immortals*. Honolulu, HI: University of Hawai'i Press.

Wesley, Michael. (2007). Jealous suitors: Sino–Japanese competitive regionalism and the future of East Asia. In Michael Heazle and Nick Knight (Eds.). *China–Japan relations in the twenty-first century: creating a future past?* (pp. 207–221). Cheltenham, UK: Edward Elgar.

Williams P. and Wallace D. (1989). *Unit 731: the Japanese Army's secret of secrets*. London: Hodder and Stoughton.

Wishnick, Elizabeth. (2009). Competition and cooperative practices in Sino–Japanese Energy and environmental relations: towards an energy security 'risk community'? *The Pacific Review*, 22(4), 401–428.

Xing, Yuqing. (2008). Sino–Japanese relations: the dimensions of trade and FDI. *International University of Japan IRI Working Papers*, No. 2. Retrieved from http://nirr.lib.niigata-u.ac.jp/bitstream/10623/31284/1/EMS_2008_06.pdf, access date 1 August 2014.

Xu, Bin and Xiaoyu Pu. (2010). Dynamic statism and memory politics: a case analysis of the Chinese War reparations movement. *China Quarterly*, 201, 156–175.

Xu, Xianfen. (2007). The study of Sino–Japanese relations in Japan and China, 1990–2005. *Modern Asian Studies Review* (Tokyo: Toyo Bunko, 2007), 12, 79–113.

Yahuda, Michael. (2006). The limits of economic interdependence: Sino–Japanese relations. In Alastair Iain Johnston and Robert S. Ross (Eds.). *New directions in the study of China's foreign policy* (pp. 162–185). Stanford, CA: Stanford University Press.

Yahuda, Michael. (2013). *Sino–Japanese relations after the Cold War: two tigers sharing a mountain*. London: Routledge.

Yamazaki, Jane. (2005). *Japanese apologies for World War II*. London: Routledge.

Yang, Daqing. (1999). Convergence or divergence? Recent historical writings on the Rape of Nanjing. *American Historical Review*, 104(3), 842–865.

Yang, Daqing. (2002). Mirror for the future or the history card? Understanding the 'history problem'. In Marie Soderberg (Ed.). *Chinese–Japanese relations in the twenty-first century: complementarity and conflict* (pp. 10–31). London: Routledge.

Yang, Daqing, Liu, Jie, Mitani, Hiroshi, Gordon, Andrew, Esselstrom, Erik, Fogel, Joshua A. ... Yang, Zhihui (Eds.). (2012). *Toward a history beyond borders: contentious issues in Sino–Japanese relations*. Cambridge, MA: Harvard University Press.

Yoshida, Takashi. (2006). *The making of the 'Rape of Nanking': history and memory in Japan, China, and the United States*. Oxford, UK: Oxford University Press.

Yoshimi, Yoshiaki. (2000). *Comfort women: sexual slavery in the Japanese military during World War II.* New York, NY: Columbia Press.

Zhao, Quansheng. (1993). *Japanese policymaking: the politics behind politics: informal mechanisms and the making of China policy.* Westport, CT: Praeger.

Zhang, Jian. (2007). The influence of Chinese nationalism on Sino–Japanese relations. In Michael Heazle and Nick Knight (Eds.). *China–Japan relations in the twenty-first century: creating a future past?* (pp. 15–34). Cheltenham, UK: Edward Elgar.

Zhang, Ming and Montaperto, Ronald N. (1998). *A triad of another kind: the United States, China and Japan.* Basingstoke, UK: Macmillan.

PART V

Economy

27

The Japanese Economy

Marcus Rebick

INTRODUCTION

Japan's economy, during its rapid growth from the 1950s to the 1980s was regarded as a model for the world, and during the 1980s much credit was given to its economic and political institutions (Vogel, 1979; Johnson, 1982; Aoki, 1988; Womack et al., 1991). On the other hand, during the 1990s, a period of much slower growth and stagnation, Japan's institutions were criticised by many (e.g. Porter and Takeuchi, 1999; Blomström et al., 2003). Today, with other countries in East Asia having different institutions showing similar capacities for rapid growth, we have a more balanced view and, without denying some unique cultural aspects, Japan's economic institutions do not appear to be that exceptional from the perspective of a European economist. Students of the 'varieties of capitalism' approach, for example, would regard Japan as one example of a country with a coordinated market economy (or CME) along with Germany, the Netherlands and others (Hall and Soskice, 2001). In contrast to liberal market economies, such as those of the USA and UK, CMEs are said to rely less on the market mechanism to allocate resources and reward participants, and more on long-term relationships. Their financial systems and corporate-governance arrangements are less open to pressure from market forces and firms are less sensitive to

short-term fluctuations in their share price. This chapter will provide a basic overview of Japanese economic institutions with some attention to the welfare state. It will then discuss macroeconomic developments including the effects of the global financial crisis of 2008/9 and the disasters of March 2011. Before beginning this description, however, I will present some basic information about Japan's economy and events in the past couple of decades that have had a major impact on it.

Table 27.1 shows some basic statistics about Japan in comparison with selected other countries. Japan's total economic output in 2010 was roughly 479 trillion yen or 4 million yen per capita. To make comparisons with other economies one could use market exchange rates, but these suffer from two problems: first, currency values are prone to short-term fluctuations and second, there is a bias against poorer countries because the cost of non-traded goods and services in those economies is less than in more developed economies. For this reason, many economists prefer to use exchange rates based on the purchasing power of the currency for a similar basket of goods. Using this method to make conversions into US dollars, Japan has the third largest economy in the world after the USA and China, and the Japanese level of per capita income is similar to that of the UK, other major European countries and South Korea, although lower than that of the USA.

Table 27.1   Size and National Income in 2010

	USA	UK	Japan	China	South Korea
Population (Millions)	309	61	127	1,341	49
GDP ($ Billions)	14,447	2,262	5,459	5,878	1,044
GDP PPP ($ Billions)	14,447	2,221	4,299	10,086	1,422
GDP/Capita PPP ($)	46,588	35,716	33,751	6,778*	29,101

Source: OECD Statistics
* Figure for 2009

Japan's economic output grew very rapidly in the period from the 1950s to the beginning of the 1990s, with growth rates reaching as high as 12.5 per cent per annum in the 1960s. In the space of about 20 years from 1953 to 1973 Japan was dramatically transformed from a poor country to one where personal incomes were comparable with those of most western European countries. The period from 1992 to 2002, however, referred to by economists as the 'Lost Decade' because of the lost opportunity for growth, saw average growth rates plummet to an average of just 1 per cent per year. Recovery followed with a long expansion beginning in 2002 and growth rates averaged some 2 per cent per year, a level comparable to that of the major European economies. Most recently Japan was severely affected by the financial crisis and global slowdown of 2008, and GDP per annum fell by 6.5 per cent in real terms over the period 2008–2009 due to a 25 per cent drop in its exports. Although the economy made up much of the lost ground in 2010, the disasters associated with the Northeast Japan earthquake of March 2011 led to a drop of around 1 per cent in 2011. As a result of the stagnation of the Lost Decade, and the setbacks since 2008, Japanese government debt has also reached very high levels, with gross debt at more than twice the size of GDP. Japan's government is unlikely to default on its debt obligations, however. For one thing, when the government's assets are taken into account the net debt is only about the level of annual GDP. Second, the Japanese have had trade surpluses since the early 1980s and thus are net savers; they have not been dependent on the rest of the world to finance their government deficits. Thus the problems that have afflicted some of the peripheral Eurozone countries have not appeared in Japan so far.

Relational Contracting and Commitment

Before discussing the different aspects of Japan's economy in more detail I would like to emphasise the importance of relational contracting and long-term relationships for major markets – for capital, for labour and for goods. Relational contracting refers to (often informal) contracts where the specific identities of the buyer and seller are of great importance as trust is an important element in doing business (Aoki 1988; Sako, 1992) In the case of capital Japan has relied on banks to finance much of investment in addition to the stock and bond markets. Unlike the stock market, where it is possible for anonymous investors to exit quickly by selling stock, bank loans typically involve a degree of commitment to the borrower. In 'stock market capitalism', it is difficult for the small investor to influence the management of the company, whereas in Japan's case banks can be in a powerful position with respect to their clients.[1] Japanese banks are also patient with their borrowers, often helping them to overcome difficulties rather than calling in their loans and forcing the company into bankruptcy. The labour market shows a similar kind of long-term commitment between firms and their employees. Japanese employees (especially men) have long tenures compared with most of the other OECD countries – they have not been as mobile as their counterparts elsewhere – and the remuneration of employees may be based partly on the length of service to the firm. Finally, the goods market also places importance on long-term relationships between suppliers of both final and intermediate goods and their customers. Purchases are not necessarily based on price alone but on long-term reliability and satisfaction.

The view just given of the Japanese economy is to some extent a caricature – there is great variety in Japan as well. Some firms behave much more like Anglo-American firms, starting of course with foreign-firm affiliates themselves. Smaller firms may be unable to provide long-term job security to their employees and deregulation of goods markets has meant that competitive pressures are forcing firms to pay more attention to the short run. The Lost Decade placed a great deal of strain on the economy and many long-term relationships have been scuttled. The stock market appears to have a greater influence on corporate behaviour than in the past. Nevertheless, it is better to start with the stylised view just presented than to assume that markets operate for the short term as in the most basic economic theory. I will begin the detailed discussion by looking at the financial system.

THE FINANCIAL SYSTEM AND CORPORATE GOVERNANCE

There are many different kinds of financial institutions, ranging from the giant banks Mitsubishi-Tokyo, Mizuho, Sumitomo-Mitsui Financial Group (SMFG) and the Japan Post Bank (undergoing privatisation) to small agricultural cooperatives. Life insurance companies and securities firms also play a major role in the financial sector. Deregulation in the 1980s and 1990s has erased some of the distinctions between these institutions and allowed them to offer a greater range of products than in the past (Hoshi and Kashyap, 2004).

The main characteristic of the Japanese financial system that strikes the Anglo-American observer is the importance of indirect finance in the large-firm sector. In indirect finance the savings of households are channelled through financial institutions which then lend or invest in firms. This is in contrast to direct finance where the direct purchase of shares (possibly through a fund) is the principal way in which firms raise funds. In Japan in 2008 55 per cent of household financial assets were held in the form of currency and deposits whereas in the USA the figure was only 15 per cent (BOJ, 2009). The use of financial intermediaries that primarily make loans to businesses has great implications for the governance of corporations. Until the 2000s many Japanese firms were less concerned with the performance of their shares on the stock market than with working closely with banks to secure finance.

The most widely accepted theory about Japanese corporate governance suggests that, while several financial institutions may make loans to a particular firm, one bank, known as the 'main bank', is in charge of monitoring the behaviour of the firm. These are typically large banks, such as the giant banks just mentioned, that were recently formed through mergers, and the major regional banks. The main bank for a firm is generally the bank with the greatest share of loans in the firm (although this is not a strict rule) and will often be one of the largest shareholders in the firm as well. The main bank is usually at the centre of an enterprise group (*kigyō shūdan*) that is comprised of large firms in different industries. These large firms (especially financial firms) also hold shares in other firms in the group, thus stabilising the shareholding and possibly preventing hostile takeovers from taking place. This insulates the firm from the pressures of the stock market, but this means there is a need for some other disciplinary device to prevent the firm

from abusing its funds. This is where the main bank comes in.

The main bank is typically involved in the underwriting of bond issuance by the firm and usually the firm's business transactions are run through the bank. The main bank may also send some of its staff to sit on the firm's board of directors. Thus the main bank has an informational advantage and this means that out of all the firm's creditors it is most able to assess the risks involved in an investment. This was particularly true in Japan up to the end of the 1990s because there was not a great deal of transparency about company business and there was variance in accounting methods so having inside information was advantageous. In extreme cases, if the firm is in serious financial trouble, rather than allowing for bankruptcy the main bank may undertake a rescue of the firm. Extra personnel will be dispatched to the board of directors and the management of the firm may be replaced. Supporters of the main-bank theory point to examples of successful rescues, such as that of Mazda in 1974 when the automobile manufacturer faced a serious crisis after the first oil shock (Hoshi and Kashyap, 1999).

There is a large literature on the main bank. Many empirical studies show that, given particular criteria for identifying a main bank (e.g. largest lender to a firm), firms that have a main bank behave differently from other firms, and that banks also behave differently towards firms for which they are main banks compared with other firms (Aoki and Patrick, 1994; Flath, 2005). Other studies have examined how main banks behave when the firm is facing difficulties – for example, finding that more staff are sent to the boards of directors of these firms (Sheard, 1994). On the other hand, Miwa and Ramseyer (2006) assert that there are no such things as main banks and that the entire theory is unsound.

Whatever one thinks of main banks there is no doubt that the last 30 years have had a major impact on Japanese finance and corporate governance. First, there has been major deregulation in the financial sector culminating in the 'Big Bang' of 1997. The government's supervision of the financial sector has also undergone a transformation, with the new Financial Services Agency taking over supervision of banks from the Ministry of Finance. Second, it should be noted that since the 1980s many large firms have been less dependent on banks for raising capital, finding that issuing stock or bonds is a cheaper source of finance that also leaves their management with greater independence. The large banks have therefore increasingly been drawn into the financing of smaller firms, which had previously been financed solely by smaller financial institutions. Another major change was the reduction in shareholding in non-financial firms by financial institutions during the 1990s. Institutional investors such as life-insurance companies and foreign investors have become more important sources of capital. Accounting standards have been changed and there is much greater transparency in the firm's accounts. The firm's share price is more sensitive to its short-term business prospects and the firm is more concerned about the share price (as it affects the cost of raising funds on the markets). These changes mean that banks are less important in monitoring firms than in the past (Dore, 2007; Jackson and Miyajima, 2007). There is now a great deal of variation in finance, with some firms apparently maintaining main bank relationships while others do not (Jackson and Miyajima, 2007).

No overview of the financial system would be complete without mentioning the role of the Japanese Post Office, which offered both postal savings accounts and life insurance. Now undergoing privatisation the Japan Post Bank is the world's largest bank and in the past as much as 20 per cent of all deposits were held in postal accounts. Before the 2000s postal savings were controlled by the Ministry of Finance, which used them to fund the Fiscal Investment and Loan Program, a major source of government finance for infrastructure projects.[2] Today the Japan Post Bank is independent of the MOF and does not directly transfer its funds to the government but instead buys government bonds which are then used to finance government investment. Thus the Japan Post Bank's portfolio of investments is very different from that of other major banks. The future of the bank is not yet clear but it is likely to continue to invest in low-risk assets such as government bonds.

CORPORATE GROUPS

Turning now to industrial organisation, the most celebrated feature is the corporate group often referred to as a *keiretsu*. Unfortunately, there is much confusion about the term *keiretsu*. Some authors use it to refer to any kind of corporate group, some restrict its use to refer to vertical production chains. In this chapter I will make a distinction between horizontal groups (*kigyō shūdan*), which consist of a number of large firms, in different industries that are usually centred around a main bank, and other financial institutions and *vertical keiretsu*, which are subcontracting groups.

Horizontal Groups

Some of the horizontal groups and their banks have a history reaching back to the pre-war conglomerates known as *zaibatsu*. The *zaibatsu* were, generally, family-owned conglomerates where the various

major firms in the group were owned and controlled through a holding company. These were dissolved by the American Occupation in the late 1940s and the groups that reformed after the Occupation ended were much more loosely constructed. In particular, the holding companies that were at the centre of the *zaibatsu* were banned after the war and have only been permitted again since 1999. The groups that exist today are characterised by cross-shareholding, interlocking boards of directors, regular meetings of the company presidents and reliance on the group's set of financial institutions. They may also share some preference for trading with other members of the group but this is a weaker tie than the others. In fact, the primary functions of the group appear to be two-fold – some sharing of risk and the prevention of outside interference by holding significant shares of stock within the group.

As with main banks, there have been many studies on the corporate groups to try and determine the role that they play. Some of these empirical studies find the surprising fact that firms in horizontal groups earn lower profits than independent firms (Nakatani, 1984; Lincoln and Gerlach, 2004). It may be the case that membership in a group offers greater insurance against risk, as the main bank and other financial institutions in the group may come to the aid of a firm that is in trouble. The firms in the group would have to pay the banks a premium for this insurance and thus profits would be lower. However, it should be noted that other studies have found the opposite – firms in these groups are more profitable (Miwa and Ramseyer, 2006).

Most studies have used some kind of arbitrary definition to determine which firms belong to a particular group. For example, a group may be defined by membership in the presidents' club (*shachōkai*), or those firms which have a certain percentage of their loans coming from financial institutions in the group, or by those firms which have a defined minimum of their shares held by other firms within the group (see Nakatani, 1984) for an early example of this). In a rigorous study, Lincoln and Gerlach (2004) use a sophisticated computational technique known as 'block modelling' to determine membership in various groups. This procedure allows them to consider relationships in finance, shareholding and trade simultaneously, and their results show a more nuanced and complicated pattern than that shown by other studies. On the other hand, just as with main banks, Miwa and Ramseyer (2006) deny that these groups exist at all. Although their view appears to be extreme, it is the case that the definition of these groups is ambiguous and the results of empirical studies appear to vary according to definition and time period used.

Corporate groups have also been undergoing change, such as the aforementioned unwinding of cross-shareholding between financial and non-financial institutions. Lincoln and Gerlach (2006), using groups defined by membership in *shachōkai*, examine the extent to which ties have weakened in finance, trade, cross-shareholding and directorships. They find that the corporate group networks are weakening but that firms are developing new ties with other firms outside their original corporate groups, including foreign firms. New corporate groups are also forming in Japan, most famously the Softbank group in IT services. So, although the older corporate groups are in general weakening, relational contracting remains important in Japan.

Vertical keiretsu

The other type of corporate grouping is the vertical *keiretsu*, principally found in manufacturing, which consists of a parent firm and chains of subsidiaries. Each firm in the chain may be a part or total owner of the supplier firms immediately below it, although some are financially independent. Although subcontracting is part of the economy in all countries, it is more extensive and developed in Japan. For example, most of the value of an automobile in Japan is not created by the automobile manufacturer but by the subcontracting firms that produce various parts. The theorist Masahiko Aoki (1988) argues that this arrangement works well because it fosters competition among the various suppliers. According to this theory, suppliers win contracts not by being the lowest bidder but by being reliable and producing high-quality parts. A good supplier will be 'promoted' and gain a larger share of the business of the parent firm, and a supplier that is less reliable will lose some business, but not be cast off completely. The parent firm also works together with its subsidiaries to help them develop new technology, often organising them into groups (Sako, 2006).

There is another role that subcontracting plays, however. In general, the lower down the supply chain one goes the lower the value added per worker in the production process. This is partly because the smaller firms have less physical capital than the large firms and partly because the workers themselves are less skilled (have less human capital). Subcontracting, then, provides a way for a firm to save on costs and pay its less productive workers a lower wage than its union would allow if all the workers were incorporated into the large firm. If the wages were equalised this would lead to a situation where, from the point of view of economic efficiency, higher-value workers would be underpaid and lower value workers overpaid. A large firm that tried to vertically integrate would either be less profitable (paying less able workers more) or unable to attract the best talent (paying everyone a lower wage). This brings us to the subject of labour institutions in Japan.

LABOUR MARKETS AND INSTITUTIONS

As with capital markets and industrial organisation, Japanese labour markets and institutional arrangements support the theory of a coordinated market economy. Most male workers enjoy a long-term relationship with their firm provided that the firm is large enough to be able to provide job security. These workers develop firm-specific skills over an extended period of in-firm training and thus they become more valuable to the firm than outsiders with the same number of years of experience acquired elsewhere. The firm is partly able to protect these insiders with a buffer of less protected workers. In the past, with steady economic growth, this was a less important feature of the labour market but the slow growth of recent years has led firms to increase the size of this buffer, particularly by increasing the number of temporary workers.

Japan's labour market is thus characterised by a dual structure with highly protected and well paid regular employees in large firms on the one hand, and more poorly paid part-time workers, temporary workers and workers in smaller firms on the other. This dual structure has a long history and dates back to the 1920s when large industrial firms faced a shortage of skilled labour and were compelled to pay their workers higher wages in order to keep them in the firm (Minami, 1986: 318). The firm-size gap in earnings has fluctuated in size over the years but remains a feature of the labour economy. The latter part of the twentieth century also saw a steady rise in the number of part-time workers (mainly women). Although the average part-time worker works about 20 hours per week, part-time workers in Japan can work nearly as many hours as regular employees and many of them work 40 or more hours per week. The main features of part-time status is that pay is much lower (per hour) than for regular workers and part-time workers usually do not share in the semi-annual bonuses that make up 20–30 per cent of the regular workers' total cash compensation. Part-time workers may still enjoy job protection similar to that of full-time workers, but this is not the case for temporary workers. The proportion of temporary workers in the workforce rose from 10 to 14 per cent between 1995 and 2006, and the newly legalised temporary agency workers made up 2.5 per cent of the workforce in 2009 (JIL, 2009: 120, 122)

Japanese regular employees enjoy high levels of job protection for a number of reasons. First, as already mentioned, Japanese firms invest heavily in training their workers and some of the skills developed over a worker's career are firm-specific. This makes it difficult for the firm to make workers redundant and then hire back workers with similar skills when times are good. Second, unions in Japan have chosen to put job security ahead of demands for higher wages. Third, Japanese workers can be moved to different departments in the firm if their job is phased out. Workers are usually willing to accept postings that are in different locations if necessary, even going so far as to live separately from their families for a year or two. Fourth, Japanese law has precedents that mean firms can only make workers redundant if they are suffering from severe financial distress and there is no way for them to move workers to another part of the company.

In the past workers in most companies could expect their earnings to increase with the length of time they spent in the company. This 'seniority wage' system did not account for all of the raises received by employees – favourable appraisals, the development of better skills or earlier promotion to a higher rank could also increase earnings above the normal annual raise. However, in recent years, the pay packet received by white-collar workers has downplayed the importance of seniority and in many firms there is now no component of the wage that is based directly on seniority.

Japanese industrial relations are characterised by enterprise unionism, where each unionised firm has its own union with which it bargains independently. However, bargaining is highly coordinated with company unions banding together in industrial associations and, ultimately, in peak federations of which Rengō is today by far the largest. Japanese firms also band together in industry associations and then in the peak federation *Keidanren*. Bargaining is almost always for an annual agreement and is conducted simultaneously across federations culminating in the spring – hence the name Spring Offensive, or *shuntō*. Most Japanese workers do not belong to a union, however. The unionisation rate or union density has fallen from around 35 per cent of the non-agricultural workforce in the early 1970s to around 18 per cent today. Despite this, many companies set their annual across-the-board wage increases in line with those of the unionised firms in their industry, and before the Lost Decade there was not much difference between union and non-union wages.[3] During the Lost Decade, however, non-unionised firms failed to keep up with unionised workers, mainly because they were unable to resist wage cuts. As a result, a gap opened up between union and non-union workers' pay – 7 to 9 per cent according to some estimates – and thus the *shuntō* lost its role as an industry-wide wage setter (Hata and Kawaguchi, 2008). Japanese unions have tried to stem the decline in their membership by recruiting part-time workers, but most part-time workers (mainly women) are not interested – their wages relative to those of men are unlikely to be a high priority for the union and the union dues would be an unwanted tax on their pay.

To an outside observer one of the most notable aspects of the Japanese labour market is the large gender gap in earnings. Full-time women workers earn on average only 67 per cent as much as men for an hour's work (JIL, 2009: 181) and if part-time workers are considered the gap is much greater. The fact that many working women work part-time is partly a matter of choice and not in itself that unusual. However, the Japanese case stands out because the demands of full-time work are less compatible with the demands of family life. Japanese work is often organised as teamwork and it is difficult for full-time workers to take time off to look after family members in cases of ill health. It is also the case that many Japanese workers are called upon to work overtime without any notice and may be transferred to distant locations at very short notice. These factors all combine to create a situation where women are heavily disadvantaged in the labour market.[4] One of the challenges for Japan, if it is to develop the use of its women in the workforce, is to restructure work so that there is a better work-life balance.

SOCIAL WELFARE

In a highly-influential work Esping-Anderson (1990) defined three types of welfare state: a liberal type, which provides minimal, usually means-tested benefits and places much of the lifetime risk on the individual; a conservative state, where much of the social welfare is channelled through employers in a male breadwinner society; and a social-democratic state with universal benefits that are seen as a citizens' basic rights. The US, Canada and Australia are examples of the liberal type, Germany and Austria the conservative type and the Scandinavian countries the social-democratic type. Japan would mainly appear to be a conservative type of state in this classification scheme. Health care, as in most of the countries of the OECD, is a universal entitlement, but pension benefits are much higher for employees than for the self-employed and highest for workers in larger firms and the public sector. Japan has also, like Germany, introduced a long-term care-insurance system for the elderly funded by contributions from residents over the age of 40. On the other hand, Japan resembles the liberal welfare states in that unemployment benefits are among the lowest in the OECD, especially in terms of the length of time that one can receive benefits. Benefits for the poorest (Public Assistance) are very strictly means-tested. As in other East Asian countries, the family is considered to be the ultimate bearer of risk, and relatives (including aunts and uncles) can be forced to assist family members that are needy (Goodman et al., 1998). As a result, the overall tax burden (including pension and insurance contributions) on Japanese is amongst the lowest in the OECD.

Although pensions for regular workers in large firms and the public sector are adequate to maintain a good standard of living after retirement, the self-employed, workers in small firms and women who are not married to someone with a good pension are not so well off. This is one of the reasons why many Japanese retire from the labour market at a late age. Also, to receive any pension at all, one must work for at least 25 years and this is a problem for many women. Consequently, there are still high rates of poverty among the elderly, and lone elderly women are especially at risk.

Since pensions are so important for an ageing population, and because there is a disparity in the coverage, a bit more should be said about them. Japan has a three-tiered pension system. There is the National Pension (*kokumin nenkin*), which is designed to cover all of the population. This is a relatively small benefit, however – the average monthly benefit is just over 50,000 yen (£260). For many Japanese this is their entire pension income, and it is lower than the benefits given to the very poor through the Public Assistance system (*seikatsu hogo*). Employees, however, enjoy a second, employees' pension, a government-run occupational pension that provides earnings-related benefits, by which the highly paid receive larger pensions (and make larger contributions when they are working). These pensions are quite generous and levels rival those of other OECD countries with similar occupational pensions – average monthly benefits are around 170,000 yen (£850), and this figure will rise as more retirees make the full 40 years of contributions.[5] Finally, there is a third tier provided by companies (and public employers) that adds to the employee pension,

sometimes in the form of a lump-sum payment made at mandatory retirement.

MACROECONOMIC PERFORMANCE

Turning now to macroeconomic performance, Japan enjoyed very rapid growth from the mid 1950s until the first oil shock of 1973, then, after 1974, slower but still high levels of growth through to 1992 before it entered the Lost Decade. Growth averaged 1 per cent per annum during the Lost Decade and wage levels fell on average in real terms and unemployment levels increased. The poorly paid were most affected by this downturn and both inequality and poverty levels rose significantly. As shown in Figure 27.1, the Lost Decade actually consisted of separate periods of slow growth separated by brief recoveries in 1996 and 2000.

The immediate causes of the recession are well known (Boltho and Corbett, 2000; Ito, 2003). An enormous bubble in stock and land prices developed at the end of the 1980s. Stock prices at their peak in late 1989 were around five times the level that they were at in early 2009. Investment in plant and equipment boomed. Just prior to the collapse of the bubble the Bank of Japan raised interest rates sharply by 3 percentage points and this was the most likely trigger for the inevitable collapse. For a couple of years the economy continued to grow but it experienced a major slowdown in 1992.

It was not surprising that a slowdown followed the collapse of the bubble economy. First, many

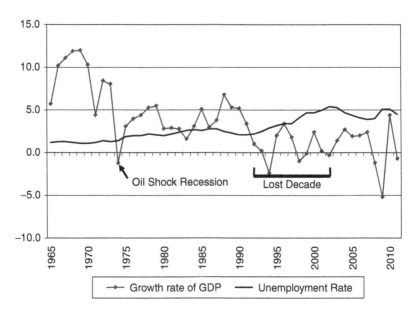

Figure 27.1   GDP growth and unemployment rates

businesses had over-invested during the boom and quickly found themselves with excess capacity once the future outlook turned bleak. Many firms outside the real-estate sector had also invested heavily in stocks or in real estate in the hopes of making a quick profit and were now saddled with debts that they could not pay. These were the principal causes of the drop in investment demand. Richard Koo (2009) goes so far as to claim that these problems in the balance sheets of all corporations (including non-financial firms) were the cause of the duration of the recession. Until firms had reduced the debt on their balance sheets they were unwilling to undertake further investment, even if banks were willing to lend to them. Financial institutions also suffered greatly as deregulation had left them free to invest heavily in real estate and stocks, either directly or through subsidiaries. Deregulation of financial markets in the 1980s was not accompanied by the establishment of proper supervision and governance. The deregulation itself gave rise to huge competitive pressures which pushed institutions into making risky investments. After the bubble burst banks and other financial institutions found that many of the loans they had made were unlikely to be repaid because the borrowers were losing money. Although all of this was a massive shock to the economy, poor government policy in the succeeding years takes much of the blame for the length of time Japan needed to recover, although external events also played a major role.

In contrast to the actions taken by the USA and the UK in the financial and economic crisis of 2008, the Japanese government did not recognise the severity of the problem at an early stage. First, the Bank of Japan, which had raised interest rates to cool down the boom, did not lower them quickly enough. One of the consequences of this may have been the deflation that took hold in Japan later in the decade. Second, government fiscal policy was weak and inconsistent (Posen 1998). In 1995 a massive stimulus package was enacted and the economy responded with strong growth in 1996. As soon as this recovery took place, however, the government reversed its fiscal policy by raising taxes, including the consumption tax which rose from 3 to 5 per cent. The economy duly slowed down again. On top of all this, 1997 brought a major financial crisis for many Asian countries. This deeply affected Japan because it supplied many of the investment goods in these countries. Failed investments in the affected countries added to the woes of Japanese financial institutions. Finally, although a short recovery appeared to take place at the very end of the 1990s, the collapse of the dotcom-investment boom in the USA in 2000 reduced the demand for Japanese exports, and sustained recovery did not take place in Japan until 2002.

Throughout this entire period the financial system struggled. A number of financial institutions

failed over the course of the decade, but some economists argue that more should have been allowed to fail (Hoshi and Kashyap, 2004). The earliest victims were the housing loan corporations, or *jūsen*, which were originally set up in the 1970s to provide mortgage financing for households. During the bubble period, however, they had lent vast quantities to real-estate speculators and were made insolvent by the collapse in property prices. The government tried some rescue packages in the hopes that property prices would rise again, but this only delayed the inevitable end, which came in 1995. A similar pattern of forbearance by the Ministry of Finance was also seen in the banking sector. The banks had huge amounts – over 70 trillion yen by one estimate – of non-performing loans, but the Ministry of Finance, which was responsible for monitoring the banks, did not reveal the true scale of the problem to the public (Hoshi and Kashyap, 1999). The banks themselves did not foreclose on their problem borrowers and this meant that the financial crisis continued much longer than necessary. The bad-loans problem was not resolved until the early 2000s, when both economic recovery and stronger pressure from the government to dispose of non-performing loans brought the banks back to health.

Unemployment also became a major issue for the first time since the 1950s. Unemployment rates remained relatively low during the first part of the Lost Decade but then rose to levels above 5 per cent after 1998. While this level does not seem particularly high from the perspective of other countries, Japan's very poor provision of unemployment benefits made this a more serious problem. Much of the unemployment and underemployment was and is found among the more poorly educated youth, but new high-school and university graduates also faced a very difficult job market from 1994 onwards. Many firms reacted to hard times by holding on to their older employees and greatly reducing their hiring of new graduates (Genda, 2003). This was a major factor in the rise of casual employment among the young, who could not find satisfactory full-time work.

The Lost Decade gave rise to considerable debate amongst economists about what the government needed to do. While some economists (e.g. Posen, 1998) have insisted that more government stimulus packages were needed, the state of government finances was a major problem. Since tax receipts fall and expenditures (such as unemployment benefits) rise naturally during a recession, the government debt ballooned during this period, reaching the high levels that exist today. There are also economists who have maintained that the stimulus packages were not that effective. This was partly because much of the additional spending was on public works, often very wasteful projects with little benefit for the public. It is also possible that Japanese households reduced their consumption because they expected future tax increases would be necessary to pay off the government debt. Koo (2009), meanwhile, argues that the fiscal stimulus was successful in preventing Japan from entering into an even deeper depression over the Lost Decade. The private sector was still unwilling to invest until balance sheets were restored to health and government stimulus packages helped keep the economy afloat. In effect, private debt was transformed into public debt during this period.

Some economists advocated monetary rather than fiscal policy. Krugman (1998) argued that the Japanese economy was caught in a Keynesian liquidity trap where conventional monetary policy was useless because interest rates were already at zero. He theorised that the way to get out of this trap was to create expectations of future inflation: if consumers and firms thought that prices would go up in the future then they would be less inclined to postpone purchases of goods or investment today. In order to do this he advocated a very strong form of inflation targeting where the Bank of Japan would commit itself to increasing the money supply until prices reached a much higher level. However, the Bank of Japan would not accept an inflation target. Instead, during the early 2000s it embarked on a program of quantitative easing which continued to push money into the financial sector. In part it did this by intervening in the foreign-exchange markets selling yen and buying US dollars.

Japan came out of its Lost Decade in 2002 and continued with steady growth of around 2 per cent per annum until 2008 when it entered a sharp recession along with the global downturn. The proximate cause of the revival in economic growth was the rapid increase in exports, especially to China. The Chinese economy had started to grow rapidly after the reforms of the 1980s and by the 2000s had become a major world economy. Its rapid growth pulled in investment goods and some intermediate goods made in Japan. Just as exports had helped Japan recover in the early 2000's, however, the 25 per cent drop in exports starting in the fourth quarter of 2008 led to a large drop in domestic output. The economy began to contract steeply.

Although the economy bounced back in 2010, the following year brought the Great Tohoko (Northeast Japan) Earthquake and Tsunami. In addition to a great loss of life approximately 17 trillion yen of capital (about 3 per cent of GDP) was wiped out and the overall growth rate was negative during 2011 (Takenaka, 2011). The Tohoko region in itself was not large enough to generate this drop in the growth rate; however, the disaster at the Fukushima Dai-ichi nuclear-power plant disrupted electricity supplies for much of eastern Japan and anxiety about nuclear safety led the government to order the temporary shutdown of virtually all nuclear-power plants across Japan. Although the Tohoko region

only accounts for some 4 per cent of Japanese GDP, it has many factories that were an integral part of the supply chain for firms outside the Tohoko region, and so the disaster had a major impact on both the automotive and electronics industries. Finally, at least some of the downturn can be attributed to a drop in consumption by Japanese outside Tohoko, who apparently felt that it was inappropriate to be spending money at a time when so many of their fellow Japanese were suffering.

Although the short-term effects for the overall economy do not seem to have been that great, the effects on the Tohoko region have been catastrophic. Entire communities were wiped out and it is unlikely that the region will ever recover fully. Tohoko was a declining region with a shrinking population even before the the events of 2011 and the disasters have served to accelerate an existing trend. More important for the national economy is the change in policy towards nuclear power. Despite recent changes in government policy the future of nuclear power appears to be very uncertain in Japan. Even if the existing plants are brought back into service it is unlikely that new plants will be built as previously planned. This will mean that Japan will have to rely to a greater extent on imported fossil fuels in the future and this will have a major effect on the balance of trade.

The economy did recover from the Lost Decade and maintained a long expansion after 2002, but its growth rate never returned to the levels seen up to the end of the 1980s. This was due to a number of factors. First, the labour force had started falling at the end of the 1990s, the ageing population and low fertility rate limiting the pace of growth to some extent. Second, total-factor-productivity growth (productivity growth coming from the more effective use of capital and labour) had slowed down. Japan now had productivity in manufacturing that matched that of other developed countries, making it difficult for it to make further advances by importing technology. In any case, manufacturing was becoming a less substantial part of the entire economy. It is much more difficult to improve productivity in services than in manufacturing – teaching, haircuts and health care remain labour-intensive activities.[6] Thus, during the 2000s, Japan's growth had slowed to levels similar to those of the major European countries.

It has not all been bad news, however. The distribution of goods has become more efficient, in part due to the information technology (IT) revolution. In the past Japan had a large number of retail stores per capita In 1990, for example, Japan had more than 13 stores per 1,000 people compared with under 10 for the USA and the major European countries (Flath, 2005: 296). In addition, distribution channels were quite complex with goods moving through multiple layers of wholesalers before reaching the retail level. This system has been challenged by the rise of convenience stores and larger retail stores that have the capacity to negotiate directly with suppliers and manufacturers, bypassing the wholesale level. Better use of IT has also led to more efficient distribution systems using supply-chain management. Previously, Japan had laws that made it difficult for large stores to open without gaining government approval, which held up the development of larger, more efficient retailers. These regulations were dismantled in the 1990s and larger stores have now become a more important part of the retail landscape.

FOREIGN TRADE AND INVESTMENT

We turn now to foreign trade and investment, where Japan has some unusual characteristics. The trade-to-GDP ratio for Japan is about 25 per cent, similar to the USA, but well below that of countries in the EU and East Asia; and Japan has run a trade surplus almost uninterrupted since the early 1980s. Much of this can be explained by the fact that Japanese domestic savings tend to be higher than domestic investment levels and so foreign investment helps to compensate for the substantial surpluses (around 2 per cent of GDP). Japan, like many other developed countries, reduced its tariffs greatly in the late 1960s, but its trading pattern has remained unusual in that it engages in relatively low levels of intra-industry trade (e.g. importing Fiats and exporting Toyotas). It primarily exports manufactured goods and imports raw materials which are scarce in Japan. These facts have been used to argue that Japan deliberately acts to block foreign-manufactured imports, generally through non-tariff barriers (Lincoln, 1990). However, a number of studies, such as Saxonhouse (1993), have suggested that Japan's trading pattern can largely be explained

by its overall size (allowing it to produce every kind of product) and its distance from other countries (making imports more expensive).

One might argue that there were barriers to trade in the 1980s, but increasingly Japan is moving towards higher levels of intra-industry trade (Flath, 2005). Japan is now importing more finished goods, such as consumer electronics and agriculture, which had been highly protected. However, a large share of these imports come through the foreign affiliates of Japanese companies (Greaney, 2005, 2009). This raises the question of why we do not see more foreign multinationals operating in Japan. Flath (2005) suggests that the Japanese language and culture make it difficult for foreign firms to enter the country, but surveys suggest that other factors are important. Foreign companies are put off by the high cost of office space, government regulations and by business practices including the complex distribution channels. The high value of the yen also discourages investment. As shown in Figure 27.2, the market value of the yen has consistently been higher than purchasing power would warrant. When foreign multinationals do enter the Japanese market it is often through a tie-up with a domestic company, and there have been an increasing number of ventures involving a merger between a Japanese company subsidiary and a subsidiary of a foreign company. However, Japan's levels of inward FDI and M&A involving foreign firms are still extremely low by international standards.

Japan's trade pattern has been the cause of some friction between the USA and Japan. This reached a peak in the 1980s when Japanese goods, including consumer electronics and automobiles, flooded the USA in response to the high value of the US dollar during the early 1980s. However, even after the yen rose sharply in value after 1985, Japan continued to run a trade surplus with the USA as Japanese firms cut prices (in yen) to remain competitive and

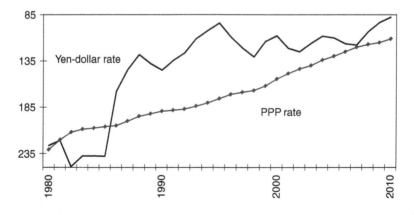

Figure 27.2   Yen–US dollar exchange rate and PPP rate

hold on to market share. It should also be noted that Japanese firms saved on the cost of raw materials after the yen appreciated. Trade friction between the USA and Japan continued through the beginning of the 1990s but became a minor issue after the Japanese economy entered its period of stagnation and the US economy boomed. The increased importance of China as a source of American imports has also been a factor in the cooling of the tension with Japan, and in fiscal 2008–09 Japan recorded a trade deficit.

POPULATION AGEING

The facts about ageing are documented elsewhere in this *handbook*, but both increased longevity and falling fertility play a role. Japan's population is experiencing the most rapid ageing in the world: by 2020 28 per cent of the population will be over the age of 65. Ageing is already having a major impact on the economy. A life-cycle model of savings behaviour, in which those of working age save while retired workers dissave, suggests that as the population ages savings rates will fall. This is part of the explanation for why Japan's savings rate has fallen over the past 20 years. A second consequence of ageing is the impact on government finances. The cost of health care will rise, as will the cost of caring for the elderly who are not cared for by their own families. In particular, at present contribution and benefit levels the long term care insurance system may not be financially sound in the future. The pension system is also on shaky ground, although recent reforms have implemented a system where benefits will be cut automatically if the low fertility rate continues. On the other hand, education expenses are likely to fall in the future. Weinstein and Broda (2005) argue that although Japan will face difficulties it should be able to manage its finances without raising taxes more than a few percentage points. In fact, successive governments (both Liberal Democratic Party and Democratic Party of Japan) considered raising the consumption tax from the current level of 5 per cent to 10 per cent but found it politically difficult to do so. The large employers' federation, *keidanren*, called for an increase to the European levels of 17 per cent, mainly to keep payroll taxes for health care and pensions low. The public response both to the introduction of a 3 per cent consumption tax in 1989 and its rise to 5 per cent in 1997 was very negative, however, with the LDP faring badly in the elections that followed. The Democratic Party of Japan similarly suffered serious losses in the 2010 Upper House elections when its leader, Prime Minister Kan Naoto, proposed an increase from 5 per cent to 10 per cent. It was only through the adoption of a cross-party agreement in 2012 and the solid majority obtained by the LDP in the 2012 general election that made it possible to implement an increase from 5 per cent to 8 per cent in April 2014 with a subsequent planned rise to 10 per cent in April 2015. Nonetheless, this percentage is still lower than sales and value added tax rates in most industrialized countries.

A likely by-product of the decline in the savings rate will be a decline in or reversal of the trade surplus that Japan has enjoyed since the early 1980s. Japan had its first trade deficit in 28 years for the fiscal year ending in March 2009, but this was mainly due to the global downturn. Nevertheless, it is likely that trade deficits will become a more regular feature in the future, and the Japanese may need to draw down on the investments they have made abroad. Ageing will also have a major effect on economic growth, with the working-age population getting smaller and the older workforce not likely to be as vigorous. However, it is not necessarily the case that growth of output per capita will slow down. There are still many sectors of the economy that are less productive than their counterparts in the USA, and Japan can most likely make better use of both IT and the abilities of women in the workplace.

CONCLUSIONS

The Japanese economy has undergone major changes since the beginning of the Lost Decade, but many of its institutional features, including long-term employment relationships, relational contracting in finance and goods production have remained more or less intact. Although Japanese institutions and low productivity in the non-traded goods sector have been subject to criticism, there have been noticeable improvements. The biggest challenge facing Japan in the future may be its ageing population. Caring for the elderly, in particular, will be a major problem and Japan may need to rethink its policies on immigration if it wishes to provide for its elderly at a reasonable cost.

NOTES

1　Institutional investors in shares such as pension funds, however, can potentially have a greater influence on the governance of the firm.
2　Using these funds, the government was able to keep taxes at lower levels than would otherwise have been possible.
3　The annual wage increases are known as the 'base-up' and are separate from any increases

workers receive for good performance or for staying with their company for an additional year.

4 Adding to the problem is the intense competition in education – women feel pressured to do everything they can to help their children do well in school.

5 Many of the oldest generation of Japanese worked in firms that were not covered by the scheme in the first part of their careers.

6 Japan did, however, share in the IT revolution and the greater productivity that it produced, but not as fully as possible (Jorgenson and Nomura, 2005).

REFERENCES

Aoki, Masahiko (1988) *Information, Incentives and Bargaining in the Japanese Economy*, Cambridge: Cambridge University Press.

Aoki, Masahiko and Patrick, Hugh (eds) (1994) *The Japanese Main Bank System*, Oxford: Oxford University Press.

Blomström, Magnus, Corbett, Jennifer, Hayashi, Fumio, and Kashyap, Anil (2003) *Structural Impediments to Growth in Japan*, Chicago: University of Chicago Press.

BOJ (Bank of Japan) (2009) Financial assets held by Japanese and US households, from flow of funds (4th quarter of 2008 – Japan and US Overview), downloaded from: www.boj.or.jp/en/type/stat/boj_stat/sj/sjhi084q.pdf on 1 June 2009. (NOTE: This data is usually only available on-line for the current quarter on a temporary basis so the link is for reference only.)

Boltho, Andrea. and Corbett, Jenny (2000) The assessment: Japan's stagnation – can policy revive the economy?, *Oxford Review of Economic Policy* 16(2), 1–17.

Dore, Ronald (2007) Insider management and board reform: for whose benefit? In Aoki Masahiko, Gregory Jackson and Hikeaki Miyajima (eds), *Corporate Governance in Japan*, Oxford: Oxford University Press, 370–395.

Esping-Andersen, Gøsta (1990) *The Three Worlds of Welfare Capitalism*, Cambridge UK: Polity Press.

Flath, David (2005) *The Japanese Economy 2nd Edition*, Oxford: Oxford University Press.

Genda, Yuji (2003) Who really lost jobs in Japan? Youth employment in an ageing Japanese society. In Seiritsu Ogura, Toshiaki Tachibanaki and David Wise (eds), *Labor Markets and Firm Benefit Policies in Japan and the USA*, Chicago: University of Chicago Press, 103–133.

Goodman, Roger, White, Gordon and Kwon, Huck-ju (1998) *The East Asian Welfare Model*, London: Routledge.

Greaney, Theresa M. (2005) Measuring network effects on trade: are Japanese affiliates distinctive?, *Journal of the Japanese and International Economies* 19, 194–214.

Greaney, Theresa M. (2009), Measuring network effects on trade: a reexamination, *Japan and the World Economy*, 21(3), 219–25.

Hall, Peter A. and Soskice, David (2001) An introduction to the varieties of capitalism. In Peter A. Hall and David Soskice (eds), *Varieties of Capitalism: The Institutional Foundations of Comparative Advantage*, Oxford: Oxford University Press, 2–15.

Hata, Hiromi and Kawaguchi, Daiji (2008) The union-wage effect in Japan, *Industrial Relations*, 47(4), 569–89.

Hoshi, Takeo and Kashyap, Anil (1999) The Japanese banking crisis: Where Did it Come from and How Will it End?, *NBER/Macroeconomics Annual* (MIT Press), 1999 – special issue, 14(2), 129–201.

Hoshi, Takeo and Kashyap, Anil (2004) Japan's financial crisis and economic stagnation, *The Journal of Economic Perspectives*, 18(1), 3–26.

Ito, Takatoshi (2003) Retrospective on the bubble period and its relationship to developments in the 1990s, *The World Economy*, 26, March, 283–300.

Jackson, Gregory and Miyajima, Hideaki (2007) Introduction: the diversity and change of corporate governance in Japan. In Masahiko Aoki, Gregory Jackson and Hikeaki Miyajima (eds), *Corporate Governance in Japan*, Oxford: Oxford University Press, 1–50.

JIL (Japan Institute of Labour Policy and Training) (2009) *Handbook of International Labour Statistics 2009*, Tokyo: Japan Institute of Labour Policy and Training.

Johnson, Chalmers (1982) *MITI and the Japanese Miracle*, Stanford: Stanford University Press.

Jorgenson, Dale and Nomura, Kojo (2005) The industry origins of Japanese economic growth, *NBER Working Paper 11800*, Cambridge MA: NBER.

Koo, Richard C (2009) *The Holy Grail of Macroeconomics: Lessons from Japan's Great Recession*, Singapore: John Wiley and Sons.

Krugman, Paul (1998) It's baaack: Japan's slump and the return of the liquidity trap, *Brookings Papers on Economic Activity*, 1998: 2, 138–205.

Lawrence, Robert Z. (1993) Japan's different trade regime: an analysis with particular reference to keiretsu, *Journal of Economic Perspectives*, 7(3), 3–19.

Lincoln, Edward J. (1990) *Japan's Unequal Trade*, Washington: Brookings Press.

Lincoln, James R. and Gerlach, Michael L. (2004) *Japan's Network Economy: Structure Persistence and Change*, Cambridge: Cambridge University Press.

Minami, Ryōshin (1986) *The Economic Development of Japan: A Quantitative Study*, New York: St Martin's Press.

Miwa, Yoshiro and Ramseyer, J. Mark (2006) *The Fable of the Keiretsu*, Chicago: University of Chicago Press.

Nakatani, Iwao (1984) The role of financial corporate grouping. In Masahiko Aoki (ed) *The Economic Analysis of the Japanese Firm*, Amsterdam: North Holland Elsevier, pp. 227–58.

Porter, Michael E. and Takeuchi, Hirotaka (1999) Fixing what really ails Japan, *Foreign Affairs*, May/June 78(3), 66–82.

Posen, Adam (1998) *Restoring Japan's Economic Growth*, Washington: Institute for International Economics.

Sako, Mari (1992) *Prices, Quality and Trust: Interfirm Relations in Britain and Japan*, Cambridge: Cambridge University Press.

Sako, Mari (2006) *Shifting Boundaries of the Firm: Japanese Company*, Japanese Labour, Oxford: Oxford University Press.

Saxonhouse, Gary (1993) What does Japanese trade structure tell us about Japanese trade policy?, *Journal of Economic Perspectives*, 7(3) 21–43.

Sheard, Paul (1994) Main banks and the governance of financial distress. In Masahiko Aoki and Hugh Patrick (eds), *The Japanese Main Bank System*, pp. 188–230.

Takenaka, Heizo (2011) The Great Disaster and the Japanese economy. In Yoichi Funabashi and Heizo Takenaka (eds) *Lessons from the Great Disaster*, Tokyo: Japan Times, pp. 117–146.

Vogel, Ezra (1979) *Japan as Number One: Lessons for America*, Cambridge MA: Harvard University Press.

Weinstein, David and Broda, Christian (2005) Happy news from the dismal science: reassessing Japanese fiscal policy and sustainability. In Ito Takatoshi, Hugh T. Patrick and David E. Weinstein (eds), *Reviving Japan's Economy: Problems and Prescriptions*, Cambridge: MIT Press. 40–78.

Womack, James P., Jones, Daniel T. and Roos, Daniel (1991) *The Machine That Changed the World*, New York: Harper Perennial.

28

Japanese Business and Management

Parissa Haghirian

INTRODUCTION

This chapter sketches the history and prospects of Japan's phenomenal economic success, setting out key features that underpinned it, reflecting on the social consequences of Japan's economic transformation, and evaluating the impact of recent events.

Japan's economic success and development is a unique phenomenon. As early as the Edo period (1603–1868) Japan had a highly developed internal market and the Japanese showed great interest in the country's economic development. As a consequence, Japan was quick to embrace Western technologies and began a rapid process of industrialization after the Meiji Restoration and its opening to international trade.

The Japanese economy was completely destroyed in 1945; but the country quickly set about reconstruction, generating long boom periods and growth rates of up to 10 percent in the 1960s. A phenomenal rate of growth was interrupted by the first oil shock of the 1970s, but by then Japan was already on a par with the Western industrialized economies. The rapid economic development was supported by Japanese economic policies, its highly motivated entrepreneurs and workforce, and the application of unique Japanese management practices.

The bursting of the real-estate bubble in the late 1980s put an end to the success story. Japan fell into a recession from which it saw only very slow recovery into the late 1990s. The recession led to massive political and economic restructuring measures; only now, at the beginning of the twenty-first century, does Japan seem to have recovered from her economic crisis and to have regained her role as a major player in the global economy. But this dominant position within international business now faces new challenges in the form of competition from its Asian neighbors, particularly China and India, and the difficulties of adapting to globalization. And in March 2011 a major earthquake and tsunami hit the north of Japan, leading to a critical incident at the nuclear plant in Fukushima which is expected to have a long-lasting effect on Japanese economic development.

INITIAL ECONOMIC DEVELOPMENT DURING THE TOKUGAWA PERIOD

Japan was a closed country (*sakoku*) until 1853. This was originally initiated by the third Tokugawa shogun, Iemitsu, who closed the islands to foreign commerce and expelled the missionaries in 1635. While the seclusion created internal peace and stability, Japan fell behind in technological development and remained a medieval state for the next two hundred years.

However, during this period – the Edo or Tokugawa period – Japan developed a highly functional and professionalized internal market: a wide variety of products and regional specialties became available throughout the country (Shimbo and Hasegawa, 1999: 185–86), and the foundations of an 'economy-minded society' were laid (Hayami, 1999) which can still be observed today. Japan had its own currency and a very efficient distribution system; and, in particular, a strong interest in technology and mechanical objects could be observed among the Tokugawa Japanese (Morris-Suzuki, 1994).

Many successful business empires were established in this period, and merchant families such as the Mitsui, Kōnoike, and Sumitomo – who 'began as samurai houses whose head changed to merchant status after the extinction of the feudal lords' (Jansen, 2000: 120) – managed to establish enormous wealth by developing new business practices (such as fixed prices or customer orientation) and marketing activities (such as printing the company name and address on umbrellas) (Linhart, 1983). Drawing on their samurai background, these companies developed strong and reliable administrations and grew into dominant merchant houses, which were accompanied by a variety of smaller businesses (Jansen, 2000). But it was not only on a managerial level that Tokugawa Japanese showed expertise: Japan manifested a variety of attributes which supported economic growth; in many rural areas farmers were already accustomed to working in a monetized economy, and goods were traded in both rural and urban areas all through Japan (Beasley, 1995: 103).

Japan's Rapid Industrialization after the Meiji Restoration

The turning point in Japanese history came in 1853 when Commodore Perry sailed to Japan with his squadron of warships and forced the country to open up its ports to the West (Reischauer and Jansen, 2005). This triggered a momentous chain of events. The shogunate fell and the Imperial Restoration in 1868 ended Japan's seclusion. The new possibilities engendered by openness gave a strong impetus to the Japanese economy. Industrial development became the overriding goal of the new Meiji government, which set out to transform Japan from a medieval empire into an industrialized state, able to match the West and deal with it on equal terms. The slogan of the new government was *fukoku kyōhei* ('Enrich the country, strengthen the military') (Linhart, 1983), and the production of weapons became a major industry. By 1885 the Meiji government was making strong efforts to create Western-style industries in Japan, a development which was supported by the fact that many traditional Japanese industries had already developed techniques ill suited to mass production (Wittner, 2007) which could be easily replaced or renewed. Not every entrepreneur in Japan, however, was excited about this venture into industry; to mitigate concerns about risk, therefore, the Japanese government founded a number of enterprises in strategically important industrial sectors such as cement, glass, sugar, beer, textiles, and heavy industry (Linhart, 1983). Two ministries were founded to facilitate the absorption of modern Western technology: the Ministry of Public Works (1870) and the Ministry of Home Affairs (1873) (Wittner, 2007).

It was in this period that the foundations of today's economic structures were laid. These were dominated by two very different types of organization: on the one hand very small, family-owned businesses; on the other large corporations. The most famous examples of the latter are the *zaibatsu*, the big conglomerates, which originated from wealthy merchant houses (such as Mitsui) or were founded by ex-samurai (such as Mitsubishi). All had strong ties with the Meiji government. Their business operations were wide ranging, including fields such as banking, heavy industry, logistics, and trade; and numerous sub-businesses were founded throughout their concerns, conferring great wealth on the owner families (Beasley, 1995). The Meiji leaders took the German *Konzern* (corporate group or conglomerate) as the model for these new corporations, and at the end of the nineteenth century four large *zaibatsu* dominated the Japanese economy: Mitsui, Mitsubishi, Yasuda, and Sumitomo. The families owning them exercised their power through a centralized holding firm which they alone controlled (Lonien, 2003).

Exports from Japan began early after the Meiji Restoration. During the Meiji (1868–1912) and Taisho (1912–26) periods economic development was based on production and export of goods in the primary and light industries, mainly textiles (Okazaki and Okuno-Fujiwara, 1999). For many years silk was the main export: 31 percent of the world's raw silk production came from Japan in the first decade of the twentieth century (Linhart, 1983). Cheap labor was the major reason why Japan was able to increase its exports so rapidly and industrialize at such a fast pace: labor costs at that time were cheaper than in India and only a tenth of the UK's. It was mainly women who worked in the newly founded factories, often under unbearable conditions. Japan's rapid industrialization was based on the exploitation of female labor (Linhart, 1983).

Private entrepreneurs soon started to play a more dominant role in Japan's economy. One example is trade with foreign countries, which in 1885 was strongly controlled by foreign merchants, mostly because Japanese merchants lacked the connections and experience needed for dealing with the outside world. However, the dominance of foreign merchants quickly decreased. For example, 90 percent of the silk trade was in foreign hands in 1887, but only 60 percent in 1900 (Beasley, 1995).

THE TWENTIETH CENTURY

During the Meiji era local and central governments played the dominant role in connecting Japanese businesses and the outside world. At the beginning of the twentieth century, however, Japanese corporations began forging stronger connections with the international technological community and became importers of industrial expertise. This led to the so-called 'second industrial revolution' in which the diffusion of electrical power and techniques of mass production supported the inflow of Western technology and led to a demand for specialists and engineers. Japanese companies started to set up their own research laboratories, and Japanese experts focused on adapting Western technology to local Japanese needs. In so doing Japan took a very different path from the other Asian economies of that time, which, generally, remained mere subsidiaries of Western firms and did not develop their own technological foundations (Morris-Suzuki, 1994) nor strengthen their ability to develop future technologies themselves. This development went hand in hand with a decline of the agricultural sector, which showed lower productivity and lower wages than the industrial sector. This trend increased over the following years (Lonien, 2003).

The build-up of heavy industries began during the economic boom of World War I and continued (with a pause during the Depression) until World War II. During this period heavy and chemical industries gained in importance, surging from 16.2 to 58.5 percent of all manufacturing. At the same time textile production fell from 36.3 to 16.8 percent (Okazaki and Okuno-Fujiwara, 1999). The *zaibatsu* ensured sustained growth by supplying military equipment in World War I. During the interwar period they focused their investments on securing raw materials from abroad for Japanese industries. In Japan they grew increasingly important in the areas of distribution and logistics (Lonien, 2003).

The invasion of other Asian nations during World War II was strongly driven by the need to supply raw materials for the ongoing industrialization of Japan. Japan invested heavily in mainland China during its occupation, often expropriating Chinese firms, and increasing the production of iron and coal (Beasley, 1995). In other occupied areas in Southeast Asia Japan secured vital resources such as oil, rubber, bauxite, and wood, while in Japan the war economists controlled most industries (Zoellner, 2006).

Post-war Development

Japan's economic resurrection did not start directly after World War II; after the defeat and destruction of 1945 the Japanese faced several years of extreme hardship and poverty under Allied Occupation. The post-war years were marked by material shortages and spiraling inflation which lasted for over four years. The government tried to curb inflation by issuing a 'new yen', imposing wage and price controls, and promoting strategic industries, but these attempts were unsuccessful in encouraging business to invest in the new economy. Meanwhile, legal market wholesale prices increased by 539 percent in the first year of occupation, and inflation could also be observed in the black market (Dower, 2000).

The Allied forces strongly influenced the economic development of Japan. They forced the country to demilitarize and made changes in the constitution and the educational system, including giving women the right to vote (Linhart, 1983). They dismantled the *zaibatsu*s, aiming to dissolve the industrial and financial forces which had supported the war. Families owning the zaibatsu were forced to give up their honorary titles and executive functions. The overall aim was divestiture of these family holdings, allowing the *zaibatsu* companies to acquire greater independence from their original owners (Lonien, 2003). The American occupation also gave many Japanese firms their first access to new technology, and new techniques became incorporated into the slowly recovering industries (Morris-Suzuki, 1994).

At the end of the Allied occupation in 1952 Japan still ranked as a less developed country. The Korean War was the first impetus towards real recovery due to the fact that the American forces received supplies from Japan and used the country as a base from which to fight the North Korean army. Japanese companies started to increase production, and found they had a young and highly motivated workforce to support them (Saito, 2000), a trend which was accompanied by the structural development of Japanese industry. Even before World War II Japan had possessed very impressive light-industry plants, with textiles and food production being the most important industries. The development of the heavy industries, such as machinery manufacturing and the chemical industry, which had started before World War II, was followed by a diversification in the industrial sector. Shipbuilding, iron and steel, synthetic textiles, domestic appliances, cars, and semiconductors became major export industries (Okazaki and Okuna-Fujiwara, 1999). The US occupation forces had to adjust their strategies to the changes in the political situation in Japan. The victory of Mao's communists in China in 1949 and the end of the Korean war led to a reconstruction of the *zaibatsu* in a slightly different style: Japan was to become a buffer zone between US capitalism and communism. The Ministry of International Trade and Industry (MITI) became responsible for organizing Japan's industrial policy and supporting the reconstruction of the former *zaibatsu* in a modified way (Lonien, 2003). The new vertical conglomerates, called *keiretsu*, focusing on large manufacturing industries, mainly on auto or electronic giants, were divided into the traditional-style *keiretsu* (the large conglomerates; for example, Mitsui and Mitsubishi), which display horizontal structures and are organized around a major industrial firm and its buyers and suppliers, and the new vertical *keiretsu*, which focus on a manufacturing firm and its key suppliers (McGuire and Dow, 2009), such as the auto or electronic giants (e.g. Honda and Matsushita).

By 1960 the Japanese economy had recovered from wartime destruction and was expanding very rapidly. Between 1955 and 1960, for instance, steel production more than doubled from 9.4 million to 22.1 million tons – 6.5 percent of the total world production – and this trend could be observed in other industrial fields. The rapid growth was also reflected in the Japanese labor market. Employment grew steadily, particularly in large-scale enterprises, and graduates were recruited in high numbers (Ohtsu, 2002).

The Boom Years

From 1953 until 1973 the Japanese economy grew at an annual growth rate of 8 to 10 percent (Nakamura, 1995), making it the first less developed country in the post-war period to graduate to developed-nation status. During the 1950s the major industries were textiles and light industries; during the 1960s the iron and steel industry and the shipbuilding industry were most dominant; in the 1970s the automotive industry rose to prominence (Linhart, 1983).

Since then production and manufacturing management have become the backbone and the major strength of Japanese corporations. In particular, Japanese automotive corporations developed very specific and efficient methods to produce cars, which later made them leaders in their field (Haghirian, 2010a). Most notable is Toyota, whose CEO Eiji Toyoda visited the USA in the 1950 to investigate their car factories. Instead of being surprised by technological improvement he and his colleagues were surprised that many production methods had not changed since the 1930s, and he returned to Japan with the intention to improve production processes. Based on their experiences in the USA, and following the teachings of W. Edwards Deming, an American quality pioneer, Toyoda and his colleagues developed the famous Toyota Production System (TPS) (Liker, 2004), which in subsequent decades became the leading production technology and is still the most influential Japanese management technique today. TPS became a role model for Western car makers – in fact, for manufacturers of all kinds of products – in terms of safety, quality, and cost effectiveness, and made Toyota one of the most successful Japanese corporations. Japanese production management incorporated the just-in-time (JIT) style of production management, in which all parts used during the production process are delivered exactly at the right time and in their proper amounts. Just-in-time management reduces waste and costs, and uses methods such as *kanban* (small cards which help the coordination of manufacturing parts) and *heijunka* (continuous control of quality during the production process as well as after the product is manufactured). The system called *Jidōka* blocks defective products from penetrating the production line. In Japanese, *jidōka* literally means 'automated'. This refers to the automated procedures of Japanese manufacturing companies and what is expected from their workers and assembly lines. The system is operated through thorough inspections conducted by workers and by a device that immediately halts the entire production system when defective products are spotted (Haghirian, 2010a). Japanese production management is based on the philosophy of *kaizen*, which refers to continuous improvement of all management and manufacturing processes with the overall goal of improving quality and customer value (Imai, 1997). These concepts allowed Japanese manufacturers to take the lead in quality and in cost, and supported the development of the Japanese economy.

Another well known Japanese management technique is the 5S system, by which production processes are structured into five stages: *seiri* (sort), *seiton* (set in order), *seiso* (clean), *seiketsu* (systematize), and *shitsuke* (standardize). In the first step, *seiri* (sort), materials and parts used in the production process are sorted and the parts not used are stored at another place; after this the parts are organized and placed in the correct order (*seiton*). All parts of the production process are kept clean and tidy (*seiso*), and the processes become a regular part of the workplace system in order to guarantee consistency and reliability in quality and results (*seiketsu*). In the fifth stage, *shitsuke*, the processes are communicated to all employees in order to support *kaizen* goals (Imai, 1997). Such practices underpin the quality and efficiency goals of Japanese manufacturers, and led to the prominence of Japan's products in world markets.

Another reason why Japan became dominant in consumer-goods production was the acquisition of foreign technology on favorable terms. Japanese companies were not initially perceived as a threat by Western firms and were able to buy licenses without restrictive conditions, drawing on the large pool of Western inventions. Even in the late 1960s many production licenses still came with no restrictions attached, allowing the export of high-tech products to the expanding East and Southeast Asian markets (Morris-Suzuki, 1994).

Other factors that influcnced the high growth rates of Japan after the war were to be found in the strong relationship between government and industry. The government promoted long-term investment in future industries and technologies while keeping expenditures on defense relatively low. More resources were put into developing industry than into the military. Economic change and development was strongly supported by the Japanese government: the MITI granted subsidies and protection to domestic corporations over foreign competitors, with the overall goal of effective permanent structural reform, abandoning industries which were not promising and supporting those which were (Lonien, 2003).The term 'Japan, Inc.' came into currency to describe the Japanese industrial system and the interaction between government and business (Abbeglen, 2002); this phrase is still in use today. The policies of Japan Inc. were highly beneficial for the automotive and electronics industries but led to disaster in the agricultural and construction sectors. These were heavily subsidized for many years (Lonien, 2003) but remain internationally uncompetitive even today.

The Japanese mentality and attitude towards work was also an important factor in the rapid development. The Japanese fascination with modern technology, and their traditional openness towards ideas from the West, led them to accept Western products and behavior relatively faster than other developing countries. The positive attitude that the Japanese public shows towards work is also said to have hastened the country's economic development.

As a result of increased production and exports during the 1960s, Japan's position in the global economy changed. By 1968 Japan ranked third after the USA and the Soviet Union in Gross National Product. From that time onward Japan also changed from a debtor to a creditor nation, a situation which strengthened its position as a foreign investor. Japan's foreign investments rose from a gross value of $1 billion in 1965 to $3.6 billion in 1970 (Nakamura, 1995).

This, then, was a period in which Japan developed distinctive management practices, and these, along with the strong cooperation between government and industry, low military expenditures, and intense interest in technology and innovation, led to unprecedented success for the Japanese economy. At the heights of its economic triumph Japanese management styles became a role model and began to influence Western business practices.

SOCIAL CHANGES

Successful industrialization also led to major changes in Japanese society. Due to the growing demand by corporations for a talented work force there was an increase in the number of Japanese working in the manufacturing and tertiary (service) sectors (Nakamura, 1995). This was accompanied by strong urbanization, which made Tokyo and Osaka the most populated areas in Japan (Reischauer and Jansen, 2005). This growing number of white-collar workers, or of the 'salaryman', (Takeda, 2002), became emblematic of the Japanese economy from then on.

During the boom years the Japanese started to become ardent consumers. With increasing incomes they were not only able to maintain high savings rates but to buy the goods being produced in Japan and, before long, goods from overseas. The purchasing power of Japanese consumers became increasingly important for Japanese economic stability (Haghirian, 2011). At the same time changes in the Japanese family structure became visible, not least the increase in nuclear families residing in Japan's big cities and a strong trend towards 'housewifization' (Debroux, 2010: 54). Japanese women, who enjoyed equal rights with men during WWII, became victims of a business system which segregated economic and social roles, making women focus on unpaid at-home labor and leaving them without social protection (Debroux, 2010). This trend was further supported by manufacturers of Japanese consumer goods, who emphasized the image of the happy housewife surrounded by an array of electronic kitchen helpers (Partner 1999: 152). In the 1960s consumption became a widespread phenomenon: *mai kā* (my car) and *mai homū* (my home) became synonyms for wealth and success (Haghirian, 2011). The boom years were accompanied by other events which made Japan more visible internationally. It hosted the Olympic Games in 1964 and the Osaka International Exhibition in 1970 (Reischauer and Jansen, 2005).

THE JAPANESE CORPORATION AND ITS MANAGEMENT PRACTICES

Japan is – at present – the only Asian economy which has managed to transform itself from a developing country into a post-industrialized nation, but there are major structural differences between the Japanese economy and other industrialized economies. Japanese business practices have been strongly influenced by Japan's centuries-long seclusion, and Japanese organizations continue to reflect these cultural particularities today.

One relic of the Meiji era is still visible today: this is, as mentioned above, the 'dual structure' of the Japanese economy, the division into big multinational corporations and small (mostly family-owned) businesses. Certain specific company structures are also characteristic of the way Japan's economy has developed: the economic landscape remains dominated by the *keiretsu*, in which financial firms, the trading company, and the key manufacturers are the main players. Japanese business is also characterized by networks of mutual stakeholding, or 'cross-shareholding': the cross-ownership of shares among groups of interrelated companies, their main creditor bank, their customers, and their suppliers in order to insulate themselves from market pressures and to strengthen ties between the members of the *keiretsu*. The bank is usually the largest lender, but also has important shareholders from other companies in the group, meaning debt-holders are often shareholders at the same time (Ozkan, 2011).

During Japan's high-growth period the rights of investors – stockholders in particular – were severely restricted; the power of stockholders was curtailed through cross-shareholding. On top of this relationships with shareholders are friendly (Kono and Clegg, 2001); the focus of these relationships lies on maintaining stability and securing the future of the *keiretsu*, but not so much on increasing the profit of the shareholders.

Another Japanese particularity is its trade unions, which have traditionally played a different role in Japanese firms than their counterparts in the West. In a Japanese firm the unions are dominant: every big company usually has their own union. Until now these unions were in charge of negotiating the annual wage increases with the firm but did not have much power. Additionally, only full-time employees were able to join their company's union. In recent years they have adopted a more Western role and increasingly support members who are facing part-time-job issues and violation of contracts (Haghirian, 2010a).

CULTURAL INFLUENCES ON JAPANESE MANAGEMENT PRACTICES

Interpersonal relationships in Japan – as well as in Asia more generally – are strongly influenced by a collectivist orientation (Schuette and Ciarlante, 1998) and play a dominant role in all business and economic relationships. Belonging to a group is very important for Japanese, and carries with it a plethora of duties. Great importance is placed on interpersonal harmony, social interaction, and relationships. This endeavor for harmony ties individuals to norms and rules and discourages them from

'sticking out'. As a consequence there is a high degree of self-restraint and reluctance to express disagreement with majority opinions (Schuette and Ciarlante, 1998). At the same time Japanese organizations grant strong support, security, and stability. However, the strong group orientation does not allow decisions to be made on an individual basis (Dunung, 1998); many parties are involved in decision-making and there is a sincere pursuit of majority acceptance of future projects (Chen, 2004). Management practices reflect this. Two major features of Japanese management are *nemawashi*, or unofficial negotiations, and the *ringi* system, a group-decision-making process. *Nemawashi* refers to communication between negotiators in a relaxed environment before an official meeting takes place. This allows participants to present their ideas and circulate them; in this way problems can be solved in advance of the final meeting, and harmony and understanding is secured. *Nemawashi* is the reason why Japanese meetings often only have an information-exchange function and simply finalize the results of the *nemawashi* process. The strong group orientation and discussion processes are often seen as a major reason why Japanese companies find it so difficult to take radical decisions and reinvent themselves. On the one hand Japanese firms have a tendency towards 'me too' behavior, applying strategies which their competitors (mostly Japanese) apply as well; on the other they are often paralyzed by long, risk-avoiding discussions and decision-making processes (Kono and Clegg, 2001), leading to slow reactions and lost business opportunities.

Japanese management has become famous for its particular way of managing knowledge and information. Japanese knowledge management strongly focuses on tacit knowledge or knowledge which is located in people and not documented in reports or data (Nonaka and Takeuchi, 1995). Lifetime employment supports this practice. Japanese companies do not have to be afraid of their employees leaving their companies and can therefore allow them to gain a high degree of company-related know-how. In many Japanese firms knowledge is therefore communicated from person to person and on-the-job training is preferred. This free flow of knowledge supports Japanese advances in new product development (Haghirian, 2011).

LIFETIME EMPLOYMENT

The roles of Japanese individuals in everyday life are well defined (Samiee and Mayo, 1990) and most interactions are based on vertical or superior–subordinate relationships. All individuals are ranked within their respective organizations. The higher the rank/status of their employer the higher they are perceived in society's hierarchy (De Mente, 1994). Japanese will usually respect those with a higher rank, and interactions between members of different ranks follow clear guidelines. Generally, customers hold all the power (Schuette and Ciarlante, 1998), which explains the strong focus of Japanese companies on meeting customer expectations. The vertical relationships within the firm guarantee stability and job safety. This is most obvious in the most notable differences from Western management practices: lifetime employment and seniority-based pay and promotion. Lifetime employment refers to the preference of Japanese corporations for hiring their employees after their graduation from university and retaining them in the company for most of their careers. Long-term fixed employment was already an integral part of Japanese human-resource management in the 1920s to avoid losing skilled workers in the Depression (Ozakaki and Okuna-Fujiwara, 1999). Lifetime employment is not a legal requirement for Japanese companies, but a post-World War II custom. The strict Japanese labor laws, which make it very difficult to lay off personnel, supported the establishment of this system (Haghirian, 2010a). Lifetime employment is strongly associated with the large Japanese firm, mostly because of the extensive company-based welfare system (Graham, 2009a).

Lifetime employment offers great advantages for the economic development of Japanese corporations. Corporations can invest in the training of their employees and support them in building up know-how over a long period of time, and lifetime employment is thought to improve employee motivation and loyalty. It also helps the company deal with fluctuations in product demand. Western companies tend to lay off workers when demand for their products goes down and have a higher turnover of employees as a result. Japanese companies, on the other hand, first run down stocks, reduce work hours, and lay off part-timers before cutting back the employment of their regular workers (Ozakaki and Okuna-Fujiwara, 1999). This is seen as a successful way to retain skilled workers until demand recovers.

Traditional Japanese corporations were strongly hierarchical systems in which career opportunities depended on length of stay in the firm. This provided a stable and reliable system for employees but could decrease motivation for ambitious workers. All relationships within the Japanese firm are based on the seniority principle.

Every team member is interwoven in a web of relationships in which older members have more power, higher status and a higher salary than younger ones. Older members are called *senpai* and younger *kōhai*. *Senpai* have to take the responsibility to train

and integrate younger members into the company, on the other hand *kōhai* are supposed to show an obedient behaviour and support their superiors while learning the job from the scratch. The seniority principle which is a major pillar of Japanese society can be still observed in Japan corporations. Even if an increasing number of Japanese companies are considering more achievement based measure for promotions and salary rises, seniority still plays a major part in how businesses in Japan are organized. The *senpai-kōhai* relationships still dominate the way people are trained in firms and influence all relationships in the *kaisha*. To achieve cost reduction, Japanese companies prefer achieving operational efficiencies such as product redesign, mass customization. (Sakano and Lewin, 1999)

WORKPLACE EQUALITY

From the 1950s the Japanese labor market was strongly divided: men were employed in paid jobs outside the house, whereas women worked unpaid in family enterprises or households. This situation started to change in the 1970s: female labor-force participation rates as well as their hourly wage has increased since then. The labor-participation rate was 52.9 percent in 1970 and rose to 59.9 percent in 2003. At the same time the percentage of women doing part-time work almost tripled to 39.7 percent (Rebick, 2005).

In 1986 the Equal Employment Opportunity Law (EEOL) came into effect, which encourages employers to provide equal opportunities for women in the workplace. It was not very effective because it did not stipulate penalties for violations of the law. After its enactment many companies began to introduce two different employment tracks to promote the careers of women with university degrees (Ohtsu, 2002): *ippanshoku*, or administrative track, and *sōgōshoku*, or managerial track (Haghirian, 2010a). The *sōgōshoku* track was supposed to treat men and women the same in the company and provide them with similar chances to both of them; but the reality in the Japanese firm looks different. Today the *ippanshoku* track is mainly reserved for women and the managerial track for men. Once in the *ippanshoku* track a woman cannot become a manager and is supposed to stay in a supportive role. Men in the managerial track, however, are allowed to climb up the organizational hierarchy and build successful careers.

Today the situation of Japanese women cannot be compared to the situation they faced in the postwar period; it is true that many labor choices which are open to women today did not exist before (Rebick, 2005). Despite this, in 1997 60 percent of Japanese women said they had witnessed sexual harassment in their workplace (Rebick, 2005) and in 2010 Japan still only ranks at 94 in the Global Gender Gap Index (Hausmann et al., 2010), and the situation is not very likely to improve. As well as discrimination there are a number of other issues which make careers difficult for Japanese women. There is still a wage gap between male and female employees, and long working hours are incompatible with family life. Japanese policy makers still promote the idea of a family (consisting of a married heterosexual couple and children) and have adapted neither family laws nor tax laws to the changes in Japanese society (Persson, 2010). The Japanese tax system, for instance, hinders women's careers because it provides tax exemptions for married women who are earning less than 1, 300, 000 yen per year (Haghirian, 2009b).

FIRST DRAWBACKS IN ECONOMIC DEVELOPMENT

Despite the success of its post-war economic rebound, Japan has suffered from events that affected its economy. In 1974 GNP decreased 1.4 percent for the first time since 1950 because of the oil crisis, and growth slowed from 10 to 3.6 percent between 1974 and 1979. Despite a weak economy from 1981 until 1983, a strong US dollar led to an increase in exports after 1983. By 1985 the surplus in Japan's balance of payments account reached 3.7 percent of GNP (Gakken, 2002). Japan's economic turnaround was complete. It had emerged as an economic powerhouse.

This was the time when Western managers and researchers developed a deeper interest in the Japanese economy and traditional Japanese management styles (Van Wolferen, 1989; Jackson, 1993; Abegglen and Stalk, 1996). Japanese management was portrayed as the superior and more people-oriented approach, an attitude supported by the strong internationalization activities of Japanese firms at the time, mainly via acquisitions of Western firms, which led to worldwide media coverage. The *nihonjinron* (theory about the Japanese) literature also dealt with the Japanese economic miracle, presenting Japanese management practices in an idealistic way, an approach which was very well received in Japan (Graham, 2009b).

BUBBLE ECONOMY

Japan's export-led economic growth first experienced difficulties after the G5 Plaza Agreement of 1985 and the rapid appreciation of the yen. Interest rates were lowered in order to increase domestic demand, and the expanded supply of domestic

capital resulted in an increase of investment in land and stocks. At the same time land values increased and finance companies increased the number of loans with real estate as security. Capital secured by such loans was used to purchase more real estate, which later became 'bad debts'. In these years Japanese companies borrowed massively from Japanese banks (which obtained their funds from the high levels of household saving). Ongoing inflation allowed them to pay their loans back without problems until 1990 when the bubble burst. Real estate purchased at high bubble prices was no longer able to pay for itself, putting pressure on the businesses that owned it. Consumers also reacted to these changes and personal consumption decreased. Many banks left with bad loans went bankrupt or were supported by government (Kobayashi, 2006).

THE 'LOST DECADE'

The 1990s – the years after the bubble burst – are known as the 'lost decade'. The recession and the lost decade significantly damaged Japan's image as an economic powerhouse. It added a layer of scepticism to the already existing difficulties of Japanese corporations in coping with globalization, not least the increasing challenge that China presented for the Japanese economy (Haghirian et al., 2008). There were difficulties in disposing of bad debts, for which interest payments were late or which were not recoverable because of bankruptcy. This inevitably forced the Japanese economy into low growth for more than a decade until 2000 (Gakken, 2002). In the 1990s Japanese firms suffered financial losses and were in need of major restructuring measures (Kono and Clegg, 2001). The year 1998 was marked by a banking crisis, which not only led to a credit crunch for firms but became a tipping point when a 'combination of economic and social crisis, global competition, and the ineffectiveness of government policies' (Schaede, 2008: 21) revealed that major changes were needed. This was the trigger for major changes within Japanese organizations (Schaede, 2008).

The reasons for this situation were manifold. Japanese companies mostly focused too much on growth and often did not base their expansion plans on thorough analysis but on the wish to copy their rivals' behavior. Japanese companies are also said to have compounded their errors rather than take corrective actions (Kono and Clegg, 2001).

CONSEQUENCES OF THE RECESSION

As a result of the recession Japan's traditional retail system was challenged. Unsettled by the economic events, Japanese consumers – traditionally equating price and quality and sticking to high-price Japanese brands which occupied up to 90 percent of department stores' retail space – developed more cost-conscious purchase-decision patterns and welcomed changes in the distribution environment, such as discount stores and hypermarkets (Fields et al., 2000). After 1995 a number of Western retailers entered the Japanese market and presented new distribution systems, such as convenience stores, discount outlets, and mail order.

Despite the gloom that overshadowed the 1990s, Japan's internationalization also received a new boost during that time. Japanese manufacturers realized that they could not compete with China's cheap production processes, and this led to the internationalization of a large number of Japanese companies, which had previously focused on the Japanese market and not yet exported their manufacturing processes. Today Japan is the most influential foreign investor in China.

Recognizing a need for improvement, the Japanese government promoted foreign investment in Japan and inaugurated the 'Invest Japan' campaign by establishing offices at each ministry, agency, and institutions concerned with international business to provide necessary information for potential foreign investors (FPC, 2004). Prime Minister Junichiro Koizumi unequivocally welcomed foreign direct investment as a way to revive the country's economy. Investors in Japan reported that the business environment was becoming less regulated and more open to foreigners with new products and different ways of doing business (ACCJ, 2004). Accordingly, foreign direct investment in Japan increased dramatically between 1997 and 2000. The main factors behind this pattern include a large increase in international mergers and acquisitions and the growing number of Japanese companies, especially in the automobile, telecommunications and financial industries, actively seeking foreign investment (Kondansha, 2003).

CHALLENGES FOR THE JAPANESE FIRM AFTER THE RECESSION

Only in 2003 did the Japanese economy start to show subtle signs of recovery. Parts of the economic recovery are based on the weak value of the yen, which boosted export sales, parts on the long-expected effects of structural reforms started in the 1990s. Not all Japanese companies, however, could manage the change and keep their leading position in international markets. But even if there are a number of new 'stars' and very successful multinational corporations, the majority of Japanese companies are still small-and medium-sized corporations, of which

many are not very professionally managed. While the total number of new entrepreneurs is decreasing, these small-and medium-sized enterprises declined by about 6 percent each year during the years 2004 to 2006 (Ministry of Economy, Trade and Industry, 2007).

Leading firms have used the strong structural changes and increasing pressure and implemented major changes in their business strategies. They have adjusted to the increasingly competitive and globalized environment by repositioning and divesting. New players in the market are not only the Japanese government with its restrictive role, but consumers, entrepreneurs, and employees (Schaede, 2008).

At the same time the country is increasingly worrying about a labor shortage in the future. Even if the ideal of 'the one-earner family' is still strongly promoted by the Japanese media, the reality looks different. The fertility rate is decreasing dramatically; Japan has the oldest population in the world. Industries which need a lot of physical labor, such as the medical field, will need foreign workers to survive. Despite this, restrictive immigration laws bar foreign labourers from entering Japan and stringent qualification requirements keep skilled foreign professionals away. In 2009 the number of registered foreigners fell for the first time since annual records were kept, shrinking 1.4 percent from the year before (Tabuchi, 2011). During 2010 Japanese firms struggled with the strength of the yen against the US dollar. and the overseas production ratio of Japanese manufacturers is higher than 30 percent (Sanchanta, 2010). The lifetime employment model, however, is still in place in many Japanese companies. The reason for this is the very strict Japanese labor laws, which make it very difficult for a company to make employees redundant (Haghirian, 2010a). Lifetime employment still remains the Japanese 'ideal' (Graham, 2009a), providing financial security and a long-term career. Having a full-time job means lifetime employment; companies who look for outstanding talent have to offer recruits this. Yet the number of part-time workers has increased dramatically. In 2008 65.4 percent of the Japanese workforce were said to be fully employed and 15.7 were working part-time, a trend which is watched with worry by Japanese media and society (Keizer, 2010). In addition, since 2000 an increasing number of Japanese employees have been changing jobs. Reasons for this development include more flexibility in the labor market, increased pressure to perform and the stronger individualisation of Japanese employees. The seniority principle is also experiencing changes: many companies are currently experimenting with new compensation practices and performance-related-pay components are becoming increasingly popular. However, these changes are mostly observed on the managerial level and less among non-managerial workers (Conrad, 2009).

All of these developments influence the consumer market in Japan, which is expected soon to resemble consumer markets in other industrialized countries and to show a greater distinction between luxury-oriented consumers and consumers who are more sensitive to price and choose cheaper products (Haghirian, 2010b).

THE EFFECTS OF THE CATASTROPHE OF MARCH 2011

At the beginning of 2011 the social and corporate climate was dominated by pessimism. The reasons for this are manifold. Even though a high number of baby boomers have retired since 2007, many decision makers in Japanese companies are older male employees, who have little experience in modern leadership. These leaders tend to avoid risk; responsibilities are shared with other members of the group, team or corporation. The discussion on Japanese leadership also included criticism of Japanese politics, particular of then prime minister Kan.

Amid the discussion on the lack of leadership, government, and the recurring weaknesses of the Japanese firm, the east of Japan was hit by a massive earthquake and a tsunami of up to 10 meters on 11 March 2011. This event also hit the nuclear-power plant in Fukushima, which was so strongly affected that the population within a radius of 40km had to be evacuated. The catastrophe, which led to a strong discussion about the processes within the company Tepco, which built and maintained the power plant in Fukushima, included managerial implications. Tepco very badly managed and did not show the transparency and open communication processes which would have been expected, and its lack of leadership and obvious helplessness led to highly critical reactions among the Japanese public.

The catastrophe and the danger of the Fukushima power plant will have a long-lasting negative impact on the Japanese economy. The series of disasters – earthquake, tsunami, nuclear alert, and power shortages – has had a major effect on Japanese manufacturers, which are famous for their low-inventory and just-in-time approaches (*The Economist*, 2011). Other negative effects could be seen in the tourism industry and the agricultural sector.

At the time of writing the consequences can only be anticipated. Scenarios run from a recurring recession which, will hurt the Japanese economy even further, to a new impetus for the Japanese economy, massive investment from overseas, and the retransfer of Japanese financial assets from overseas back to Japan. The events of March 2011 will also have a long-lasting effect on Japan's energy policy. On top of this, traditional management practices are under stress, but so far many corporations have not managed to develop or update them, a challenge which will remain.

In December 2012 Shinzō Abe assumed office as the Japanese prime minister. He advocates a new economic policy, which the media has named Abenomics. His main focus has been increased public spending and devaluation of the yen. The Japanese public responded very positively to the political change. The yen's value had declined by more than 30 percent at the end of 2013, which gave a boost to Japanese exporting businesses. Japanese companies have also started to increase their internationalization processes and focus more on training and developing their human resources. Overall, Abenomics has created a more positive attitude among Japanese businesses; however, the long-term effects of the new economic policies remain to be seen.

REFERENCES

Abbeglen, J.C. (2002). Japan, Inc. In A. Bird (Ed.) *Encyclopedia of Japanese Business and Management*, p. 474. London: Routledge.

Abbeglen, J. C. and Stalk, G. J. (1996). *Kaisha, the Japanese Corporation*. Tokyo: Charles E. Tuttle Company.

ACCJ. (2004). *The Long Road to Reform*. Retrieved November 15, 2004 from www.accj.or.jp/tmp/longroadE.pdf

Beasley, W.G. (1995). *The Rise of Modern Japan. Political, Economic and Social Change since 1850*. New York: St. Martin's Press (Revised Edition).

Chen, M. (2004). *Asian Management Systems*. London: Thompson.

Conrad, H. (2009). From Seniority to Performance Principle: The Evolution of Pay Practices in Japanese Firms since the 1990s. *Social Science Japan Journal* 13, 115–135.

Debroux, P. (2010). *Female Entrepreneurship in East and South-East Asia: Opportunities and Challenges*. Oxford: Chandos Publishing.

De Mente, B. (1994). *Japanese Etiquette and Ethics in Business*. Chicago: NTC Business Books.

Dower, J. W. (2000). *Embracing Defeat; Japan in the Wake of World War II*. New York: W.W. Norton and Company.

Dunung, S. P. (1998). *Doing Business in Asia: The Complete Guide*. San Francisco: Jossey-Bass.

The Economist. (2011). Japan and the global supply chain: Broken links http://www.economist.com/node/1848601531 March. Accessed July 28, 2014.

Fields, G., Katahira, H. and Wind, J. (2000). *Leveraging Japan: Marketing for the New Asia*. San Francisco: Jossey-Bass.

FPC. (2004). *Fact and Figures of Japan 2004*. Retrieved 25 October 2004 from www.fpcj.jp/e

Gakken. (2002). *Japan as It Is*. Tokyo: Gakken.

Graham, F. (2009a). *Inside the Japanese Company*. New Delhi: Cambridge University Press.

Graham, F. (2009b). *A Japanese Company in Crisis*. New Delhi: Cambridge University Press.

Haghirian, P. (2009a). *J-Management; Fresh Perspectives on the Japanese Firm in the 21st Century*. Bloomington: iUniverse Star.

Haghirian, P. (2009b). Japanese women in international management. *Japan Spotlight* (September–October).

Haghirian, P. (2010a). *Understanding Japanese Management Practices*. New York: Business Expert Press.

Haghirian, P. (2010b). Historical development of Japanese consumerism. In P. Haghirian (Ed.) *Japanese Consumer Dynamics*, pp. 3–17. London: Palgrave.

Haghirian, P. (2011). *Multinationals and Cross-Cultural Management: The Transfer of Knowledge within Multinational Corporations*. London: Routledge.

Haghirian, P., R. Sinkovics, and V. Bamiatzi. (2008). Japan: New business opportunities in an established market. *Global Business and Organizational Excellence* (November/December): 51–61.

Hausmann, R., Tyson, L. and Zahidi, S. (2010). *The Global Gender Gap Report*. Geneva: World Economic Forum.

Hayami, A. (1999). Introduction: The Emergence of 'Economic Society'. In Hayami, A., Saito, O. and Toby, R. P. (Eds.) *The Emergence of Economic Society in Japan* 1600–1859; *Early Modern*. Oxford: Oxford University Press, p. 1 –35.

Imai, M. (1997). *Gemba Kaizen; A Commonsense, Low-cost Approach to Management*. New York: McGrawHill.

Jackson, T. (1993). *Turning Japanese: The Fight for Industrial Control of The New Europe*. London: Harper Collins Publishers.

Jansen, M. B. (2000). *The Making of Modern Japan*. Cambridge: Harvard Business Press.

Keizer, A. B. (2010). *Changes in Japanese Employment Practices: Beyond the Japanese Model*. London: Routledge.

Kobayashi, K. (2006). *The Japanese Economy*. Tokyo: IBC Publishing.

Kondansha. (2003). *Bairingaru Nihon Jiten*. Tokyo: Kodansha International.

Kono, T. and Clegg, S. (2001). *Trends in Japanese Management: Continuing Strengths, Current Problems and Changing Priorities*. London: Palgrave.

Liker, J. K. (2004). *The Toyota Way: 14 Management Principles from the World's Greatest Manufacturer*. New York: McGraw-Hill.

Linhart, S. (1983). Japan. In L. Ladstätter and S. Linhart (Eds.) *China und Japan, Die Kulturen Ostasiens*. Wien: Ueberreuter.

Lonien, C. (2003). *The Japanese Economic and Social System: From a Rocky Past to an Uncertain Future*. Amsterdam: IOS Press.

McGuire, J. And Dow S. (2009). Japanese keiretsu: Past, present and future. *Asia Pacific Journal of Management* 26, 333–351.

Ministry of Economy, Trade, and Industry. (2007). White Paper on Small and Medium Sized Enterprises in Japan. Tokyo: Japan Small Business Research Institute. Retrieved on July 2, 2008 from www.chusho.meti.go.jp/ pamflet/hakusyoh19/download/2007 hakusho_eng.pdf

Morris-Suzuki, T. (1994). *The Technological Transformation of Japan: From the Seventeenth to the Twenty-first Century*. Cambridge: Cambridge University Press.

Nakamura, T. (1995). *The Postwar Japanese Economy: Its Development and Structure, 1937–1994*. Tokyo: Tokyo University Press.

Nonaka, I. and Takeuchi, H. (1995). *The Knowledge-creating Company*. New York: Oxford University Press.

Ohtsu, M. (2002). *Inside Japanese Business; A Narrative History 1960–2000*. Armonk: M.E. Sharpe.

Okazaki, T. and Okuno-Fujiwara, M. (1999): *The Japanese Economic System and Its Historical Origins*. Oxford: Oxford University Press.

Ozkan, E. U. (2011): The bank-based financial system and kinyu keiretsu: Political economy of the bank-centered cross-shareholding system in postwar Japan. *Ritsumeikan Journal of Asia Pacific Studies* 30, (November).

Partner, S. (1999). *Assembled in Japan: Electrical Goods and the Making of the Japanese Consumer*. Study of the East Asian Institute, Columbia University: University of California Press.

Persson, M. (2010). Empowering Women. Lecture at the Sophia Community College. April 17, 2010. Tokyo: Sophia University.

Rebick, M. (2005). *The Japanese Employment System: Adapting to a New Economic Environment*. Oxford: Oxford University Press.

Reischauer, E. O. and Jansen, M. B. (2005). *The Japanese Today: Change and Continuity*. Tokyo: Tuttle Publishing.

Saito, M. (2000). *The Japanese Economy*. Singapore: World Scientific Publishing.

Sakano, T. and Lewin, A. (1999): Impact of CEO succession in Japanese companies: A coevolutionary perspective. *Organization Science* 10 (5), 654–671.

Samiee, S., and Mayo, A. (1990). Barriers to trade with Japan: A socio-cultural perspective. *European Journal of Marketing* 24 (12), 48–66.

Sanchanta, M. (2010). Japan firms send work overseas. *The Wall Street Journal* 26 October, 1.

Schaede, U. (2008). *Choose and Focus: Japanese Business Strategies for the 21st Century*. Ithaca NY: Cornell University Press.

Schuette, H. and Ciarlante, D. (1998). *Consumer Behavior in Asia*. London: Macmillan Press.

Shimbo, H. and Hasegawa, A. (1999). 'The dynamics of market economy and production'. In A. Hayami, O. Saitō and R. P. Toby (Eds.) *The Emergence of Economic Society in Japan 1600–185; Early Modern*, pp. 159–191. Oxford: Oxford University Press.

Tabuchi, H. (2011). Japan keeps a high wall for foreign labor. *New York Times* 2 January.

Takeda, M. (2002). White-collar workers. In A. Bird (Ed.) *Encyclopedia of Japanese Business and Management*, p. 474. London: Routledge.

Van Wolferen, Karel (1989). *The Enigma of Japanese Power*. London: Macmillan.

Wittner, D. H. (2007). *Technology and the Culture of Progress in Meiji Japan*. London: Routledge.

Zoellner, R. (2006). *Geschichte Japans: Von 1800 bis zur Gegenwart*. Paderborn: Schöningh.

29

Japanese Consumers and Consumerism

Parissa Haghirian

INTRODUCTION

Consumption has long played an important role in Japanese life. Even before the Meiji Restoration (1868) the Japanese consumer had a notably wide range of products and services to choose from. The distinctive profile of contemporary consumerism, however, developed between the wars, when urban areas were reconstructed to incorporate department stores and amusement parks, and so became increasingly attractive not only for established urban shoppers but for the increasing number of Japanese who were moving from the countryside to Tokyo and other major urban centers.

The years immediately after World War II were marked by extreme poverty; but this situation changed with the USA's entry into the Korean War, which gave an initial boost to the Japanese economy. Japan went on to experience a succession of economic booms, and the rapid rate of growth – up to 10 percent – not only created increasing demand for new goods within the Japanese market but also transformed and refined Japanese shopping habits.

At the beginning of the new millennium Japan possessed the most affluent and interesting consumer market in the world. Strong segmentation has led to the development of influential new consumer groups such as the baby boomer, the new rich, single women, and the *otaku*. Consumer behavior,

however, is still idiosyncratic, and has shifted from the price-insensitive luxury shopping of the 1980s to the more price-conscious attitudes of recent years. At the same time consumers still seek a high level of quality and expect the best service in the world.

This chapter discusses the development of Japanese consumerism after World War II, describes the most prominent contemporary consumer groups in Japan, and presents an overview of Japanese consumer behavior.

THE HISTORICAL DEVELOPMENT OF JAPANESE CONSUMERISM

Japanese consumers have long been avid shoppers and shown great interest in new and innovative products. Already in the Edo-Period (1603-1868) Japan had a fully developed consumer market, and a great variety of products and regional specialties were available throughout the country (Shimbo and Hasegawa, 1999: 185–86; see also Francks, 2009).

Modern Japanese consumption, however, is rooted in the interwar period. After the 1923 earthquake Tokyo expanded rapidly (Linhart, 1983). Property developers were investing in an increasing number of commuter subway and train lines, but also in shopping areas and department stores at central stations. The places where commuters changed trains, such as Shinjuku, Shibuya, and Ikebukuro, emerged as shopping and leisure centers. The development of these new centers of consumption also changed consumption habits. The number of Western-style goods and restaurants increased during this period, providing fashionable items for the growing urban middle class (Francks, 2009).

The years following World War II presented a different picture. Unemployment, poverty, and hunger marked the post-war years: calorie-intake levels slumped beneath that of Western countries' and most Japanese struggled to put food on the table (Partner, 1999: 139). At the same time, however, many Japanese had a first glimpse of luxuries which had not been considered appropriate during wartime, but which were now displayed by the occupying Allied forces. For many Japanese this period marked their first acquaintance with Western products and consumer culture.

Things changed when the USA entered the Korean War. Starting in 1950, military procurement by the US army created demand in the Japanese market and propelled Japan's economy forward (Saito, 2000: 221). Japan began to recover from WWII: exports expanded in response to the rise in international prices and production, and employment and profits rose. The Japanese economy boomed (Nakamura, 1995). By the 1950s, with growth rates reaching 10 percent, the Japanese were beginning to show a renewed interest in consumer products.

As incomes increased Japanese households were able to spend and save at the same time (Horioka, 2006). The famous Jimmu boom of 1955–56 led to major changes in Japanese consumption and savings rates. An average urban working family saved only 2 percent of its income in 1951, but 12.5 percent in 1957 (Shinohara, 1959). At the same time Japanese people started to enjoy consuming and purchased ever greater quantities of the new consumer goods (Saito 2000: 221). In 1955 Japan returned to, and soon surpassed, pre-war levels of productivity. At the same time an increasing number of Japanese workers were leaving the agricultural sector and going to work in construction and manufacturing – a trend which continued until the 1970s (Nakamura, 1995). In the 1960s this trend also channeled a large number of workers into tertiary industries such as commerce and service trades, which started to increasingly consume products.

The 'three sacred treasures' of the 1950s (television, electric washing machine, and refrigerator) were the most popular products of the era (Partner, 1999: 138). These treasures, although expensive, entered Japanese homes very rapidly. In 1955 4 percent of households were equipped with a washing machine, while ownership of televisions and refrigerators was below 1 percent. Five years later 45 percent of Japanese households owned a washing machine, 54 percent a television, and 15 percent a refrigerator. By 1970 more than 90 percent of Japanese households owned all three (Yoshimi, 2006).

Mai hōmu (my home) and *mai kā* (my car) became the keywords of Japanese consumption in the 1960s; owning a family house and a car were the symbols of success. As the number of individual cars increased, *Mai kā* became the most popular middle-class item. Meanwhile, savings rates were still high: many people preferred to pay for consumer goods with their savings rather than pay interest on installment plans (JETRO, 1985). The longest boom (the Izanagi boom) took off in October 1965 and lasted for fifty seven months. Japanese GDP grew at over 10 percent for the five consecutive years 1966–70. As Japan continued to prosper consumers reacted by consuming even more. The favorite combination of products in this period was the 3Cs – car, cooler, and a color television (Saito, 2000: 224). The high rate of diffusion of television sets also exposed the majority of Japanese people to commercials (Ballon, 1973), providing them with even more information on consumer products.

The increasing interest in consumer products had political effects. In 1968 the government responded to public demands for a comprehensive system of consumer-protection policies (MacLachlan, 1997). The Consumer Protection Basic Law (*Shōshisha hogo kihon hō*) was the first law to assert that consumer protection was a governmental objective. 'It specified the regulatory responsibilities of all levels of government toward consumers, the responsibilities of firms to improve the quality of their products and services and to respond to consumer claims, and the obligations of consumers themselves to acquire the knowledge for making rational purchasing decisions' (Nishimura, 2006: 273).

Consumption patterns started to change at this time. The new generations of post-war Japanese were very different from their elders and started to follow new trends. The *shinjinrui* ('The New Breed'), as they were called, showed increasing hedonism in their purchasing patterns and tried to distinguish themselves from the older generations through different types of consumer behavior. They also started to prefer Western products over Japanese (De Mente, 2004: 263), and this was the period in which Western manufacturers started to show more interest in the Japanese market. As consumption became a lifestyle activity the nature of Japanese consumption also changed. This began during the 1970s with rising expenditure on items meant to increase life satisfaction. By the end of the 1970s more than four million Japanese had travelled overseas (Jansen, 2000), and the quality of goods and services became more important than their price, marking a major change from the nature of consumer demands in the 1950s and 1960s (JETRO, 1985). The 1970s saw a major expansion in the range of products available to consumers. Hand-in-hand with this development the Japanese diet started to change, increasingly including more Western components; from this time onwards Japan became the greatest food importer worldwide (Francks, 2009: 194) and today 62 percent of its food supply comes from overseas sources (Assmann, 2011).

The 1980s were dominated by the bubble economy: consumption became a lifestyle, and by the second part of the decade private consumption had become a motor of economic development (Kokumin Seikatsu Sentâ, 1997: 166; Meyer-Ohle and Fuess, 1997). The so-called 'bubble' boomed. Salaries continued to improve, many jobs were available, and a large-scale market for expensive imported products developed. As foreign travel became even more fashionable the number of Japanese traveling overseas rose to 10 million per year (Jansen, 2000). It was during these boom years that European brand manufacturers started their successful entry into the Japanese market.

When the bubble burst, however, Japanese consumer attitudes changed dramatically. With rising unemployment and the collapse of numerous Japanese corporations the national sense of security was threatened and consumers started to make more risk-averse and price-oriented buying decisions. The major influences on the retail market were the economic recession and the deregulation process, which was based on a traditional and highly complex distribution system that had been in existence since before Japan opened up to the West. 100-yen stores became a frequent sight in Japanese cities; outlet malls offered leftover products and discounted merchandise at 30 to 70 percent below the regular price. These new styles of consumption forced traditional corporations, such as the Sogo department store, out of business (Gakken, 2002).

At the beginning of the new century Japanese society had undergone a tremendous change in the ten years since the bubble burst. The economic situation was more stressful for many Japanese, and the myths of the Japanese economic miracle, such as lifetime employment and the unbeatable stability of Japanese corporations, had been called into question. The number of women entering the workforce increased, part-time work became more common, and Japanese baby boomers started to retire. The younger generation faced an insecure future (Haghirian, 2011).

The first decade of the new century saw the Japanese economy showing signs of recovery, and consumption increased once more; but this was also a time of product and food scandals, leaving Japanese consumers with concerns about the safety and ethics of their once highly admired firms. Unsurprisingly, therefore, Japanese consumers were sending very mixed messages to marketers as the new century began. 'Consumers shop around more rationally and include more options in their portfolio of alternatives (e.g., 100-yen stores, all-night auctions) and are now prepared to purchase previously owned apparel and other items, something that was anathema during the boom years' (McHardy Reid 2007: 97). A further shift could be observed away from the hedonism of the bubble years in favor of greater interest in health and health-promoting products, such as organic food, and also a rise in consumer spending on adult education. Japanese consumers expressed their individuality through creative choices among brands described as high-quality, reputable, and prestigious (Knight and Kim, 2007); luxury consumption boomed.

THE JAPANESE CONSUMER MARKET TODAY

Japanese consumers are not only one of the most influential consumer groups worldwide, they have also have astonishingly particular consumer attitudes and an almost professional – and highly demanding – interest in new products and world-class services. In many industries Japan is seen as a trend-setting market and Japanese consumer groups as the consumers of the future.

But the economic crisis of 2008 has also left its marks on Japan. At the time of writing – the beginning of 2010 – consumption in Japan is weak (*Nikkei Shimbun*, 2010) and consumer attitudes and behavior are shifting dramatically (Salsberg, 2010). Overall spending in Japan has decreased by 8 percent in comparison to the year 2000 (*Nikkei Shimbun*, 2010). Some observers have even coined the term 'consumer hatred' to explain the Japanese tendency to consume less (*New York Times*, 2010). After decades of difference from consumers in industrialized countries, eschewing low prices and preferring to shop at the high end, Japanese consumers now seem more similar to their Western counterparts, looking for value and attempting to entertain themselves at reasonable cost – 37 percent of Japanese consumers claim to have cut overall spending (Salsberg, 2010).

The reasons for this dramatic change lie in the shrinkage of the Japanese middle class. The number of households holding a 8–9 million yen annual budget shrank by 18 percent, households holding 15 million yen shrank by 30 percent, and the 10–15 million yen class by 19 percent. At the same time wages did not increase by as much as they used to. All these changes impacted strongly on spending behavior. Younger consumers are reluctant to spend money on cars or loans while they are unsure about their future income. Older consumers are reluctant because they worry about outliving their money after retirement (*Nikkei Shimbun*, 2010). This has 'bred a deep pessimism about the future and a fear of taking risks that make people instinctively reluctant to spend or invest, driving down demand – and prices – even further' (*New York Times*, 2010). The overall confidence of Japanese consumers in the future is decreasing.

Outlooks on the future of Japanese consumption, then, are pessimistic. Sawa (2010) writes that 'Although government fiscal expenditures may increase families' disposable income, the marginal propensity to consume – the proportion of additional disposable income that actually goes to consumption – is expected to remain low.' At the same time very wealthy consumers have neither changed their consumer behavior nor lost their lust for luxury. Even where they also report income cuts due to the post-2008 economic crisis, they are still spending on expensive luxury and brand products (*Nikkei Shimbun*, 2009).

PARTICULARITIES OF JAPANESE CONSUMER BEHAVIOR

At the time of writing Japan presents a very sophisticated and also very modern consumer market. Japanese consumers do not only show a pronounced affinity for high-quality products, they have been successfully segmented by Japanese marketers and targeted by specialized products and services. The following sections discuss the particularities of Japanese consumer behavior and the new consumer groups which dominate Japanese marketing today.

Collectivistic Consumer Attitudes

The most widely discussed question in studies of Japanese consumer behavior is whether the Japanese make group-oriented or individualistic purchasing decisions. Many authors refer to Japan as a collectivistic culture in which consumers show a collectivistic consumer behaviour (e.g. Schütte and Carliante 1998). In collectivist-oriented cultures, product and brand preferences are more likely to express attitudes arising from social norms than from internal drives or motives (Haghirian, 2010). 'Loyalty is a key concept in collectivistic cultures' and Asian consumers tend to 'rely more on information found in their reference group' and to 'follow the group consensus until there is significant evidence showing that the new product is better' (Usunier, 2000, p. 110). Erffmeyer et al. (1999) even assume that Japan's unique Shinto-based culture places an emphasis on the individual's responsibility to the group, including family, co-workers, employer, and society at large (Erffmeyer et al., 1999). Japanese

consumers are thus seen as collectivistic consumers, basing their purchasing decisions on whether they will find acceptance among their peers and seeking to integrate into their social groups through buying products which strengthen their positions within it.

Love for Brands

Fashion brands play an important role in the Japanese consumer market. The Japanese term *burando* (brand) only refers to luxury products such as bags and fashion, and does not apply to products which can be consumed less overtly, such as skin care or other products – even if they are themselves 'branded' (Haghirian, 2010). Japanese consumers have a high affinity for brands, and Japan is often said to possess the world's only 'mass luxury market' because – in contrast to other markets – luxury brand products are mainly purchased by the Japanese middle class. Most popular goods in this category are expensive fashion items, luxury handbags in particular. In Japan buying and wearing luxury goods has become a 'way of life' and there is no going back unless consumers simply cannot afford them anymore (Chada and Husband, 2008). Product or brand preferences 'represent expressions of what is considered socially acceptable rather than individual preferences' (Schütte and Ciarliante 1998: 71). In this manner Japan has become a mass luxury market and Japanese consumers have become highly selective in their brand purchases (Schütte and Ciarliante, 1998).The economic crisis of recent years has posed a marginal challenge to these attitudes but, nevertheless, expensive brand products remain important in signaling status and success in Japanese society.

Corporate reputations are another important factor when addressing Japanese consumers. Traditionally, they have tended to choose large, well known companies when purchasing products, and Japanese corporations have decades of experience in brand development and communication. Image-building in Japan is not limited to a brand but is in most cases linked with corporate image: the company and its reputation both have a major influence in the decision to buy (Schütte and Ciarliante, 1998). Consumers believed that they can avoid making the wrong decision or buying an inferior product by always sticking to the same company, since purchasing a new brand from an unknown company might result in dissatisfaction (Schneidewind, 1998) – thus Japanese advertisements often focus more on the company than on the product (Sanga and Nishida, 2009).

High Diffusion Rate

The collectivistic attitude of consumers is also seen as an explanation for the high rate of diffusion of new products in the Japanese market. Once a brand has gained acceptance among early adopters the rate of diffusion proceeds rapidly in societies with homogenous cultural and socio-economic backgrounds, such as Japan. The interest in new and exciting products makes Japanese consumers willing to pay a lot of money for them (Haghirian, 2010), and Japanese companies have developed great expertise in meeting this expectation. They react by constantly launching new products: new products are labelled *shinhatsubai*, a term which corresponds to the English 'new and improved, now on sale', and Japanese consumers show marked preferences for such products. The word *shinhatsubai* is composed of the character for 'new' (*shin*) followed by the character with the dynamic meaning of 'discharge, start, leave' (*hatsu*) and ends with the character for 'sell' (*bai*). The expression conveys a sense of a new movement of goods into the market place (Watts, 1998). Not all of these products, however, are real and radical innovations, nor do they offer new value for the customer: often these 'new and improved' products are simply new flavors or the same product in different packaging.

Quality Perception

One of the most important issues – indeed, probably the most important issue in selling to the Japanese – is quality (Melville, 1999: 67). Japanese quality perceptions, however, greatly differ from other nations. Consumers have long since expected to pay more for innovative, well made, and fashionable products, and demand for these goods was already rising in the late 1970s (JETRO, 1985. Even today Japanese consumers are obsessed with quality: a characteristic of the Japanese market is not to be satisfied with the rational and functional but to demand a higher level of quality and operation.

Quality in Japan is a property which must permeate every aspect of a product, including continuous attention to improvement. If Japanese customers are satisfied with the quality of the product a company is offering they might buy from the same company again; however, if the customer is dissatisfied with the quality then they will usually never again buy a product from that company, and the reputation of the firm could be spoiled for years. (Haghirian and Toussaint, 2011: 23)

Price Sensitivity

The consumers of the 1990s bubble economy were known to care little about prices; but as the recession of the 1990s wore on the Japanese became more and more price-conscious. The economic downturn after the bursting of the bubble meant that Japanese consumers 'were now being forced towards practicality even for status items', while before they had only been 'price-conscious in personal-use purchases' (Schütte and Ciarliante, 1998). This had a tremendous effect on consumption habits and led to 'an increasing focus on lifestyle resources such as personal capital and assets and an increasing conservatism in consumption. In effect, Japanese consumers have become more price-sensitive, exhibit much higher tendencies toward purchasing restraint, and "are generally leaning toward more consumptive downscaling"' (Kobayashi, 1994). At the same time many retailers started to change their distribution systems, and Japanese consumers developed a taste for cheaper products. The positive attitude towards cheap prices was mainly targeted at generic products. Designer and luxury products, on the other hand, could still be sold for a high price (Haghirian and Toussaint, 2011).

Ethnocentrism

Japanese consumers are often portrayed as being very ethnocentric in their purchasing behavior, and several studies have been conducted on Japanese consumers and their reaction to imports as opposed to Japanese goods (Nagashima, 1970, 1977; Kamins and Nagashima, 1995; Gurhan-Canli and Maheswaran, 2000). In most developed countries domestic products generally enjoy a more favorable evaluation than foreign-made products. This strong preference for domestic products can also be seen among Japanese consumers (Usunier, 2000: 157). Japanese consumers generally assume that the quality of Japanese products is higher than that of the West's and are willing to pay higher prices for them. One reason for this is the high level of service, particularly after-sale services, which is a common feature of Japanese companies. Foreign companies are often thought not to offer the same quality of service (Melville, 1999).

In Japan, quality permeates every aspect of a product and involves continuous attention to improvement (Melville, 1999). It should be noted that in Japan many of the areas where foreign firms succeed are those in which Japan has traditionally not been competitive: certain agricultural products – like wine or cheese from Europe – and high-fashion brands are cases in point. In these areas Japanese consumers are unlikely to perceive a lack of Japanese quality and are more likely to accept imports. Many otherwise ethnocentric consumers are also often conscious of the role of imported items as status symbols and are therefore more likely to buy them (Rice and Wongtada, 2007). When it comes to televisions and other electronic goods, and also cars, foreign products are more likely to be seen as threatening and are therefore eschewed unless they fall into the luxury category and are desired as status symbols. Threatening goods being imported from neighboring countries are even more likely to elicit a negative response – for example, Korean televisions or Chinese computers (Nijssen and Douglas, 2004).

JAPAN'S NEW CONSUMER GROUPS

As we have seen, Japanese consumers have played an increasingly important role in the economic development of the country. Since the 1980s the Japanese consumer market has proved to be a successful stimulus for Japanese firms, many of which still focus exclusively on the Japanese market. Japanese companies have therefore long been careful to develop products that closely match the tastes of their customers, screening and investigating the Japanese market very intensely. The importance of Japanese consumers has led to strong segmentation within the market, and many consumer groups which are not yet fully recognized in many other industrialized countries have generated a lot of interest among Japanese marketers and marketing scientists. The following sections discuss the most prominent consumer groups in the modern Japanese market in detail.

Baby Boomers

The most widely discussed group among Japanese consumers are the baby boomers, or the 'silver market'. Among the industrialized nations Japan has the highest percentage of older citizens and the fastest-aging population. In 2009 the population of elderly citizens (65 years and over) was 29.01 million, constituting 22.7 percent of the total population and marking record highs both in absolute and relative terms. The proportion of people who are older than 60 years is projected to rise to more than 31.8 percent by 2030, and 39.6 percent by 2050 (Ministry of Internal Affairs and Communication, 2010). The term 'baby boomer' refers to Japanese who were born between 1947 and 1949. They are the 'classic' Japanese 'salarymen', the backbone of the Japanese economic miracle. In 2007 they started to retire, which presented not only a managerial problem for Japanese firms – because of the tacit corporate knowledge they took with them – but also a financial one. Many baby boomers are entitled to retirement money of up to 38 months of salary, having worked in their companies for a lifetime. These payments amount to up to 28 million yen (equivalent to 246,000 euros as of October 2010) per person. According to government data

households headed by people in their sixties have average savings of 22.88 million yen and debt of 2.17 million yen, resulting in net savings of 20.71 million yen. These households also benefit from pension payments that do not decrease with deflation (*Nikkei Weekly*, 2010a). It is believed that Japanese older than 50 years hold more than 80 percent of a total of 1,439 quadrillion yen of financial assets (*Nikkei Weekly*, 2010a).

Older Japanese are seen – despite their age – as one of the most promising groups of customers, and Japan's senior citizens not only make up a very high proportion of the total population they have the highest life expectancy. According to the Statistics Bureau (2010) Japanese men born in 2007 have a life expectancy of 79.19 years and women of 85.99 years. The retirement of Japanese workers will inevitably have a major impact on the consumer market (Ishiwata, 2006); many of the retired baby boomers will spend their time taking care of hobbies and interests. According to a study by the Nihon Keizai Research Institute 78.4 percent of 9,513 surveyed members of the baby-boomer generation aim to devote their spare time to hobbies: in first place are domestic trips (78.6 percent), foreign travel (72.2 percent) comes second, followed by gardening and housework (40.5 percent), outdoor activities (39.7 percent), sports (36.5 percent), and cultural activities (34.9 percent (Nagao, 2006: 129). The retirees are therefore a lucrative target for different industries. They are well educated, have an average of more than twenty years of retirement ahead of them, and plenty of interests.

Women

Female consumers are the next most frequently discussed target group in the Japanese media. In the Japanese family women usually make the purchasing decisions and manage the finances. In their role as consumers and as family managers they are taken very seriously by Japanese marketing managers and have long been the object of promotional activities by Japanese companies. 'In Japan the wife often also has fiscal responsibility within the family' (Schütte and Ciarliante, 1998); 'she receives her husband's pay cheque and maintains the family budget, pays the bills and manages savings' (Usunier, 2000). Indeed, it is said that 'over 60 percent of housewives control the family budget' (Schütte and Ciarliante, 1998: 52).

In recent years Japanese women have also been assigned more importance as independent consumers. As the marriage age in Japan increases and the number of single households rises the number of women controlling their own income is rising as well. Due to the changing role of women in Japanese society their financial power is now more considerable than ever: as well as managing the family's finances they contribute an increasing share of it themselves (Lasserre and Schütte, 1999).

There are several reasons for these developments. The traditional Japanese family model – in which the man earns the money and the woman takes care of the family and the household – is losing its popularity, although for many Japanese it still remains the ideal for now. Changes in attitudes towards traditional marriage have led to a greater number of women entering the Japanese labor market and also wanting to remain in employment (Schad-Seifert, 2006: 240). Since the early 1970s the women's movement, in particular, has influenced more and more women to strive to find employment in a corporation. This was partly the result of increased interest in better educational opportunities. Instead of attending short university courses in expectation of a life as a housewife and mother, since the 1990s more women have been taking four-year university degrees (Chiavacci, 2006: 196).

Japanese women, however, have a tough time in the labor market. Their career opportunities remain dim. In 1970 women accounted for 52.9 percent of the workforce; in 2003 it was 59.9 percent (Rebick, 2005). Among part-time employees the percentage of women is still above average at 76.4 percent (Schad-Seifert, 2006: 240), but the number of women rising to management positions is not large (Rebick, 2005: 118). To face the threat of a labor shortage, however, the Japanese government plans to increase the number of married women in employment. Currently, measures are being discussed that aim to integrate up to 70 percent of married Japanese women between 25 and 44 into working life by the year 2017 (Howard 2007: 29).

Although we cannot speak of gender equality and equal access to economic opportunities, a growing number of Japanese women have an independent income. And while they may not have gained more influence in the corporate world they have definitely gained influence as powerful consumers. Japan's rapid economic growth since World War II has transformed Japanese women into the world's most visible and highly regarded consumers (McCreery, 2000). They have more economic and social freedom and independence than ever before and – since many put off marriage until their late twenties – can enjoy their single years with high disposable incomes (Skov and Moeran, 1995; Schütte and Ciarliante, 1998; Solomon and Askegaard, 1999). And Japanese women have increasing influence on major consumer trends in Asia (Schütte and Ciarliante, 1998).

Unmarried women have been the center of media attention. Single working women in Japan are often referred to as 'parasite singles', which refers to the fact that they often live with their parents and have the means to spend a much higher amount on fashion and leisure than their Western counterparts. They are between 20 and 24 years old and employed in full-time jobs, which means that they have few or no living costs and can spend most of their income on consumer goods, travel, or restaurant visits. Eight percent of Japanese women aged between 20 and 24 belong to this group (Howard 2007: 29). In Japan public discussion on single women has been dominated by their 'unorthodox lifestyle', a debate which was fanned by a 1999 book by Masahiro Yamada, *Parasaito shingoru no jidai (The Age of Parasite Singles)*. Junko Sakai's *Makeinu no Toboe (The Howl of the Loser Dog)*, published in 2003, heated the debate even more: in this best-seller the author deals with the lives of working women singles in their 30s, called *makeinu*, or 'loser dogs' (Japan Market Research Network, 2007). Sakai's book has provoked strong reactions in the Japanese media and led to single working women in Japan being portrayed as losing out on happiness and family life.

Japanese marketers, however, have recognized single women with an independent income as an interesting new target group. This does not seem surprising, since the average income of Japanese women who work has continuously increased in recent years. Since 1980 they have increased their average income by 2.9 million per year (Moore and Smith, 2004) – an increasingly important target group for companies in the areas mentioned above (Howard 2007: 29).

Today the discussion of single women in Japan has lost its aggressiveness. One reason for this is the increasing number of individuals living alone; and these are not only women. Other singleton customer groups under discussion at the moment are the so-called ARAFO ('around forty'): female consumers who have spent more than a decade in the workforce and often have very high incomes. The number of people living alone among the silver consumers is also increasing (Collins, 2011).

With increasing numbers of them working, women's consumption behavior is changing. It no longer focuses on the family but on women's consumer products and, especially, high-quality brand products. Working women, as a new consumer group, have become increasingly interesting for the consumer-goods industry. The target group of wealthy women between 20 and 40 years old is particularly interested in social advancement. They generally reside in one of the more elegant districts of Tokyo, and their careers and work environment are stimulating and have high status (May, 2007). In addition to brands they are interested in international travel (Ishiwata, 2006) and on services that facilitate daily life, such as assistance in financial management (May, 2007).

In the first decade of this century their influence became obvious even for very traditional Japanese corporations. In the 1990s, for instance,

Japanese banks only reluctantly gave loans to single women, expecting them to get married, become housewives, and lose their regular incomes. Over the past decade many banks have recognized the financial power of single women in Japan and have developed new products which, among other things, have allowed them to buy property more easily (Haghirian, 2007).

The 'New Rich'

The changes in Japanese society have led to an increase in class difference, and have produced a growing number of very wealthy Japanese (Usui, 2006: 52). Both the groups discussed above – the baby boomers and single women with income – fall into the category of the 'new rich': *nyū richi* or *fuyūsō*. These are consumers who have assets of 100 million yen or more (Miyamoto et al., 2006: 2). The *nyū richi* and their interest in high-quality and luxury products has also led to an increase in market entries by Western luxury brands.

Japanese consumers are famous for their wealth, and interest in luxury and brand products. The fact that there are so many wealthy consumers has resulted in them becoming a focus of attention for Japanese corporations, and the rich are widely discussed in the Japanese media. A household is considered part of the *fuyūsō* if its financial assets exceed 100 million yen (Miyamoto and Yonemura, 2008). If they exceed 500 million yen then a member of this household would be considered a HNWI (High Net Worth Individual). Households with financial assets falling in the bracket of 500 million to 100 million yen are considered affluent; 100 million to 50 million yen, mass affluent. Households in the bracket of 50 million to 30 million yen are considered the upper mass-retail layer, and below 30 million yen is the mass-retail layer. In 2006 approximately 813,000 households were counted as *fuyūsō* and approximately 52,000 HNWIs.

Up until 2008 Japan's *nyū richi* kept spending on luxuries. 'Despite a sluggish economy, tepid retail sales and a weak yen, demand for super-luxury goods and services is up' (ABC News, 2008); but the appeal of luxury and expensive products changed very quickly. Japan's market for imported luxury goods fell 10 percent to 11.9 billion US dollars (1.06 trillion yen) from 2007. In 2009–10 it is expected to shrink to 992.7 billion yen, compared to its peak of 1.9 trillion yen in 1996 (*New York Times*, 2009). Atsmon et al. (2009) identify three reasons for the sudden change: the economic crisis in 2008, a 'luxury bubble' between 2004 and 2007, and underlying channel trends and longer-term shifts in consumer attitudes and behavior that began six to eight years ago.

The economic crisis which hit the world economy in 2008 had the most tremendous effect on the spending of Japanese luxury lovers. The crisis coincided with the bursting of a 'luxury bubble', which had initially taken off with the enormous interest in foreign luxury brands. This led to a high number of foreign entries into the Japanese market. Successful brands were forced to open up branches within short time intervals. But since most famous brands have European origins the appreciation of the euro increased the prices of the goods on offer (Atsmon et al., 2009); meanwhile, Japanese consumers were being offered an increasing array of luxury products, which might have made them less interesting as a whole.

Consumer attitudes have also changed. In 2007 the Japan Market Resource Network issued a prognosis of increased confidence and a change in the character of consumer values, such as a new mix of 'high' and 'low' lifestyles, or an increasing acceptance of mixing luxury brands with less prestigious and even lower-quality products. The Japanese consumer seemed to be more confident about purchasing products with lower brand value. Lower-priced items and discount shops became increasingly socially accepted (Japan Market Resource Network, 2007).

At the same time, however, Japan's super rich have not changed their purchasing behavior. A recent survey of consumers with financial assets of more than 10 million yen (112,300 US dollars) reveals that the spending habits of Japan's wealthiest consumers appear relatively unaffected by the economic downturn, and that rich consumers are still looking for exclusive shopping experiences. And the wealthiest Japanese – those owning more than 100 million yen in financial assets or deriving at least 30 million yen in annual household income – are increasingly interested in buying real estate and Western luxury items, such as watches and cars (*Nikkei Shimbun*, 2009).

Otaku

Another widely discussed group is the *otaku* or 'enthusiastic consumers', who are overwhelmingly occupied with their hobbies and invest a lot of money in them. Their purchasing power and creativity has also led to reactions from Japanese marketing firms. The word 'otaku' in standard Japanese is a very formal way of saying 'you' – roughly equivalent to the English 'thou'. It was adopted by hard-core Japanese fans of *manga* and *anime* (comics and animation respectively) in the early 1980s as a slang term referring to themselves. The term has broadened in recent years to refer to fanatics of any number of hobbies, from car enthusiasts to collectors of *manga*-inspired dolls.

The stereotypical *otaku* is an unmarried male professional, usually working in a technology-related field; this stereotype is hardly universal, however, and, in fact, *otaku* can be young or old, male or female, and their hobbies vary widely. The most stereotypical *otaku* hobbies and industries are those which have, traditionally, drawn fanatical followers: comics and animation, video games, and electronics of all types. The *otaku* market is not a single market segment, however, but consists of many small niche markets which serve the particular tastes of the fanatics of that specific interest. But there is one common theme for all the varied *otaku* groups: they spend liberally in pursuit of their hobby.

Over 2.85 million Japanese could be categorized as *otaku*, and this market segment generates over 2.6 billion US dollars annually. Furthermore, comic books (the largest of the *otaku* markets, at over 350,000 people) generate revenues to the tune of 83 billion yen per year. The bulk of the *otaku* market is made up of five major classifications: comics (100 billion yen annually), animation (20 billion), idols (60 billion), games (78 billion), and PC assembly (32 billion) (Kitabayashi, 2004).

There are several subgroups within the category of *otaku*. For instance, comic (*manga*) *otaku* purchases include the comics themselves but also comic-themed products ranging from model figures of their favorite characters, trading cards, posters, and clothing, to accessories and trinkets (bags, cell-phone tassels, pens, and stationary) (Agulhon, 2011). Animation *otaku* have similar shopping habits to (and a significant overlap with) comic *otaku*, with animation DVDs replacing the comics but the secondary purchases remaining similar. On the other hand game *otaku* will purchase games, but many prefer first-run, limited or special editions of games (often purchasing the same core game many times for additional content). Game *otaku* also overlap heavily with the previous two classifications, purchasing comics and animation based on their favorite games. Game *otaku* who favor 'network games' tend to overlap into the PC assembly group, custom-building their PCs to play their favorites. The PC assembly market purchases cutting-edge, boutique parts and builds PCs to meet their specific interests, be it a silent PC or one which has colored fans and wiring inside with custom-case artwork outside. Finally, idol *otaku* are extreme fans of pop musicians (their 'idols'), who attend concerts and purchase first-run or special-edition CDs, books, magazines, DVDs, and any other material concerning their idolized performers (Kitabayashi, 2004).

Young Japanese Men

A new consumer group which has also became prominent over recent years is young men who do not purchase the way their fathers did: that is, they do not purchase the classic male goods such as cars and alcohol but show more cost-oriented consumer behavior and a taste for fashion items and beauty products (Toussaint, 2011). This group is known as the *soshoku danshi* (grass eaters). One reason for their behavior is their pessimistic view of the future: young Japanese who grew up in times of economic stagnation and deflation refuse to buy big-ticket items like cars or televisions; fewer choose to study abroad in America (*New York Times*, 2010); and their marriage age has been put back, leaving them with more control over their spending habits and more time to develop distinctive tastes and self-confidence in their purchase decisions (Toussaint, 2011).

CONCLUSION

At the end of the first decade of the twenty-first century the Japanese consumer market is still one of the most important in the world. Not only do the Japanese still have high purchasing power they have assumed a role as worldwide trend-setters and drivers of product development. At the same time the Japanese consumer market shows all the features of a post-industrial and super-mature consumer society: Japanese consumers have highly specific preferences, their buying decisions are sophisticated and particular, and they have divided into distinctive consumer groups, which, it can reasonably be supposed, will develop in other industrialized markets in the near future.

The particularity of the Japanese consumer market, however, also makes it very difficult to predict its future development. At the moment it is not clear how Japanese consumers will react to a recovery of the economic situation nor whether they will retain their position as one of the world's most influential and trend-setting consumer groups. At this point we can only speculate on how the Japanese consumer market will develop in the near future; but we can assume that the Japanese market will become more similar to other industrialized markets in which class differences are clearly visible and consumption more dependent on price perceptions and purchasing power. As the number of middle-class consumers decreases the Japanese consumer market may also come to show a clear distinction between wealthy and lower-income consumers. Despite this, the Japanese consumer market will keep its role as the 'retail model market of the future'.

REFERENCES

ABC News Online (2008). Japan's New Rich Spend Big on Luxuries, available at www.abc.net.au/

news/stories/2008/01/07/ 2133589.htm, accessed on 26 March 2010.

Agulhon, V. (2011). Sony Playstation 3 (PS3): Phoenix from the Flames?. In P. Haghirian and P. Gagnon (eds.), *Case Studies in Japanese Management*. Singapore: World Scientific Press, pp. 147–59.

Assmann, S. (2011). Beyond Sushi and Tempura: An Overview on the Japanese Food Market. In P. Haghirian (ed.), *Japanese Consumer Dynamics*. London: Palgrave Macmillan, pp. 163–82.

Atsmon, Y., Salsberg, B. and Yamanashi, H. (2009). Luxury Goods in Japan: Momentary Sigh or Long Sayonara? How Luxury Companies can Succeed in a Changing Market, *McKinsey Asia Consumer and Retail*, available at www.csia.mckinsey.com/~/media/Extranets/Consumer%20Shopper%20Insights/Reports/LUXURY_GOODS_IN_JAPAN.ashx, accessed on 14 December 2009.

Ballon, R. (1973). *Marketing in Japan*. Tokyo: Sophia University in cooperation with Kodansha International Ltd.

Chadha, R. and Husband, P. (2008). *The Cult of the Luxury Brand*. London and Boston: Nicholas Brealy International.

Chiavacci, D. (2006). Schwarze Schiffe in der japanischen Arbeitswelt – Wahrnehmung und Popularität von ausländischen Unternehmen als Arbeitgeber. In Haak, R. (Ed.), *Japanstudien – Jahrbuch des Deutschen Instituts für Japanstudien 2006 – Arbeitswelten in Japan (Band 18)*. Tokyo: Deutsches Institut für Japanstudien, pp. 111–48.

Collins, K. (2011). The Single Market. In P. Haghirian (ed.), *Japanese Consumer Dynamics*. London: Palgrave Macmillan, pp. 89–105.

De Mente, B. (2004). *Japan's Cultural Code Words: Key Terms That Explain the Attitudes and Behavior of the Japanese*. Tokyo: Tuttle Publishing.

Erffmeyer, R.C., Keillor, B. and Thorne LeClair, D. (1999). An Empirical Investigation of Japanese Consumer Ethics, *Journal of Business Ethics*, 18, 35–50.

Francks, P. (2009). *The Japanese Consumer: The Alternative Economic History of Modern Japan*. Cambridge: Cambridge University Press.

Gakken (2002). *Japan as It Is: A Bilingual Guide*. Tokyo: Gakken Corporation.

Gurhan-Canli, Z. and Maheswaran, D. (2000). Cultural Variations in Country of Origin, *Journal of Marketing Research*, 37, 309–17.

Haghirian, P. (2007). *Markteintritt in Japan*. Vienna: LexisNexis.

Haghirian, P. (2010). Innovative Marketings-strategien japanischer Unternehmen [Japanese Companies develop Innovative Marketing Strategies]. *Japan MARKT*, August 2007, 8–10, downloaded from www.parisshaghirian.com/publications/non-refereed-journal-paper/ accessed on 14 December 2009.

Haghirian, P. (2011). Historical Development of Japanese Consumerism. In P. Haghirian (ed.),

Japanese Consumer Dynamics. London: Palgrave Macmillan, pp. 3–17.

Haghirian, P. and Toussaint, A. (2011). Japanese Consumer Behavior. In P. Haghirian (ed.), *Japanese Consumer Dynamics*. London: Palgrave Macmillan, pp. 18–30.

Horioka, C. Y. (2006). Are the Japanese Unique? An Analysis of Consumption and Saving Behavior in Japan. In S. Garon. and P. L. Maclachlan, (eds.), *The Ambivalent Consumer: Questioning Consumption in East Asia and the West*. London: Cornell University Press, pp. 113–36.

Howard, D. (2007). Japanese Consumers: From Homogeneity to Diversity. *Nikkei Weekly*, 4 June 2007, 29.

Ishiwata, Y. (2006). Trends among Japanese Consumers and Promising Targets, Presentation of the Center of Consumer Studies. Tokio: Dentsu Corporation, downloaded from www.hawaiitourismauthority.org/pdf/Japan%20Cnsmr%20Trends.pdf on 12 April 2007.

Jansen, M. B. (2000). *The Making of Modern Japan*. Harvard: Harvard University Press.

Japan Market Resource Network (2007). JMRN August 2007 Consumer Survey, Attitudes towards Luxury Brands. Tokyo: Japan Market Research Network.

JETRO (1985). *Selling in Japan: The World's Second Largest Market*. Tokyo: Japan External Trade Organization (JETRO).

Kamins, M. A. and Nagashima, A. (1995). Perceptions of Products Made in Japan Versus Those Made in the United States among Japanese and American Executives: A Longitudinal Perspective, *Asia Pacific Journal of Management*, 12(1), 49–68.

Kitabayashi, K. (2004). The Otaku Group from a Business Perspective: Revaluation of Enthusiastic Consumers. Nomura Research Institute, downloaded from www.nri.co.jp/english/opinion/papers/2004/pdf/np200484.pdf on 10 January 2008.

Knight, D. K. and Kim, E. Y. (2007). Japanese Consumers' Need for Uniqueness: Effects on Brand Perceptions and Purchase Intention, *Journal of Fashion Marketing and Management*, 11(2), 270–280.

Kobayashi, F. (1994). Changing Lifestyles. In Y. Yamaguchi (ed.), *Japan 1994 Marketing and Advertising Yearbook*. Tokyo: Dentsu, Inc.

Kokumin Seikatsu Sentā. (1997). *Sengo shōshisha undōsha* [History of the Post-war Consumer Movement]. Tokyo: Ôkurashō Insatsukyoku.

Lasserre, P., & Schuette, H. (1999). *Strategies of Asia Pacific, Beyond the Crisis* (Revised and Updated Paperback Edition ed.). Houndmills: MacMillan Press Ltd.

Linhart, S. (1983). Japan. In L. Ladstätter and S. Linhart (eds.), *China und Japan, Die Kulturen Ostasiens*. Wien: Ueberreuter.

MacLachlan, P. (1997). The Seikatsusha and the Fight for Consumer Rights: Consumer Movement Activism in Postwar Japanese Society. In H. Meyer-Ohle and H. Fuess (eds.), *Japanstudien 9, Dienstleistung und Konsum in the 1990er Jahren*. Munich: iudicium Verlag, pp. 113–28.

May, R. (2007). A Look at the Essential Consumer Lifestyles. Insights from JMR, downloaded from www.jmrlsi.co.jp/english/ on 14 May 2007.

McCreery, J. (2000). *Japanese Consumer Behaviour: From Worker Bees to Wary Shoppers (Consumasian)*. Honolulu: University of Hawaii Press.

McHardy Reid, D. (2007). Consumer Change in Japan: A Longitudinal Study, *Thunderbird International Business Review*, 49(1), 77–101.

Melville, I. (1999). *Marketing in Japan*. Butterworth-Heinemann.

Meyer-Ohle, H. and Fuess, H. (1997). Konsum und Dienstleistung im Japan der 1990er Jahre: Einleitung. In H. Meyer-Ohle and H. Fuess (eds), *Japanstudien*, 9, 15–23.

Ministry of Internal Affairs and Communication. (2010). Chapter 2, Population, downloaded from www.stat.go.jp/english/data/handbook/c02cont.htm#cha2_2, accessed on 14 December 2009.

Miyamoto, H., Mutoh, M. and Ogimoto, Y. (2006). Marketing for Wealthy New Clients: Targeting the Mass Affluent, Nomura Research Institute, available at www.nri.co.jp, accessed on 12 December 2006.

Miyamoto, H. and Yonemura, T. (2008). New Wave of Retail Asset Management Business: From Private Banking to Sales at Bank Branches, Nomura Research Papers 129, available at www.nri.co.jp, accessed on 20 October 2010.

Moore, K. and Smith, M. (2004). Taking global brands to Japan, *Across the Board*, 41(1), 39.

Nagao, K. (2006). Dankai sedai ga hiraku atarashi shinia shijo. In S. Kobayashii, (ed.): *Dankai māketto*. Tokyo: Nihon keizai kenkyū sentā, pp. 118–61.

Nagashima, A. (1970). A Comparison of Japanese and U.S. Attitudes Toward Foreign Products, *Journal of Marketing* 34, January, 68–77.

Nagashima, A. (1977). A Comparative 'Made in' Product Image Survey Among Japanese Businessmen, *Journal of Marketing*, July, 95–100.

Nakamura, T. (1995). *The Postwar Japanese Economy: Its Development and Structure, 1937–1994*. Tokyo: University of Tokyo Press.

New York Times. (2009). Versace to Close Its Japanese Stores, *The New York Times*, 8 October.

New York Times. (2010). Japan Goes from Dynamic to Disheartened, 19 October, available at www.nytimes.com/2010/10/17/world/asia/17japan.html?_r=3&page wanted=1, accessed on 20 December 2009.

Nijssen, E. J. and Douglas, S. P. (2004). Examining the Animosity Model in a Country with a High Level of Foreign Trade, *International Journal of Research in Marketing*, 21, 23–38.

Nikkei Shimbun. (2009). Rich Classes Still Want to Spend: Despite Economic Downturn, Moneyed Consumers Still Looking for Luxury, 14 December.

Nikkei Shimbun. (2010). Shrinkage of Middle Class Hits Consumption, 10 May.

Nikkei Weekly. (2010a). Boomers Wield Financial Clout, 11 January 2010, 3.

Nikkei Weekly. (2010b). Older Generations Carry Consumption, 12 April 2010, 5.

Nishimura, T. (2006). Household Debt and Consumer Education in Postwar Japan. In S. Garon and P. L. Maclachlan (eds.), *The Ambivalent Consumer: Questioning Consumption in East Asia and the West*. London: Cornell University Press, pp. 260–280.

Partner, S. (1999). *Assembled in Japan: Electrical Goods and the Making of the Japanese Consumer*. Study of the East Asian Institute, Columbia University: University of California Press.

Rebick, M. (2005). *The Japanese Employment System: Adapting to a New Economic Environment*. New York: Oxford University Press.

Rice, G. and Wongtada, N. (2007). Conceptualizing Inter-attitudinal Conflict in Consumer Response to Foreign Brands, *Journal of International Consumer Marketing*, 20(1), 31–65.

Saito, M. (2000). *The Japanese Economy*. Singapore: World Scientific Pub.

Sakai, J. (2003). *Makeinu no Toboe* (The Howl of the Loser Dog). Tokyo: Kodansha.

Salsberg, B. (2010). The New Japanese Consumer, *McKinsey Quarterly*, March. http://www.mckinsey.com/insights/marketing_sales/beyond_paid_media_marketings_new_vocabulary, accessed on 28 July 2014.

Sanga, A. and Nishida, J. (2009). Marketing. In P. Haghirian (ed.), *J-Management: Fresh Perspectives on the Japanese Firm in the 21st Century*. Bloomington: iUniverse Press, pp. 180–203.

Sawa, T. (2010). Japan's Economy Will Grow on Eco-consumption, Immigration, *Japan Times* (9 February). Download from http://www.japantimes.co.jp/opinion/ 2010/02/09/commentary/japans-economy-will-grow-on-eco-consumption-immigration/#.U9T86bHEeSo

Schad-Seifert, A. (2006). Japans kinderarme Gesellschaft – die niedrige Geburtenrate und das Gender-Problem. In: M. Pohl and I. Wieczorek (eds.): *Japan 2006 Politik und Wirtschaft*. Hamburg: Institut für Asienkunde, pp. 221–44.

Shinohara, M. (1959). The Structure of Saving and the Consumption Function in Postwar Japan, *Journal of Political Economy*, 67(6): 589–603.

Schneidewind, D. (1998). *Shinhatsubai*. Munich: Beck.

Schütte, H. and Carliante, D. (1998). *Consumer Behavior in Asia*. London: Palgrave Macmillan.

Shimbo, H. and Hasegawa, A. (1999). The Dynamics of Market Economy and Production. In A. Hayami, O. Saitō and R. P. Toby (eds.), *The Emergence of*

Economic Society in Japan 1600–1859. Oxford: University Press, pp. 159–91.

Skov, L. and Moeran, B. (1995). *Women, Media and Consumption in Japan.* Honolulu: University of Hawaii Press.

Solomon, M., Bamossy, G. and Askegaard, S. (1999). *Consumer Behaviour, A European Perspective.* New York: Prentice Hall Europe.

Statistics Bureau (2010). Trends of Average Age Expectation of Life by Age (1891–2007', available at www.stat.go.jp/data/nenkan/zuhyou/y0212000. xls, downloaded on 19 October 2010.

Toussaint, A. (2011). Male Order: Resonating with Today's Young Male Japanese Consumers. In P. Haghirian (ed.): *Japanese Consumer Dynamics.* London: Palgrave Macmillan, pp. 119–43.

Usui, H. (2006). *Nihon no Fuyūsō,* Tokyo: Takashimasha.

Usunier, J. C. (2000). *Marketing Across Cultures.* Harlow: Pearson Education Limited.

Watts, J. (1998). Soccer Shinhatsubai: What are Japanese Consumers Making of the J. League? In D. P. Martinez (ed.), *The Worlds of Japanese Popular Cultures: Gender, Shifting Boundaries and Global Cultures.* Cambridge: Cambridge University Press, pp. 181–201.

Yamada, M. (1999). Parasaito shinguru no jidai (The Age of 'Parasite' Singles) [Japanese]. Tokyo: Chikuma Shobō.

Yoshimi, S. (2006). Consuming America, Producing Japan. In S. Garon and P. L. Maclachlan (eds.), *The Ambivalent Consumer: Questioning Consumption in East Asia and the West.* London: Cornell University Press, 63–84.

30

Labor Relations[1]

Akira Suzuki

INTRODUCTION

Cooperative enterprise unionism is often regarded as the dominant feature of labor relations in Japan. Enterprise unions often give priority to the market competitiveness of the enterprise over immediate demands of union members, such as higher wages and shorter working hours. Leaders of these unions have justified such policies by emphasizing that only better corporate performance will bring about higher wages and improved working conditions. Cooperative industrial relations were seen as one of the major reasons for the rapid economic growth in the 1960s and for the global competitiveness of Japan's export industries in the 1970s and 1980s. Even after the Japanese economy went into long-term recession in the early 1990s, and employers of even big enterprises started to downsize their workforce, enterprise-based cooperative industrial relations seemed to remain stable.

The Japanese labor movement, however, has not always been dominated by cooperative enterprise unionism. From the late 1940s to the mid 1960s labor unions adopted various policy orientations ranging from moderate to radical, and competed among themselves for the dominant position in the labor movement at the enterprise and national levels. This chapter examines how the 'balance' among various policy orientations of

the labor movement has changed from the 1950s to the 2000s by analyzing how these changes occurred in response to the political and economic contexts of each period as well as to the internal political dynamics of the labor movement. The first section of the chapter discusses the four types of policy orientation of the labor movement based on the two dimensions: 'method of seeking policy goals' and 'level of activities and focus of demand'. The typology of the policy orientations will serve as a 'template' for the subsequent analysis of the labor movement. The second section briefly examines the development of the Japanese labor movement prior to the early 1950s, outlining the early development of the labor movement and the institutions of industrial relations. The third, fourth, and fifth sections examine the development of the labor movement in Japan in the 1950s, from the early 1960s to the mid 1970s, and from the mid 1970s to the late 1980s. These chapters show how the four types of policy orientation were formed in each period and how their balance changed from one period to the next. The sixth section examines how the labor movement suffered from and/or coped with the changing economic and political contexts since the early 1990s. This section also considers how labor researchers evaluated the development of the labor movement since the 1990s when Japan went into severe economic recession.

TYPES OF POLICY ORIENTATION OF THE LABOR MOVEMENT

Types of Policy Orientation Based on Two Dimensions

The policy orientations of the labor movement can be classified into two dimensions: 'method of seeking policy goals' and 'level of activities and focus of demand'. The first dimension consists of the two aspects of the labor movement – as a 'movement' and as an 'institutional actor'. The labor movement is an actor of formal or informal rules (industrial-relations institutions) that define the relationship between labor unions, management and government, as well as an actor in the social movement designed to improve the status of workers at workplaces or in society as a whole. When the labor movement focuses on its 'movement' aspect the labor unions mobilize union members and their supporters for assemblies and strikes or for daily labor struggles to press for and seek concessions from its negotiating partners such as management and government. It often involves conflicts and tense relations between the negotiating parties. When the labor movement focuses on institutions, meanwhile, labor unions place their emphasis on seeking a compromise from or agreement with the negotiating parties through collective bargaining and labor–management consultations. Negotiations are led by union leaders, labor unions tending to run their organizations via a top-down (control) approach rather than a bottom-up (mobilization) approach.

The second dimension refers to the level of labor-movement activities. Since the labor movement engages in activities in both the economic and political spheres, the activities in the former can be classified as the corporate/industrial level, those in the latter as the national/social level. The levels of activities are linked to the central demands of the labor movement. Corporate/industrial-level activities focus on economic demands, such as wages and working conditions, while national/social-level activities focus on political demands, such as the promotion of policy formulation and improvement.

Four Types of Policy Orientation of the Labor Movement

The policy orientations of the labor movement can be classified into four types based on the above two dimensions (see Table 30.1). The first type is 'militant political unionism', which focuses on the movement aspect and involves national/social-level activities. This type of policy orientation is likely to be the main characteristic of the labor movement when the government represses the labor movement

or gives it only 'passive approval', which refers to the conditions in which the government accepts the organizing of labor unions but does not provide sufficient legal protection (Marks, 1989). This policy orientation is also likely to develop when the labor movement is regarded as a political outsider or is politically marginal, and its influence on formal policy-making processes is very limited. For the labor movement to exert its political influence on this 'closed' structure of political opportunities it is necessary to mobilize as many workers as possible to attend large-scale public assemblies and organize strikes (such as general strikes) to pressure the government. Massive mobilization requires, as a precondition, that many union members share a sufficient sense of solidarity to respond to calls for political mobilization.

The second type is 'political exchange', which focuses on the institutional aspects while acting at the national/social level. The labor movement, when it adopts this policy orientation, focuses on winning labor and social-policy demands by negotiation between union leaders and political elites (political exchanges) rather than through pressuring the government by mobilizing union members. For negotiations between labor and political elites to start the labor movement needs to have political influence that cannot be ignored by the government, or to have an established position as a political insider to have access to policy-making processes (Marks, 1989). A typical example is the corporatist system often seen in Western Europe. For the labor movement to exert its influence effectively as a political insider the movement needs to be recognized as an important actor that broadly represents the interests of workers in civil society.

The third type is 'militant economic unionism', which focuses on policies that are based on mobilization of union members for strikes at the corporate/industrial level and daily activities at workplaces. This type of policy orientation, in many cases, is implemented in combination with the first type, 'militant political unionism', since it centers on mobilization. However, while the former focuses on negotiating items on an economic agenda, such as wages and working conditions, with the management (or employer associations), the latter focuses on negotiating the political agenda with the government. Labor unions adopting this policy orientation seek concessions, such as wage increases and improved working conditions, from the management through the pressure of mass mobilization of union members for collective actions such as strikes. The members of labor unions with this type of policy orientation are not closely integrated into management and have a sufficient sense of solidarity to respond to mobilization orders from their leaders. This type of policy orientation, in many cases, is likely to develop

Table 30.1   Types of policy orientations of the labor movement

		Main methods of seeking policy goals	
		Focus on movement aspect: Mobilization of unions members and supporters (often involving conflicts and tension with counterparts of negotiations)	Focus on institutional aspects: Seeking a compromise from or agreement with the negotiating parties through deals
Level of activities and focus of demands	National/social level: Focus on political demands	(1) Militant political unionism (political unionism with unions as outsiders)	(2) Political exchange (political unionism with unions as insiders)
	Corporate/ industrial level: Focus on economic demands	(3) Militant economic unionism	(4) Business unionism or cooperative unionism

under conflictual labor–management relationships in which the management takes hard-line positions against demands made by the union, which in turn reacts combatively to the hard-line management.

The fourth type is 'business unionism' or 'cooperative unionism', which focuses on negotiations over an economic agenda through institutionalized relationships between labor and management (or employer associations) at the corporate/industrial level. The distinction between the two sub-types can be made based on whether labor unions have 'arm's-length' relations with management (business unionism) or are integrated into 'firms' decision making' (cooperative unionism) (Turner, 1991). 'Business unionism' can typically be found in labor–management relationships in the USA, where labor unions are organized as 'local unions' at the corporate level. Although organized at the corporate level, they are regarded by management as a part of external industrial unions. Local unions are supposed to contribute to stable industrial relations by negotiating and signing collective agreements with the management that stipulate wages and other working conditions and by dealing with complaints from union members through grievance procedures provided in the agreements. On the other hand, unions adopting 'cooperative unionism' (a typical example is enterprise unions in Japan) base their labor–management relationships on 'mutual trust' between labor and management. Such relationships have non-contract-based and informal elements, unlike the contract-based relations of 'business unionism'. These unions try to maintain stable labor–management relationships through close communication between union leaders and management. They also exert control over union members by keeping mobilization to a minimum to ensure that labor disputes do not affect corporate performance.

In the following section the chapter discusses the development of the postwar labor movement in Japan by period. The characteristics of the

labor movement in each period and the changes in characteristics from one period to the next can be represented by the balance or changes in the balance among the four types of policy orientations shown in Table 30.1. Table 30.2 illustrates the labor movement from the 1950s to the end of the 1980s in terms of the types described in Table 30.1. The general trend shows that, despite some differences in timing between each of the national confederations and sectors, the policy orientation shifted from 'militant political unionism' to 'political exchanges' at the national/social level (Table 30.2 (1) to (2)) and from 'militant economic unionism' to 'cooperative unionism' at the corporate/industrial level (Table 30.2 (3) to (4)). In terms of the relationship between the national/social-level activities and corporate/industrial-level activities, the influence of the former on the latter was strong when the labor movement was politicized in response to contentious national political debates up to the early 1970s (Table 30.2 (1) to (3)). For example, the economic demands of the spring offensive for wage hikes (*shunto*) in this period were linked to political issues. With the institutionalization of industrial relations, however, the influence of corporate-level activities on the national/social-level activities increased (Table 30.2 (4) to (2)). For example, industry-level union federations in export-oriented industries, representing the corporate-level economic interests of enterprise unions, formed a loose confederation in the mid 1970s so that these enterprise unions could make public-policy (i.e. political) demands (such as tax reductions and subsidies to enterprises for the maintenance of employment security) to the government more effectively.

The general trend of the labor movement in Japan is characterized by the movement aspect weakening under the increased influence of the institutional aspect. It should be noted, however, there are some exceptions to this general trend. Since the mid 1980s a new type of labor union, called 'community unions', has gained some, though limited, influence

Table 30.2 Types of policy orientations of the labor movement in Japan after the 1950s (1950s–80s)

		Main methods of seeking policy goals	
		Focus on movement aspect	Focus on institutional aspects
Level of activities and focus of demands	National/social level	(1) Political struggles led by Sohyo (From 1950s to the first half of the 1970s), the public-sector labor movement	(2) The 'Social Contract-based Labor Movement,' the demand for policy changes and institutional reforms (after the mid-1970s)
	Corporate/ industrial level	(3) Industry-level coordinated struggles during spring wage offensives (*Shunto*), shop-floor struggles, struggles against rationalization	(4) Industrial relations based on mutual trust (enterprise unions in large firms after the mid-1960s)

in the labor movement. Community unions are individually affiliated unions with a regional, rather than enterprise-based, representation structure. Although the total membership of community unions is a tiny fraction of the total number of union members (less than 1 percent), these unions opt for movement-based, rather than institutional-based, union policies, thus constituting the 'counter-trend' to the institutionalization of the labor movement in general.

DEVELOPMENT OF THE LABOR MOVEMENT UNDER POSTWAR DEMOCRATIC REFORMS[2]

The most significant event for the labor movement was the legalization of labor unions, implemented as part of the democratic reforms by General Headquarters (GHQ) during the US Occupation. The Labor Union Law, promulgated on 22 December 1945 and enforced on 1 March 1946, was the first law in Japan to stipulate rights for workers to organize labor unions, engage in collective bargaining with management, and go on strike if the negotiations failed. The Labor Relations Adjustment Law (enforced in the autumn of 1946), which stipulates a procedure for settling disputes between labor and management, introduced the system of mediation and arbitration by the Labor Commission. The Labor Standards Law, which regulates working conditions such as wages, working hours, and safety and health, was promulgated in April 1947 and fully enforced in November 1947. The labor laws introduced in the postwar reforms were advanced in nature and 'enhanced the legal environment of the labor movement to similar or better than that of the advanced capitalist countries at a stroke' (Kurita, 1994: 52–53).

Given the political changes accruing from the democratic reforms, the number of labor unions increased sharply. Most of the newly organized labor unions were enterprise-based or plant-based labor unions. Enterprise or plant unions were comprised of regular employees working at certain companies or plants, and many were so-called 'mixed unions', which include both clerical and factory workers (white-collar and blue-collar workers) at their companies. An 'enterprise union' was set up for a company with one plant, while a 'plant union' was formed per plant in a company with multiple plants (both are hereafter collectively called 'enterprise unions'). Industry-level union federations were also organized, along with the enterprise unions, but were basically 'alliances where enterprise unions could join or withdraw at their own discretion' (Kurita, 1994: 56). In addition to the enterprise unions and their industry-level federations nationwide labor-union organizations were also formed. Both Sodomei (Japan Confederation of Trade Unions) and Sanbetsu-kaigi (All Japan Congress of Industrial Unions) were formed in August 1946 and represented the rightist and leftist labor movements, respectively. The Sodomei was formed mainly by pre-war rightist and middle-faction union leaders and boasted about 1,700 labor unions with 855,000 members. The Sanbetsu-kaigi, on the other hand, had 21 industry-level union federations with about 1.56 million members. Many of the leaders were Japanese Communist Party (JCP) members and the organization was under the strong influence of the JCP. The Congress of Industrial Unions of Japan, rather than Sodomei, took the initiative in the labor movement in Japan for some years after its inauguration.

The policy orientations of the labor movement at the corporate as well as at the national/social levels were characterized by 'militant economic unionism' and 'militant political unionism', respectively (Table 30.1 (1) and (3)). Enterprise unions demanded large-scale wage hikes and the establishment of 'management councils' through which the unions had a strong say in corporate management. To put pressure on management the unions engaged in strikes and 'production-control struggle' (the struggle for the unions to occupy the management mechanism and to continue daily corporate activities instead of halting them). The national-level union movement and the public-sector unions with nationwide networks (e.g. the unions of postal and railway workers) linked their economic demands with political demands such as the overthrow of the government.

The US Occupation forces changed their policy in Japan from democratization to economic recovery after the Cold War started, and tried to suppress the increasingly combative labor movement. Ordinance No. 201 issued by the Japanese government in July 1948, based on the letter from General MacArthur, banned civil servants (public-sector workers) from striking and deprived them of the right to sign collective agreements with the government authorities. However, government-operated enterprises such as Japanese National Railways were designated as public corporations, and workers were granted the right to engage in collective bargaining with the authorities of the public corporations. The revised Labor Union Law of June 1949 included provisions purportedly to increase the autonomy of the unions by excluding 'people representing the interests of employers' (i.e., mid-management-level workers) from becoming union members and by prohibiting employers from paying salaries to full-time union officials. Another provision of the revised Labor Union Law, the provision to limit the validity of labor agreements to three years or less and ban automatic renewals, led to the termination of labor agreements without valid dates (many of them advantageous to labor unions) by management (Hyodo, 1997: 82–83).

In addition the economic policies of the US Occupation had indirect 'repressive' effects on the labor movement. For example, the occupation forces stipulated the Nine Principles for Economic Stability for the recovery of the Japanese economy, and Joseph Dodge (an economic advisor to the occupation forces) laid down the 'Dodge Line' to carry them out in March 1949. The fiscal constraints imposed by the Dodge Line forced administrative organizations and public corporations to cut personnel in large numbers (administrative restructuring). Private companies also came under severe pressure, as many of them relied on government subsidies and loans, and they implemented corporate restructuring by sharply reducing their personnel. Such personnel cuts in the public and private sectors dealt a serious blow to the labor movement as the cuts included many leftist unionists.

As the Korean War started the occupied forces launched the 'Red Purge' in July 1950 targeted at the newspaper and broadcasting industries. The Red Purge spread to the public and private sectors in general, resulting in the dismissal of a total of 13,000 people by the end of the year. Many leaders and activists from the enterprise unions who led the 'militant economic unionism' were dismissed either through the corporate and administrative restructuring or the Red Purge and, as a result, their unions were severely weakened or forced to disband. The impact of these suppressive policies was felt in the reduced number of labor unions and union members as well as the rate of union density. From 1949 to 1951 the number of labor unions declined by 20 percent, from 34,688 to 27,644. The number of union members declined by 15 percent and union density fell by 13.2 percentage points.

LABOR-MOVEMENT EFFORTS TO OVERCOME ENTERPRISE UNIONISM (THE 1950S)

Labor Policies and Political and Economic Contexts

The labor movement was weakened at the national as well as the corporate level due to the repressive policies against labor unions by GHQ and the government, and by management. However, the government maintained the framework of the Labor Union Law, which was introduced as part of the postwar democratization efforts, and neither restricted nor abolished the legalization of labor unions in the private sector. It also did not intervene in labor–management relationships at the corporate level. For the labor movement in the public sector, on the other hand, the government maintained the restrictive framework even after the US Occupation ended in 1951, and the legal system regulating public-sector labor relations was established separately from the system regulating private-sector labor relations. The Revised National Civil Service Law and the Local Civil Service Law sharply restricted the right for collective bargaining by national and local public employees and abolished the right to strike. The Public Corporations and Government Enterprises Labor Relations Law recognized the right for collective bargaining but banned strikes by employees of three public corporations (Japan National Railways (JNR), Japan Tobacco and Salt Public Corporation, and Nippon Telegraph and Telephone Public Corporation) and five government-operated enterprises (including the postal and forestry services). These very different legal frameworks for the private and public sectors of the labor movement had a strong influence on its development.

Major political events for the labor movement in the 1950s included political disputes and conflicts over a peace treaty to end the US Occupation, the military alliance with the USA, the rearmament of Japan, the 'reversed course' policy to correct 'excessiveness' in the postwar democratization reforms, the constitutional revision and the revision of the Japan–US Security Treaty. Such events helped revive active labor movements at the national level. Sohyo (General Council of Trade Unions of Japan, the national confederation established in July 1950 by the forces that opposed the strong influence of communists in the labor movement and aimed to establish a unified confederation encompassing centrist labor unions) played a central role in bolstering the active labor movement.

The Japanese economy, which had remained sluggish since the implementation of the Dodge Line, emerged from the recession due to the extra demand triggered by the Korean War, but plunged into a slump once again when the 'Korean War economic boom' waned in 1952. However, signs of economic turnaround began to appear in the latter half of 1954, and the balance of international payments drastically improved in 1955, with mining and industrial production and capital spending increasing sharply. Although the Japanese economy experienced a short recession in 1957, it started to recover in the autumn of 1958. The period of high economic growth, which lasted until the early 1970s, had started.

Sohyo's 'Shift to the Left' and the 'Takano Line'

Sohyo grew into an organization of 3.77 million members, or two-thirds of all unionized workers, by integrating labor unions participating in the anti-communist movement of Sanbetsu Kaigi, unions affiliated with Sodomei, and major independent unions. However, the trend for unifying the labor movement centering on Sohyo did not last long due to the impact of the Korean War and the intensified East-West conflict, which triggered internal conflicts of opinion within the labor movement. The second Sohyo convention, held in March 1951, after heated discussions, adopted the 'Four Peace Principles' – opposition to rearmament, maintaining neutrality, opposition to establishing military bases in Japan, and the overall peace treaty. It also rejected joining the International Confederation of Free Trade Unions (ICFTU), which had supported the USA in the Korean War. Thus, Sohyo, against the will of the USA, changed its political stance from friendship with the West to neutrality, siding neither with the USA nor the Soviet Union. The reasons for this change in Sohyo's political stance included a strengthened alliance among mid-level left-leaning union leaders of the major member unions of Sohyo, including Kokuro (National Railway Workers' Union), Zentei (Japan Postal

Workers' Union) and Nikkyoso (Japan Teachers' Union), and the spontaneous spread of support for pacifism among young union members who had had direct experience of World War II. On the other hand, a group consisting of union leaders who opposed the adoption of the Four Peace Principles and supported the ICFTU also strengthened its unity. As a result the anti-communist centrist forces, which supported the foundation of Sohyo, split into rightist and leftist factions over these political issues (Hyodo, 1997: 100; Carlile, 2005: 177, 179).

The split further deepened as three industry-level union federations Kaiin Kumiai (All Japan Seamen's Union), Zensen Domei (Japan Federation of Textile Industry Workers' Union), and Zeneien (Japan Motion Picture and Theatrical Workers' Union) seceded from Sohyo following the third Sohyo convention in 1953. These unions, together with affiliates of the 'reconstructed' Sodomei, formed Zenro (the Japan Trade Union Congress, 0.8 million members) in April 1954 (Sodomei split in November 1950 between a leftist group, which called for the disbandment of Sodomei and integration into Sohyo, and a rightist group, which rejected the disbandment of Sodomei and called for the formation of a new 'reconstructed' Sodomei). Zenro adopted a policy which focused on its affiliation with the ICFTU and struggles in the economic rather than political arena. The ICFTU, however, did not approve Zenro's request for affiliation because the international confederation still hoped for the affiliation of a unified national confederation based on a reconciliation between Sohyo and Zenro, and was hesitant to give Zenro, whose membership was much smaller than that of Sohyo, privileged status as the only ITUC-affiliated national confederation in Japan. Giving Zenro such status would have further alienated Sohyo and its affiliates from the ICFTU (Nakakita, 2008:127–134).

Sohyo in the early 1950s adopted a militant political unionist policy under the leadership of General Secretary Minoru Takano (Table 30.1 (1)). Based on the 'Takano Line' policy, Sohyo played a central role in a national movement, which called for peace and democracy, and engaged in a political struggle against regressive policies such as the Subversive Activities Prevention Law (1952). Sohyo also revitalized the labor movement at the corporate level through a bottom-up approach, associating the political agenda of the national movement with the economic demands (such as wage hikes and opposition to personnel cuts) of the enterprise unions (Shimizu, 1982: 319; Carlile, 2005: 216–217; Shinoda, 2005). For corporate-level struggles Sohyo adopted 'gurumi (joint) struggle' tactics, in which local community members and families of union members joined the struggles. Joint-struggle tactics were applied in the Amagasaki Steel dispute and the Nikko-Muroran dispute (both in 1954), which were reactions to wage reductions and personnel cuts in the economic recession following the end of the Korean War economic boom. The disputes were prolonged, involving local community members and families of union members, but the labor unions eventually lost both (Kamada and Kamada, 1993).

The Shift to the 'Ohta/Iwai Line' and the Start of the Spring Offensive

In the mid 1950s Kaoru Ohta, a chairman of Goka Roren (National Federation of Synthetic Chemical Industry Workers Unions), and others advocated a tactic which focused on wage struggles, unlike the joint-struggle tactics, which focused on a political agenda. Under the initiative of Ohta and other union leaders who were critical of the Takano Line, industry-level union federations started the spring offensive, or *shunto*, a jointly organized struggle for wage hikes. At the end of 1954 the joint council comprised five industry-level union federations belonging to Sohyo, including Goka Roren and Shitetsu Soren (General Federation of Private Railway Workers' Unions of Japan). Three other industry-level union federations including Denki Roren (All Japan Federation of Electric Machine Workers' Unions, not a member of Sohyo) joined the joint council later, developing the council into the Joint Council of Eight Industry-level Union Federations. The joint council staged three rounds of unified strikes and all the participating organizations won wage hikes.

The labor unions focused on wage struggles because of intensified suppression of wage hikes by employers. Nikkeiren (Japan Federation of Employers' Associations, one of the major employers' associations established in 1948) started insisting that it would not allow 'wage hikes without improved productivity', and that wage hikes should be limited to regular pay hikes. The spring offensive aimed at strengthening ties among labor unions at the industrial level through joint industrial struggles to counter the 'suppressive wage hike policy'; at reversing the weakening negotiating power of the enterprise unions at companies where managerial authority had strengthened; and at winning an increase in the basic wage rate in addition to regular pay hikes (Kurita, 1994: 131; Hyodo, 1997: 124–125). At the sixth Sohyo convention, held after the 1955 spring wage offensive, Akira Iwai from Kokuro was elected as general secretary, while Kaoru Ohta was elected as vice chairman. The executive committee of Sohyo thus shifted from the 'Takano Line' to the 'Ohta/Iwai Line'.

Sohyo's executive committee under the 'Ohta/Iwai Line' focused on economic struggles in the spring offensive based on militant economic unionism (Table 30.1 (3)). It did not give the political agenda a central role but did not totally depart from militant political unionism (Table 30.1 (1)). Playing coordinating roles for popular actions, Sohyo called on its member industry-level union federations to mobilize their union members for such political struggles as the campaign against the expansion of the Sunagawa Base of the US Air Force (1955–56), the struggle against the revision of the Police Official Duties Execution Law that aimed at giving police officers an authority to disperse mass rallies (1958), and the struggle against the revision of the US–Japan Security Treaty (1959–60) (Hyodo, 1997: 198–199).

Enterprise Unions' Militant Economic Unionism

The power of the enterprise unions was considerably weakened as a result of the repressive policies of GHQ/government and management in the late 1940s. However, in the 1950s, many enterprise unions regained their combativeness. After many leftist executive leaders and activists were dismissed as a result of corporate restructuring and the Red Purge, moderate members took over the executive committees of the enterprise unions. As Sohyo leaned toward the left, however, some moderate leaders and activists began to advocate militant economic unionism (Table 30.1 (3)). Leaders and activists advocating militant economic unionism tried to overcome the weakness of the enterprise unions mainly through two different approaches. First, through participation in the struggles of the spring offensives organized by industry-level union federations, enterprise unions tried to strengthen their negotiating power against management. Enterprise unions, coordinating their actions through industry-level union federations, made unified demands for wage hikes under the same collective bargaining schedules and went on unified strikes if the negotiations failed. Second, the enterprise unions tried to maintain and improve working conditions by democratizing the authoritarian relationship between management and labor through struggles at workplaces and by holding back the pace of rationalization (Shimizu, 1982: 334–336). Some enterprise unions, such as Nissan Local of Zenji (All Japan Automobile Workers' Union), the union of Hokuriku Railroad (Hokuriku Railroad Workers' Union), and the union of Miike Coal Mine (Miike Union), formed powerful organizations at their workplaces to regulate the working conditions of union members (Kamii, 1994; Hirai, 2000). Few other enterprise unions were able to stage effective struggles at their workplaces, but they tried to revitalize their unions through the bottom-up approach by mobilizing union members at the workplace level.

While enterprise unions followed the militant economic–unionism policy to gain autonomy for the labor-union movement, management did not recognize the autonomy of the unions. Management promoted 'second unions', which cooperated with management by intervening with labor unions during protracted labor disputes over wage hike demands and rationalization proposals. Examples of protracted labor disputes which resulted in splits of labor unions included the Nissan dispute (1953), the Nikko-Muroran dispute (1954), the Oji Paper dispute (1958), the Mitsui-Miike dispute (1959–60) and the Shin Nihon Chisso dispute (1962–63). The second unions were described in two contrasting ways: as a 'second personnel department' subordinate to the management, and as an organization with some degree of spontaneity on the side of the workers with a strong sense of enterprise consciousness. Some observers pointed to instances of 'excessively' cooperative attitudes taken by second unions toward management policies (Yamamoto, 1981), but the fact that the second unions represented a majority of workers, with the 'first unions' being relegated to a minority status, gives due weight to the opposite view as well (Kurita, 1994; Hisamoto, 1998).

Intensified Conflict between Public-sector Unions and Government

The public-sector unions, led by the JCPU (Joint Council of Public-sector Unions, hereafter the JCPU), participated in the spring offensive starting in 1956. Kokuro and Zentei began to engage in de facto strikes, which crossed the legal boundaries of the Public Corporations and Government Enterprises Labor Relations Law through such actions as 'assemblies at workplaces', 'rejecting overtime work', and 'work-to-rule tactics'. In the 1957 spring wage offensive the JCPU, led by Kokuro, escalated their collective actions, causing delays and disruptions to many national railway train services. Public-sector unions such as Kokuro adopted militant strategies despite the legal restrictions, mainly for two reasons. First, employees of public corporations and government enterprises (e.g. the national railways and postal services), whose working conditions were similar to those of blue-collar workers in the private sector, felt that they had been unfairly deprived of their right to strike by the government ordinance no. 201 during the US Occupation, and they made the restoration of their right to strike one of the most important policy goals of the unions. Second, although the

Public Corporations and Government Enterprises Labor Relations Law provided the arbitration system (the committee that made binding arbitration awards when the unions and the authorities of public corporations/government enterprises could not settle wage negotiations by themselves), the system did not function smoothly because the government did not fully comply with the arbitration awards. This made it necessary for public-sector workers to take extra-legal actions to put pressure on the government.

The confrontation between the public-sector unions and the government intensified because of the 'retaliation' by the latter against the former. The government and public corporations punished the JCPU unions for the strikes in the 1957 spring offensive on a record scale, dismissing 19 people, suspending, reducing wages, and reprimanding about other 700 people within Kokuro. Kokuro staged a struggle against this punishment on a scale in excess of the spring offensive, and the government and public corporations responded by further punishing union members on a massive scale. Relations between the public-sector unions and the government plunged into a vicious circle of struggles against punishment and further punishments. Kokuro selected three dismissed union members as executives at its convention in June 1957 and, in response, the JNR authority refused any collective bargaining with Kokuro, giving 'a lack of lawful representatives' as their rationale. After being unable to engage in any collective bargaining for four months Kokuro selected unpunished members as its chairman and vice chairman to lift the deadlock between labor and management. Kokuro and the Zentei (Zentei went on strike in the 1958 spring offensive and the government imposed massive punishments and rejected any collective bargaining) regarded the punishments and the rejection of any collective bargaining as suppression of the unions by the government, and further intensified the militant political-unionist policy (Table 30.1 (1)). To counter the government's suppressive policies Zentei and Sohyo jointly filed complaints with the International Labour Organization (ILO) to proceed with the struggle for ratification of the ILO Convention 87 (Freedom of Association and Protection of the Right to Organise Convention).

Struggles against Revision of the Security Treaty and Massive Mobilization for the Mitsui–Miike Dispute

The Japanese labor movement was tilted toward militant political and economic unionism in 1959 and 1960 as the Sohyo-led labor movement engaged in struggles in the political arena (struggles against the revision of the US–Japan Security Treaty) as well as in the economic arena (the labor dispute at the Mitsui–Miike Coal Mine).

The struggle against the revision of the US–Japan Security Treaty was a political struggle joined by a broad range of the labor movement, including private-sector labor unions. The revision of the treaty was designed to enhance mutual obligations, including Japan's obligation to cooperate in wars fought by US forces in the Far East. The labor movement, led by Sohyo, formed the National Conference Against Security Treaty Revisions in March 1959 with 13 organizations. The national movement against the revision culminated after the House of Representatives forced through the ratification of the treaty on 19–20 May 1960. Following the forced vote on the ratification demonstrations against the revision took place almost every day around the Diet building, the prime minister's office and the US embassy. Massive political strikes against the revision were organized in the 17th unified action on 4 June, which were joined by 4.6 million members. Kokuro and Doro (National Railway Locomotive Engineers' Union), which played leading roles in the united actions, staged an 'assembly at workplaces' from 5am to 7am, causing many train services to be delayed or canceled. Massive political strikes were also held on 15 and 22 June. However, the movement gradually faded as the new security treaty was ratified automatically on 19 June, and Prime Minister Kishi announced his resignation on 23 June, the day the treaty came into force.

At around the same time the biggest labor dispute in Japan's postwar history took place at the Mitsui–Miike Coal Mine. In August 1959 the Mitsui Mine Company announced a restructuring plan, including about 2,000 personnel reductions at the mine. In those days the Miike Union staged active struggles at workplaces and regulated the pace of restructuring and working conditions. As the number of miners who responded to the voluntary-retirement offer fell far short of the company's target it designated 1,278 workers, including about 300 workplace activists, for dismissal in December as a strategy for weakening the regulating power of the Miike Union. In protest against these targeted dismissals the union staged intermittent strikes. However, because the company started a lock-out in January 1960 the union went on indefinite strike (Hirai, 2000). Sohyo and Tanro (Japan Coal Miners' Union, the industry-level union federation with which the Miike Union was affiliated) gave full support and advice to the Miike Union during the rest of the strike.

During the strike groups critical of the strike seceded from the Miike Union, calling for the cancellation of the strike and the resumption of coal production. They later formed the second labor union (Miike Shinro, or New Miike Union) in March. The New Miike Union signed a labor agreement with the company that included the restarting of production, and began work again by breaking the picket line in violent clashes with Miike Union members. However, the Miike Union members then occupied the coal-storage sites (the hoppers) to prevent mined coal from being shipped out. The hoppers were occupied not only by Miike Union members but also by other union members gathered from around the country to support the Miike Union members, swelling the number of occupying union members and supporters to as many as 20,000. To remove these occupying union members and supporters from the hoppers 10,000 police were gathered in July. Amid increasing concerns over casualties if clashes were to occur, the Miike Union and management agreed to give carte blanche to a mediation plan by the chairman of the Central Labor Committee, just barely averting deadly clashes. The mediation plan offered in August only replaced the designated dismissals with voluntary retirement, virtually accepting the dismissals of workers designated by the company. However, conscious of the limits of the movement, Tanro decided after heated discussions to accept the mediation plan. The Miike Union accepted Tanro's decision, eventually ending the Miike dispute. After the dispute was settled the strength of the Miike Union waned as the company adopted hostile labor policies against the union, and the New Miike Union, which accepted and cooperated with the company's restructuring plan, gained the labor leadership instead.

DEVELOPMENT OF THE LABOR MOVEMENT DURING THE HIGH-ECONOMIC-GROWTH PERIOD (FROM 1960 TO THE MID 1970S)

Political and Economic Contexts of the Labor Movement

In the aftermath of the heated struggle against the revision of the US–Japan Security Treaty the Ikeda administration adopted a low-profile political agenda. Prime Minister Ikeda tried to stabilize his Liberal Democratic Party (LDP) administration by pursuing the high-economic-growth strategy, including his renowned plan to double the national income. However, this did not mean that political disputes disappeared: the labor movement, led by Sohyo, staged a struggle against the Anti Political Violence Law in 1961, a struggle against the Treaty on Basic Relations between Japan and the Republic of Korea in 1965, and a unified strike against the Vietnam War in 1966. However, the scale of mobilization for these political struggles fell far short of that for the struggles against the revision of the security treaty. The conflicts between the government and the public-sector labor unions eased to some extent after the 'Ikeda–Ohta Meeting' in 1964 on public-sector wages (see below). The Japanese Diet also ratified ILO Convention 87 in 1965, as demanded by public-sector unions. However, the government continued to oppose granting the right to strike to workers of public corporations and government enterprises.

The high pace of economic growth in Japan accelerated further in the 1960s. The annual real economic growth rate topped 10 percent from 1960 to 1969 except for 1962 and 1965. Being exposed to severe international competition as a result of the trade and capital liberalizations in the early 1960s, Japanese companies rapidly increased their capital spending to enhance their competitiveness, causing labor shortages (especially for young workers). The job-openings ratio had hovered at around 1 percent since 1967, and the demand for workers outpaced the supply until 1974. Given this labor-market situation, wages increased at every spring offensive (Lee, 2000: 34). The high-economic-growth period ended with the First Oil Shock in the autumn of 1973, but labor unions increased their demands for wage hikes as inflation rapidly took over. In the 1974 spring offensive labor unions mobilized the highest number of union members and won the largest wage hikes in the history of the spring offensive.

Sohyo's Declining Influence in the Private Sector and Domei's Expansion

The shift in the stance of the labor movement for major private companies from militant economic unionism to cooperative unionism started in some companies in the 1950s and accelerated further in the 1960s, especially among export-oriented enterprise unions. This shift took the following forms: the secession of enterprise unions as a whole from a Sohyo-affiliated industry-level union federation after the leadership change at an enterprise union; or the split of a labor union into a majority group in favor of cooperative unionism and a minority group in favor of militant economic unionism due to a dispute over secession from Sohyo. Such secessions and splits were conspicuous, especially among enterprise unions in the ship-building, chemical, paper-pulp, and metal-machinery industries (Kinoshita, 1992: 17–32; see Ueda, 1999 for a case study of the ship-building industry). Many of the enterprise unions that seceded from Sohyo joined industry-level union federations affiliated with Domei (Japanese Confederation of Labor), whose policy was oriented to cooperative industrial

relations. Domei was a national confederation established in 1964 as a successor organization to Zenro and Sodomei.

This policy shift occurred for the following reasons. First, given the severe market situation their companies were facing, these enterprise unions opted to cooperate with, rather than fight, the management so that their companies could survive competition from abroad. Second, the management at major private companies intervened in the internal affairs of their labor unions with the overriding aim of establishing a leadership cooperative with management. And, third, the industry-level union federations affiliated with Domei actively made approaches to the labor unions affiliated with Sohyo to make the policy change. As a result Domei overtook Sohyo in its number of private-sector-worker members in 1967 (see Gordon, 1998 for a case study of the role played by management in consolidating the leadership advocating cooperative unionism in one of the major steel companies).

'Pattern Bargaining' in the Spring Offensive

The spring offensive, which started in 1955, adopted militant economic unionism to demand large-scale wage hikes from management by staging unified struggles coordinated by the industry-level union federations. It was in 1964 or later that the spring offensive started to adopt a mechanism by which the levels of wage hikes between different industries were determined by 'pattern bargaining'. Before then the spring offensive could not set clear patterns for wage hikes, and the relationship between private-sector wages and public-sector wages was uncertain. However, it was agreed at the 'Ikeda–Ohta Meeting' (a meeting between Prime Minister Ikeda and Sohyo Chairman Ohta) held during the 1964 spring offensive that the wages of workers in the public sector should mirror those of workers in the private sector. As a result major private companies (especially in the heavy chemical industry) became pattern setters in the ensuing spring offensives, which were followed by wage settlements in other industries/sectors in this order: private railway companies, public corporations, national public employees, and local public employees (Hayakawa, 1992: 246). Moreover, the spring offensive started to influence wages of non-unionized companies as it served as a yardstick for wage hikes in mid-and small-sized companies and companies in local industries with low rates of union density.

In the spring offensives after the 1960s the industry-level union federations belonging to the Japan Council of Metalworkers' Unions (IMF-JC) increased their influence in wage negotiations.

The IMF-JC was founded in 1964 by labor unions of companies in export industries to cope with trade liberalization. It was joined by industry-level union federations in the metal-machinery industries (steel, electric machine, ship-building, automobile, and machinery) that were beyond the existing frameworks of the national confederations such as Sohyo and Domei. The IMF-JC played the role of pattern setter in the 1967 spring offensive for the first time, and the industry-level union federations affiliated with the IMF-JC played leading roles in setting the pattern of wage hikes in the spring offensives that followed. Among them the industry-level union federation of the steel industry (Tekko Roren (Japanese Federation of Iron and Steel Workers' Unions, hereafter the JFSWU)) strengthened its influence as the pattern setter because the business performance of the materials industry was relatively stable (Lee, 2000: 33).

Sohyo's Efforts to Give the Spring Offensive a Political Agenda

Sohyo in the early 1970s not only made economic demands in the spring offensive but also political demands related to the living standards of a broad range of people, urging the government, through massive mobilization of their union members, to implement their proposed policies. Although the spring offensive was institutionalized, starting in 1964, in terms of wage hikes through pattern bargaining, it also tended to become a political struggle (Table 30.1 (1)). The 'Major 15 Demands' advocated by Sohyo in the 1970 spring offensive included a broad range of demands for policy changes and institutional reforms, such as a unified national minimum wage, anti-pollution measures, measures against traffic disaster, tax reductions, and improvements in social security systems, as well as large-scale wage hikes and shorter working hours. In the 1973 spring offensive 53 industry-level union federations belonging to the joint spring offensive committee, which had 3.5 million members, staged unified 'pension' strikes and mass meetings across the country, demanding improvements of the pension system, particularly the introduction of a sliding scale based on wages.

The 1974 spring offensive, which took place against the backdrop of skyrocketing prices caused by the First Oil Shock, was the height of the massive mobilization-style strategy. Sohyo regarded the spring offensive as a 'struggle to seek changes in the economic and political regimes through solidarity between the labor unions and the people', and demanded wage hikes of over 30,000 yen, under the banner of the 'People's spring offensive to defend the nation's standards of living from inflation', while demanding that the government implement

the policies aimed at improving people's livelihoods, such as price controls, tax reductions, and an increase in assistance to low-income families. The biggest numbers of strikes in the history of the spring offensive were staged in early to mid April. The two assemblies held in March by the People's Joint Fight against Inflation attracted 230,000 to 250,000 people in Tokyo and 1.3 to 1.4 million people nationwide. The spring offensive attracted this large number of people due to public complaints against declining living standards caused by inflation and public resentment of moves by companies that further fueled inflation (Shinkawa, 1993: 201–202; Hyodo, 1997: 307–308). The 1974 spring offensive marked a record number of dispute cases at 5,375 and triggered the highest wage hikes in history of the spring offensive – 32.9 percent – at major private companies.

Striking for the Right to Strike by the JCPU

Two major events that changed the trend of the labor movement took place in 1975. One of them was the 1975 spring offensive, which we will discuss in the next section. The other event was the 'strike for the right to strike' by the JCPU, which was held for eight days between November and December 1975. The strike for the right to strike was a political strike organized by nine public-sector unions belonging to the JCPU, including Kokuro, Zentei and Zendentsu (Telecommunication Workers' Union of Japan), to demand the government revive the right to strike banned by the Public Corporations and Government Enterprises Labor Relations Law. It was also the last case of the large-scale labor movement adopting the militant-political-unionism policy (Table 30.1 (1)) in the public sector. Faced with the strike, the government, insisting that parliamentary democracy could not be maintained at the same time as illegal strikes, announced that it would respect a written recommendation by an expert committee (an advisory body to the Cabinet Secretariat designed to discuss the issue of right to strike), which was negative about granting the right to strike. Thus, the government maintained its stance against granting the right to strike to public-sector workers. The JCPU protested against this government announcement, but faced with mounting public criticism of the prolonged strikes it decided to cancel them. The JCPU failed to gain any concessions from the government and the strike for the right to strike ended in defeat (Hyodo, 1997: 316; Kumazawa, 1982: 509).

The significance of the strike for the right to strike in the context of the labor movement is the fact that the strike revealed a difference in opinion between the public and private sectors. Domei, strongly influenced by the private-sector labor unions, strongly opposed political strikes. During the strike members of the Tetsuro (the Railway Workers' Union, a minority union within the JNR, affiliated with Domei) cooperated in running the train services together with managers. Even the private-sector labor unions that had had cooperative relations with the JCPU, such as Shitetsu Soren and Unyu Roren (All Japan Federation of Transport Workers' Unions), showed little interest in supporting the strike. Thus, the strike for the right to strike gained little support, with only a few exceptions, and turned into an isolated struggle by the JCPU. The private-sector labor unions showed little interest in supporting the strike because many of them had immediate concerns over their members' employment amid the recession following the oil shock and the streamlining measures imposed by management. They were also skeptical about the class-struggle-oriented rhetoric emphasized by the JCPU (Kumazawa, 1982: 502–503; Shinkawa, 1993: 149; Inoue, 1997: 195–196). Following the defeat the influence of the public-sector labor movement within Sohyo and the labor movement as a whole declined.

THE LABOR MOVEMENT IN THE LOW-GROWTH PERIOD AND THE UNIFICATION OF THE LABOR MOVEMENT (FROM 1975 TO THE LATE 1980S)

Political and Economic Contexts of the Labor Movement

Fearful of cost-push inflation caused by the large-scale wage hikes in spring offensives (especially in 1974), the government adopted several countermeasures for the 1975 spring offensive. While refraining from adopting formal income policies (presenting formal guidelines on wage hikes to be observed by unions and management at the corporate level), the government had unofficial discussions about wage hikes with business leaders and some private-sector union leaders, especially the leaders of the JFSWU (which had played the important role of pattern setter in spring offensives). The government also implemented measures to control total demand through financial tightening, reducing both the corporate ability to pay wages and labor unions' militancy (Shinkawa, 1993: 203–204, 211).

In the 1980s the government adopted the policy of administrative reform. The government launched the Temporary Research Committee on Public Administration (*Rincho*) in 1979, from which the government received a recommendation in 1982 (on the privatization of JNR, the Nippon Telegraph and Telephone Public Corporation (NTT) and the Japan Tobacco and Salt Public Corporation). The government, based on the recommendation from the Japan National Railways Reconstruction Management Committee and the Japan National Railways Reform Law legislated in 1986, divided and privatized JNR into nine new JR companies in April 1987. The divestiture and privatization of JNR considerably weakened the influence of Kokuro, which had played central roles in Sohyo and the public-sector labor movement in the past.

The economic growth rate during the second half of 1970s and the 1980s, following the First Oil Shock, hovered around a very low 3 to 5 percent. The economic recovery in Japan depended closely on restructuring, cost reductions, and quality improvement by export-oriented companies to increase their international competitiveness. Labor unions of major private companies reacted swiftly to the economic situation and increased their cooperation with management to increase their corporate competitiveness. Hit hard by the recession, mid- and small-sized companies suffered more severe conditions than their larger counterparts. Labor unions of mid- and small-sized companies, which used to stage militant movements against restructuring, shifted their 'anti-rationalization' policy to a more 'realistic' one, given that the survival of their companies was at stake (Inoue, 1997).

Transformation of the Spring Offensive and the Leadership of Export-industry Labor Unions

Given the large-scale wage hikes in the 1974 spring offensive, Nikkeiren (Japanese Federation of Employers' Associations) announced a guide for wage hikes of 15 percent or less in the 1975 spring offensive, with the firm determination to restrain them. Responding to the government and business circles' concerns about cost-push inflation, leaders of the private-sector labor movement such as the JFSWU and the Domei recommended accepting wage-hike restraints. For example, at the Domei Convention in January 1975 Chairman Amaike proposed a 'Social Contract-based Labor Movement', which called for the government to contain inflation while labor unions restrained their demands for wage hikes. At the previous year's convention JFSWU Chairman Miyata suggested it would be difficult for the labor unions to continue with the practice of the 'previous year's wage-hike achievements plus a bit extra', a conventional method of demanding wage hikes, as the Japanese economy was transforming from the period of high economic growth to the 'stable growth period' (Hyodo 1997: 292–293).

The JFSWU as a pattern setter compromised with the 14.9 percent offer by management in the 1975 spring offensive, and the wage hikes won in the ensuing wage-hike negotiations by the other industries were lower than the levels set by the JFSWU. The JFSWU setting a wage-hike cap marked a 'virtual' end to the pattern of private-sector labor unions (up to the 1974 spring offensive) winning further increases in the ensuing wage-hike negotiations from the levels won initially by the pattern setter (i.e. the JFSWU). The wage hikes at major private-sector companies were less than half of the previous year's levels (13.1 percent on average), which were within the guide presented by Nikkeiren. The number of strikes staged in the 1975 spring offensive declined by 30 percent from the previous year because private-sector labor unions were increasingly concerned about the economic recession and changed their strategy from focusing on wage hikes to maintaining employment. Since government and management did not make any policy commitments, such as anti-inflation measures or job security, in return for voluntary acceptance of wage-hike restraints by labor unions, the 'Social Contract-based Labor Movement' was dubbed 'Self-restraint without a Contract' (Inoue, 1997: 174–175).

The wage hikes declined further in the 1976 spring offensive to one-digit figures. In the spring offensives in the late 1970s the IMF-JC, which consisted mainly of export-oriented industry-level union federations, increased its weight. In the 1976 spring offensive, four of the IMF-JC-affiliated industry-level union federations (steel, shipbuilding, electrics, and automobile) adopted the 'Intensive Negotiation by JC4 Industry-level Union Federations' (hereafter the 'Intensive Negotiation') strategy, in which the four organizations demanded decisions on wage hikes from management on the same day. The 'Intensive Negotiation' strategy was designed to 'win the maximum wage hikes' through an enhanced alliance among industry-level union federations affiliated with the IMF-JC. However, the actual effect of the strategy was for the unions of export-oriented industries to set a cap on wage hikes for all industries which was commensurate with improved productivity in the export sectors directly exposed to market competition. The 'Intensive Negotiation' strategy had this effect because the labor unions in the export sector reacted sensitively to competitive market pressures. For example, the 'economic consistency' theory, which was advocated by the JFSWU and affected the entire policy of the IMF-JC, argued that the wage-hike demands needed to be consistent with the real economic and market situations. The transformation of the spring offensives made obsolete the past wage-hike negotiations of mobilizing union members for strikes, which characterized the spring offensives up to

1974. The transformation also promoted top-level negotiations. After 1975 the negotiating process for determining wage hikes in the spring offensive became less visible to ordinary union members as the negotiations were held only at the 'top level', resulting in the further institutionalization of the spring offensive (Hyodo, 1997: 301, 322; Sako, 1997: 250; Lee, 2000: 44, 51–52).

Attempts to Have a Stronger Say in Government Policy-making through Demands for Policy Changes and Institutional Reforms

The 'Social Contract-based Labor Movement' advocated by Domei and the other private-sector labor unions that accepted wage-hike restraints in the 1975 spring offensive became, effectively, 'Self-Restraint without Contracts', and no formal agreement on the 'political exchange' (Table 30.1 (2)) was reached between the labor movement and the government. However, unofficial ties were formed between union leaders and the government, and through such ties the private-sector labor unions sought to increase their influence on government policies. The private-sector labor unions engaged in the demand for policy changes and institutional reforms because labor-union leaders were increasingly convinced that concentrating only on economic demands at the corporate level would not be sufficient to maintain the living standards of workers (Hyodo, 1997: 298). Sixteen industry-level union federations established Seisui Kaigi (Trade Union Council for Policy Promotion) in 1976. Seisui Kaigi made policy demands on the government and the ruling and opposition parties in four policy areas (economic policy, employment, prices, and taxes). As the unemployment worsened in industries suffering the structural recession, such as ship-building and textiles, Seisui Kaigi also demanded that the government formulate industrial policies and measures to support the unemployed (Hyodo, 1997: 418–419). A formal discussion forum for representatives of the government, management, and labor unions, Sanrokon (the Round Table Discussion Meeting of Industrial Labor Problems), had been established in 1970. During the 1975 spring offensive and after Sanrokon gained increasing attention as a venue for 'political exchange'. Labor-union representatives demanded increased authority and functions for Sanrokon as an organ for corporatism. However, Sanrokon remained just one of the advisory councils to the Minister of Labor and was said to have 'failed to gain any authority whatsoever to influence national policies' (Shinkawa, 1993: 222).

Development of Labor–management Consultation Systems and Enhancement of Mutual Trust

Enterprise unions at major private companies enhanced their cooperative unionism after the mid 1970s. As mentioned earlier, the labor unions of export-sector companies, as represented by the IMF-JC, voluntarily restrained their demands for wage hikes in response to their companies' severe market situations and in line with the 'economic consistency' theory. They also responded flexibly to drastic restructuring plans, which were required to enhance corporate competitiveness. Such moves by the enterprise unions were criticized as being 'too acquiescent' to management demands, but the enterprise unions made some efforts to make their presence clearly felt.

First, they made efforts to defend the employment of their workers in compensation for 'sacrifices', such as limited wage hikes and reallocation of the labor force within companies due to restructuring plans. The commitment by management to stable employment was believed to have been maintained at least until the early 1990s at major private companies. However, measures to cope with the excessive labor force accruing from corporate restructuring plans shifted gradually from the reallocation of the labor force within companies to the transfer to affiliated companies within corporate groups. Second, labor union leaders adopted the 'Deep Involvement in Management' strategy in which they voiced and exchanged opinions on restructuring and management plans in detail with the management through labor–management consultations within the general framework of cooperation. The labor–management consultation system was designed to smooth out labor–management communications through exchanges of opinions between representatives of the enterprise union and the management on working conditions, employment and personnel affairs, welfare, production plans, and management policies. The consultation system was different from collective bargaining, which, if it failed, could result in strikes (Kurita, 1994: 182–183; also see Nitta, 1988 for a case study of the consultation system at one of the major steel companies). A survey in 1984 by the Ministry of Labor indicated that about 65 percent of companies had some form of labor–management consultation body, with a higher percentage at larger companies. A survey conducted in 1992–93 among enterprise unions in the private sector revealed that about 60 percent of labor unions had an 'effective say in the management strategy', with a higher percentage at larger companies. About 60 percent of the labor unions started to have such a say in the early 1980s (Inagami, 1995: 10, 298–299). However, some argue that involvement with management by enterprise unions was only

'procedural' and had no actual impact on management strategies (Kamii, 1994: 9–10).

The 'Deep Involvement in Management' strategy through the labor–management consultation system also had some side effects. As mutual trust deepened between the enterprise-union leaders and the management, and they started to share high-level management information, the gap between labor-union leaders and ordinary members widened. For example, labor-union leaders and the management held unofficial prior consultations over personnel restructuring that were not disclosed to general members. The agreement made at the unofficial meeting was 'discussed' between union and management representatives at the official consultation, as shown in the case of a major steel company (Mori, 2003). There may have been some cases where the management made modifications to their original restructuring plans based on the opinions of labor-union leaders at unofficial consultations. However, general union members knew the content of the unofficial meetings only when they were discussed at official meetings, and labor–management agreements had already been reached by then. As a result, the sense of being a party to the running of their union waned among the general members of the unions, reducing their interest in union activities.

Move toward the Unification of the Labor Movement and Internal Conflict within Sohyo

The movement to unify the labor movement under one dominant confederation became increasingly active from the end of the 1970s to the early 1980s. This movement was led by private-sector labor unions. Due to the economic changes since the mid 1970s, and to the active pursuit of the 'Deep Involvement in Management' strategy by many private-sector enterprise unions, the differences in policy orientations among member unions of major labor confederations such as Sohyo, Domei, and the Churitsu Roren (Federation of Independent Unions of Japan, the confederation of industry-level union federations not affiliated with either Sohyo or Domei) became narrow. In other words, the policy orientations of these confederations started to converge on cooperative unionism (Table 30.1 (4)). In addition the major confederations were in agreement on the necessity of demanding policy changes and institutional reforms, thus strengthening their voice in political exchanges with the government (Table 30.1 (2)).

The conventions of the Domei, the JFSWU (a major affiliate of Sohyo), and Zensen Domei (a major affiliate of Domei) in 1978 advocated the labor-unification movement led by private-sector unions (hereafter called 'the labor unification').

As a result of consultations among the major national confederations, the Labor Unification Promotion Council was formed in 1980, which consisted of representatives from six industry-level union federations in the private sector. After 13 rounds of discussions the council released the 'Basic Plan for Labor Unification' in June 1981. The basic plan argued that conditions for the labor unification were favourable due to the deepening of the 'mutual relationship' among industry-level union federations in the private sector. The necessity of labor unification included the fact that the split of the national confederations prevented the labor movement in Japan from exerting its influence when demanding that the government make policy changes and institutional reforms, and the fact that labor unification enabled the labor movement in Japan to participate actively in the international labor movement by reinforcing the alliance between the national labor movement and the ICFTU. For the 'approach to the unification' the basic plan advocated launching the Preparatory Conference for Labor Unification, which consisted of industry-based labor unions committed to participating in the new national confederation. The basic plan took a firm stand against any groups and organizations which criticized the labor unification led by the private-sector unions as being a 'rightist-oriented reorganization' by saying it would 'respond resolutely' to them.

Domei supported the basic plan by saying 'it followed our policy in general', while opinions within Sohyo were split among those who supported the basic plan, those who opposed the selective conditions for joining the preparatory conference while supporting the basic plan, and those who opposed the basic plan per se. After four months of internal disputes over the basic plan Sohyo approved the Preparatory Conference for Labor Unification on the condition that 'the preparatory conference should be open to all the industry-level union federations which supported the labor unification'. As a result, the preparatory conference was established in December 1981 with 39 industry-level union federations, which led to the inauguration of Zenmin Rokyo (Japanese Private Sector Trade Union Council) in 1982 and Minkan Rengo (Japanese Private Sector Trade Union Council) in November 1987. Following the establishment of the Minkan Rengo all the national labor confederations except Sohyo disbanded themselves. Sohyo continued to be a national labor organization, mainly for the public-sector unions. However, Sohyo decided to dissolve itself and merged into Minkan Rengo (overall unification) in 1989 – and Rengo (Japanese Trade Union Confederation) was formed in November.

One of the reasons for the development of labor unification was a policy change by Sohyo.

The Sohyo leadership, after their defeat in the strike for the right to strike in 1975, started to realize that its past policies of militant political unionism and militant economic unionism had had only limited effects, and switched their policies to cooperative unionism and political exchange (demand for policy changes and institutional reforms) as advocated by the IMF-JC and Domei (see Table 30.1). These changes in policy orientation by Sohyo were also affected by the fact that the enterprise unions in the private sector affiliated with Sohyo (including those of mid-and small-sized firms), facing the hardship caused by the drastic restructuring processes under the severe economic conditions following the First Oil Shock, started to insist that Sohyo adopt a more realistic economic policy instead of the anti-restructuring policy (Inoue, 1997: 209–213; Shinkawa, 1993: 215).

Sohyo had to overcome internal conflict for it to be able change its policy and integrate with the labor unification led by the private-sector unions. Sohyo underwent two major internal conflicts. First, there was a conflict between the public- and private-sector unions. Labor unions in the public sector were experiencing a situation that was politically and economically different from that experienced by unions in the private sector. The public sector unions were in conflict with the government over the right to strike but were not directly exposed to market competition. Thus, they did not show much interest in the private-sector labor unions' need to respond flexibly to the severe economic conditions and restructuring plans. However, the Sohyo leadership, fearful that the Sohyo movement would become isolated from the rest of the labor movement by maintaining its anti-restructuring policy, virtually retracted its anti-restructuring policy at the end of the 1970s despite strong opposition from the public-sector unions (Inoue, 1997: 218–219).

Second, there was a conflict over which political parties it should support (the mainstream group supported the Japan Socialist Party while the anti-mainstream group advocated the 'freedom to support political parties' (this actually meant supporting the Japan Communist Party). This conflict was evident in the dispute over the 'Basic Plan for Labor Unification'. While the mainstream industry-level union federations supported or accepted the basic plan, the anti-mainstream industry-level union federations affiliated with the Toitsu Rosokon (The Council for Promoting Labor Movement Unification, a minority faction within Sohyo consisting of those industry-level union federations that supported the 'freedom to support political parties') opposed the plan, denouncing it as 'anti-communist separatism' or 'labor unification centered on major companies'. Supporters of Toitsu Rosokon established oppositional groups within some of Sohyo's major affiliates, such as Nikkyoso (Japan Teachers' Union) and Jichiro (All Japan Prefectural and Municipal Workers' Unions). Sohyo initially opposed the selective policy of labor unification that virtually excluded the unions affiliated with Toitsu Rosokon, but later accepted such exclusion. As a result, when Rengo was founded in 1989, Zenroren (National Confederation of Trade Unions) was also formed mainly by industry-level union federations affiliated with Toitsu Rosokon. The conflict within Nikkyoso and Jichiro deepened between the mainstream group, which intended to join Rengo, and the anti-mainstream group (supporters of Toitsu Rosokon), which opposed joining Rengo. The anti-mainstream groups eventually withdrew from their respective unions and formed their own industry-based organizations, which became members of Zenroren. A small minority of 'left socialist' unions led by Kokuro, which opposed joining Rengo while also refusing to join Zenroren, formed another, much smaller, confederation called Zenrokyo (National Trade Union Council) in 1989.

Kokuro's Weakening Influence in the Process of the Divestiture and Privatization of JNR

Another reason that Sohyo lost its unique presence as a national confederation during the process of labor unification was the weakening influence of the public-sector labor movement, which had previously had a strong influence at Sohyo. A significant example is that of Kokuro, which had played a central role in the public-sector labor movement, but which lost most of its influence during the process of divestiture and privatization of the JNR in 1987.

Kokuro lost its influence due to a mass exodus of members concerned for their employment after divestiture and privatization, and to a split within Kokuro. After the Japan National Railways Reconstruction Management Committee presented its detailed privatization plan in July 1985 the JNR authority implemented policies to isolate Kokuro, which opposed the JNR reform plan, from two other major JNR unions (Tetsuro and Doro), which supported the reforms (the 'Isolation Policy'). The 'Isolation Policy' adopted by the national railway authority took the form of refusing to renew the Employment Stability Agreement with Kokuro in November 1985 (while renewing it with the two other unions) and presenting a draft Joint Labor–management

Declaration in January 1986, which helped split the labor unions between those that supported the reform from those that opposed it (Kokuro refused to sign the declaration, while the other two unions signed it). The Joint Declaration included provisions for the unions to 'exercise self-restraint on strikes' after privatization, to positively support restructuring plans, and to implement measures to downsize the workforce based on labor–management cooperation. The expiration of the employment agreement and the refusal to sign the Joint Declaration put Kokuro at a disadvantage in the competition among competing labor unions in the National Railways immediately before its privatization. Many Kokuro members began to feel that their jobs were at risk, and the number of people leaving Kokuro increased rapidly in January 1986. The mass exodus began to threaten the status of Kokuro as the largest union in the JNR (see Mochizuki, 1993 for a general overview of the impact of privatization on the labor movement at JNR).

As the Japan National Railways Reform Law became certain to pass through the Diet, due to the victory of the ruling LDP in the House of Councilors and House of Representatives elections in July 1986, the Kokuro executive board leaned towards accepting the Joint Declaration by citing a 'need for bold compromise', but the plan by the executive board to sign the Joint Declaration was rejected due to the strong influence of a group opposing the JNR reforms within Kokuro at its convention in October 1986. As a result the group opposing the JNR reforms took the initiative at the executive board of Kokuro. The mainstream group, which used to be at the helm of Kokuro, left Kokuro and formed Tetsusan Soren (General Federation of Railway Industry Labor Unions). In June 1987, after divestiture and privatization, the biggest labor union at the new JR companies was Tetsudo Roren (All Japan General Federation of Railway Workers Unions, a federation of labor unions led by Tetsuro and Doro, which supported the JNR reforms, of about 110,000 members), which opted for cooperative unionism, while the number of union members at Kokuro declined by 75 percent from June of the previous year to about 41,000. Kokuro thus became the minority labor union.

As mentioned above, after the First Oil Shock the private-sector labor movement, due to strong market pressure, increasingly adopted a cooperative unionist policy. Meanwhile, the labor movement at JNR, which was under relatively weak market pressure, adopted a cooperative unionist policy because of the political processes of divestiture and privatization, and the isolationist policy by the JNR authority against Kokuro.

DEVELOPMENT OF THE LABOR MOVEMENT AFTER THE 1990s – LABOR-MOVEMENT SETBACKS AND THE SEARCH FOR NEW WAYS FORWARD

Changes in Labor Policies and the Economic Environment Surrounding the Labor Movement

Following the collapse of the 'bubble economy' in 1990, the Japanese economy plunged into the 'Heisei Recession', the biggest recession in its postwar history. The average GDP growth rate declined from 4.6 percent per year in the five-year period between 1985 and 1989 to 2.2 percent in the five-year period (1990–94) following the Heisei Recession, and to 1.2 percent in the five-year period after that (1995–99). The impact of the recession on the labor market and the labor movement was felt in the increased unemployment rate and an increase in the number of unemployed people; an increase in the number of non-regular workers; personnel cuts (so-called 'restructuring') at major companies through voluntary retirement and preferential early retirement; a decline in wage hikes in the spring offensive; and a decline in the union density and the number of union members.

Given the dire state of the economy, management reviewed 'Japanese-style management', which assumed long-term employment and seniority-based wages. The '"Japanese-style management" in the new era', announced by Nikkeiren in 1995, symbolized this move. The report advocated a drastic review of the employment system while maintaining the basic principles of Japanese-style management. Specifically, the report argued that the employment system should be divided into three categories ('a group of workers with long-accumulated expertise', 'a group of workers with highly specialized expertise', and 'a group of workers with flexible employment'), and that an 'employment portfolio customized to each company' should be developed based on an effective combination of the three categories. The treatments of the three groups were quite different. The first group benefited from 'unlimited-term employment contracts' with regular pay raises, while the second and the third groups were relegated to 'limited-term employment contracts' without regular pay raises.

The government promoted the deregulation of the labor market. Through a series of legal revisions at the end of the 1990s the government implemented a thorough review of postwar labor-related laws which focused on worker protection. The government, along with the revision of the Equal Employment Opportunity Law in 1997, revised the Labor Standards Law, abolishing the 'Women's Protection Provision', which banned night work, and restricted late-night overtime by female workers. The Labor Standards Law was revised again in 1998, expanding the occupational categories eligible for discretionary work arrangements to include the majority of white-collar workers, deregulating requirements for the variable working-hours scheme, and extending the maximum fixed-term employment contract for workers with highly specialized skills and expertise from one year to three years. The revised Worker Dispatching Law, enacted in 1999, liberalized the use of dispatched workers, 'with only a few exceptions in port, transport, construction, guard services and others designated by the Cabinet Order' (Japan Labor Bulletin, 1999). The Worker Dispatching Law was revised again in 2003, extending the dispatch period from one year to three and lifting a ban on dispatching workers in manufacturing jobs. The Labor Standards Law, revised in the same year, extended the maximum fixed-term employment contract to three years in principle (five years for workers with highly specialized skills and expertise) and eased requirements and procedures for the introduction of the discretionary work arrangements of white-collar workers.

The promotion of labor-market deregulation reached a limit after the mid 2000s as the general public began to recognize negative effects of the deregulation policies, most obviously an increase in the number of workers (particularly among young people) with precarious employment and low wages. Another side effect of the deregulation policies was the polarization of working hours: while full-time workers' hours increased, due to the reduction in the numbers of full-time workers assigned to each workplace, the hours of precariously employed workers were reduced as these workers were flexibly dispatched or deployed to companies and workplaces in response to market fluctuations. The government tried to deal with the working-hours issue by further deregulation, with the introduction of 'the white-collar exemption'. The Ministry of Health, Labor and Welfare took the position that, while overtime payment should be raised to discourage long working hours, white-collar workers (with high annual salaries) who satisfied certain conditions should be exempt from the uniform application of working-hours provisions. The government intended to include the provision on the white-collar exemption in the revised Labor Standards Law, but the bill submitted to the Diet in March 2007 did not include the exemption due to strong public opposition. The opposition was based on the public's apprehension that the white-collar exemption would further increase the working hours of already overworked white-collar workers.

As in other industrialized countries the economic and financial crisis of 2008 created havoc in labor markets, causing a large increase in the unemployment rate (from 4.0 percent in 2008 to 5.1 percent in 2009) and a drastic decline in the job-openings ratio (from 0.88 in 2008 to 0.47 in 2009). Precariously employed workers, particularly dispatched workers in manufacturing jobs, took the brunt of the deterioration of employment conditions as many employment contracts were cancelled or not renewed. The government started to consider the re-regulation of the Worker Dispatching Law in 2006, and the deterioration of labor-market conditions in late 2008 intensified the debate (Igarashi, 2010). The newly elected government led by the Democratic Party of Japan (the DPJ) submitted the bill for the revised Worker Dispatching Law to the Diet in April 2010. The proposed revision tightened the regulations on manpower-dispatch businesses (temporary-staff agencies) by prohibiting the dispatch of workers to manufacturing jobs and registration-type worker dispatching (registration-type workers are paid only when they are dispatched to workplaces). The proposed revision met with strong opposition from business associations. The DPJ, whose political influence had declined after its defeat in the House of Councilors election in July 2010, made a compromise with the two major opposition parties (the LDP and New Komeito) on a much watered-down bill. The new revision bill, passed by the Diet in March 2012, did not include the provisions to prohibit dispatching workers to manufacturing jobs and registration-type worker dispatching.

Declining Influence of the Labor Movement on Policy Formulation

Rengo, which was founded in 1989 through labor unification, grew into a dominant confederation, with its membership accounting for 62 percent of organized workers as of 1990, and was expected, on behalf of union members and workers as a whole, to engage in 'political exchanges' with government (Table 30.1 (2)). Rengo did, in fact, put the demand for policy changes and institutional reforms at the top of its agenda, dispatching labor representatives to advisory committees attached to government ministries (*shingikai*) and holding meetings with government agencies, the Cabinet, and the ruling party to discuss policy issues. However, at the very moment that Rengo embarked on enhancing its organizational presence in the political field the Japanese economy plunged into deep recession and the government embraced neo-liberal and deregulatory policies even more closely. Rengo, while opposing the deregulation of the labor market by the government, could not exert any influence on the formulation of such policies.

The major route for Rengo to participate in policy formulations as representatives of the interests of labor was to attend advisory committees set up

at ministerial level. Rengo and the affiliated organizations had dispatched a total of 290 people to 70 committees as of 1997. These committees discussed labor, social security, education, the economy, and gender equality. Rengo focused on those that dealt with labor policies. The former Ministry of Labor set up a total of 11 committees, most of whose members consisted of three parties (representing labor, employers, and the public interest). The committees most important for labor-related policy formulations were the Central Labor Standards Committee (CLSC), which discussed labor standards, and the Central Employment Security Committee (CESC), which discussed employment issues.

Until the early 1990s these committees discussed policies being considered by the government and made recommendations and reports to the Ministry of Labor based on the principles of the three-party agreement. When opinions between the representatives of labor and employers differed members representing the public interest played an intermediary role. The members representing the public interest developed recommendations and reports by taking the opinions of both labor and management into consideration, and members from unions and employers accepted them, allowing a compromise to be reached. However, as mentioned above, the government started to pursue deregulation of the labor market in the late 1990s, making it difficult for the councils to maintain the principle of agreement among the three parties. The revised Labor Standards Law in 1998 and the revised Worker Dispatching Act in 1999 were discussed at the CLSC and CESC, respectively. The representatives of labor were adamantly opposed to applying the discretionary work arrangements to the majority of white-collar workers and to the liberalization of the worker-dispatching practice. The representatives of the employers, meanwhile, strongly supported deregulation and so did the representatives of the public interest. The CLSC and CESC did not respect the opinions of the labor side, and presented reports saying that the proposed revisions of the laws were generally reasonable. The collapse of the principle of three-party agreement suggested the declining influence (compared with the influence they had exerted when the principle of three-party agreement had worked) of the labor unions on policy formulation under the government's neo-liberal policies (Suzuki, 2004).

State of Enterprise Unions and Evaluations of their Functions

Although the environment surrounding the labor movement changed radically in the 1990s, the cooperative unionism characteristic of enterprise unions persisted. Corporate restructuring and personnel cuts implemented by companies under severe economic pressure seemed to help increase formal and informal communication between labor and management through the labor-management-consultation system. A 2006 Rengo Soken (Research Institute for Advancement of Living Standards (RENGO-RIALS)) survey conducted among enterprise unions provides some snapshots of the current state of enterprise unions. The survey asked about changes in the frequency and content of labor–management consultations in the previous five years. As for the 'frequency' of consultations, while the largest number of unions reported that it was 'unchanged' at 61 percent, the number of unions which answered 'increased' (28 percent) exceeded the number of 'decreased' (10 percent). As for the 'complexity' of agendas, the largest number of unions reported that it was 'unchanged' at 54 percent, but those which answered 'becoming more complex' also accounted for 44 percent. Concerning the number of unofficial labor–management consultations, the number of unions which answered 'increased' from five years ago (29 percent) exceeded the number of those which answered 'decreased' (7 percent). The survey also asked whether labor–management relations had changed during consultations in the previous five years. While the largest number of unions reported that it was 'unchanged' at 71 percent, the number of unions which answered 'becoming more cooperative' (21 percent) exceeded the number of 'becoming confrontational' (6 percent). Concerning the level of understanding among ordinary union members of the agenda discussed at labor–management consultations, the largest number of unions said 'unchanged' from five years ago (72 percent), and the number of those who answered 'decreased' (17 percent) exceeded the number of those who said 'increased' (10 percent). The survey reported that 'ordinary union members were being left behind by the cooperative industrial relations of labor–management consultations' (RENGO-RIALS, 2007: 57–61, 170).

Labor researchers evaluated the current state of enterprise unions in positive and negative ways. On the positive side Inagami and Whittaker, based on a case study of industrial relations at Hitachi, argued that the 'overlapping interests' of labor and management, which had developed under cooperative industrial relations in the period of rapid economic growth, continued to exist even in the 1990s (Inagami and Whittaker, 2005). By 'overlapping interests,' they meant that 'the union was bound to give ultimate priority to the continued prosperity of the company, as jobs and livelihoods depended on this', and that 'managers internalized the importance of protecting jobs and livelihoods' (Ingami and Whittaker, 2005: 199). They pointed out that, although the Hitachi Union and other enterprise unions in the late 1990s were not able to exercise their influence to prevent corporate restructuring and to win wage hikes (or prevent wage reductions), '(in) the case of Hitachi… union engagement in the reforms was able to bring about a greater emphasis on "high road" (i.e. high value added, high wages) measures' because the union was actively involved in the HRM reforms through the system of labor–management consultations (Inagami and Whitaker, 2005: 211, 213). Sako, in her study of the shifting boundaries of enterprise unions (from factory, to enterprise, and to corporate group) and their internal structures (centralization and decentralization), argued that, although enterprise unions changed their boundaries and internal structures largely in response to corporate restructuring and to changes in HRM policies, they also had some degree of autonomy in making strategic choices in deciding their boundaries (Sako, 2006). For example, her case study shows that the Matsushita Union, in response to the company's move to create 'divisional companies' (*bunsha*) in the late 1990s, reorganized its internal structure to make 'branch groups' that corresponded with divisional companies. This reorganization was based on the union's strategy to strengthen its participation in the labor-management-consultation system at the level of newly created divisional companies (Sako, 2006: 85).

To the author's knowledge there are no book-length studies that examine the functions of enterprise unions since the early 1990s from critical perspectives. The reason for the absence of such studies was not so much that researchers had lost interest in studying the current state of enterprise unions as that they found it increasingly difficult to get access to enterprise unions' materials and data. Enterprise unions seemed not to be willing to cooperate with those researchers whom they deemed to be critical of their activities. One study of the earlier activity of enterprise unions from a critical perspective well known among non-Japanese labor scholars is that by Kawanishi (Kawanishi, 1992). The study, an English translation of a book originally published in Japanese in 1989 (Kawanishi, 1989), was based mainly on the research of the Hitachi Union in the late 1960s in which Kawanishi participated as a member of the research team. Examining workplace-level industrial relations, Kawanishi argued that enterprise unions at Hitachi and other large private-sector companies had lost independence from management and came to function 'as administrative bodies for management'. According to Kawanishi, workplace-level organizations of the Hitachi Union did not represent the interests of rank-and-file members vis-à-vis management. Although rank-and-file members had grievances over labor intensification, long working hours, and the difficulties of taking paid leave, workplace-level union representatives could do little to address these grievances because these representatives also held supervisory positions and were under great pressure to meet production goals. The top union leaders, in the meantime, embraced cooperative industrial relations, accepting the management's policy to rationalize production processes and streamline workforces. It should be noted that Dore's comparative study between Hitachi and English Electric (Dore, 1973) was based on the same materials and data that Kawanishi used but evaluated the Hitachi Union in a more positive way (Kawanishi, 1992: 182).

There are some article-length studies that examine the recent development of enterprise unions. For example, Yamagaki, in his study of the cooperative unionism of enterprise unions in steel industry from the 1970s to the 1990s, criticized the excessively concessionary policies of the enterprise unions (Yamagaki, 2000). The leadership of the unions justified their cooperative policies by emphasizing that the unions' cooperation in rationalization and productivity increase (e.g. the unions' acceptance of labor intensification and tight staffing) would be reciprocated by management in terms of wage hikes and employment security. Based on financial reports of steel companies and other official statistical sources, he analyzed product outputs, corporate profits, retained earnings, wage levels, labor share, labor productivity, and employee numbers. According to Yamagaki, although the companies made profits and increased retained earnings by 'aggressively' rationalizing production, labor's share actually decreased because real wages of union members did not increase commensurately with an increase in value-added labor productivity. Moreover, the very premise of cooperative labor–management relations – employment security – was itself considerably weakened in the 1980s and 1990s as companies downsized their workforces by temporary or permanent transfers of workers to other companies, and by early retirement schemes. The critical appraisal of enterprise unions made by Yamagaki and other labor scholars can be summarized as follows: the more severe economic conditions became the more deeply enterprise unions became embedded in the logic of corporate management; and they lost their capacity to consult with management as representatives of union members, and instead assumed the role of persuading union members to accept what was decided in labor–management consultations between union leaders and management (Suzuki, 2001, 2009; Takahashi, 2010).

Decline in Union Density and Membership

One of the reasons for the declining influence of the labor movement at the national/social and corporate levels is a decline in the union density and the number of union members. Union density started to decline after 1975: it declined from 34.4 percent in 1975 to 29.7 percent in 1983 and to 19.6 percent in 2003. The number of union members continued to increase until 1994 but started to decline in 1995. Union density in the private sector was below the overall rate, which included the public sector, falling below 20 percent at 19.8 percent in 1997. The private-sector union density was at its lowest in 2006 at 16.0 percent, but increased slightly to 17.0 percent in 2010 (see Table 30.3).

There were several reasons for declining union density. The first is changes in industrial structure: while employment in manufacturing, with a relatively high rate of union density, declined, employment in service industries, with a relatively low union density, increased. The second reason is a structural change in employment, such as the increased ratio of part-time workers and female workers. Since nonregular workers, such as part-time workers (many of whom are women), are not members of enterprise unions (enterprise unions normally are comprised solely of regular workers), the increase in the number of the non-regular workers reduced union density. The third reason attributes the decline to the lack of organizing efforts by labor unions rather than to the external environments of unions. The lack of organizing efforts can be discussed at two levels: the enterprise unions and the industry-level union federations. At the corporate level enterprise unions are basically comprised of regular workers at specific companies and have little incentive to organize non-regular workers at the same companies. This attitude was reinforced by union shop agreements signed with management, which allowed enterprise unions to organize newly hired regular workers automatically. The industry-level union federations are expected to help organize workers of companies with no labor organizations in their respective industries, but, except for some federations, they do not have sufficient human and financial resources to undertake serious organizing efforts (for discussions of union-organizing issues see Tsuru, 2002 and Suzuki, 2006).

National confederations took seriously the declining influence of the labor movement, due to declining union density and membership, since they represent workers as a whole in the political arena and in civil society. At every convention both Rengo and Zenroren stressed the necessity of organizing new members but started to make serious efforts to encourage and assist organizing efforts of affiliated federations only after 2000. Rengo put 'efforts to organize new members' at the top of the agenda at its 2001 convention and announced its 'Action Plan 21', which was designed to recruit 600,000 new numbers in two years. The target figure was based on the numbers presented and targeted by

Table 30.3   Union members and union density (overall and private sector)

	Union members (in thousands)	Overall union density (%)	Private sector union density (%)
1990	12,265	25.2	21.9
1991	12,397	24.5	21.4
1992	12,541	24.4	21.3
1993	12,663	24.2	21.3
1994	12,699	24.1	21.2
1995	12,614	23.8	20.8
1996	12,451	23.2	20.2
1997	12,285	22.6	19.8
1998	12,093	22.4	19.6
1999	11,825	22.2	19.4
2000	11,539	21.5	18.7
2001	11,212	20.7	18.0
2002	10,801	20.2	17.5
2003	10,531	19.6	17.1
2004	10,309	19.2	16.8
2005	10,138	18.7	16.4
2006	10,041	18.2	16.0
2007	10,080	18.1	16.2
2008	10,065	18.1	16.5
2009	10,078	18.5	16.9
2010	10,054	18.5	17.0

(Ministry of Labor, Ministry of Health, Labor and Welfare, *Basic Survey on Labor Unions*, each year)

each member organization. To achieve this target Rengo allocated over 20 percent of its budget, or about 1 billion yen, and assigned 20 staff members to the newly installed 'Center for Organizing New Members'. Zenroren also decided at its council meeting in 2001 to set up a 200-million-yen 'Fund for Organizing New Members' with which union organizers were newly hired (Hayakawa, 2006).

Development of Community Unions and Recent Studies on the Revitalization of the Labor Movement

An alternative form of union organization called 'community unions' has undertaken the organization of workers at the 'margin' of labor markets. These unions have a regional representational structure, with members drawn from a number of firms. Often referred to as 'community unions', they cover those workers who fall outside the coverage of enterprise unions, such as part-time and other non-regular workers, workers in small firms, and foreign workers. Community unions were first organized in the first half of the 1980s by regional labor councils (*chikuro*), semi-autonomous regional federations of labor unions affiliated with Sohyo. Some of these

councils were active in organizing workers in their respective regions, particularly part-time workers and workers in small firms. They established community unions in order to represent the workers in collective bargaining with their respective employers. By 1989 the number of community unions had increased to about 50. In 1990 60 community unions representing 10,000 workers established a loose nationwide network called the CUNN (Community Union Nationwide Network). Currently the CUNN has 74 affiliates and represents about 15,000 workers (for details see Suzuki, 2008). Besides community unions affiliated with the CUNN (many of them are not affiliated with either of the two major national confederations, Rengo and Zenroren) there are community unions established by the regional organizations of the two national confederations. Rengo adopted a new organizing policy in 1996 and gave its prefecture-level organizations authority to establish community unions. As of 2009 45 prefecture-level organizations established community unions with total membership of about 15,000 (Takasu, 2010: 50, 53). Zenroren, the leftist confederation, adopted a policy promoting the establishment of community unions in 2002. As of 2009 there are 135 Zenroren-affiliated community unions with a membership of

10,000 (Takasu, 2010: 57–58). Besides these three groups of community unions there are community unions affiliated with Zenrokyo, and individually affiliated unions established by some industrial-level union federations. The total number of community unions in Japan is estimated to be about 300 (for cases studies of community unions see Urano and Stewart, 2007; Suzuki, 2008; Weathers, 2010).

The policy orientation of community unions tends to be 'militant economic unionism' (Table 30.1 (3)). These unions typically address the complaints that individual workers have with their employers and any ensuing disputes. Community unions usually organize new members by offering counseling services on labor issues to workers in dispute with employers. When these workers become union members the unions engage in collective bargaining on their behalf to resolve disputes concerning dismissals, overdue wages, poor working conditions, and harassment and discrimination at the workplace. These activities and the organizational form of community unions are possible because the Japanese labor law has liberal union-recognition procedures: any group of workers, in principle, can form a labor union without notifying the public authority. Thus, community unions can organize members from multiple firms even if these workers are in a minority as union members in their respective firms; and the unions are entitled to engage in collective bargaining with these firms (Suzuki, 2008). But despite the legal entitlement to collective bargaining, employers sometimes refuse to engage in collective bargaining with community unions. In such cases community unions mobilize union members (not only members directly involved in a dispute but other union members) and supporters for protest rallies (often in front of the offices of employers) to put pressure on management to start collective bargaining. Even when employers do agree to engage in collective bargaining with community unions the bargaining process tends to be adversarial because the unions represent workers who have specific grievances with employers.

Community unions also participate in mobilization-based actions against government labor-market-deregulation policies and thus have the policy orientation of 'militant political unionism' (Table 30.1 (1)). Although the size of each community union is small, community unions actively form networks among themselves. The CUNN is a typical example of networks among community unions. It is a loose nationwide network of 74 community unions without any hierarchical relationship between its headquarters and member unions. Some networks were formed to tackle policy issues, such as labor deregulation, and social issues, such as an increase in working poor. These networks were often based on loose personal

networks among activists of community unions, and those of labor-related NGOs, labor lawyers, and academics. One such network organized a campaign called 'Say No to the Revision of the Labor Standards Law' against the 1998 revision, organizing numerous rallies and other forms of collective action all over Japan. Two rallies held in Tokyo in November 1997 and April 1998 gathered 3,000 and 4,000 participants, respectively (Takasu, 2010: 48). At the end 2008 and beginning of 2009 a network of community-union and NGO activists played an important role in the movement to set up an emergency camp at Hibiya Park in the center of Tokyo (called *haken mura* – literally, a village of (jobless) dispatched workers). The emergency camp provided food and shelter for about 500 unemployed non-regular workers, who had lost their jobs and homes because of the economic and financial crisis. This movement drew wide media attention and put strong pressure on the government to reconsider its neo-liberal labor-market policies, particularly deregulation of manpower-dispatch businesses (for details see Shinoda, 2009; Endo, 2009).

How will the new movement led by community unions influence the labor movement as a whole? Will it have a revitalizing effect on enterprise unions? Some labor researchers take such a view. For example, Kinoshita argued that community unions have the potential to transform enterprise unions by introducing a different organizing principle (individual-based affiliation) to their members from outside (Kinoshita, 2007). A similar view was expressed by the Rengo Assessment Committee, a committee of seven external members (one lawyer, three academics, one journalist, one NGO activist, and one writer) in its final report submitted to Rengo in September 2003. The report criticized mainstream unions (i.e. enterprise unions) for not being capable of adapting themselves to rapid social and economic changes, and called upon the labor movement to shed enterprise unionism and become more independent as a social movement. To realize this goal the report proposed that Rengo adopt a new organizing policy that would promote the establishment of labor unions that organized workers across enterprises, such as unions of part-time workers, craft unions, and community unions, and that Rengo and its affiliates revise membership rules to allow their members to join two unions (e.g. enterprise unions and community unions) at the same time (Rengo, 2003).

Other labor scholars take the view that enterprise unions, rather than community unions, should play a leading role in revitalizing the labor movement. For example, Hashimoto, based on a case study of enterprise unions that had organized non-regular workers, argued that enterprise unions would benefit from organizing non-regular workers in two ways. First, the morale of non-regular workers would improve because of smoother workplace-level communication, and the resulting decline in the turnover of non-regular workers would contribute to the improved productivity of the companies. Second, enterprise unions would become revitalized as the organization of non-regular workers stimulated union activities at the workplace level and gave birth to a new cadre of union activists among non-regular workers (Hashimoto, 2009: 49). Nakamura too has stressed the importance for enterprise unions to 'break the wall' between regular and non-regular workers. He argued that unless enterprise unions organize non-regular workers these workers might seek assistance from 'outside unions' (i.e. community unions). If rival unions are run by non-regular workers, he suggested, the voice of enterprise unions would weaken, and the maintenance of harmonious industrial relations would become difficult (Nakamura, 2009).

CONCLUSION

This chapter has examined the historical changes in policy orientations of the labor movement from the 1950s to the present. The period from the 1950s to the 1980s can be characterized as the transition from mobilization-based to institution-based policies. Labor unions both at the corporate/industrial and national/social levels, in response to changes in economic and political environments as well as to the shift in internal union politics (in which management played no small part), moderated their stances and routinized their relationship with management and the government. The timing of and the force behind the institutionalization of labor unions were different between the private and public sectors. The private-sector unions became institutionalized in the mid 1960s at the corporate level and in the mid 1970s at the political level. The spring offensives, which can be seen as industry-level activities of labor unions, started to be institutionalized in the mid 1960s as a result of the development of pattern bargaining, and became fully institutionalized after the 1975 spring offensive as the 'economic consistency' advocated by the IMF-JC became the defining principle of wage hikes. The public-sector unions, relatively isolated from the economic conditions influencing private-sector unions, maintained the policy of militant political unionism well into the 1980s. Although the defeat of the JCPU in the strike for the right to strike somewhat moderated the policy of public-sector unions, unions such as Kokuro maintained the stance of militant political unionism until the mid 1980s. It took the political intervention, in the form of the divestiture and privatization and the 'isolation policy' against Kokuro, to weaken the union and to

establish the cooperative labor relations of the privatized railway companies. Although cooperative enterprise unionism is the dominant feature of labor relations in Japan, it should be noted that its dominance in the labor movement as a whole was not accomplished until the late 1980s.

The process of enterprise unions becoming cooperative with management seems to be irreversible, as union leaders strengthened their commitment to cooperative unionism under the severe economic conditions starting in the early 1990s. As shown above, some labor researchers who focused on the extent of information sharing in labor–management consultations evaluated the functions of enterprise unions positively, while others who focused on the extent of representation evaluated them critically. The strong commitment to cooperative unionism had the side effects of bureaucratizing the enterprise unions and of increasing the indifference of rank-and-file members to union activities, which may have hollowing-out effects on union organizations in a long run. Some signs of the re-emergence of militant unionism (both economic and political) seem to have developed at the 'margin' of the labor movement, as community unions increase their numbers and form networks among themselves and with other movement organizations. However, it is still too early to tell whether community unions will revitalize the labor movement because the membership of these movement-oriented unions is a tiny fraction (estimated to be somewhere between 30,000 and 40,000) of total union membership (10 million). However, if the 'irreversible process' of cooperative unionism continues, the relative influence of enterprise unions may decline in the future. And if precariously employed workers, whose numbers keep increasing, begin to seek resolutions of their grievances with employers more proactively, greater opportunities will be created for community unions and other alternative forms of workers' organizations (such as labor-issue NGOs) to expand their sphere of influence in the labor movement.

NOTES

1   This chapter is a substantially modified version of a book chapter originally published in Japanese (Suzuki, 2010).
2   Unless otherwise noted, the historical description of the labor movement in this chapter is based on the reference materials published by the Ohara Institute for Social Research, Hosei University. The materials include *Nihon Rodo Nenkan* (*Japan Labor Yearbook*, published each year), *Shakai Rodoundo Dai Nenpyo* (*Chronicle of Social and Labor Movements, published in 1995*), *Nihon no Rodokumiai 100nen* (*One Hundred Years of*

the *Japanese Labor Unions*, published in 1999), and *Nihon Rodoundo Shiryo Shusei* (*Collections of Historical Materials of the Japanese Labor Movement*, 14 volumes, published from 2005 to 2007). All the reference materials were published by Junposha.

REFERENCES

Carlile, Lonny E. 2005. *Divisions of Labor: Globality, Ideology, and War in the Shaping of the Japanese Labor Movement*. Honolulu: University of Hawaii Press.

Dore, Ronald. 1973. *British Factory, Japanese Factory: The Origins of National Diversity in Industrial Relations*. Oxford, England: University of California Press.

Endo, Koshi. 2009. Toshikoshi Hakenmurano Daiseiko. [Big Achievement of Hibiya Tent Village for the Jobless.] *Keizai Ronshu* (Meiji University) 56 (3–4): 97–109.

Gordon, Andrew. 1998. *Wages of Affluence: Labor and Management in Postwar Japan*. Cambridge: Harvard University Press.

Hashimoto, Shuichi. 2009. Kigyobetu Kumiai niokeru Hiseiki Jugyoin Soshikika no Jirei ga Shimesu Koto. [What Cases of Enterprise Unions Organizing Non-regular workers Imply.] *Nihon Rodo Kenkyu Zasshi* 591: 41–50.

Hayakawa, Seiichiro. 1992. Shunto no Tenkai to Henbo. [The Development and Transformation of Shunto.] In Hosei Daigaku Ohara Shakaimondai Kenkyujo, ed., *Rengo Jidai no Rodo Undo*. Tokyo: Sogo Rodo Kenkyujo.

Hayakawa, Seiichiro. 2006. Rengo to Zenroren no Soshikikakudai Senryaku. [Organizing Strategies of Rengo and Zenroren.] In Akira Suzuki and Seiichiro Hayakawa, eds., *Rodokumiai no Soshiki Kakudai Senryaku*. Tokyo: Ochanomizu Shobo.

Hirai, Yoichi. 2000. *Miike Sogi*. [Miike Dispute.] Kyoto: Minerva Shobo.

Hisamoto, Norio. 1998. *Kigyonai Roshikankei to Jinzai Keisei*. [Industrial Relations within the Enterprise and the Development of Human Resources.] Tokyo: Uhikaku.

Hyodo, Tsutomu. 1997. *Rodo no Sengoshi*. [Postwar History of the Labor Movement.] Tokyo: University of Tokyo Press.

Igarashi, Jin. 2010. Rodo Saikisei ni Mukete no Kozokaikaku Rosen karano Hanten. [A Change in Policy Orientation from Structural Reforms to Re-regulation of Labor.] In Akira Suzuki, ed., *Shinjiyushugi to Rodo*. Tokyo: Ochanomizu Shobo.

Inagami, Takeshi, ed. 1995. *Seijuku Shakai no Nakano Kigyobetu Kumiai*. [Enterprise Unions in Mature Society.] Tokyo: Nihon Rodo Kenkyu Kiko.

Inagami, Takeshi and Whittaker, D. Hugh. 2005. *The New Community Firm: Employment, Governance and Management Reform in Japan*. Cambridge: Cambridge University Press.

Inoue, Masao. 1997. *Shakai Hendo to Rodo: Rengo no Seritsu to Taishushakai no Seijuku*. [Organized Labor in Social Transformation: The Establishment of Rengo and the Development of Mass Society.] Tokyo: Bokutakusha.

Japan Labor Bulletin. 1999. Revised Worker Dispatching Law: Worker Dispatching Has Generally Been Liberated. September 1.

Kamada, Tesuhiro and Kamada, Toshiko. 1993. *Nikko Mororan Sogi 30nengo no Shogen*. [Testimonies of the Nikko-Murosan Dispute, 30 Years after the Dispute.] Tokyo: Ochanomizu Shobo.

Kamii, Yoshihiko. 1994. *Rodokumiai no Shokuba Kisei*. [Shopfloor Regulations by Labor Unions.] Tokyo: University of Tokyo Press.

Kawanishi, Hirosuke. 1989. *Kigyoubetu Kumiai no Riron: Mohitotsu no Nihonteki Roshikankei*. [Theories of Enterprise Unionism: Another Approach to Japanese-style Industrial Relations.] Tokyo: Nihon Hyoronsha.

Kawanishi, Hirosuke. 1992. *Enterprise Unionism in Japan*. (Translated by Ross E. Mouer.) London: Kegan Paul International.

Kinoshita, Takeo. 1992. Sangyobetu Zenkokusoshiki no Bunretsu Saihen to Minkan 'Rengo' eno Michinori. [The Splits and Restructuring of Industrial-level Union Federations and a Path to the Formation of Private-sector Rengo.] In Hosei Daigaku Ohara Shakaimondai Kenkyujo, ed., *Rengo Jidai no Rodo Undo*. Tokyo: Sogo Rodo Kenkyujo.

Kinoshita, Takeo. 2007. *Kakusha Shakai ni Idomu Yunion*. [Community Unions Challenging an Unequal Society.] Tokyo: Kadensha.

Kumazawa, Makoto. 1982. Sutoken Suto 1975 Nihon. [The Strike for the Right to Strike and Japan in 1975.] In Shizo Shimizu, ed., *Sengo Rodokumiai Undoshiron*. Tokyo: Nihon Hyoronsha.

Kurita, Ken. 1994. *Nihon no Rodo Shakai*. [Japanese Workers' Societies.] Tokyo: University of Tokyo Press.

Lee, Minjin. 2000. *Chingin Kettei Seido no Kannichi Hikaku*. [Korea-Japan Comparison of Wage Determination Systems.] Chiba: Azusa Shuppansha.

Marks, Gary. 1989. *Unions in Politics: Britain, Germany, and the United States in the Nineteenth and Early Twentieth Centuries*. Princeton: Princeton University Press.

Mochizuki, Mike. 1993. Public Sector Labor and the Privatization Challenge: The Railway and Telecommunications Unions. In Garry D. Allison and Yasunori Sone, eds., *Political Dynamics in Contemporary Japan*. Ithaca: Cornell University Press.

Mori, Tateshi. 2003. Shokuba no Roshikankei no Kozo. [The Structures of Industrial Relations in Workplaces.] In Kazuo Saguchi and Shuichi

Hashimoto, eds., *Jinjiromukanri no Shiteki Bunseki*. Kyoto: Minerva Shobo.

Nakakita, Koji. 2008. *Nihon Rodoseiji no Kokusai Kankeishi*. [History of Japanese Labor Politics in the Context of International Relations.] Tokyo: Iwanami Shoten.

Nakamura, Keisuke. 2009. *Kabe o Kowasu* [Breaking the Wall Separating Regular and Non-regular Workers.] Tokyo: Daiichi Shorin.

Nitta, Michio. 1988. *Nihon no Rodosha Sanka*. [Workers' Participation in Japan.] Tokyo: University of Tokyo Press.

Rengo. 2003. Rengo Hyoka Iinnkai Saishu Hokoku. [The Final Report of the Rengo Assessment Committee.] Tokyo: Rengo.

RENGO-RIALS. 2007. 'Rodosha Sanka, Roshi Komunyukeshon ni kansuru Chosa' Houkokusho. [Report on 'Workers' Participation and Labor–management Communication.] Tokyo: Rengo Research Institute for Advancement of Living Standards.

Sako, Mari. 1997. Shunto: The Role of Employer and Union Coordination at the Industry and Inter-sectoral Levels. In Mari Sako and Hiroki Sato, eds., *Japanese Labour and Management in Transition; Diversity, flexibility and participation*. London: Routledge.

Sako, Mari. 2006. *Shifting Boundaries of the Firm: Japanese Company–Japanese Labour*. New York: Oxford University Press.

Shimizu, Shizo. 1982. Sohyo 30nen no Baransu Shito. [Balance Sheet of 30 Years' History of Sohyo.] In Shizo Shimizu, ed., *Sengo Rodokumiai Undoshiron*. Tokyo: Nihon Hyoronsha.

Shinkawa, Toshimitsu. 1993. *Nihongata Fukushi no Seiji Keizaigaku*. [Political Economy of the Japanese-style Welfare System.] Tokyo: Sanichi Shobo.

Shinoda, Toru. 2005. Shimin Shakai no Shakai Undo e. [Toward a Social Movement in Civil Society.] In Jiro Yamaguchi, Taro Miyamoto, Minoru Tsubogo, eds., *Posuto Fukushi Kokka to Sosharu Gabanansu*. Kyoto: Minerva Shobo.

Shinoda, Toru. 2009. Which Side Are You On?: Hakenmura and the Working Poor as a Tipping Point in Japanese Labor Politics. *The Asia Pacific Journal*: www.japanfocus.org/-Toru-SHINODA/3113 (accessed 27 March 2012)

Suzuki, Akira. 2001. Roshi Kankei: Jidosha/Tekkogyo wo chushinto shite. [Industrial Relations, Mainly in the Auto and Steel industries.] *Ohara Shakaimondai Kenkyujo Zasshi* [Journal of Ohara Institute for Social Research] 507: 11–28.

Suzuki, Akira. 2004. The Rise and Fall of Interunion Wage Coordination and Tripartite Dialogue in Japan. In Harry Charles Katz, Wonduck Lee and Joohee Lee, eds., *The New Structure of Labor Relations: Tripartism and Decentralization*. Ithaca: Cornell University Press.

Suzuki, Akira. 2006. Sangyobetu Soshikino Soshiki Kakudai Senryaku. [Organizing Strategies of

Industry-level Union Federations: Their Institutional Contexts and Mediating Factors.] In Akira Suzuki and Seiichiro Hayakawa, eds., *Rodokumiai no Soshiki Kakudai Senryaku*. Tokyo: Ochanomizu Shobo.

Suzuki, Akira. 2008. Community Unions in Japan: Similarities and Differences of Region-based Labour Movements between Japan and Other Industrialized Countries. *Economic and Industrial Democracy* 29 (4): 492–520.

Suzuki, Akira. 2009. Nihon no Rodo Undo: Sai Kasseika no Kanosei to Rodoundo Shidosha no Gensetu Bunseki. [The Labor Movement in Japan: An Examination of its Possible Revitalization Based on the Discourse Analysis of Union Leaders.] In Toshimitsu Shinkawa and Toru Shinoda, eds., *Rodo to Fukushi Kokkano Kanosei: Rodoundo Saisei no Kokusai Hikaku*. Kyoto: Minerva Shobo.

Suzuki, Akira. 2010. Rodo Undo. [Labor Movement.] In Norio Hisamoto and Tamai Kingo, eds., *Shai Seisaku 1: Waku Lifu Baransu to Shakai Seisaku*. Kyoto: Horitsu Bunkasha.

Takahashi, Yukichi. 2010. 'Kigyoshakai' Saiko: Shin Jiyushugi no Kaikaku to 'Kigyoshakai' no Henyo. [Re-examination of 'Corporate Society' under Neo-liberal Reforms.] In Akira Suzuki, ed., *Shinjiyushugi to Rodo*. Tokyo: Ochanomizu Shobo.

Takasu, Hirohiko. 2010. Yunion Undo no Keisei to Genjo. [The Formation and the Current State of the (Community) Union Movement.] *Nihon Rodo Nenkan* [Ohara Institute for Social Research, Hosei University] 80: 40–68.

Turner, Lowell. 1991. *Democracy at Work: Changing World Markets and the Future of Labor Unions*. Ithaca: Cornell University Press.

Tsuru, Yasushi. 2002. *Roshi Kankei no Non-union Ka*. [Non-unionization of Industrial Relations.] Tokyo: Toyo Keizai Shinpo sha.

Ueda, Osamu. 1999. *Keiei Gorika to Roshi Kankei*. [Corporate Rationalization and Labor Unions.] Kyoto: Minerva Shobo.

Urano, Edison I. and Stewart, Paul. 2007. Including the Excluded Workers? The Challenges of Japan's Kanagawa City Union. *Working USA* 10 (1): 103–123.

Weathers, Charles. 2010. The Rising Voice of Japan's Community Unions. In Henk Vinken, Yuko Nishimura, Bruce White, Masayuki Deguchi, eds., *Civic Engagement in Contemporary Japan: Established and Emerging Perspectives*. New York: Springer Science Business Media.

Yamagaki, Masahiro. 2000. Nihongata 'Rodokumiai Undo' to Sono Kiketsu. [Japanese-style 'Trade Unionism' and its Consequences.] *Ohara Shakai Mondai Kenkyujo Zasshi* [the Journal of Ohara Institute for Social Research] 498: 19–42.

Yamamoto, Kiyoshi. 1981. *Jidosha Sangyo no Roshi Kankei*. [Labor-capital Relations in the Auto Industry.] Tokyo: University of Tokyo Press.

31

Foreign Workers in Japan[1]

Gabriele Vogt

INTRODUCTION

Japan for many years has been an outlier case to students of international labor migration. It is one of the wealthiest countries of its region offering wages to workers much higher than those most of its neighboring countries can; it also provides stable political conditions, thus guaranteeing secure living and working conditions. The push/pull model of international labor migration states that these kind of economically powerful and politically solid states tend to receive much international labor migration (pull), particularly so when neighboring states fall short of offering the same qualities (push). According to this model, international labor migration to Japan could be expected to take place on a large scale. Yet it can hardly be witnessed at all. The percentage of registered foreign residents in Japan amounts to a mere 1.6 percent of the overall population (MOJ, 2013a). Compared to other OECD nations (UK 7.7 percent, Germany 8.5 percent, Spain 12.4 percent) Japan's figure stands out as an extremely low one (OECD, 2013).[2] Exploring the background to this low figure will be an interesting task. I will do so by analyzing Japan's migration policy over the course of the past two decades, thereby arguing that we need to 'bring the state back in' (Hollifield, 2000: 137) when aiming at understanding the global flows of international labor migration.[3]

OUTLINE

Through a qualitative content analysis of government statistics and documentations as well as expert interviews I will demonstrate the existence of a significant gap between policy output (official immigration policies) and policy outcome (on-the-ground results of these policies) in Japan's migration policy. The policy output insists that international labor migration to Japan comprises only highly skilled and only on a temporary basis – in a nutshell: 'Japan is not an immigration country'. The policy outcome, however, paints a different picture: it is predominantly foreign workers who are not highly skilled and who have a long-term-resident perspective who are employed in Japan as foreign workers. Their number, however, also remains relatively miniscule. Yet the role of foreign workers for Japan's economic performance is much larger than could be assumed by simply looking at their population's percentage of the total population of Japan.

Conceptually this paper draws on the 'gap hypotheses' of Cornelius et al. (2004), which they introduced into migration research in the mid 1990s. A gap in migration policy pinpoints a significant divergence between policy output and policy outcome. There are two kinds of policy gaps: '(1) those caused by the unintended consequences of policy, and (2) those caused by inadequate implementation or enforcement of policy.'

(Cornelius and Tsuda, 2004: 5). As for the question of how and why policy gaps originate, they name four causes: flawed policies, macro-structural frameworks, domestic and international political constraints, and ambiguous policy intentions (Cornelius and Tsuda, 2004: 7–15).

They call Japan an 'extreme case' (Cornelius and Tsuda, 2004: 14) when it comes to ambiguous policy intentions. The quantity and positions of major political actors (single politicians, political parties, bureaucracy, interest groups etc.) in migration-policy-making in Japan is broad, and migration policy over the past decades has to some degree always looked like a compromise solution trying to incorporate vastly diverse political ideas.[4] This paper's main concern, however, lies with the first kind of policy gap Cornelius and Tsuda identify: those gaps caused by the unintended consequences of policy. Cornelius and Tsuda mention that in some cases the 'unintended consequences' of immigration-control policies may not be so unintended, or may in fact be fully intended' (Cornelius and Tsuda, 2004: 6).

In this paper I argue that the persisting gaps between migration policy output and outcome in Japan are, in fact, government policy. I also argue that one of the most recent policy reforms, the introduction of sector-specific and nation-specific migration channels via Economic Partnership Agreements (EPA),[5] symbolizes a shift toward adjusting policy output to an already existing policy outcome. We therefore witness a significant but almost invisible policy shift. The result of this policy shift is nothing more than what we already see on the ground: a domestic labor market partially opened to sector-specific and nation-specific international labor migration. What this policy reform will probably not bring about is a change in migrants' life and work; they will still be confined to the margins of the labor market and excluded largely from societal, political, and economic integration unless a real migration-policy change and a change in mindset follow. It is time for Japan to give up its state of denial and face the reality of being an immigration country, much more so given the accelerating need for foreign workers in the light of demographic change.

DEMOGRAPHIC AND PROFESSIONAL COMPOSITION OF THE FOREIGN-WORKER POPULATION

This section highlights the milestones of the historical development of labor-migration flows to Japan since World War II and introduces the three largest ethnic groups of registered foreign residents with regard to their demographic and professional composition.

A Look into History

By the end of 2012 the number of registered foreign residents in Japan stood at roughly 2.04 million persons (2,038,159), which amounted to 1.6 percent of the total population. Their number had been steadily on the rise from the postwar years until 2008, when there were 2,217,426 foreign residents.[6] The subsequent decline is attributed to the global economic downturn of 2008–09, which resulted in a significant out-migration of the Brazilian community in particular.[7] Also, the unassertive crisis-management and a general decrease in trust in the Japanese government, as a result of its handling of the Fukushima nuclear crisis in the aftermath of the 11 March 2011 earthquake and tsunami, is another reason for the decline of Japan's foreign population (Roberts, 2012: 49–50).

Data released by Japan's Ministry of Justice (MOJ) tell us that more than 600,000 foreign nationals (641,482) had already registered as residents of Japan by 1955 (Figure 31.1). Most of them were former colonial subjects of the Japanese Empire, which brought them to the Japanese 'mainland' as forced laborers: by 1945 the number of Koreans living in Japan had exceeded two million; the population of mainland Chinese and Taiwanese in Japan had risen to almost 60,000 over the wartime period. Many of them returned to their homelands after the end of the war, but some hundred thousand – in particular Koreans – for personal or professional reasons remained in Japan (Morris-Suzuki, 2008).[8] Migration literature calls these early migrants to Japan 'old-comers'.

The first wave of 'new-comers' reached Japan in the late 1970s. For this period sociologist Hiroshi Komai[9] distinguishes four types of migration. First, female migration mainly from the Philippines, Korea, Taiwan, and Thailand. Many of these migrants worked on so-called entertainer visas (*kōgyō*) in Japan's sex industry.[10] Second, Komai mentions the Indochinese refugees from Vietnam, Cambodia, and Laos; and, third, the second- and third-generation descendants of Japanese who, at the end of World War II, had been left in China. In the final group of new-comer migrants are business professionals from Europe and North America (Komai, 2001: 16–17). Despite the broad range of newcomers with regard to their nationality and motives for coming to Japan, the total number of registered foreign residents in Japan remained small: by 1980 it stood at below 800,000 persons (782,910). It was only from the late 1980s on and in particular since 1990 that the number of registered foreign residents in Japan rose speedily (MOJ, 2008).

The reasons behind this development are structural. In the late 1980s Japan entered a period of relatively high economic growth (the so-called

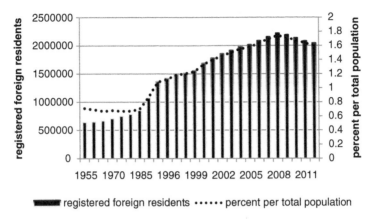

Figure 31.1 Registered foreign residents in Japan, 1955–2012

Source: MOJ 2008; MOJ 2009; MOJ 2010; MOJ 2011; MOJ 2012, MOJ 2013a.

bubble economy), which attracted workers on the global labor market. Then with the 1990 revision of Japan's Immigration Control and Refugee Recognition Act the legal framework for labor migration – at least for some specific groups – was put into action.

Japan's high-economic-growth era of the late 1980s and the high value of the yen coincided with a significant decline in oil production in the Middle East. Labor migrants, in particular from Bangladesh, Pakistan, and Iran who had been working in the oil industry, started to look for new destination countries. South Korea, Taiwan, and Japan were attractive (Kuwahara, 2005: 30–31) for laborers willing to engage in 3K jobs: that is, jobs that are *kitanai* (dirty), *kiken* (dangerous), and *kitsui* (severe). Most of these jobs come with an additional 3K, which makes them even less attractive to educated natives who in times of high economic growth have the luxury of picking their employment carefully. These are: *kyūryō ga yasui* (doesn't pay well), *kyūka ga sukunai* (little vacation), and *kakkō ga warui* (bad image). Workers from Bangladesh, Pakistan, and Iran largely worked in these 3K jobs. The number of irregular migrants (mostly visa-overstayers)[11] from these countries did, however, increase rapidly in the early 1990s. The number of irregular Iranians, for example, increased from 764 in July 1990 to 32,994 by November 1992 (Shimada, 1994: 26). The Japanese government reacted to this trend by revoking the visa-exemption agreements (*sashō sōgo menjo torikime*) with Iran in 1992; since then the numbers of regular and irregular Iranians in Japan have fallen sharply.[12]

The second and more central reason for the increase of registered foreign residents in Japan since the early 1990s is the revision of the Immigration Control and Refugee Recognition

Act (*shutsunyūkoku kanri oyobi nanmin ninteihō*). The act is based on the initial 1951 Immigration Ordinance (*shutsunyūkoku kanri rei*) and had come into effect in 1981. Its main purpose is to regulate the entry and stay of foreign nationals in Japan. It defines 27 visa categories (Table 31.1). Only four of these categories allow for unconditional work activities, five do not allow their holders to work,[13] and one – technical intern training (*ginō jisshū*) – comprises on-the-job training and subsequent employment.[14] Seventeen of these categories include a work permit for designated activities. These 17 all are closely knit with specific professions, such as professor, manager, and engineer. Excluded from work in Japan, amid the lack of an appropriate visa category, are unskilled workers (*tanjun rōdō*).[15] All of these 17 work-related visa categories are limited to a maximum of three respectively five years; an option for renewal and/or extension is provided, though. The guideline of Japan's migration policy is 'labor migration only of the highly skilled and only on a temporary basis'.

The four categories that allow for unconditional work in Japan are: permanent resident (*eijūsha*), spouse or child of Japanese national (*nihonjin no haigūsha*), spouse or child of permanent resident (*eijūsha no haigūsha*), and long-term resident (*teijūsha*). Looking at the proportion of holders of these visas within the total population of registered foreign residents in Japan it becomes clear that three out of these four categories – the exception being 'spouse or child of permanent resident' – are listed among the top-ranking categories for 2012. Permanent residents comprise 49.5 percent of all registered foreign residents in Japan, long-term residents amount to 8.1 percent, and spouses or children of Japanese nationals to 8.0 percent (Figure 31.2). Add to this another 1.1 percent for the category of spouse or child of permanent resident

Table 31.1 Visa categories and work permission in Japan

Visa Category	Work Permission		
	Without Limitation	Designated Activities	None
Diplomatic visa (gaikō)		✓	
Official visa (kōyō)		✓	
Professor (kyōju)		✓	
Artist (geijutsu)		✓	
Religious activities (shūkyō)		✓	
Journalist (hōdō)		✓	
Investor/Business manager (tōshi/keiei)		✓	
Legal/Accounting services (hōritsu/kaikei gyōmu)		✓	
Medical Services (iryō)		✓	
Researcher (kenkyū)		✓	
Instructor (kyōiku)		✓	
Engineer (gijutsu)		✓	
Specialist in Humanities/International Services (jinbun chishiki, kokusai gyōmu)		✓	
Intracompany Transferee (kigyōnai tenkin)		✓	
Entertainer (kōgyō)		✓	
Skilled Labor (ginō)		✓	
Technical Intern Training (ginō jisshū)		✓	
Cultural Activities (bunka katsudō)			✓
Temporary Visitor (tanki taizai)			✓
College Student (ryūgaku)			✓
Trainee (kenshū)			✓
Dependent (kazoku taizai)			✓
Designated Activities (tokutei katsudō)		✓	
Permanent Residents (eijūsha)	✓		
Spouse or Child of Japanese National (nihonjin no haigūsha)	✓		
Spouse or Child of Permanent Resident (eijūsha no haigūsha)	✓		
Long-term Resident (teijūsha)	✓		

Source: Data by § 2 II and § 19 Immigration Control and Refugee Recognition Act.

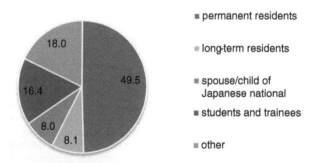

- permanent residents
- long-term residents
- spouse/child of Japanese national
- students and trainees
- other

Figure 31.2 Registered foreign residents in Japan by visa categories (2012)

Source: MOJ 2013a.

and it is fair to say that two thirds (66.7 percent) of all registered foreign nationals in Japan do not have any restriction on their permission to work (MOJ, 2013a) and with the exception of long-term residents there is no limit on the duration of their stay in Japan. Both of these aspects – 'unconditioned work permit and unlimited duration of stay' – run counter to the basic principles of Japan's migration policy. The gap between policy output and policy outcome becomes obvious.

This gap was further institutionalized by the 1990 law revision. The visa category of 'long-term resident' in the 1990 law revision was expanded specifically to include descendants of Japanese nationals up to the third generation. The so-called *nikkeijin,* Latin Americans, mostly from Brazil and Peru, make most use of this new migration option, as data of registered foreign residents according to nationality show. By the end of 2007 a total of 268,604 long-term resident permits had been issued;[16] 55.3 percent of these permits (148,528) had been issued to Brazilian residents in Japan (MOJ, 2008). This opportunity for residence for descendants of Japanese nationals, as well as preparations for an expansion of Japan's trainee program, which proceeded in two steps (the 1990 expansion of the trainee system's availability to small businesses and the 1993 introduction of a specialized trainee program (*senmon kenshū*)), must be understood as the two fundamental changes of the 1990 revision. Both changes had an immediate impact on the numerical rise within Japan's largest foreign residents' communities. They also increased Japan's migration-policy gap, a schizophrenic approach to international labor migration among Japan's politicians and general public alike.

Largest Ethnic Groups: Koreans, Chinese, Brazilians

Figure 31.3 shows the largest ethnic groups in Japan in 2011: the Korean, Chinese, and Brazilian communities. In 2012, however, the Filipino community with 10 percent of Japan's foreign population surpassed the Brazilian community, which stood at 9.5 percent. Since the numerical rise and fall of Japan's Brazilian community is linked with several milestones in Japan's migration-policy reforms, this community, rather than the Filipino, is included in this chapter.

Koreans

Four out of the five largest groups of registered foreign residents in Japan experienced steady growth in the decade and a half to 2011 (Figure 31.3). Only the Korean community's numbers declined. Their number fell from its peak in 1992 (688,144 persons) to 530,421 in 2012 (MOJ, 2013a). In 2007 the Korean community was no longer the largest ethnic group among registered foreign nationals in Japan; and they are now second to the Chinese community. The numerical decline of the Korean community reflects a decline specifically among the Korean 'old-comers': that is, persons who came (who often were forced to come) to Japan as workers before the end of World War II and their descendants. Since Japan regained political sovereignty in 1952 they have been residing in Japan as 'special permanent residents' (*tokubetsu eijūsha*). It is the number of Koreans registered as 'special permanent residents' that is on the decline: from 471,756 persons in 2003 to 377,350 in 2012 (MIC, 2013a). There are two main reasons for this: first, the old-age mortality of the original 'old-comer' generation of Korean migrants; and, second, the

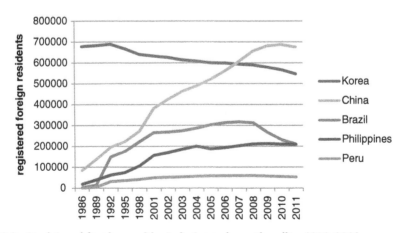

Figure 31.3   Registered foreign residents in Japan by nationality, 1986–2011

Source: MOJ 2008; MOJ 2009; MOJ 2012.

descendant generation of Koreans who were brought up and socialized in Japanese society opt for naturalization in increasing numbers. Soo Im Lee, Professor of Business Administration at Ryukoku University, speaks of an average of 10,000 naturalizations per year (Lee, 2008; 2012).[17] An increasing number of 'new-comer' Koreans who mainly come to Japan as 'college students' (17,874 in 2012) cannot (yet) make up for the decrease in 'old-comer' Koreans (MIC, 2013a; MIC, 2013b).[18]

Chinese

The Chinese community with 653,004 registered members in 2012 is the largest foreign ethnic group in Japan (MOJ, 2013a). Their numbers have seen a sharp increase since the early 1990s. In contrast with the Korean community, the bulk of the current Chinese community is 'new-comer' migrants.[19] They mainly come to Japan as 'college students' (113,984 in 2012) or 'trainees' (111,851 in 2012). Increasing numbers of Chinese also decide to settle in Japan, for example, as 'spouse or child of a Japanese national' (34,771) or as 'spouse of a permanent resident' (8,792). Another path that Chinese students in Japan often choose after graduation is changing their student visa to a working visa, predominantly that of 'engineer' (20,933)[20] before applying for 'permanent residency' after a minimum of five years in stable employment (191,946) (MIC, 2013a).[21] 'The Chinese community in Japan is evenly composed' (Liu-Farrer, 2009a: 121–122) of holders of a variety of visa categories. The community is predominantly female (58.45 percent are women) and young (only 1.98 percent are over 65 years). Many of these young female members of Japan's Chinese community are transnational employees or entrepreneurs, who build close-knit business partnerships between Japanese and Chinese small- and medium-sized companies, thereby playing an enormously important role as cultural mediators for the expansion of Japan's overseas market activities (Liu-Farrer, 2009b). Furthermore, 'these transnational practices' – services that Japanese cannot provide that smoothly – 'also represent immigrants' strategies to overcome their marginality in a society they perceive as [...] closed to outsiders' (Liu-Farrer, 2009a: 134). Sociologist Gracia Liu-Farrer (2009a: 123) argues that the 'rapid increase in the number of naturalized citizens and permanent residents among the Chinese in Japan indicates the maturation and stabilization of the Chinese community in Japan'.

While this is undoubtedly true for a certain segment of the Chinese community in Japan – the well educated segment – another large and growing part of the community is being socially and economically marginalized and operates in the low-wage sectors of the Japanese business world. The most prominent group of this part of the Chinese community is 'trainees'. Since the 1990 MOJ promulgation to grant access to Japan's state-regulated internship program to small firms of less than 20 employees the number of trainees has risen rapidly. This rise was further accelerated in 1993 when a specialized trainee program (*senmon kenshū*) was added to the existing one, and then again in 2009 through an amendment to the Immigration Control and Refugee Recognition Act. The new program allowed companies to employ their trainees for another year after they had completed a two-year internship. Initiated as a means of foreign aid that would grant a knowledge spillover to developing countries, this addition to the trainee system meant employers could plan for the long-term in the knowledge that they had a supply of low-wage labor. Violations of workers' and human rights as well as blunt ignorance of legal standards of minimum wages occur all too often, many social movement-leaders bemoan (Yano, 2006; Torii, 2007), but the trainee system has been tremendously popular with young Chinese, who see it as yet another (next to student visas) avenue by which they can relocate to Japan. Of the 153,391 trainees residing in Japan in 2012, 111,851 were Chinese. This equals 72,9 percent or almost three quarters of all trainees in Japan (MIC, 2013a).

Brazilians

The trainee system is a side door through which unskilled workers can migrate to Japan. It is just one of the side doors that were opened in the early 1990s due to an increasing demand for low-wage labor in Japanese industry. The other group that saw a steep numerical increase as a result of in Japan's domestic labor shortage is descendants (up to the third generation) of Japanese nationals. Most of these so-called *nikkeijin* are descendants of Japanese emigrants to Brazil and, in much smaller numbers, to Peru. Then Senior Vice Minister of Justice, Tarō Kōno (Liberal Democratic Party (LDP)), in an interview with the author in February 2006, acknowledged that making available the 'long-term resident' visa category to *nikkeijin* had very pragmatic beginnings. Despite the political discourse of the time – that *nikkeijin* should be given the opportunity to visit their family in Japan and work a bit on the side to support their stay and travel in the land of their ancestors – the policy reform had more to do with Japan's need for workers in its low-wage manufacturing sector, particularly the automobile and electric industries. Opening this migration side door to *nikkeijin* specifically, and not to low-wage laborers in general, helped to keep up the appearance that there was no migration of unskilled workers to Japan. Furthermore, many politicians were apparently convinced that having *nikkeijin* come to live and work in Japan would not require any integration measures – after all, they were 'Japanese'.

Jumping to the conclusion that a blood-line relationship with the country of destination would compensate for comprehensive integration measures was a huge mistake, as Kōno (2006) pointed out.[22]

Comprehensive ethnographic research projects, for example by Roth (2002) and Tsuda (2003), highlight the manifold discriminations *nikkeijin* face in their daily lives and at their workplaces. Quarrels between the Japanese and comparatively large *nikkeijin* communities over faulty garbage disposal, noisy youngsters hanging out in the evenings, and wildly-parking cars[23] indeed occur frequently, as mayors of towns in Aichi, Shizuoka, Mie, and Gunma prefectures – many of which have a high concentration of *nikkeijin* residency – lament.[24] These prefectures represent Japan's manufacturing belt and so far have drawn the bulk of Japan's Brazilian and Peruvian *nikkeijin* communities. There is no data available on *nikkeijin* communities per se; we do, however, know from Tsuda's (2009: 207) ethnographic data that in the heyday of *nikkeijin* migration to Japan, around 2007, their number was 'well over 330,000'. In his own research Tsuda works with data for registered Brazilian residents in Japan as equal to that of the Brazilian *nikkeijin* community. This move seem just given the fact that 97.4 percent of Brazilians (192,173 in 2012) reside in Japan either as 'long-term resident' (53,044), 'permanent resident' (114,632) or 'spouse or child of Japanese national' (19,519) – with the second and third being common 'follow-up visas' to the 'initial *nikkeijin* visa.' The data show – after a continuous increase in numbers since 1989 – a slight decrease in numbers more recently: from its peak of 316,967 in 2007, down to 312,582 in 2008 – that is, just below the 2006 level – and to 192,173 in 2012 (MOJ, 2008, 2009; MIC, 2013a).

This decrease is closely connected to the economic downturn that reached Japan in fall 2008 and hit the automobile industry particularly hard; in fact, the decrease was particularly pronounced in 2009 when the medium-term impact of the downturn and the Japanese government's handling of the crisis had become more obvious. Foreign temporary workers were the first to be laid off;[25] losing employment in many cases also meant losing apartments. In most cases not being covered by social-security systems immediately translated into a very severe situation. In January 2009 the Cabinet Office reacted to the hardships Brazilian *nikkeijin* workers faced in Japan by publishing a six-page appeal to companies employing *nikkeijin* and other foreign workers (*Nikkeijin nado no gaikokujin rōdōsha o koyō suru jigyōshu no minasama e*).[26] The Cabinet Office appealed to employers of foreign workers not to have them evacuate the company dormitories the day they are laid off, but to grant them a certain grace period, to assist them with skill-up retraining programs, including Japanese language

classes, and to offer them a realistic perspective for re-employment once the economic situation improved. While this Cabinet Office program was aimed at assisting *nikkeijin* workers to stay on in Japan despite the increasing unemployment rate that hit them particularly heftily, the Ministry of Health, Labour and Welfare initiated another program to assist *nikkeijin* with repatriation to their homelands. As of April 2009 *nikkeijin* who had lost their jobs and wanted to return to their homelands were granted government assistance of 300,000 yen per person plus an additional 200,000 yen per family member – under the condition that they would not attempt to return to Japan as 'long-term residents' (MHLW, 2009c). After receiving much public criticism, only one month after its introduction the system was changed to a 'three-year waiting period before possible re-entrance on a long-term visa' (Roberts, 2012: 53). Yet social-activist Debito Arudou calls these payments 'race-based benefits' and 'golden parachutes'; he also argues that they represent the failure of Japan's labor migration policy directed at *nikkeijin* (Arudou, 2009). 'By the program's end on March 31, 2010, 21,675 nikkei Brazilians (92.5 percent), Peruvians (4.2 percent) and others (3.3 percent) had repatriated under this scheme'. (Roberts, 2012: 53). The drop in resident numbers clearly shows in Figure 31.3. At this point the future of Japan's *nikkeijin*-centered migration policy is indeed insecure; a revival seems unlikely, in particular so new forms of regulated labor migration to Japan – sector-specific and nation-specific channels – are currently being tested.

LABOR-MARKET PARTICIPATION OF THE FOREIGN-WORKER POPULATION

While the labor-market participation of specific ethnic groups has already been introduced to some degree, this section will focus on providing an overview of the figures and facts involved when addressing the general labor-market participation of regular and irregular migrants.

Regular Migrants

The figures introduced in the sections above are based on data provided by Japan's Immigration Bureau, subordinate to MOJ. A revision to the Immigration Control and Refugee Recognition Act in summer 2009 strengthened the already leading role of MOJ in administering data related to registered foreign residents. Tasks that had been under the administration of municipalities – in particular social services such as health insurance – were placed under MOJ administration, thereby strengthening MOJ's role in immigration control and migration-policy implementation (Matsutani, 2009). Most recently, in 2012 and 2013, MOJ also took over a central position in the agenda-setting phase of Japan's migration policy. Its so-called 'Points-based Preferential Immigration Treatment for Highly Skilled Foreign Professionals' (MOJ, 2013c) specifically targets the upper end of the global labor market by granting highly skilled foreign professionals in Japan – a status that is determined by their level of education, Japanese-language proficiency, employment status, and income – a number of special rights, such as resident permits for members of their extended family, resident permits for maids, and, most prominently, a quicker route to permanent residency. With the introduction of this system Japan has joined what sociologist David Chiavacci has previously called the 'global war for talent' (2012: 27).

The other government body involved in administering the life and work of foreign residents in Japan is the Ministry of Health, Labour and Welfare (MHLW). MHLW is the leading authority when it comes to the labor-market participation of foreign residents. MHLW conducts yearly surveys among Japanese companies on their hiring of foreign workers. In October 2007 participation in these surveys became mandatory for all companies (the maximum fine for non-compliance is 300,000 yen); before that date companies' cooperation was voluntary, with a rather low return rate (in 2006, the final year of voluntary participation, the return rate stood at 59.59 percent). Another feature of the 2007 system change is an expanded survey sample. The sample now includes all companies, even those of less than 50 employees, which had previously not been surveyed. Due to these shifts in the survey system, a longitudinal analysis of foreign workers' labor-market participation is impossible. We see, for example, for 2006 that 30,488 companies reported that they employed foreign workers. Only two years later, in 2008, the figure stands at 76,811 companies: that is, two and a half times more than in 2006 (MHLW, 2006; MHLW, 2009a). In 2012, 119,731 companies hired 682,450 foreign workers in total (MHLW, 2013). Of course, we cannot conclude that the number of companies employing foreign workers rose drastically; neither can we argue that the companies that did not respond to the survey while it was still voluntary employ relatively more foreign workers than the early respondents, nor that it is particular companies with less than 50 employees that have a high share of foreign workers. In order to draw any of these conclusions we would need more in-depth, longitudinal and comprehensive data. What we can observe, however, from the MHLW data available are the

following characteristics of foreign workers' labor-market participation in 2012:

- 682,450 foreign workers were employed in Japanese companies;
- 24.8 percent (169,057) of all reported foreign workers were employed via (domestic or foreign) subcontractors;
- 43.4 percent of all reported foreign workers were Chinese, followed by Brazilians (14.9 percent) and Filipinos/as (10.7 percent);
- 45.2 percent of all reported foreign workers were holders of a visa category they obtained on grounds of their personal history (bottom four categories in Table 31.1); 18.2 percent were holders of a visa category based on their professional skills (top 14 categories in Table 31.1 with the exemption of diplomats and government officials);
- 99.4 percent of all Brazilians reported as foreign workers in Japan were holders of a visa category they obtained on grounds of their personal history;
- 26.2 percent of all reported foreign workers resided in Tokyo; 8.3 percent in Aichi; 6.6 percent in Osaka; 6.3 percent in Kanagawa; 4.3 percent in Saitama; 3.8 percent in Chiba;
- 28.8 percent of all reported foreign workers were employed in the manufacturing sector; 13.3 percent in restaurants and hotels; 16.1 percent in small businesses; 7.6 percent in the service sector; 4.8 percent in information technology; 3.7 percent in education;
- Chinese (36.4 percent) and Brazilians (57.3 percent) often worked in the manufacturing sector; so did 61.3 percent of Vietnamese, 52.7 percent of Peruvians, and 47.5 percent of Filipinos; Koreans (19.0 percent) worked in small businesses; and nationals of G8 nations (45.6 percent) in education (MHLW, 2013).

The difference between reported foreign workers and registered foreign residents in Japan is striking. Are only 682,450 of the registered 2,038,159 foreign residents (33.5 percent) employed in Japanese companies? Once again Japan shows us an extremely low figure considering that roughly half of all global migration streams occur for the purpose of work. Possible explanations for this low percentage include the following. a) We need to deduct the number of registered foreign nationals below the age of 15 and above the age of 64 in order to get data on the working-age foreign population before doing our math. This data, however, is provided neither by MHLW nor by MOJ. b) Some foreign workers may not be employed by Japanese but by foreign companies that are not required to respond to this survey. This would also explain the low figure of holders of a visa category that is based on migrants' professional skills (in particular 'intra-company transferees'). c) Japan's Korean minority seems not to be reported via this survey system; otherwise they would have had to show up in the records of large ethnic groups in the workforce. 43.4 percent of all reported foreign workers were Chinese; the Korean community is almost as large as the Chinese. Given their different age structures – predominantly young Chinese 'new-comer' migrants and ageing Korean 'old-comer' migrants – we can expect to see fewer Koreans than Chinese in the workforce, but they would still show up in relatively high numbers. We may suspected that the Korean minority has blended in so well that they are simply not being reported as 'foreign' workers.

With regard to the composition of Japan's foreign workers, we see an unsurprising concentration of foreign workers in the Kantō and Kansai regions; we also see nation-specific and sector-specific divisions, and a division with regard to the visa categories that grant permission to stay and work in Japan. In line with the MOJ data presented in Figure 31.2, we can also see that the majority of foreign workers in Japan reside in the country using a visa category they obtain on grounds of their personal life history – family relations in many cases. It is fair to conclude from this data that Japan's foreign workers' communities are not only relatively small but also centered around persons who have settled in Japan for the long-term rather than the typical transmigrants who stop by to make money and then embark again on their migration journey. All the more surprising, then, that foreign workers seem not to have been well integrated into Japanese

society. I would argue that the public and political discourse on foreigner crime over the course of the past two decades has been too prevalent to allow for foreigners' full integration as workers and citizens in their communities. Marginalization of foreign residents and workers has evolved around the topic of irregular migrants living undocumented lives in Japan and supporting themselves by committing crimes (Yamamoto, 2004).

Irregular Migrants

In the Japanese context there are two main backdoors through which irregular migration occurs: a) visa-overstayers: that is, migrants not leaving Japan although the duration of their visa has expired; and b) illegal workers: that is, migrants who engage in work that they are not eligible for according to their visa status.[27]

Based on the calculations of Japan's Immigration Bureau the number of visa-overstayers amounted to 62,009 persons as of 1 January 2013. This is down by 236,637 persons (79.2 percent) from the record high of 298,646 visa-overstayers on 1 May 1993. We observe a decline in visa-overstayers for all nationalities[28] (Figure 31.4) with the Koreans (25.2 percent) forming the largest group among them, followed by the Chinese (12.5 percent), Filipinos as (9.2 percent), Thai (5.7 percent), Taiwanese (6.5 percent), and Malaysians (3.5 percent) (MOJ, 2013b). Similarly, with regard to the valid visa the overstayers were on before becoming irregulars we can observe a decline in all categories. It is striking, however, that in 2013 (and before) more than two thirds of visa-overstayers (70.9 percent) used the category of 'temporary visitor' to enter

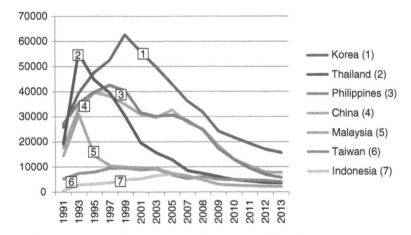

Figure 31.4 Visa-overstayers in Japan by nationality, 1991–2013

Source: MOJ 2013b.

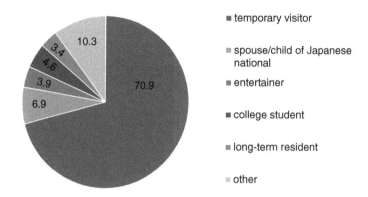

Figure 31.5   Visa-overstayers in Japan by category of last valid visa, 2013

Source: MOJ 2013b.

Japan initially (Figure 31.5) (MOJ 2013b). This is surprising because the MOJ upholds the public and political discourse of Chinese college and pre-college students over-staying their visas as the most immediate threat to Japan's border-control efforts.[29]

The relatively rapid decrease in the number of visa-overstayers in the second half of the data period is partly a result of the aggressive campaign against illegal work by foreigners (*fuhō shūrō gaikokujin taisaku kyanpēn*) which MOJ launched in 2004. In this campaign MOJ does not distinguish between visa-overstayers and illegal workers. In fact, MOJ uses the term *fuhō shūrō gaikokujin* (illegal foreign workers) in the title and the explanatory text of its campaign flyers while in the very same flyers it uses the numbers for visa-overstayers and not illegal workers.[30] The Ministry may have chosen to do so deliberately since the number of visa-overstayers is far more eye-catching than that of illegal workers. Compare the 220,552 visa-overstayers of 2003 (the data used by MOJ when launching the campaign) with the 34,325 illegal workers that came to light the same year (MOJ, 2008). The MOJ campaign against illegal foreign workers is still in place, albeit limited to active campaigning in the month of June. At a Shinagawa-station pathway that you need to cross when changing from an incoming train to the bus that brings you to the Tokyo branch of the Immigration Bureau – the busiest of all the branches in the country – you simply cannot miss a huge banner warning against the illegal employment of foreigners (Figure 31.6).

The total number of illegal foreign workers in Japan stood at 8,979 persons in 2012; it has been on the decline ever since 2005. The majority of illegal foreign workers in Japan come from Asian countries (84.7 percent in 2012), followed by Latin American (4.2 percent) countries. Workers from

the top five countries of the MOJ statistics – China, Philippines, Korea, Thailand and Vietnam – make up 77.7 percent of all illegal foreign workers in Japan. We do, however, see clear differences along gender lines. The ratio of female illegal workers exceeded that of their male counterparts for nationals of the Philippines and Korea. Male illegal workers occupied the largest proportion for nationals of China, Thailand, Vietnam, Indonesia, Peru, Brazil, and Nepal. We also see gender differences with regard to type of work. While the majority of factory and construction workers were male, hostesses and waitresses were in most cases female. Factory work is the largest (18.1 percent) profession illegal foreign workers are employed in (Figure 31.7). As with the visa-overstayers, we can identify the Chinese as the largest ethnic group among illegal foreign workers. Another similarity between the two categories of irregular migrants is that the number of illegal foreign workers is also on the decline. It reached a peak in 2005 with 45,935 cases of illegal employment, and by 2012 the figure stood at 8,979 cases (MOJ, 2013b).

Evolving irregularities in labor-migration structures often reflect an increasing gap between the economic demand for, in most cases, low-wage labor and the supply of this labor on the national market. This gap in Japan has been very pronounced – yet not officially acknowledged – since the late 1980s. Policy-makers aimed at bridging the gap by accepting the existence of a different kind of gap: that between policy output and policy outcome. While the output still was framed as 'Japan does not need and does not want international labor migration', the outcome had long been to accept foreign workers as part of Japan's labor market. The extremely low number of irregular migrants in Japan is largely a result of the tolerated existence of this second gap.

Figure 31.6 Banner warning against illegal employment of foreign workers

Source: Picture taken by the author at Shinagawa station in June 2009.

A NEW CHANNEL OF INTERNATIONAL LABOR MIGRATION TO JAPAN

After the publication of a United Nations Population Division report on 'Replacement Migration: Is it a Solution to Declining and Ageing Populations?' in 2000 the public, scholarly and political discourse on international labor migration to Japan started evolving around what proved to become a new strong pull-factor for migration to Japan: the issue of demographic change (UNPD, 2000). Japan's

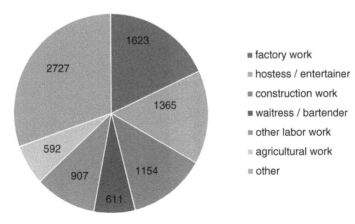

- factory work
- hostess / entertainer
- construction work
- waitress / bartender
- other labor work
- agricultural work
- other

Figure 31.7 Illegal foreign workers in Japan by type of work, 2012

Source: MOJ 2013b.

society is ageing and declining rapidly. While the working-age population (15–64 years) is predicted to decline from 63.8 percent of total population in 2010 to 50.9 percent by 2060, the old-age population (older than 65 years) over the same period of time will increase from 23.0 percent of total population to 39.9 percent, and the total population will shrink from 128.06 million in 2010 to 86.74 million in 2060 (NIPSSR, 2013).

Japan is reacting to this challenge of population ageing and decline in manifold ways,[31] including introducing bilateral Economic Partnership Agreements (EPA) that allow for nation-specific and sector-specific labor migration of health-care workers to Japan. Nurses and caregivers from Indonesia (from August 2008) and the Philippines (from May 2009) have been granted access to Japan's health-care labor market.[32] This sector already sees tremendous labor shortages, a trend that is expected to become even more severe as the population ages further and more elderly people will need professional health care. As the workforce declines fewer people will be available to work as health-care professionals. It is no coincidence that the health-care sector is at the forefront of Japan's latest migration-policy reform (Vogt, 2010; Vogt, 2011).

Finding a common position among the stakeholders involved in formulating Japan's draft for the EPA negotiations with Indonesia and the Philippines was no easy task. The positions brought to the table by MOJ, MHLW, and the Ministry of Economy, Trade and Industry (METI) were extremely diverse. While MOJ bluntly refused any agreement that would allow for nation-specific and sector-specific labor migration to Japan, METI – strongly pushed by the Japan Business Federation (*Keidanren*) – was an outspoken supporter of the EPA framework. In fact, *Keidanren* supports an expansion of the EPA framework to more business sectors and more partner nations. In this situation MHLW was pushed into a central position within the intra-Japanese negotiations. The main concern of MHLW had long been to improve working conditions in the health-care sector in order to ensure that Japanese nurses and care-givers who had left the sector due to low pay, low prestige, and long working hours with inflexible schedules would return to their professions. The thought of admitting foreign workers to this sector was closely connected with a fear of deteriorating work standards and a declining wage level. MHLW, strongly lobbied by the Japan Nursing Association, was hesitant to support the EPA framework. In the end they did support it, in particular as a countermeasure to the severe labor shortage in the sector. However, MHLW also pushed through a condition within the EPA framework that makes this channel of labor migration a rather bumpy road for interested foreign workers. EPA labor migrants will need to take Japan's

national care-giver examination three to four years after their arrival to Japan. The exam is to be taken in the Japanese language. Passing the exam equals a permission to stay and work in Japan; failing the exam results in the visa and work permit being revoked.[33] This high hurdle to a professional career in Japan may be the main reason why numbers of applicants from both partner nations have so far remained below the 1,000 persons per nation per year threshold Japan has set for EPA-channeled labor migration (Vogt, 2010; Vogt, 2011).

Nevertheless, this new channel of international labor migration to Japan marks a milestone for Japan's migration policy. For the first time Japan has *officially* opened its national labor market to a workforce that is not highly skilled and offered them a long-term-settlement perspective. This has been the *outcome* of Japan's migration policy for some time; what is new, however, is that this is now a policy *output*. In other words, with the EPA Japan's gap between migration-policy output and outcome has finally been bridged. Since, at this point, any fundamental revision of the Immigration Control and Refugee Recognition Act that would institutionalize the new policy output is not yet in sight we need to be cautious when classifying the significance of this – admittedly huge – policy change. It might be fair to talk about this being the test phase of a political paradigm shift.

BRIDGING THE GAP?

This study on foreign workers in Japan has brought to light two different gap scenarios. First, the number of registered foreign residents in Japan – and even more the number of foreign workers in Japan – is very low compared to other OECD nations. This is surprising because there are severe labor shortages in some sectors of Japan's economy, shortages which seemingly cannot be filled via the domestic labor market. Second, there is a gap between policy output (labor migration is exclusively of the highly skilled and on a temporary basis only) and policy outcome (labor migration includes those who are not highly skilled and offers a long-term perspective) in Japan's migration policy. This gap was institutionalized with the 1990 revision of Japan's Immigration Control and Refugee Recognition Act, which opened the side doors for *nikkeijin* labor migration to Japan, and also for trainees to enter the Japanese workforce. Both channels – albeit not coherent with official political guidelines – helped to bridge the first gap mentioned above, the gap between economic demand and labor supply. One of the most recent moves in Japan's migration policy, the implementation of a new channel for international labor migration to Japan via bilateral Economic Partnership Agreements with selected nations, is a first move to bridge the second gap, that between policy output and policy outcome. The EPA framework helps to reformulate policy output and policy outcome. As argued above, along with Cornelius and Tsuda's assumption that '"unintended consequences" of immigration control policies may not be so unintended, or may in fact be fully intended' (Cornelius and Tsuda, 2004: 6), Japan has intentionally pursued a gap policy in its migration framework. The existing gaps have allowed economic demands to be met without officially acknowledging the existence of these demands. The newly formed EPA channel, however, represents a new age of migration policy in Japan: due to the impacts of a rapidly ageing and declining population, the economic need for foreign workers has been officially acknowledged for the first time. This policy shift reflects the enormity of the impact demographic change is having on the composition of Japan's national and international workforce. Should Japan decide to walk further down the path of labor immigration, the question of how Japan will meet the demands of a growing foreign population will have to be asked. It is the social, political, and economic integration of foreign workers and residents that poses an immediate challenge to Japan. Adequately addressing this challenge may mean bridging a third gap: the gap between national-level policy formulation and local-level policy implementation. A more closely knit network between different-level political actors throughout all phases of the policy process promises to be not only a valuable addition to Japan's political system, but perhaps a necessary one.

NOTES

1 The realities and policies of migration are in constant flux. When substantial updates to an earlier version of this chapter became necessary Ruth Achenbach agreed to join me in rolling Sisyphus' boulder uphill. For this I am very grateful.

2 On Japan's migration and integration policies in comparative perspective to Germany, France and Canada see, for example, Vogt and Roberts (2011).

3 Political-economist James Hollifield writes: 'What's missing from these accounts [push/pull-model] is a theory of the state and the way in which it influences population movements'. (Hollifield, 2000: 146).

4 For the case study of care-giver migration to Japan the negotiating process of the Japanese position among a variety of political actors has been demonstrated, for example, in Vogt 2007.

5 Details on the EPA-administered migration scheme, in effect since 2008, can be found in later in this chapter.

6 If one were to apply the revised method of calculating Japan's foreign residents (in effect since 2013), which deducts the number of short-term visas, the 2008 figure would still constitute the numerical peak of Japan's foreign population. It would then stand at 2,144,682 persons in 2008 (MOJ, 2013a).

7 The composition of the Brazilian community in Japan is addressed later in the chapter.

8 Further information on migration to Japan in the early postwar years can be obtained from Morris-Suzuki (2006).

9 Komai, a former University of Tsukuba professor of sociology, is the author of numerous books on international migration to Japan. He is, however, also a contentious figure, often criticized as a supporter of 'cultural singularity' (Ishiwata, 2004: 93).

10 Table 31.1 provides an overview over visa categories and related work permissions.

11 See later in the chapter.

12 In 1989 visa-exemption agreements with Bangladesh and Pakistan had also been revoked (Tsuda and Cornelius, 2004: 457).

13 College students, for example, are, allowed to work part-time up to 20 hours per week during the term and 28 hours per week between terms to finance their tuition and living expenses.

14 This visa category will be discussed in more detail and with regard to Japan's Chinese population, later in the chapter.

15 The exclusion of unskilled foreign workers from Japan's labor market has long been criticized by business representatives. Most recently, with the upcoming 2020 Tokyo Olympic Games, the business world seems to have won an ally in Prime Minister Shinzō Abe, who publicly toyed with the idea of giving contracts to unskilled workers from abroad to support Japan's construction industry. In this context, he also raised the possibility of an extension of the technical intern training program from a maximum of three years residence in Japan to five years (*Toyo Keizai*, 2014).

16 By the end of 2012 164,945 long-term-resident permit holders resided in Japan (MOJ, 2013a). This drop in numbers corresponds to a drop in the share of the long-term-resident visa category from 11.7 percent in 2008 to the aforementioned 8.1 percent of all visas holders in Japan in 2012 (MOJ, 2009; MOJ, 2013a). The story behind these figures, again, is closely connected to the significant drop in Japan's Brazilian community, which will be elaborated on further in this chapter.

17 See also Lee (2012: 8).

18 The trend of a declining 'old-comer' population and a growing 'new-comer' population among Japan's Korean residents is reflected in growing discontents of identity and ideology within the community (Lie, 2008).

19 Only 2,116 Chinese in Japan are registered as 'special permanent residents', a category that immediately identifies them as 'old-comers' (MIC, 2013a).

20 In 2012 42,287 foreign nationals resided in Japan on the visa category of 'engineer'; 20,933 (49.5 percent) of them were Chinese nationals (MIC, 2013a).

21 LeBail (2011) provides detailed information on the integration of Chinese students into Japan's society and labor market.

22 See also Tsuda (2009: 208).

23 Tsuda (2009: 210) arugues that these quarrels are nurtured by 'social class prejudice' and 'considerable cultural prejudice toward the Japanese–Brazilians based on a negative evaluation of their "Brazilian" behavior'.

24 Mayors of towns with a foreign population above the national average (top ranking Oizumi-chō reported a foreign population of 14.5 percent in 2013) formed a committee under this very name (*Gaikokujin shūjū toshi kaigi*) in 2001. By 2013, the committee had grown to 27 member cities and towns. Their mayors meet once a year to discuss issues relevant to integration measures; they also formulate policy proposals which they pass on to representatives of national-level ministries concerned with migration-policy-making (GSTK, 2013).

25 Between November 2008 and February 2009 more than 9,000 foreign nationals turned to the Ministry of Health, Labour and Welfare's Hello Work unemployment agency. This is eleven times the figure for the same period a year earlier (Arudou, 2009). For more information on the impacts of the economic downturn on foreign workers in Japan see Rau and Vogt (2009).

26 The program was to be implemented by the Ministry for Health, Labour and Welfare. The program outline can be accessed via the MHLW website (MHLW, 2009b).

27 While violations of the Immigration Control Act by 'illegal entry' – that is, entering the country without a valid passport or valid visa in the first place – is the most prominent contravention of migration laws in many industrialized countries, the numbers of 'illegal entries' to Japan remain relatively low: In 2007 Japan saw 7,454 illegal entries, down 28.6 percent from the previous year; 32.3 percent of those charged with 'illegal entry' came from China, 21.8 percent from the Philippines, and 9.1 percent from Thailand (MOJ, 2008). The downward-trend has been continuous: in 2012 1,875 illegal entries were registered, 28.4 percent coming from China, 27.7 percent from the Philippines, and 9.5 percent from Korea (MOJ, 2013b).

28 Visa-overstayers from Vietnam are an exception: while their number in 2012 stood at 1,014 persons, by 2013 it had risen to 1,110 persons (MOJ, 2013b).

29 The 'Chinese threat' was also stressed by Kōno (2006).

30 MOJ, in this campaign, which was launched in 2004, kept referring to 220,000 visa-overstayers, which in fact is the 2003 figure (MOJ, 2013b). See also, for example, the 2006 edition of the campaign pamphlet (MOJ, 2006).

31 The various impacts of Japan's demographic change on the nation's society, culture, politics, and economics as well as multiple actors' reactions toward these impacts are introduced in Coulmas et al. (2008).

32 Nurses and caregivers from Vietnam joined them in Japan in February 2014 (*VietnamPlus*, 2013).

33 For additional information on the EPA negotiations and the EPA system of international labor migration see, for example, Vogt (2007).

REFERENCES

Arudou, Debito (2009). 'Golden Parachutes' Mark Failure of Race-based Policy. In *The Japan Times* (2009/04/07). www.japantimes.co.jp/community/2009/04/07/community/golden-parachutes-mark-failure-of-race-based-policy/#.UuuDnLTO9UE (accessed 2014/01/31).

Chiavacci, David (2012). Japan in the 'Global War for Talent': Changing Concepts of Valuable Foreign Workers and Their Consequences. In *ASIEN, The German Journal on Contemporary Asia*, July 2012 (no. 124), pp. 27–47.

Cornelius, Wayne A. and Takeyuki Tsuda (2004). Controlling Immigration. The Limits of Government Intervention. In Cornelius, Wayne A., Takeyuki Tsuda, Philip L. Martin and James F. Hollifield (eds.): *Controlling Immigration. A Global Perspective* (2nd edition). Stanford, CA: Stanford University Press, pp. 3–48.

Coulmas, Florian, Harald Conrad, Annette Schad-Seifert and Gabriele Vogt (eds.) (2008). *The Demographic Change. A Handbook about Japan.* Leiden / Boston: Brill.

GSTK, Gaikokujin shūjū toshi kaigi (2013). *Kaiin toshi* (Member cities). www.shujutoshi.jp/member/index.htm (accessed 2014/01/29).

Hollifield, James F. (2000). The Politics of International Migration. How Can We 'Bring the State Back In?'. In Brettell, Caroline B. and James F. Hollifield (eds.): *Migration Theory, Talking across Disciplines.* New York / London: Routledge, pp. 137–185.

Ishiwata, Eric (2004). Re-made in Japan: Nikkeijin Disruptions of Japan's Ethno-Spacial Boundaries. In Germer, Andrea and Andreas Moerke (eds.): *Grenzgänge. (De-)Konstruktion kollektiver*

Identitäten in Japan. Japanstudien 16. Jahrbuch des Deutschen Instituts für Japanstudien. Munich: iudicium, pp. 91–117.

Komai, Hiroshi (2001). *Foreign Migrants in Contemporary Japan*. Melbourne: Trans Pacific Press.

Kōno, Tarō (Senior Vice Minister of Justice (2005/06). personal conversation, Tokyo, 2006/02/20.

Kuwahara, Yasuo (2005). Migrant Workers in the Post-war History of Japan. In *Japan Labor Review. Special Edition: Foreign Workers*. Vol. 2, No. 4 (Autumn 2005). Tokyo: The Japan Institute for Labour Policy and Training, pp. 25–47.

LeBail, Hélène (2011). Integration of Chinese students into Japan's society and labour market. In Roberts, Glenda and Gabriele Vogt (eds.): *Migration and Integration – Japan in Comparative Perspective*. Munich: iudicium, pp. 72–88.

Lee, Soo Im (Ryukoku University). personal conversation, Tokyo, 2008/09/08.

Lee, Soo Im (2012). Diversity of *Zainichi* Koreans and Their Ties to Japan and Korea. In *Studies on Multicultural Societies No. 8 (Working Paper Series)*. Kyoto: Ryukoku University, Afrasian Research Centre. http://afrasia.ryukoku.ac.jp/publication/upfile/WP008.pdf (accessed 2014/01/31).

Lie, John (2008) Zainichi Recognitions: Japan's Korean Residents' Ideology and Discontents. In *The Asia-Pacific Journal: Japan Focus*. www.japanfocus.org/-John-Lie/2939 (accessed 2014/01/31).

Liu-Farrer, Gracia (2009a). Creating a Transnational Community. Chinese Newcomers in Japan. In Weiner, Michael (ed.): *Japan's Minorities. The Illusion of Homogeneity* (2nd edition). London / New York: Routledge, pp. 116–138.

Liu-Farrer, Gracia (2009b). *Making Careers in the Occupational Niche: Chinese Students in Corporate Japan's Transnational Business*. Unpublished paper presented at the DIJ Social Science Study Group, Tokyo.

Matsutani, Minoru (2009). Diet OKs Bill to Up Foreigner Controls. In: *The Japan Times* (2009/07/09). www.japantimes.co.jp/news/2009/07/09/news/diet-oks-bills-to-up-foreigner-controls/#.UuuD5LTO9UE (accessed 2014/01/31).

MHLW, Ministry of Health, Labour and Welfare (2006). *Gaikokujin koyō jōkyō hōkoku kisha happyō heisei 5-18* (Press release on the registration of information about employing foreign nationals 1993–2006). www.mhlw.go.jp/bunya/koyou/gaikokujin09/index.html (accessed 2014/01/31).

MHLW, Ministry of Health, Labour and Welfare (2009a). *Gaikokujin koyō jōkyō no todokede jōkyō heisei 20 nen 10 gatsumatsu genzai ni tsuite* (On the registration of information about employing foreign nationals as of end of October 2008). www.mhlw.go.jp/houdou/2009/01/dl/h0116-9a.pdf (accessed 2014/01/31).

MHLW, Ministry of Health, Labour and Welfare (2009b). *Nikkeijin nado no gaikokujin rōdōsha o koyō suru jigyōshu no minasama e* (To the company leaders who employ nikkeijin and other foreign workers). www.mhlw.go.jp/bunya/koyou/other34/dl/01.pdf (accessed 2014/01/31).

MHLW, Ministry of Health, Labour and Welfare (2009c). *Nikkeijin rishokusha ni tai suru kikoku shienjigyō no gaiyō* (Outline of the program to support repatriation of unemployed nikkeijin and other foreigners). www.mhlw.go.jp/houdou/2009/03/dl/h0331-10a.pdf (accessed 2014/01/31).

MHLW, Ministry of Health, Labour and Welfare (2013). *Gaikokujin koyō jōkyō no todokede jōkyō matome (heisei 24 nen 10 gatsumatsu genzai)* (Compendium on registration of information about employing foreign nationals as of end of October 2012). www.mhlw.go.jp/stf/houdou/2r9852000002ttea.html (accessed 2014/01/29).

MIC, Ministry of Justice (2013a). *Kokuseki, chiiki-betsu zairyū shikaku (zairyū mokuteki) betsu sō zairyū gaikokujin* (Overall number of foreign residents by nationality, residence title [goal of stay]). www.e-stat.go.jp/SG1/estat/List.do?lid=000001111233 (accessed 2014/01/29)

MIC, Ministry of Justice (2013b). *Kokuseki, chiiki-betsu nenrei – danjo-betsu sō zairyū gaikokujin* (Overall number of foreign residents by nationality, age and sex). www. e-stat.go.jp/SG1/estat/List.do?lid= 000001111233 (accessed 2014/01/29).

MOJ, Ministry of Justice (2006). *Fuhō shūrō gaikokujin taisaku kyanpēn* (Campaign against illegal employment of foreigners). www.moj.go.jp/NYUKAN/campaign18nen.html (accessed 2009/09/01).

MOJ, Ministry of Justice (2008). *Heisei 20 nen-hatsu shutsunyūkoku kanri* (Immigration Control 2008 edition). www.moj.go.jp/NYUKAN/nyukan78.html (accessed 2014/ 01/29).

MOJ, Ministry of Justice (2009). *Heisei 20 nenmatsu genzai ni okeru gaikokujin tōrokusha tōkei ni tsuite* (Statistics on registered foreign residents as of end of 2008). www.moj.go.jp/PRESS/090710-1/090710-1.html (accessed 2014/01/29).

MOJ, Ministry of Justice (2010). *Heisei 21 nenmatsu genzai ni okeru gaikokujin tōrokusha tōkei ni tsuite* (Statistics on registered foreign residents as of end of 2009). www.moj.go.jp/nyuukokukanri/kouhou/nyuukokukanri04_00005.html (accessed 2014/ 01/29).

MOJ, Ministry of Justice (2011). *Heisei 22 nenmatsu genzai ni okeru gaikokujin tōrokusha tōkei ni tsuite* (Statistics on registered foreign residents as of end of 2010). www. moj.go.jp/nyuukokukanri/kouhou/ nyuukantourokusyatoukei110603.html (accessed 2014/01/29).

MOJ, Ministry of Justice (2012). *Heisei 23 nenmatsu genzai ni okeru zairyū gaikokujin kazu ni tsuite* (On the number foreign residents as of end of 2011).

www.moj.go.jp/nyuukokukanri/kouhou/nyuu-kokukanri04_00021.html (accessed 2014/01/29).

MOJ, Ministry of Justice (2013a). *Heisei 24 nenmatsu genzai ni okeru zairyū gaikokujin kazu ni tsuite* (On the number foreign residents as of end of 2012). www.moj.go.jp/nyuukokukanri/kouhou/nyuu-kokukanri04_00030.html (accessed 2014/01/29).

MOJ, Ministry of Justice (2013b). *Heisei 25 nen-hatsu shutsunyūkoku kanri* (Immigration Control 2013 edition). www.moj.go.jp/nyuukokukanri/kouhou/nyuu-kokukanri06_ 00041.html (accessed 2014/01/29).

MOJ, Ministry of Justice (2013c). *Points-based Preferential Immigration Treatment for Highly Skilled Foreign Professionals*. www.immi-moj.go.jp/newimmiact_3/en/index.html (accessed 2014/01/31).

Morris-Suzuki, Tessa (2006). Invisible Immigrants: Undocumented Migration and Border Controls in Early Postwar Japan. In *The Asia-Pacific Journal: Japan Focus*. www.japanfocus.org/-Tessa-Morris_Suzuki/2210 (accessed 2014/01/29).

Morris-Suzuki, Tessa (2008). Migrants, Subjects, Citizens: Comparative Perspectives on Nationality in the Prewar Japanese Empire. In *The Asia-Pacific Journal: Japan Focus*. www.japanfocus.org/-Tessa-Morris_Suzuki/ 2862 (accessed 2014/01/29).

NIPSSR, National Institute of Population and Social Security Research (2013). *Population Statistics of Japan 2012*. www.ipss.go.jp/index-e.html (accessed 2014/01/31).

OECD, Organisation for Economic Co-Operation and Development (2013). *International Migration Outlook 2013*. www.oecd-ilibrary.org/social-issues-migration-health/ international-migration-outlook-2013_migr_outlook-2013-en (accessed 2014/01/29).

Rau, Florence and Gabriele Vogt (2009). Below the Surface. Japan's Foreign Workforce. In *J@pan.Inc*, Spring 2009, pp. 20–21.

Roberts, Glenda (2012). Vocalizing the "I" Word: Proposals and Initiatives on Immigration to Japan from the LDP and Beyond. In *ASIEN, The German Journal on Contemporary Asia*, July 2012 (no. 124), pp. 48–68.

Roth, Joshua Hotaka (2002). *Brokered Homeland, Japanese Brazilian Migrants in Japan*. Ithaca / London: Cornell University Press.

Shimada, Haruo (1994). *Japan's 'Guest Workers'. Issues and Public Policies*. Tokyo: University of Tokyo Press.

Torii, Ippei (2007/10/24). *The Controversial Debate on Admitting More Immigrants to Japan*. Unpublished paper presented at the DIJ International Symposium 'Migration and Integration – Japan in Comparative Perspective', Tokyo.

Toyo Keizai (2014/01/09). Abe seiken, 'gaikokujin rōdōsha' no gakudai o kentō. Tanjunrōdōsha ukeiremo (Abe administration studies expansion of 'foreign workers'. Also acceptance of unskilled workers). http://otakomu.jp/archives/38402.html (accessed 2014/01/31).

Tsuda, Takeyuki (2003). *Strangers in the Ethnic Homeland, Japanese Brazilian Return Migration in Transnational Perspective*. New York: Columbia University Press.

Tsuda, Takeyuki (2009). Japanese–Brazilian Ethnic Return Migration and the Making of Japan's Newest Immigration Minority. In Weiner, Michael (ed.): *Japan's Minorities. The Illusion of Homogeneity* (2nd edition). London / New York: Routledge, pp. 206–227.

Tsuda, Takeyuki and Wayne A. Cornelius (2004). Japan: Government Policy, Immigration Reality. In Cornelius, Wayne A., Takeyuki Tsuda, Philip L. Martin and James F. Hollifield (eds.): *Controlling Immigration. A Global Perspective* (2nd edition). Stanford, CA: Stanford University Press, pp. 438–476.

UNPD, United Nations Population Division (2000). *Replacement Migration. Is it a Solution to Declining and Ageing Populations?* www.un.org/esa/population/publications/migration/migration.htm (accessed 2014/ 01/31).

VietnamPlus (2013/12/10). More Vietnamese Nurses and Orderlies to Work in Japan. www.en.vietnamplus.vn/Home/More-Vietnamese-nurses-and-orderlies-to-work-in-Japan/201312/43204.vnplus (accessed 2014/01/31).

Vogt, Gabriele (2007). Closed Doors, Open Doors, Doors Wide Shut? Migration Politics in Japan. In: *Japan Aktuell. Journal of Current Japanese Affairs.* 5/2007, pp. 3–30.

Vogt, Gabriele (2010). Care-Giver Migration to Graying Japan. In Salzmann, Thomas, Barry Edmonston and James Raymer (eds.): *Demographic Aspects of Migration*. Wiesbaden: VS Research, pp. 327–348.

Vogt, Gabriele (2011). The Political Economy of Health-care Migration: A Japanese Perspective. In Coulmas, Florian and Ralph Lützeler (eds.): *Imploding Populations in Japan and Germany: A Comparison*. Leiden / Boston: Brill, pp. 323–346.

Vogt, Gabriele and Glenda S. Roberts (eds.) (2011). *Migration and Integration – Japan in Comparative Perspective*. Munich: iudicium.

Yamamoto, Ryoko (2004). Alien Attack? The Construction of Foreign Criminality in Contemporary Japan. In Germer, Andrea and Andreas Moerke (eds.): *Grenzgänge. (De-)Konstruktion kollektiver Identitäten in Japan. Japanstudien 16. Jahrbuch des Deutschen Instituts für Japanstudien*. Munich: iudicium, pp. 27–57.

Yano, Manami (Co-founder and then chairperson of *Ijuren*). personal conversation, Tokyo, 2006/04/10. (*Ijuren*: www.migrants.jp/).

32

Agriculture

Aurelia George Mulgan

INTRODUCTION

Agriculture in Japan is a declining industry. Two essential factors of production – land and labour – are contracting at an alarming rate. Between 1961 and 2013 Japan lost 1.55 million hectares (ha) of land under cultivation, a 25 per cent fall.[1] The agricultural working population dropped even more dramatically, slumping from a peak of 14.54 million in 1960 to just 2.27 million in 2014, an 84 per cent decline, while the number of farm households decreased almost 60 per cent from 6.18 million to 2.53 million, with only 1.41 million commercial farms[2] (Nōrinsuisanshō, 2014). Japanese agriculture is also facing a severe demographic crisis. In 2013 the average age of the agricultural working population was 66.2 yrs, while in 2014, 64 per cent were 65 yrs or over (Nōrinsuisanshō, 2014). Many farmers of retirement age have no successors[3] and have simply abandoned cultivation.[4] Other negative trends include an almost continuous contraction in public and private investment in the farm industry, and in the value of gross agricultural output[5] and in agricultural income produced.[6] In 2012 the farm sector's share of GDP was only 1 per cent compared with 9 per cent in 1960, while over the same period Japan's self-sufficiency in food, measured in calories, trended continuously downwards from 79 per cent to 39 per cent, the lowest among major developed countries (Nōrinsuisanshō, 2014; Yamashita, 2008a).

The fundamental cause of the decline of Japanese agriculture is the lack of agricultural reform, particularly the government's failure to adopt structural adjustment policies leading to a sector in which more efficient large-scale operations predominate (OECD, 2009). The average size of farms grew from 0.9 ha in 1960 to 2.45 ha in 2014 (Nōrinsuisanshō, 2014; Yamashita, 2005), which is well short of the 10 ha required for full-time farming (Godo, 2006: 134). Less than a third of commercial farms are full-time professional operations. The rest are part-time, the vast majority earning more income from non-agricultural jobs than from farming. For them agriculture is a spare-time occupation and subsidiary business with just under 60 per cent of all commercial farm households earning less than ¥1 million per year from farm sales (Nōrinsuisanshō, Daijin Kanbō Tōkeibu, 2012). Numbers of non-farming landowners are also rising, with over a million households owning farmland but not engaged in agriculture, preferring instead to retain the land for future capital gain. Indeed, abandoned farmland is often held for resale as land for non-agricultural purposes, which attracts higher profits and is a major obstacle to consolidating land for large-scale farming (Godo, 2008; Godo and Takahashi, 2008; Yamazaki, 2004).

The 'smallness' of Japanese agriculture underlies its relative lack of productivity, efficiency and profitability. Farm size has not increased sufficiently to capture economies of scale. High-cost and internationally uncompetitive small farms remain supported by regulated markets, subsidies and import protection. With the TSE (Total Support Estimate)[7] surpassing the total value-added amount from agriculture, it could be argued that the Japanese economy would be better off without its agricultural sector (Godo, 2008). International comparisons by the OECD put Japanese agriculture as among the most highly protected in the developed world (OECD, 2008a).

Almost every aspect of Japan's agricultural economy is controlled, administered and supported by means of laws and policies, public and semi-public organisations, annual budgetary outlays and public investment. Presiding over this vast apparatus of regulatory, allocatory and direct market intervention is the Ministry of Agriculture, Forestry and Fisheries, or MAFF (Nōrinsuisanshō) (George Mulgan, 2005a), a bureaucracy that gives agriculture the distinction of being 'the most intervened sector' in the Japanese economy (Honma, 2000a: 1).

THE FIVE LEGAL PILLARS OF POSTWAR AGRICULTURAL POLICY

Five laws have formed the core of agricultural legislation in the postwar period: the 1942 Food Control (FC) Law (Shokuryō Kanrihō, or Shokkanhō), the 1947 Agricultural Cooperative Union Law (Nōgyō Kyōdō Kumiaihō), the 1949 Land Improvement Law (Tochi Kairyōhō), the 1952 Agricultural Land Law (Nōchihō) and the 1961 Agricultural Basic Law (Nōgyō Kihonhō) (Kajii, 1991). The consequences of these laws have been profound.

The 1942 FC Law established the Food Control (FC) system, which regulated the distribution and pricing of staple foods (rice, wheat and barley) and which was administered by the MAFF's Food Agency. The law provided a direct link from rice producers to the government and then to consumers, prohibiting in principle any other system of distributing rice (Tashiro, 1998). Its original purpose was to protect consumers by instituting a system of equitable distribution of staple food during the war. However, its main policy purpose changed in the late 1950s to one of increasing farmers' incomes by raising the price at which the government bought rice from farmers – the so-called 'producer rice price' (seisansha beika).

This became the principal mechanism for supporting farmers' incomes.

The effects of high producer rice prices were myriad and deleterious. They 'were crucial in the spread of part-time farming in the postwar years' (Jussaume, 2003, 199) and in keeping small-scale farmers in agriculture, which hindered the development of large-scale, business-oriented farms and the structural reform of agriculture (Yamashita, 2005). High rice prices also discouraged farmers from switching to other products and stimulated continuing surpluses,[8] prompting the government to introduce a rice acreage reduction scheme (gentan) in 1970.[9] When the scheme was first introduced, Watanabe Michio, MAFF Minister at the time, described it as 'like using an air-cooler and heater at the same time' (Yamashita, 2009a) because rice price supports stimulated production at the same time as the gentan suppressed it. The policy contributed to budget deficits (including losses on state trading, surplus rice storage and disposal, and subsidies to run the gentan, as well as to convert rice production to wheat, soybeans etc.), blocked the structural adjustment of agriculture by discouraging scale expansion in rice production and prevented the agricultural sector from responding sufficiently to the Westernisation of the Japanese diet,[10] thus assisting the decline in the country's food self-sufficiency rate.[11] Curtailing rice production also contributed to the abandonment of agricultural land, which represented a loss of agricultural resources, further undermining Japan's food security (Yamashita, 2008b).

The 1947 Agricultural Cooperative Union Law provided for the establishment of a nationwide system of farm cooperatives (nōgyō kyōdō kumiai), or Nōkyō (now JA, short for Japan Agricultural Cooperatives). The cooperatives' designated legal purpose is to promote the livelihood and agricultural production activities of farmers through self-help and mutual cooperation. JA grew into a mammoth farm trading, finance and insurance organisation as well as an agricultural interest group, encompassing practically all farm families and serving almost all their production, business and consumer needs. Under the FC system JA's principal task was to collect the rice produced by farmers for sale to the government.

The 1949 Land Improvement Law authorises large-scale, government-subsidised agricultural public works geared to the development of agricultural land. Projects include the provision of irrigation and drainage to rice paddies, reclaiming land for paddy field development, levelling farmland in order to form large cultivation plots, and the development of upland fields, all with a view to expanding agricultural production, lifting productivity and consolidating land holdings.

The land improvement industry became one of the principal public works industries in farming areas (George Mulgan, 2005a). It not only played a central role in the development of paddy-field farming but also helped to expand production in the livestock and horticultural sectors (Motosugi, 2003).

The 1952 Agricultural Land Law (ALL) sought to consolidate the fruits of the 1946 agricultural land reform (Yamashita, 2008c), which transferred land ownership from landlords to tillers of the soil, enabling tenant farmers to become small owner-cultivators without changing farm size, thus preserving the traditional agricultural production structure from prewar days (Kawagoe, 1999). The law aimed to maintain and improve agricultural production capacity and expand agricultural land through the owner-farmer principle (*jisakunō shugi*) (Yamazaki, 2004), which 'reinforced the ideology of household land ownership' (Jussaume, 2003, 206). Restrictions on land transfers were imposed by limiting the conversion of farmland to other uses as well as the transfer of ownership rights to persons other than owner-farmers, although central and local governments were permitted to purchase farmland for public works, and agricultural land could be entrusted to agricultural cooperatives because they were groups of farmers (Hatta et al., 2011: 18).

The law also restricted the ability of farmers to lease their land while providing guarantees for tenants against the cancellation of leases. Farmers were increasingly motivated to hold on to their land for future capital gain as land prices rose and as loose enforcement of the zoning regulations provided opportunities for land conversion (Yamashita, 2009b). As a result, the original purpose of the ALL to expand productive farmland and to develop the country's agriculture was subverted (Yamazaki, 2004). Rather than providing a means of expanding the scale of production, agricultural land was sold at great profit for non-agricultural purposes (Godo, 2008; Godo and Takahashi, 2008).

Although the ALL was amended from time to time to encourage leasing, the government retained its conservative stance towards separating 'ownership' and 'use' (Egaitsu, 1985). An amendment to the ALL in 2009 allowed private firms to lease agricultural land, but revisions to the initial bill because of strong political opposition from within both the ruling and opposition parties made conditions on borrowers of farmland stricter (for example, at least one member of an agricultural production corporation had to be engaged in farming full-time) and deregulation of farmland ownership was passed up. In combination with artificially high rice prices and the preferences of salaried landowners to retain their land for future profit, the continuing obstacles to mobilising agricultural land ownership helped to preserve the small-scale structure of agriculture and prevent other capable and motivated farmers from expanding their operations (Godo, 2008; Yamashita, 2008c). Moreover, because many farmers held on to their land for capital gain rather than to earn a living from farming, they lost their motivation for engaging in productive farming (Egaitsu, 1985).

The 1961 Agricultural Basic Law (ABL) had its origins in the turning point that agriculture passed in the early 1960s, when postwar economic growth was accompanied by the relative decline of agriculture as an industrial sector. The ABL was implemented to change the focus of the country's agricultural policy from supporting landed farmers and increasing output to fostering the productivity and efficiency of agriculture (Shimomura, 2004; Shimizu, 1985a). The scenario envisaged under the law by its main architect, MAFF Administrative Vice-Minister Ogura Takekazu, was that viable family farms (*jiritsu keiei nōka*) would accumulate land relinquished by farmers leaving agriculture to take up jobs in other industries. By expanding the amount of land they worked, farmers who were serious about making a living from agriculture could generate income on a par with workers in other industries. According to this vision, parity of productivity and income between the agricultural sector and the non-agricultural sector would be achieved mainly through rationalisation of farming structure (Ogura, 1982). However, the ruling Liberal Democratic Party (LDP), anxious to distribute income benefits directly to its farm supporters, injected a provision into the law enabling the government to take measures to stabilise prices of farm products in response to demand, supply, production and other economic conditions (George Mulgan, 2006a).

Structural policy and price policy became the twin pillars of 'Basic Law agricultural policy' (*Kihonhō nōsei*) (Hemmi and Katō, 1985). In practice, however, structural policy was undermined by price policy, which encouraged the growth of part-time farming, which in turn limited the mobilisation of farmland. The ABL thus achieved the opposite of what was intended: price policy was used to achieve parity of income between workers in manufacturing and agriculture, and viable family farms became a myth (Gomi, 2001). By 1980 81 per cent of agricultural commodities were covered by the price support and stabilisation system, up from 61 per cent in 1960 (Katō, 1985: 157, 158). The income gap between urban and rural households diminished rapidly and by the mid-1970s average incomes in farm households were higher than in urban households (Godo, 2001).

EXPLAINING AGRICULTURAL SUPPORT AND PROTECTION

Why did the government choose to support and protect agriculture rather than impose structural adjustment on the sector in order to make it more efficient and internationally competitive? Detailed empirical, historical and institutional analysis has revealed that the explanation for agricultural support and protection in Japan is complex and multifactorial, with diverse electoral, organisational, party-political, policymaking, bureaucratic, institutional and ideological factors helping to shape agricultural policy (George Mulgan, 2000, 1997a). Moreover, political pressures opposing agricultural support and protection are weak.

Electoral Factors

Farmers have been a potent political constituency, exercising much greater electoral influence than the contribution of agriculture to the national economy would suggest. Farmers' voting power has been inflated by an electoral system skewed towards disproportionate representation of rural areas. Because the decline in the number of rural voters was not accompanied by a corresponding redistribution of seats, urbanisation empowered rural voters at the expense of their urban counterparts. The failure to adjust voting values to match shifts in population mitigated the electoral impact of a gradually shrinking agricultural electorate (George Mulgan, 1997a).

Furthermore, the party connections of the agricultural sector have, historically, been stable. Farmers formed the mainstay of the conservative-dominated power structure under the ruling Liberal Democratic Party (LDP) from 1955 until 2009. Over this period the vast majority of farm politicians were affiliated to the LDP, while the LDP was the predominant party representing rural and semi-rural electorates (George Mulgan, 2005b, 2000, 1997a; Shimomura, 2004). Given the party's stable support base among agricultural voters, LDP politicians designed policies to retain the allegiance of farmers, particularly small-scale farmers, because structural reform of the industry would hasten the decline in numbers of farm voters (Godo and Takahashi, 2008; George Mulgan, 1997a). Farmers living in close-knit rural communities with strongly cooperative norms were also easier to mobilise for political purposes.

Organisational Factors

The farm sector has been highly organised by a spectrum of agricultural groups with JA acting as the dominant farmers' organisation (George Mulgan, 2000).[12] Led by its peak body, the Central Union of Agricultural Cooperatives, or JA-Zenchū, JA's strength as an agricultural interest group has been due to a number of factors.

First, the scope of JA's services is all-encompassing, including the marketing of farm produce, the purchasing of production supplies and machinery, the provision of banking and insurance facilities, and the conduct of a number of consumer-related businesses and social services (George Mulgan, 2000). Second, JA's membership rate is extremely high, embracing a large majority of farmers as well as a relatively high proportion of non-farmers residing in the geographic zones covered by the local co-ops, who may join as associate members and who now outnumber regular farm members.[13] Third, JA has directly penetrated government through the twin processes of corporatisation and direct political representation (George Mulgan, 2011b).

Corporatisation has two main aspects. First, as an organisation legislated into existence, JA performs various administrative functions for the government in exchange for commissions, subsidies and guaranteed monopolies, such as rice collection under the FC Law as well as sales of farm machinery and fertiliser (Godo, 2001). In addition, JA has acted as a channel for the payment of government monies to farmers, including rice purchase payments and other subsidies (George Mulgan, 2000). Rather than being an 'independent' agricultural organisation, JA's functioning has been firmly anchored in the government's administrative system (Uraki and Ishida, 1985) as an adjunct of state intervention in the agricultural sector (Francks, 2000). JA-Zenchū has been called 'the ōtemachi branch of the MAFF' (Kawakita and Onoue, 2001: 121) because it is always under pressure to follow MAFF policy directives (Koide, 2009).

Second, JA is incorporated into processes of agricultural policymaking, including a legal right to make representations to 'administrative authorities' on matters affecting the agricultural cooperatives. It is automatically consulted as the principal spokesperson for farmers and is represented in government advisory councils as well as in negotiations with the agricultural bureaucracy and ruling party, including in formal committee deliberations (George Mulgan, 2001, 2000).

Direct political representation involves former executives and staff from JA and related organisations standing for electoral office at all levels of government. JA members, executives and staff provide campaign, voting, financial and organisational backup for these candidates as well as for other pro-farmer candidates. The National League of Farmers' Agricultural Policy Campaign Organisations (Zenkoku Nōgyōsha Nōsei Undō

Soshiki Renmei, or Zenkoku Nōseiren) acts as JA's political arm. Its branches, or farmers' political leagues (*nōmin seiji renmei*, or *nōseiren*), operate in all 47 prefectures. JA has been able to deliver bloc votes to candidates because of its high levels of organisational mobilisation and its extremely high membership rate in which JA's farmer members are virtually synonymous with farm household voters. Furthermore, JA's organisational structure corresponds to existing administrative units (national, prefectural and municipal), making the agricultural cooperatives 'territorial organisations' for electoral purposes (George Mulgan, 1997a; Goto and Imamura, 1993).

Although it maintains an official stance of political neutrality, JA has been the most reliable source of votes (*hyōden*) for the LDP (Nakamura, 2001) and the LDP's biggest vote-gathering machine (George Mulgan, 1997a). The vast majority of candidates receiving electoral endorsement and other forms of support from JA organisations have been from the LDP (George Mulgan, 2001; 2005b).

JA's electoral activities (*senkyo undō*) are complemented by orthodox lobbying, or 'agricultural policy activities' (*nōsei katsudō*), as a farm interest group. JA-Zenchū executives lobby MAFF officials as well as Diet members from all political parties, but particularly those from the LDP during its long rule. JA's main policy focus is on policies that impact on farmers' incomes ('administrative' prices, agricultural trade policy and budget subsidies for farm assistance programs) as well as those that affect JA's businesses. For example, because JA's role in the FC system was central to its marketing operations and provided guaranteed profits, JA long had a vested interest in the preservation of rice market control (Kawasaki, 1992). JA-Zenchū annually issued a 'demand rice price' (*yōkyū beika*), which became an important factor in the annual political drama leading to the MAFF Minister's decision on the Food Agency's buying price. Zenkoku Nōseikyō also mobilised JA executives, staff and farmer members behind the organisation's agricultural policy and electoral goals.

However, whether JA's organisational interests coincide with those of agriculture and the farmers themselves is contested. JA has developed a vested interest in small-scale, part-time farming because it remains the principal source of its economic, political and organisational power. Part-time farmers who rely on single-package cooperative services and facilities are less motivated to cut production costs and push for lower marketing commissions than full-time professional farmers. They comprise the majority of Japanese farmers and 'just do what they are told by JA' (Koide, 2009). Not only do they help to preserve the size of JA's membership and business base but they are also privileged organisationally within JA by the one-member-one-vote system. Hence their views are more strongly reflected in JA's business priorities and policy interests, which are antipathetic to structural reform of agriculture because this would inevitably reduce JA's membership size, business volume and profits. Moreover, in designing many agricultural policy reforms the MAFF has sought to protect the interests of JA and small-scale farmers and, as a result, the scale expansion of farmland has not made any progress (Kishi, 2011).

Party-political Factors

Politicians linked to agriculture and forestry (*nōrin kankei giin*) have been variously called 'farm politicians' (*nōson giin*), 'agriculture and forestry Diet members' (*nōrin giin*), 'agricultural cooperative Diet members' (*nōkyō giin*) and agricultural and forestry tribe members (*nōrin zoku*). Most have been LDP politicians. They have combined one or more of the following attributes: electoral representation of a rural constituency; former employment in the MAFF; previous or existing positions in agricultural organisations, including JA; support from farmers' groups and agricultural organisations in elections; active roles in parliamentary and party committees on agriculture; and close ties to MAFF officials (George Mulgan, 2005b, 2000, 1997a).

The *nōrin zoku* are the most expert and influential members of the LDP in agricultural policymaking, best known for promoting its 'subsidy-scattering' (*baramaki*) agricultural policies (Koide, 2009). They appeared on the scene in the 1960s and became increasingly engaged in pressuring the government to raise the producer rice price. Thereafter they successfully intervened in all aspects of agricultural policymaking while extending their spheres of patronage and influence into areas of bureaucratic discretion (the designation of farm and rural infrastructure projects in regional areas) and developing clientelistic ties with construction companies bidding for public works contracts (George Mulgan, 2006b). In fact, agricultural and rural public works spending formed a huge pork barrel on which farm politicians, including the *nōrin zoku*, concentrated their lobbying efforts, while construction companies became a major source of political funding (George Mulgan, 2006b) and votes for LDP candidates.

Policymaking Factors

The *nōrin zoku* can be identified by their executive roles in LDP agricultural policy committees as well as in Diet standing committees on agriculture, forestry and fisheries. They project a strong image of the farm sector as one where the political convention of 'prior examination and approval' (*jizen shinsa • shōnin*) of government policy by the ruling LDP was entrenched. For major agricultural policy initiatives the MAFF submitted its draft proposals to an advisory council (*shingikai*), which helped to legitimise its policy recommendations and provide a veneer of broader consultation among community-wide groups and interests such as academic experts, consumer organisations and trade unions (Schwartz, 1998). Draft policies and legislation were then submitted to the deliberations of agricultural policy committees of the LDP's Policy Affairs Research Council (PARC), which acted as a political filter and customary veto point, usually amending reform proposals to protect the interests of small-scale farmers, the organisational interests of JA and the political interests of farm politicians.

MAFF officials played the primary coordinating (*chōsei*) role in policy deliberations among *nōrin zoku*, JA representatives and themselves. This tripartite policymaking system formed an institutionalised and semi-autonomous agricultural policy subgovernment or 'triangle' (George Mulgan, 2011b, 2001; Yamashita, 2009a), in which MAFF bureaucrats and *nōrin zoku* representing the government and ruling party (*seifu-yotō*) respectively made the final decisions on proposed legislation and policy.

Institutional Factors

The MAFF's own establishment law grants it broad discretionary authority to intervene in the agricultural sector while other agricultural laws and ordinances provide institutional, administrative and policy instruments for that intervention and the agricultural budget provides the necessary funds (George Mulgan, 2005a). Among institutional tools for intervention is the vast apparatus of auxiliary agencies (*gaikaku dantai*), which assist the main ministry in administering the agricultural sector and which are staffed mainly by retired MAFF officials or 'old boys' (OBs).

The primary determinant of MAFF policy is, arguably, its desire to maximise bureaucratic intervention in the agricultural sector (George Mulgan, 2005a, 2006a). Intervention bestows benefits on the MAFF as an organisation and on its officials, both as administrative functionaries and as private individuals. Benefits include power, status and other perks, as well as employment opportunities in lucrative post-retirement jobs in MAFF auxiliary agencies (which themselves develop a vested interest in agricultural support and protection) and in agricultural, food and construction

companies (George Mulgan, 2006a, 2001, 1997b). Agricultural support and protection in Japan should therefore be seen not only as politically demand-driven but also as bureaucratically supply-driven irrespective of demand (George Mulgan, 2005a).

Widely known as a 'bastion of conservatism' (*hoshushugi no gajō*), the MAFF has a reputation for persecuting reform-minded bureaucrats (Yamashita, 2009c). While it maintains an official standpoint of promoting a modern agriculture dominated by a limited number of larger-scale, independent farmers, the reality is that the MAFF has worked to sustain the traditional structure of Japanese agriculture dominated by small-scale, intervention-dependent farmers (Godo, 2008; George Mulgan, 2006a). However, over the years, the ministry has had to accommodate both domestic and international pressures for agricultural policy reform and liberalisation of the sector, which has mandated an effort to constrain the more extreme demands of politically vested interests in agricultural support and protection (George Mulgan, 2006a).

Ideological Factors

The special benefits and concessions granted to farmers have been legitimated by an ideology of agricultural support and protection, a modern-day version of pre-war agricultural fundamentalism (*nōhon shugi*), which held that farmers were the foundation of the state. The present variant purveyed by the leaders of agricultural organisations, farm politicians and MAFF bureaucrats, and even incorporated into agricultural legislation, has been developed specifically to justify the maintenance of agricultural subsidies and trade protection, which imposes considerable budgetary costs on taxpayers as well as high food prices on consumers.[14] The ideology of agricultural support and protection underscores the value of farming to the nation by identifying the public goods it provides, the national interests it promotes and the strategic needs it fulfils.

The most important national interest is food security (*shokuryō anpo*), which is equated with food self-sufficiency (*shokuryō jikyūritsu*), and which plays on fears of import dependence among both the public and politicians regardless of party. The unilateral US ban on soybean exports in 1973 (from where Japan sourced 95 per cent of its soybean demand) and the world food crisis in 1973 have often been cited as examples of the dangers of relying on imports for staple food. The MAFF also developed the concept of 'basic foodstuffs' to defend against rice market opening in the Uruguay Round of the General Agreement on Tariffs and

Trade (GATT), arguing that for a nation with a lower level of food self-sufficiency, securing a certain level of domestic production of basic foods was essential to a nation's livelihood (Tsukada, 1989). It subsequently stuck to the concept of food security as its principal defence against agricultural trade liberalisation in WTO (World Trade Organization) negotiations. In arguing for high levels of import protection, the MAFF has routinely pointed to public opinion polls supporting higher rates of self-sufficiency and concern with food safety as well as unanimous Diet resolutions on food self-sufficiency. Food security rhetoric has become even more hyped in recent years, with a 'food crisis' discourse emerging, exploited politically by the MAFF and emerging as a shibboleth in the manifestos of all political parties.

The multifunctionality of agriculture is another concept central to the ideology of agricultural support and protection. It encompasses the environmental public goods of helping to provide a green environment, maintain national land, prevent floods, soil erosion and landslides (by pointing to the role of rice paddies in holding water), and sustaining Japan's regional society as well as its dietary and cultural traditions (Tashiro, 1992). Central to this ideology, rice farming as the basis for agricultural society has become the last fortress of Japanese agriculture (Gomi, 2001; Francks, 2000). The MAFF has valued the external benefits of agriculture at ¥8 trillion (MAFF, 2003).

Weak Opposing Pressures

Consumer groups, labour unions, business organisations and opposition parties, which might have been expected to adopt an anti-agriculture stance because of the impact of high food prices on household budgets and on wage demands, have not mobilised politically against food prices, exerting only weak countervailing pressure to agricultural support and protection. While increasingly urbanised consumers have periodically expressed dissatisfaction at inflation-inducing hikes in the rice price and at price differentials for agricultural products between Japan and other countries, consumer groups have prioritised food safety and food security over food prices. Their calls for greater food self-sufficiency have been accompanied by declarations of opposition to agricultural trade liberalisation (Vogel, 1999; Bullock, 1995).

Groups representing large-scale manufacturing firms have periodically voiced objections to agricultural producer prices leading to wage rises, and have pressed the government on trade

reform fearing both retaliation and discrimination against Japan's manufactured exports in overseas markets. The Japan Business Federation (Nippon Keidanren) has been the principal spokesperson for these interests, making formal proposals to government at crucial junctures during international trade negotiations. As a result, from time to time it has had to wear the accusation of 'agriculture bashing'. Generally speaking, however, business organisations have not campaigned forcefully and consistently for agricultural policy reform, including trade reform (Bullock, 1995).

Opposition parties – the Japan Socialist Party (now the Social Democratic Party), Japan Communist Party, and more latterly, the Democratic Party of Japan (DPJ) – have tended to reflect the voice of urban consumers and labour unions in politics, but in an attempt to wrest farm votes from the LDP have consistently offered more generous concessions to agricultural interests as the true defenders of small-scale inefficient farmers as well as advocating a self-sufficiency policy on food that appeals to many farmers, agricultural cooperatives and consumer groups (Yoshioka, 1989). The DPJ's offer to grant direct income subsidies to all commercial farms, regardless of size, prior to the 2007 Upper House election was more generous than the existing scheme and helped a number of DPJ candidates to victory in rural prefectural seats. The policy was retained for the 2009 Lower House election and proved equally successful in attracting farmers' votes.

The lack of strong countervailing power to the farm lobby has provided the foundation for a public choice explanation of Japanese agricultural support and protection. Economists espousing a self-styled 'political market' approach have argued that it is a typical case of concentrated benefits versus diffused costs in which the rational self-interests of farmers, consumers, industry and politicians prevail. As this explanation goes, farmers have a strong incentive to organise effectively to demand government intervention because the benefits are large in terms of increased income from agricultural production. On the other hand, because the costs in terms of higher food prices are diffused across a large number of consumers and represent a relatively small proportion of total household expenditure, consumers are not motivated to lobby strongly against support for farmers. The political calculus of government politicians reflects these considerations: they are motivated to supply agricultural protection in response to the political demands of organised farm interests, while largely ignoring the interests of unorganised consumers and taxpayers. Opposition from other potential losers such as industry is also muted because the costs of agricultural support and protection to individual firms in terms of the higher wages paid to their workers and possible trade repercussions are not sufficiently concentrated for them to engage in organised lobbying against farm protection policies (George Mulgan, 2008; Anderson et al., 1986).

To some extent the public choice explanation of Japan's agricultural support and protection is borne out by the facts, although the motivations of non-agricultural groups that might be expected to oppose farm protection are not always grounded in rational economic self-interest (as public choice theory would predict) but in other non-economic, social and cultural motivations and values. While it is certainly true that farmers have organised to demand agricultural support and protection, and farm politicians have been willing to supply it out of political self-interest, single-factor explanations such as the public choice approach do not provide a full account, as the above multifactorial explanation suggests.

MAJOR SHIFTS IN AGRICULTURAL POLICY

Initially the dominant trend in agricultural policy was increasing government assistance to farmers to boost food production, agricultural productivity and farmers' incomes. In the late 1970s, however, domestic and international pressures for agricultural reform began to build. The government's response to these pressures for change was very measured. There was a gradual shift towards less government intervention, including deregulation, retrenchment (a reduction in subsidies, including price supports), privatisation (a wind-back of direct government participation in agricultural markets) and market opening. However, the Japanese farm sector remained well short of full marketisation, notwithstanding the fact that official reform goals advocated an expansion in farm scale, cuts in production costs – bringing domestic prices closer to international levels – and increasing market access for agricultural imports (Yoshioka, 1989). What occurred was predominantly a change in modes of intervention rather than a concerted reduction in levels of intervention (George Mulgan, 2006a).

Easing Controls on Rice Distribution and Pricing

A series of steps partially liberalised the FC system over the period 1951 to 1994, when it was abolished. The reforms gradually deregulated rice distribution, with freer marketing permitted through non-government channels. The 1994 New Food Law[15] cut back further the Food Agency's role in the rice market, introducing an element of deregulation and competition into distribution and price formation, with a shift from government-controlled pricing to a mixture of public and private management of pricing. However, the Food Agency retained a sufficient level of direct participation in the market (purchasing, importing and selling) to preserve its price-maintenance function to some extent. Even the non-government market remained administratively 'managed' (George Mulgan, 2006a).

As a production cartel, the *gentan* was legislated into existence when the New Food Law was passed as a measure to restrict the supply of domestically produced rice and thus prevent producer rice prices from plummeting in a freer domestic rice market. In fact, the *gentan* and government manipulation of rice stocks replaced the *seisansha beika* as the principal means of supporting the producer price and farmers' incomes.

The Shift from Price Supports to Public Works

In the early 1970s the LDP engineered a shift to a 'comprehensive agricultural policy', or CAP (*sōgō nōsei*), adopted as a measure to cope with the huge overproduction of rice (Motosugi, 2003). The CAP substituted public works expenditure for regular increases in the producer rice price (Shimomura, 2004). The proportion spent on price, distribution and income measures in the agricultural budget declined relative to expenditure on agricultural public works, known as 'agricultural production base adjustment works' (*nōgyō seisan kiban seibi jigyō*) (George Mulgan, 2005a; Shimizu, 1985b). The aim was to maintain agricultural spending levels and farmers' political support at the same time as ameliorating urban and business dissatisfaction with high rice prices (Shimomura, 2004). Over the years the content of agricultural policy evolved more and more into expenditure on agricultural and rural public works, rising from 30–40 per cent of the agriculture, forestry and fisheries budget in the 1970s to 40–50 per cent in the 1980s, over 50 per cent in the 1990s and 40–50 per cent in the 2000s (George Mulgan, 2006b, 2001; Yamazaki, 2004; Nōrinsuisanshō, Daijin Kanbō Tōkeibu, 2008b: 70, Nōrinsuisanshō Tōkeibu, 2003: 76).

Coupled with the *sōgō nōsei*, politically strategic distributive politics, with its heavy emphasis on public works in rural areas in the name of 'equal development' by narrowing the gap in living infrastructure investment per capita between urban and rural areas (based on Tanaka's concept of 'remodelling the Japanese archipelago'), became a key LDP strategy (Shimomura, 2004). Agricultural public works were supplemented by expanding investment in 'rural life and related issues' through the introduction of so-called 'rural adjustment works' (*nōson seibi jigyō*) (Shimizu, 1985b). These were designed to improve living conditions in rural areas by funding 'non-agricultural infrastructure and community development' (Goto and Imamura, 1993: 24). This meant that over time the focus of spending in the agricultural sector shifted from industrial infrastructure to living infrastructure, with the budget share of agricultural public works decreasing as allocations to rural public works rose (Motosugi, 2003; George Mulgan, 1997a). Government funding financed the construction of agricultural and rural roads, development projects in hilly and mountainous areas, and the provision of social infrastructure for rural dwellers, including sewage services, community halls, parks, gymnasiums etc. (Motosugi, 2003).

The decision to channel public works subsidies to whole towns and villages, including farming and non-farming residents, reflected a shift in LDP priorities away from purely emphasising farmers' votes to wooing the wider interests of farm households and non-farm rural dwellers in regional cities, towns and villages (Hirose, 1981). The political interests of the farmers also changed from agriculture-related policies to influencing politicians to bring public works and business projects to their areas so they could make a profit on land sales for non-farming purposes (Godo, 2008). This in turn weakened agriculture by encouraging the shift to side-job farming and increasing the reliance of the country's rural areas and agricultural industry on the construction industry (Shimomura, 2004). Rural public works became a common interest binding both farmers and ordinary rural dwellers, while construction became a major alternative to farming in rural areas (George Mulgan, 2001).

Trends in Agricultural Support and Stabilisation Prices

Trends in administered agricultural prices shifted from large, regular increases in the 1960s and early 1970s to smaller increases in the late 1970s, price freezes in the early 1980s, cuts in the late 1980s and incremental declines thereafter. The most politically significant reduction was the decrease in the producer rice price in 1987. Henceforth, the *seisansha beika* was subject to regular, annual declines, which also gave a lead to other administrative prices (George Mulgan, 2006a). Budget allocations to price support measures drastically decreased (by 50 per cent between 1984 and 1989, for example) (Tsukada, 1989: 8).

Cuts to agricultural prices were designed to encourage farmers to become more efficient and internationally competitive in anticipation of market-opening concessions in trade negotiations at the GATT Uruguay Round as well as in response to higher levels of imports consequent upon earlier liberalisation of beef, pork and citrus markets in the late 1980s and early 1990s, which undermined domestic price support systems.

The New Basic Law

The 1999 Food, Agriculture and Rural Areas Basic Law (*Shokuryō, Nōgyō, Nōson Kihonhō*), commonly known as the New Basic Law, or NBL, replaced the 1961 ABL. The NBL espoused market principles as the main determinant of agricultural prices and committed the government to further privatisation of agricultural trading systems and deregulation of agricultural pricing arrangements. However, on balance, it was heavily weighted in favour of agricultural support and protection as opposed to agricultural deregulation and liberalisation (George Mulgan, 2001). Its policy axioms of 'securing stable food supply', 'fulfilling the multifunctional roles of agriculture', 'sustainable agricultural development' and 'development of rural areas' were new ways of rationalising continuing support and protection for producers on food security and environmental grounds as well as continuing high levels of expenditure on agricultural and rural public works (George Mulgan, 2006a, 2001). The new law was also designed to provide a solid ideological, legal and policy defence against further liberalisation of Japan's agricultural market in WTO trade negotiations (George Mulgan, 2001). Much political disputation centred on the food self-sufficiency target incorporated into the 2000 Basic Plan to implement the law because of the utility of such targets in justifying both import barriers and increased support for agriculture. The 2000 Basic Plan incorporated a food self-sufficiency target of 45 per cent (on a calorie basis) by fiscal 2010. This target was maintained in the 2005 Basic Plan but the target date was changed to 2015. Then in August 2008, a new package of emergency measures for agriculture announced a new target of 50 per cent within 10 years (Honma, 2009a). This has now become the target for 2020.

Declines in Agricultural Import Barriers

Japan's agricultural trade liberalisation has been negotiated through international market access agreements (the GATT/WTO as well as bilateral or regional Free Trade Agreements, or FTAs).[16]

Under the aegis of the GATT, which Japan joined in 1955, agricultural trade liberalisation began in 1960, proceeding in a series of incremental steps thereafter. Agricultural trade policy reforms included tariff reductions, abolition of import quotas and greater participation of private companies in import trades either alongside or in lieu of state trading agencies. Between 1962 and 1986 the number of agricultural commodities subject to quantitative import restrictions fell substantially from 103 to 22 (Eto, 1987: 11).[17] Another significant liberalisation occurred in 1988 when Japan agreed to expand import quotas for key products such as beef and citrus, then to abolish quotas altogether and reduce tariffs in 1991.

In 1994 Japan agreed to the Uruguay Round Agreement on Agriculture (URAA) of the GATT, which represented a modest victory for the principles of free trade and multilateralism (George Mulgan, 1997a). The URAA replaced quantitative import barriers with tariffs, except for rice, for which Japan negotiated a separate 'minimum access' (MA) deal, obligating it to import certain fixed quantities annually over the term of the six-year agreement (1994–2000).

Despite the series of market-opening steps over a number of decades, Japan retains one of the world's most protected farm sectors (Godo, 2008). Its nominal protection rate for agricultural commodities is one of the highest among developed nations (Godo and Takahashi, 2008). This restrictive agricultural import regime is marked not only by high tariffs for key products,[18] which are retained to keep the domestic prices of these products high (Yamashita, 2008d), but also by complex import arrangements that curb the import of cheaper foreign agricultural products and impose higher costs on domestic consumers.

Japan's request for exceptional treatment for sensitive items and general resistance to further opening of its agricultural market has led to friction in trade liberalisation negotiations. It helped to block a successful outcome from the Doha Round of WTO negotiations and delayed or limited the potential of FTAs to liberalise trade fully between Japan and other countries (George Mulgan, 2014a, 2008, 2006a, 2005a; Yamashita, 2005). Agricultural protectionism remains the most significant barrier to the evolution of Japan's FTA strategy (Yamazaki, 2004).

The Shift to Market Determination of Prices

Implementing the URAA and the 1999 New Basic Law brought about changes to agricultural pricing policy. First, under the URAA Japan agreed to reduce its Aggregate Measurement of Support (AMS) by trimming trade-distorting support (so-called 'amber box' support in WTO parlance) for agriculture and by transforming traditional-type agricultural subsidies to decoupled-type ones (subsidies that would assist farmers but not impact on production directly, such as price supports). Japan reduced its amber box support by nearly 80 per cent between 1995 and 2000, largely by removing rice from the amber box in 1998 (Godo and Takahashi, 2008). This was done by changing the nature of support for rice farmers, which moved some agricultural support from the amber box into the blue box, another WTO category of agricultural support that permits subsidies tied to programs that limit production (i.e. the *gentan*). By allowing rice prices largely to reflect the market principle while making compensation for falls in the rice price conditional on farmers cutting rice production and diverting to other crops,[19] the MAFF was able to effect this change. It also enabled the government to dramatically cut the AMS it reported to the WTO without reducing permitted support to rice farmers. The shift in agricultural policy approach revealed a loophole in the URAA market price support AMS system, whereby a change in official policy actually resulted in a minimal change in the actual level of support (Hart and Beghin, 2004).

Second, the 1999 NBL sanctioned an across-the-board switch from price support to income compensation for farmers (so-called 'farm management stabilisation measures'), which were extended to products other than rice such as wheat, milk for processing and soybeans (George Mulgan, 2006a). Prices for these commodities were determined primarily by market forces with farm incomes supplemented mainly through less trade-distorting direct payments.

The Shift to Direct Income Support for Farmers

The New Basic Plan of 2005 took these developments further by announcing a policy of fully-fledged direct payments to farmers in line with the WTO principle of decoupling. The scheme was implemented in 2007 for producers of rice, wheat, barley, soybeans, sugar beet and starch potatoes. It compensated farmers 'for 90% of the loss of income compared with the average income of the preceding five years (excluding the highest and lowest years) to mitigate income instabilities caused by price fluctuations'[20] (OECD, 2009: 72). Funding was provided by both the government (75 per cent) and participating producers (OECD, 2009).

The MAFF originally proposed restricting direct payments to certified farmers with 4 ha or more (10 ha in Hokkaido) as a gesture towards structural reform. However, under pressure from JA and LDP farm politicians the scheme was broadened to embrace community-based farming 'collectives' of 20 ha or more, which encompassed part-time farmers, leading in some cases to the cancellation of leases to full-time farmers so that part-time farmers would qualify for direct income support (Yamashita, 2008e). Moreover, JA organised some small farms into these collectives for the sole purpose of receiving the government subsidy to benefit itself as well as the farmers (Godo and Takahashi, 2008).[21]

Even this enlarged scheme proved unpopular compared with the more liberal scheme touted by the DPJ.[22] Under direct pressure from LDP farm politicians the government's scheme was dramatically revised in the wake of the 2007 election to make more farms eligible, including small-scale farms, by allowing each municipality to approve exceptions to the official qualifications (Yamashita, 2008e). The direct payments policy thus ceased to be an instrument of structural reform.

MAJOR SOURCES OF AGRICULTURAL POLICY REFORM

Several factors have contributed both to a gradual erosion in the power of Japanese farmers and increasing pressure on the government to embrace agricultural policy reform.

The Shrinking Farm Electorate

Farmers' voting power is declining because numbers of farm household voters continue to fall, although the absolute size of the national agricultural electorate has contracted at a slower pace than might have been expected because of the continuing predominance of part-time farming (George Mulgan, 2005b). In 1960 farmers comprised 37 per cent of the national electorate, falling to 15 per cent in 1990 and 7 per cent in 2005, (calculated from data in Nōrinsuisanshō, Daijin Kanbō Tōkeibu, 2008a: 64–76; Ministry of Internal Affairs and Communications, 2009a; George Mulgan, 1997a: 878).[23] In 2010 farm household voters comprised 5 per cent of the national voting population (calculated from data in Nōrinsuisanshō, Daijin Kanbō Tōkeibu, 2012; Sōmushō, 2012).

The decline in farm voters has been reflected in the changing socio-economic profiles of electorates, very few of which could now be called 'agricultural', with 20 per cent or more voters resident in farm households. The fall has also registered in the shrinking representation of agricultural interests in the Diet. The number of nōkyō giin, for example, peaked at 51 in 1971, falling to five in the Lower House after the 2009 election and four in the Upper House after the 2010 Upper House election.[24]

Most notable were the electoral losses sustained by groups of LDP farm politicians in the 2004 and 2007 Upper House elections. Six veteran nōrin zoku and nōrin giin lost their prefectural or proportional representation seats in 2004 and 10 lost in 2007 (including five who had held the position of MAFF deputy minister or parliamentary secretary), with several others supported by Zenkoku Nōseiren also unsuccessful (George Mulgan, 2011b: 117). Overall, only half of the candidates recommended by Zenkoku Nōseiren won seats in the 2007 election (Yamashita, 2009d). The 2009 elections completed the picture with key nōrin zoku losing their seats and only 100 of the 281 (36 per cent) of candidates recommended by Zenkoku Noseiren victorious (Nōsei Undō Jyānaru, 2009: 2–13). One bright spot in this bleak landscape was the 2007 victory of JA's own organisational representative (soshiki daihyō) – a former top executive from JA-Zenchū – with just under 450,000 personal votes (gaining second place among the LDP's proportional representation candidates) mobilised from among JA's staff of 250,000 and their family members (Yamashita, 2009d).

Over the same period farmers' overwhelming support for the LDP began to erode. What was formerly a 'hard' pro-LDP rural vote gradually grew 'softer' with the 2007 and 2009 elections showing a clear shift in farmers' support for the DPJ, with an increasing number of DPJ Diet candidates, including those with agricultural expertise (as MAFF OBs, for example) and connections, winning seats in rural constituencies (George Mulgan, 2011a). On the other hand, the DPJ adopted several anti-JA positions, seeking to curtail the organisation's economic and political power, given its openly pro-LDP bias (Yamashita, 2009d).

The 1994 Electoral Reforms

The influence of the 1994 electoral reforms on farmers' voting power was mixed. On the one hand, malapportionment in the Lower House electoral system was significantly reduced, with the disparity in voting values at the extreme falling from 5:1 to a little over 2:1,[25] thus moderating the electoral bias in favour of less densely populated areas (i.e. rural and farm voters).[26] The conversion of what were previously multi-member constituencies into single-member districts in the Lower House also worked against politicians representing a narrow sectoral interest such as agriculture (George Mulgan, 2005b, 2001, 2000, 1997a). In order to win a plurality in single-member districts politicians had to cater to a wider range of interests including business people and consumers, not just farmers. In this way the reformed electoral system undermined the incentives for policy specialisation among LDP Diet members (George Mulgan, 2001), and hence posed a threat to the entire *zoku* system (George Mulgan, 2005b, 2001; Krauss and Pekkanen, 2004).

On the other hand, the need for a plurality put a greater premium on candidates enlisting the support of organisations that could generate reliable voting blocs, such as JA. Moreover, because electoral reform shrank the size of constituencies their socio-economic profiles became more homogeneous (George Mulgan, 1997a). Many districts in rural and regional areas became more uniformly rural and agricultural than before, which strengthened the agricultural orientation of some Diet members (George Mulgan, 2006b).

Organisational Decline

The shrinking agricultural electorate has been accompanied by a general erosion of JA's organisational powers, with a gradually declining membership, reduced patronage of its services and a shrinking capacity for political mobilisation. The 2009 election campaign was unprecedented in the discord within the organisation over which party and candidates to support. While JA groups officially endorsed LDP candidates in most electorates, some prefectural organisations either gave their members a free vote or endorsed DPJ candidates. By the time of the 2010 elections a more balanced pattern of party support was in evidence, with Zenkoku Nōseiren recommending six prefectural constituency candidates from the DPJ in addition to nine from the LDP and one from New Kōmeitō.

JA's marketing and purchasing businesses have also suffered. Some farmers are choosing to operate outside of the agricultural cooperative system because of the high commissions it charges and its prioritising of organisational profits over membership benefits. The losses in the farm-trading and material-supply businesses of many local cooperatives are only being made up by the profits on their banking and insurance operations. This is not preventing closures of local JA branches in towns and villages, while four of JA's major businesses

are in long-term decline: loans, long-term insurance holdings, marketing and purchasing. Only JA's saving business is expanding – bolstered by farmland sales – although JA's peak finance body, the Central Bank for Agriculture and Forestry (Nōrinchūkin), sustained huge losses in the 2008–09 financial crisis. As a result, JA may not be able to rely so heavily in the future on its financial businesses to make up the deficits in its agriculture-related businesses (Yamashita, 2009d).

Changes to the Policymaking System

The general developmental trend in Japanese policymaking has been towards stronger top-down executive-style authority at the expense of the bottom-up special-interest policy communities. Cabinet functions have been strengthened and the institutional structures supporting prime ministerial policy direction have been buttressed, including the Prime Minister's Official Residence (Kantei), Cabinet Secretariat, Cabinet Office and Cabinet Office councils, including the Council on Economic and Fiscal Policy (CEFP).[27]

Prime Minister Koizumi (2001–06) actively pursued structural reform of the policymaking system focusing on weakening the role of LDP politicians as representatives of special interests. The dual structure of LDP-bureaucracy policymaking was partially displaced by the shift towards a much more prime minister-centred policymaking system. The DPJ consolidated these changes by abolishing the DPJ's Policy Research Council (PRC) and promising to eliminate the vested interests of Diet members representing special interests (*zoku giin*) and to increase the number of politicians holding government posts such as minister, senior vice-minister and parliamentary secretary in an attempt to subordinate both ruling party backbenchers and the bureaucracy to the prime minister and cabinet on policy matters. These changes initially challenged the previously pervasive influence of the agricultural policy community. However, after the revival of the DPJ's PRC the ruling party once more asserted decisive pressure on agriculture-related policy (George Mulgan, 2014b).

Budgetary and Other 'Transcendental' Policy Pressures

'Transcendental' policy pressures under which successive administrations endeavoured to reform all relevant sectors without any 'sacred areas' (*seiiki naki*) impacted on the government's delivery of agricultural support and protection.

Transmitted via bodies such as the Kantei and prime ministerial advisory councils, including the CEFP, as well as the Ministry of Finance (MOF), these pressures targeted issues such as administrative reform (*gyōsei kaikaku*), fiscal reconstruction (*zaisei saiken*), market liberalisation (*jiyūka*), privatisation (*mineika*), and deregulation (*kisei kanwa*) (George Mulgan, 2006a, 1997b).

Budgetary pressures were critical in reducing the government's role in the FC system as well as in its final abolition, in reducing price supports for agricultural products (particularly rice), in the introduction of the *gentan* to reduce rice surpluses and in the shift in MAFF budget spending away from price supports to agricultural and rural public works (George Mulgan, 2006a; Shimomura, 2004). Fiscal constraints imposed particularly severe strictures on the agricultural budget during the fiscal reconstruction decade from the late 1970s until the late 1980s, again from the late 1990s and under the Koizumi administration of 2001–06, with the cuts falling most heavily in the area of public works (George, 2006c, 1993), which fell by 36 per cent from 2002 to 2008, while non-agricultural public works-related spending fell by only 8 per cent (Nōrinsuisanshō, Daijin Kanbō Tōkeibu, 2008b: 70). The overall proportion of the national General Account (GA) budget allocated to agriculture, forestry and fisheries declined by 23 per cent from a peak of ¥3.43 trillion in 2000 to ¥2.64 trillion in 2008. Over the same period local government expenditure on agriculture, forestry and fisheries also fell by more than a third and special account expenditure by 25 per cent. In relative terms expenditure on agriculture, forestry and fisheries in the GA budget declined from 4 per cent to 3.2 per cent (Nōrinsuisanshō, Daijin Kanbō Tōkeibu, 2008b: 70, 72, 74; Nōrinsuisanshō Tōkeibu, 2003: 76, 78, 80).

Pressures for deregulation were significant in the passage of the New Food Law and associated abolition of the FC system, which were offered up by the MAFF as a major deregulatory reform freeing up rice marketing and distribution (George Mulgan, 1997b), and in limited farmland deregulation in 2003, which permitted corporate entities, including private companies, to lease previously abandoned farmland in so-called 'structural reform special zones', an initiative of the Koizumi administration (George Mulgan, 2006a).

Administrative reform resulted in some cutbacks in MAFF staff numbers (George Mulgan, 1997b), although the MAFF was not affected by the 2001 amalgamations in the restructuring of the bureaucracy in that year. The MAFF retained its name and functions but was reorganised internally, with its various bureaus, departments and sections reorganised and renamed (George Mulgan,

2005a, 2001). In 2003 another MAFF reorganisation saw the abolition of the Food Agency and the creation of a new Food Safety and Consumer Affairs Bureau in recognition of the MAFF's self-styled 'new emphasis' on consumers and food safety. In spite of the 4,500 staff working to assure food safety and peace of mind, very serious food safety scandals continued to beset the MAFF and Japanese consumers.

External Pressure (Gaiatsu)

International market opening pressure, particularly from major agricultural exporting countries such as the United States and Australia, has played an important role in opening Japanese agricultural markets (George Mulgan, 2005a, 1997c; Davis, 2007, 2003). *Gaiatsu* exerted through bilateral trade negotiations in the 1970s and 1980s realised a number of victories for foreign exporters in the United States and Australia in relation to specific products such as beef and citrus. Once achieved, the US goal shifted to partial liberalisation of Japan's rice market, which became a major trade issue between the United States and Japan at the GATT Uruguay Round (Tsukada, 1989).

The URAA was another significant step signed under international pressure. It also required certain policy adjustments behind the border. For example, it promoted domestic reform of the FC system (the enactment of the New Food Law and abolition of the FC Law) (Mishima, 2001) as well as changes to agricultural price support systems and the shift to direct income support for farmers.

Nevertheless, the government always managed to limit the concessions it made to its negotiating partners, or to protect agriculture in other ways. Even after URAA, for example, key products remained protected by means of tariff rate quotas (TRQs),[28] high secondary duties (over-quota tariffs) and state trading (for in-quota imports of rice, wheat, barley, skim milk powder, butter, silk and sugar),[29] while rice was made an exception to tariffication under the MA import arrangement. The MAFF accepted the URAA because of this exceptional treatment for rice, which allowed the Food Agency to control rice imports and prevent them from having any impact on the demand and supply of domestic rice (MA rice was stored for use as food aid) (Yamashita, 2008d), and because import arrangements for other products under tariffication enabled the government to limit import quantities just as effectively as before (Honma 2000a, 2000b). Of the 28 commodities that Japan converted from non-tariff protection to tariffs under the URAA, TRQs were created for

19 of them (Choi and Sumner, 2000), with Japan having the highest average over-quota rate, at 388 per cent, for agricultural products in the WTO (Gibson et al., 2001).

Moreover, the government further compensated the rural sector with a six-year ¥6.01 trillion package of spending, directed mainly towards rice farming, with 53 per cent put aside for public works in agricultural regions (George Mulgan, 2005a, 2001). Rice tariffication was subsequently permitted in 1999 in order to reduce Japan's rice-import obligations (George Mulgan, 2006a; Honma, 2000b), allowing the MAFF to reduce rice stocks.

On balance Japan's market opening concessions by no means equated with free trade or even a remote approximation to it. What international agreements prompted were changes in the methodology of agricultural protection and some adjustments to domestic policies to conform to the terms of negotiated agreements. The agricultural policy community consented to trade agreements because one form of agricultural protection was substituted for another, because the MAFF could often utilise additional sources of funding from new import mark-ups and tariffs, because farm and rural interests were handsomely compensated and because exceptions to trade liberalisation could be negotiated for 'sensitive items'. Furthermore, while the GATT/WTO package-negotiation structure might have been conducive to cross-sector linkage between business and agriculture (Davis, 2003), in the Japanese case, such linkages were not the facilitating factor in Japan's agreeing to the URAA.

The Continuing Failure to Reform

The DPJ's direct income subsidy policy was introduced for all commercial rice farms in fiscal 2010. It compensated farmers for the difference between their cost of production and the sales price of their rice.[30] It was restricted to farms participating in rice production adjustment, which helped to maintain higher rice prices and prevent efficient farmers from increasing production and reducing production costs. The scheme was expanded to include wheat and soybeans in fiscal 2011. In failing to restrict payments to larger farms the policy continued incentives for small-scale, inefficient farm households to remain in farming, thus exacerbating the agricultural sector's major structural problem.

At the same time the DPJ promised to promote the liberalisation of trade through multilateral (WTO) and bilateral (FTA) negotiations – and later, under the Kan and Noda governments, to explore the possibility of participating in the regional free trade grouping, the Trans-Pacific Partnership (TPP). These trade agreements were all predicated on some level of agricultural market opening, particularly the TPP, which aimed to abolish all tariffs on farm products within 10 years. In theory, the direct income subsidy scheme was designed to facilitate market opening by providing a safety net for farmers. However, in the absence of agricultural trade liberalisation, which was opposed by a large number of DPJ politicians for reasons of short-term political advantage (George Mulgan, 2014b), it became a typical *baramaki* policy designed to secure farmers votes (George Mulgan, 2011a: 29).

The new LDP government under Prime Minister Abe went further and faster than the DPJ in suddenly announcing Japan's participation in the TPP negotiations in March 2013. This placed greater urgency on making the domestic agricultural sector more internationally competitive. Despite government assurances that it would achieve structural reform of the industry, agricultural 'reform' plans revealed more bureaucratic intervention and government spending in the farm sector not less, thus giving the appearance of reform without delivering the substance (George Mulgan, 2013a, 2013b).

THE FUTURE OF JAPANESE AGRICULTURE

The prognoses for Japanese agriculture are dire, ranging from 'notably bad' (Godo, 2008: 14) to 'completely collapsing' (Yamazaki, 2004: 128). The problems besetting the sector are a product of policy failure, described in general terms as a 'convoy system of protecting the weaker farmers' (*Nihon Nōgyō Shinbun*, 22 November 2003). No government in the postwar period has successfully dealt with the long-standing problem of high production costs and lack of international competitiveness. The immediate agricultural policy agenda facing the Japanese government includes:

- dealing with the large numbers of small-scale, part-time farmers cultivating micro-sized, unprofitable, scattered plots and non-farming landholders who are blocking the consolidation of farmland and thus preventing greater economies of scale in the industry. Government policies need to be reconfigured to provide opportunities and incentives for larger-scale farms to expand their operations.
- preventing farmers' continuing manipulation of agricultural land regulations to make a speculative profit on the sale of their farmland for resi-

dential, industrial, commercial and public works developments (Godo, 2009, 2008, 2007, 2006; Godo and Takahashi, 2008; Yamashita, 2008c) rather than for the enlargement of farms to improve efficiency and productivity. The degradation of Japan's agricultural land base is a primary threat to its food security (Yamashita, 2008b; Godo and Takahashi, 2008). Legal reform is also needed to deregulate farmland ownership and to change the owner-farmer principle, as well as tax reform to eliminate tax incentives for people who own farmland and to increase fixed assets tax and inheritance tax. Such reforms would induce small-scale, part-time farmers to lease or sell their land to full-time professional farmers and would encourage young people and joint-stock companies into the farm sector.

- lowering barriers to imports, including high tariffs and state trading, which not only limit Japan's prospects of signing bilateral, regional and multilateral trade agreements, but which also reduce prospects of agreements offering greater access to the Japanese market. Policies are needed to prepare the farm sector for agricultural trade liberalisation in the context of bilateral and multilateral trade agreements.

Japan's agriculture retains potential for growth as an industrial sector, with plans being mapped out by agricultural policy experts emphasising Japan's superior agricultural land, technology and skills (Oizumi, 2009; Honma, 2009a, 2009b). However, unless its myriad problems are seriously tackled by a government prepared to override objections from farmers, JA, politicians and bureaucrats with a vested interest in small-scale, subsidy-dependent farming, this potential will never be realised.

NOTES

1 In 1961 land under cultivation peaked at 6.09 million hectares (ha), falling to 4.54 million ha in 2013 (Nōrinsuisanshō, 2014).
2 Farm household figures are those for 2010 because of the unavailability of 2014 figures. Commercial farms have 30a (ares) or more of cultivated land under management or have annual sales of agricultural products of ¥500,000 or more.
3 Farms can only be inherited by members of the same family.
4 The area of abandoned farmland rose to 400,000 ha in 2010 (Nōrinsuisanshō, 2014). This amounted to 3,960 sq km, an area larger than

Saitama Prefecture, and almost three times the area abandoned in 1985 (*Japan Times*, 2011).
5 The value of agricultural production fell from a peak of ¥11.7 trillion in 1984 to ¥8.5 trillion in 2012 (Nōrinsuisanshō, 2014).
6 Income from agriculture shrank by 50% between 1992 and 2006 (*Tōkyō Shinbun*, 14 August 2009) and from ¥5 trillion to ¥3 trillion between 1995 and 2010 (Kishi, 2011).
7 The Total Support Estimate (TSE) is a measure of the annual monetary value of total transfers from taxpayers and consumers arising from policy measures that support agriculture (less budgetary receipts), regardless of the measures' objectives and their impact on farm production and income, and on consumption of farm products (OECD, 2008b).
8 The annual rice crop peaked at 14.45 million tonnes in 1967 (Yamashita, 2008a).
9 Introduced in 1970, the area of rice acreage reduction expanded annually to 1.1 million ha, or 40% of the country's total rice acreage of 2.5 million ha, equivalent to 5 million tonnes annually, while over 7 million tonnes of wheat is imported (Yamashita, 2008a).
10 Farmers had little incentive to move out of rice into other crops requiring land-intensive cultivation, such as wheat, barley and feed grains, to support the increasing consumption of livestock products. Wheat production, for example, declined from 3.83 million tons in 1960 to 460,000 tons in 1975, while consumption increased from 6 million tons in 1960 to 8.5 million tons currently, 90 per cent of which is supplied by the United States, Canada and Australia (Yamashita, 2008a).
11 Per capita rice consumption declined continuously from a peak of 118.3kg in 1962 to 56.3kg in 2012, with total rice consumption falling from 13.3 million tonnes in 1963 to 8.74 million tonnes in 2005 (Nōrinsuisanshō, 2014;Yamashita, 2008a).
12 The other major farmers' groups are the land improvement groups, the agricultural mutual aid associations and the agricultural committee system, as well as associations of commodity producers and the farmers' unions.
13 In 2012 there were 4.6 million regular farm members of JA compared with 5.3 million associate members (Norinsuisanshō, 2014).
14 Prices received by farmers were 2.6 times higher than world market prices in 1986–88 and 1.9 times higher in 2005–07 (OECD, 2008a: 70).
15 The full title is Law for Stabilisation of Supply-Demand and Price of Staple Food (*Shuyō Shokuryō no Jikyū oyobi Kakaku no Anteihō*), also referred to as the new Staple Food Law (*Shokuryōhō*).

16 The preferred terminology in Japan is Economic Partnership Agreement (EPA).

17 Yoshioka claims the 1962 figure was 104, falling to 22 in 1984, 'of which 19 are agricultural products' (Yoshioka, 1986: 24).

18 On agricultural products Japan has 142 tariff-lines in excess of 100 per cent (mega-tariffs). Mega-tariffs account for 63 per cent of all tariff-lines in the dairy sector, with 20 of these rates exceeding 500 per cent. Mega-tariffs on various categories of rice range from 710 per cent to 1,364 per cent. A large number of mega-tariffs also applied on imports of meats and sweetening products. The highest Japanese tariff is 2000 per cent on konjac (*konnyaku*) (Gibson et al., 2001, 29).

19 The title of the new policy was the 'Rice Farming Income Stabilisation Program'.

20 In the case of wheat, barley, soybeans, sugar beet and starch potatoes, the program also provided two other types of direct payments – for 'historical area planted'and 'on commodity output' (OECD, 2009; 72).

21 In order to be eligible for the direct payments these farm collectives 'must aim to consolidate more than two-thirds of the land in the community, have written rules of association, unify financial accounts, set a target income for participating farmers and have a plan to become an Agricultural Production Corporation' (OECD, 2009: 62).

22 Only about 10 per cent of rice farmers were eligible for the income support because 90 per cent (1.5 million out of 1.66 million) owned fields of 3 ha or less (Oosu, 2010), which made the scheme very unpopular.

23 The figures for 1990, 2005 and 2010 are for voters resident in commercial farm households.

24 These figures were calculated from the author's personal database on farm and JA politicians.

25 By 2012 the disparity in the value of votes in the Lower House had risen to 2.48:1 between Koichi (3) and Chiba (4).

26 The disparity in the value of votes in the Upper House remains much higher. In the 2010 Upper House elections it was 5:1 in prefectural constituencies.

27 The CEFP was abolished when the DPJ came to power in September 2009.

28 This is a two-level tariff, with limited import volumes permitted at the lower tariff level (in-quota), with all imports exceeding the quota charged at a higher rate. TRQs are regarded as playing an important role in agricultural protection by protecting sensitive agricultural sectors.

29 State trading delivers not only controls over imports but income from profits on import trades, which are directed by the importing agencies (the Food Agency, and Agriculture and Livestock Industries Corporation, or ALIC) into production and price subsidies for producers.

30 A subsidy of ¥15,000 per 10a (the gap between the average rice price over the previous three years and the average production cost over the previous seven years) and a variable subsidy to cover the gap between the actual price received by farmers and the average rice price were paid.

REFERENCES

Anderson, Kym, Hayami, Yujiro, George, Aurelia, Honma, Masayoshi, Otsuka, Keijiro, Saxon, Eric, Shei, Shunyi and Tyers, Rodney, 1986. *The political economy of agricultural protection: East Asia in international perspective*, Sydney: Allen and Unwin.

Bullock, Bob, 1995. *Explaining rice liberalization in Japan*, Occasional Paper 95–01, Program on US–Japan Relations, Harvard University.

Choi, Jung-Sup and Sumner, Daniel A., 2000. Opening markets while maintaining protection: Tariff rate quotas in Korea and Japan, *Agricultural and Resource Economics Review*, 29(1), April, 91–102.

Davis, Christina, 2007. Repeal of the rice laws in Japan: The role of international pressure to overcome vested interests, *Comparative Politics*, 40(1), October, 21–40.

Davis, Christina, 2003. *Food fights over free trade: How international institutions promote agricultural trade liberalization*, Princeton: Princeton University Press.

Egaitsu, Norio, 1985. Kōzō seisaku to kengyō nōka [Structural policy and part-time farms]. In Kenzō Hemmi and Yuzuru Katō (eds), *Kihonhō nōsei no keizai bunseki [An economic analysis of Basic Law agricultural policy]*, Tokyo: Meibun Shobō, 431–452.

Eto, Taku, 1987. *The agricultural policies of Japan, the United States, and the European Community*, Occasional Paper 87–20, Program on US–Japan Relations, Harvard University.

Francks, Penelope, 2000. Japan and an East Asia model of agriculture's role in industrialization, *Japan Forum*, 12(1), 43–52.

George Mulgan, Aurelia, 2014a. The politics of trade policy. In Jeff Kingston (ed.), *Critical issues in contemporary Japan*, London and New York: Routledge, 24–36.

George Mulgan, Aurelia, 2014b. Bringing the party back in: How the DPJ diminished prospects for Japanese agricultural trade liberalization under the TPP, *Japanese Journal of Political Science*, 15(1), March, 1–22.

George Mulgan, Aurelia, 2013a. Same old, same old: Farm reform shell game, *The Oriental Economist Report*, 81(12), December, 13–14.

George Mulgan, Aurelia, 2013b. Abe's 'growth' strategy for agriculture in Japan, *East Asia Forum*, 5 June, www.eastasiaforum.org/2013/06/05/abes-growth-strategy-for-agriculture-in-japan/, accessed on 22 August, 2014.

George Mulgan, Aurelia, 2011a. Agricultural politics and the Democratic Party of Japan, *Japanese Studies Online*, (2), 22–30, http://japaninstitute.anu.edu.au/sites/default/files/u5/Japan_Agricultural_Politics_DPJ.pdf, accessed on 22 August, 2014.

George Mulgan, Aurelia, 2011b. The farm lobby. In Takashi Inoguchi and Purnendra Jain (eds), *Japanese politics today*, New York: Palgrave, 109–126.

George Mulgan, Aurelia, 2008. Japan's FTA politics and the problem of agricultural trade liberalisation, *Australian Journal of International Affairs*, 62(2), June, 164–178.

George Mulgan, Aurelia, 2006a. *Japan's agricultural policy regime*, London and New York: Routledge.

George Mulgan, Aurelia, 2006b. *Power and pork: A Japanese political life*, Canberra: ANU Press.

George Mulgan, Aurelia, 2006c. *Agriculture and political reform in Japan: The Koizumi legacy*, Pacific Economic Papers No. 360, Australia–Japan Research Centre, ANU.

George Mulgan, Aurelia, 2005a. *Japan's interventionist state: The role of the MAFF*, London and New York: RoutledgeCurzon.

George Mulgan, Aurelia, 2005b. Where tradition meets change: Japan's agricultural politics in transition, *Journal of Japanese Studies*, 31(2), Summer, 261–298.

George Mulgan, Aurelia, 2001. *Japan Inc' in the agricultural sector: Reform or regression*, Pacific Economic Papers No. 314, Australia–Japan Research Centre, ANU.

George Mulgan, Aurelia, 2000. *The politics of agriculture in Japan*, London and New York: Routledge.

George Mulgan, Aurelia, 1997a. Electoral determinants of agrarian power: Measuring rural decline in Japan, *Political Studies*, XLV(5), December, 875–899.

George Mulgan, Aurelia, 1997b. The politics of deregulation and Japanese agriculture. In Pempel, T. J., Warren, Tony, George Mulgan, Aurelia, Lesbirel, S. Hayden, Jain, Purnendra and Tabusa, Keiko, *The politics of economic reform in Japan*, Pacific Economic Papers No. 270, Australia–Japan Research Centre, ANU, 3.1–3.38.

George Mulgan, Aurelia, 1997c. The role of foreign pressure (*gaiatsu*) in Japan's agricultural trade liberalization, *The Pacific Review*, 10(2), 165–209.

George Mulgan, Aurelia, 1993. The politics of public spending in the Japanese agriculture, forestry and fisheries sector. In Takekazu Ogura (ed.), *Japanese agricultural policy reconsidered*, Tokyo: Food and Agriculture Policy Research Center, 165–218.

Gibson, Paul, Waino, John, Whitley, Daniel and Bohman, Mary, 2001. *Profiles of tariffs in global agricultural markets*, Economic Research Service, United States Department of Agriculture No. 796, 25 January.

Godo, Yoshihisa, 2009. Kieru nōchi: Kome kanzei teppai de 'gisō nōka' no ego o tate [Disappearing farmland: Breaking the ego of 'fake farmers' by abolishing the rice tariff], *Wedge*, February, 10–12.

Godo, Yoshihisa, 2008. Shokuryō jikyūritsu kōjō to Nihon shakai no byōri ['The food self-sufficiency discourse and the pathology of Japanese society']. *Kokusai Mondai*, 577, December, 14–23.

Godo, Yoshihisa, 2007. *The puzzle of small farming in Japan*, Pacific Economic Papers No. 365, Australia–Japan Research Centre, ANU.

Godo, Yoshihisa, 2006. *Nihon no shoku to nō [Food and agriculture in Japan]*, Tokyo: NTT Shuppan.

Godo, Yoshihisa, 2001. *The changing economic performance and political significance of Japan's agricultural cooperatives*, Pacific Economic Papers No. 318, Australia–Japan Research Centre, ANU.

Godo, Yoshihisa and Takahashi, Daisuke, 2008. *Japan: Shadow WTO agricultural domestic support notifications*, Discussion Paper No. 822, International Food Policy Research Institute. Retrieved 5 April 2009 from www.ifpri.org/pubs/dp/ifpridp00822.asp

Gomi, Hisatoshi, 2001. Kōsatsu shitai: Nōgyō no iji saisei ninau shutai [I want to examine: The main entities that will undertake the roles of maintaining and reviving agriculture], *JA Com, Shōhyō*. Retrieved 14 April 2009 from http://www.jacom.or.jp/archive02/document/shohyou/books00/01091306.html

Goto, Junko and Imamura, Naraomi, 1993. Japanese agriculture: characteristics, institutions, and policies. In Luther Tweeten, Cynthia L. Dishon, Wen S. Chern, Naraomi Imamura and Masaru Morishima (eds), *Japanese & American agriculture: Tradition and progress in conflict*, Boulder CO: Westview Press.

Hart, Chad E. and Beghin, John C., 2004. *Rethinking agricultural domestic support under the World Trade Organization*, Briefing Paper 04-BP 43, November, Center for Agricultural and Rural Development, Iowa State University.

Hatta, Tatsuo, Matsumoto, Hiroyuki and Yamashita, Kazuhito, 2011. Teidan: TPP o ki ni, utte deru nōgyō e [Tripartite talk: Shift to agriculture that sallies forth using the TPP as an opportunity], *Keizai Seminar* (660), June/July, 10–25.

Hemmi, Kenzō and Katō, Yuzuru, 1985. Hashigaki [Introduction]. In Kenzō Hemmi, and Yuzuru Katō (eds), *Kihonhō nōsei no keizai bunseki [An economic analysis of Basic Law agricultural policy]*, Tokyo: Meibun Shobō, 1–4.

Hirose, Michisada, 1981. *Hojokin to seikentō* [*Subsidies and the ruling party*], Tokyo: Asahi Shinbunsha.

Honma, Masayoshi, 2009a. Paving the way to large-scale farming, *Japan Echo*, 36(3), June, 20–25.

Honma, Masayoshi, 2009b. Japan's grand strategy for agriculture in globalized world, *Japan Spotlight*, Japan Economic Foundation, July/August. Retrieved 20 June 2009 from www.jef.or.jp/journal/index.html

Honma, Masayoshi, 2000a. Political economy and agricultural policy reform in Japan, Paper presented to the workshop on 'Some Key Issues for the East Asian Food Sector', Australian National University, 2 May.

Honma, Masayoshi, 2000b. Japan's agricultural policy and WTO negotiations. In *Some key issues for the East Asian food sector*, Pacific Economic Papers No. 305, Australia–Japan Research Centre, ANU.

Japan Times, 2011. Editorial: Strengthening primary industries, 1 November. Retrieved 27 August 2012 from www.japantimes.co.jp/text/ed20111101a1.html

Jussaume, Raymond, A. Jr, 2003. Part-time farming and the structure of agriculture in postwar Japan. In Ann Waswo and Yoshiaki Nishida (eds), *Farmers and village life in twentieth-century Japan*, London and New York: RoutledgeCurzon.

Kajii, Isoshi, 1991. Nōgyō kōshō no zasetsu to Nihon nōgyō no saihensei [The failure of the agricultural negotiations and the reorganisation of Japanese agriculture]. In Tsutomu Ōuchi and Naomi Saeki (eds), *GATTO nōgyō kōshō to Nihon nōgyō* [*The GATT agricultural negotiations and Japanese agriculture*], Nihon Nōgyō Nenpō 37, Tokyo: Nōrin Tōkei Kyōkai, 112–182.

Katō, Yuzuru, 1985. Nōsanbutsu kakaku seisaku no tenkai [The development of agricultural price policy]. In Kenzō Hemmi and Yuzuru Katō (eds), *Kihonhō nōsei no keizai bunseki* [*An economic analysis of Basic Law agricultural policy*], Tokyo: Meibun Shobō, 151–181.

Kawagoe, Toshihiko, 1999. Abstract. In *Agricultural land reform in postwar Japan: Experiences and issues*, The World Bank. Retrieved 16 July 2014 from http://elibrary.worldbank.org/doi/pdf/10.1596/1813-9450-2111

Kawasaki, Isonobu, 1992. *Shokuryōchō-dono: Watashi wa yamigomeya desu* [*Mr Food Agency: I am running a black market rice shop*], Tokyo: Gendai Shorin.

Kawakita, Takao and Onoue, Yukio, 2001. *Nōrinsuisanshō* [*The Ministry of Agriculture, Forestry and Fisheries*], Tokyo: Intamedia.

Kishi, Hiroyuki, 2011. TPP to Ōsaka W senkyo no kyōtsūten [What the TPP and the double election in Osaka have in common], *Diamond Online*, No. 163, 10 November. Retrieved 16 July 2014 from http://diamond.jp/articles/-/14810

Koide, Yasunari and Editorial Department, 2009. 2-nen buri no kome bōraku de baramaki nōsei fukkatsu no bu [The revival of the subsidy-scattering agricultural policy with the slump in the rice price after two years as the excuse?], *Diamond Online*, 22 June. Retrieved 16 July 2014 from http://diamond.jp/articles/-/979

Krauss, Ellis and Pekkanen, Robert, 2004. Explaining party adaptation to electoral reform: The discreet charm of the LDP, *Journal of Japanese Studies*, 30(1), Winter, 17–23.

Mainichi Shinbun, 2009. Zenkoku Nōseiren suisen kōho ga kettei, 31 August: 2–13.

Ministry of Agriculture, Forestry and Fisheries, 2003. *Why agriculture needs different treatment in trade rules? Japan's policy reform and WTO negotiations*, May. Retrieved 16 July 2009 from http://www.maff.go.jp/e/pdf/fact_sheet.pdf

Ministry of Internal Affairs and Communications, 2009a. *Japan statistical yearbook 2009*. Retrieved 11 February 2009 from www.stat.go.jp/english/data/nenkan/1431-24.htm

Mishima, Tokuzō, 2001. Koizumi kōzō kaikaku no honshitsu: Itami ni taeta kekka wa dō naru ka [The essence of Koizumi's structural reform: The consequences of 'enduring pain'], *JA Com, Nōgyō Jiron*, 17 October. Retrieved 19 July 2014 from http://www.jacom.or.jp/archive02/document/ronsetsu/jiron/jiron01/01101705.html

Motosugi, Akio, 2003. The farmland and rural improvement project budget under the Agriculture Basic Law in Japan, *Paddy and Water Environment*, 1, 59–63.

Nakamura, Yasuhiko, 2001. *Nōrin zoku* [*Agricultural tribe Diet members*], Tokyo: Bunshun Shinsho.

Nikkei Weekly, 2009. New seeds of potential lie beneath Japan's shrivelling agriculture biz, 5 October.

Nōrinsuisanshō, 2014. Sōgō nōkyō issei chōsa kekka' (Heisei 24 jigyō nendo) [Complete research results for general purpose agricultural cooperatives (2014 business year)], Retrieved 16 July 2014 from http://www.maff.go.jp/j/keiei/sosiki/kyosoka/k_tokei/pdf/1gaiyou.pdf

Nōrinsuisanshō, 2011. Nōrinsuisan kihon dētashū [Agriculture, forestry and fisheries basic data collection]. Retrieved 11 January 2011 from www.maff.go.jp/j/tokei/sihyo/index.html

Nōrinsuisanshō, Daijin Kanbō Tōkeibu, 2012. *Dai 86-ji Nōrinsuisanshō tōkeihyō* [*The 86th statistical yearbook of Ministry of Agriculture, Forestry and Fisheries*], 2010–2011. Retrieved 15 August 2012 from www.maff.go.jp/j/tokei/kikaku/nenji/86nenji/index.html#ns002

Nōrinsuisanshō, Daijin Kanbō Tōkeibu, 2008a. *Dai 82-ji Nōrinsuisanshō tōkeihyō* [*The 82nd statistical* yearbook of Ministry of Agriculture, Forestry and Fisheries], 2006–2007, Tokyo: Nōrinsuisanshō, Daijin Kanbō Tōkeibu.

Nōrinsuisanshō, Daijin Kanbō Tōkeibu, 2008b. Poketto nōrinsuisan tōkei 2008 [Pocket agriculture, forestry and fisheries statistics 2008], Tokyo: Nōrin Tōkei Kyōkai.

Nōrinsuisanshō Tōkeibu, 2003. Poketto nōrinsuisan tōkei 2003 [Pocket agriculture, forestry and fisheries statistics 2003], Tokyo: Nōrin Tōkei Kyōkai.

Ogura, Takekazu, 1982. Can Japanese agriculture survive? Tokyo: Agricultural Policy Research Center, 3rd Edition.

Oizumi, Ikkan, 2009. Nihon no nōgyō wa seicho sangyō ni kaereru [Japan's agriculture can be changed into a growth industry], Tokyo: Yosensha.

Oosu, Shinji, 2010. Will the income compensation program for rice farmers actually restore Japanese agriculture?, ChuoOnline. Retrieved 9 January 2010 from www.yomiuri.co.jp/adv/chuo/dy/opinion/20100705.htm

Organisation for Economic Co-operation and Development (OECD), 2009. Evaluation of agricultural policy reforms in Japan. Retrieved 15 December 2009 from www.oecd.org/dataoecd/26/45/42791674.pdf

Organisation for Economic Co-operation and Development (OECD), 2008a. Agricultural policies in OECD countries at a glance, Paris: OECD.

Organisation for Economic Co-operation and Development (OECD), 2008b. OECD Glossary of statistical terms, Paris: OECD

Schwartz, Frank, 1998. Advice and consent: The politics of consultation in Japan, Cambridge MA: Cambridge University Press.

Shimizu, Ryōhei, 1985a. Kihonhō nōsei ka ni okeru tochi kairyō seisaku no henyō ni tsuite [Concerning the evolution of land improvement policy under the Basic Law agricultural policy]. In Kenzō Hemmi and Yuzuru Katō (eds), Kihonhō nōsei no keizai bunseki [An economic analysis of Basic Law agricultural policy], Tokyo: Meibun Shobō, 348–368.

Shimizu, Junichi, 1985b. Nōgyō zaisei shishutsu no kōzō to kinō [The structure and function of fiscal expenditure on agriculture]. In Kenzō Hemmi and Yuzuru Katō (eds), Kihonhō nōsei no keizai bunseki [An economic analysis of Basic Law agricultural policy], Tokyo: Meibun Shobō, 527–555.

Shimomura, Taichi. 2004. Sengo nōsei no tenkan to rieki seiji: 'Sōgō Nōsei' to Tanaka Kakuei [The transformation of the postwar agricultural policy and pork barrel in Japan: The 'Comprehensive Agricultural Policy' and Kakuei Tanaka], Hokudai Nōgaku Ronshū 55(3), 1077–1117.

Sōmushō, 2012. Dai22kai Sangiingiin tsūjō senkyo kekkachō [Results of the 22nd regular election of House of Councillors Diet members]. Retrieved 15 August 2012 from www.soumu.go.jp/senkyo/senkyo_s/data/sangiin22/index_1.html

Tashiro, Shōichi, 1998. The rice management system under the Staple Food Law, Memoirs of the Faculty of Agriculture, Kagoshima University, 34, 143–148. Retrieved 16 July 2014 from http://ci.nii.ac.jp/els/110004910588.pdf?id=ART0008063393&type=pdf&lang=en&host=cinii&order_no=&ppv_type=0&lang_sw=&no=1405758569&cp=

Tashiro Yōichi, 1992. An environmental mandate for rice self-sufficiency, Japan Quarterly, 39(1), 34–44.

Tsukada, Minoru, 1989. From rice to reform: Internationalization of the Japanese agriculture industry, Speaking of Japan, 10(102), June, 6–9.

Uraki, Shinichi and Ishida, Masaaki, 1985. Nōgyō kōzō seisaku to chihō gyōzaisei [Structural policy and local administrative and fiscal policy]. In Kenzō Hemmi and Yuzuru Katō (eds), Kihonhō nōsei no keizai bunseki [An economic analysis of Basic Law agricultural policy], Tokyo: Meibun Shobō, 611–628.

Vogel, Steven, 1999. When interests are not preferences: The cautionary tale of Japanese consumers, Comparative Politics, 31, January, 187–207.

Yamashita, Kazuhito, 2009a. Minshutō no seiken dasshugo ni otozureru 'Nōgyō Kaikoku' no rasuto chansu [The last chance for 'Opening Agriculture' coming with a DPJ administration], Diamond Online, 1 July. Retrieved 16 July 2014 from http://diamond.jp/articles/-/3453

Yamashita, Kazuhito, 2009b. Heisei no nōsei kaikaku to yobu ni wa hodotōi: Nōchihō kaisei wa 'Shōwa no natsumero' da [Far from Heisei agricultural policy reform: The amended Land Law is full of 'Shōwa nostalgia'], Diamond Online, 20 May. Retrieved 19 June 2009 from http://diamond.jp/articles/-/6816

Yamashita, Kazuhito, 2009c. Nōkyō toraianguru ga tsui ni hōkai? Gentan minaoshi no hata o tateta Ishiba no kake [The 'JA triangle' finally collapsing? Ishiba's gamble with the flag of abolishing the acreage reduction program], Diamond Online, 30 January. Retrieved 12 June 2009 from http://diamond.jp/articles/-/3860

Yamashita, Kazuhito, 2009d. The agricultural cooperatives and farming reform in Japan (2), The Tokyo Foundation. Retrieved 26 March 2009 from http://www.tokyofoundation.org/en/articles/2008/the-agricultural-cooperatives-and-farming-reform-in-japan-2/?searchterm=Yamashita%20Kazuhito

Yamashita, Kazuhito, 2008a. Dai 3-kai 'Nihon no shokuryō jikyūritsu wa naze teika shita no ka? [No. 3 'Why has Japan's food self-sufficiency declined?'], Seisaku Kenkyū, Tōkyō Zaidan. 26 August. Retrieved 15 February 2009 from www.tkfd.or.jp/research/sub1.php?id=174

Yamashita, Kazuhito, 2008b. The perilous decline of Japanese agriculture, The Tokyo Foundation.

Retrieved 8 February 2009 from http://www.toky-ofoundation.org/en/articles/2008/the-perilous-decline-of-japanese-agriculture-1/?searchterm=Yamashita%20Kazuhito

Yamashita, Kazuhito, 2008c. Let corporations play a role in reviving Japanese agriculture, The Tokyo Foundation, 2 December. Retrieved 11 February 2009 from http://www.tokyofoundation.org/en/articles/2008/let-corporations-play-a-role-in-reviving-japanese-agriculture/?searchterm=Yamashita%20Kazuhito

Yamashita, Kazuhito, 2008d. Dai 5-kai 'Jikomai ga abaku nōsei no konponteki na mujun' ['No. 5 'Tainted rice reveals the fundamental contradictions in agricultural policy'], *Seisaku Kenkyū*, Tōkyō Zaidan, 25 September. Retrieved 13 March 2009 from www.tkfd.or.jp/research/sub1.php?id=188

Yamashita, Kazuhito, 2008e. The Agricultural Cooperatives and Farming Reform in Japan (1), The Tokyo Foundation. Retrieved 26 March 2009 from http://www.tokyofoundation.org/en/articles/2008/the-agricultural-cooperatives-and-farming-reform-in-japan-1/?searchterm=Yamashita%20Kazuhito

Yamashita, Kazuhito, 2005. The mistakes in agricultural policy that have hindered structural reforms and the merits and demerits of JA agricultural cooperatives, Research Institute of Economy, Trade and Industry (RIETI). Retrieved 12 December 2008 from www.rieti.go.jp/en/papers/contribution/yamashita/06.html

Yamazaki, Yasuyo, 2004. Nōgyō wa saisentan sangyō ni naru: 'Heisei no nōchi kaikaku' de denen kara no sangyō kakumei o [Agriculture as a frontier industry: 'Heisei land reform' for an industrial revolution from farmland], *Chūō Kōron*, March, 128–147.

Yoshioka, Yutaka, 1989. Reforming Japan's agricultural policy: A perspective on significant changes. *Speaking of Japan*, 10(103), July, 22–26.

Yoshioka, Yutaka, 1986. Business before politics, *Speaking of Japan*, 7(65), May, 22–26.

Zenkoku Nōseiren suisen kōho ga kettei 2009. [National Farmers' League decides its recommended candidates], *Nōsei Undō Jyānaru*, No. 86, August, 2–13.

33

Energy

Alexandru P. Luta and Paul Midford

INTRODUCTION

Ever since Japan began industrializing in the late nineteenth century the country has been bereft of sufficient energy resources to cover its needs. In 2010 Japan imported 81 percent of its energy needs, with an overwhelming dependence on imported fossil fuels. Beginning in the 1960s, and especially since the oil crises of the 1970s, nuclear power has been promoted as the main means for reducing Japan's dependence on energy imports (along with efforts to increase energy efficiency). However, the Great East Japan Earthquake of 11 March 2011, which triggered a massive tsunami and a major nuclear accident, undermined Japan's existing energy policy. A national debate on the future of Japan's energy policy, especially the role of nuclear power and renewables in supplying electricity, has emerged as a result. The final outcome of this debate, and the nature and scope of the resulting changes, have started to emerge, yet remain far from certain and may even reverse.

At the heart of the current turmoil in Japanese energy policy lies electricity production. As shown in Graph 33.1 electricity represented 25.9 percent of Japan's final energy consumption in 2010, outstripping every other form of energy consumption, including the use of fossil fuels in transportation.

More relevantly, circa 43.6 percent of the country's total primary energy supply[1] is used up in the conversion of different energy sources, such as fossil fuels, fissile material and natural energy sources, into electricity (IEEJ, 2012).

When the US hegemon's implicit guarantee of Japan's oil imports collapsed during the 1973 Arab oil embargo the country faced a severe energy crisis that sent the economy into a significant recession and marked a watershed in Japan's energy policy. As hydro power had already been exploited to the point at which the marginal costs of further growth rapidly increased (Scalise, 2011: 143), the Japanese strategy to cope with the energy challenges posed by the country's paucity of fossil fuel resources, and by its need to import energy from distant and often unstable or unfriendly regions, has been to expand the role of nuclear power. In 2010 nuclear power supplied 24.9 percent of all the electricity generated in the country – a percentage that was meant to rise further in the coming decades (METI, 2011a). This expansion, which was already facing significant hurdles due to local opposition and growing national unease about nuclear power, became impossible to pursue in light of the nuclear accident in Fukushima.

The challenge for Japanese energy policy from now on is to find a new energy mix for electricity generation that will placate both a population

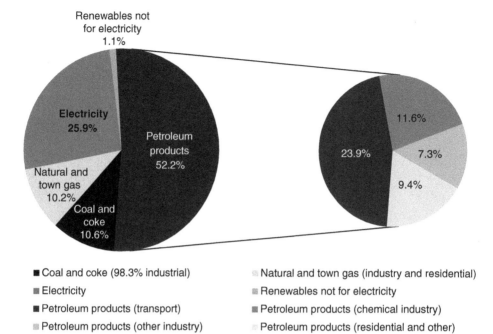

Coal and coke (98.3% industrial)

Electricity

Petroleum products (transport)

Petroleum products (other industry)

Natural and town gas (industry and residential)

Renewables not for electricity

Petroleum products (chemical industry)

Petroleum products (residential and other)

Graph 33.1   Total final energy consumption in fiscal year 2010 by energy source and type of final use

Source: Adapted from Handbook of Energy and Economic Statistics in Japan (2012).

worried about the safety of nuclear power and a business sector keenly concerned about keeping energy costs down and supply stable. Despite efforts to reduce reliance on expensive fossil-fuel imports in the wake of the oil crises of the 1970s, in 2010 export-oriented Japan was still reliant on fossil fuels to generate 66.7 percent of its electricity (see Table 33.2). Meanwhile, renewable energy had gained only a limited role in electricity generation, as electric power companies had been unwilling to facilitate it due to perceptions about high generation costs and problematic grid integration (Kimura and Suzuki, 2006). Consequently, these new technologies still have a long road ahead, full of significant policy challenges, before they can replace the generation capacity that nuclear power provided before 3-11.

The 1973 oil embargo is the starting point for this chapter's analysis of Japan's current energy usage, security, and policy. The rest of this chapter is divided into four sections. The next section demonstrates how the 1973 crisis represented a watershed in Japan's energy policy and markets, stimulating a shift in the country's industrial structure, the promotion of energy efficiency, and the accelerated development of a nuclear-power industry ambitious both in scale and in scope. The following section examines how a series of nuclear accidents globally and

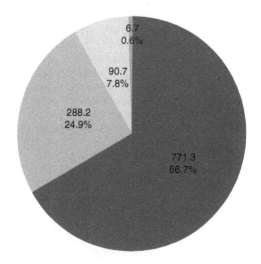

Thermal   Nuclear   Hydro   Other renewables

Graph 33.2   Breakdown of electricity generation in fiscal year 2010 by energy source in TWh and percentages of total

Source: Adapted from METI, Handbook of Electric Power Industry in Japan (2012).

inside Japan gradually undermined public support and the policy environment for expanding nuclear power. As the policy of nuclear-power expansion slowed and eventually stopped due to increasing local opposition and national skepticism, some tentative steps were taken toward supporting renewable forms of energy, such as solar, wind, geothermal, biomass, and even tidal energy. Nonetheless, we show how the virtual deadlock in nuclear-power policy negatively affected renewables as well. The penultimate section examines the impact of the March 2011 earthquake, tsunami, and especially the Fukushima Dai-ichi accident on nuclear-power policy and renewables. We argue that the impact of the Fukushima accident was largely to break the deadlock about energy policy, with a consensus emerging about the need to move away from nuclear power and toward renewable energy. Nonetheless, significant policy conflicts and even policy paralysis continue to hinder a complete overhaul of electricity policy, especially the questions of whether to restart some of Japan's idled nuclear plants in the short-run, how quickly and completely to move away from nuclear power and toward reliance on renewable power, and whether and to what extent to separate the ownership and control over the electric grid from producing companies. In the final sections we assess the extent to which the techno-industrial complex embodied by the 'nuclear village' and the regional electric-power companies continue to exert influence versus other stakeholders.

THE OIL SHOCKS OF THE 1970S

Although Japan exploited its domestic coal reserves to help fuel its early industrialization, these reserves were far from sufficient to meet demand. Already before the outbreak of the Pacific War Japan had become dependent on imported oil, and energy security had become a pressing concern for Japanese leaders. Indeed, the US decision to impose an oil embargo on Japan in the fall of 1941 played a large role in Japan's decision to go to war against the USA and the UK simultaneously and seize the oil fields of the Dutch East Indies (now Indonesia). After the war, as Japan shut down its coal industry due to declining viability in the 1960s, it expanded large-scale hydro-electricity production by building a number of dams, and tried to stem its growing dependence on imported oil for transportation by expanding and electrifying its commuter and regional rail networks. The inauguration of the Bullet Train system in October 1964 is the most well known manifestation of this. Japan also began developing a nuclear-power industry, as discussed below. Nonetheless, Japan's dependence on imported oil continued to increase.

With the Yom Kippur War escalating into a full-blown OPEC oil embargo the so-called Japanese post-war miracle of exceptionally high economic growth, a period lasting from approximately 1955 to 1973, came to an end (Katz, 1998: 165–166). The economy, which had grown by more than 8 percent from 1972 to 1973, contracted in 1974 by more than 1.2 percent (UN, 2013). Although the economy quickly recovered from this recession, it never returned to the path of high economic growth that had characterized Japan's miracle years. Instead growth rates halved from the 8–10 percent range down to an average of 4 percent in the years following the 1973 oil shock (Katz, 1998: 165–167). The oil shock of 1979 had a similar impact. While the Japanese economy had grown by nearly 5.5 percent in 1979, with the eruption of the Iranian Revolution that same year, triggering the second oil crisis of the 1970s, Japanese growth slumped to around 2.8 percent in 1980.

In the long-term the 1970s oil shocks left a deep impression on public opinion and elites. The 1973 oil embargo is best remembered for causing Japan to run out of toilet paper (many Japanese horde toilet paper to this day in anticipation of a future oil crisis). How much of the impact of the crisis was caused by the actual embargo and how much by the government's response can be debated. The late oil-economist Morris Adelman argued that policy responses, far more than the embargo, were responsible for fuel shortages in the USA at that time (Adelman, 2008: 110–112, 139).[2] No comparable study has examined whether this was the case with Japan. Nonetheless, the conviction of both elites and the public has been that the shortages Japan suffered were the direct result of the embargo, and that this demonstrated Japan's profound energy insecurity. With reliance on oil in the total primary energy supply during 1970–1979 swinging between 71.8 percent and 77.7 percent, practically all of which was imported, Japan, regardless of the reason, experienced a tremendous energy supply-side shock.

Japan adopted two major policies in response to these oil crises.[3] First, Tokyo embarked on a drive to increase energy efficiency and reduce economic reliance on energy-intensive industries. Second, diversification away from oil, which had displaced coal between 1960 and 1980, came to be seen as imperative. Coal, gas and nuclear energy recorded impressive growth from 1979 to 1989, in both absolute and relative terms, as seen in Table 33.1. These two policy approaches were tremendously successful, improving Japanese energy efficiency by 23.9% between 1979 and 1989. Policy-makers especially favored nuclear power since it could provide a stable supply of energy while largely avoiding reliance on geographically concentrated and politically unpredictable sellers.

Table 33.1 Japan's changing primary energy consumption 1979–1989

Year	1979		1989	
Energy Source	Mtoe	Percentage	Mtoe	Percentage
Coal	51.2	14.5	73.2	17.8
Gas	18.6	5.3	40.6	9.9
Nuclear	18.3	5.2	47.7	11.6
Oil	256.8	72.8	235.1	57.2

Source: Beyond 20/20 Database (IEA), Energy balances, Japan, Total primary energy supply.

Note: Mtoe = Million tons oil equivalent.

* Authors' own calculation, tracking the improvement in the ratio between the total primary energy supply and GDP measured in purchasing power parity terms. Source: Energy Balances of OECD Nations, 2013 edition, Beyond 20/20 database, IEA.

Additionally, nuclear power could be considered a cheap energy source, if back-end costs, especially related to the nuclear-fuel cycle and spent-fuel disposal, are omitted or socialized away through government policy instead of being directly charged to consumers.

Improving Energy Effiency

One way Japan improved its energy efficiency was by gradually de-emphasizing energy-intensive materials industries such as aluminum and steel, which had hitherto been promoted as part of Japan's economic development, in favor of less energy-intensive industries such as manufacturing (Katz, 1998: 167–169, 173). Specific policy responses in these areas included the foundation of the New Energy and Industrial Technology Development Organization (NEDO) in 1982, consolidating two earlier research initiatives: one on new and renewable forms of energy, and one on energy conservation (Kanekiyo, 2006). The 1979 Act on the Rational Use of Energy granted governmental agencies powers to encourage investment in energy-saving facilities, set fuel-efficiency standards, and establish standards for the level and structure of energy consumption of actors in a number of economic sectors. This legal stick was complemented with carrots, including tax breaks and depreciation schemes offered to companies in the wake of the second oil shock to improve their energy efficiency, and low-interest loans from the Japan Development Bank for energy conservation projects in factories (Fukasaku, 1995).

This 1979 act received a number of amendments in the wake of the 1997 adoption of the Kyoto Protocol. The government gained the right

Table 33.2 Trends in the absolute values and shares of total final energy consumption of Japan's industrial, and commercial and residential sectors*

Sectors	1990		2006	
	Mtoe	%	Mtoe	%
Industry	104.9	34.4%	101.9	29.0%
Commercial and residential	84.0	27.5%	116.3	33.1%

Source: Beyond 20/20 Database (IEA), Energy balances, total final consumption.

*Omitted sectors are agriculture and transportation.

to impose certain energy-efficiency improvements upon companies. In 2002 energy-efficiency rules were extended to newly built office buildings and buildings undergoing major renovation work, while in 2005 new regulations affecting the freight sector and residential buildings were drafted. The combination of government efforts to promote energy efficiency succeeded in significantly reducing the ratio of energy to GDP, and did so faster than was the case in other advanced economies.

In order to target smaller scale consumers Japan introduced the Top Runner program, forcing manufacturers to match the energy efficiency of their products with the best practices in their sector. It was established under the above act in 1998 and by 2010 it covered 23 product lines, with energy-efficiency improvements of between 14 and 85 percent (METI, 2010b). Yet the large purchasing power of Japanese consumers has led to a fast diffusion of most appliances, largely offsetting the energy-efficiency gains in the household and commercial sectors with increasing electricity demand. According to one study, Japan's per capita energy consumption in 2009 was 10 percent higher than for the EU as a whole (ABB, 2010).

In fact, by 2006 industry's share of total final energy consumption was noticeably falling, while that of the residential and commercial sectors was rising, which is why that year saw the introduction of the Energy Conservation Frontrunner Plan under the New National Energy Strategy, setting a target to improve energy efficiency by at least a further 30 percent by 2030.

Developing Other Energy Sources

Japan's second major response to the 1970s oil shocks was to develop new energy sources. As the first crisis developed the Ministry of International Trade and Industry (MITI) was able to appropriate 2.5 billion yen in 1974 for an R&D program called the Sunshine Program, which covered coal liquefaction, geothermal power and hydrogen, along with solar technologies – both solar thermal power and photovoltaics (PV). When the second oil crisis erupted, this program received a budgetary boost in the form of a special account for alternative-energy development, financed from taxes on coal use and electricity. The establishment of NEDO in 1982 involved consolidating the Sunshine Program with the Moonlight Program, which dealt with energy conservation (Kanekiyo, 2006).

Yet the most noticeable policy change was the ramping up of nuclear power. Japan had launched its peacetime nuclear-power program in the mid 1950s. At that time nuclear power, although explicitly limited to peaceful purposes, was nonetheless tied to great-power nationalism. Yasuhiro Nakasone, then a young Diet member became a leading advocate for Japan developing nuclear power for peaceful purposes, and explicitly linked this with a nationalist agenda. Nakasone would subsequently write that at the time he thought 'Nuclear power is the greatest discovery of the twentieth century, and if Japan cannot use it for peaceful purposes, the country will forever have to content itself with being a fourth rate power' (*Asahi Shimbun*, 2011).[4] Japan turned on its first commercial nuclear reactor in 1966 (Aldrich, 2008: 125).

Within a year of the 1973 oil embargo the Tanaka Cabinet passed new laws on electricity generation that greatly increased subsidies for nuclear power, offering them at double the going rate for thermal plants (Samuels, 2013: 114; Suzuki, 2000: 6). Richard Katz's observation that 'the shock effect of the 1973 oil crisis was the initial impetus for the new wave of retrograde protectionism that gripped Japan' (Katz 1998: 167) may thus have validity in the non-traded electricity sector as well. Japan's nuclear-power industry grew rapidly thereafter,

with nuclear-power generation doubling between 1981 and 1986, and again between 1986 and 1998 (see Graph 33.1), becoming one of Japan's baseload power sources (Aldrich, 2013). Graph 33.2 shows almost the same pattern in terms of nuclear power's share of Japan's total electricity production: between 1980 and 1986 nuclear power's share of total electricity production increased by two thirds but then dipped significantly from 1987. This dip ended in 1989 and nuclear's share increased again, from approximately 23 percent to 32 percent by 1998, after which nuclear's share declined, oscillating between 25 percent and 30 percent of generation through 2010.

The Basic Energy Plans

More recently the government of Japan has attempted to develop a structure for the long-term planning of Japanese energy policy. To this end in 2002 the Diet passed the Basic Act on Energy Policy, mandating that Ministry of Economy, Trade and Industry (METI) draft Basic Energy Plans at regular intervals. These plans provide the overarching framework spelling out the Japanese government's vision for future developments in the energy sector. So far, the plans, drafted in 2003, 2007, and 2010, listed three principles in accordance with which this sector was to be ideally managed: stability of energy supply, compatibility between the economy and the environment, and the application of market principles. It should be noted that, due to Japan's intense reliance on imported energy sources, supply stability has been an overriding concern of Japanese decision-makers, matched in its importance only by the need to keep energy prices in check in order to

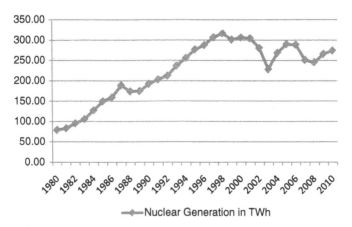

Graph 33.3. Nuclear-power generation in TWh

Source: U.S. Energy Information Administration International Energy Statistics.
Accessed at http://www.eia.gov/cfapps/ipdbproject/iedindex3.cfm?tid=2&pid=27&aid=12&cid=regions&syid=2007&eyid=2011&unit=BKWH

maintain Japan's export-dependent industries' international competitiveness.

The plans all reflected the lessons that Japanese policy-makers drew from the oil crises of the 1970s by emphasizing the need for bilateral diplomacy to ensure crucial supplies of oil. While acknowledging its drawbacks related to greenhouse gases (GHG), they praise coal, along with more climate-friendly natural gas for being distributed more evenly across the globe, ensuring easier access.

There is a strong contrast in the attitude towards nuclear power relative to renewable energy. The 2010 Plan states that Japan would 'continue its steady pursuit [of nuclear power] as an unshakeable national strategy, without faltering over the mid- or long-term' (METI, 2010a: 27) since it fulfills the plans' three guiding principles. Preoccupation with the safety of this technology and the public's understanding of the need for it feature prominently in all three documents, with the stated attitude towards its continued development, such as the nuclear fuel cycle, being that 'the state shall take the initial step' (METI, 2010a: 27). Conversely, renewable energies are depicted in the 2003 and 2007 versions as energy sources plagued by high costs and unstable supply, fulfilling only a supplementary role and requiring further technological development and demonstration projects before further deployment. This basic description was still present in the 2010 version compiled under the new Democratic Party of Japan (DPJ) administration, despite it being published after a law had been enacted promoting renewable energy with a feed-in tariff 'appropriate to Japan's actual circumstances' (METI 2010a: 25). The promotion of renewables was justified as steming from their low environmental impact, potential for job creation, and role in diversifying the energy supply.

Despite this shift in favor of renewables the priority in 2010 still lay with nuclear power. Unlike its previous two iterations, the 2010 plan mentioned certain explicit numerical targets, most relevantly the goal of achieving a ratio of zero-emission sources for electricity generation of more than 50 percent of all electricity by 2020, and approximately 70 percent by 2030, by adding (new construction or replacement) nine new reactors by 2020 and a total of at least 14 or more reactors by 2030 (METI, 2010a: 27). Conversely, the goal for all renewable energies, including hydro (both large and small), biomass, and waste, was placed at 10 percent of the total primary energy supply (METI, 2010a: 23) – a much smaller percentage of a much larger amount.

Despite official government support, nuclear power was not universally accepted in Japan. What Graphs 33.3 and 33.4 show is that nuclear power enjoyed tremendous growth during the first half of the 1980s but then suffered a reversal following the 1986 Chernobyl nuclear accident in the Soviet Union as public and especially local concerns about safety began to rise, fueling opposition to building new nuclear reactors and dampening opposition to safety measures that reduced utilization rates. This forced Japan's Electric Power Companies (EPCOs) and the national government to redouble efforts to overcome opposition, often through increased subsidies to communities where nuclear-power plants were based. For example, in 1994 MITI began eliminating caps on the subsidies offered to host communities (Aldrich, 2008: 139).

By 1989 the nuclear industry had begun to regain momentum, although not to the same extent as it achieved in the early 1980s. Nonetheless, a series of nuclear accidents and cover-ups in the 1990s, such as the one that effectively shuttered the experimental

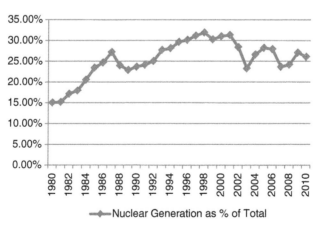

Graph 33.4. Nuclear-electricity generation as a percentage of total electricity generation

Source: Based on data from the U.S. Energy Information Administration International Energy Statistics. Accessed at ttp://www.eia.gov/cfapps/ipdbproject/iedindex3.cfm?tid=2&pid=27&aid=12&cid=regions&syid=2007&eyid=2011&unit=BKWH

Monju fast breeder reactor indefinitely and especially the Tokaimura nuclear accident in 1999 (Aldrich, 2008: 125, 139), brought this second nuclear golden age to an end. Although the Tokaimura accident occurred at a nuclear-fuel-processing plant rather than at a power plant, it was at the time the worst nuclear accident in Japan, having caused a significant release of radiation locally and several plant workers to suffer radiation-sickness-related injuries, leading to two deaths. Before this accident around two thirds of Tokaimura residents regarded nuclear power as more or less safe, but after it only 15 percent answered so (Samuels, 2013: 113). After the Tokaimura accident the expansion of nuclear-power generation came to a halt (see Graphs 33.3 and 33.4).[5] Although a majority of Japanese continued to support nuclear power, growing safety concerns, revelations about repeated EPCO cover-ups of (albeit generally small) nuclear-plant accidents, and a resurgence in local opposition stifled further expansion of nuclear power during the twelve years separating the Tokaimura accident from the Fukushima-Dai-ichi nuclear accident in March 2011. Fifteen months before 3–11 a Cabinet Office poll found 59.9 percent supporting nuclear power; nonetheless, 53.9 percent, an increase of more than 12 percent from the previous Cabinet Office poll, expressed concern about the safety of using nuclear power due to accident cover-ups and a general lack of transparency (*Asahi Shimbun*, 2009). Consequently, the best way to characterize public attitudes toward using nuclear power on the eve of the March 2011 earthquake and tsunami was ambivalence.

JAPAN'S ELECTRICITY SECTOR IN THE DECADE BEFORE 3–11

The electricity sector is dominated by the 10 vertically integrated regional EPCOs (*ippan denki jigyōsha*), effectively regional monopolies, which have remained unchanged and largely unchallenged since the division of Nippon Hassoden in 1951 under the US occupation (the tenth utility, Okinawa EPCO, formally became one of the 10 only in 1972, when the USA returned the Ryukyu Islands to Japan). Furthermore, historical accident has led to the three eastern utilities (Hokkaido, Tohoku, and Tokyo) being on a different frequency – 50 Hz – from the seven western ones (Okinawa, Kyushu, Shikoku, Chugoku, Kansai, Chubu, and Hokuriku), which use 60 Hz. There are only very limited interconnections between the individual utilities' service areas and the two frequency areas.[6] These features have greatly limited the flexibility with which the Japanese energy system can respond to sudden shocks, such as the 11 March 2011 earthquake that led to the multiple meltdown at the Fukushima Dai-ichi nuclear plant.

A number of actors other than the 10 EPCOs are active in the Japanese electricity sector. There are two wholesale power utilities that are allowed to sell electricity to the EPCOs alone; a great number of auto-producers, which are companies generating electricity mainly for their own needs, but who also have the potential to sell excess power to the grid; and around 70 smaller power producers and suppliers (PPS) and specific electric utilities (METI, 2011a).

All nuclear-power plants in operation or under construction in Japan belong either to the EPCOs or the wholesale utilities. Of the 1,156.9 TWh of electricity generated in Japan in 2010, 821.9 TWh (71.0 percent) was generated by the EPCOs, 85.8 TWh (7.4 percent) was generated by the wholesale companies and sold to the EPCOs, and 238.6 TWh (20.6 percent) was generated by auto-producers, leaving less than 1 percent to the other actors (METI, 2011a).

Japan was no exception to the wave of regulatory reform in the electricity sector worldwide. The first round occurred in 1995 when, most importantly, auto-producers and trading companies were allowed to enter wholesale arrangements with EPCOs as independent power producers. SEUs, consisting mostly of railroad companies, were also allowed to sell power in circumscribed areas, as they possessed their own transmission and distribution networks. The second round, occurring in 2000, introduced among other things the first liberalization of the retail sector, enabling PPSs to sell electricity larger than 2 MW to consumers. However, since PPSs do not own their own transmission and distribution infrastructure, they purchased usage rights from EPCOs, paying so-called wheeling charges for transmission. The third round in 2003 led to the creation of the Japan Electric Power Exchange (JEPX), a wholesale spot and forward market for electricity. The liberalized section of the market was also expanded: consumers with loads as low as 50kW could purchase electricity, amounting to 63 percent of all electric power traded in Japan. An attempt was made at unbundling EPCOs but, in the wake of the California electricity crisis and the Enron bankruptcy, it became politically untenable to move further than account unbundling. The most recently completed round, the fourth, was launched in 2008 but failed to liberalize the captive-consumer segment below 50kW.

While the Japanese electricity market is largely liberalized de jure, only 0.7 percent of the electricity consumed in Japan was traded on JPEX in 2011. With the rest of the electricity being traded in bilateral contracts, primarily between EPCOs and consumers, the impact of the wholesale market on tariffs in Japan has been minimal. Given the strong ownership of installations for the generation, transmission, and distribution of electricity by the

10 EPCOs and the nearly complete dominance of sales to all customers within their service areas, the Japanese case can be said to be a textbook example of vertically integrated local monopolies. Japanese electricity prices, calculated in terms of purchasing parity, were 24 percent higher in 2010 than the OECD average (Scalise, 2012b: 25),[7] and it is said that a significant reason for this is the near complete lack of competition in this sector (DeWit et al., 2012).

POST-FUKUSHIMA POLITICS AROUND NUCLEAR ENERGY

The Aftermath of the Accident

The earthquake that struck Japan on 11 March 2011 was of unprecedented scale for Japan in the era of modern seismology. At magnitude 9 it triggered a tsunami that reached 40 meters at its highest point and swept as far as 10 km inland (Koh, 2011). The disaster took approximately 24.8 GW worth of generating capacity offline, 11.3 GW of which came from nuclear power alone (Nakayama, 2011). The most severe accidents occurred at Tokyo Electric Power's (TEPCO) Fukushima Dai-ichi nuclear-power plant. All four active reactors had their reactor buildings destroyed by hydrogen explosions, and three experienced full meltdowns (McCurry, 2011). TEPCO was left facing vast compensation payments for the evacuated population in the vicinity, the clean-up of the irradiated areas, and the decommissioning of the reactors, forcing the government to effectively nationalize it (Kyodo 2012b).

Immediately after the accident utilities raised concerns that a gap might emerge between peak demand and maximum available supply in the range of 10 to 15 GW during the summer peak of Japanese electricity consumption (July to September 2011) (Someno, 2011). In addition, parts of Tokyo and other areas in East Japan were subjected to planned (but nonetheless highly disruptive) rolling blackouts during the first few weeks following 3–11 in order to prevent unplanned blackouts caused by demand outstripping the greatly reduced supply.

To make up for the shortfall the Tohoku and Tokyo EPCOs were forced to restart mothballed thermal plants, to lease emergency gas-fired generators from abroad (Energy Central, 2011), and to prevail on auto-producers, such as steel mills (*Nikkei*, 2011a) and pulp-and-paper factories (*Nikkei*, 2011b), to feed power into the grid. METI also issued an administrative order to Japan's largest consumers to reduce their peak consumption by 15 percent from the previous year.

The massive damage and significant numbers of refugees resulting from the Fukushima Dai-ichi accident, the slow pace at which reliable information

became available about why the safety measures had proven so inadequate, and uncertainty about when the Fukushima reactors would be finally brought under control provoked heightened public concern about the safety of nuclear power, concern that penetrated all levels of government. Thus, even though all nuclear reactors need to undergo routine maintenance shutdowns every eighteen months, when reactors throughout the country entered their regularly scheduled maintenance shutdowns after the Fukushima accident utilities were unable to persuade local governments to agree to their restart once maintenance was completed. Utilities again voiced concerns about impending blackouts ahead of summer 2012 as the last nuclear reactors went offline on 5 May, leaving the country without any nuclear power for the first time in over forty years (Warnock, 2012). The DPJ government of Noda Yoshihiko ordered the restart of two reactors in the town of Oi, Fukui prefecture, a little over a month later, citing a likely power shortage in the Kansai region. Japan managed to weather the summer without significant shortages, and data after the fact showed that Kansai could have got by without restarting the Oi reactors, albeit without much margin to spare in the case of an unforseen event (*Asahi Shimbun*, 2012).[8]

The New Politics of Energy

Prime Minister Kan Naoto of the DPJ responded to the increasingly negative public attitudes towards nuclear power and ordered a fundamental revision of the country's Basic Energy Plan in mid May. By mid July Kan was ready to call for abandoning Japan's reliance on nuclear power in favor of renewable energy (Scalise, 2012a: 140; DeWit et al., 2012: 160). His party had been experiencing difficulty transforming into law the electoral pledges from its spectacular victory in 2009 against the LDP, but Kan's shift on nuclear power was well supported by the public, making it difficult for the LDP to stand in the way; indeed, the LDP was beginning to rethink its support for nuclear power (*Japan Times*, 2011). Kan brokered a deal with the LDP and other opposition parties under which he agreed to step down as prime minister in September 2011 in exchange for the passage of a package of laws that included a generalized feed-in tariff (FIT) for renewable energy.

Noda, Kan's successor, launched a national debate about the future direction of Japan's Basic Energy Plan in the autumn of 2011 through a body called the Committee on Basic Energy Issues. However, the committee remained deadlocked for months in an acrimonious stand-off between proponents and opponents of nuclear power. The political pressure continued rising during the summer of 2012, when

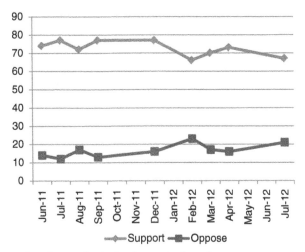

Graph 33.5. Support for the gradual phasing out of nuclear power

Note: These results were obtained in answer to the following question: 'Do you favor gradually reducing nuclear generation of electricity and eliminating it in the future? Are you opposed?'

Source: Asahi Shimbun, June 13, 2011, August 7, 2011, September 10, 2011, December 13, 2011, February 14, 2012, April 18, 2012, July 10, 2012, June 26, 2013, November 12, 2013.

protestors gathered in the largest demonstrations in Tokyo since the 1960s to voice their opposition to continued reliance on nuclear power. The Noda administration was caught between its desire for a pragmatic policy, allowing it to take maximum advantage of Japan's existing nuclear-generation capacity on the one hand, and the protestors on the other. According to unofficial estimates on some occasions the numbers of demonstrators approached 170,000 (Narioka, 2012), most of whom supported the immediate elimination of nuclear power from Japan's energy mix. Of far greater significance for the Noda administration, as indicated by Graph 33.5, a clear and stable majority of Japanese had come to favor the gradual elimination of nuclear power, thereby effectively endorsing the non-nuclear vision that Kan had laid out a year earlier.

Eliminating nuclear power completely, even over the mid-term, would be a valiant undertaking. Apparently reflecting this reality, the general public has been less opposed to restarting some nuclear plants in the short-run, with nearly as many respondents supporting as opposing restarts in a February 2012 *Nikkei* poll (*Nikkei*, 2012).[9] In 2010, the last year before the triple calamity, nuclear power generated approximately 24.9 percent of all electricity in Japan (METI, 2011a). Even under conditions of restrained demand, utilities were forced to divert financial resources into purchasing huge quantities of fossil fuels to generate power from thermal-power plants, as indicated by Graph 33.6. Unlike nuclear power, which is typically used for baseload generation

and runs uninterrupted for months at a time, the costs of continuously combusting fuel to generate electricity make thermal plants economical for only a limited amount of time as load-following and peaking plants. Besides TEPCO seven of Japan's power utilities had already reported net losses as a result of this fuel substitution during the winter of 2012 (Yahoo!News, 2012), leading to a string of applications by the utilities to METI for permission to raise the rates they charge their captive consumers (*Nikkei*, 2013b). The scale of Japanese fossil-fuel procurement ballooned to such an extent that the export-driven economy recorded its first trade deficit since 1980 (*The Guardian*, 2012), a trend that only worsened over the course of 2012 and into 2013.

Caught between tremendous political pressures pushing it in opposing directions, the Noda administration was unable to construct a fully consistent policy on energy. Based on one of the three scenarios drafted by the Committee on Basic Energy Issues and debated at a series of nationwide public hearings during the summer of 2012, a minister-level committee placed under the Cabinet decided on 14 September 14 2012 to eliminate Japan's reliance on nuclear power by the 2030s thereby effectively realizing Kan's call from July of the previous year to eliminate reliance on nuclear power. The Noda cabinet called for eliminating nuclear power through the implementation of three principles: cap nuclear-reactor lifetimes at 40 years; no restart of reactors without the safety approval of the new Nuclear Regulation Authority (NRA); and no construction of additional reactors. It mandated replacing nuclear

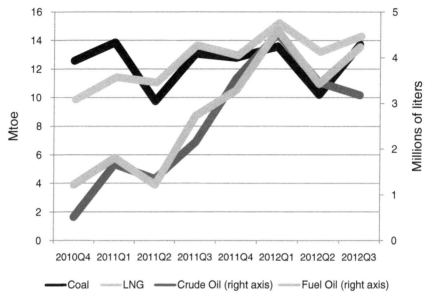

Graph 33.6.   Fossil-fuel consumption of 10 Japanese utilities since 2010 Q4

Source: Energy Indicators of Japan (March 2012 and March 2013), Institute of Energy Economics, Japan.

power with a threefold increase in renewables from 110 TWh to 300 TWh – or an eightfold increase from 25 TWh to 190 TWh if large-scale hydro generation excluded (Energy and Environment Council, 2012).

This momentous decision, widely reported in the media, caused consternation among domestic business associations, local governments, and foreign capitals close to nuclear interests. Consequently, the Noda Cabinet limited itself to a brief statement pledging to take the Council's decision 'into account... with flexibility' when 'reviewing and re-examining' its 'future policies on energy and the environment' – thereby refraining from adopting it as a Cabinet decision (Cabinet of Japan, 2012). Rather, the decision is like a Chief Cabinet Secretary *danwa* or statement that nonetheless carries significant weight. However, exceptions to this policy quickly emerged. On 15 September, a mere day after the council's decision, METI minister Edano Yukio announced that the ban on 'new construction' did not include plants that were already under construction, and that he intended to allow construction work on two nearly completed nuclear reactors to resume. If the forty-year lifetime rule for these two new plants were to be applied this would mean that the Noda Cabinet's decision to phase out all nuclear power by the end of the 2030s would be delayed for at least 15 years, until around 2055[10] (see Graph 33.7). Despite these contradictions and the lower level of legal force in the Cabinet's decision, Prime Minister Noda Yoshihiko himself, while

addressing the United Nations General Assembly on September 26, declared that Japan aimed at realizing zero reliance on nuclear power by the 2030s.

Due to these inconsistencies work on the new Basic Energy Plan fell into abeyance until after the December 2012 Lower House elections that Noda felt compelled to call in November. The main opposition party, the LDP, led by the controversial Abe Shinzō (who had resigned amid controversy while serving as prime minister in September 2007), was able to frame the election in terms of economic and foreign policies but, above all, as about governing competence. The LDP hardly touched on energy policy and failed to take a clear stand for or against the gradual elimination of nuclear power (Jimintō, 2012).

Although the LDP and its coalition partner, New Komeito, emerged victorious from the election with a combined two-thirds majority in the Lower House, the election turnout was very low, and in terms of votes received the LDP did not do especially well. In the contest for 180 proportional-representation seats the LDP expanded its share of the vote by just under 1 percent in comparison with 2009 (and actually received fewer votes) when the party was trounced. The LDP did somewhat better in terms of votes received in the 300 single-member districts, but overall it is more accurate to say that the DPJ lost rather than that the LDP won. The disunited DPJ had disappointed voters with its inability to deliver on many of the

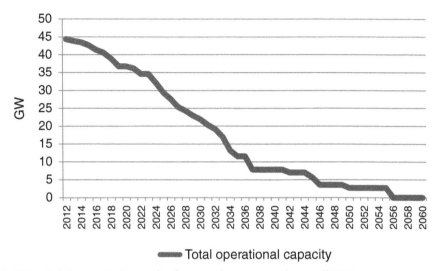

Total operational capacity

Graph 33.7. Total expected capacity from nuclear generation until 2060

Source: Authors' own calculations based on construction data for Japanese reactors from the World Nuclear Database. Assumptions: Completion of Shimane-3 and Ohma reactors, complete decommissioning of Fukushima Dai-ichi, a conservative reactor retirement age of 40, and no further nuclear accidents.

electoral pledges it had made in its 2009 election manifesto, and by creating an image of incompetence in government. The non-LDP vote, which in 2009 had converged on voting for the DPJ, scattered in 2012 among several new parties, causing the LDP to win significantly more seats than it would have won had there been no boom in new-party candidates (Reed et al., 2012).

Nuclear Power as Hot Potato

With an eye towards winning the regular Upper House elections, scheduled for July of 2013, the LDP pushed an economic-stimulus package and monetary policy aggressively onto the agenda, while keeping energy issues at arm's length. The coalition agreement between the LDP and New Komeito entrusts the issue of restarting idle nuclear reactors to the NRA, an agency set up by the DPJ under the Ministry of Environment in an attempt to correct perceived collusion between METI, which had previously had jurisdiction for nuclear regulation, and the power utilities. Furthermore, both parties, in line with their 2012 election manifestos, pledged to accelerate the introduction of renewable and energy-efficiency measures, and to reduce reliance on nuclear power as far as possible.

The inclination and ability of the LDP to move away from the DPJ government's policy of gradually eliminating nuclear power remains unclear. Public opinion overwhelmingly supports phasing out nuclear power, even while a plurality in many

polls is tolerant of restarting some nuclear plants in the short-run. The LDP chose not to stake out a position against nuclear phase-out in its 2012 election manifesto, although it included a statement that appeared to endorse the phase-out, declaring that the party 'aimed to establish a socio-economic structure that could be strong even without nuclear power'. On the other hand, the LDP did not promise to phase out nuclear power (Jimintō, 2012: 23). New Komeito ran on a platform advocating the entire elimination of nuclear power as soon as possible. Moreover, New Komeito explicitly promised not to allow any new nuclear plants to be constructed (Komeito, 2012: 7).

In short, the Lower House elections did not give the coalition partners any mandate on energy policy However, the pull of the old status quo and the economic realities of rising electricity bills due to fossil-fuel imports are difficult to resist. The LDP quietly dropped the most vocally anti-nuclear committee members from the Committee on Basic Energy Issues in January 2013. Consequently, once the NRA's laborious process of drafting new safety guidelines was completed, and geological and other technical surveys of the 50 remaining operable reactors[11] were done, the need to reopen the political discussion on reactor restarts resurfaced in 2014. The NRA signaled in July 2014 that two reactors at the Sendai plant on the southern island of Kyushu could be restarted as early as fall 2014. However, none of the other 17 reactors that are under review for safety approval are likely to be restarted before 2015, or later, if ever, due to the very laborious and strict safety standards and the high costs of meeting these standards. (Nagata and Yoshida, 2014).

The question of new builds is only likely to be addressed after the first restarts. The political barriers to building new nuclear-power plants are likely to be formidable, as a large majority of between two thirds and three quarters of the public favors phasing out nuclear power, a position backed by New Komeito.

PROMOTING RENEWABLES

Clearly, the multiple meltdowns at Fukushima Dai-ichi have raised the salience of renewable energy as a form of electricity generation in Japan. Yet the future of renewable-energy policy inherits the legacy of its checkered past. Broadly, three periods can be identified: an initial period of uncoordinated policy initiatives, a second period when a comprehensive instrument, a renewable portfolio standard (RPS), was introduced for the first time, and a third period post-3/11 when the Kan administration passed the FIT law.

Uncoordinated Technology Policies

The Ministry of International Trade and Industry (MITI) became interested in renewable energy when it started promoting solar energy even before the first oil crisis as a means of reducing the country's dependence on imported oil and creating a new high-technology industry. Generous government support and numerous demonstration projects for solar photovoltaics (PV) through the Sunshine Program, launched as the oil crises unfolded, attracted attention from a host of private manufacturers, who eventually suceeded in improving efficiency and decreasings the cost of solar modules. When, by the early 1990s, the programs' cumulative expenses had reached 600 billion yen without any major commercial successes to show for it, MITI took new measures to promote the commercial take-off of PV technology, such as devising technical standards for grid connection, persuading electric utilities to launch a voluntary net-metering system, simplifying installation and providing subsidies for the installation of residential systems. With these measures in place the Japanese solar market took off in earnest (Kimura and Suzuki, 2006).

By contrast, wind power was not promoted by the Japanese government because it had not been considered a technology that could spawn a major export industry. Investment incentives were eventually introduced for wind farms in 1997, but their abolition in 2007 discouraged additional investments. This is not only because wind projects face much tougher environmental impact assessments

and construction standards than is the case with solar, but also because they require extensive investments for grid connections as optimal sites often are located far away from demand centres – and no straightforward mechanism for sorting out how to split these costs between developers and the grid-owning utilities has been developed. This stands in marked contrast with residential PV systems, which are installed on the rooftops of homes that are already connected to the grid (Moe, 2011).

Although geothermal power, like solar and wind, is a method for generating electricity that has been more costly than non-renewable conventional generation technologies, unlike solar and wind it has the advantage of producing a stable output of electricity, allowing it to serve as a baseload power source. Consequently, geothermal does not create grid-integration problems like solar and wind. As a highly volcanic land Japan possesses the world's third largest potential for geothermal energy after the USA and Indonesia, estimated at 23.5 GW, which is more than half of Japan's current installed nuclear capacity (Think GeoEnergy, 2011). However, Japan has only 18 geothermal power plants in operation nationwide so far, with an installed capacity of 530 megawatts (*Asahi Shimbun*, 2010),[12] due to two reasons unrelated to generation costs. First, the areas with the greatest geothermal potential are generally located in national parks, where Ministry of Environment (MOE) regulations inhibit development. Second, geothermal energy faces unexpected challenges from Japan's traditional hot-springs industry, which, despite a lack of examples to support its claims, has thus far been successful in asserting that the construction of geothermal electricity projects would damage operations at nearby hot springs (Ehara, 2013). However, even before 3–11 METI was cooperating with MOE to ease the regulations inhibiting geothermal plant development.[13] Following 3–11, deregulation efforts were redoubled, with anti-nuclear LDP politician Taro Kono and others negotiating an inter-ministerial agreement between MOE, METI, and the Home Affairs Ministry to relax regulations for geothermal projects in national parks (Kyodo, 2012a; Kono, 2011).

Sluggish Growth under the RPS

Efforts to promote renewable energy more systematically in Japan had already started by the late 1990s. Inspired by the early success of Germany's FIT in advancing renewables, a network of green NGOs promoted a Parliamentary Initiative for Renewable Energy Promotion aimed at creating a similar policy instrument in Japan. In response to this legislator-sponsored bill MITI, concerned that the FIT might lead to an uncontrollable rise in renewables and spiraling costs, introduced a competing bill

Table 33.3 Targets for the Japanese RPS scheme in TWhs

2003	2004	2005	2006	2007	2008	2009	2010	2011	2012	2013	2014
7.32	7.66	8.00	8.34	8.67	9.27	10.33	12.20	13.15	14.10	15.05	16.00
						(10.38)	(12.43)	(12.82)	(14.21)	(15.73)	(17.33)

Note: Bracketed figures refer to a 2009 upgrade of targets by METI.

Source: METI 2011.

laying out the bare bones of a renewable portfolio standard (RPS) (Suwa and Jupesta, 2012).

This MITI bill eventually became the 2002 Act on Special Measures Concerning New Energy Use by Electric Operators, obligating EPCOs, PPSs and SEUs to use a certain amount of 'new energy' set by ministerial notice every four years (see Table 33.3). 'New energy' under this law included wind, solar, biomass (including waste incineration), geothermal, and hydro (within certain limits).

The law allowed companies to achieve their targets through trading between obligated entities, including saving and borrowing of certificates between compliance periods, and to reduce targets by realizing certain energy-efficiency measures. While flexibility in the design of a policy instrument is usually a desirable feature, the scheme designed by METI did not lead to a diffusion of renewable technologies comparable to that in other countries.

The failure of the RPS to promote renewable energy difusion in Japan soon became apparent even in the case of PV. Japanese companies had pioneered solar-cell technologies that dominated the world market in the early 2000s. Government-financed assistance payments between 1994 and 2005 for the installation of rooftop solar panels had helped Japanese manufacturers achieve this dominance, but by 2004 the FITs introduced in multiple European

countries had helped promote the growth of their solar companies even as Japan ending its assistance to Japanese companies. Unsurprisingly, new solar orders fell sharply in Japan and Japanese solar makers' world market share declined (PV News, 2013).

In the face of this and rising energy prices the LDP responded in 2009, passing the Act on the Promotion of the Use of Non-Fossil Energy Sources and Efficient Use of Fossil Energy Sources by Energy Businesses. Based on this law a ministerial order re-established subsidies for solar energy – this time in FIT form, which started in November 2009. Although this was only a net FIT, purchasing only the electricity produced by an installation in excess of its owners' electricity consumption, the instrument soon elicited a response in Japan's domestic market. The total amount of solar panels shipped in terms of generation capacity grew nearly three-fold from 2008 to 2009, and fivefold by 2010. Nonetheless, this FIT instrument was limited strictly to 'non-commercial' use, set a low ceiling for maximum capacity, and failed to provide any assistance to energy technologies other than PV (see Table 33.5).

A Breakthrough under the DPJ?

In August 2009 the LDP, which had been in power as the leading governing party for all but nine

Table 33.4 Track record of Japan's RPS scheme.

	2004	2005	2006	2007	2008	2009	2010	2011
Total electricity generation (TWh)	1,137.3	1,157.9	1,161.1	1,195.0	1,146.2	1,112.6	1,156.8	880.4
…of which renewables (TWh)	107.8	91.3	102.5	89.9	89.2	90.3	118.3	105.1
…excluding hydro power (TWh)	4.6	4.9	5.2	5.6	5.7	6.5	27.6	28.2
…further excluding geothermal (TWh)[1]	1.3	1.7	2.1	2.6	2.9	3.6	25.0	26.2
…further excluding biomass (TWh)[2]	1.3	1.7	2.1	2.6	2.9	3.6	4.0	4.6
Renewables as a percentage of all	9.5%	7.9%	8.8%	7.5%	7.8%	8.1%	10.2%	11.9%
…excluding hydro power	0.4%	0.4%	0.5%	0.5%	0.5%	0.6%	2.4%	3.2%
…further excluding geothermal	0.1%	0.2%	0.2%	0.2%	0.3%	0.3%	2.2%	3.0%
…further excluding biomass	0.1%	0.2%	0.2%	0.2%	0.3%	0.3%	0.3%	0.5%

Source: METI, Agency of Natural ReSources and Energy, Power Survey Statistics, available at http://www.enecho.meti.go.jp/info/statistics/denryoku/result-2.htm

[1] There were no investments in new geothermal projects in Japan between 2003 and 2012.

[2] From 2010, waste incineration was included with biomass instead of thermal generation, hence the large jump in biomass for that year.

Table 33.5 Rates under the net FIT system for solar PV

	Domestic use		Non-domestic use	
	Only solar	Double generation	Only solar	Double generation*
<10 kW	JPY 48	JPY 39	JPY 24	JPY 20
>10 kW	JPY 24	JPY 20		

Source: http://www.meti.go.jp/ press/20110330003/20110330003.pdf

Note: Double generation refers to generating electricity not only from solar panels, but also using a second technology, such as gas generators. The double generation tariff was lower because it was thought that households would end up consuming the stable electricity output from these other technologies and end up feeding in larger amounts of electricity from variable output PV, with potential negative effects on the grid.

months (in 1993-94) since 1955, was cleanly swept from office by voters, and the the DPJ was swept into power. The DPJ had promised as part of its ambitious package on climate change to extend the previous LDP administration's FIT to other renewable-energy technologies beyond solar. Although the government had hardly begun implementing the net FIT that the LDP had past earlier the same year, November 2009 witnessed the establishment of a DPJ government project team for creating an extended feed-in tariff for renewable energy that would pay operators for the total amount of electricity generated across a wide spectrum of renewable energy technologies, in other words a gross FIT. The

Kan Cabinet adopted a METI-drafted bill for submission to the Diet on the morning of 11 March 2011, mere hours before the massive earthquake struck Japan's north-eastern coast.

Although the bill did not contain any concrete provisions for either the tariff level or the length of the coverage period, it quickly became a flash point of contention as popular discontent with Japan's reliance on nuclear power soared. The bill was modified in committee, giving the Diet, not METI, the right to appoint the members of the tariff-setting committee, the tariff, and the coverage period – a right that politicians chose to exercise vigorously once the law was passed in August 2011 by rejecting a slate of experts seen as potentially hostile toward renewable energy. As a result, even though the initial project team had envisaged tariffs in the case of PV of around 20 yen, the actual tariffs introduced on 1 July 2012, were much higher – in some cases the highest in the world (see Table 33.6).

These tariffs are calculated with a given profit margin in mind, but as the market for renewable technologies increases and competition between manufacturers and service providers intensifies, overall system costs are expected to decline significantly. Consequently, Japan's FITs are set to decrease gradually over time (Johnston, 2012; *Japan Times*, 2012), as per the German FIT model. However, system costs will not come down unless a number of ancillary measures are taken. Siting remains an extremely time-consuming affair for large-scale facilities, as areas with great generation potential are often located far away from grids, or even in national parks. A recent political compromise has made it possible to install solar panels on

Table 33.6 Tariff levels per kWh decreed in July 2012

Technology	Subdivision	Tariff (JPY)	Tariff (EUR €)	Coverage (years)
Solar	< 10kW	42	41.34	10
Solar	<10kW, "double generation"	34	33.47	10
Solar	>10kW	42	41.34	20
Wind	<20kW	57.75	56.85	20
Wind	>20kW	23.1	22.74	20
Hydro	<200kW	35.7	35.14	20
Hydro	>20kW, <1MW	30.45	29.97	20
Hydro	>1MW, <30MW	25.2	24.81	20
Geothermal	<15MW	42	41.34	15
Geothermal	>15MW	27.3	26.87	15
Biomass	Methane fermentation, gasification	40.95	40.31	20
Biomass	Unused thinned timber	33.6	33.08	20
Biomass	Other wood materials, husks and straw	25.2	24.81	20
Biomass	Waste	17.85	17.57	20
Biomass	Wood from construction waste	13.65	13.44	20

Source: http://www.enecho.meti.go.jp/saiene/kaitori/dl/120522setsumei.pdf

top of agricultural land, but similar initiatives with other types of renewable technologies are required. Similarly, Environmental Impact Assessments (EIA) have been waved for PV, but wind and geothermal require EIAs of two to four years, pushing project lead times to almost 10 years, which slows down expansion considerably. Indeed, from October 2012 wind-farm projects are required to go through the same EIA as a thermal- or nuclear-power plant, a process that can take five to nine years (*Asahi Shimbun*, 2013). Furthermore, red tape in the approval of installations for the FIT are hampering competition between suppliers, which keeps generation costs up.

CONCLUSION: THE HURDLES AHEAD

Overall, the future of renewables in Japan is no longer tied to the question of generation costs. Already a 2011 report of the Cabinet's Energy and Environment Council found that the generation costs for renewables were within range of conventional generation costs based on thermal and nuclear technologies (see Table 33.7). The generalized FIT has since July 2012 allowed independent investments to stream into these technologies – although the results are overwhelmingly concentrated in solar so far.

The biggest hurdle to the diffusion of renewables remains the issue of connecting renewables to the

Table 33.7 Modelled generation costs for new plants in 2030

Technology	Generation costs (JPY/kWh)
Nuclear power	>8.9
Coal-fired thermal	10.3–10.6
LNG-fired thermal	10.9–11.4
Onshore wind	8.8–17.3
Offshore wind	8.6–23.1
Geothermal	9.2–11.6
Small-scale hydro	19.1–22.0
Wood-based biomass	17.4–32.2
Oil-fired thermal (50% capacity factor)	25.1–28.0
Oil-fired thermal (10% capacity factor)	38.9–41.9
Rooftop solar	9.9–20.0
Gas cogeneration	20.1–21.1 (reducible to 11.5–12.0 once sales of heat are taken into account)

Source: Report of the Cost Investigation Committee, Energy and Environment Council, Cabinet of Japan (2011).

grid. Utilities have been voicing reservations about renewables since the 1990s, claiming solar and wind are not only intermittent but also unpredictable, which creates technical challenges for maintaining the frequency of the alternating current within grids, and about the need to strike a balance with conventional energy or chemical batteries in the short-run, and develop electricity-storage infrastructure in the long-run.[14] Although the 2011 FIT law stipulates that utilities need to buy up electricity from renewable-power producers, utilities retain the right to refuse connection to applicants if a utility fears that doing so would cause damage to its grid. This is in marked contrast to the provisions of the German FIT law, which obligates grid companies to connect applicants and give their electricity priority access to the transmission and distribution networks. Renewable-energy developers in Japan have complained that the EPCOs, owning both generation and transmission infrastructure, restrict access to transmission networks in a non-transparent manner in order to protect the profitability of their own generation assets. This has given rise to calls for further unbundling of Japanese utilities, which merely keep separate financial accounts for their different divisions in generation, transmission and distribution.

After the Fukushima accident METI's Expert Committee on the Reform of the Power System did not manage to produce more than a document spelling out the directions for the re-regulation of the electricity sector under the Noda Cabinet. However, this debate did not fade away once the LDP had won a majority in the December 2012 Lower House election. Instead, the same committee managed to produce a timetable for reform, which is to proceed in three main steps. First, by 2015 a national grid regulatory organization is to be set up and new rules regarding transmission and the operation of the wholesale market are to be drawn up. Second, by 2016, the retail sector is to be liberalized, enabling small-scale consumers, including households, to select their electricity provider, and restrictions on sales of electricity between various actors are to be lifted. Finally, in 2018–2020, the present electricity-tariff system is to be abandoned and legal unbundling introduced, eliminating the system of vertically integrated monopolies that has made some see Japan as a unique case among developed, and even most developing, nations (Kyodo, 2013a; DeWit et al., 2012: 157).

Legal unbundling would create subsidiary companies in generation and transmission that would have to be financially viable on their own. Legal unbundling is less radical than ownership unbundling, which would force the current EPCOs to spin off their grid divisions entirely. These proposals were submitted as a bill to the regular Diet session of 2013, but were very controversial, both within the Diet overall and the LDP. Nonetheless, the EPCOs had reason to compromise on grid divestiture for the sake of obtaining an agreement to turn at least some of Japan's nuclear reactors back on at an early date. Eventually, the bill was passed in the fall 2013 Diet session, with the continued support of the Abe Cabinet (Kyodo 2013b).

Whatever the outcome of the policy process, the issue of grid management is going to be of great importance for the diffusion of renewables in Japan over the next decade, as it is in other OECD economies. The vast majority of grid assets are old and in need of replacement within 20 years (Scalise, 2012b: 27). The skewed distribution of sites with high renewable-energy potential relative to load centres also means that investment in expanded inter-regional grid connections is required in addition to regular renewal. Furthermore, as demonstrated by the aftermath of the Fukushima accident, the interconnectivity between the eastern and western frequency areas needs to be enhanced to avoid bottlenecks in transmission that seriously limit flexiblity in response to crises. Proposals have also been floated for Japan to develop grid connections with South Korea, and perhaps Russia, to allow for electricity imports, and to move toward a more decentralized grid as power generation becomes less centralized and more distributed with the increase in renewables.[15]

It is important to note that greenhouse-gas emissions have surged as a consequence of the Fukushima accident, with data from March 2013 suggesting CO2 emissions from Q4 of 2011 until Q3 of 2012 had risen by 7.4 percent to 1,198.5 metric tons from the previous equivalent one-year period. However, even though the DPJ's first prime minister, Hatoyama Yukio, had pledged that by 2020 Japan would reduce its emissions by 25 percent relative to 1990, this had never been more than a conditional pledge to be transformed into an official target upon the creation of 'a new global, comprehensive, fair and effective framework, in which all major economies would participate'. As neither the USA nor China has joined such a framework, Japan has in effect no real commitment to anything – even less so since Tokyo has chosen not to participate in the Kyoto Protocol's second commitment period.

Once the impacts of the Fukushima accident started rippling through Japan's energy sector the Kan and Noda governments quietly acknowledged that this pledge would have to be revised – and since then Japanese negotiators have made no secret of this during annual climate negotiations. The new LDP government has already intimated that mitigation targets will only be articulated when the room for pursuing such goals becomes clear upon the adoption of a 'best energy mix', a goal the party explicitly put off in its 2012 election manifesto, where it called for spending up to ten years to determine the 'best mix' for electricity generation (Jimintō, 2012:

23). Hatoyama's ambitious target was predicated on the expansive nuclear-building program spelled out in the 2010 Basic Energy Plan that Kan cancelled. Japan's new climate-mitigation target will only be settled once the country's energy mix has been negotiated and not the other way around.

The question of how great a role renewables should play in Japan's electricity generation remains far from settled even though all major political parties, including the LDP, support expanding renewable energy. Nonetheless, the LDP's 2012 election manifesto, which called for 'introducing renewable energy as much as possible' (Jimintō, 2012: 23), obviously begs the question of how much actually is possible. As of mid 2013 no new long-term target for the diffusion of renewables has been formally announced by the government to replace the Noda administration's goal of generating 35 percent of electricity from renewables by 2030 (Oppenheim, 2013: 95). Keenly aware of the impact that making any rash pronouncements on energy policy could have on its prospects of winning the upcoming Upper House elections, the LDP refused to say more than is in its 2012 election manifesto and its coalition agreement with the New Komeito: that is, to promote renewables and energy efficiency and to entrust nuclear restarts to the Nuclear Regulatory Agency. Furthermore, the renewable technologies to be promoted strategically are still the same ones declared by the DPJ, namely offshore wind, biomass, geothermal and ocean wave energy. For example, in early March 2013 the Abe Cabinet announced new measures to facilitate the development of tidal-wave electricity plants by interceding with fishing associations and local governments that might oppose them (*Nikkei*, 2013a).

The further diffusion of renewables and of the resilience of nuclear power will depend on the political will to maintain the policy framework put in place by the Kan and Noda administrations, eliminate existing policy hurdles, and reap the benefits from electricity-market and grid reform. The debate on the future of the architecture of the electricity market, the nature of the players to be accepted into it, and the relationships among them still does not provide an answer to the question of what the overall balance between fossil, nuclear, and renewable-energy sources will be in the future. Yet without a clear sense of direction organizing the necessary investments in a timely manner will be difficult.

As was the case in the 1970s, Japan again stands at an energy crossroads. Having again suffered a devastating crisis that revealed the country's acute energy insecurity, the lessons that are drawn from this crisis will likely shape energy policy for decades to come, as was the case with the 1970s oil shocks. By no later than the next Lower House election, which must be held by the end of 2016, Japan's new direction should be clear.

NOTES

1 Total primary energy refers to domestic energy production plus energy imports.

2 For a more recent iteration of what is called the 'energy insecurity myth' see Cohen and Kirshner (2011).

3 Additionally, Japan began stockpiling oil to deal with temporary disruptions.

4 On the early history of nuclear power in Japan in general see Samuels (1987: chapter 6).

5 Although several new nuclear reactors were completed after the Tokaimura accident, reactor retirements, and aggravated concerns over safety increased nuclear-reactor downtimes that reduced utilization rates, meaning that this new capacity failed to translate into increased power generation.

6 Chubu EPCO has the capacity to convert up to 1 GW of 50 Hz power to 60 Hz, and vice versa, a bottleneck that hindered power balancing after 3–11. See Scalise (2011) and Williams (2011).

7 Scalise calculates a weighted average price in Japan of 16.4 yen per kWh versus 13.4 yen per kWh average for the OECD as a whole (Scalise, 2012b: 25).

8 The same data also showed that the government had underestimated the amount of solar electricity produced on the day the electricity reserve margin was at its lowest (3 August) by a factor of three, although solar's overall contribution to supply was still modest (*Asahi Shimbun*, 2012).

9 Polling results were more negative to restarts in a number of other polls (e.g. see Yomiuri 2012), but opposition to nuclear restarts in the short-run was always far less than to maintaining nuclear power in the long run.

10 However, the Noda government's decision to eliminate nuclear power by 2039 at latest would seem to imply that newer nuclear reactors would also have to be shut down before reaching 40 years of age (see Graph 33.5).

11 Although the Japanese government recognizes 50 operable reactors, this number includes Fukushima reactors 5 and 6, which, although largely undamaged by 3–11, are unlikely ever to be restarted.

12 In 2007 these geothermal plants generated 3.1 TWh, surpassing wind-power production for that year (*Asahi Shimbun*, 2010). In addition to electricity generation Japan uses heat from geothermal sources to heat buildings, roads, and for aquaculture. Japan is estimated to use 1,000 Terajoules of direct geothermal heat every year (New Energy Foundation, 2012).

13 In addition to regulations hindering development in or near national parks, geothermal plants were treated like conventional fossil-fuel thermal plants, requiring trained specialists for pressures and temperatures far beyond those actually found at geothermal plants (*Asahi Shimbun*, 2010).

14 Two of the most discussed forms of storage are flywheel storage, currently used commercially in Okinawa and New York state (a new 20 Mw plant is being constructed in Pennsylvannia), and hydrogen storage. See www.beaconpower.com/ and www.scotland.gov.uk/Publications/2010/10/28091356/4 (Accessed July 17, 2014). It is also worth noting that wind and solar luminence are predictable, with precision rising as the time horizon shortens.

15 Regarding distributed power see DeWit et al. (2012: 163–165).

REFERENCES

ABB (2010). Trends in global energy efficiency 2011: Country reports – Japan, accessed at www05.abb.com/global/scot/scot316.nsf/veritydisplay/5a74498fcc9fbabbc1257864005160e4/$file/Japan.pdf on May 1, 2013.

Adelman, M.A. (2008). *Genie out of the Bottle: World Oil since 1970*. Cambridge, M.A.: MIT Press.

Aldrich, D. (2008). *Site Fights: Divisive Facilities and Civil Society in Japan and the West*. Ithaca: Cornell University Press.

Aldrich, D. (2013). Post-Fukushima Nuclear Politics in Japan, Part I, *The Monkey Cage* (April 1), Accessed 3 April, 2013 at http://themonkeycage.org/2013/04/01/post-fukushima-nuclear-policies

Asahi Shimbun (2009). 'Genpatsu, kuni ni fushinkan' zō naikakufu yoronchōsa (November 27): 37.

Asahi Shimbun (2010). Deregulation eyed for geothermal power (Febuary 17): accessed at www.asahi.com/english/TKY201002160499.html on February 22, 2011.

Asahi Shimbun (2011). Genshiryoku bei wo otte (July 17): 3.

Asahi Shimbun (2012). Sore demo 'saikadō ha datō (September 5): 5.

Asahi Shimbun (2013). Saisei ene kisei ga habamu (March 25): 3.

Cabinet of Japan (2012). Future Policies for Energy and the Environment. Cabinet of Japan, September 19, 2012.

Cohen, D. and Kirshner J. (2011). Myth-telling: The cult of energy insecurity and China-US relations. *Global Asia*, retrieved from http://www.globalasia.org/Issue/ArticleDetail/272/myth-telling-the-cult-of-energy-insecurity-and-china-us-relations.html on July 30, 2014.

DeWit, A., Iida T. and Kaneko, M. (2012). Fukushima and the political economy of power policy in Japan. In Jeff Kingston, ed., *Natural Disaster and Nuclear Crisis in Japan: Response and Recovery after Japan's 3/11*. Abingdon: Routledge. pp. 156–172.

Ehara, S. (2013). The case of geothermal energy. Presentation given at the closed-door Expert

Workshop, REvision 2013, Japan Renewable Energy Foundation, February 25.

Energy and Environment Council (2011). Kosuto nado kenshō iinkai hōkokusho]. Cabinet of Japan, December 19, 2011. Accessed at http://www.cas. go.jp/jp/seisaku/npu/policy09/pdf/20111221/ hokoku.pdf on August 17, 2014.

Energy and Environment Council (2012). Kakushinteki enerugii-kankyō senryaku. Cabinet of Japan, September 14, 2012. Accessed at www.kantei. go.jp/jp/noda/actions/201209/14kaigi.html on September 16, 2012.

Energy Central (2011). Aggreko mobilises 200 MW emergency power for Japan, retrieved from www. energycentral.com/generationstorage/fossilandbiomass/news/vpr/10732/Aggreko-mobilises-200-MW-emergency-power-for-Japan on April 14, 2013.

Fukasaku, Y. (1995) Energy and environmental policy integration – the case of energy conservation policies and technologies in Japan. *Energy Policy*, 23(12): 1063–1076.

Guardian (2012). Japan to report first trade deficit since 1980 following Fukushima disaster (January 24): accessed at www.guardian.co.uk/world/2012/jan/24/japan-trade-deficit-fukushima-disaster on January 25, 2012.

Institute of Energy Economics, Japan (2012). *EDMC Handbook of Energy & Economic Statistics in Japan*. Tokyo, Japan: The Energy Conservation Center, The Institute of Energy Economics, Japan.

Japan Times (2011). LDP planning major energy policy rethink (July 6): accessed at www.japantimes.co.jp/news/2011/07/06/national/ldp-planning-major-energy-policy-rethink/#. UZDqn8rpGSo on May 11, 2013.

Japan Times (2012). Amping up renewable energy (July 17): accessed at www.japantimes.co.jp/text/ed20120717a1.html on July 19, 2012.

Jimintō (2012). Jūten seisaku 2012: Nihon wo torimodosu: accessed at www.jimin.jp/policy/manifest/ on 3 January 2013.

Johnston, E. (2012). New feed-in tariff system a rush to get renewables in play. *Japan Times*, May 29, accessed at www.japantimes.co.jp/text/nn20120529i1.html on May 29, 2012.

Kanekiyo, K. (2006). Lowering energy intensity toward sustainable development. Institute of Energy Economics, Japan, February: accessed at http://eneken.ieej.or.jp/data/en/data/pdf/314.pdf on June 16, 2010.

Kaneko K. (2011). Tsunawatari tsudzuku konka no denryoku jukyū: 'keikaku teiden nash' ha gensoku, *Nikkei BP Net*, May 10, accessed at: www.eco.nik-keibp.co.jp/article/report/20110502/106454/ on July 19, 2011.

Katz, R. (1998). *Japan: The System that Soured -The Rise and Fall of the Japanese Economic Miracle*. Armonk: M.E. Sharpe.

Kimura, O. and T. Suzuki. (2006). 30 years of solar energy development in Japan. Paper presented at the Berlin Conference on the Human Dimensions of Global Environmental Change.

Koh, Y. (2011). Another post-quake controversy: evacuee housing, *Japan Real Time*, May 8: retrieved from http://blogs.wsj.com/japanrealtime/2011/05/08/another-post-quake-controversy-evacuee-housing-2/ on July 17, 2014.

Komeito (2012). *Manifesto 2012*, accessed at www.komei.or.jp on 4 January, 2013.

Kono, T. (2011). The politics of renewable power in Japan. Keynote address before 2011 NTNU Seminar: Renewables and Energy Security in Japan, East Asia and Norway, 9–10 November.

Kyodo (2012a). Renewable energy reforms unveiled, *Japan Times* (March 31), accessed at www.japantimes.co.jp/news/2012/03/31/business/renewable-energy-reforms-unveiled/#.UYQl98p7pac on May 3, 2012.

Kyodo (2012b). Tepco to be nationalized on July 25 with yen 1 trillion transaction, *Japan Times* (May 22), accessed at www.japantimes.co.jp/news/2012/05/22/national/tepco-to-be-nationalized-on-july-25-with-1-trillion-transaction/#.UY41ksrpGSo on May 11, 2013.

Kyodo (2013a). Electricity market to be freed up in '16, *Japan Times* (April 2), accessed at www.japantimes.co.jp/news/2013/04/02/business/electricity-market-to-be-freed-up-in-16/#.UY7NTcrpGSo on May 11, 2013.

Kyodo (2013b) New law paves way to break up electricity monopolies, Japan Times (November 13), accessed at http://www.japantimes.co.jp/news/2013/11/13/national/new-law-paves-way-to-break-up-electricity-monopolies/#.U90p__l_uSo on July 30, 2014.

McCurry, J. (2011). Japan nuclear plant confirms meltdown of two more reactors, *The Guardian* (May 24), retrieved from www.guardian.co.uk/world/2011/may/24/japan-nuclear-plant-more-meltdowns?CMP=twt_gu on July 19, 2011.

METI (2010a). Basic energy Plan. June 2010. Accessed at www.enecho.meti.go.jp/topics/kihonkeikaku/new_index.htm on May 6, 2013.

METI (2010b). Top runner program: Developing the world's best energy-efficient appliances. Revised edition, March 2010. Accessed at http://enecho.meti.go.jp/policy/saveenergy/toprunner2011.03en-1103.pdf on May 8, 2013.

METI. (2011a). Denki jigyō binran heisei 23 nenban.

METI. (2011b). On the implementation of the act on special measures concerning new energy use by electric operators for FY2010, July 15: 4.

Moe, E. (2011) Vested interests, energy efficiency and renewables in Japan, *Energy Policy* 40: 260–273.

Nagata, Kazuaki, and Reiji Yoshida (2014). Sendai nuclear plant gets first restart OK, *Japan Times* (July 16), retrieved from http://www.japantimes.co.jp/news/2014/07/16/national/sendai-reactors-get-regulators-ok-restart-first-since-fukushima/#.U90tuPl_uSo July 30, 2014.

Nakayama, M. (2011). Japanese power plants damaged, closed by quake, tsunami, *Bloomberg* (April 27), retrieved from www.bloomberg.com/news/2011-04-27/japanese-power-plants-damaged-closed-by-quake-tsunami-table-.html on May 14, 2011.

Narioka, Kosaku (2012). Fukushima Watch: Tokyo Protesters Stage Largest Anti-Nuclear Rally So Far, *The Wall Street Journal*: Japan Real Time, accessed at http://blogs.wsj.com/japanrealtime/2012/07/16/fukushima-watch-tokyo-protesters-stage-largest-anti-nuclear-rally-so-far/ on May 2, 2013.

New Energy Foundation (2012). Geothermal plants in Japan, accessed at http://nef.or.jp/english/new/pre_geo.html on April 24, 2012.

Nikkei (2011a). Shin'nittetsu, jika-hatsu no saikadō saidai un'yō de Tōden Tōhoku-den ni kyōkyū, *Nikkei BP Net* (April 27), retrieved from http://eco.nikkeibp.co.jp/article/news/20110427/106432/ on May 18, 2011.

Nikkei (2011b). Nihonseishi gurūpu, natsu no denryoku busoku taiō de jika hatsuden wo furu katsuyō shite Tōden nado ni kyōkyū, *Nikkei BP Net* (May 11), retrieved from http://eco.nikkeibp.co.jp/article/news/20110511/106487/ on May 13, 2011.

Nikkei (2012). Genpatsu saikadō, sanpi ga kikkō, *Nihon Keizai Shimbun* (February 20): 2.

Nikkei (2013a). Kaiyō hatsuden, kaiiki wo kōbo: seifu shūnai ni 14 nendo, jishō jikken, *Nihon Keizai Shinbun* (March 10): 1.

Nikkei (2013b). Power utilities facing smaller rate hikes than hoped, *Nikkei Shimbun* (April 3), accessed at http://e.nikkei.com/e/ac/TNKS/Nni20130402D0204A03.htm on April 23, 2013.

Oppenheim, R. (2013). Japan's energy crossroads: nuclear, renewables, and the quest for a new energy mix. In D. Al-Badri and G. Berends, eds., *After The Great East Japan Earthquake: Political and policy Change in Post-Fukushima Japan*. Copenhagen: Nordic Institute for Asian Studies Press, pp. 83–105.

PV News (2013) 29th Annual Cell and Module Cell Data Collection Results, 32 (5).

Reed, S. R., Scheiner, E., Smith, Daniel M. and Thies, M. (2012). The Japanese general election of 2012: Sometimes, lucky is better than popular, *The Monkey Cage* (December 27), accessed at www.themonkeycage.org/blog/2012/12/27/the-japanese-general on December 28, 2012.

Samuels, R. J. (2013). *3.11: Disaster and Change in Japan*. Cornell: Cornell University Press.

Samuels, R. J. (1987). *The Business of the Japanese State: Energy Markets in Comparative Historical Perspective*. Ithaca: Cornell University Press

Scalise P. J. (2011). Three scenarios for economic impact: A legacy from the 1800s leaves Tokyo facing blackouts, *The Oriental Economist* (April): 8–9.

Scalise, P. J. (2012a). Hard choices: Japan's post-Fukushima energy policy in the twenty-first century. In Jeff Kingston, ed., *Natural Disaster and Nuclear Crisis in Japan: Response and Recovery after Japan's 3/11*. Abingdon: Routledge.

Scalise, P. J. (2012b). Japan's distribution challenge: Lessons from abroad. In Economist Intelligence Unit, *Powering ahead: Perspectives on Japan's energy future*. London: The Economist, pp. 24–28.

Someno, K. (2011). Preparing for the Summer Energy Crisis, The Tokyo Foundation (May 2), Accessed 10 October 2014 at http://www.tokyofoundation.org/en/articles/2011/summer-energy-crisis

Suwa, A. and Jupesta J. (2012). Policy innovation for technology diffusion: A case-study of Japanese renewable energy public support programs, *Sustainability Science* 7(2): 185-197.

Suzuki, T. (2000). Nuclear power generation and energy security: The challenges and possibilities of regional cooperation, report published by the James A. Baker Institute for Public Policy, Rice University (May).

Think GeoEnergy (2011). Japan's geothermal resources could help to replace nuclear capacity, *Geothermal Energy News*, accessed at www.think-geoenergy.com/archives/7346 on April 23, 2012.

UN (2013). UN Data, accessed at www.data.un.org/ on May 13, 2013.

Yahoo!News (2012). Tōden nozoku denryoku 9-sha, 4 ~ 12 tsukiki wa nenryō-hi zōdai de 7-sha saishū akaji, genpatsu teishi hibiku (February 1), accessed at http://headlines.yahoo.co.jp/hl?a=20120131-00000003-fsi-bus_all on February 10, 2012.

Warnock, E. (2012). With or without Oi: Summer power shortages in Kansai?, *Japan Real Time* (June 6), accessed at http://blogs.wsj.com/japanrealtime/2012/06/06/with-or-without-oi-summer-power-shortages-in-kansai on July 17, 2014.

Williams, M. (2011). A legacy from the 1800s leaves Tokyo facing blackouts, *Computer world* (March 18), accessed at www.computerworld.com/s/article/9214758/A_legacy_from_the_1800s_leaves_Tokyo_facing_blackouts on April 30, 2013.

Yomiuri Shimbun (2012). Naikaku shijiritsu geraku 30%, honsha zenkoku yoron cho'sa kekka, (February 14, 2012).

Index

Page numbers in **bold** indicate tables, in *italic* indicate figures and followed by a letter n indicate end of chapter notes.